# DR. BURGESS'S ATLAS OF MARINE AQUARIUM FISHES

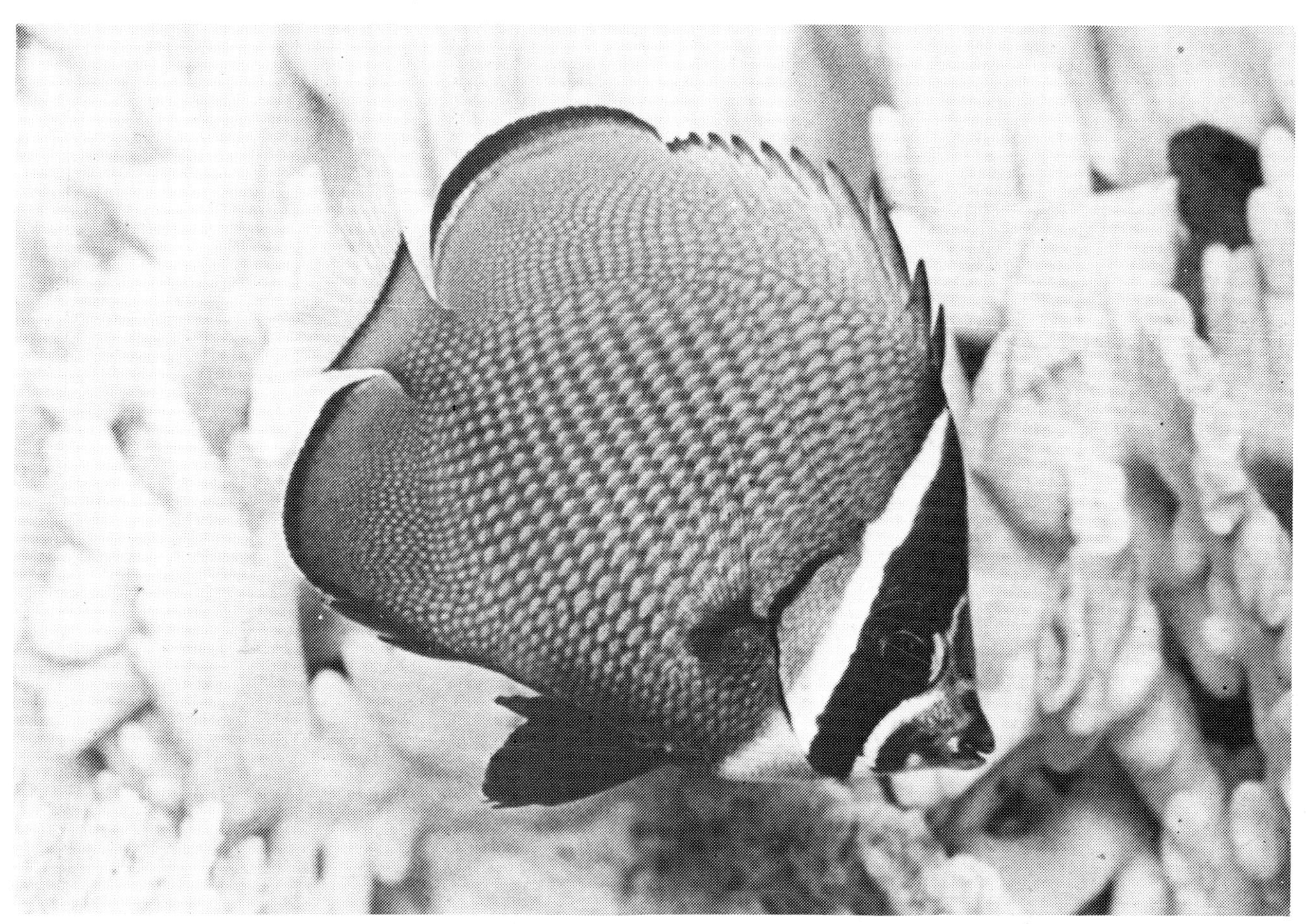

DR. WARREN E. BURGESS

DR. HERBERT R. AXELROD

RAYMOND E. HUNZIKER III

Title page photo of *Chaetodon collare* by K. Paysan.

Distributed in the UNITED STATES by T.F.H. Publications, Inc., One T.F.H. Plaza, Neptune City, NJ 07753; in CANADA to the Pet Trade by H & L Pet Supplies Inc., 27 Kingston Crescent, Kitchener, Ontario N2B 2T6; Rolf C. Hagen Ltd., 3225 Sartelon Street, Montreal 382 Quebec; in CANADA to the Book Trade by Macmillan of Canada (A Division of Canada Publishing Corporation), 164 Commander Boulevard, Agincourt, Ontario M1S 3C7; in ENGLAND by T.F.H. Publications, The Spinney, Parklands, Portsmouth PO7 6AR; in AUSTRALIA AND THE SOUTH PACIFIC by T.F.H. (Australia) Pty. Ltd., Box 149, Brookvale 2100 N.S.W., Australia; in NEW ZEALAND by Ross Haines & Son, Ltd., 82 D Elizabeth Knox Place, Panmure, Auckland, New Zealand; in the PHILIPPINES by Bio-Research, 5 Lippay Street, San Lorenzo Village, Makati, Rizal; in SOUTH AFRICA by Multipet Pty. Ltd., Box 235, New Germany, South Africa 3620. Published by T.F.H. Publications, Inc. Manufactured in the United States of America by T.F.H. Publications, Inc.

# Table of Contents

Introduction ........ 5
Aquaristic Section ........ 7
Caption Explanation ........ 21
Systematic List of Fish Families ........ 24
Acknowledgments ........ 26
Photographers ........ 27
Table of Metric and English Weights and Measures ........ 29

SYSTEMATIC PICTORIAL IDENTIFICATION SECTION

Jawless Fishes *(Plates #1 & 2; pp. 33 & 34)* ........ Text: page 658
Sharks, Rays and Chimaeras *(Plates #1-16; pp. 33–49)* ........ Text: page 658
The Coelacanth *(Plate #17; p. 50)* ........ Text: page 661
Tarpons, Ladyfish, and Bonefish *(Plate #17; p. 50)* ........ Text: page 661
Eels *(Plates #18–29; pp. 51–64)* ........ Text: page 661
Herrings and Herring-like Fishes *(Plates #30–32; pp. 65–69)* ........ Text: page 662
Milkfish *(Plate #32; p. 68)* ........ Text: page 662
Smelts and Noddlefishes *(Plate #33; p. 68)* ........ Text: page 663
Deep-sea Bristlemouths and Viperfishes *(Plate #33; p. 68)* ........ Text: page 663
Lizardfishes and Their Relatives *(Plates #34–37; pp. 71-75)* ........ Text: page 663
Lanternfishes *(Plate #37; p. 75)* ........ Text: page 663
Codfishes and Rattails *(Plates #38 & 39; pp. 76–79)* ........ Text: page 664
Cusk Eels, Pearlfishes, and Their Relatives *(Plates #40 & 41; pp. 79–81)* ........ Text: page 664
Toadfishes and Anglerfishes *(Plates 42–51; pp. 82–93)* ........ Text: page 664
Clingfishes *(Plates #52–54; pp. 94–97)* ........ Text: page 665
Flyingfishes, Halfbeaks, and Needlefishes *(Plates #55 & 56; pp. 98–100)* ........ Text: page 666
Silversides and Their Relatives *(Plate #57; p. 102)* ........ Text: page 666
Opah and Related Fishes *(Plate #58; p. 103)* ........ Text: page 666
Squirrelfishes, Lanternfishes, Pineconefishes, and Their Relatives *(Plates #58–69; pp.101, 103–116)* ........ Text: page 667
Dories and Boarfishes *(Plate #70; p. 118)* ........ Text: page 667
Tubesnouts and Sticklebacks *(Plate #70; p. 118)* ........ Text: page 668
Sea Moths *(Plate #71; p. 119)* ........ Text: page 668
Sea Horses, Pipefishes, and Their Relatives *(Plates #71–82; pp. 117, 119–133)* ........ Text: page 668
Flying Gurnards *(Plate #83; p. 137)* ........ Text: page 669
Scorpionfishes, Sea Robins, Sculpins, and Their Relatives *(Plates #34, 83–114; pp. 72, 134–169)* ........ Text: page 669
Snooks and Glassfishes *(Plates #115, 254; pp. 170, 323)* ........ Text: page 671
Groupers and Their Relatives *(Plates #116–158; pp. 171–215)* ........ Text: page 671
Grunters or Tigerperches and Aholeholes *(Plates #159–161; pp.216–219)* ........ Text: page 672

Bigeyes *(Plates #161 & 162; pp. 219 & 220)* .......... Text: page 672
Cardinalfishes *(Plates #163–178, 254; pp. 221–237, 323)* .......... Text: page 673
Tilefishes and Smelt-whitings
*(Plates #179–181, 429; pp. 238–241, 511)* .......... Text: page 673
Jacks, Cobias, Remoras, Etc.
*(Plates #182–192, 194; pp. 242–255, 257)* .......... Text: page 673
Moonfishes and Slipmouths *(Plate #193; p. 256)* .......... Text: page 674
Pomfrets *(Plate #194; p. 257)* .......... Text: page 675
Australian Salmons *(Plate #194; p. 257)* .......... Text: page 675
Rovers, Snappers, and Fusiliers
*(Plates #195–209; pp. 258-273)* .......... Text: page 675
Tripletails *(Plate #209; p. 273)* .......... Text: page 675
Mojarras *(Plates #210 &211; pp. 274–276)* .......... Text: page 676
Grunts, Porgies, and Their Relatives
*(Plates #212–242, 245; pp. 277–308, 313)* .......... Text: page 676
Drums and Croakers *(Plates #242–244; pp. 308–311)* .......... Text: page 676
Goatfishes *(Plates #245–251; pp. 312–319)* .......... Text: page 677
Moonfishes *(Plates #252 & 344; pp. 320–321, 418)* .......... Text: page 677
Sweepers *(Plates #252–254; pp. 321–323)* .......... Text: page 677
Butterflyfishes, Angelfishes, and Their Allies
*(Plates #255–296; pp. 324–367)* .......... Text: page 677
Knifejaws *(Plate #297; pp. 368 & 369)* .......... Text: page 678
Surfperches *(Plates #297–298; pp. 368–370)* .......... Text: page 678
Damselfishes and Clownfishes
*(Plates #299–336; pp. 371–409)* .......... Text: page 679
Hawkfishes and Their Relatives
*(Plates #337–344; pp. 410–419)* .......... Text: page 679
Bandfishes and Owstoniids *(Plate #345; p. 420)* .......... Text: page 679
Mullets, Barracudas, and Threadfins
*(Plates #345–347; pp. 420–423)* .......... Text: page 680
Wrasses, Parrotfishes, and Odacids
*(Plates #348–415; pp. 424–493)* .......... Text: page 680
Eelpouts, Pricklebacks, and Their Relatives
*(Plates #416–417; pp. 494–495)* .......... Text: page 681
Jawfishes, Stargazers, Sandperches, and
Their Relatives *(Plates #418–424; pp. 496–505)* .......... Text: page 681
Blennies and Their Relatives
*(Plates #425–452; pp. 506–534)* .......... Text: page 682
Dragonets *(Plates #453–456; pp. 535–539)* .......... Text: page 683
Gobies and Their Relatives
*(Plates #429, 457–495; pp. 511, 540–580)* .......... Text: page 683
Surgeonfishes *(Plates #496–509; pp. 581–595)* .......... Text: page 684
Rabbitfishes *(Plates #510–513; pp. 596–600)* .......... Text: page 684
Tunas, Mackerels, Billfishes, and Their Relatives
*(Plates #514–517; pp. 601–605)* .......... Text: page 685
Driftfishes, Butterfishes, and Medusafishes
*(Plate #518; pp. 605–606)* .......... Text: page 685
Flatfishes *(Plates #519–525; pp. 607–615)* .......... Text: page 685
Puffers, Triggerfishes, Boxfishes, and Their Relatives
*(Plates #526–563; pp. 616–656)* .......... Text: page 686
INDEX .......... 689

# INTRODUCTION

This *Atlas of Marine Fishes* is designed mainly as a pictorial aid for the identification of marine fishes. The thousands of photographs are all that will be needed for most aquarists to identify species that they are keeping in their tanks or that they have seen in their local marine fish store. They will also be able to find for the most part fishes that they are likely to collect along their own shores, including those that occur only in the cooler waters of temperate coasts. Further, many fishes are included that are too big for hobbyists but will be seen in the ever-popular public aquariums where large reef tanks or oceanariums house larger fishes, including sharks. Whenever possible, different aspects of a single species are shown. That is, where juveniles are different from adults or males differ from females, both (or even all three) are shown. Ichthyologists have even been fooled by some species that appear so different as a juvenile or as one or the other sex. This has prompted additional names for fishes that had already been named previously. The name applied to the fishes in these photographs is the name that as far as known is the currently accepted name for the fish and supersedes any name applied to it in our previous publications. The most recent scientific papers and books were used to determine the correct names. However, certain obstacles are always present that prevent identifying some of the species with absolute certainty. First of all, since the fish is represented in a photograph only and not "in the flesh" where some of the diagnostic counts or measurements could be made, educated guesses must be made using what available information there is. This information may be color pattern, geographic locality, or even identifications by a photographer who is knowledgeable in fish systematics and has actually seen the fish itself.

Whenever possible color proofs were sent to experts in the field for identification. Dr. Gerald R. Allen kindly identified members of the family Pomacentridae, Dr. Victor G. Springer did the same for the blennies, Dr. Guido Dingerkus identified the elasmobranchs, Dr. William N. Eschmeyer did the scorpionfishes, Dr. William F. Smith-Vaniz did the carangids and some blennies, and Dr. Douglas Hoese tackled the gobies. Unfortunately, some plates were not available to these experts at the time so these identifications were accomplished to the best of my (W.E.B.) ability and should not reflect on the expertise of these scientists.

The common names applied to these fishes were taken from current scientific literature whenever possible. Unfortunately, in some instances (as also happened in the scientific names) there was disagreement (even by the same author in two papers), so that one or the other name was selected. Space does not permit the inclusion of alternate common names or scientific synonyms.

In keeping with the intent of this book to provide the best means to identify the marine fishes, a section is devoted to presenting an outline drawing of a representative of many of the families. As a further aid to aquarists, a short description of the best means of keeping fishes of each family accompanies each drawing. Carrying this one step further, along with the scientific name under each photograph can be seen numerical and pictorial symbols giving a brief account of the species's basic requirements for living, a number indicating the range, and a family number so that each fish can be easily placed in its systematic position. An aquarist recognizing his fish in the photographs can utilize the information in the caption or can refer to the information in the general family care write-ups in the front part of this book. The fishes are presented in systematic order according to Nelson (1984, *Fishes of the World,* John Wiley & Sons, NY), with the cartilaginous fishes first and the plectognaths last.

The range given is approximate. This is partially due to inadequate knowledge of the true range of certain species as well as the limitations dictated by the space available in this book. For example, a species that is found only in the Hawaiian Islands unfortunately must be indicated as a "6" even though Hawaii encompasses only a small portion of the area covered by that number. On the other hand, when a species infringes only a small distance into the adjoining numbered range only the number for the greater area is given. For example, a Caribbean species that occasionally extends its range along the U.S. coastline to, perhaps, the Carolinas, will be indicated only as a "2". A map showing the numbered areas appears on page 23.

The symbols are also approximations. Depicting the type of feeding by a single symbol is virtually impossible. An omnivorous fish that is not particular about its diet should be accorded every feeding symbol. But space limitations force us to indicate only the most likely food(s) of a given fish. It should be remembered that a well-balanced diet is always best.

Like most things, there are sure to be changes, especially in the nomenclature of the fishes. Even so, this book should prove to be the standard for identifying marine aquarium fishes for some time to come.

## AQUARISTIC SECTION

This section is provided as an introductory guide to the maintenance of marine fishes in the aquarium. Habits and requirements are given for each family, or in some cases related groups of families. Included are data such as temperament and compatibility, water conditions, relative hardiness, size, aquascape type, and feeding habits. The family listings (names and numbers) are based on the systematic listing by Nelson (1984), which is found on pages 24-25.

For families that have representatives common in the aquarium hobby, a generalized drawing is included to help with identification. Each drawing immediately precedes the corresponding written entry. After narrowing an unidentified fish down to the family level using these drawings, turning to the pictorial section of the book should give you a good chance of identifying it down to the species level. The selection of families illustrated by drawings may seem somewhat arbitrary, but effort was made to include only those that often appear in pet shops or are commonly collected by hobbyists in coastal areas.

Not all of the families listed here are suitable for home aquaria, and the writeups indicate the reasons why—many are simply too large, others too delicate, others too dangerous! In general, fishes that commonly reach an adult size in excess of a foot or so are suitable only for large public aquaria, and information on many of these species is included for the benefit of such aquaria.

It should be noted that these entries are only generalizations; individual species of some families vary widely with regard to their aquarium care. The butterflyfishes of the family Chaetodontidae are a good example—some species are very hardy, eat almost anything, and are good fishes for the beginner. Others eat only live coral and other hard-to-get items, and these are almost impossible for the average hobbyist to maintain. It is always best to research each individual species, preferably before a specimen is purchased. A good reference for this purpose is *Exotic Marine Fishes* (T.F.H. H-938), as well as much of the scientific literature.

### 1) MYXINIDAE

Hagfishes. Ravenous predators and scavengers, consuming dead and dying fishes. Usually found in groups. Produce large volumes of mucus that may be troublesome in small systems. Not compatible with any other fishes. Dark tank, cool water.

### 2) PETROMYZONTIDAE

Lampreys. Parasitic predators on living fishes. Cool, well-oxygenated water. Not compatible with fishes not intended as prey.

### 4) CHIMAERIDAE

Chimaeras. Cool water, dim light. Foods include benthic invertebrates and fishes. Good aquarium foods include chopped fish, crab, and shrimp. Most are too large for home aquaria, though young specimens are sometimes kept. Compatible with fishes too large to be easy prey.

### 6) CHLAMYDOSELACHIDAE

Frilled sharks. Dark, cold tank. Foods include benthic invertebrates and fishes. Too large for home aquaria; rarely kept even by public aquaria.

### 7) HEXANCHIDAE

Sixgill sharks. Dark, cold tank. Sensitive to changes in water conditions. Eat fishes, crabs, shrimp. Will outgrow home aquaria but are unlikely to be seen outside of public aquaria anyway.

### 8) HETERODONTIDAE

Horn sharks. Relatively inactive, often resting on the bottom. Provide shaded grottos for shelter. Eat fishes, crustaceans. In captivity will accept live goldfish, chopped clam, shrimp, crab. Peaceful with fishes too large to swallow whole. Spines can cause injury; handle with care.

## 9) RHINCODONTIDAE

Whale sharks. Peaceful plankton feeders. Too large for any aquarium.

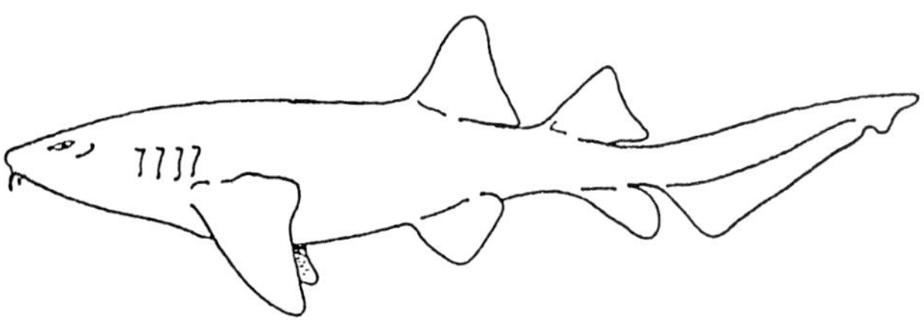

## 10) ORECTOLOBIDAE

Nurse sharks and relatives. Feed on benthic invertebrates. Good aquarium foods include live goldfish, chopped clam, crab, shrimp. Warm, well-lit tank. Peaceful with fishes too large to swallow, but should not be kept with any invertebrates not intended as food. Active and fast-growing, reaching a large size; large tank necessary. Relatively hardy.

## 11) ODONTASPIDAE

Sand tiger sharks. Aggressive fish eaters. Large tank needed, only suitable for public aquaria.

## 12) LAMNIDAE

Mackerel sharks. Pelagic. Very large, often aggressive. Wide variety in diet within this family; various species feed on plankton, fishes, marine mammals. Not suitable for home aquaria and not yet kept with success in public aquaria.

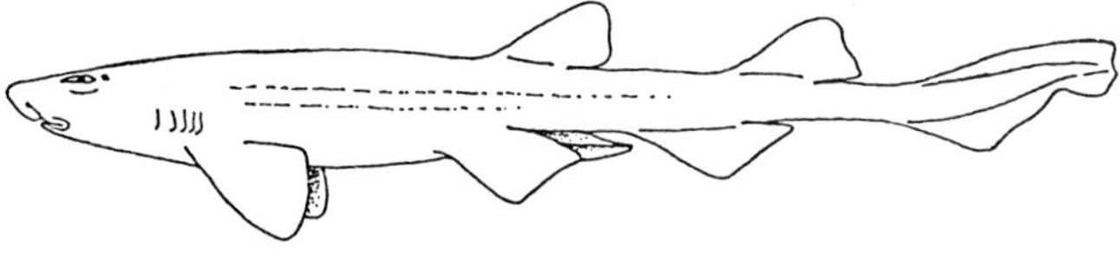

## 13) SCYLIORHINIDAE

Catsharks. Among the best sharks for home aquaria. Somewhat sensitive to adverse changes in water quality, but otherwise hardy. Many are quite attractive, and many remain moderately small. Goldfish, shrimp or prawn, chopped clam, and beef heart are good foods. Large tanks with caves preferred. Peaceful with most fishes, but may attempt to eat many invertebrates.

## 14) CARCHARHINIDAE

Requiem sharks. Active, aggressive predators with powerful jaws and sharp teeth. Very sensitive and generally make poor captives. Very large tanks with no sharp corners are required; these sharks swim tirelessly. Will eat live or chopped fish as well as squid, shrimp, crab.

## 15) SPHYRNIDAE

Hammerhead sharks. Pelagic, extremely poor survival in captivity. Extended head lobes easily damaged. Very sensitive to any change in water conditions. Fish eaters, will also take squid.

## 16) SQUALIDAE

Dogfish sharks. Fairly hardy in captivity; not terribly prone to disease and not too sensitive to changes in water quality. Venomous dorsal spines in some species; handle with care. Good foods include goldfish or chopped fish, chopped clam, squid, shrimp, crab. Large tanks with no sharp edges and few obstructions. Peaceful with fishes of like size.

## 19) PRISTIDAE

Sawfishes. Very large, and small specimens are fast-growing, thus generally unsuitable for home aquaria but are often kept in public aquaria. Sensitive; "saw" is easily injured. Fish eaters, will accept chopped fish and squid. Soft substrate needed, as these rays will sometimes bury themselves.

## 20) TORPEDINIDAE

Torpedo rays. Sluggish bottom dwellers and sand burrowers. Not overly sensitive to water quality. Eat small fishes and benthic invertebrates—foods: chopped fish, crab, shrimp, prawn, squid. Electric organs present, which can deliver a startling but sublethal shock.

## 21) RHINOBATIDAE

Guitarfishes. Inactive rays; need soft substrate for burying. Fairly hardy and not disease-prone. Like dim light. Eat mostly benthic invertebrates; almost any crustacean meat and chopped fish will be accepted. Some rather large—big tanks needed. Peaceful with most other fishes.

## 22) RAJIDAE

Skates. Bottom dwellers, need soft sand for burying themselves. Eat shellfish and crustaceans; good foods include crab, shrimp, prawn, chopped clam, squid. Peaceful with other fishes. Large tanks necessary—many grow large. Fairly hardy and not too sensitive to changes in water quality.

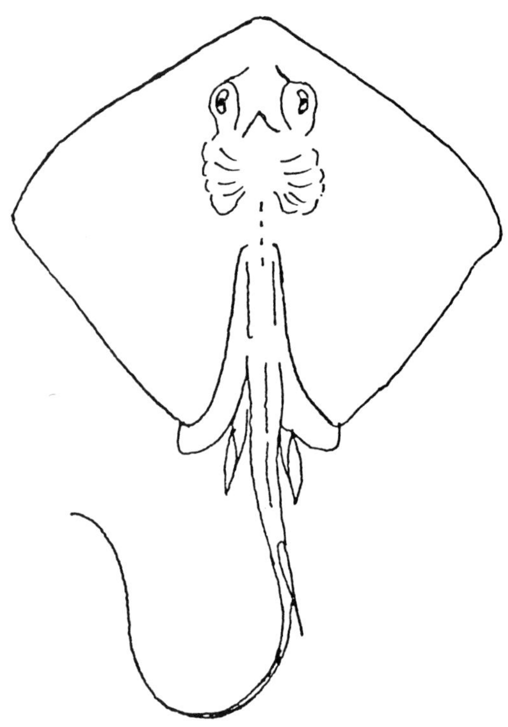

## 23) DASYATIDAE

Stingrays. Bottom dwellers, need soft substrate. Most grow very large and require big tanks. Barbed tail spine is dangerous—handle with extreme care. Will eat most meaty foods and will devour any tankmate small enough to swallow.

## 26) MYLIOBATIDAE

Eagle rays. Pelagic, often schooling. Unsuitable for all but the largest public aquaria. Foods include most shellfish and crustaceans. Warm water, very sensitive to any change in water quality. Venomous tail spines present.

### 27) MOBULIDAE

Mantas. Huge, plankton-eating pelagic rays. Very peaceful. Very sensitive, not suitable for aquaria.

### 31) LATIMERIIDAE

Coelacanth. Never kept in aquaria. Dim light preferred. Eats fishes, crustaceans.

### 43) ELOPIDAE

Ladyfishes. Fast-moving schooling fishes. Large, spacious aquaria needed. Warm water, eat crustaceans and small fishes. Peaceful. Somewhat sensitive in captivity.

### 44) MEGALOPIDAE

Tarpons. Very active; brightly lit large tanks with no obstructions needed. Eat any fishes small enough to swallow. Hardy and long-lived. Peaceful with fishes of like size. Very large; large tanks needed.

### 45) ALBULIDAE

Bonefish. Large and spacious aquaria needed. Soft substrate a must; bonefish root about for benthic invertebrates. Foods: shrimp, crab, chopped clam, small live feeder fish. Peaceful, but very nervous and sensitive to the slightest environmental change.

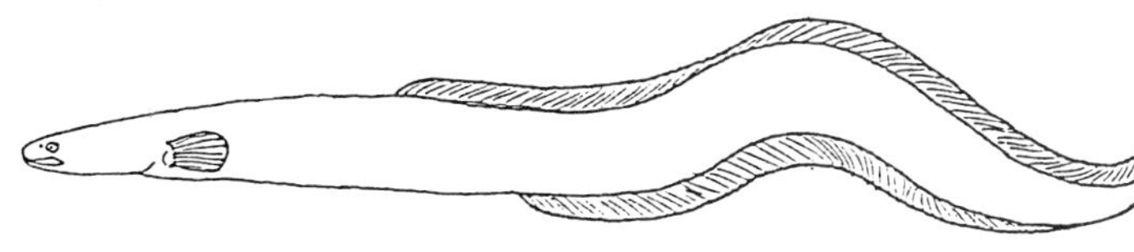

### 49) ANGUILLIDAE

Eels. Very hardy, not disease prone. Will eat anything remotely edible. Relatively peaceful with fishes too large to swallow. Relish many invertebrates, however. Grow very quickly and will outgrow many home aquaria. Not sensitive to water quality, and can withstand any salinity from freshwater to full marine.

### 51) MORINGUIDAE

Small, wormlike burrowing eels. Feed mostly on worms and small crustaceans. Delicate; rarely seen in captivity.

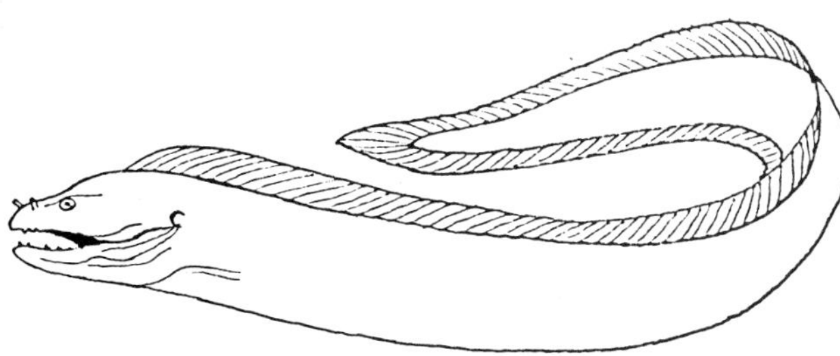

### 54) MURAENIDAE

Moray eels. Large, with powerful jaws and teeth. Can bite; handle with care. Warm water. Hardy, not disease prone. Large tanks needed for most species. Will eat any fishes or crustaceans that can be captured, but generally peaceful with larger fishes. Foods: goldfish, chopped fish, scallops, shrimp, crab, squid. Provide caves and rockwork for shelter.

### 58) OPHICHTHIDAE

Snake eels. Large but shyer than morays. Many burrow; provide soft sand or fine gravel. Peaceful but may eat small fishes. Primarily crustacean and mollusc eaters. Very hardy.

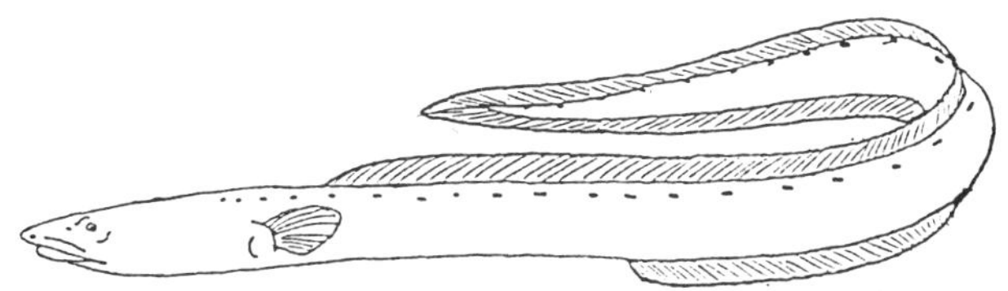

### 62) CONGRIDAE

Conger eels. Large, active, aggressive. Provide rockwork for shelter. Mainly fish eaters. Good foods for captives include feeder fish, chopped fish, scallops, clam, shrimp, squid. Large tanks necessary.

### 69) CLUPEIDAE

Herrings. Active schooling fishes. Keep in large groups in large, spacious tank. Delicate scales and fins easily damaged. Very disease prone. Eat mostly planktonic crustaceans—live brine shrimp is a good substitute for captives. Peaceful.

### 70) ENGRAULIDAE

Anchovies. Pelagic schooling fishes, need to be kept in large groups in large tanks. Delicate and easily stressed; difficult to keep. Eat planktonic crustaceans; feed live brine shrimp. Peaceful.

### 72) CHANIDAE

Milkfish. Large and active, do not take well to aquaria. Feed on crustaceans, small fishes, algae.

### 137) OSMERIDAE

Smelts. Large schools, large tanks. Delicate and disease prone. Will eat small fishes or chopped fish or crustacean meat.

### 139) SALANGIDAE

Lancelike smelt allies. Delicate in captivity. Large schools, large tanks. Eat planktonic crustaceans.

### 144) GONSTOMATIDAE, 147) CHAULINODONTIDAE, 148) STOMIIDAE, 150) MELANOSTOMIIDAE

Viperfishes, dragonfishes, and allies. Deepsea fishes. Toothy predators. Because of need for darkness, cold, and pressure, never kept in captivity.

### 153) AULOPIDIDAE

Benthic predators similar to lizardfishes. Will eat all fishes small enough to swallow; may attack larger ones. Also eat crustaceans. Good foods for captives include chopped fish and shrimp. Large tanks necessary for many species.

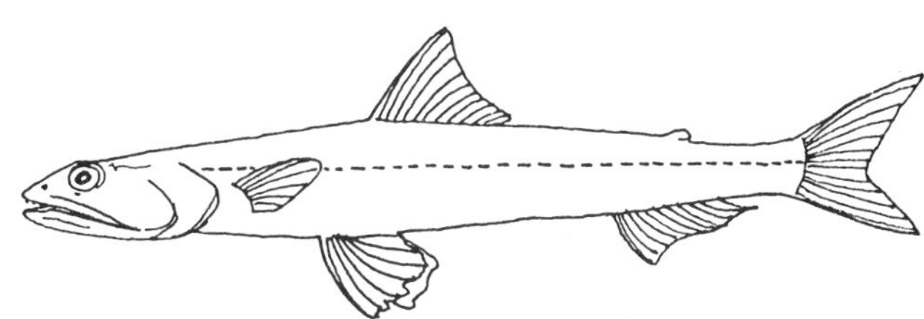

### 157) SYNODONTIDAE

Lizardfishes. Benthic predators, often lie partly buried in soft sand. Very aggressive; will eat most fish and crustaceans. Live fish and shrimp preferred as food—will rarely accept nonliving foods. Very delicate and subject to transport shock—acclimate as gently as possible. Water quality must be excellent.

### 163) ALEPISAURIDAE

Lancetfishes. Pelagic predators. Rarely kept even in public aquaria and unlikely to adapt to captivity.

### 166) MYCTOPHIDAE

Lanternfishes. Bioluminescent midwater fishes; superficially sardine-like. Very delicate; sensitive to water quality and rather disease prone. Plankton feeders—live brine shrimp is a good substitute.

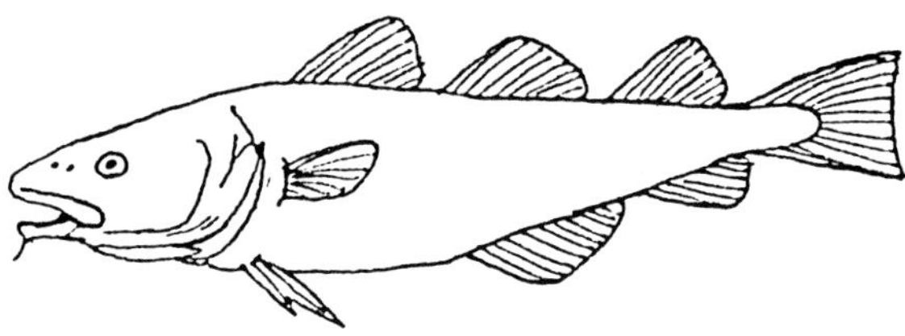

### 171) MORIDAE, 174) GADIDAE, 176) MACROURIDAE

Codfishes and allies. Mostly coldwater, often deepwater, often large. Spacious tanks required. Groups preferred. Foods: fish, crustaceans. Most somewhat delicate but some are kept in public aquaria.

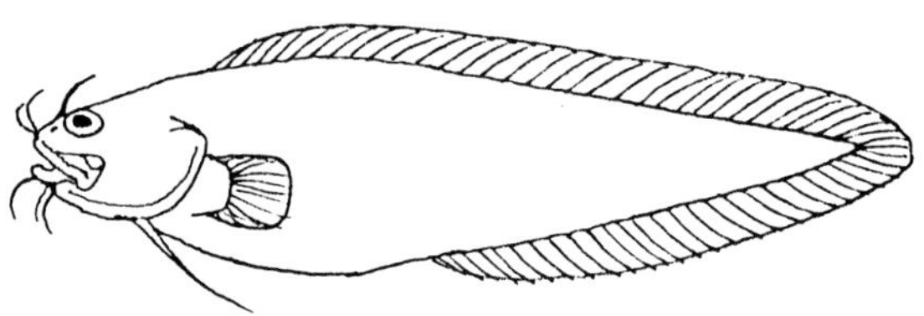

### 177) OPHIDIIDAE

Cusk eels and brotulids. Usually sluggish bottom dwellers. Food mostly benthic invertebrates; feed shrimp, crab, chopped clam, squid. Dim tank with caves and other hollows preferred. Usually peaceful with fishes too large to swallow.

### 178) CARAPIDAE

Pearlfishes. Inhabit body cavities of sea cucumbers and sometimes molluscs. Emerge to feed on small invertebrates; good foods would be brine shrimp, bloodworms, glassworms. Peaceful but delicate and shy.

### 179) BYTHITIDAE

Livebearing brotulas. Benthic; peaceful; fairly hardy. Will eat chopped clam, shrimp, bloodworms, brine shrimp, prepared foods. Dim tank with hollows.

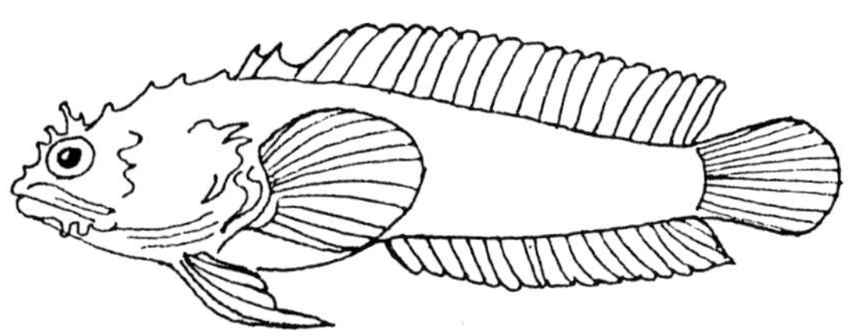

### 181) BATRACHOIDIDAE

Toadfishes. Big-headed benthic predators; will eat anything that can be swallowed. Large teeth and strong jaws—handle with care. Especially fond of crustaceans and molluscs. Like hollows, but place decor with care, as toadfishes like to dig and may undermine decorations.

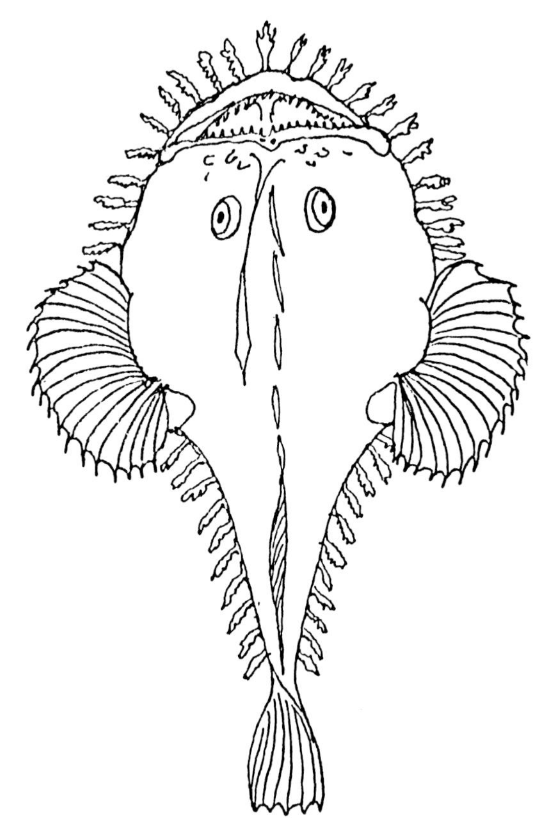

### 182) LOPHIIDAE

Goosefishes. Large, toothy anglerfishes—handle with care. Will eat anything—no compatible tankmates. Very large. Need soft substrate. Not too sensitive to water quality variations.

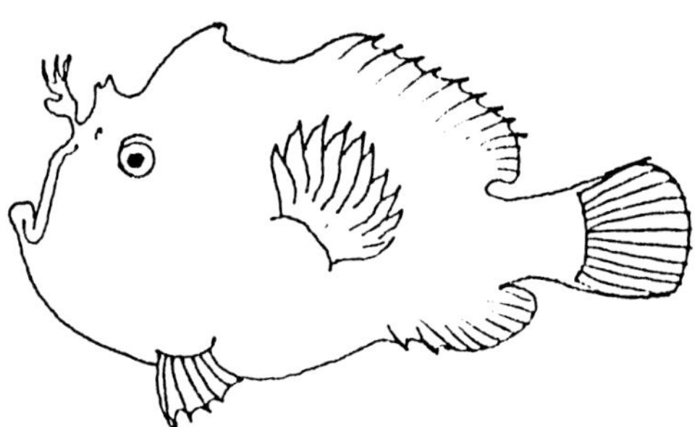

### 183) ANTENNARIIDAE

Frogfishes. Lethargic benthic anglerfishes that lure and ambush passing fishes. Can swallow prey nearly as large as themselves. Cannibalistic. Hardy, but prone to hunger strikes if overfed. Provide coral ledges for perching.

## 186) OGCOCEPHALIDAE

Batfishes. Slow moving, benthic. Very peaceful and shy. Food mostly small crustaceans and polychaete worms but also "angle" for small fishes. Many refuse to feed in captivity, but sometimes live brine shrimp or glass shrimp will be accepted. Cannot compete with faster-moving fishes. Dim tank with soft substrate preferred.

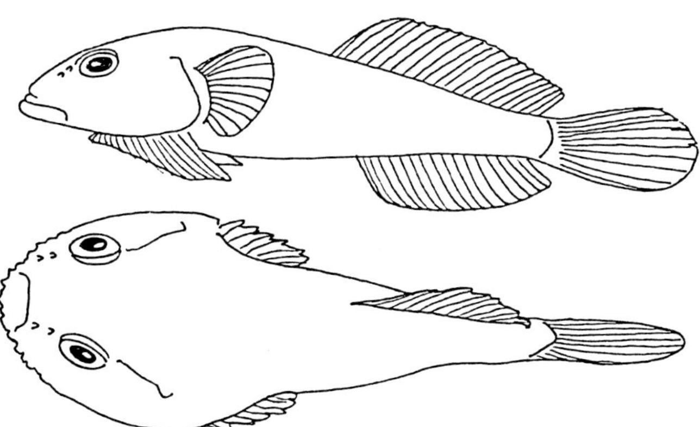

## 198) GOBIESOCIDAE

Clingfishes. Benthic. Very hardy. Very tolerant of water quality changes; very resistant to disease. Generally peaceful, but very small fishes may be eaten. Often become tame. Foods: prawn, brine shrimp, bloodworms, chopped clam, chopped squid.

## 200) EXOCOETIDAE

Flyingfishes. Not easily confined, but small specimens sometimes adapt to aquaria. Jumpers; keep tank tightly covered. Peaceful, but will eat small fishes. Wide, shallow tank without obstructions. Feed bloodworms, brine shrimp, glassworms, flake foods.

## 201) HEMIRAMPHIDAE, 202) BELONIDAE

Halfbeaks and needlefishes. Swift surface predators. Good jumpers. Very delicate and prone to capture and transport shock. Elongate bills easily damaged. Very nervous and prone to panic in aquaria. Round tanks with no sharp corners preferable.

## 213) ATHERINIDAE, 214) ISONIDAE

Silversides and relatives. Surface-to-midwater planktivores. Large schools preferred. Large, spacious tanks needed. Very sensitive to any change in water quality. Deciduous scales easily damaged. Very prone to fungus. Easily killed by transport shock. Foods: brine shrimp, bloodworms, glassworms.

## 218) LAMPRIDIDAE

Opahs. Warmwater, very large. Feed mostly on small fishes. Poorly known.

## 223) REGALECIDAE

Oarfishes. Elongate, very delicate. Feed on small fishes and planktonic invertebrates. Never kept.

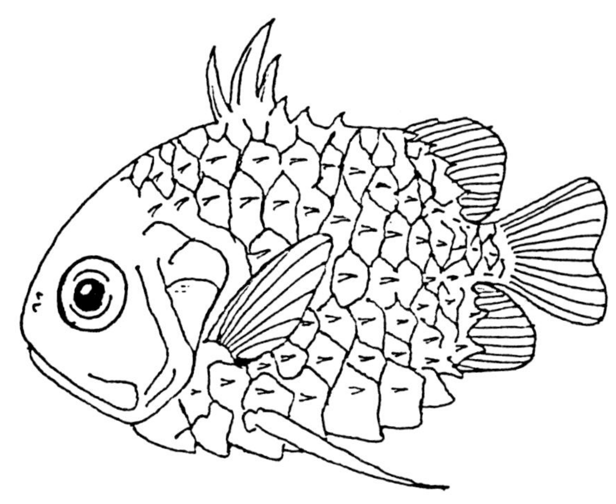

## 229) MONOCENTRIDIDAE

Pinecone fishes. Warmwater, very slow, peaceful, and shy. Rather sensitive to water quality. Possess bioluminescent organs; prefer dim tank. Feed mostly on small crustaceans, but often refuse to feed in captivity. Try live brine shrimp, live glass shrimp, bloodworms, glassworms.

## 230) TRACHICHTHYIDAE

Slimeheads. Similar to squirrelfishes; nocturnal predators. Generally peaceful but may eat small fish and crustaceans. Hardy. May be aggressive with conspecifics.

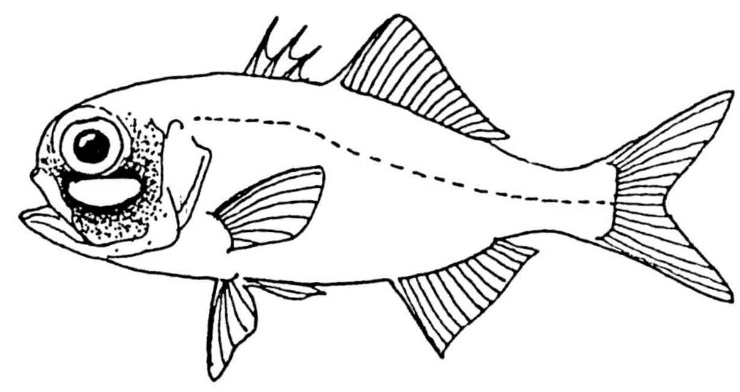

## 231) ANOMALOPIDAE

Flashlight fishes. Possess bioluminescent organs; dim tank. Prefer to be kept in groups. Not overly sensitive. Feed on small crustaceans, fishes. Peaceful. Feed guppies, brine shrimp, bloodworms, prepared foods.

## 234) BERYCIDAE

Alfonsinos. Squirrelfish-like. Peaceful but will eat small fishes and crustaceans. Foods: guppies, brine shrimp, prepared foods. Hardy.

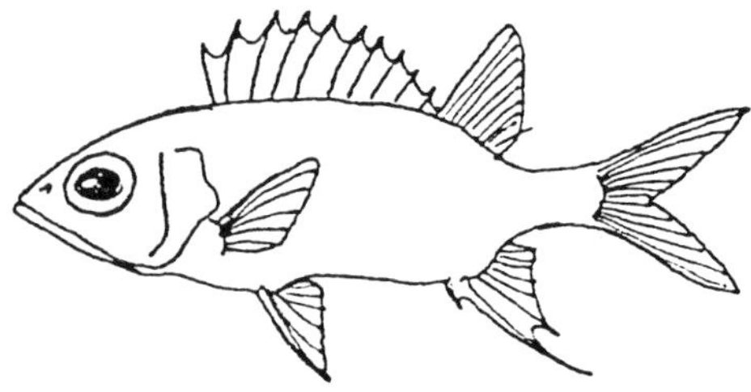

## 235) HOLOCENTRIDAE

Squirrelfishes. Generally peaceful, but will eat small fishes and crustaceans. Nocturnal; provide shaded hollows. Very hardy and tolerant of water quality variations. Most species school. Some become quite large. Foods: small feeder fishes, chopped clam, prawn, brine shrimp, bloodworms, all prepared foods.

## 236) POLYMIXIIDAE

Beardfishes. Generally similar to squirrelfishes in temperament and care.

## 244) MACRUROCYTTIDAE, 245) ZEIDAE, 248) CAPROIDAE

Dories, boarfishes, and allies. Rarely seen in aquaria, but are fairly hardy. Many grow quite large. Feed on fishes and crustaceans but are usually peaceful with tankmates too large to swallow.

## 250) AULORHYNCHIDAE, 251) GASTEROSTEIDAE

Tubesnouts and sticklebacks. Often coolwater fishes. Very easy to keep but are territorial and fight viciously with conspecifics if crowded. Peaceful with other species. Hardy. Very tolerant of salinity variations; many species can stand fresh water. Planted tank. Foods: Brine shrimp, bloodworms, glassworms, prepared foods.

## 253) PEGASIDAE

Sea moths. Slow-moving bottom fishes. Peaceful, not competitive; do not keep with swifter fishes. Not disease prone, but often difficult to feed. Prefer small living invertebrates; try brine shrimp, bloodworms.

## 254) AULOSTOMIDAE, 255) FISTULARIDAE

Trumpetfishes and cornetfishes. Generally warmwater. Fairly hardy. Ambush predators. Prefer planted tank for hiding. Eat small fishes, crustaceans; feed guppies, goldfish, prawn.

## 256) MACRORHAMPHOSIDAE, 257) CENTRISCIDAE

Snipefishes and shrimpfishes. Armored but slow and shy. Do not compete well with other species. Not prone to disease, but sometimes difficult to feed. Eat mostly small invertebrates; try live brine shrimp, bloodworms, glassworms.

## 258) SOLENOSTOMIDAE

Ghost pipefishes. Habits and care same as family Syngnathidae.

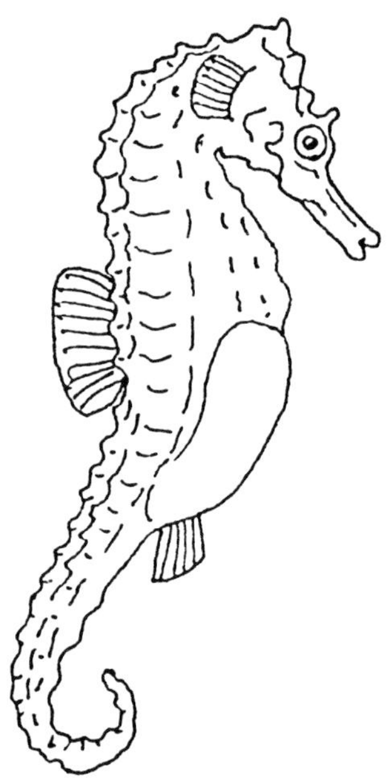

## 259) SYNGNATHIDAE

Seahorses and pipefishes. Very slow and shy—do not keep with competitive species. Have bred in aquaria. Branched corals, sea fans, plants needed for shelter or anchorage. Not disease prone but very sensitive to any decline in water quality. Sometimes difficult to feed, as tubular mouths accommodate only tiny foods, like brine shrimp, bloodworms, glassworms, livebearer fry.

## 260) DACTYLOPTERIDAE

Flying gurnards. Benthic; generally peaceful. Large pectoral fins easily damaged—transport with care. Eat mostly bottom invertebrates, small fishes. Hardy.

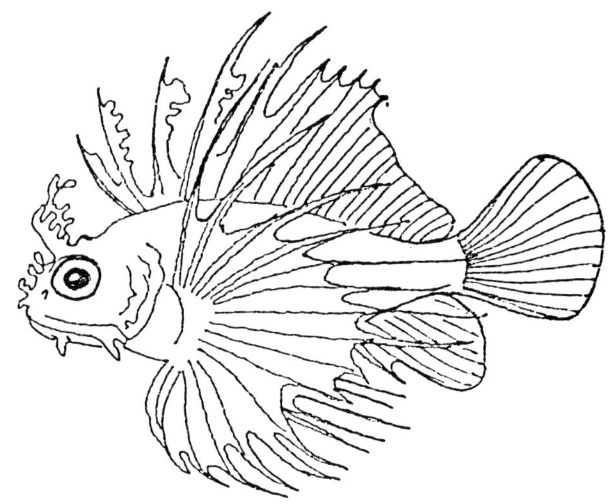

**262) SCORPAENIDAE**
Scorpionfishes. Venomous; handle with extreme care. Usually very hardy; not sensitive to water variations, not disease prone. Can swallow fishes nearly their own size, but peaceful with fishes too large to eat. Prefer coral-aquascaped tanks with ledges and caves. Many grow large. Foods: goldfish, prawn.

**263) SYNANCEIIDAE**
Stonefishes. Similar in care to scorpionfishes, but venom is deadly to humans. Best not kept at all!

**264) CARACANTHIDAE, 265) APLOACTINIDAE, 266) PATAECIDAE**
Velvetfishes. Benthic, Generally peaceful and small. Good for reef tanks, as plants and invertebrates supply good camouflage. Feed small feeder fishes, prawn. Generally hardy but uncommon in captivity.

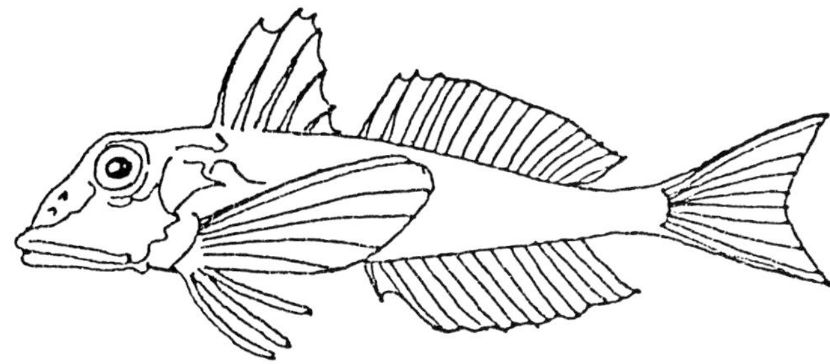

**268) TRIGLIDAE**
Searobins. Active benthic predators. Like a fairly open substrate area on which to "crawl" around. Spiny but nonvenomous. Will eat anything that can be swallowed. Sometimes aggressive with conspecifics. Very hardy.

**269) PLATYCEPHALIDAE**
Flatheads. Similar in care to searobins.

**271) ANOPLOPOMATIDAE,**
**272) HEXAGRAMMIDAE**
Sablefishes and greenlings. Large, midwater or benthic. Often coldwater species that require large tanks. Feed mostly on crustaceans, molluscs, fishes; good captive foods include chopped fish or clam, shrimp, crab, squid. Rocky tanks with plants.

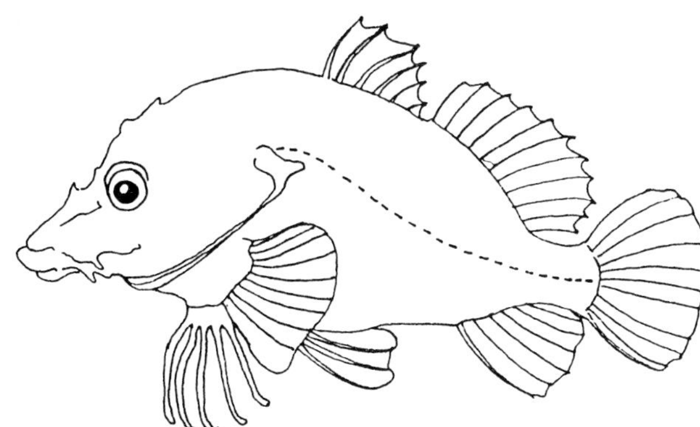

**276) COTTIDAE**
Sculpins. Generally small (but there are exceptions), very territorial with conspecifics but relatively peaceful with other species. Spiny; handle with care. Usually very tolerant of environmental variations, and many are very adaptable to salinity changes. Like plenty of hiding places and a cool, dim tank. Will eat small fishes and invertebrates; good foods include guppies or goldfish, brine shrimp, bloodworms, glassworms, chopped clam, prawn.

**280) AGONIDAE**
Poachers. Coldwater, benthic. Peaceful. Sensitive to variations in water quality. Generally eat small invertebrates: try brine shrimp, bloodworms, glassworms, small prepared foods.

**281) CYCLOPTERIDAE**
Lumpfishes and snailfishes. Benthic, coldwater. Need water that is heavily aerated. Some rather large. Very hardy; few disease problems. Peaceful with anything too large to swallow. Foods: chunks of clam, squid, shrimp, crab, also brine shrimp and bloodworms for smaller species.

**282) CENTROPOMIDAE**
Snooks. Large shallow water, estuarine predators; too big for most tanks. Require plenty of open swimming room. Eat mostly live fishes but may accept chunks of fish, mollusc, crustacean meats. Fairly tolerant of salinity variations. Fairly hardy. Related family (Ambassidae—often considered subfamily of Centropomidae) includes the small, planktivorous glassfishes, which are peaceful and harmless.

**283) PERCICHTHYIDAE**
Temperate basses. Very large, generally suitable only for large public aquaria. Very active fish eaters. Sensitive to water quality fluctuations.

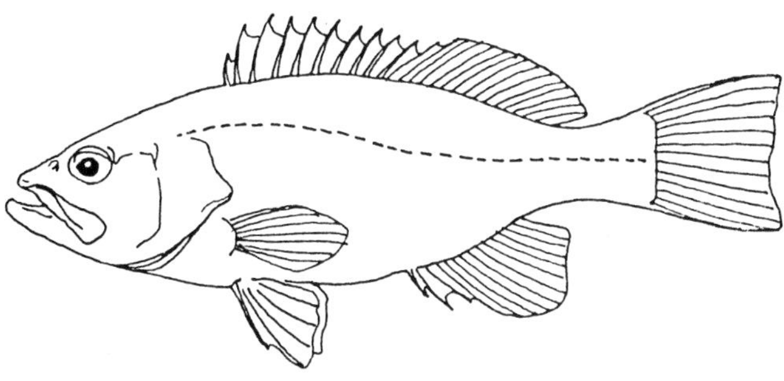

**284) SERRANIDAE**
Groupers and sea basses. Large-mouthed predators, often aggressive with conspecifics but peaceful with other fishes if they cannot be swallowed. Will eat crustaceans and some molluscs but leave most other invertebrates alone. Like to dig in bottom substrate. Coral aquascape with shadowy grottos preferred. Many very large when full-grown. Foods: feeder fishes, chopped clam, squid, shrimp, crab. Very hardy.

**285) GRAMMISTIDAE**
Soapfishes. Peaceful but will eat small fishes. Hardy, disease resistant. However, when stressed or attacked, may release a toxic mucus that can kill tankmates. Shy; coral caves preferred. Often tame easily. All foods accepted.

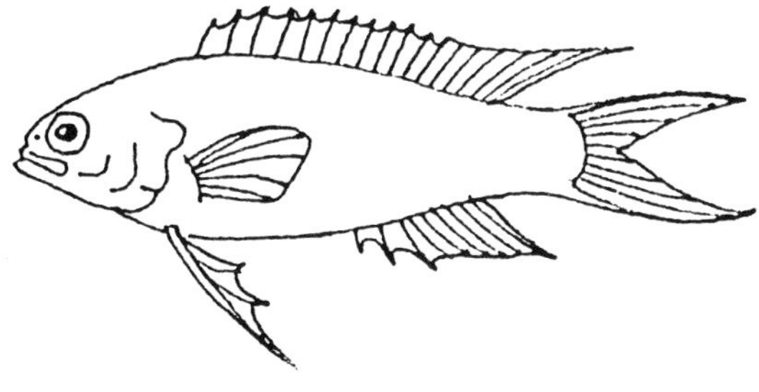

## 286) PSEUDOCHROMIDAE, 287) GRAMMIDAE

Dottybacks and basslets respectively. Mostly tropical. Small, peaceful grouper-like fishes, generally do not bother fish or invertebrate tankmates. May be aggressive with conspecifics, however. Prefer heavily aquascaped tanks with lots of hiding places. Good in reef aquaria. Most are hardy fishes. Small foods: brine shrimp, bloodworms, glassworms, small slivers of chopped clam or shrimp. Most will learn to take flake foods and other prepared diets.

## 288) PLESIOPIDAE

Devilfishes or roundheads. Shy at first, but very hardy. Like shadowy grottos. May be aggressive with conspecifics. Usually slow to feed at first—start with live guppies and wean over to brine shrimp, prawn, chopped clam, prepared foods. Very disease resistant.

## 289) ACANTHOCLINIDAE

Habits and care as for dottybacks (Pseudochromidae).

## 290) GLAUCOSOMATIDAE

Similar to serranids in appearance, habits, and care.

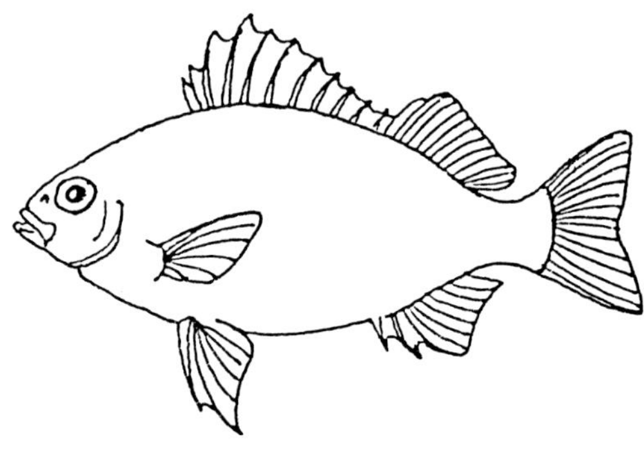

## 291) TERAPONIDAE, 293) KUHLIIDAE

Grunters and aholeholes. Schools preferred. Large, spacious aquaria. Very hardy; not prone to disease; very tolerant of water quality fluctuations. Wide salinity tolerance. Foods: brine shrimp, bloodworms, prawn, all prepared foods, feeder fishes.

## 296) PRIACANTHIDAE

Bigeyes. Nocturnal predators, peaceful and shy with all they cannot swallow. Prefer dark overhangs and grottos in their tanks. Hardy, but some too large for average home aquaria.

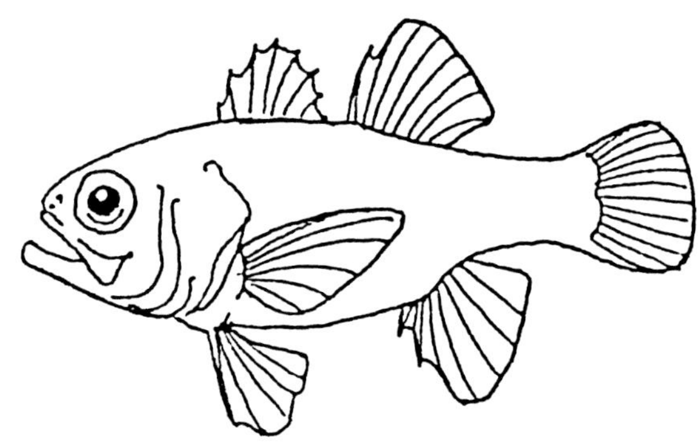

## 297) APOGONIDAE

Cardinalfishes. Most small and peaceful. Good for reef tanks. Somewhat light-shy. Many are schooling fishes. Have spawned in aquaria. Mostly tropical temperatures. Hardy and resistant to disease and water quality variations. Foods: brine shrimp, bloodworms, glassworms, chopped clam, shrimp. Large species will accept small guppies.

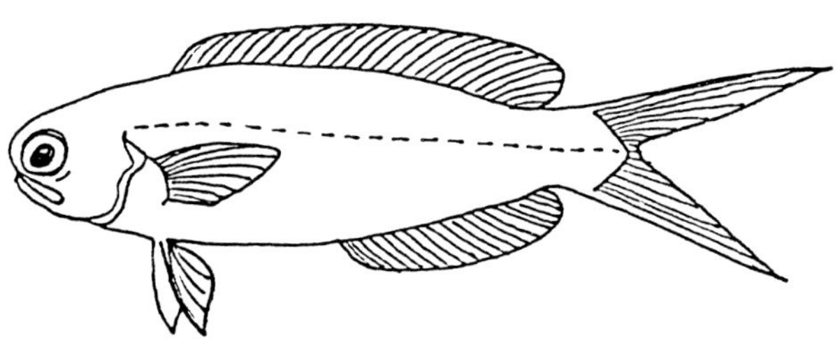

## 299) SILLAGINIDAE, 300) MALACANTHIDAE

Smelt-whitings and tilefishes. Most aquarium species are small, colorful, and shy. Feed mostly on small invertebrates. Good for reef aquaria. Often feed poorly, but good foods would include live brine shrimp, bloodworms, glassworms, chopped clam. They are very sensitive to any fluctuation in water quality. Prone to transport shock; acclimate with care.

## 301) LABRACOGLOSSIDAE, 302) LACTARIIDAE

False trevallies and relatives. Midwater schooling fishes; large spacious tank needed. Feed mostly on small fishes; incompatible with smaller fishes.

## 303) POMATOMIDAE

Bluefishes. Ravenous schooling predators; incompatible with all other species. Very large tanks needed. Fairly hardy. Wide salinity tolerance.

## 304) RACHYCENTRIDAE

Cobia. Active, very large. Feed on fishes and crustaceans, so incompatible with most other species.

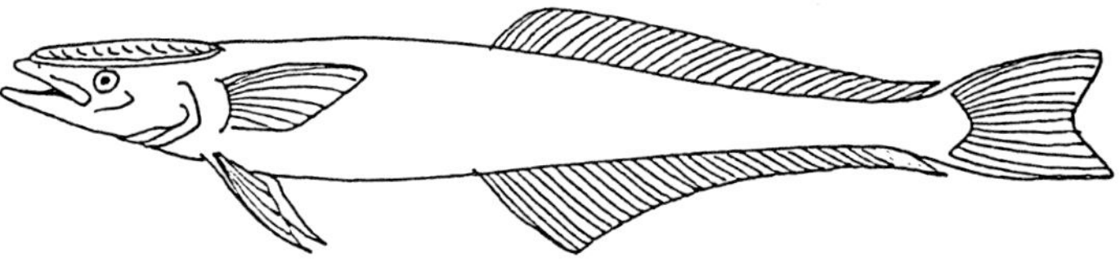

## 305) ECHENEIDIDAE

Remoras. Very hardy in aquaria. May attach to larger fishes with sucker disc (for transport only; no injury is involved). However, this does annoy some fishes. Best hosts are sharks. Live, frozen, prepared foods accepted with gusto.

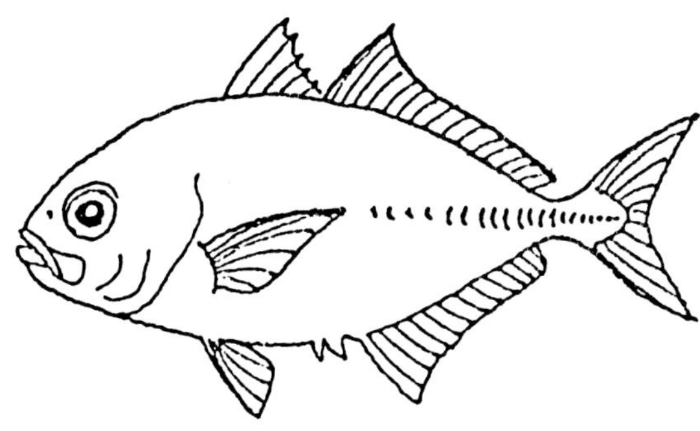

## 306) CARANGIDAE

Jacks. Fast-moving schooling fishes. Fairly hardy but require large tanks. Somewhat prone to transport shock. Many species have wide salinity tolerance. Will eat small fishes but are usually peaceful with those of like size. Foods: fish, chopped clam, prawn, squid.

## 307) NEMATISTIIDAE

Roosterfish. Care similar to Carangidae.

## 308) CORYPHAENIDAE

Dolphinfishes. Young specimens sometimes kept but are delicate; feed brine shrimp, bloodworms. Adults are swift, pelagic—not suitable for any but large public aquaria.

## 309) APOLECTIDAE

Habits and care similar to Carangidae.

## 310) MENIDAE, 311) LEIOGNATHIDAE, 312) BRAMIDAE

Moonfish, slipmouths, pomfrets, respectively. Mostly oceanic schooling fishes. Peaceful but active; spacious tanks necessary. Sensitive to fluctuations in water quality. Foods: small fishes, brine shrimp, bloodworms, squid, chopped clam.

## 314) ARRIPIDAE

Australian salmon. Midwater schoolers feeding on small fishes. Cool water, large tanks. Hardy but seldom seen.

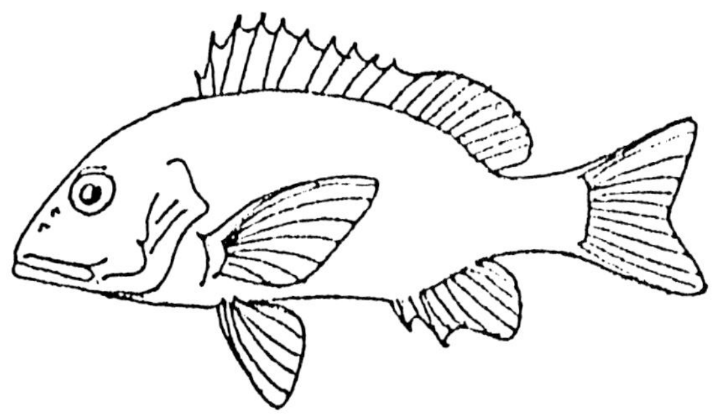

## 315) EMMELICHTHYIDAE, 316) LUTJANIDAE, 317) CAESIONIDAE

Rovers, snappers, fusiliers, respectively. Bottom to midwater schooling fishes. Very hardy, not prone to disease. Not sensitive to water quality fluctuations, and many species are euryhaline. Peaceful with fishes too large to swallow. Many species grow large and need big tanks. Coral/rock aquascape. All foods accepted.

## 318) LOBOTIDAE

Tripletails. Very hardy, euryhaline. Young specimens need planted tanks for camouflage. Peaceful with large fishes, will eat small ones. Most grow large but are fairly sedentary; provide caves for shelter.

## 319) GERREIDAE

Mojarras. Small, active schooling fishes. Peaceful, relatively hardy, euryhaline. Need plenty of open swimming room. Feed on planktonic crustaceans—live brine shrimp is a good substitute.

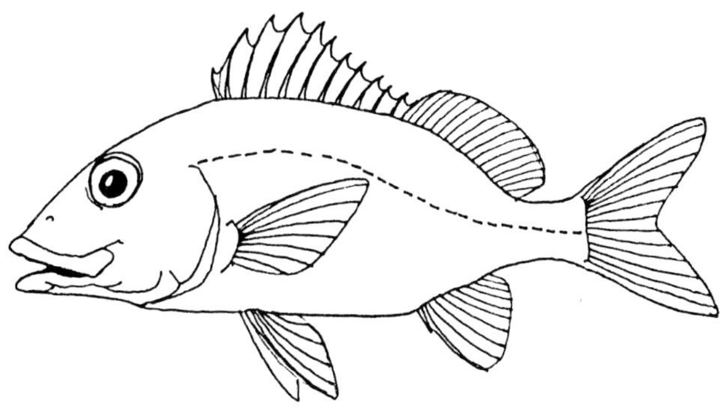

## 320) HAEMULIDAE, 321) INERMIIDAE, 322) SPARIDAE

Grunts, bonnetmouths, porgies, respectively. Generally, snapper-like fishes. Midwater- to bottom-schoolers. Very hardy; disease resistant; tolerant of variations in water quality. Coral/rock/plant aquascapes. Often aggressive. All foods taken, but many species also graze on algae.

## 324) LETHRINIDAE, 325) NEMIPTERIDAE

Emperors and threadfin breams. Similar in appearance, behavior, and requirements to snappers.

## 326) SCIAENIDAE

Drums. Bottom dwellers feeding on benthic invertebrates. Fairly hardy, but tropical species are prone to *Cryptocaryon* infection. Most species (except the very largest) are peaceful and shy. Coral/rock aquascape. Prefer groups of same species. Foods: brine shrimp, bloodworms, glassworms, chopped clam, frozen prepared foods.

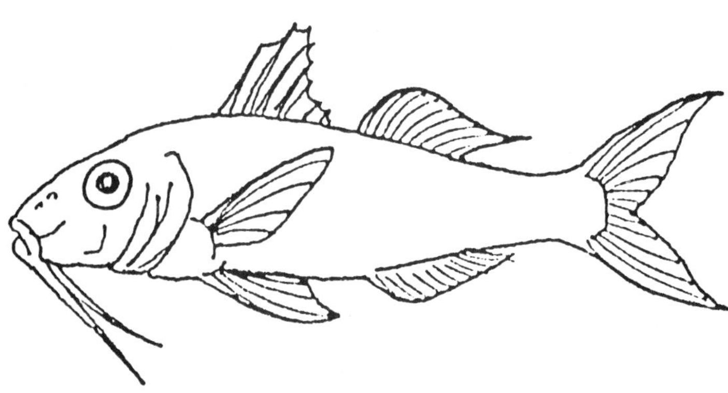

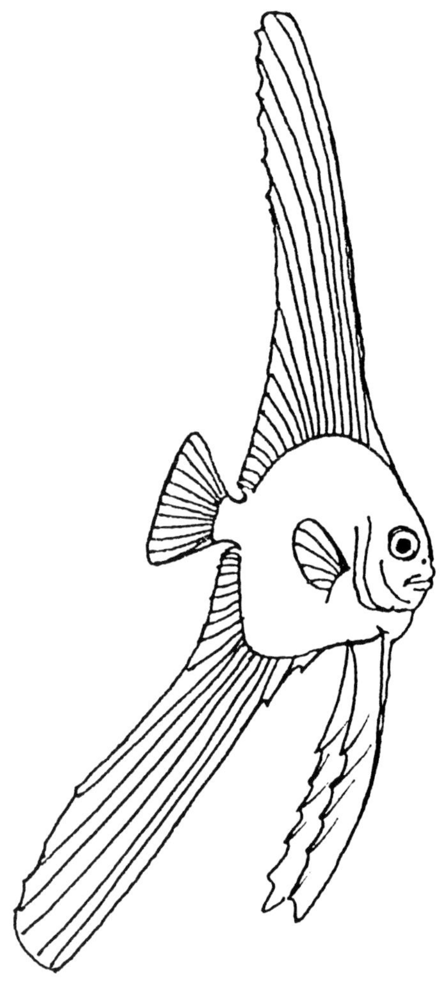

## 327) MULLIDAE

Goatfishes. Use barbels to find benthic invertebrates. Excellent scavengers. Hardy when acclimated, but very prone to transport shock. Peaceful. Soft substrate preferable. Foods: chopped clam, prawn, crab, brine shrimp, bloodworms, all prepared foods.

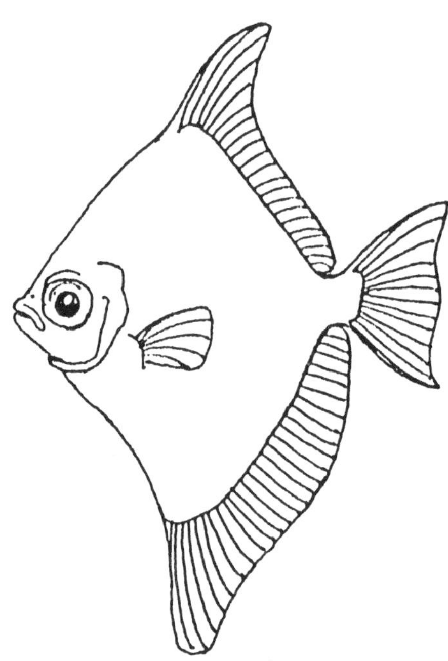

## 335) EPHIPPIDIDAE

Spadefishes and batfishes. Very hardy (with the exception of *Platax pinnatus*) but grow quite large. Very peaceful. Young prefer plant thickets for camouflage. Need very deep tanks. Coral/rock aquascape for mature specimens. All foods taken vigorously.

## 328) MONODACTYLIDAE

Monos. Brackish to marine. Planted aquaria, roots and rocks as decorations. Prefer groups of same species, but tend to be scrappy. Generally peaceful with other species. Not overly sensitive to water quality, but prone to ich. Foods: bloodworms, brine shrimp, glassworms, prepared foods.

## 329) PEMPHERIDIDAE

Sweepers. Small fishes, school in massive shoals in open water adjoining reefs; large tanks necessary. Very delicate and sensitive; not often seen in the hobby. Feed on planktonic invertebrates—try brine shrimp and bloodworms.

## 334) KYPHOSIDAE

Sea chubs. Open-water schoolers; large tanks. Often reach a large size. Very hardy. Peaceful but will eat small fishes. Algae necessary in diet. Other foods include clam, squid, crab, prawn.

## 336) SCATOPHAGIDAE

Scats. Brackish to marine; very hardy but prone to lymphocystis. Not overly aggressive but sometimes nip at fins. Prefer schools but are often scrappy with conspecifics. Algae necessary in diet. Other foods: brine shrimp, bloodworms, prepared foods.

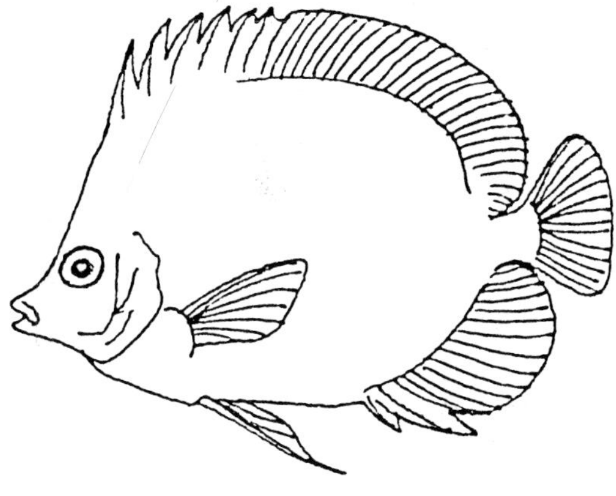

## 338) CHAETODONTIDAE

Butterflyfishes. Very beautiful reef fishes. Of variable hardiness. Some feed only on live corals and are almost impossible to keep alive in captivity. Most are sensitive to any change in water quality, and some are fairly disease-prone. Butterflyfishes are very peaceful with other species but may be aggressive with conspecifics, except for mated pairs collected together. Foods: brine shrimp, bloodworms, glassworms, chopped clam, frozen prepared foods.

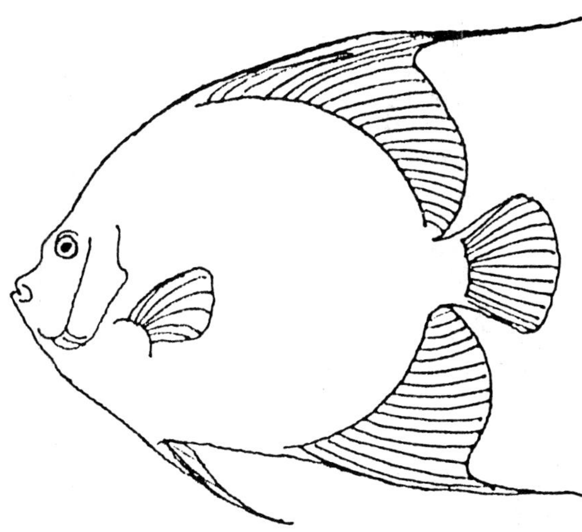

## 339) POMACANTHIDAE

Angelfishes. Hardy with relatively few exceptions. Not sensitive to most variations in water quality, but some suffer in the presence of high nitrates. Most are fairly disease-resistant but some species are prone to lymphocystis. Generally peaceful, but large specimens are often dominant fishes. Often aggressive with conspecifics. Coral/rock aquascape with lots of nooks will partition territories. Algae very necessary in diet. Other foods: brine shrimp, bloodworms, glassworms, chopped clam, prawn, boiled spinach.

## 340) ENOPLOSIDAE

Oldwife. Hardy, accepts all foods.

## 343) OPLEGNATHIDAE

Knifejaws. Peaceful but may eat small fishes. Will consume most crustaceans and many molluscs. Coral/rock aquascape. Foods: shrimp, crab, chopped clam.

## 345) EMBIOTOCIDAE

Surfperches. Most need cool aquaria, but are otherwise hardy. Some reach a large size. Livebearers. Peaceful but will eat small fishes. Algae necessary in diet. Rock/plant aquascape.

## 346) POMACENTRIDAE

Damselfishes (including anemonefishes). Very hardy and resistant to disease. Very scrappy with conspecifics, and very territorial in relations with other species. Lots of coral decorations will help to break up territories. Among the easiest of marine fishes to breed; they are parental-guarding substrate spawners. Anything edible will be accepted. Algae is also welcome.

## 348) CIRRHITIDAE

Hawkfishes. Benthic predators. Like high coral heads as "perches" and vantage points. Some species grow rather large. Peaceful, extremely hardy. Coral/rock aquascape. Foods: guppies, bloodworms, brine shrimp, chopped clam, prepared foods.

## 350) APLODACTYLIDAE, 351) CHILODACTYLIDAE, 352) LATRIDIDAE

Morwongs and relatives. Generally similar to hawkfishes in habits and care, but most are somewhat larger.

## 353) OWSTONIIDAE, 354) CEPOLIDAE

Owstoniids and bandfishes. Somewhat delicate, not generally available. Feed on small invertebrates.

## 355) MUGILIDAE

Mullets. Fast-swimming schoolers. Euryhaline. Excellent jumpers—tank must be well-covered. Feed on small invertebrates in substrate, but will accept most aquarium foods. Sensitive to fungal infections. Prone to transport shock; acclimate carefully. Large spacious tanks necessary.

## 356) SPHYRAENIDAE

Barracudas. Large midwater predators. Some are schooling fishes. Very large tanks needed. Toothy; handle with care. Usually accept only live fishes, but acclimated specimens will sometimes accept chunks of fish. Hardy and long-lived, but aggressive and difficult to house with other fishes.

## 357) POLYNEMIDAE

Threadfins. Benthic fishes. Peaceful, active. Feed on small fishes and crustaceans.

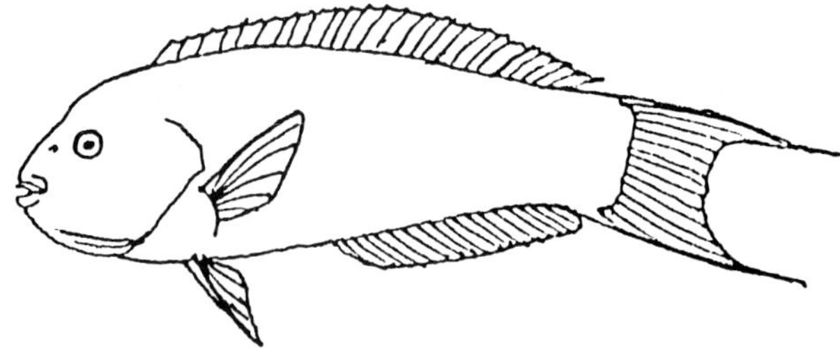

## 358) LABRIDAE

Wrasses. Most very hardy and peaceful. Most are at least territorial with conspecifics—provide plenty of room. Most invertebrates will not be molested except for small crustaceans. Many burrow in sand; soft substrate needed. Coral aquascape. With few exceptions, all foods will be taken. Good for reef aquaria.

## 359) ODACIDAE

Weed whitings. Wrasselike, care similar. Cool water and plant/rock aquascape. Seldom seen.

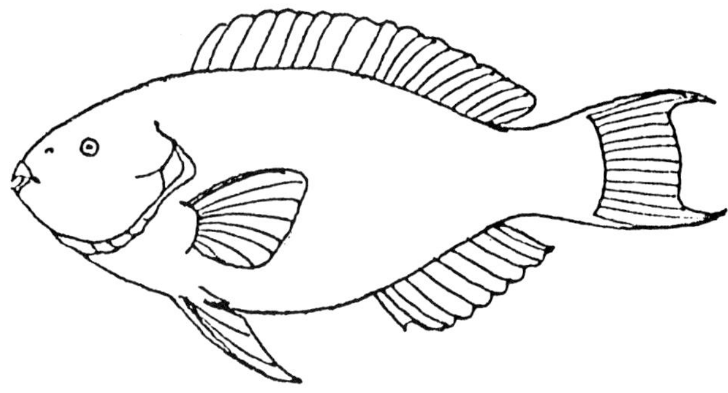

## 360) SCARIDAE

Parrotfishes. Moderately hardy, but some species are delicate. Often difficult to feed. Coral heads heavily encrusted with algae necessary in diet. Other foods: brine shrimp, chopped clam, bloodworms. Peaceful with other fishes but sometimes aggressive with conspecifics. Some species very large and need big tanks.

## 361) BATHYMASTERIDAE, 362) ZOARCIDAE, 363) STICHAEIDAE, 365) PHOLIDIDAE, 366) ANARHICHADIDAE

Eelpouts, wolffishes, and relatives. Bottom dwellers, some very large. Cool to cold water. Most eat benthic invertebrates, but fishes that can be caught will also be eaten. Rock aquascape with caves preferred. Very hardy. Foods: whole or chopped fish, clam, squid, also shrimp and crab.

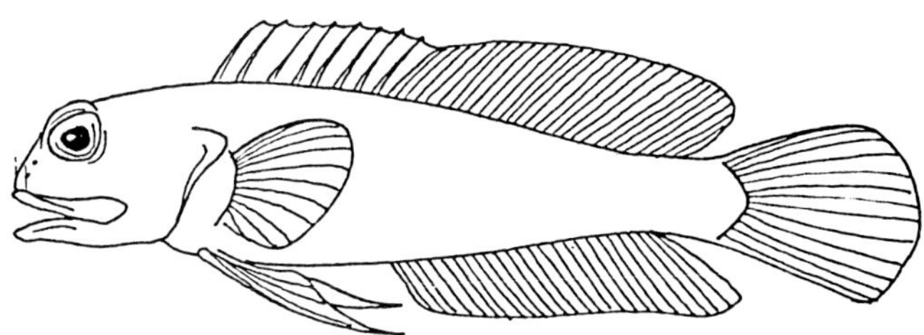

## 375) OPISTOGNATHIDAE

Jawfishes. Secretive. Excavate burrows in sand and gravel bottoms. Very territorial with conspecifics, but conflicts are largely bluff. Peaceful with other species. Good with most invertebrates; excellent in reef aquaria. Hardy. Foods: brine shrimp, bloodworms, glassworms, prepared foods.

## 376) CONGROGADIDAE

Eelblennies. Very hardy. Some are euryhaline. Aggressive; will eat many tankmates (both fish and invertebrate). Bred in captivity. Foods: goldfish, chopped clam, prawn. Rocks and caves needed for shelter.

## 379) NOTOGRAPTIDAE

Similar to eelblennies in habits and care.

## 380) PHOLIDICHTHYIDAE

Convict blenny. Hardy. Prefers groups of conspecifics. Coral/rock aquascape with shady hollows. Peaceful. All foods accepted.

## 381) TRICHODONTIDAE

Sandfishes. Ambush predators. Need soft sand for burying. Incompatible with fishes small enough to swallow. Somewhat delicate and disease prone. Food: Small feeder fishes.

## 382) TRACHINIDAE

Weeverfishes. Venomous, some lethally so. Ambush predators. Seldom kept.

## 383) URANOSCOPIDAE

Stargazers. Capable of delivering startling but sublethal electrical shock. Ambush predators; soft sand needed for burrowing. Will eat any fishes and crustaceans small enough to swallow. Some quite large and need big tanks. Foods: small live fishes as well as shrimp and crab meat. Very hardy.

## 384) TRICHONOTIDAE, 385) CREEDIIDAE, 386) LEPTOSCOPIDAE, 388) MUGILOIDIDAE

Sanddivers, sandperches, and relatives. Similar to sandfishes and lizardfishes in habits and care.

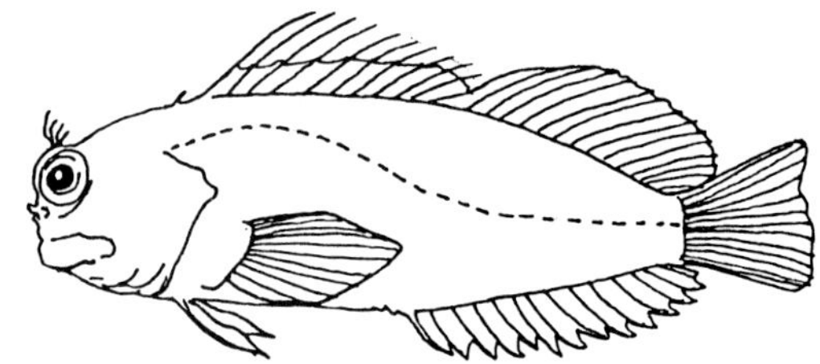

## 390) TRIPTERYGIIDAE, 391) DACTYLOSCOPIDAE, 392) LABRISOMIDAE, 393) CLINIDAE, 394) CHAENOPSIDAE, 395) BLENNIIDAE

Blennies and their relatives. Most are small, benthic fishes. Often very territorial with both conspecifics and other species; provide plenty of room. Extremely hardy, disease resistant, and tolerant of variations in water quality. Provide rocky caves and plenty of plants. Most eat small invertebrates, and algae is an important dietary item to many species. Other foods: brine shrimp, bloodworms, glassworms, chopped clam, most prepared foods including flake food.

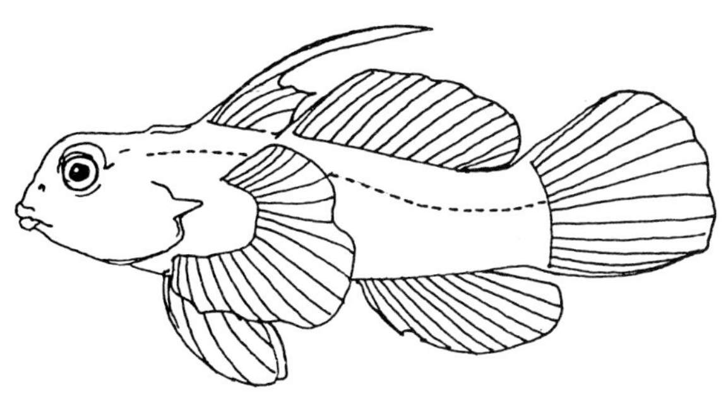

## 399) CALLIONYMIDAE

Dragonets. Benthic micropredators. Some hardy, others very delicate. Excellent for reef tanks. Very peaceful with other fishes, but may fight among themselves. Very slow-moving, deliberate feeders that cannot compete with voracious feeders like damselfishes. Foods: brine shrimp, bloodworms, glassworms.

## 402) ELEOTRIDIDAE

Sleeper gobies. Ambush predators. Euryhaline. Lethargic; need shadowy holes for shelter. Very hardy and disease resistant. Many grow large; big tanks needed. Rocks, plants, driftwood. Foods: small fishes, chunks of beef heart, clam, squid, shrimp.

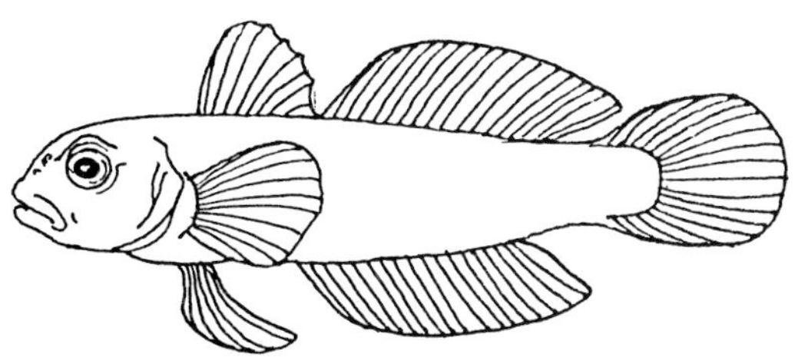

## 403) GOBIIDAE

Gobies. Benthic micropredators. Most small and peaceful, but territorial with their own species. Most fairly hardy. Some commonly bred in captivity (especially *Gobiosoma* sp.). Coral aquascape including empty mollusc shells. Excellent in reef tanks. Foods: brine shrimp, bloodworms, glassworms, prepared foods.

## 404) GOBIOIDIDAE, 405) TRYPAUCHENIDAE, 407) MICRODESMIDAE

Eel-like gobies. Some are burrowers; soft substrate needed. Feed on small benthic invertebrates. Delicate and seldom seen.

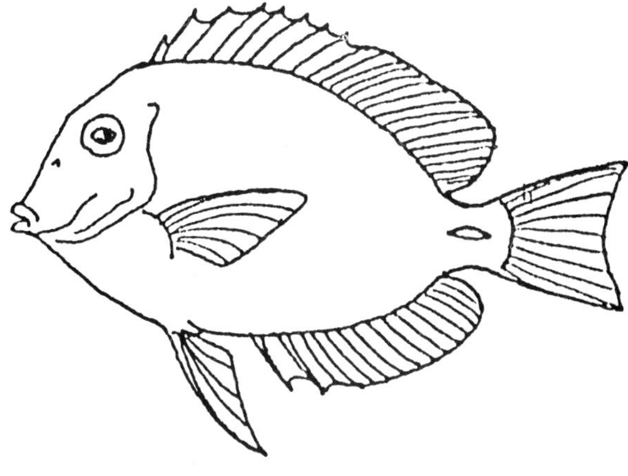

## 409) ACANTHURIDAE

Surgeonfishes. Algal grazers. Peaceful with other species; may be aggressive with conspecifics. Generally hardy but somewhat prone to *Oodinium* and *Cryptocaryon*. Coral aquascape. Foods: boiled spinach and vegetable-based prepared foods, brine shrimp, bloodworms, chopped clam.

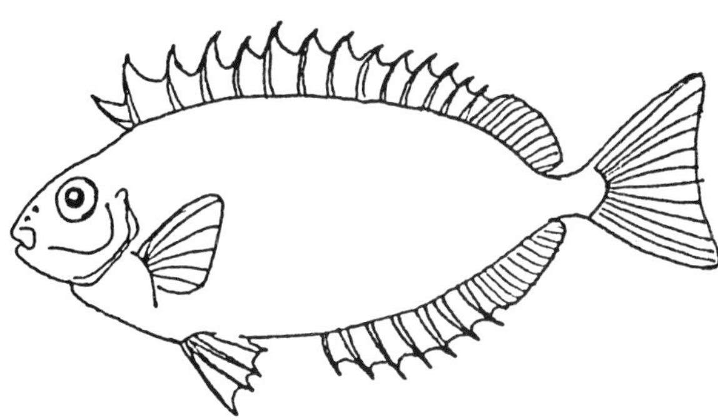

## 410) SIGANIDAE

Rabbitfishes. Dorsal spines venomous; handle with care. Habits and care as for Acanthuridae.

## 412) GEMPYLIDAE, 413) TRICHIURIDAE

Snake mackerels and cutlassfishes. Elongate, pelagic, often deepwater. Piscivorous. Delicate; never kept.

## 414) SCOMBRIDAE

Tunas and mackerels. Extremely active pelagic schooling fishes. Too large except for public aquaria. Delicate and prone to shock. Many very large. Food almost exclusively small fishes.

## 415) XIPHIIDAE, 417) ISTIOPHORIDAE

Swordfishes. Pelagic piscivores. Do not adapt well to captivity—bills easily damaged.

## 419) CENTROLOPHIDAE, 420) NOMEIDAE

Medusafishes and driftfishes. Often commensal with jellyfishes or other pelagic cnidarians. Usually small and peaceful, but other fishes will be in danger from cnidarian host. Somewhat delicate and sensitive to water quality variations. Feed on planktonic invertebrates; good substitutes are brine shrimp and bloodworms.

## 423) STROMATEIDAE

Butterfishes. Open-water schooling fishes. Delicate; prone to transport injury and shock. Foods: brine shrimp, bloodworms.

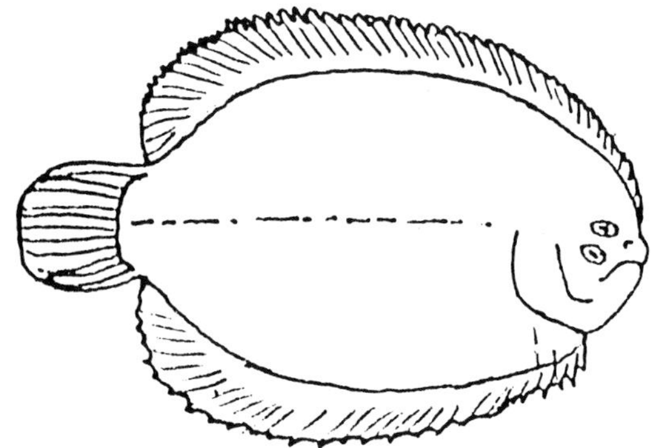

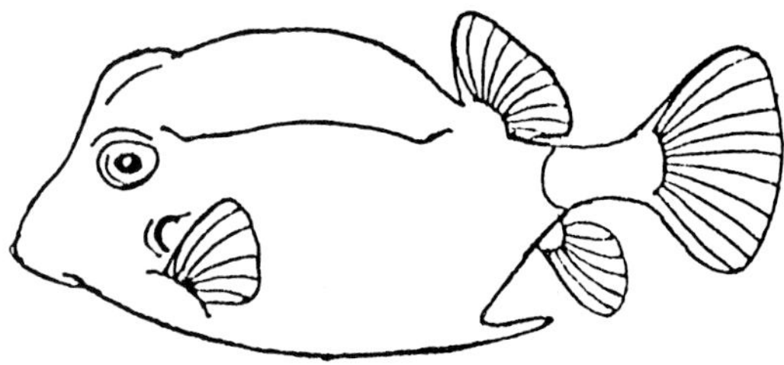

## 432) PSETTODIDAE, 434) BOTHIDAE, 435) PLEURONECTIDAE, 436) CYNOGLOSSIDAE, 437) SOLEIDAE

Flatfishes. Benthic; need soft sand for burying. Some very large. Often euryhaline. Tropical as well as coldwater species. Generally peaceful with other fishes but will eat most benthic invertebrates. Fairly hardy. Foods: Chopped fish, shrimp, crab, squid.

## 438) TRIACANTHODIDAE, 439) TRIACANTHIDAE

Spikefishes and triplespines. Relatively peaceful. Feed on small benthic invertebrates. Seldom kept.

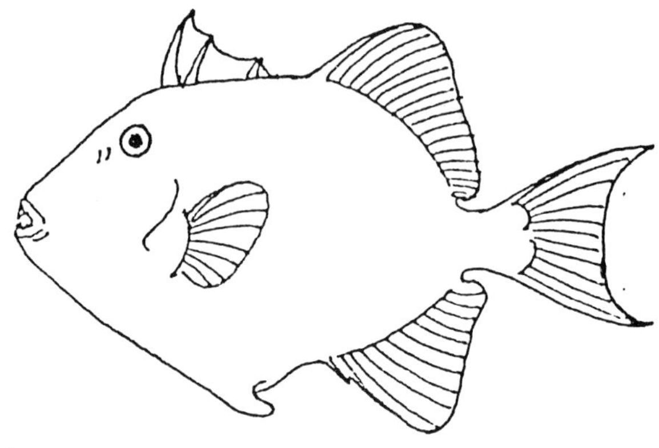

## 440) BALISTIDAE

Triggerfishes and filefishes. Triggers are aggressive, sometimes downright vicious. Files are a bit more peaceful but still may be nippy. Teeth and jaws powerful; large specimens may bite. Given to rearranging aquascape. Large triggers may attack heaters, filters, etc. Incompatible with most other species, and usually aggressive with conspecifics. Will eat anything remotely edible and may sample things that are not!

## 441) OSTRACIONIDAE

Boxfishes. Very peaceful and shy. Slow moving; do not compete well with more active fishes. Some species will exude toxins when stressed, so acclimate with care. Fairly hardy but may be slow to begin feeding. Foods: brine shrimp, bloodworms, chopped clam.

## 442) TRIODONTIDAE

Three-toothed puffer. Habits and care as for Tetraodontidae.

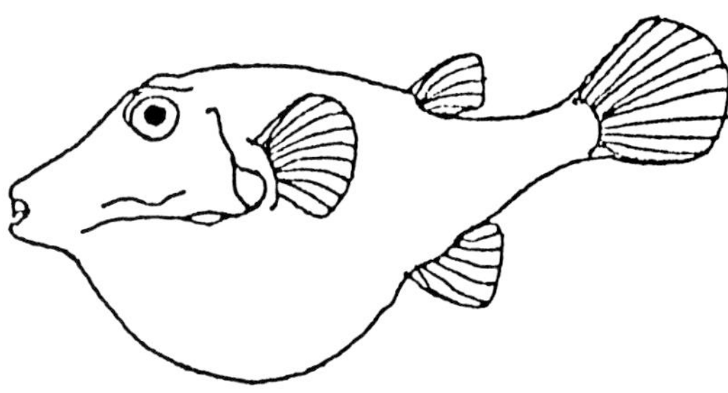

## 443) TETRAODONTIDAE

Puffers. Very hardy. May be nippy. May inflate when disturbed. If inflated with air, deflation often troublesome. All foods taken.

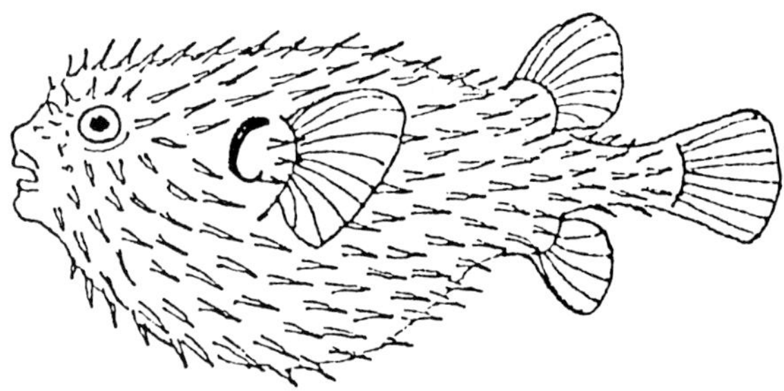

## 444) DIODONTIDAE

Porcupinefishes. Habits and care as for Tetraodontidae.

## 445) MOLIDAE

Molas. Huge, never kept. Feed mostly on jellyfishes.

# CAPTIONS

The captions, where possible, identify the fishes, the family they belong to, their range, feeding habits, aquarium lighting, temperament, aquarium decor, and swimming habits, as well as the specific gravity of the water that best suits them, optimum temperature, greatest size, and the minimum capacity of the aquarium that best suits them.

## SYMBOLS:

**Feeding:**

represents prepared foods, usually frozen. Very few marine fishes will do well on flake food although some types are quite nutritious.

represents invertebrates. Although the symbol is obviously a worm, most marine fishes prefer crustaceans and/or molluscs. Many fishes have specific diets and must be supplied certain invertebrates or they will decline (ex. some butterflyfishes need live coral polyps). Please refer to the family write-ups in this book as well as other TFH marine fish books for more detailed information.

represents live fishes.

represents plant matter. This is usually in the form of algae and can be provided rather easily by growing your own in the tank or buying prepared algal foods from your dealer.

**Light:** These symbols represent the amount of light recommended for the tank. Remember, however, that some fishes are nocturnal and will be seen only when light levels are low. Others are at their best during the days, showing their colors off in direct sunlight.

Bright with occasional sunlight

Bright, no sunlight

As dark as possible as long as fishes are visible

**Aggressiveness/Compatibility:** Here again there is commonly no cut-and-dried distinction. A fish may be quite peaceful when small, but its appetite grows with its size and it may soon be foraging on the other tankmates. Others may be aggressive only during spawning seasons.

♥ Peaceful community fish

Not recommended for beginners

**Tank Decoration:**

represents a tank that should be supplied with plant life (normally algae). In some instances algae must be supplied because the inhabitants of the tank feed on it; in others it is decorative.

represents coral for the tropical tanks and rocks for the more temperate aquaria.

represents a balance between the two where corals (or rocks) are used along with plants for decoration. The new reef tanks would come under this designation.

represents a sand or gravel bottom. Sand is required by some fishes (burrowers, etc.), while marine aquarists use dolomite or similar material in order to maintain the proper pH balance.

**Tank Level:** Fish Locality: Many species are tied to one area of the tank. There are bottom species (like flatfishes) and surface fishes (like needlefishes) and some that will stay just about in the middle range all the time. Most species of marine fishes are wanderers and will swim pretty much around the tank investigating every corner.

Bottom swimmer

Swims in middle of water

No special swimming level

Top swimmer

**°C:** the temperature in degrees centigrade at which the species is most comfortable. There is of course a range at which the fish will live that extends above and below this figure.

**sg:** specific gravity. Again, this is an optimum figure. Specific gravity can be easily obtained by use of a simple hydrometer.

**cm:** the length of a fish (standard length). This is the maximum length a fish is said to attain. Most specimens seen are normally much smaller, and aquarium specimens are generally smaller yet. Many species grow so large only juveniles are kept by aquarists. An inch equals 2.54 cm.

**L:** the smallest possible size of the tank needed for an average adult of that particular species, given in liters. A gallon is equal to about 3.8 liters.

**Range Number:**

Range numbers give approximate ranges of the species. Ex. Indo-Pacific = 6-9; Indo-West Pacific = 7-9.

**Family Number:**

Family numbers follow the species name. The list of families is given on pp. 24 and 25.

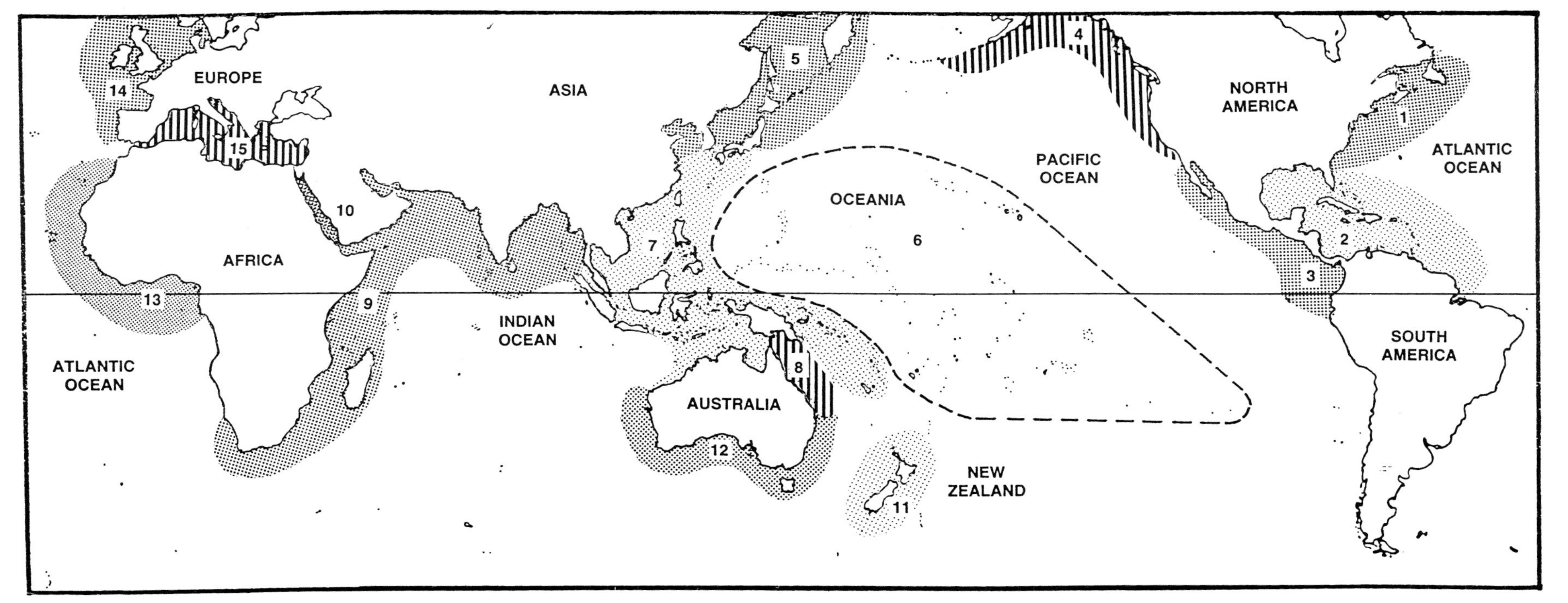


Geographic regions are keyed to numbers for easy species caption reference. These regions are highly arbitrary and many species do not confine themselves to these limits. Also species may inhabit only a small portion of the delimited area. But this does give a reasonable approximation of the fishes' range which should help aquarists determine the environment needed for proper maintenance of the fishes.

1. Temperate Western Atlantic.
2. Tropical Western Atlantic.
3. Tropical Eastern Pacific.
4. Temperate Eastern Pacific.
5. Temperate Western Pacific.
6. Oceania.
7. Tropical Western Pacific.
8. Great Barrier Reef.
9. Northern and Western Indian Ocean.
10. Red Sea.
11. New Zealand.
12. Temperate Australia.
13. Tropical Eastern Atlantic.
14. Temperate Eastern Atlantic.
15. Mediterranean Sea.

# Systematic List of the Families of Fishes of the World (after Nelson, 1984)

**Myxiniformes**
1 Myxinidae
**Petromyzontiformes**
2 Petromyzontidae
**Chimaeriformes**
3 Callorhynchidae
4 Chimaeridae
5 Rhinochimaeridae
**Hexanchiformes**
6 Chlamydoselachidae
7 Hexanchidae
**Heterodontiformes**
8 Heterodontidae
**Lamniformes**
9 Rhincodontidae
10 Orectolobidae
11 Odontaspididae
12 Lamnidae
13 Scyliorhinidae
14 Carcharhinidae
15 Sphyrnidae
**Squaliformes**
16 Squalidae
17 Pristiophoridae
18 Squatinidae
**Rajiformes**
19 Pristidae
20 Torpedinidae
21 Rhinobatidae
22 Rajidae
23 Dasyatidae
24 Potamotrygonidae
25 Hexatrygonidae
26 Myliobatididae
27 Mobulidae
**Ceratodontiformes**
28 Ceratodontidae
**Lepidosireniformes**
29 Lepidosirenidae
30 Protopteridae
**Coelacanthiformes**
31 Latimeriidae
**Polypteriformes**
32 Polypteridae
**Acipenseriformes**
33 Acipenseridae
34 Polyodontidae
**Lepisosteiformes**
35 Lepisosteidae
**Amiiformes**
36 Amiidae
**Osteoglossiformes**
37 Osteoglossidae
38 Pantodontidae
39 Hiodontidae
40 Notopteridae
41 Mormyridae
42 Gymnarchidae
**Elopiformes**
43 Elopidae
44 Megalopidae
45 Albulidae
46 Halosauridae
47 Notacanthidae
48 Lipogenyidae
**Anguilliformes**
49 Anguillidae
50 Heterenchelyidae
51 Moringuidae
52 Xenocongridae
53 Myrocongridae
54 Muraenidae
55 Nemichthyidae
56 Cyematidae
57 Synaphobranchidae
58 Ophichthidae
59 Nettastomatidae
60 Colocongridae
61 Macrocephenchelyidae
62 Congridae
63 Derichthyidae
64 Serrivomeridae
65 Saccopharyngidae
66 Eurypharyngidae
67 Monognathidae
**Clupeiformes**
68 Denticipitidae
69 Clupeidae
70 Engraulididae
71 Chirocentridae
**Gonorynchiformes**
72 Chanidae
73 Gonorynchidae
74 Kneriidae
75 Phractolaemidae
**Cypriniformes**
76 Cyprinidae
77 Psilorhynchidae
78 Homalopteridae
79 Cobitididae
80 Gyrinocheilidae
81 Catostomidae
**Characiformes**
82 Citharinidae
83 Hemiodontidae
84 Curimatidae
85 Anostomidae
86 Erythrinidae
87 Lebiasinidae
88 Gasteropelecidae
89 Ctenoluciidae
90 Hepsetidae
91 Characidae
**Siluriformes**
92Diplomystidae
93 Ictaluridae
94 Bagridae
95 Cranoglanididae
96 Siluridae
97 Schilbidae
98 Pangasiidae
99 Amblycipitidae
100 Amphiliidae
101 Akysidae
102 Sisoridae
103 Clariidae
104 Heteropneustidae
105 Chacidae
106 Olyridae
107 Malapteruridae
108 Ariidae
109 Plotosidae
110 Mochokidae
111 Doradidae
112 Auchenipteridae
113 Pimelodidae
114 Ageneiosidae
115 Helogenidae
116 Cetopsidae
117 Hypophthalmidae
118 Aspredinidae
119 Trichomycteridae
120 Callichthyidae
121 Loricariidae
122 Astroblepidae
**Gymnotiformes**
123 Sternopygidae
124 Rhamphichthyidae
125 Hypopomidae
126 Apteronotidae
127 Gymnotidae
128 Electrophoridae
**Salmoniformes**
129 Esocidae
130 Umbridae
131 Argentinidae
132 Bathylagidae
133 Opisthoproctidae
134 Alepocephalidae
135 Searsiidae
136 Lepidogalaxiidae
137 Osmeridae
138 Plecoglossidae
139 Salangidae
140 Sundasalangidae
141 Retropinnidae
142 Galaxiidae
143 Salmonidae
**Stomiiformes**
144 Gonostomatidae
145 Sternoptychidae
146 Photichthyidae
147 Chauliodontidae
148 Stomiidae
149 Astronesthidae
150 Melanostomiidae
151 Malacosteidae
152 Idiacanthidae
**Aulopiformes**
153 Aulopididae
154 Chlorophthalmidae
155 Scopelarchidae
156 Notosudidae
157 Synodontidae
158 Giganturidae
159 Paralepididae
160 Anotopteridae
161 Evermannellidae
162 Omosudidae
163 Alepisauridae
164 Pseudotrichonotidae
**Myctophiformes**
165 Neoscopelidae
166 Myctophidae
**Percopsiformes**
167 Percopsidae
168 Aphredoderidae
169 Amblyopsidae
**Gadiformes**
170 Muraenolepididae
171 Moridae
172 Melanonidae
173 Bregmacerotidae
174 Gadidae
175 Merlucciidae
176 Macrouridae
**Ophidiiformes**
177 Ophidiidae
178 Carapidae
179 Bythitidae
180 Aphyonidae
**Batrachoidiformes**
181 Batrachoididae
182 Lophiidae
183 Antennariidae
184 Brachionichthyidae
185 Chaunacidae
186 Ogcocephalidae
187 Caulophrynidae
188 Ceratiidae
189 Gigantactinidae
190 Neoceratiidae
191 Linophrynidae
192 Oneirodidae

193 Thaumatichthyidae
194 Centrophrynidae
195 Diceratiidae
196 Himantolophidae
197 Melanocetidae

**Gobiesociformes**
198 Gobiesocidae
199 Alabetidae

**Cyprinodontiformes**
200 Exocoetidae
201 Hemiramphidae
202 Belonidae
203 Scomberesocidae
204 Oryziidae
205 Adrianichthyidae
206 Horaichthyidae
207 Aplocheilidae
208 Cyprinodontidae
209 Goodeidae
210 Anablepidae
211 Jenynsiidae
212 Poeciliidae

**Atheriniformes**
213 Atherinidae
214 Isonidae
215 Melanotaeniidae
216 Neostethidae
217 Phallostethidae

**Lampriformes**
218 Lampridae
219 Veliferidae
220 Lophotidae
221 Radiicephalidae
222 Trachipteridae
223 Regalecidae
224 Stylephoridae
225 Ateleopodidae
226 Mirapinnidae
227 Eutaeniophoridae
228 Megalomycteridae

**Beryciformes**
229 Monocentrididae
230 Trachichthyidae
231 Anomalopidae
232 Diretmidae
233 Anoplogastridae
234 Berycidae
235 Holocentridae
236 Polymixiidae
237 Stephanoberycidae
238 Melamphaidae
239 Gibberichthyidae
240 Rondeletiidae
241 Barbourisiidae
242 Cetomimidae

**Zeiformes**
243 Parazenidae
244 Macrurocyttidae
245 Zeidae
246 Oreosomatidae
247 Grammicolepididae
248 Caproidae

**Gasterosteiformes**
249 Hypoptychidae
250 Aulorhynchidae
251 Gasterosteidae

**Indostomiformes**
252 Indostomidae

**Pegasiformes**
253 Pegasidae

**Syngnathiformes**
254 Aulostomidae
255 Fistulariidae
256 Macrorhamphosidae
257 Centriscidae
258 Solenostomidae
259 Syngnathidae

**Dactylopteriformes**
260 Dactylopteridae

**Synbranchiformes**
261 Synbranchidae

**Scorpaeniformes**
262 Scorpaenidae
263 Synanceiidae
264 Caracanthidae
265 Aploactinidae
266 Pataecidae
267 Congiopodidae
268 Triglidae
269 Platycephalidae
270 Hoplichthyidae
271 Anoplopomatidae
272 Hexagrammidae
273 Zaniolepididae
274 Normanichthyidae
275 Ereuniidae
276 Cottidae
277 Cottocomephoridae
278 Comephoridae
279 Psychrolutidae
280 Agonidae
281 Cyclopteridae

**Perciformes**
282 Centropomidae
283 Percichthyidae
284 Serranidae
285 Grammistidae
286 Pseudochromidae
287 Grammidae
288 Plesiopidae
289 Acanthoclinidae
290 Glaucosomatidae
291 Teraponidae
292 Banjosidae
293 Kuhliidae
294 Centrarchidae
295 Percidae
296 Priacanthidae
297 Apogonidae
298 Dinolestidae
299 Sillaginidae
300 Malacanthidae
301 Labracoglossidae
302 Lactariidae
303 Pomatomidae
304 Rachycentridae
305 Echeneididae
306 Carangidae
307 Nematistiidae
308 Coryphaenidae
309 Apolectidae
310 Menidae
311 Leiognathidae
312 Bramidae
313 Caristiidae
314 Arripidae
315 Emmelichthyidae
316 Lutjanidae
317 Caesionidae
318 Lobotidae
319 Gerreidae
320 Haemulidae
321 Inermiidae
322 Sparidae
323 Centracanthidae
324 Lethrinidae
325 Nemipteridae
326 Sciaenidae
327 Mullidae
328 Monodactylidae
329 Pempherididae
330 Leptobramidae
331 Bathyclupeidae
332 Toxotidae
333 Coracinidae
334 Kyphosidae
335 Ephippididae
336 Scatophagidae
337 Rhinoprenidae
338 Chaetodontidae
339 Pomacanthidae
340 Enoplosidae
341 Pentacerotidae
342 Nandidae
343 Oplegnathidae
344 Cichlidae
345 Embiotocidae
346 Pomacentridae
347 Gadopsidae
348 Cirrhitidae
349 Chironemidae
350 Aplodactylidae
351 Cheilodactylidae
352 Latrididae
353 Owstoniidae
354 Cepolidae
355 Mugilidae
356 Sphyraenidae
357 Polynemidae
358 Labridae
359 Odacidae
360 Scaridae
361 Bathymasteridae
362 Zoarcidae
363 Stichaeidae
364 Cryptacanthodidae
365 Pholididae
366 Anarhichadidae
367 Ptilichthyidae
368 Zaproridae
369 Scytalinidae
370 Bovichthyidae
371 Nototheniidae
372 Harpagiferidae
373 Bathydraconidae
374 Channichthyidae
375 Opistognathidae
376 Congrogadidae
377 Chiasmodontidae
378 Champsodontidae
379 Notograptidae
380 Pholidichthyidae
381 Trichodontidae
382 Trachinidae
383 Uranoscopidae
384 Trichonotidae
385 Creediidae
386 Leptoscopidae
387 Percophidae
388 Mugiloididae
389 Cheimarrhichthyidae
390 Tripterygiidae
391 Dactyloscopidae
392 Labrisomidae
393 Clinidae
394 Chaenopsidae
395 Blenniidae
396 Icosteidae
397 Schindleriidae
398 Ammodytidae
399 Callionymidae
400 Draconettidae
401 Rhyacichthyidae
402 Eleotrididae
403 Gobiidae
404 Gobioididae
405 Trypauchenidae
406 Kraemeriidae
407 Microdesmidae
408 Kurtidae
409 Acanthuridae
410 Siganidae
411 Scombrolabracidae
412 Gempylidae
413 Trichiuridae
414 Scombridae
415 Xiphiidae
416 Luvaridae
417 Istiophoridae
418 Amarsipidae
419 Centrolophidae
420 Nomeidae
421 Ariommatidae
422 Tetragonuridae
423 Stromateidae
424 Anabantidae
425 Belontiidae
426 Helostomatidae
427 Osphronemidae
428 Luciocephalidae
429 Channidae
430 Mastacembelidae
431 Chaudhuriidae

**Pleuronectiformes**
432 Psettodidae
433 Citharidae
434 Bothidae
435 Pleuronectidae
436 Cynoglossidae
437 Soleidae

**Tetraodontiformes**
438 Triacanthodidae
439 Triacanthidae
440 Balistidae
441 Ostraciidae
442 Triodontidae
443 Tetraodontidae
444 Diodontidae
445 Molidae

## ACKNOWLEDGMENTS

We wish to thank the many people who have helped with every aspect of the formation of this book. We particularly acknowledge Lourdes A. Burgess, Mary Ellen O'Donnell, and Ray Weigand for their contributions in researching the material used in the writing of the captions, and to Jerry Walls for reading most of the material and making relevant suggestions for its improvement.

Many thanks to those who have helped in other ways such as continuing to provide reprints of their papers or by identifying the color proofs sent to them. Unfortunately, lack of time prevented others from completing this task and they must accept our identifications based on the literature at hand. Hopefully future editions will be able to carry any corrections made in the interim.

# *PHOTOGRAPHERS*

We are indebted to the following photographers, many of whom are certainly of world-class caliber and have taken some of the finest fish portraits that have ever graced the pages of any book. We sincerely apologize to anybody who has been inadvertently omitted from this list.

*Robert Abrams*
*Ray Allard*
*Dr. Gerald R. Allen*
*Paul Allen*
*Neil Armstrong*
*Charles Arneson*
*Glen S. Axelrod*
*Dr. Herbert R. Axelrod*
*Wayne Baldwin*
*Heiko Bleher*
*Guy van den Bossche*
*Dr. Martin R. Brittan*
*Dr. Warren E. Burgess*
*Taylor Cafferey*
*Bruce Carlson*
*Kok-Hang Choo*
*Neville Coleman*
*Dr. Patrick L. Colin*
*Walter Deas*
*Helmut Debelius*
*Dr. Guido Dingerkus*
*Wade Doak*
*Douglas Faulkner*
*Stanislav Frank*
*U. Erich Friese*
*Karl Frogner*
*Michio Goto* (Marine Life Documents)
*Daniel W. Gotshall*
*Dirk Grossman*
*Hilmar Hansen* (Aquarium Berlin)
*Edmund Hobson*
*Scott Johnson*
*Earl Kennedy*
*Alex Kerstitch*
*Karl Knaack*
*Alexandr Kochetov*
*Sergei Kochetov*
*Rudie Kuiter*
*Pierre Laboute*
*Dr. Roger Lubbock*
*Ken Lucas* (Steinhart Aquarium)
*Gerhard Marcuse*
*George Miller*
*Robert F. Myers*
*Arend van den Nieuwenhuizen*
*Aaron Norman*
*James H. O'Neill*
*Brian J. Parkinson*
*Klaus Paysan*
*Nicholas Polunin*
*Allan Power*
*Dr. John E. Randall*
*Andre Roth*
*Barry C. Russell*
*Dr. Shih-Chieh Shen*
*Dr. Victor G. Springer*
*Dr. Walter A. Starck II*
*Roger Steene*
*William Stephens*
*Katsumi Suzuki*
*Yoshio Takemura*
*Dr. Denis Terver*
*Dr. R. E. Thresher*
*Gene Wolfsheimer*
*Dr. Loren P. Woods*
*Dr. Fujio Yasuda*

In addition, illustrations were made by the Japanese artists Tomita, Arita, and Kumada. Additional illustrations are from the Smithsonian Institution *Albatross* Expedition, from Bleeker's *Atlas Ichthyologique,* and from the *Philippine Journal of Science.*

The line drawings of family representatives were accomplished by Mr. John Quinn.

# WEIGHTS & MEASURES

## CUSTOMARY U.S. MEASURES AND EQUIVALENTS

### LENGTH

| | | |
|---|---|---|
| 1 inch (in) | | = 2.54 cm |
| 1 foot (ft) | = 12 in | = .3048 m |
| 1 yard (yd) | = 3 ft | = .9144 m |
| 1 mile (mi) | = 1760 yd | = 1.6093 km |
| 1 nautical mile | = 1.152 mi | = 1.853 km |

### AREA

| | | |
|---|---|---|
| 1 square inch ($in^2$) | | = 6.4516 $cm^2$ |
| 1 square foot ($ft^2$) | = 144 $in^2$ | = .093 $m^2$ |
| 1 square yard ($yd^2$) | = 9 $ft^2$ | =.8361 $m^2$ |
| 1 acre | = 4840 $yd^2$ | = 4046.86 $m^2$ |
| 1 square mile ($mi^2$) | = 640 acre | = 2.59 $km^2$ |

### WEIGHT

| | | |
|---|---|---|
| 1 ounce (oz) | = 437.5 grains | = 28.35 g |
| 1 pound (lb) | = 16 oz | = .4536 kg |
| 1 short ton | = 2000 lb | = .9072 t |
| 1 long ton | = 2240 lb | = 1.0161 t |

### VOLUME

| | | |
|---|---|---|
| 1 cubic inch ($in^3$) | | = 16.387 $cm^3$ |
| 1 cubic foot ($ft^3$) | = 1728 $in^3$ | = .028 $m^3$ |
| 1 cubic yard ($yd^3$) | = 27 $ft^3$ | = .7646 $m^3$ |
| 1 fluid ounce (fl oz) | | = 2.957 cl |
| 1 liquid pint (pt) | = 16 fl oz | = .4732 l |
| 1 liquid quart (qt) | = 2 pt | = .946 l |
| 1 gallon (gal) | = 4 qt | = 3.7853 l |
| 1 dry pint | | = .5506 l |
| 1 bushel (bu) | = 64 dry pt | = 35.2381 l |

## METRIC MEASURES AND EQUIVALENTS

### LENGTH

| | | |
|---|---|---|
| 1 millimeter (mm) | | = .0394 in |
| 1 centimeter (cm) | = 10 mm | = .3937 in |
| 1 meter (m) | = 1000 mm | = 1.0936 yd |
| 1 kilometer (km) | = 1000 m | = .6214 mi |

### AREA

| | | |
|---|---|---|
| 1 sq centimeter ($cm^2$) | = 100 $mm^2$ | = .155 $in^2$ |
| 1 sq meter ($m^2$) | = 10,000 $cm^2$ | = 1.196 $yd^2$ |
| 1 hectare (ha) | = 10,000 $m^2$ | = 2.4711 acres |
| 1 sq kilometer ($km^2$) | = 100 ha | = .3861 $mi^2$ |

### WEIGHT

| | | |
|---|---|---|
| 1 milligram (mg) | | = .0154 grain |
| 1 gram (g) | = 1000 mg | = .0353 oz |
| 1 kilogram (kg) | = 1000 g | = 2.2046 lb |
| 1 tonne (t) | = 1000 kg | = 1.1023 short tons |
| 1 tonne | | = .9842 long ton |

### VOLUME

| | | |
|---|---|---|
| 1 cubic centimeter ($cm^3$) | | = .061 $in^3$ |
| 1 cubic decimeter ($dm^3$) | = 1000 $cm^3$ | = .353 $ft^3$ |
| 1 cubic meter ($m^3$) | = 1000 $dm^3$ | = 1.3079 $yd^3$ |
| 1 liter (l) | = 1 $dm^3$ | = .2642 gal |
| 1 hectoliter (hl) | = 100 l | = 2.8378 bu |

## TEMPERATURE

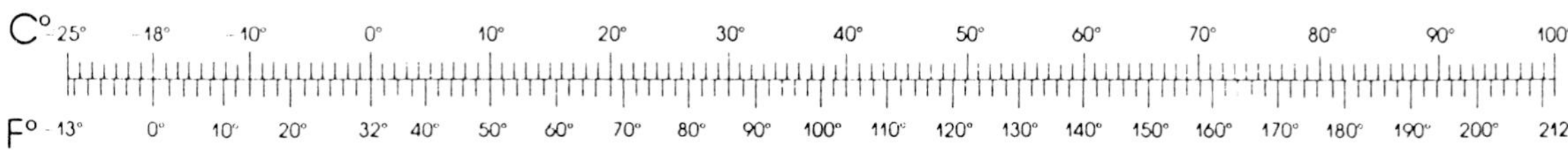


CELCIUS° = 5/9 (F° −32°)  FAHRENHEIT° = 9/5 C° +32°

# PICTORIAL IDENTIFICATION SECTION

The following pictorial identification section includes thousands of photographs of marine fishes from around the world. The families are in systematic sequence according to Nelson (1984), or as close to that as practical. (See pages 24 and 25.) The individual photos are coded with a family number for ready reference. In some cases some photos are out of sequence due to reasons beyond our control, but the family numbers should make it easy to place these "orphans" in their proper sequence.

Aquarists can scan through these pages until they find the correct family for the fish they are trying to identify. They can then look more carefully at the species depicted until they find the photo that most closely resembles their fish. One has to remember that differences in size, sex, geography, and even temperament may cause the fish to look different. However, in most cases an identification can be made with reasonable certainty. Once a correct name is arrived at the species can be researched in other references or the caption may provide all the information needed.

The captions are set up as follows:

Line 1: Scientific name and family number

Line 2: Range number (or, in the case of fishes with worldwide distribution, the abbreviation for "circumtropical"), feeding symbol, light symbol, compatibility symbol, tank decor symbol, tank level symbol, temperature in degrees Celsius, specific gravity, size of fish, capacity of tank. (Full text dealing with symbols found in the captions begins on page 21.)

*Eptatretus stouti* 1
4 14°C sg: 1.022 64 cm 500L

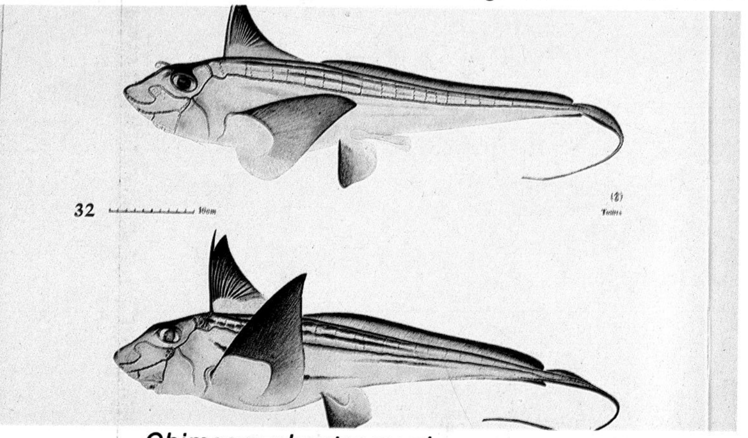

*Chimaera phantasma* 4
5 14°C sg: 1.022 100 cm 1200L

*Notorynchus cepedianus* 7
Antitropical 20°C sg: 1.022 200 cm 3000L

*Heterodontus japonicus* 8
7-9 26°C sg: 1.022 150 cm 2000L

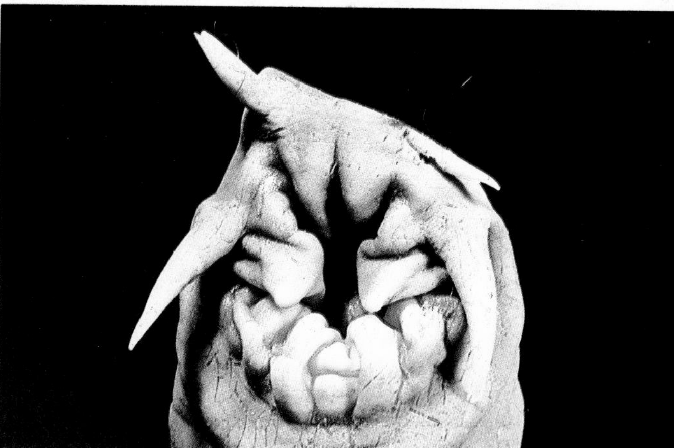

*Eptatretus* sp. (*stouti*?) 1
4 14°C sg: 1.022 64 cm 500L

*Chlamydoselachus anguineus* 6
1, 4, 11, 14 14°C sg: 1.022 200 cm 2000L

*Heptranchias perlo* 7
Circumtropical 25°C sg: 1.022 137 cm 3500L

*Heterodontus portusjacksoni* 8
12 26°C sg: 1.022 138 cm 3500L

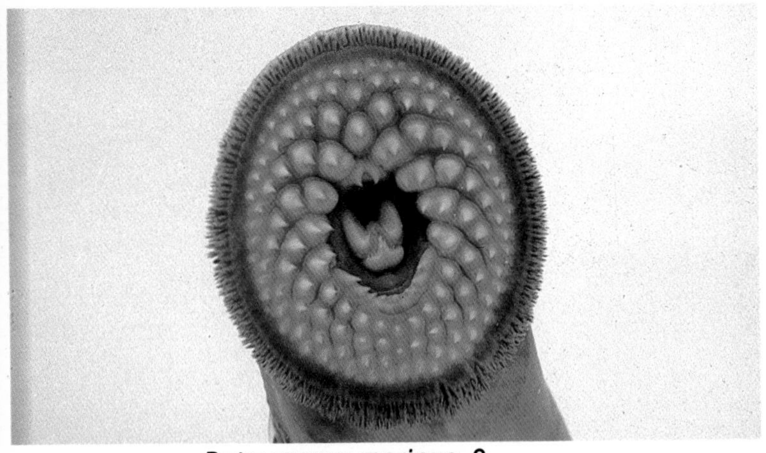

*Petromyzon marinus* 2
1 14°C sg: 1.020 100 cm 500L

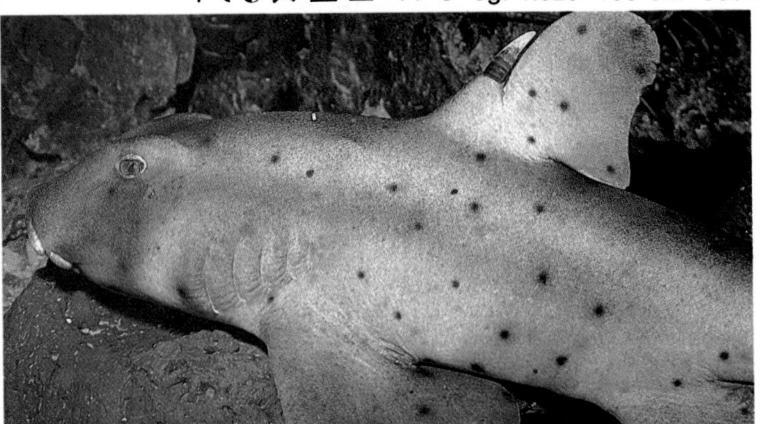

*Heterodontus francisci* 8
3-4 26°C sg: 1.022 96 cm 1000L

*Heterodontus mexicanus* 8
3 26°C sg: 1.022 96 cm 1000L

*Stegostoma varium* 10
7-9 26°C sg: 1.022 230 cm 2500L

*Hydrolagus colliei* 4
4 14°C sg: 1.022 96 cm 1000L

*Heterodontus zebra* 8
7 26°C sg: 1.022 100 cm 1000L

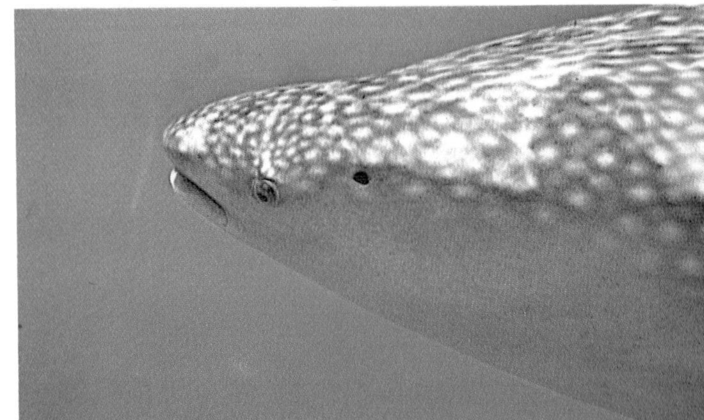

*Rhincodon typus* 9
circumtropical 26°C sg: 1.022 1000-1200 cm

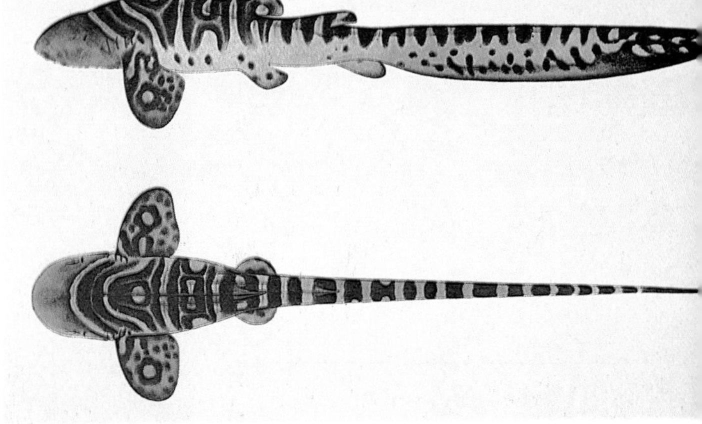

*Stegostoma varium* 10
7-9 26°C sg: 1.022 230 cm 2500L

*Ginglymostoma cirratum* 10
1-3 26°C sg: 1.022 430 cm 5000L

*Ginglymostoma cirratum* 10
1-3 26°C sg: 1.022 430 cm 5000L

*Nebrius concolor* 10
7-9 26°C sg: 1.022 300 cm 3500L

*Hemiscyllium trispeculare* 10
7-8 26°C sg: 1.022 62 cm 1000L

*Hemiscyllium ocellatum* 10
8 26°C sg: 1.022 92 cm 1000L

*Orectolobus maculatum* 10
12 26°C sg: 1.022 320 cm 5000L

*Orectolobus japonicus* 10 ♂
7 26°C sg: 1.022 100 cm 1200L

*Orectolobus japonicus* 10 ♂
7 26°C sg: 1.022 100 cm 1200L

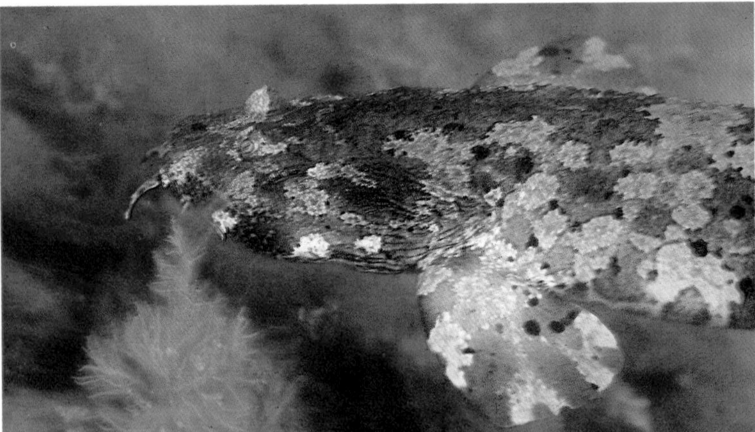

*Orectolobus ornatus* 10
8 26°C sg: 1.020 215 cm 3000L

*Sutorectus wardi* 10
12 24°C sg: 1.022 50 cm 500L

*Eucrossorhinus dasypogon* 10
7-8 26°C sg: 1.022 120 cm 2000L

*Eucrossorhinus dasypogon* 10
7-8 26°C sg: 1.022 120 cm 2000L

*Chiloscyllium confusum* 10
7-9 25°C sg: 1.022 220 cm 3000L

*Chiloscyllium griseum* 10
7-9 25°C sg: 1.022 240 cm 3000L

*Chiloscyllium plagiosum* 10
7-9 25°C sg: 1.022 100 cm 2000L

*Chiloscyllium punctatum* 10
7 26°C sg: 1.022 110 cm 2000L

*Odontaspis taurus* 11
Circumtropical 26°C sg: 1.022 318 cm 5000L

*Cetorhinus maximus* 12
Circumtemperate 18°C sg: 1.022 900 cm >5000L

*Isurus oxyrinchus* 12
Circumtemperate 24°C sg: 1.022 300 cm >5000L

*Halaelurus buergeri* 13
7-9 26°C sg: 1.022 50 cm 500L

*Odontaspis ferox* 11
Circumtropical 26°C sg: 1.022 360 cm 5000L

*Isurus oxyrinchus* 12
Circumtemperate 24°C sg: 1.022 300 cm >5000L

*Alopias superciliosus* 12
Circumtropical 26°C sg: 1.022 450 cm >5000L

*Galeus sauteri* 13
7 26°C sg: 1.022 40 cm 500L

*Scyliorhinus canicula* 13
13-14 24°C sg: 1.022 80 cm 1000L

*Chiloscyllium punctatum* 10
7 26°C sg: 1.022 110 cm 1500L

*Cephaloscyllium ventriosum* 13
3-4 23°C sg: 1.023 100 cm 1500L

*Atelomycterus macleayi* 13
8 26°C sg: 1.022 62 cm 1000L

*Mustelus henlei* 14
3-4 25°C sg: 1.022 94 cm 2000L

*Mustelus manazo* 14
7 26°C sg: 1.022 150 cm 3000L

*Triaenodon apicalis* 14
6, 7 26°C sg: 1.022 120 cm 3000L

*Triaenodon obesus* 14
7-10 26°C sg: 1.022 250 cm 5000L

*Triakis scyllia* 14
5, 7 25°C sg: 1.022 100 cm 1200L

*Triakis semifasciatus* 14
4 24°C sg: 1.023 200 cm 2500L

*Galeocerdo cuvieri* 14
Circumtrop. 26°C sg: 1.022 730 cm >5000L

*Carcharhinus amblyrhynchos* 14
6-9 26°C sg: 1.022 250 cm 2500L

*Carcharhinus melanopterus* 14
6-10 26°C sg: 1.020 200 cm 2000L

*Carcharhinus plumbeus* 14
Circumtrop. 26°C sg: 1.020 220 cm 2000L

*Carcharhinus wheeleri* 14
9-10 26°C sg: 1.020 170 cm 2000L

*Negaprion brevirostris* 14
1-2, 13 26°C sg: 1.020 340 cm 3500L

#8

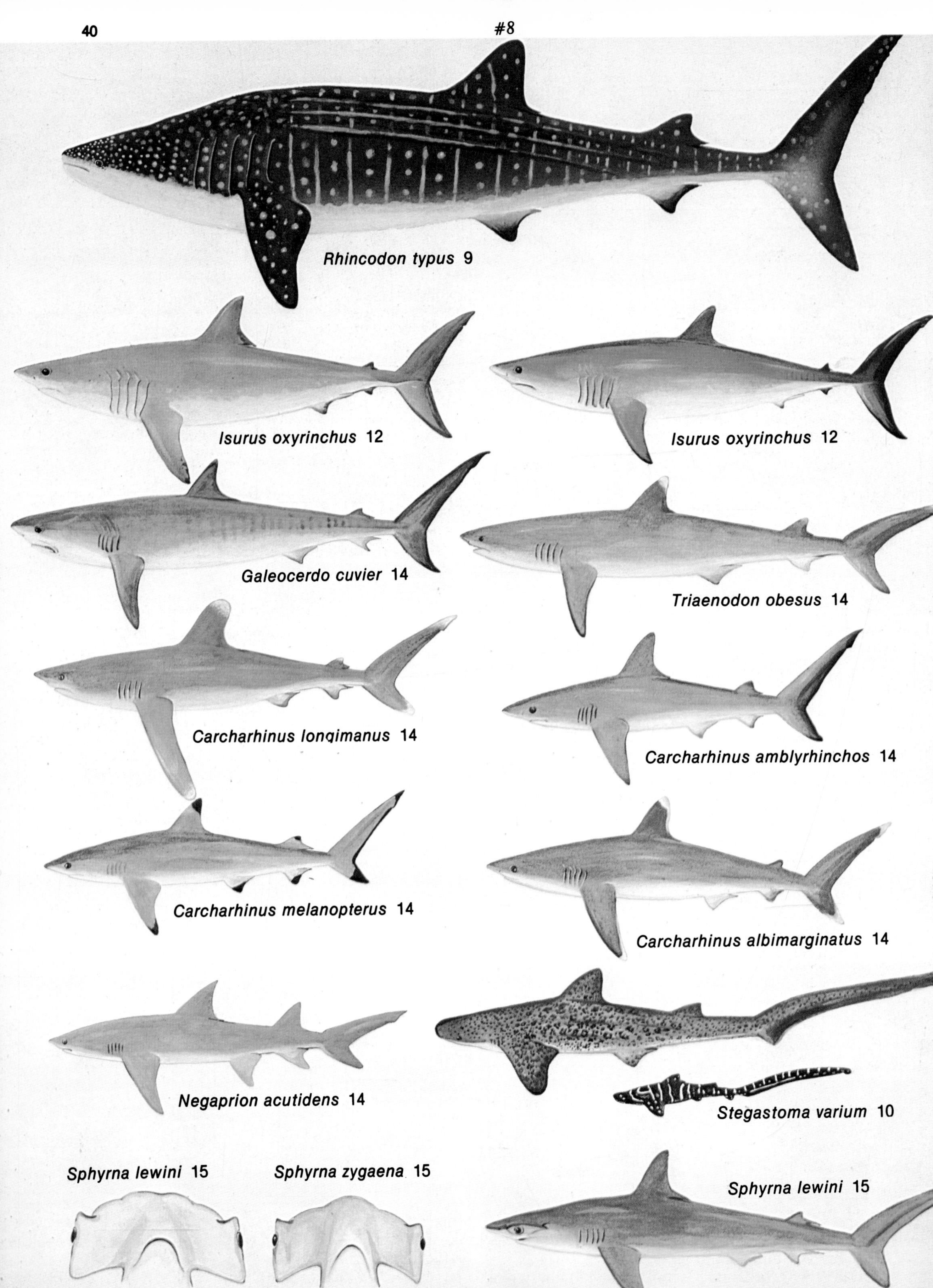
Rhincodon typus 9
Isurus oxyrinchus 12
Isurus oxyrinchus 12
Galeocerdo cuvier 14
Triaenodon obesus 14
Carcharhinus longimanus 14
Carcharhinus amblyrhinchos 14
Carcharhinus melanopterus 14
Carcharhinus albimarginatus 14
Negaprion acutidens 14
Stegastoma varium 10
Sphyrna lewini 15
Sphyrna zygaena 15
Sphyrna lewini 15

*Sphyrna lewini* 15
Circumtrop. 26°C sg: 1.022 300 cm >5000L

*Sphyrna lewini* 15
Circumtrop. 26°C sg: 1.022 300 cm >5000L

*Centroscyllium ritteri* 16
5 24°C sg: 1.023 100 cm 2000L

*Squatina californica* 18
4 21°C sg: 1.023 150 cm 2000L

*Sphyrna zygaena* 15
Circumtemp. 26°C sg: 1.022 >300 cm >5000L

*Squalus mitsukurii* 16
All oceans 26°C sg: 1.022 100 cm 2000L

*Squalus suckleyi* 16
24°C sg: 1.023 75 cm 1500L

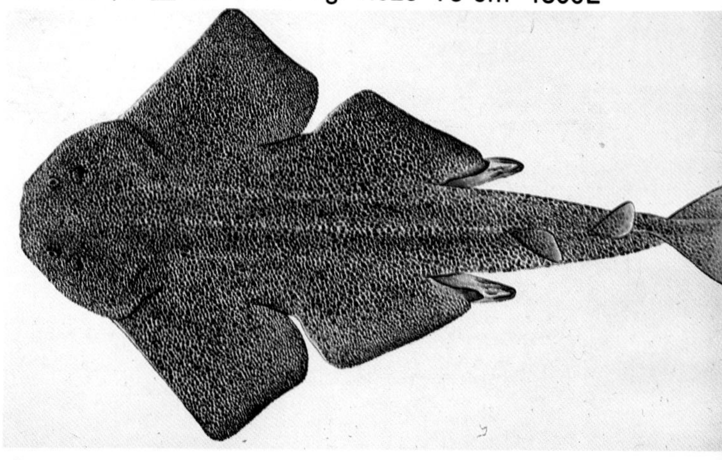

*Squatina japonica* 18
7 25°C sg: 1.022 300 cm 5000L

*Anoxypristis cuspidata* 19
6-7, 9-10 26°C sg: 1.022 >5000L

*Diplobatos ommata* 20
3 26°C sg: 1.022 20 cm 300L

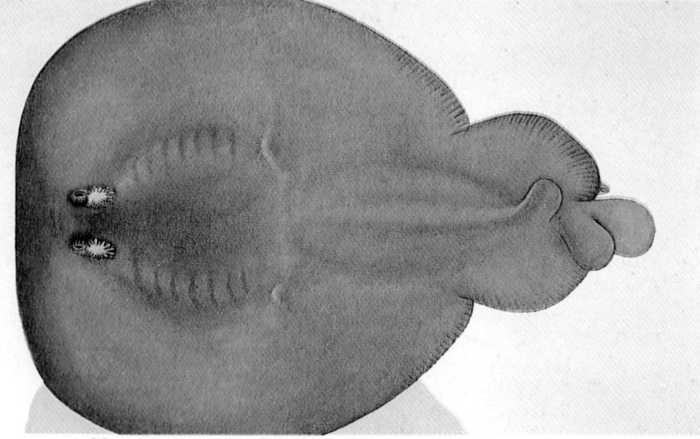

*Hypnos subnigrum* 20
8, 12 *24°C sg: 1.022 70 cm 800L*

*Narke japonica* 20
7 26°C sg: 1.022 40 cm 500L

*Pristis pectinata* 19
Trop. Atl. 26°C sg: 1.022 600 cm >5000L

*Hypnos monopterygium* 20
12 22°C sg: 1.020 70 cm 800L

*Narcine brunneus* 20
9 26°C sg: 1.022 20 cm 300L

*Narcine brasiliensis* 20
1-2 26°C sg: 1.022 45 cm 500L

*Torpedo nobiliana* 20
1, 13-15 25°C sg: 1.022 180 cm 3500L

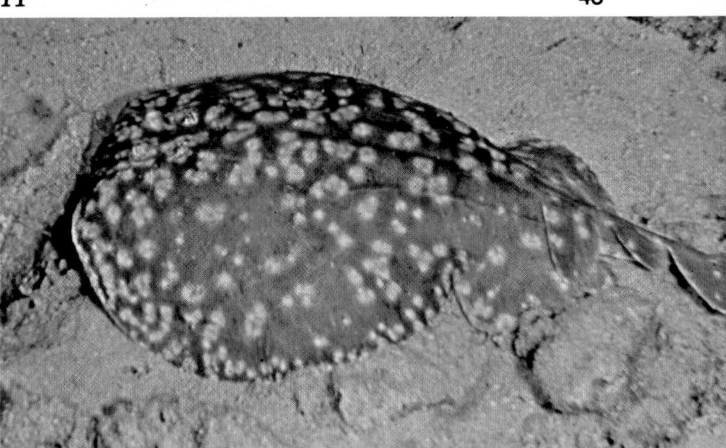

*Torpedo sinuspersici* 20
9-10 26°C sg: 1.022 130 cm 2500L

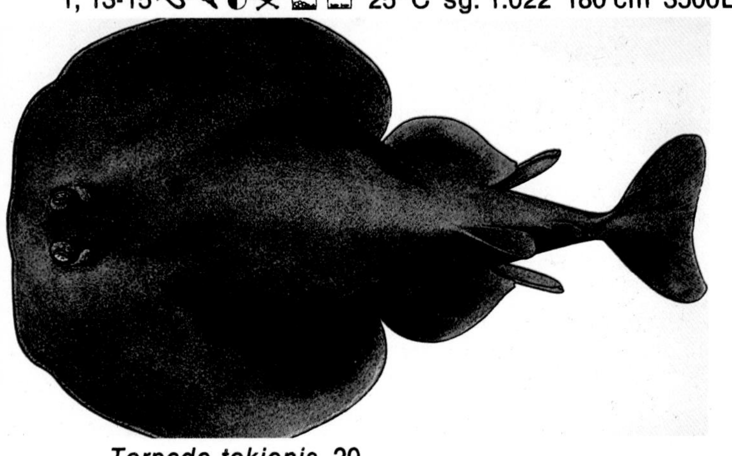

*Torpedo tokionis* 20
7 26°C sg: 1.022 100 cm 1500L

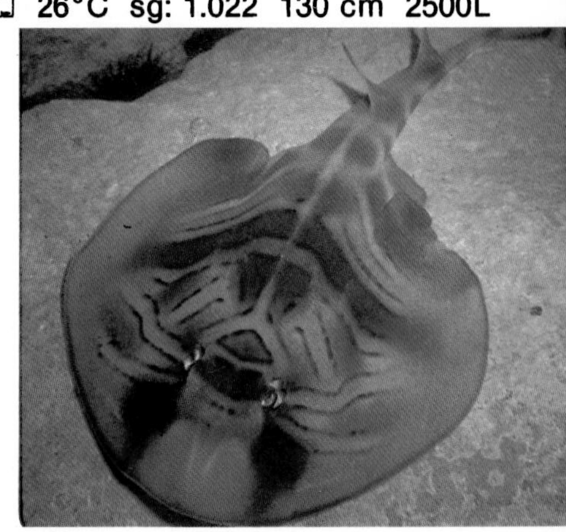

*Trygonorhina fasciata* 21
7-8 26°C sg: 1.020 100 cm 1500L

*Platyrhina sinensis* 21
5 24°C sg: 1.023 70 cm 700L

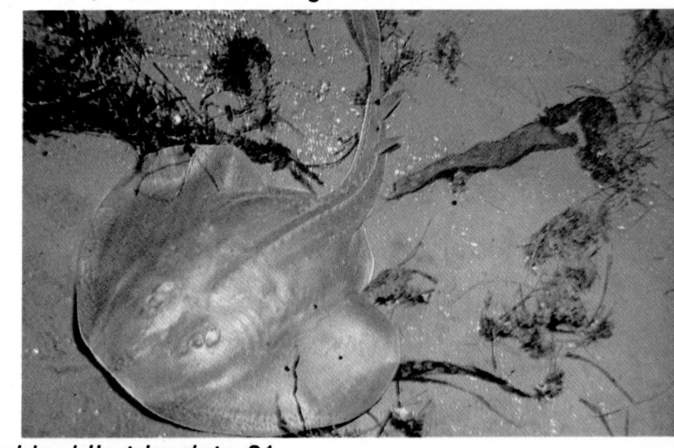

*Platyrhinoidis triseriata* 21
4 16°C sg: 1.024 91 cm 1500L

*Zapteryx exasperata* 21
3 26°C sg: 1.022 91 cm 1500L

*Rhinobatos productus* 21
4 18°C sg: 1.024 170 cm 3500L

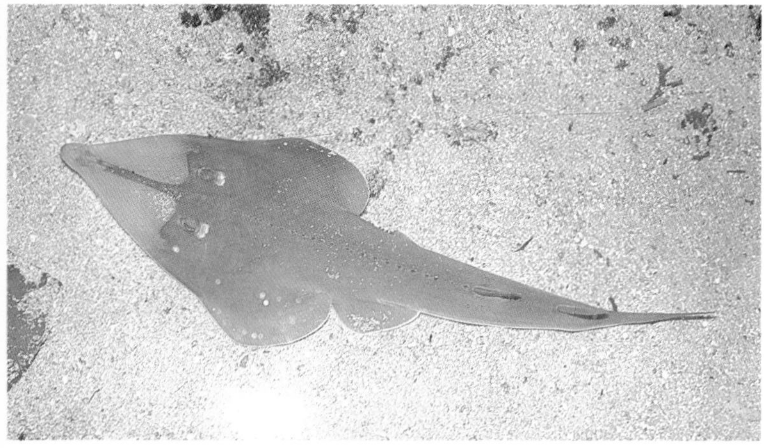

*Rhinobatos armatus* 21
7-9 ∿ ◐ ♥ ▣ ▢ 26°C sg: 1.022 120 cm 1200L

*Rhinobatos formosensis* 21
7 ∿ ◐ ♥ ▣ ▢ 26°C sg: 1.022 100 cm 1000L

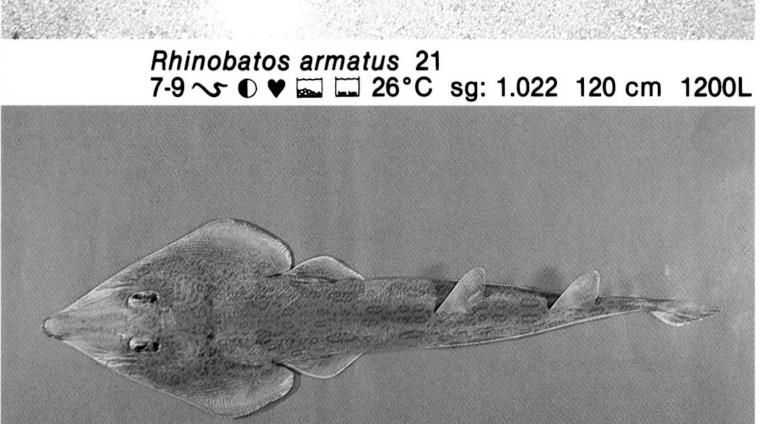

*Rhinobatos hynnicephalus* 21
7 ∿ ◐ ♥ ▣ ▢ 26°C sg: 1.022 100 cm 1000L

*Rhinobatos schlegeli* 21
7, 9 ∿ ◐ ♥ ▣ ▢ 26°C sg: 1.022 100 cm 1000L

*Rhinobatos vincentiana* 21
12 ∿ ◐ ♥ ▣ ▢ 23°C sg: 1.024 100 cm 1000L

*Raja porosa* 22
7 ∿ ◐ ♥ ▣ ▢ 26°C sg: 1.022 50 cm 500L

*Taeniura lymma* 23
7-10 ∿ ◐ ♥ ▣ ▢ 26°C sg: 1.022 25 cm 250L

*Trygonoptena testaceus* 23
7-8, 12 ∿ ◐ ♥ ▣ ▢ 26°C sg: 1.022 60 cm 600L

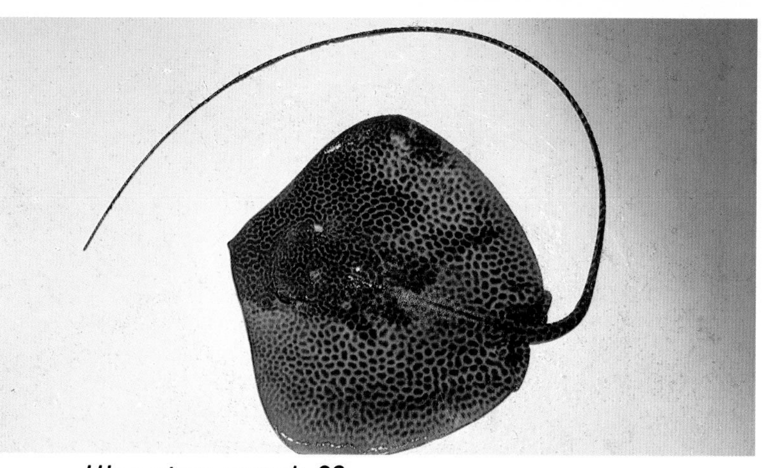

*Himantura uarnak* 22
6-10 26°C sg: 1.022 200 cm 3500L

*Amphotistius kuhlii* 22
7-10 26°C sg: 1.022 50 cm 1500L

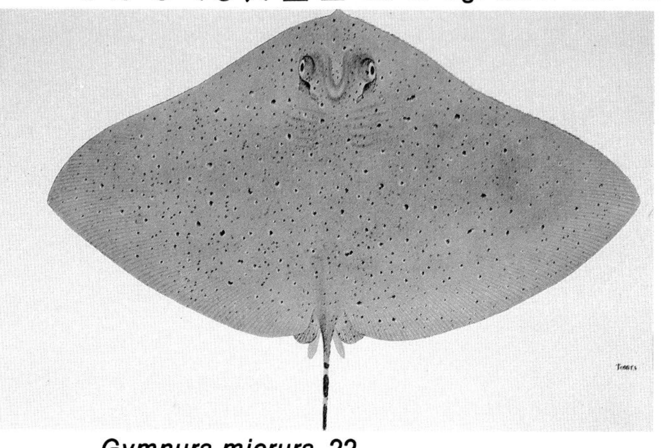

*Gymnura micrura* 22
7, 9 26°C sg: 1.020 44 cm 1500L

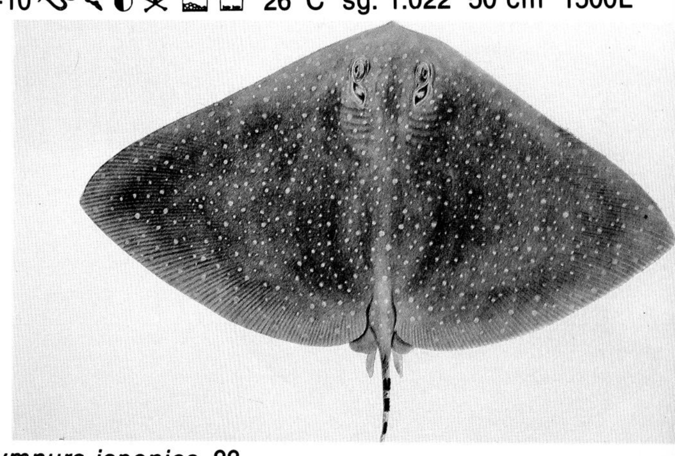

*Gymnura japonica* 22
5, 7, 9 26°C sg: 1.022 180 cm 3500L

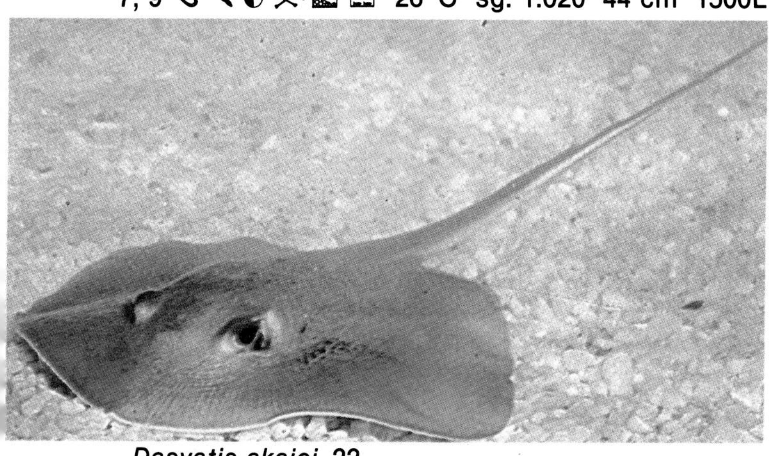

*Dasyatis akajei* 22
5, 7 25°C sg: 1.022 45 cm 800L

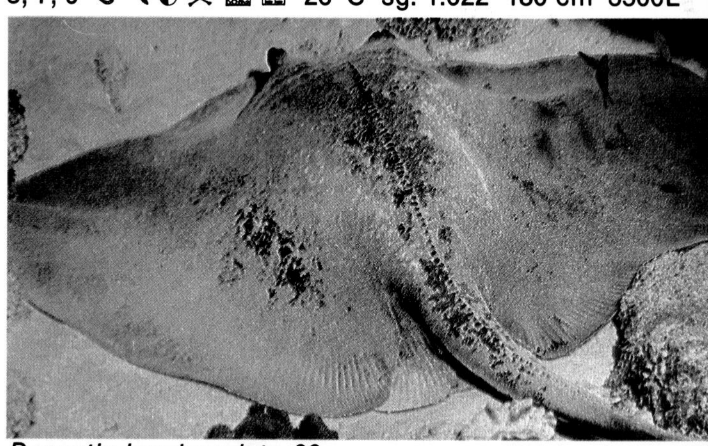

*Dasyatis brevicaudata* 22
9, 11-12 26°C sg: 1.022 210 cm 3500L

*Dasyatis hawaiiensis* 22
6 26°C sg: 1.022 120 cm 1500L

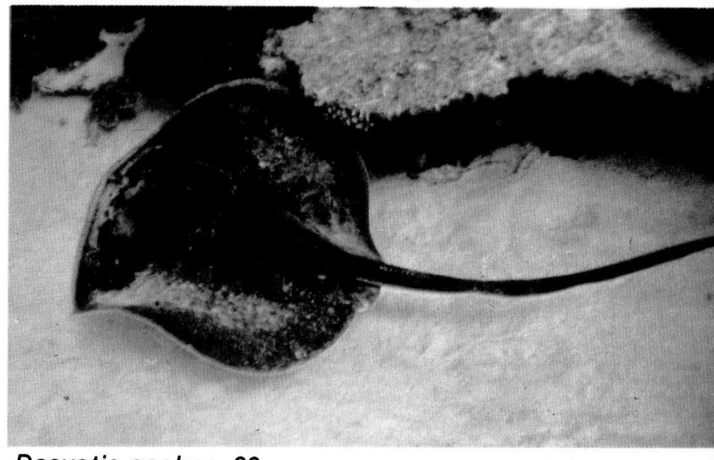

*Dasyatis sephen* 22
5, 7-9 26°C sg: 1.022 200 cm 3500L

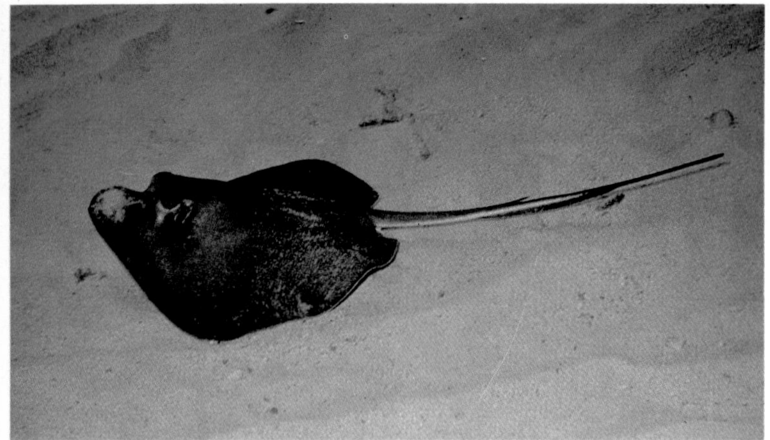

*Dasyatis americana* 22
2 24°C sg: 1.022 90 cm 1500L

*Urogymnus africanus* 22
9 26°C sg: 1.022 100 cm 1500L

*Urolophus aurantiacus* 22
5 24°C sg: 1.022 40 cm 800L

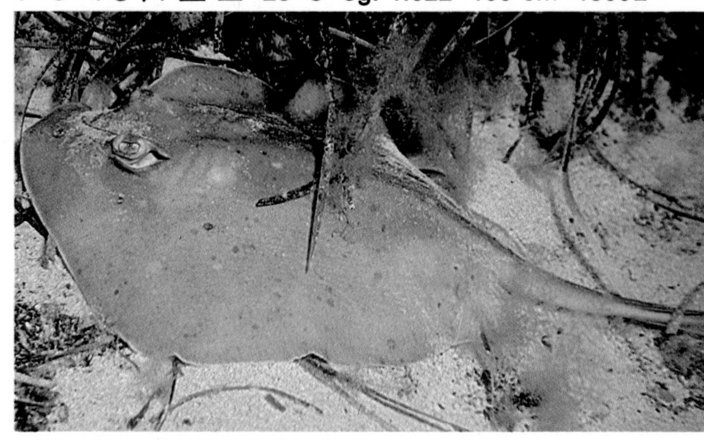

*Urolophus mucosus* 22
12 22°C sg: 1.022 35 cm 700L

*Urolophus halleri* 22
3 26°C sg: 1.022 56 cm 800L

*Urolophus jamaicensis* 22
2 26°C sg: 1.022 62 cm 800L

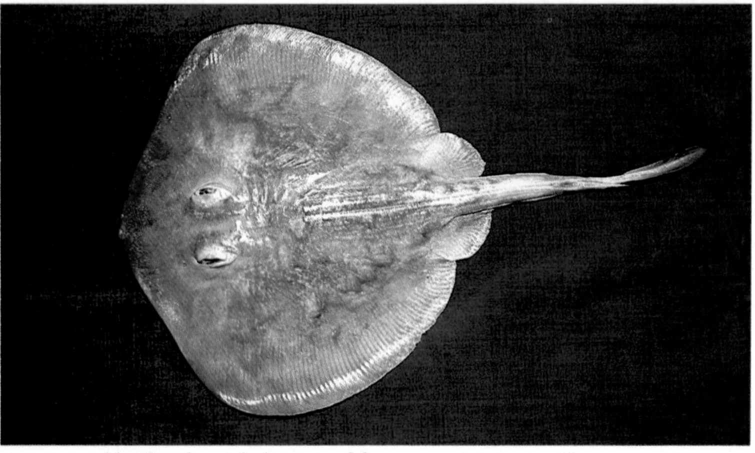

*Urolophus lobatus* 22
12 23°C sg: 1.024 200 cm 3500L

*Urolophus concentricus* 22
3 26°C sg: 1.022 45 cm 800L

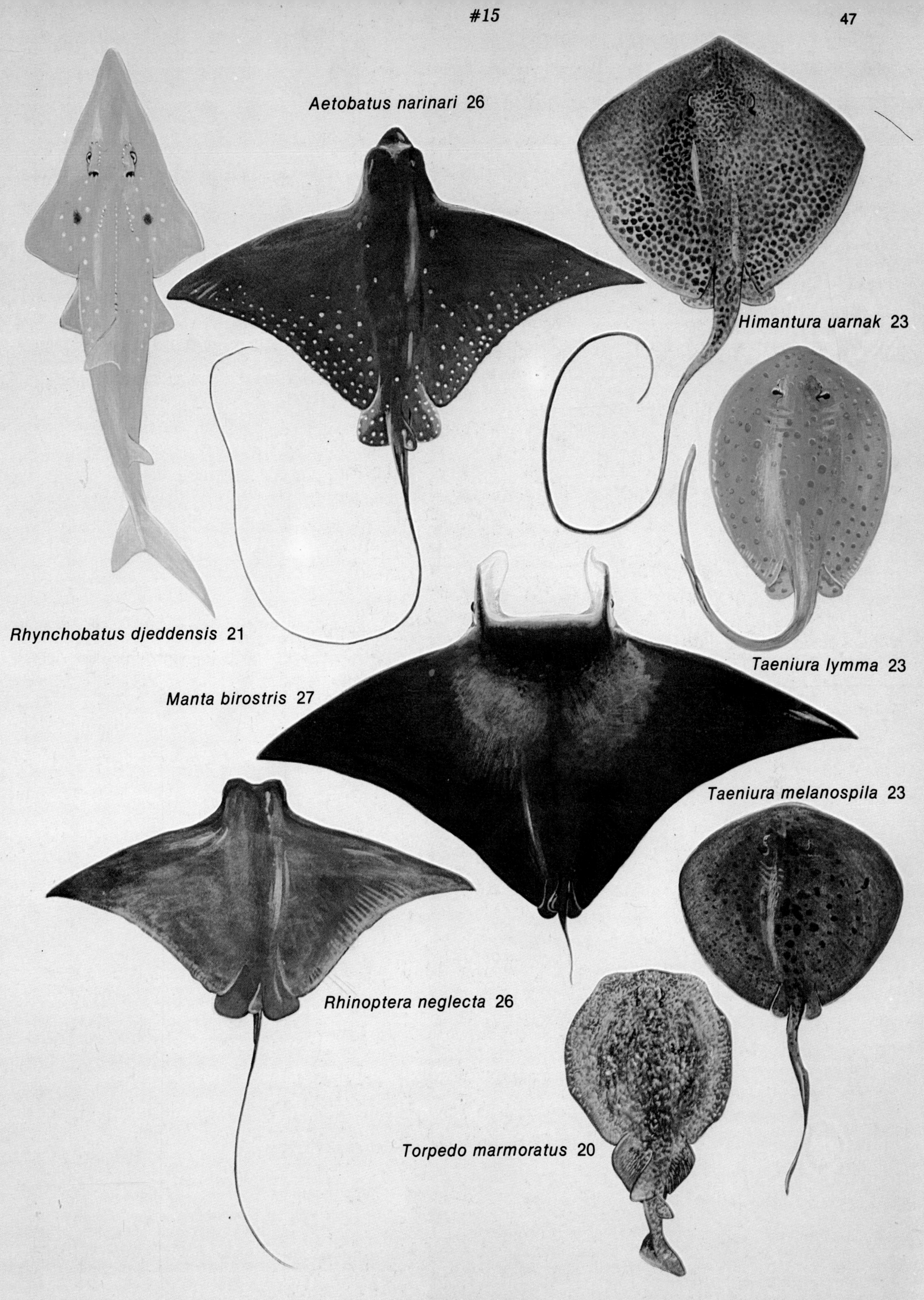
Aetobatus narinari 26
Himantura uarnak 23
Rhynchobatus djeddensis 21
Taeniura lymma 23
Manta birostris 27
Taeniura melanospila 23
Rhinoptera neglecta 26
Torpedo marmoratus 20

*Aetobatus narinari* 26
Circumtrop. 26°C sg: 1.022 230 cm ⟩5000L

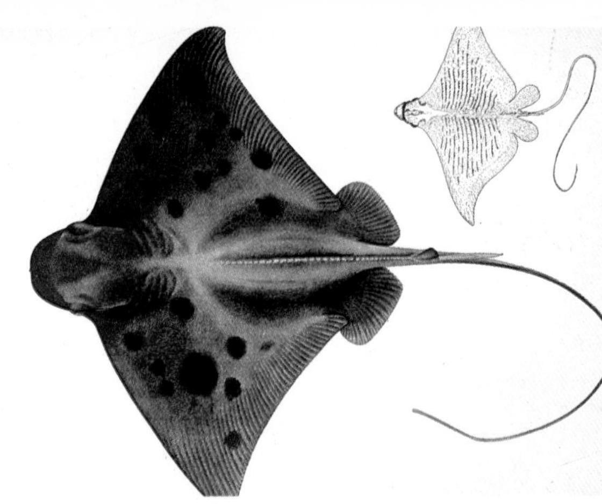

*Myliobatis tobijei* 26
7 26°C sg: 1.022 130 cm 4000L

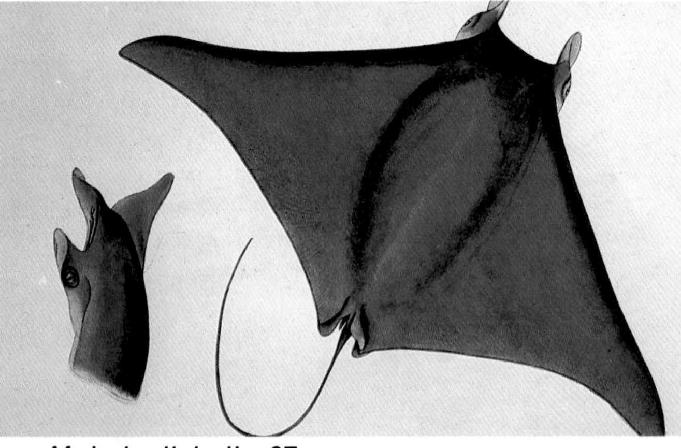

*Mobula diabolis* 27
7-12 26°C sg: 1.022 178 cm ⟩5000L

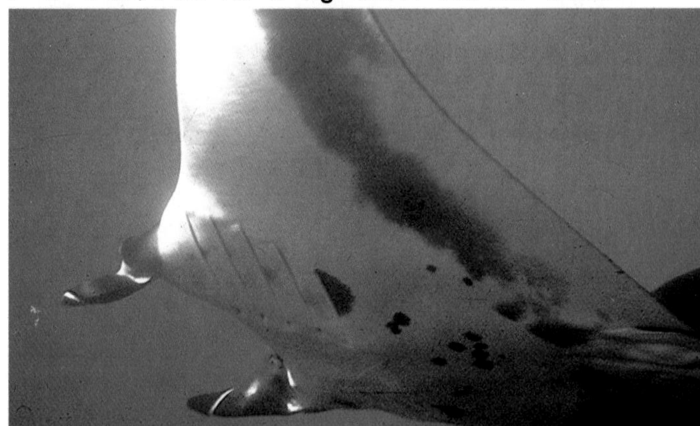

*Manta hamiltoni* 27
3, 6-9 26°C sg: 1.022 670 cm ⟩5000L

*Manta birostris* 27
Circumtrop. 26°C sg: 1.022 670 cm ⟩5000L

*#16A*

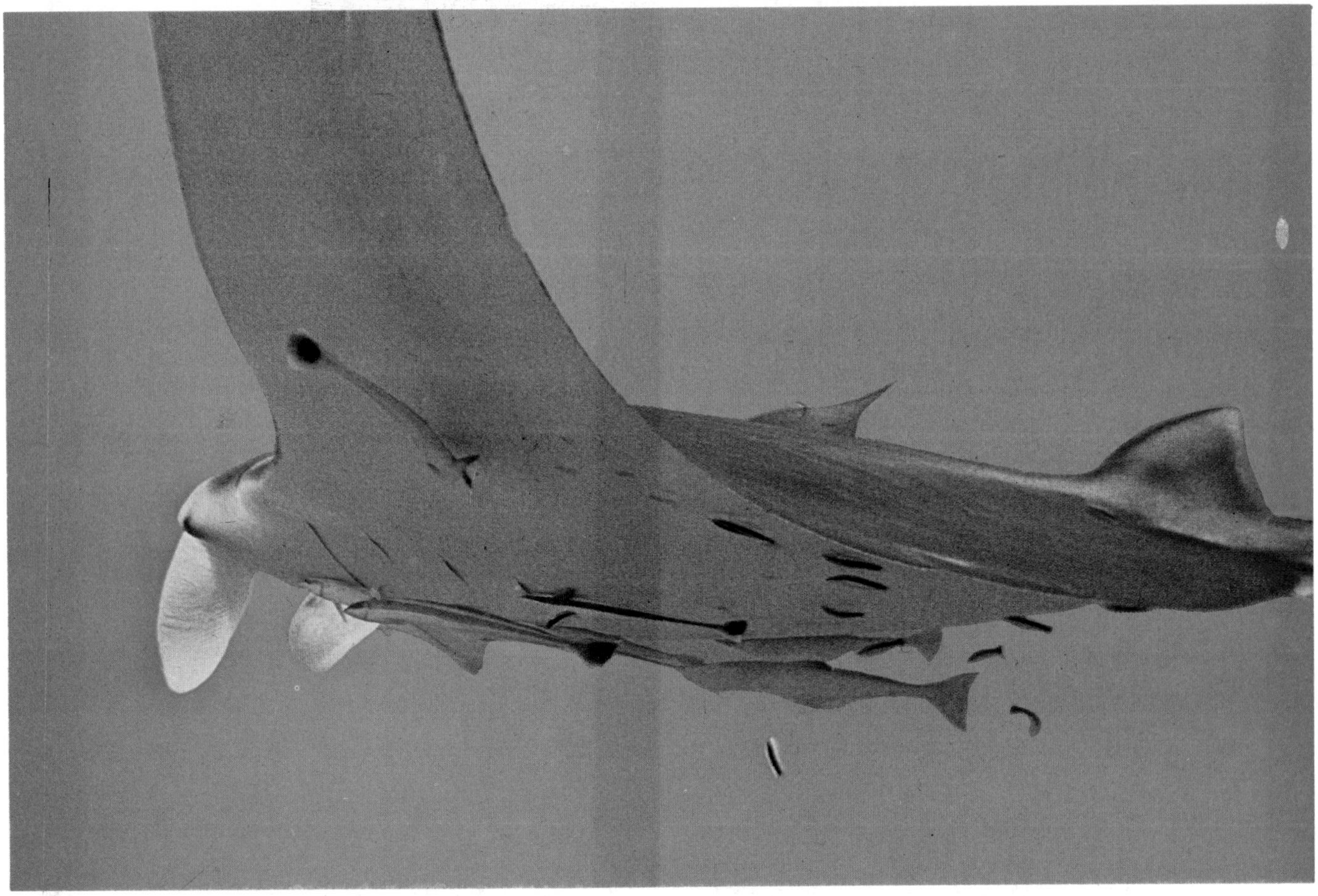

*Manta birostris* 27
Circumtrop. ∿ ↘ ◐ ♥ ⊡ 26°C sg: 1.022 670 cm >5000L

*Aetobatus narinari* 26
Circumtrop. ∿ ↘ ◐ ☠ ⊡ 26°C sg: 1.022 230 cm >5000L

*Latimeria chalumnae* 31
9 21°C sg: 1.023 135 cm ⟩5000L

*Elops machnata* 43
6-9 26°C sg: 1.022 80 cm 2000L

*Megalops cyprinoides* 44
12 26°C sg: 1.018 150 cm 2500L

*Pterothrissus gissu* 45
5 24°C sg: 1.023 60 cm 1500L

*Elops hawaiiensis* 43
6, 7 26°C sg: 1.022 60 cm 1500L

*Megalops atlanticus* 44
2, 13 26°C sg: 1.018 240 cm 5000L

*Megalops atlanticus* 44
2, 13 26°C sg: 1.018 240 cm 5000L

*Albula vulpes* 45
Circumtrop. 26°C sg: 1.018 60 cm 1500L

#18

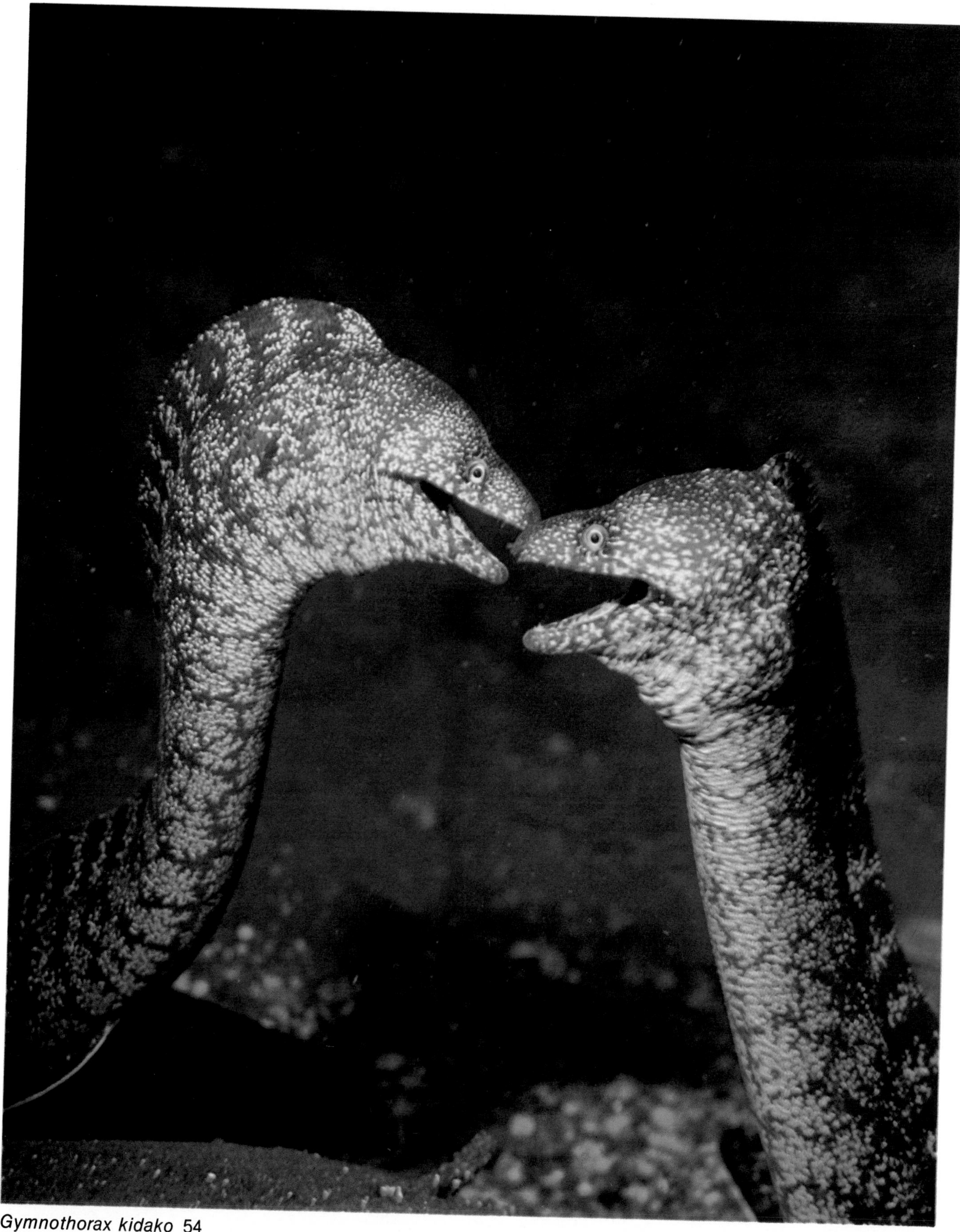

*Gymnothorax kidako* 54
5, 7 26°C sg: 1.022 80 cm 400L

*Rhinomuraena quaesita* 54
7 26°C sg: 1.022 120 cm 1000L

*Gymnothorax* sp. 54
6-9 26°C sg: 1.022 200 cm 800L

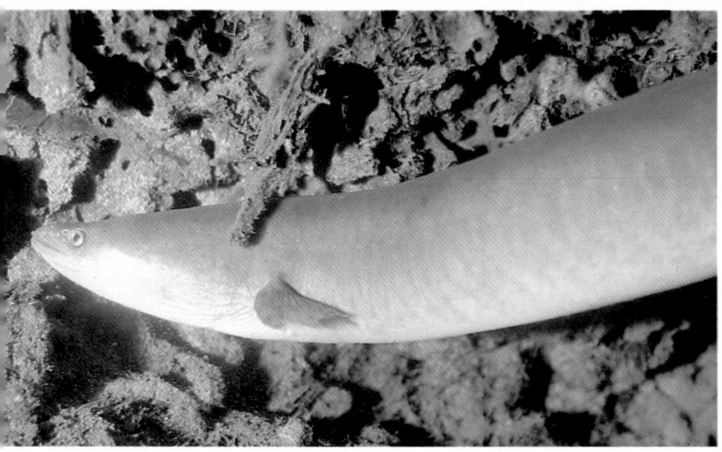

*Anguilla dieffenbachii* 49
11-12 ~ ↘ ◐ ✲ ▣ ◻ 24°C sg: 1.018 90 cm 1000L

*Anguilla anguilla* 49
13, 14 ~ ↘ ◐ ✲ ▣ ◻ 21°C sg: 1.018 90 cm 1000L

*Anguilla japonica* 49
5 ~ ↘ ◐ ✲ ▣ ◻ 22°C sg: 1.018 100 cm 1000L

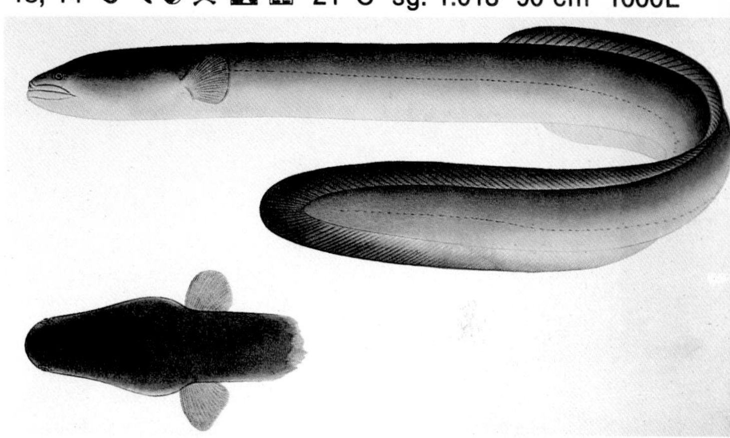

*Anguilla australis* 49
12 ~ ↘ ◐ ✲ ▣ ◻ 23°C sg: 1.018 100 cm 1000L

*Moringa microchir* 51
7, 9 ~ ◐ ♥ ▣ ◻ 26°C sg: 1.020 39 cm 400L

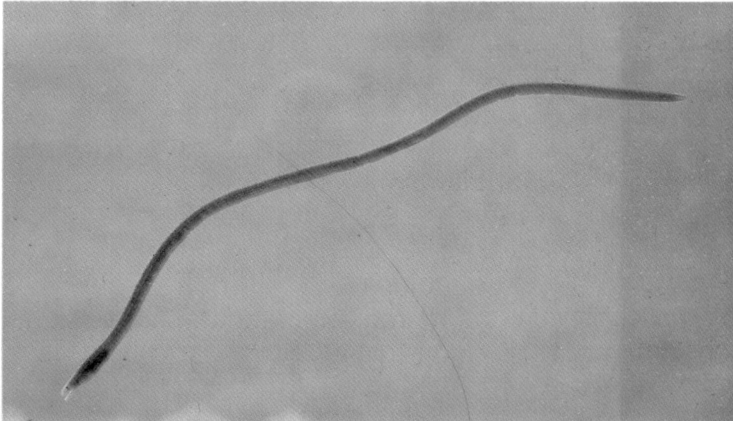

*Muraenichthys* sp. 58
6, 7 ~ ↘ ◐ ♥ ▣ ◻ 26°C sg: 1.020 30 cm 300L

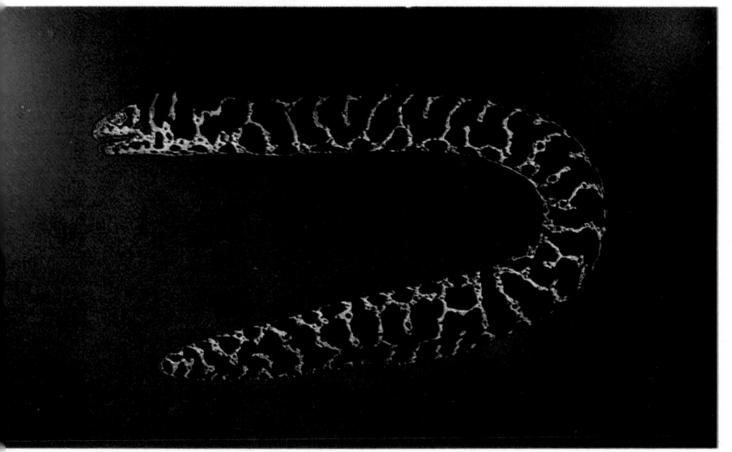

*Echidna catenata* 54
2 ~ ↘ ◐ ✲ ▣ ◻ 26°C sg: 1.020 70 cm 500L

*Echidna pozyzona* 54
7 ~ ↘ ◐ ✲ ▣ ◻ 26°C sg: 1.022 60 cm 500L

*Gymnomuraena zebra* 54
3, 6, 7 26°C sg: 1.022 90 cm 500L

*Gymnothorax fimbriatus* 54
9 26°C sg: 1.022 80 cm 500L

*Gymnothorax rueppelliae* 54
6-10 26°C sg: 1.022 55 cm 300L

*Gymnothorax thyrsoideus* 54
7 26°C sg: 1.022 80 cm 500L

*Gymnothorax eurostus* 54
5-7, 9 26°C sg: 1.022 80 cm 500L

*Uropterygius concolor* 54
7, 9 26°C sg: 1.022 32 cm 300L

*Gymnothorax steindachneri* 54
6 25°C sg: 1.023 91 cm 700L

*Gymnothorax woodwardi* 54
12 26°C sg: 1.022 75 cm 500L

*Gymnothorax flavimarginatus* 54
3, 6-9 26°C sg: 1.022 100 cm 500L

*Gymnothorax moringa* 54
2 26°C sg: 1.022 70 cm 400L

*Gymnothorax castaneus* 54
3 26°C sg: 1.022 120 cm 500L

*Gymnothorax panamensis* 54
3 26°C sg: 1.022 30 cm 200L

*Siderea picta* 54
6-9 26°C sg: 1.022 68 cm 400L

*Gymnothorax vicinus* 54
2 26°C sg: 1.022 120 cm 500L

*Gymnothorax funebris* 54
1, 2 26°C sg: 1.022 240 cm 800L

*Gymnothorax mordax* 54
3-4 26°C sg: 1.023 200 cm 800L

*Gymnothorax flavimarginatus* 54
3, 6-9 26°C sg: 1.022 80 cm 400L

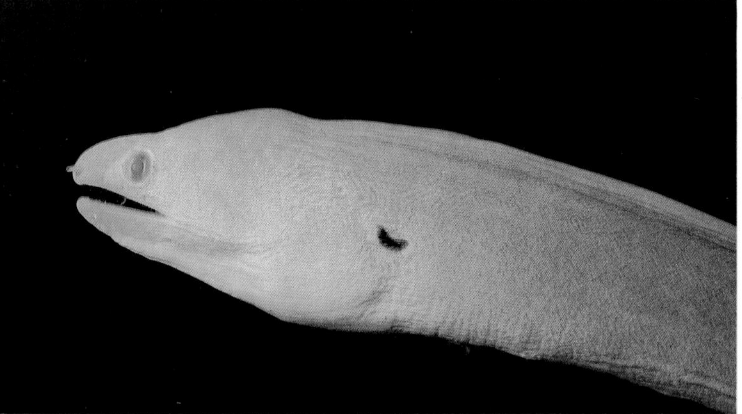

*Gymnothorax melatremus* 54
9 26°C sg: 1.022 26 cm 120L

*Gymnothorax nudivomer* 54
6, 10 26°C sg: 1.022 100 cm 400L

*Gymnothorax flavimarginatus* 54
3, 6-9 26°C sg: 1.022 80 cm 400L

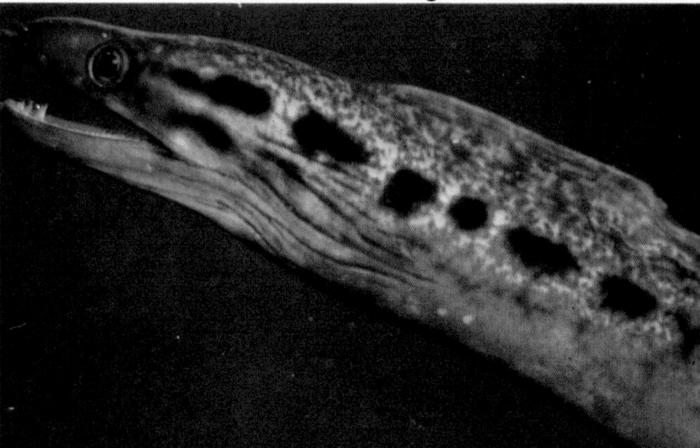

*Gymnothorax margaritophorus* 54
7, 9 26°C sg: 1.022 36 cm 200L

*Gymnothorax meleagris* 54
7, 9 26°C sg: 1.022 90 cm 400L

*Gymnothorax permistus* 54
9 26°C sg: 1.022 75 cm 300L

*Gymnothorax* sp. 54
12 26°C sg: 1.022 60 cm 300L

*Gymnothorax nubilis* 54
11 26°C sg: 1.022 50 cm 500L

*Gymnothorax obesus* 54
11 24°C sg: 1.024 178 cm 2000L

*Gymnothorax ramosus* 54
11 24°C sg: 1.024 80 cm 800L

*Gymnothorax leucostigma* 54
5, 7 26°C sg: 1.022 100 cm 500L

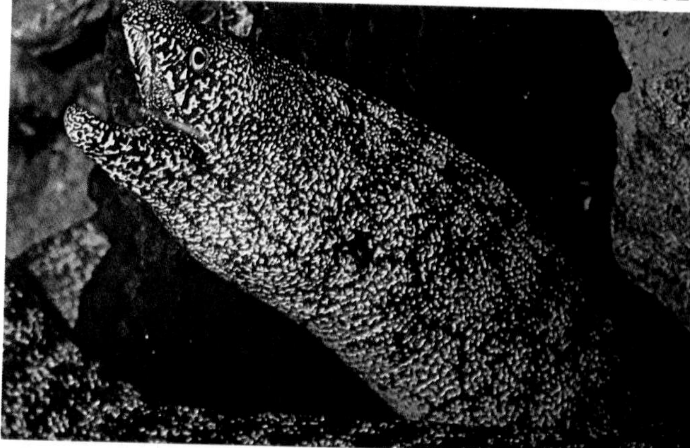

*Gymnothorax kidako* 54
5, 7 26°C sg: 1.022 80 cm 400L

*Gymnothorax prionodon* 54
11-12 24°C sg: 1.024 80 cm 800L

*Muraena melanotis* 54
13 26°C sg: 1.022 140 cm 1400L

*Siderea picta* 54
6-9 26°C sg: 1.022 68 cm 300L

*Gymnothorax undulatus* 54
6-9 26°C sg: 1.022 150 cm 500L

*Gymnothorax zonipectus* 54
6-9 26°C sg: 1.022 31 cm 100L

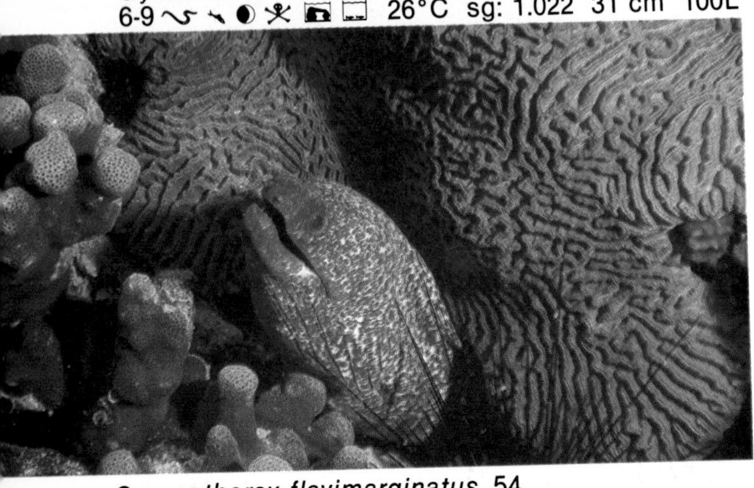

*Gymnothorax flavimarginatus* 54
3, 6-9 26°C sg: 1.022 80 cm 400L

*Gymnothorax favagineus* 54
6-9 26°C sg: 1.022 250 cm 800L

*Gymnothorax flavimarginatus?* 54
3, 6-9 26°C sg: 1.022 80 cm 400L

*Gymnothorax prasinus* 54
12 26°C sg: 1.022 30 cm 100L

*Muraena pardalis* 54
6-9 26°C sg: 1.022 100 cm 400L

*Echidna nebulosa* 54
6-9 26°C sg: 1.022 70 cm 300L

*Gymnothorax breedeni* 54
6-9 26°C sg: 1.022 65 cm 300L

*Siderea grisea* 54
9-10 26°C sg: 1.022 38 cm 400L

*Echidna nebulosa* 54
6-9 26°C sg: 1.022 70 cm 300L

*Enchelycore bayeri* 54
7, 9 26°C sg: 1.022 70 cm 300L

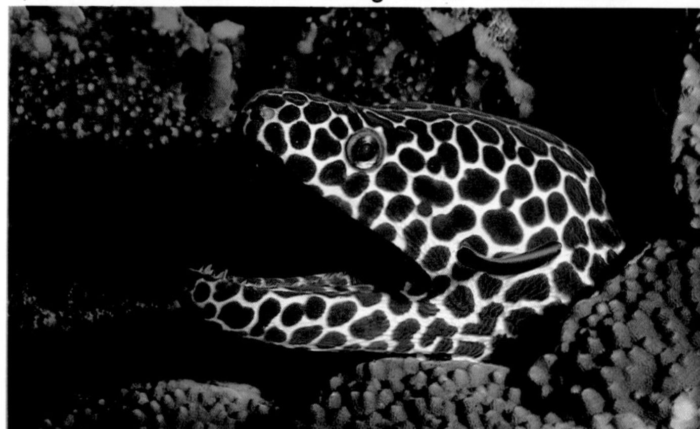

*Gymnothorax favagineus* 54
6-9 26°C sg: 1.022 250 cm 2500L

*Gymnothorax javanicus* 54
6-10 26°C sg: 1.022 250 cm 1000L

*Gymnothorax javanicus* 54
6-10 26°C sg: 1.022 250 cm 1000L

*Gymnothorax prasinus* 54
11 26°C sg: 1.022 100 cm 400L

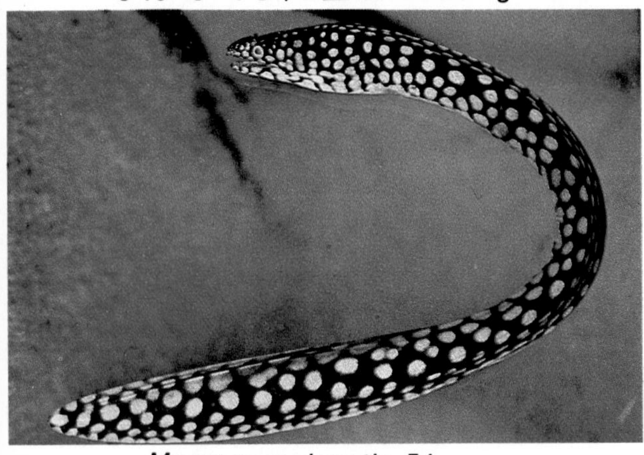

*Muraena melanotis* 54
13 26°C sg: 1.022 100 cm 400L

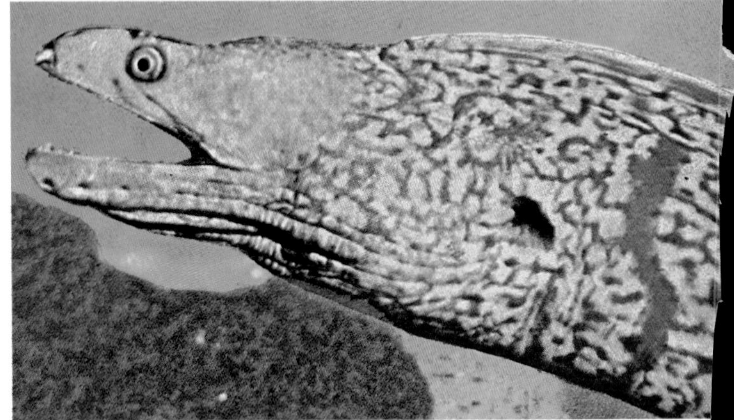

*Muraena helena* 54
13 26°C sg: 1.022 50 cm 400L

*Muraena lentiginosa* 54
3 26°C sg: 1.022 60 cm 400L

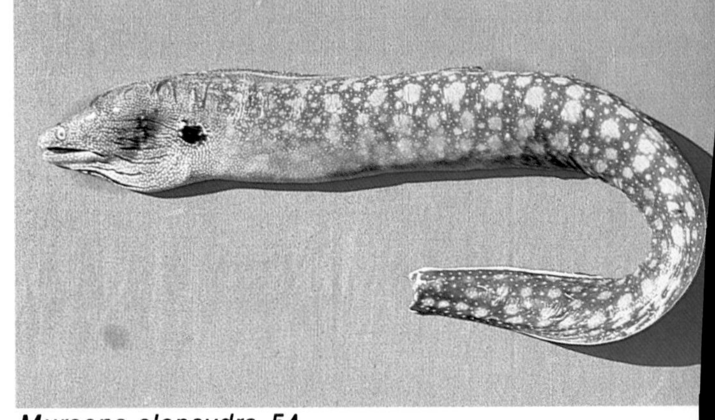

*Muraena clepsydra* 54
3 26°C sg: 1.022 50 cm 400L

*Muraena miliaris* 54
2, 13 26°C sg: 1.022 60 cm 400L

*Uropterygius tigrinus* 54
6 26°C sg: 1.022 120 cm 800L

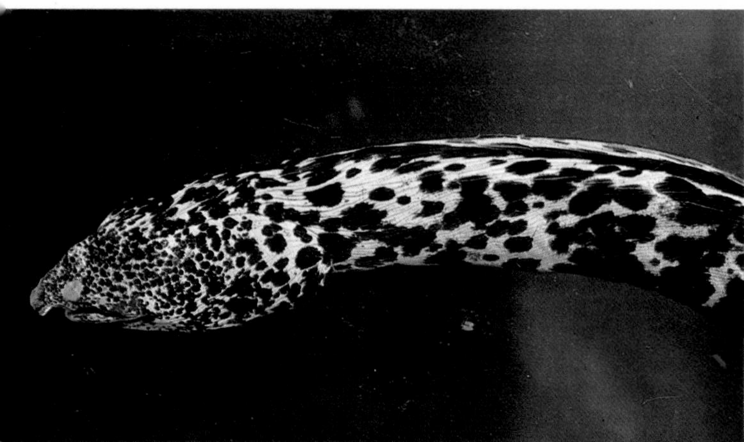

*Callechelys marmoratus* 58
6-9 26°C sg: 1.022 57 cm 600L

*Pisodonophis cancrivorus* 58
7, 9 25°C sg: 1.022 100 cm 1000L

*Muraenichthys tasmaniensis* 58
12 25°C sg: 1.023 35 cm 300L

*Leiuranus semicinctus* 58
6-9 26°C sg: 1.022 60 cm 500L

*Myrichthys aciminatus* 58
2 26°C sg: 1.022 102 cm 1000L

*Myrichthys colubrinus* 58
7-9 26°C sg: 1.022 75 cm 750L

*Myrichthys maculosus* 58
3, 6-9 26°C sg: 1.022 100 cm 1000L

*Myrichthys oculatus* 58
2 26°C sg: 1.022 100 cm 1000L

*Ophichthus ophis* 58
1-2 24°C sg: 1.022 122 cm 1200L

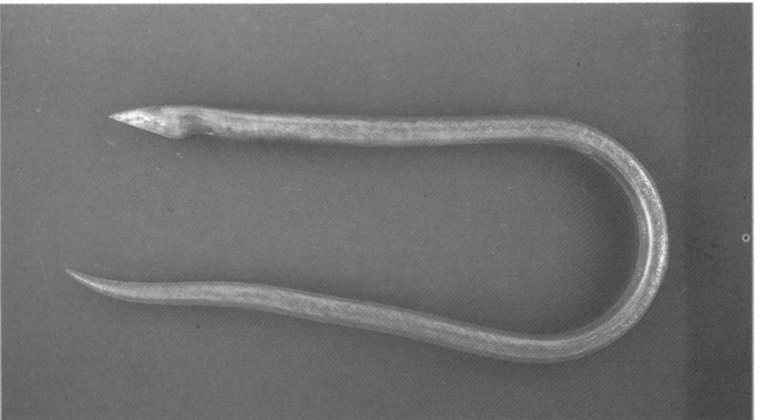

*Apterichtus ansp* 58
2 25°C sg: 1.022 54 cm 500L

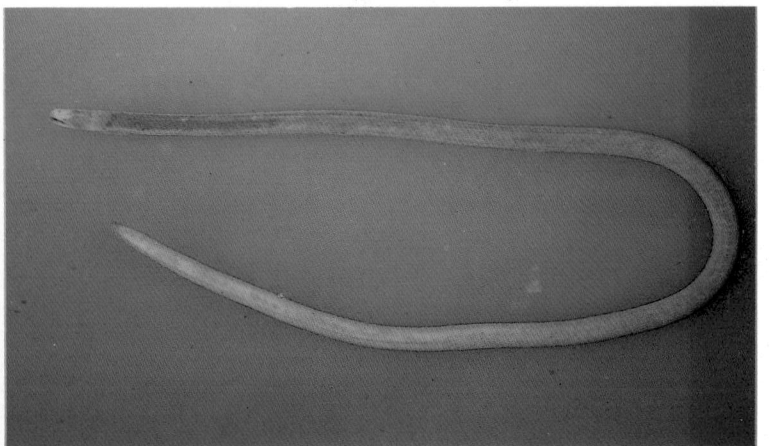

Ophichthid eel 58
2 26°C sg: 1.022 45 cm 500L

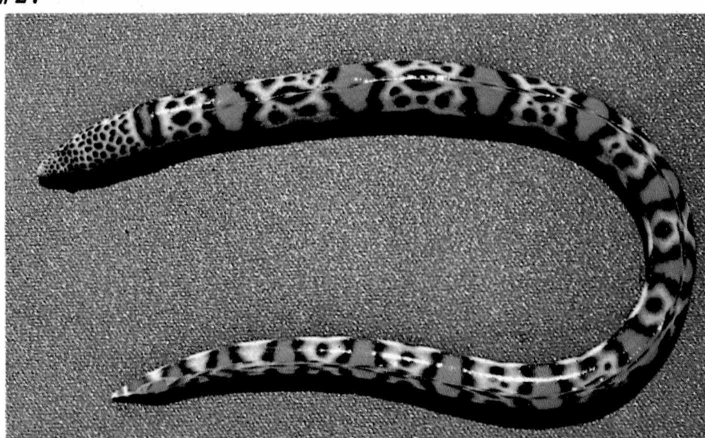

*Quassiremus notochir* 58
3 26°C sg: 1.022 85 cm 1000L

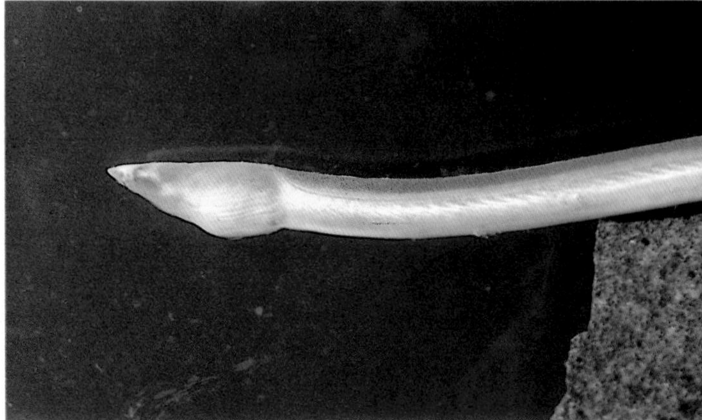

*Sphagebranchus flavicauda* 58
7 ♥ 25°C sg: 1.022 30 cm 300L

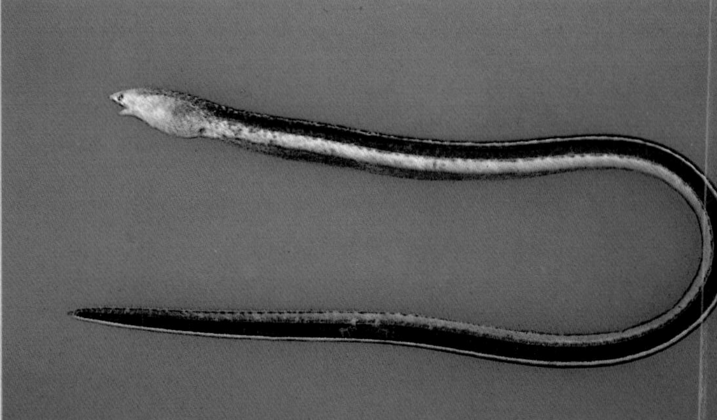

*Aprognathodon platyventris* 58
2 26°C sg: 1.022 23 cm 300L

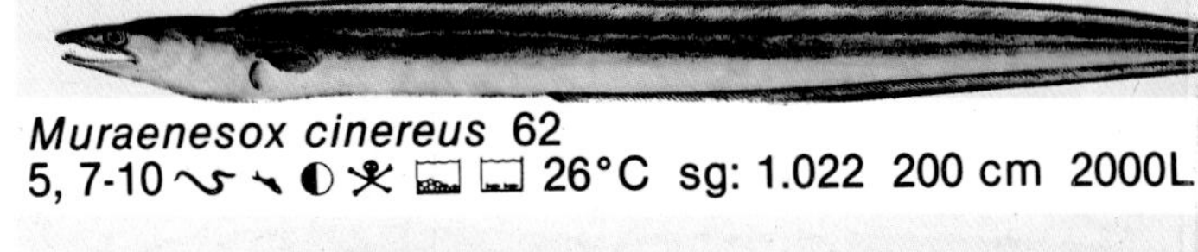

*Muraenesox cinereus* 62
5, 7-10 26°C sg: 1.022 200 cm 2000L

*Gnathophis nystromi* 62
5, 7 26°C sg: 1.022 45 cm 450L

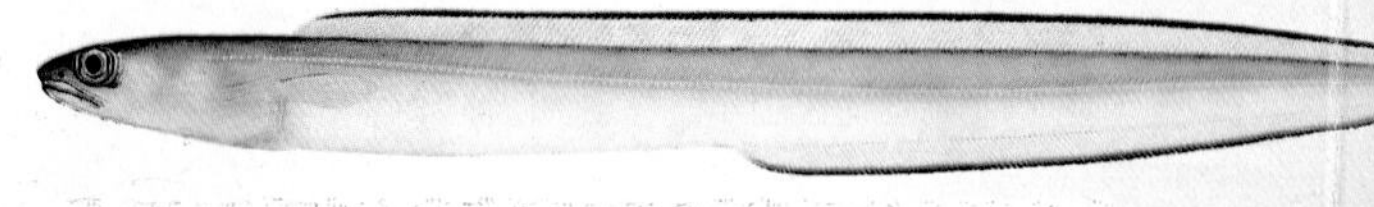

*Anago anago* 62
6-9 26°C sg: 1.022 60 cm 600L

*Conger japonicus* 62
5 26°C sg: 1.022 240 cm 2500L

*Conger cinereus* 62
7, 9 26°C sg: 1.022 103 cm 1000L

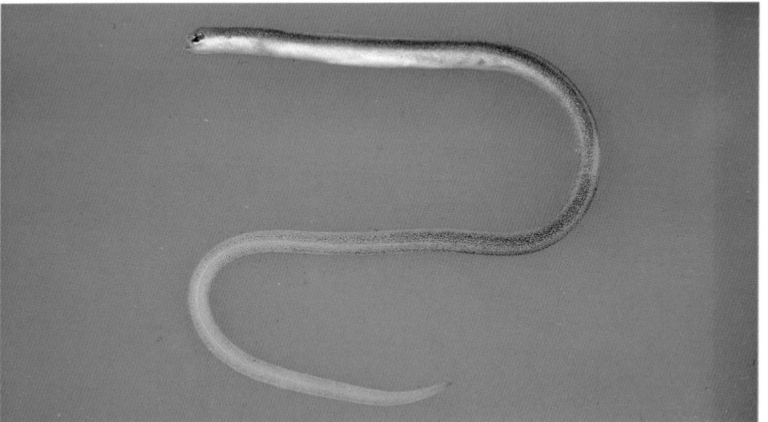

*Heteroconger halis* 62
2 26°C sg: 1.022 51 cm 500L

*Taenioconger digueti* 62
3 26°C sg: 1.022 63 cm 600L

*Ariosoma impressa* 62
2 26°C sg: 1.022 18 cm 200L

*Conger wilsoni* 62
7, 9 26°C sg: 1.022 150 cm 1500L

*Gorgasia preclara* 62
7, 9 26°C sg: 1.022 40 cm 400L

*Taenioconger* sp 62
7 26°C sg: 1.022 30 cm 300L

*Rhinomuraena quaesita* 54
7 26°C sg: 1.022 120 cm 1000L

*Myrichthys maculosus* 58
3, 6-9 26°C sg: 1.022 100 cm 1000L

*Gorgasia preclara* 62
7, 9 26°C sg: 1.022 40 cm 400L

*Gorgasia maculata* 62
9 26°C sg: 1.022 25 cm 300L

*Rhinomuraena quaesita* 54
7 26°C sg: 1.022 120 cm 1000L

*Brachysomophis cirrhocheilus* 58
7, 9 26°C sg: 1.022 110 cm 1200L

*Taenioconger hassi* 62
7, 9 26°C sg: 1.022 36 cm 400L

#30

*Dussumieria hasselti* 69
7 ~ ◐ ♥ ▭ ▭ 26°C sg: 1.022 15 cm 200L

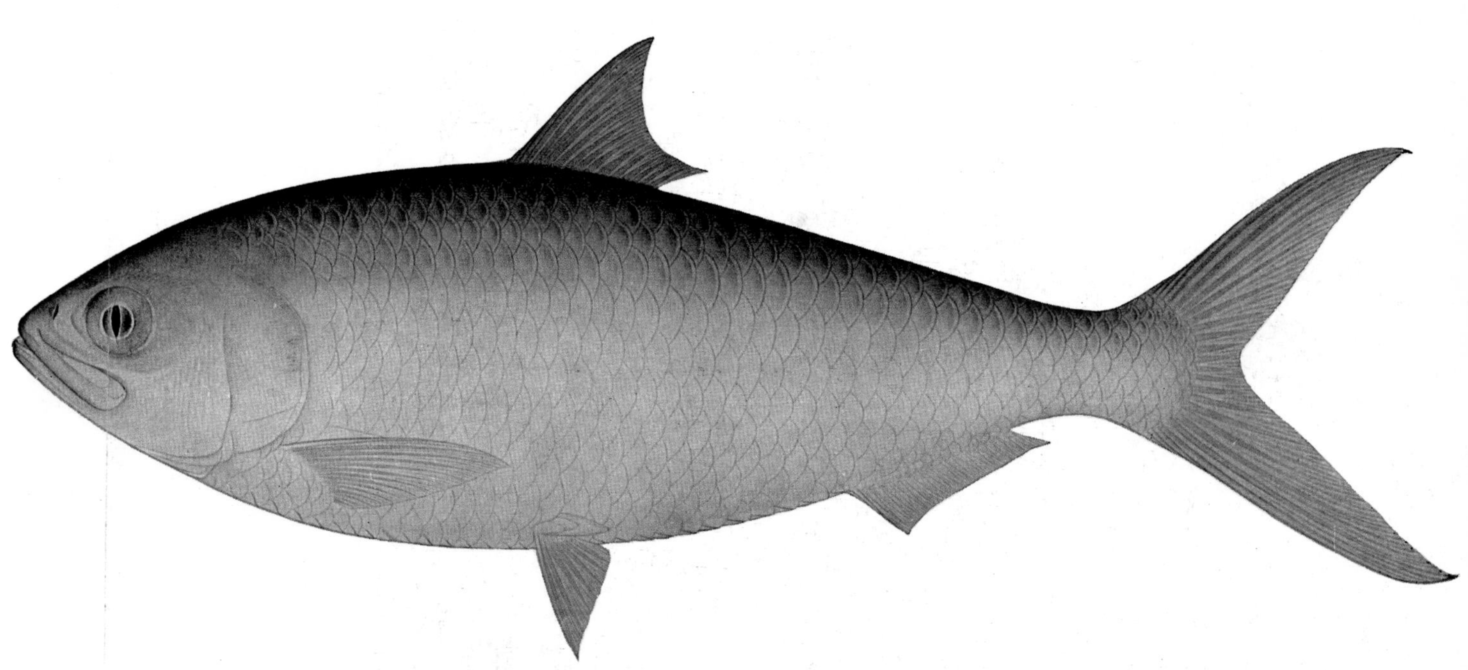

*Hilsa reevesii* 69
7 ~ ◐ ♥ ▭ ▭ 26°C sg: 1.022 25 cm 250L

*Amblygaster leiogaster* 69
7, 9-10 ∿ ◐ ♥ ▭ ▭ 26°C sg: 1.022 25 cm 300L

*Spratelloides japonicus* 69
6-10 ∿ ◐ ♥ ▭ ▭ 26°C sg: 1.022 10 cm 100L

*Clupea harengus pallasi* 69
4-7 ∿ ◐ ♥ ▭ ▭ 26°C sg: 1.022 35 cm 400L

*Sardinella* cf *jussieu* 69
7-10 ∿ ◐ ♥ ▭ ▭ 26°C sg: 1.022 18 cm 200L

*Amblygaster sirm* 69
7, 9 ∿ ◐ ♥ ▭ ▭ 26°C sg: 1.022 25 cm 300L

*Spratelloides robustus* 69
8, 12 ∿ ◐ ♥ ▭ ▭ 26°C sg: 1.022 10 cm 100L

*Etrumeus teres* 69
Circumtrop. ∿ ◐ ♥ ▭ ▭ 26°C sg: 1.022 30 cm 300L

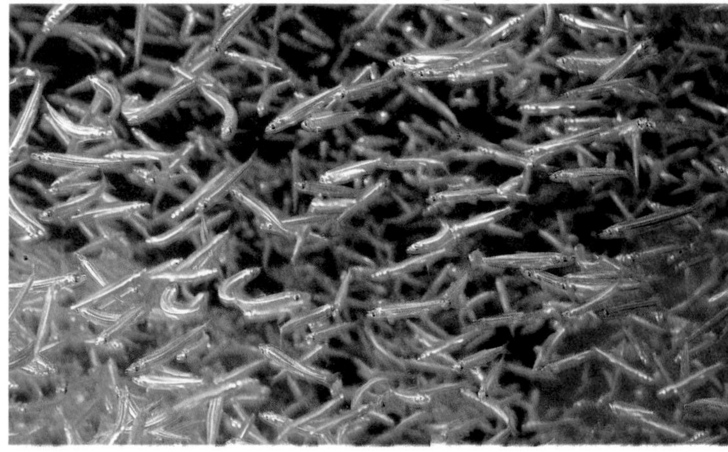

*Jenkinsia* sp. 69
2 ∿ ◐ ♥ ▭ ▭ 26°C sg: 1.022 7 cm 80L

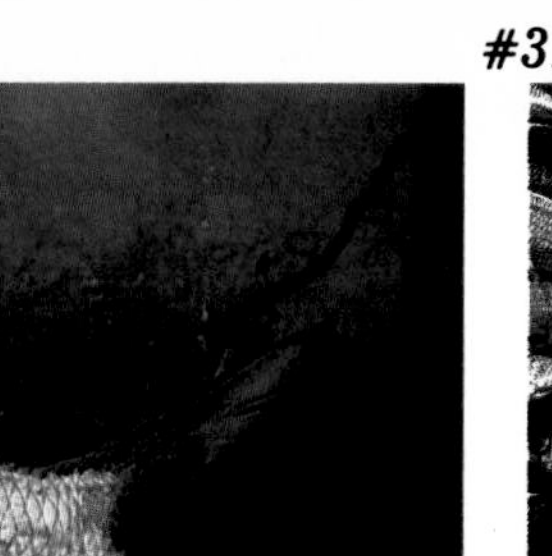

*Anodontostoma chacunda* 69
7, 9 ◐ ♥ 26°C sg: 1.022 17 cm 200L

*Dorosoma petenense* 69
1-2 ◐ ♥ 24°C sg: 1.023 22 cm 250L

*Konosirus punctatus* 69
5-9 ◐ ♥ 24°C sg: 1.023 30 cm 300L

*Nematalosa japonica* 69
5, 7 ◐ ♥ 22°C sg: 1.024 25 cm 300L

*Opisthonema libertate* 69
3 ◐ ♥ 26°C sg: 1.022 23 cm 200L

*Opisthopterus tartoor* 69
3, 6-9 ◐ ♥ 26°C sg: 1.022 23 cm 250L

*Harengula koningsbergeri* 69
7 ◐ ♥ 26°C sg: 1.022 13 cm 150L

*Ilisha elongata* 69
7, 9 ◐ ♥ 26°C sg: 1.022 30 cm 300L

*Engraulis mordax* 70
4 22°C sg: 1.024 13 cm 150L

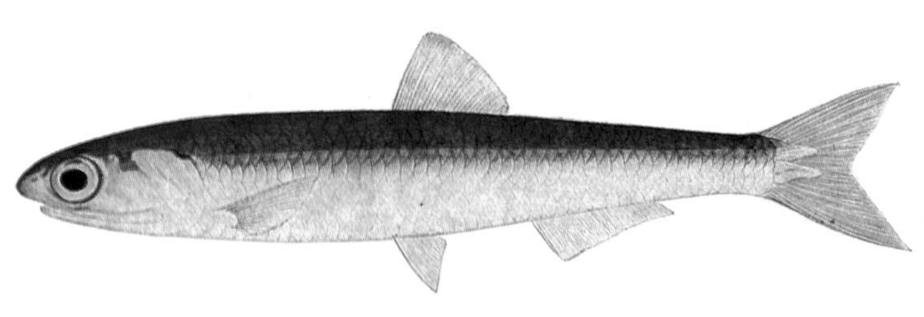

*Engraulis japonicus* 70
5, 7, 9 26°C sg: 1.022 13 cm 150L

*Thryssa hamiltoni* 70
7-9, 12 25°C sg: 1.022 25 cm 250L

*Chanos chanos* 72
5-10 26°C sg: 1.022 180 cm 2000L

*Anchoviella* sp. 70
15 26°C sg: 1.024 8 cm 80L

*Anchovia commersoniana* 70
7, 9 26°C sg: 1.022 13 cm 150L

*Setipinna breviceps* 70
5, 7, 9 25°C sg: 1.022 15 cm 150L

*Chirocentrus nudus* 71
7, 12 26°C sg: 1.022 45 cm 500L

*#32A*

*Engraulis mordax* 70
4 ◐ ♥ 22°C sg: 1.024 13 cm 150L

*Opisthonema oglinum* 69
2 ◐ ♥ 26°C sg: 1.022 30 cm 300L

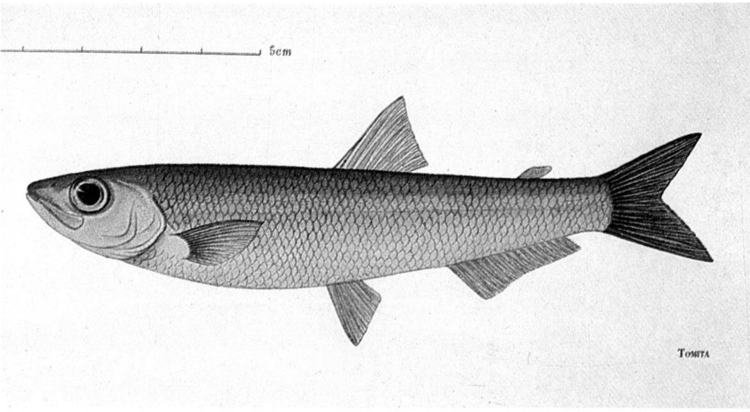


*Hypomesus olidus* 137
4, 5 23°C sg: 1.024 7 cm 80L

*Hypomesus pretiosus japonicus* 137
5 24°C sg: 1.023 5 cm 50L

*Spirinchus lanceolatus* 137
5 23°C sg: 1.024 10 cm 100L

*Salangichthys microdon* 139
5 24°C sg: 1.023 10 cm 100L

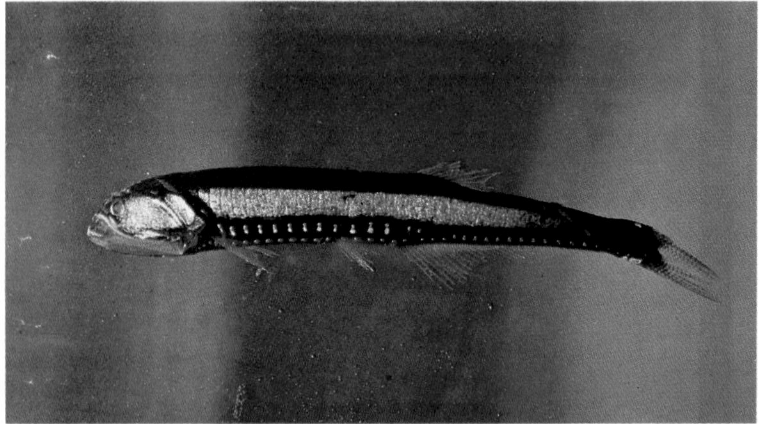

*Gonostoma elongatum* 144
Circumtrop. 20°C sg: 1.024 27 cm 300L

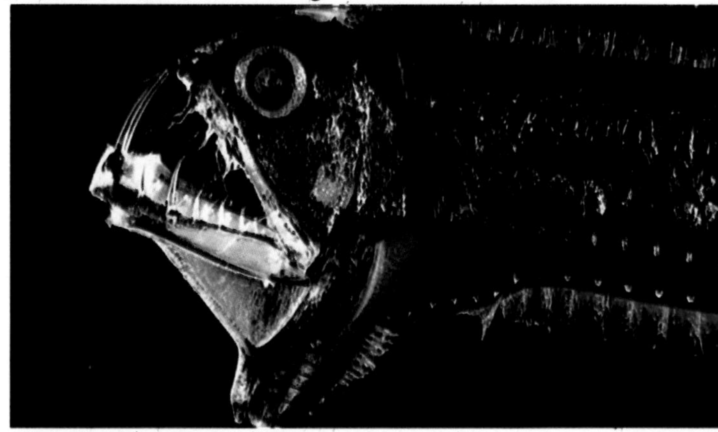

*Chauliodus sloani* 147
Circumtemp. 20°C sg: 1.024 30 cm 300L

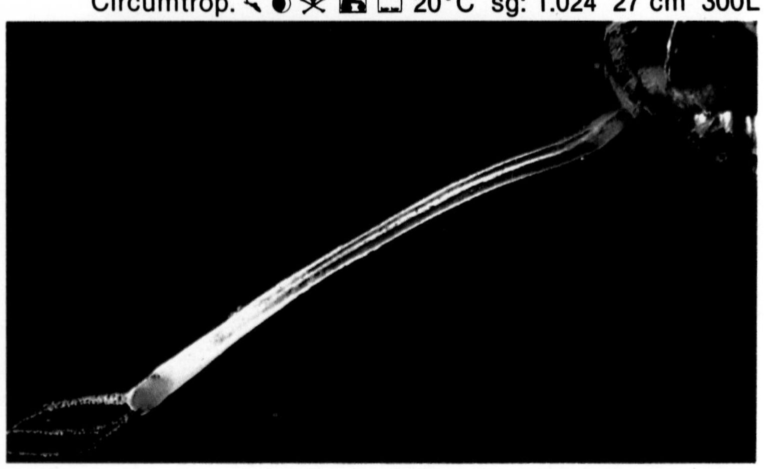

? *Stomias* sp. 148
6 20°C sg: 1.024 18 cm 200L

? *Melanostomias* sp. 150
Circumtemp. 20°C sg: 1.024 26 cm 300L

#34

*Aulopus purpurissatus* 153
7-8, 12 26°C sg: 1.022 60 cm 600L

*Synodus* sp. 157
2 26°C sg: 1.022 30 cm 300L

*Cociella crocodila* 269
5, 7-10 26°C sg: 1.022 25 cm 300L

*Aulopus purpurissatus* 153
7-8, 12 26°C sg: 1.022 60 cm 600L

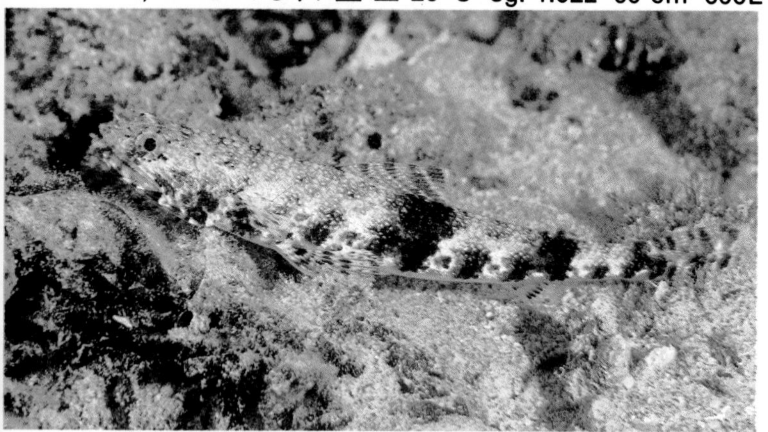

*Saurida gracilis* 157
7-10 26°C sg: 1.023 20 cm 200L

*Synodus variegatus* 157
6-7 26°C sg: 1.022 22 cm 200L

*Platycephalus haackei* 269
7-8 26°C sg: 1.022 40 cm 400L

*Aulopus purpurissatus* 153
7-8, 12 26°C sg: 1.022 60 cm 600L

*Synodus jaculum* 157
7, 9 26°C sg: 1.022 15 cm 150L

*Synodus variegatus* 157
6-7 26°C sg: 1.022 22 cm 200L

*Aulopus japonicus* 153
5 24°C sg: 1.023 20 cm 200L

*Trachinocephalus myops* 157
Circumtrop. 26°C sg: 1.022 30 cm 300L

*Saurida dermatogenys* 157
6 26°C sg: 1.022 30 cm 300L

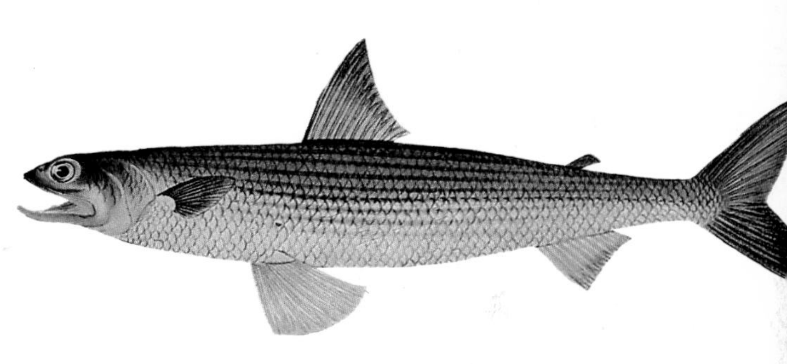

*Saurida undosquamis* 157
7-10 26°C sg: 1.022 30 cm 300L

*Harpadon microchir* 157
5 24°C sg: 1.023 50 cm 500L

*Harpadon translucens* 157
7, 9 26°C sg: 1.022 60 cm 600L

*Synodus synodus* 157
2, 13 26°C sg: 1.022 30 cm 300L

*Synodus intermedius* 157
1-2 24°C sg: 1.023 45 cm 500L

#36

*Synodus rubromarmoratus* 157
5, 7-8 ◐ 26°C sg: 1.022 7.5 cm 100L

*Synodus ulae* 157
5-7 ◐ 26°C sg: 1.022 25 cm 300L

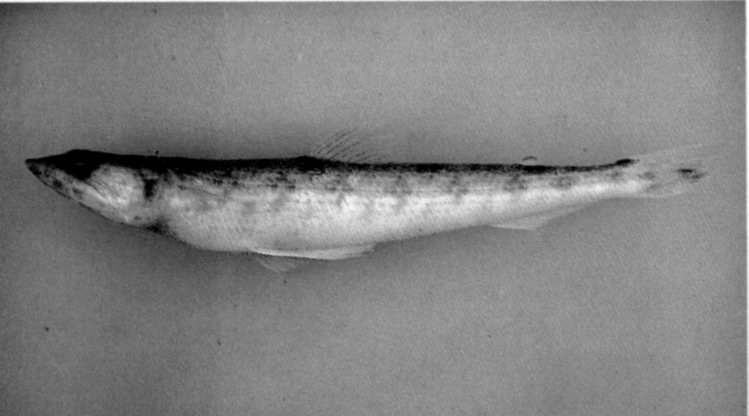

*Synodus foetens* 157
2 ◐ 26°C sg: 1.022 40 cm 400L

*Synodus synodus* 157
2, 13 ◐ 26°C sg: 1.022 30 cm 300L

*Synodus engelmani* 157
6-9 ◐ 26°C sg: 1.022 20 cm 200L

*Saurida normani* 157
1-2 ◐ 26°C sg: 1.022 25 cm 300L

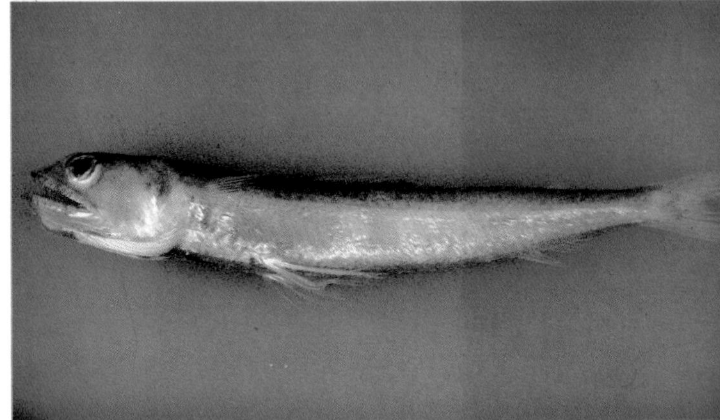

*Synodus poeyi* 157
1-2 ◐ 24°C sg: 1.023 30 cm 300L

*Synodus intermedius* 157
1-2 ◐ 24°C sg: 1.023 45 cm 500L

*Synodus synodus* 157
2, 13 26°C sg: 1.022 30 cm 300L

*Synodus lacertinus* 157
3 26°C sg: 1.022 10 cm 100L

*Synodus* sp. 157
8 26°C sg: 1.022 15 cm 150L

*Alepisaurus borealis* 163
3, 6-7 20°C sg: 1.024 300 cm 3000L

*Synodus* sp. 157
8 26°C sg: 1.022 15 cm 150L

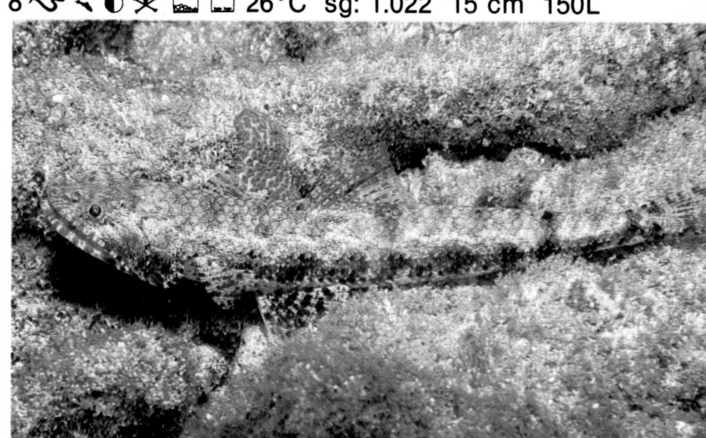

*Saurida gracilis* 157
7-10 26°C sg: 1.022 20 cm 200L

*Synodus* sp. 157
8 26°C sg: 1.022 15 cm 150L

Myctophid 166
All Oceans 22°C sg: 1.023 10 cm 100L

#38

*Pollachius pollachias* 174
14 20°C sg: 1.024 52 cm 500L

*? Lotella* sp. 171
12 ∿ ↘ ◐ ✱ ▣ ▭ 23°C sg: 1.024 50 cm 500L

*Lotella fuliginosa* 171
12 ∿ ◐ ♥ ▣ ▭ 24°C sg: 1.024 10 cm 100L

*Lotella rhacinus* 171
11 ∿ ↘ ◐ ✱ ▣ ▭ 22°C sg: 1.024 45 cm 500L

*Physiculus maximowiczi* 171
5 ∿ ◐ ♥ ▣ ▭ 23°C sg: 1.024 10 cm 100L

*Pseudophycis breviusculus* 171
12 ∿ ◐ ♥ ▣ ▭ 24°C sg: 1.024 7 cm 80L

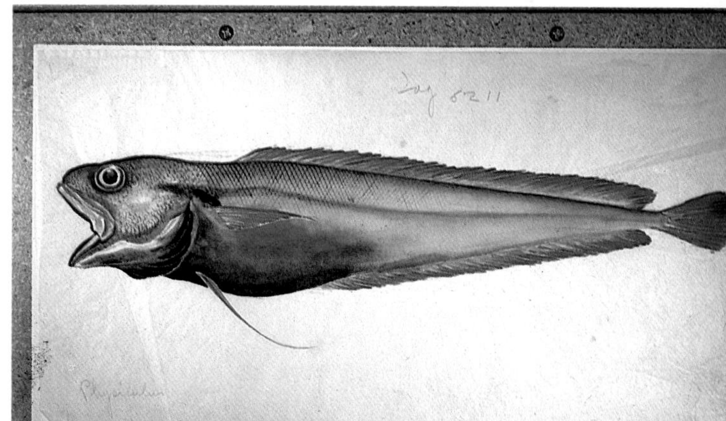

*Physiculus* sp. 171
?7 ∿ ◐ ♥ ▣ ▭ 26°C sg: 1.022 25 cm 250L

*Eleginus gracilis* 174
5 ∿ ◐ ♥ ▣ ▭ 22°C sg: 1.024 10 cm 100L

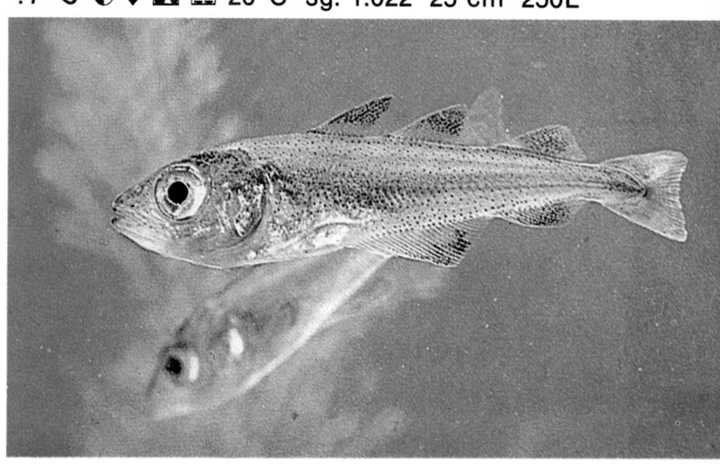

*Pollachius pollachius* 174
14 ∿ ↘ ◐ ✱ ▣ ▭ 20°C sg: 1.024 52 cm 500L

*Gadus macrocephalus* 174
1, 4-5 23°C sg: 1.024 100 cm 1000L

*Theragra chalcogramma* 174
5 26°C sg: 1.024 10 cm 100L

*Gaidropsarus ensis* 174
1-2 26°C sg: 1.022 30 cm 300L

*Coelorhinchus tokiensis* 176
5 24°C sg: 1.023 10 cm 100L

*Gadus morhua* 174
1, 14 22°C sg: 1.024 150 cm 1500L

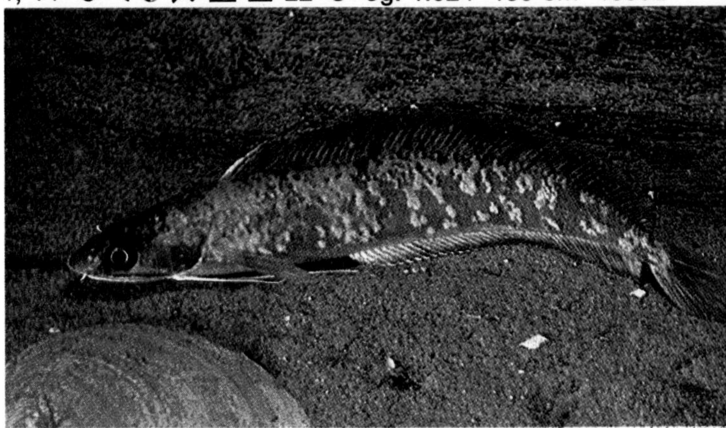

*Urophycis chuss* 174
1 22°C sg: 1.024 52 cm 500L

*Coryphaenoides asper* 176
5 23°C sg: 1.024 10 cm 100L

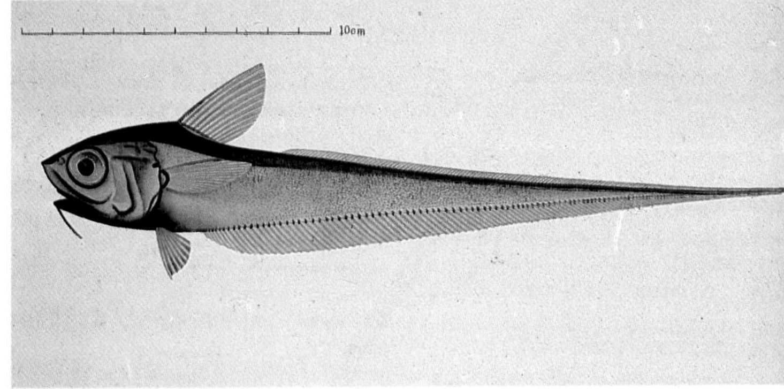


*Hymenocephalus gracilis* 176
5 24°C sg: 1.024 20 cm 200L

#40

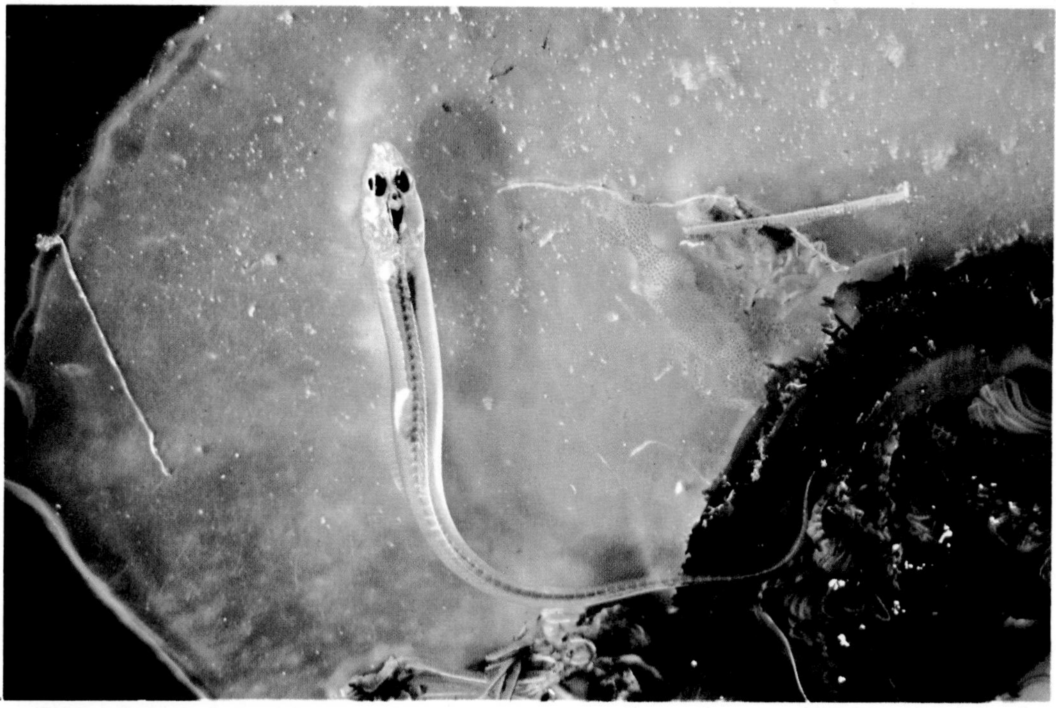

*Onuxodon margaritiferae* 178
7, 9 26°C sg: 1.022 9 cm 100L

*Carapus bermudensis* 178

2 26°C sg: 1.022 20 cm 200L

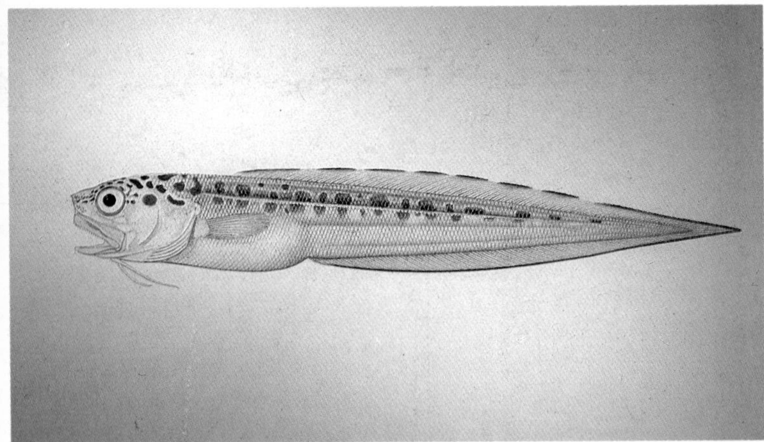

*Lepophidium* sp. 177
3 ◐ 26°C sg: 1.022 25 cm 300L

*Lepophidium prorates* 177
3 ◐ 26°C sg: 1.022 27 cm 300L

*Brotula barbata* 177
6-10 ◐ 26°C sg: 1.022 100 cm 1000L

*Brotula multibarbata* 177
6-10 ◐ 26°C sg: 1.022 100 cm 1000L

*Chilara taylori* 177
3 ◐ 26°C sg: 1.022 36 cm 400L

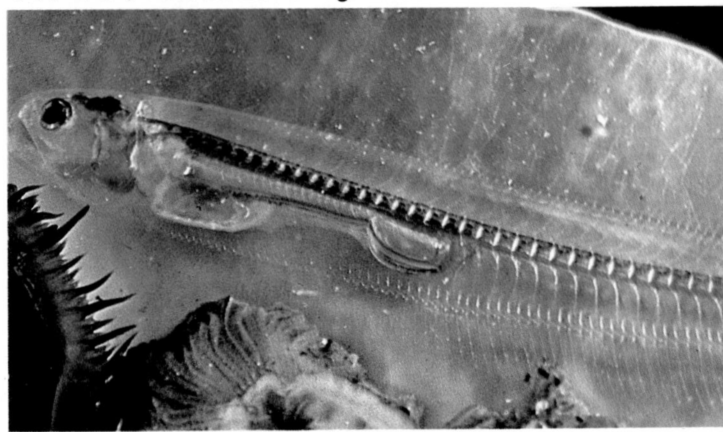

*Onuxodon margaritiferae* 178
7, 9 ◐ ♥ 26°C sg: 1.022 9 cm 100L

*Carapus bermudensis* 178
2 ◐ ♥ 26°C sg: 1.022 20 cm 200L

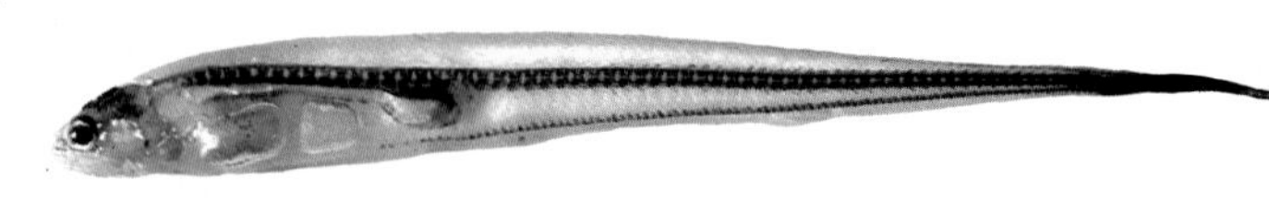

*Carapus homei* 178
8 ◐ ♥ 26°C sg: 1.022 17 cm 200L

*Encheliophis gracilis* 178
7, 9 26°C sg: 1.022 30 cm 300L

*Dinematichthys dasyrhynchus* 179
12 24°C sg: 1.023 8 cm 100L

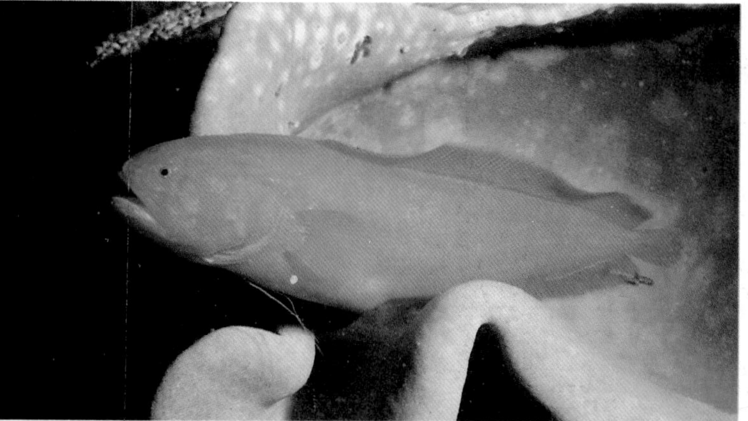

*Brotula erythrea?* 179
7 26°C sg: 1.022 12cm 150L

*Brosmophycis marginata* 179
3-4 26°C sg: 1.022 46 cm 500L

*Stygnobrotula latibricola* 179
2 26°C sg: 1.022 8 cm 80L

*Brotulina fusca* 179
7, 9 26°C sg: 1.022 12 cm 120L

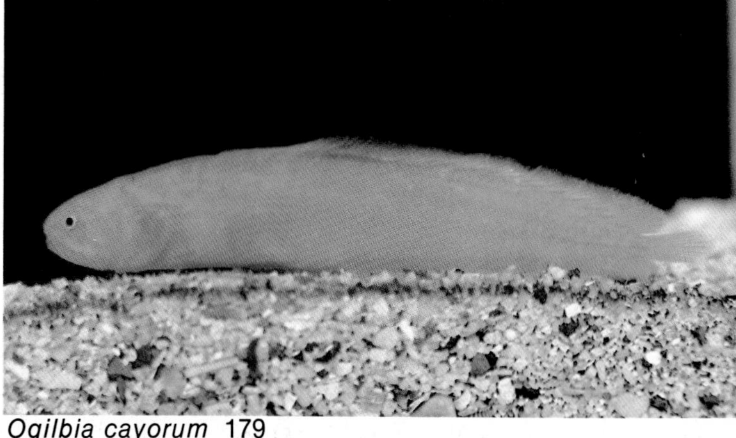

*Ogilbia cayorum* 179
2 26°C sg: 1.022 10 cm 100L

*Ogilbia* sp. 179
3 26°C sg: 1.022 10 cm 100L

#42

*Antennarius striatus* 183
1, 2, 6-13 26°C sg: 1.022 15.5 cm 200L

*#42A*

*Antennarius hispidus* 183
7-9 26°C sg: 1.022 15 cm 200L

*Halophryne diemensis* 181
7-9 26°C sg: 1.022 30 cm 300L

*Halophryne diemensis* 181
7-9 26°C sg: 1.022 30 cm 300L

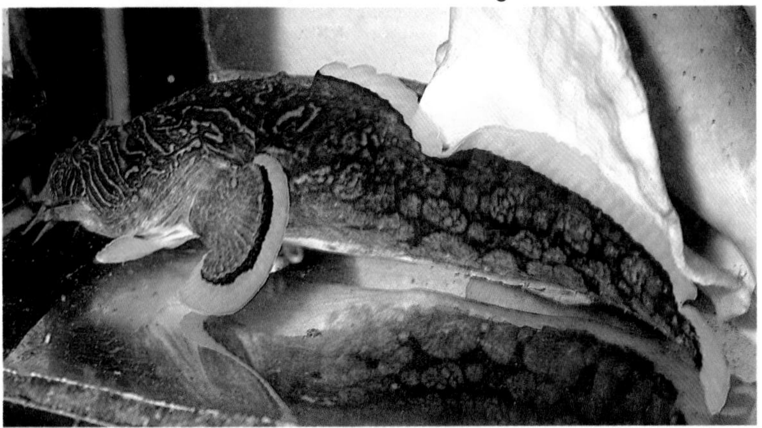

*Sanopus splendidus* 181
2 26°C sg: 1.022 20 cm 200L

*Sanopus splendidus* 181
2 26°C sg: 1.022 20 cm 200L

*Porichthys notatus* 181
3-4 26°C sg: 1.022 38 cm 400L

*Porichthys margaritatus* 181
3 26°C sg: 1.022 11.3 cm 100L

*Batrachomoeus trispinosus* 181
7, 9 26°C sg: 1.022 20 cm 200L

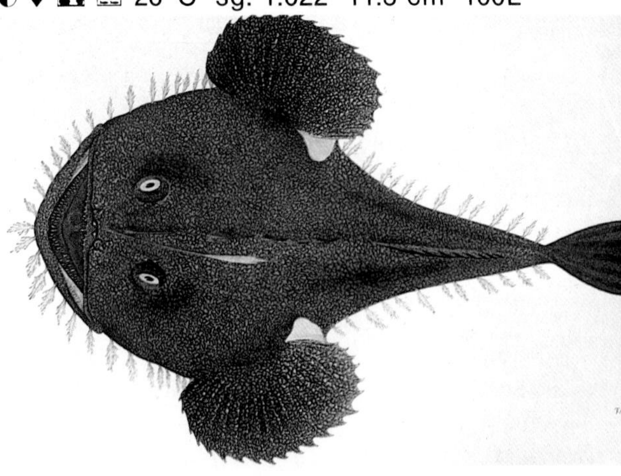

*Lophiomus setigerus* 182
7 26°C sg: 1.022 35 cm 400L

*Lophiocharon trisignatus* 183
7 26°C sg: 1.022 15 cm 200L

*Histophryne bougainvillei* 183
8, 12 25°C sg: 1.022 6.4 cm 100L

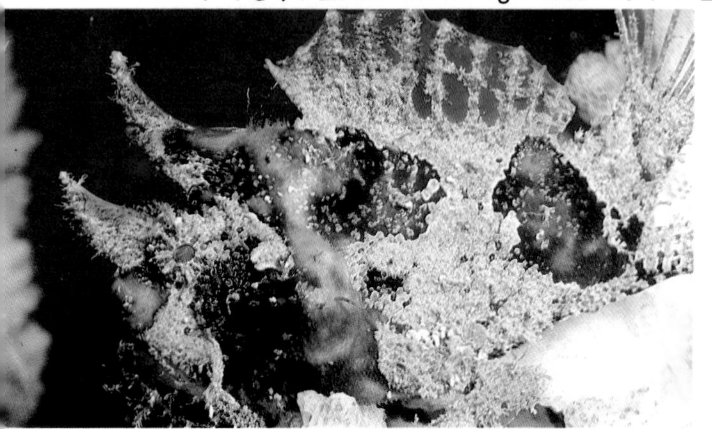

*Tathicarpus butleri* 183
7, 8, 12 25°C sg: 1.022 10 cm 100L

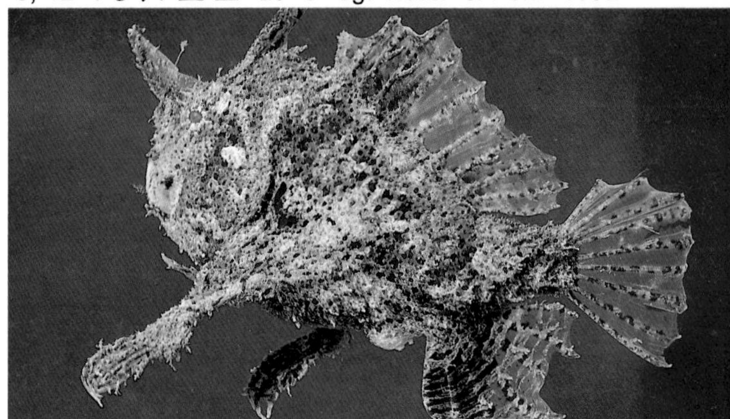

*Tathicarpus butleri* 183
7, 8, 12 26°C sg: 1.022 10 cm 100L

*Rhycherus gloveri* 183
12 24°C sg: 1.022 11.5 cm 100L

*Histrio histrio* 183
1-2, 7-10, 13 26°C sg: 1.022 14 cm 100L

*Antennarius maculatus* 183
7, 9 26°C sg: 1.022 8.5 cm 100L

*Antennarius biocellatus* 183
7 26°C sg: 1.018 12 cm 100L

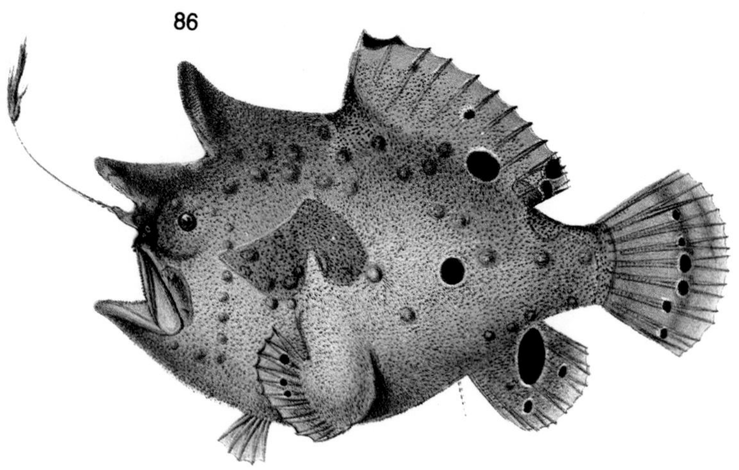

*Antennarius maculatus* 183

*Antennarius maculatus* 183

*Antennarius maculatus* 183

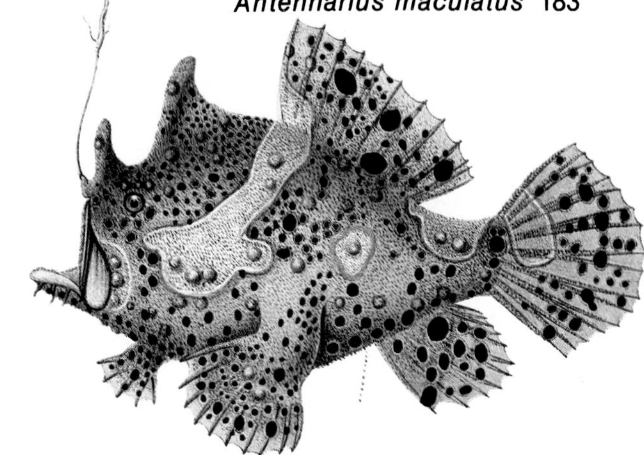

*Antennarius maculatus* 183

*Antennarius maculatus* 183

*Antennarius striatus* 183

*Antennarius maculatus* 183

*Antennarius coccineus* 183

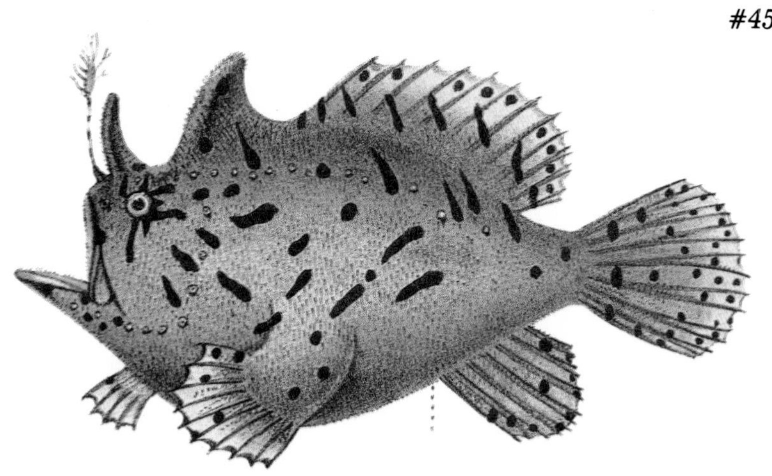

*Antennarius hispidus* 183

*Antennarius hispidus* 183

*Antennarius commersoni* 183

*Antennarius commersoni* 183

*Antennarius pictus* 183

*Antennarius pictus* 183

*Antennarius biocellatus* 183

*Antennarius biocellatus* 183

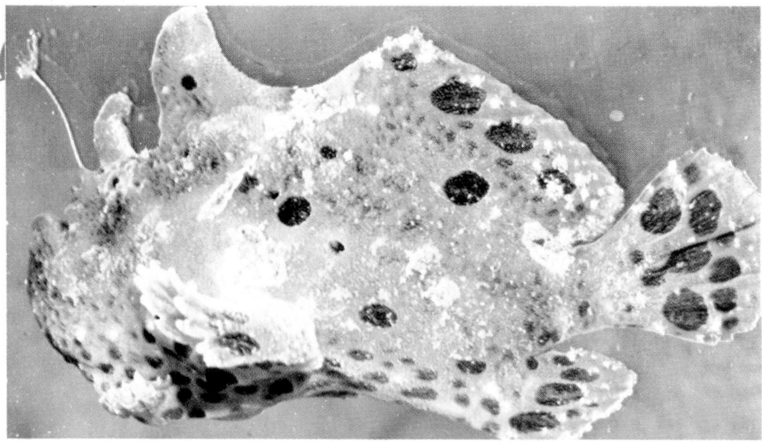

*Antennarius pardalis* 183
13 26°C sg: 1.022 10 cm 100L

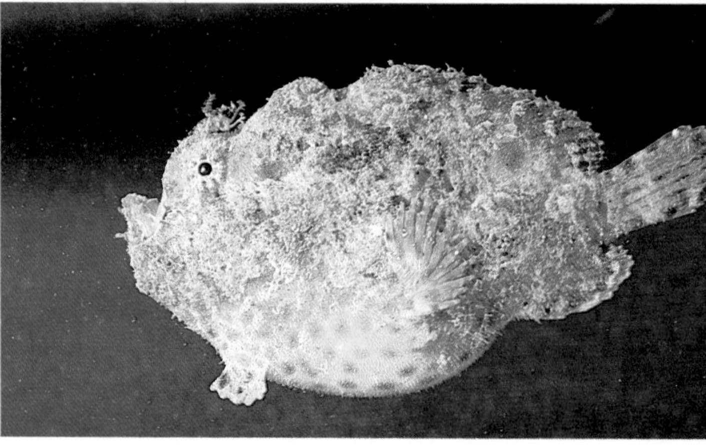

*Antennarius sanguineus* 183
3 26°C sg: 1.022 8 cm 100L

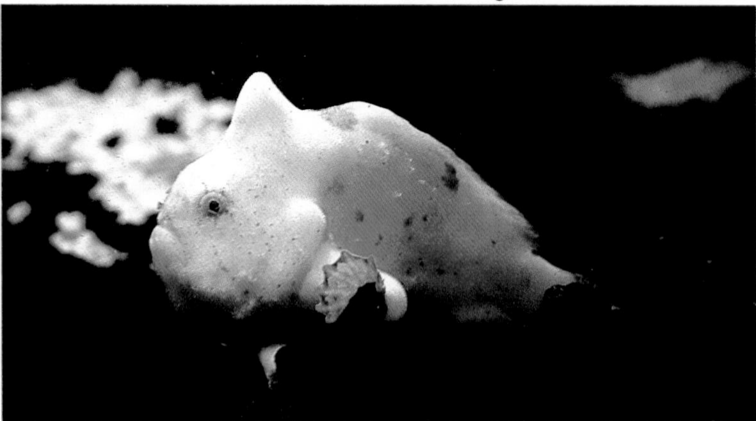

*Antennarius strigatus* 183
3 26°C sg: 1.022 8 cm 100L

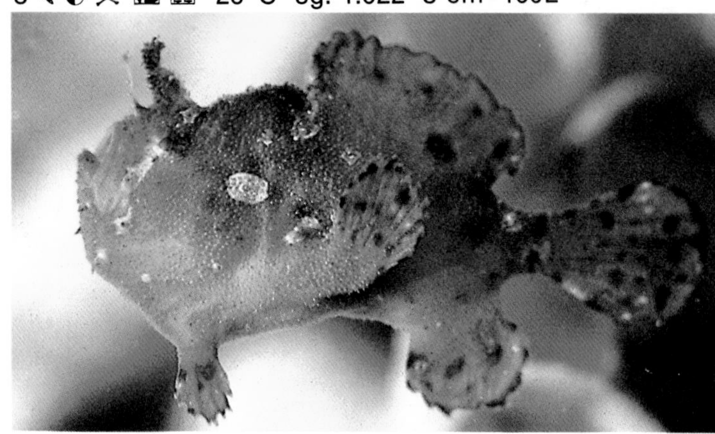

*Antennarius avalonis* 183
3 26°C sg: 1.022 33 cm 300L

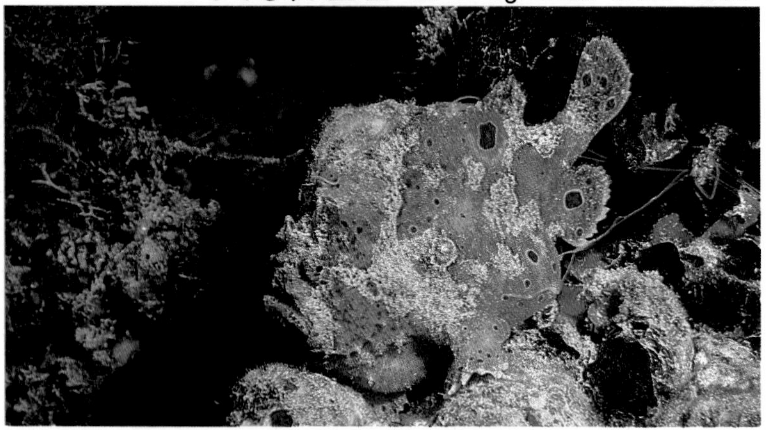

*Antennarius multiocellatus* 183
2, 13 26°C sg: 1.022 11 cm 100L

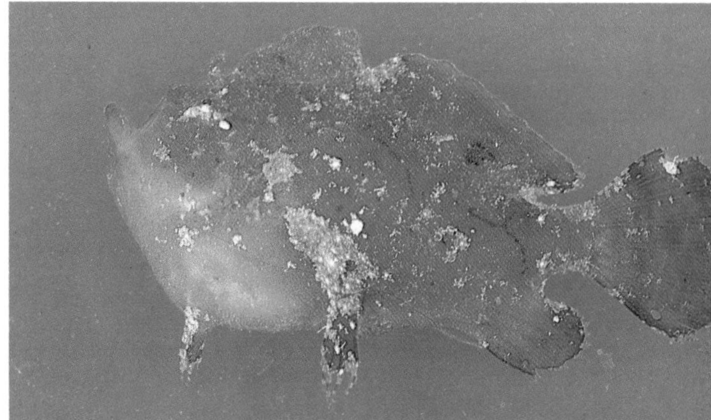

*Antennarius pauciradiatus* 183
2 26°C sg: 1.022 4 cm 50L

*Antennarius ocellatus* 183
2 26°C sg: 1.022 32 cm 300L

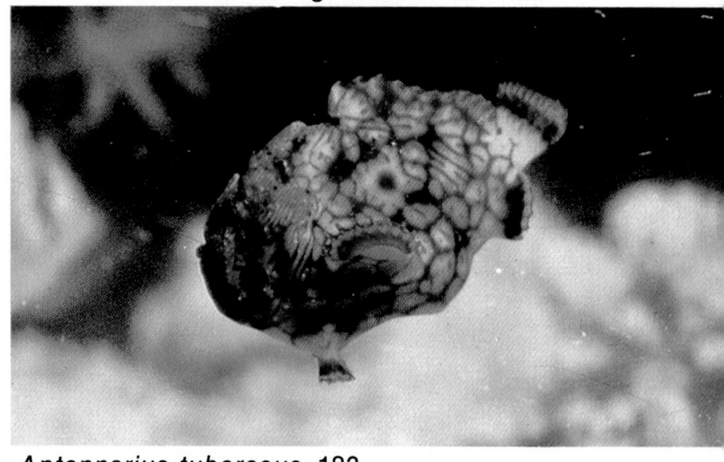

*Antennarius tuberosus* 183
6-10 26°C sg: 1.022 7 cm 100L

*Antennarius maculatus* 183
7, 9 ◐ 26°C sg: 1.022 8.5 cm 100L

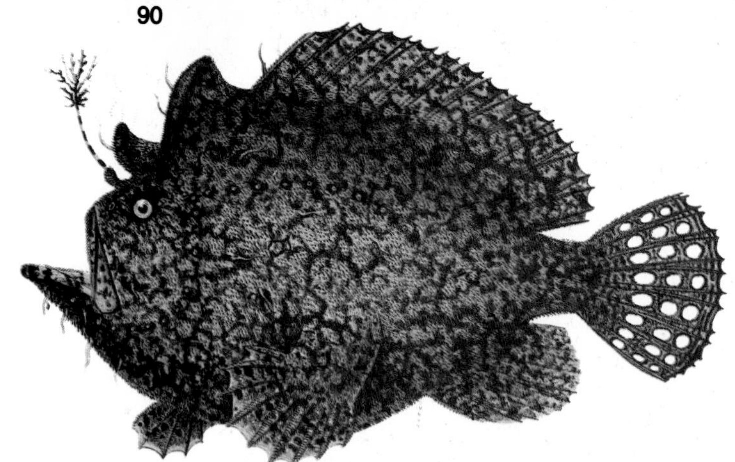

*Lophiocharon trisignatus* 183

*Antennarius commersoni* 183

*Antennarius striatus* 183

*Antennarius striatus* 183

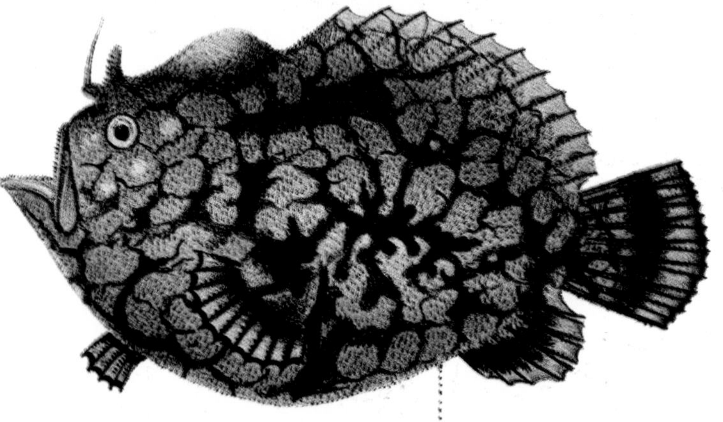

*Antennarius tuberosus* 183

*Antennarius biocellatus* 183

*Antennarius pictus* 183

*Antennarius nummifer* 183

*Antennarius hispidus* 183
7-9 26°C sg: 1.022 15 cm 200L

*Antennarius commersoni* 183
3, 6-10 26°C sg: 1.022 29 cm 300L

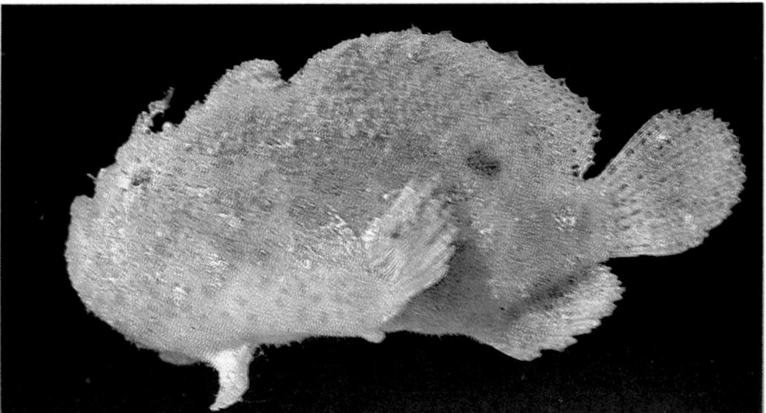

*Antennarius nummifer* 183
3, 6-10 26°C sg: 1.022 29 cm 300L

*Antennarius commersoni* 183
3, 6-10 26°C sg: 1.022 29 cm 300L

*Antennarius striatus* 183
1-2, 6-13 26°C sg: 1.022 15.5 cm 200L

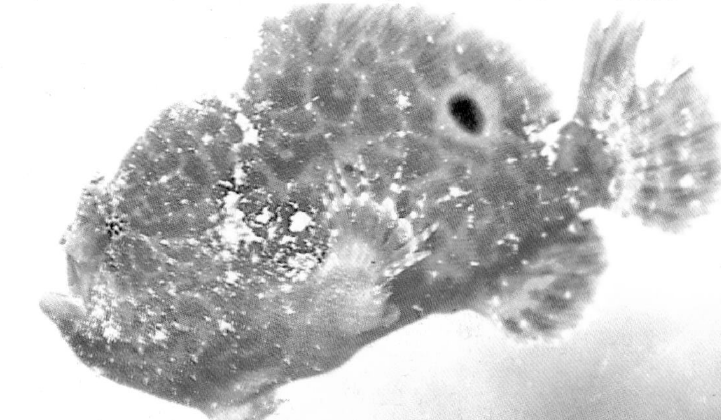

*Antennarius coccineus* 183
6-10 26°C sg: 1.022 9 cm 100L

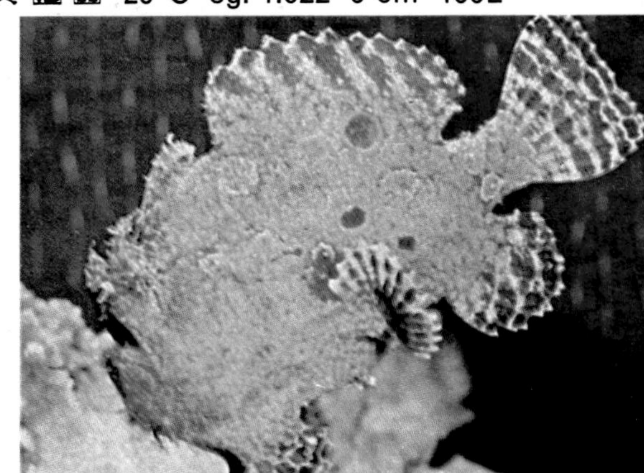

*Antennarius indicus* 183
9 26°C sg: 1.022 19 cm 200L

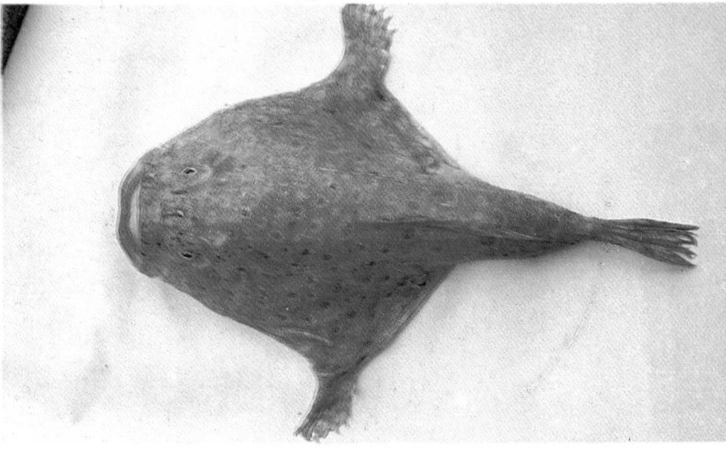

*Chaunax abei* 185
5-7 24°C sg: 1.022 30 cm 300L

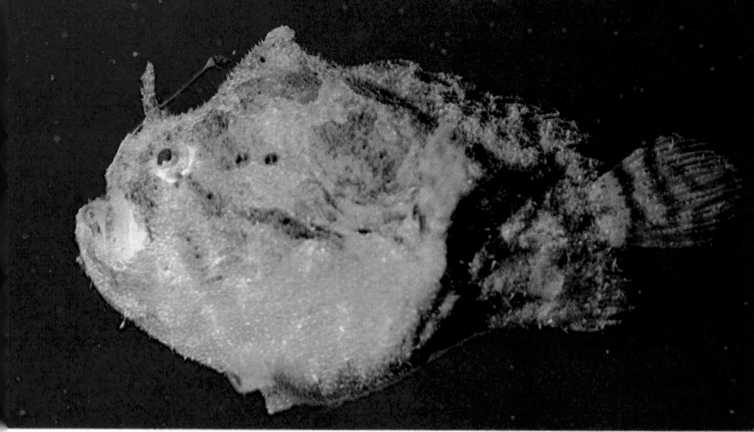

*Antennarius analis* 183
6-8, 12 26°C sg: 1.022 8 cm 100L

*Antennarius commersoni* 183
3, 6-10 26°C sg: 1.022 29 cm 300L

*Antennarius maculatus* 183
7, 9 26°C sg: 1.022 8.5 cm 100L

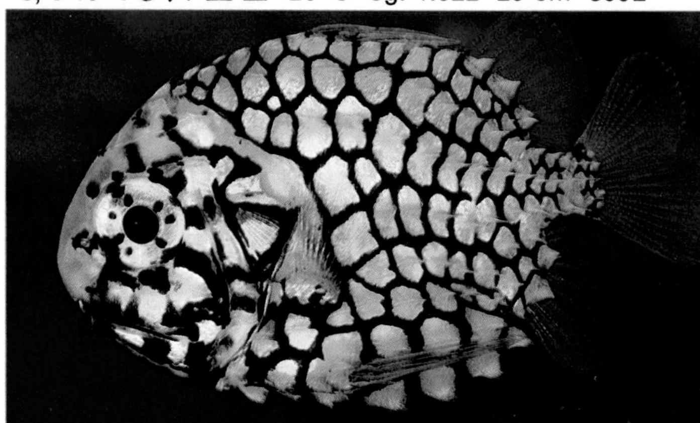

*Monocentris japonicus* 253
7-10 26°C sg: 1.022 16 cm 200L

*Eurypegasus draconis* 229
7-9 26°C sg: 1.022 10 cm 100L

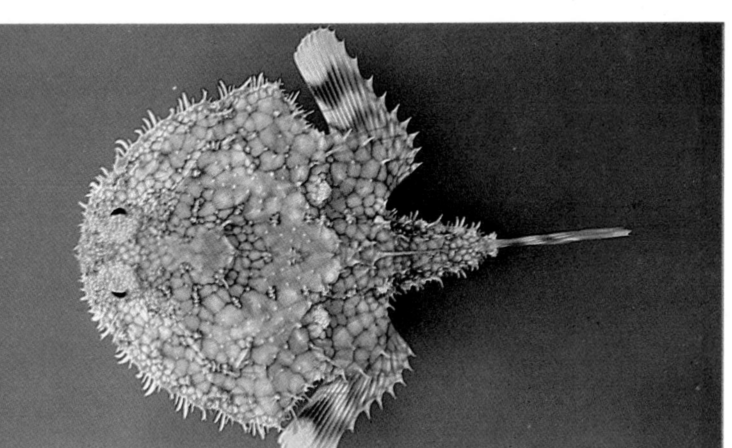

*Halieutichthys aculeatus* 186
2 ◐ ♥ 26°C sg: 1.022 10 cm 100L

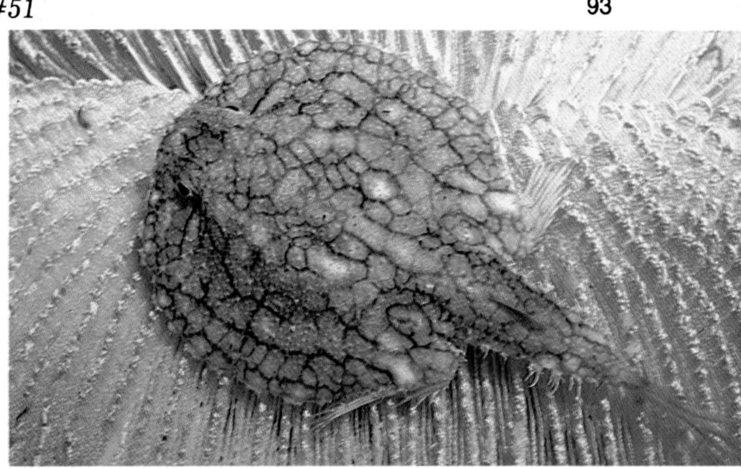

*Halieutaea retifera* 186
6 (HI) ◐ ♥ 26°C sg: 1.022 10 cm 100L

*Halieutaea stellata* 186
7, 9 ◐ ♥ 26°C sg: 1.022 30 cm 300L

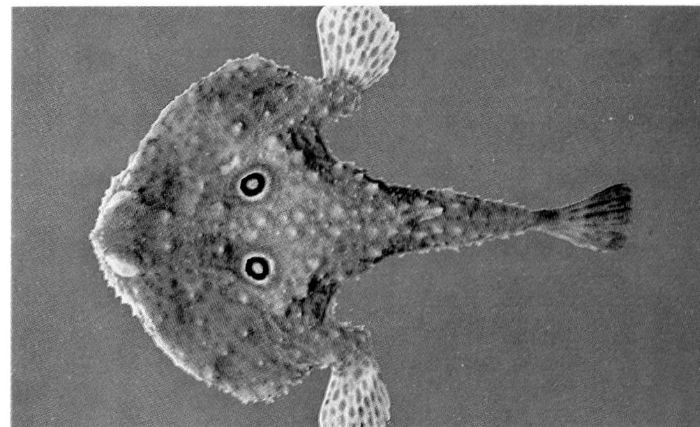

*Zalieutes elator* 186
3 ◐ ♥ 26°C sg: 1.022 15 cm 200L

*Ogcocephalus nasutus* 186
2 ◐ ♥ 26°C sg: 1.022 38 cm 400L

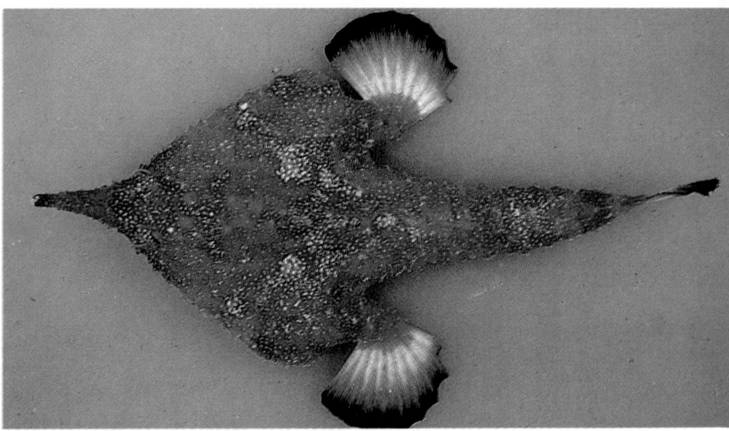

*Ogcocephalus corniger* 186
2 ◐ ♥ 26°C sg: 1.022 23 cm 200L

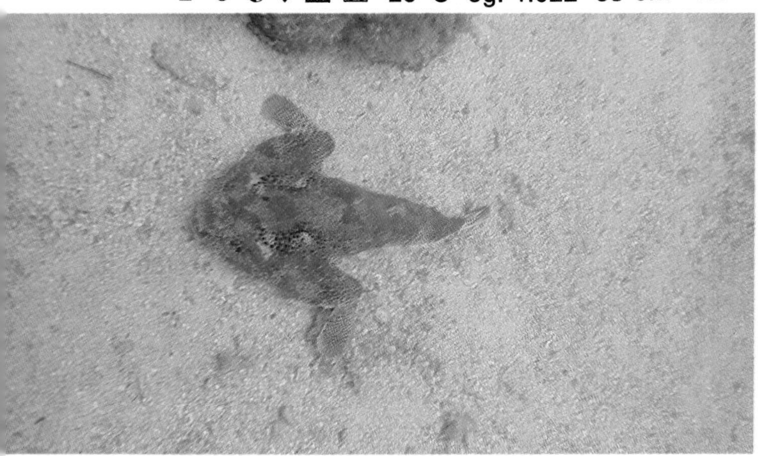

*Ogcocephalus radiatus* 186
2 ◐ ♥ 26°C sg: 1.022 38 cm 400L

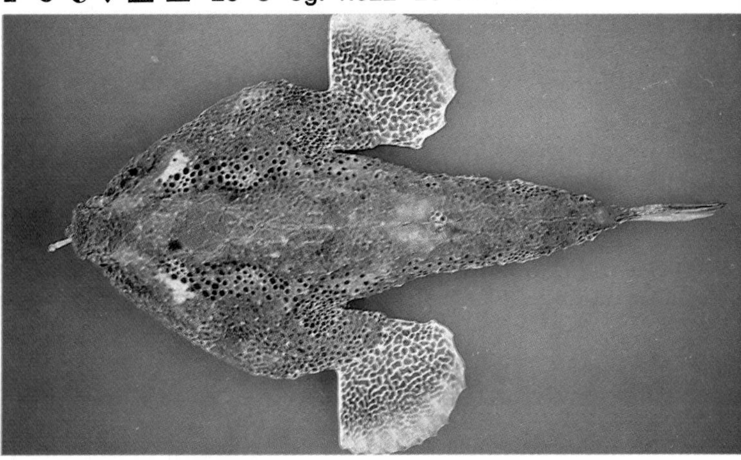

*Ogcocephalus radiatus* 186
2 ◐ ♥ 26°C sg: 1.022 38 cm 400L

#52

*Discotrema crinophila* 198
6-9 ↝ ◐ ♥ 26°C sg: 1.022 5 cm 50L

*Discotrema* sp. 198
6-9 ↝ ◐ ♥ 26°C sg: 1.022 5 cm 50L

*Diademichthys lineatus* 198
7-9 ◐ ♥ 26°C sg: 1.022 5 cm 50L

*Discotrema crinophila* 198
6-9 ◐ ♥ 26°C sg: 1.022 5 cm 50L

*Lepadichthys lineatus* 198
9-10 ◐ ♥ 26°C sg: 1.022 31 cm 300L

Undescribed Gobiesocid 198
12 ~ ◐ ♥ ⌂ ▭ 24°C sg: 1.023 2.5 cm 50L

Undescribed Clingfish? 198
12 ~ ◐ ♥ ⌂ ▭ 24°C sg: 1.023 2.5 cm 50L

*Cochleoceps spatula* 198
12 ~ ◐ ♥ ⌂ ▭ 24°C sg: 1.023 2.5 cm 50L

*Aspasmogaster tasmaniensis* 198
12 ~ ◐ ♥ ⌂ ▭ 24°C sg: 1.023 1.5 cm 50L

*Sicyases sanguineus* 198
3 ~ ⚓ ◐ ✕ ⌂ ▭ 26°C sg: 1.022 22 cm 200L

*Sicyases sanguineus* 198
3 ~ ⚓ ◐ ✕ ⌂ ▭ 26°C sg: 1.022 22 cm 200L

*Arcos robiginosus* 198
2 ~ ◐ ♥ ⌂ ▭ 26°C sg: 1.022 3.5 cm 50L

*Aspasmichthys ciconiae* 198
5, 7 ~ ◐ ♥ ⌂ ▭ 26°C sg: 1.022 8 cm 100L

*Lepadogaster candollei* 198
13, 15 ◐ ♥ 26°C sg: 1.024 12 cm 120L

*Lepadogaster lepadogaster* 198
15 ◐ ♥ 26°C sg: 1.024 10 cm 100L

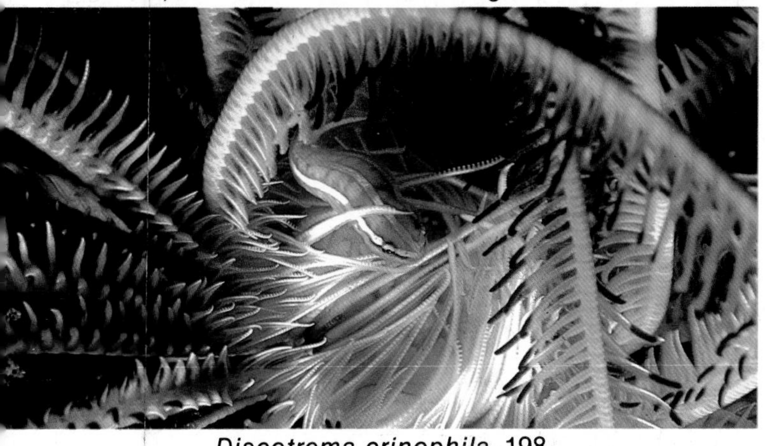

*Discotrema crinophila* 198
6-9 ◐ ♥ 26°C sg: 1.022 5 cm 50L

*Lepadichthys frenatus* 198
5 ◐ ♥ 24°C sg: 1.023 3 cm 50L

*Tomicodon humeralis* 198
3 ◐ ♥ 26°C sg: 1.022 8.3 cm 100L

*Gobiesox maeandricus* 198
3-4 ◐ ♥ 24°C sg: 1.023 16 cm 200L

*Gobiesox adustus* 198
3 ◐ ♥ 26°C sg: 1.022 5 cm 50L

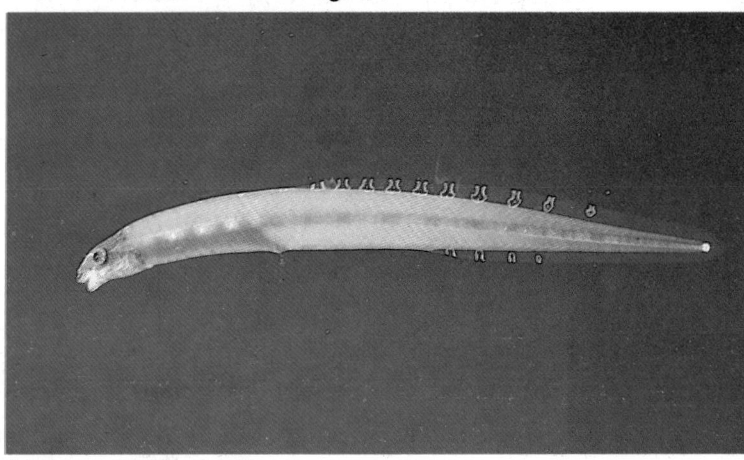

*Alabes parvulus* 199
12 ◐ ♥ 24°C sg: 1.023 3.2 cm 50L

*#55*

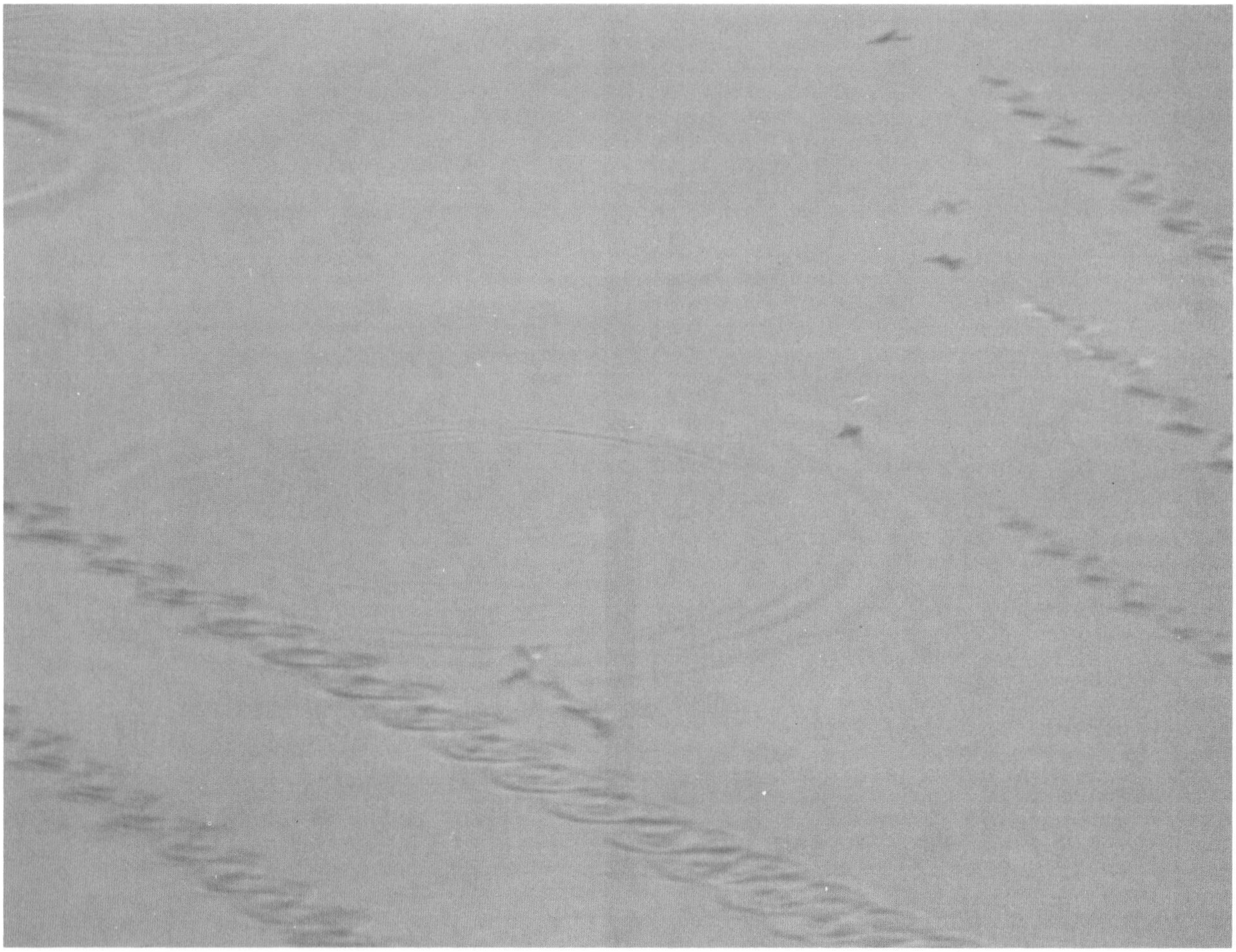

Exocoetidae 200
6-9 ∿ ↘ ◐ ♥ ☐ 26°C sg: 1.022 27 cm 300L

Exocoetidae 200
6-9 ∿ ↘ ◐ ♥ ☐ 26°C sg: 1.022 27 cm 300L

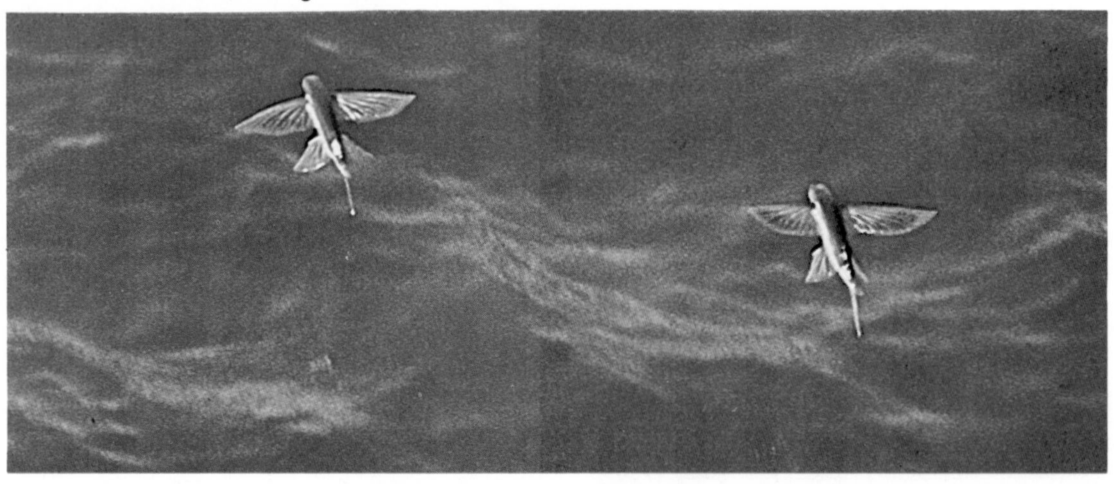

*Cheilopogon atrisignis* 200
7, 9 ∿ ➘ ◐ ♥ ☐ 26°C sg: 1.022 25 cm 300L

*Hirundichthys* sp. 200
6-7 ∿ ➘ ◐ ♥ ☐ 26°C sg: 1.022 26 cm 300L

*Cypselurus poecilopterus* 200
6, 7 ∿ ➘ ◐ ♥ ☐ 26°C sg: 1.022 30 cm 300L

*Cheilopogon pinnatibarbatus japonicus* 200
7 ∿ ➘ ◐ ♥ ☐ 26°C sg: 1.022 30 cm 300L

*Cheilopogon suttoni* 200
7, 9 ∿ ➘ ◐ ♥ ☐ 26°C sg: 1.022 25 cm 300L

*Cypselurus hiraii* 200
7 ∿ ➘ ◐ ♥ ☐ 26°C sg: 1.022 30 cm 300L

*Hemiramphus far* 201
7, 9 ➘ ◐ ⚔ ☐ 26°C sg: 1.022 65 cm 800L

*Hemiramphus far* 201
7, 9 ➘ ◐ ⚔ ☐ 26°C sg: 1.022 65 cm 800L

*Hyporhamphus dussumieri* 201
6-9 26°C sg: 1.022 40 cm 400L

*Hyporhamphus melanochir* 201
12 23°C sg: 1.024 25 cm 300L

*Hemiramphus brasiliensis* 201
1-2, 13 26°C sg: 1.022 40 cm 400L

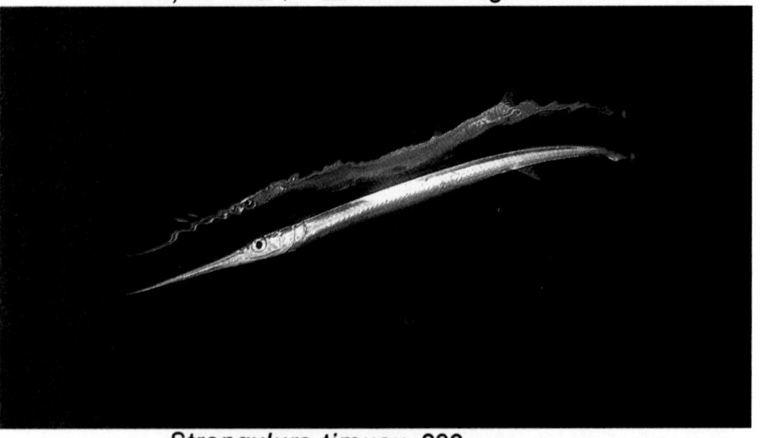

*Strongylura timucu* 202
1 23°C sg: 1.024 100 cm 1000L

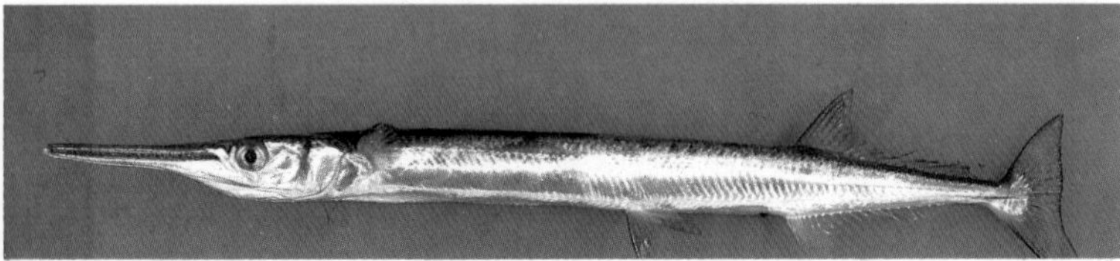

*Tylosurus crocodilus* 202
Circumtrop. 26°C sg: 1.022 100 cm 1000L

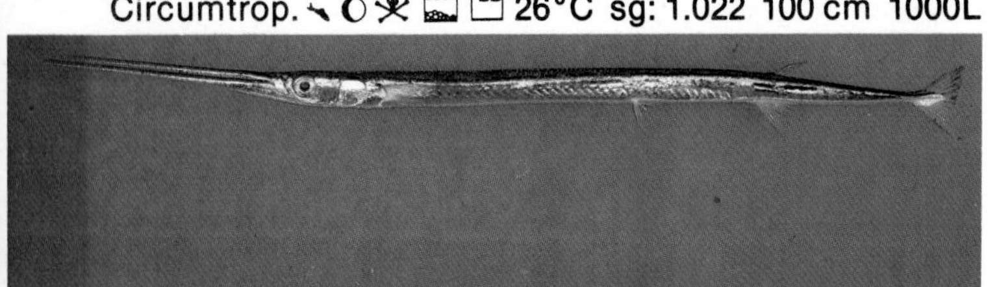

*Platybelone argalus* 202
6, 7 26°C sg: 1.022 50 cm 500L

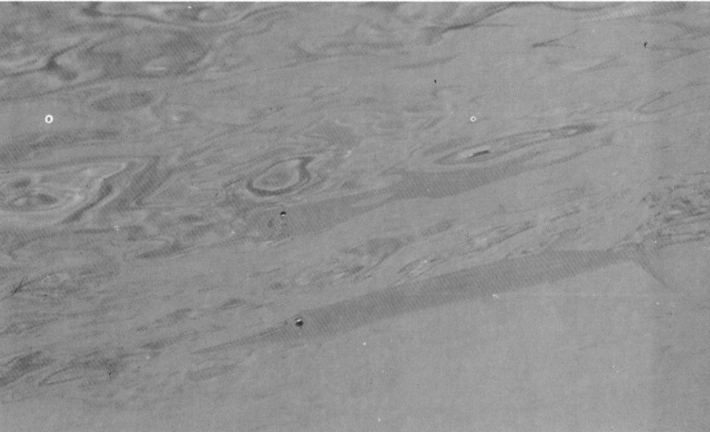

*Tylosurus crocodilus* 202
Circumtrop. 26°C sg: 1.022 100 cm 1000L

*Hyporhamphus sajori* 201
7 26°C sg: 1.022 45 cm 500L

*Cololabias saira* 203
3-5 26°C sg: 1.022 40 cm 400L

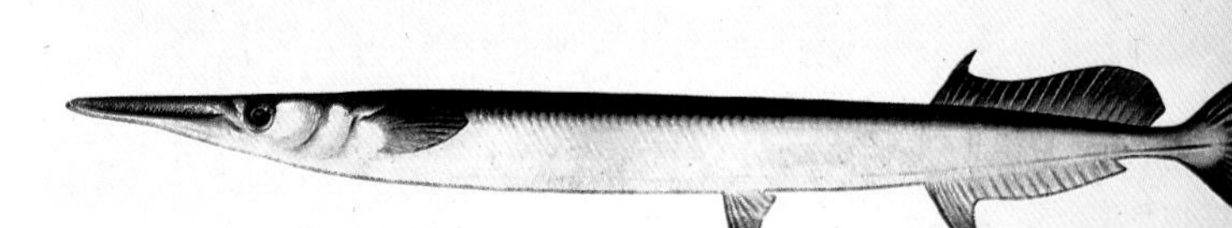

*Tylosurus crocodilus* 202
Circumtrop. 26°C sg: 1.022 100 cm 1000L

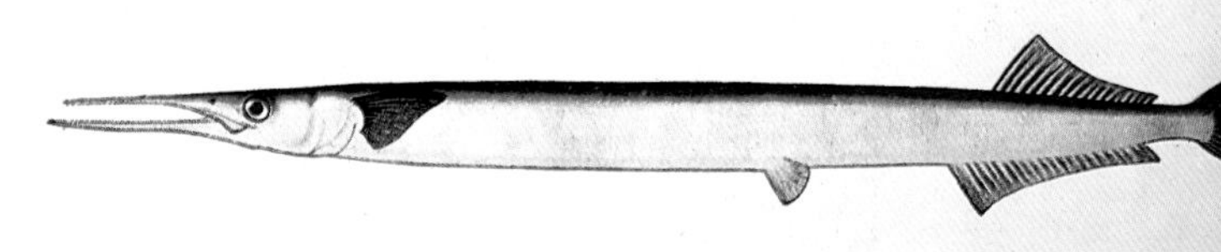

*Strongylura anastomella* 202
5, 7 26°C sg: 1.022 100 cm 1000L

*Tylosurus leiurus* 202
7 26°C sg: 1.022 100 cm 1000L

*Ablennes hians* 202
Circumtrop. 26°C sg: 1.022 120 cm 1500L

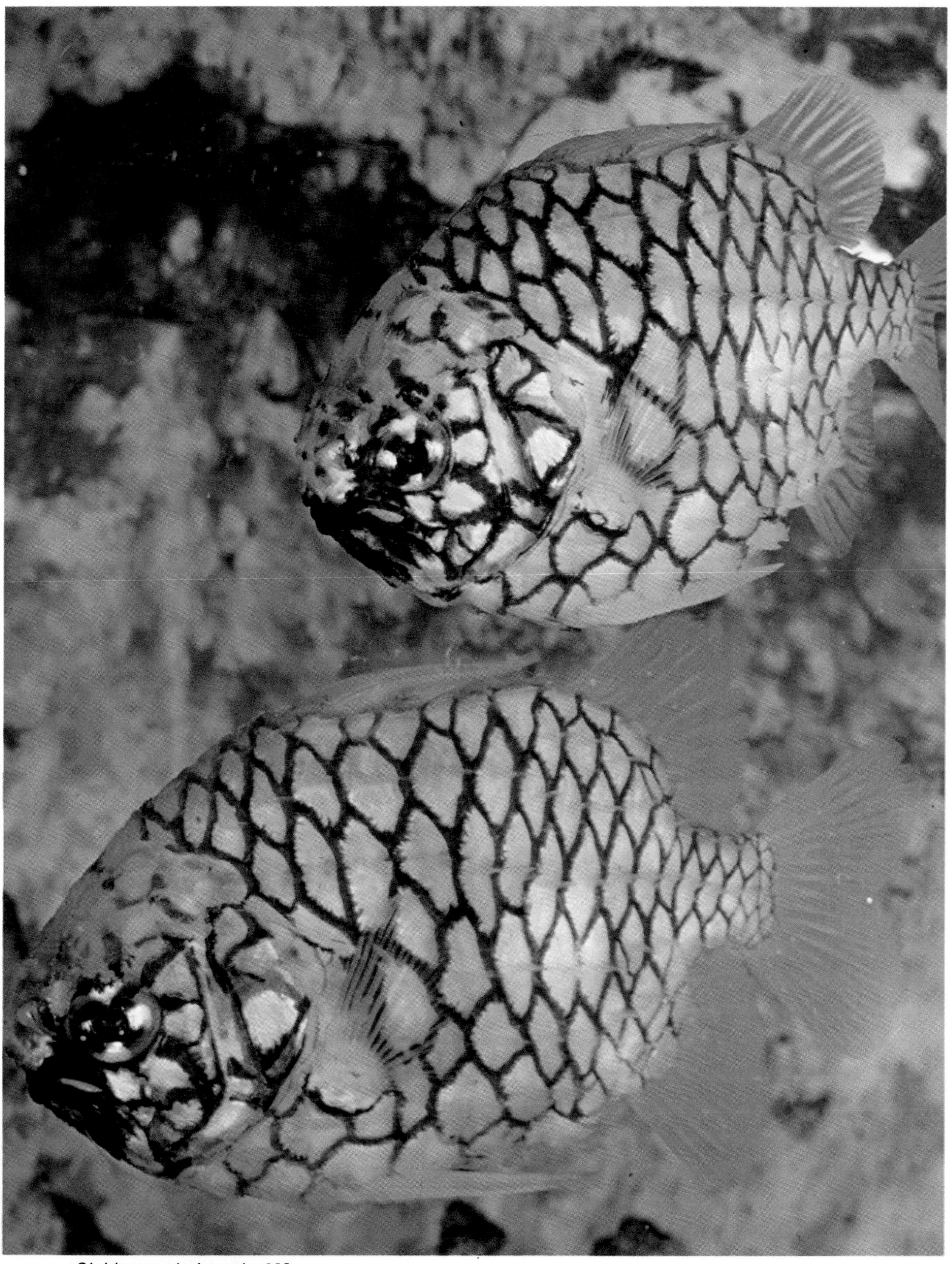

*Cleidopus gloriamaris* 229
12 ~ ◐ ♥ [icon] [icon] 23°C sg: 1.024 28 cm 300L

*Atherinops affinis* 213
3 ∿ ◐ ♥ 26°C sg: 1.022 38 cm 400L

*Atherinosoma elongata* 213
7-8 ∿ ◐ ♥ 26°C sg: 1.022 8 cm 80L

*Atherina boyeri* 213
15 ∿ ◐ ♥ 26°C sg: 1.024 10 cm 100L

*Craterocephalus pauciradiatus* 213
7 ∿ ◐ ♥ 26°C sg: 1.022 7 cm 80L

*Atherinomorus ogilbyi* 213
7-8 ∿ ○ ♥ 26°C sg: 1.022 17 cm 200L

*Atherinomorus lacunosus* 213
7-8 ∿ ◐ ♥ 26°C sg: 1.022 12.5 cm 150L

*Atherinomorus endrachtensis* 213
7-8, 12 ∿ ○ ♥ 26°C sg: 1.022 10 cm 100L

*Iso rhothophilus* 214
12 ∿ ◐ ♥ 24°C sg: 1.023 3 cm 50L

*Lampris guttatus* 218
Circumtrop. 26°C sg: 1.022 200 cm 2500L

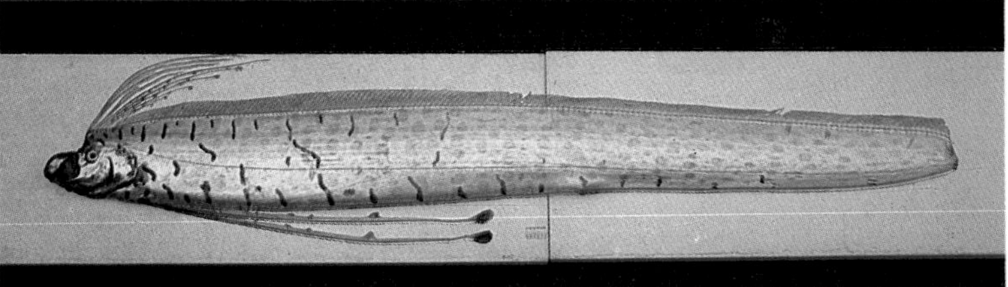

*Regalecus glesne* 223
Circumtrop. 25°C sg: 1.022 1000 cm 5000L

*Gephyroberyx japonicus* 230
5 24°C sg: 1.023 100 cm 1000L

*Sorosichthys ananassa* 230
12 23°C sg: 1.024 3 cm 50L

*Monocentrus japonicus* 229
7, 9 25°C sg: 1.022 16 cm 200L

*Cleidopus gloriamaris* 229
12 23°C sg: 1.024 28 cm 300L

*Hoplostethus elongatus* 230
11 22°C sg: 1.024 12 cm 150L

*Trachichthys australis* 230
12 22°C sg: 1.024 12 cm 150L

#58A

*Myripristis* sp. 235
6-10 26°C sg: 1.022 15 cm 200L

*Sargocentron spiniferum* 235
6-9 26°C sg: 1.022 45 cm 500L

*#58B*

*Sargocentron violaceum* 235
7, 9 [symbols] 26°C sg: 1.022 25 cm 300L

*Anomalops katoptron* 231
7 26°C sg: 1.022 30 cm 300L

*Photoblepharon palpebratus* 231
7, 9-10 26°C sg: 1.022 11 cm 100L

*Beryx decadactylus* 234
Cosmopol. 26°C sg: 1.022 60 cm 600L

*Beryx splendens* 234
2, 6-9, 13 26°C sg: 1.022 50 cm 500L

*Trachichthodes affinis* 230
8, 11-12 24°C sg: 1.023 45 cm 500L

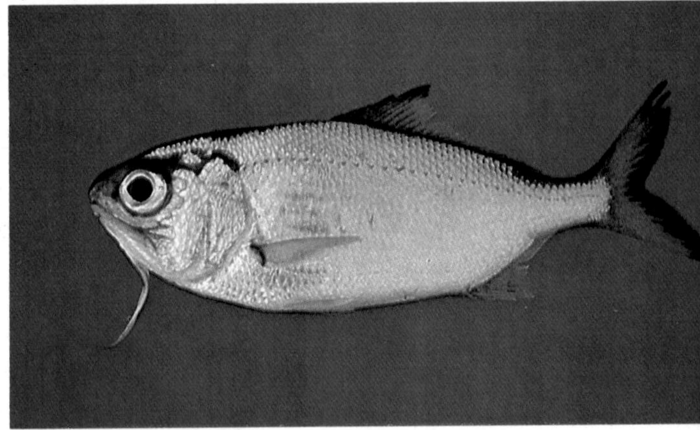

*Polymixia lowei* 236
1-2 26°C sg: 1.022 20 cm 200L

*Corniger spinosus* 238
2 26°C sg: 1.022 20 cm 200L

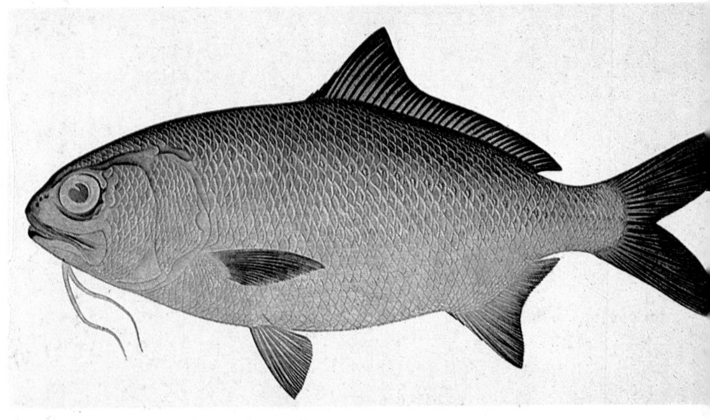

*Polymixia berndti* 236
6-7, 9 26°C sg: 1.022 15 cm 150L

*Sargocentron diadema* 235
6-9 26°C sg: 1.022 23 cm 300L

*Sargocentron xantherythrus* 235
6 26°C sg: 1.022 18 cm 200L

*Sargocentron violaceum* 235
7, 9 26°C sg: 1.022 25 cm 300L

*Sargocentron coruscum* 235
2 26°C sg: 1.022 10 cm 100L

*Sargocentron ittodai* 235
7 26°C sg: 1.022 20 cm 200L

*Sargocentron tieroides* 235
6-7 26°C sg: 1.022 30 cm 300L

*Sargocentron bullisi* 235
1-2 25°C sg: 1.022 13 cm 150L

*Sargocentron vexillarium* 235
2 26°C sg: 1.022 12.6 cm 150L

*Sargocentron diadema* 235
6-9 26°C sg: 1.022 23 cm 300L

*Sargocentron microstoma* 235
6 26°C sg: 1.022 18 cm 200L

*Sargocentron seychellensis* 235
9 26°C sg: 1.022 18 cm 200L

*Neoniphon sammara* 235
6-10 26°C sg: 1.022 30 cm 300L

*Sargocentron caudimaculatum* 235
7, 9-10 26°C sg: 1.022 25 cm 300

*Sargocentron spiniferum* 235
6-9 26°C sg: 1.022 45 cm 500L

*Sargocentron tiere* 235
6, 7 26°C sg: 1.022 30 cm 300L

*Neoniphon opercularis* 235
6-9 26°C sg: 1.022 35 cm 400L

*Holocentrus hastatus* 235
13 26°C sg: 1.022 10 cm 100L

*Holocentrus rufus* 235
2 26°C sg: 1.022 26 cm 300L

*Sargocentron rubrum* 235
6-10 26°C sg: 1.022 36 cm 400L

*Sargocentron lepros* 235
7 26°C sg: 1.022 12 cm 150L

*Holocentrus ascensionis* 235
1-2 26°C sg: 1.022 30 cm 300L

*Sargocentron caudimaculatum* 235
7-10 26°C sg: 1.022 25 cm 300L

*Sargocentron suborbitalis* 235
3 26°C sg: 1.022 25 cm 300L

*Sargocentron punctatissimum* 235
6-9 26°C sg: 1.022 16 cm 200L

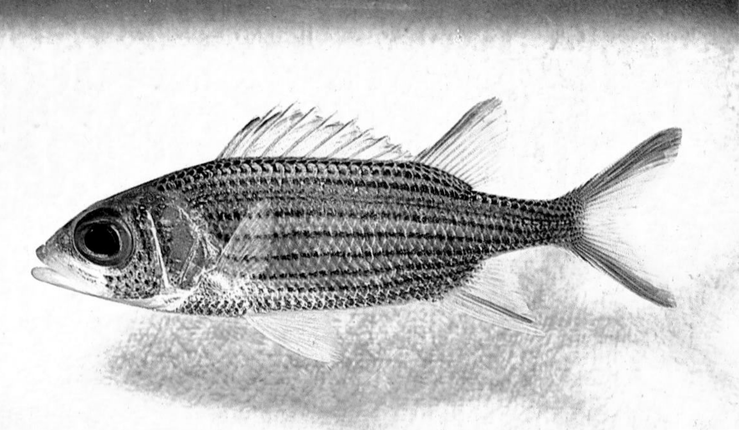

*Neoniphon argenteus* 235
7, 9 26°C sg: 1.022 24 cm 300L

*Neoniphon opercularis* 235
6-9 26°C sg: 1.022 35 cm 400L

*Sargocentron ensifer* 235
6 26°C sg: 1.022 22.5 cm 300L

*Sargocentron melanospilos* 235
6, 7 26°C sg: 1.022 27 cm 300L

*Neoniphon marianus* 235
2 26°C sg: 1.022 17 cm 200L

*Neoniphon sammara* 235
6-10 26°C sg: 1.022 30 cm 300L

*Neoniphon scythrops* 235
6 26°C sg: 1.022 25 cm 300L

*Neoniphon aurolineatus* 235
6-7 26°C sg: 1.022 22 cm 200L

*Sargocentron diadema* 235
6-10 26°C sg: 1.022 18 cm 200L

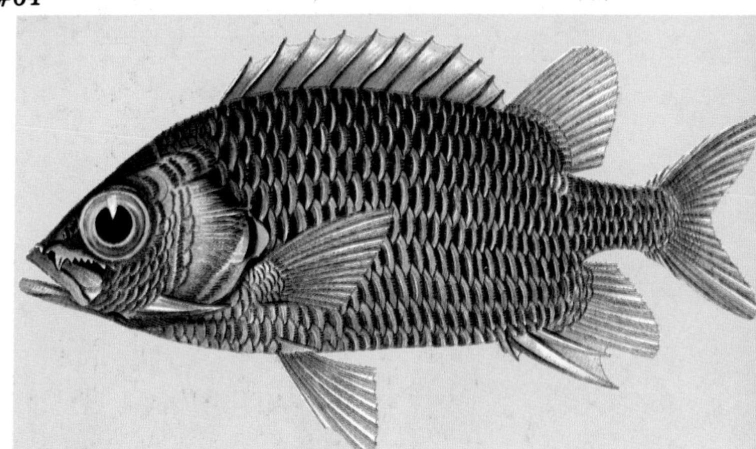

*Sargocentron violaceum* 235
6-7, 9 26°C sg: 1.022 20 cm 200L

*Sargocentron caudimaculatum* 235
7-10 26°C sg: 1.022 25 cm 300L

*Neoniphon laeve* 235
9 26°C sg: 1.022 30 cm 300L

*Sargocentron tiere* 235
6, 7 26°C sg: 1.022 30 cm 300L

*Sargocentron melanospilos* 235
6, 7 26°C sg: 1.022 27 cm 300L

*Neoniphon sammara?* 235
5-10 26°C sg: 1.022 30 cm 300L

*Sargocentron lacteoguttatus* 235
6-7, 9 26°C sg: 1.022 15 cm 150L

*Myripristis violacea* 235
6-7, 9 ~ ↘ ◐ ✻ ▣ ▭ 26°C sg: 1.022 20 cm 200L

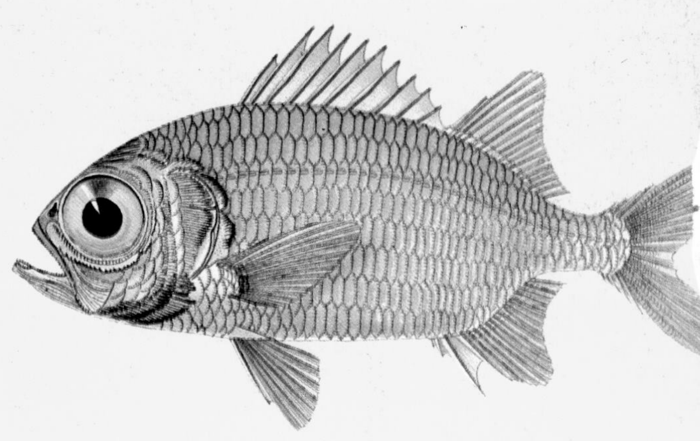

*Myripristis pralinus* 235
7, 9 ~ ↘ ◐ ✻ ▣ ▭ 26°C sg: 1.022 20 cm 200L

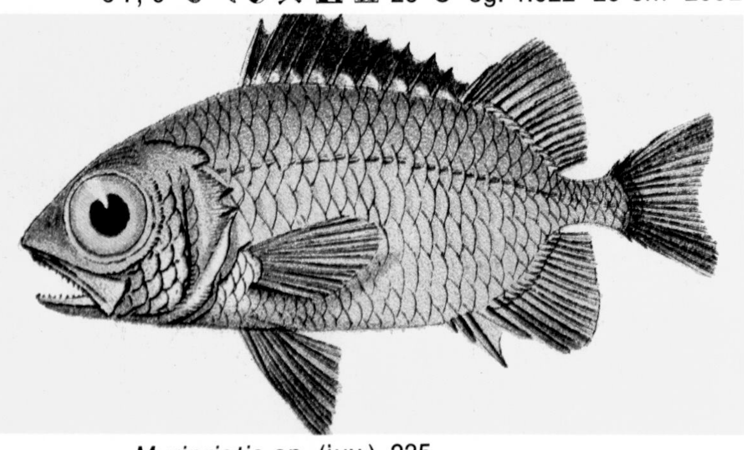

*Myripristis* sp. (juv.) 235
6-9 ~ ↘ ◐ ✻ ▣ ▭ 26°C sg: 1.022 20 cm 200L

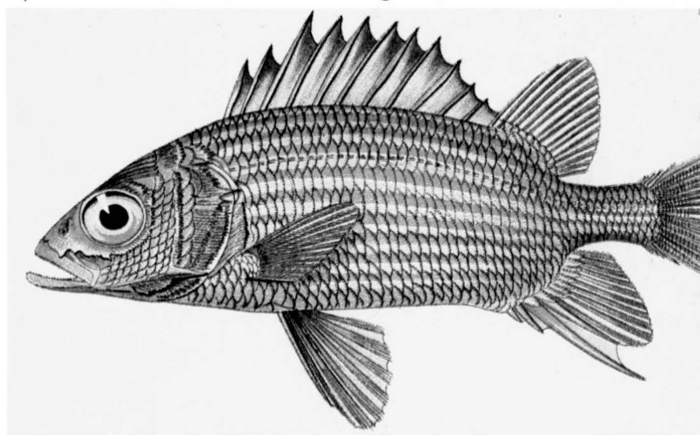

*Neoniphon argenteus* 235
7, 9 ~ ↘ ◐ ✻ ▣ ▭ 26°C sg: 1.022 24 cm 250L

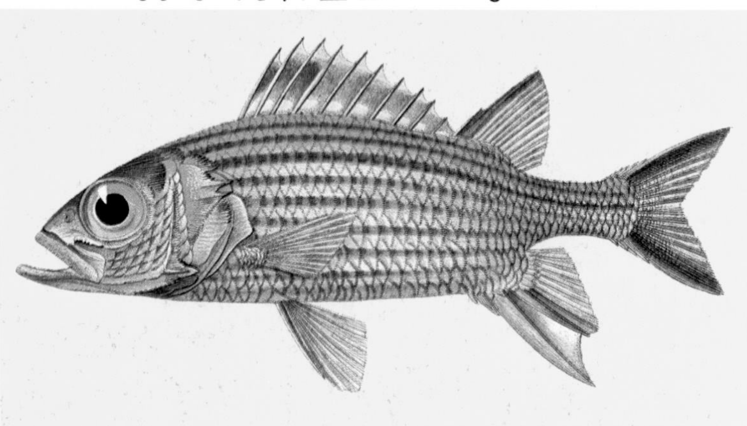

*Neoniphon sammara* 235
6-10 ~ ↘ ◐ ✻ ▣ ▭ 26°C sg: 1.022 30 cm 300L

*Neoniphon opercularis* 235
7, 9 ~ ↘ ◐ ✻ ▣ ▭ 26°C sg: 1.022 35 cm 400L

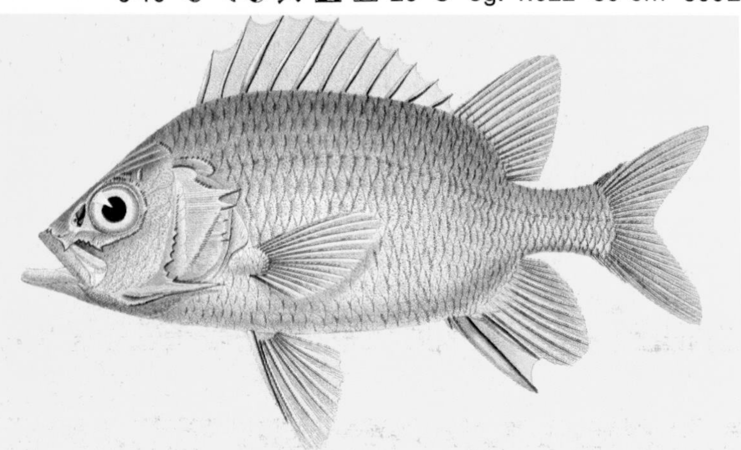

*Sargocentron spiniferum* 235
7, 9-10 ~ ↘ ◐ ✻ ▣ ▭ 26°C sg: 1.022 45 cm 500L

*Sargocentron caudimaculatum* 235
7-10 ~ ↘ ◐ ✻ ▣ ▭ 26°C sg: 1.022 25 cm 250L

*Plectrypops retrospinis* 235
2 26°C sg: 1.022 10 cm 100L

*Pristilepis oligolepis* 235
6-9 26°C sg: 1.022 30 cm 300L

*Myripristis leiognathus* 235
3 26°C sg: 1.022 17.5 cm 200L

*Myripristis adustus* 235
6-7, 9 26°C sg: 1.022 32 cm 300L

*Plectrypops lima* 235
6 26°C sg: 1.022 17.5 cm 200L

*Ostichthys japonicus* 235
6-7, 9 26°C sg: 1.022 45 cm 500L

*Myripristis jacobus* 235
1-2, 13 26°C sg: 1.022 20 cm 200L

*Myripristis* sp. 235
6 26°C sg: 1.022 17 cm 200L

*Myripristis adustus* 235
6-7, 9 26°C sg: 1.022 32 cm 300L

*Myripristis kuntee* 235
6-10 26°C sg: 1.022 15 cm 200L

*Myripristis murdjan* 235
7-10 26°C sg: 1.022 24 cm 250L

*Myripristis vittatus* 235
7, 9 26°C sg: 1.022 20 cm 200L

*Myripristis hexagonatus* 235
6-7, 9 26°C sg: 1.022 20 cm 200L

*Myripristis melanostictus* 235
7, 9 26°C sg: 1.022 30 cm 300L

*Myripristis violacea* 235
6-7, 9 26°C sg: 1.022 20 cm 200L

*Myripristis adustus* and *Myripristis vittata* 235
7, 9 26°C sg: 1.022 32 cm 250L

*Myripristis axillaris* 235
7-10 26°C sg: 1.022 27 cm 300L

*Myripristis xanthacrus* 235
10 26°C sg: 1.022 17 cm 200L

*Myripristis pralinia* 235
7, 9 26°C sg: 1.022 20 cm 200L

*Myripristis kuntee* 235
6-10 26°C sg: 1.022 15 cm 200L

*Myripristis violacea* 235
6-7, 9 26°C sg: 1.022 20 cm 200L

*Myripristis berndti* 235
7, 9 26°C sg: 1.022 30 cm 300L

*Myripristis berndti* 235
7, 9 26°C sg: 1.022 30 cm 300L

*Myripristis amaenus* 235
6 26°C sg: 1.022 30 cm 300L

*Myripristis melanostictus* 235
7, 9 26°C sg: 1.022 30 cm 300L

*Myripristis adustus* 235
7, 9 26°C sg: 1.022 32 cm 300L

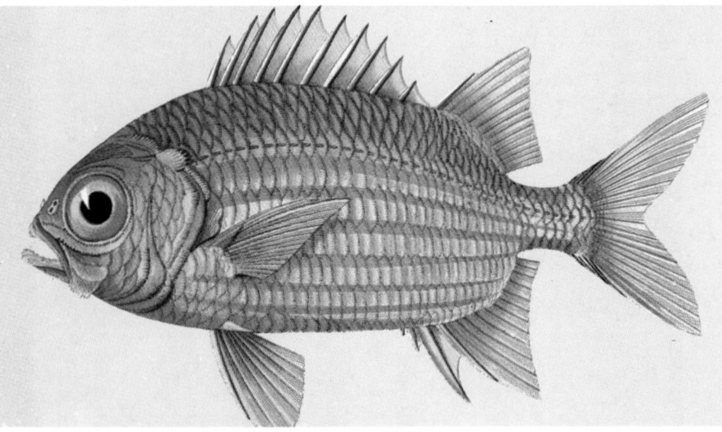

*Myripristis hexagonus* 235
6-7, 9 26°C sg: 1.022 20 cm 200L

*Myripristis murdjan* 235
7-10 26°C sg: 1.022 24 cm 250L

*Myripristis trachyacron* 235
7 26°C sg: 1.022 16 cm 200L

*Myripristis melanostictus* 235
7, 9 26°C sg: 1.022 30 cm 300L

*Myripristis murdjan* 235
7-10 26°C sg: 1.022 24 cm 250L

*Myripristis murdjan* 235
7-10 26°C sg: 1.022 24 cm 250L

#70

*Aulostomus chinensis* 254
7, 9 26°C sg: 1.022 100 cm 1000L

*Cyttopsis rosea(?)* 245
Circumtrop. 26°C sg: 1.022 22 cm 200L

*Zenion hololepis* 244
7, 9 26°C sg: 1.022 10 cm 100L

*Zeus japonicus* 245
5-9 26°C sg: 1.022 50 cm 500L

*Zenopsis nebulosa* 245
5-7 26°C sg: 1.022 50 cm 500L

*Antigonia capros* 248
1-2, 6-9, 13 26°C sg: 1.022 25 cm 300L

*Aulichthys japonicus* 250
5 24°C sg: 1.023 15 cm 150L

*Aulorhynchus flavidus* 250
3 26°C sg: 1.022 18 cm 200L

*Spinachia spinachia* 251
14 22°C sg: 1.024 19 cm 200L

*Parapegasus natans* 253
5, 7-8, 12 25°C sg: 1.022 18 cm 200L

*Parapegasus* sp.? 253
7, 9 26°C sg: 1.022 12 cm 120L

*Aulostomus chinensis* 254
7, 9 26°C sg: 1.022 100 cm 1000L

*Fistularia commersonii* 255
Circumtrop. 26°C sg: 1.022 160 cm

*Pegasus volitans* 253
5, 7, 9 26°C sg: 1.022 17.5 cm 200L

*Aulostomus maculatus* 254
2 26°C sg: 1.022 91 cm 1000L

*Aulostomus chinensis* 254
7, 9 26°C sg: 1.022 100 cm 1000L

*Fistularia tabacaria* 255
1-2 24°C sg: 1.023 180 cm 2000L

#71A

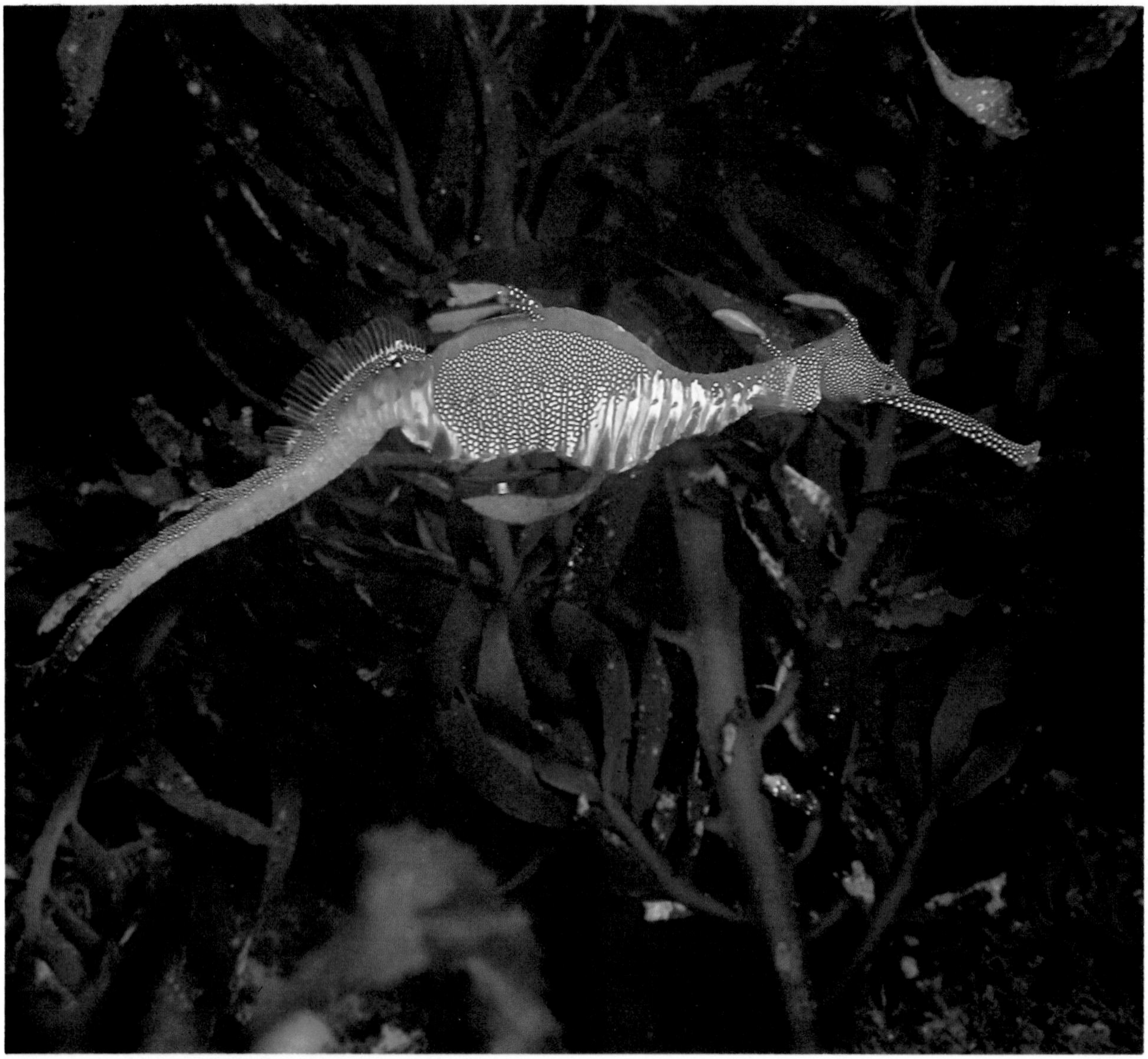

*Phyllopteryx taeniolatus* 259
12 ∿ ◐ ♥ 24°C sg: 1.023 23 cm 250L

*Solenostomus paradoxus* 258
5, 7, 9 ∿ ◐ ♥ 26°C sg: 1.022 16.5 cm 200L

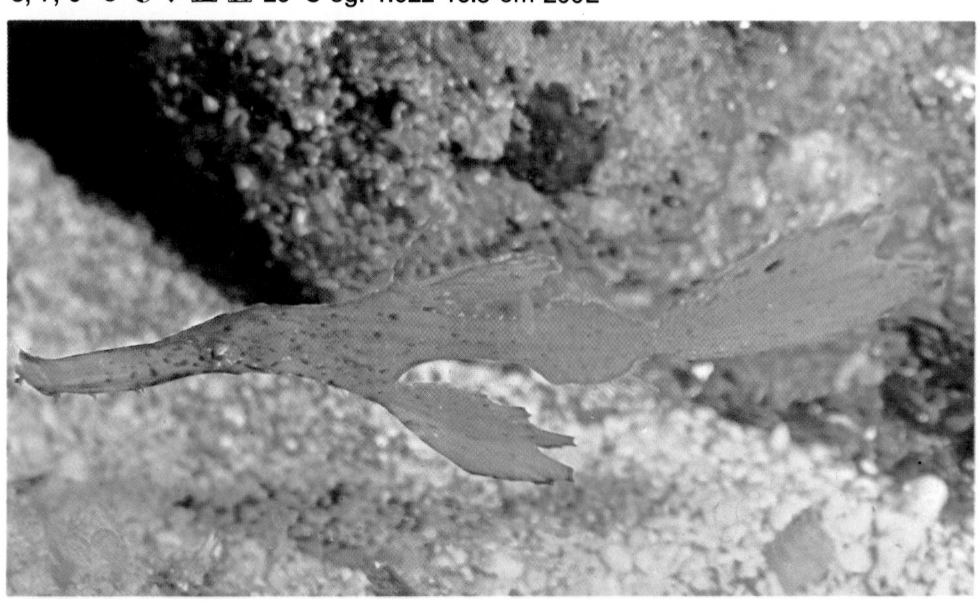

*#71B*

*Phycodorus eques* 259
12 ~ ◐ ♥ 24°C sg: 1.023 35 cm 400L

*Aeoliscus strigatus* and *A. punctulatus* 257
7-10 ◐ ♥ 26°C sg: 1.022 15 cm 150L

*Macrorhamphosus scolopax* 256
Circumtrop. ∿ ◐ ♥ 26°C sg: 1.022 20 cm 200L

*Solenostomus paegnius* 258
5, 7, 9 ∿ ◐ ♥ 26°C sg: 1.022 10 cm 100L

*Solenostomus paradoxus* 258
5, 7, 9 ∿ ◐ ♥ 26°C sg: 1.022 16.5 cm 200L

*Centriscus scutatus* 257
7-9 ∿ ◐ ♥ 24°C sg: 1.023 15 cm 200L

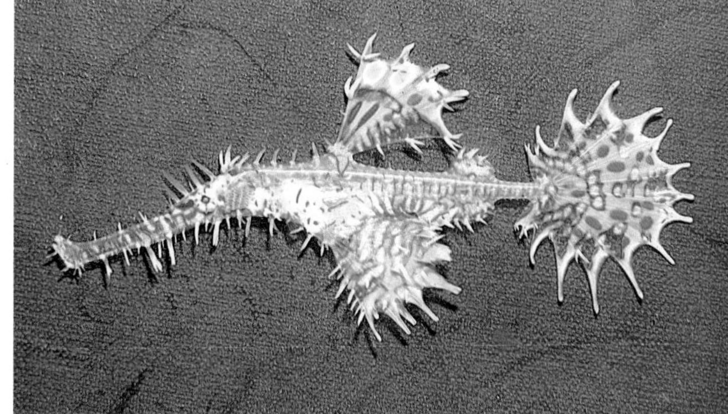

*Solenostomus cyanopterus* 258
5, 7, 9 ∿ ◐ ♥ 26°C sg: 1.022 17 cm 200L

*Solenostomus paradoxus* 258
5, 7, 9 ∿ ◐ ♥ 26°C sg: 1.022 16.5 cm 200L

*Solenostomus paradoxus* 258
5, 7, 9 ∿ ◐ ♥ 26°C sg: 1.022 16.5 cm 200L

#74

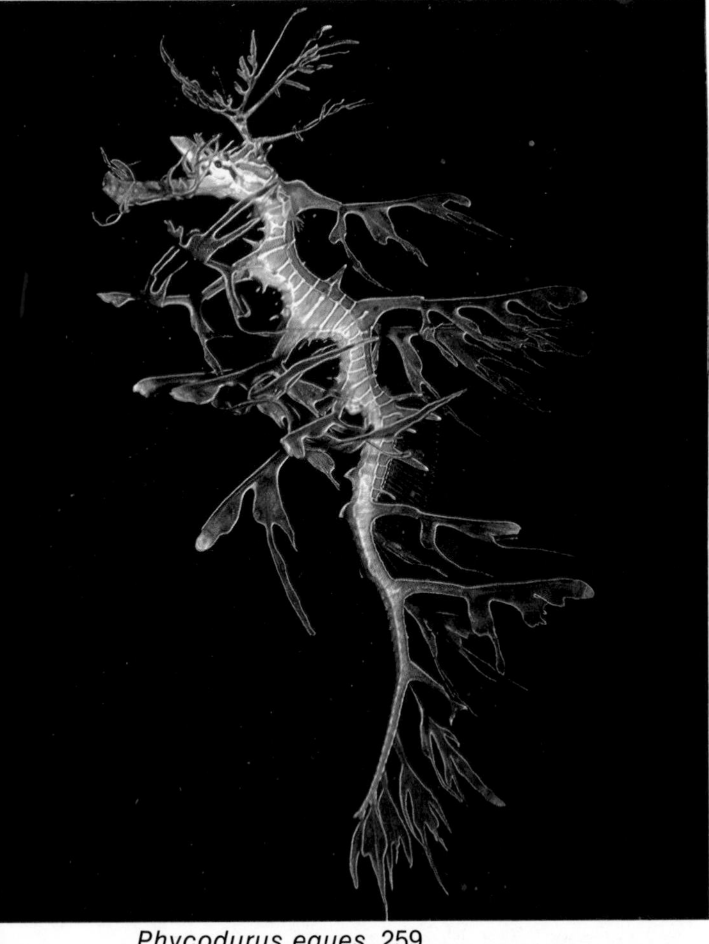

*Phycodurus eques* 259
12 ~ ◐ ♥ 24°C sg: 1.023 35 cm 400L

*Phyllopteryx taeniolatus* 259
12 ~ ◐ ♥ 24°C sg: 1.023 23 cm 250L

*Phycodurus eques* 259
12 ~ ◐ ♥ 24°C sg: 1.023 35 cm 400L

*Phyllopteryx taeniolatus* 259
12 ~ ◐ ♥ 24°C sg: 1.023 23 cm 250L

*Solenostomus armatus* 258
7 ~ ◐ ♥ 26°C sg: 1.022 12 cm 120L

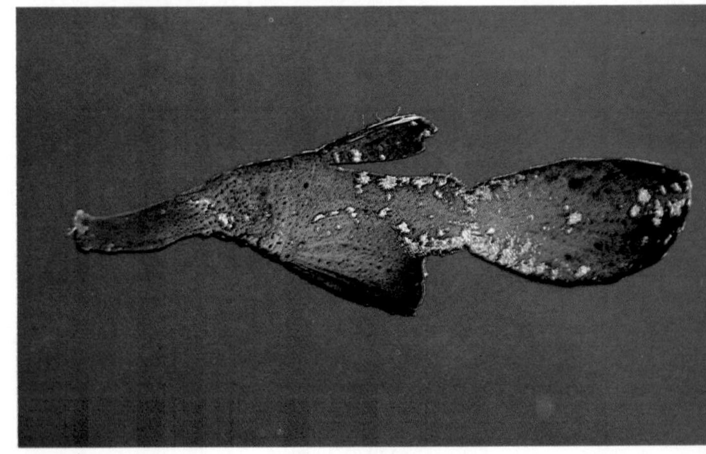

*Solenostomus cyanopterus* 258
5, 7, 9 ~ ◐ ♥ 26°C sg: 1.022 17 cm 200L

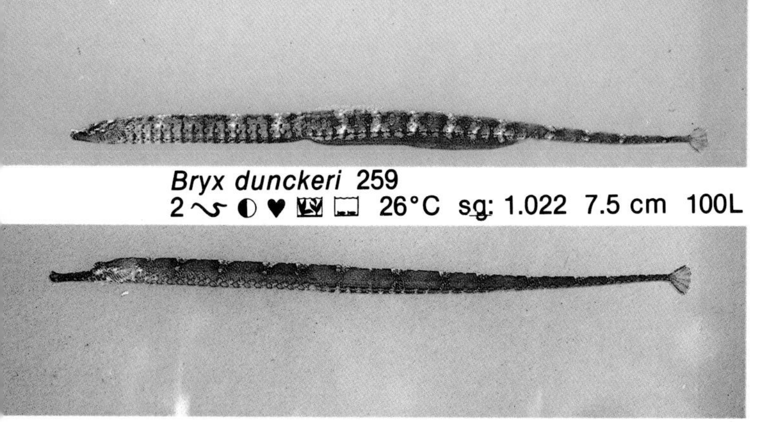

*Bryx dunckeri* 259
2 ∿ ◐ ♥ 26°C sg: 1.022 7.5 cm 100L

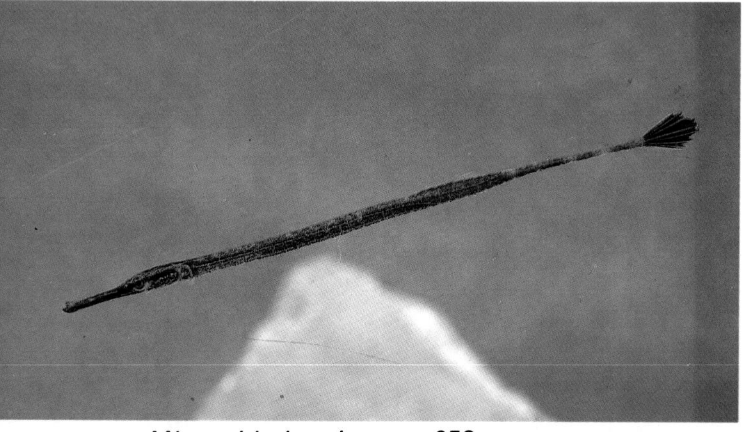

*Syngnathus louisianae* 259
2 ∿ ◐ ♥ 26°C sg: 1.022 38 cm 400L

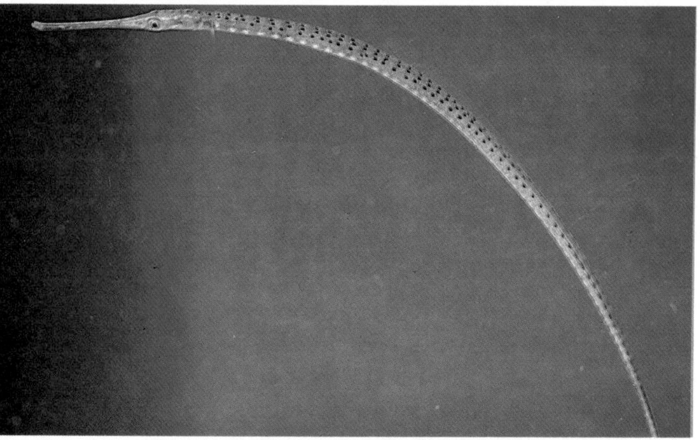

*Microphis brachyurus* 259
6-9 ∿ ◐ ♥ 26°C sg: 1.022 20 cm 200L

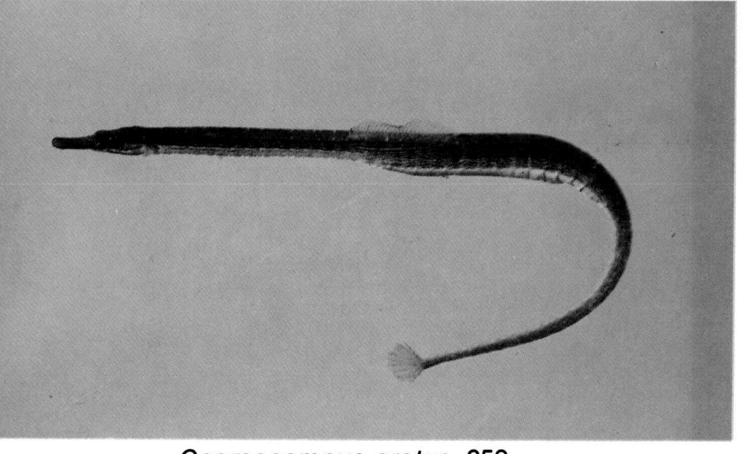

*Stigmatopora argus* 259
12 ∿ ◐ ♥ 26°C sg: 1.022 27 cm 300L

*Cosmocampus arctus* 259
3 ∿ ◐ ♥ 26°C sg: 1.022 9 cm 100L

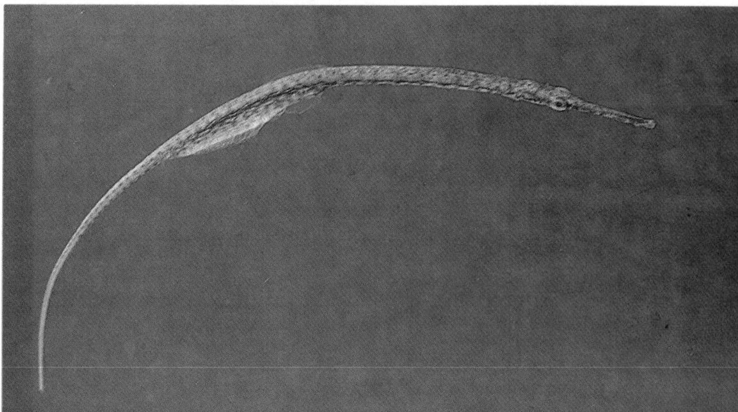

*Micrognathus ensenadae* 259
2 ∿ ◐ ♥ 26°C sg: 1.022 12.5 cm 100L

*Stigmatopora nigra* 259
8, 11 ∿ ◐ ♥ 26°C sg: 1.022 17.3 cm 200L

*Syngnathoides biaculeatus* 259
7-10 ∿ ◐ ♥ 26°C sg: 1.022 30 cm 300L

*Syngnathus* sp. 259
7-10 ∿ ◐ ♥ 26°C sg: 1.022 25 cm 150L

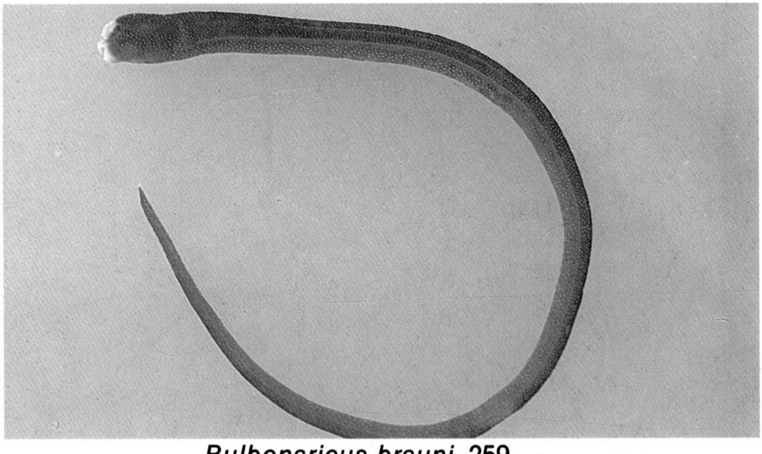

*Bulbonaricus brauni* 259
7 ∿ ◐ ♥ ▩ ▭ 26°C sg: 1.022 5.5 cm 50L

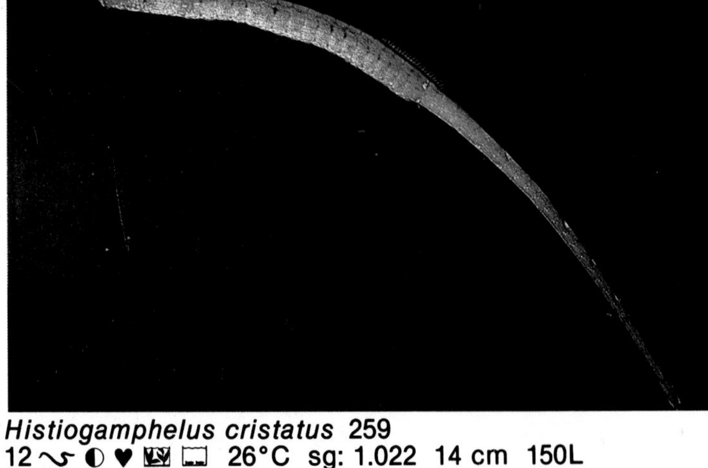

*Histiogamphelus cristatus* 259
12 ∿ ◐ ♥ ▩ ▭ 26°C sg: 1.022 14 cm 150L

*Lissocampus caudalis* 259
12 ∿ ◐ ♥ ▩ ▭ 24°C sg: 1.022 13 cm 100L

*Hippichthys penicillus* 259
7, 9 ∿ ◐ ♥ ▩ ▭ 26°C sg: 1.022 8.0 cm 100L

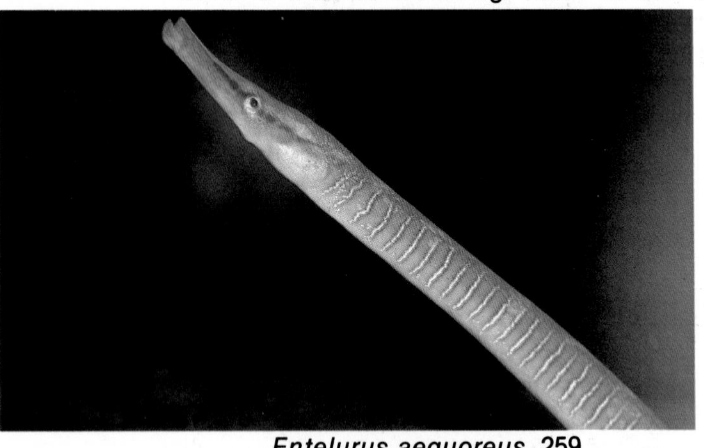

*Entelurus aequoreus* 259
13 ∿ ◐ ♥ ▩ ▭ 26°C sg: 1.022 150L

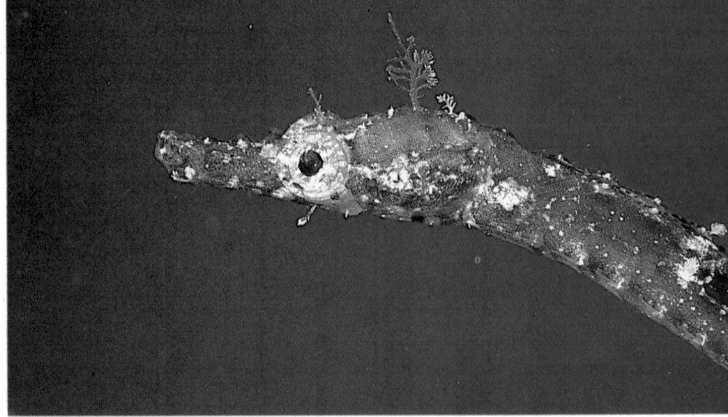

*Halicampus grayi* 259
7-9 ∿ ◐ ♥ ▩ ▭ 26°C sg: 1.022 20 cm 200L

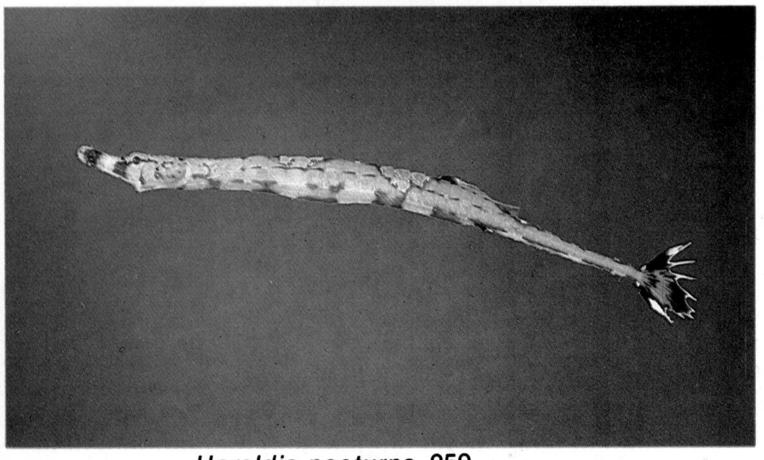

*Heraldia nocturna* 259
12 ∿ ◐ ♥ ▩ ▭ 24°C sg: 1.022 9 cm 100L

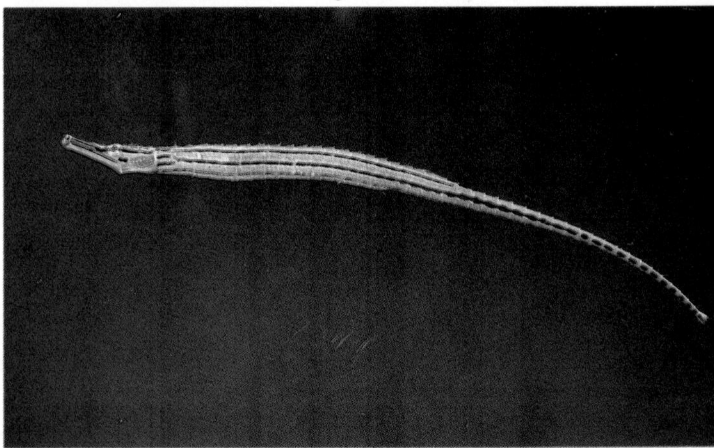

*Maroubra perserrata* 259
12 ∿ ◐ ♥ ▩ ▭ 24°C sg: 1.022 7 cm 100L

*Doryrhamphus dactyliophorus* 259
6-7, 9-10 ◐ ♥ 26°C sg: 1.022 18 cm 200L

*Doryrhamphus janssi* 259
7, 8 ◐ ♥ 26°C sg: 1.022 13 cm 100L

*Doryrhamphus japonicus* 259
5 ◐ ♥ 26°C sg: 1.022 8 cm 100L

*Doryrhamphus e. excisus* 259
3, 6-9 ◐ ♥ 26°C sg: 1.022 7 cm 100L

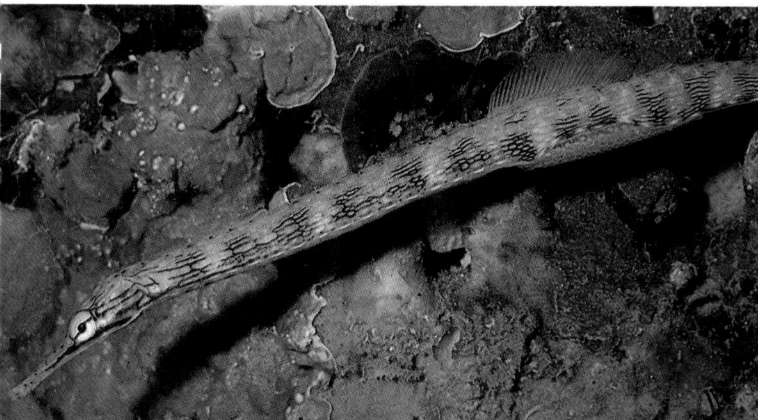

*Corythoichthys intestinalis* 259
6, 7 ◐ ♥ 26°C sg: 1.022 16 cm 200L

*Corythoichthys paxtoni* 259
8 ◐ ♥ 26°C sg: 1.022 14 cm 100L

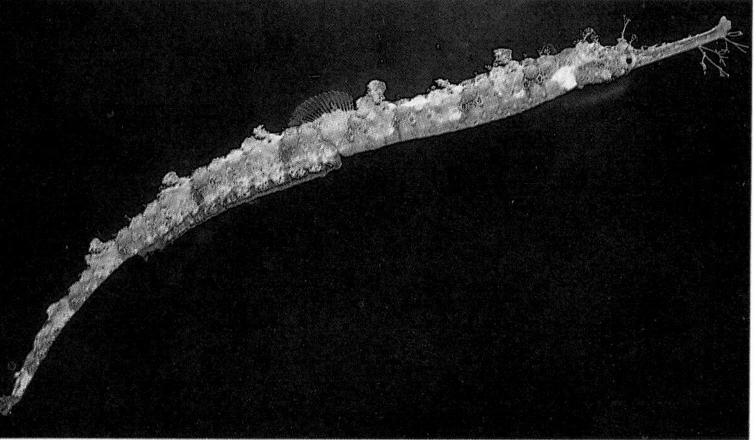

*Halicampus macrorhynchus* 259
7-10 ◐ ♥ 26°C sg: 1.022 13.5 cm 150L

*Corythoichthys amplexus* 259
6-9 ◐ ♥ 26°C sg: 1.022 9 cm 100L

*Corythoichthys amplexus* 259
6-9 ∿ ◐ ♥ 26°C sg: 1.022 9 cm 100L

*Corythoichthys schultzi* 259
6-10 ∿ ◐ ♥ 26°C sg: 1.022 15 cm 150L

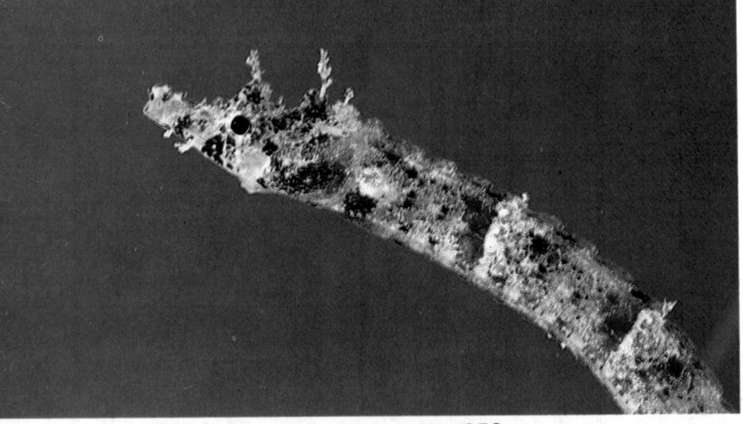

*Halicampus spinirostris* 259
7-9 ∿ ◐ ♥ 26°C sg: 1.022 12 cm 100L

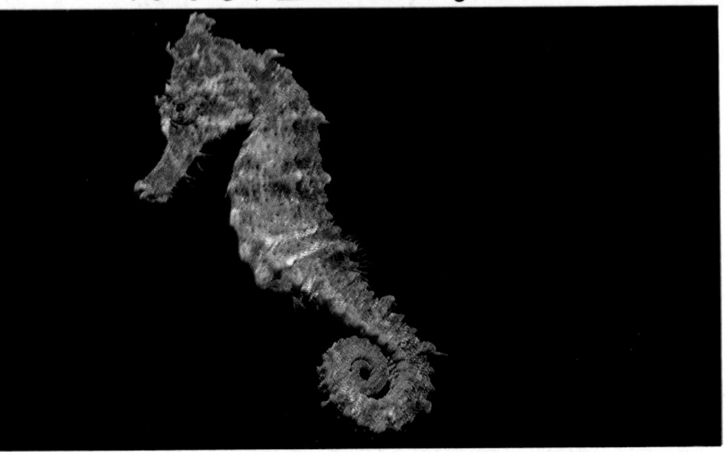

*Hippocampus kuda* 259
7 ∿ ◐ ♥ 26°C sg: 1.022 18 cm 200L

*Corythoichthys haematopterus* 259
6-9 ∿ ◐ ♥ 26°C sg: 1.022 20 cm 200L

*Doryrhamphus multiannulatus* 259
9-10 ∿ ◐ ♥ 26°C sg: 1.022 18 cm 200L

*Hippocampus angustus* 259
12 ∿ ◐ ♥ 24°C sg: 1.023 10 cm 100L

*Hippocampus abdominalis* 259
12 ∿ ◐ ♥ 24°C sg: 1.023 10 cm 100L

*Hippocampus breviceps* 259
12 ∿ ◐ ♥ 24°C sg: 1.022 6.5 cm 60L

*Hippocampus bargibanti* 259
6 ∿ ◐ ♥ 26°C sg: 1.022 5 cm 50L

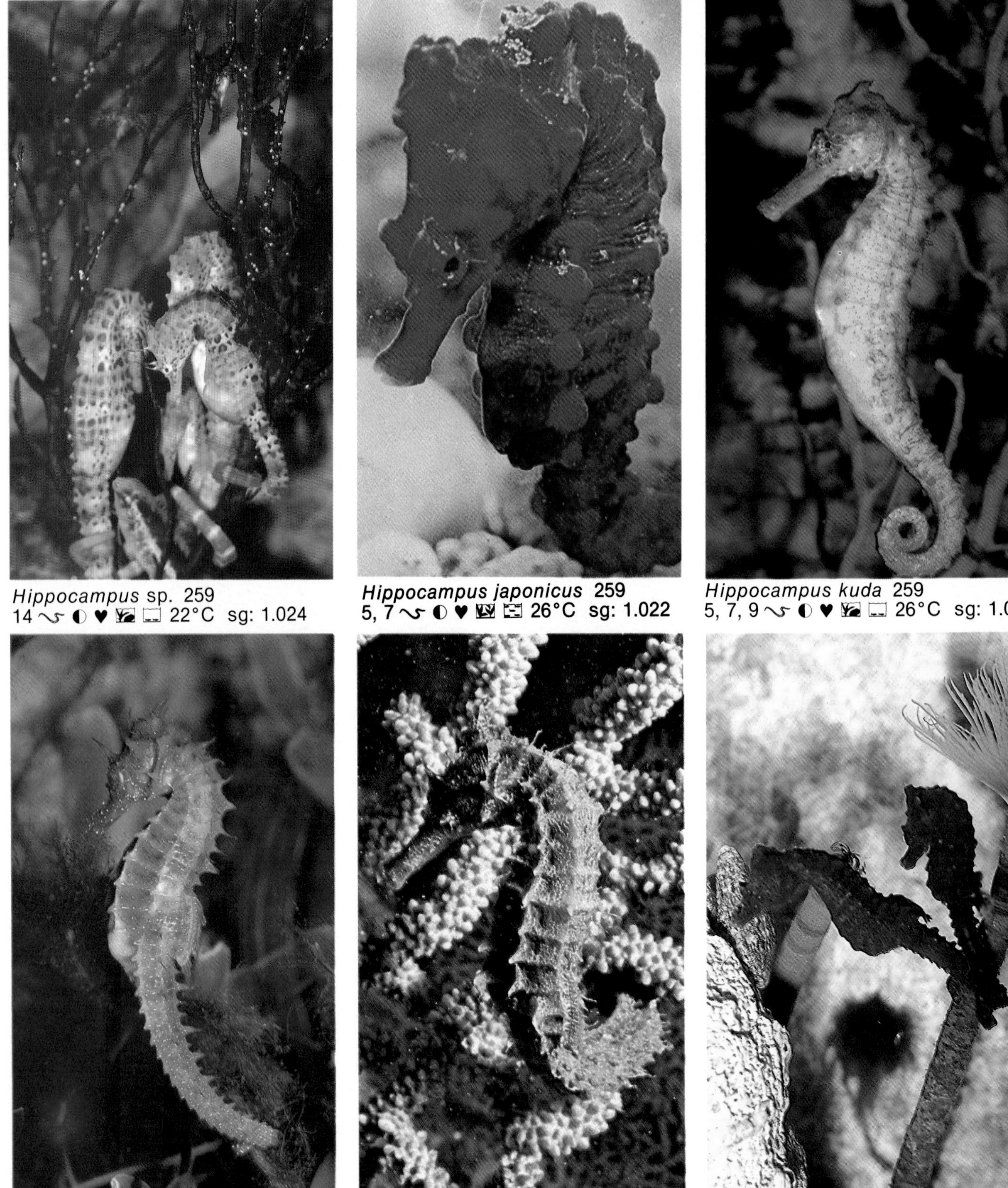

*Hippocampus* sp. 259
14 ◐ ♥ 22°C sg: 1.024

*Hippocampus japonicus* 259
5, 7 ◐ ♥ 26°C sg: 1.022

*Hippocampus kuda* 259
5, 7, 9 ◐ ♥ 26°C sg: 1.02

*Hippocampus ramulosus* 259
13, 15 ◐ ♥ 26°C sg: 1.024

*Hippocampus ingens* 259
3 ◐ ♥ 26°C sg: 1.022

*Hippocampus hippocampus* 259
14, 15 ◐ ♥ 26°C sg: 1.0

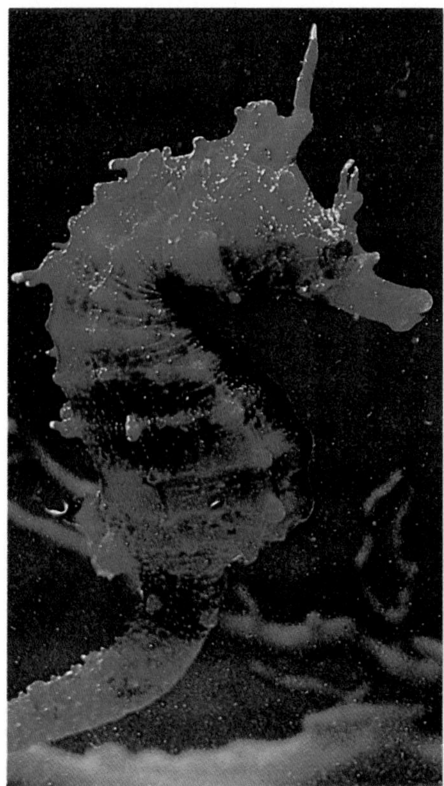

*Hippocampus coronatus* 259
5, 7 ∿ ◐ ♥ ▣ ▣ 24°C sg: 1.023

*Hippocampus reidi* 259
1-2 ∿ ◐ ♥ ▣ ▣ 24°C sg: 1.023

*Hippocampus erectus* 259
1-2 ∿ ◐ ♥ ▣ ▣ 23°C sg: 1.024 15 cm 200L

*Hippocampus erectus*, family Syngnathidae (259).

#82A

*Hippocampus kuda* 259
7 ~ ◐ ♥ ▣ ▭ 26°C sg: 1.022 18 cm 200L

#83

*Pterois volitans* 262
7-8 ◐ 26°C sg: 1.022 35 cm 400L

#83A

*Inimicus filamentosus* 263
9-10 26°C sg: 1.022 18 cm 200L

*#83B*

*Scorpaenopsis oxycephala* 262
6-10 ◐ 26°C sg: 1.022 30 cm 300L

*Dactyloptena orientalis* 260
7-9 ◐ ♥ 26°C sg: 1.022 35 cm 400L

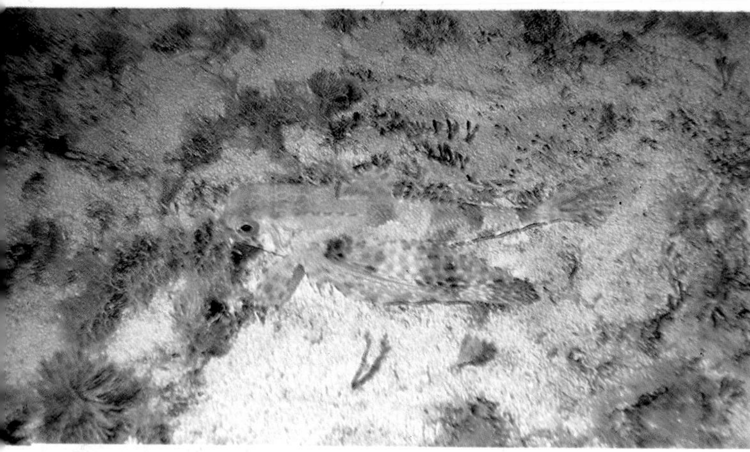

*Dactylopterus volitans* 260
1-2, 13-14 26°C sg: 1.022 45 cm 500L

*Dactyloptena peterseni* 260
7, 9 26°C sg: 1.022 30 cm 300L

*Apistus carinatus* 262
6-9 26°C sg: 1.022 15 cm 150L

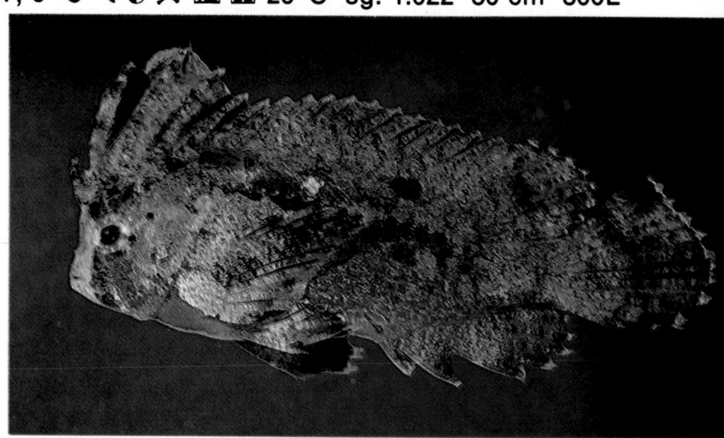

*Ablabys taenianotus* 262
7, 9 26°C sg: 1.022 9 cm 100L

*Peristrominous dolosus* 265
7, 12 26°C sg: 1.022 8 cm 80L

*Neosebastes pandus* 262
12 24°C sg: 1.023 30 cm 300L

*Centropogon australis* 262
12 23°C sg: 1.024 10 cm 100L

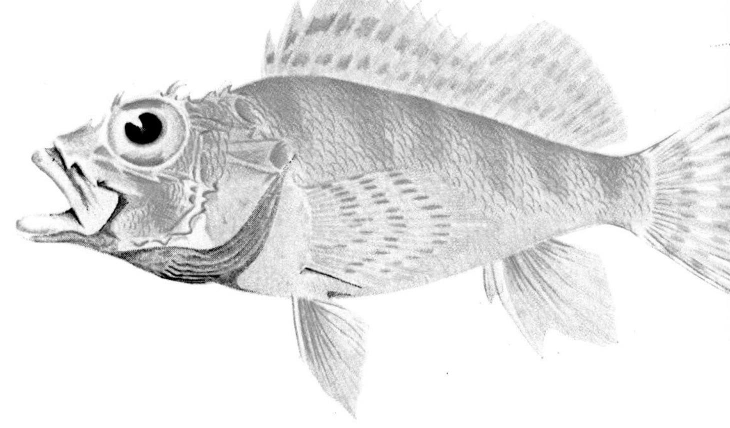

*Pontinus nematophthalmus* 262
2 25°C sg: 1.022 14 cm 150L

*Helicolenus hilgendorfi* 262
5 23°C sg: 1.024 20 cm 200L

*Helicolenus papillosus* 262
11 24°C sg: 1.023 30 cm 300L

*Sebastolobus macrochir* 262
5 24°C sg: 1.023 30 cm 300L

*Sebastolobus alascanus* 262
4 23°C sg: 1.024 75 cm 750L

*Sebasticus albofasciatus* 262
5 24°C sg: 1.023 25 cm 250L

*Sebasticus marmoratus* 262
5, 7 24°C sg: 1.023 34 cm 350L

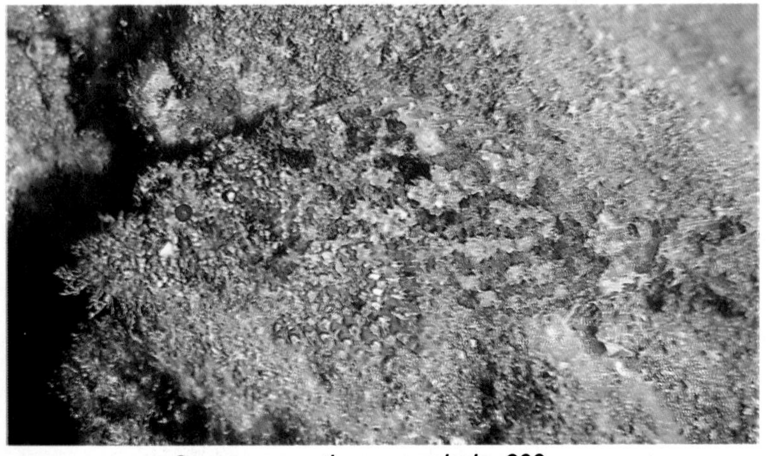

*Scorpaenopsis oxycephala* 262
6-10 26°C sg: 1.022 30 cm 300L

*Scorpaena cardinalis* 262
8 26°C sg: 1.022 45 cm 500L

*Rhinopias eschmeyeri* 262
9 ◐ 26°C sg: 1.022 19 cm 200L

*Rhinopias frondosa* 262
6-9 ◐ 26°C sg: 1.022 25 cm 300L

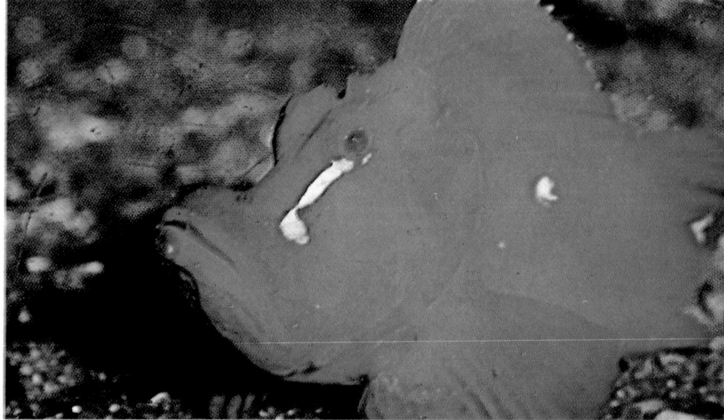

*Rhinopias argoliba* 262
5 ◐ 24°C sg: 1.023 17 cm 200L

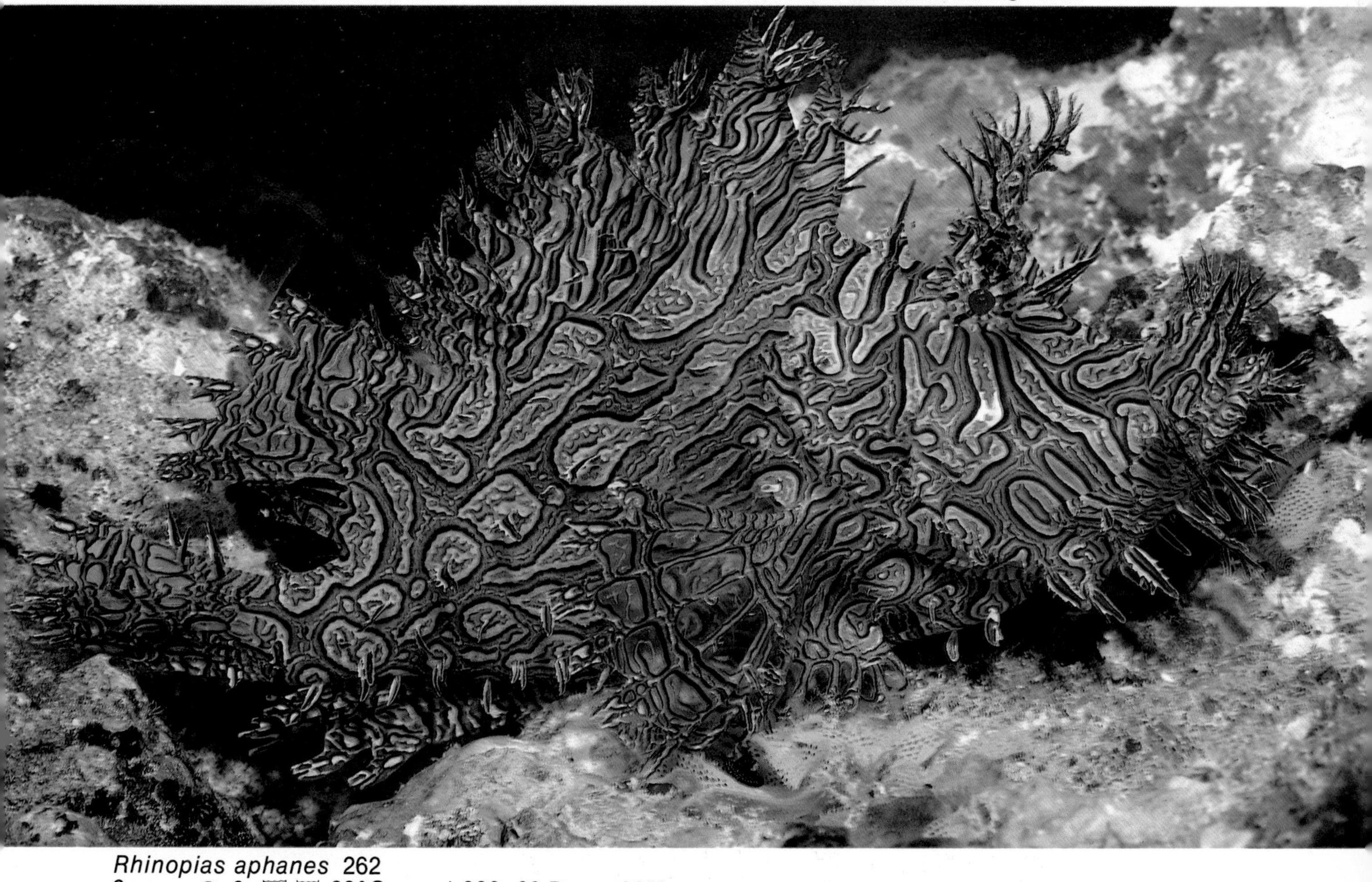

*Rhinopias aphanes* 262
6 ◐ 26°C sg: 1.022 23.5 cm 300L

*Parapterois heterurus* 262
5, 7, 9 26°C sg: 1.022 15 cm 150L

*Dendochirus barberi* 262
6 26°C sg: 1.022 10.8 cm 100L

*Pterois volitans* 262
7-8 26°C sg: 1.022 35 cm 400L

*Pterois sphex* 262
6 26°C sg: 1.022 25 cm 300L

*Dendrochirus zebra* 262
7-10 26°C sg: 1.022 30 cm 300L

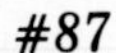

*Pterois antennata* 262
6-9 26°C sg: 1.022 20 cm 200L

*Pterois antennata* 262
7-9 26°C sg: 1.022 30 cm 300L

*Pterois antennata* 262
7-9 26°C sg: 1.022 30 cm 300L

*Pterois volitans* 262
7-8 26°C sg: 1.022 35 cm 400L

*Pterois miles* 262
9, 10 26°C sg: 1.022 31 cm 300L

*Pterois radiata* 262
6-10 26°C sg: 1.022 20 cm 200L

*Dendrochirus zebra* 262
7-10 26°C sg: 1.022 30 cm 300L

*Dendrochirus biocellatus* 262
7 26°C sg: 1.022 12 cm 120L

*Taenianotus triacanthus* 262
6-9 26°C sg: 1.022 10 cm 100L

*Scorpaenodes steenei* 262
12 24°C sg: 1.022 18 cm 200L

*Dendrochirus brachypterus* 262
6-10 26°C sg: 1.022 18 cm 200L

*Taenianotus triacanthus* 262
6-9 26°C sg: 1.022 10 cm 100L

*Scorpaenodes parvipinnis* 262
9 26°C sg: 1.022 15 cm 150L

*Scorpaena notata* 262
13-15 26°C sg: 1.024 30 cm 300L

*Scorpaena scrofa* 262
13-15 26°C sg: 1.024 30 cm 300L

*Scorpaena grandicornis* 262
2 26°C sg: 1.022 25 cm 300L

*Scorpaena porcus*
13-15 26°C sg: 1.024 30 cm 300L

*Scorpaena plumieri plumieri* 262
1-2, 13 26°C sg: 1.023 30 cm 300L

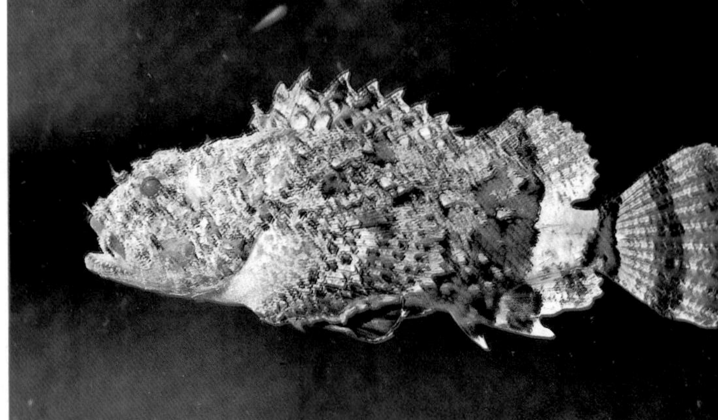

*Scorpaena plumieri mystes* 262
3 26°C sg: 1.023 30 cm 300L

*Scorpaena plumieri* (juv.) 262
1-3, 13 26°C sg: 1.023 30 cm 300L

*Scorpaena plumieri* 262
1-3, 13 26°C sg: 1.022 30 cm 300L

*Scorpaena sonorae* 262
3 26°C sg: 1.022 12 cm 120L

*Scorpaena guttata* 262
4 22°C sg: 1.024 43 cm 400L

*Scorpaena inermis* 262
2 26°C sg: 1.022 11 cm 100L

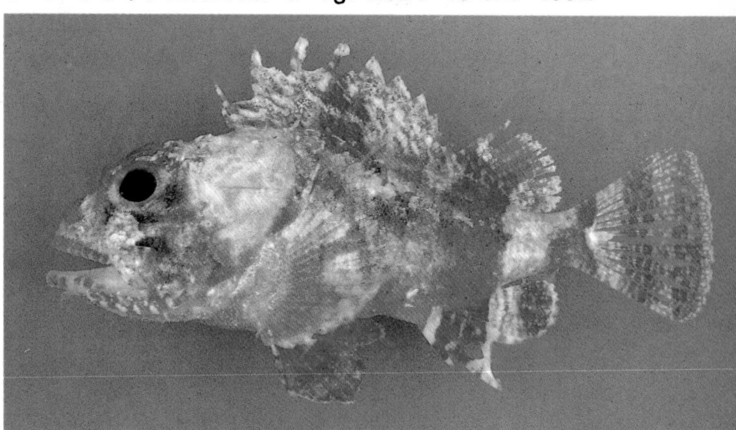

*Scorpaena elachys* 262
2 26°C sg: 1.022 64 cm 700L

*Scorpaena albifimbria* 262
2 26°C sg: 1.022 75 cm 800L

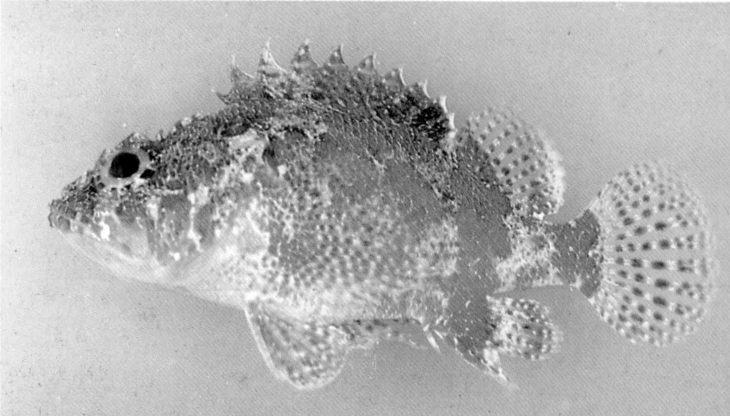

*Scorpaenodes tredecimspinosus* 262
2 26°C sg: 1.022 10 cm 100L

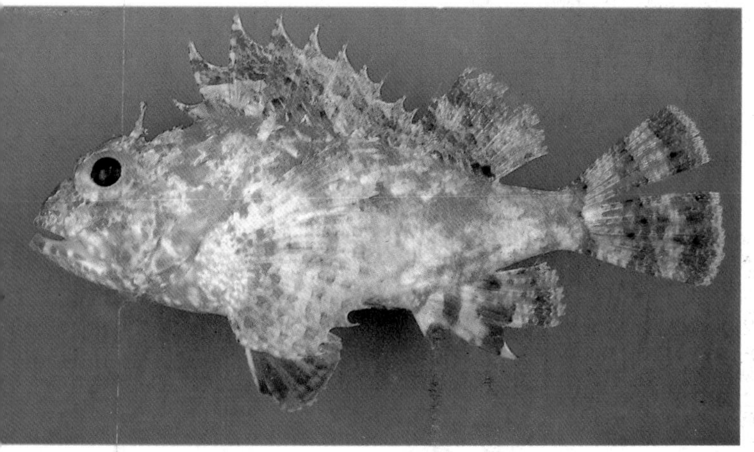

*Scorpaena* 262
2 26°C sg: 1.024 23 cm 250L

*Scorpaena bergi* 262
1-2 24°C sg: 1.023 75 cm 800L

*Scorpaena coniorta* 262
6 26°C sg: 1.022 7.5 cm 80L

*Sebastapistes cyanostigma* 262
6-10 26°C sg: 1.022 8 cm 80L

*Scorpaena* sp. 262
12 24°C sg: 1.022 10 cm 100L

*Scorpaena neglecta* 262
5, 7 26°C sg: 1.022 30 cm 300L

*Scorpaenopsis* sp. 262
11-12 26°C sg: 1.022 10 cm 100L

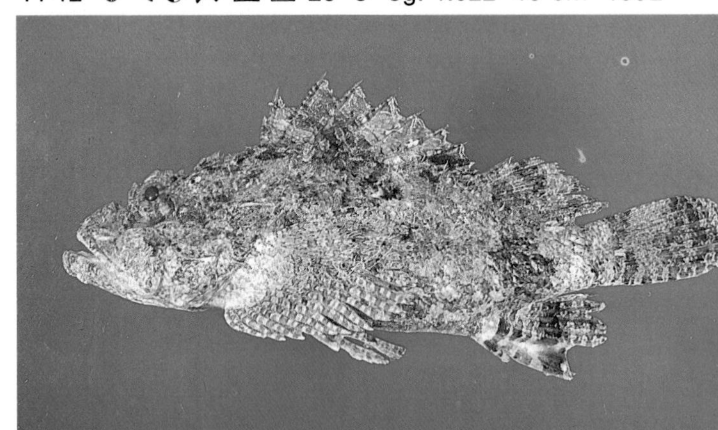

*Scorpaenopsis oxycephala* 262
6-10 26°C sg: 1.022 30 cm 300L

*Scorpaena sumptuosa* 262
12 24°C sg: 1.023 30 cm 300L

*Pontinus macrocephalus* 262
6-7 26°C sg: 1.022 13 cm 150L

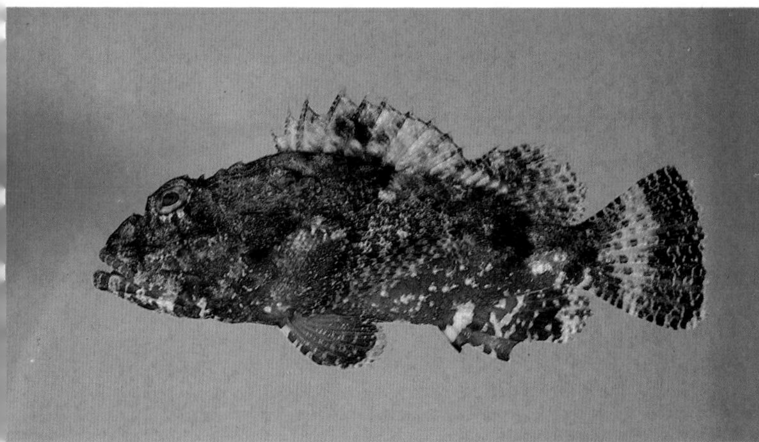

*Scorpaenopsis brevifrons* 262
6-7, 9 26°C sg: 1.022 10.5 cm 100L

*Scorpaenopsis gibbosa* 262
9-10 26°C sg: 1.022 10 cm 100L

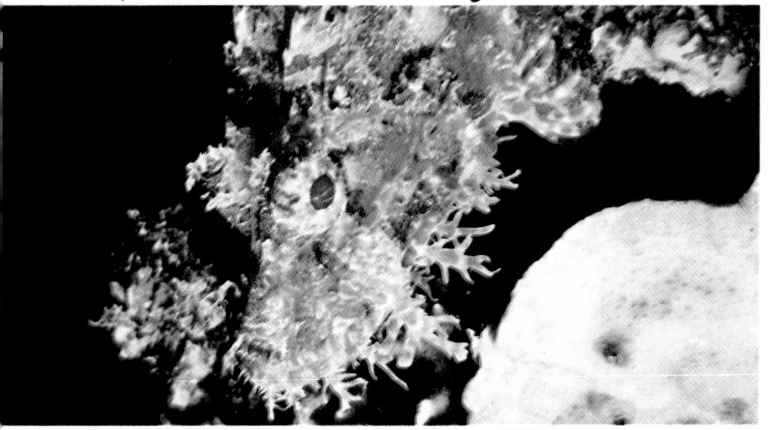

*Scorpaenopsis oxycephala* 262
6-10 26°C sg: 1.022 30 cm 300L

*Scorpaenopsis oxycephala* 262
6-10 26°C sg: 1.022 30 cm 300L

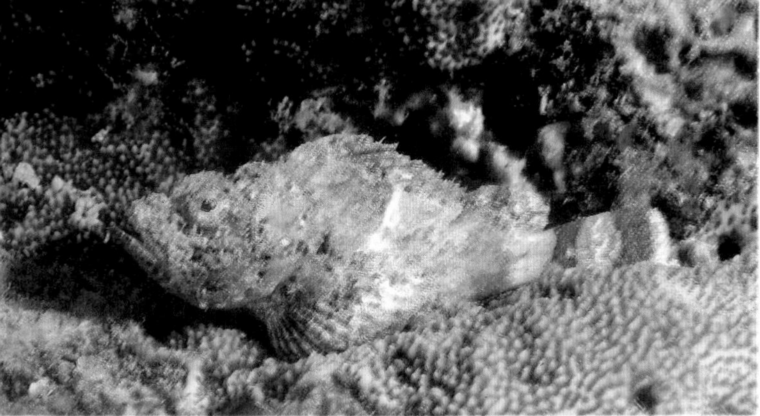

*Scorpaenopsis diabolus* 262
6-10 26°C sg: 1.022 30 cm 300L

*Scorpaenopsis barbatus* 262
9-10 26°C sg: 1.022 22 cm 200L

*Sebastapistes strongia* 262
7-9 26°C sg: 1.022 10 cm 100L

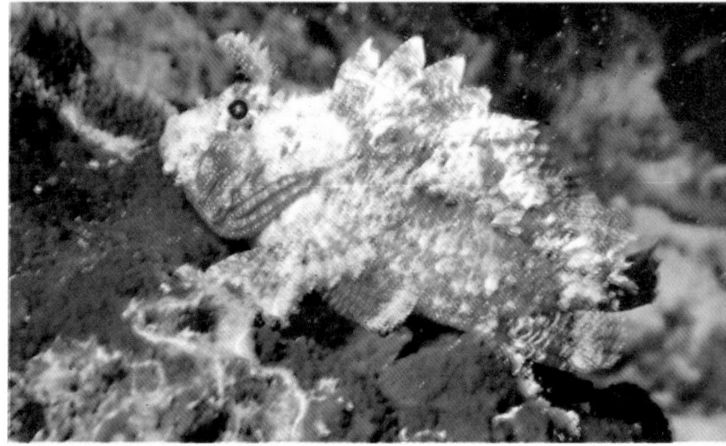

*Sebastapistes* sp. 262
7 26°C sg: 1.022 10 cm 100L

*Iracundus signifier* 262
6-9 26°C sg: 1.022 10 cm 100L

*Sebastapistes cyanostigma* 262
6-9 26°C sg: 1.022 7 cm 80L

*Scorpaenopsis* sp. 262
7, 9 26°C sg: 1.022 8 cm 80L

*Scorpaenopsis* sp. 262
7, 9 26°C sg: 1.022 18 cm 200L

*Scorpaena picta* 262
5, 7-9, 12 26°C sg: 1.022 12 cm 150L

*Scorpaena* sp. 262
7, 12 26°C sg: 1.022 22 cm 200L

*Scorpaenopsis* sp. 262
7, 9 26°C sg: 1.022 20 cm 200L

*Scorpaenopsis diabolus* 262
6-10 26°C sg: 1.022 30 cm 300L

*Sebastes atrovirens* 262
3, 4 24°C sg: 1.023 42 cm 500L

*Sebastes carnatus* 262
4 23°C sg: 1.023 40 cm 400L

*Sebastes chrysomelas* 262
4 22°C sg: 1.024 39 cm 400L

*Sebastes dallii* 262
4 22°C sg: 1.024 20 cm 200L

*Sebastes auriculatus* 262
3, 4 25°C sg: 1.022 55 cm 600L

*Sebastes caurinus* 262
4 24°C sg: 1.022 40 cm 400L

*Sebastes constellatus* 262
4 24°C sg: 1.023 30 cm 300L

*Sebastes maliger* 262
4 24°C sg: 1.023 60 cm 600L

*Sebastes mystinus* 262
4 22°C sg: 1.024 53 cm 500L

*Sebastes nigrocinctus* 262
4 22°C sg: 1.024 61 cm 600L

*Sebastes paucispinis* 262
3, 4 22°C sg: 1.024 90 cm 1000L

*Sebastes rosaceus* 262
3, 4 22°C sg: 1.024 36 cm 400L

*Sebastes melanops* 262
4 22°C sg: 1.024 60 cm 600L

*Sebastes nebulosus* 262
4 22°C sg: 1.024 43 cm 400L

*Sebastes pinniger* 262
4 22°C sg: 1.024 76 cm 800L

*Sebastes ruberrimus* 262
4 21°C sg: 1.024 91 cm 1000L

*Sebastes serriceps* 262
4 23°C sg: 1.024 41 cm 400L

*Sebastes rubrivinctus* 262
4 22°C sg: 1.024 51 cm 500L

*Sebastes miniatus* 262
4 23°C sg: 1.024 76 cm 800L

*Sebastes umbrosus* 262
4 22°C sg: 1.024 27 cm 300L

*Sebastes serranoides* 262
4 23°C sg: 1.024 61 cm 600L

*Sebastes marinus* 262
1, 14 22°C sg: 1.024 51 cm 500L

*Sebastes flavidus* 262
4 23°C sg: 1.024 20 cm 200L

*Sebastes* sp. 262
4 22°C sg: 1.024 50 cm 500L

*Sebastes trivittatus* 262
5 23°C sg: 1.024 40 cm 400L

*Sebastes joyneri* 262
5 23°C sg: 1.024 20 cm 200L

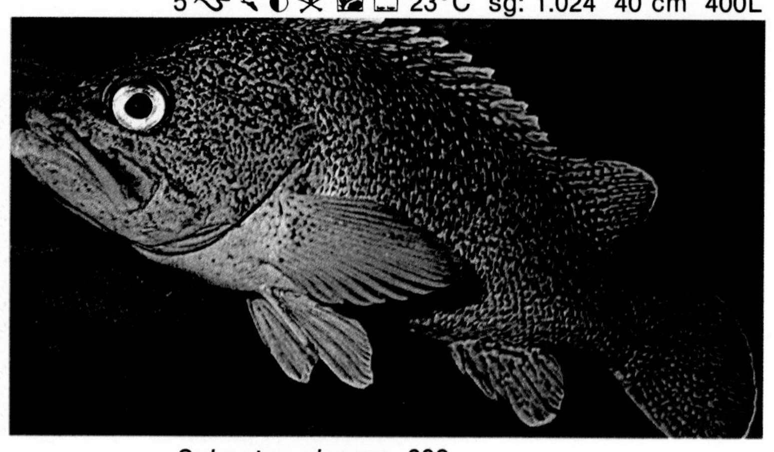

*Sebastes nivosus* 262
5 23°C sg: 1.024 40 cm 400L

*Sebastes inermis* 262
5 23°C sg: 1.024 35 cm 400L

*Sebastes baramenuke* 262
5 23°C sg: 1.024 45 cm 500L

*Sebastes pachycephalus* 262
5 23°C sg: 1.024 40 cm 400L

*Sebastes oblongus* 262
5 23°C sg: 1.024 40 cm 400L

*Sebastes matsubarae* 262
5 23°C sg: 1.024 70 cm 700L

*Scorpaenodes scaber* 262
6-8, 12 25°C sg: 1.022 63 cm 600L

*Scorpaenodes* sp. 262
7-8, 12 25°C sg: 1.022 12 cm 150L

*Scorpaenodes carribbaeus* 262
2 26°C sg: 1.023 10 cm 100L

*Scorpaenodes xyris* 262
3, 4 26°C sg: 1.023 15 cm 200L

*Scorpaenodes varipinnis* 262
7-8, 12 25°C sg: 1.022 5 cm 50L

*Scorpaenodes* sp. 262
7-8, 12 25°C sg: 1.022 8 cm 100L

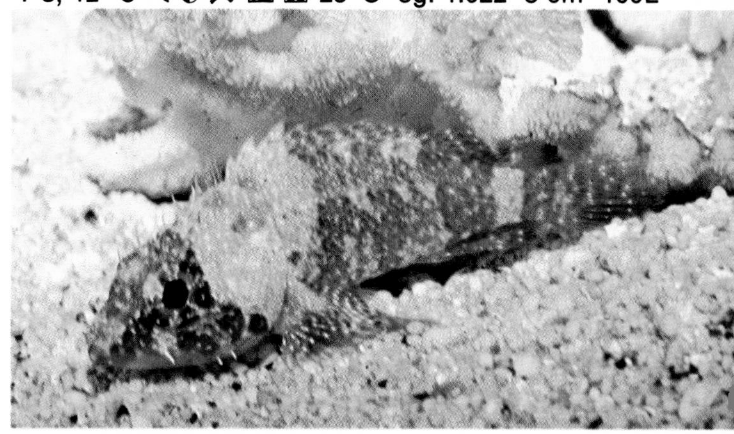

*Scorpaenodes insularis* 262
13 26°C sg: 1.022 6.5 cm 80L

*Scorpaenopsis* sp. 262
8 26°C sg: 1.022 15 cm 200L

*Scorpaenopsis diabolus* 262
6-10 26°C sg: 1.022 30 cm 300L

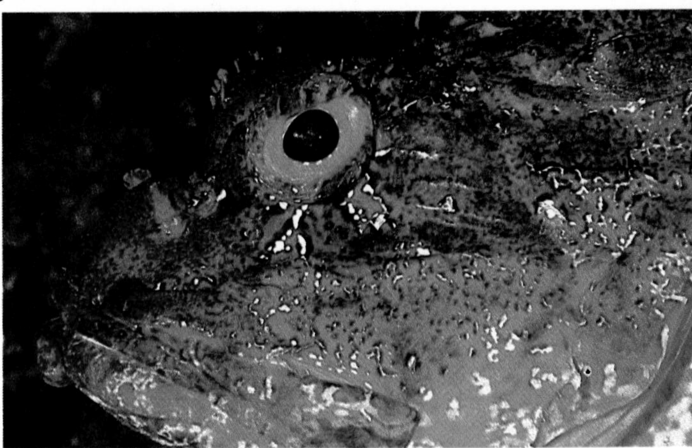

*Scorpaena cooki* 262
12 24°C sg: 1.023 26 cm 300L

*Scorpaena ballieui* 262
6 26°C sg: 1.022 10 cm 100L

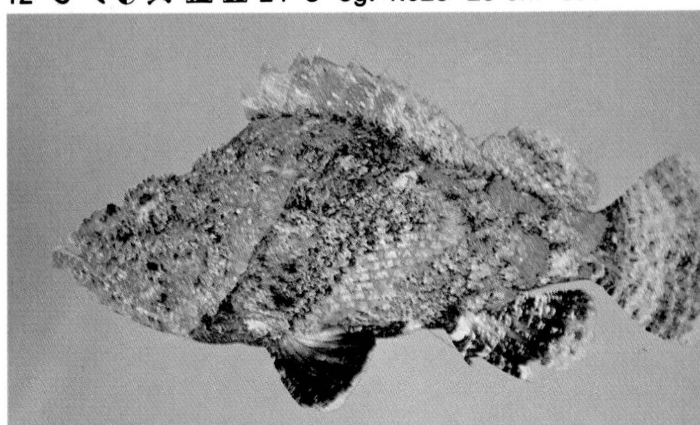

*Scorpaenopsis diabolus* 262
6-10 24°C sg: 1.023 30 cm 300L

Scorpionfish 262
3? 26°C sg: 1.022 15 cm 200L

*Scorpaenodes* sp. 262
7 26°C sg: 1.022 10 cm 100L

*Scorpaenodes kelloggi* 262
6-7, 9 26°C sg: 1.022 5 cm 60L

*Scorpaenodes littoralis* 262
7 26°C sg: 1.022 15 cm 200L

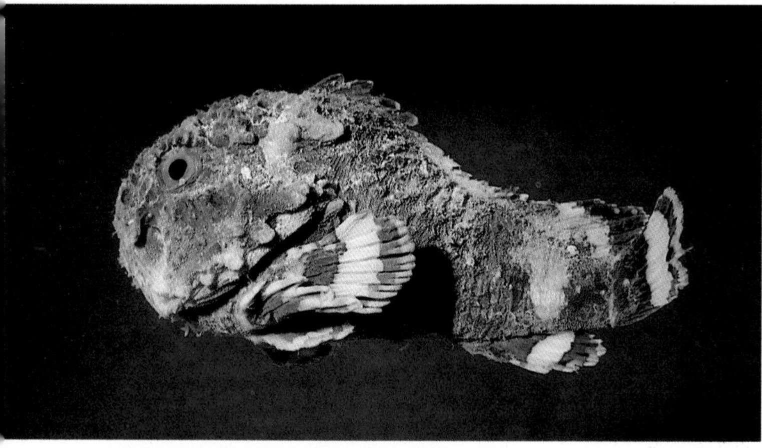

*Dampierosa daruma* 263
12 24°C sg: 1.023 16 cm 200L

*Erosa erosa* 263
8 26°C sg: 1.022 15 cm 200L

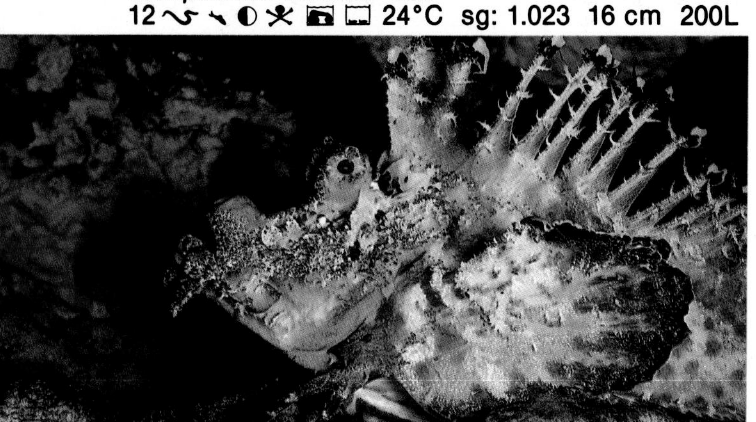

*Inimicus filamentosus* 263
9-10 26°C sg: 1.022 18 cm 200L

*Inimicus filamentosus* 263
9-10 26°C sg: 1.022 18 cm 200L

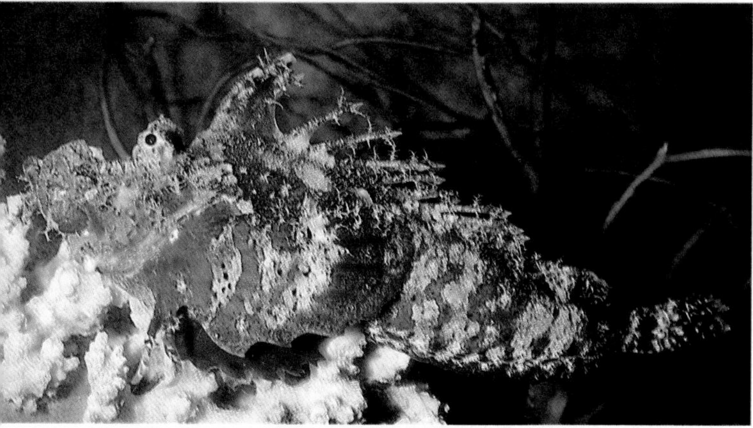

*Inimicus caledonicus* 263
7-9 26°C sg: 1.022 12 cm 150L

*Inimicus* sp. 263
8 26°C sg: 1.022 15 cm 200L

*Minous versicolor* 263
12 26°C sg: 1.022 8 cm 100L

*Minous quincarinatus* 263
7 26°C sg: 1.022 15 cm 200L

*Hipposcorpaena* sp. 262
5, 7, 9 26°C sg: 1.022 23 cm 300L

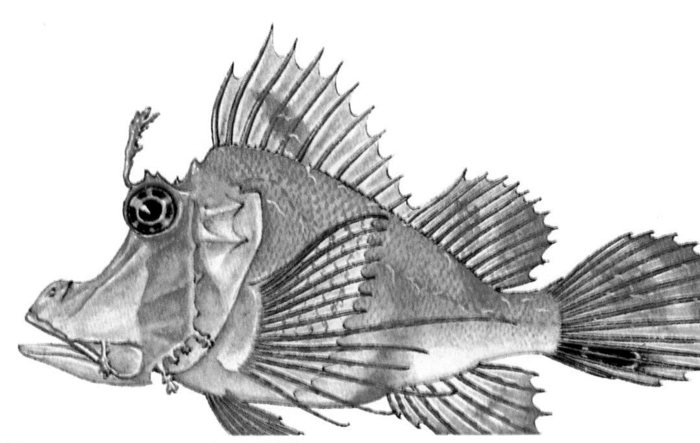

*Hipposcorpaena* sp. 262
5, 7, 9 26°C sg: 1.022 23 cm 300L

*Inimicus didactylus* 263
6-8 26°C sg: 1.022 20 cm 200L

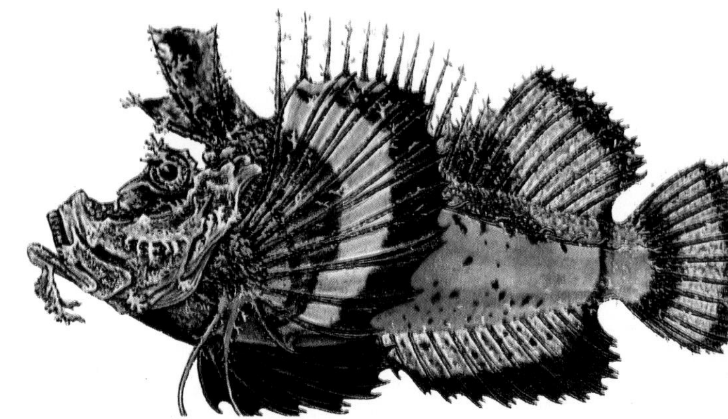

*Inimicus didactylus* 263
6-8 26°C sg: 1.022 20 cm 200L

*Aploactis aspera* 265
5 24°C sg: 1.023 10 cm 100L

*Erosa erosa* 263
8 26°C sg: 1.022 15 cm 150L

*Cocotropus dermacanthus* 265
7 26°C sg: 1.022 4 cm 50L

*Hypodytes longispinis* 262
7-9 26°C sg: 1.022 10 cm 100L

*Synanceia verrucosa*
6-10 ⁓ ↘ ◐ ✕ ▣ ☐ 26°C sg: 1.022 35 cm 400L

*Synanceia alula* 263
7 ◐ 26°C sg: 1.022 85 cm 1000L

*Inimicus sinensis* 263
7-9, 12 ◐ 26°C sg: 1.022 25 cm 300L

*Perryena leucometopon* 267
12 ◐ 24°C sg: 1.024 16 cm 200L

*Caracanthus maculatus* 264
6-7 ◐ ♥ 26°C sg: 1.022 5.5 cm 600L

*Synanceia verrucosa* 263
7, 9-10 ◐ 26°C sg: 1.022 35 cm 400L

*Glyptauchen panduratus* 262
12 ◐ 26°C sg: 1.022 10 cm 100L

*Amblyapistus taenionotus* 267
7 ◐ 26°C sg: 1.022 12 cm 150L

*Caracanthus madagascariensis* 264
9 ◐ ♥ 26°C sg: 1.022 5 cm 50L

*Paraploactis obbesi?* 265
7 26°C sg: 1.022 5 cm 50L

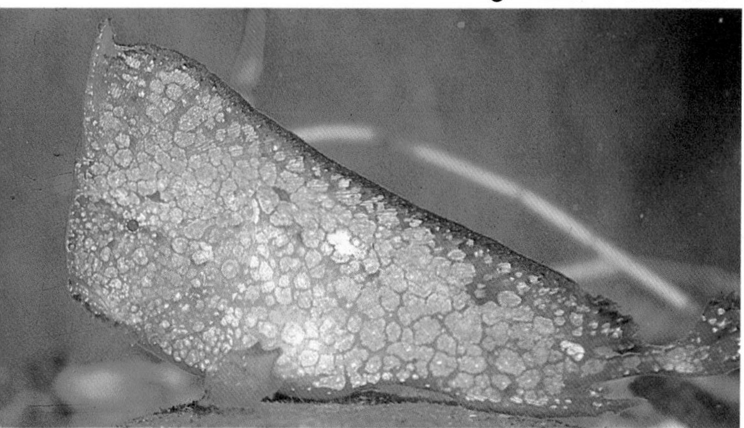

*Neopataecus waterhausi* 266
12 26°C sg: 1.022 6.0 cm 60L

*Hypodytes rubripinnis* 262
7 26°C sg: 1.022 11 cm 100L

*Paracentropogon vespa* 262
7-8 26°C sg: 1.022 9 cm 100L

*Pataecus fronto* 266
12 24°C sg: 1.023 12 cm 150L

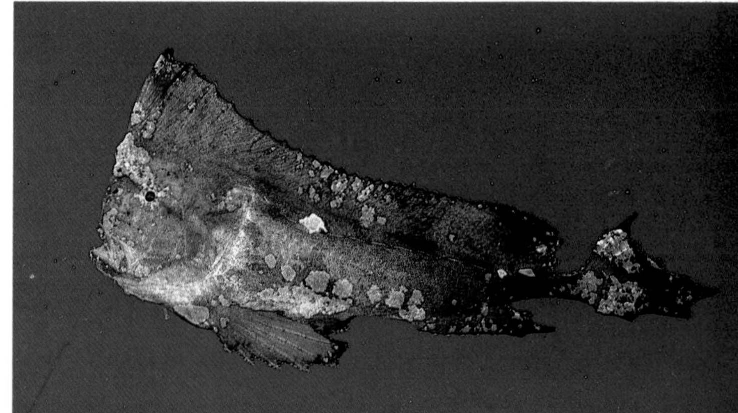

*Neopataecus waterhausi* 266
12 24°C sg: 1.023 6.0 cm 60L

*Hypodytes* sp. 262
7, 9 26°C sg: 1.022 5 cm 50L

*Hypodytes leucogaster* 262
7-9 26°C sg: 1.022 5 cm 50L

*Bellator gymnostethus* 268
3 26°C sg: 1.022 9 cm 100L

*Chelidonichthys spinosus* 268
7 26°C sg: 1.022 40 cm 400L

? *Peristedion* sp. 268
7 26°C sg: 1.022 15 cm 200L

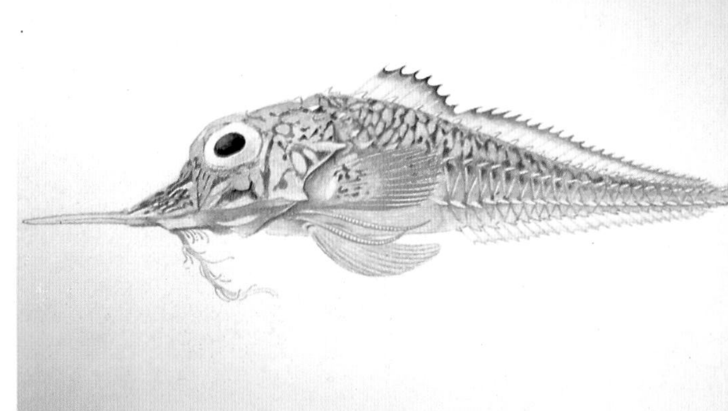

*Satyrichthys laticephalus* 268
5 24°C sg: 1.023 30 cm 300L

*Dixiphichthys hoplites* 268
7 26°C sg: 1.022 20 cm 200L

*Pterygotrigla multiocellatus* 268
5, 7 26°C sg: 1.022 35 cm 300L

*Lepidotrigla microptera* 268
7 24°C sg: 1.022 30 cm 300L

*Paratrigla vanessa* 268
7-9, 11-12 26°C sg: 1.022 50 cm 500L

*Prionotus ophryas* 268
2 26°C sg: 1.022 23 cm 300L

*Prionotus scitulus* 268
1-2 24°C sg: 1.023 25 cm 300L

*Prionotus carolinus* 268
1 24°C sg: 1.023 38 cm 400L

*Prionotus rubio* 268
2 26°C sg: 1.022 23 cm 300L

*Bembras japonicus* 269
7 24°C sg: 1.022 30 cm 150L

*Cociella crocodila* 269
7, 9-10 26°C sg: 1.022 50 cm 500L

*Onigocia spinosa* 269
5 24°C sg: 1.022 10 cm 100L

*Thysanophrys otaitensis* 269
6-9 26°C sg: 1.022 25 cm 300L

*Platycephalus indicus* 269
7-10, 15 26°C sg: 1.022 100 cm 1000L

*Inegocia guttata* 269
5, 7 25°C sg: 1.022 50 cm 500L

*Onigocia macrolepis* 269
5, 7 25°C sg: 1.022 12 cm 150L

*Onigocia macrolepis* 269
5, 7 25°C sg: 1.022 12 cm 150L

*Anoplopoma fimbria* 271
3-5 23°C sg: 1.024 76 cm 800L

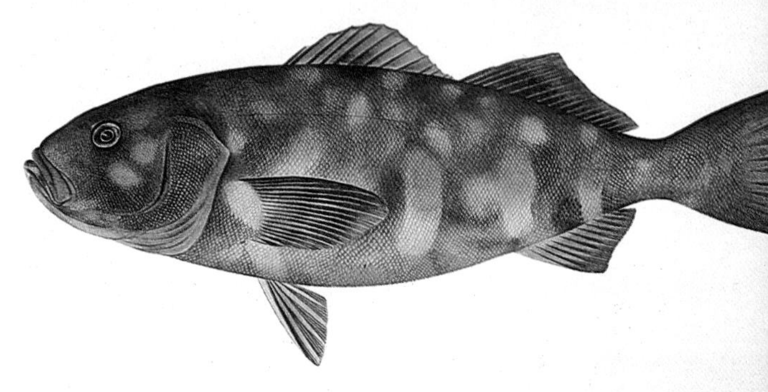

*Erilepis zonifer* 271
4, 5 25°C sg: 1.022 183 cm 2000L

*Hexagrammos otaki* 272
5 24°C sg: 1.023 40 cm 400L

*Hexagrammos* sp. 272
4 24°C sg: 1.023 40 cm 400L

*Hexagrammos decagrammus* 272
4 23°C sg: 1.023 50 cm 500L

*Hexagrammos decagrammus* 272
4 23°C sg: 1.023 50 cm 500L

*Oxylebius pictus* 272 ♀
4 24°C sg: 1.023 15 cm 200L

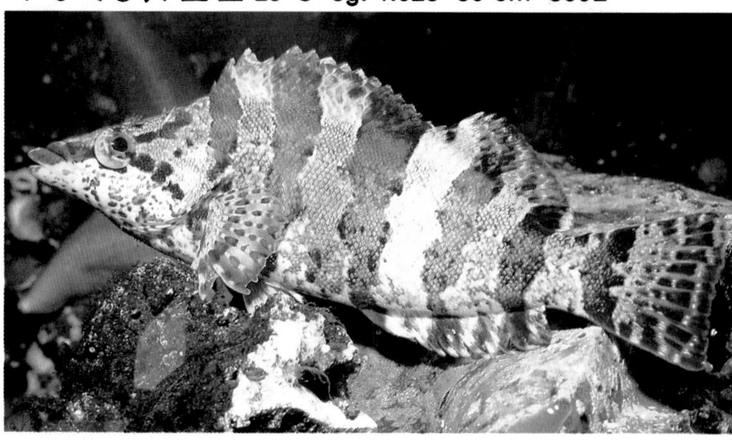

*Oxylebias pictus* 272
4 24°C sg: 1.023 15 cm 200L

*Ophiodon elongatus* 272
4 23°C sg: 1.024 152 cm 1500L

*Pleurogrammus azonus* 272
5 24°C sg: 1.023 70 cm 800L

*Zaniolepis frenata* 273
4 24°C sg: 1.023 10 cm 100L

*Zaniolepis latipinnis* 273
4 24°C sg: 1.023 30 cm 300L

*Artedius harringtoni* 276
4 23°C sg: 1.024 10 cm 100L

*Clinocottus analis* 276
3-4 26°C sg: 1.022 18 cm 200L

*Cottus kazika* 276
5 24°C sg: 1.023 5 cm 50L

*Cottus pollux* 276
5 24°C sg: 1.023 15 cm 200L

*Enophrys diceraus* 276
4 23°C sg: 1.023 37 cm 400L

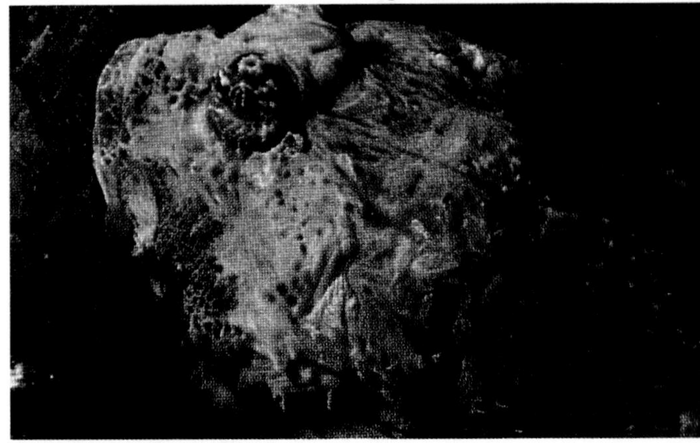

*Enophrys bison* 276
4 23°C sg: 1.023 37 cm 400L

*Gymnocanthus detrisus* 276
5 24°C sg: 1.023 10 cm 100L

*Gymnocanthus herzensteini* 276
5 24°C sg: 1.023 10 cm 100L

*Hemilepidotus gilberti* 276
5 24°C sg: 1.023 36 cm 400L

*Hemilepidotus hemilepidotus* 276
4 22°C sg: 1.024 50 cm 500L

*Hemitripteris americanus* 276
1 22°C sg: 1.024 40 cm 400L

*Hemitripteris villosus* 276
5 22°C sg: 1.024 40 cm 400L

*Jordania zonope* 276
4 23°C sg: 1.024 15 cm 150L

*Leiocottus hirundo* 276
3 26°C sg: 1.022 25 cm 300L

*Myoxocephalus aeneus* 276
4 16°C sg: 1.024 60 cm 600L

*Myoxocephalus scorpius* 276
Circumpolar 16°C sg: 1.024 60 cm 600L

*Rhamphocottus richardsoni* 276
4-5 23°C sg: 1.024 8 cm 80L

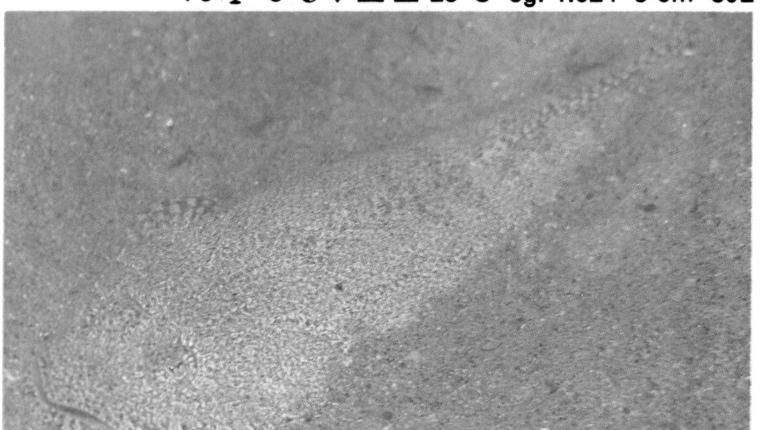

*Platycephalus* sp. 269
26°C sg: 1.022

*Argyrocottus zanderi* 276
5 23°C sg: 1.024 9 cm 100L

*Blepsias* sp. 276
23°C sg: 1.024

*Porocottus allisi* 276
5 23°C sg: 1.024 7 cm 70L

*Scorpaenichthys marmoratus* 276
4 23°C sg: 1.024 30 cm 300L

*Pseudoblennius percoides* 276
5 23°C sg: 1.024 20 cm 200L

*Nautichthys oculafasciatus* 276
4 23°C sg: 1.024 20 cm 200L

*Dasycottus japonicus* 279
5 23°C sg: 1.024 10 cm 100L

*Scorpaenichthys marmoratus* 276
4 23°C sg: 1.024 30 cm 300L

*Pseudoblennius cottoides* 276
5 23°C sg: 1.024 7 cm 80L

*Taurulus bubalis* 276
14-15 20°C sg: 1.024 17 cm 200L

*Psychrolutes paradoxus* 279
4-5 24°C sg: 1.023 6.4 cm 80L

*Agonomalus proboscidalis* 280
5 24°C sg: 1.023 20 cm 200L

*Agonomalus proboscidalis* 280
5 24°C sg: 1.023 20 cm 200L

*Agonus acipenserinus* 280
4 24°C sg: 1.023 30 cm 300L

*Occella verrucosa* 280
4 24°C sg: 1.023 30 cm 300L

*Podothecus sachi* 280
5 24°C sg: 1.023 50 cm 500L

*Cyclopterus lumpus* 281
14 24°C sg: 1.023 56 cm 6[illegible]

*Liparis pulchellus* 281
4-5 24°C sg: 1.023 30 cm 300L

*Liparis ochotenis* 281
5 24°C sg: 1.023 40 cm 400L

#114A

*Pseudoblennius cottoides* 276
5 23°C sg: 1.024 7 cm 80L

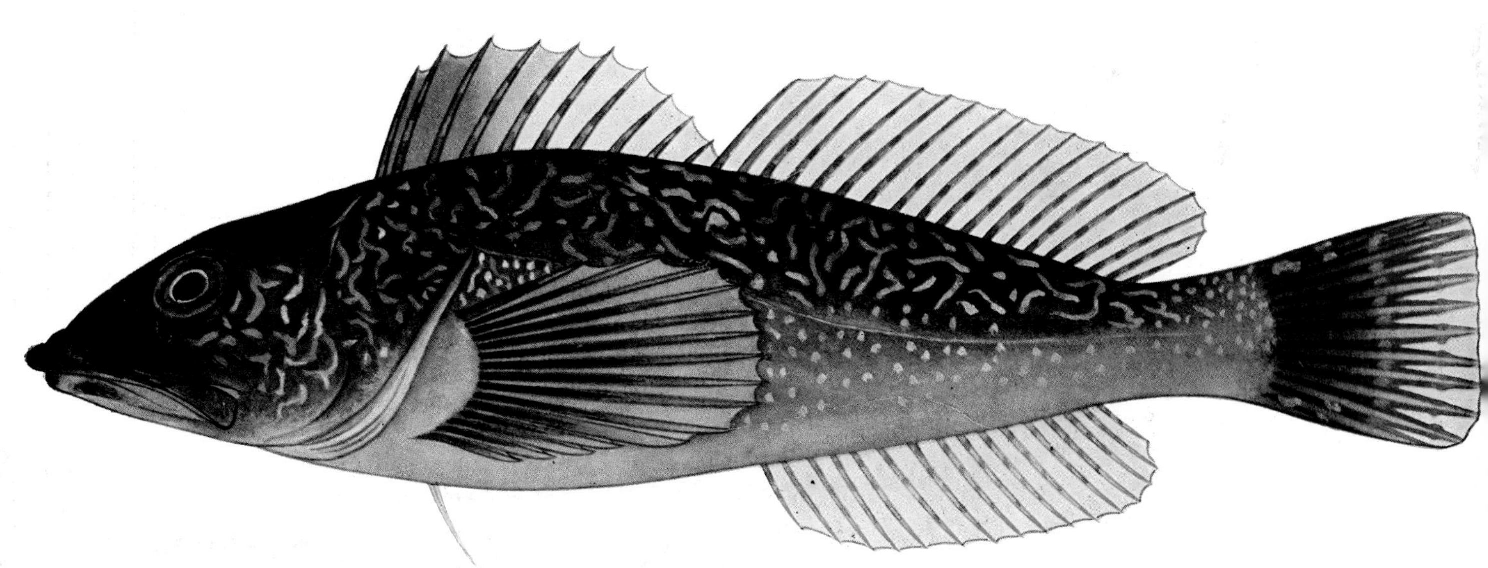

*Pseudoblennius percoides* 276
5 23°C sg: 1.024 20 cm 200L

*Centropomus undecimalis* 282
1-2 26°C sg: 1.022 110 cm 1200L

*Centropomus nigrescens* 282
3 26°C sg: 1.022 100 cm 1000L

*Psammoperca waigiensis* 282
7, 9 26°C sg: 1.022 35 cm 400L

*Lates calcarifer* 282
7-9 26°C sg: 1.022 150 cm 2000L

*Ambassis macracanthus* 282
9 26°C sg: 1.022 15 cm 200L

*Chanda ranga* 282
9 26°C sg: 1.022 8 cm 80L

*Ambassis interruptus* 282
7, 9 26°C sg: 1.022 8 cm 80L

*Dicentrarchus labrax* 283
14-15 21°C sg: 1.024 100 cm 1000L

#116

*Mirolabrichthys dispar* 284
6-7 26°C sg: 1.022 10 cm 100L

#116A

*Stereolepis gigas* 283
4-5 25°C sg: 1.022 220 cm 2500L

*Coreoperca kawamebari* 283
5 21°C sg: 1.016 11 cm 150L

*Doederleinia berycoides* 283
5 24°C sg: 1.023 40 cm 400L

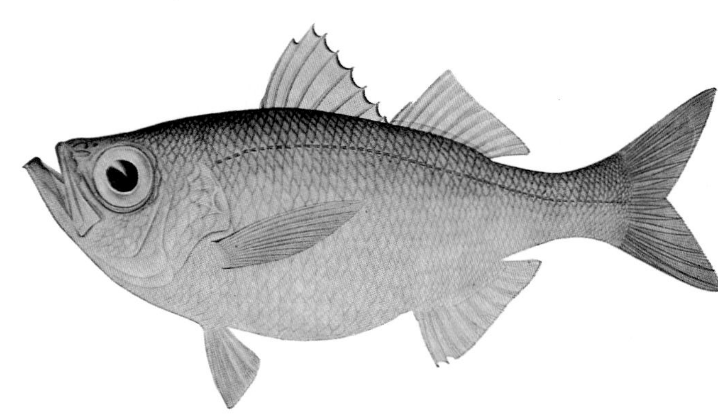

*Malakichthys wakiyai* 283
5 26°C sg: 1.022 48 cm 500L

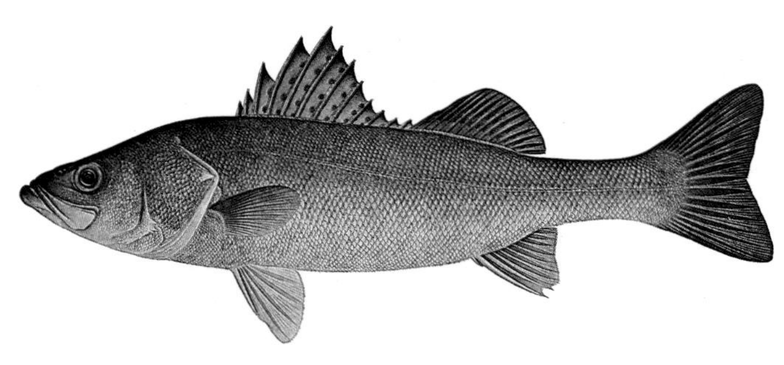

*Lateolabrax japonicus* 283
5 24°C sg: 1.023 150 cm 1500L

*Morone saxatilis* 283
1, 4 24°C sg: 1.023 183 cm 2000L

*Niphon spinosus* 283
7 26°C sg: 1.022 100 cm 1000L

*Polyprion oxygeneiosus* 283
11 22°C sg: 1.024 220 cm 2500L

*Stereolepis gigas* 283
4-5 25°C sg: 1.022 220 cm 2500L

*Stereolepis ischinagi* 283
5 24°C sg: 1.023 200 cm 2000L

*Pseudanthias kashiwae* 284 ♂
7 ◐ ♥ 26° sg: 1.022 11 cm 100L

*Pseudanthias kashiwae* 284 ♀
7 ◐ ♥ 26° sg: 1.022 11 cm 100L

*Mirolabrichthys bicolor* 284
7, 9 ◐ ♥ 26°C sg: 1.022 13 cm 150L

*Mirolabrichthys ignitus* 284
7, 9 ◐ ♥ 26°C sg: 1.022 10 cm 100L

*Pseudanthias* sp. 284
9 ◐ ♥ 26° sg: 1.022 10 cm 100L

*Pseudanthias truncatus* 284
7 ◐ ♥ 26° sg: 1.022 10 cm 100L

*Pseudanthias luzonensis* 284 ♂
7-8 ◐ ♥ 26° sg: 1.022 10 cm 100L

*Pseudanthias luzonensis* 284 ♀
7-8 ◐ ♥ 26° sg: 1.022 10 cm 100L

*Nemanthias carberryi* 284
9 ♀ ~ ◐ ♥ ▨ ⊟ 26°C sg: 1.022 7 cm 80L

*Nemanthias carberryi* 284
9 ♀ ~ ◐ ♥ ▨ ⊟ 26°C sg: 1.022 7 cm 80L

*Nemanthias carberryi* 284
9 ♀ ~ ◐ ♥ ▨ ⊟ 26°C sg: 1.022 7 cm 80L

*Mirolabrichthys evansi* 284
5, 7-9 ♀ ~ ◐ ♥ ▨ ⊟ 26°C sg: 1.022 10.5 cm 100L

*Mirolabrichthys imeldae* 284
7 ♀ ~ ◐ ♥ ▨ ⊟ 26°C sg: 1.022 10 cm 100L

***Anthias anthias*** **284**
**15 ◐ ♥ ⊟ 26°C sg: 1.022 25 cm 250L**

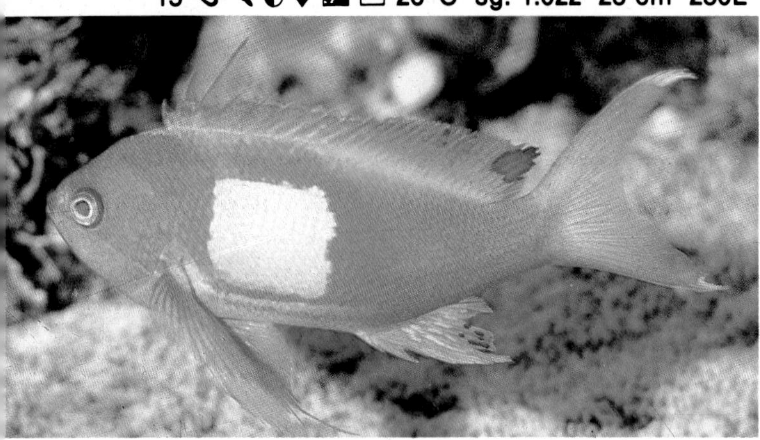

*Pseudanthias pleurotaenia* 284
7-8 ◐ ♥ ⊟ 26° sg: 1.022 10 cm 100L

***Mirolabrichthys thompsoni*** **284**
**6 ◐ ♥ ⊟ 26°C sg: 1.022 19 cm 200L**

*Pseudanthias squamipinnis* 284 ♀
6-10 ◐ ♥ ⊟ 26° sg: 1.022 10.5 cm 100L

*Pseudanthias ventralis ventralis* 284
6 ◐ ♥ ⊟ 26° sg: 1.022 7 cm 70L

*Pseudanthias rubrizonatus* 284
7 ◐ ♥ ⊟ 26° sg: 1.022 12 cm 150L

*Pseudanthias ventralis hawaiiensis* 284
6 ◐ ♥ ⊟ 26° sg: 1.022 8 cm 80L

*Pseudanthias squamipinnis* 284 ♂
6-10 ◐ ♥ ⊟ 26° sg: 1.022 10.5 cm 100L

*Pseudanthias hutchi* 284
7 26° sg: 1.022 10 cm 100L

*Pseudanthias taeniatus* 284
10 26° sg: 1.022 13 cm 100L

*Pseudanthias* sp. 284
10 26° sg: 1.022 10 cm 100L

*Pseudanthias fasciatus* 284
5, 7 24° sg: 1.023 9 cm 80L

*Pseudanthias taira* 284
5 24° sg: 1.022 10 cm 60L

*Pseudanthias engelhardi* 284
8 26° sg: 1.022 4 cm 50L

*Pseudanthias tenuis* 284
2 26° sg: 1.022 10 cm 100L

*Pseudanthias pictilis* 284
12 24° sg: 1.023 9 cm 100L

*Mirolabrichthys bartletti* 284
6 〰 ⸜ ◐ ♥ 🖼 ⊟ 26°C sg: 1.022 17 cm 200L

*Pseudanthias pleurotaenia* 284 ♀
7-8 〰 ⸜ ◐ ♥ 🖼 ⊟ 26° sg: 1.022 10 cm 100L

*Mirolabrichthys tuka* 284
7 〰 ⸜ ◐ ♥ 🖼 ⊟ 26°C sg: 1.022 13 cm 150L

*Mirolabrichthys pascalus* 284
6 〰 ⸜ ◐ ♥ 🖼 ⊟ 26°C sg: 1.022 17 cm 200L

*Mirolabrichthys tuka* (juv.) 284
7 〰 ⸜ ◐ ♥ 🖼 ⊟ 26°C sg: 1.022 13 cm 150L

*Mirolabrichthys imeldae* 284
7 〰 ⸜ ◐ ♥ 🖼 ⊟ 26°C sg: 1.022 9 cm 100L

*Paranthias colonus* 284
3 〰 ⸜ ◐ ♥ 🖼 ⊟ 26°C sg: 1.022 30 cm 300L

*Paranthias furcifer* 284
2 〰 ⸜ ◐ ♥ 🖼 ⊟ 26°C sg: 1.022 38 cm 400L

*Mirolabrichthys smithvanizi* 284
7, 9 ◐ ♥ 26°C sg: 1.022 6 cm 60L

*Pseudanthias squamipinnis* 284
6-10 ◐ ♥ 26° sg: 1.022 10.5 cm 100L

*Acanthistius pardalotus* 284
12 ◐ ♥ 26°C sg: 1.022 20 cm 200L

*Anyperodon leucogrammicus* 284
7, 9-10 ◐ 26°C sg: 1.022 50 cm 500L

*Mirolabrichthys dispar* 284
6-7 ◐ ♥ 26°C sg: 1.022 10 cm 100L

*Pseudanthias squamipinnis* 284
6-10 ◐ ♥ 26° sg: 1.022 10.5 cm 100L

*Aethaloperca rogaa* 284
7, 9-10 ◐ ♥ 26°C sg: 1.022 60 cm 600L

*Anyperodon leucogrammicus* 284
7, 9-10 ◐ ♥ 26°C sg: 1.022 50 cm 500L

*Sacura parva* 284
7, 12 26°C sg: 1.022 7 cm 80L

*Serranocirrhitus latus* 284
7 26°C sg: 1.022 8 cm 80L

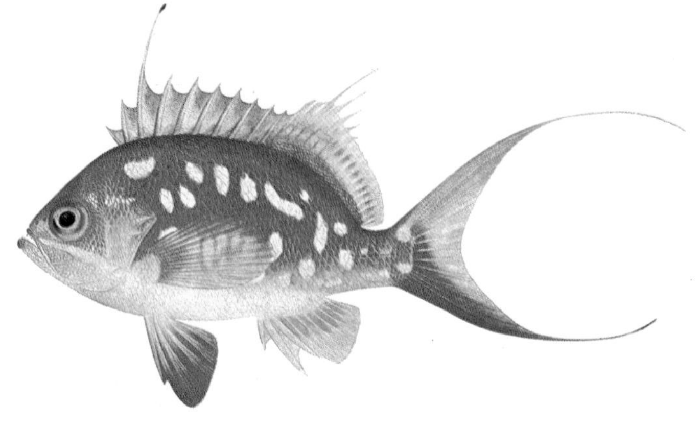

*Sacura margaritacea* 284 ♂
5, 7 26°C sg: 1.022 13 cm 150L

*Sacura margaritacea* 284 ♀
5, 7 24°C sg: 1.023 13 cm 150L

*Odontanthias fuscipinnis* 284
6 26°C sg: 1.022 19 cm 200L

*Odontanthias elizabethae* 284
6 26°C sg: 1.022 17 cm 150L

*Holanthias martinicensis* 284
2 26°C sg: 1.022 20 cm 200L

*Holanthias borbonius* 284
7, 9, 12 23°C sg: 1.024 10 cm 100L

*Caesioperca rasor* 284 ♀
12 ~ ↘ ◐ ♥ ▨ ▭ 24°C sg: 1.023 18 cm 200L

*Caesioperca rasor* 284 ♂
12 ~ ↘ ◐ ♥ ▨ ▭ 24°C sg: 1.023 18 cm 200L

*Caprodon schlegeli* 284
3, 5-8 ~ ↘ ◐ ✲ ▨ ▭ 26°C sg: 1.022 40 cm 400L

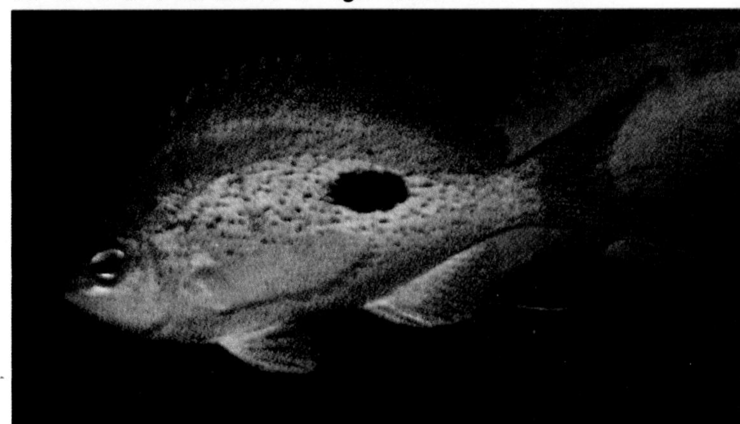

*Caesioperca lepidoptera* 284
11 ~ ↘ ◐ ✲ ▨ ▭ 22°C sg: 1.024 30 cm 300L

*Caprodon longimanus* 284
11, 12 ~ ↘ ◐ ♥ ▨ ▭ 22°C sg: 1.024 3.5 cm 50L

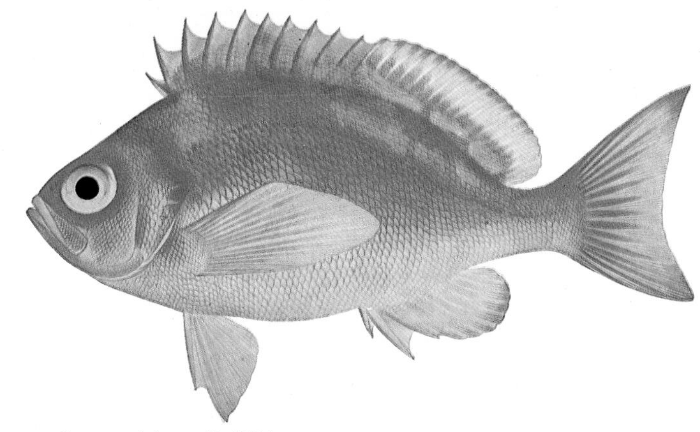

*Caprodon schlegeli* 284
3, 5-8 ~ ↘ ◐ ✲ ▨ ▭ 26°C sg: 1.022 3.5 cm 50L

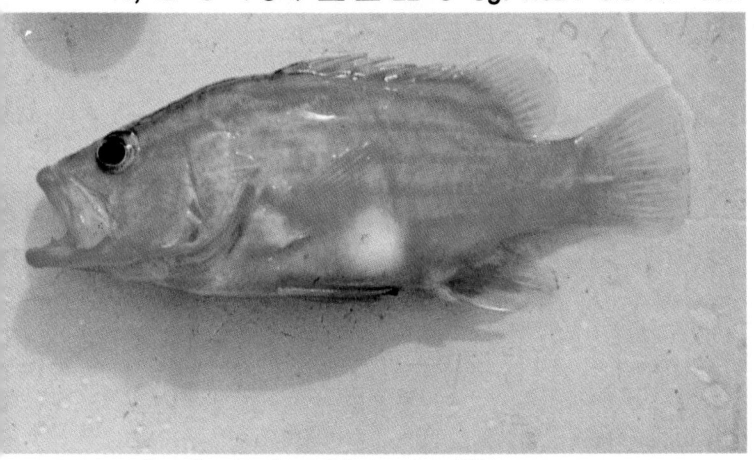

*Gonioplectrus hispanus* 284
2 ~ ↘ ◐ ✲ ▨ ▭ 26°C sg: 1.022 30 cm 300L

*Plectranthias japonicus* 284
7 ~ ↘ ◐ ✲ ▨ ▭ 23°C sg: 1.024 100 cm 100L

*Gracila albomarginata* 284
7, 9 26°C sg: 1.022 50 cm 500L

*Cephalopholis argus* 284
6-10 26°C sg: 1.022 50 cm 500L

*Cephalopholis pachycentron* 284
7, 9 26°C sg: 1.022 30 cm 300L

*Cephalopholis aurantia* 284
9 26°C sg: 1.022 60 cm 600L

*Cephalopholis polleni* 284
7, 9 26°C sg: 1.022 35 cm 400L

*Cephalopholis boenack* 284
6-9 26°C sg: 1.022 35 cm 400L

*Cephalopholis leopardus* 284
7, 9 26°C sg: 1.022 20 cm 200L

*Cephalopholis nigripinnis* 284
9 26°C sg: 1.022 25 cm 300L

*Cephalopholis miniata* 284
7, 9-10 26°C sg: 1.022 45 cm 500L

*Cephalopholis sonnerati* 284
6-7, 9 26°C sg: 1.022 57 cm 600L

*Cephalopholis urodelus* 284
7, 9 26°C sg: 1.022 25 cm 300L

*Cephalopholis miniata* 284
7, 9-10 26°C sg: 1.022 45 cm 500L

*Cephalopholis sexmaculata* 284
6-10 26°C sg: 1.022 50 cm 500L

*Cephalopholis sonnerati* 284
6-7, 9 26°C sg: 1.022 57 cm 600L

*Cephalopholis urodelus* 284
7, 9 26°C sg: 1.022 25 cm 300L

*Cephalopholis panamensis* 284
3 26°C sg: 1.022 30 cm 300L

*Cephalopholis fulva* 284
2 26°C sg: 1.022 30 cm 300L

*Cephalopholis analis* 284
6 26°C sg: 1.022 60 cm 600L

*Cephalopholis taeniops* 284
13 26°C sg: 1.022 30 cm 300L

*Cephalopholis cruentatus* 284
2 26°C sg: 1.022 30 cm 300L

*Cephalopholis fulva* 284
2 26°C sg: 1.022 30 cm 300L

*Cephalopholis hemistiktos* 284
9-10 26°C sg: 1.022 25 cm 300L

*Epinephelus fasciatus* 284
6-10 26°C sg: 1.022 35 cm 350L

*Cephalopholis sexmaculata* 284
6-10 26°C sg: 1.022 47 cm 500L

*Epinephelus damelii* 284
8, 12 25°C sg: 1.022 180 cm 2000L

*Epinephelus awoara* 284
7 24°C sg: 1.023 45 cm 500L

*Callanthias japonica* 284
7 25°C sg: 1.022 20 cm 200L

*Callanthias allporti* 284
11 21°C sg: 1.024 20 cm 200L

*Epinephelus corallicola* 284
7, 9 26°C sg: 1.022 45 cm 500L

*Epinephelus merra* 284
6-9 26°C sg: 1.022 45 cm 500L

*Epinephelus merra* 284
6-9 26°C sg: 1.022 45 cm 500L

*Callanthias allporti* 284
11 21°C sg: 1.024 20 cm 200L

*Epinephelides armatus* 284
12 24°C sg: 1.022 30 cm 400L

*Epinephelus fario* 284
7, 9 26°C sg: 1.022 38 cm 400L

*Epinephelus fuscoguttatus* 284
6-9 26°C sg: 1.022 90 cm 1000L

*Epinephelus hexagonatus* 284
5, 7, 9 26°C sg: 1.022 25 cm 300L

*Epinephelus caeruleopunctatus* 284
7, 9 26°C sg: 1.022 75 cm 800L

*Epinephelus fasciatus* 284
7, 9 26°C sg: 1.022 35 cm 400L

*Epinephelus rivulatus* 284
5, 7, 9 26°C sg: 1.022 35 cm 400L

*Epinephelus rivulatus* 284
5, 7, 9 26°C sg: 1.022 35 cm 400L

*Epinephelus tauvina* 284
7, 9-10 26°C sg: 1.022 70 cm 800L

*Epinephelus tauvina* 284
7, 9-10 26°C sg: 1.022 70 cm 800L

*Epinephelus* sp. 284
7 26°C sg: 1.022 40 cm 400L

*Epinephelus tukula* 284
7, 9 26°C sg: 1.022 200 cm 2000L

*Epinephelus malabaricus* 284
7, 9-10 26°C sg: 1.022 150 cm 1500L

*Epinephelus undulosus* 284
7, 9 26°C sg: 1.022 75 cm 800L

*Epinephelus multinotatus* 284
9 26°C sg: 1.022 100 cm 1000L

*Epinephelus socialis* 284
6 26°C sg: 1.022 22.5 cm 300L

*Epinephelus merra* 284
7-9 26°C sg: 1.022 45 cm 500L

*Epinephelus truncatus* 284
5, 7, 9 26°C sg: 1.022 40 cm 400L

*Epinephelus maculatus* 284
7-8 26°C sg: 1.022 60 cm 600L

*Epinephelus diacanthus* 284
9 26°C sg: 1.022 55 cm 600L

*Epinephelus septemfasciatus* 284
5, 7, 9 26°C sg: 1.022 100 cm 1000L

*Epinephelus microdon* 284
5, 7-10 26°C sg: 1.022 90 cm 1000L

*Epinephelus moara* 284
5, 7 26°C sg: 1.022 100 cm 1000L

*Epinephelus megachir* 284
8 26°C sg: 1.022 55 cm 600L

*Epinephelus epistictus* 284
7 26°C sg: 1.022 30 cm 500L

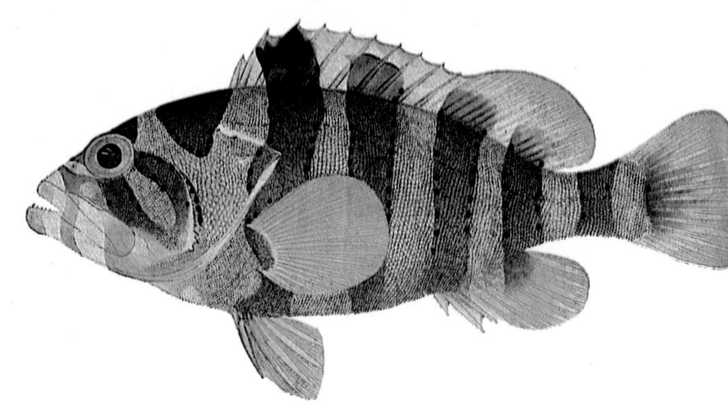

*Epinephelus amblycephalus* 284
5, 7, 9 26°C sg: 1.022 40 cm 500L

*Epinephelus akaara* 284
5, 7, 9 26°C sg: 1.022 40 cm 500L

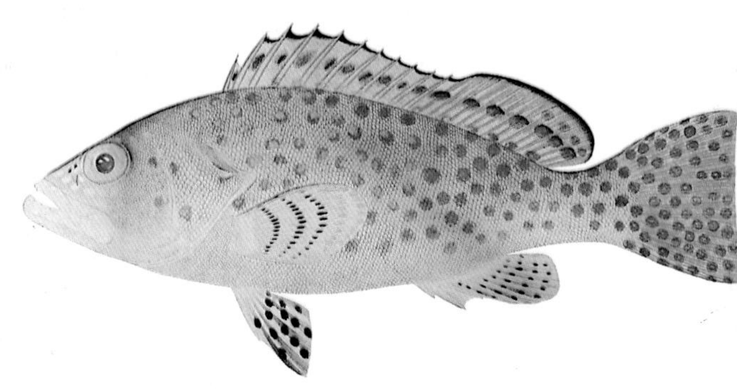

*Epinephelus areolatus* 284
7, 9-10 26°C sg: 1.022 50 cm 500L

*Epinephelus flavocoeruleus* 284
7, 9 26°C sg: 1.022 70 cm 800L

*Epinephelus latifasciatus* 284
5, 7, 9 26°C sg: 1.022 40 cm 500L

*Epinephelus cyanopodus* 284
6-9 26°C sg: 1.022 80 cm 800L

*Epinephelus cometae* 284
5, 7-9 26°C sg: 1.022 80 cm 800L

*Epinephelus labriformis* 284
3 26°C sg: 1.022 51 cm 500L

*Epinephelus niveatus* 284
1-3 26°C sg: 1.022 90 cm 1000L

*Epinephelus dermatolepis* 284
3 26°C sg: 1.022 110 cm 1200L

*Epinephelus dermatolepis* 284
3 26°C sg: 1.022 110 cm 1200L

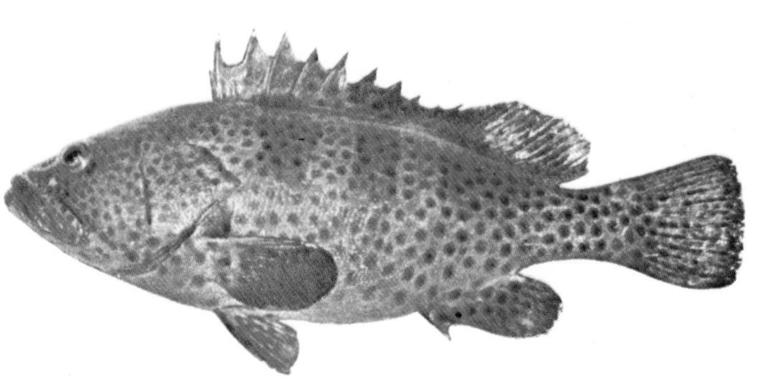

*Epinephelus analogus* 284
3 26°C sg: 1.022 80 cm 800L

*Epinephelus acanthistius* 284
3 26°C sg: 1.022 71 cm 800L

*Epinephelus labriformis* 284
3 26°C sg: 1.022 51 cm 500L

*Epinephelus itajara* 284
3 26°C sg: 1.022 240 cm 2500L

*Epinephelus guttatus* 284
1-2 24°C sg: 1.022 38 cm 400L

*Epinephelus guttatus* 284
1-2 24°C sg: 1.023 60 cm 600L

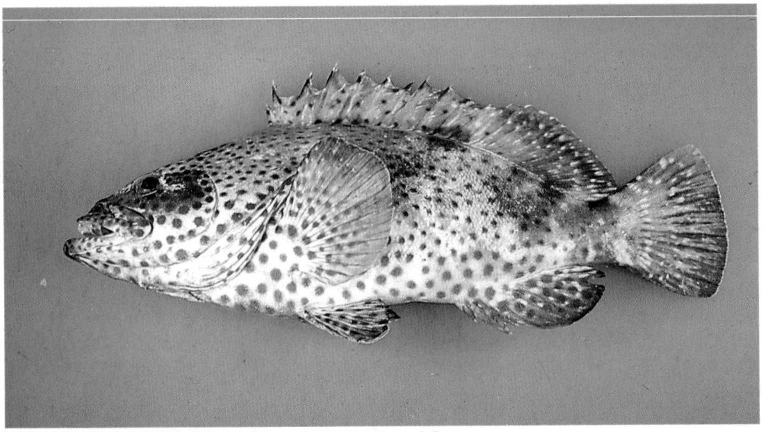

*Epinephelus adscensionis* 284
1-2, 13 24°C sg: 1.023 60 cm 600L

*Epinephelus mystacinus* 284
1-2 26°C sg: 1.022 150 cm 1500L

*Epinephelus striatus* 284
1-2 24°C sg: 1.023 30 cm 300L

*Epinephelus striatus* 284
1-2 23°C sg: 1.023 30 cm 300L

*Epinephelus morio* 284
1-2 23°C sg: 1.023 110 cm 1200L

*Epinephelus inermis* 284
1-2 24°C sg: 1.023 91 cm 1000L

*Mycteroperca bonaci* 284
2 24°C sg: 1.023 130 cm 1500L

*Mycteroperca interstitialis* 284 (juv.)
1-2 24°C sg: 1.022 76 cm 800L

*Mycteroperca rosacea* (rare golden form) 284
3 26°C sg: 1.022 100 cm 1000L

*Mycteroperca rubra* 284
2 26°C sg: 1.022 68 cm 800L

*Mycteroperca prionura* 284
3 26°C sg: 1.022 80 cm 1000L

*Mycteroperca interstitialis* 284
1-2 26°C sg: 1.022 68 cm 800L

*Mycteroperca rosacea* 284
3 26°C sg: 1.022 100 cm 1000L

*Mycteroperca venenosa* 284
1-2 26°C sg: 1.022 90 cm 1000L

*Mycteroperca tigris* 284
1-2 26°C sg: 1.022 100 cm 1000L

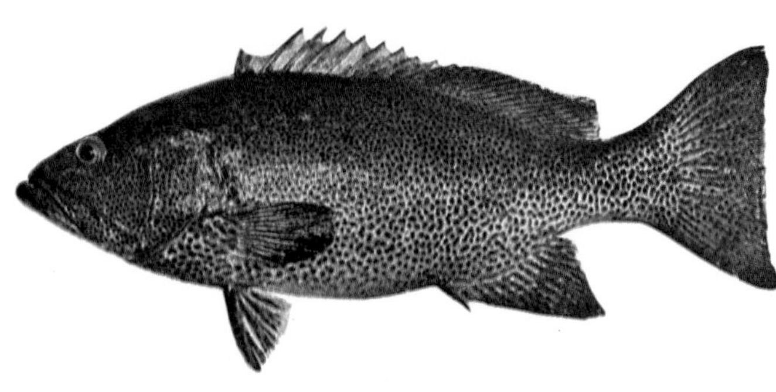

*Mycteroperca rosacea* 284
3 26°C sg: 1.022 100 cm 1000L

*Mycteroperca rosacea* (golden phase) 284
3 26°C sg: 1.022 100 cm 1000L

*Cromileptes altivelis* 284
7-9 26°C sg: 1.022 65 cm 800L

*Mycteroperca tigris* (juv.) 284
1-2 26°C sg: 1.022 100 cm 1000L

*Mycteroperca microlepis* 284
1-2 24°C sg: 1.023 60 cm 600L

*Epinephelus lanceolatus* 284
7, 9 26°C sg: 1.022 270 cm 3000L

*Cephalopholis pachycentron* 284
7, 9 26°C sg: 1.022 25 cm 300L

*Cromileptes altivelis* 284
7-9 26°C sg: 1.022 70 cm 700L

*Serranus phoebe* 284
1-2 26°C sg: 1.022 15 cm 150L

*Serranus tortugarum* 284
2 26°C sg: 1.022 80 cm 800L

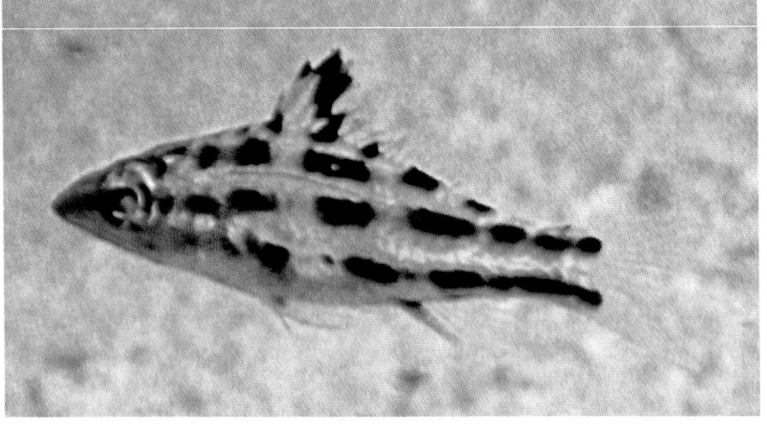

*Serranus luciopercanus* 284
2 26°C sg: 1.022 12 cm 150L

*Serranus cabrilla* 284
10, 14-15 26°C sg: 1.022 25 cm 300L

*Serranus hepatus* 284
13-15 26°C sg: 1.022 13 cm 150L

*Serranus scriba* 284
14-15 26°C sg: 1.022 25 cm 300L

*Serraniculus pumilio* 284
1-2 26°C sg: 1.022 7.5 cm 80L

*Serranus heterurus* 284
13 26°C sg: 1.022 22 cm 200L

*Serranus fasciatus* 284
3 26°C sg: 1.022 18 cm 150L

*Serranus annularis* 284
2 26°C sg: 1.022 8 cm 80L

*Serranus flaviventris* 284
2 26°C sg: 1.022 7.5 cm 80L

*Serranus chionaraia* 284
2 26°C sg: 1.022 5 cm 100L

*Serranus baldwini* 284
2 26°C sg: 1.022 5 cm 50L

*Serranus tigrinus* 284
2 26°C sg: 1.022 10 cm 100L

*Serranus subligarius* 284
2 26°C sg: 1.022 15 cm 150L

*Serranus tabacarius* 284
2 26°C sg: 1.022 18 cm 200L

*Liopropoma carmabi* 284
2 ◐ ♥ 26°C sg: 1.022 5 cm 100L

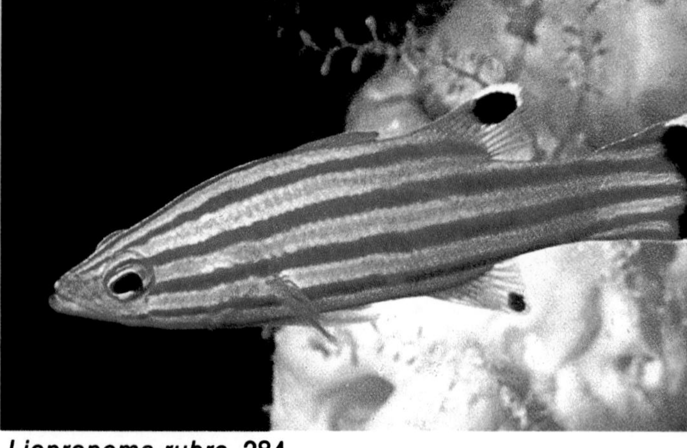

*Liopropoma rubre* 284
2 ◐ ♥ 26°C sg: 1.022 8 cm 150L

*Liopropoma fasciatum* 284
3 ◐ ♥ 26°C sg: 1.022 15 cm 150L

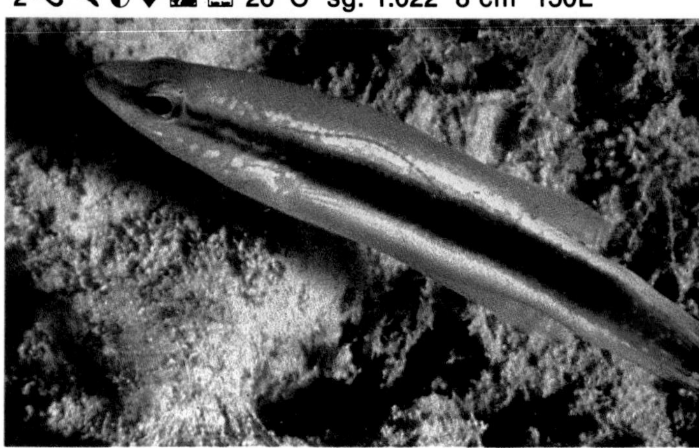

*Liopropoma eukrines* 284
2 ◐ ♥ 26°C sg: 1.022 5 cm 100L

*Liopropoma mowbrayi* 284
2 ◐ ♥ 26°C sg: 1.022 8 cm 100L

*Liopropoma swalesi* 284
7 ◐ ♥ 26°C sg: 1.022 6 cm 100L

*Liopropoma lineata* 284
6-7 ◐ ♥ 26°C sg: 1.022 7 cm 100L

*Liopropoma susumi* 284
6-7 ◐ ♥ 26°C sg: 1.022 8 cm 100L

*Liopropoma pallidum* 284
6-7 26°C sg: 1.022 15 cm 150L

*Liopropoma* sp. 284
7 26°C sg: 1.022 15 cm 150L

*Hypoplectrodes nigrorubrum* 284
12 24°C sg: 1.023 9 cm 100L

*Ellerkeldia annulata* 284
12 24°C sg: 1.023 20 cm 80L

*Ellerkeldia hunti* 284
11-12 22°C sg: 1.024 38 cm 400L

*Ellerkeldia maccullochi* 284
12 23°C sg: 1.024 20 cm 200L

*Ellerkeldia rubra* 284
12 23°C sg: 1.024 9 cm 100L

*Ellerkeldia wilsoni* 284
12 24°C sg: 1.023 20 cm 200L

*Rainfordia opercularis* 285
12 24°C sg: 1.022 12 cm 150L

*Luzonichthys waitei* 284
7 26°C sg: 1.022 7 cm 150L

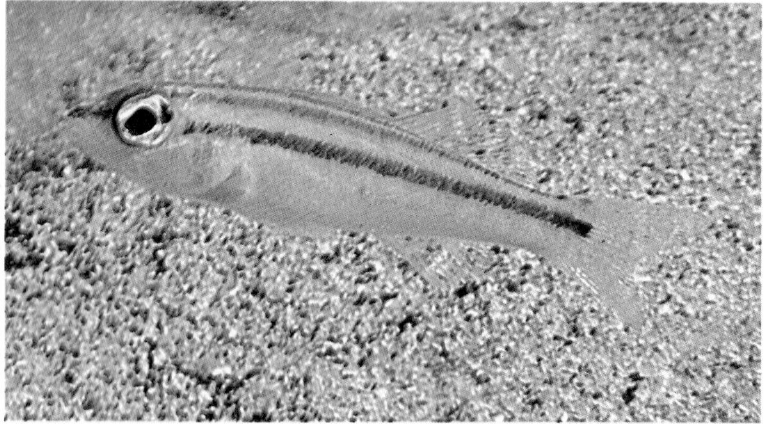

*Diplectrum formosum* 284
1-2 26°C sg: 1.022 30 cm 300L

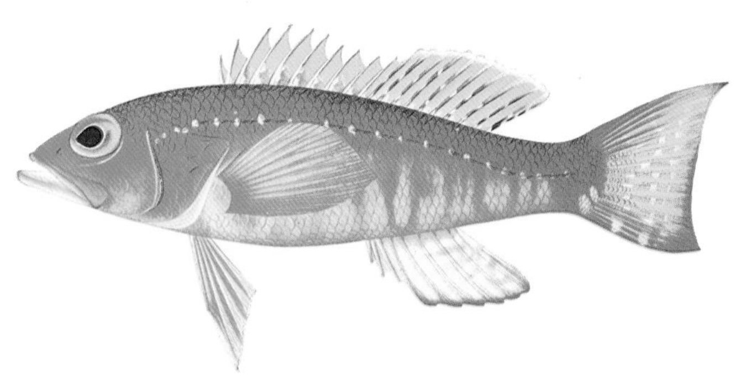

*Chelidoperca hirundinacea* 284
7 26°C sg: 1.022 15 cm 200L

*Pikea aurora* 284
6 26°C sg: 1.022 18 cm 200L

*Schultzea beta* 284
2 26°C sg: 1.022 10 cm 150L

*Diplectrum pacificum* 284
3 26°C sg: 1.022 15 cm 150L

*Rabaulichthys altipinnis* 284
7-8 26°C sg: 1.022 5 cm 100L

*Hypoplectrus indigo* 284
2 26°C sg: 1.022 15 cm 200L

*Hypoplectrus gummigutta* 284
2 26°C sg: 1.022 13 cm 150L

*Hypoplectrus nigricans* 284
2 26°C sg: 1.022 15 cm 200L

*Hypoplectrus unicolor* 284
2 26°C sg: 1.022 10 cm 100L

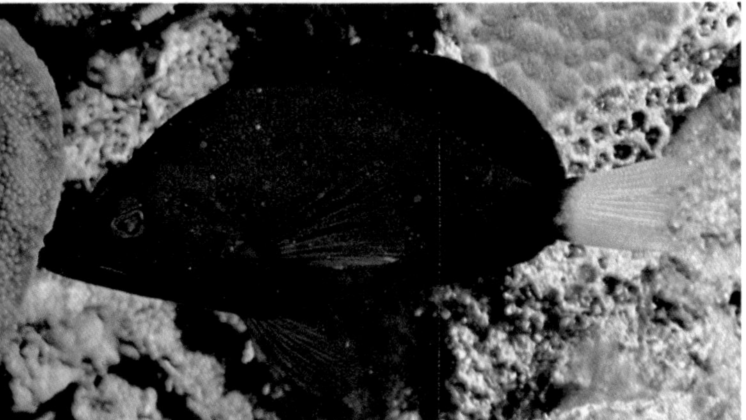

*Hypoplectrus chlorurus* 284
2 26°C sg: 1.022 12.5 cm 150L

*Hypoplectrus guttavarius* 284
2 26°C sg: 1.022 11.3 cm 100L

*Hypoplectrus gemma* 284
2 26°C sg: 1.022 11 cm 100L

*Hypoplectrus puella* 284
2 26°C sg: 1.022 11.5 cm 100L

*Acanthistius serratus* 284
8, 12 25°C sg: 1.023 45 cm 500L

*Acanthistius cinctus* 284
9, 11-12 24°C sg: 1.023 50 cm 500L

*Trachypoma macracantha* 284
11 22°C sg: 1.023 22 cm 200L

*Trisotropis dermopterus* 284
5 26°C sg: 1.022 45 cm 500L

*Paralabrax clathratus* 284
3 26°C sg: 1.022 45 cm 500L

*Paralabrax nebulifer* 284
3 26°C sg: 1.022 50 cm 500L

*Paralabrax auroguttatus* 284
3 26°C sg: 1.022 30 cm 300L

*Paralabrax maculatofasciatus* 284
3 26°C sg: 1.022 56 cm 600L

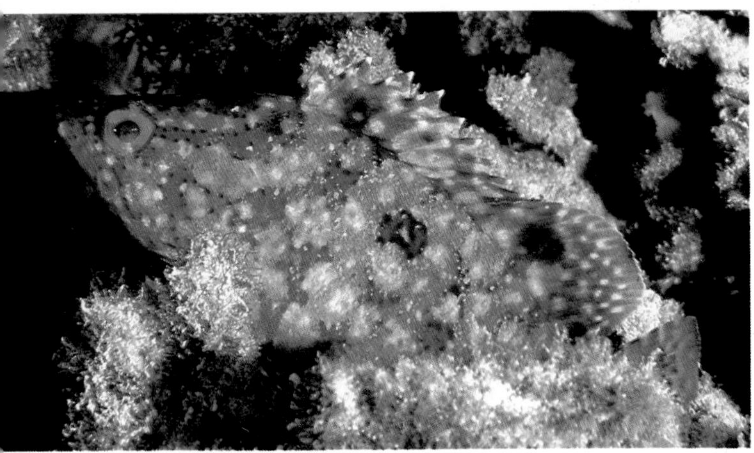

*Alphestes afer* 284
2 26°C sg: 1.022 27 cm 300L

*Alphestes multiguttatus* 284
3 26°C sg: 1.022 20 cm 200L

*Variola albomarginata* 284
7, 9 26°C sg: 1.022 65 cm 600L

*Variola louti* 284
7-10 26°C sg: 1.022 80 cm 800L

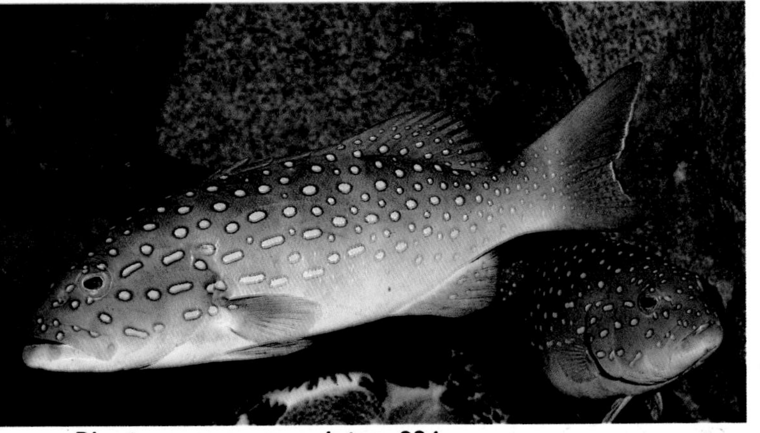

*Plectropomus maculatus* 284
8, 12 24°C sg: 1.022 60 cm 600L

*Plectropomus leopardus* 284
7-9 26°C sg: 1.022 65 cm 800L

*Plectropomus oligacanthus* 284
8 26°C sg: 1.022 55 cm 600L

*Plectropomus areolatus* 284
5-10 26°C sg: 1.022 53 cm 600L

*Variola louti* 284
7-10 26°C sg: 1.022 80 cm 800L

*Plectropomus laevis* 284
5, 7, 9 26°C sg: 1.022 100 cm 1000L

*Plectropomus leopardus* 284
7-9 26°C sg: 1.022 66 cm 800L

*Aulacocephalus temmincki* 285
5, 7, 9 26°C sg: 1.022 25 cm 250L

*Variola louti* 284
7-10 26°C sg: 1.022 80 cm 800L

*Plectropomus laevis* 284
5, 7, 9 26°C sg: 1.022 100 cm 1000L

*Pogonoperca punctata* 285
6-7, 9 26°C sg: 1.022 35 cm 400L

*Grammistes sexlineatus* 285
7, 9-10 26°C sg: 1.022 27 cm 300L

*Epinephelus multinotatus* 284
9 26°C sg: 1.022 100 cm 1200L

*Cromileptes altivelis* 284
7-9 26°C sg: 1.022 70 cm 800L

*Ellerkeldia wilsoni* 284
12 23°C sg: 1.024 20 cm 200L

*Othos dentex* 284
12 24°C sg: 1.023 70 cm 800L

*Epinephelus summana* 284
7, 9 26°C sg: 1.022 48 cm 500L

*Dinoperca petersi* 284
9 26°C sg: 1.022 62 cm 800L

*Luzonichthys microlepis* 284
9 26°C sg: 1.022 6 cm 60L

*Belonoperca chabanaudi* 285
7, 9 26°C sg: 1.022 14.5 cm 150L

*Diploprion bifasciatus* 285
5, 7, 9 26°C sg: 1.022 25 cm 300L

*Diploprion bifasciatus* (juv.) 285
5, 7, 9 26°C sg: 1.022 25 cm 300L

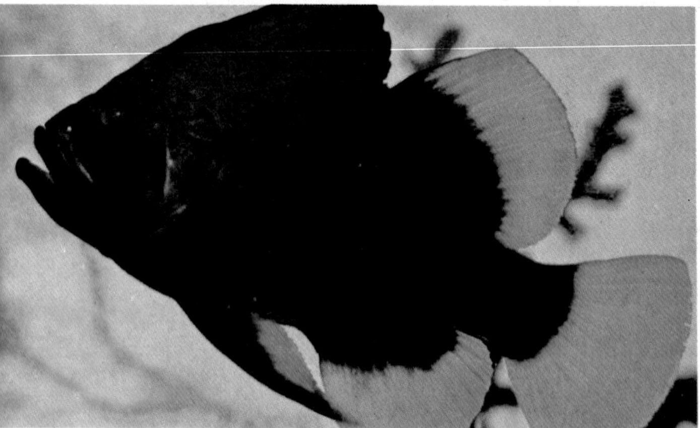

*Diploprion bifasciatus* (var.) 285
5, 7, 9 26°C sg: 1.022 25 cm 300L

*Diploprion drachi* 285
9-10 26°C sg: 1.022 14 cm 150L

*Grammistes sexlineatus* 285
7-10 26°C sg: 1.022 27 cm 300L

*Grammistops ocellatus* 285
7, 9 26°C sg: 1.022 10 cm 100L

*Pseudogramma polyacantha* 285
6-9 26°C sg: 1.022 7 cm 80L

*Pseudogramma gregoryi* 285
1-2 24°C sg: 1.023 7.5 cm 80L

*Epinephelus multinotatus* 284
9 26°C sg: 1.022 100 cm 1200L

*Cromileptes altivelis* 284
7-9 26°C sg: 1.022 70 cm 800L

*Ellerkeldia wilsoni* 284
12 23°C sg: 1.024 20 cm 200L

*Othos dentex* 284
12 24°C sg: 1.023 70 cm 800L

*Epinephelus summana* 284
7, 9 26°C sg: 1.022 48 cm 500L

*Dinoperca petersi* 284
9 26°C sg: 1.022 62 cm 800L

*Luzonichthys microlepis* 284
9 26°C sg: 1.022 6 cm 60L

*Belonoperca chabanaudi* 285
7, 9 26°C sg: 1.022 14.5 cm 150L

*Diploprion bifasciatus* 285
5, 7, 9 26°C sg: 1.022 25 cm 300L

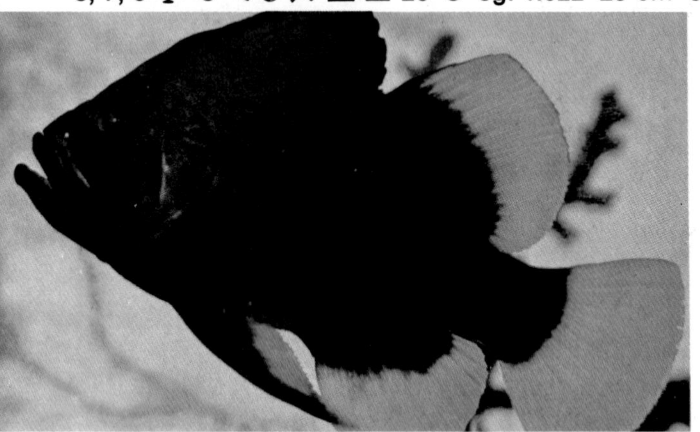

*Diploprion bifasciatus* (var.) 285
5, 7, 9 26°C sg: 1.022 25 cm 300L

*Grammistes sexlineatus* 285
7-10 26°C sg: 1.022 27 cm 300L

*Pseudogramma polyacantha* 285
6-9 26°C sg: 1.022 7 cm 80L

*Diploprion bifasciatus* (juv.) 285
5, 7, 9 26°C sg: 1.022 25 cm 300L

*Diploprion drachi* 285
9-10 26°C sg: 1.022 14 cm 150L

*Grammistops ocellatus* 285
7, 9 26°C sg: 1.022 10 cm 100L

*Pseudogramma gregoryi* 285
1-2 24°C sg: 1.023 7.5 cm 80L

*Suttonia lineata* 285
6 ◐ ♥ 26°C sg: 1.022 12.5 cm 150L

*Rypticus bistrispinus* 285
2 ◐ ♥ 26°C sg: 1.022 15 cm 150L

*Rypticus subbifrenatus* 285
2, 13 ◐ ♥ 26°C sg: 1.022 18 cm 200L

*Rypticus saponaceus* 285
1-2, 13 ◐ 26°C sg: 1.022 33 cm 400L

*Rypticus bicolor (?)* 285
3 ◐ 26°C sg: 1.022 33 cm 400L

*Labracinus cyclophthalmus* 286
7 ◐ ♥ 26°C sg: 1.022 14 cm 150L

*Pseudoplesiops rosae* 286
12 ◐ ♥ 24°C sg: 1.023 5 cm 50L

*Pseudochromis luteus* 285
7 ◐ ♥ 26°C sg: 1.022 5 cm 50L

*Pseudochromis tapeinosoma* 286
7-8, 12 ♥ 26°C sg: 1.022 5 cm 50L

*Pseudochromis wilsoni* 286
7-8, 12 ♥ 26°C sg: 1.022 6 cm 60L

*Pseudochromis marshallensis* 286
7-8, 12 ♥ 26°C sg: 1.022 7 cm 80L

*Pseudochromis veliferus* 286
8 ♥ 26°C sg: 1.022 7 cm 80L

*Pseudochromis cyanotaenia* 286
7-8, 12 ♥ 26°C sg: 1.022 5 cm 50L

*Pseudochromis xanthochir* 286
7-8, 12 ♥ 26°C sg: 1.022 7 cm 80L

*Pseudochromis marshallensis* 286
7-8, 12 ♥ 26°C sg: 1.022 7 cm 80L

*Pseudochromis veliferus* 286
8 ♥ 26°C sg: 1.022 7 cm 80L

*Pseudochromis bitaeniata* 286
7-8, 12 26°C sg: 1.022 6 cm 80L

*Pseudochromis novaehollandiae* 286
7-8, 12 26°C sg: 1.022 19 cm 200L

*Pseudochromis aureus* 286
7-8 26°C sg: 1.022 10 cm 100L

*Pseudochromis aureus* 286
7-8 26°C sg: 1.022 10 cm 100L

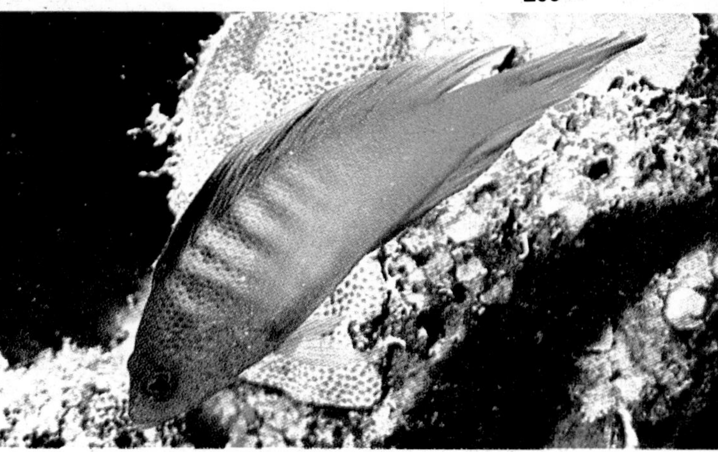

*Pseudochromis longipinnis* 286
8 26°C sg: 1.022 9.6 cm 100L

*Pseudochromis mccullochi* 286
7-8, 12 26°C sg: 1.022 10 cm 100L

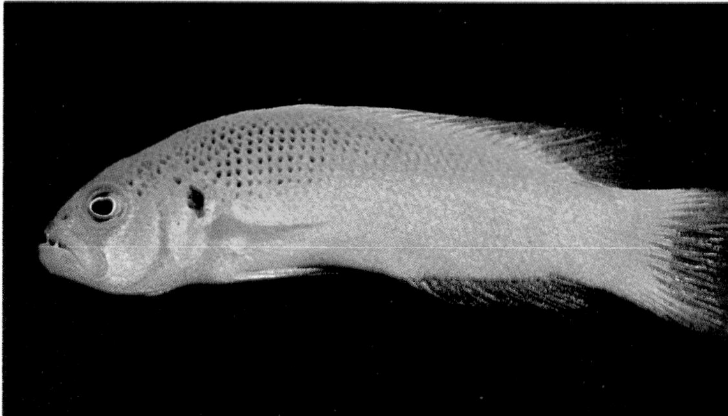

*Pseudochromis moorei* 286
7 26°C sg: 1.022 10 cm 100L

*Pseudochromis fuscus* 286
9 26°C sg: 1.022 10 cm 100L

*Pseudochromis dilectus* 286
9 ◐ ♥ 26°C sg: 1.022 7 cm 80L

*Pseudochromis paranox* 286
7 ◐ ♥ 26°C sg: 1.022 3.5 cm 50L

*Pseudochromis melanotaenia* 286
6, 7 ◐ ♥ 26°C sg: 1.022 6 cm 60L

*Pseudochromis sankeyi* 286
9-10 ◐ ♥ 26°C sg: 1.022 7.4 cm 80L

*Pseudochromis dilectus* 286
9 ◐ ♥ 26°C sg: 1.022 7 cm 80L

*Pseudochromis springeri* 286
10 ◐ ♥ 26°C sg: 1.028 5.5 cm 60L

*Pseudochromis pesi* 286
10 ◐ ♥ 26°C sg: 1.028 8 cm 80L

*Pseudochromis dixurus* 286
10 ◐ ♥ 26°C sg: 1.028 9 cm 100L

*Pseudochromis porphyreus* 286
7 26°C sg: 1.022 5.5 cm 60L

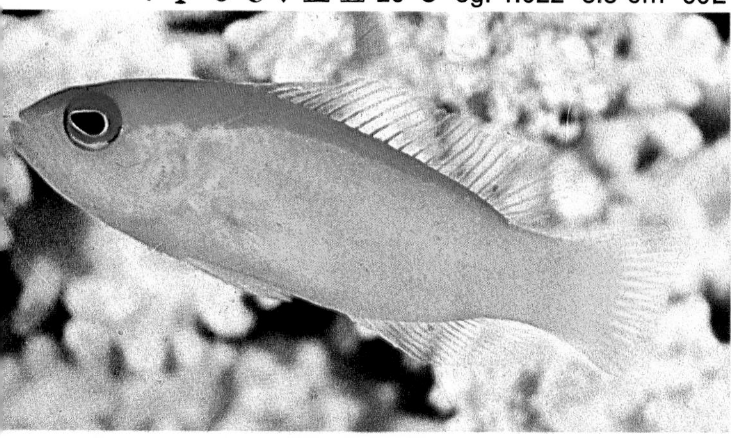

*Pseudochromis diadema* 286
7 26°C sg: 1.022 27.4 cm 300L

*Pseudochromis cyanotaenia* 286
12 24°C sg: 1.023 5 cm 50L

***Pseudochromis olivaceus*** **286**
**9-10 26°C sg: 1.022 9.2 cm 100L**

*Pseudochromis paccagnellae* 286
7-8 26°C sg: 1.022 5 cm 50L

*Pseudochromis perspicillatus* 286
7 26°C sg: 1.022 12 cm 150L

*Pseudochromis flammicauda* 286
8 26°C sg: 1.022 5.5 cm 60L

*Pseudoplesiops inornatus* 286
9 26°C sg: 1.022 10 cm 100L

*Pseudochromis dutoiti* 286
9 26°C sg: 1.022 8.8 cm 100L

*Pseudochromis fridmani* 286
10 26°C sg: 1.028 6 cm 60L

*Labracinus lineatus* 286
7-8, 12 25°C sg: 1.022 14 cm 150L

*Belonepterygion fasciolatum* 289
12 23°C sg: 1.024 5 cm 50L

*Pseudochromis flavivertex* 286
9-10 26°C sg: 1.022 7 cm 80L

*Pseudochromis melas* 286
9 26°C sg: 1.022 9 cm 100L

*Glaucosoma hebraicum* 290
12 24°C sg: 1.023 60 cm 600L

*Belonepterygion fasciolatum(?)* 289
12 23°C sg: 1.024 5 cm 50L

*Lipogramma regia* 287
2 ◐ ♥ 26°C sg: 1.022 2.5 cm 50L

*Lipogramma klayi* 287
2 ◐ 26°C sg: 1.022 4 cm 50L

*Lipogramma trilineata* 287
2 ◐ ♥ 26°C sg: 1.022 3.5 cm 50L

*Gramma loreto* 287
2 ◐ 26°C sg: 1.022 7.5 cm 80L

*Gramma linki* 287
1-2 ◐ 24°C sg: 1.023 6.5 cm 60L

*Gramma melacara* 287
2 ◐ 26°C sg: 1.022 10 cm 100L

*Assessor flavissimus* 288
8 ◐ ♥ 26°C sg: 1.022 8 cm 80L

*Assessor macneilli* 288
8 ◐ 26°C sg: 1.022 8 cm 80L

*Calloplesiops altivelis* 287
7-10 26°C sg: 1.022 16 cm 200L

*Calloplesiops argus* 288
7 26°C sg: 1.022 16 cm 200L

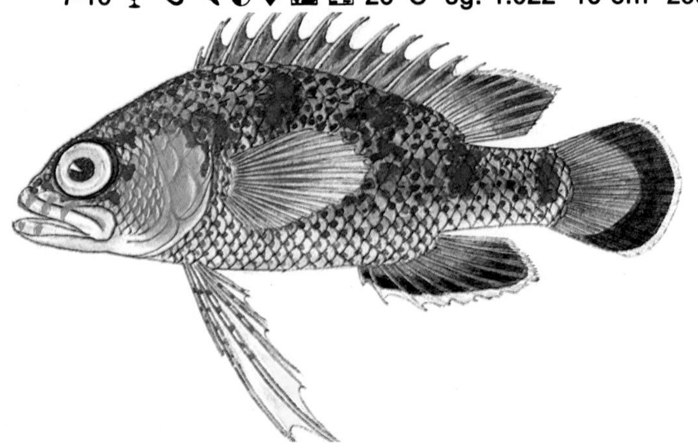

*Plesiops oxycephalus* 287
7 26°C sg: 1.022 10 cm 100L

*Plesiops corallicola* 288
7, 9 26°C sg: 1.022 15 cm 200L

*Plesiops cephalotaenia* 287
12 23°C sg: 1.024 3.5 cm 50L

*Paraplesiops poweri* 288
8 26°C sg: 1.022 20 cm 200L

*Trachinops noarlungae* 288
12 23°C sg: 1.024 9 cm 100L

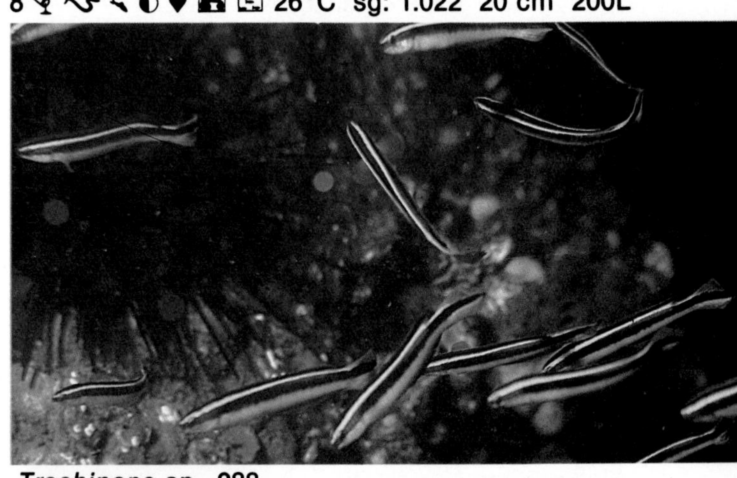

*Trachinops* sp. 288
8 26°C sg: 1.022 8 cm 100L

*Paraplesiops meleagris* 288
12 22°C sg: 1.024 25 cm 300L

*Calloplesiops altivelis* 288
7-10 26°C sg: 1.022 16 cm 200L

*Trachinops brauni* 288
12 24°C sg: 1.023 6 cm 60L

*Paraplesiops meleagris* 288
12 22°C sg: 1.024 25 cm 300L

#159

*Terapon jarbua* 291
7, 9 ~ ↘ ◐ ✂ ▨ ⊟ 26°C sg: 1.022 23 cm 400L

*Terapon theraps* 291
6-10 ~ ↘ ◐ ✂ ▨ ⊟ 26°C sg: 1.022 30 cm 300L

*Terapon jarbua* 291
7, 9 26°C sg: 1.022 23 cm 400L

*Kuhlia mugil* 293
3, 6-9 26°C sg: 1.022 20 cm 200L

*Pelates sexlineatus* 291
7-10 9-10 26°C sg: 1.022 25 cm 300L

*Pelates quadrilineatus* 291
7, 9 26°C sg: 1.022 24 cm 300L

*Mesopristes argenteus* 291
7 26°C sg: 1.016 25 cm 300L

*Amniataba caudavittatus* 291
12 23°C sg: 1.023 9 cm 100L

*Terapon theraps* 291
7-10 26°C sg: 1.022 25 cm 300L

*Rhyncopelates oxyrhynchus* 291
7, 9 26°C sg: 1.022 30 cm 300L

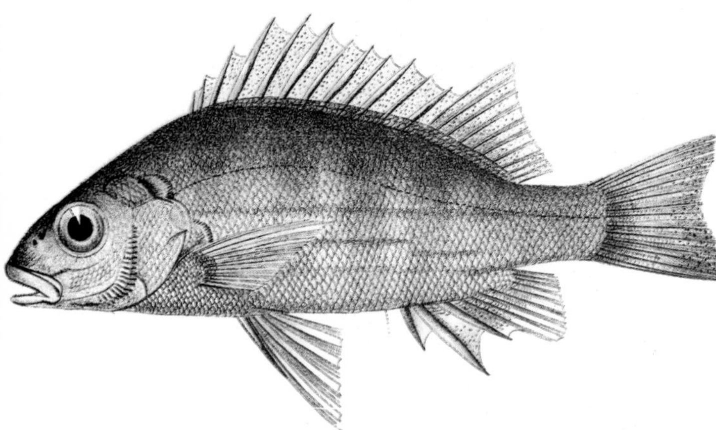

*Mesopristes cancellatus* 291
7 26°C sg: 1.022 20 cm 200L

*Mesopristes cancellatus* 291
7 26°C sg: 1.022 20 cm 200L

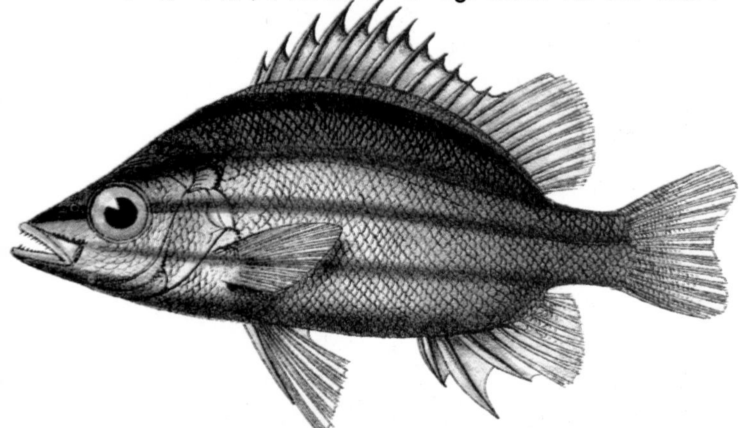

*Mesopristes argenteus* 291
7 26°C sg: 1.022 25 cm 300L

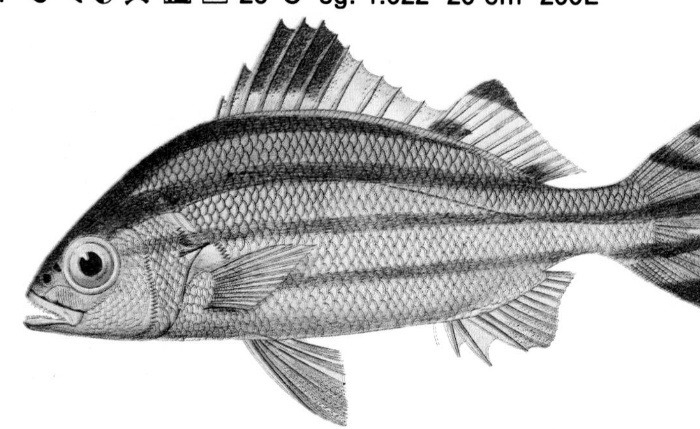

*Terapon theraps* 291
6-10 26°C sg: 1.022 30 cm 300L

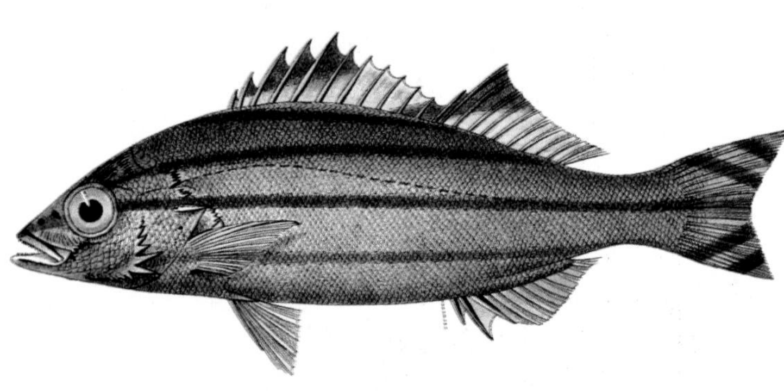

*Terapon theraps* 291
6-10 26°C sg: 1.022 30 cm 300L

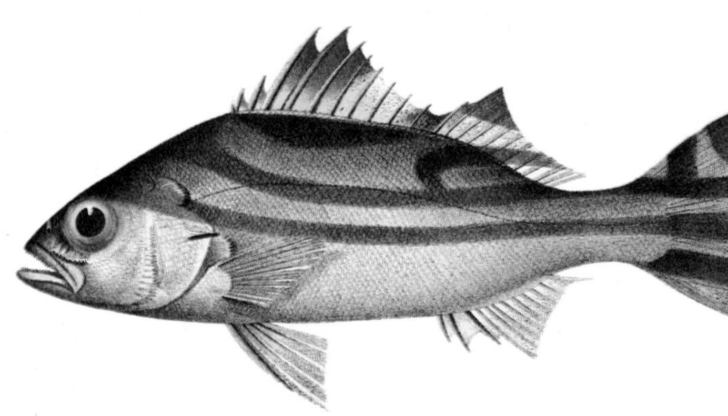

*Terapon jarbua* 291
7, 9 26°C sg: 1.022 33 cm 400L

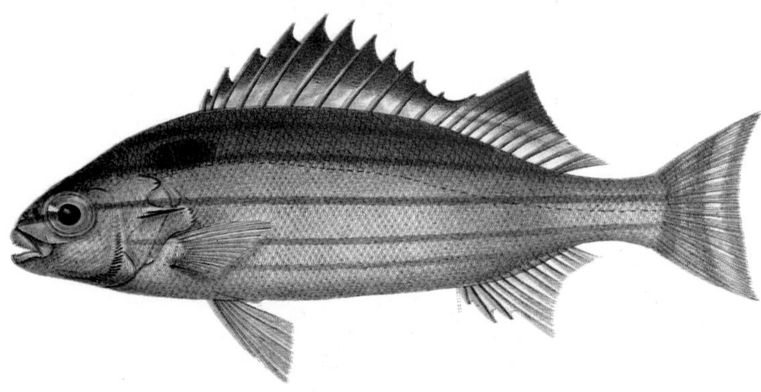

*Pelates sexlineatus* 291
7 26°C sg: 1.022 20 cm 200L

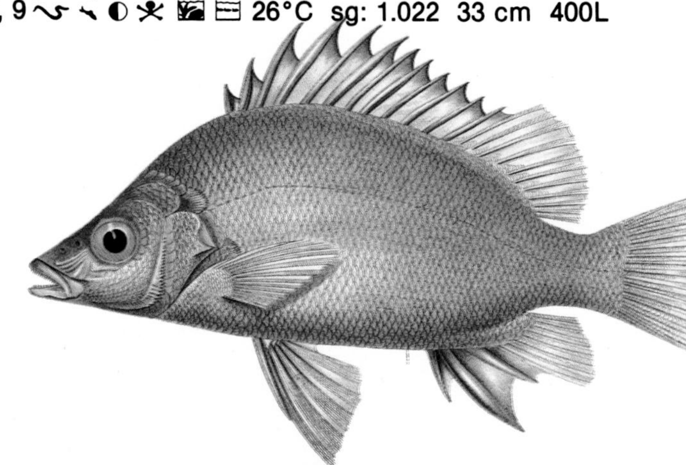

*Mesopristes argenteus* 291
7 26°C sg: 1.022 25 cm 300L

*Kuhlia marginata* 293
6-8 26°C sg: 1.022 21.5 cm 250L

*Kuhlia mugil* 293
3, 6-9 26°C sg: 1.022 20 cm 200L

*Pristigenys multifasciata* 296
5, 7 26°C sg: 1.022 27 cm 300L

*Pristigenys serrula* 296
3 26°C sg: 1.022 15 cm 200L

*Kuhlia rupestris* 293
7-9 26°C sg: 1.022 40.5 cm 400L

*Kuhlia sandvicensis* 293
6 26°C sg: 1.022 30 cm 300L

*Pristigenys alta* 296
1, 2 25°C sg: 1.022 30 cm 300L

*Pristigenys niphonia* 296
7, 9 26°C sg: 1.022 26 cm 300L

*Priacanthus hamrur* 284
6-10 26°C sg: 1.022 45 cm 500L

*Priacanthus macracanthus* 296
7-8 26°C sg: 1.022 23 cm 300L

*Priacanthus arenatus* 296
2, 13 26°C sg: 1.022 40 cm 400L

*Heteropriacanthus cruentatus* 296
Circumtrop. 26°C 30.5 cm 300L

*Priacanthus tayenus* 296
7-8 26°C sg: 1.022 27.5 cm 300L

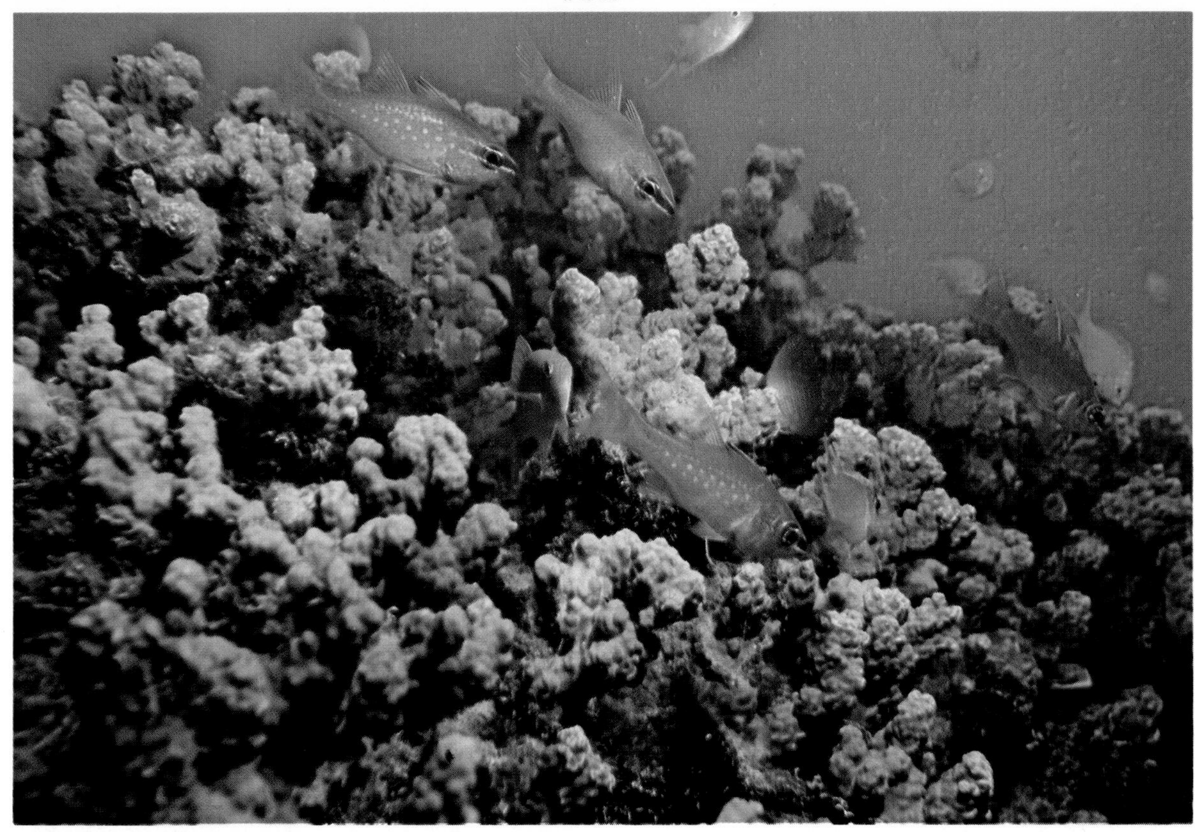

*Apogon apogonides* 297
7, 9 ◐ ♥ 26°C sg: 1.022 10 cm 100L

*Sphaeramia nematoptera* 297
7, 9 ◐ ♥ 26°C sg: 1.022 10 cm 100L

*Apogon cyanosoma* 297
7-8 ◐ ♥ 26°C sg: 1.022 7 cm 80L

*Rhabdamia gracilis* 297
7, 9 ◐ ♥ 26°C sg: 1.022 6 cm 60L

*Rhabdamia cypselurus* 297
7-8 ◐ ♥ 26°C sg: 1.022 5 cm 50L

*Gymnapogon urospilotus* 297
5, 7 ◐ ♥ 26°C sg: 1.022 3 cm 50L

*Rhabdamia* sp. 297
12 ◐ ♥ 24°C sg: 1.022 4 cm 50L

*Apogon angustatus* 297
6-10 26°C sg: 1.022 8 cm 80L

*Apogon cyanosoma* 297
7-8 26°C sg: 1.022 7 cm 80L

*Apogon robustus* 297
9 26°C sg: 1.022 6 cm 60L

*Apogon robustus* 297
9 26°C sg: 1.022 6 cm 60L

*Apogon cooki* 297
7-8 26°C sg: 1.022 6 cm 60L

*Apogon victoriae* 297
7-12 26°C sg: 1.022 8 cm 80L

*Apogon fraenatus* 297
7-10 26°C sg: 1.022 10 cm 100L

*Apogon nitidus* 297
9 26°C sg: 1.022 8 cm 80L

*Apogon nigrofasciatus* 297
7-8 26°C sg: 1.022 10 cm 100L

*Apogon novemfasciatus* 297
7-10 26°C sg: 1.022 8 cm 100L

*Apogon fasciatus* 297
7-8 26°C sg: 1.022 11.5 cm 100L

*Apogon endekataenia* 297
7, 9 26°C sg: 1.022 10 cm 100L

*Apogon compressus* 297
7-8 26°C sg: 1.022 11.5 cm 100L

*Apogon doederleini* 297
7 26°C sg: 1.022 7 cm 80L

*Apogon cookii* 297
7-9 26°C sg: 1.022 10 cm 100L

*Apogon margaritiphora* 297
6-7 26°C sg: 1.022

*Apogon hartzfeldii* 297
7-8 ◐ ♥ 26°C sg: 1.022 11.5 cm 100L

*Apogon chrysotaenia* 297
7 ◐ ♥ 26°C sg: 1.022 12 cm 150L

*Apogon* sp. 297
7 ◐ ♥ 26°C sg: 1.022 10 cm 100L

*Apogon novaeguinea* (? = *cyanosoma*) 297
8 ◐ ♥ 26°C sg: 1.022 10 cm 100L

*Apogon* sp. 297
7 ◐ ♥ 26°C sg: 1.022 7 cm 80L

*Apogon* sp. 297
7-8 ◐ ♥ 26°C sg: 1.022 10 cm 100L

*Apogon semiornatus* 297
7, 9 ◐ ♥ 26°C sg: 1.022 7 cm 80L

*Apogon* sp. 297
6 ◐ ♥ 26°C sg: 1.022 8 cm 100L

*Apogon exostigma* 297
6-7 ◐ ♥ 26°C sg: 1.022 10 cm 100L

*Apogon kallopterus* 297
7-10 ◐ ♥ 26°C sg: 1.022 15 cm 150L

*Apogon notatus* 297
7 ◐ ♥ 26°C sg: 1.022 10 cm 100L

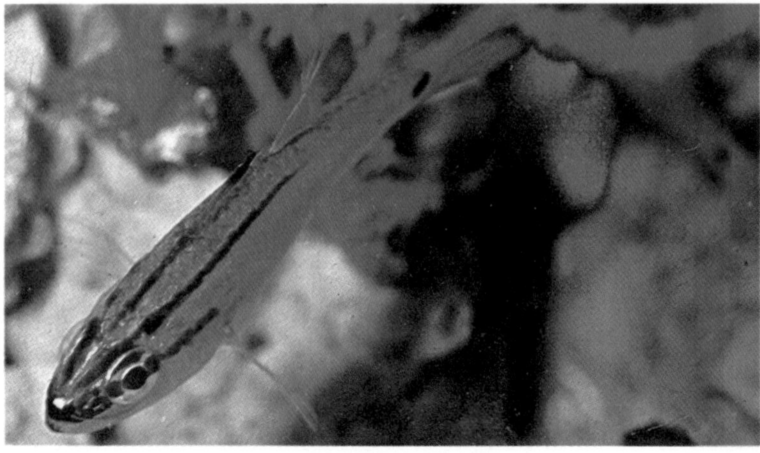

*Apogon semilineatus* 297
5, 7 ◐ ♥ 26°C sg: 1.022 8 cm 80L

*Apogon kallopterus* 297
7-10 ◐ ♥ 26°C sg: 1.022 15 cm 150L

*Apogon kallopterus* 297
7-10 ◐ ♥ 26°C sg: 1.022 15 cm 150L

*Apogon gilberti* 297
5, 7, 9 ◐ ♥ 26°C sg: 1.022 4 cm 50L

*Apogon ishigakiensis* 297
5, 7 ◐ ♥ 26°C sg: 1.022 60 cm 60L

*Apogon sangiensis* 297
7-8 ◐ ♥ 26°C sg: 1.022 9 cm 100L

*Apogon* sp. 297
7-8 ◐ ♥ 26°C sg: 1.022 7 cm 100L

*Apogon ceramensis* 297
7-8 ◐ ♥ 26°C sg: 1.022 10 cm 100L

*Apogon thermalis* 297
7, 9 ◐ ♥ 26°C sg: 1.022 8 cm 80L

*Apogon hyalosoma* 297
7 ◐ ♥ 26°C sg: 1.022 17 cm 200L

*Apogon amboinensis* 297
7-8 ◐ ♥ 26°C sg: 1.022 10 cm 100L

*Apogon kiensis* 297
7-10 ◐ ♥ 26°C sg: 1.022 5 cm 50L

*Apogon sealei* 297
6-8 ◐ ♥ 26°C sg: 1.022 10 cm 100L

*Apogon taeniatus* 297
7-10 26°C sg: 1.022 10 cm 100L

*Apogon trimaculatum* 297
7 26°C sg: 1.022 15 cm 150L

*Apogon niger* 297
5, 7 24°C sg: 1.022 15 cm 150L

*Apogon leptacanthus* 297
7, 9 26°C sg: 1.022 6 cm 60L

*Apogon lineatus* 297
5, 7 24°C sg: 1.023 13 cm 150L

*Apogon dispar* 297
7 26°C sg: 1.022 4.5 cm

*Apogon darnleyensis* 297
7, 12 25°C sg: 1.022 5 cm 50L

*Apogon melas* 297
7 26°C sg: 1.022 12 cm 80L

*Apogon taeniopterus* 297
6 26°C sg: 1.022 10 cm 100L

*Apogon menesemus* 297
6 26°C sg: 1.022 10 cm 100L

*Apogon savayensis* 297
6-10 26°C sg: 1.022 10 cm 100L

*Apogon guamensis* 297
7-10 26°C sg: 1.022 10 cm 100L

*Apogon quadrifasciatus* 297
7-10 26°C sg: 1.022 10 cm 100L

*Apogon maculifera* 297
6 26°C sg: 1.022 15 cm 150L

*Apogon ruppelli* 297
12 26°C sg: 1.022 10 cm 100L

*Apogon norfolcensis* 297
11-12 26°C sg: 1.022 15 cm 150L

*Apogon pseudomaculatus* 297
2 ◐ ♥ 26°C sg: 1.022 8 cm 80L

*Apogon maculatus* 297
2 ◐ ♥ 25°C sg: 1.022 15 cm 150L

*Apogon quadrisquamatus* 297
2 ◐ ♥ 26°C sg: 1.022 8 cm 80L

*Apogon aurolineatus* 297
2 ◐ ♥ 26°C sg: 1.022 5 cm 50L

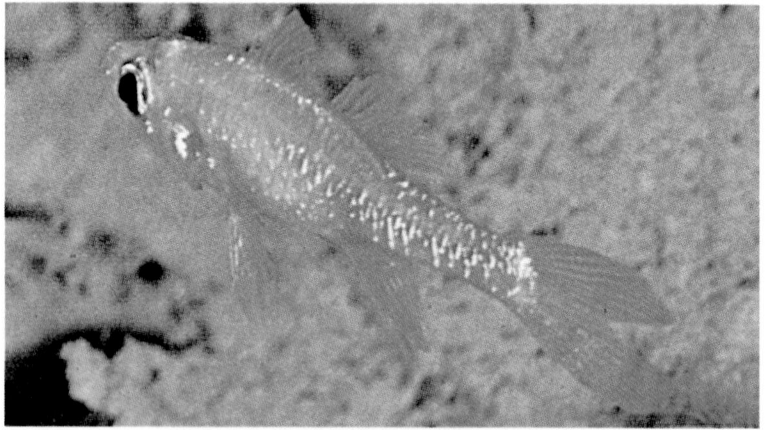

*Apogon leptocaulus* 297
7, 9 ◐ ♥ 26°C sg: 1.022 6 cm 60L

*Apogon retrosella* 297
3 ◐ ♥ 26°C sg: 1.022 10 cm 100L

*Apogon pacifici* 297
3 ◐ ♥ 26°C sg: 1.022 8 cm 80L

*Apogon dovii* 297
3 ◐ ♥ 26°C sg: 1.022 7.5 cm 80L

*Apogon binotatus* 297
2 24°C sg: 1.022 13 cm 150L

*Apogon robinsi* 297
2 26°C sg: 1.022 13 cm 150L

*Apogon pillionatus* 297
2 26°C sg: 1.022 7 cm 80L

*Apogon anisolepis* 297
2 26°C sg: 1.022 6 cm 60L

*Apogon planifrons* 297
2 26°C sg: 1.022 11 cm 100L

*Apogon townsendi* 297
2 26°C sg: 1.022 7.5 cm 80L

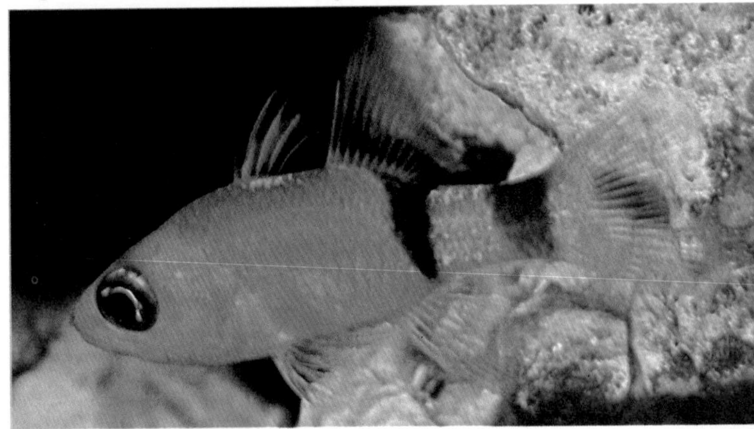

*Apogon phenax* 297
2 26°C sg: 1.022 8 cm 80L

*Apogon lachneri* 297
2 26°C sg: 1.022 11 cm 100L

*Apogon crassiceps* 297
6-7 ◐ ♥ 25°C sg: 1.022 10 cm 100L

*Apogon* sp. 297
7 ◐ ♥ 26°C sg: 1.022 8 cm 80L

*Apogon nigripes* 297
9-10 ◐ ♥ 26°C sg: 1.022 7 cm 80L

*Apogon elliotti* 297
7 ◐ ♥ 26°C sg: 1.022 12 cm 150L

*Apogon coccineus* 297
6-10 ◐ ♥ 26°C sg: 1.022 5 cm 50L

*Apogon evermanni* 297
6 ◐ ♥ 26°C. sg: 1.022 10 cm 100L

*Apogon* sp. 297
7 ◐ ♥ 26°C sg: 1.022 7.5 cm 80L

*Sphaeramia nematoptera* 297
7, 9 ◐ ♥ 26°C sg: 1.022 10 cm 100L

*Apogon apogonides* 297
7, 9 ◐ ♥ 26°C sg: 1.022 10 cm 100L

*Apogon kallopterus* 297
6-10 ◐ ♥ 26°C sg: 1.022 15 cm 150L

*Apogon* sp. 297
7 ◐ ♥ 26°C sg: 1.022 6 cm 60L

*Cheilodipterus artus* 297
9 ◐ ♥ 26°C sg: 1.022 12 cm 150L

*Apogon aureus* 297
7, 9-10 ◐ ♥ 26°C sg: 1.022 12 cm 150L

*Apogon taeniatus* 297
9-10 ◐ ♥ 26°C sg: 1.022 10 cm 100L

*Cheilodipterus quinquelineatus* 297
6-10 ◐ ♥ 26°C sg: 1.022 12 cm 150L

*Cheilodipterus lineatus* 297
6-10 ◐ ♥ 26°C sg: 1.022 22 cm 200L

*Cheilodipterus macrodon* 297
6-10 24°C sg: 1.022 24 cm 200L

*Cheilodipterus lachneri* 297
9-10 26°C sg: 1.022 12 cm 150L

*Cheilodipterus* sp. 297
7 26°C sg: 1.022 8 cm 80L

*Cheilodipterus* sp. 297
6 26°C sg: 1.022 12 cm 150L

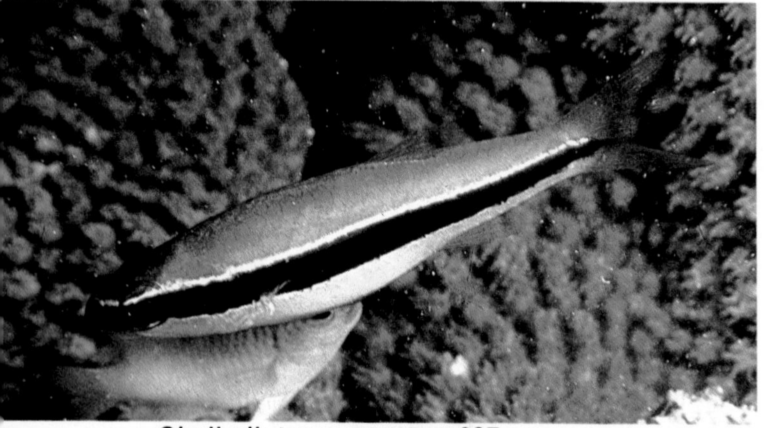

*Cheilodipterus zonatus* 297
7, 8 26°C sg: 1.022 9 cm 100L

*Apogon affinis* 297
2 26°C sg: 1.022 10 cm 100L

*Foa fo* 297
6-8 24°C sg: 1.023 3 cm 50L

*Fowleria variegata* 297
6-10 26°C sg: 1.022 5 cm 50L

*Archamia leai* 297
7-8 25°C sg: 1.022 8 cm 80L

*Archamia zosterophora* 297
7, 9 25°C sg: 1.022 6 cm 60L

*Archamia melasma* 297
7-8 25°C sg: 1.022 7 cm 80L

*Archamia fucata* 297
7, 9-10 25°C sg: 1.022 8 cm 80L

*Archamia lineolata* 297
7-10 25°C sg: 1.022 9 cm 100L

*Archamia biguttata* 297
6-7 25°C sg: 1.022 7 cm 50L

*Fowleria* cf *variegata* 297
6-10 25°C sg: 1.022 5 cm 50L

*Fowleria aurita* 297
7, 9-10 25°C sg: 1.022 9 cm 100L

*Astrapogon stellatus* 297
2 25°C sg: 1.022 6.5 cm 200L

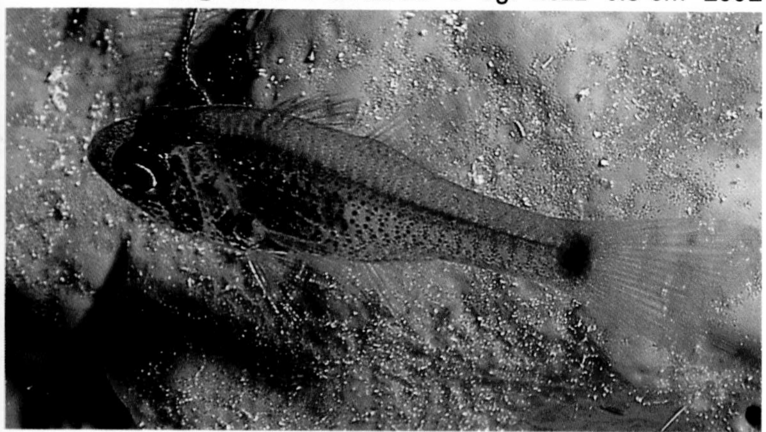

*Phaeoptyx xenus* 297
2 26°C sg: 1.022 7.5 cm 75L

*Pterapogon mirifica* 297
7 25°C sg: 1.022 8 cm 80L

*Vincentia* sp. 297
7, 12 24°C sg: 1.022 4.5 cm 50L

*Astrapogon punticulatus* 297
2 25°C sg: 1.022 6.5 cm 80L

*Phaeoptyx pigmentaria* 297
2 26°C sg: 1.022 6.5 cm 70L

*Phaeoptyx conklini* 297
2 25°C sg: 1.022 6.5 cm 80L

*Vincentia punctatus* 297
7, 12 25°C sg: 1.022 10 cm 100L

*Pseudamia gelatinosa* 297
7, 9 26°C sg: 1.022 7 cm 80L

*Pseudamia amblyuroptera* 297
7 26°C sg: 1.022 7.5 cm 80L

*Siphamia versicolor* 297
6-10 26°C sg: 1.022 4 cm 50L

*Siphamia fuscolineata* 297
7-8 26°C sg: 1.022 4 cm 50L

*Siphamia cephalotes* 297
7, 12 25°C sg: 1.022 4 cm 50L

*Siphamia* sp. 297
7 26°C sg: 1.022 4 cm 50L

*Apogonichthys ocellatus* 297
7, 9 26°C sg: 1.022 6 cm 60L

*Siphamia mossambica* (?) 297
9 26°C sg: 1.022 4 cm 50L

#179

*Hoplolatilus starcki* 300
6 ~ ◐ ♥ 26°C sg: 1.022 11 cm 100L

*Hoplolatilus fronticinctus* 300
7-9 ~ ◐ ♥ 26°C sg: 1.022 21 cm 200L

*Sillago sihama* 299
6-9 26°C sg: 1.022 30 cm 300L

*Sillago macrolepis* 299
7 26°C sg: 1.022 20 cm 200L

*Caulolatilus princeps* 300
3-4 25°C sg: 1.022 45 cm 500L

*Sillago maculata* 299
8 26°C sg: 1.022 30 cm 300L

*Branchiostegus* sp. 300
7 26°C sg: 1.022 40 cm 400L

*Lopholatilus chameleonticeps* 300
1-2 23°C sg: 1.024 42 cm 400L

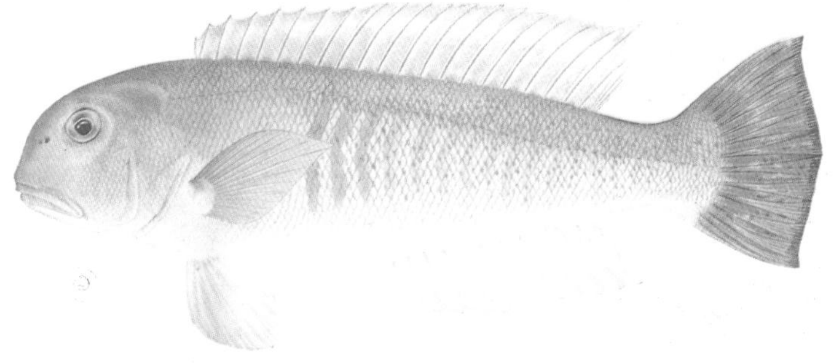

*Branchiostegus albus* 300
5, 7 24°C sg: 1.023 40 cm 400L

*Branchiostegus japonicus* 300
5, 7 26°C sg: 1.022 45 cm 500L

*Hoplolatilus cuniculus* 300
6 ◐ ♥ 26°C sg: 1.022 9 cm 100L

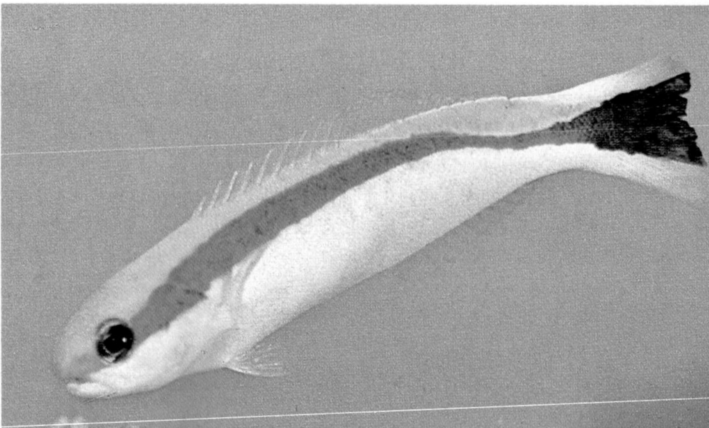

*Hoplolatilus marcosi* 300
7 ◐ ♥ 26°C sg: 1.022 20 cm 200L

*Hoplolatilus starcki* 300
6 ◐ ♥ 26°C sg: 1.022 11 cm 100L

*Hoplolatilus starcki* 300
6 ◐ ♥ 26°C sg: 1.022 11 cm 100L

*Hoplolatilus fourmanoiri* 300
7 ◐ ♥ 26°C sg: 1.022 20 cm 200L

*Hoplolatilus purpureus* 300
7 ◐ ♥ 26°C sg: 1.022 15 cm 200L

*Hoplolatilus chlupatyi* 300
7 ◐ ♥ 26°C sg: 1.022 15 cm 200L

*Hoplolatilus chlupatyi* 300
7 ◐ ♥ 26°C sg: 1.022 15 cm 200L

*Malacanthus latovittatus* 345
5, 7, 9 ◐ ♥ 26°C sg: 1.022 45 cm 500L

*Malacanthus latovittatus* 300
5, 7, 9 ◐ 26°C sg: 1.022 45 cm 500L

*Malacanthus plumieri* 300
1-2, 13 ◐ ♥ 26°C sg: 1.022 60 cm 600L

*Malacanthus brevirostris* 300
6-10 ◐ 26°C sg: 1.022 60 cm 600L

*Labracoglossa argentiventris* 301
5 ◐ 23°C sg: 1.024 25 cm 300L

*Malacanthus brevirostris* 300
6-10 ◐ 26°C sg: 1.022 60 cm 600L

*Lactarius lactarius* 302
7 ◐ 24°C sg: 1.023 20 cm 200L

*Pomatomus saltatrix* 303
Worldwide ◐ 26°C sg: 1.022 90 cm 1000L

*#182*

*Alectis indicus* 306
5, 7 [symbols] 26°C sg: 1.022 50 cm 500L

#182A

*Pseudocaranx dentex* 306
5, 7 ~ ↘ ◐ ✕ ▭ ▭ 25°C sg: 1.022 95 cm 1000L

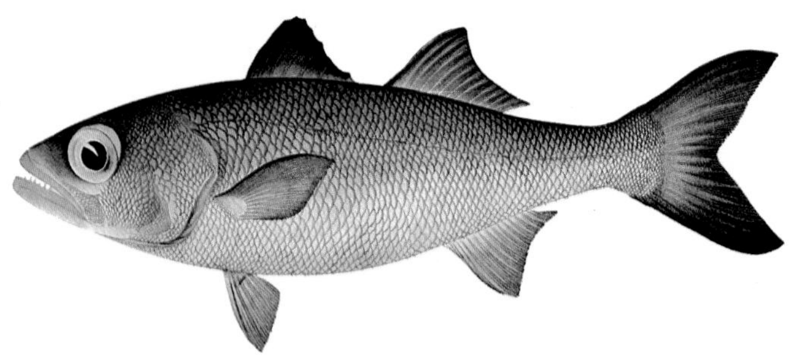

*Scombrops gilberti* 303
5 23°C sg: 1.024 100 cm 1000L

*Scombrops boops* 303
5 24°C sg: 1.023 110 cm 1200L

*Rachycentron canadum* 304
Circumtrop. 26°C sg: 1.022 180 cm 2000L

*Rachycentron canadum* 304
Circumtrop. 26°C sg: 1.022 180 cm 2000L

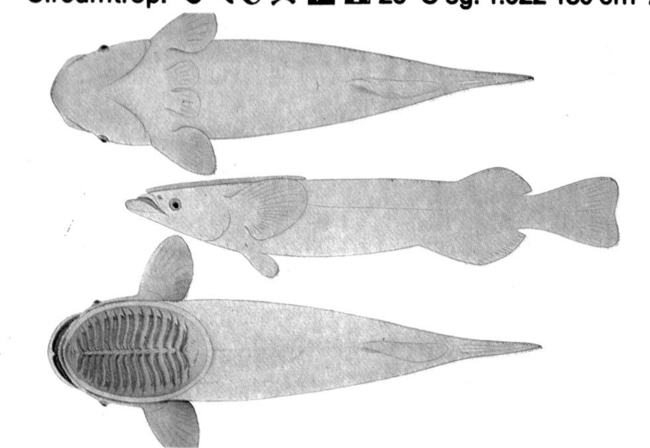

*Remorina albescens* 305
1-15 26°C sg: 1.022 30 cm 300L

*Echeneis naucrates* 305
Worldwide 26°C sg: 1.022 100 cm 1000L

*Echeneis naucratoides* 305
Circumtrop. 26°C sg: 1.022 100 cm 1000L

*Echeneis* sp. 305
Worldwide 26°C sg: 1.022 100 cm 1000L

*Selar crumenophthalmus* 306
Circumtrop. 26°C sg: 1.022 30 cm 300L

*Selar crumenophthalmus* 306
Circumtrop. 26°C sg: 1.022 30 cm 300L

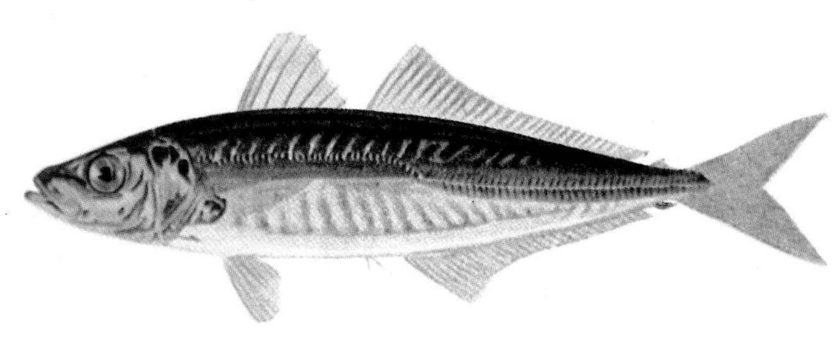

*Decapterus punctatus* 306
1, 2 25°C sg: 1.022 60 cm 600L

*Trachurus japonicus* 306
5-7 24°C sg: 1.023 50 cm 500L

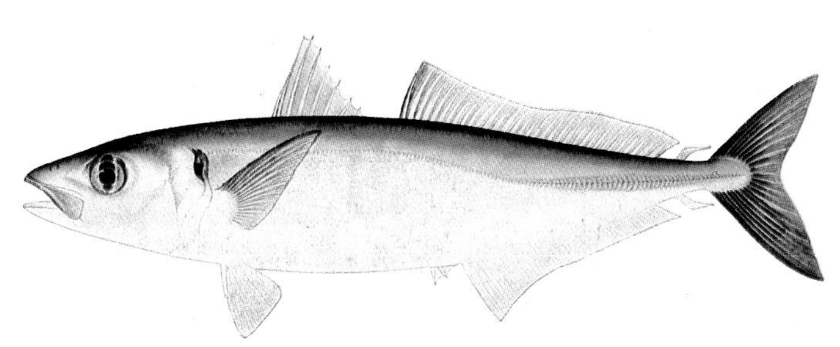

*Decapterus muroadsi* 306
6-7 26°C sg: 1.022 35 cm 400L

*Decapterus tabl* 306
Circumtrop. 26°C sg: 1.022 30 cm 300L

*Elagatis bipinnulata* (juv.) 306
Circumtrop. 26°C sg: 1.022 100 cm 1000L

*Elagatis bipinnulata* 306
Circumtrop. 26°C sg: 1.022 100 cm 1000L

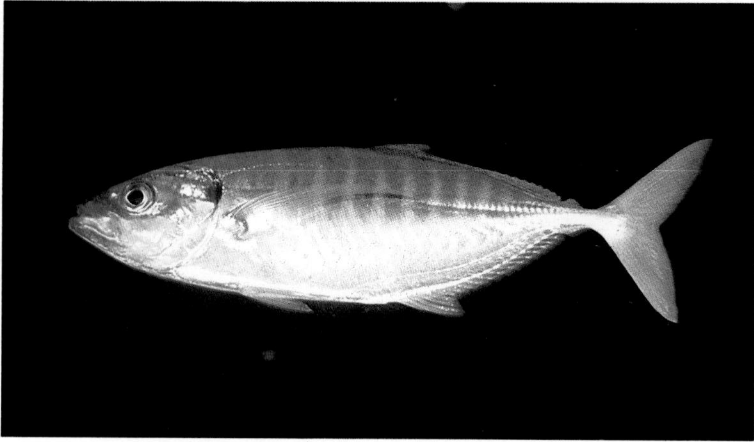

*Atule mate* 306
5, 7, 9 26°C sg: 1.022 30 cm 300L

*Carangoides vinctus* 306
3 26°C sg: 1.022 30 cm 300L

*Carangoides equula* 306
5-7 26°C sg: 1.022 40 cm 400L

*Carangoides* sp. 306
8 26°C sg: 1.022 65 cm 800L

*Gnathanodon speciosus* 306
5-10 26°C sg: 1.022 90 cm 1200L

*Carangoides orthogrammus* 306
5-10 26°C sg: 1.022 40 cm 400L

*Carangoides dinema* (juv.) 306
7 26°C sg: 1.022

*Uraspis helvola* 306
5, 7 26°C sg: 1.022 75 cm 800L

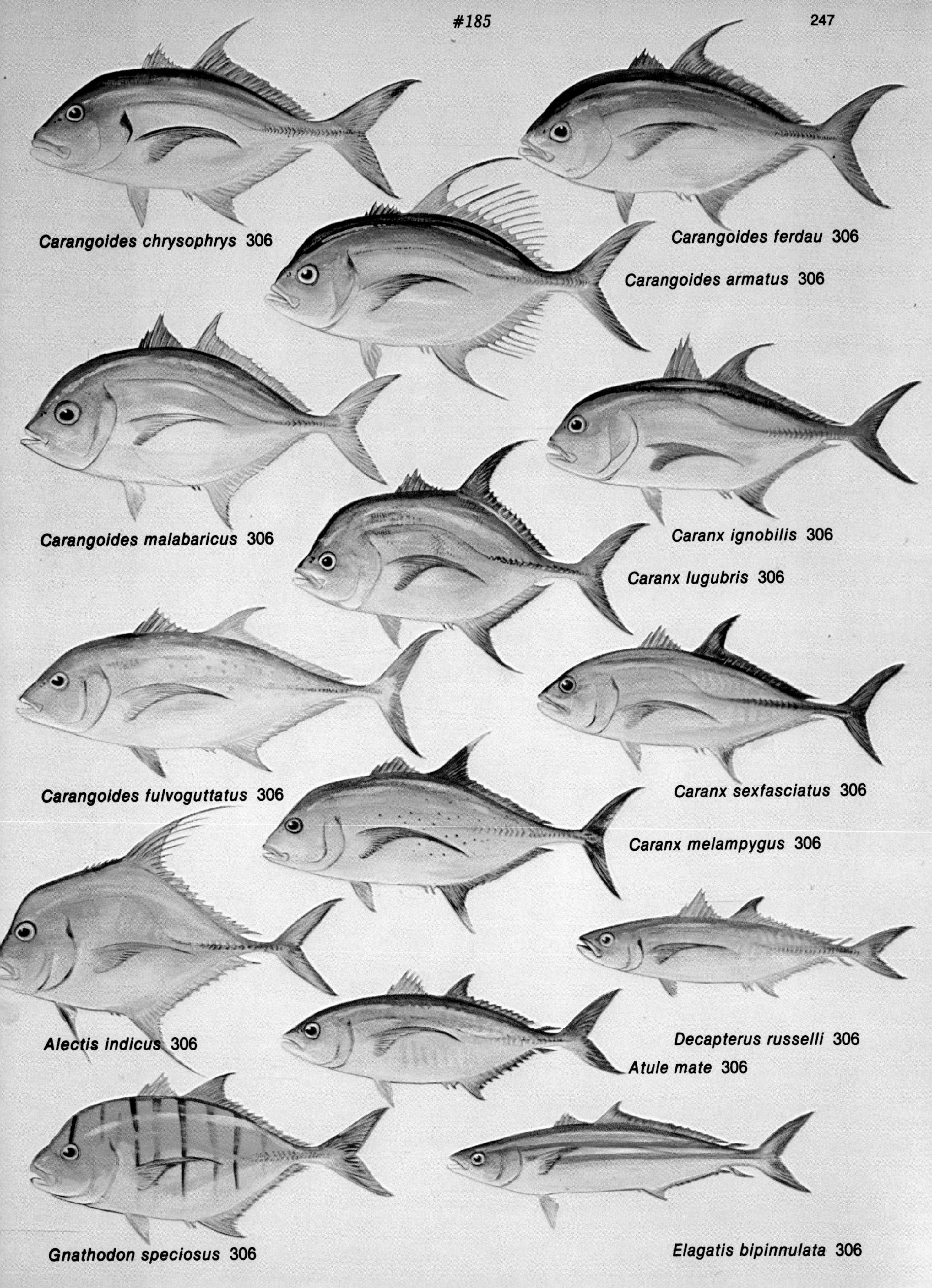
Carangoides chrysophrys 306
Carangoides ferdau 306
Carangoides armatus 306
Carangoides malabaricus 306
Caranx ignobilis 306
Caranx lugubris 306
Carangoides fulvoguttatus 306
Caranx sexfasciatus 306
Caranx melampygus 306
Alectis indicus 306
Decapterus russelli 306
Atule mate 306
Gnathodon speciosus 306
Elagatis bipinnulata 306

*Caranx melampygus* 306
3, 6-10 26°C sg: 1.022 80 cm 800L

*Caranx bucculentus* 306
7 26°C sg: 1.022 25 cm 300L

*Carangoides* sp. *(?armatus)* (juv.) 306
7-9 26°C sg: 1.022 55 cm 300L

*Carangoides ruber* 306
1-2 26°C sg: 1.022 28 cm 300L

*Caranx melampygus* 306
3, 6-10 26°C sg: 1.022 80 cm 800L

*Caranx lugubris* 306
Circumtrop. 26°C sg: 1.022 93 cm 1000

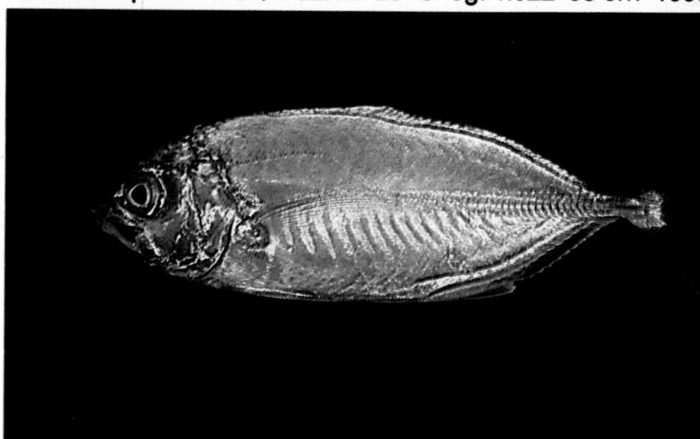

*Caranx crysos* 306
1-2, 13 25°C sg: 1.023 58 cm 600L

*Carangoides ferdau* 306
6-10 26°C sg: 1.022 60 cm 800L

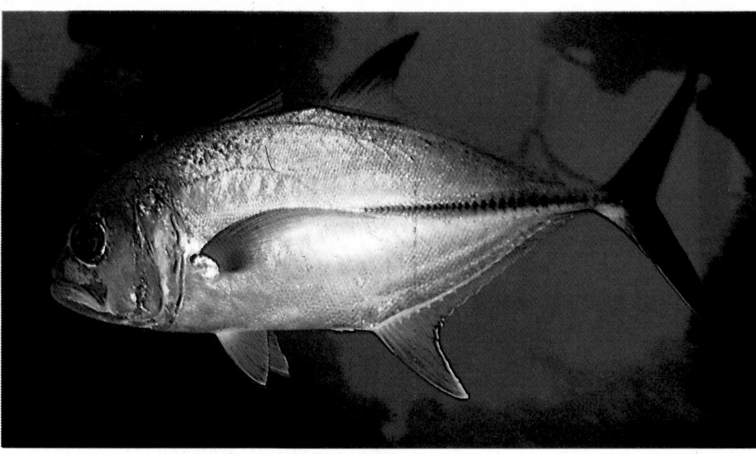

*Caranx latus* 306
1-2 25°C sg: 1.022 75 cm 800L

*Caranx sexfasciatus* 306
3, 6-10 26°C sg: 1.022 85 cm 1000L

*Caranx ignobilis* 306
7-10 26°C sg: 1.022 100 cm 1000L

*Caranx hippos* and *C. caballus* 306
Circumtrop. 26°C sg: 1.022 90 cm 1000L

*Carangoides coeruleopinnatus* 306
7-9 26°C sg: 1.022 40 cm 400L

*Carangoides fulvoguttatus* 306
7-10 26°C sg: 1.022 100 cm 1000L

*Carangoides bartholomei* 306
1-2 26°C sg: 1.022 100 cm 1000L

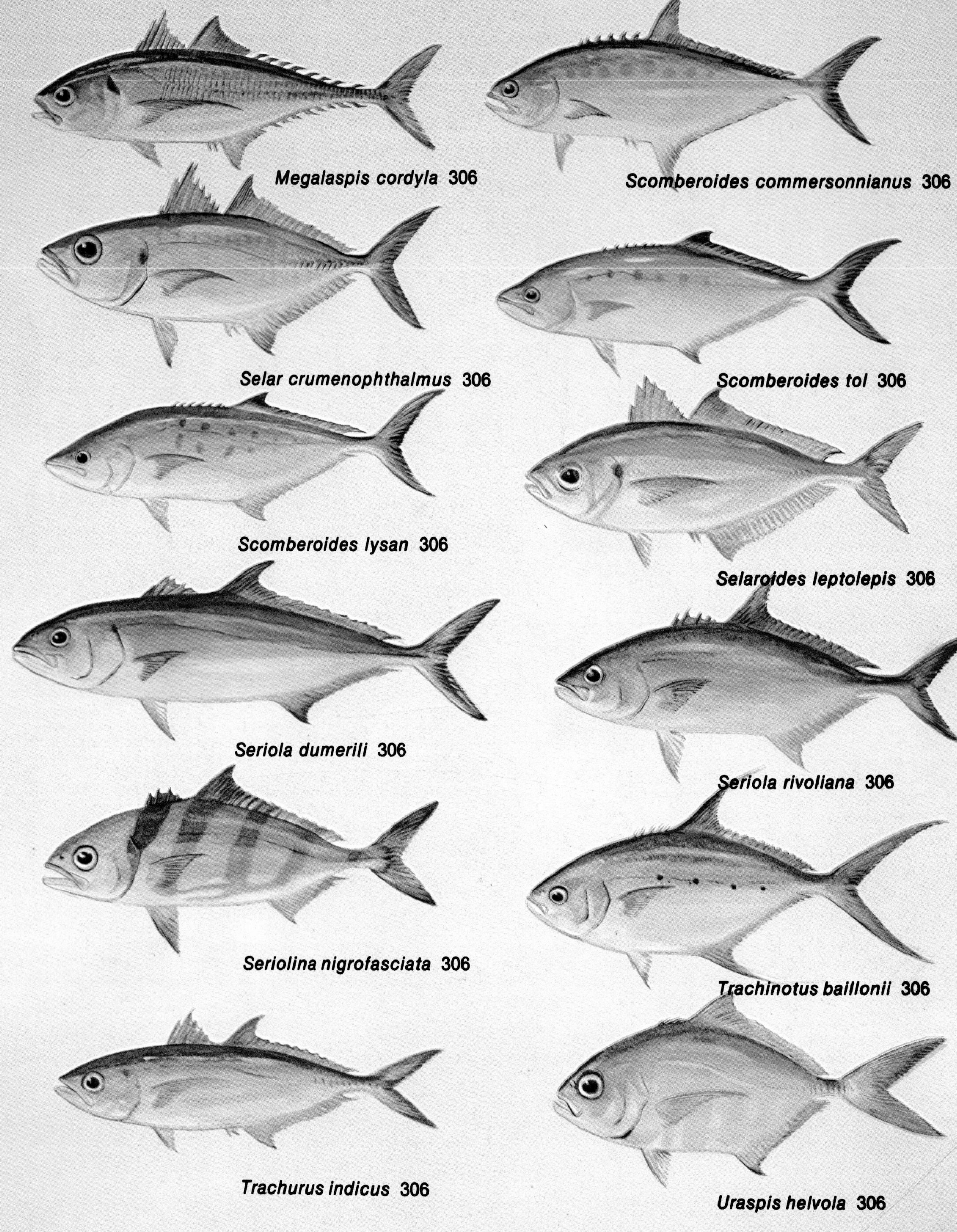

Megalaspis cordyla 306

Scomberoides commersonnianus 306

Selar crumenophthalmus 306

Scomberoides tol 306

Scomberoides lysan 306

Selaroides leptolepis 306

Seriola dumerili 306

Seriola rivoliana 306

Seriolina nigrofasciata 306

Trachinotus baillonii 306

Trachurus indicus 306

Uraspis helvola 306

*Alectis ciliaris* 306 1200L
Circumtrop. 26°C sg: 1.022 110 cm

*Alectis indicus* 306
5, 7 26°C sg: 1.022 50 cm 500L

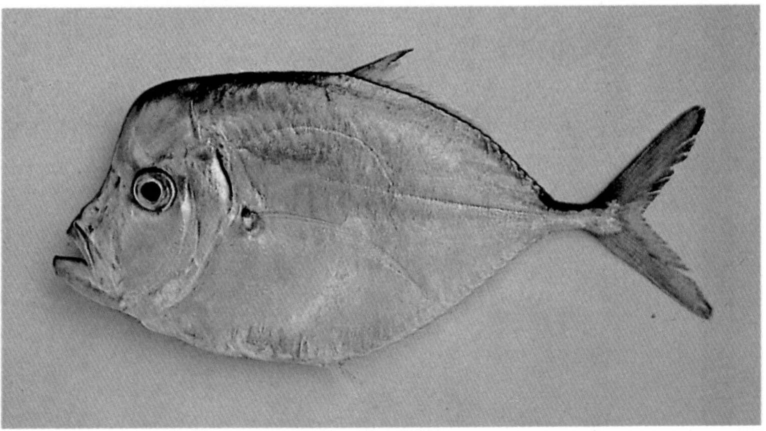

*Selene setapinnis* .306
2 26°C sg: 1.022 30 cm 300L

*Selene brevoortii* 306
3 26°C sg: 1.022 30 cm 300L

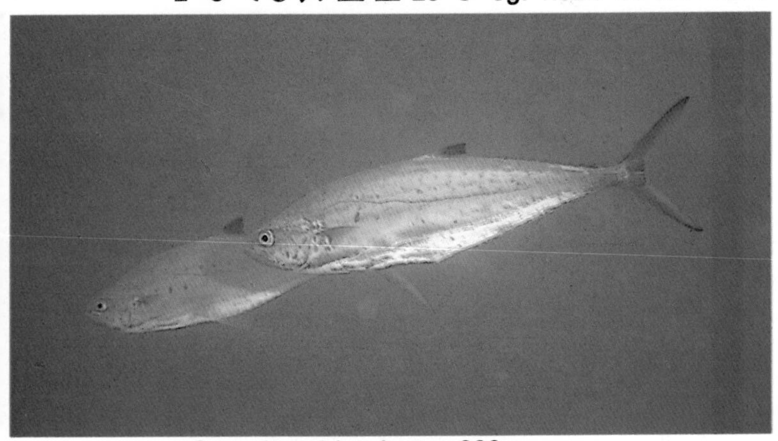

*Scomberoides lysan* 306
6-9 26°C sg: 1.022 60 cm 600L

*Selene vomer* 306
1-2, 13-14 26°C sg: 1.022 30 cm 300L

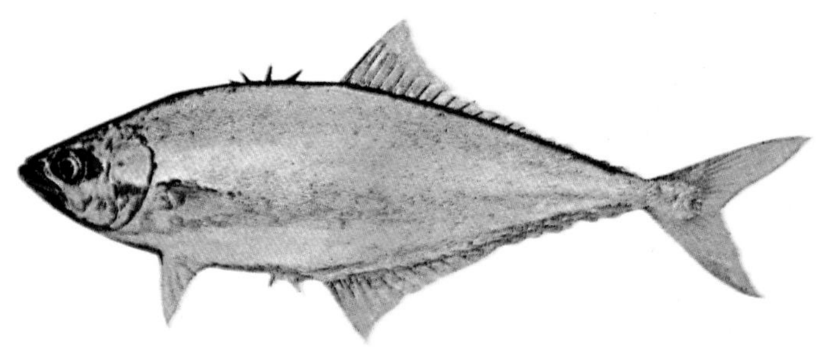

*Oligoplites saurus* 306
2-3 26°C sg: 1.022 30 cm 300L

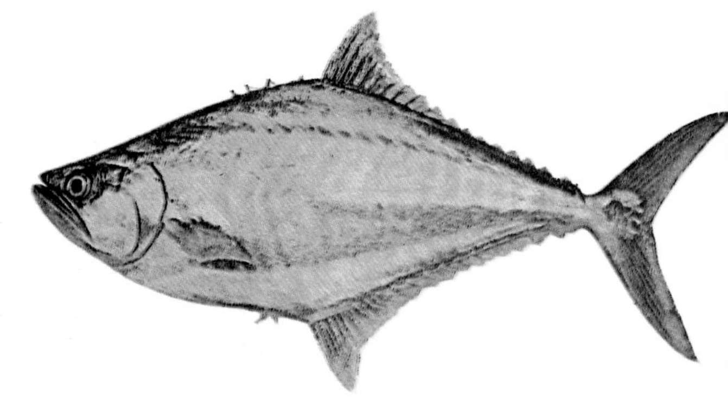

*Oligoplites altus* 306
3 26°C sg: 1.022 31 cm 300L

*Seriola hippos* 306
7-8 26°C sg: 1.022 100 cm 1000L

*Seriola rivoliana* 306
Circumtrop. 26°C sg: 1.022 100 cm 1000L

*Seriola lalandi lalandi* 306
7-8, 11-12 23°C sg: 1.024 90 cm 1000L

*Seriola dumerili* (juv.) 306
Circumtrop. 24°C sg: 1.022 180 cm 2000L

*Seriola lalandi dorsalis* 306
3, 4 25°C sg: 1.022 90 cm 1000L

*Seriola rivoliana* 306
Circumtrop. 26°C sg: 1.022 100 cm 1000L

*Seriola quinqueradiata* 306
5 23°C sg: 1.024 100 cm 1000L

*Seriola dumerili* 306
Circumtrop. 24°C sg: 1.022 180 cm 2000L

*Naucrates ductor* 306
Circumtrop. 26°C sg: 1.022 60 cm 600L

*Seriola zonata* 306
2 26°C sg: 1.022 80 cm 800L

*Seriolina nigrofasciata* 306
Circumtrop. 26°C sg: 1.022 90 cm 1000L

*Seriolina nigrofasciata* (juv.) 306
Circumtrop. 26°C sg: 1.022 90 cm 1000L

*Chloroscombrus chrysurus* 306
1-2 26°C sg: 1.022 30 cm 300L

*Pantolabus radiatus* 306
8, 12 26°C sg: 1.022 25 cm 300L

*Megalaspis cordyla* 306
6-9 26°C sg: 1.022 95 cm 1000L

*Pseudocaranx dentex* 306
5, 7 25°C sg: 1.022 95 cm 1000L

*Trachinotus goodei* 306
1, 2 26°C sg: 1.022 32 cm 300L

*Trachinotus baillonii* 306
7-10 26°C sg: 1.022 60 cm 600L

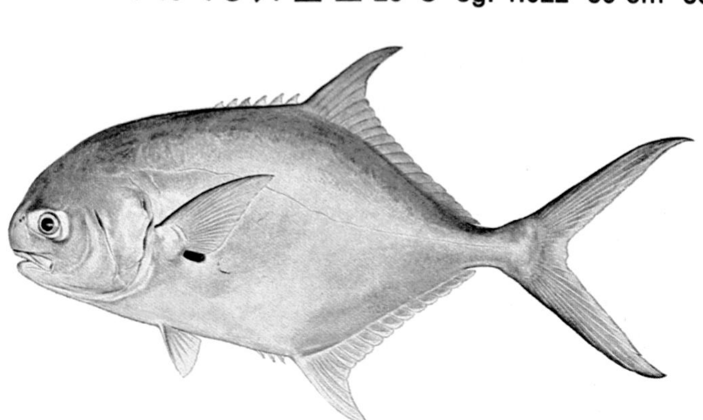

*Trachinotus kennedyi* 306
3 26°C sg: 1.022 61 cm 600L

*Trachinotus falcatus* 306
1-2, 13-14 26°C sg: 1.022 140 cm 1500L

*Trachinotus rhodopus* 306
3 26°C sg: 1.022 60 cm 600L

*Trachinotus blochii* 306
7, 9 26°C sg: 1.022 60 cm 600L

*Trachinotus carolinus* 306
1, 2 26°C sg: 1.022 60 cm 600L

*Trachinotus blochii* 306
7, 9 26°C sg: 1.022 60 cm 600L

*Naucrates ductor* 306
Circumtrop. 26°C sg: 1.022 60 cm 600L

*Seriola zonata* 306
2 26°C sg: 1.022 80 cm 800L

*Seriolina nigrofasciata* 306
Circumtrop. 26°C sg: 1.022 90 cm 1000L

*Seriolina nigrofasciata* (juv.) 306
Circumtrop. 26°C sg: 1.022 90 cm 1000L

*Chloroscombrus chrysurus* 306
1-2 26°C sg: 1.022 30 cm 300L

*Pantolabus radiatus* 306
8, 12 26°C sg: 1.022 25 cm 300L

*Megalaspis cordyla* 306
6-9 26°C sg: 1.022 95 cm 1000L

*Pseudocaranx dentex* 306
5, 7 25°C sg: 1.022 95 cm 1000L

*Trachinotus goodei* 306
1, 2 26°C sg: 1.022 32 cm 300L

*Trachinotus rhodopus* 306
3 26°C sg: 1.022 60 cm 600L

*Trachinotus baillonii* 306
7-10 26°C sg: 1.022 60 cm 600L

*Trachinotus blochii* 306
7, 9 26°C sg: 1.022 60 cm 600L

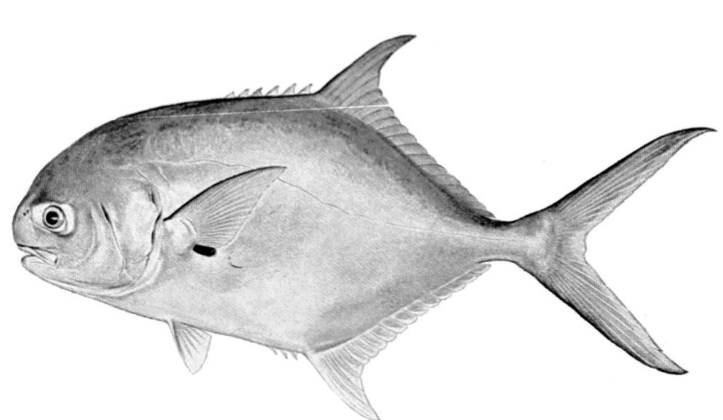

*Trachinotus kennedyi* 306
3 26°C sg: 1.022 61 cm 600L

*Trachinotus carolinus* 306
1, 2 26°C sg: 1.022 60 cm 600L

*Trachinotus falcatus* 306 1500L
1-2, 13-14 26°C sg: 1.022 140 cm

*Trachinotus blochii* 306
7, 9 26°C sg: 1.022 60 cm 600L

#192A

*Trachinotus blochii* 306
7, 9 ◐ 26°C sg: 1.022 60 cm 600L

*Trachinotus goodei* 306
1, 2 ◐ 26°C sg: 1.022 32 cm 300L

*Mene maculata* 310
5-7, 9 26°C sg: 1.022 30 cm 300L

*Gazza minuta* 311
7, 9 26°C sg: 1.022 15 cm 200L

*Leiognathus nuchalis* 311
5, 7 26°C sg: 1.022 17 cm 200L

*Leiognathus equulus* 311
7, 9-10 26°C sg: 1.022 30 cm 300L

*Secutor ruconius* 311
7, 9 26°C sg: 1.022 10 cm 100L

*Leiognathus fasciata* 311
7, 9 26°C sg: 1.022 20 cm 200L

*Leiognathus nuchalis* 311
5, 7 26°C sg: 1.022 17 cm 200L

*Leiognathus rivulatus* 311
5, 7 26°C sg: 1.022 10 cm 100L

*Nematistius pectoralis* 307
3 26°C sg: 1.022 122 cm 1200L

*Parastromateus niger* 309
7-8 26°C sg: 1.022 55 cm 600L

*Taractichthys steindachneri* 312
3, 6-9 26°C sg: 1.022 60 cm 600L

*Arripes trutta* 314
11-12 22°C sg: 1.024 76 cm 800L

*Coryphaena hippurus* 308
Circumtrop. 26°C sg: 1.022 150 cm 1500L

*Brama japonicus* 312
4-5 23°C sg: 1.024 122 cm 1200L

*Pterycombus petersii* 312
6-9, 13 23°C sg: 1.024 31 cm 300L

*Arripes georgianus* 314
12 23°C sg: 1.024 70 cm 800L

#195

*Lutjanus biguttatus* 316
6-7 [symbols] 26°C sg: 1.022 28 cm 300L

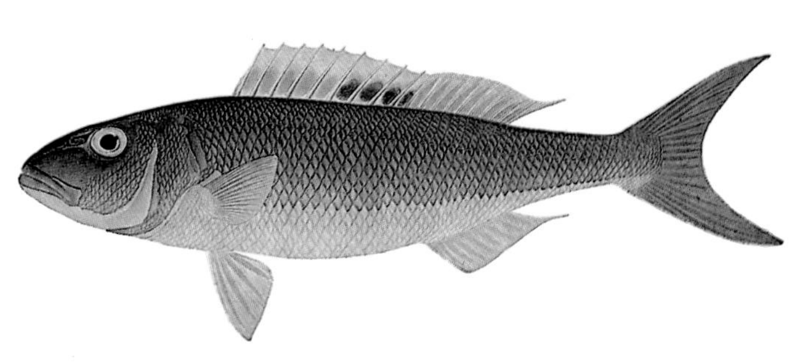

*Aprion virescens* 316
6-9 26°C sg: 1.022 100 cm 1000L

*Paracaesio xanthura* 316
12 23°C sg: 1.023 38 cm 400L

*Etelis marshi* 316
6, 7 26°C sg: 1.022 90 cm 1000L

*Etelis oculatus* 316
2 26°C sg: 1.022 91 cm 1000L

*Apsilus dentatus* 316
2 26°C sg: 1.022 46 cm 500L

*Rhomboplites aurorubens* 316
1, 2 26°C sg: 1.022 60 cm 600L

*Apsilus fuscus* 316
13 26°C sg: 1.022 75 cm 800L

*Aphareus furcatus* 316
7 26°C sg: 1.022 40 cm 400L

*Lutjanus bengalensis* 316
9 26°C sg: 1.022 13 cm 150L

*Lutjanus notatus* 316
9 26°C sg: 1.022 22 cm 200L

*Lutjanus argentimaculatus* 316
6-10 26°C sg: 1.022 60 cm 600L

*Lutjanus decussatus* 316
7 26°C sg: 1.022 30 cm 300L

*Lutjanus kasmira* 316
5-10 26°C sg: 1.022 40 cm 400L

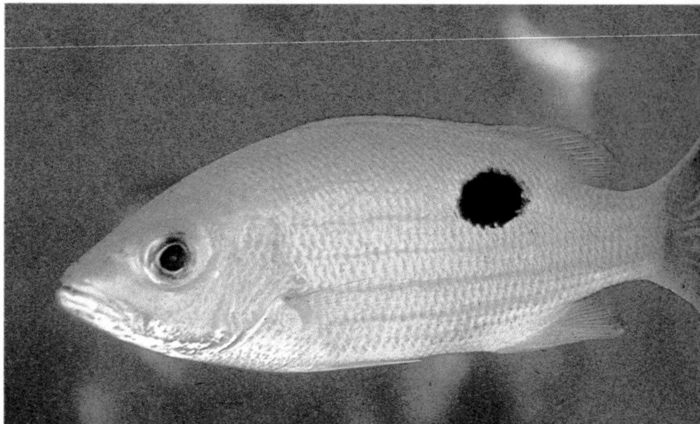

*Lutjanus ehrenbergii* 316
7-10 26°C sg: 1.022 30 cm 300L

*Lutjanus fulviflammus* 316
7-10 26°C sg: 1.022 30 cm 300L

*Lutjanus carponotatus* 316
6-8, 12 25°C sg: 1.022 40 cm 400L

*Lutjanus lutjanus* 316
5-9 26°C sg: 1.022 25 cm 300L

*Lutjanus rufolineatus* 316
7 26°C sg: 1.022 22 cm 200L

*Lutjanus argentimaculatus* 316
6-10 26°C sg: 1.022 60 cm 600L

*Lutjanus carponotatus* 316
6-8, 12 25°C sg: 1.022 40 cm 400L

*Lutjanus vitta* 316
7, 9 26°C sg: 1.022 37.5 cm 400L

*Lutjanus quinquelineatus* 316
7, 9 26°C sg: 1.022 40 cm 400L

*Lutjanus adetii* 316
6-7 26°C sg: 1.022 40 cm 400L

*Lutjanus bohar* 316
7-10 26°C sg: 1.022 90 cm 1000L

*Lutjanus monostigma* 316
7-10 26°C sg: 1.022 60 cm 600L

*Lutjanus madras* 316
9 26°C sg: 1.022 20 cm 200L

*Lutjanus gibbus* 316
7-10 26°C sg: 1.022 40 cm 400L

*Lutjanus fulvus* 316
6-9 26°C sg: 1.022 60 cm 600L

*Lutjanus lunulatus* 316
8 26°C sg: 1.022 25 cm 300L

*Lutjanus biguttatus* 316
6-7 26°C sg: 1.022 28 cm 300L

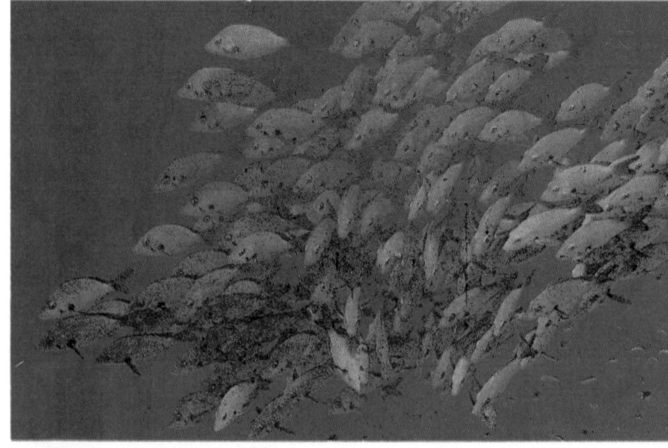

*Lutjanus gibbus* 316
7-10 26°C sg: 1.022 50 cm 500L

*Lutjanus vaigiensis* 316
9 26°C sg: 1.022 60 cm 600L

*Lutjanus russelli* 316
7, 9 26°C sg: 1.022 50 cm 500L

*Lutjanus stellatus* 316
7 26°C sg: 1.022 35 cm 400L

*Lutjanus timorensis* 316
7 26°C sg: 1.022 20 cm 200L

*Lutjanus bohar* 316
7, 9 26°C sg: 1.022 90 cm 1000L

*Lutjanus russelli* 316
7, 9 26°C sg: 1.022 50 cm 500L

*Lutjanus monostigma* 316
7, 9, 10 26°C sg: 1.022 60 cm 600L

*Lutjanus malabaricus* 316
9 26°C sg: 1.022 47.5 cm 500L

*Lutjanus synagris* 316
2 26°C sg: 1.022 35 cm 400L

*Lutjanus mahogoni* 316
2 26°C sg: 1.022 36 cm 400L

*Lutjanus vivanus* 316
2 26°C sg: 1.022 90 cm 1000L

*Lutjanus guttatus* (juv) 316
3 26°C sg: 1.022 60 cm 600L

*Lutjanus jocu* 316
1, 2 24°C sg: 1.023 100 cm 1000L

*Lutjanus mahogoni* 316
2 26°C sg: 1.022 36 cm 400L

*Lutjanus viridis* 316
3 26°C sg: 1.022 30 cm 300L

*Lutjanus guttatus* 316
3 26°C sg: 1.022 60 cm 600L

*Lutjanus campechanus* 316
2 26°C sg: 1.022 60 cm 600L

*Lutjanus buccanella* 316
1, 2 26°C sg: 1.022 75 cm 800L

*Lutjanus apodus* 316
1, 2 24°C sg: 1.023 60 cm 600L

*Lutjanus cyanopterus* 316
2 26°C sg: 1.022 150 cm 1500L

*Lutjanus analis* 316
1, 2 24°C sg: 1.023 65 cm 800L

*Lutjanus buccanella* (juv.) 316
1, 2 26°C sg: 1.022 75 cm 800L

*Lutjanus apodus* 316
1, 2 24°C sg: 1.023 60 cm 600L

*Lutjanus griseus* 316
1, 2 24°C sg: 1.023 60 cm 600L

*Lutjanus rivulatus* 316
7 26°C sg: 1.022 70 cm 800L

*Lutjanus erythropterus* 316
6-10 26°C sg: 1.022 60 cm 600L

*Lutjanus gibbus* 316
7-10 26°C sg: 1.022 50 cm 500L

*Lutjanus semicinctus* 316
7, 9 26°C sg: 1.022 30 cm 300L

*Lutjanus argentimaculatus* 316
7-10 26°C sg: 1.022 60 cm 600L

***Lutjanus erythropterus*** **(juv.) 316**
**6-10 26°C sg: 1.022 60 cm 600L**

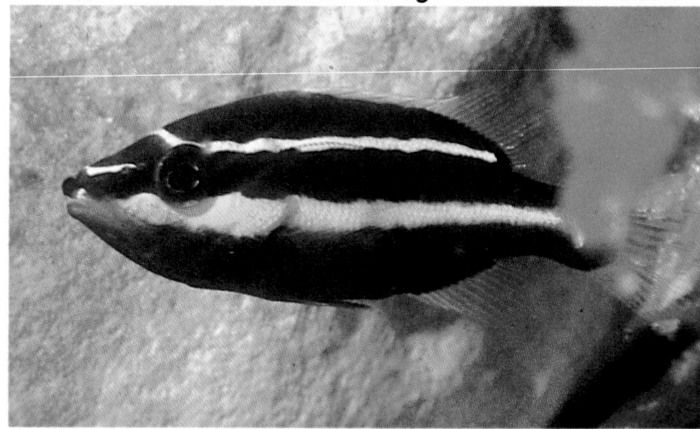

*Lutjanus* sp. (*lemniscatus?*) 316
7, 9 26°C sg: 1.022 45 cm 500L

*Lutjanus lemniscatus* 316
7, 9 26°C sg: 1.022 45 cm 500L

*Symphorichthys spilurus* 316
7 [icons] 26°C sg: 1.022 50 cm 500L

*Symphorichthys spilurus* (juv.) 316
7 26°C sg: 1.022 50 cm 500L

*Symphorichthys spilurus* (adult) 316
7 26°C sg: 1.022 50 cm 500L

*Lutjanus aratus* 316
3 26°C sg: 1.022 75 cm 800L

*Symphorus nematophorus* 316
7 26°C sg: 1.022 80 cm 800L

*Lutjanus novemfasciatus* 316
3 26°C sg: 1.022 120 cm 1200L

*Lutjanus colorado* 316
3 26°C sg: 1.022 75 cm 800L

*Lutjanus peru* 316
3 26°C sg: 1.022 38.5 cm 400L

*Lutjanus peru* 316
3 26°C sg: 1.022 38.5 cm 400L

*Pristipomoides macrophthalmus* 316
7 26°C sg: 1.022 50 cm 500L

*Ocyurus chrysurus* 316
1-2 24°C sg: 1.023 60 cm 1000L

*Pristipomoides filamentosus* 316
7 26°C sg: 1.022 80 cm 800L

*Pristipomoides multidens* 316
7 26°C sg: 1.022 90 cm 1000L

*Tropidinus zonatus* 316
7 26°C sg: 1.022 30 cm 300L

*Macolor niger* (juv.) 316
7-10 26°C sg: 1.022 75 cm 800L

*Hoplopagrus guentheri* 316
3 26°C sg: 1.022 75 cm 800L

*Hoplopagrus guentheri* (juv.) 316
3 26°C sg: 1.022 75 cm 800L

*Lutjanus sebae* 316
7, 9 26°C sg: 1.022 90 cm 1000L

*Macolor niger* (juv.) 316
7-10 26°C sg: 1.022 75 cm 800L

*Macolor niger* 316
7-10 26°C sg: 1.022 75 cm 800L

*Caesio varilineata* 317
9 26°C sg: 1.022 30 cm 300L

*Lutjanus vitta* 316
7-8 26°C sg: 1.022 37.5 cm 400L

*Macolor niger* (juv.) 316
7-10 26°C sg: 1.022 75 cm 800L

*Symphorus nematophorus* 316
7 26°C sg: 1.022 80 cm 800L

*Caesio xanthonota* 317
7, 9 26°C sg: 1.022 40 cm 400L

*Caesio teres* 317
9 ◐ 26°C sg: 1.022 30 cm 300L

*Pterocaesio chrysozona* 317
7, 9 ◐ ♥ 26°C sg: 1.022 18 cm 200L

*Pterocaesio tile* 317
7, 9 ◐ ♥ 26°C sg: 1.022 30 cm 300L

*Pterocaesio randalli* 317
7, 9 ◐ ♥ 26°C sg: 1.022 18 cm 200L

*Pterocaesio trilineata* 317
9 ◐ ♥ 26°C sg: 1.022 18 cm 200L

*Pterocaesio lativittata* 317
7, 9 ◐ ♥ 26°C sg: 1.022 18 cm 200L

*Pterocaesio tile* 317
7, 9 ◐ ♥ 26°C sg: 1.022 30 cm 300L

*Caesio caerulaurea* 317
7, 9 ◐ ♥ 26°C sg: 1.022 18 cm 200L

*Caesio erythrogaster* 317
7-9 ◐ 26°C sg: 1.022 36 cm 400L

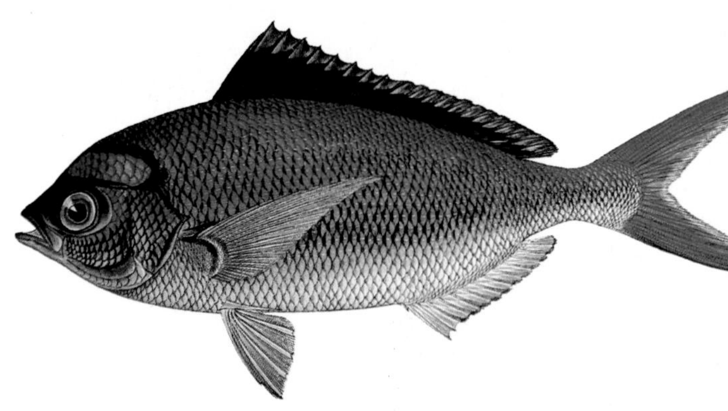

*Caesio lunaris* 317
7, 9 ◐ 26°C sg: 1.022 30 cm 300L

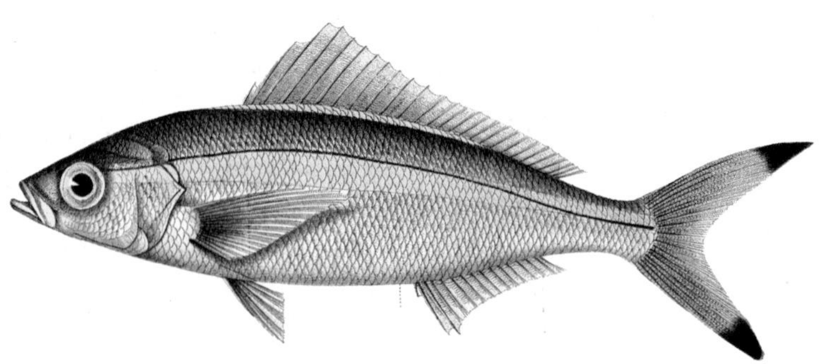

*Pterocaesio chrysozona* 317
7, 9 ◐ ♥ 26°C sg: 1.022 18 cm 200L

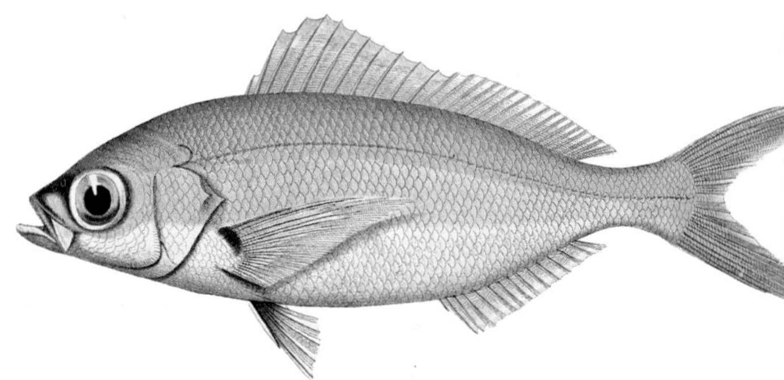

*Caesio xanthonotus* 317
7, 9 ◐ 26°C sg: 1.022 40 cm 400L

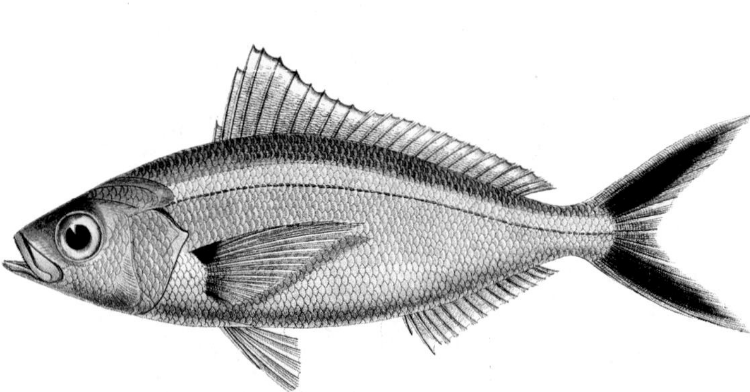

*Caesio caerulaurea* 317
7, 9 ◐ ♥ 26°C sg: 1.022 18 cm 200L

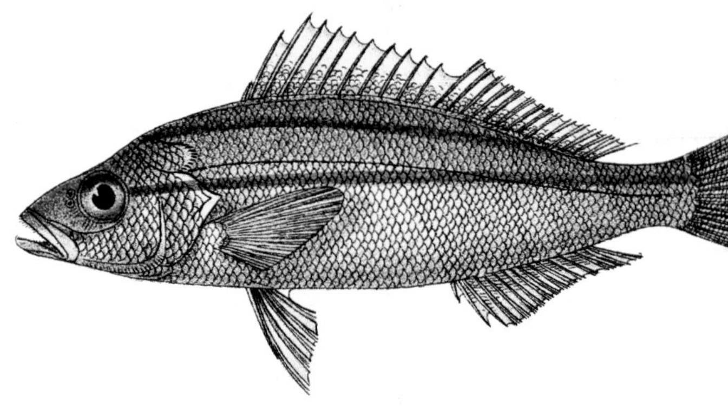

*Pterocaesio digramma* 317
7 ◐ ♥ 26°C sg: 1.022 25 cm 300L

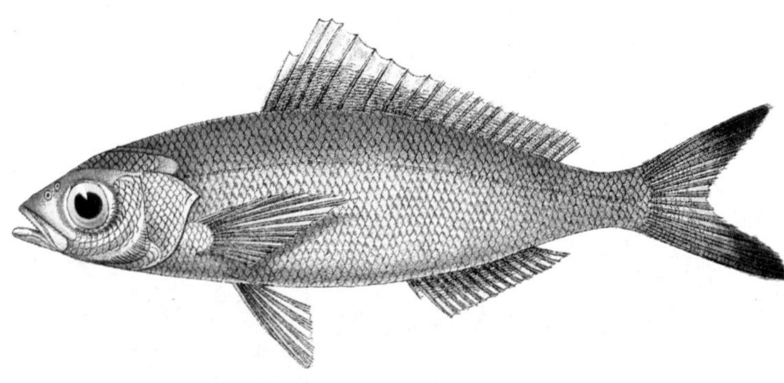

*Caesio pisang* 317
5, 7 ◐ ♥ 26°C sg: 1.022 20 cm 200L

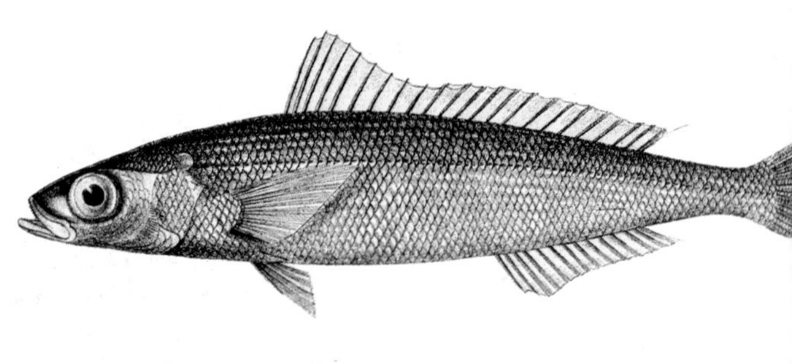

*Gymnocaesio gymnopterus* 317
7, 9 ◐ ♥ 26°C sg: 1.022 16 cm 200L

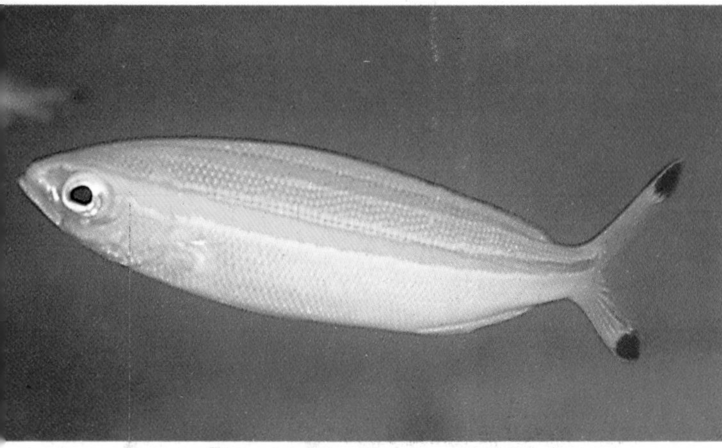

*Pterocaesio digramma* 317
7 26°C sg: 1.022 25 cm 300L

*Caesio cuning* 317
7 26°C sg: 1.022 40 cm 400L

*Caesio teres* 317
9 26°C sg: 1.022 30 cm 300L

***Caesio lunaris*** **317**
**7, 9 26°C sg: 1.022 30 cm 300L**

***Caesio pisang*** **317**
**5, 7 26°C sg: 1.022 20 cm 200L**

*Caesio caerulaurea* 317
7, 9 26°C sg: 1.022 18 cm 200L

*Lobotes surinamensis* 317
Circumtrop. 26°C sg: 1.022 96 cm 1000L

*Lobotes surinamensis* 317
Circumtrop. 26°C sg: 1.022 96 cm 1000L

*#210*

*Gerres oyena* 319
7, 9 26°C sg: 1.022 25 cm 300L

*Gerres baconensis* 319
7 26°C sg: 1.022 25 cm 300L

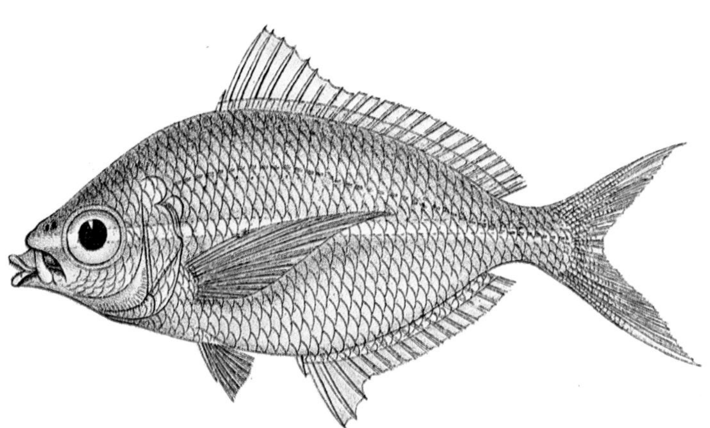

*Pentaprion longimanus* 319
7, 9 ~ ◐ ♥ ▣ ⊡ 26°C sg: 1.022 27 cm 300L

*Parequula melbournenses* 319
12 ~ ◐ ♥ ▣ ⊡ 26°C sg: 1.022 10 cm 100L

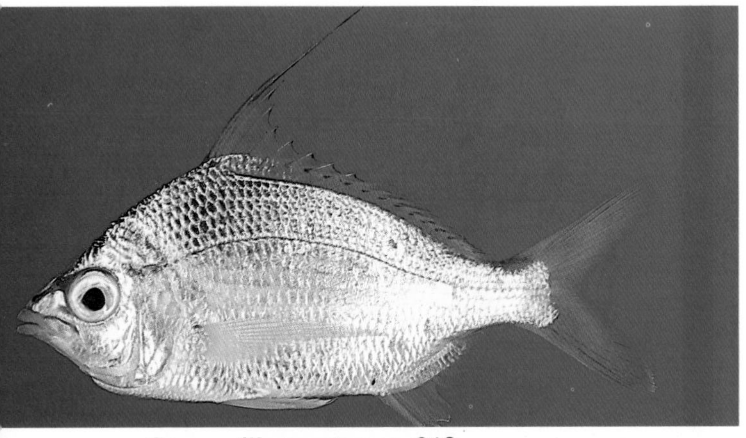

*Gerres filamentosus* 319
7, 9 ~ ◐ ♥ ▣ ⊡ 26°C sg: 1.022 27 cm 300L

*Gerres acinaces* 319
7, 9 ~ ◐ ♥ ▣ ⊡ 26°C sg: 1.022 25 cm 300L

*Eucinostomus gracilis* 319
3 ~ ◐ ♥ ▣ ⊡ 26°C sg: 1.022 20 cm 200L

*Gerres cinereus* 319
2 ~ ◐ ♥ ▣ ⊡ 26°C sg: 1.022 20 cm 200L

*Eucinostomus argenteus* 319
1-3 ~ ◐ ♥ ▣ ⊡ 26°C sg: 1.022 20 cm 200L

*Eucinostomus gula* 320
1-2 ~ ◐ ♥ ▣ ⊡ 25°C sg: 1.022 18 cm 200L

*Gerres filamentosus* 319
7, 9 ◐ ♥ 26°C sg: 1.022 27 cm 300L

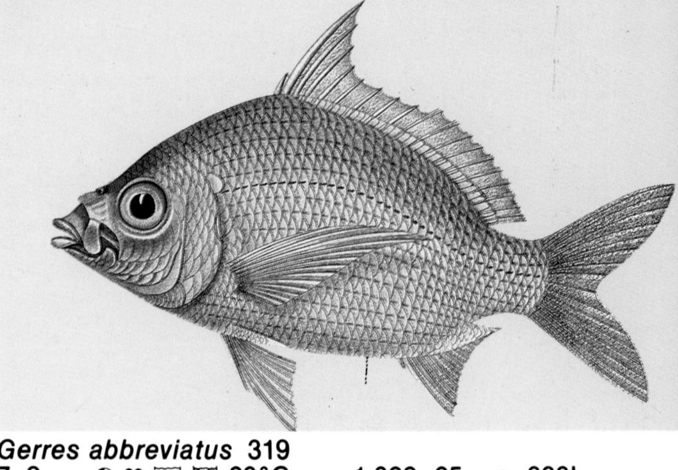

*Gerres abbreviatus* 319
7, 9 ◐ ♥ 26°C sg: 1.022 25 cm 300L

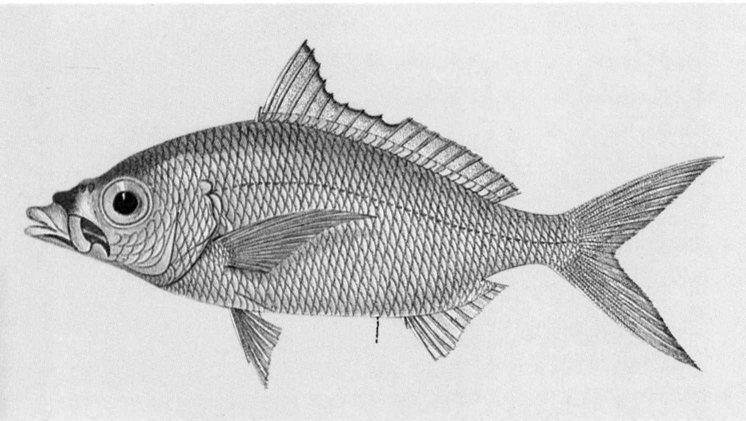

*Gerres macrosoma* 319
7 ◐ ♥ 26°C sg: 1.022 25 cm 300L

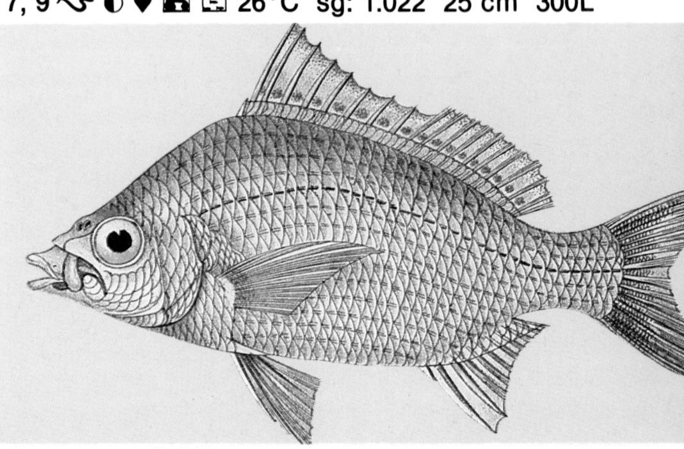

*Gerres poeti* 319
7 ◐ ♥ 26°C sg: 1.022 23 cm 300L

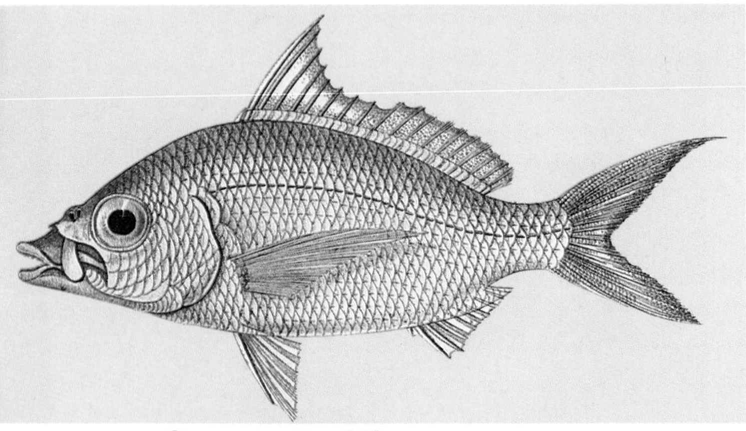

*Gerres oyena* 319
7, 9 ◐ 26°C sg: 1.022 25 cm 300L

*Gerres kapas* 319
7 ◐ ♥ 26°C sg: 1.022 17.5 cm 200L

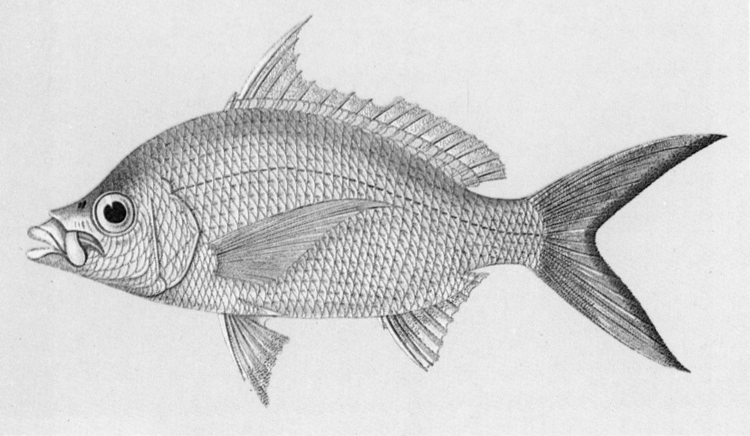

*Gerres acinaces* 319
7, 9 ◐ ♥ 26°C sg: 1.022 25 cm 300L

*Gerres macracanthus* 319
7 ◐ ♥ 26°C sg: 1.022 17 cm 200L

*Haemulon flavolineatum* 320
2 [symbols] 26°C sg: 1.022 30 cm 300L

*Haemulon parrai* 320
2 26°C sg: 1.022 40 cm 400L

*Haemulon melanurum* 320
26°C sg: 1.022 33 cm 350L

*Haemulon sciurus* 320
2 26°C sg: 1.022 18 cm 200L

*Haemulon plumieri* 320
2 26°C sg: 1.022 45 cm 500L

*Haemulon flavolineatum* 320
2 26°C sg: 1.022 30 cm 300L

*Haemulon flavolineatum* 320
2 26°C sg: 1.022 30 cm 300L

*Haemulon flavolineatum* 320
2 26°C sg: 1.022 30 cm 300L

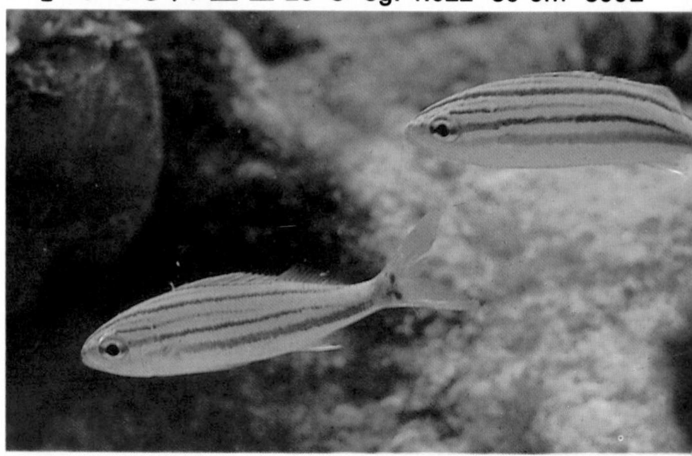

*Haemulon striatum* 320
2 26°C sg: 1.022 28 cm 300L

*Haemulon chrysargyreum* 320
2 26°C sg: 1.022 23 cm 300L

*Haemulon album* 320
2 26°C sg: 1.022 60 cm 600L

*Haemulon macrostomum* 320
2 26°C sg: 1.022 43 cm 500L

*Haemulon aurolineatum* 320
1-2 25°C sg: 1.022 25 cm 300L

*Haemulon aurolineatum* 320
2 26°C sg: 1.022 36 cm 400L

*Haemulon sciurus* 320
2 26°C sg: 1.022 30 cm 300L

*Haemulon sciurus* 320
2 26°C sg: 1.022 30 cm 300L

*Haemulon sexfasciatum* 320
3 26°C sg: 1.022 33 cm 500L

*Haemulon flaviguttatum* 320
3 26° sg: 1.022 30 cm 300L

*Anisotremus surinamensis* (juv.) 320
2 26°C sg: 1.022 60 cm 600L

*Anisotremus surinamensis* 320
2 26°C sg: 1.022 60 cm 600L

*Anisotremus davidsonii* 320
3 26°C sg: 1.022 58 cm 600L

*Anisotremus taeniatus* 320
3 26°C sg: 1.022 25 cm 250L

*Anisotremus virginicus* 320
2 26°C sg: 1.022 38 cm 400L

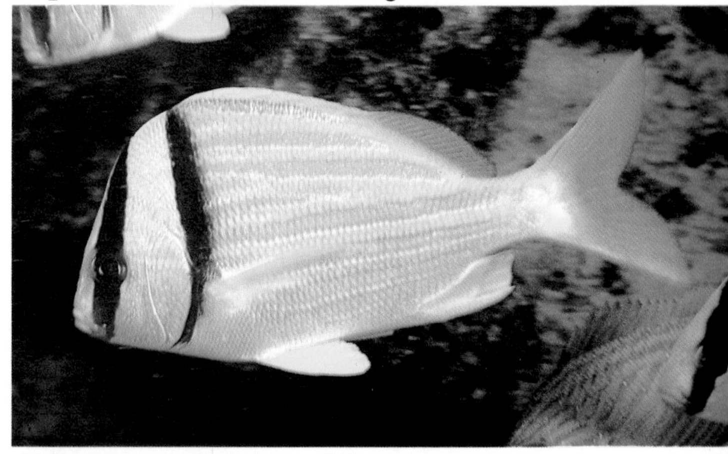

*Anisotremus virginicus* 320
2 26°C sg: 1.022 38 cm 400L

*Parapristipoma trilineatum* 320
7 26°C sg: 1.022 40 cm 400L

*Conodon nobilis* 320
2 26°C sg: 1.022 30 cm 300L

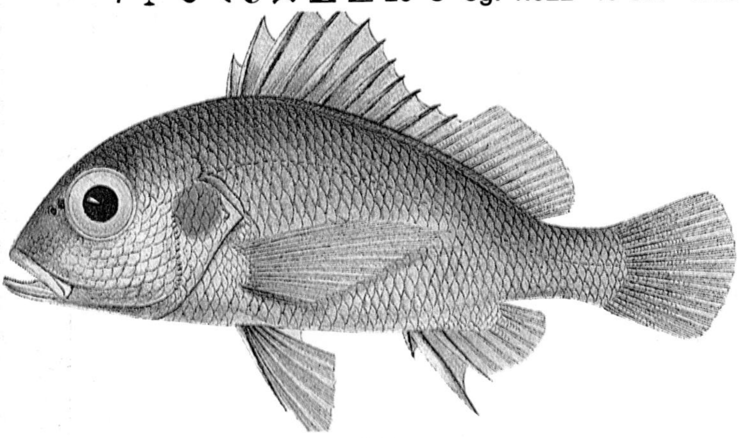

*Pomadasys argyreus* 320
7, 9 26°C sg: 1.022 20 cm 200L

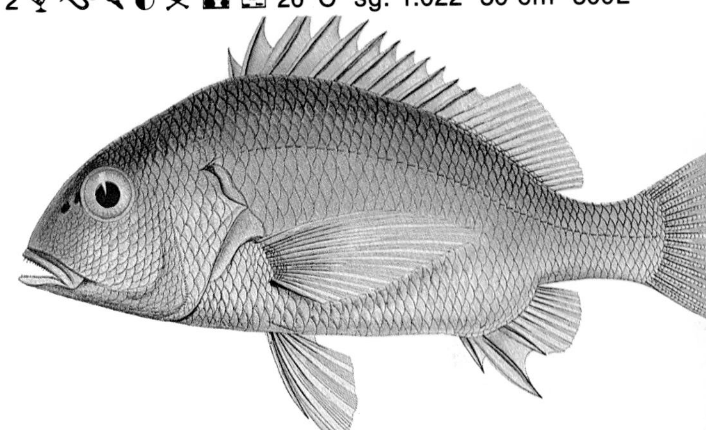

*Pomadasys argyreus* 320
7, 9 26°C sg: 1.022 20 cm 200L

*Pomadasys maculatum* 320
7 26°C sg: 1.022 15 cm 200L

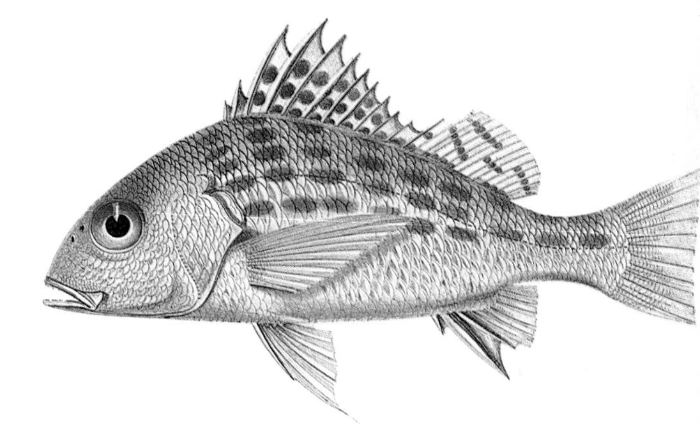

*Pomadasys hasta* 320
6-10 26°C sg: 1.022 40 cm 400L

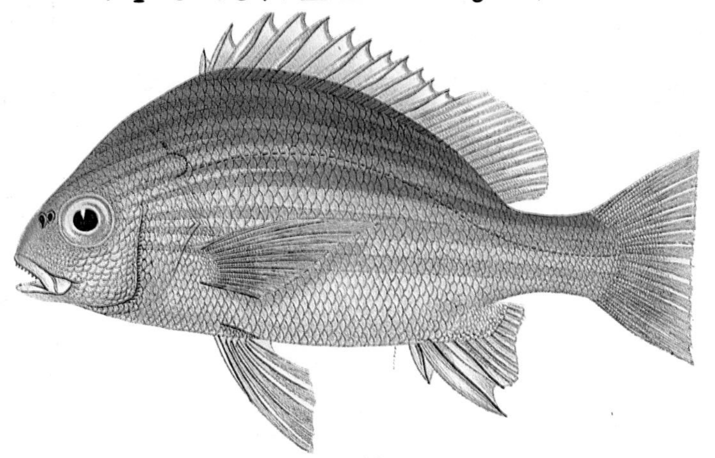

*Pomadasys furcatus* 320
7-9 26°C sg: 1.022 50 cm 500L

*Pomadasys corvinaeformis* 320
2 26°C sg: 1.022 25 cm 300L

*Scolopsis ghanam* 325
9-10 26°C sg: 1.022 25 cm 300L

*Plectorhinchus chaetodonoides* (juv.) 320
7 26°C sg: 1.022 60 cm 600L

*Plectorhinchus chaetodonoides* 320
7 26°C sg: 1.022 60 cm 600L

*Plectorhinchus gaterinus* 320
9-10 26°C sg: 1.022 60 cm 600L

*Scolopsis ghanam* 325
9-10 26°C sg: 1.022 25 cm 300L

*Plectorhinchus chaetodonoides* 320
7 26°C sg: 1.022 60 cm 600L

*Plectorhinchus flavomaculatus* 320
7, 9-10 26°C sg: 1.022 60 cm 600L

*Plectorhinchus schotaf* 320
7-9 26°C sg: 1.022 60 cm 600L

*Plectorhinchus albovittatus* 320
7, 9-10 ◐ ♥ 26°C sg: 1.022 20 cm 200L

*Plectorhinchus albovittatus* (juv.) 320
7, 9-10 ◐ ♥ 26°C sg: 1.022 20 cm 200L

*Plectorhinchus flavomaculatus* 320
7, 9-10 ◐ ♥ 26°C sg: 1.022 60 cm 600L

*Plectorhinchus multivittatus* 320
7, 12 ◐ ♥ 26°C sg: 1.022 60 cm 600L

*Plectorhinchus picus* 320
7, 9 ◐ ♥ 26°C sg: 1.022 60 cm 600L

*Plectorhinchus chaetodonoides* 320
7 ◐ ♥ 26°C sg: 1.022 60 cm 600L

*Hapalogenys nigripinnis* 320
5, 7 ◐ ☠ 26°C sg: 1.022 60 cm 600L

*Hapalogenys mucronatus* 320
5-7 ◐ ☠ 26°C sg: 1.022 30 cm 300L

*Plectorhinchus celebicus* 320
7 26°C sg: 1.022 50 cm 500L

*Plectorhinchus diagrammus* 320
7, 9 26°C sg: 1.022 50 cm 500L

*Plectorhinchus schotaf* 320
7-9 26°C sg: 1.022 60 cm 600L

*Plectorhinchus cinctus* 320
7, 9 26°C sg: 1.022 60 cm 600L

*Plectorhinchus goldmanni* 320
6-7 26°C sg: 1.022 60 cm 600L

*Plectorhinchus diagrammus* 320
7, 9 26°C sg: 1.022 50 cm

*Plectorhinchus nigrus* 320
7, 9-10 26°C sg: 1.022 60 cm 600L

*Plectorhinchus sordidus* 320
9-10 26°C sg: 1.022 60 cm 600L

*Plectorhinchus gaterinus* 320
9-10 ◐ ♥ 26°C sg: 1.022 60 cm 600L

*Plectorhinchus sordidus* 320
9-10 ◐ ♥ 26°C sg: 1.022 60 cm 600L

*Plectorhinchus lineatus* 320
7, 9 ◐ ♥ 26°C sg: 1.022 35 cm 400L

*Plectorhinchus lineatus* 320
7, 9 ◐ 26°C sg: 1.022 35 cm 400L

*Plectorhinchus picus* 320
7, 9 ◐ ♥ 26°C sg: 1.022 60 cm 600L

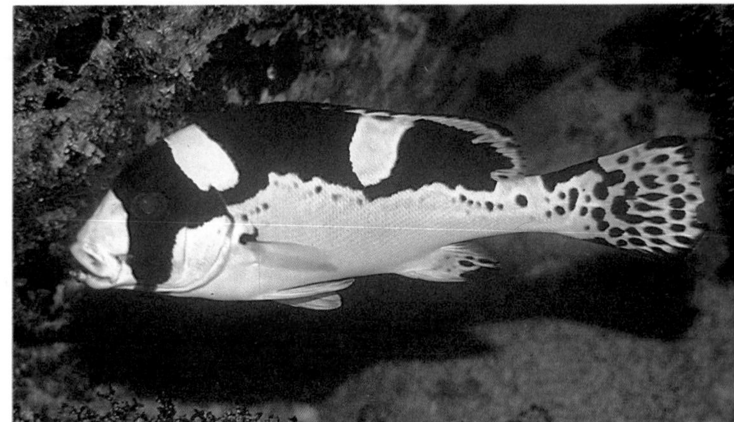

*Plectorhinchus picus* 320
7, 9 ◐ ♥ 26°C sg: 1.022 60 cm 600L

*Plectorhinchus picus* 320
7, 9 ◐ ♥ 26°C sg: 1.022 60 cm 600L

*Plectorhinchus pictus* 320
7, 9-10 ◐ ♥ 26°C sg: 1.022 90 cm 1000L

*Plectorhinchus lineatus* 320
7, 9 26°C sg: 1.022 35 cm 400L

*Plectorhinchus lineatus* 320
7, 9 26°C sg: 1.022 35 cm 400L

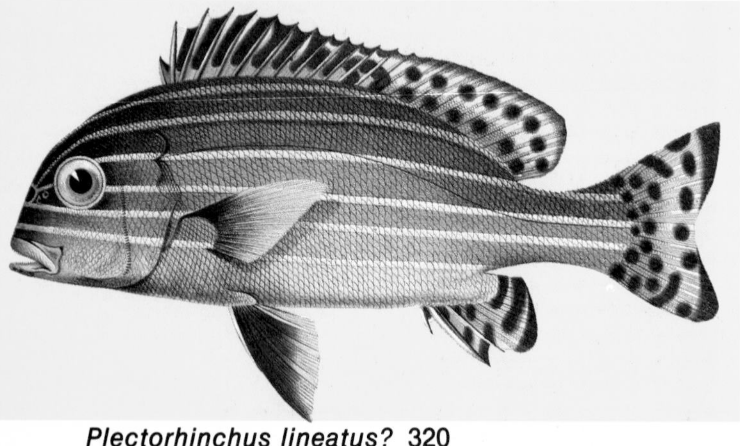

*Plectorhinchus lineatus?* 320
7, 9 26°C sg: 1.022 35 cm 400L

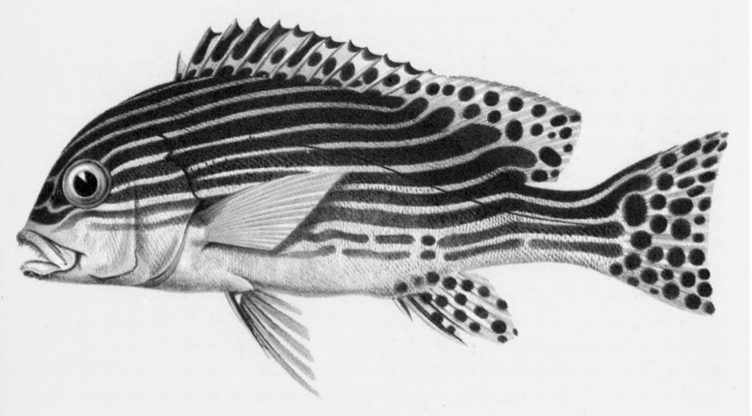

*Plectorhinchus goldmanni?* 320
6-7 26°C sg: 1.022 50 cm 500L

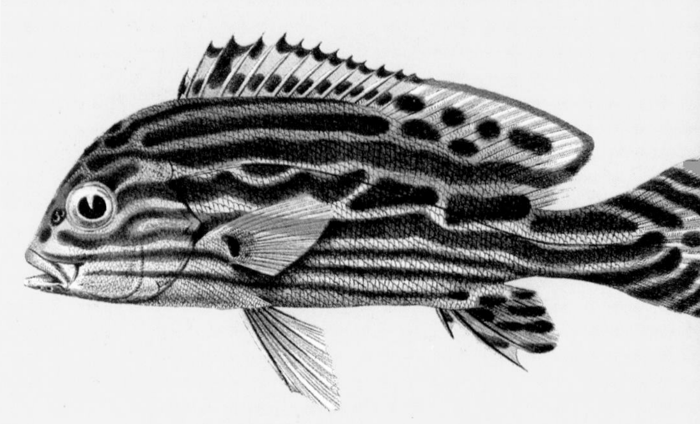

*Plectorhinchus lineatus* 320
7, 9 26°C sg: 1.022 35 cm 400L

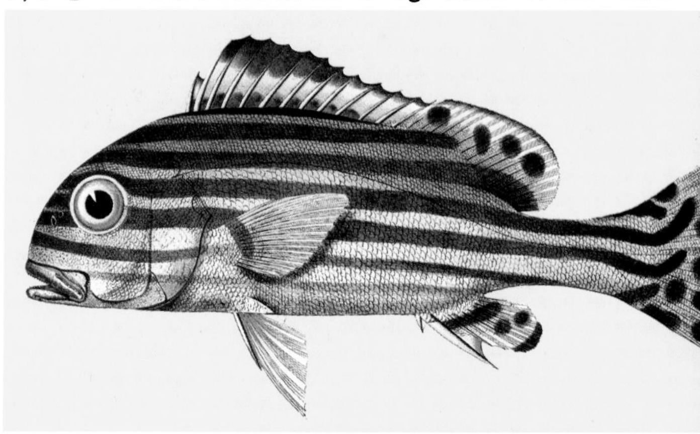

*Plectorhinchus lineatus* 320
7, 9 26°C sg: 1.022 35 cm 400L

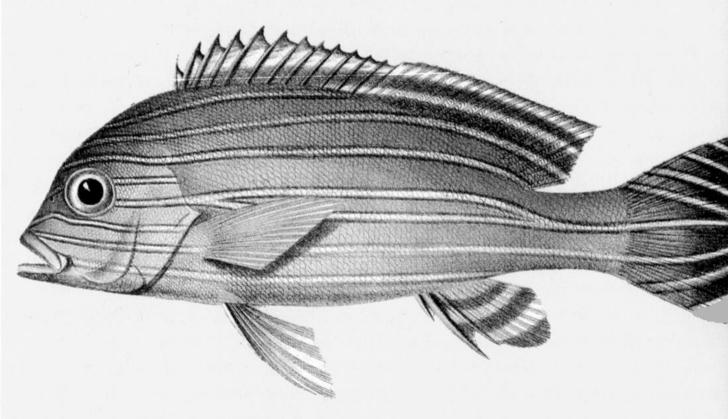

*Plectorhinchus polytaenia* 320
7, 9 26°C sg: 1.022 50 cm 500L

*Plectorhinchus goldmanni* 320
6-7 26°C sg: 1.022 50 cm 500L

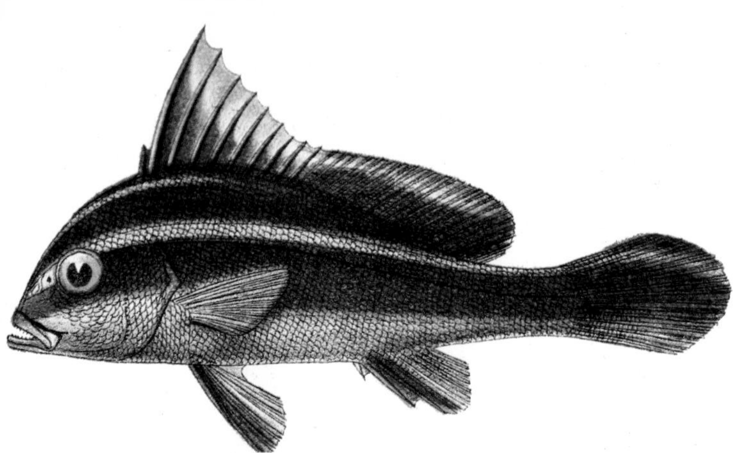

*Plectorhinchus pictus* 320
7, 9-10 26°C sg: 1.022 90 cm 1000L

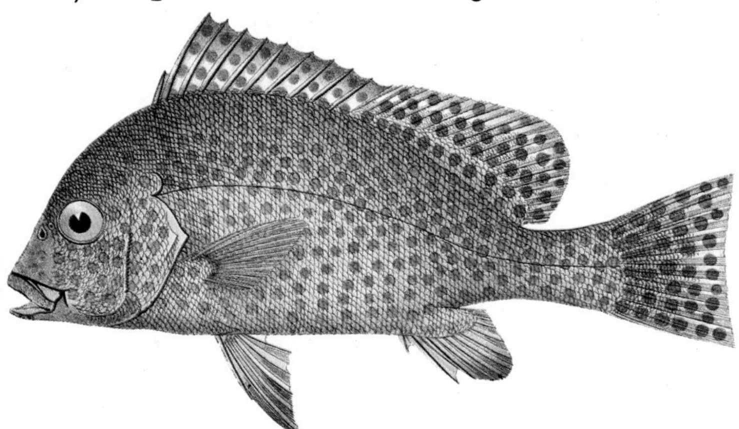

*Plectorhinchus pictus* 320
7, 9-10 26°C sg: 1.022 90 cm 1000L

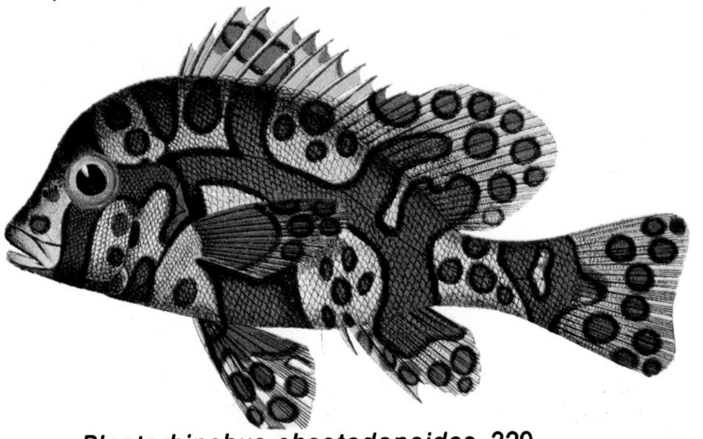

*Plectorhinchus chaetodonoides* 320
7 26°C sg: 1.022 60 cm 600L

*Plectorhinchus chaetodonoides* 320
7 26°C sg: 1.022 60 cm 600L

*Plectorhinchus pictus* 320
7, 9-10 26°C sg: 1.022 90 cm 1000L

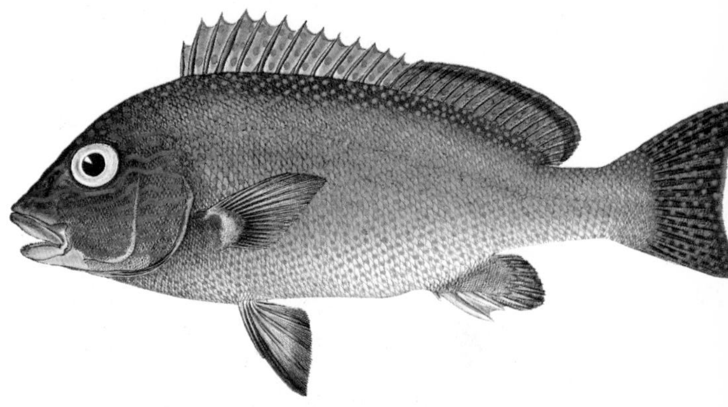

*Plectorhinchus flavomaculatus* 320
7, 9-10 26°C sg: 1.022 60 cm 600L

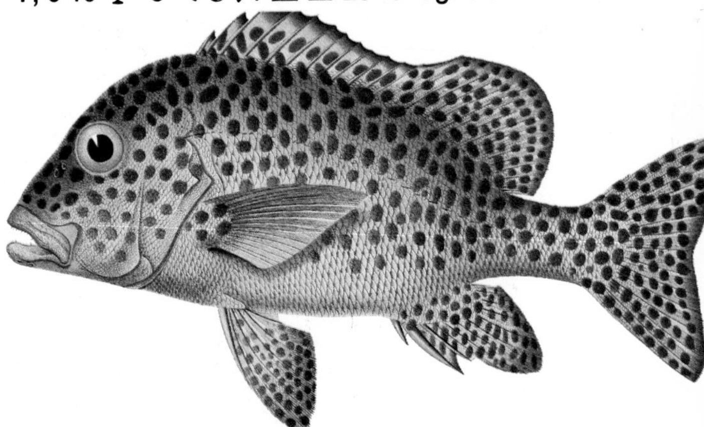

*Plectorhinchus chaetodonoides* 320
7 26°C sg: 1.022 60 cm 600L

*Plectorhinchus picus* 320
7, 9 26°C sg: 1.022 60 cm 600L

*Inermia vittata* 321
2 26°C sg: 1.022 13 cm 150L

*Spicara maena flexuosa* 323
15 26°C sg: 1.022 21 cm 200L

*Boops salpa* 322
13-15 26°C sg: 1.022 45 cm 500L

*Diplodus bermudensis* 322
2 26°C sg: 1.022 30 cm 300L

*Emmelichthyops ruber* 315
2 26°C sg: 1.022 13 cm 150L

*Diplodus puntazzo* 322
13, 15 26°C sg: 1.022 45 cm 500L

*Lithognathus mormyrus* 322
9-10, 15 26°C sg: 1.022 55 cm 600L

*Diplodus vulgaris* 322
13, 15 26°C sg: 1.022 30 cm 300L

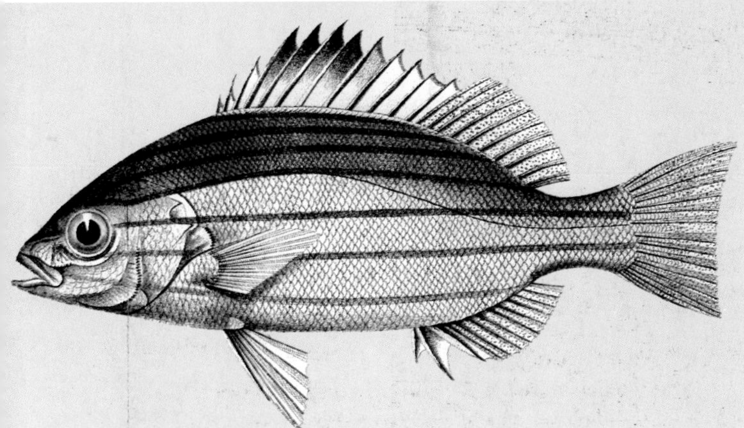

*Pelates quadrilineatus* 291
7-10 26°C sg: 1.022 25 cm 300L

*Pelates quadrilineatus* 291
7-10 26°C sg: 1.022 25 cm 300L

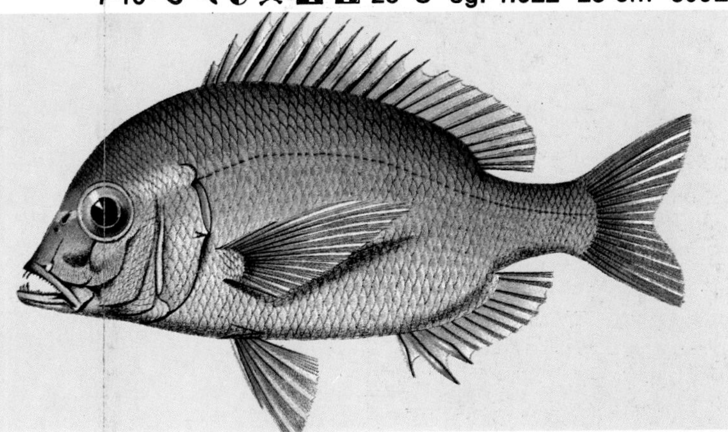

*Dentex tumifrons* 322
5, 7 26°C sg: 1.022 35 cm 400L

*Evynnis japonica* 322
5, 7 26°C sg: 1.022 45 cm 500L

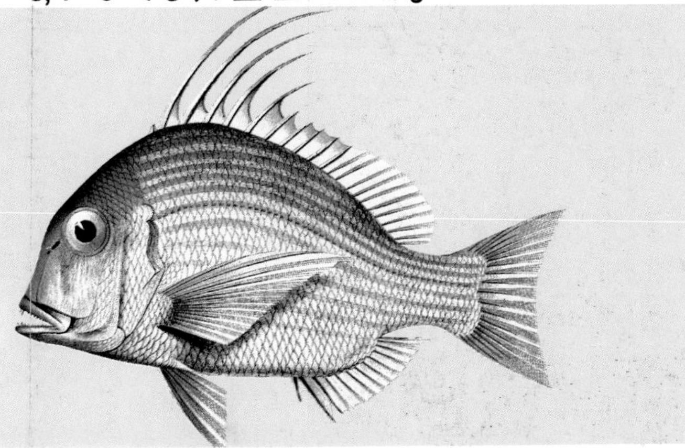

*Argyrops bleekeri* 322
7 26°C sg: 1.022 50 cm 500L

*Argyrops spinifer* 322
7 26°C sg: 1.022 50 cm 500L

*Acanthopagrus berda* 322
7, 9-10 26°C sg: 1.022 50 cm 500L

*Acanthopagrus berda* 322
7, 9-10 26°C sg: 1.022 50 cm 500L

*Argyrops bleekeri* 322
7 ∿ ↘ ◐ ✲ ▨ ▣ 26°C sg: 1.022 50 cm 500L

*Pagrus major* 322
5, 7 ∿ ↘ ◐ ✲ ▨ ▣ 26°C sg: 1.022 70 cm 800L

*Pagrus auratus* 322
7-8, 12 ∿ ↘ ◐ ✲ ▨ ▣ 26°C sg: 1.022 100 cm 1000L

*Pagrus major* 322
5, 7 ∿ ↘ ◐ ✲ ▨ ▣ 26°C sg: 1.022 70 cm 800L

*Gymnocranius japonicus* 324
6-7 ∿ ↘ ◐ ✲ ▨ ▣ 26°C sg: 1.022 50 cm 500L

*Gymnocranius bitorquatus* 322
7-8 ∿ ↘ ◐ ✲ ▨ ▣ 26°C sg: 1.022 41 cm 400L

*Pagellus acarne* 322
14-15 ∿ ↘ ◐ ✲ ▨ ▣ 26°C sg: 1.022 35 cm 400L

*Gymnocranius lethrinoides* 322
6-7 ∿ ↘ ◐ ✲ ▨ ▣ 26°C sg: 1.022 50 cm 500L

*Calamus bajonado* 322
2 ♀ ∿ ⟍ ◐ ✲ ▣ ☰ 26°C sg: 1.022 60 cm 600L

*Calamus pennatula* 322
2 ♀ ∿ ⟍ ◐ ✲ ▣ ☰ 26°C sg: 1.022 35 cm 400L

*Calamus calamus* 322
2 ♀ ∿ ⟍ ◐ ✲ ▣ ☰ 26°C sg: 1.022 41 cm 400L

*Calamus nodosus* 322
2 ♀ ∿ ⟍ ◐ ✲ ▣ ☰ 26°C sg: 1.022 46 cm 500L

*Calamus brachysomus* 322
3 ♀ ∿ ⟍ ◐ ✲ ▣ ☰ 26°C sg: 1.022 60 cm 600L

*Pagrus pagrus* 322
2, 13 ♀ ∿ ⟍ ◐ ✲ ▣ ☰ 26°C sg: 1.022 90 cm 1000L

*Evynnis cardinalis* 322
7 ♀ ∿ ⟍ ◐ ✲ ▣ ☰ 26°C sg: 1.022 40 cm 400L

*Evynnis japonica* 322
5, 7 ♀ ∿ ⟍ ◐ ✲ ▣ ☰ 26°C sg: 1.022 45 cm 500L

*Archosargus probatocephalus* 322
2 26°C sg: 1.022 91 cm 1000L

*Archosargus probatocephalus* 322
2 26°C sg: 1.022 91 cm 1000L

*Acanthopagrus latus* 322
7, 9-10 26°C sg: 1.022 50 cm 500L

*Lagodon rhomboides* 322
2 26°C sg: 1.022 35 cm 400L

*Acanthopagrus schlegeli* 322
5, 7 26°C sg: 1.022 50 cm 500L

*Acanthopagrus bifasciatus* 322
9-10, 13 26°C sg: 1.022 50 cm 500L

*Rhabdosargus sarba* 322
5, 7, 9-10 26°C sg: 1.022 46 cm 500L

*Acanthopagrus australis* 322
6-7 26°C sg: 1.022 55 cm 600L

*Chrysoblephus anglicus* 322
9 26°C sg: 1.022 100 cm 1000L

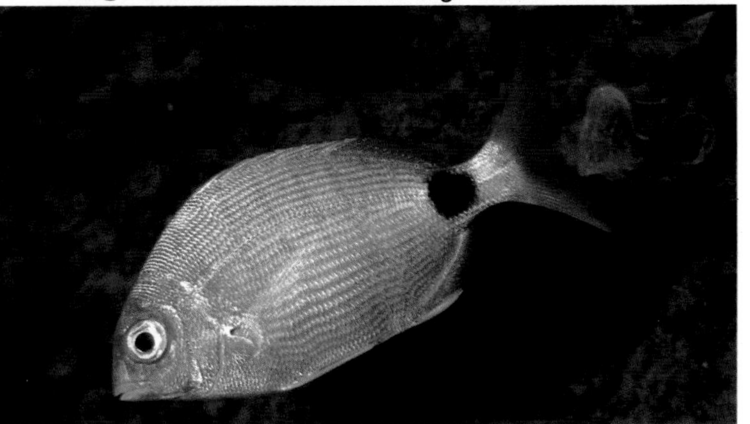

*Diplodus sargus* 322
14-15 26°C sg: 1.022 40 cm 400L

*Rhabdosargus thorpei* 322
9 26°C sg: 1.022 40 cm 400L

*Monotaxis grandoculus* 324
7, 9-10 26°C sg: 1.022 45 cm 500L

*Diplodus cervinus* 322
13-15 26°C sg: 1.022 55 cm 600L

*Porcostoma dentata* 322
9 26°C sg: 1.022 30 cm 300L

*Gymnocranius griseus* 324
5, 7, 9 26°C sg: 1.022 50 cm 500L

*Monotaxis grandoculis* 324
7, 9-10 26°C sg: 1.022 45 cm 500L

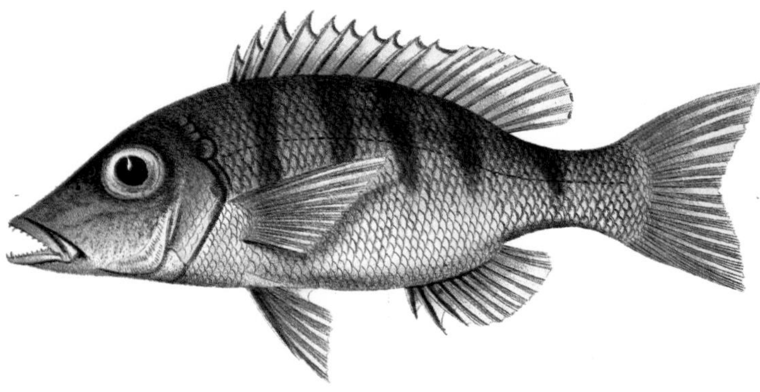

*Lethrinus crocineus* 324
7-9 26°C sg: 1.022 60 cm 600L

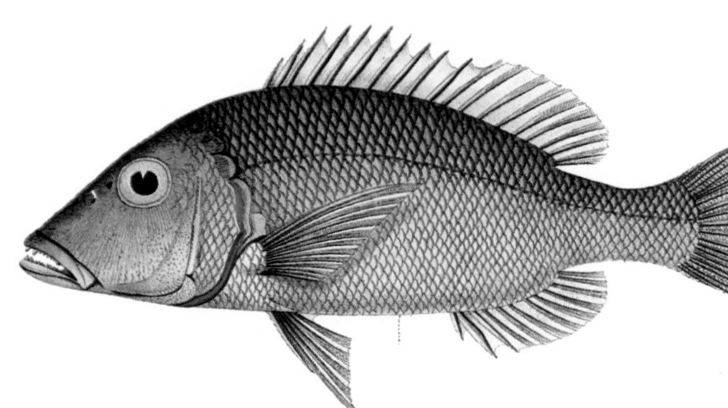

*Lethrinus lentjan* 324
6-10 26°C sg: 1.022 50 cm 500L

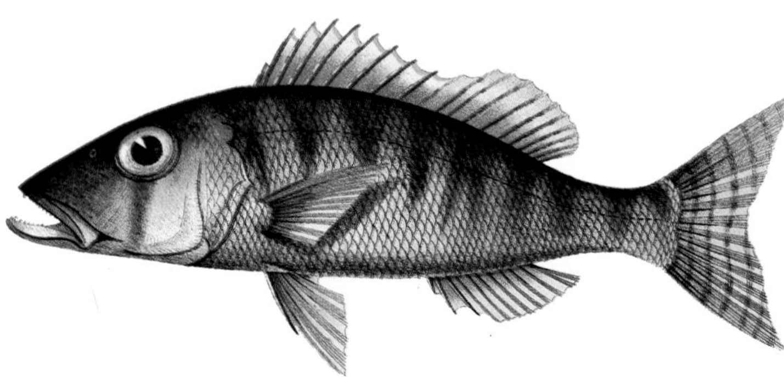

*Lethrinus variegatus* 324
6-9 26°C sg: 1.022 60 cm 600L

*Lethrinus variegatus* 324
6-9 26°C sg: 1.022 60 cm 600L

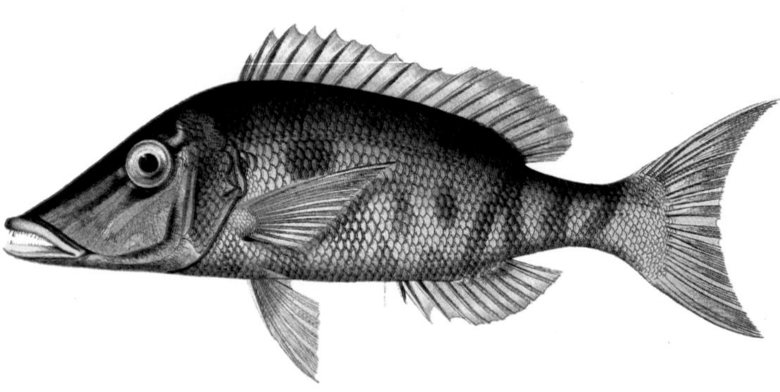

*Lethrinus rostratus* 324
7 26°C sg: 1.022 60 cm 600L

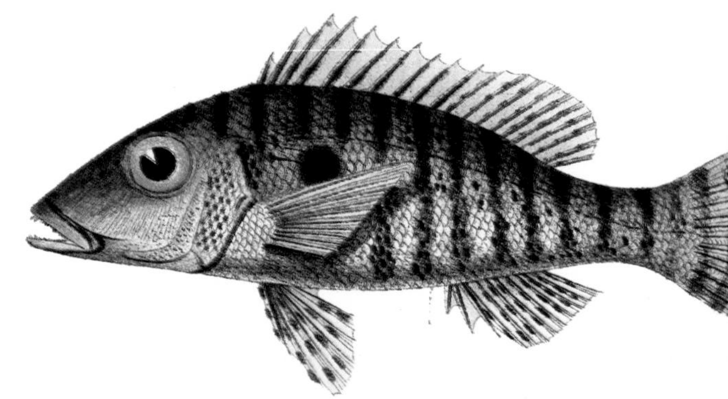

*Lethrinus amboinensis* 324
6-7 26°C sg: 1.022 70 cm 800L

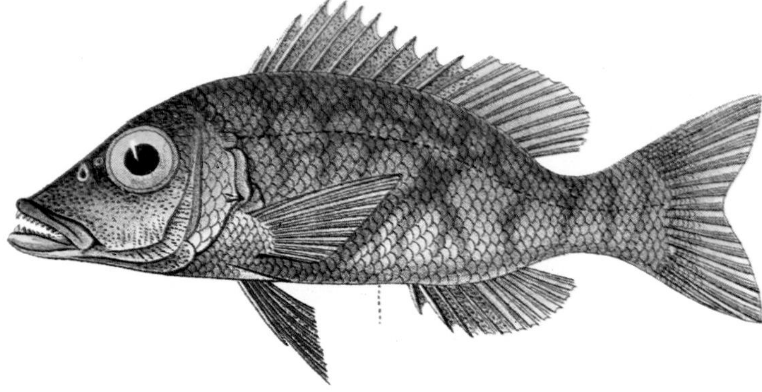

*Lethrinus reticulatus* 324
7-8 26°C sg: 1.022 40 cm 400L

*Lethrinus variegatus?* 324
6-9 26°C sg: 1.022 60 cm 600L

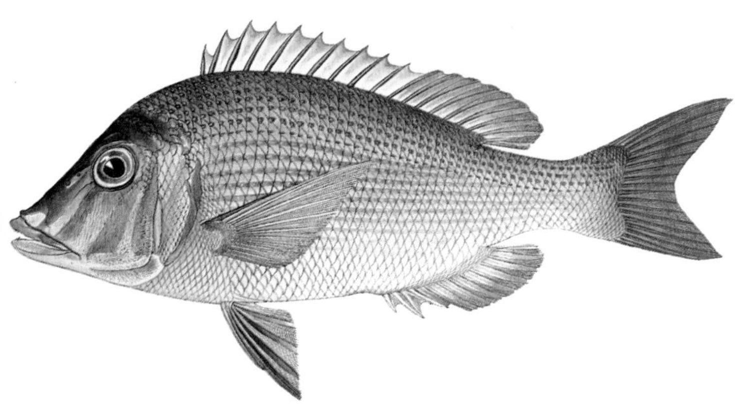

*Lethrinus nebulosus* 324
7-10 26°C sg: 1.022 90 cm 1000L

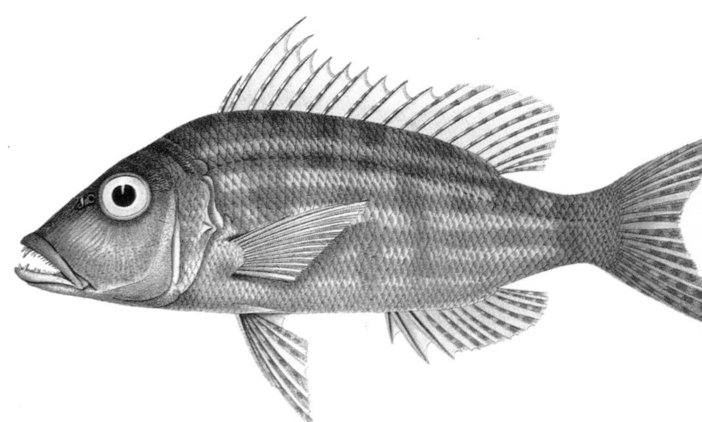

*Lethrinus nematacanthus* 324
7 26°C sg: 1.022 25 cm 300L

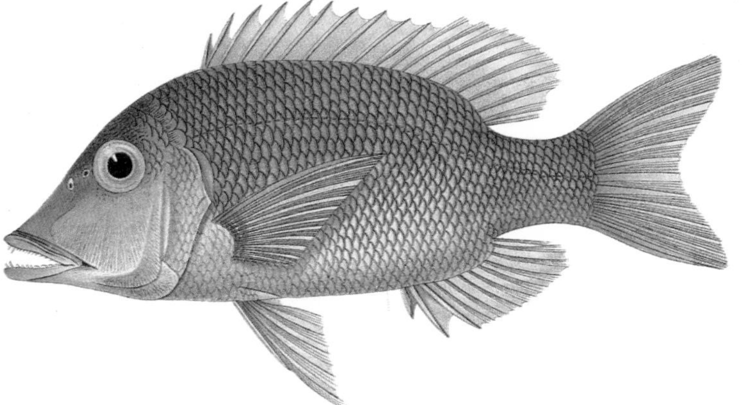

*Lethrinus hypselopterus* 324
7-9 26°C sg: 1.022 50 cm 500L

*Lethrinus kallopterus* 324
7, 9 26°C sg: 1.022 80 cm 800L

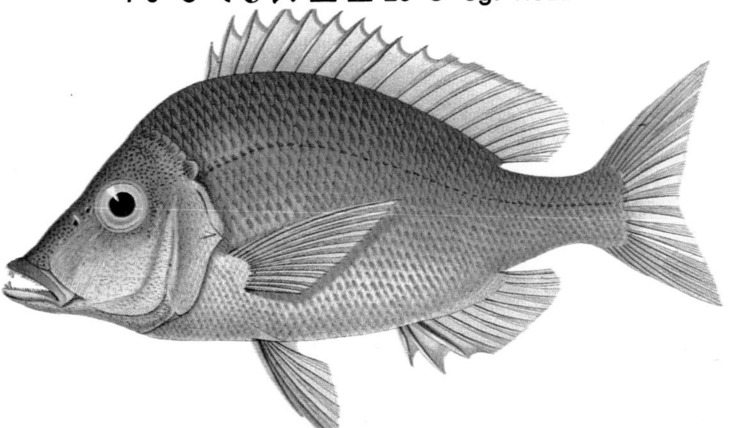

*Lethrinus haematopterus* 324
7 26°C sg: 1.022 45 cm 500L

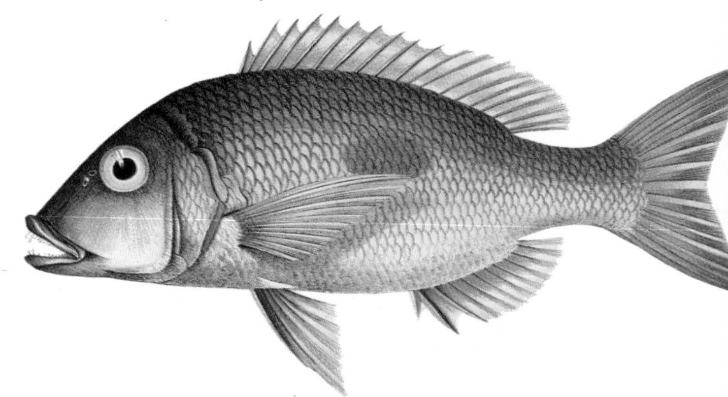

*Lethrinus harak* 324
6-10 26°C sg: 1.022 60 cm 600L

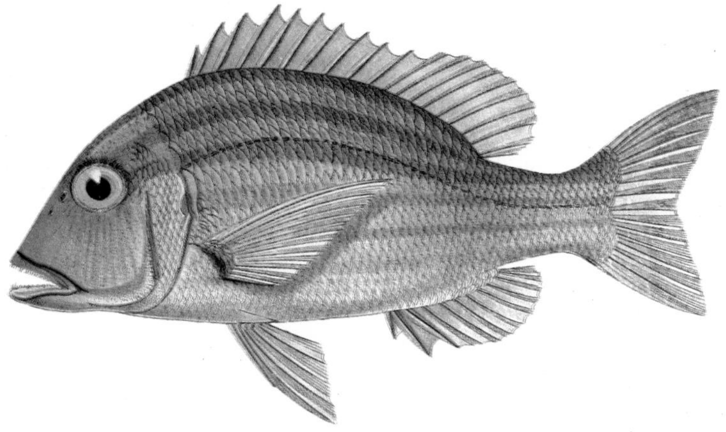

*Lethrinus ornatus* 324
7 26°C sg: 1.022 45 cm 500L

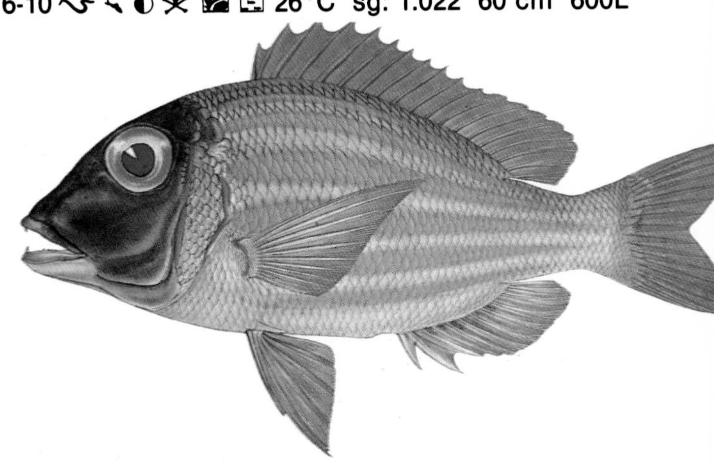

*Lethrinus ornatus* 324
7 26°C sg: 1.022 45 cm 500L

*Lethrinus mahsena* 324
7-10 26°C sg: 1.022 50 cm 500L

*Lethrinus ornatus* 324
7 26°C sg: 1.022 45 cm 500L

*Monotaxis grandoculis* 324
7, 9-10 26°C sg: 1.022 8 cm 80L

*Gymnocranius lethrinoides* 324
7 26°C sg: 1.022 50 cm 500L

*Lethrinus nebulosus* 324
7-10 26°C sg: 1.022 90 cm 1000L

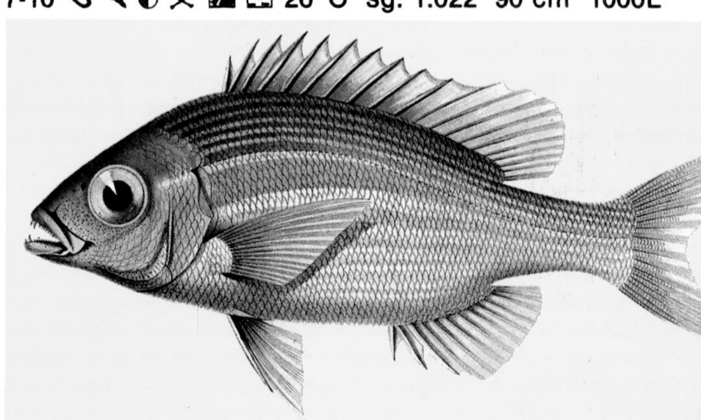

*Gnathodentex aurolineatus* 324
5, 7, 9 26°C sg: 1.022 45 cm 500L

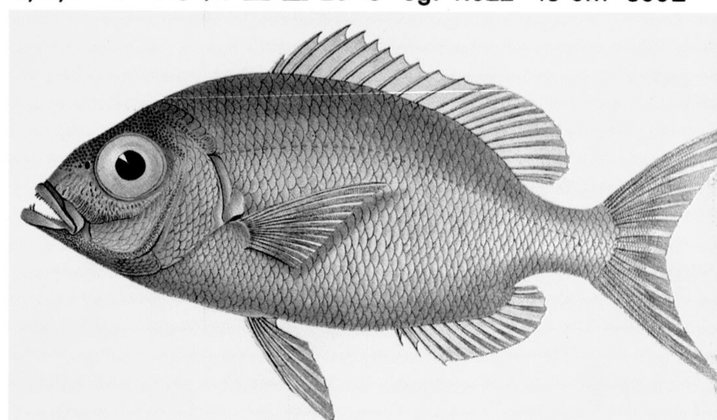

*Gymnocranius griseus* 324
5, 7, 9 26°C sg: 1.022 50 cm 500L

*Gymnocranius griseus* 324
5, 7, 9 26°C sg: 1.022 50 cm 500L

*Lethrinus nebulosus* 324
5, 7, 9-10 26°C sg: 1.022 100 cm 1000L

*Lethrinus ramak* 324
7-9 26°C sg: 1.022 60 cm 600L

*Lethrinus lentjan* 324
6-10 26°C sg: 1.022 50 cm 500L

*Lethrinus mahsena?* 324
7-10 26°C sg: 1.022 50 cm 500L

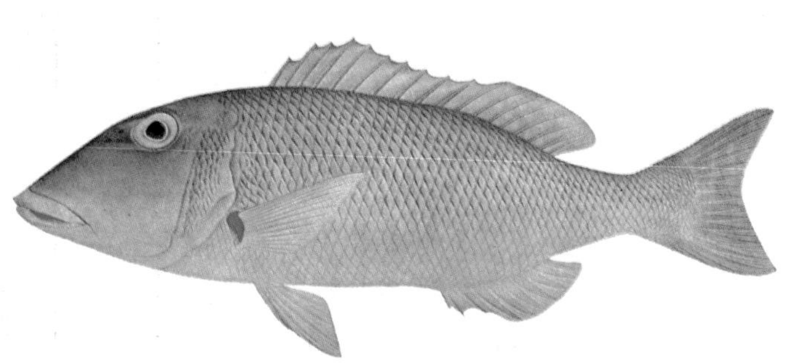

*Lethrinus xanthochilus* 324
7-10 26°C sg: 1.022 80 cm 800L

*Lethrinus rubrioperculatus* 324
5, 7, 9 26°C sg: 1.022 60 cm 600L

*Lethrinus hypselopterus* 324
7-9 26°C sg: 1.022 50 cm 500L

*Lethrinus miniatus* 324
7, 9-10 26°C sg: 1.022 100 cm 1000L

*Lethrinus chrysostomus* 324
7-8 26°C sg: 1.022 91 cm 1000L

*Lethrinus harak* 324
6-7, 9-10 26°C sg: 1.022 60 cm 600L

*Lethrinus variegatus* 324
5, 7, 9 26°C sg: 1.022 60 cm 600L

*Gnathodentex aurolineatus* 324
5, 7, 9 26°C sg: 1.022 45 cm 500L

*Lethrinus enigmaticus* 324
9 26°C sg: 1.022 40 cm 400L

*Lethrinus kallopterus* 324
7, 9 26°C sg: 1.022 80 cm 800L

*Lethrinus variegatus* 324
5, 7, 9 26°C sg: 1.022 60 cm 600L

*Gnathodentex aurolineatus* 324
5, 7, 9 26°C sg: 1.022 45 cm 500L

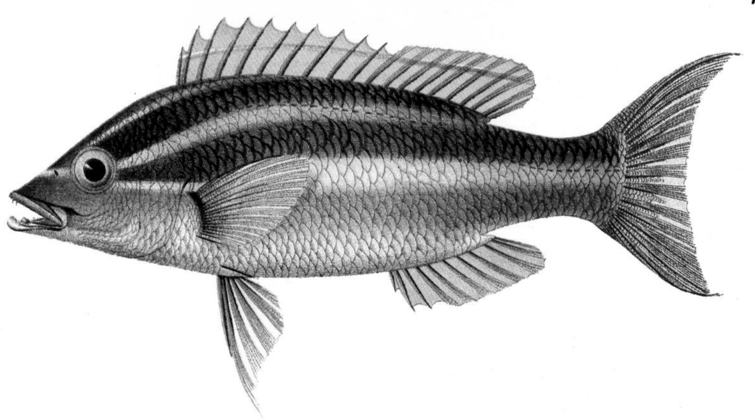

*Pentapodus caninus* 325
7 26°C sg: 1.022 28 cm 300L

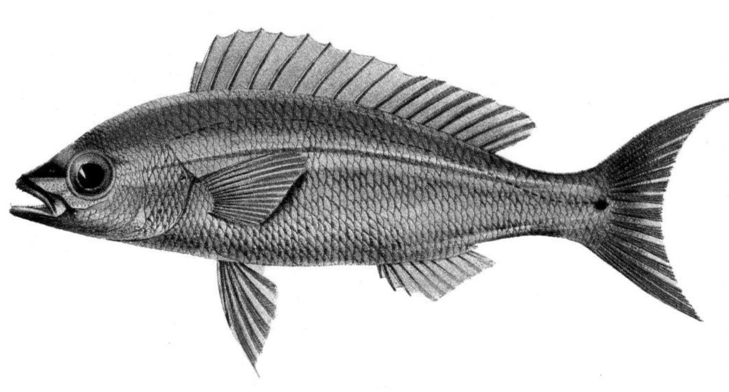

*Pentapodus setosus* 325
7-8, 12 26°C sg: 1.022 35 cm 400L

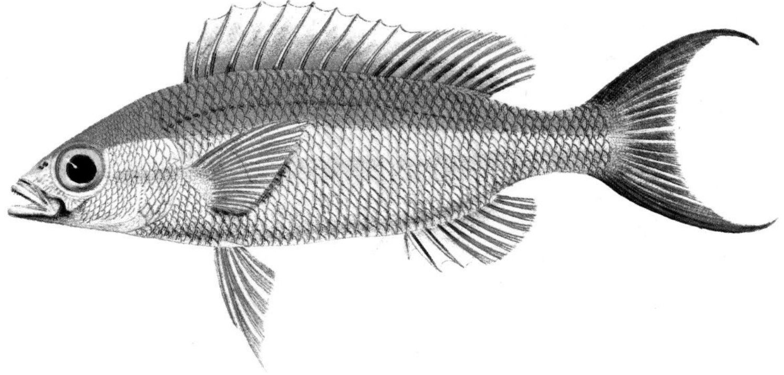

*Pentapodus microdon* 325
7 26°C sg: 1.022 20 cm 200L

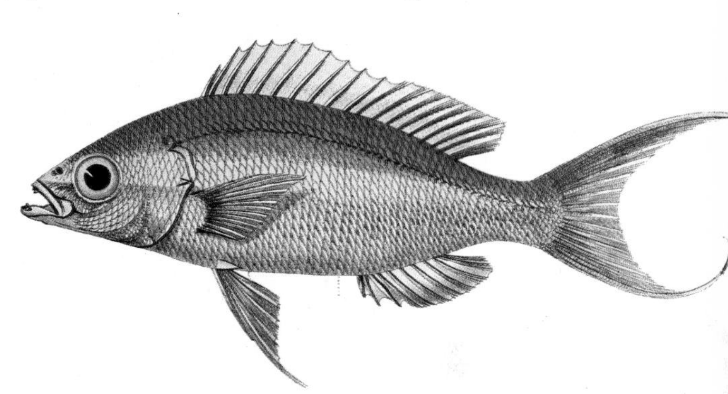

*Pentapodus macrurus* 325
7 26°C sg: 1.022 35 cm 400L

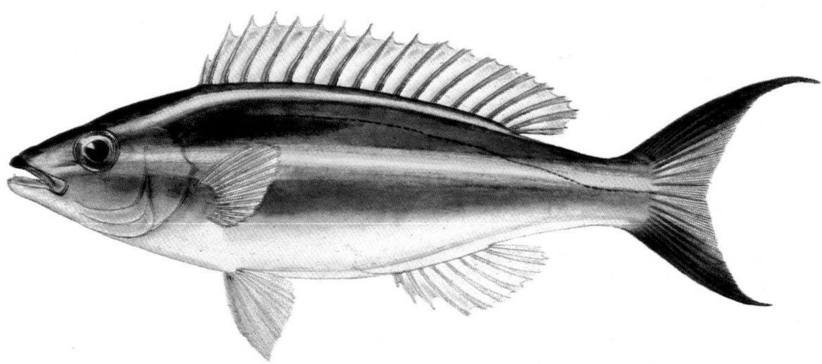

*Pentapodus nemurus* 325
7 26°C sg: 1.022 46 cm 500L

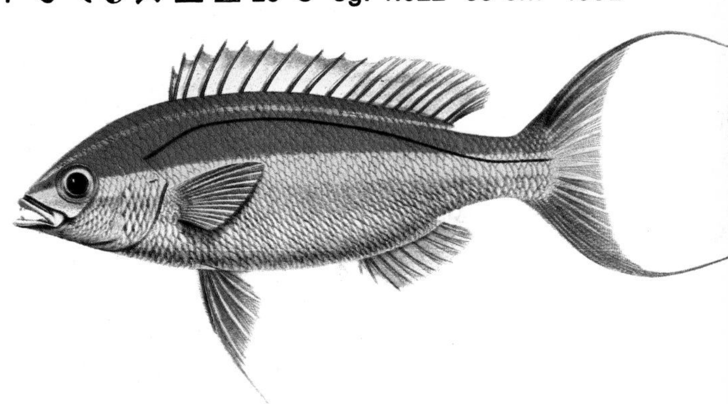

*Pentapodus nemurus* 325
7 26°C sg: 1.022 46 cm 500L

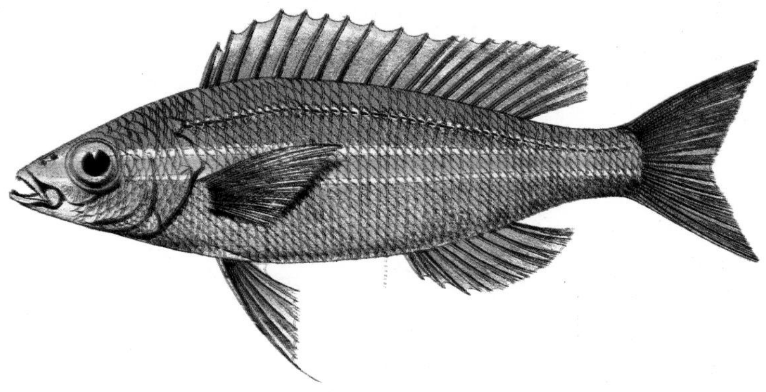

*Pentapodus hellmuthi* 325
7 26°C sg: 1.022 20 cm 200L

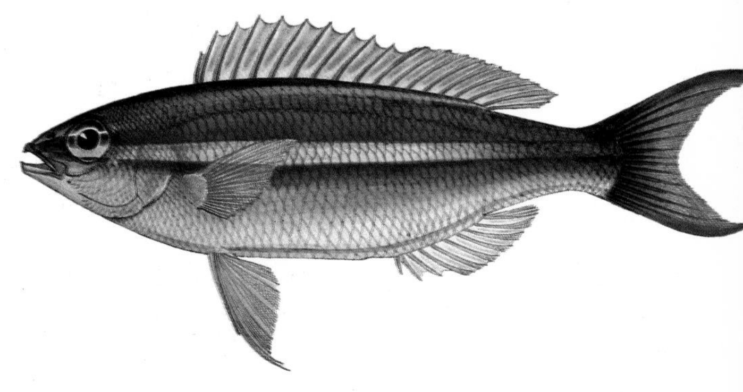

*Pentapodus* sp. 325
7 26°C sg: 1.022 35 cm 400L

*Pentapodus caninus* 325
7 26°C sg: 1.022 28 cm 300L

*Pentapodus vitta* 325
7-8, 12 26°C sg: 1.022 14 cm 150L

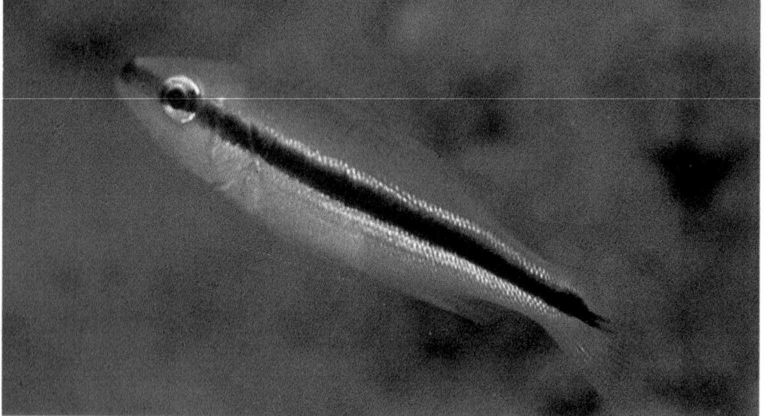

*Pentapodus* sp. 325
7-8 26°C sg: 1.022 25 cm 300L

*Pentapodus* sp. 325
8 26°C sg: 1.022 20 cm 200L

*Pentapodus nemurus* 325
7 26°C sg: 1.022 46 cm 500L

*Pentapodus porosus* 325
7 26°C sg: 1.022 25 cm 300L

*Pentapodus setosus* 325
7-8, 12 26°C sg: 1.022 35 cm 400L

*Pentapodus* sp. 325
7 26°C sg: 1.022 20 cm 200L

*Pentapodus vitta* 325
7-8, 12 26°C sg: 1.022 14 cm 150L

*Scolopsis bilineatus* 325
7, 9 26°C sg: 1.022 25 cm 300L

*Scolopsis bimaculatus* 325
9-10 26°C sg: 1.022 30 cm 300L

*Scolopsis bimaculatus?*
9-10 26°C sg: 1.022 30 cm 300L

*Scolopsis frenatus* 325
9 26°C sg: 1.022 31 cm 300L

*Scolopsis frenatus*
9 26°C sg: 1.022 31 cm 300L

*Scolopsis ciliatus* 325
7 26°C sg: 1.022 20 cm 200L

*Scolopsis vosmeri* 325
7-10 26°C sg: 1.022 25 cm 300L

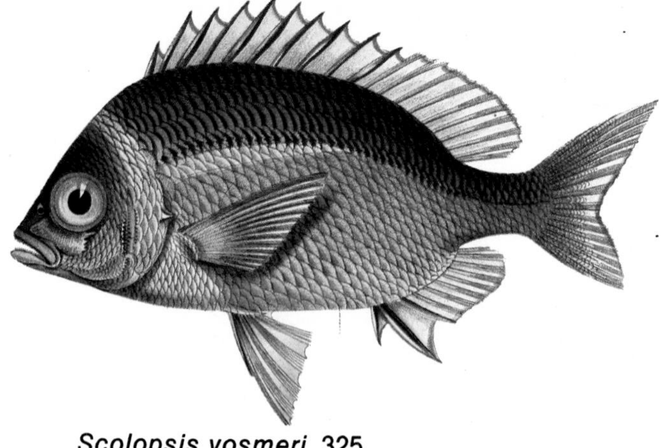

*Scolopsis vosmeri* 325
7-10 ◐ ♥ 26°C sg: 1.022 25 cm 300L

*Scolopsis vosmeri* 325
7-10 ◐ ♥ 26°C sg: 1.022 25 cm 300L

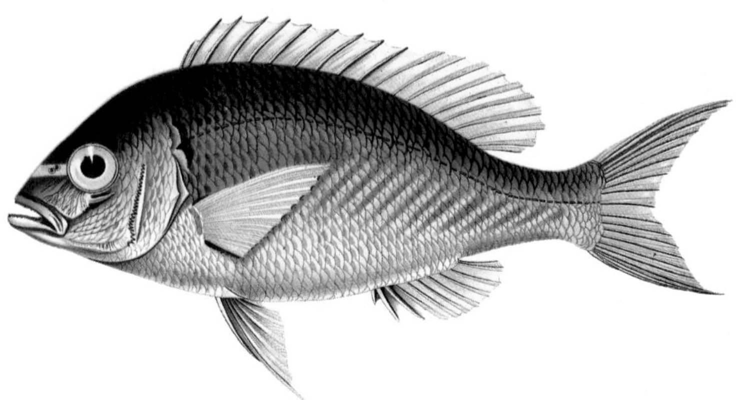

*Scolopsis monogramma* 325
7 ◐ ♥ 26°C sg: 1.022 31 cm 300L

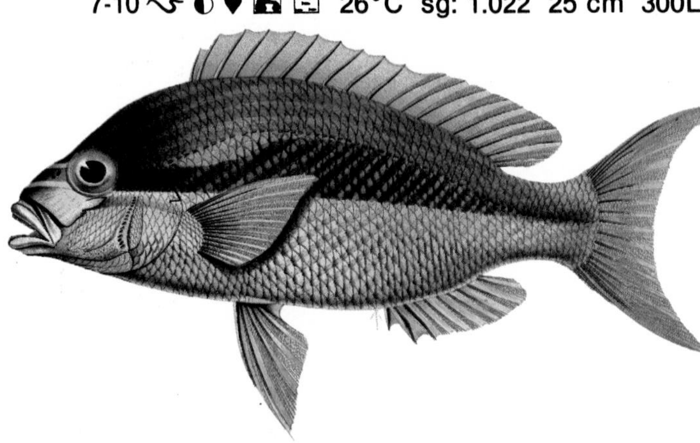

*Scolopsis dubiosus* 325
7 ◐ ♥ 26°C sg: 1.022 40 cm 400L

*Scolopsis bilineatus* 325
7 ◐ ♥ 26°C sg: 1.022 25 cm 300L

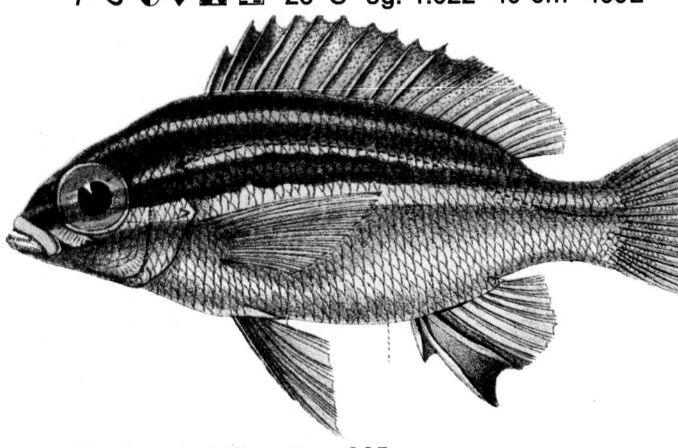

*Scolopsis bilineatus* 325
7-8 ◐ ♥ 26°C sg: 1.022 25 cm 300L

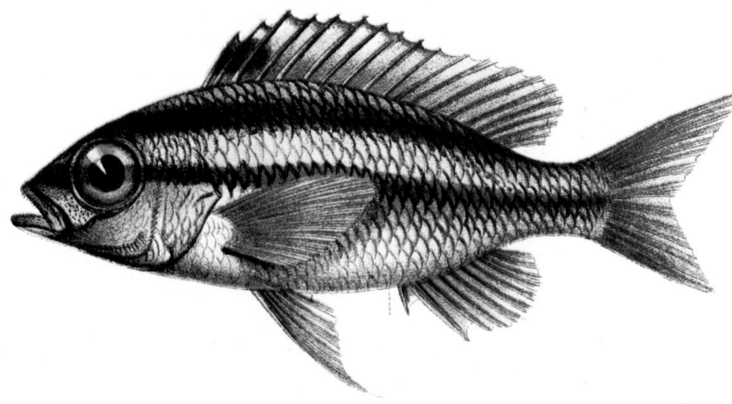

*Scolopsis leucotaenia* 325
7, 9 ◐ ♥ 26°C sg: 1.022 12 cm 100L

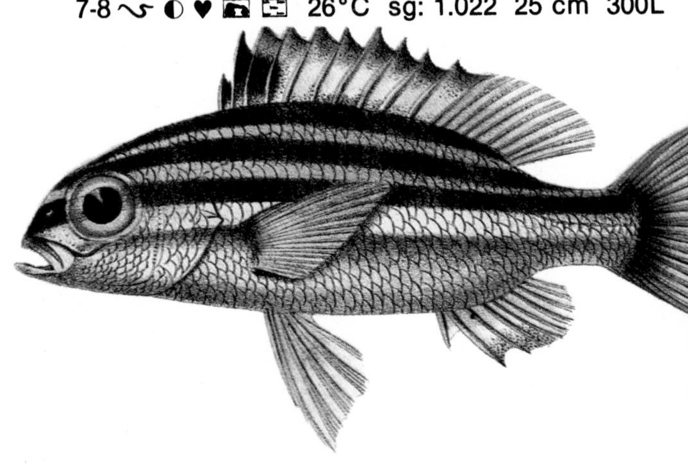

*Scolopsis bleekeri* 325
8 ◐ ♥ 26°C sg: 1.022 25 cm 300L

*Pentapodus vitta* 325
7-8, 12 26°C sg: 1.022 14 cm 150L

*Scolopsis bimaculatus* 325
9-10 26°C sg: 1.022 30 cm 300L

*Scolopsis frenatus* 325
9 26°C sg: 1.022 31 cm 300L

*Scolopsis ciliatus* 325
7 26°C sg: 1.022 20 cm 200L

*Scolopsis bilineatus* 325
7, 9 26°C sg: 1.022 25 cm 300L

*Scolopsis bimaculatus?*
9-10 26°C sg: 1.022 30 cm 300L

*Scolopsis frenatus*
9 26°C sg: 1.022 31 cm 300L

*Scolopsis vosmeri* 325
7-10 26°C sg: 1.022 25 cm 300L

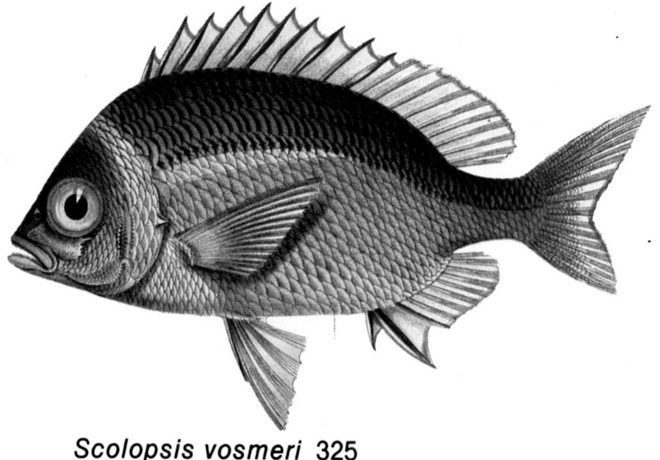

*Scolopsis vosmeri* 325
7-10 ~ ◐ ♥ 26°C sg: 1.022 25 cm 300L

*Scolopsis vosmeri* 325
7-10 ~ ◐ ♥ 26°C sg: 1.022 25 cm 300L

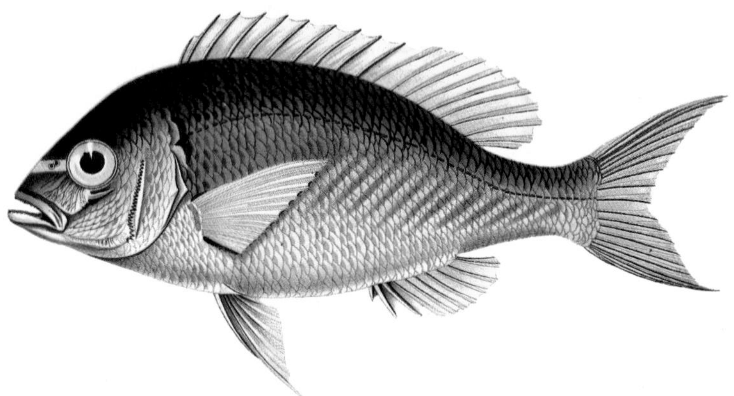

*Scolopsis monogramma* 325
7 ~ ◐ ♥ 26°C sg: 1.022 31 cm 300L

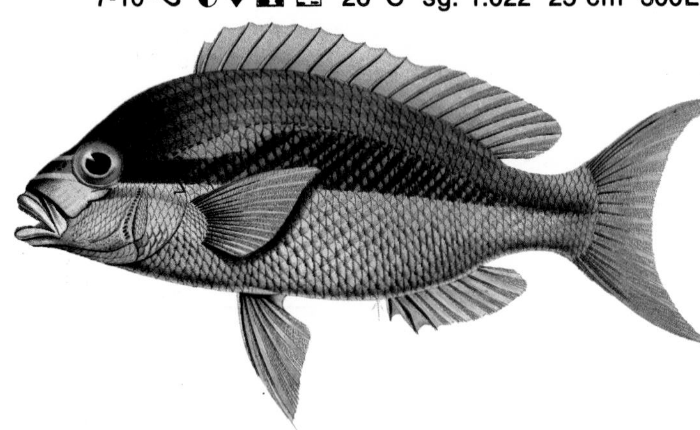

*Scolopsis dubiosus* 325
7 ~ ◐ ♥ 26°C sg: 1.022 40 cm 400L

*Scolopsis bilineatus* 325
7 ~ ◐ ♥ 26°C sg: 1.022 25 cm 300L

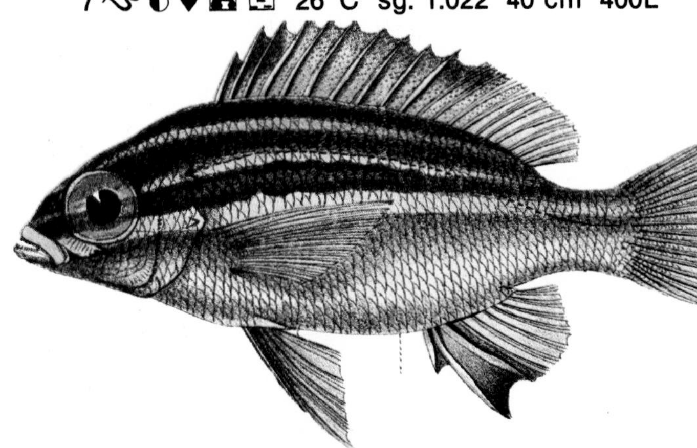

*Scolopsis bilineatus* 325
7-8 ~ ◐ ♥ 26°C sg: 1.022 25 cm 300L

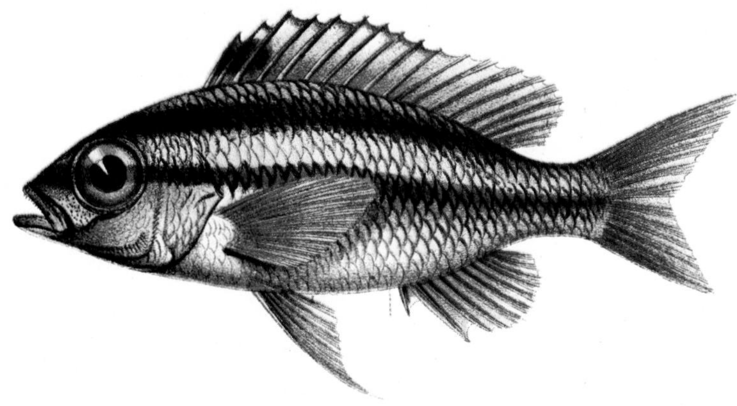

*Scolopsis leucotaenia* 325
7, 9 ~ ◐ ♥ 26°C sg: 1.022 12 cm 100L

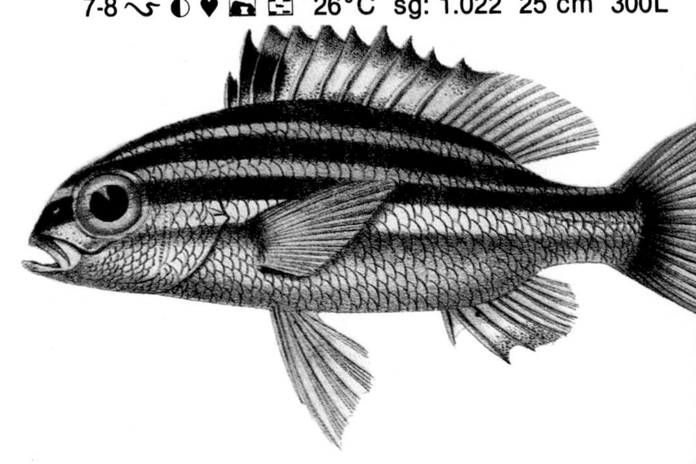

*Scolopsis bleekeri* 325
8 ~ ◐ ♥ 26°C sg: 1.022 25 cm 300L

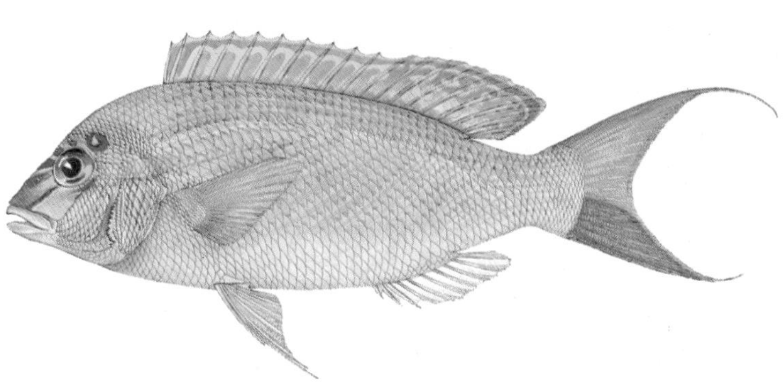

*Scolopsis temporalis* 325
7 26°C sg: 1.022 33 cm 400L

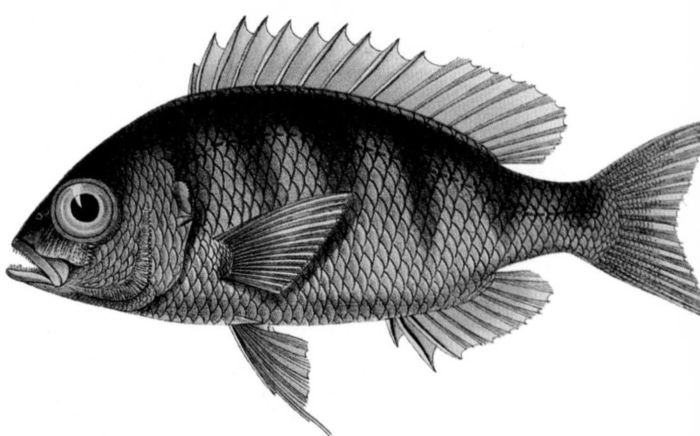

*Scolopsis inermis* 325
7-9 26°C sg: 1.022 30 cm 300L

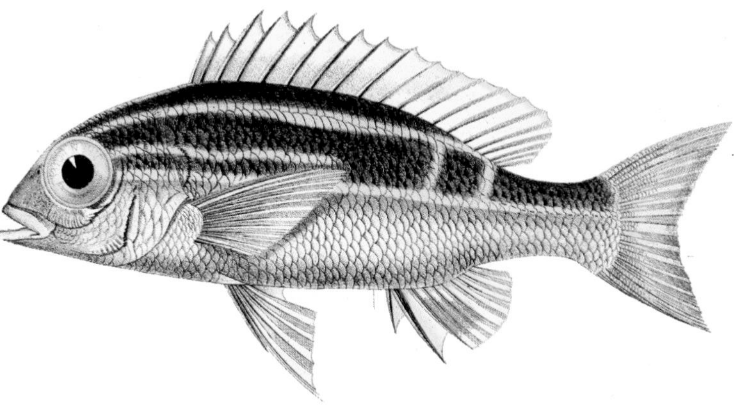

*Scolopsis cancellatus* 325
7 26°C sg: 1.022 25 cm 300L

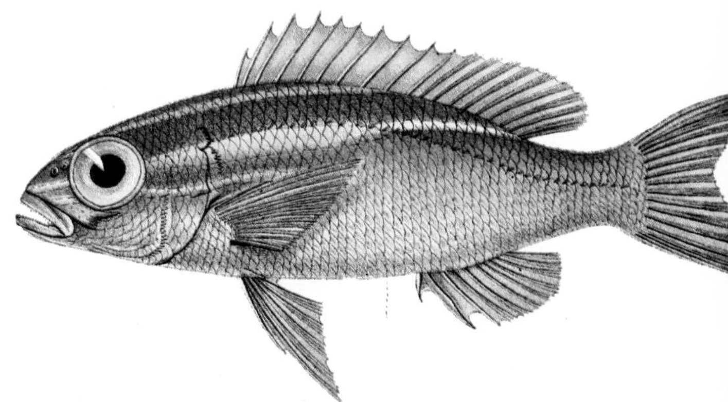

*Scolopsis trilineatus* 325
7 26°C sg: 1.022 20 cm 200L

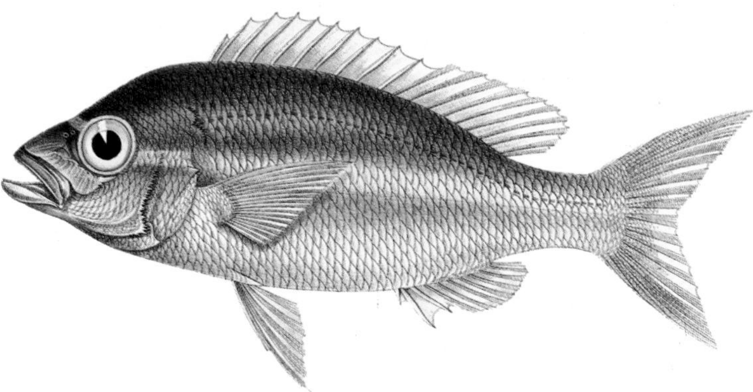

*Scolopsis personatus* 325
7 26°C sg: 1.022 20 cm 200L

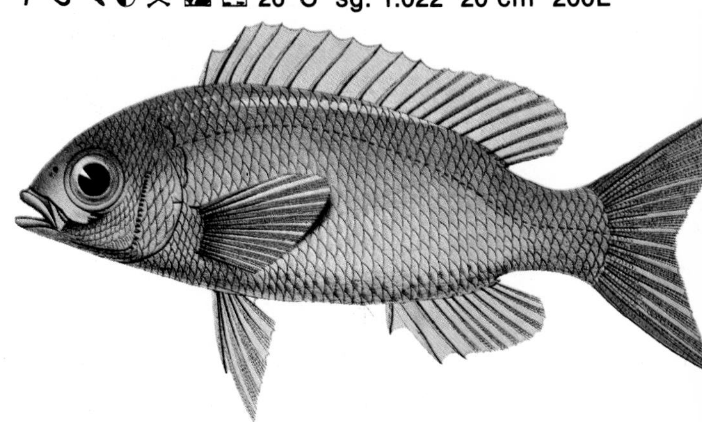

*Scolopsis ciliatus* 325
7 26°C sg: 1.022 20 cm 200L

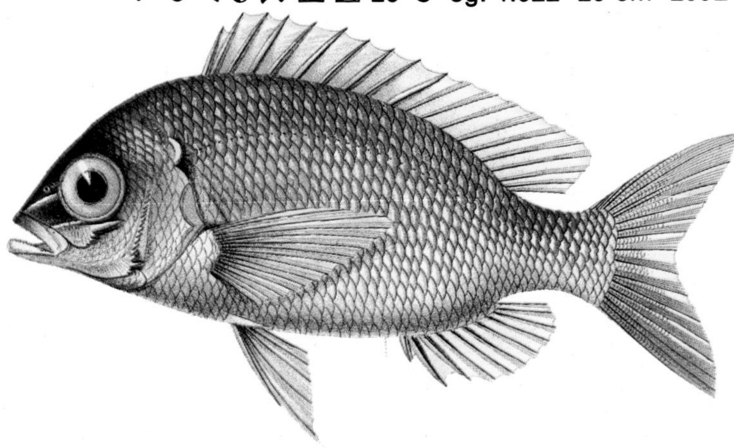

*Scolopsis margaritifera* 325
7 26°C sg: 1.022 25 cm 300L

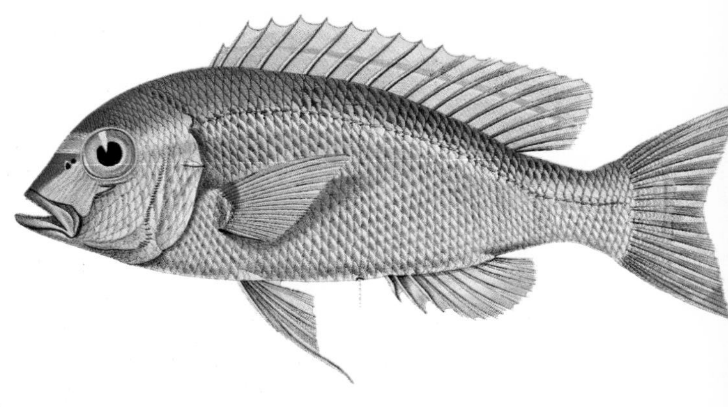

*Scolopsis taeniopterus* 325
7 26°C sg: 1.022 25 cm 300L

*Scolopsis dubiosus* 325
7 ~ ◐ ♥ 26°C sg: 1.022 40 cm 400L

*Scolopsis monogramma* 325
7 ~ ◐ ♥ 26°C sg: 1.022 31 cm 300L

*Scolopsis bilineatus* 325
7-8 ~ ◐ ♥ 26°C sg: 1.022 25 cm 300L

*Scolopsis bilineatus* 325
7 ~ ◐ ♥ 26°C sg: 1.022 25 cm 300L

*Scolopsis xenochrous* 325
7 ~ ◐ ♥ 26°C sg: 1.022 11 cm 100L

*Scolopsis bleekeri* 325
8 ~ ◐ ♥ 26°C sg: 1.022 25 cm 300L

*Scolopsis cancellatus* 325
7 ~ ◐ ♥ 26°C sg: 1.022 25 cm 300L

*Scolopsis cancellatus* 325
7 ~ ◐ ♥ 26°C sg: 1.022 25 cm 300L

*Nemipterus upeneoides* 325
7-8 ◐ ♥ 26°C sg: 1.022 16 cm 200L

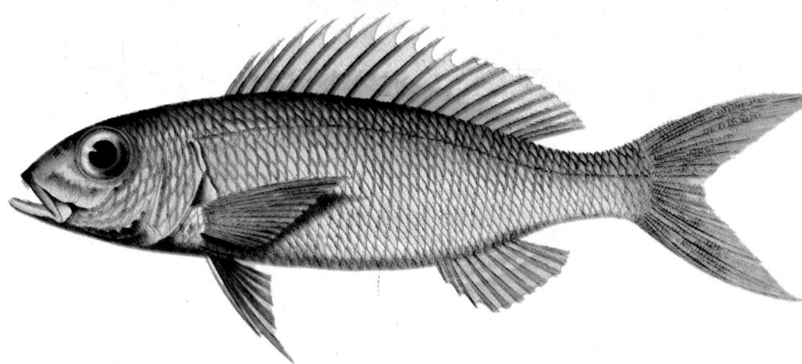

*Nemipterus tolu* 325
7, 9 ◐ ♥ 26°C sg: 1.022 30 cm 300L

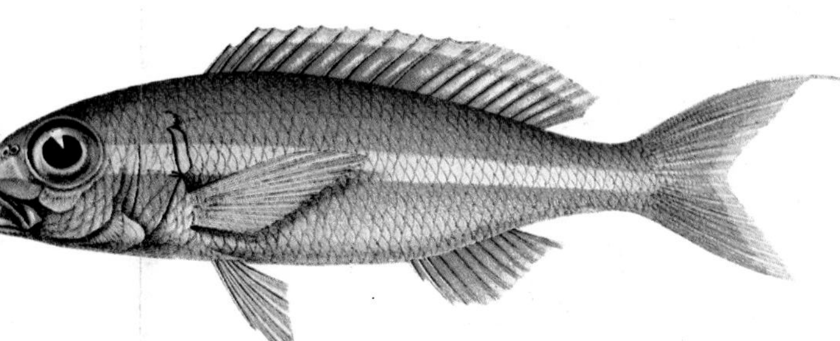

*Nemipterus balinensis* 325
7 ◐ ♥ 26°C sg: 1.022 15 cm 200L

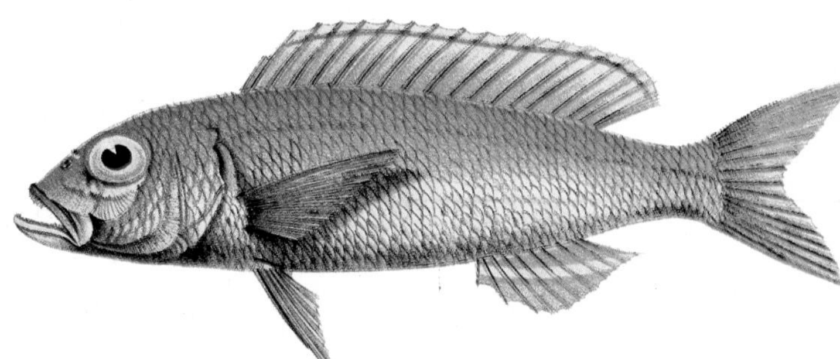

*Nemipterus zysron* 325
7 ◐ ♥ 26°C sg: 1.022 17 cm 200L

*Nemipterus ovenii* 325
7 ◐ ♥ 26°C sg: 1.022 19 cm 200L

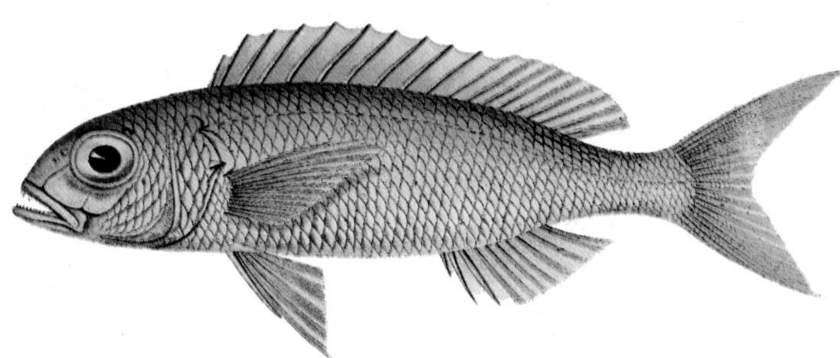

*Nemipterus metopias* 325
7 ◐ ♥ 26°C sg: 1.022 25 cm 300L

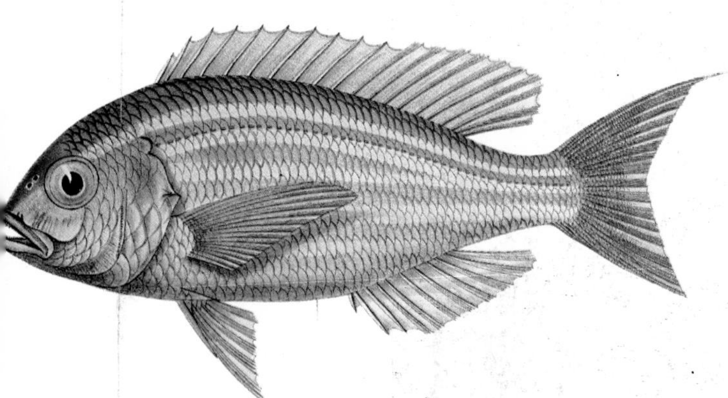

*Nemipterus japonicus* 325
7 ◐ ♥ 26°C sg: 1.022 30 cm 300L

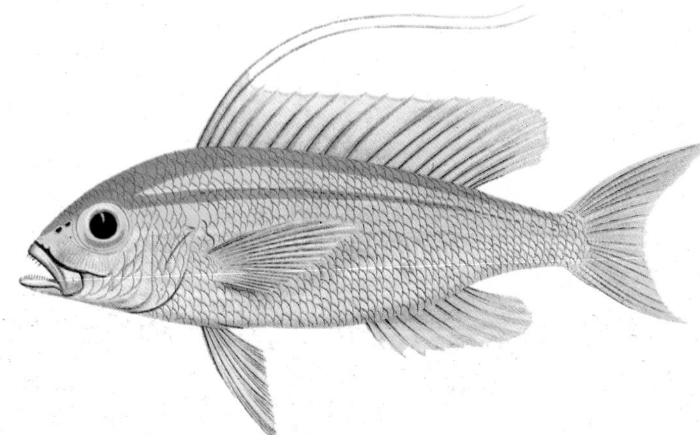

*Nemipterus nematophorus* 325
7 ◐ ♥ 26°C sg: 1.022 25 cm 300L

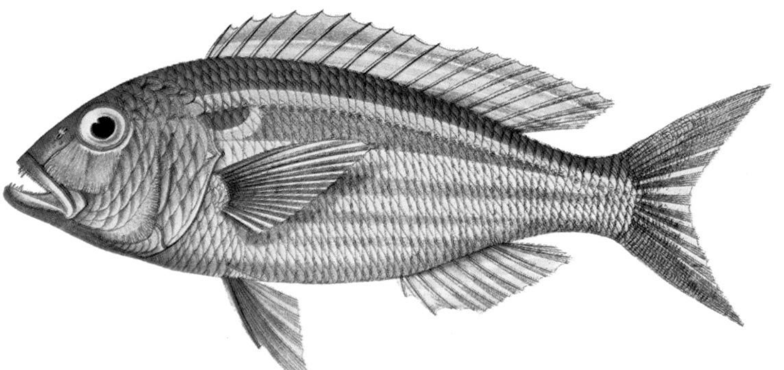

*Nemipterus hexodon* 325
7 ∿ ◐ ♥ 26°C sg: 1.022 30 cm 300L

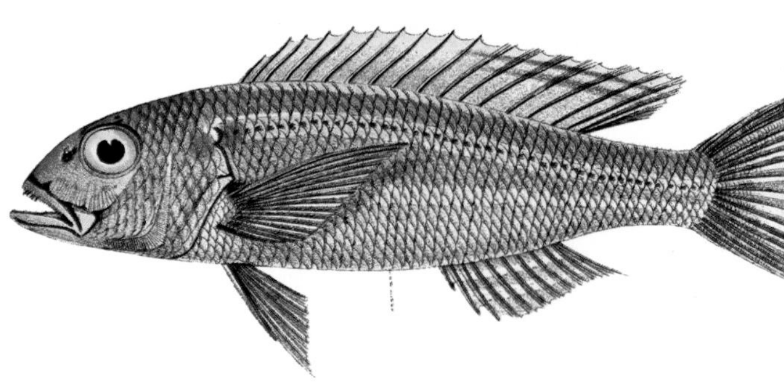

*Nemipterus mesoprion* 325
7, 9 ∿ ◐ ♥ 26°C sg: 1.022 20 cm 200L

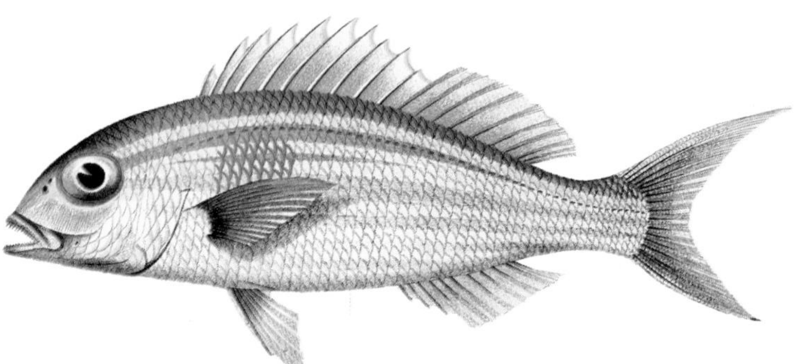

*Nemipterus tolu* 325
7, 9 ∿ ◐ ♥ 26°C sg: 1.022 30 cm 300L

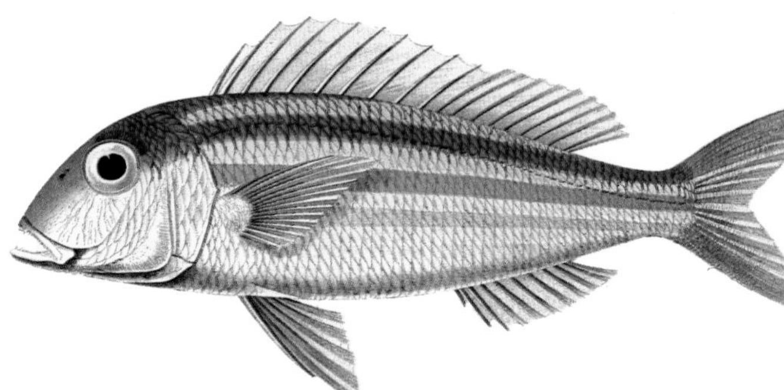

*Nemipterus peronii* 325
7, 9, 10 ∿ ◐ ♥ 26°C sg: 1.022 25 cm 300L

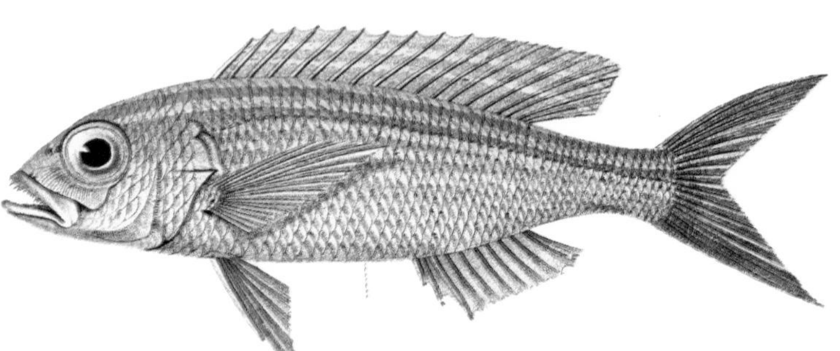

*Nemipterus sumbawensis* 325
7 ∿ ◐ ♥ 26°C sg: 1.022 16 cm 200L

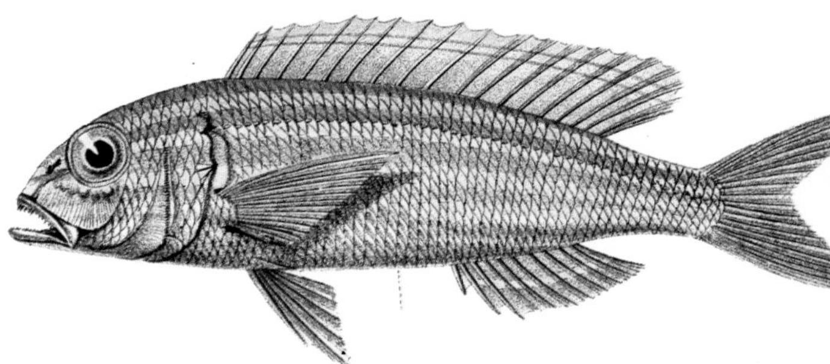

*Nemipterus tambuloides* 325
7 ∿ ◐ ♥ 26°C sg: 1.022 30 cm 300L

*Nemipterus gracilis* 325
7 ∿ ◐ ♥ 26°C sg: 1.022 18 cm 200L

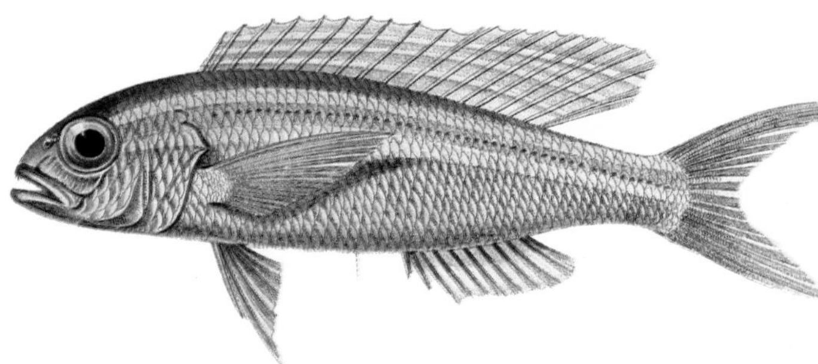

*Nemipterus marginatus* 325
7 ∿ ◐ ♥ 26°C sg: 1.022 30 cm 300L

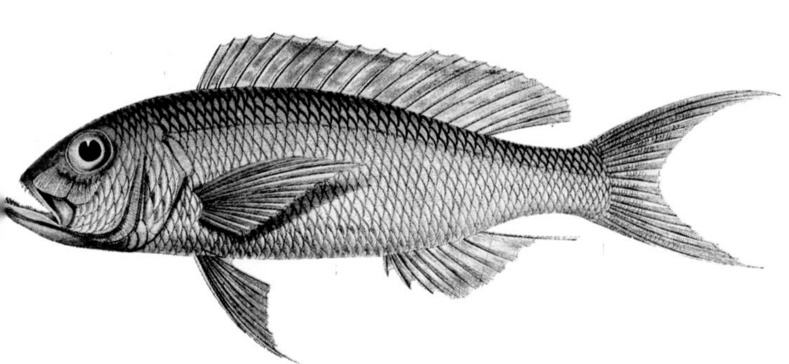

*Nemipterus hexodon* 325
7 ◐ ♥ 26°C sg: 1.022 30 cm 300L

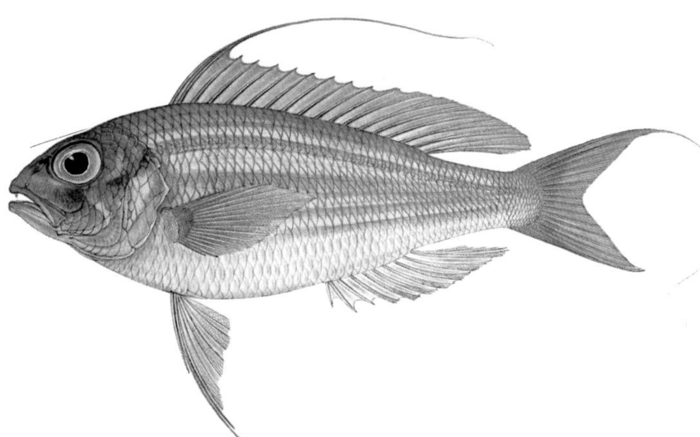

*Nemipterus nematophorus* 325
7 ◐ ♥ 26°C sg: 1.022 25 cm 300L

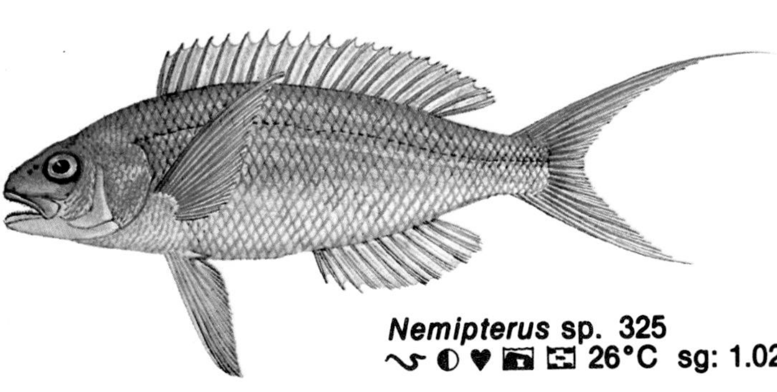

*Nemipterus* sp. 325
◐ ♥ 26°C sg: 1.022

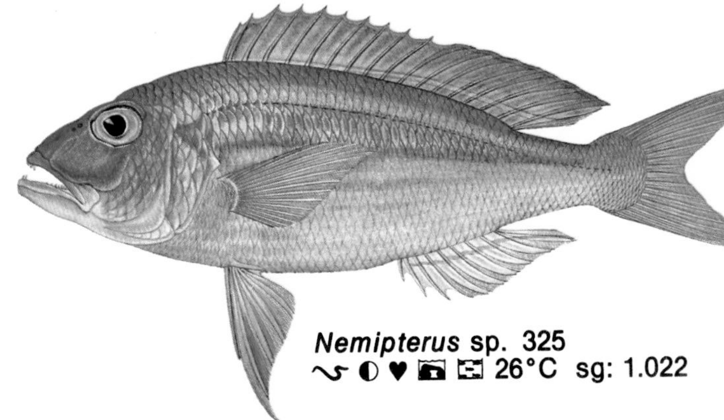

*Nemipterus* sp. 325
◐ ♥ 26°C sg: 1.022

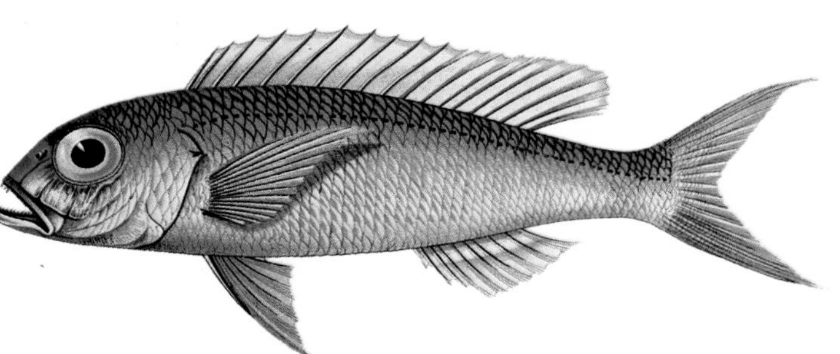

*Nemipterus nemurus* 325
7 ◐ ♥ 26°C sg: 1.022 25 cm 300L

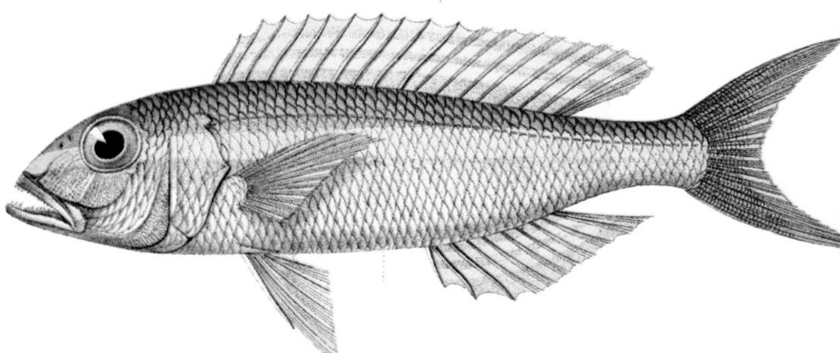

*Nemipterus celebicus* 325
7 ◐ ♥ 26°C sg: 1.022 20 cm 200L

*Pentapodus caninus* (juv.) 325
7, 9 ◐ ♥ 26°C sg: 1.022 28 cm 300L

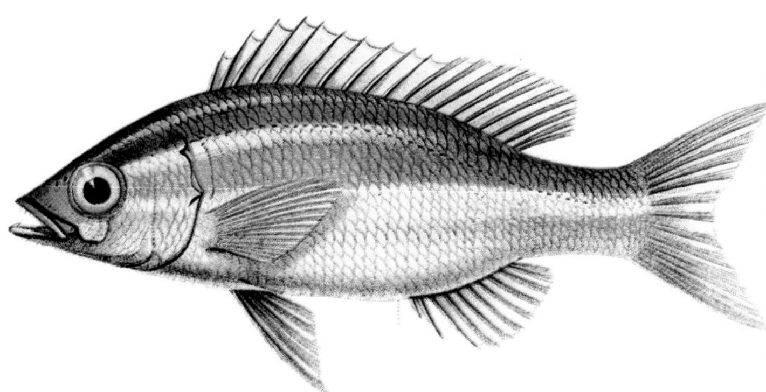

*Pentapodus bifasciatus* 325
7 ◐ ♥ 26°C sg: 1.022 20 cm 200L

*Scolopsis margaritifera* 325
7 26°C sg: 1.022 25 cm 300L

*Scolopsis margaritifera* 325
7 26°C sg: 1.022 25 cm 300L

*Nemipterus virgatus* 325
7, 9 26°C sg: 1.022 30 cm 300L

*Nemipterus hexodon* 325
7 26°C sg: 1.022 30 cm 300L

*Equetus acuminatus* 326
2 26°C sg: 1.022 23 cm 300L

*Equetus acuminatus* 326
2 26°C sg: 1.022 23 cm 300L

*Equetus acuminatus* 326
2 26°C sg: 1.022 23 cm 300L

*Equetus umbrosus* 326
2 26°C sg: 1.022 25 cm 300L

#242A

*Equetus umbrosus* 326
2 ◐ ♥ 26°C sg: 1.022 25 cm 300L

*Equetus punctatus* 326
2 ◐ ♥ 26°C sg: 1.022 25 cm 300L

*Equetus lanceolatus* 326
2 26°C sg: 1.022 25 cm 300L

*Equetus punctatus* 326
2 26°C sg: 1.022 25 cm 300L

*Equetus viola* 326
3 26°C sg: 1.022 25 cm 300L

*Equetus punctatus* 326
2 26°C sg: 1.022 25 cm 300L

*Equetus lanceolatus* (juv.) 326
2 26°C sg: 1.022 25 cm 300L

*Equetus punctatus* 326
2 26°C sg: 1.022 25 cm 300L

*Equetus viola* 326
3 26°C sg: 1.022 25 cm 300L

*Equetus viola* 326
3 26°C sg: 1.022 25 cm 300L

*Menticirrhus undulatus* 326
3 ◐ ♥ 26°C sg: 1.022 71 cm 800L

*Umbrina roncador* 326
3 ◐ ♥ 26°C sg: 1.022 51 cm 500L

*Roncador stearnsi* 326
3 ◐ ♥ 26°C sg: 1.022 69 cm 800L

*Genyonemus lineatus* 326
3 ◐ ♥ 26°C sg: 1.022 41 cm 400L

*Nibea mitsukurii* 326
7 ◐ ♥ 26°C sg: 1.022 75 cm 800L

*Odontoscion dentex* 326
2 ◐ ♥ 26°C sg: 1.022 20 cm 200L

*Johnius diacanthus* 326
8 ◐ ♥ 26°C sg: 1.022 150 cm 2500L

*Bairdiella batabana* 326
2 ◐ ♥ 26°C sg: 1.022 20 cm 200L

#245

*Parupeneus atrocingulatus* 327
6-7 ◐ ♥ 26°C sg: 1.022 25 cm 300L

*Upeneichthys porosus* 327
8, 11-12 ◐ ♥ 26°C sg: 1.022 30 cm 300L

*Plectorhinchus pictus* 320
5, 7, 9-10 26°C sg: 1.022 90 cm 1000L

*Plectorhinchus pictus* 320
5, 7, 9-10 26°C sg: 1.022 90 cm 1000L

*Pomadasys commersoni* 320
9 26°C sg: 1.022 80 cm 800L

*Pomadasys* sp. 320
9 26°C sg: 1.022 35 cm 400L

*Parupeneus rubescens* 327
7-10 26°C sg: 1.022 42 cm 500L

*Parupeneus rubescens* 327
7-10 26°C sg: 1.022 42 cm 500L

*Parupeneus macronema* 327
7 26°C sg: 1.022 35 cm 400L

*Upeneus tragula* 327
7, 9 26°C sg: 1.022 25 cm 300L

*Upeneichthys lineatus* 327
11-12 ∿ ◐ ♥ ▭ ▭ 23°C sg: 1.024 35 cm 400L

*Upeneichthys porosus* 327
11, 12 ∿ ◐ ♥ ▭ ▭ 26°C sg: 1.022 25 cm 300L

*Upeneus bensasi* 327
5, 7, 9 ∿ ◐ ♥ ▭ ▭ 26°C sg: 1.022 20 cm 200L

*Upeneus moluccensis* 327
7, 9 ∿ ◐ ♥ ▭ ▭ 26°C sg: 1.022 23 cm 300L

*Upeneus tragula* 327
7, 9 ∿ ◐ ♥ ▭ ▭ 26°C sg: 1.022 25 cm 300L

*Upeneus vittatus* 327
7, 9-10 ∿ ◐ ♥ ▭ ▭ 26°C sg: 1.022 30 cm 300L

*Pseudupeneus grandisquamis* 327
3 ∿ ◐ ♥ ▭ ▭ 26°C sg: 1.022 30 cm 300L

*Pseudupeneus maculatus* 327
2 ∿ ◐ ♥ ▭ ▭ 26°C sg: 1.022 30 cm 300L

*Mulloides dentatus* 327
3 26°C sg: 1.022 30.5 cm 400L

*Mulloides pflugeri* 327
7 26°C sg: 1.022 30 cm 300L

*Parupeneus multifasciata* 327
7 26°C sg: 1.022 30 cm 300L

*Pseudupeneus prayensis* 327
13 26°C sg: 1.022 21 cm 200L

*Mulloides martinicus* 327
2 26°C sg: 1.022 40 cm 400L

*Mulloides flavolineatus* 327
7-10 26°C sg: 1.022 40 cm 400L

*Parupeneus atrocingulatus* 327
6-7 26°C sg: 1.022 25 cm 300L

*Parupeneus pleurostigma* 327
6-10 26°C sg: 1.022 25 cm 300L

*Parupeneus atrocingulatus* 327
6-7 26°C sg: 1.022 25 cm 300L

*Parupeneus cinnabarinus* 327
9-10 26°C sg: 1.022 28 cm 300L

*Parupeneus forsskalii* 327
9-10 26°C sg: 1.022 28 cm 300L

*Parupeneus indicus* 327
5-7 26°C sg: 1.022 40 cm 400L

*Parupeneus chrysopleuron* 327
7 26°C sg: 1.022 30 cm 300L

*Parupeneus cyclostomus* 327
7-10 26°C sg: 1.022 50 cm 500L

*Parupeneus pleurotaenia* 327
6-7 26°C sg: 1.022 35 cm 300L

*Parupeneus porphyreus* 327
6-7 26°C sg: 1.022 31 cm 300L

*Mulloides vanicolensis* 327
6-7, 9-10 26°C sg: 1.022 38 cm 400L

*Mulloides vanicolensis* 327
6-7, 9-10 26°C sg: 1.022 38 cm 400L

*Parupeneus barberinoides* 327
6-7 26°C sg: 1.022 25 cm 300L

*Parupeneus barberinus* 327
7-10 26°C sg: 1.022 50 cm 500L

*Parupeneus bifasciatus* 327
7 26°C sg: 1.022 40 cm 400L

*Parupeneus cyclostomus* 327
7, 9 26°C sg: 1.022 52 cm 500L

*Parupeneus cyclostomus* 327
7, 9 26°C sg: 1.022 52 cm 500L

*Upeneus sulphureus* 327
7-9 ∿ ◐ ♥ 26°C sg: 1.022 20 cm 200L

*Upeneus vittatus* 327
7, 9-10 ∿ ◐ ♥ 26°C sg: 1.022 30 cm 300L

*Upeneus tragula* 327
7, 9 ∿ ◐ ♥ 26°C sg: 1.022 25 cm 300L

*Upeneus moluccensis* 327
7 ∿ ◐ ♥ 26°C sg: 1.022 17 cm 200L

*Mulloides flavolineatus* 327
5, 7, 9-10 ∿ ◐ ♥ 26°C sg: 1.022 30 cm 300L

*Upeneus sundaicus* 327
7 ∿ ◐ ♥ 26°C sg: 1.022 22 cm 200L

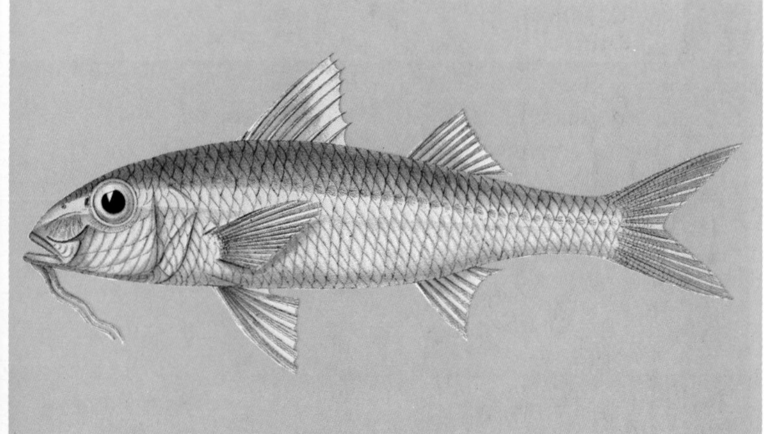

*Mulloides flavolineatus* 327
5, 7, 9-10 ∿ ◐ ♥ 26°C sg: 1.022 30 cm 300L

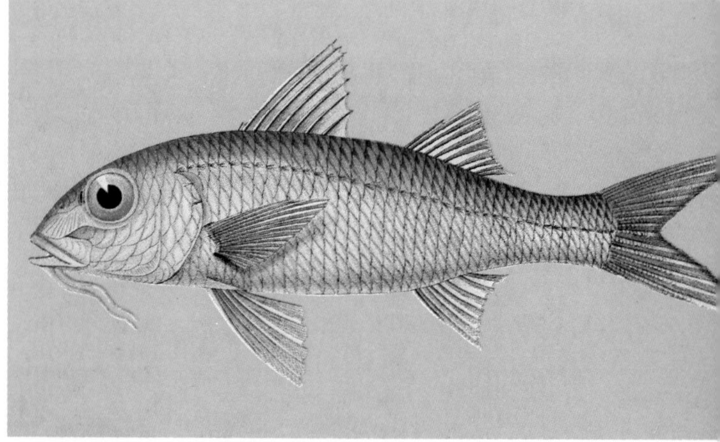

*Mulloides vanicolensis* 327
6-7, 9-10 ∿ ◐ ♥ 26°C sg: 1.022 38 cm 400L

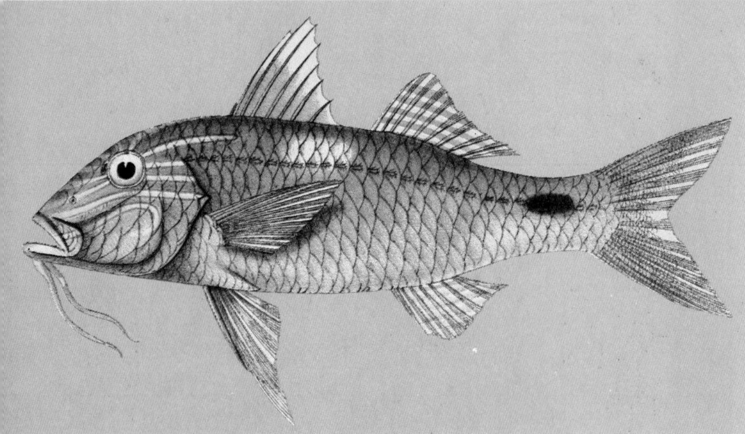

*Parupeneus indicus* 327
5-9 26°C sg: 1.022 40 cm 400L

*Parupeneus pleurostigma* 327
6-10 26°C sg: 1.022 25 cm 300L

*Parupeneus barberinus* 327
7-10 26°C sg: 1.022 50 cm 500L

*Parupeneus macronema* 327
7 26°C sg: 1.022 35 cm 400L

*Parupeneus pleurospilus* 327
7-10 26°C sg: 1.022 30 cm 300L

*Parupeneus pleurospilus* 327
7-10 26°C sg: 1.022 30 cm 300L

*Parupeneus barberinoides* 327
6-7 26°C sg: 1.022 25 cm 300L

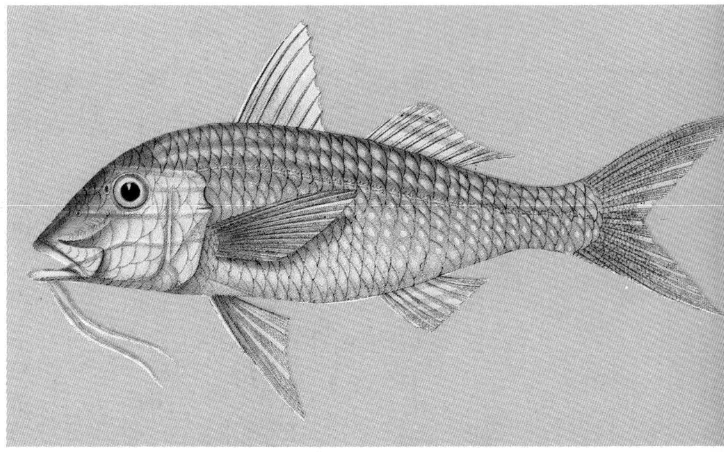

*Parupeneus luteus* 327
7 26°C sg: 1.022 30 cm 300L

#252

*Monodactylus argenteus* 328
6-10 26°C sg: 1.017 23 cm 250L

*Monodactylus argenteus* 328
6-10 26°C sg: 1.017 23 cm 250L

*Schuettea woodwardi* 328
12 24°C sg: 1.023 6 cm 100L

*Parapriacanthus unwini* 329
12 24°C sg: 1.023 7 cm 100L

*Monodactylus sebae* 328
9 26°C sg: 1.018 20 cm 200L

*Pempheris oualensis* 329
6-7, 9 26°C sg: 1.022 20 cm 200L

*Parapriacanthus dispar* 329
11-12 23°C sg: 1.024 8 cm 100L

*Pempheris analis* 329
12 24°C sg: 1.023 12 cm 100L

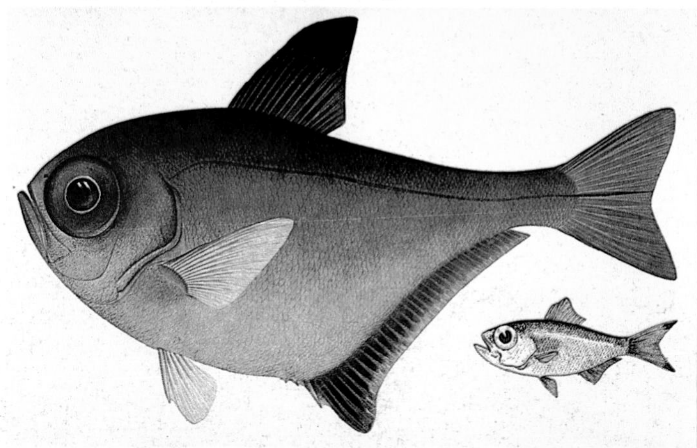

*Pempheris japonica* 329
5, 7 26°C sg: 1.022 18 cm 200L

*Pempheris multiradiata (juv.)* 329
12 23°C sg: 1.024 16 cm 80L

*Pempheris adspersa* 329
11-12 23°C sg: 1.023 16 cm 80L

*Pempheris* cf *japonicus* 329
5, 7 26°C sg: 1.022 18 cm 200L

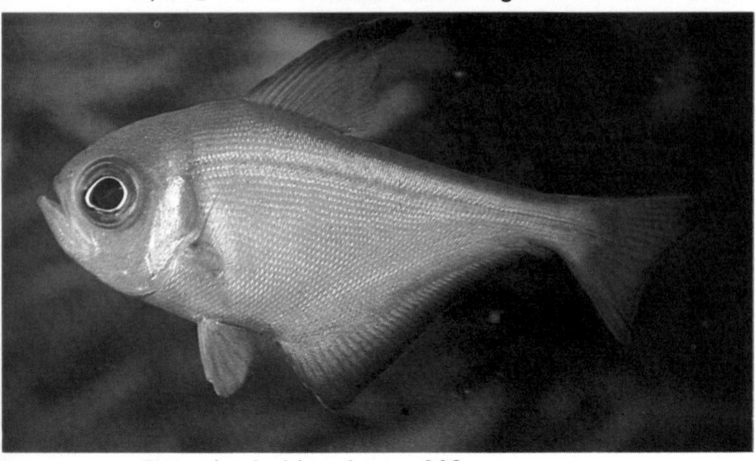

*Pempheris klunzinger* 329
12 26°C sg: 1.022 16 cm 200L

*Pempheris schomburgki* 329
2 25°C sg: 1.022 15 cm 200L

*Pempheris analis* 329
12 24°C sg: 1.023 12 cm 100L

*Pempheris compressa* 329
12 23°C sg: 1.022

*Pempheris schwenki* 329
7-9 26°C sg: 1.022 15 cm 200L

*Archamia mozambiquensis* 297
9 26°C sg: 1.022 8 cm 800L

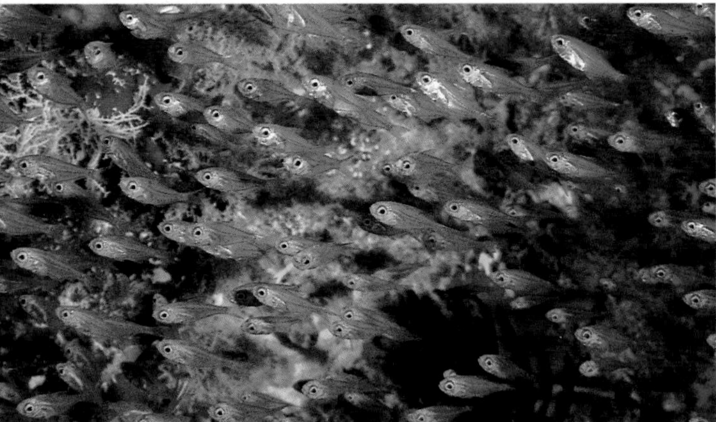

*Parapriacanthus ransonneti* 329
5-10 26°C sg: 1.022 75 cm 800L

*Pempheris vanicolensis* 329
7 26°C sg: 1.022 20 cm 200L

*Pempheris oualensis* 329
6-7, 9 26°C sg: 1.022 30 cm 300L

*Sphaeramia orbicularis* 297
7-9 26°C sg: 1.022 12 cm 150L

*Parapriacanthus ransonneti* 329
5-10 26°C sg: 1.022 75 cm 800L

*Pempheris vanicolensis* 329
7 26°C sg: 1.022 20 cm 200L

*Ambassis natalensis* 329
9 26°C sg: 1.022 9 cm 100L

#255

*Microcanthus strigatus* 334
5-7 🍸 ∿ ⚘ ◐ ♥ ▨ ☷ 26°C sg: 1.022 20 cm 200L

*#255A*

*Atypichthys latus* 334
11-12 24°C sg: 1.023 13 cm 150L

*Girella tricuspidatus* 334
11 23°C sg: 1.022 50 cm 500L

*Atypichthys strigatus* 334
11-12 ◐ ♥ 23°C sg: 1.024 15 cm 200L

*Atypichthys latus* 334
11-12 ◐ ♥ 24°C sg: 1.023 13 cm 150L

*Girella punctata* 334
5, 7 ◐ ♥ 24°C sg: 1.023 55 cm 600L

*Girella nigricans* 334
3 ◐ ♥ 26°C sg: 1.022 66 cm 800L

*Girella tephraeops* 334
12 ◐ ♥ 24°C sg: 1.023 15 cm 200L

*Girella simplicidens* 334
3 ◐ ♥ 26°C sg: 1.022 46 cm 500L

*Girella mezina* 334
6-7 ◐ ♥ 25°C sg: 1.022 11 cm 100L

*Hermosilla azurea* 334
3 ◐ ♥ 26°C sg: 1.022 44 cm 500L

*Tilodon sexfasciatum* 334
12 ◐ ♥ 23°C sg: 1.024 30 cm 300L

*Kyphosus cornelii* 334
12 ◐ ♥ 23°C sg: 1.024 38 cm 400L

*Girella zebra* 334
12 ◐ ♥ 23°C sg: 1.024 30 cm 300L

*Neatypus obliquus* 334
12 ◐ ♥ 23°C sg: 1.024 14 cm 150L

*Tilodon sexfasciatum* 334
12 ◐ ♥ 23°C sg: 1.024 30 cm 300L

*Kyphosus sydneyanus* 334
12 ◐ ♥ 23°C sg: 1.024 80 cm 1000L

*Microcanthus strigatus* 334
5-7 ◐ ♥ 26°C sg: 1.022 20 cm 200L

*Scorpis georgianus* 334
12 ◐ ♥ 23°C sg: 1.022 35 cm 400L

*Medialuna californiensis* 334
3 26°C sg: 1.022 48 cm 500L

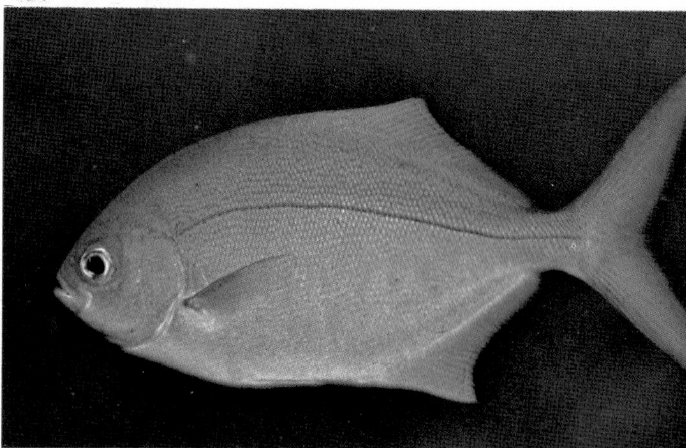

*Scorpis aequipinnis* 334
11 22°C sg: 1.024 40 cm 400L

*Kyphosus analogus* 334
3 26°C sg: 1.022 45 cm 500L

*Kyphosus elegans* 334
2 26°C sg: 1.022 38 cm 400L

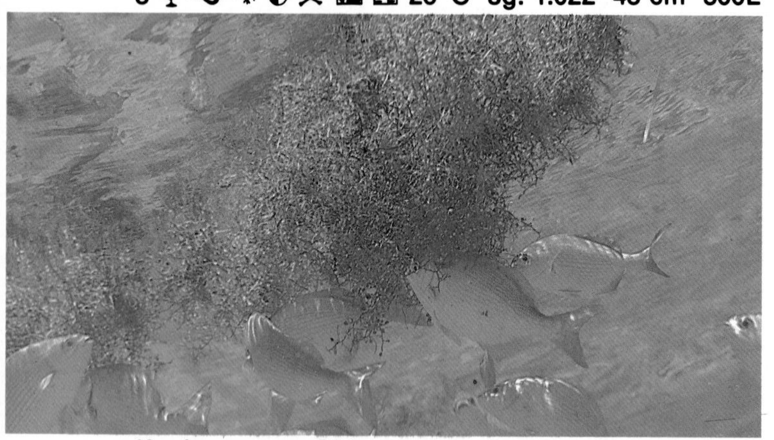

*Kyphosus* sp. 334
2 26°C sg: 1.022 32 cm 300L

*Kyphosus cinerascens* (golden form) 334
7-10 26°C sg: 1.022 50 cm 500L

*Kyphosus incisor* 334
2 26°C sg: 1.022 30 cm 300L

*Kyphosus sectatrix* 334
2 26°C sg: 1.022 35 cm 800L

*Kyphosus fuscus* 334
6 ◐ 26°C sg: 1.022 60 cm 600L

*Kyphosus gibsoni* 334
7 ◐ 26°C sg: 1.022 20 cm 200L

*Kyphosus fuscus* 334
6 ◐ 26°C sg: 1.022 60 cm 600L

*Kyphosus sydneyanus* 334
12 ◐ ♥ 23°C sg: 1.024 80 cm 1000L

*Scatophagus argus* 336
7, 9 ◐ 26°C sg: 1.015 35 cm 400L

*Scatophagus tetracanthus* 336
7, 9 ◐ ♥ 26°C sg: 1.022 40 cm 400L

*Selenotoca multifasciata* 336
7 ◐ 26°C sg: 1.015 40 cm 400L

*Scatophagus argus* 336
7, 9 ◐ ♥ 26°C sg: 1.015 35 cm 400L

*Chaetodipterus faber* 335
1-2 ◐ ♥ 26°C sg: 1.022 91 cm 1000L

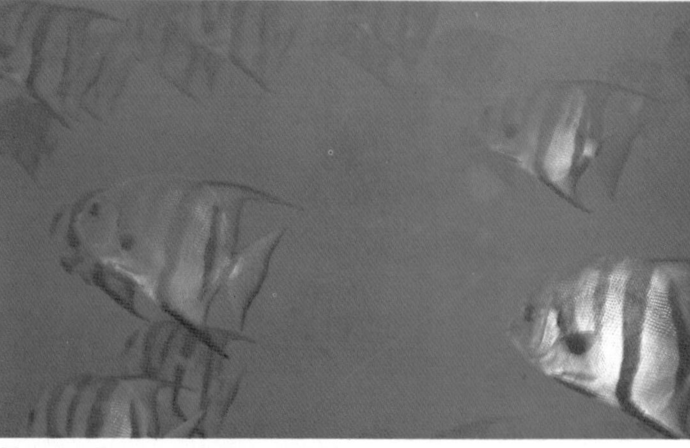

*Chaetodipterus faber* 335
1-2 ◐ ♥ 26°C sg: 1.022 91 cm 1000L

*Chaetodipterus zonatus* 335
3 ◐ ♥ 26°C sg: 1.022 65 cm 800L

*Drepane punctata* 335
7, 9 ◐ ♥ 26°C sg: 1.022 40 cm 400L

*Ephippus orbis* 335
7, 9 ◐ ♥ 26°C sg: 1.022 25 cm 300L

*Zabidius novemaculeatus* 335
7-8 ◐ ♥ 26°C sg: 1.022 20 cm 200L

*Platax orbicularis* 335
7-10 ◐ ♥ 26°C sg: 1.022 50 cm 500L

*Platax pinnatus* 335
7, 9-10 ◐ ♥ 26°C sg: 1.022 40 cm 400L

*Platax batavianus* 335
7-8 ~ ◐ ♥ ▨ ⊟ 26°C sg: 1.022 50 cm 500L

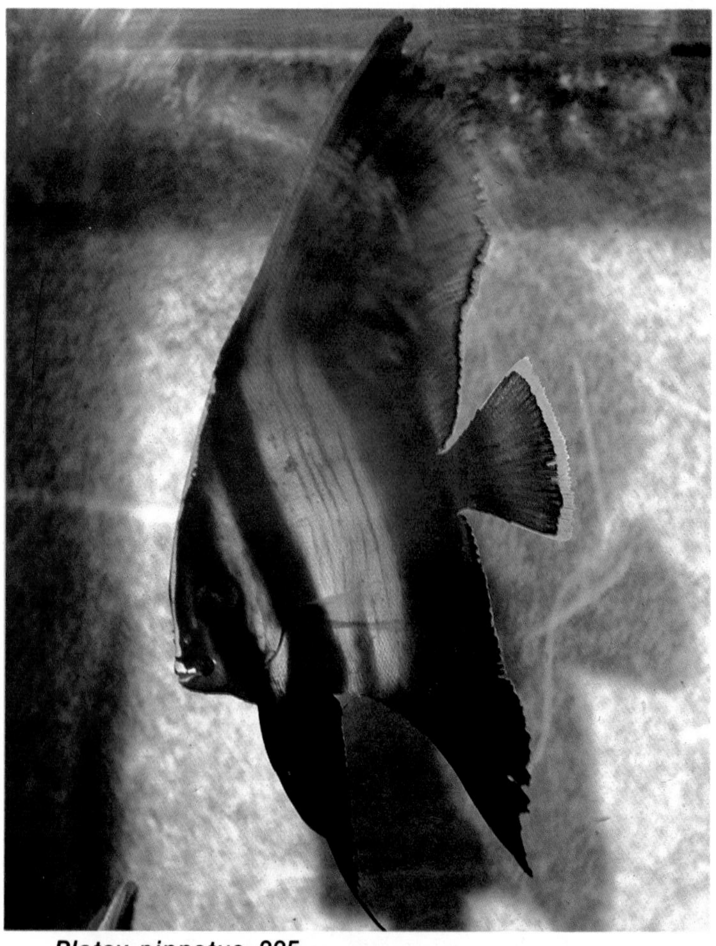

*Platax pinnatus* 335
7, 9-10 ♀ ~ ◐ ♥ ▣ ☰ 26°C sg: 1.022 40 cm 500L

*Platax pinnatus* 335
7, 9-10 ♀ ~ ◐ ♥ ▣ ☰ 26°C sg: 1.022 40 cm 500L

*Platax batavianus* 335
7-8 ♀ ~ ◐ ♥ ▣ ☰ 26°C sg: 1.022 50 cm 600L

*Platax orbicularis* 335
7-10 ♀ ~ ◐ ♥ ▣ ☰ 26°C sg: 1.022 50 cm 600L

*Platax orbicularis* 335
7-10 ♀ ~ ◐ ♥ ▣ ▤ 26°C sg: 1.022 50 cm 500L

*Enoplosus armatus* 340
12 ♥ 23°C sg: 1.024 12 cm 150L

*Pentaceropsis recurvirostris* 341
12 ♥ 23°C sg: 1.024 50 cm 500L

*Drepane punctata* 335
7, 9 ♥ 26°C sg: 1.022 40 cm 400L

*Platax teira* 335
7-10 ♥ 26°C sg: 1.022 50 cm 500L

*Platax teira* 335
7-10 ♥ 26°C sg: 1.022 50 cm 500L

*Platax teira* 335
7-10 ♥ 26°C sg: 1.022 50 cm 500L

*Chaetodon daedalma* 338
5, 7 ◐ ♥ 25°C sg: 1.022 15 cm 200L

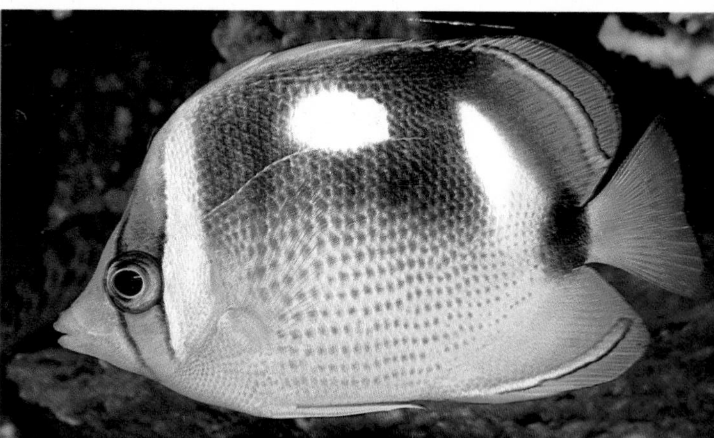

*Chaetodon quadrimaculatus* 338
6 ◐ ♥ 26°C sg: 1.022 15 cm 200L

*Chaetodon ocellatus* 338
2 ◐ ♥ 26°C sg: 1.022 19 cm 200L

*Chaetodon robustus* 338
13 ◐ ♥ 26°C sg: 1.022 15 cm 200L

*Zanclistius elevatus* 341
11 ◐ ♥ 22°C sg: 1.022 30 cm 300L

*Pentaceros japonicus* 341
7-8 ◐ ♥ 26°C sg: 1.022 25 cm 300L

*Evistias acutirostris* 341
5-6 ◐ ♥ 26°C sg: 1.022 55 cm 600L

*Evistias acutirostris* 341
5-6 ◐ ♥ 26°C sg: 1.022 55 cm 600L

#265

*Chaetodon declevis* 338
6 ~ ◐ ♥ ▨ ⊡ 26°C sg: 1.022 15 cm 200L

*Chaetodon argentatus* 338
7 ~ ◐ ♥ ▨ ⊡ 26°C sg: 1.022 13 cm 200L

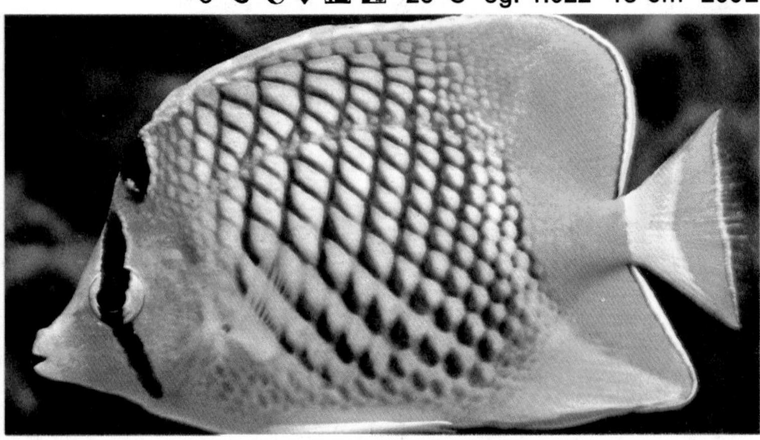

*Chaetodon xanthurus* 338
7 ~ ◐ ♥ ▨ ⊡ 26°C sg: 1.022 15 cm 200L

*Chaetodon mertensii* 338
6-8 ~ ◐ ♥ ▨ ⊡ 26°C sg: 1.022 14 cm 200L

*Chaetodon trifascialis* 338
6-10 ~ ◐ ♥ ▨ ⊡ 26°C sg: 1.022 15 cm 200L

*Chaetodon baronessa* 338
6-8 ~ ◐ ♥ ▨ ⊡ 26°C sg: 1.022 15 cm 200L

*Chaetodon trifasciatus* 338
6-10 ~ ◐ ♥ ▨ ⊡ 26°C sg: 1.022 17 cm 200L

*Chaetodon reticulatus* 338
6-7 ~ ◐ ♥ ▨ ⊡ 26°C sg: 1.022 18 cm 200L

*Chaetodon triangulum* 338
9 25°C sg: 1.022 14 cm 200L

*Chaetodon leucopleura* 338
9 26°C sg: 1.022 19 cm 200L

*Chaetodon paucifasciatus* 338
9-10 26°C sg: 1.023 15 cm 200L

*Chaetodon melannotus* 338
6-10 25°C sg: 1.022 17 cm 200L

*Chaetodon larvatus* 338
9, 10 26°C sg: 1.023 14 cm 200L

*Chaetodon trifascialis* 338
6-10 26°C sg: 1.022 15 cm 200L

*Chaetodon madagascariensis* 338
9 26°C sg: 1.022 15 cm 200L

*Chaetodon ocellicaudus* 338
6-7, 9 26°C sg: 1.022 13 cm 200L

*Chaetodon wiebeli* 338
7 26°C sg: 1.022 19 cm 200L

*Chaetodon auripes* 338
5, 7 26°C sg: 1.022 19 cm 200L

*Chaetodon flavirostris* 338
6, 8, 12 26°C sg: 1.022 18 cm 200L

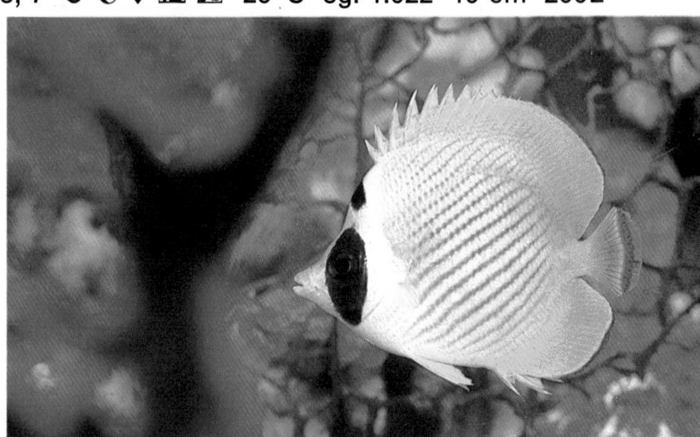

*Chaetodon adiergastos* 338
7 26°C sg: 1.022 19 cm 200L

*Chaetodon nigropunctatus* 338
9 26°C sg: 1.022 16 cm 200L

*Chaetodon mesoleucos* 338
10 26°C sg: 1.030 15 cm 200L

*Chaetodon selene* 338
7 26°C sg: 1.022 18 cm 200L

*Chaetodon gardneri* 338
9 26°C sg: 1.022 12 cm 200L

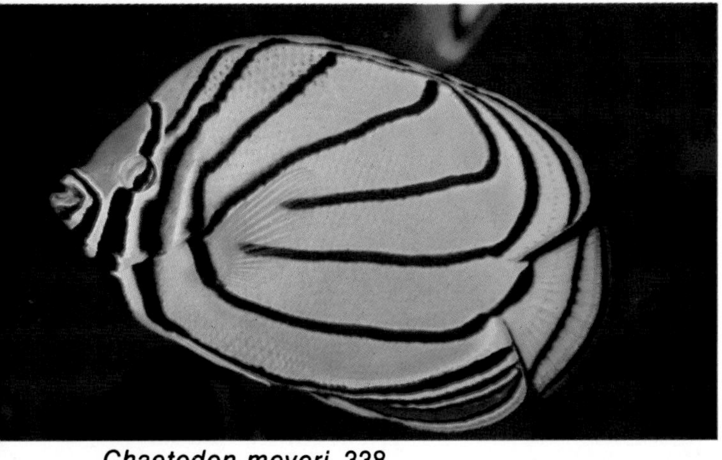

*Chaetodon meyeri* 338
6-7, 9 26°C sg: 1.022 18 cm 200L

*Chaetodon nigropunctatus* 338
9 26°C sg: 1.022 16 cm 200L

*Chaetodon lineolatus* 338
6-10 26°C sg: 1.022 29 cm 400L

*Chaetodon plebeius* 338
6-9 26°C sg: 1.022 19 cm 200L

*Chaetodon ornatissimus* 338
6-8 26°C sg: 1.022 19 cm 200L

*Chaetodon octofasciatus* 338
7-9 26°C sg: 1.022 13 cm 200L

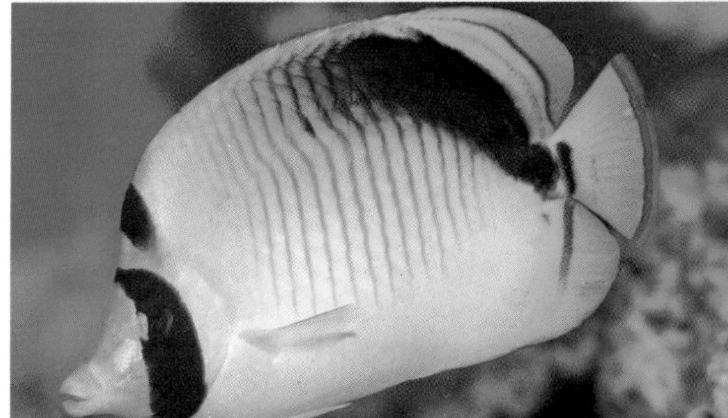

*Chaetodon oxycephalus* 338
7,9 26°C sg: 1.022 22 cm 300L

*Chaetodon plebeius* 338
6-9 26°C sg: 1.022 19 cm 200L

*Chaetodon aureofasciatus* 338
7-8 ◐ ♥ 26°C sg: 1.022 14 cm 200L

*Chaetodon blackburnii* 338
9 ∼ ◐ ♥ 26°C sg: 1.022 13 cm 200L

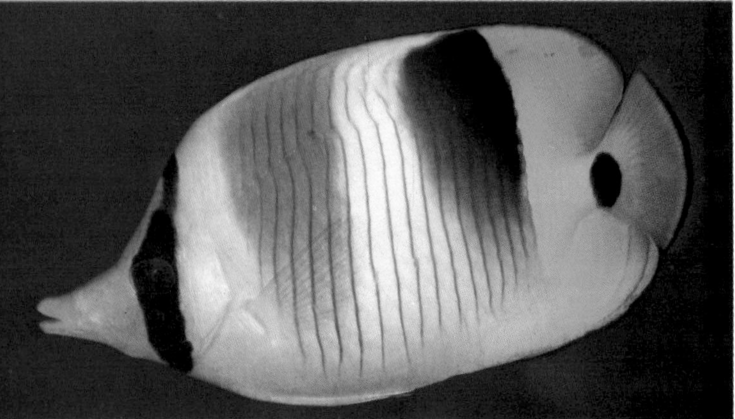

*Chaetodon ulietensis* 338
6-8 ∼ ◐ ♥ 26°C sg: 1.022 17 cm 200L

*Chaetodon falcula* 338
9 ∼ ◐ ♥ 26°C sg: 1.022 29 cm 400L

*Chaetodon fasciatus* 338
10 ∼ ◐ ♥ 26°C sg: 1.030 20 cm 200L

*Chaetodon lunula* 338
6-9 ∼ ◐ ♥ 26°C sg: 1.022 21 cm 200L

*Chaetodon flavocoronatus* 338
6 ∼ ◐ ♥ 26°C sg: 1.022 13 cm 200L

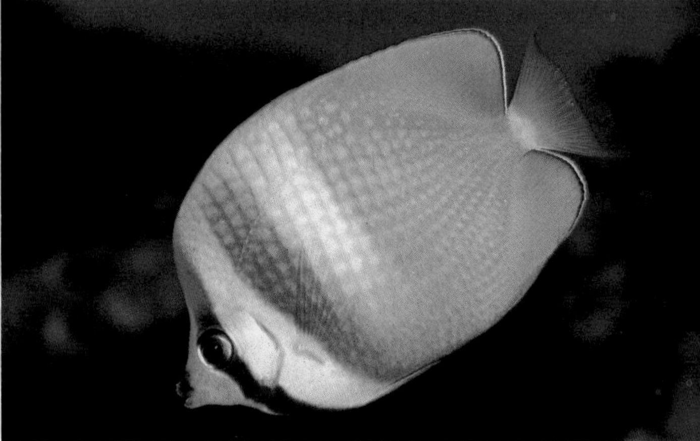

*Chaetodon kleini* 338
6-10 ∼ ◐ ♥ 26°C sg: 1.022 15 cm 200L

*Chaetodon assarius* 338
7,12 ◐ ♥ 26°C sg: 1.022 14 cm 200L

*Chaetodon melapterus* 338
9-10 ~ ◐ ♥ 26°C sg: 1.022 14 cm 200L

*Chaetodon bennetti* 338
6-9 ~ ◐ ♥ 26°C sg: 1.022 15 cm 200L

*Chaetodon citrinellus* 338
6-9 ~ ◐ ♥ 26°C sg: 1.022 13 cm 200L

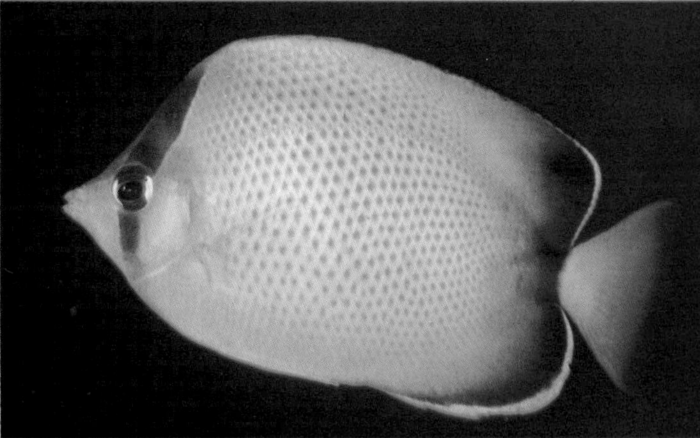

*Chaetodon dolosus* 338
9 ~ ◐ ♥ 26°C sg: 1.022 14 cm 200L

*Chaetodon austriacus* 338
10 ~ ◐ ♥ 26°C sg: 1.030 16 cm 200L

*Chaetodon trifasciatus* 338
6-9 ~ ◐ ♥ 26°C sg: 1.022 17 cm 200L

*Chaetodon collare* 338
7, 9 ~ ◐ ♥ 26°C sg: 1.022 18 cm 200L

*Chaetodon sedentarius* 338
2 ∿ ◐ ♥ 26°C sg: 1.022 17 cm 200L

*Chaetodon sanctaehelenae* 338
13 ∿ ◐ ♥ 26°C sg: 1.022 18 cm 200L

*Chaetodon trichrous* 338
6 ∿ ◐ ♥ 26°C sg: 1.022 14 cm 200L

*Chaetodon fremblii* 338
6 ∿ ◐ ♥ 26°C sg: 1.022 18 cm 200L

*Chaetodon litus* 338
Easter Is. ∿ ◐ ♥ 26°C sg: 1.022 15 cm 200L

*Chaetodon hemichrysus* 338
6 ∿ ◐ ♥ 26°C sg: 1.022 19 cm 200L

*Chaetodon pelewensis* 338
6-7 ∿ ◐ ♥ 26°C sg: 1.022 13 cm 200L

*Chaetodon multicinctus* 338
6 ∿ ◐ ♥ 26°C sg: 1.022 15 cm 200L

*Chaetodon rainfordi* 338
8 ◐ ♥ 26°C sg: 1.030 15 cm 200L

*Chaetodon striatus* 338
2 ◐ ♥ 26°C sg: 1.022 14 cm 200L

*Chaetodon humeralis* 338
3 ◐ ♥ 26°C sg: 1.022 18 cm 200L

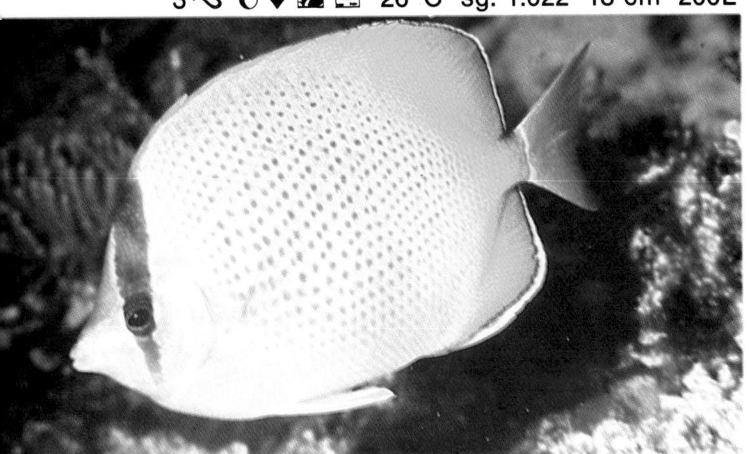

*Chaetodon guentheri* 338
7-8 ◐ ♥ 26°C sg: 1.022 15 cm 200L

*Chaetodon tricinctus* 338
11, 12 ◐ ♥ 23°C sg: 1.022 20 cm 200L

*Chaetodon capistratus* 338
2 ◐ ♥ 26°C sg: 1.022 13 cm 200L

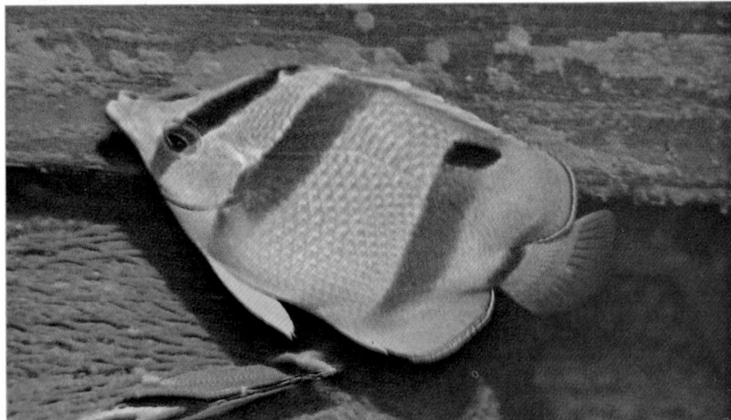

*Chaetodon hoefleri* 338
13 ◐ ♥ 26°C sg: 1.022 18 cm 200L

*Chaetodon miliaris* 338
6 ◐ ♥ 26°C sg: 1.022 17 cm 200L

*Chaetodon guttatissimus* 338
9-10 ~ ◐ ♥ 26°C sg: 1.022 15 cm 200L

*Chaetodon semilarvatus* 338
10 ~ ◐ ♥ 26°C sg: 1.030 19 cm 200L

*Chaetodon speculum* 338
7-8 ~ ◐ ♥ 26°C sg: 1.022 16 cm 200L

*Chaetodon decussatus* 338
9 ~ ◐ ♥ 26°C sg: 1.022 17 cm 200L

*Chaetodon punctatofasciatus* 338
6-7 ~ ◐ ♥ 26°C sg: 1.022 13 cm 200L

*Chaetodon semeion* 338
6-7,9 ◐ ♥ 26°C sg: 1.022 22 cm 300L

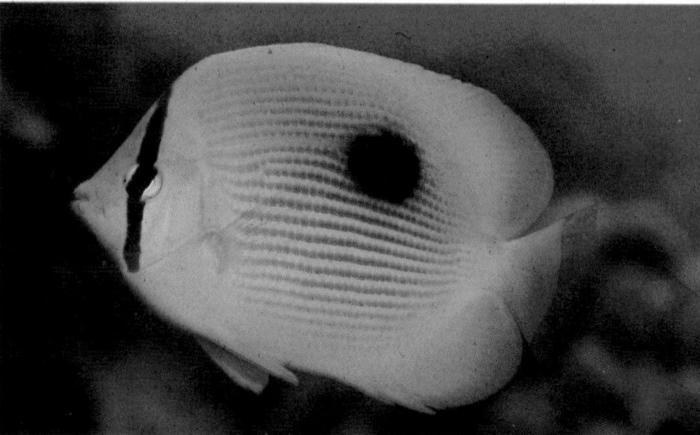

*Chaetodon zanzibariensis* 338
9 ~ ◐ ♥ 26°C sg: 1.022 16 cm 200L

*Chaetodon vagabundus* 338
6-10 ~ ◐ ♥ 26°C sg: 1.022 17 cm 200L

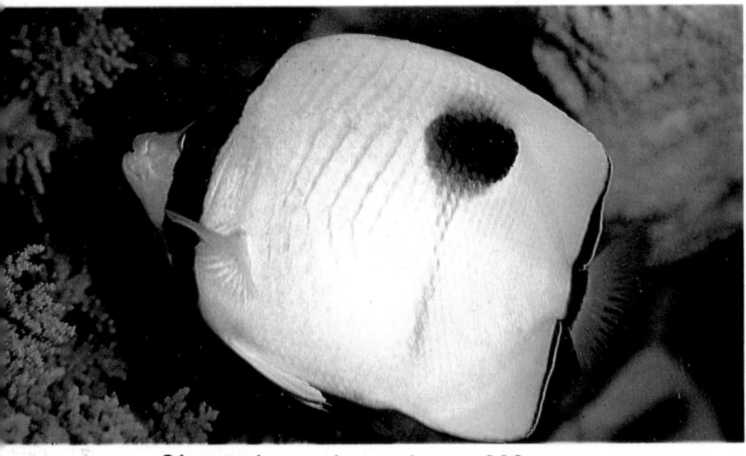

*Chaetodon unimaculatus* 338
6-9 ∿ ◐ ♥ 26°C sg: 1.022 20 cm 200L

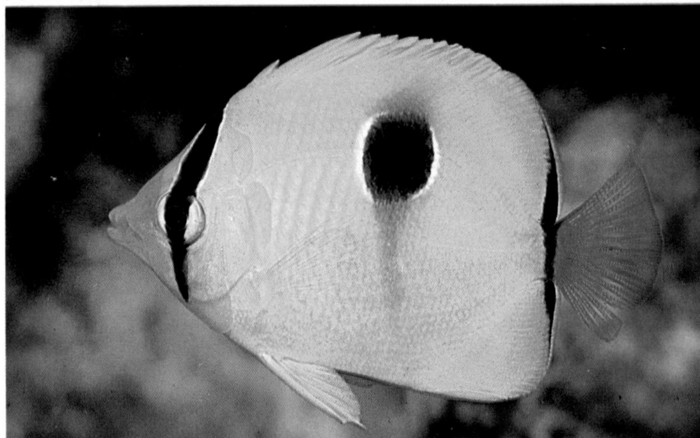

*Chaetodon unimaculatus* 338
6-9 ∿ ◐ ♥ 26°C sg: 1.022 20 cm 200L

*Chaetodon mitratus* 338
9 ∿ ◐ ♥ 26°C sg: 1.022 14 cm 200L

*Chaetodon marleyi* 338
9 ∿ ◐ ♥ 26°C sg: 1.022 28 cm 300L

*Chaetodon xanthocephalus* 338
9 ∿ ◐ ♥ 26°C sg: 1.022 21 cm 200L

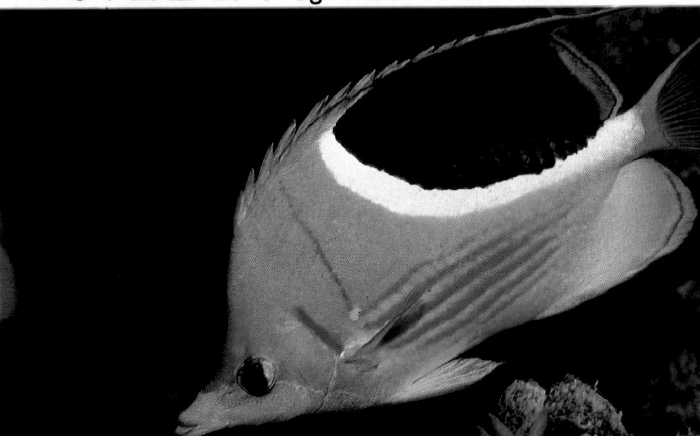

*Chaetodon ehippium* 338
6-9 ∿ ◐ ♥ 26°C sg: 1.022 21 cm 300L

*Chaetodon auriga* 338
6-10 ∿ ◐ ♥ 26°C sg: 1.022 19 cm 200L

*Chaetodon rafflesi* 338
6-9 ∿ ◐ ♥ 26°C sg: 1.022 17 cm 200L

*Chaetodon dichrous* 338
13 ∿ ◐ ♥ 26°C sg: 1.022 15 cm 200L

*Chaetodon aculeatus* 338
2 ∿ ◐ ♥ 26°C sg: 1.022 12 cm 150L

*Chaetodon nippon* 338
5, 7 ∿ ◐ ♥ 26°C sg: 1.022 17 cm 200L

*Chaetodon modestus* 338
5, 7 ∿ ◐ ♥ 26°C sg: 1.022 16 cm 200L

*Chaetodon excelsa* 338
6 ∿ ◐ ♥ 25°C sg: 1.022 15 cm 200L

*Chaetodon jayakari* 338
9 ∿ ◐ ♥ 26°C sg: 1.022 14 cm 200L

*Chaetodon burgessi* 338
6 ∿ ◐ ♥ 25°C sg: 1.022 11 cm 150L

*Chaetodon tinkeri* 338
6 ∿ ◐ ♥ 26°C sg: 1.022 16 cm 200L

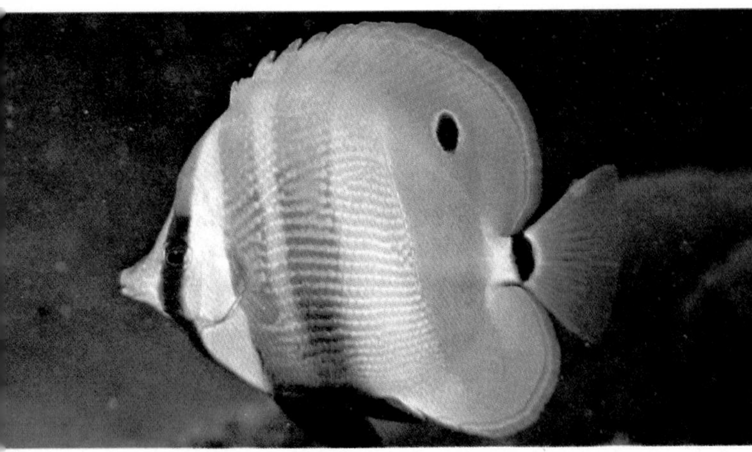

*Coradion chrysozonus* 338
7 26°C sg: 1.022 12 cm 150L

*Pseudochaetodon nigrirostris* 338
3 26°C sg: 1.022 18 cm 200L

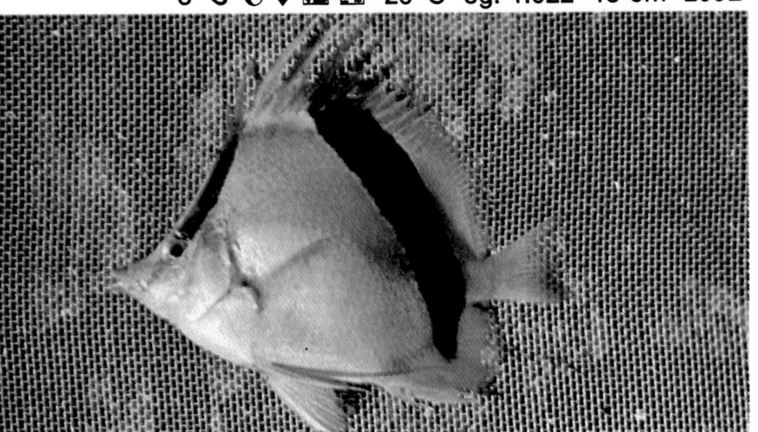

*Chaetodon aya* 338
2 26°C sg: 1.022 15 cm 200L

*Chaetodon guyanensis* 338
2 26°C sg: 1.022 15 cm 200L

*Coradion altivelis* 338
7-8 26°C sg: 1.022 15 cm 200L

*Coradion melanopus* 338
7 26°C sg: 1.022 15 cm 200L

*Chaetodon falcifer* 338
3 26°C sg: 1.022 19 cm 200L

*Chaetodon marcellae* 338
13 26°C sg: 1.022 15 cm 200L

#277

*Heniochus pleurotaenia* 338
9 ∿ ◐ ♥ ▨ ▣ 26°C sg: 1.022 16 cm 200L

*Heniochus acuminatus* 338
6-10 ∿ ◐ ♥ ▨ ▣ 26°C sg: 1.022 20 cm 200L

*Chelmon marginalis* 338
7, ∿ ◐ ♥ ▨ ▣ 26°C sg: 1.022 10 cm 100L

*Parachaetodon ocellatus* 338
6-9 ∿ ◐ ♥ ▨ ▣ 26°C sg: 1.022 17 cm 200L

*Chelmonops truncatus* 338
8, 12 ∿ ◐ ♥ ▨ ▣ 23°C sg: 1.022 23 cm 250L

*Coradion chrysozonus* 338
7 ∿ ◐ ♥ ▨ ▣ 26°C sg: 1.022 12 cm 150L

*Chelmon rostratus* 338
6-9 ~ ◐ ♥ ▣ ▣ 26°C sg: 1.022 20 cm 200L

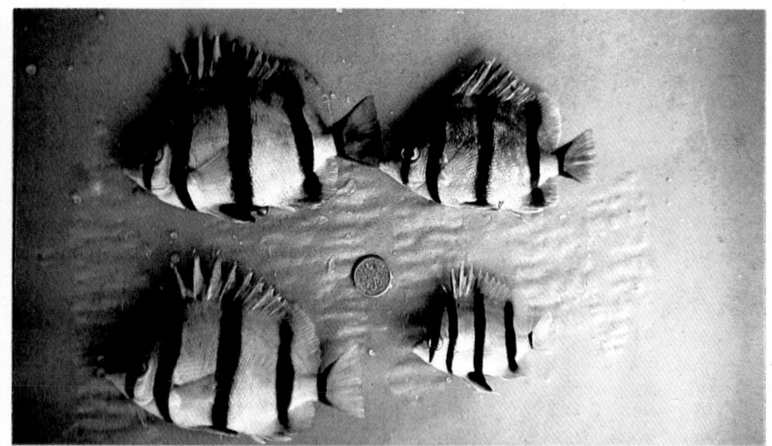

*Amphichaetodon melbae* 338
3 ∿ ◐ ♥ 23°C sg: 1.022 16 cm 200L

*Chelmonops truncatus* 338
8, 12 ∿ ◐ ♥ 23°C sg: 1.022 23 cm 250L

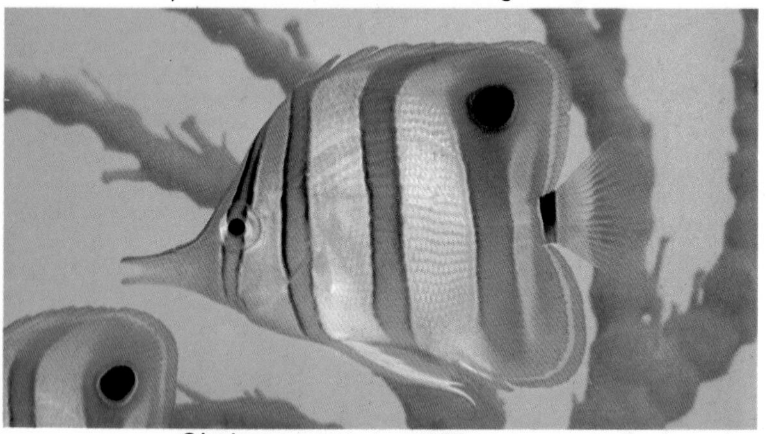

*Chelmon rostratus* 338
6-9 ∿ ◐ ♥ 26°C sg: 1.022 20 cm 200L

*Chelmon rostratus* 338
6-9 ∿ ◐ ♥ 26°C sg: 1.022 20 cm 200L

*Amphichaetodon howensis* 338
11-12 ∿ ◐ ♥ 23°C sg: 1.022 20 cm 200L

*Chelmonops truncatus* 338
8, 12 ∿ ◐ ♥ 23°C sg: 1.022 23 cm 250L

*Chelmon muelleri* 338
7-8 ∿ ◐ ♥ 26°C sg: 1.022 15 cm 150L

*Parachaetodon ocellatus* 338
6-9 ∿ ◐ ♥ 26°C sg: 1.022 17 cm 200L

*Forcipiger longirostris* 338
6-7, 9 ∽ ◐ ♥ 26°C sg: 1.022 27 cm 300L

*Forcipiger longirostris* 338
6-7, 9 ∽ ◐ ♥ 26°C sg: 1.022 27 cm 300L

*Forcipiger longirostris* 338
6-7, 9 ∽ ◐ ♥ 26°C sg: 1.022 27 cm 300L

*Forcipiger flavissimus* 338
3, 5-10 ♀ ∽ ◐ ♥ 26°C sg: 1.022 26 cm 300L

*Hemitaurichthys polylepis* 338
8 ∽ ◐ ♥ 26°C sg: 1.022 18 cm 200L

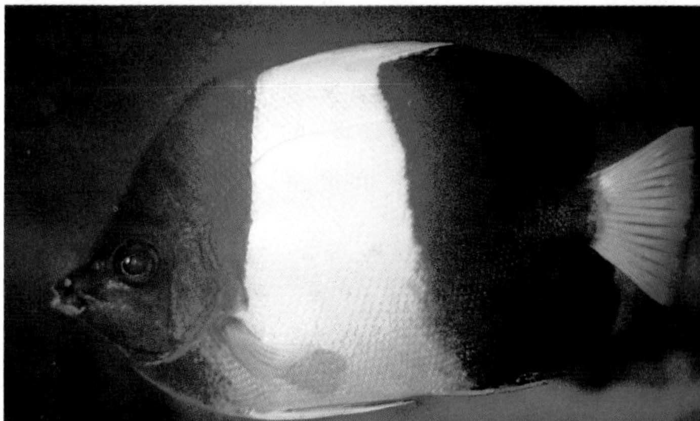

*Hemitaurichthys zoster* 338
9 ∽ ◐ ♥ 26°C sg: 1.022 20 cm 200L

*Hemitaurichthys thompsoni* 338
6 ∽ ◐ ♥ 26°C sg: 1.022 22 cm 300L

*Hemitaurichthys multispinus* 338
6 ∽ ◐ ♥ 26°C sg: 1.022 21 cm 200L

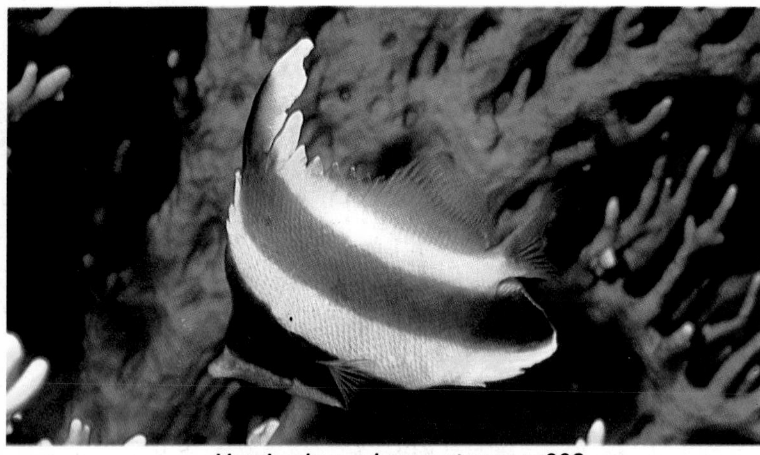

*Heniochus chrysostomus* 338
6-8 ∿ ♥ 26°C sg: 1.022 18 cm 300L

*Heniochus intermedius* 338
9-10 ∿ ◐ ♥ 26°C sg: 1.030 20 cm 200L

*Heniochus monoceros* 338
6-7, 9 ∿ ◐ ♥ 26°C sg: 1.022 19 cm 200L

*Heniochus singularius* 338
7 ∿ ◐ ♥ 26°C sg: 1.022 24 cm 300L

*Heniochus varius* 338
6-8 ∿ ◐ ♥ 26°C sg: 1.022 17 cm 200L

*Heniochus varius* 338
6-8 ∿ ◐ ♥ 26°C sg: 1.022 17 cm 200L

*Heniochus acuminatus* 338
6-10 ∿ ◐ ♥ 26°C sg: 1.022 25 cm 300L

*Heniochus monoceros* 338
6-7, 9 ∿ ◐ ♥ 26°C sg: 1.022 19 cm 200L

*Pygoplites diacanthus* 339
6-10 ~ ⚘ ◐ ♥ ▣ ☷ 26°C sg: 1.022 25 cm 300L

*Apolemichthys trimaculatus* 339
7-9 26°C sg: 1.022 30 cm 300L

*Centropyge acanthops* 339
9 26°C sg: 1.022 8 cm 80L

*Centropyge bispinosus* 339
7-9 26°C sg: 1.022 12 cm 150L

*Centropyge flavopectoralis* 339
9 26°C sg: 1.022 25 cm 300L

*Apolemichthys xanthurus* 339
9 26°C sg: 1.022 15 cm 150L

*Centropyge bicolor* 339
7 26°C sg: 1.022 15 cm 150L

*Centropyge eibli* 339
9 26°C sg: 1.022 15 cm 150L

*Centropyge multispinis* 339
9 26°C sg: 1.022 14 cm 150L

*Centropyge shepardi* 339
6 ◐ ♥ 26°C sg: 1.022 12 cm 150L

*Centropyge ferrugatus* 339
7 ◐ ♥ 26°C sg: 1.022 10 cm 100L

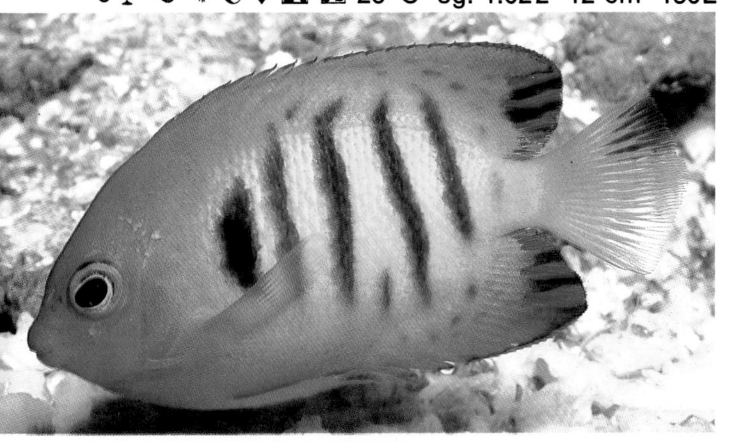

*Centropyge loriculus* 339
7 ◐ ♥ 26°C sg: 1.022 12 cm 150L

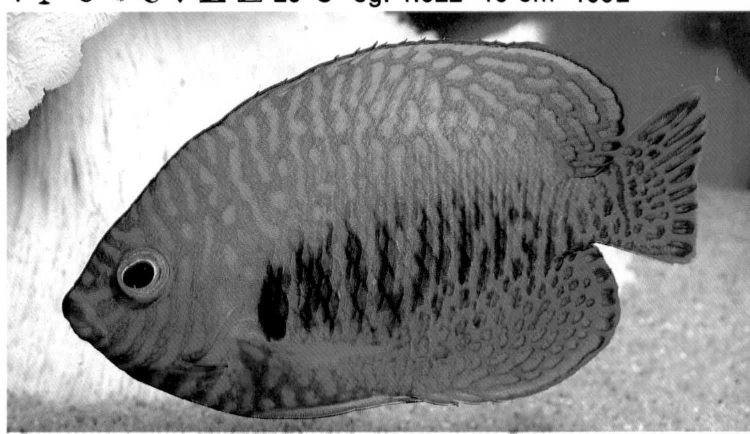

*Centropyge potteri* 339
6 ◐ ♥ 26°C sg: 1.022 10 cm 100L

*Centropyge nox* 339
7 ◐ ♥ 26°C sg: 1.022 11 cm 100L

*Centropyge colini* 339
6 ◐ ♥ 26°C sg: 1.022 7 cm 80L

*Centropyge heraldi* 339
7 ◐ ♥ 26°C sg: 1.022 12 cm 150L

*Centropyge heraldi* (var.) 339
7 ◐ ♥ 26°C sg: 1.022 12 cm 150L

*Centropyge resplendens* 339
13 26°C sg: 1.022 7 cm 100L

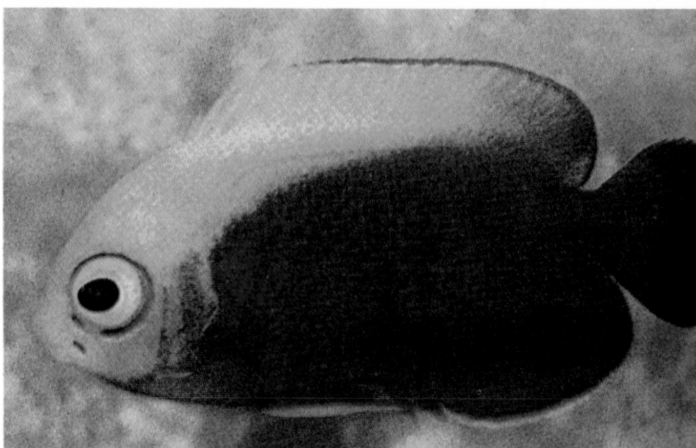

*Centropyge aurantonotus* 339
2 26°C sg: 1.022 6 cm 60L

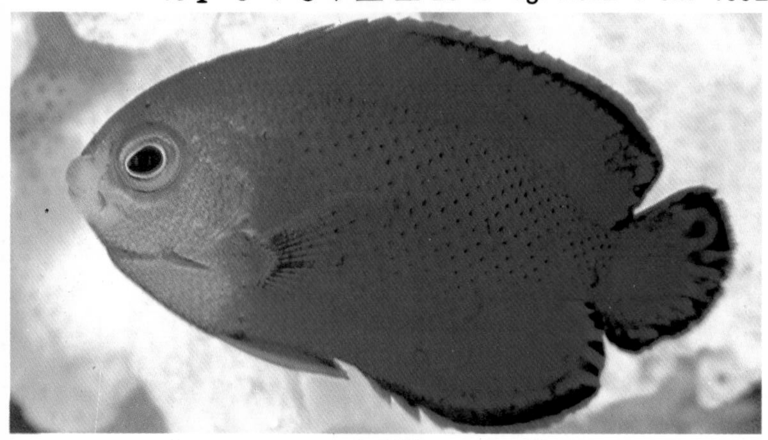

*Centropyge argi* 339
2 26°C sg: 1.022 7 cm 100L

*Centropyge fisheri* 339
6 26°C sg: 1.022 10 cm 100L

*Centropyge hotumatua* 339
6 26°C sg: 1.022 9 cm 100L

*Centropyge multicolor* 339
6 26°C sg: 1.022 8 cm 80L

*Centropyge interruptus* 339
5-7 26°C sg: 1.022 16 cm 200L

*Centropyge flavicauda* 339
7 26°C sg: 1.022 8 cm 80L

*Centropyge flavissimus* 339
6-7 ♥ 26°C sg: 1.022 9 cm 100L

*Centropyge multifasciatus* 339
6-7 ♥ 26°C sg: 1.022 15 cm 150L

*Centropyge tibicin* 339
7 ♥ 26°C sg: 1.022 19 cm 200L

*Genicanthus caudovittatus* (male) 339
10 ♥ 26°C sg: 1.022 20 cm 200L

*Centropyge flavissimus* 339
6-7 ♥ 26°C sg: 1.022 9 cm 100L

*Centropyge joculator* 339
9 ♥ 26°C sg: 1.022 15 cm 150L

*Centropyge vroliki* 339
7 ♥ 26°C sg: 1.022 10 cm 100L

*Genicanthus caudovittatus* 339 ♀
10 ♥ 26°C sg: 1.022 20 cm 200L

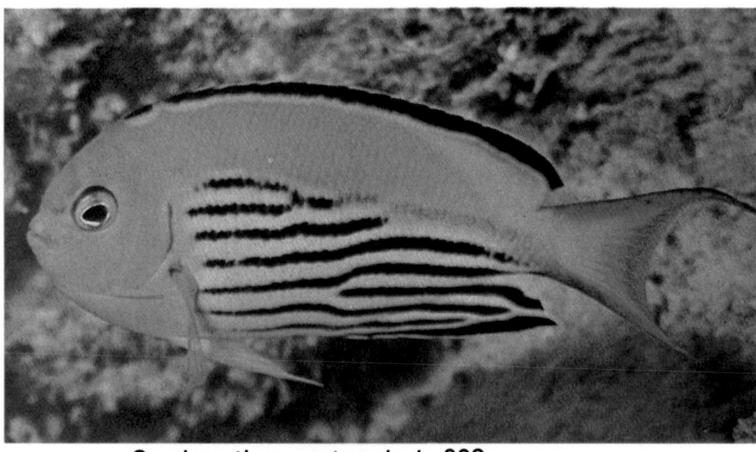

*Genicanthus watanabei* 339 ♂
7 ∿ ◐ ♥ 26°C sg: 1.022 10 cm 100L

*Genicanthus watanabei* 339 ♀
7 ∿ ◐ ♥ 26°C sg: 1.022 10 cm 100L

*Genicanthus semifasciatus* 339 ♂
7 ∿ ◐ ♥ 26°C sg: 1.022 10 cm 100L

*Genicanthus semifasciatus* 339 ♀
7 ∿ ◐ ♥ 26°C sg: 1.022 10 cm 100L

*Genicanthus melanospilus* 339 ♂
7 ∿ ◐ ♥ 26°C sg: 1.022 21 cm 200L

*Genicanthus melanospilus* 339 ♀
7 ∿ ◐ ♥ 26°C sg: 1.022 21 cm 200L

*Genicanthus semicinctus* 339 ♂
11 ∿ ◐ ♥ 26°C sg: 1.022 10 cm 100L

*Genicanthus semicinctus* 339 ♀
11 ∿ ◐ ♥ 26°C sg: 1.022 10 cm 100L

*Genicanthus personatus* 339 ♂
6 26°C sg: 1.022 21 cm 200L

*Genicanthus personatus* 339 ♀
6 26°C sg: 1.022 21 cm 200L

*Genicanthus lamarck* 339 ♀
7, 9 26°C sg: 1.022 24 cm 300L

*Genicanthus bellus* 339 ♂
7 26°C sg: 1.022 13 cm 150L

*Genicanthus bellus* 339 ♀
7 26°C sg: 1.022 13 cm 150L

*Chaetodontoplus melanosoma* (juv.) 339
7 26°C sg: 1.022 20 cm 200L

*Chaetodontoplus melanosoma* 339
7 26°C sg: 1.022 20 cm 200L

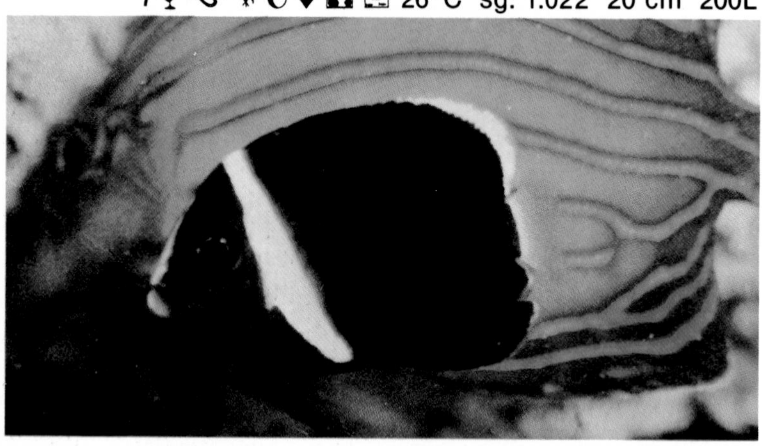

*Chaetodontoplus septentrionalis* (juv.) 339
7 26°C sg: 1.022 22 cm 200L

*Chaetodontoplus septentrionalis* 339
7 26°C sg: 1.022 22 cm 200L

*Chaetodontoplus duboulayi* 339
7-8 26°C sg: 1.022 22 cm 200L

*Chaetodontoplus chrysocephalus* 339
7 26°C sg: 1.022 22 cm 200L

*Chaetodontoplus personifer* 339 ♀
7-8 26°C sg: 1.022 23 cm 250L

*Chaetodontoplus personifer* 339 ♂
7-8 26°C sg: 1.022 23 cm 250L

*Chaetodontoplus cyanopunctatus* 349
7 26°C sg: 1.022 13 cm 150L

*Chaetodontoplus conspicillatus* 339
8 26°C sg: 1.022 25 cm 300L

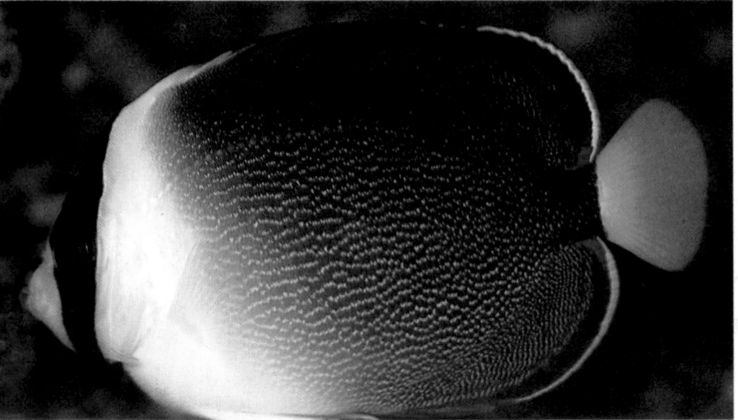

*Chaetodontoplus mesoleucus* 339
7 26°C sg: 1.022 15 cm 150L

*Chaetodontoplus mesoleucus* 339
7 26°C sg: 1.022 15 cm 150L

*Euxiphipops navarchus* 339 (juv.)
7 26°C sg: 1.022 25 cm 300L

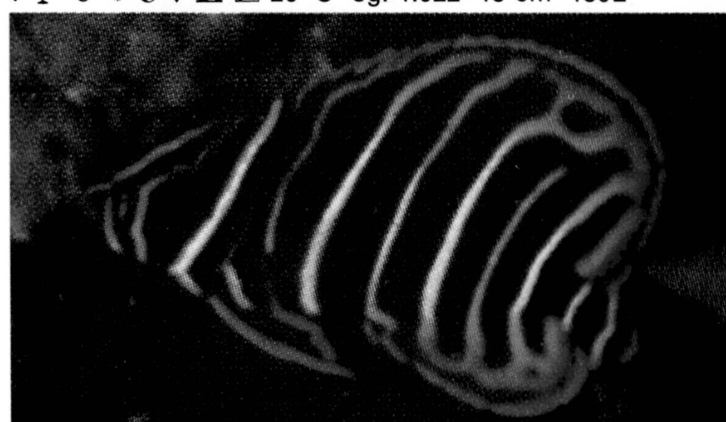

*Euxiphipops xanthometopon?* (juv.) 339
7-9 26°C sg: 1.022 45 cm 500L

*Euxiphipops xanthometopon* 339
7-9 26°C sg: 1.022 45 cm 500L

*Pygoplites diacanthus* (juv.) 339
7, 9-10 26°C sg: 1.022 30 cm 300L

*Pomacanthus zonipectus* 339
3 26°C sg: 1.022 30 cm 300L

*Pomacanthus zonipectus* (juv.) 339
3 26°C sg: 1.022 30 cm 300L

*Pomacanthus paru* 339
2, 13 26°C sg: 1.022 40 cm 400L

*Pomacanthus paru* (juv.) 339
2, 13 26°C sg: 1.022 40 cm 400L

*Pomacanthus arcuatus* 339
2 26°C sg: 1.022 36 cm 400L

*Pomacanthus arcuatus* 339 (juv.)
2 26°C sg: 1.022 36 cm 400L

*Pomacanthus semicirculatus* 339 (juv.)
7-10 26°C sg: 1.022 45 cm 500L

*Pomacanthus maculosus* 339 (juv.)
9-10 26°C sg: 1.024 40 cm 400L

*Pomacanthus annularis* 339 (juv.)
9 26°C sg: 1.022 25 cm 250L

*Pomacanthus annularis* 339
9 26°C sg: 1.022 25 cm 250L

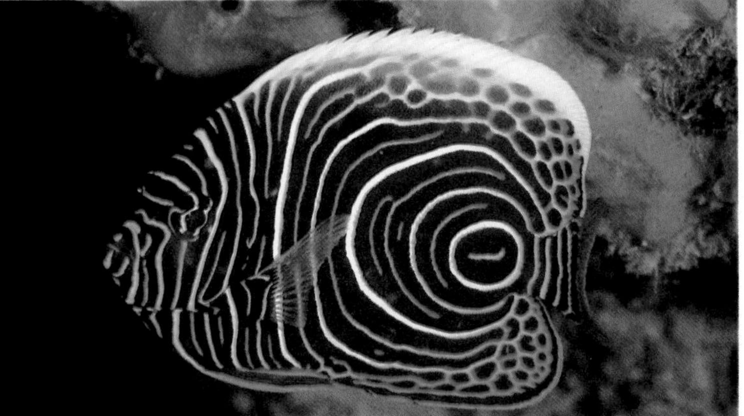

*Pomacanthus imperator* 339 (juv.)
6-10 26°C sg: 1.022 38 cm 400L

*Pomacanthus imperator* 339
6-10 26°C sg: 1.022 38 cm 400L

*Pomacanthus maculosus* 339
9-10 26°C sg: 1.024 40 cm 400L

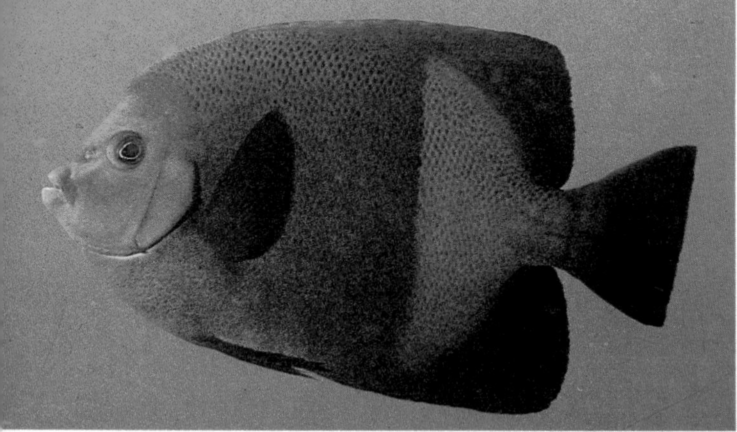

*Pomacanthus striatus* 339
9 26°C sg: 1.022 45 cm 500L

*Pomacanthus chrysurus* 339
7, 9 26°C sg: 1.022 33 cm 300L

*Euxiphipops navarchus* 339
7 26°C sg: 1.022 25 cm 300L

*Pygoplites diacanthus* 339
7, 9-10 26°C sg: 1.022 30 cm 300L

*Pomacanthus semicirculatus* 339
7-10 26°C sg: 1.022 45 cm 500L

*Euxiphipops sexstriatus* 339
7-9 26°C sg: 1.022 50 cm 500L

*Euxiphipops xanthometapon* 339
7-9 26°C sg: 1.022 45 cm 500L

*Arusetta asfur* 339
9-10 26°C sg: 1.022 35 cm 400L

*Pomacanthus semicirculatus* 339
7-9 26°C sg: 1.022 40 cm 400L

*Apolemichthys arcuatus* 339
6 26°C sg: 1.022 17.5 cm 200L

*Apolemichthys xanthopunctatus* 339
6 26°C sg: 1.022 25 cm 300L

*Holacanthus tricolor* (juv.) 339
2 26°C sg: 1.022 25 cm 300L

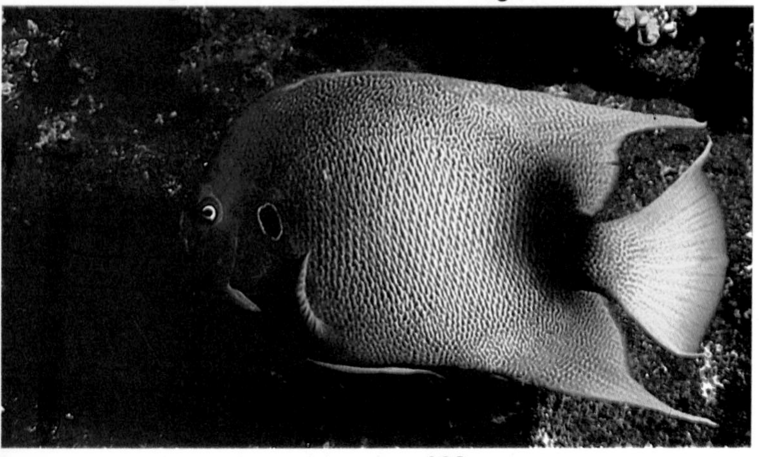

*Holacanthus africanus* 339
13 26°C sg: 1.022 18 cm 200L

*Apolemichthys xanthotis* 339
10 26°C sg: 1.028 20 cm 200L

*Holacanthus venustus* 339
7 26°C sg: 1.022 11 cm 100L

*Holacanthus tricolor* 339
2 26°C sg: 1.022 25 cm 300L

*Holacanthus africanus* 339 (juv.)
13 26°C sg: 1.022 18 cm 200L

*Girella tricuspidatus* 334
11 ◐ ♥ 23°C sg: 1.022 50 cm 500L

*Oplegnathus fasciatus* 343
5 ◐ 24°C sg: 1.022 80 cm 1000L

*Oplegnathus punctatus* 343
5-7 ◐ 26°C sg: 1.022 86 cm 1200L

*Oplegnathus punctatus* 343
5-7 ◐ 26°C sg: 1.022 86 cm 1200L

*Amphistichus rhodoterus* 345
3 ◐ 26°C sg: 1.022 41 cm 400L

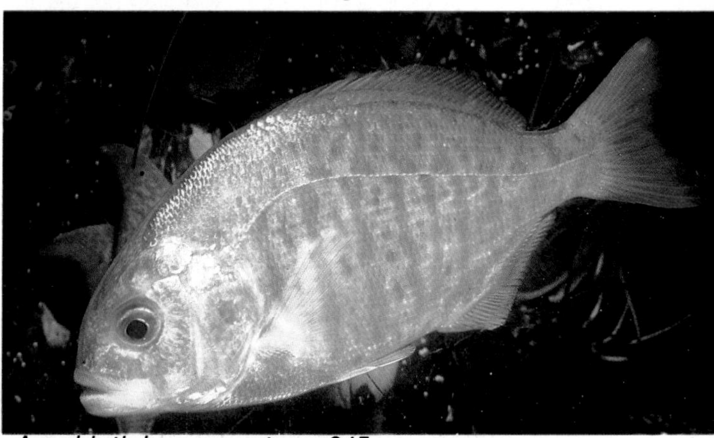

*Amphistichus argenteus* 345
3 ◐ 26°C sg: 1.022 43 cm 500L

*Cymatogaster aggregata* 345
3-4 ◐ ♥ 26°C sg: 1.022 18 cm 200L

*Ditrema temmincki* 345
5 ◐ 26°C sg: 1.022 30 cm 300L

*Embiotoca jacksoni* 345
3 ~ ◐ ✕ ▨ ☷ 26°C sg: 1.022 39 cm 500L

*Hypsurus caryi* 345
3 ~ ◐ ✕ ▨ ☷ 26°C sg: 1.022 30 cm 300L

*Micrometrus aurora* 345
3 ~ ◐ ✕ ▨ ☷ 26°C sg: 1.022 18 cm 200L

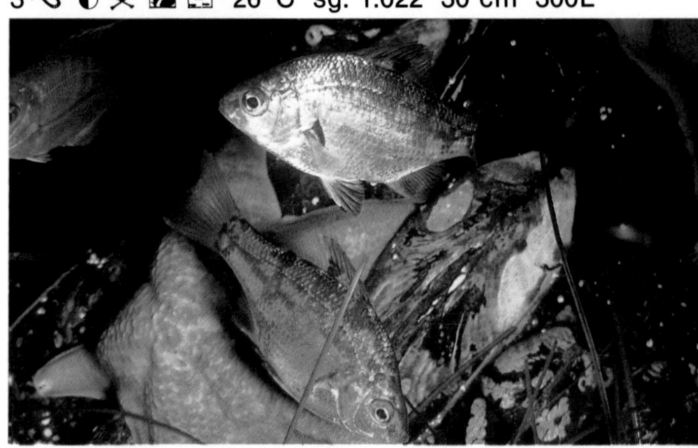

*Micrometrus minimus* 345
3 ~ ◐ ✕ ▨ ☷ 26°C sg: 1.022 16 cm 200L

*Damalichthys vacca* 345
3 ~ ◐ ✕ ▨ ☷ 26°C sg: 1.022 44 cm 500L

*Hyperprosopon ellipticum* 345
3 ~ ◐ ✕ ▨ ☷ 26°C sg: 1.022 30 cm 300L

*Neoditrema ransonneti* 345
5 ~ ◐ ✕ ▨ ☷ 24°C sg: 1.022 15 cm 200L

*Phanerodon furcatus* 345
3-4 ~ ◐ ✕ ▨ ☷ 26°C sg: 1.022 32 cm 300L

#299

*Dascyllus flavicauda* 346
6 26°C sg: 1.022 10 cm 100L

*Chromis viridis* 346
6 26°C sg: 1.022 10 cm 100L

*Premnas biaculeatus* 346
6-9 26°C sg: 1.022 18 cm 200L

*Amphiprion leucokranos* 346
6-7 26°C sg: 1.022 12 cm 150L

*Amphiprion latezonatus* 346
8, 12 24°C sg: 1.023 12 cm 100L

*Amphiprion akindynos* 346
6, 8, 12 26°C sg: 1.022 12 cm 150L

*Premnas biaculeatus* 346
6-9 26°C sg: 1.022 18 cm 200L

*Amphiprion percula* 346
6, 8 26°C sg: 1.022 11 cm 100L

*Amphiprion polymnus* 346
5-7 26°C sg: 1.022 10 cm 100L

*Amphiprion akindynos* 346 (juv.)
6, 8, 12 26°C sg: 1.022 12 cm 150L

*Amphiprion akallopisos* 346
7, 9 26°C sg: 1.022 9 cm 100L

*Amphiprion allardi* 346
9 26°C sg: 1.022 11 cm 100L

*Amphiprion chrysogaster* 346
9 26°C sg: 1.022 11 cm 100L

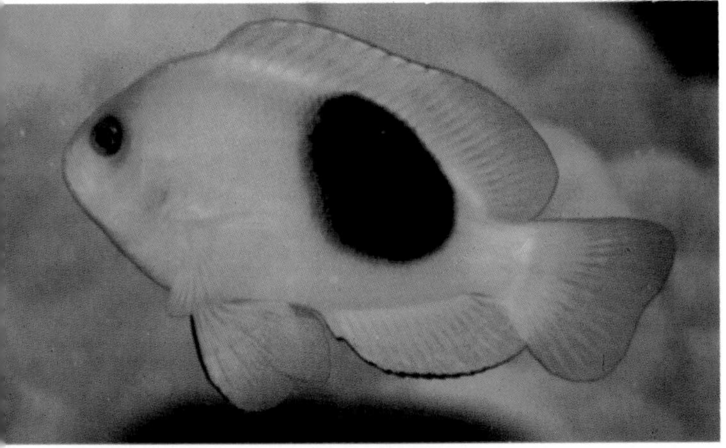

*Amphiprion ephippium* 346
7, 9 26°C sg: 1.022 7 cm 80L

*Amphiprion akallopisos* 346
7, 9 26°C sg: 1.022 9 cm 100L

*Amphiprion clarkii* 346
5-7, 9 26°C sg: 1.022 10 cm 100L

*Amphiprion chrysogaster* 346
9 26°C sg: 1.022 11 cm 100L

*Amphiprion fuscocaudatus* 346
9 26°C sg: 1.022 13 cm 150L

*Amphiprion mccullochi* 346
11-12 26°C sg: 1.022 13 cm 150L

*Amphiprion melanopus* 346
6-8 26°C sg: 1.022 13 cm 150L

*Amphiprion melanopus* 346
6-8 26°C sg: 1.022 13 cm 150L

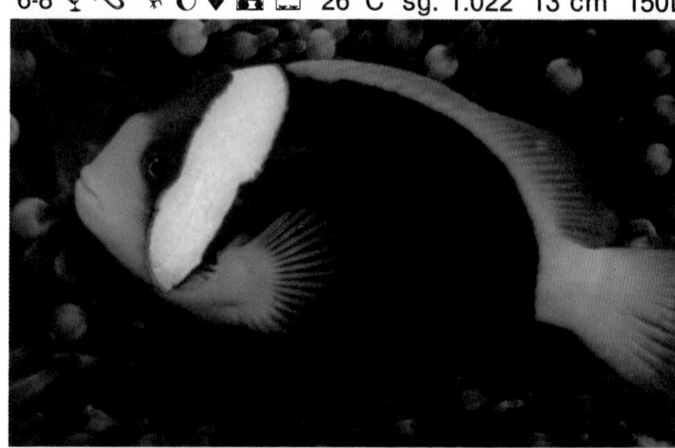

*Amphiprion melanopus* (var)
6-8 26°C sg: 1.022 13 cm 150L

*Amphiprion ephippium* 346
7, 9 26°C sg: 1.022 10 cm 100L

*Amphiprion ephippium* 346
7, 9 26°C sg: 1.022 10 cm 100L

*Amphiprion bicinctus* 346 (juv.)
6 26°C sg: 1.022 14 cm 150L

*Amphiprion thiellei* 346
7 26°C sg: 1.022 8 cm 100L

*Amphiprion perideraion* 346
6-8 [symbols] 26°C sg: 1.022 11 cm 100L

*Amphiprion sandaracinos* 346
6-7 26°C sg: 1.022 14 cm 150L

*Amphiprion perideraion* 346
6-8 26°C sg: 1.022 11 cm 100L

*Amphiprion tricinctus* 346
6 26°C sg: 1.022 14 cm 150L

*Amphiprion chrysopterus* 346
6-7 26°C sg: 1.022 12.5 cm 150L

*Amphiprion rubrocinctus* 346
6-8, 12 25°C sg: 1.022 14 cm 150L

*Amphiprion rubrocinctus* 346
6-8, 12 25°C sg: 1.022 14 cm 150L

*Amphiprion frenatus* 346
7, 9 26°C sg: 1.022 10 cm 100L

*Amphiprion frenatus* 346
7, 9 26°C sg: 1.022 10 cm 100L

*Amphiprion nigripes* 346
9 26°C sg: 1.022 12 cm 150L

*Amphiprion nigripes* 346
9 26°C sg: 1.022 12 cm 150L

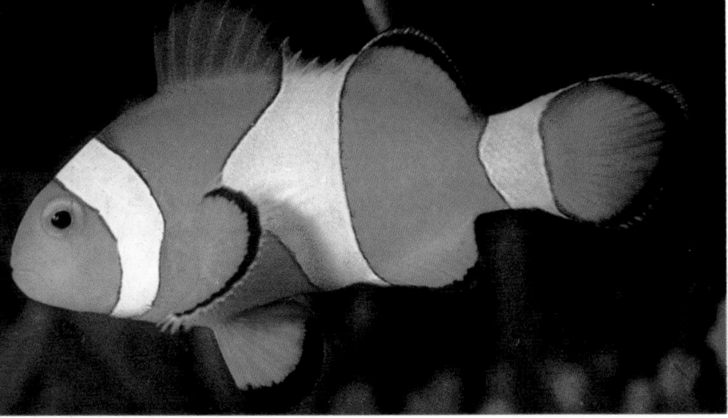

*Amphiprion ocellaris* 346
6-7 26°C sg: 1.022 15 cm 200L

*Amphiprion sebae* 346
7, 9 26°C sg: 1.022 14 cm 150L

*Dascyllus carneus* 346
7 26°C sg: 1.022 10 cm 50L

*Dascyllus aruanus* 346
6-7 26°C sg: 1.022 10 cm 100L

*Dascyllus trimaculatus* 346
6-7 26°C sg: 1.022 14 cm 150L

*Parma bicolor* 346
12 26°C sg: 1.022 20 cm 200L

*Dascyllus albisella* 346
6 ♥ 26°C sg: 1.022 13 cm 200L

*Dascyllus trimaculatus* 346
6-7 ♥ 26°C sg: 1.022 14 cm 200L

*Dascyllus flavicauda* 346
6 ♥ 26°C sg: 1.022 10 cm 100L

*Dascyllus strasburgi* 346
6 ♥ 26°C sg: 1.022 14 cm 200L

*Dascyllus melanurus* 346
6-7 ♥ 26°C sg: 1.022 10 cm 100L

*Dascyllus marginatus* 346
9-10 ♥ 26°C sg: 1.022 12 cm 100L

*Dascyllus reticulatus* 346
6-7 ♥ 26°C sg: 1.022 10 cm 100L

*Dascyllus carneus* 346
7 ♥ 26°C sg: 1.022 10 cm 50L

*Parma oligolepis* 346
8, 12 26°C sg: 1.022 20 cm 200L

*Parma microlepis* 346
11 23°C sg: 1.024 30 cm 300L

*Parma alboscapularis* 346
11 23°C sg: 1.023 20 cm 200L

*Parma polylepis* 346
6, 8, 12 25°C sg: 1.022 21 cm 200L

*Parma mccullochi* 346
12 23°C sg: 1.023 12 cm 50L

*Parma microlepis* 346 (juv.)
11 23°C sg: 1.024 30 cm 300L

*Parma victoriae* 346
11 23°C sg: 1.024 20 cm 200L

*Parma occidentalis* 346
11 23°C sg: 1.023 30 cm 300L

*Abudefduf vaigiensis* 346
7 ◐ ♥ 26°C sg: 1.022 20 cm 200L

*Abudefduf troscheli* 346
3 ◐ ♥ 26°C sg: 1.022 23 cm 200L

*Abudefduf declevifrons* 346
3 ◐ ♥ 26°C sg: 1.022 25 cm 200L

Abudefduf taurus 346
2 ◐ ♥ 26°C sg: 1.022 25 cm 300L

*Abudefduf saxatilis* 346
Circumtrop. ◐ ♥ 26°C sg: 1.022 15 cm 200L

*Abudefduf troscheli* 346 ♂
3 ◐ ♥ 26°C sg: 1.022 23 cm 200L

*Abudefduf sordidus* 346
6-9 ◐ ♥ 26°C sg: 1.022 20 cm 200L

*Abudefduf taurus* 346
2 ◐ ♥ 26°C sg: 1.022 25 cm 300L

*Abudefduf bengalensis* 346
7-8 26°C sg: 1.022 17 cm 200L

*Abudefduf notatus* 346
5-7 26°C sg: 1.022 17 cm 200L

*Abudefduf sparoides* 346
9 26°C sg: 1.022 16 cm 200L

*Amblyglyphidodon leucogaster* 346
6-10 26°C sg: 1.022 13 cm 150L

*Abudefduf margariteus* 346
9 26°C sg: 1.022 16 cm 80L

*Abudefduf sexfasciatus* 346
9-10 26°C sg: 1.022 15 cm 200L

*Amblyglyphidodon flavilatus* 346
9-10 26°C sg: 1.022 25 cm 300L

*Lepidozygus tapeinosoma* 346
6-7 26°C sg: 1.022 12 cm 150L

*Abudefduf whitleyi* 346
8 26°C sg: 1.022 18 cm 200L

*Abudefduf septemfasciatus* 346
6-7 26°C sg: 1.022 23 cm 300L

*Abudefduf lorenzi* 346
6 26°C sg: 1.022 12 cm 150L

*Abudefduf abdominalis* 346
6 26°C sg: 1.022 19 cm 200L

*Amblyglyphidodon leucogaster* 346
6-10 26°C sg: 1.022 13 cm 150L

*Amblyglyphidodon curacao* 346
6-7 26°C sg: 1.022 14 cm 200L

*Amblyglyphidodon ternatensis* 346
6-7 26°C sg: 1.022 14 cm 150L

*Amblyglyphidodon aureus* 346
6-7 26°C sg: 1.022 13 cm 150L

*Chromis atripectoralis* 346
6-7, 9, 12 25°C sg: 1.022 13 cm 150L

*Chromis axillaris* 346
9 26°C sg: 1.022 13 cm 150L

*Chromis viridis* 346
6 26°C sg: 1.022 10 cm 100L

*Chromis dimidiata* 346
9-10 26°C sg: 1.022 9 cm 100L

*Chromis elerae* 346
6-7 26°C sg: 1.022 10 cm 100L

*Chromis klunzingeri* 346
12 24°C sg: 1.023 10 cm 100L

*Chromis nigrura* 346
9 26°C sg: 1.022 5 cm 50L

*Chromis opercularis* 346
9 26°C sg: 1.022 16 cm 200L

*Chromis flavomaculata* 346
7 26°C sg: 1.022 12 cm 150L

*Chromis* sp. 346
6 26°C sg: 1.022 10.5 cm 150L

*Chromis randalli* 346
6 26°C sg: 1.022 17 cm 200L

*Chromis cinerascens* 346
7 26°C sg: 1.022 10 cm 100L

*Chromis enchrysura* 346
1-2 25°C sg: 1.022 10 cm 100L

*Chromis ovalis* 346
6 26°C sg: 1.022 19 cm 200L

*Chromis westaustralis* 346
12 24°C sg: 1.023 7 cm 100L

*Chromis notata* 346
5 23°C sg: 1.022 4 cm 50L

*Chromis lineata* 346
6-7 26°C sg: 1.022 9 cm 100L

*Chromis acares* 346
6 26°C sg: 1.022 9 cm 100L

*Chromis analis* 346
6-7, 9 26°C sg: 1.022 13 cm 150L

*Chromis mirationis* 346
5 26°C sg: 1.022 12 cm 150L

*Chromis vanderbilti* 346
6, 8 26°C sg: 1.022 10 cm 100L

*Chromis agilis* 346
6-8 26°C sg: 1.022 12 cm 150L

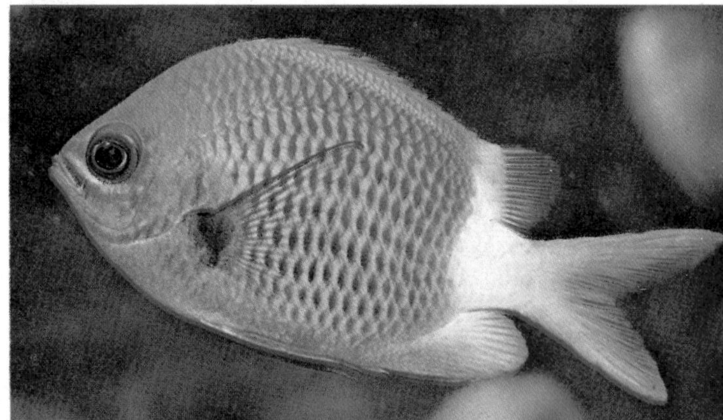

*Chromis chrysura* 346
5-6, 8-9 26°C sg: 1.022 15 cm 200L

*Chromis verater* 346
6 26°C sg: 1.022 20 cm 200L

*Chromis amboinensis* 346
6-7 26°C sg: 1.022 11 cm 100L

*Chromis ternatensis* 346
6-7, 9 26°C sg: 1.022 12 cm 100L

*Chromis fumea* 346
7-8, 11-12 26°C sg: 1.022 9 cm 100L

*Chromis opercularis* 346
9 26°C sg: 1.022 16 cm 200L

*Chromis atripes* 346
6-8 26°C sg: 1.022 5 cm 50L

*Chromis lepidolepis* 346
6-7 26°C sg: 1.022 12 cm 150L

*Chromis hypselepis* 346
11-12 23°C sg: 1.024 13 cm 150L

*Chromis weberi* 346
6-7, 9 26°C sg: 1.022 19 cm 200L

*Chromis nitida* 346
8, 12 26°C sg: 1.022 12 cm 150L

*Chromis bicolor* 346
6-7 26°C sg: 1.022 11 cm 100L

*Chromis hanui* 346
6 26°C sg: 1.022 11 cm 100L

*Chromis leucura* 346
6 26°C sg: 1.022 10 cm 100L

*Chromis retrofasciata* 346
6-8 26°C sg: 1.022 9 cm 100L

*Chromis xanthura* 346
6-7 26°C sg: 1.022 16 cm 200L

*Chromis iomelas* 346
6, 8 26°C sg: 1.022 10 cm 100L

*Chromis* sp. "D" 346
6 26°C sg: 1.022 6 cm 100L

*Chromis insolatus* 346
2 26°C sg: 1.022 10 cm 100L

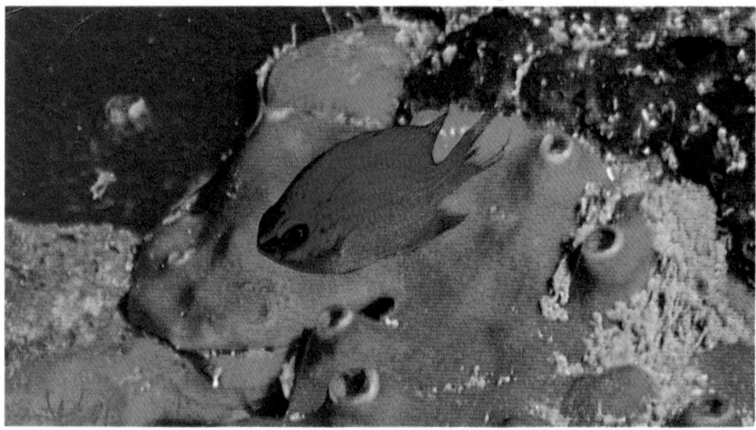

*Chromis scotti* 346
2 26°C sg: 1.022 10 cm 100L

*Chromis cauta (?)* 346
13 26°C sg: 1.022 11 cm 100L

*Chromis chromis* 346
13-15 26°C sg: 1.024 12 cm 150L

*Chromis cyaneus* 346
2 26°C sg: 1.022 13 cm 150L

*Chromis scotti* 346
2 26°C sg: 1.022 10 cm 100L

*Chromis flavicauda* 346
2 26°C sg: 1.022 8 cm 100L

*Chromis cadenati* 346
13 26°C sg: 1.022 12 cm 100L

*Chromis limbaughi* 346
3 26°C sg: 1.022 10 cm 100L

*Chromis limbaughi* 346
3 26°C sg: 1.022 10 cm 100L

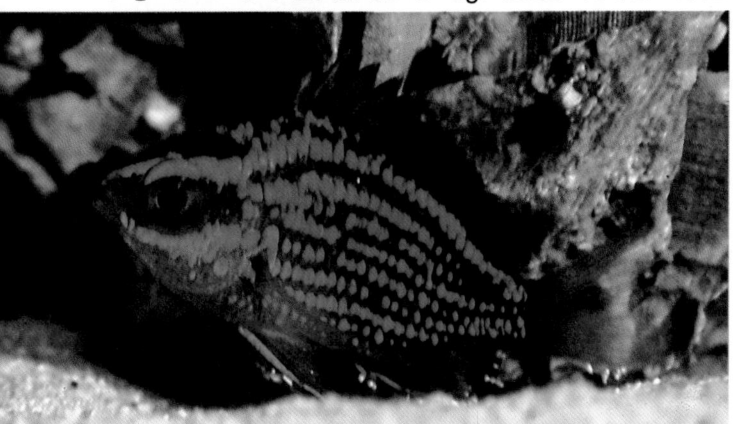

*Chromis altus* 346
3 26°C sg: 1.022 9 cm 100L

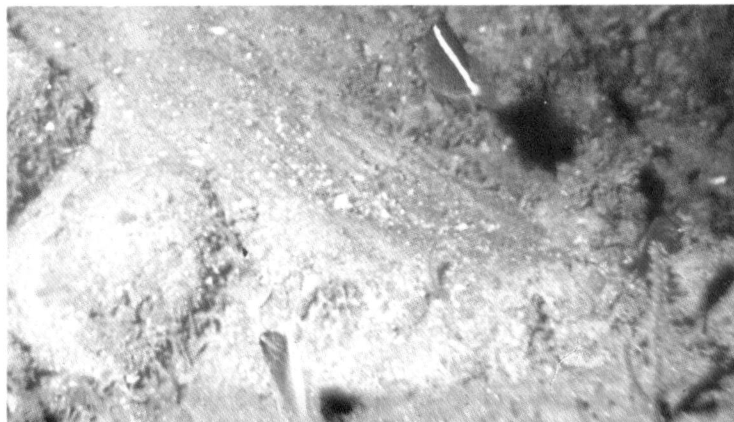

*Chromis altus* 346
3 26°C sg: 1.022 9 cm 100L

*Chromis multilineatus* 346
2 26°C sg: 1.022 16 cm 200L

*Chromis punctipinnis* 346
3 26°C sg: 1.022 30 cm 300L

*Chromis viridis* 346
6 26°C sg: 1.022 10 cm 100L

*Chromis atrilobata* 346
3 26°C sg: 1.022 7 cm 80L

*Chrysiptera notialis* 346
26°C sg: 1.022 6.5 cm 100L

*Chrysiptera rapanui* 346
6 25°C sg: 1.022 11 cm 100L

*Chrysiptera melanomaculata* 346
6, 11-12 26°C sg: 1.022 7 cm 100L

*Chrysiptera galba* 346
6 26°C sg: 1.022 12 cm 150L

*Chrysiptera glauca* 346
6-7 26°C sg: 1.022 12 cm 100L

*Chrysiptera rex* 346
6-8 26°C sg: 1.022 11 cm 100L

*Chrysiptera niger* 346
8 26°C sg: 1.022 10 cm 100L

Unidentified Damselfish (nuptial pattern) 346
6-7 26°C sg: 1.022 12 cm 100L

*Chrysiptera leucopoma* 346
6-7 26°C sg: 1.022 12 cm 150L

*Chrysiptera caeruleolineata* 346
6-7 26°C sg: 1.022 9 cm 100L

*Chrysiptera traceyi* 346
6-7 26°C sg: 1.022 10 cm 100L

*Chrysiptera annulata* 346
9-10 26°C sg: 1.024 7 cm 80L

*Chrysiptera leucopoma* 346 (juv.)
6-7 26°C sg: 1.022 12 cm 150L

*Paraglyphidodon* sp. (juv.) 346
8 26°C sg: 1.022 10 cm 150L

*Chrysiptera talboti* 346
6-8 26°C sg: 1.022 10 cm 100L

*Chrysiptera tricincta* 346
6 26°C sg: 1.022 10 cm 100L

*Chrysiptera flavipinnis* 346
6, 8 26°C sg: 1.022 11 cm 100L

*Chrysiptera cyanea* 346 ♀
6-7 26°C sg: 1.022 8 cm 100L

*Chrysiptera taupou* 346
6 26°C sg: 1.022 75 cm 100L

*Chrysiptera springeri* 346
7 26°C sg: 1.022 10 cm 100L

*Chrysiptera starcki* 346
6-8 26°C sg: 1.022 10 cm 100L

*Chrysiptera cyanea* 346 ♂
6-7 26°C sg: 1.022 8 cm 100L

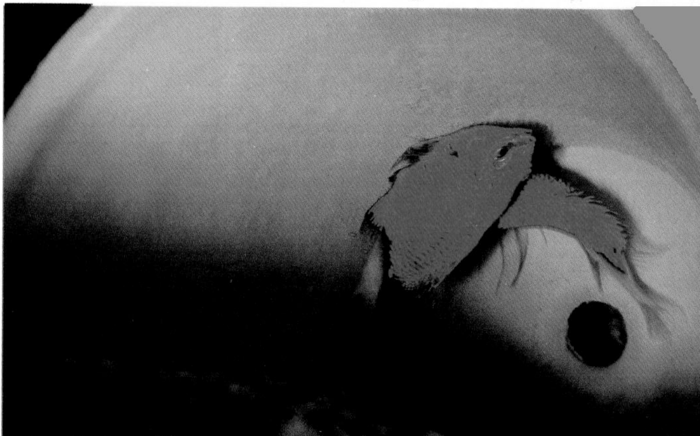

*Chrysiptera parasema* 346
7 26°C sg: 1.022 8 cm 50L

*Chrysiptera rollandi* 346
6, 8 26°C sg: 1.022 9 cm 100L

*Chrysiptera hemicyanea* 346
7 26°C sg: 1.022 20 cm 200L

*Chrysiptera biocellata* 346
6-7 26°C sg: 1.022 12 cm 150L

*Chrysiptera unimaculata* 346
6-8 26°C sg: 1.022 11 cm 100L

*Chrysiptera rollandi* 346
6, 8 26°C sg: 1.022 9 cm 100L

*Plectroglyphidodon leucozona* 346
6-9 26°C sg: 1.022 9 cm 100L

*Chrysiptera glauca* 346
6-7 26°C sg: 1.022 12 cm 100L

*Chrysiptera unimaculata* 346
6-8 26°C sg: 1.022 11 cm 100L

*Neopomacentrus miryae* 346
10 26°C sg: 1.028 11 cm 100L

*Plectroglyphidodon phoenixensis* 346
6 26°C sg: 1.022 7 cm 100L

*Plectroglyphidodon dickii* 346
7-9 26°C sg: 1.022 13 cm 150L

*Plectroglyphidodon johnstonianus* 346
6-8 26°C sg: 1.022 12 cm 150L

*Plectroglyphidodon imparipennis* 346
6-7 26°C sg: 1.022 10 cm 100L

*Plectroglyphidodon sindonis* 346
6 26°C sg: 1.022 15 cm 200L

*Pomachromis exilis* 346
6 26°C sg: 1.022 11 cm 100L

*Pomachromis guamensis* 346
6 26°C sg: 1.022 12 cm 150L

*Pomachromis fuscidorsalis* 346
6 26°C sg: 1.022 11 cm 100L

*Pomachromis richardsoni* 346
6-8 26°C sg: 1.022 11 cm 100L

*Paraglyphidodon nigroris* 346
6-7 ♀ ∿ ⚘ ◐ ♥ 26°C sg: 1.022 15 cm 200L

*Paraglyphidodon nigroris* 346 (juv.)
6-7 ♀ ∿ ⚘ ◐ ♥ 26°C sg: 1.022 15 cm 200L

*Paraglyphidodon melas* 346
6-10 ♀ ∿ ⚘ ◐ ♥ 26°C sg: 1.022 17 cm 200L

*Paraglyphidodon melas* 346 (juv.)
6-10 ♀ ∿ ⚘ ◐ ♥ 26°C sg: 1.022 17 cm 200L

*Paraglyphidodon polyacanthus* 346
6, 11-12 ♀ ∿ ⚘ ◐ ♥ 24°C sg: 1.023 17 cm 200L

*Paraglyphidodon polyacanthus* 346
6, 11-12 ♀ ∿ ⚘ ◐ ♥ 24°C sg: 1.023 17 cm 200L

*Paraglyphidodon lacrymatus* 346
6-7 ♀ ∿ ⚘ ◐ ♥ 26°C sg: 1.022 13 cm 150L

*Paraglyphidodon oxyodon* 346
7 ♀ ∿ ⚘ ◐ ♥ 26°C sg: 1.022 5 cm 50L

*Hypsypops rubicunda* 346
3 24°C sg: 1.023 36 cm 500L

*Hypsypops rubicunda* 346 (juv.)
3 24°C sg: 1.023 36 cm 500L

*Acanthochromis polyacanthus* 346
6-7 26°C sg: 1.022 10 cm 100L

*Acanthochromis polyacanthus* (juv.) 346
6-7 26°C sg: 1.022 10 cm 100L

*Hemiglyphidodon plagiometopon* 346
6-7, 9 26°C sg: 1.022 19 cm 200L

*Hemiglyphidodon plagiometopon* 346
6-7, 9 26°C sg: 1.022 19 cm 200L

*Cheiloprion labiatus* 346
6-7, 9 26°C sg: 1.022 11 cm 100L

*Amblypomacentrus breviceps* 346
6-7 26°C sg: 1.022 8 cm 100L

*Neopomacentrus taeniurus* 346
6-7 26°C sg: 1.018 11 cm 100L

*Neopomacentrus cyanomos* 346
6-7, 9 26°C sg: 1.022 12 cm 150L

*Neopomacentrus violascens* 346
5-7 26°C sg: 1.022 10 cm 100L

*Neopomacentrus metallicus* 346
6 26°C sg: 1.022 6 cm 80L

*Neopomacentrus taeniurus* 346
6-7 26°C sg: 1.018 11 cm 100L

*Neopomacentrus azysron* 346
6-7 26°C sg: 1.022 6 cm 80L

*Neopomacentrus nemurus* 346
6-7 26°C sg: 1.022 11 cm 100L

*Neopomacentrus filamentosus* 346
7 26°C sg: 1.022 7 cm 80L

*Pomacentrus philippinus* 346
6-8 26°C sg: 1.022 13 cm 150L

*Pomacentrus trichourus* 346
9 26°C sg: 1.022 10 cm 100L

*Pomacentrus caeruleus* 346
7-9 26°C sg: 1.022 10 cm 100L

*Pomacentrus alleni* 346
7-9 26°C sg: 1.022 8 cm 50L

*Pomacentrus coelestis* 346
6-8 26°C sg: 1.022 12 cm 150L

*Pomacentrus australis* 346
8 26°C sg: 1.022 11 cm 100L

*Pomacentrus coelestis* 346
6-8 26°C sg: 1.022 12 cm 150L

*Pomacentrus lepidogenys* 346
6-8 26°C sg: 1.022 12 cm 150L

*Pomacentrus reidi* 346
6-8 26°C sg: 1.022 14 cm 150L

*Pomacentrus chrysurus* 346
6-8 26°C sg: 1.022 12 cm 150L

*Dischistodus pseudochrysopoecilus* 346
6-8 26°C sg: 1.022 19 cm 200L

*Pomacentrus tripunctatus* 346
6-8 26°C sg: 1.022 11 cm 100L

*Pomacentrus emarginatus* 346
6-7 26°C sg: 1.022 13 cm 150L

*Pomacentrus brachialis* 346
7 26°C sg: 1.022 8 cm 100L

*Pomacentrus arenarius* 346
11-12 26°C sg: 1.022 8 cm 100L

*Pomacentrus albimaculus* 346
7 26°C sg: 1.022 12 cm 150L

*Pomacentrus wardi* 346
8 26°C sg: 1.022 13 cm 150L

*Pomacentrus nigromarginatus* 346
6-8 26°C sg: 1.022 12 cm 150L

*Pomacentrus nigromanus* 346
6-8 26°C sg: 1.022 12 cm 150L

*Pomacentrus philippinus* 346
6-8 26°C sg: 1.022 13 cm 150L

*Pomacentrus stigma* 346
7 26°C sg: 1.022 12 cm 150L

*Pomacentrus amboinensis* 346
6-8 26°C sg: 1.022 12 cm 150L

*Pomacentrus smithi* 346
6-7 26°C sg: 1.022 10 cm 100L

*Pomacentrus grammorhynchus* 346
6-8 26°C sg: 1.022 13 cm 150L

*Pomacentrus sulfureus* 346
9-10 26°C sg: 1.022 10 cm 100L

*Pomacentrus amboinensis* 346 (juv.)
6-8 26°C sg: 1.022 12 cm 150L

*Pomacentrus vaiuli* 346
6-8 26°C sg: 1.022 8 cm 100L

*Pomacentrus bankanensis* 346
6-8 26°C sg: 1.022 11 cm 100L

*Pomacentrus moluccensis* 346
6-7 26°C sg: 1.022 11 cm 100L

*Pomacentrus chrysurus* 346
6-8 26°C sg: 1.022 12 cm 150L

*Pomacentrus pavo* 346
6-9 26°C sg: 1.022 13 cm 150L

*Pomacentrus pikei* 346
9 26°C sg: 1.022 12 cm 150L

*Pomacentrus trilineatus* 346
10 26°C sg: 1.022 7 cm 100L

*Pomacentrus* sp. 346
9 26°C sg: 1.022 10 cm 150L

*Stegastes fasciolatus* 346
6 26°C sg: 1.022 13 cm 150L

*Stegastes* sp. 346
7, 9 26°C sg: 1.022 9 cm 100L

*Stegastes* sp. 346
9 26°C sg: 1.022 8 cm 100L

*Stegastes albifasciatus* 346
6-7 26°C sg: 1.022 13 cm 150L

*Stegastes lividus* 346
6-10 26°C sg: 1.022 15 cm 150L

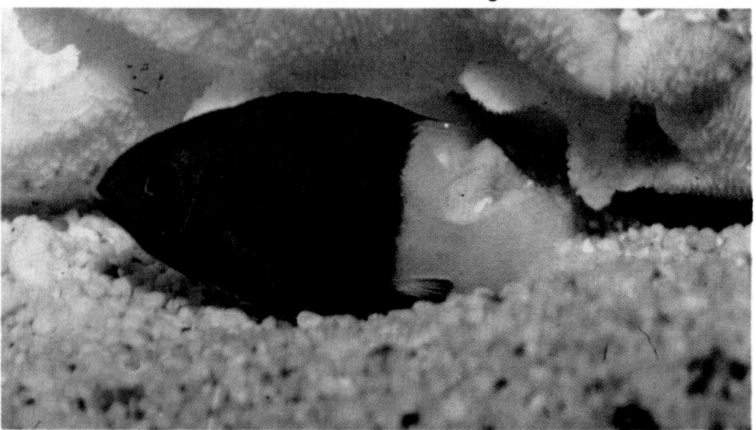

*Stegastes* sp. 346
3 24°C sg: 1.023 12 cm 150L

*Pomacentrus milleri* 346
7 26°C sg: 1.022 7 cm 80L

*Stegastes apicalis* 346
8 26°C sg: 1.022 15 cm 150L

*Stegastes fasciolatus* 346
6 26°C sg: 1.022 13 cm 150L

*Stegastes simsiang* 346
7 26°C sg: 1.022 15 cm 150L

*Pomacentrus milleri* 346
7 26°C sg: 1.022 7 cm 80L

Stegastes rectifraenum 346
3 26°C sg: 1.022 10 cm 100L

Stegastes rectifraenum 346
3 26°C sg: 1.022 10 cm 100L

Stegastes gascoynei 346
6, 11-12 26°C sg: 1.022 15 cm 150L

Stegastes leucorus 346
3 26°C sg: 1.022 50 cm 500L

Stegastes aureus 346
6 26°C sg: 1.022 13 cm 150L

Stegastes emeryi 346
6 26°C sg: 1.022 11 cm 100L

Stegastes nigricans 346
6-7 26°C sg: 1.022 15 cm 150L

Stegastes obreptus 346
7 26°C sg: 1.022 12 cm 150L

*Stegastes partitus* 346
2 26°C sg: 1.022 10 cm 100L

*Stegastes partitus* 346
2 26°C sg: 1.022 10 cm 100L

*Stegastes planifrons* 346
2 26°C sg: 1.022 13 cm 150L

*Stegastes planifrons* 346
2 26°C sg: 1.022 13 cm 150L

*Stegastes dorsopunicans* 346
2 26°C sg: 1.022 15 cm 150L

*Stegastes dorsopunicans* 346
2 26°C sg: 1.022 15 cm 150L

*Stegastes redemptus* 346
3 26°C sg: 1.022 12 cm 150L

*Stegastes redemptus* 346
3 26°C sg: 1.022 12 cm 150L

*Stegastes diencaeus* 346
2 26°C sg: 1.022 13 cm 150L

*Stegastes mellis* 346
2 26°C sg: 1.022 12.5 cm 800L

*Stegastes variabilis* 346
2 26°C sg: 1.022 13 cm 150L

*Stegastes variabilis* 346
2 26°C sg: 1.022 13 cm 800L

*Stegastes imbricata* 346
13 26°C sg: 1.022 13 cm 150L

*Stegastes leucostictus* 346
2 26°C sg: 1.022 10 cm 100L

*Stegastes flavilatus* 346
3 26°C sg: 1.022 5 cm 50L

*Stegastes flavilatus* 346
3 26°C sg: 1.022 5 cm 50L

*Microspathodon dorsalis* 346
3 26°C sg: 1.022 31 cm 300L

*Microspathodon chrysurus* 346
2 26°C sg: 1.022 20 cm 200L

*Microspathodon bairdi* 346
3 26°C sg: 1.022 20 cm 200L

*Pristotis jerdoni* 346
7-8 26°C sg: 1.022 11 cm 100L

*Microspathodon dorsalis* 346
3 26°C sg: 1.022 31 cm 300L

*Microspathodon chrysurus* 346
2 26°C sg: 1.022 20 cm 200L

*Microspathodon frontalis* 346
13 26°C sg: 1.022 25 cm 300L

*Pristotis cyanostigma* 346
10 26°C sg: 1.022 10 cm 100L

*Dischistodus prosopotaenia* 346
6-9 26°C sg: 1.022 15 cm 150L

*Dischistodus pseudochrysopoecilus* 346
6-7 26°C sg: 1.022 16 cm 200L

*Dischistodus chrysopoecilus* 346
6-7 26°C sg: 1.022 16 cm 200L

*Dischistodus perspicillatus* 346
6-9 26°C sg: 1.022 16 cm 200L

*Dischistodus prosopotaenia* 346
6-9 26°C sg: 1.022 15 cm 150L

*Dichistodus fasciatus* 346
7-8 26°C sg: 1.022 11.5 cm 150L

*Dischistodus melanotus* 346
6, 11-12 24°C sg: 1.022 10 cm 100L

*Mecaenichthys immaculatus* 346
12 23°C sg: 1.024 10 cm 100L

#337

*Paracirrhites forsteri* 348
6-10 ◐ ♥ 26°C sg: 1.022 25 cm 300L

*Cirrhitichthys aprinus* 348
6-9 ◐ ♥ 26°C sg: 1.022 7 cm 80L

*Cirrhitichthys oxycephalus* 348
3-10 26°C sg: 1.022 8 cm 100L

*Cirrhitichthys bleekeri* 348
9 26°C sg: 1.022 10 cm 100L

*Cirrhitichthys aprinus* 348
6-9 26°C sg: 1.022 7 cm 80L

*Cirrhitichthys guichenoti* 348
9 26°C sg: 1.022 11 cm 100L

*Cirrhitichthys oxycephalus* 348
3-10 26°C sg: 1.022 8 cm 100L

*Cirrhitichthys aureus* 348
5-7 26°C sg: 1.022 13 cm 150L

*Cirrhitichthys falco* 348
7 26°C sg: 1.022 5 cm 50L

*Cirrhitus rivulatus* 348
3 26°C sg: 1.022 52 cm 500L

*Cirrhitus rivulatus* 348
3 26°C sg: 1.022 50 cm 500L

*Cirrhitus splendens* 348
11-12 26°C sg: 1.022 20 cm 200L

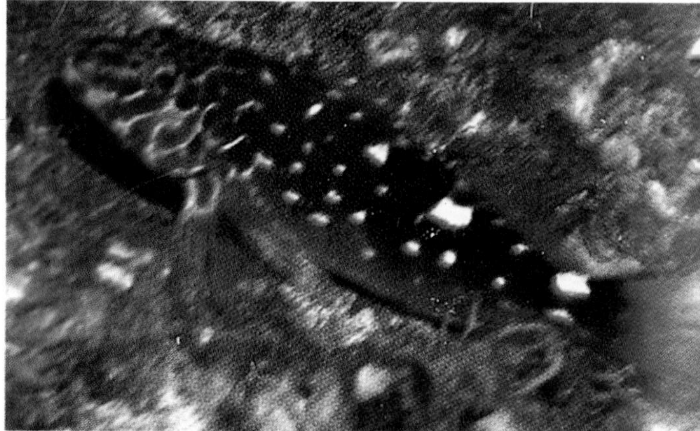

*Cirrhitus atlanticus* 348
13 24°C sg: 1.023 19 cm 200L

*Neocirrhitus armatus* 348
6, 8 26°C sg: 1.022 7.5 cm 80L

*Cyprinocirrhites* sp. 348
6 25°C sg: 1.022 12 cm 150L

*Cirrhitops fasciatus* 348
6-9 ◐ ♥ 26°C sg: 1.022 13 cm 150L

*Cyprinocirrhites polyactus* 348
6-9 ◐ ♥ 25°C sg: 1.022 12 cm 150L

*Paracirrhites arcatus* 348
6-9 ◐ ♥ 26°C sg: 1.022 14 cm 150L

*Paracirrhites forsteri* 348
6-10 ◐ ♥ 26°C sg: 1.022 25 cm 300L

*Paracirrhites hemistictus* 348
6 ◐ ♥ 26°C sg: 1.022 18 cm 200L

*Paracirrhites hemistictus* 348
6 ◐ ♥ 26°C sg: 1.022 18 cm 200L

*Cirrhitus pinnulatus* 348
6-10 ◐ ♥ 26°C sg: 1.022 25 cm 300L

*Oxycirrhitus typus* 348
3, 6-10 ◐ ♥ 26°C sg: 1.022 13 cm

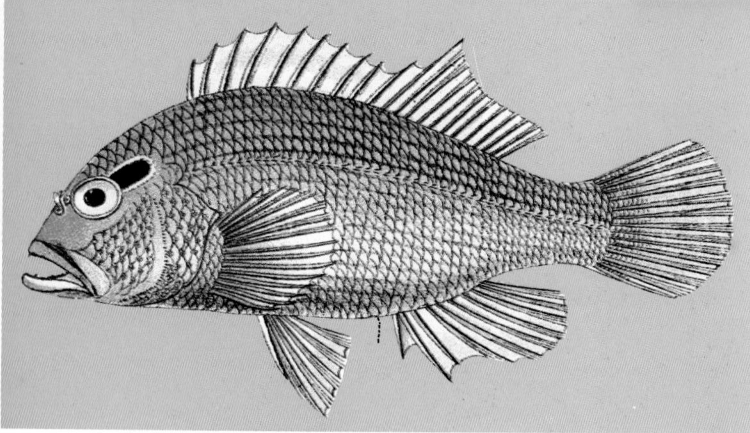

*Paracirrhites arcatus* 348
6-9 26°C sg: 1.022 14 cm 150L

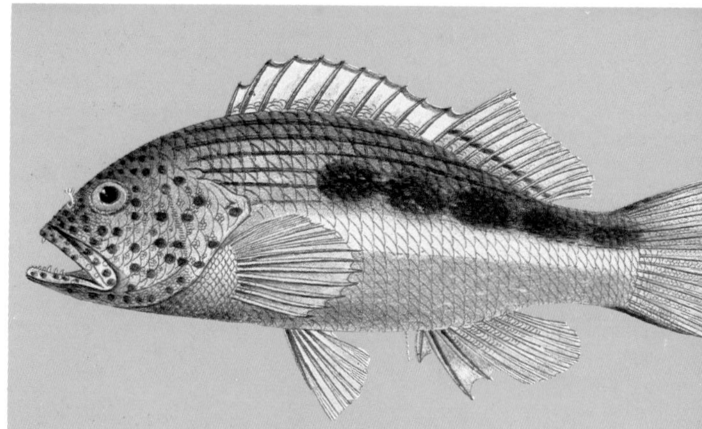

*Paracirrhites forsteri* 348
6-10 26°C sg: 1.022 25 cm 300L

*Cirrhites pinnulatus* 348
6-10 26°C sg: 1.022 25 cm 300L

*Cirrhitus pinnulatus* 348
6-10 26°C sg: 1.022 25 cm 300L

*Cirrhitichthys aprinus* 348
6-9 26°C sg: 1.022 7 cm 80L

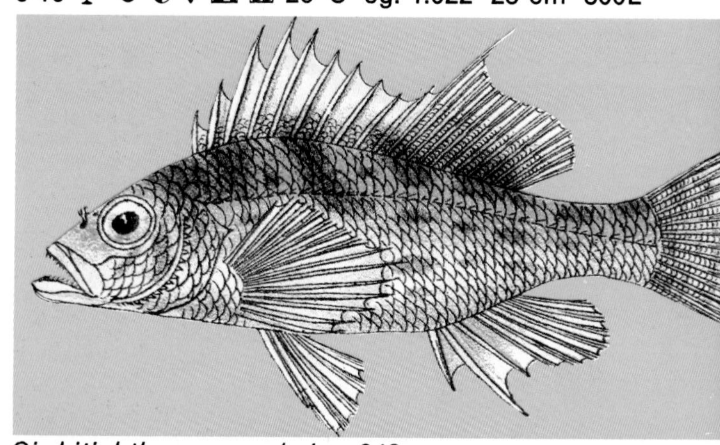

*Cirrhitichthys oxycephalus* 348
3-10 26°C sg: 1.022 8 cm 100L

*Amblycirrhitus oxyrhynchus* 348
7 26°C sg: 1.022 8 cm 50L

*Oxycirrhites typus* 348
3, 6-10 26°C sg: 1.022 13 cm 150L

*Amblycirrhitus pinos* 348
2, 13 26°C sg: 1.022 68 cm 700L

*Amblycirrhitus earnshawi* 348
13 26°C sg: 1.022 18 cm· 200L

*Paracirrhites forsteri* 348
7-10 26°C sg: 1.022 25 cm 300L

*Chironemus marmoratus* 349
11 21°C sg: 1.024 35 cm 350L

*Amblycirrhites bimacula* 348
6-9 26°C sg: 1.022 7 cm 80L

*Paracirrhites xanthus* 348
6 26°C sg: 1.022 51 cm 500L

*Paracirrhites forsteri* 348
7-10 26°C sg: 1.022 25 cm 300L

*Threpterius maculosus* 349
12 24°C sg: 1.024 12 cm 150L

*Aplodactylus meandritus* 350
11 22°C sg: 1.024 38 cm 400L

*Cheilodactylus zonatus* 351
6, 7 25°C sg: 1.022 45 cm 500L

*Nemadactylus macropterus* 351
11 22°C sg: 1.024 58 cm 600L

*Cheilodactylus douglasi* 351
11 22°C sg: 1.024 70 cm 700L

*Nemadactylus valenciennesi* 351
11 22°C sg: 1.024 70 cm 700L

*Cheilodactylus fuscus* 351
8, 12 22°C sg: 1.024 46 cm 500L

*Cheilodactylus spectabilis* 351
11-12 23°C sg: 1.024 20 cm 200L

*Latridopsis ciliaris* 352
11 22°C sg: 1.024 105 cm 1200L

*Cheilodactylus gibbosus* 351
8, 12 ♀ ~ ◐ ♥ ▣ ▭ 24°C sg: 1.022 30 cm 300L

*Cheilodactylus gibbosus* 351
8, 12♀ ~ ◐ ♥ ▣ ▭ 26°C sg: 1.022 30 cm 300L

*Cheilodactylus ephippium* 351
11-12 ♀ ~ ◐ ♥ ▣ ▭ 23°C sg: 1.024 20 cm 200L

*Cheilodactylus vittatus* 351
6-7♀ ~ ◐ ♥ ▣ ▭ 26°C sg: 1.022 25 cm 300L

*Cheilodactylus vittatus* 351
6-7♀ ~ ◐ ♥ ▣ ▭ 26°C sg: 1.022 25 cm 300L

*Cheilodactylus quadricornis* 351
5, 7♀ ~ ◐ ♥ ▣ ▭ 25°C sg: 1.022 40 cm 400L

*Cheilodactylus gibbosus* 351
8, 12♀ ~ ◐ ♥ ▣ ▭ 25°C sg: 1.022 30 cm 300L

*Cheilodactylus vittatus* 351
6-7♀ ~ ◐ ♥ ▣ ▭ 26°C sg: 1.022 25 cm 300L

*Cheilodactylus nigripes* 351
12 23°C sg: 1.024 24 cm 250L

*Cheilodactylus rubrolabiatus* 351
12 24°C sg: 1.022 50 cm 500L

*Dactylosargus* sp. 350
7, 12 26°C sg: 1.022 40 cm 500L

*Dactylophora nigricans* 351
12 24°C sg: 1.024 120 cm 1200L

*Chirodactylus brachydactylus* 351
9 26°C sg: 1.022 40 cm 400L

*Chirodactylus brachydactylus* 351
9 26°C sg: 1.022 40 cm 400L

*Monodactylus argentus* 328
6-10 26°C sg: 1.017 23 cm 250L

*Monodactylus falciformes* 328
9-10 26°C sg: 1.017 31 cm 300L

*Cheilodactylus zonatus* 351
6, 7 ♀ ∿ ◐ ♥ ▣ ▭ 25°C sg: 1.022 45 cm 500L

*Owstonia grammodon (?)* 353
7 ◐ 26°C sg: 1.022 23 cm 250L

*Acanthocepola limbata* 354
7 ◐ 26°C sg: 1.022 41 cm 400L

*Cepola australis* 354
12 ◐ 26°C sg: 1.022 38 cm 400L

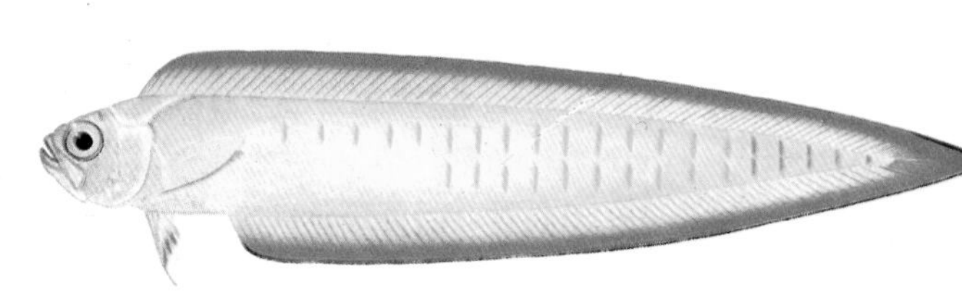

*Acanthocepola indica* 354
7 ◐ 26°C sg: 1.022 35 cm 400L

*Polydactylus* sp. 357
7 ◐ 26°C sg: 1.022 30 cm 300L

*Polydactylus virginicus* 357
2 ◐ ♥ 26°C sg: 1.022 30 cm 300L

*Eleutheronema tetradactylum* 357
7 ◐ 26°C sg: 1.022 22 cm 200L

*Polydactylus sexfilis* 357
7-9 ◐ ♥ 26°C sg: 1.022 100 cm 1000L

*Liza vaigiensis* 355
7-9 26°C sg: 1.020 60 cm 600L

*Liza oligolepis* 355
7 26°C sg: 1.017 30 cm 300L

*Liza saliens* 355
15 26°C sg: 1.010 40 cm 400L

*Liza* sp. 355
15 26°C sg: 1.020 35 cm 400L

*Liza vaigiensis* 355
7-9 26°C sg: 1.020 60 cm 600L

*Mugil cephalus* 355
2 26°C sg: 1.020 50 cm 500L

*Liza vaigiensis* 355
7-9 26°C sg: 1.020 60 cm 600L

*Aldrichetta forsteri* 355
11 26°C sg: 1.020 50 cm 500L

*Sphyraena obtusata* 356
7-10 26°C sg: 1.022 90 cm 1000L

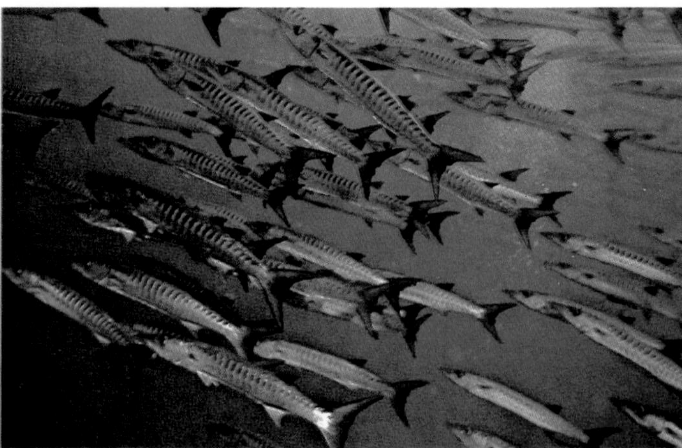

*Sphyraena jello* 356
7-10 26°C sg: 1.022 125 cm 1500L

*Sphyraena barracuda* (juv.) 356
1-2, *7-10* 25°C sg: 1.022 30 cm 2000L

*Sphyraena barracuda* 356
1-2, 7-10 25°C sg: 1.022 200 cm 2000L

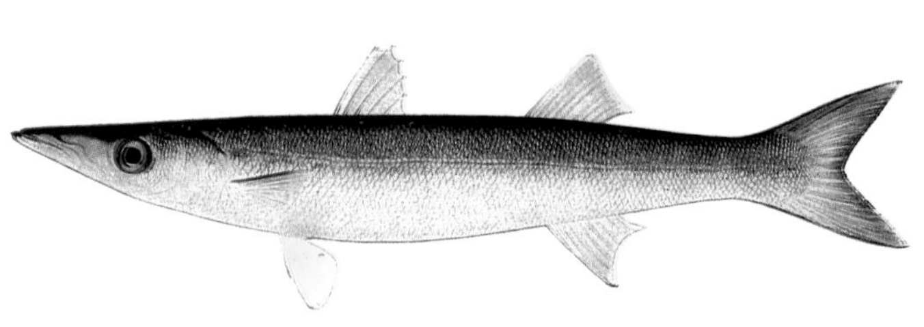

*Sphyraena pinguis* 356
5-7 26°C sg: 1.022 30 cm 300L

*Sphyraena qenie* 356
7-10 26°C sg: 1.022 115 cm 1200L

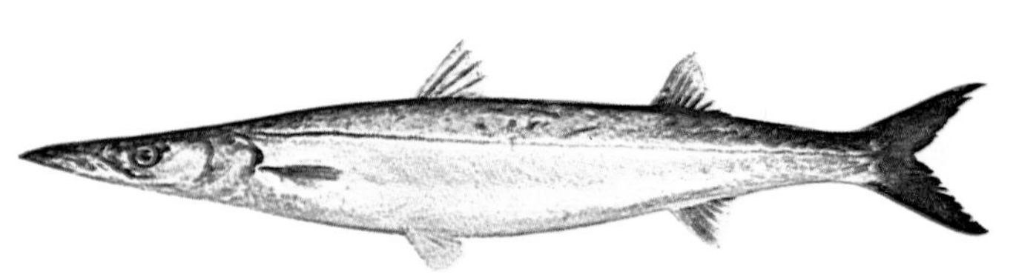

*Sphyraena argentea* 356
3-4 26°C sg: 1.022 110 cm 1200L

*Sphyraena flavicauda* 356
7-9 26°C sg: 1.022 50 cm 500L

#347A

*Sphyraena barracuda* 356
1-2, 7-10 25°C sg: 1.022 200 cm 2000L

*Sphyraena barracuda* 356
1-2, 7-10 25°C sg: 1.022 200 cm 2000L

#348

*Paracheilinus filamentosus* 358
7 ~ ◐ ♥ ▣ ☷ 26°C sg: 1.022 8 cm 100L

*Anampses caeruleopunctatus* 358
6-10 ∿ ◐ ♥ ▣ ▣ 26°C sg: 1.020 40 cm 300L

*Anampses meleagrides* 358
7-10 ∿ ◐ ♥ ▣ ▣ 26°C sg: 1.020 22 cm 200L

*Anampses cuvier* 358 ♂
6 ∿ ◐ ♥ ▣ ▣ 26°C sg: 1.020 38 cm 300L

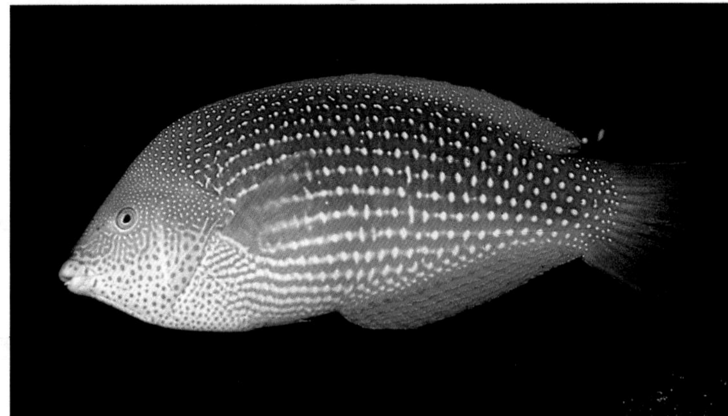

*Anampses cuvier* 358 ♀
6 ∿ ◐ ♥ ▣ ▣ 26°C sg: 1.020 38 cm 300L

*Anampses chrysocephalus* 358 ♂
6 ∿ ◐ ♥ ▣ ▣ 26°C sg: 1.020 16 cm 200L

*Anampses chrysocephalus* 358 ♀
6 ∿ ◐ ♥ ▣ ▣ 26°C sg: 1.020 16 cm 200L

*Anampses geographicus* 358
6-9 ∿ ◐ ♥ ▣ ▣ 26°C sg: 1.020 25 cm 250L

*Anampses neoguinaicus* 358
7-8 ∿ ◐ ♥ ▣ ▣ 25°C sg: 1.020 14 cm 150L

*Anampses caeruleopunctatus* 358
6-10 ∿ ◐ ♥ 26°C sg: 1.020 40 cm 300L

*Anampses lineatus* 358
9-10 ∿ ◐ ♥ 26°C sg: 1.020 12 cm 150L

*Bodianus opercularis* 358
7-9 ◐ ♥ 26°C sg: 1.020 12 cm 150L

*Bodianus axillaris* 358 (juv.)
6-9 ◐ ♥ 26°C sg: 1.020 20 cm 250L

*Anampses lennardi* 358
7 ∿ ◐ ♥ 25°C sg: 1.020 25 cm 300L

*Anampses twisti* 358
6-10 ∿ ◐ ♥ 26°C sg: 1.020 18 cm 200L

*Bodianus bimaculatus* 358
7 ◐ ♥ 26°C sg: 1.020 9 cm 100L

*Bodianus axillaris* 358
6-9 ◐ ♥ 26°C sg: 1.020 20 cm 250L

*Anampses lennardi* 358
7 25°C sg: 1.020 25 cm 300L

*Anampses femininus* 358
6 26°C sg: 1.020 21 cm 200L

*Pseudocoris bleekeri* 358
7 26°C sg: 1.022 15 cm 200L

*Anampses elegans* 358
11-12 26°C sg: 1.020 28 cm 300L

*Bodianus* sp. 358
9 25°C sg: 1.020 21 cm 200L

*Bodianus oxycephalus* 358
7, 9 25°C sg: 1.020 27 cm 300L

*Bodianus speciosus* 358
13 26°C sg: 1.022 80 cm 800L

*Bodianus masudai* 358
5, 7 26°C sg: 1.020 12 cm 200L

*Bodianus bilunulatus* 358
6-9 26°C sg: 1.020 55 cm 600L

*Bodianus macrourus* 358
7-9 26°C sg: 1.020 40 cm 500L

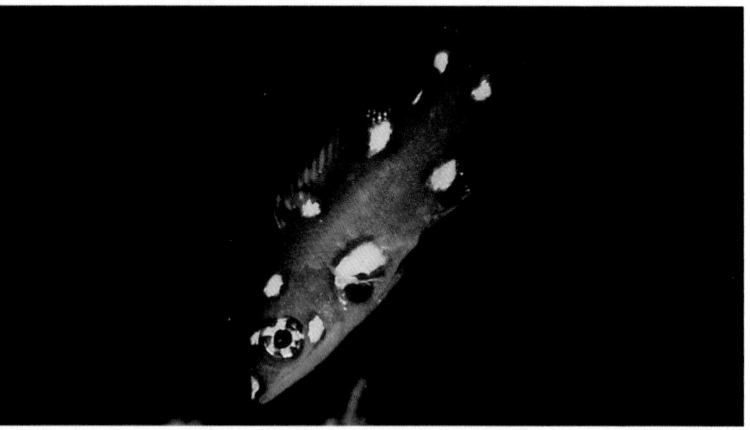

*Bodianus mesothorax* 358 (juv.)
7 26°C sg: 1.020 30 cm 300L

*Bodianus mesothorax* 358
7 26°C sg: 1.020 30 cm 300L

*Bodianus diana* 358 (juv.)
7-10 26°C sg: 1.020 25 cm 300L

*Bodianus diana* 358 (juv.)
7-10 26°C sg: 1.020 25 cm 300L

*Bodianus perdito* 358
6-9 26°C sg: 1.020 80 cm 800L

*Bodianus perdito* 358
6-9 26°C sg: 1.020 80 cm 800L

(juv.)
*Bodianus bilunulatus* 358
6-9 26°C sg: 1.020 55 cm 600L

*Bodianus bilunulatus* 358
6-9 26°C sg: 1.020 55 cm 600L

*Bodianus anthioides* 358
6-10 26°C sg: 1.020 21 cm 200L

*Bodianus diana* 358
7-10 26°C sg: 1.020 25 cm 300L

*Bodianus frenchii* 358
7-9 26°C sg: 1.020 50 cm 500L

*Bodianus macrourus* 358
7-9 26°C sg: 1.020 40 cm 500L

*Choerodon rubescens* 358
12 25°C sg: 1.020 75 cm 800L

*Achoerodus gouldii* 358
8, 12 26°C sg: 1.020 125 cm 2000L

*Bodianus rufus* 358
2 26°C sg: 1.020 50 cm 500L

*Bodianus rufus* 358
2 26°C sg: 1.020 50 cm 500L

(juv.)
*Bodianus pulchellus* 358
2 26°C sg: 1.020 23 cm 300L

*Bodianus pulchellus* 358
2 26°C sg: 1.020 23 cm 300L

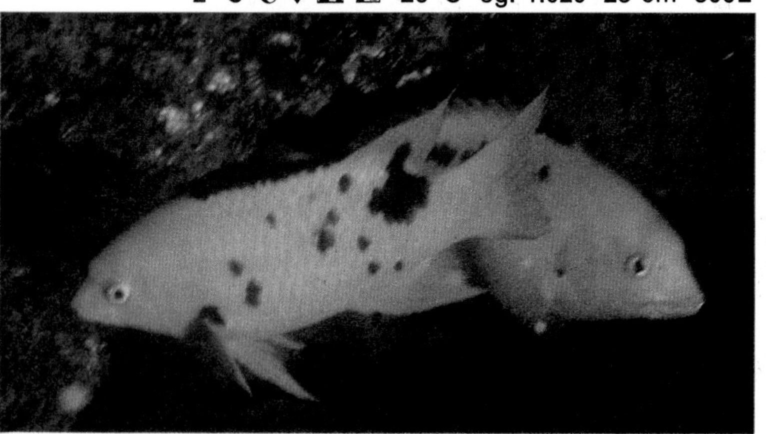

*Bodianus eclancheri* 358
3 26°C sg: 1.020 25 cm 300L

*Bodianus eclancheri* 358
3 26°C sg: 1.020 25 cm 300L

*Bodianus diplotaenia* 358 ♀
3 26°C sg: 1.020 76 cm 800L

*Bodianus diplotaenia* 358 ♂
3 26°C sg: 1.020 76 cm 800L

*Choerodon cyanodus* 358
12 26°C sg: 1.020 30 cm 300L

*Choerodon anchorago* 358
7-9 26°C sg: 1.020 25 cm 300L

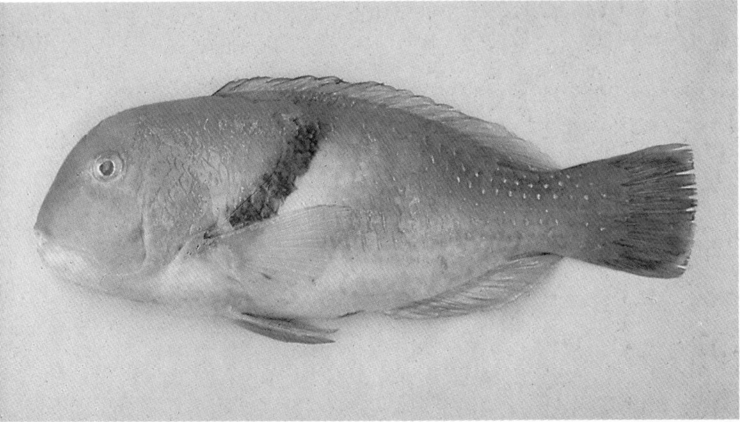

*Choerodon azurio* 358
7 26°C sg: 1.020 40 cm 500L

*Choerodon jordani* 358
7 *26°C sg: 1.020 14 cm 200L*

*Choerodon schoenleinii* 358
7 26°C sg: 1.020 100 cm 2000L

*Choerodon schoenleinii* 358
7 26°C sg: 1.020 100 cm 2000L

*Cheilinus oxycephalus* 358
7-9 26°C sg: 1.020 17 cm 200L

*Cheilinus unifasciatus* 358
6-7 26°C sg: 1.020 30 cm 300L

*Cheilinus bimaculatus* 358
7-9 26°C sg: 1.020 15 cm 200L

*Cheilinus digrammus* 358
6-10 26°C sg: 1.020 35 cm 400L

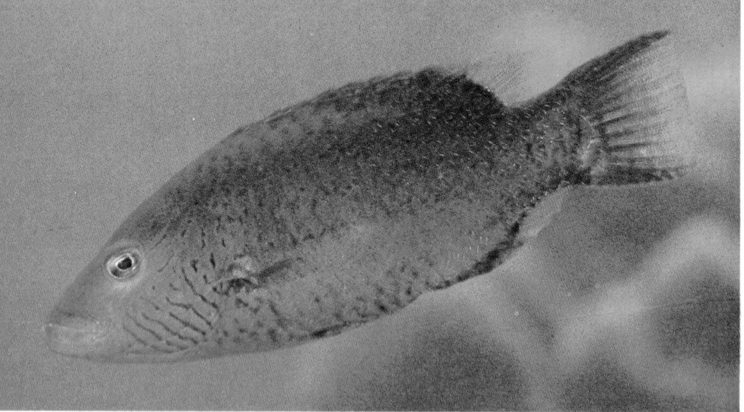

*Cheilinus digrammus* 358
6-10 26°C sg: 1.020 35 cm 400L

*Cheilinus lunulatus* 358
10 27°C sg: 1.020 50 cm 500L

*Cheilinus bimaculatus* 358
7-9 26°C sg: 1.020 15 cm 200L

*Cheilinus digrammus* 358
6-10 26°C sg: 1.020 35 cm 400L

*Cheilinus fasciatus* 358
6-9 26°C sg: 1.020 35 cm 400L

*Cheilinus trilobatus* 358
6-9 26°C sg: 1.020 40 cm 400L

*Cheilinus undulatus* 358 ♂
6-10 26°C sg: 1.022 230 cm 5000L

*Cheilinus digrammus* 358
6-10 26°C sg: 1.020 35 cm 400L

*Cheilinus chlorourus* 358
6-9 26°C sg: 1.020 36 cm 400L

*Cirrhilabrus* sp. 358 ♂
9 26°C sg: 1.020 10 cm 100L

*Cirrhilabrus cyanopleura* 358 ♀
7 25°C sg: 1.020 15 cm 200L

*Cirrhilabrus cyanopleura* 358 ♂
7 25°C sg: 1.020 15 cm 200L

♂ *Cirrhilabrus exquisitus* 358
6-9 26°C sg: 1.020 11 cm 150L

*Cirrhilabrus exquisitus* 358
6-9 26°C sg: 1.020 11 cm 150L ♀

♂ *Cirrhilabrus rubriventralis* 358
10 ∿ ◐ ♥ 26°C sg: 1.030 7.5 cm 100L

*Cirrhilabrus melanomarginatus* 358
7 ∿ ◐ ♥ 26°C sg: 1.022 13 cm 100L ♂

*Cirrhilabrus* sp. 358
7-8 ∿ ◐ ♥ 26°C sg: 1.022 10 cm 100L

*Cirrhilabrus temmincki* 358
7, 12 ∿ ◐ ♥ 26°C sg: 1.022 10 cm 100L ♂

*Cirrhilabrus laboutі* 358
7-8 ∿ ◐ ♥ 26°C sg: 1.022 10 cm 100L

*Cirrhilabrus* sp. "D." 358
7-8 ∿ ◐ ♥ 26°C sg: 1.022 10 cm 100L ♂

♂ *Cirrhilabrus lineatus* 358
7-8 ∿ ◐ ♥ 26°C sg: 1.022 10 cm 100L

*Cirrhilabrus cyanopleura* 358
5, 7 ∿ ◐ ♥ 26°C sg: 1.022 9 cm 100L ♂

*Cirrhilabrus jordani* 358
6 ∿ ◐ ♥ 26°C sg: 1.022 10 cm 100L

*Cirrhilabrus scottorum* 358
6 ∿ ◐ ♥ 26°C sg: 1.022 8 cm 100L

*Cirrhilabrus lubbocki* 358
7 ∿ ◐ ♥ 26°C sg: 1.022 7 cm 100L

*Cirrhilabrus rubripinnis* 358
7 ∿ ◐ ♥ 26°C sg: 1.022 7 cm 100L

*Verriculus sanguineus* 358
6 ∿ ◐ ♥ 26°C sg: 1.022 20 cm 150L

*Conniella apterygia* 358 ♂
12 ◐ ♥ 24°C sg: 1.020 8 cm 100L

*Coris caudimacula* 358
7-10 ◐ ♥ 26°C sg: 1.020 20 cm 200L

*Coris auricularis* 358 ♂
12 ◐ ♥ 24°C sg: 1.020 32 cm 400L

*Coris auricularis* 358 (juv.)
12 ◐ ♥ 24°C sg: 1.020 32 cm 400L

*Coris aygula* 358 (juv.)
6-10 ◐ ♥ 26°C sg: 1.020 120 cm 2000L

*Coris aygula* 358 ♂
6-10 ◐ ♥ 26°C sg: 1.020 120 cm 2000L

*Coris variegata* 358
6-10 ◐ ♥ 26°C sg: 1.020 20 cm 200L

*Coris variegata* 358
6-10 ◐ ♥ 26°C sg: 1.020 20 cm 200L

*Coris julis* 358 ♀
15 ◐ ♥ 26°C sg: 1.022 25 cm 300L

*Coris julis* 358 ♂
15 ◐ ♥ 26°C sg: 1.022 25 cm 300L

*Coris pictoides* 358
7, 12 ◐ ♥ 24°C sg: 1.020 15 cm 200L

*Coris bulbifrons* 358 ♂
11-12 ◐ ♥ 26°C sg: 1.020 30 cm 400L

*Coris picta* 358 (juv.)
7-8, 11-12 ◐ ♥ 26°C sg: 1.020 25 cm 300L

*Coris picta* 358 ♂
7-8, 11-12 ◐ ♥ 26°C sg: 1.020 25 cm 300L

*Coris sandageri* 358 (juv.)
11-12 ◐ ♥ 25°C sg: 1.020 25 cm 300L

*Coris dorsomacula* 358 ♂
7-8 ◐ ♥ 26°C sg: 1.020 15 cm 200L

*Coris auricularis* 358 (juv.)
12 🍸 ◐ ♥ ▦ ▤ 24°C sg: 1.020 32 cm 400L

*Coris auricularis* 358
12 🍸 ◐ ♥ ▦ ▤ 24°C sg: 1.020 32 cm 400L ♀

*Coris flavovittata* 358 ♂
6 🍸 ◐ ♥ ▦ ▤ 26°C sg: 1.020 45 cm 500L

*Coris flavovittata* 358
6 🍸 ◐ ♥ ▦ ▤ 26°C sg: 1.020 45 cm 500L ♀

*Coris caudimacula* 358 ♀
7-10 🍸 ◐ ♥ ▦ ▤ 26°C sg: 1.020 20 cm 200L

*Coris caudimacula* 358
7-10 🍸 ◐ ♥ ▦ ▤ 26°C sg: 1.020 20 cm 200L ♂

*Coris venusta* 358 ♂
6 🍸 ◐ ♥ ▦ ▤ 26°C sg: 1.020 15 cm 200L

*Coris ballieui* 358
6 🍸 ◐ ♥ ▦ ▤ 26°C sg: 1.020 35 cm 400L

*Coris gaimard africana* 358 ♂
9 ◐ ♥ 26°C sg: 1.020 35 cm 400L

*Coris formosa* 358 ♀
9 ◐ ♥ 26°C sg: 1.020 60 cm 800L

*Coris formosa* 358 ♂
9 ◐ ♥ 26°C sg: 1.020 60 cm 800L

*Diproctacanthus xanthurus* 358
7 ◐ ♥ 26°C sg: 1.020 10 cm 100L

*Coris gaimard africana* 358 (juv.)
9 ◐ ♥ 26°C sg: 1.020 35 cm 400L

*Coris formosa* 358 (juv.)
9 ◐ ♥ 26°C sg: 1.020 60 cm 800L

*Epibulus insidiator* 358
6-10 ◐ ♥ 26°C sg: 1.022 35 cm 400L

*Gomphosus varius* 358
7-9 ◐ ♥ 26°C sg: 1.020 30 cm 300L

*Halichoeres biocellatus* 358
7 ◐ ♥ 26°C sg: 1.020 10 cm 100L

*Halichoeres trispilus* 358
9 ◐ ♥ 26°C sg: 1.020 10 cm 100L

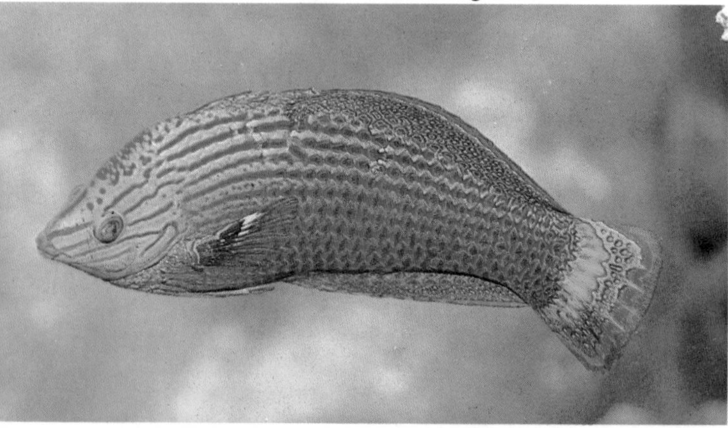

*Halichoeres marginatus* 358 ♂
6-10 ◐ ♥ 26°C sg: 1.020 18 cm 200L

*Halichoeres scapularis* 358 ♀
9-10 ◐ ♥ 26°C sg: 1.020 20 cm 200L

*Halichoeres chrysus* 358
7 ◐ ♥ 26°C sg: 1.020 10 cm 100L

*Halichoeres nebulosus* 358
7-9 ◐ ♥ 26°C sg: 1.020 11 cm 100L

*Halichoeres marginatus* 358 ♀
6-10 ◐ ♥ 26°C sg: 1.020 18 cm 200L

*Halichoeres scapularis* 358 ♂
9-10 ◐ ♥ 26°C sg: 1.020 20 cm 200L

*Halichoeres prosopeion* 358 (juv.)
7 ◐ ♥ 26°C sg: 1.020 17 cm 200L

*Halichoeres prosopeion* 358
7 ◐ ♥ 26°C sg: 1.020 17 cm 200L

*Halichoeres zeylonicus* 358
9 ◐ ♥ 26°C sg: 1.020 17 cm 200L

*Halichoeres hartzfeldii* 358
7 ◐ ♥ 26°C sg: 1.020 18 cm 200L

*Halichoeres trispilus* 358
9 ◐ ♥ 26°C sg: 1.020 10 cm 100L

*Halichoeres iridis* 358 (juv.)
9 ◐ ♥ 26°C sg: 1.020 11 cm 100L

*Halichoeres brownfieldi* 358 (juv.)
12 ◐ ♥ 26°C sg: 1.020 15 cm 200L

*Halichoeres brownfieldi* 358
12 ◐ ♥ 26°C sg: 1.020 15 cm 200L

*Halichoeres pelicieri* 358 ♀
9 ◐ ♥ 26°C sg: 1.020 15 cm 200L

*Halichoeres melasmopomas* 358 ♀
7, 9 ◐ ♥ 26°C sg: 1.020 12 cm 100L

*Halichoeres cosmetus* 358 ♀
9 ◐ ♥ 26°C sg: 1.020 11 cm 100L

*Halichoeres timorensis* 358 ♂
7 ◐ ♥ 26°C sg: 1.020 20 cm 200L

*Halichoeres timorensis* 358 (juv.)
7 ◐ ♥ 26°C sg: 1.020 20 cm 200L

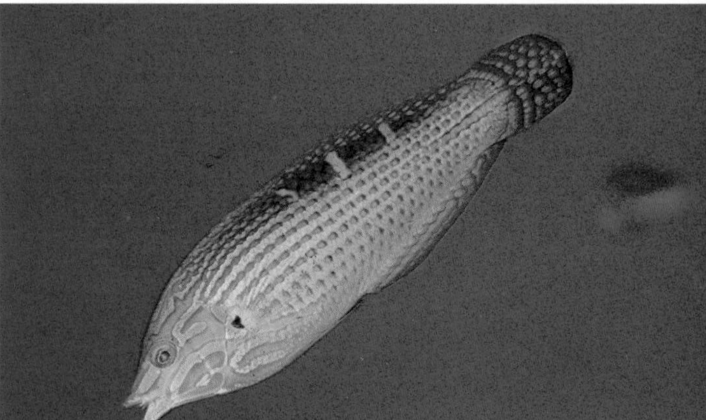

*Halichoeres melanurus* 358
7 ◐ ♥ 26°C sg: 1.020 12 cm 100L ♂

*Halichoeres iridis* 358 (juv.)
9 ◐ ♥ 26°C sg: 1.020 11 cm 100L

*Halichoeres melanochir* 358
7 ◐ ♥ 26°C sg: 1.020 18 cm 200L

*Halichoeres argus* 358 (juv.)
7 26°C sg: 1.020 12 cm 100L

*Halichoeres biocellatus* 358 (juv.)
7 26°C sg: 1.020 10 cm 100L

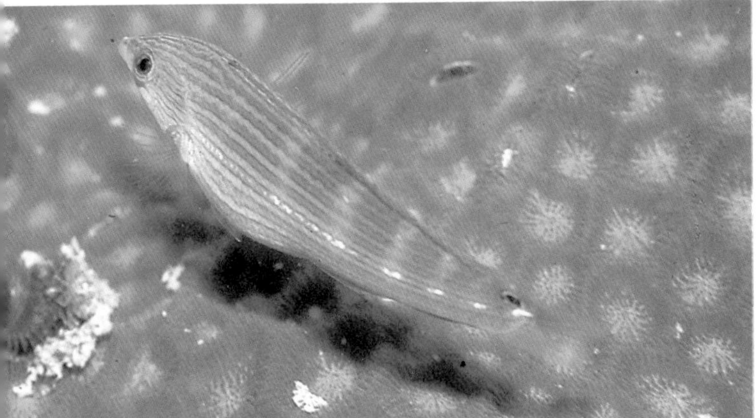

*Halichoeres hoeveni* 358 (juv.)
6-7 26°C sg: 1.020 12 cm 100L

*Halichoeres bimaculatus* 358
7, 9 26°C sg: 1.020 12 cm 100L

*Halichoeres argus* 358
7 26°C sg: 1.020 12 cm 100L ♂

*Halichoeres biocellatus* 358
7 26°C sg: 1.020 10 cm 100L

*Halichoeres melanurus* 358 ♂
7 26°C sg: 1.020 12 cm 100L

*Halichoeres chloropterus* 358
7 26°C sg: 1.020 15 cm 200L

*Halichoeres nigrescens* 358
7, 12 ◐ ♥ 26°C sg: 1.020 30 cm 400L

*Halichoeres marginatus* 358 (juv.)
6-10 ◐ ♥ 26°C sg: 1.020 18 cm 200L

*Halichoeres poecilopterus* 358 ♀
7 ◐ ♥ 26°C sg: 1.020 34 cm 400L

*Halichoeres poecilopterus* 358 ♂
7 ◐ ♥ 26°C sg: 1.020 34 cm 400L

*Halichoeres margaritaceus* 358 ♂
6-8 ◐ ♥ 26°C sg: 1.020 12 cm 100L

*Halichoeres margaritaceus* 358 ♀
6-8 ◐ ♥ 26°C sg: 1.020 12 cm 100L

*Halichoeres nebulosus* 358
7-9 ◐ ♥ 26°C sg: 1.020 11 cm 100L

*Halichoeres trimaculatus* 358 ♂
7 ◐ ♥ 26°C sg: 1.020 18 cm 200L

*Halichoeres chloropterus* 358 (juv.)
7 ◐ ♥ 26°C sg: 1.020 15 cm 200L

*Halichoeres chloropterus* 358
7 ◐ ♥ 26°C sg: 1.020 15 cm 200L

*Halichoeres hortulanus* 358 (juv.)
6-10 ◐ ♥ 26°C sg: 1.020 22 cm 300L

*Halichoeres hortulanus* 358 ♂
6-10 ◐ ♥ 26°C sg: 1.020 22 cm 300L

*Halichoeres melanochir* 358
7 ◐ ♥ 26°C sg: 1.020 18 cm 200L

*Halichoeres podostigma* 358
6-7 ◐ ♥ 26°C sg: 1.020 16 cm 200L

*Halichoeres miniatus* 358
7-8 ◐ ♥ 26°C sg: 1.020 10 crn 100L

*Halichoeres ornatissimus* 358
6-7 ◐ ♥ 26°C sg: 1.020 18 cm 200L

*Halichoeres cyanocephalus* 358 (juv.)
2 ◐ ♥ 26°C sg: 1.020 30 cm 300L

*Halichoeres cyanocephalus* 358 ♂
2 ◐ ♥ 26°C sg: 1.020 30 cm 300L

*Halichoeres maculipinna* 358 ♀
2 ◐ ♥ 26°C sg: 1.020 18 cm 200L

*Halichoeres maculipinna* 358 ♂
2 ◐ ♥ 26°C sg: 1.020 18 cm 200L

*Halichoeres poeyi*, (juv.) 358
2 ◐ ♥ 26°C sg: 1.020 20 cm 200L

*Halichoeres poeyi* 358 ♂
2 ◐ ♥ 26°C sg: 1.020 20 cm 200L

*Halichoeres bathyphilus* 358
2 ◐ ♥ 26°C sg: 1.020 23 cm 300L

*Halichoeres pictus* 358 ♂
2 ◐ ♥ 26°C sg: 1.020 13 cm 150L

*Halichoeres garnoti* 358
2 ◐ ♥ 26°C sg: 1.020 19 cm 200L

*Halichoeres garnoti* 358 (juv.)
2 ◐ ♥ 26°C sg: 1.020 19 cm 200L

*Halichoeres bivittatus* 358 ♂
2 ◐ ♥ 26°C sg: 1.020 22 cm 300L

*Halichoeres garnoti* 358 ♂
2 ◐ ♥ 26°C sg: 1.020 19 cm 200L

*Halichoeres bivittatus* 358 ♂
2 ◐ ♥ 26°C sg: 1.020 22 cm 300L

*Halichoeres bivittatus* 358 ♀
2 ◐ ♥ 26°C sg: 1.020 22 cm 300L

*Halichoeres radiatus* 358
2 ◐ ♥ 26°C sg: 1.020 46 cm 500L

*Halichoeres radiatus* 358 ♂
2 ◐ ♥ 26°C sg: 1.020 46 cm 500L

*Halichoeres semicinctus* 358
3 24°C sg: 1.020 36 cm 400L

*Halichoeres chierchiae* 358
3 26°C sg: 1.020 20 cm 200L ♂

*Halichoeres nicholsi* 358 ♀
3 26°C sg: 1.020 38 cm 400L

*Halichoeres nicholsi* 358 ♂
3 26°C sg: 1.020 38 cm 400L

*Halichoeres nicholsi* 358 (juv.)
3 26°C sg: 1.020 38 cm 400L

*Halichoeres* sp. 358
3 26°C sg: 1.020 12 cm 100L

*Halichoeres dispilus* 358 ♀
3 26°C sg: 1.020 20 cm 200L

*Halichoeres dispilus* 358
3 26°C sg: 1.020 20 cm 200L ♂

*Gomphosus varius* 358
7-9 26°C sg: 1.020 30 cm 300L

*Gomphosus caeruleus* 358
9-10 26°C sg: 1.020 28 cm 300L

*Gomphosus varius* 358 (juv.)
7-9 26°C sg: 1.020 30 cm 300L

*Hologymnosus annulatus* 358 (juv.)
7-10 26°C sg: 1.020 40 cm 400L

*Epibulus insidiator* 358
6-10 26°C sg: 1.022 35 cm 400L

*Epibulus insidiator* 358 (juv.)
6-10 26°C sg: 1.022 35 cm 400L

*Pteragogus flagellifer* 358
9 26°C sg: 1.020 20 cm 200L

*Pteragogus pelycus* 358
9 26°C sg: 1.020 15 cm 200L

*Hemigymnus fasciatus* (juv.) 358
7-10 26°C sg: 1.020 40 cm 400L

*Hemigymnus melapterus* 358
6-10 26°C sg: 1.020 90 cm 1000L

*Hologymnosus doliatus* 358 (juv.)
6-10 26°C sg: 1.020 45 cm 500L

*Hologymnosus doliatus* 358 ♂
6-10 26°C sg: 1.020 45 cm 500L

*Hemigymus fasciatus* 358
7-10 26°C sg: 1.020 40 cm 400L

*Hologymnosus annulatus* 358
7-10 26°C sg: 1.020 40 cm 400L

*Hologymnosus doliatus* 358 ♀
6-10 26°C sg: 1.020 45 cm 500L

*Pteragogus pelycus* 358
9 26°C sg: 1.020 15 cm 200L

*Labrichthys unilineatus* 358 (juv.)
6-10 26°C sg: 1.020 18 cm 200L

*Labropsis xanthonota* 358
6-9 26°C sg: 1.020 10 cm 100L

*Macropharyngodon bipartitus* 358
9-10 26°C sg: 1.020 11 cm 100L

*Macropharyngodon ornatus* 358
7-9 26°C sg: 1.020 12 cm 100L

*Labrichthys unilineatus* 358
6-10 26°C sg: 1.020 18 cm 200L

*Larabicus quadrilineatus* 358
10 27°C sg: 1.030 12 cm 100L

*Macropharyngodon cyanoguttatus* 358
9 26°C sg: 1.020 12 cm 100L

*Cheilio inermis* 358
6-10 26°C sg: 1.020 50 cm 500L

*Lienardella fasciata* (juv.) 358
7-8 ♥ 26°C sg: 1.020 30 cm 300L

*Lienardella fasciata* (adult) 358
7-8 ♥ 26°C sg: 1.020 30 cm 300L

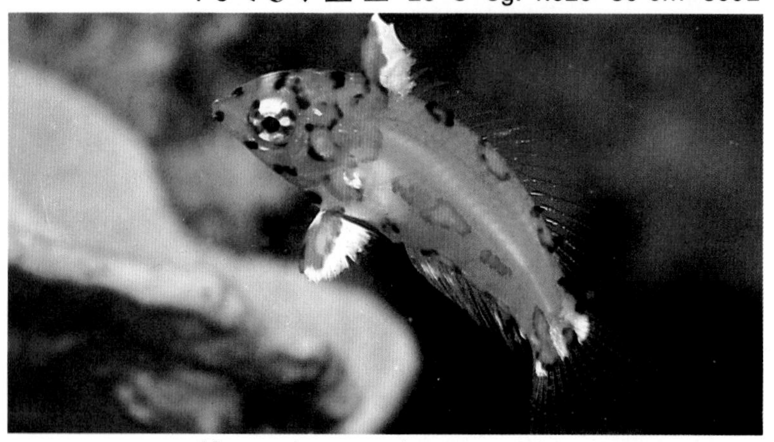

*Macropharyngodon choati* (juv.) 358
8 ♥ 26°C sg: 1.020 10 cm 100L

*Macropharyngodon choati* (adult) 358
8 ♥ 26°C sg: 1.020 10 cm 100L

*Macropharyngodon negrosensis* 358
7 ♥ 26°C sg: 1.020 12 cm 100L

*Macropharyngodon geoffroyi* 358
6-7 ♥ 26°C sg: 1.020 15 cm 200L

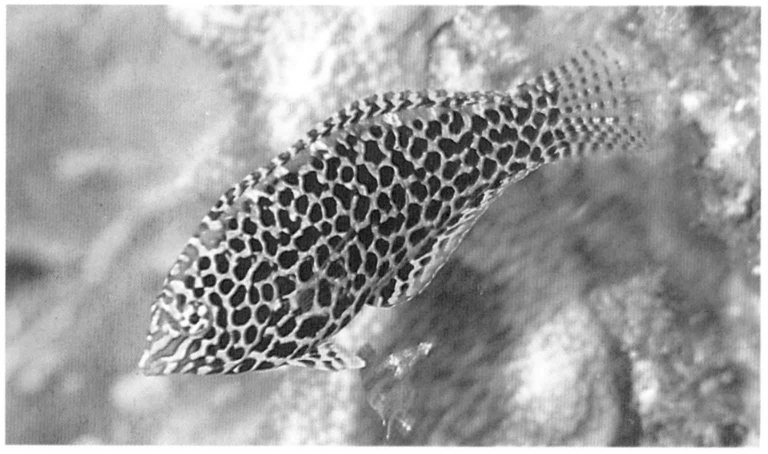

*Macropharyngodon meleagris* 358 ♀
6-9 ♥ 26°C sg: 1.020 15 cm 200L

*Macropharyngodon meleagris* 358 ♂
6-9 ♥ 26°C sg: 1.020 15 cm 200L

*Lienardella fasciata*(adult) 358
7-8 ⬊ ◐ ♥ 26°C sg: 1.020 30 cm 300L

*Stethojulis interrupta* 358 ♀
7-9 ◐ ♥ 26°C sg: 1.020 13 cm 100L

*Stethojulis interrupta* 358 ♂
7-9 ◐ ♥ 26°C sg: 1.020 13 cm 100L

*Stethojulis strigiventer* 358 ♀
6-9 ◐ ♥ 26°C sg: 1.022 15 cm 200L

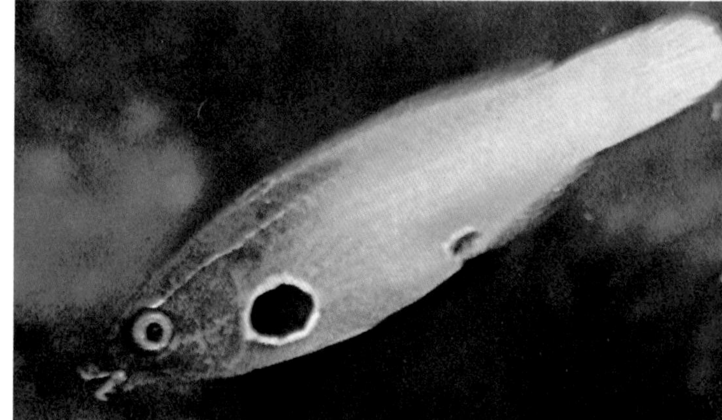

*Labropsis alleni* 358
6-7 ◐ ♥ 26°C sg: 1.020 8 cm 100L

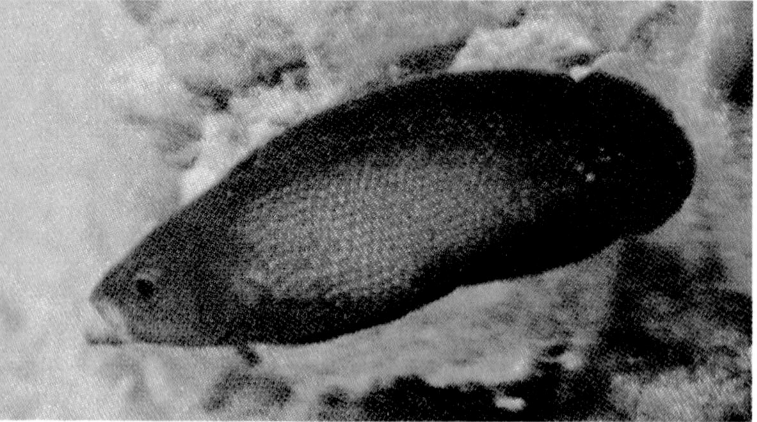

*Labropsis micronesica* 358
6 ◐ ♥ 26°C sg: 1.020 8 cm 100L

*Labropsis xanthonota* 358
6-9 ◐ ♥ 26°C sg: 1.020 10 cm 100L

*Wetmorella nigropinnata* 358
6-10 ◐ ♥ 26°C sg: 1.020 7 cm 100L

*Labropsis manabei* 358
7 ◐ ♥ 26°C sg: 1.020 12 cm 100L

*Stethojulis balteata* 358 ♀
7 〜 ◐ ♥ ▨ ▤ 26°C sg: 1.022 14 cm 100L

*Stethojulis balteata* 358 ♂
7 〜 ◐ ♥ ▨ ▤ 26°C sg: 1.022 14 cm 100L

*Stethojulis bandanensis* 358 ♀
7 〜 ◐ ♥ ▨ ▤ 26°C sg: 1.022 15 cm 200L

*Stethojulis bandanensis* 358 ♂
7 〜 ◐ ♥ ▨ ▤ 26°C sg: 1.022 15 cm 200L

*Stethojulis trilineata* 358 ♀
7-10 〜 ◐ ♥ ▨ ▤ 26°C sg: 1.022 15 cm 200L

*Stethojulis trilineata* 358 ♂
7-10 〜 ◐ ♥ ▨ ▤ 26°C sg: 1.022 15 cm 200L

*Stethojulis albovittata* 358 ♀
9-10 〜 ◐ ♥ ▨ ▤ 26°C sg: 1.022 13 cm 100L

*Stethojulis albovittata* 358 ♂
9-10 〜 ◐ ♥ ▨ ▤ 26°C sg: 1.022 13 cm 100L

#379

*Xyrichthys splendens* 358 ♀
2 ~ ◐ ♥ 26°C sg: 1.022 14 cm 100L

*Xyrichthys novacula* 358
2, 13 ~ ◐ ♥ 26°C sg: 1.022 22 cm 200L

*Xyrichthys splendens* 358 ♂
2 ~ ◐ ♥ 26°C sg: 1.022 14 cm 100L

*Xyrichthys martinicensis* 358 ♂
2 ~ ◐ ♥ 26°C sg: 1.022 15 cm 200L

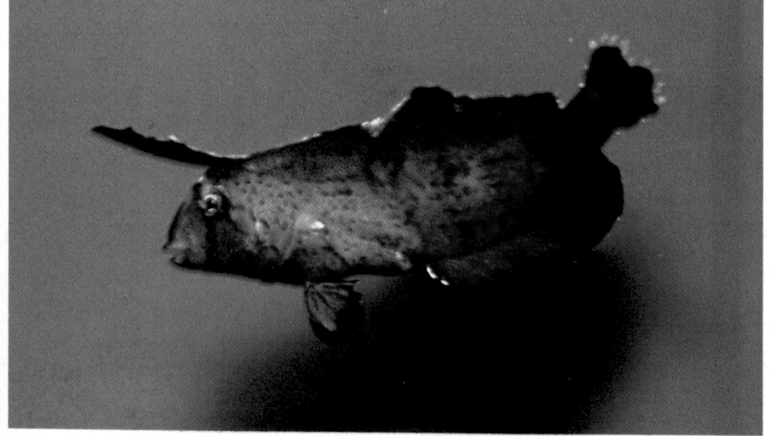

*Xyrichthys pavo (juv.)* 358
3, 6-10 ~ ◐ ♥ 26°C sg: 1.022 35 cm 400L

*Xyrichthys martinicensis* 358
2 ~ ◐ ♥ 26°C sg: 1.022 15 cm 200L

*Xyrichthys pavo* 358
3, 6-10 ∿ ◐ ♥ 26°C sg: 1.022 35 cm 400L

*Xyrichthys pavo* 358
3, 6-10 ∿ ◐ ♥ 26°C sg: 1.022 35 cm 400L

*Xyrichthys pentadactylus* 358 ♀
7-10 ∿ ◐ ♥ 26°C sg: 1.022 25 cm 300L

*Xyrichthys verrens* 358
7 ∿ ◐ ♥ 26°C sg: 1.022 30 cm 300L

*Xyrichthys* sp. 358
6 ∿ ◐ ♥ 26°C sg: 1.022 12 cm 100L

*Xyrichthys dea* (juv.) 358
7 ∿ ◐ ♥ 26°C sg: 1.022 30 cm 300L

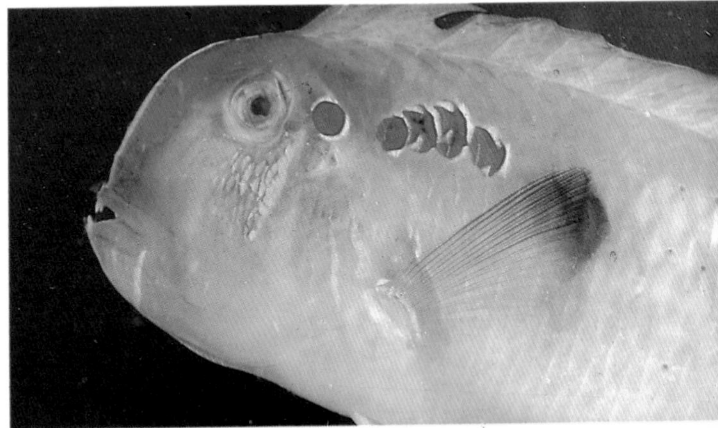

*Xyrichthys pentadactylus* 358 ♂
7-10 ∿ ◐ ♥ 26°C sg: 1.022 25 cm 300L

*Xyrichthys aneitensis* 358
6-7 ∿ ◐ ♥ 26°C sg: 1.022 25 cm 300L

*Xyrichthys pavo* 358 (juv.)
3, 6-10 ◐ ♥ 26°C sg: 1.022 35 cm 400L

*Novaculichthys taeniourus* 358
6-10 ◐ 26°C sg: 1.022 27 cm 300L

*Novaculichthys macrolepidotus* 358
7-10 ◐ ♥ 26°C sg: 1.022 13 cm 100L

*Pseudocheilinus hexataenia* 358
6-10 ◐ ♥ 26°C sg: 1.022 10 cm 100L

*Xyrichthys pavo* 358
3, 6-10 ◐ ♥ 26°C sg: 1.022 35 cm 400L

*Novaculichthys taeniourus* 358 (juv.)
6-10 ◐ 26°C sg: 1.022 27 cm 300L

*Pseudocheilinus evanidus* 358
6-10 ◐ ♥ 26°C sg: 1.022 8 cm 100L

*Pseudocheilinus octotaenia* 358
6-10 ◐ ♥ 26°C sg: 1.022 12 cm 100L

*Paracheilinus filamentosus* 358 ♂
7 ∿ ◐ ♥ 26°C sg: 1.022 8 cm 100L

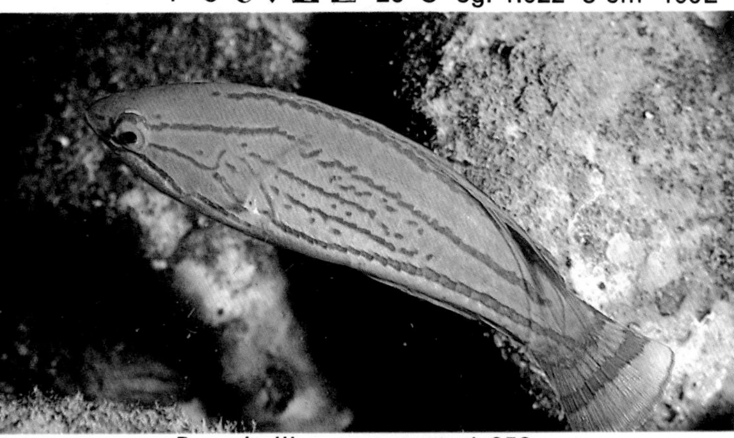

*Paracheilinus carpenteri* 358
7 ∿ ◐ ♥ 26°C sg: 1.022 7 cm 100L

*Paracheilinus lineopunctatus* 358 ♂
7 ∿ ◐ ♥ 26°C sg: 1.022 7 cm 100L

*Pseudocoris yamashiroi* 358
5, 7 ∿ ◐ ♥ 26°C sg: 1.022 15 cm 200L

*Minilabrus striatus* 358
10 ∿ ◐ ♥ 26°C sg: 1.030 4 cm 50L

*Paracheilinus octotaenia* 358
10 ∿ ◐ ♥ 27°C sg: 1.030 9 cm 100L

*Pseudocoris yamashiroi* 358
7 ∿ ◐ ♥ 26°C sg: 1.022 15 cm 200L

*Ophthalmolepis lineolatus* 358 ♂
12 ◐ ♥ 24°C sg: 1.020 40 cm 400L

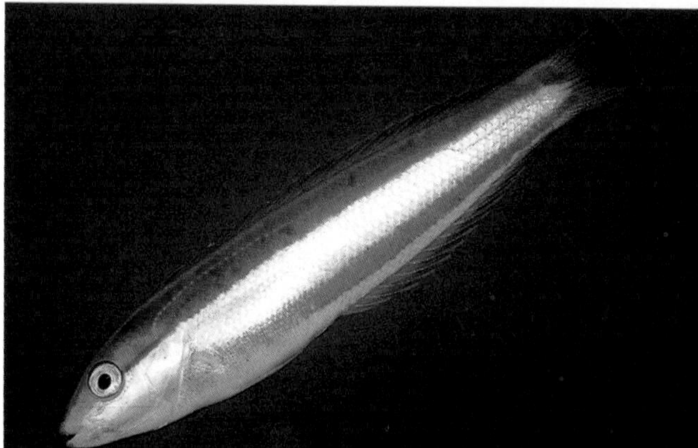

*Ophthalmolepis lineolatus* 358 ♀
12 ◐ ♥ 24°C sg: 1.020 40 cm 400L

*Pseudojuloides erythrops* 358 ♀
9 ∿ ◐ ♥ 26°C sg: 1.022 9 cm 100L

*Pseudojuloides erythrops* 358 ♂
9 ∿ ◐ ♥ 26°C sg: 1.022 9 cm 100L

*Pseudojuloides trifasciatus* 358
9 ∿ ◐ ♥ 26°C sg: 1.022 9 cm 100L

*Pseudojuloides cerasinus* 358
6-9 ∿ ◐ ♥ 26°C sg: 1.022 12 cm 100L

*Pseudojuloides* sp. 358
7 ~ ◐ ♥ 26°C sg: 1.022 10 cm 100L

*Pseudojuloides cerasinus* 358 ♂
6-9 ~ ◐ ♥ 26°C sg: 1.022 12 cm 100L

*Pseudojulis melanotus* 358
3 ~ ◐ ♥ 26°C sg: 1.022 20 cm 200L

*Pseudojuloides elongatus* 358 ♂
7-8, 12 ~ ◐ ♥ 25°C sg: 1.022 14 cm 100L

*Pseudojulis notospilus* 358 ♀
3 ~ ◐ ♥ 26°C sg: 1.022 25 cm 300L

*Pseudojulis notospilus* 358 ♂
3 ~ ◐ ♥ 26°C sg: 1.022 25 cm 300L

*Pseudocheilinus* sp. 358
6 ~ ◐ ♥ 26°C sg: 1.022 13 cm 100L

*Pseudocheilinus tetrataenia* 358
6 ~ ◐ ♥ 26°C sg: 1.022 12 cm 100L

#385

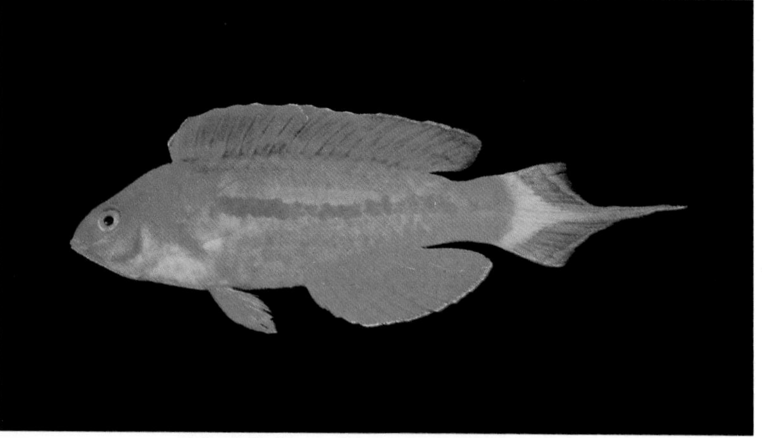

*Cirrhilabrus blatteus* 358 ♂
10 ∿ ◐ ♥ 26°C sg: 1.028 10 cm 100L

*Cirrhilabrus blatteus* 358 ♀
10 ∿ ◐ ♥ 26°C sg: 1.028 10 cm 100L

*Leptojulis cyanopleura* 358
6-7 ∿ ◐ ♥ 26°C sg: 1.022 9 cm 200L

*Leptojulis chrysotaenia* 358
7 ∿ ○ ♥ 26°C sg: 1.022 6 cm

*Pictilabrus* sp. 358
7, 12 ∿ ◐ ♥ 26°C sg: 1.022 14 cm 150L

*Pictilabrus laticlavius* 358
7, 12 ∿ ○ ♥ 26°C sg: 1.022 20 cm 200L

*Pseudolabrus biserialis* 358
7 ∿ ◐ ♥ 25°C sg: 1.022 20 cm 200L

*Pictilabrus laticlavius* 358
7, 12 ∿ ○ ♥ 26°C sg: 1.022 20 cm 200L

*Semicossyphus pulcher* 358 ♂
3-4 ◐ 22°C sg: 1.024 91 cm 1500L

*Semicossyphus pulcher* 358 ♀
3-4 ◐ 22°C sg: 1.024 91 cm 1500L

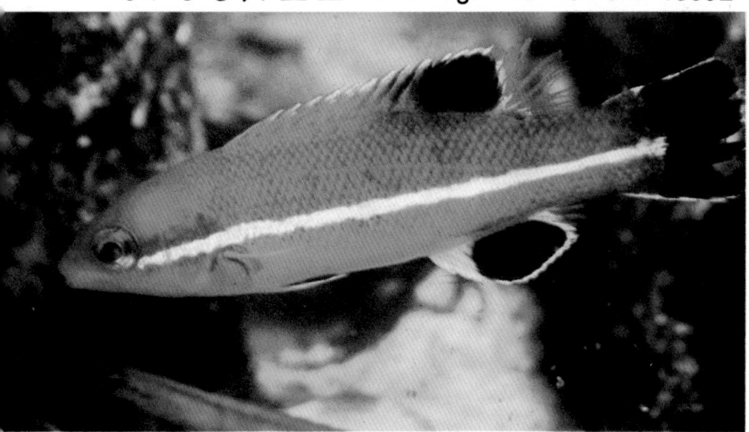

*Semicossyphus reticulatus* 358 (juv.)
7 ◐ 26°C sg: 1.022 100 cm 2000L

*Semicossyphus reticulatus* 358
7 ◐ 26°C sg: 1.022 100 cm 2000L

*Pseudolabrus milesi* 358
11-12 ◐ ♥ 22°C sg: 1.024 38 cm 400L

*Eupetrichthys angustipes* 358
12 ◐ ♥ 22°C sg: 1.024 15 cm 400L

*Dotalabrus aurantiacus* 358
12 ◐ ♥ 23°C sg: 1.022 20 cm 200L

*Dotalabrus* sp. 358
12 ◐ ♥ 23°C sg: 1.022 9 cm 100L

*Suezichthys gracilis* 358 ♀
5, 7, 8, 12 ◐ ♥ 26°C sg: 1.022 15 cm 200L

*Suezichthys gracilis* 358
5, 7, 8, 12 ◐ ♥ 26°C sg: 1.022 15 cm 200L

*Pseudolabrus gymnogenis* 358 ♀
12 ◐ ♥ 26°C sg: 1.022 38 cm 450L

*Pseudolabrus luculentus* 358
11-12 ◐ ♥ 26°C sg: 1.022 24 cm 300L

*Pseudolabrus inscriptus* 358
11 ◐ ♥ 26°C sg: 1.022 25 cm 300L

*Pseudolabrus celidotus* 358
11 ◐ ♥ 26°C sg: 1.022 24 cm 300L

*Pseudolabrus japonicus* 358
5, 7 ◐ ♥ 26°C sg: 1.022 25 cm 300L

*Pseudolabrus guntheri* 358
8 ◐ ♥ 26°C sg: 1.022 18 cm 200L

*Pseudolabrus biserialis* 358
12 24°C sg: 1.022 20 cm 200L

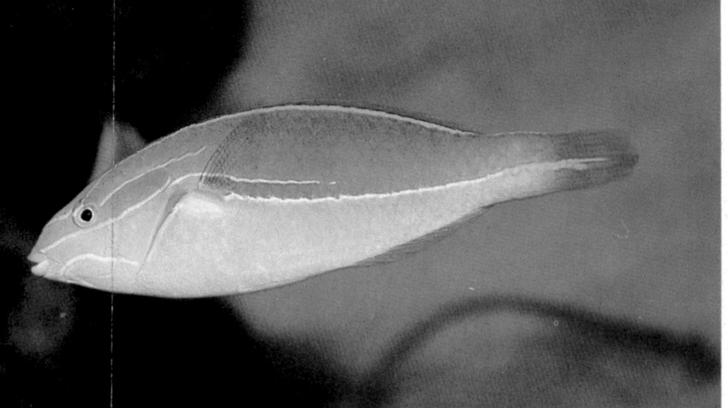

*Stethojulis bandanensis* 358 ♂
7 26°C sg: 1.022 15 cm 200L

*Thalassoma amblycephalum* 358 ♂
7-9 26°C sg: 1.022 16 cm 200L

*Thalassoma genivittatum* 358 ♂
9 26°C sg: 1.022 20 cm 200L

*Pseudolabrus parilus* 358
12 26°C sg: 1.022 45 cm 500L

*Stethojulis strigiventer* 358 ♀
6-9 26°C sg: 1.022 15 cm 200L

*Thalassoma amblycephalum* 358 ♀
7-9 26°C sg: 1.022 16 cm 200L

*Thalassoma hardwicke* 358 ♂
7-9 26°C sg: 1.022 18 cm 200L

*Thalassoma lucasanum* 358 (juv.)
3 ◐ ♥ 26°C sg: 1.022 15 cm 200L

*Thalassoma lucasanum* 358 ♂
3 ◐ ♥ 26°C sg: 1.022 15 cm 200L

*Thalassoma bifasciatum* 358
2 ◐ ♥ 26°C sg: 1.022 15 cm 200L

*Thalassoma bifasciatum* 358
2 ◐ ♥ 26°C sg: 1.022 15 cm 200L

*Thalassoma jansenii* 358
7 ◐ ♥ 26°C sg: 1.022 20 cm 200L

*Thalassoma bifasciatum* 358 ♂
2 ◐ ♥ 26°C sg: 1.022 15 cm 200L

*Thalassoma ballieui* 358
6 ◐ ♥ 26°C sg: 1.022 45 cm 500L

*Thalassoma duperreyi* 358
6 ◐ ♥ 26°C sg: 1.022 30 cm 300L

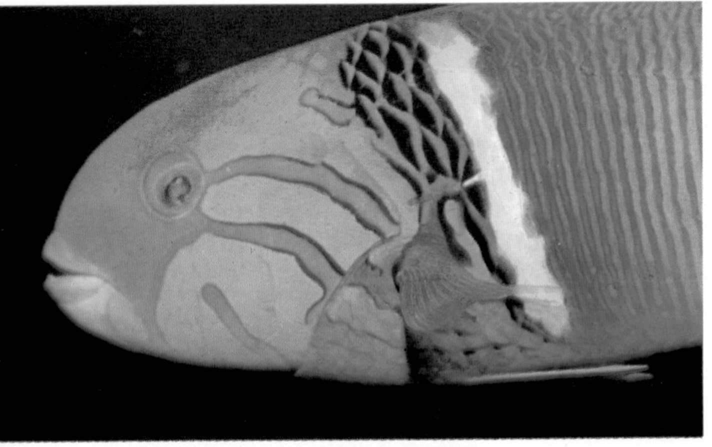

*Thalassoma hebraicum* 358
7-9 ◐ ♥ 26°C sg: 1.022 18 cm 200L

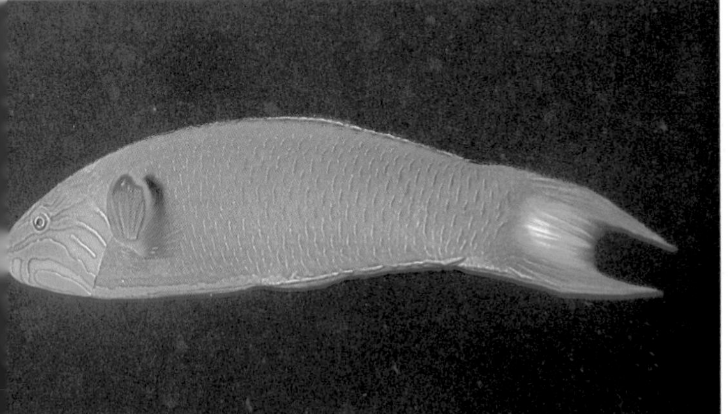

*Thalassoma lunare* 358 ♂
6-10 ◐ ♥ 26°C sg: 1.022 25 cm 300L

*Thalassoma quinquevittatum* 358 ♂
6-9 ◐ ♥ 26°C sg: 1.022 17 cm 200L

*Thalassoma genivittatum* 358
9 ◐ ♥ 26°C sg: 1.022 20 cm 200L

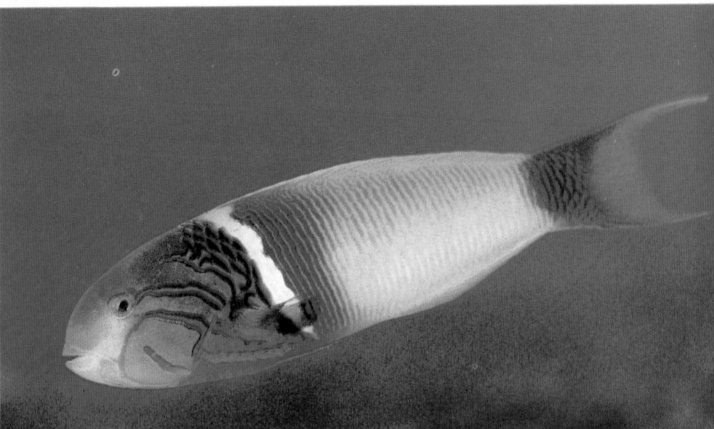

*Thalassoma hebraicum* 358 ♂
7-9 ◐ ♥ 26°C sg: 1.022 18 cm 200L

*Thalassoma lutescens* 358 ♂
7 ◐ ♥ 26°C sg: 1.022 15 cm 200L

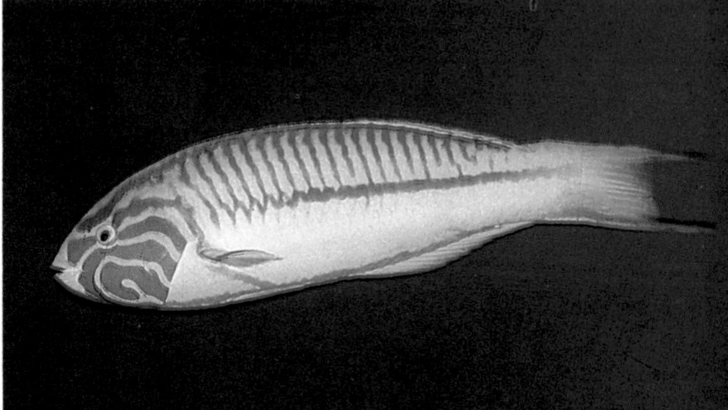

*Thalassoma klunzingeri* 358 ♂
10 ◐ ♥ 26°C sg: 1.030 20 cm 200L

*Pseudodax moluccanus* 358
6-10 ◐ ♥ 26°C sg: 1.022 25 cm 300L

*Thalassoma purpureum* 358
6-9 ◐ ♥ 26°C sg: 1.022 43 cm 500L

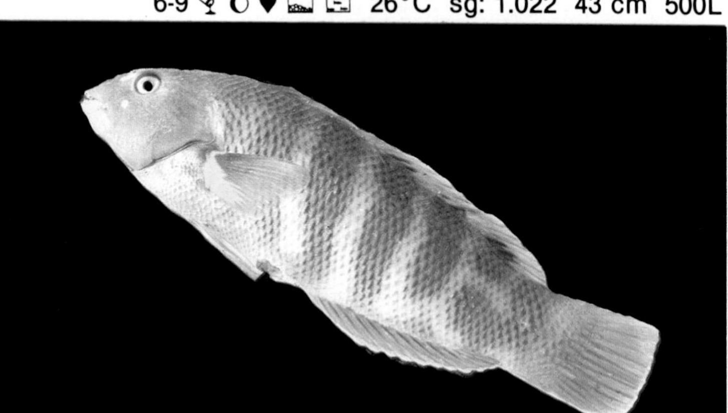

*Thalassoma septemfasciatum* 358 ♀
7, 12 ◐ ♥ 26°C sg: 1.022 23 cm 300L

*Tautogolabrus adspersus* 358
1 ◐ ♥ 26°C sg: 1.022 38 cm 400L

*Suezichthys* sp. 358 ♂
11 ◐ ♥ 26°C sg: 1.022 16 cm 200L

*Thalassoma lutescens* 358
7 ◐ ♥ 26°C sg: 1.022 15 cm 200L

*Thalassoma septemfasciatum* 358 ♂
7, 12 ◐ ♥ 26°C sg: 1.022 23 cm 300L

*Thalassoma trilobatum* 358
6-9 ◐ ♥ 26°C sg: 1.022 30 cm 300L

*Suezichthys* sp. 358 ♀
11 ◐ ♥ 20°C sg: 1.024 16 cm 200L

*Labroides dimidiatus* 358
6-10 26°C sg: 1.022 12 cm 150L

*Labroides phthirophagus* 358
6 26°C sg: 1.022 10 cm 100L

*Labroides rubrolabiatus* 358
6 26°C sg: 1.022 6 cm 100L

*Labroides pectoralis* 358
7-8 26°C sg: 1.022 12 cm 100L

*Labroides bicolor* 358
7-9 26°C sg: 1.022 14 cm 150L

*Xenojulis margaritaceous* 358
7, 12 25°C sg: 1.023 12 cm 100L

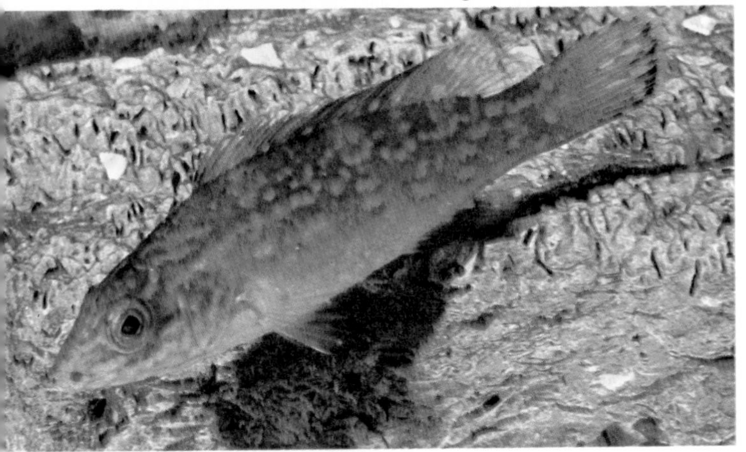

*Labrus bergylta* 358
13-15 26°C sg: 1.022 60 cm 800L

*Labrus merula* 358
13-15 26°C sg: 1.022 45 cm 500L

#393

*Lachnolaimus maximus* 358
2 ◯ 26°C sg: 1.022 91 cm 1500L

*Lachnolaimus maximus* 358
2 ◯ 26°C sg: 1.022 91 cm 1500L

*Clepticus parrae* 358
2 ◯ ♥ 26°C sg: 1.022 30 cm 300L

*Clepticus parrae* 358
2 ◯ ♥ 26°C sg: 1.022 30 cm 300L

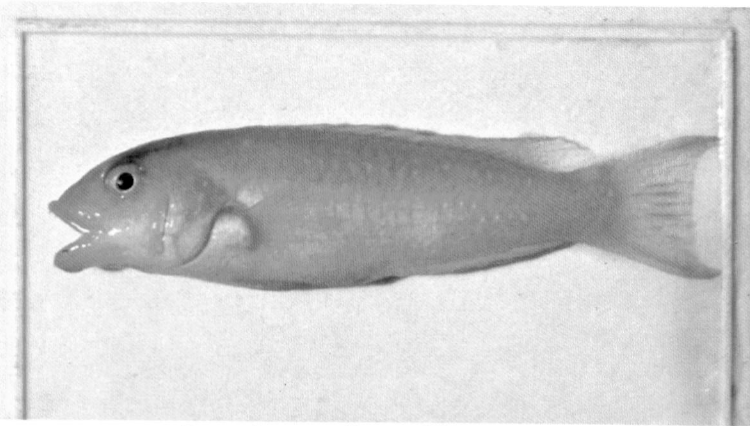

*Decodon puellaris* 358
2 ◐ ♥ 26°C sg: 1.022 15 cm 200L

*Decodon melasma* 358
3 ◐ ♥ 26°C sg: 1.022 20 cm 200L

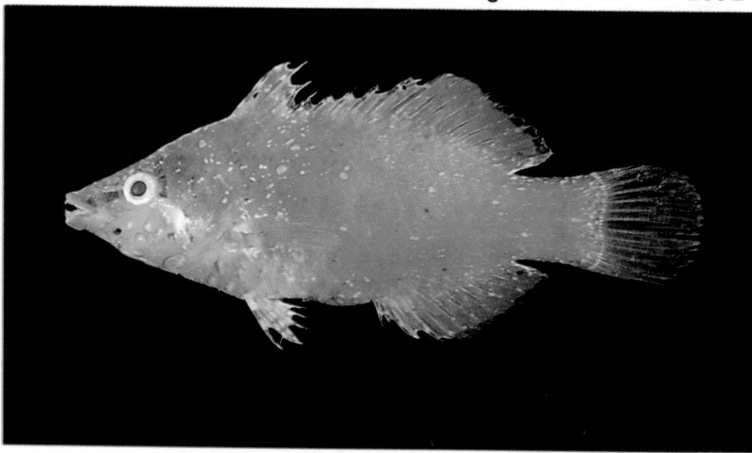

*Doratonotus megalepis* 358
2 ◐ ♥ 24°C sg: 1.022 7.5 cm 100L

*Oxyjulis californica* 358
3-4 ◐ ♥ 22°C sg: 1.023 25 cm 300L

*Symphodus melanocercus* 358 ♀
15 25°C sg: 1.022 14 cm 150L

*Symphodus ocellatus* 358 ♂
15 25°C sg: 1.022 12 cm 100L

*Symphodus doderleini* 358
15 25°C sg: 1.022 10 cm 100L

*Symphodus tinca* 358
14-15 24°C sg: 1.022 35 cm 400L

*Symphodus cinereus* 358
14-15 24°C sg: 1.022 15 cm 200L

*Symphodus mediterraneus* 358
14-15 25°C sg: 1.022 15 cm 200L

*Symphodus roissali* 358 ♀
14-15 24°C sg: 1.022 17 cm 200L

*Symphodus rostratus* 358
15 24°C sg: 1.022 13 cm 150L

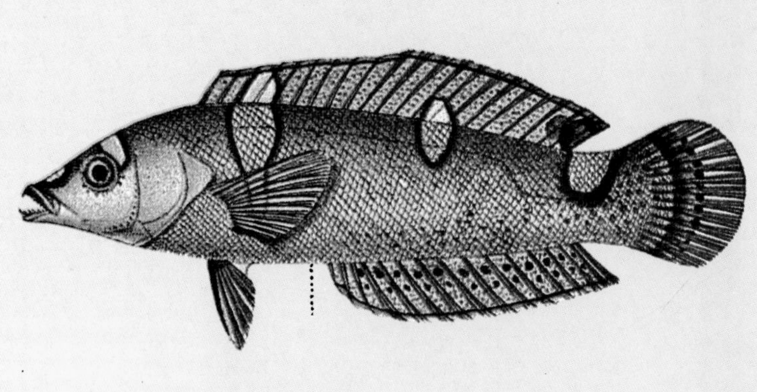

*Coris gaimard* 358
6-10 ♥ 26°C sg: 1.022 45 cm 500L

*Cheilio inermis* 358
6-10 26°C sg: 1.022 50 cm 500L

*Novaculichthys macrolepidotus* 358
7-10 ♥ 26°C sg: 1.022 15 cm 150L

*Halichoeres scapularis* 358
6-10 ♥ 26°C sg: 1.022 20 cm 200L

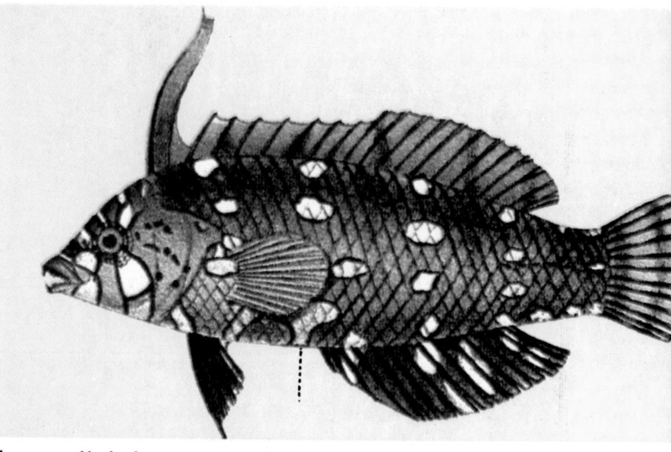

*Novaculichthys taeniourus* (juv.) 358
7-10 26°C sg: 1.022 27 cm 300L

*Novaculichthys taeniourus* (adult) 358
7-10 26°C sg: 1.022 27 cm 300L

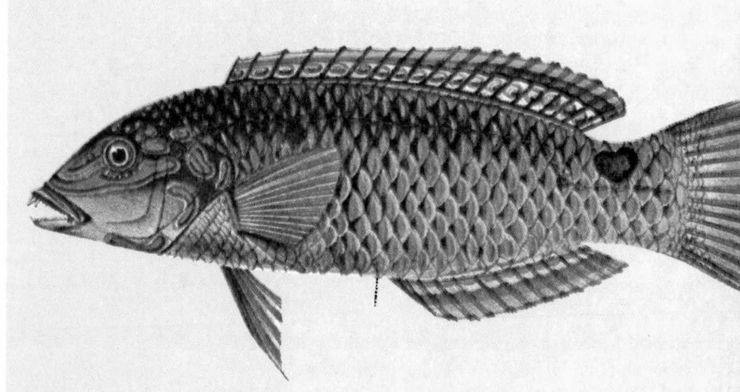

*Halichoeres trimaculata* 358
7-10 ♥ 26°C sg: 1.022 18 cm 200L

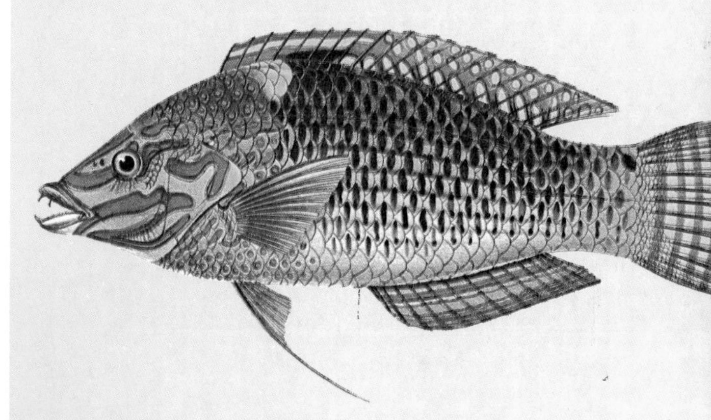

*Halichoeres hortulanus* 358
7-10 ♥ 26°C sg: 1.022 27 cm 300L

*Halichoeres nebulosus* 358
6-10 26°C sg: 1.022 12 cm 150L

*Halichoeres prosopeion* 358
7 26°C sg: 1.022 18 cm 200L

*Halichoeres amboinensis* 358
7 26°C sg: 1.022 14 cm 150L

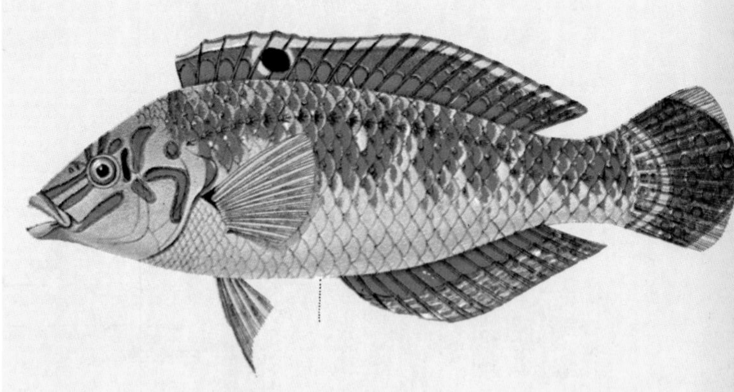

*Halichoeres nigrescens* 358
7-10 26°C sg: 1.022 30 cm 300L

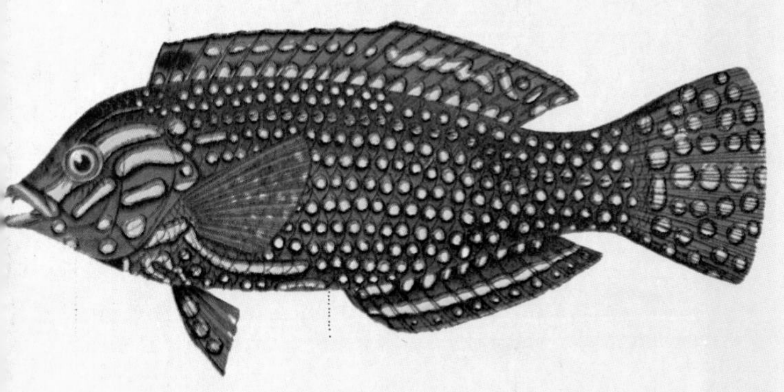

*Macropharyngodon meleagris* 358
6-7 26°C sg: 1.022 15 cm 150L

*Bodianus diana* 358
7, 9-10 26°C sg: 1.022 25 cm 300L

*Bodianus anthioides* 358
7-10 26°C sg: 1.022 21 cm 200L

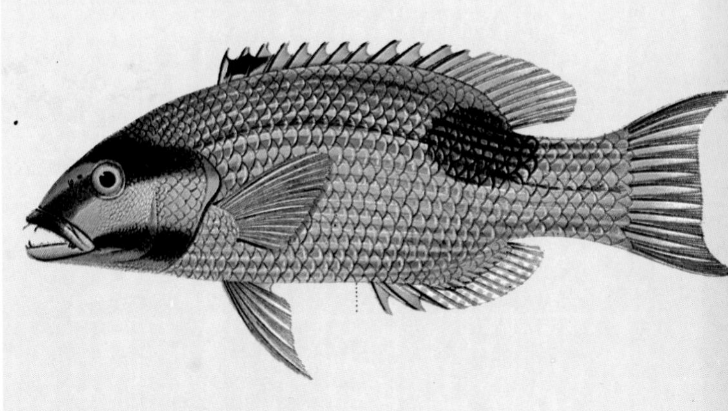

*Bodianus bilunulatus* 358
7, 9 26°C sg: 1.022 55 cm 600L

*Choerodon anchorago* (juv.) 358
7-9 26°C sg: 1.020 25 cm 300L

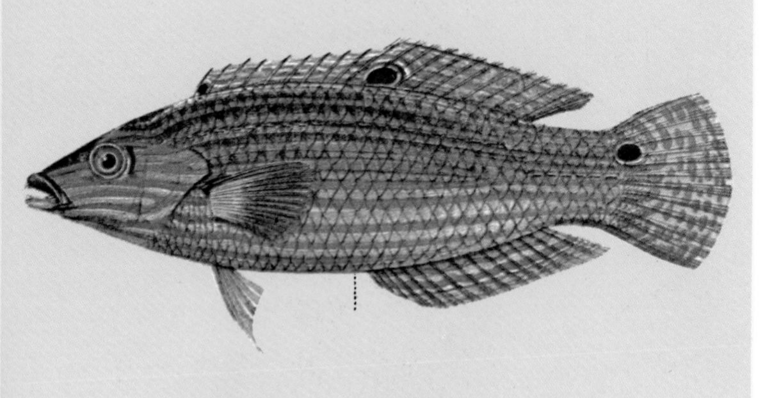

*Halichoeres hoevenii* 358
6-7 26°C sg: 1.020 12 cm 100L

*Halichoeres argus* 358
7 26°C sg: 1.020 12 cm 100L

*Stethojulis strigiventer* 358
6-9 26°C sg: 1.022 15 cm 200L



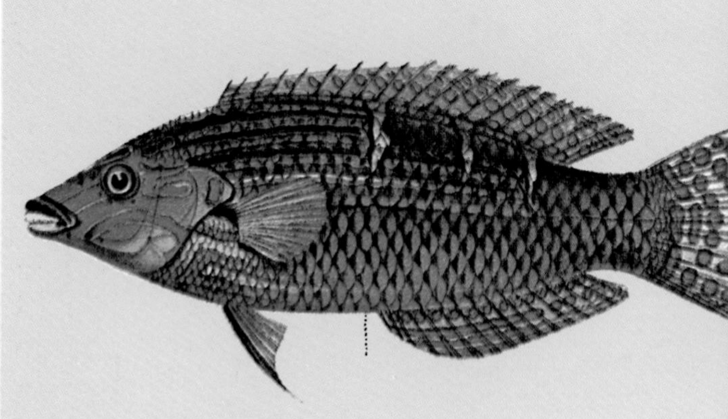

*Halichoeres hoevenii* 358
6-7 26°C sg: 1.020 12 cm 100L

*Halichoeres kallochroma* 358
7 26°C sg: 1.020 15 cm 100L

*Stethojulis strigiventer* 358
6-9 26°C sg: 1.022 15 cm 200L

*Stethojulis trilineata* 358
7-10 26°C sg: 1.022 15 cm 200L

*Halichoeres chloropterus* 358
7 ◐ ♥ 26°C sg: 1.020 15 cm 200L

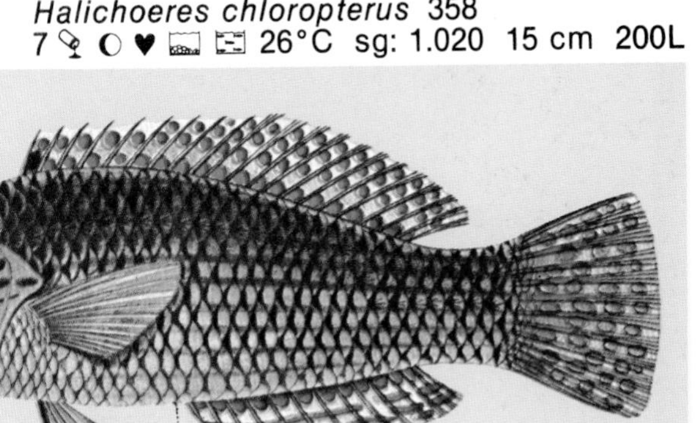

*Halichoeres pardaleocephalus* 358
7, 9 ◐ ♥ 26°C sg: 1.020 9 cm 100L

*Coris caudimacula* 358
7-10 ◐ ♥ 26°C sg: 1.020 20 cm 200L

*Coris variegata* 358
6-10 ◐ ♥ 26°C sg: 1.020 20 cm 200L

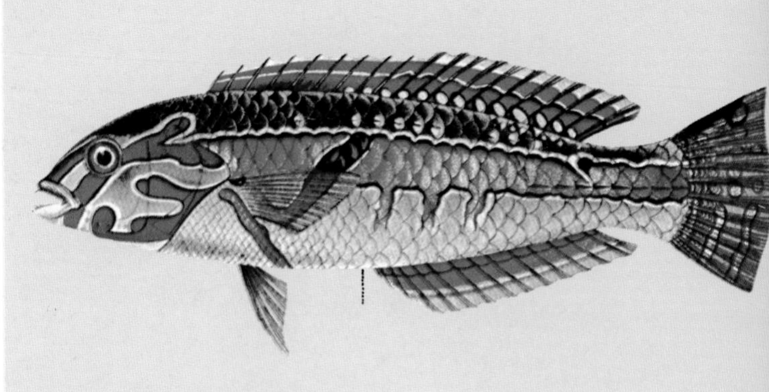

*Halichoeres hartzfeldii* 358
7 ◐ ♥ 26°C sg: 1.020 18 cm 200L

*Leptojulis cyanopleura* 358
6-7 ◐ ♥ 26°C sg: 1.022 9 cm 200L

*Coris batuensis* 358
7 ◐ ♥ 26°C sg: 1.022 11 cm 150L

*Leptojulis cyanopleura* 358
6-7 ◐ ♥ 26°C sg: 1.022 9 cm 200L

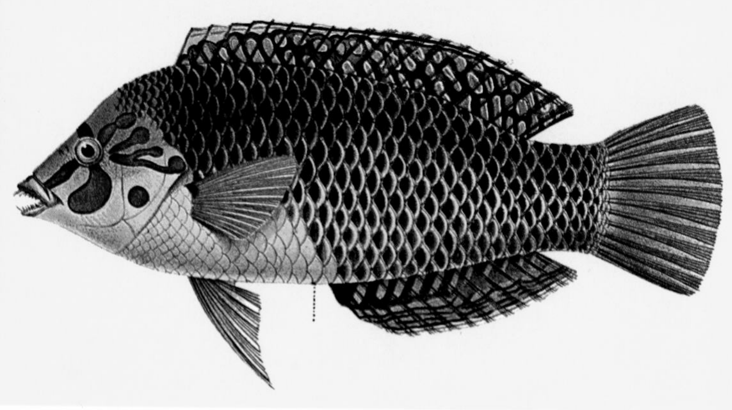

*Halichoeres podostigma* 358
7 ♀ ∽ ◐ ♥ 26°C sg: 1.022 18.5 cm 200L

*Thalassoma cupido* 358
5, 7 ♀ ∽ ◐ ♥ 26°C sg: 1.022 15 cm 150L

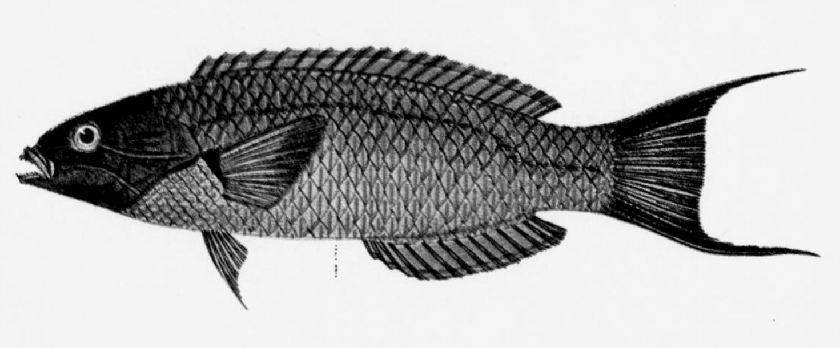

*Thalassoma amblycephalus* 358
7, 9 ♀ ∽ ◐ ♥ 26°C sg: 1.022 16 cm 200L

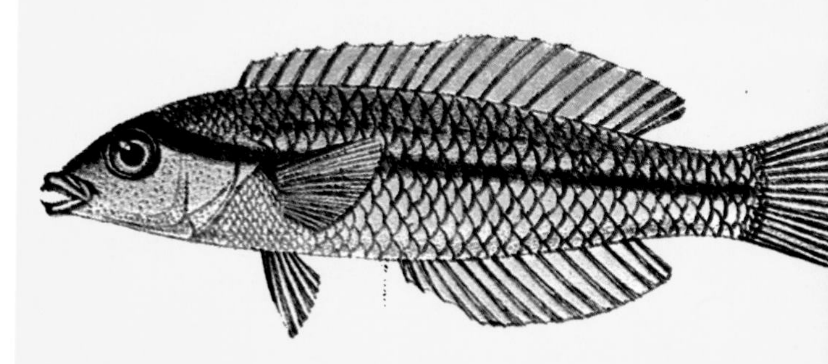

*Pseudojulis girardi* 358
7 ♀ ∽ ◐ ♥ 26°C sg: 1.022 10 cm 100L

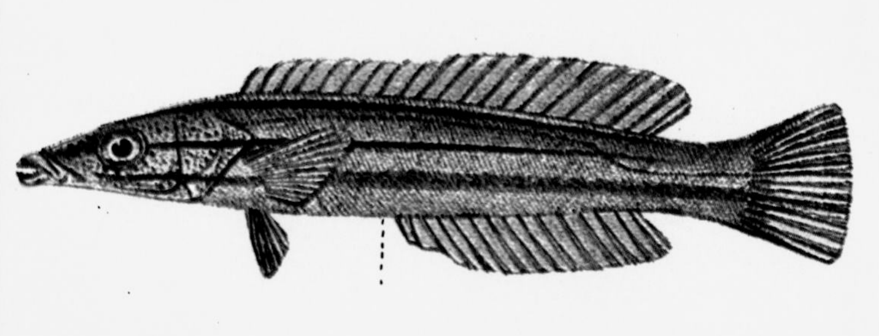

*Hologymnosus doliatus* 358
6-9, 12 ♀ ∽ ◐ ♥ 26°C sg: 1.022 32 cm 300L

*Thalassoma lunare* 358
7, 9 ♀ ∽ ◐ ♥ 26°C sg: 1.022 25 cm 300L

*Thalassoma amblycephalus* 358
7, 9 ♀ ∽ ◐ ♥ 26°C sg: 1.022 16 cm 200L

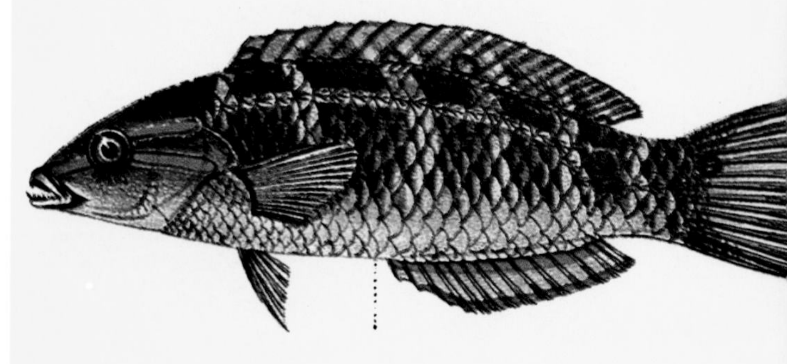

*Thalassoma schwanefeldi* 358
6, 7 ♀ ∽ ◐ ♥ 26°C sg: 1.022 10 cm 100L

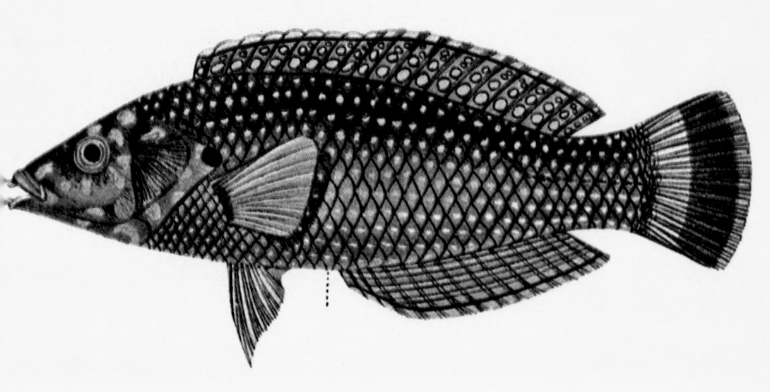

*Anampses melanurus melanurus* 358
6-7 ~ ◐ ♥ 26°C sg: 1.020 12 cm 150L

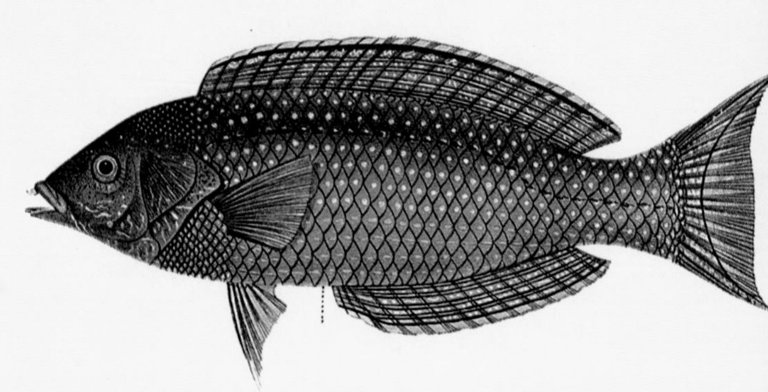

*Anampses meleagrides* 358
7, 9 ~ ◐ ♥ 26°C sg: 1.020 20 cm 200L

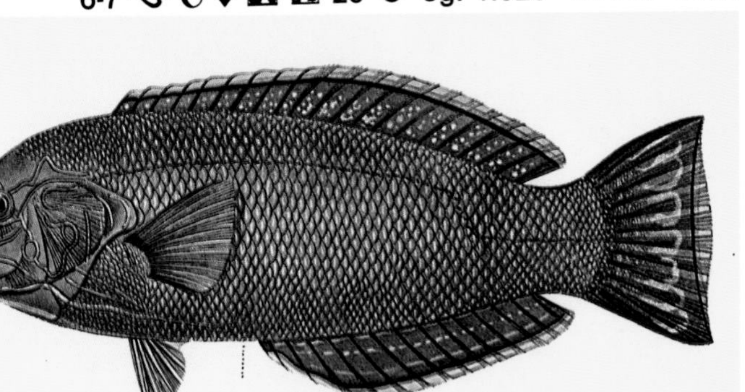

*Anampses geographicus* 358
6-9 ~ ◐ ♥ 26°C sg: 1.020 25 cm 250L

*Anampses twistii* 358
6-10 ~ ◐ ♥ 26°C sg: 1.020 18 cm 200L

*Cheilinus digrammus* 358
6-10 ~ ◐ ♥ 26°C sg: 1.020 35 cm 400L

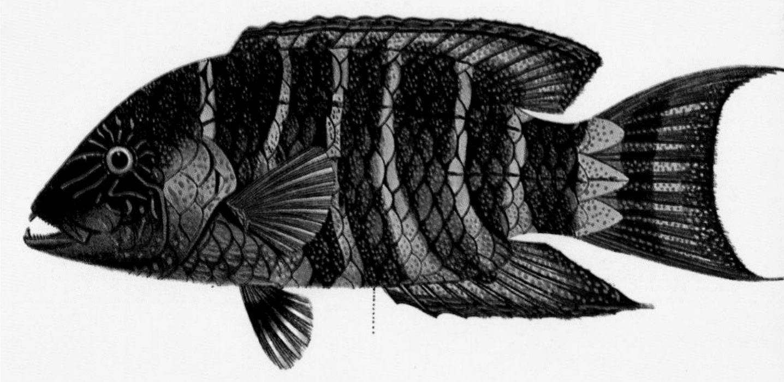

*Cheilinus fasciatus* 358
6-9 ◐ ♥ 26°C sg: 1.020 35 cm 400L

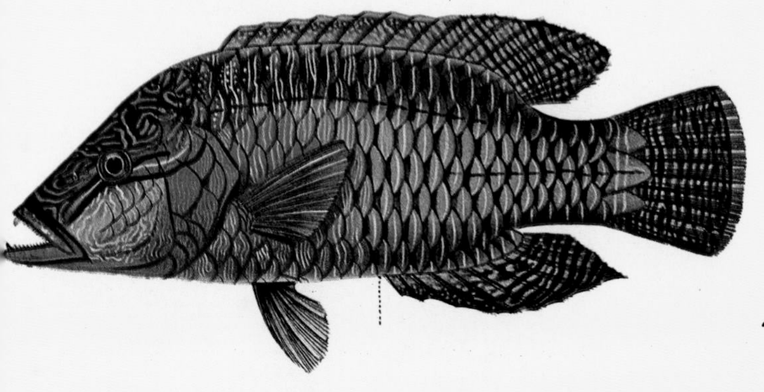

*Cheilinus undulatus* 358
6-10 ~ ◐ 26°C sg: 1.022 230 cm 5000L

*Cheilinus celebicus* 358
7 ◐ ♥ 26°C sg: 1.020 20 cm 200L

*Odax acroptilus* 359 ♀
12 23°C sg: 1.023 25 cm 300L

*Odax acroptilus* 359 ♂
12 23°C sg: 1.023 25 cm 300L

*Odax cyanomelas* 359
12 24°C sg: 1.023 45 cm 500L

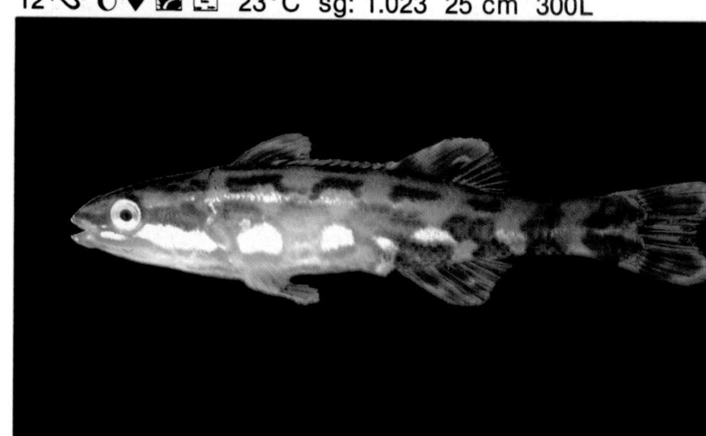

*Odax cyanomelas* 359
12 24°C sg: 1.023 45 cm 500L

*Neoodax balteatus* 359
7, 12 24°C sg: 1.022 7 cm 100L

*Siphonognathus radiatus* 359
12 24°C sg: 1.023 12 cm

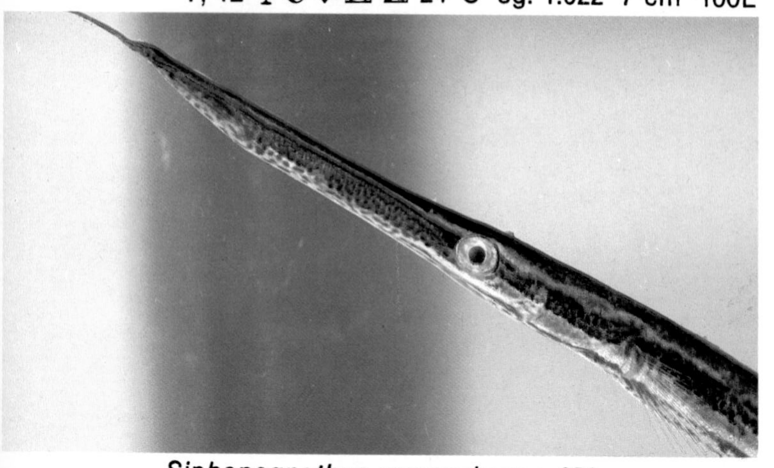

*Siphonognathus argyrophanes* 359
6, 7 26°C sg: 1.022 30 cm 300L

*Siphonognathus beddomei* 359
12 23°C sg: 1.023 13 cm 100L

*Scarus frenatus* 360
5, 7 ~ ✢ ◐ ♥ ▨ ☷ 26°C sg: 1.022 40 cm 400L

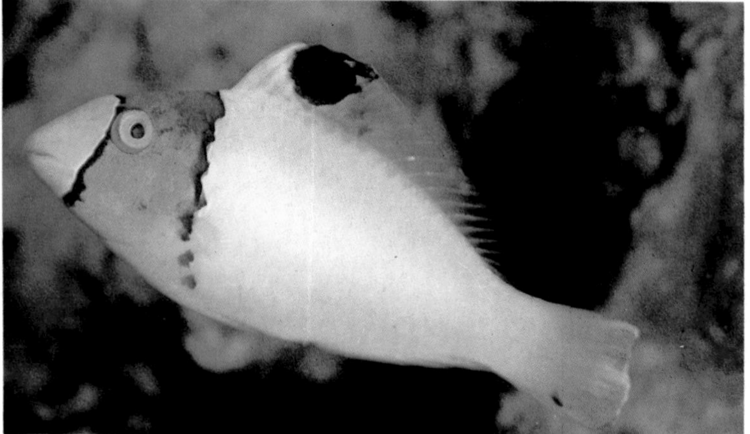

*Cetoscarus bicolor* 360 (juv.)
6-10 26°C sg: 1.022 80 cm 1000L

*Cetoscarus bicolor* 360 ♂
6-10 26°C sg: 1.022 80 cm 1000L

*Hipposcarus harid* 360
9-10 26°C sg: 1.022 75 cm 1000L

*Scarus gibbus* 360 ♂
7-10 26°C sg: 1.022 70 cm 1000L

*Scarus gibbus* 360 ♀
7-10 26°C sg: 1.022 70 cm 1000L

*Scarus prasiognathos* 360 ♂
5-7, 15 ∿ ⚘ ◐ ♥ ▣ ▣ 26°C sg: 1.022 70 cm 800L

*Scarus niger* 360 ♀
7-10 ∿ ⚘ ◐ ♥ ▣ ▣ 26°C sg: 1.022 40 cm 500L

*Scarus cyanescens* 360
9 ∿ ⚘ ◐ ♥ ▣ ▣ 26°C sg: 1.022 50 cm 500L

*Scarus rubroviolaceus* 360 ♂
3, 6-9 ∿ ⚘ ◐ ♥ ▣ ▣ 26°C sg: 1.022 66 cm 800L

*Scarus niger* 360
7-10 ∿ ⚘ ◐ ♥ ▣ ▣ 26°C sg: 1.022 40 cm 500L

*Scarus niger* 360 ♂
7-10 ∿ ⚘ ◐ ♥ ▣ ▣ 26°C sg: 1.022 40 cm 500L

*Scarus psittacus* 360 ♂
7-10 ∿ ⚘ ◐ ♥ ▣ ▣ 26°C sg: 1.022 27 cm 300L

*Scarus rubroviolaceus* 360 ♀
3, 6-9 ∿ ⚘ ◐ ♥ ▣ ▣ 26°C sg: 1.022 66 cm 800L

*Scarus atrilunula* 360
9 ♥ 26°C sg: 1.022 30 cm 300L

*Scarus sordidus* 360 ♂
5-10, 15 ♥ 26°C sg: 1.022 50 cm 500L

*Scarus gibbus* 360
7-10 ♥ 26°C sg: 1.022 70 cm 1000L

*Scarus ghobban* 360
7-10 ♥ 26°C sg: 1.022 80 cm 800L

*Scarus dimidiatus* 360 ♀
7, 9 ♥ 26°C sg: 1.022 35 cm 400L

*Scarus venosus* 360 ♀
7, 9 ♥ 26°C sg: 1.022 50 cm 500L

*Hipposcarus caudovittatus* 360
9 ♥ 26°C sg: 1.022 30 cm 300L

*Scarus frenatus* 360
5, 7 ♥ 26°C sg: 1.022 40 cm 400L

*Scarus brevifilis* 360 ♂
6, 7 26°C sg: 1.022 45 cm 500L

*Scarus frontalis* 360 ♂
6, 7 26°C sg: 1.022 50 cm 500L

*Scarus rubroviolaceus* 360 ♂
7-9 26°C sg: 1.022 60 cm 600L

*Scarus ferrugineus* 360 ♂
9-10 26°C sg: 1.022 41 cm 500L

*Scarus bleekeri* 360 ♂
6, 7 26°C sg: 1.022 25 cm 300L

*Scarus perspicillatus* 360 ♂
6 26°C sg: 1.022 62 cm 600L

*Scarus* sp. 360
6 26°C sg: 1.022 50 cm

*Scarus perspicillatus* 360 ♀
6 26°C sg: 1.022 62 cm 600L

*Bolbometopon muricatus* 360 ♂
7-10 ~ ⚘ ◐ ♥ 26°C sg: 1.022 150 cm 2000L

*Scarus dubius* 360
5, 7, 9 ~ ⚘ ◐ ♥ 26°C sg: 1.022 50 cm 500L

*Scarus gibbus* 360
7-10 ~ ⚘ ◐ ♥ 26°C sg: 1.022 70 cm 1000L

*Scarus gibbus* 360 ♂
7-10 ~ ⚘ ◐ ♥ 26°C sg: 1.022 70 cm 1000L

*Scarus schlegeli* 360
5, 7, 9 ~ ⚘ ◐ ♥ 26°C sg: 1.022 50 cm 500L

*Scarus flavipectoralis* 360
6 ~ ⚘ ◐ ♥ 26°C sg: 1.022 15 cm 250L

*Scarus tricolor* 360
5, 7, 9 ~ ⚘ ◐ ♥ 26°C sg: 1.022 50 cm 500L

*Scarus* sp. 360
6 ~ ⚘ ◐ ♥ 26°C sg: 1.022 25 cm 250L

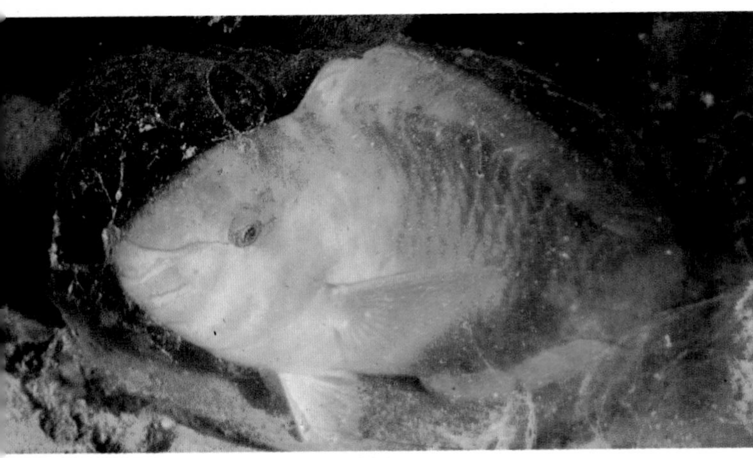

*Scarus psittacus* 360
7-10 ◐ ♥ 26°C sg: 1.022 27 cm 300L

*Scarus ghobban* 360
6-10 ◐ ♥ 26°C sg: 1.022 80 cm 800L

*Scarus ferrugineus* 360
10 ◐ ♥ 26°C sg: 1.022 41 cm 400L

*Scarus prasiognathos* 360
6-9 ◐ ♥ 26°C sg: 1.022 70 cm 800L

*Scarus frenatus* 360
5, 7 ◐ ♥ 26°C sg: 1.022 40 cm 400L

*Scarus frenatus* 360
5, 7 ◐ ♥ 26°C sg: 1.022 40 cm 400L

*Scarus guacamaia* 360
2 ◐ ♥ 26°C sg: 1.022 93 cm 1000L

*Scarus perrico* 360
3 ◐ ♥ 26°C sg: 1.022 80 cm 800L

#409

*Scarus croicensis* 360 ♀
2 26°C sg: 1.022 25 cm 300L

*Scarus croicensis* 360 ♂
2 26°C sg: 1.022 25 cm 300L

*Scarus vetula* 360 ♀
2 26°C sg: 1.022 71 cm 1000L

*Scarus vetula* 360 ♂
2 26°C sg: 1.022 71 cm 1000L

*Scarus coelestinus* 360 ♂
2 26°C sg: 1.022 106 cm 1500L

*Scarus taeniopterus* 360 ♂
2 26°C sg: 1.022 30 cm 300L

*Scarus taeniopterus* 360 ♀
2 26°C sg: 1.022 30 cm 300L

*Scarus coeruleus* 360 ♂
1-2 26°C sg: 1.022 90 cm 1000L

*Sparisoma atomarium* 360 ♂
2 ◐ ♥ 26°C sg: 1.022 10 cm 100L

*Sparisoma atomarium* 360 ♀
2 ◐ ♥ 26°C sg: 1.022 10 cm 100L

*Sparisoma aurofrenatum* 360 ♂
2 ◐ ♥ 26°C sg: 1.022 28 cm 300L

*Sparisoma aurofrenatum* 360 ♀
2 ◐ ♥ 26°C sg: 1.022 28 cm 300L

*Sparisoma chrysopterum* 360 ♂
2 ◐ ♥ 26°C sg: 1.022 50 cm 500L

*Sparisoma chrysopterum* 360 ♀
2 ◐ ♥ 26°C sg: 1.022 50 cm 500L

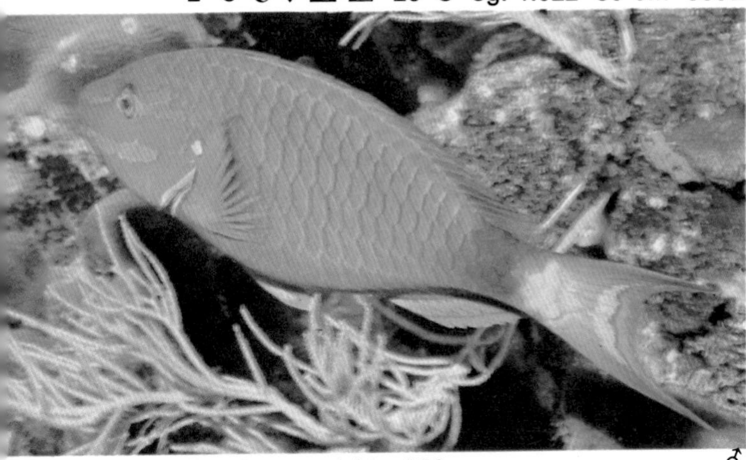

*Sparisoma viride* 360 ♂
2 ◐ ♥ 26°C sg: 1.022 51 cm 500L

*Sparisoma viride* 360 ♀
2 ◐ ♥ 26°C sg: 1.022 51 cm 500L

*Cryptotomus roseus* 360
2 25°C sg: 1.022 7 cm 100L

*Calotomus japonicus* 360
6-9 26°C sg: 1.022 60 cm 600L

*Leptoscarus vaigiensis* 360
7-9 26°C sg: 1.022 35 cm 400L

*Sparisoma radians* 360
2, 13 26°C sg: 1.022 13.5 cm 200L

#411

*Calotomus zonarchia* 360
6 26°C sg: 1.022 35 cm 400L

*Calotomus spinidens* 360
7, 9 26°C sg: 1.022 19 cm 200L

*Nicholsina denticulata* 360
3 26°C sg: 1.022 7 cm 100L

*Sparisoma rubripinne* 360
2, 13 26°C sg: 1.022 46 cm 500L

*Hipposcarus harid* 360
9 ◐ ♥ 26°C sg: 1.022 75 cm 750L

*Cetoscarus bicolor* 360
6-9 ◐ ♥ 26°C sg: 1.022 60 cm 600L

*Scarus oviceps* 370
7 ◐ ♥ 26°C sg: 1.022 35 cm 400L

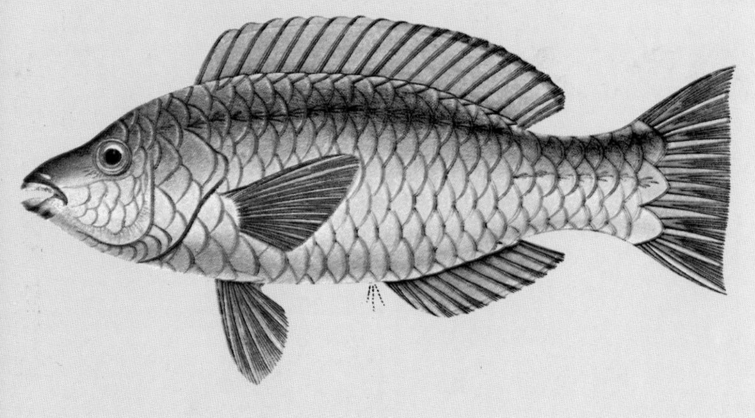

*Scarus moensi* 360
6-9 ◐ ♥ 26°C sg: 1.022 20 cm 200L

*Scarus niger* 360
7-10 ◐ ♥ 26°C sg: 1.022 40 cm 500L

*Scarus psittacus* 360
7-10 ◐ ♥ 26°C sg: 1.022 27 cm 300L

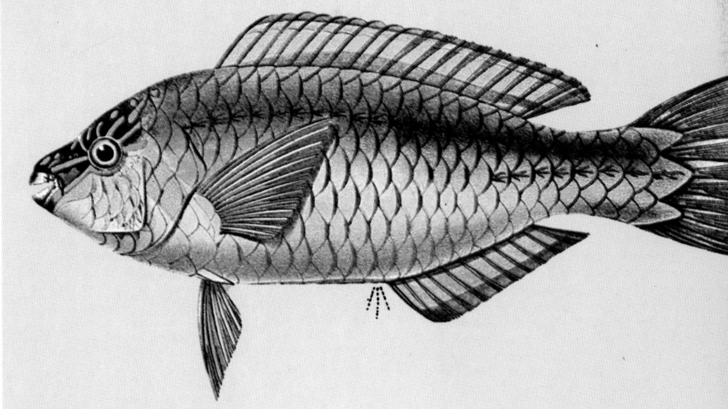

*Scarus javanicus* 360
7 ◐ ♥ 26°C sg: 1.022 28 cm 300L

*Scarus psittacus* 360
7-10 ◐ ♥ 26°C sg: 1.022 27 cm 300L

*Scarus bataviensis* 360
7, 9 26°C sg: 1.022 35 cm 400L

*Scarus oktodon* 360
7, 9 26°C sg: 1.022 33 cm 300L

*Cetoscarus bicolor* 360
6-9 26°C sg: 1.022 60 cm 600L

*Scarus sordidus* 360
6-9 26°C sg: 1.022 50 cm 500L

*Scarus prasiognathos* 360
6-9 26°C sg: 1.022 70 cm 800L

*Scarus rubroviolaceus* 360
3, 6-9 26°C sg: 1.022 66 cm 800L

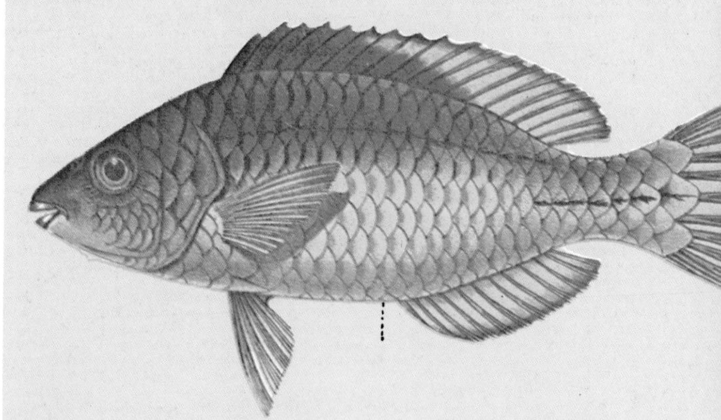

*Scarus macrocheilus* 360
7, 9 26°C sg: 1.022 12 cm 200L

*Scarus erythrodon* 360
7, 9 26°C sg: 1.022 40 cm 400L

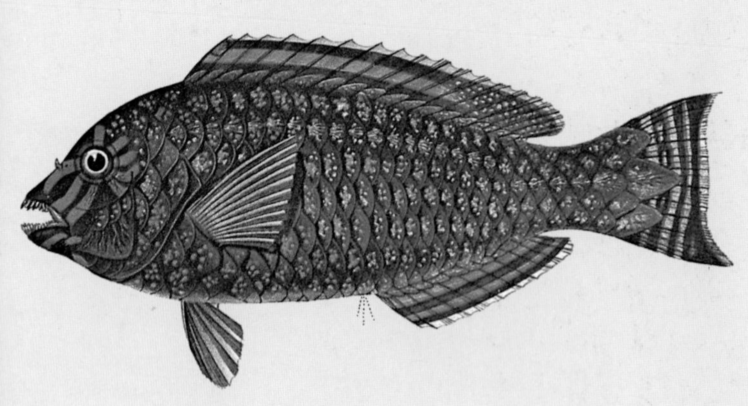

*Calotomus spinidens* 360
7, 9 26°C sg: 1.022 19 cm 200L

*Leptoscarus vaigiensis* 360
7-9 26°C sg: 1.022 35 cm 400L

*Leptoscarus vaigiensis* 360
7-9 26°C sg: 1.022 35 cm 400L

*Calotomus spinidens* 360
7, 9 26°C sg: 1.022 19 cm 200L

*Calotomus spinidens* 360
7, 9 26°C sg: 1.022 19 cm 200L

*Calotomus spinidens* 360
7, 9 26°C sg: 1.022 19 cm 200L

*Calotomus spinidens* 360
7, 9 26°C sg: 1.022 19 cm 200L

*Scarus gibbus* 360
7-10 26°C sg: 1.022 70 cm 1000L

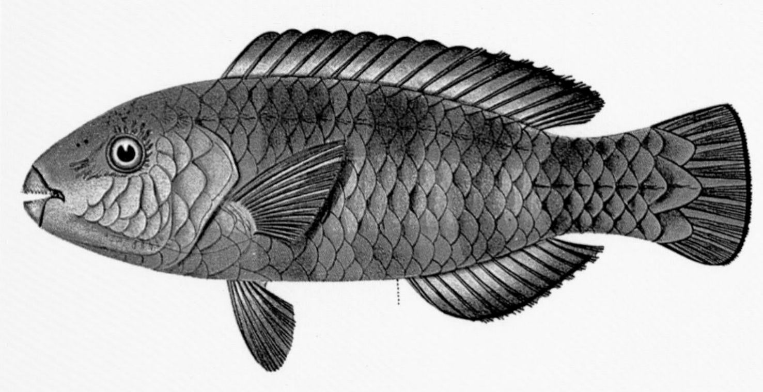

*Scarus rhodoropterus* 360
7 ◐ ♥ 26°C sg: 1.022 25 cm 250L

*Scarus microcheilus* 360
6, 7 ◐ ♥ 26°C sg: 1.022 30 cm 300L

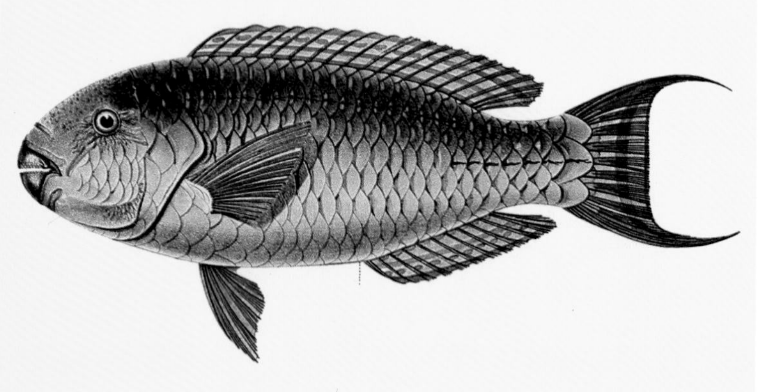

*Scarus gibbus* 360
7-10 ◐ ♥ 26°C sg: 1.022 70 cm 1000L

*Scarus prasiognathos* 360
6-9 ◐ ♥ 26°C sg: 1.022 70 cm 800L

*Scarus cyanotaenia* 360
7-8 ◐ ♥ 26°C sg: 1.022 21 cm 250L

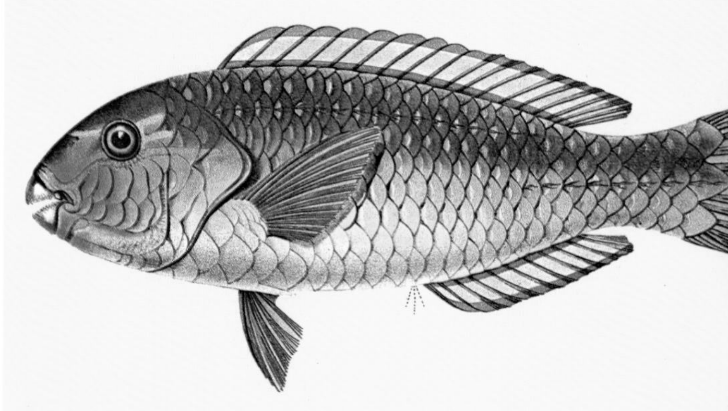

*Scarus japanensis* 360
6-7 ◐ ♥ 26°C sg: 1.022 30 cm 300L

*Scarus bleekeri* 360
6, 7 ◐ ♥ 26°C sg: 1.022 25 cm 300L

*Scarus psittacus* 360
7-10 ◐ ♥ 26°C sg: 1.022 27 cm 300L

#415A

*Scarus* sp. 360
7-10 26°C sg: 1.022 70 cm 1000L

*Scarus bleekeri* 360
6, 7 26°C sg: 1.022 25 cm 300L

*Rathbunella hypoplecta* 361
3-4 23°C sg: 1.024 30 cm 300L

*Bathymaster derjugini* 361
3-4 23°C sg: 1.024 25 cm 300L

*Lycodes pacificus* 362
4 23°C sg: 1.024 30 cm 300L

*Macrozoarces americanus* 362
1 23°C sg: 1.024 110 cm 1500L

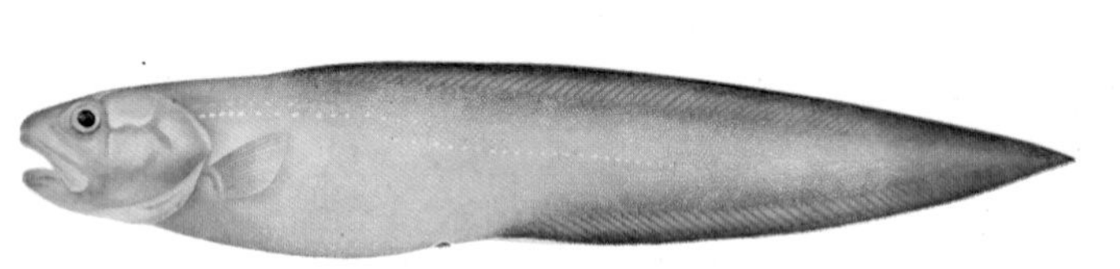

*Lycogramma zesta* 362
5 24°C sg: 1.023 10 cm 100L

*Zoarchias veneficus* 362
14 20°C sg: 1.024 25 cm 300L

*Dictyosoma burgeri* 363
5 24°C sg: 1.023 6 cm 60L

*Ernogrammus hexagrammus* 363
5, 7 24°C sg: 1.023 15 cm 150L

*Chirolophis japonicus* 363
5 23°C sg: 1.024 55 cm 500L

*Chirolophis decoratus* 363
4 22°C sg: 1.024 42 cm 400L

*Chirolophis nugator* 363
4 23°C sg: 1.024 42 cm 500L

*Cebidichthys violaceus* 363
4 26°C sg: 1.022 50 cm 500L

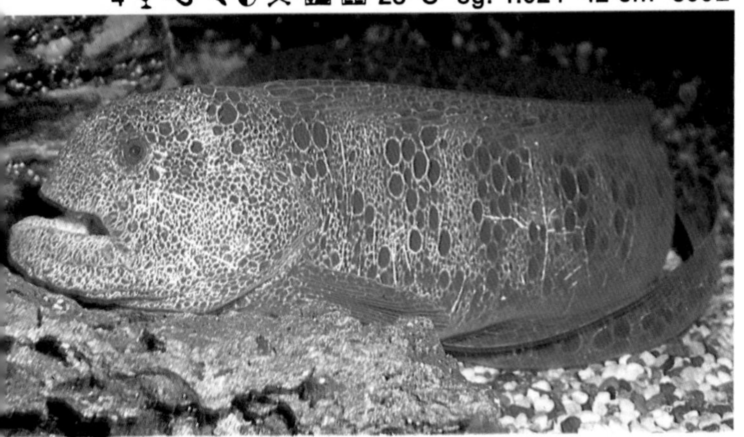

*Anarrhichthys ocellatus* 366
4-5 24°C sg: 1.023 200 cm 2000L

*Anarhichas lupus* 366
4-5 23°C sg: 1.024 200 cm 2000L

*Liocranium praepositum* 267
8 26°C sg: 1.022 10 cm 100L

*Pholis gunnellus* 365
1, 14 23°C sg: 1.024 20 cm 200L

*#418*

*Opistognathus gilberti* 375
2 ∿ ◐ ♥ ▣ ⊔ 26°C sg: 1.022 5 cm 50L

*Opistognathus gilberti* 375
2 ∿ ◐ ♥ ▣ ⊔ 26°C sg: 1.022 5 cm 50L

#419

*Opistognathus rhomaleus* 375
3-4 24°C sg: 1.023 50 cm 500L

*Opistognathus* sp. 375
3 26°C sg: 1.022 10 cm 100L

*Opistognathus aurifrons* 375
2 26°C sg: 1.022 10 cm 100L

*Opistognathus rhomaleus* 375
3-4 24°C sg: 1.023 50 cm 500L

*Lonchopisthus micrognathus* 375
2 26°C sg: 1.022 10 cm 100L

*Opistognathus darwiniensis* 375
8 26°C sg: 1.022 23 cm 250L

*Opistognathus lonchurus* 375
8 26°C sg: 1.022 12 cm 150L

*Tandya latitabunda* 375
8 26°C sg: 1.022 26 cm 250L

*Opistognathus* sp. 375
3 26°C sg: 1.022 10 cm 100L

*Opistognathus* sp. 375
3 ◐ ♥ 26°C sg: 1.022 10 cm 100L

*Opistognathus aurifrons* 375
2 ◐ ♥ 26°C sg: 1.022 10 cm 100L

*Opistognathus* sp. 375
2 ◐ ♥ 26°C sg: 1.022 11 cm 100L

*Opistognathus scops* 375
3-4 ◐ 26°C sg: 1.022 15 cm 150L

*Opistognathus gilberti* 375
2 ◐ ♥ 26°C sg: 1.022 5 cm 50L

*Opistognathus* sp. 375
2 ◐ ♥ 26°C sg: 1.022 11 cm 100L

*Opistognathus whitehursti* 375
2 ◐ ♥ 26°C sg: 1.022 7.5 cm 80L

*Opistognathus macrognathus* 375
2 ◐ 26°C sg: 1.022 20 cm 200L

*Haliophis guttatus* 376
9-10 ◐ ♥ 26°C sg: 1.024 12 cm 150L

*Blennodesmus scapularis* 376
8 ◐ ♥ 26°C sg: 1.022 5 cm 50L

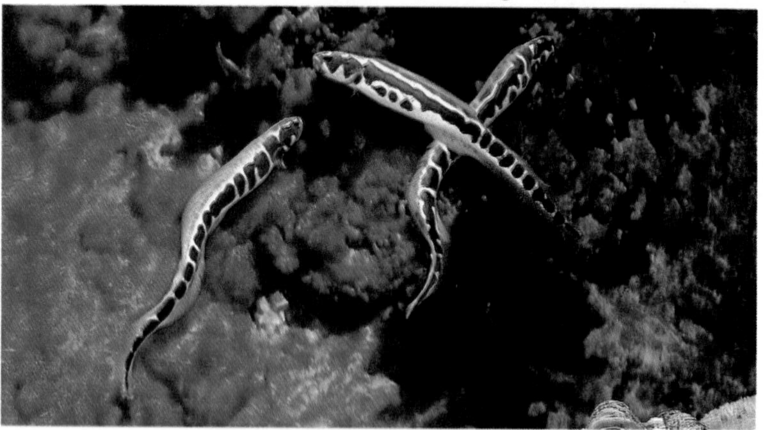

*Pholidichthys leucotaenia* (juv.) 380
7 ◐ ♥ 26°C sg: 1.022 6 cm 60L

*Pholidichthys leucotaenia* 380
7 ◐ ♥ 26°C sg: 1.022 6 cm 60L

*Arctoscopus japonicus* 381
4-5 ◐ 23°C sg: 1.023 22 cm 200L

*Notograptus livingstonei* 379
8 ◐ ♥ 26°C sg: 1.022 7 cm 80L

*Kathetostoma averruncus* 383
3-4 ◐ 24°C sg: 1.023 31 cm 300L

*Ichthyoscopus lebeck* 383
5 ◐ ♥ 23°C sg: 1.024 40 cm 400L

*Uranoscopus bicinctus* 383
5 23°C sg: 1.024 10 cm 100L

*Uranoscopus asper* 383
7 26°C sg: 1.022 15 cm 150L

*Gnathagnus elongatus* 383
5 24°C sg: 1.023 35 cm 400L

*Uranoscopus japonicus* 383
5, 7 24°C sg: 1.022 18 cm 200L

*Creedia alleni* 385
7, 12 25°C sg: 1.023 5 cm 50L

*Limnichthys fasciatus* 385
7, 12 26°C sg: 1.022 5 cm 50L

*Crapatalus arenarius* 386
8 26°C sg: 1.022 9 cm 100L

*Stichaeus grigorjewi* 363
5 23°C sg: 1.024 10 cm 100L

*Parapercis aurantica* 388
5, 7 24°C sg: 1.023 15 cm 150L

*Parapercis sexfasciata* 388
5, 7 24°C sg: 1.022 12 cm 100L

*Parapercis pulchella* 388
5, 7 24°C sg: 1.023 12 cm 150L

*Parapercis multifasciata* 388
5, 7 24°C sg: 1.022 15 cm 150L

*Parapercis* sp. 388
7, 9 26°C sg: 1.022 13 cm 150L

*Parapercis schuinslandi* 388
5, 7 24°C sg: 1.023 20 cm 200L

*Parapercis xanthozona* 388
7 26°C sg: 1.022 8.5 cm 100L

*Parapercis nebulosa* 388
8 26°C sg: 1.022 32 cm 350L

*Parapercis snyderi* 388
7 ∿ ↘ ◐ ✂ ▣ ▭ 26°C sg: 1.022 10 cm 100L

*Parapercis cephalopunctata?* 388
7, 9 26°C sg: 1.022 17 cm 200L

*Parapercis bivittata* 388
9 26°C sg: 1.022 20 cm 200L

*Parapercis hexophthalma* 388
7-10 26°C sg: 1.022 25 cm 250L

*Parapercis trispilota* 388
9 26°C sg: 1.022 15 cm 150L

*Parapercis cephalopunctata* 388
7-9 26°C sg: 1.022 17 cm 150L

*Parapercis haackei* 388
7 26°C sg: 1.022 15 cm 150L

*Parapercis tetracantha* 388
7, 9 26°C sg: 1.022 20 cm 200L

*Parapercis* sp. (juv. *cylindrica?)* 388
7, 9 26°C sg: 1.022 17 cm 150L

*Parapercis tetracantha* 388
7, 9 26°C sg: 1.022 20 cm 200L

*Parapercis snyderi* 388
7 26°C sg: 1.022 10 cm 100L

*#425A*

*Plagiotremus rhinorhynchos* 395
6-10 ∿ ◐ ♥ ▨ ⊔ 26°C sg: 1.022 12 cm 100L

*Vauclusella* sp. 390
12 ◐ ♥ 24°C sg: 1.023 3 cm 50L

*Helcogramma decurrens* 390
7 ◐ ♥ 26°C sg: 1.022 5 cm 50L

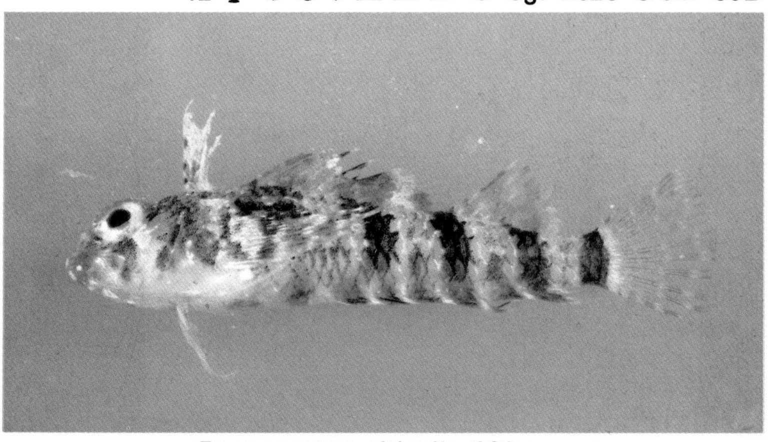

*Enneanectes altivelis* 390
2 ◐ ♥ 26°C sg: 1.022 4 cm 50L

*Norfolkia* sp. 390
12 ◐ ♥ 24°C sg: 1.023 3 cm 50L

*Enneanectes boehlkei* 390
2 ◐ ♥ 26°C sg: 1.022 4 cm 50L

*Enneanectes pectoralis* 390
2 ◐ ♥ 26°C sg: 1.022 4 cm 50L

*Enneanectes sexmaculatus* 390
3 ◐ ♥ 26°C sg: 1.022 2.5 cm 50L

*Enneanectes* sp. 390
2 ◐ ♥ 26°C sg: 1.022 4 cm 50L

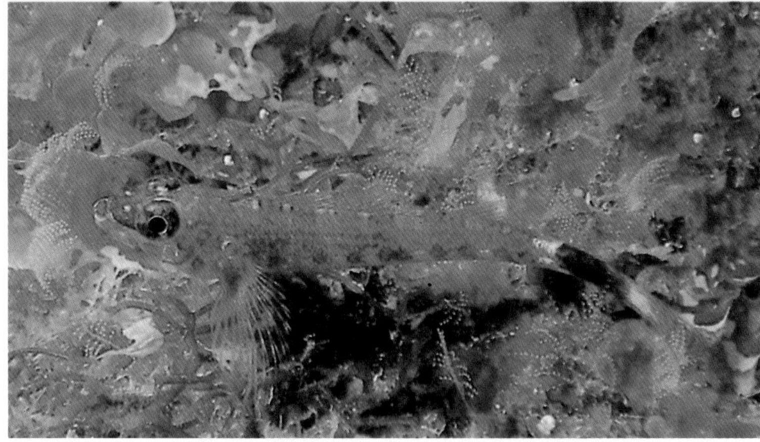

*Undescribed Tripterygiid* 390
3 ◐ ♥ 25°C sg: 1.023 8 cm 80L

*Lepidoblennius marmoratus* 390
7 ◐ ♥ 26°C sg: 1.022 9 cm 100L

*Enneanectes atrorus* 390
2 ◐ ♥ 26°C sg: 1.022 3.3 cm 50L

*Gilloblennius tripennis* 390
11 ◐ ♥ 22°C sg: 1.024 5 cm 50L

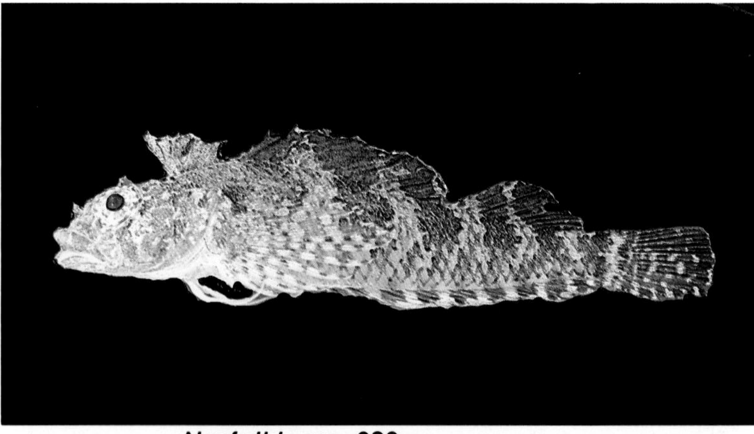

*Norfolkia* sp. 390
12 ◐ ♥ 26°C sg: 1.022 5 cm 50L

*Vauclusella* sp. 390
12 ◐ ♥ 24°C sg: 1.023 3 cm 50L

*Norfolkia brachylepis* 390
7 ◐ ♥ 26°C sg: 1.022 3.5 cm 50L

*Helcogramma* sp. 390
7 ◐ ♥ 26°C sg: 1.022 3 cm 50L

*Tripterygion tripteronotus* 390
15 ⚲ ∿ ◐ ♥ ▨ ⊔ 26°C sg: 1.024 8 cm 80L

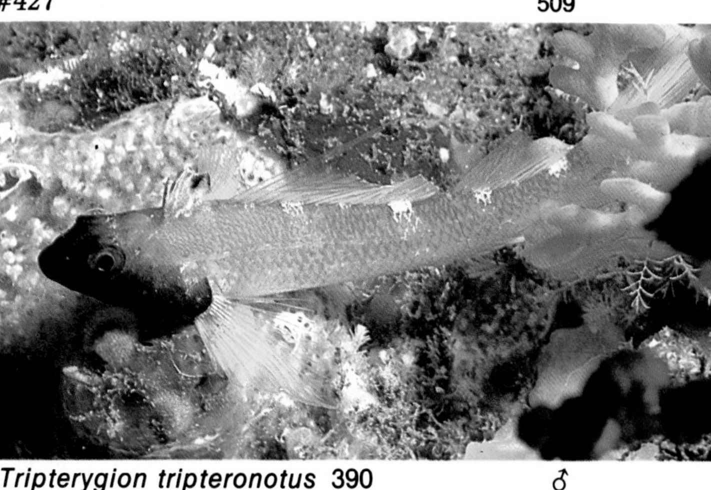

*Tripterygion tripteronotus* 390 ♂
15 ⚲ ∿ ◐ ♥ ▨ ⊔ 26°C sg: 1.024 8 cm 80L

*Tripterygion* sp. 390
3 ⚲ ∿ ◐ ♥ ▨ ⊔ 26°C sg: 1.024 3.8 cm 50L

*Tripterygion tripteronotus* 390
15 ⚲ ∿ ◐ ♥ ▨ ⊔ 26°C sg: 1.024 8 cm 80L

*Enneapterygius etheostomus* 390
5 ⚲ ∿ ◐ ♥ ▨ ⊔ 24°C sg: 1.023 4 cm 50L

*Tripterygion* sp. 390
11 ⚲ ∿ ◐ ♥ ▨ ⊔ 22°C sg: 1.024 8 cm 80L

*Tripterygiid* 390
8 ⚲ ∿ ◐ ✱ ▨ ⊔ 26°C sg: 1.024 4 cm 40L

Tripterygiid 390
8 ⚲ ∿ ◐ ♥ ▨ ⊔ 25°C sg: 1.024 4 cm 40L

*Tripterygion* sp. 390
11 ~ ◐ ♥ ▣ ▭ 24°C sg: 1.023 6 cm 60L

*Tripterygion bucknilli* 390
11 ~ ◐ ♥ ▣ ▭ 22°C sg: 1.024 8 cm 80L

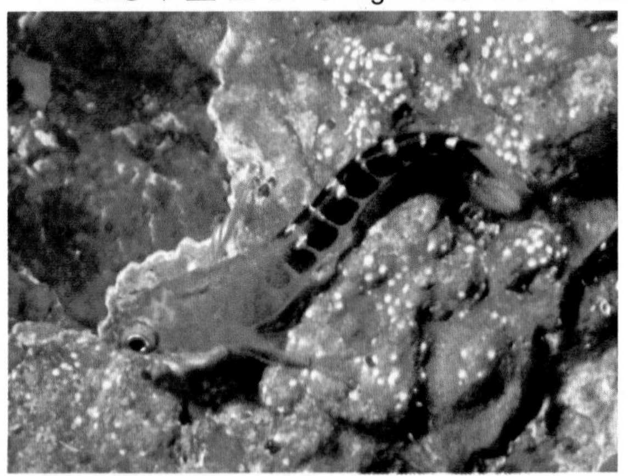

*Tripterygion* sp. 390
11 ~ ◐ ♥ ▣ ▭ 24°C sg: 1.023 6 cm 60L

*Tripterygion* sp. B. 390
11 ~ ◐ ♥ ▣ ▭ 22°C sg: 1.024 8 cm 80L

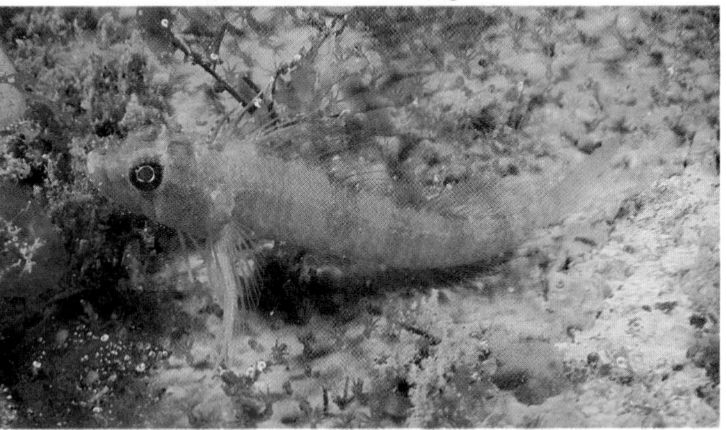

*Norfolkia cristata* 390
12 ~ ◐ ♥ ▣ ▭ 24°C sg: 1.023 5 cm 50L

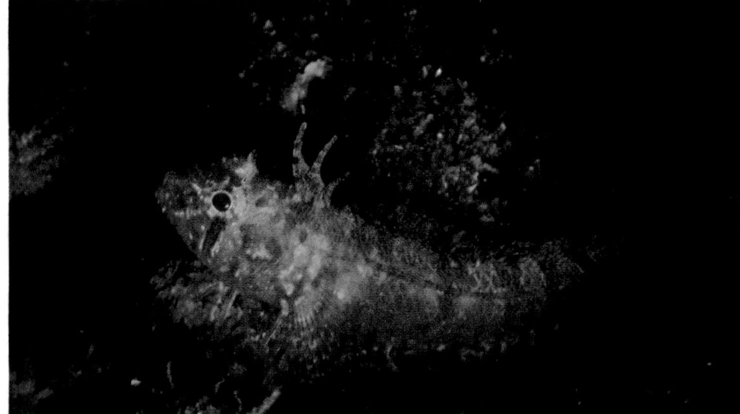

*Norfolkia incisa* 390
12 ~ ◐ ♥ ▣ ▭ 24°C sg: 1.023 3 cm 40L

*Norfolkia clarkei* 390
12 ~ ◐ ♥ ▣ ▭ 24°C sg: 1.023 6 cm 60L

*Apopterygion alta* 390
12 ~ ◐ ♥ ▣ ▭ 24°C sg: 1.023 4.4 cm 50L

*Helcogramma striata* 390
7 ~ ◐ ♥ 25°C sg: 1.022 3 cm 50L

*Helcogramma decurrens* 390
12 ~ ◐ ♥ 24°C sg: 1.023 5 cm 50L

*Helcogramma decurrens* 390
12 ~ ◐ ♥ 24°C sg: 1.023 5 cm 50L

*Helcogramma* sp. 390
9 ~ ◐ ♥ 26°C sg: 1.020 3 cm 50L

*Gunnelichthys curiosus* 407
6 ~ ◐ ♥ 26°C sg: 1.022 11 cm 100L

*Gunnelichthys monostigma* 407
13 ~ ◐ ♥ 26°C sg: 1.022 7.5 cm 80L

*Malacanthus brevirostris* 300
3, 6-10 ~ ◐ ♥ 26°C sg: 1.022 30 cm 300L

*Hoplolatilus cuniculus* 300
6 ~ ◐ ♥ 26°C sg: 1.022 9 cm 100L

*Heteristius rubrocinctus* 391
2 ~ ◐ ♥ 26°C sg: 1.022 6.0 cm 60L

*Dactyloscopus pectoralis* 391
3 ~ ◐ ♥ 26°C sg: 1.022 7.5 cm 80L

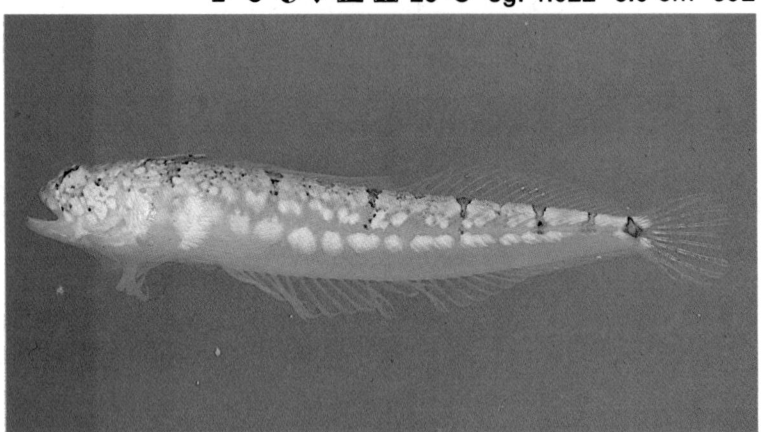

*Gillelus greyae* 391
2 ~ ◐ ♥ 26°C sg: 1.022 7.5 cm 80L

*Exerpes asper* 392
3 ~ ◐ ✕ 26°C sg: 1.022 5 cm 50L

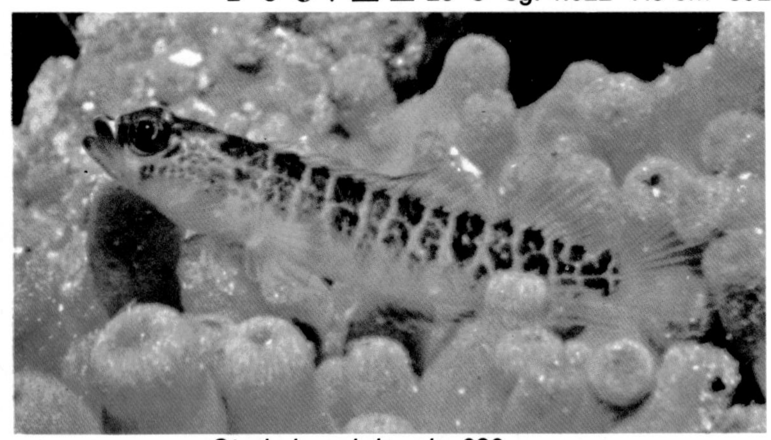

*Starksia spinipenis* 392
3 ~ ◐ ♥ 26°C sg: 1.022 5 cm 50L

*Neoclinus bryope* 392
5 ~ ◐ ♥ 26°C sg: 1.022 6 cm 60L

*Starksia ocellata* 392
2 ~ ◐ ♥ 26°C sg: 1.022 5 cm 50L

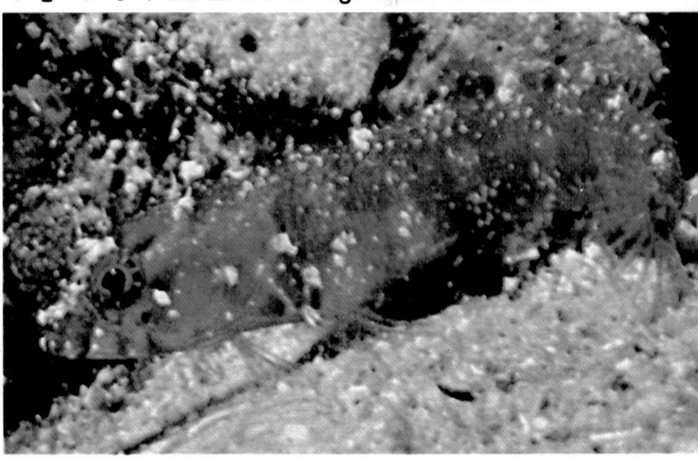

*Starksia* sp. 392
3 ~ ◐ ♥ 26°C sg: 1.022 5 cm 50L

*Labrisomus nuchipinnis* 392
1-2, 13 ♀ ~ ◐ ✕ ▣ ▭ 26°C sg: 1.022 23 cm 300L

*Labrisomus filamentosus* 392
2 ♀ ~ ◐ ♥ ▣ ▭ 26°C sg: 1.022 8.0 cm 80L

*Labrisomus bucciferus* 392
1-2 ♀ ~ ◐ ♥ ▣ ▭ 25°C sg: 1.022 9 cm 100L

*Labrisomus nigricinctus* 392
2 ♀ ~ ◐ ♥ ▣ ▭ 26°C sg: 1.022 7.5 cm 80L

*Labrisomus nuchipinnis* 392
1-2, 13 ♀ ~ ◐ ✕ ▣ ▭ 26°C sg: 1.022 23 cm 300L

*Labrisomus kalisherae* 392
2 ♀ ~ ◐ ♥ ▣ ▭ 26°C sg: 1.022 7.5 cm 80L

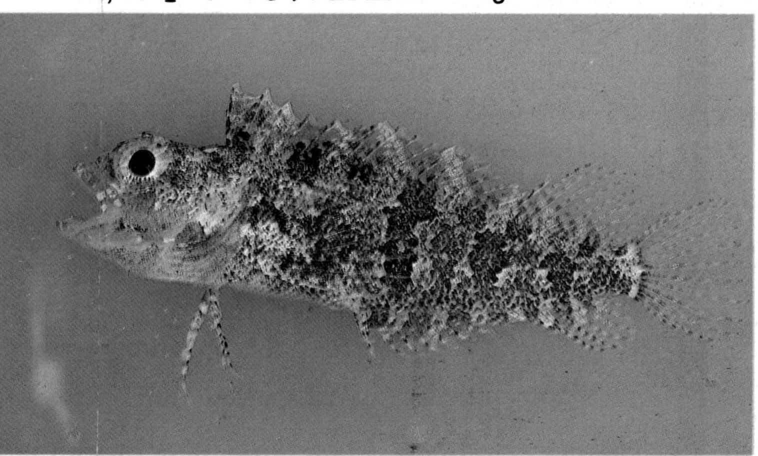

*Labrisomus haitiensis* 392
2 ♀ ~ ◐ ♥ ▣ ▭ 26°C sg: 1.022 7.5 cm 80L

*Starksia starcki* 392
2 ♀ ~ ◐ ♥ ▣ ▭ 26°C sg: 1.022 4 cm 50L

*Malacoctenus gigas* 392
3 ~ ◐ ♥ 26°C sg: 1.022 13 cm 150L

*Malacoctenus tetranemus* 392
3 ~ ◐ ♥ 26°C sg: 1.022 120 cm 150L

*Malacoctenus ebisui* 392
3 ~ ◐ ♥ 26°C sg: 1.022 12 cm 150L

*Malacoctenus tetranemus* 392
3 ~ ◐ ♥ 26°C sg: 1.022 12 cm 150L

*Paraclinus mexicanus* 392
3 ~ ◐ ♥ 26°C sg: 1.022 4 cm 40L

*Malacoctenus margaritae* 392
3 ~ ◐ ♥ 26°C sg: 1.022 12 cm 150L

*Malacoctenus zonifer* 392
3 ~ ◐ ♥ 26°C sg: 1.022 12 cm 150L

*Malacoctenus triangulatus* 392
2 26°C sg: 1.022 6.5 cm 80L

*Malacoctenus gilli* 392
2 26°C sg: 1.022 4.7 cm 50L

*Malacoctenus macropus* 392
2 24°C sg: 1.023 5.5 cm 60L

*Malacoctenus boehlkei* 392
2 26°C sg: 1.022 6 cm 60L

*Paraclinus marmoratus* 392
2 26°C sg: 1.022 10 cm 100L

*Dialommus fuscus* 392
3 26°C sg: 1.022 7.0 cm 80L

*Paraclinus fasciatus* 392
2 26°C sg: 1.022 6.5 cm 80L

*Paraclinus nigripinnis* 392
1-2 26°C sg: 1.023 5 cm 50L

*Clinus superciliosus* 393
9 26°C sg: 1.020 30 cm 250L

*Sticharium dorsale* 393
12 26°C sg: 1.022 5 cm 50L

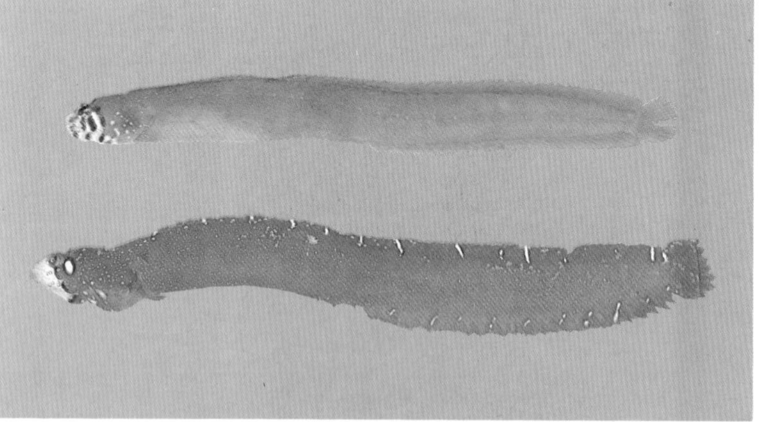

*Stathmonotus hemphilli* 392
2 26°C sg: 1.022 5 cm 50L

*Stathmonotus sinuscalifornici* 392
3 26°C sg: 1.022 7.5 cm 80L

*Gibbonsia metzi* 393
4 26°C sg: 1.022 24 cm 250L

*Heterostichus rostratus* 393
3-4 26°C sg: 1.022 61 cm 600L

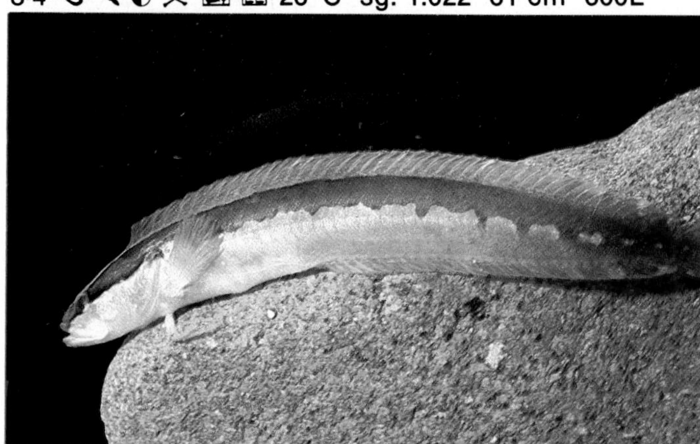

*Ophiclinus gracilis* 392
7 26°C sg: 1.022 6 cm 80L

*Xenomedia rhodopyga* 392
3 26°C sg: 1.022 6 cm 80L

*Heteroclinus whitleyi* 393
12 ~ ◐ ♥ 24°C sg: 1.022 6 cm 60L

*Heteroclinus eckloniae* 393
12 ~ ◐ ♥ 24°C sg: 1.022 3 cm 50L

*Springeratus xanthosoma* 393
7 ~ ◐ ✕ 26°C sg: 1.022 7 cm 80L

*Cristiceps australis* 393
7, 12 ~ ◐ ♥ 26°C sg: 1.022 10 cm 100L

*Heteroclinus* sp. cf. *roseus* 393
12 ~ ◐ ♥ 24°C sg: 1.022 8.5 cm 80L

*Heteroclinus roseus* 393
12 ~ ◐ ♥ 24°C sg: 1.022 7 cm 80L

*Heteroclinus adelaidae* 393
12 ~ ◐ ♥ 24°C sg: 1.022 7 cm 80L

*Cristiceps aurantiacus* 393
12 ~ ◐ ♥ 24°C sg: 1.022 4 cm 50L

*Acanthemblemaria macrospilus* 394
3 ∿ ◐ ♥ ▨ ▭ 26°C sg: 1.022 5 cm 50L

*Acanthemblemaria balanorum* 394
3 ∿ ◐ ♥ ▨ ▭ 26°C sg: 1.022 5 cm 50L

*Acanthemblemaria aspera* 394
2 ∿ ◐ ♥ ▨ ▭ 26°C sg: 1.022 4 cm 50L

*Acanthemblemaria spinosa* 394
2 ∿ ◐ ♥ ▨ ▭ 26°C sg: 1.022 5 cm 50L

*Acanthemblemaria hancocki* 394
3 ∿ ◐ ♥ ▨ ▭ 26°C sg: 1.022 4 cm 50L

*Acanthemblemaria crockeri* 394
3 ∿ ◐ ♥ ▨ ▭ 26°C sg: 1.022 5 cm 50L

*Acanthemblemaria exilispinis* 394
3 ∿ ◐ ♥ ▨ ▭ 26°C sg: 1.022 4 cm 50L

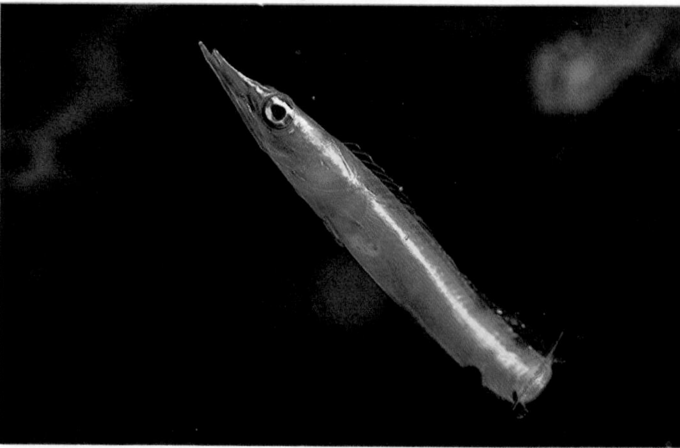

*Lucayablennius zingaro* 394
2 ∿ ◐ ♥ ▨ ▭ 26°C sg: 1.022 4 cm 50L

*Chaenopsis alepidota* 394
3 ~ ◐ ♥ ▨ ⊡ 26°C sg: 1.022 15 cm 100L

*Ekemblemaria* sp. (*myersi*?) 394
3 ~ ◐ ♥ ▨ ⊡ 26°C sg: 1.022 3.5 cm 50L

*Chaenopsis ocellata* 394
2 ~ ◐ ♥ ▨ ⊡ 26°C sg: 1.022 12.5 cm 100L

*Coralliozetus micropes* 394
3 ~ ◐ ♥ ▨ ⊡ 26°C sg: 1.022 4 cm 50L

*Chaenopsis limbaughi* 394
3 ~ ◐ ♥ ▨ ⊡ 26°C sg: 1.022 8.5 cm 100L

*Coralliozetus angelica* 394
3 ~ ◐ ♥ ▨ ⊡ 26°C sg: 1.022 4 cm 50L

*Hemiemblemaria simulus* 394
2 ~ ◐ ♥ ▨ ⊡ 26°C sg: 1.022 10 cm 100L

*Emblemaria walkeri* 394
3 ∿ ◐ ♥ ▨ ▭ 26°C sg: 1.022 6 cm 60L

*Emblemaria pandionis* 394
2 ∿ ◐ ♥ ▨ ▭ 26°C sg: 1.022 5 cm 50L

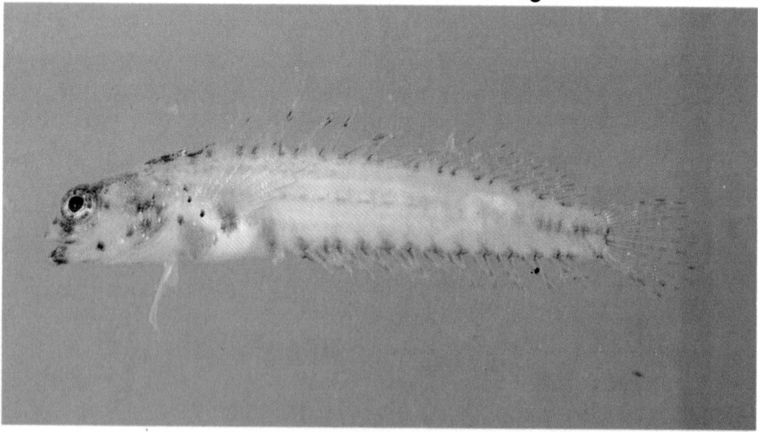

*Coralliozetus diaphanus* 394
2 ∿ ◐ ♥ ▨ ▭ 26°C sg: 1.022 4 cm 50L

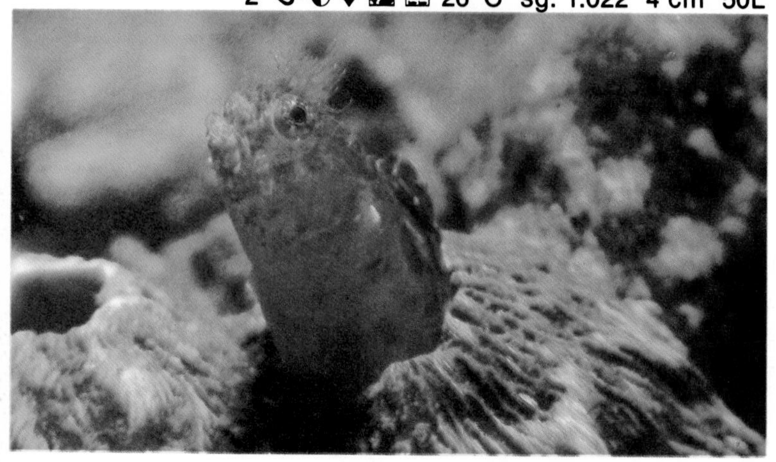

*Protemblemaria bicirrhis* 394
3 ∿ ◐ ♥ ▨ ▭ 26°C sg: 1.022 3.5 cm 50L

*Emblemaria piratula* 394
2 ∿ ◐ ♥ ▨ ▭ 26°C sg: 1.022 5 cm 50L

*Emblemaria hypacanthus* 394
3 ∿ ◐ ♥ ▨ ▭ 26°C sg: 1.022 5 cm 50L

*Emblemaria bottomei* 394
2 ∿ ◐ ♥ ▨ ▭ 26°C sg: 1.022 5 cm 50L

*Protemblemaria lucasana* 394
3 ∿ ◐ ♥ ▨ ▭ 26°C sg: 1.022 4.5 cm 50L

*Plagiotremus phenax* 395
9 ◐ ♥ 26°C sg: 1.022 8 cm 80L

*Plagiotremus laudandus flavus* 395
6 ◐ ♥ 26°C sg: 1.022 6 cm 60L

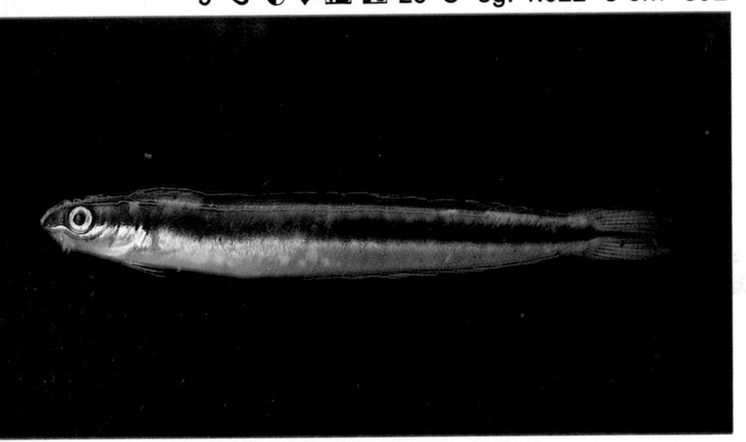

*Plagiotremus azaleus* 395
3 ◐ ♥ 26°C sg: 1.022 7.5 cm 80L

*Plagiotremus goslinei* 395
6 ◐ ♥ 26°C sg: 1.022 7.5 cm 75L

*Plagiotremus rhinorhynchos* 395
6-10 ◐ ♥ 26°C sg: 1.022 12 cm 100L

*Plagiotremus rhinorhynchos* 395
6-10 ◐ ♥ 26°C sg: 1.022 12 cm 100L

*Plagiotremus townsendi* 395 ♂
10 ◐ ♥ 26°C sg: 1.024 6 cm 60L

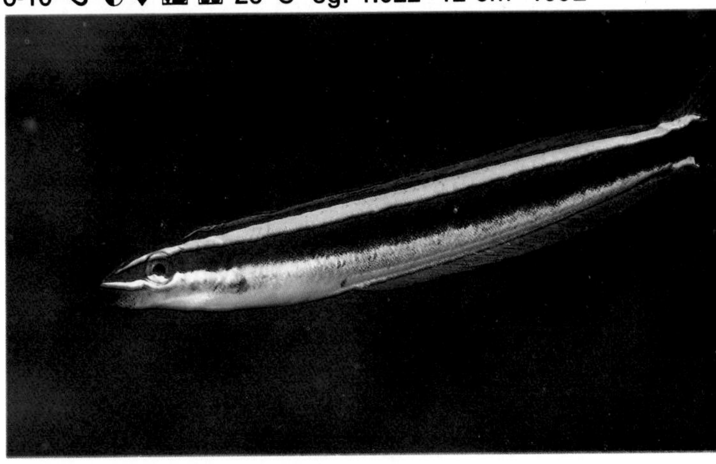

*Plagiotremus rhinorhynchos* 395
6-10 ◐ ♥ 26°C sg: 1.022 12 cm 100L

*Meiacanthus lineatus* 395
7 ~ ◐ ♥ ▨ ▭ 26°C sg: 1.022 8 cm 80L

*Meiacanthus grammistes* 395
7 ~ ◐ ♥ ▨ ▭ 26°C sg: 1.022 8cm 80L

*Meiacanthus kamoharai* 395
7 ~ ◐ ♥ ▨ ▭ 26°C sg: 1.022 8 cm 80L

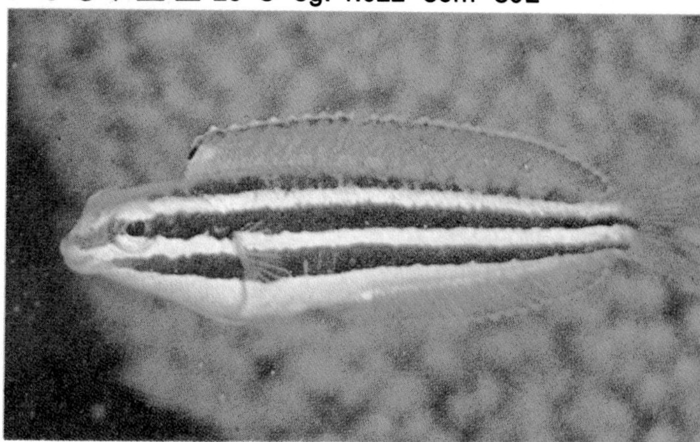

*Petroscirtes fallax* 395
7-8 ~ ◐ ♥ ▨ ▭ 26°C sg: 1.022 9 cm 100L

*Petroscirtes xestus* 395
8 ~ ◐ ♥ ▨ ▭ 26°C sg: 1.022 12 cm 100L

*Petroscirtes breviceps* 395
7-8 ~ ◐ ♥ ▨ ▭ 26°C sg: 1.022 10 cm 100L

*Petroscirtes breviceps* 395
7-8 ~ ◐ ♥ ▨ ▭ 26°C sg: 1.022 10 cm 100L

*Aspidontus taeniatus* 395
7-10 ~ ◐ ♥ ▨ ▭ 26°C sg: 1.022 13 cm 150L

*Meiacanthus atrodorsalis* 395
6-9 ∿ ◐ ♥ ▨ ⊡ 26°C sg: 1.022 7.5 cm 80L

*Meiacanthus oualanensis* 395
6 ∿ ◐ ♥ ▨ ⊡ 26°C sg: 1.022 7.5 cm 80L

*Ecsenius gravieri* (left), *Meiacanthus nigrolineatus* (right) 395
10 ∿ ◐ ♥ ▨ ⊡ 26°C sg: 1.022 9.5 cm 100L

*Meiacanthus atrodorsalis* 395
6-9 ∿ ◐ ♥ ▨ ⊡ 26°C sg: 1.022 7.5 cm 80L

*Meiacanthus bundoon* 395
6 ∿ ◐ ♥ ▨ ⊡ 26°C sg: 1.022 9 cm 100L

*Meiacanthus smithii* 395
9 ∿ ◐ ♥ ▨ ⊡ 26°C sg: 1.022 8.5 cm 90L

*Meiacanthus anema* 395
6-7 ∿ ◐ ♥ ▨ ⊡ 26°C sg: 1.022 9 cm 100L

*Meiacanthus vittatus* 395
7-8 ∿ ◐ ♥ ▨ ⊡ 26°C sg: 1.022 7.5 cm 80L

*Aidablennius sphynx* 395 ♀
15 ◐ ♥ 26°C sg: 1.024 7 cm 80L

*Aidablennius sphynx* 395 ♂
15 ◐ ♥ 26°C sg: 1.024 7 cm 80L

*Parablennius tentacularis* 395
15 ◐ ♥ 26°C sg: 1.024 16 cm 200L

*Salaria pavo* 395
13 ◐ ♥ 26°C sg: 1.022 13 cm 150L

*Lipophrys adriaticus* 395
15 ◐ ♥ 26°C sg: 1.024 10 cm 100L

*Parablennius sanguinolentus* 395
15 ◐ ♥ 26°C sg: 1.024 20 cm 200L

*Lipophrys dalmatinus* 395 ♂
15 ◐ ♥ 26°C sg: 1.024 6 cm 60L

*Parablennius rouxi* 395
15 ◐ ♥ 26°C sg: 1.024 8 cm 100L

*Parablennius incognitus* 395
15 ◐ ♥ 26°C sg: 1.024 8 cm 100L

*Lipophrys canevae* 395 ♂
15 ◐ ♥ 26°C sg: 1.024 8 cm 100L

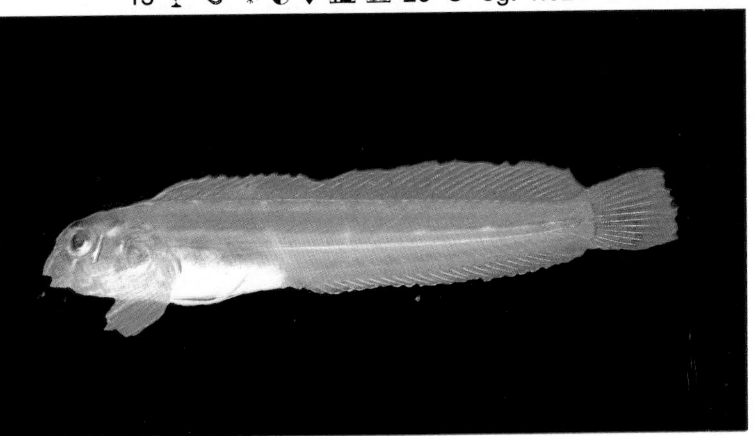

*Omobranchus ferox* 395
7, 9 ◐ ♥ 26°C sg: 1.022 6 cm 60L

*Omobranchus germaini* 395
7 ◐ ♥ 26°C sg: 1.022 6 cm 60L

*Lipophrys nigriceps* 395
15 ◐ ♥ 23°C sg: 1.022 5.5 cm 75L

*Lipophrys canevae* 395 ♂
15 ◐ ♥ 26°C sg: 1.024 8 cm 100L

*Parablennius zvonimiri* 395
15 ◐ ♥ 23°C sg: 1.023 7 cm 80L

*Omobranchus elegans* 395
5 ◐ ♥ 24°C sg: 1.023 7 cm 80L

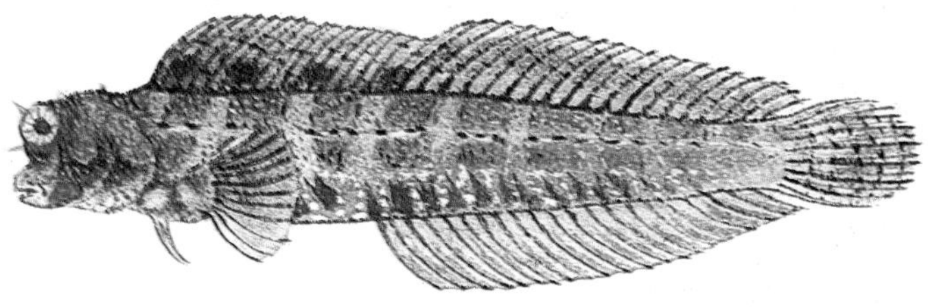

*Salarias* sp. 395
7 ∿ ◐ ♥ 26°C sg: 1.022 10 cm 100L

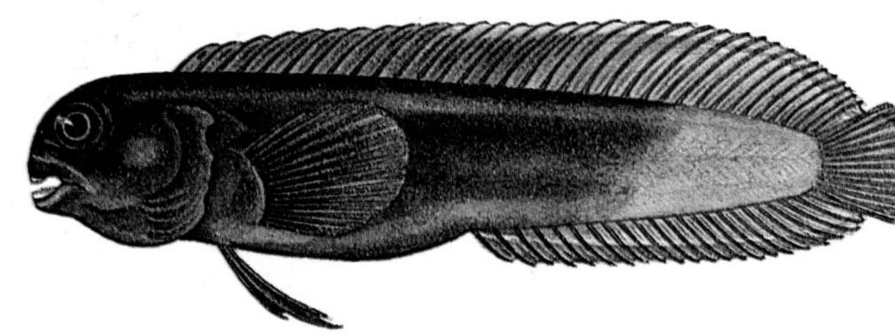

*Enchelyurus flavipes* 395
7 ∿ ◐ ♥ 26°C sg: 1.022 8 cm 80L

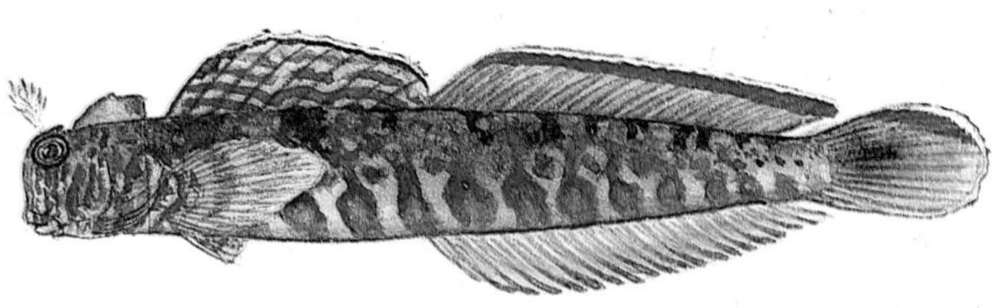

*Istiblennius* sp. 395
7 ∿ ◐ ♥ 26°C sg: 1.022 12 cm 100L

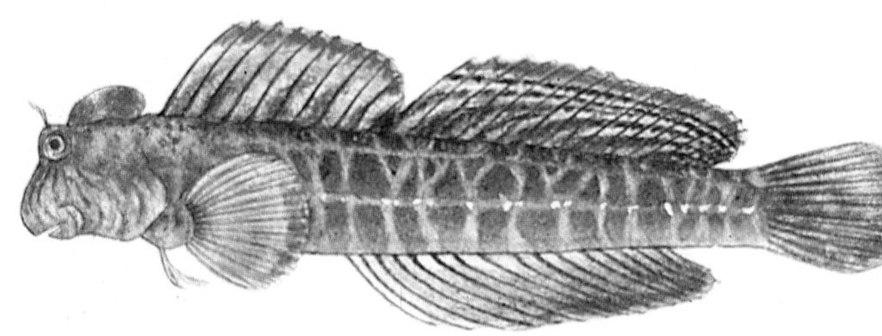

*Istiblennius* sp. 395
7 ∿ ◐ ♥ 26°C sg: 1.022 12 cm 100L

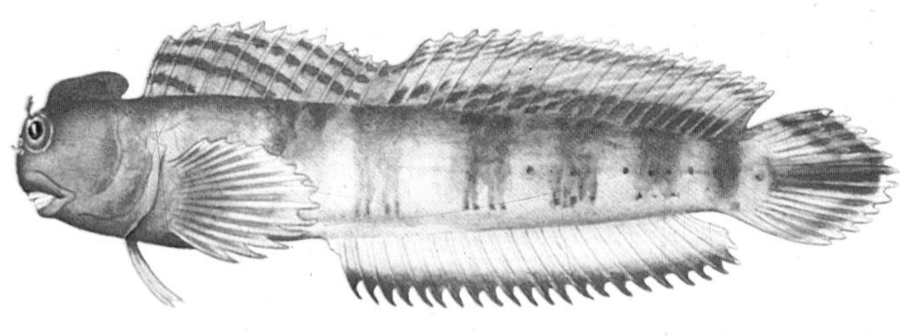

*Istiblennius dussumieri* 395
7 ∿ ◐ ♥ 26°C sg: 1.022 13 cm 100L

*Salarias fasciatus* 395
7, 9 ∿ ◐ ♥ 26°C sg: 1.022 10 cm 100L

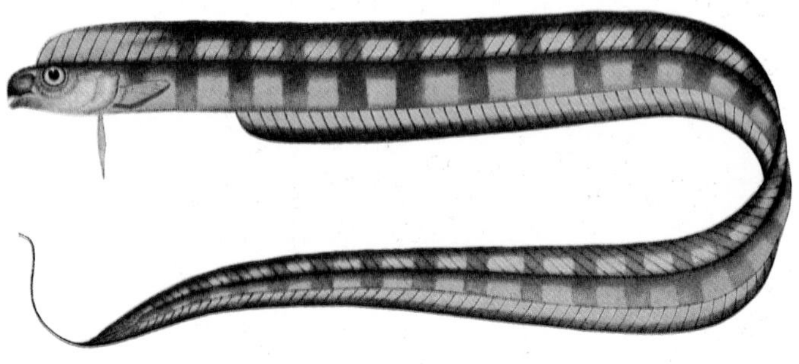

*Xiphasia setifer* 395

7, 9 ∿ ◐ ♥ 26°C sg: 1.022 50 cm 500L

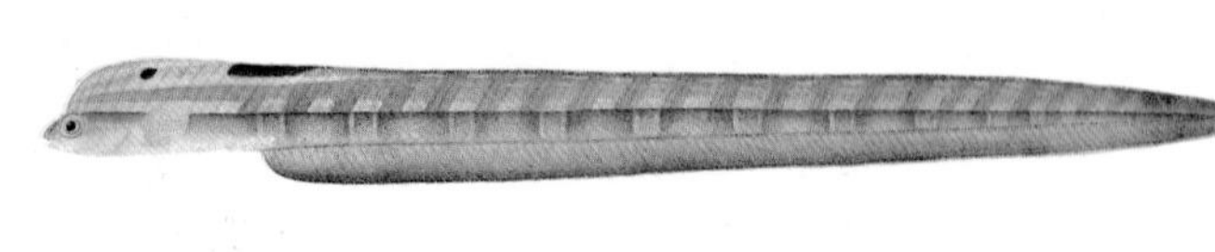

*Xiphasia setifer* 395
7, 9 ∿ ◐ ♥ 26°C sg: 1.022 50 cm 500L

*Laiphognathus multimaculatus* 395
7-9 26°C sg: 1.022 4 cm 40L

*Glyptoparus delicatulus* 395
6-7, 9 26°C sg: 1.022 3.5 cm 40L

*Salarias* sp. 395
7 26°C sg: 1.022 10 cm 100L

*Salarias guttatus* 395
7 26°C sg: 1.022 7 cm 80L

*Salarias fasciatus* 395
6-9 26°C sg: 1.022 15 cm 150L

*Salarias irroratus* 395
7 26°C sg: 1.022 7 cm 80L

*Atrosalarias fuscus* 395
7-8 26°C sg: 1.022 15 cm 150L

*Atrosalarias fuscus* (juv.) 395
7-8 26°C sg: 1.022 15 cm 150L

*Ophioblennius steindachneri* 395
3 ◐ ♥ 26°C sg: 1.022 15 cm 150L

*Ophioblennius atlanticus* 395
1, 2 ◐ ♥ 24°C sg: 1.023 13 cm 150L

*Cirripectes stigmaticus* 395
6-8 ◐ ♥ 26°C sg: 1.022 10 cm 100L

*Cirripectes stigmaticus* 395
6-8 ◐ ♥ 26°C sg: 1.022 10 cm 100L

*Cirripectes castaneus* 395
7, 9 ◐ ♥ 26°C sg: 1.022 10 cm 100L

*Cirripectes filamentosus* 395
7 ◐ ♥ 26°C sg: 1.022 8 cm 80L

*Cirripectes alboapicalis* 395
6 ◐ ♥ 26°C sg: 1.022 8 cm 100L

*Cirripectes chelomatus* 395
8 ◐ ♥ 26°C sg: 1.022 8 cm 100L

*Salarias* sp. 395
13 ◐ ♥ 26°C sg: 1.022 10 cm 100L

*Salarias fasciatus* 395
6-9 ◐ ♥ 26°C sg: 1.022 15 cm 150L

*Cirripectes stigmaticus* 395
6-8 26°C sg: 1.022 10 cm 100L

*Cirripectes* sp. 395
8 26°C sg: 1.022 10 cm 100L

*Ecsenius gravieri* 395
9-10 26°C sg: 1.022 8 cm 100L

*Meiacanthus nigrolineatus* 395
10 26° sg: 1.022 9.5 cm 100L

*Ecsenius gravieri* 395
9-10 26°C sg: 1.022 8 cm 100L

*Ecsenius gravieri* 395
9-10 26°C sg: 1.022 8 cm 100L

*Ecsenius aroni* 395
10 26°C sg: 1.028 4 cm 50L

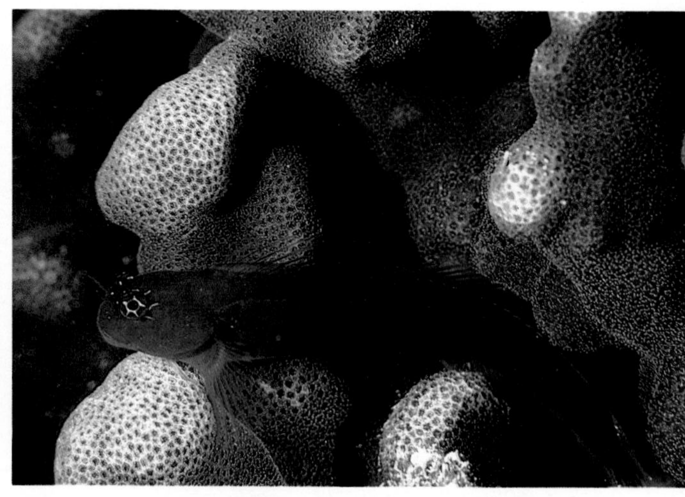

*Ecsenius pulcher* 395
9 26°C sg: 1.022 7 cm 70L

*Ecsenius pulcher* 395
9 26°C sg: 1.022 7 cm 70L

*Ecsenius pulcher* 395
9 26°C sg: 1.022 7 cm 70L

*Ecsenius lividanalis* 395
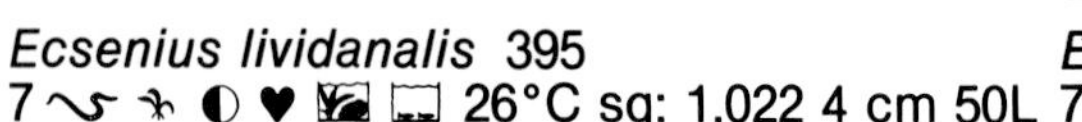
7 26°C sg: 1.022 4 cm 50L

*Ecsenius lividanalis* 395
7 26°C sg: 1.022 4 cm 50L

*Ecsenius melarchus* 395
7 ◐ ♥ 26°C sg: 1.022 5 cm 50L

*Ecsenius melarchus* 395
7 ◐ ♥ 26°C sg: 1.022 5 cm 50L

*Ecsenius midas* 395
9-10 ◐ ♥ 26°C sg: 1.022 13 cm 150L

*Ecsenius midas* 395
9-10 ◐ ♥ 26°C sg: 1.022 13 cm 150L

*Ecsenius midas* 395
9-10 ◐ ♥ 26°C sg: 1.022 13 cm 150L

*Ecsenius midas* 395
9-10 ◐ ♥ 26°C sg: 1.022 13 cm 150L

*Ecsenius stigmatura* 395
7 ◐ ♥ 26°C sg: 1.022 6 cm 60L

*Ecsenius stigmatura* 395
7 ◐ ♥ 26°C sg: 1.022 6 cm 60L

*Ecsenius frontalis* 395
10 ◐ ♥ 26°C sg: 1.026 8 cm 80L

*Ecsenius frontalis* 395
10 ◐ ♥ 26°C sg: 1.026 8 cm 80L

*Ecsenius frontalis* 395
10 ◐ ♥ 26°C sg: 1.026 8 cm 80L

*Ecsenius bicolor* 395
6-9 ◐ ♥ 26°C sg: 1.022 8 cm 100L

*Ecsenius bicolor* 395
6-9 26°C sg: 1.022 8 cm 100L

*Ecsenius bicolor* 395
6-9 26°C sg: 1.022 8 cm 100L

*Ecsenius bicolor* 395
6-9 26°C sg: 1.022 8 cm 100L

*Ecsenius bicolor* 395
6-9 26°C sg: 1.022 8 cm 100L

*Ecsenius namiyei* 395
7 26°C sg: 1.022 9 cm 100L

*Ecsenius namiyei* 395
7 26°C sg: 1.022 9 cm 100L

*Ecsenius namiyei* 395
7 ◐ ♥ 26°C sg: 1.022 9 cm 100L

*Ecsenius lineatus* 395
7 ◐ ♥ 26°C sg: 1.022 8 cm 100L

*Ecsenius lineatus* 395
7 ◐ ♥ 26°C sg: 1.022 8 cm 100L

*Ecsenius lineatus* 395
7 ◐ ♥ 26°C sg: 1.022 8 cm 100L

*Ecsenius lineatus* 395
7 ◐ ♥ 26°C sg: 1.022 8 cm 100L

*Ecsenius lineatus* 395
7 ◐ ♥ 26°C sg: 1.022 8 cm 100L

*Ecsenius oculatus* 395
7, 9, 12 ∿ ⚘ ◐ ♥ ▨ ⊔ 26°C sg: 1.022 6 cm 60L

*Ecsenius paroculus* 395
7 ∿ ⚘ ◐ ♥ ▨ ⊔ 26°C sg: 1.022 4 cm 50L

*Ecsenius oculus* 395
6-7 ♀ ∿ ⚘ ◐ ♥ ▨ ⊔ 26°C sg: 1.022 7 cm 80L

*Ecsenius monoculus* 395
7 ♀ ∿ ⚘ ◐ ♥ ▨ ⊔ 26°C sg: 1.022 5 cm 50L

*Ecsenius tessera* 395
8 ♀ ∿ ⚘ ◐ ♥ ▨ ⊔ 26°C sg: 1.022 5 cm 50L

*Ecsenius pardus* 395
6 ♀ ∿ ⚘ ◐ ♥ ▨ ⊔ 26°C sg: 1.022 5 cm 50L

*Ecsenius pardus* 395
6 ◐ ♥ 26°C sg: 1.022 5 cm 50L

*Ecsenius portenoyi* 395
6 ◐ ♥ 26°C sg: 1.022 5 cm 50L

*Ecsenius portenoyi* 395
6 ◐ ♥ 26°C sg: 1.022 5 cm 50L

*Ecsenius dentex* 395
10 ◐ ♥ 26°C sg: 1.026 5 cm 50L

*Ecsenius nalolo* 395
9-10 ◐ ♥ 26°C sg: 1.022 7 cm 80L

*Ecsenius nalolo* 395
9-10 ◐ ♥ 26°C sg: 1.022 7 cm 80L

*Ecsenius yaeyamaensis* 395
7, 9 ♀ ~ ✈ ◐ ♥ ▣ ▭ 26°C sg: 1.022 5 cm 50L

*Ecsenius yaeyamaensis* 395
7, 9 ♀ ~ ✈ ◐ ♥ ▣ ▭ 26°C sg: 1.022 5 cm 50L

*Ecsenius yaeyamaensis* 395
7, 9 ♀ ~ ✈ ◐ ♥ ▣ ▭ 26°C sg: 1.022 5 cm 50L

*Ecsenius minutus* 395
9 ♀ ~ ✈ ◐ ♥ ▣ ▭ 26°C sg: 1.022 4 cm 50L

*Ecsenius stictus* 395
8 ♀ ~ ✈ ◐ ♥ ▣ ▭ 26°C sg: 1.022 5 cm 50L

*Ecsenius stictus* 395
8 ♀ ~ ✈ ◐ ♥ ▣ ▭ 26°C sg: 1.022 5 cm 50L

*Ecsenius axelrodi* 395
7 26°C sg: 1.022 5 cm 50L

*Ecsenius axelrodi* 395
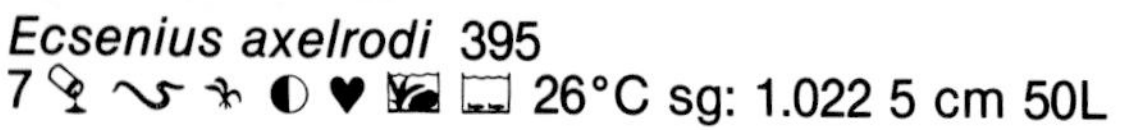
7 26°C sg: 1.022 5 cm 50L

*Ecsenius axelrodi* 395
7 26°C sg: 1.022 5 cm 50L

*Ecsenius tigris* 395
8 🍸 ~ ✢ ◐ ♥ ▨ ▭ 26°C sg: 1.022 4 cm 50L

*Ecsenius dilemma* 395
7 🍸 ~ ✢ ◐ ♥ ▨ ▭ 26°C sg: 1.022 4 cm 50L

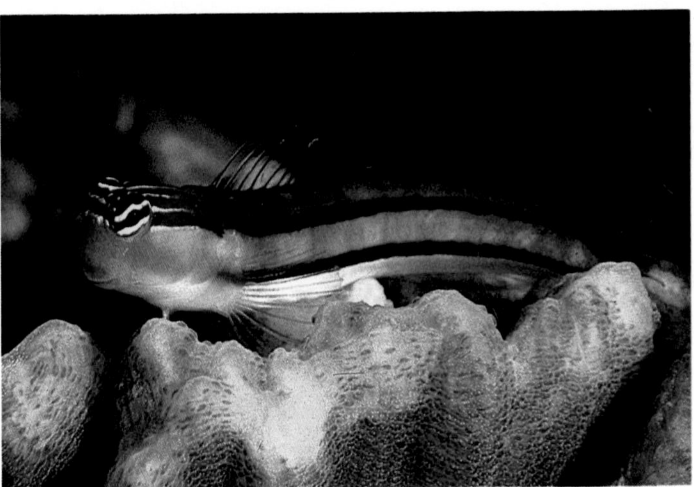

*Ecsenius dilemma* 395
7 🍸 ~ ✢ ◐ ♥ ▨ ▭ 26°C sg: 1.022 4 cm 50L

*Ecsenius dilemma* 395
7 🍸 ~ ✢ ◐ ♥ ▨ ▭ 26°C sg: 1.022 4 cm 50L

*Ecsenius bathi* 395
7 🍸 ~ ✢ ◐ ♥ ▨ ▭ 26°C sg: 1.022 4 cm 50L

*Ecsenius bathi* 395
7 🍸 ~ ✢ ◐ ♥ ▨ ▭ 26°C sg: 1.022 4 cm 50L

*Ecsenius alleni* 395
7 ⚲ ∿ ✢ ◐ ♥ ▨ ▭ 26°C sg: 1.022 4 cm 50L

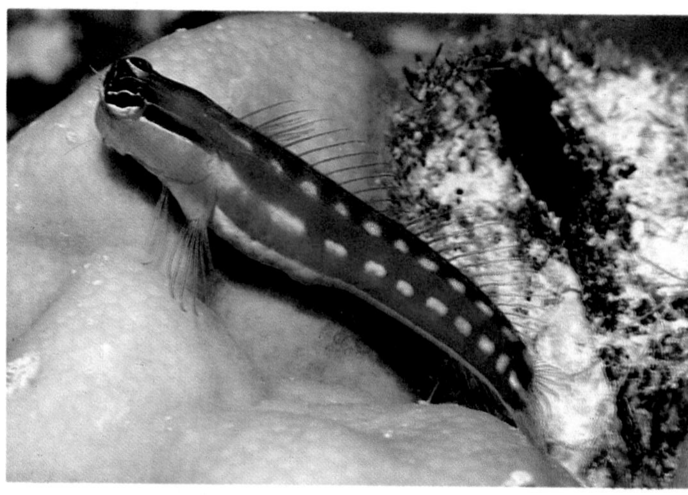

*Ecsenius australianus* 395
8 ⚲ ∿ ✢ ◐ ♥ ▨ ▭ 26°C sg: 1.022 4 cm 50L

*Ecsenius fijiensis* 395
6 ⚲ ∿ ✢ ◐ ♥ ▨ ▭ 26°C sg: 1.022 4 cm 50L

*Ecsenius fourmanoiri* 395
6, 8 ⚲ ∿ ✢ ◐ ♥ ▨ ▭ 26°C sg: 1.022 5 cm 50L

*Ecsenius opsifrontalis* 395
6 ⚲ ∿ ✢ ◐ ♥ ▨ ▭ 26°C sg: 1.022 4 cm 50L

*Ecsenius opsifrontalis* 395
6 ⚲ ∿ ✢ ◐ ♥ ▨ ▭ 26°C sg: 1.022 4 cm 50L

*Ecsenius isos*
6, 8 ◐ ♥ 26°C sg: 1.022 4 cm 50L

*Ecsenius trilineatus* 395
7 ◐ ♥ 26°C sg: 1.022 4 cm 50L

*Ecsenius pictus* 395
7 ◐ ♥ 26°C sg: 1.022 5 cm 50L

*Ecsenius pictus* 395
7 ◐ ♥ 26°C sg: 1.022 5 cm 50L

*Ecsenius bandanus* 395
7 ◐ ♥ 26°C sg: 1.022 4 cm 50L

*Ecsenius bimaculatus* 395
7 ◐ ♥ 26°C sg: 1.022 3 cm 50L

*Ecsenius collettei* 395
7 26°C sg: 1.022 4 cm 50L

*Ecsenius prooculus* 395
7 26°C sg: 1.022 4 cm 50L

*Ecsenius aequalis* 395
8 26°C sg: 1.022 4 cm 50L

*Ecsenius aequalis* 395
8 26°C sg: 1.022 4 cm 50L

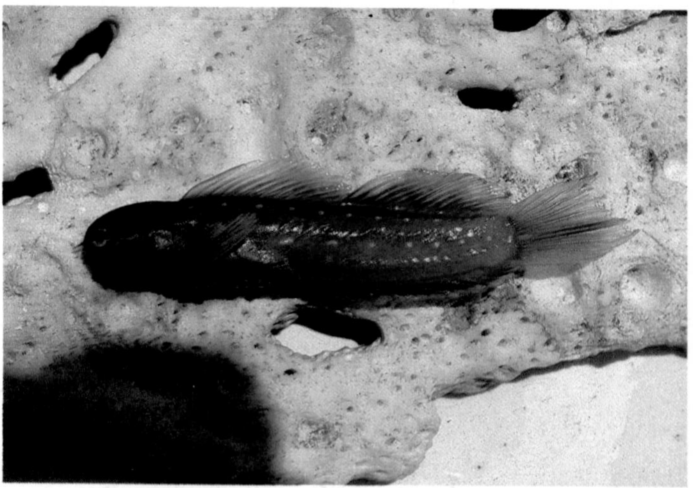

*Ecsenius mandibularis* 395
8 26°C sg: 1.022 5 cm 50L

*Ecsenius schroederi* 395
7 26°C sg: 1.022 4 cm 50L

*Entomacrodus striatus* 395
6-7, 9 ◐ ♥ 26°C sg: 1.022 9 cm 100L

*Entomacrodus decussatus* 395
6-7 ◐ ♥ 26°C sg: 1.022 17 cm 200L

*Scartella cristata* 395
2, 13 ◐ ♥ 26°C sg: 1.022 11 cm 100L

*Entomacrodus nigricans* 395
2 ◐ ♥ 26°C sg: 1.022 8 cm 100L

*Parablennius marmoreus* 395
2 ◐ ♥ 26°C sg: 1.022 8 cm 100L

*Parablennius tasmanianus* 395
12-13 ◐ ♥ 23°C sg: 1.024 13 cm 150L

*Parablennius marmoreus* 395
2 ◐ ♥ 26°C sg: 1.022 8 cm 100L

*Parablenneus marmoreus* 395
2 ◐ ♥ 26°C sg: 1.022 8 cm 100L

*Hypsoblennius brevipinnis* 395
3 ◐ ♥ 26°C sg: 1.022 12 cm 150L

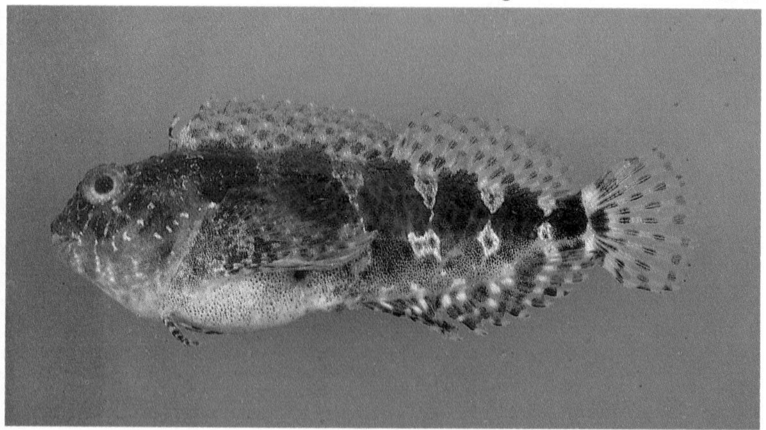

*Hypleurochilus bermudensis* 395
1-2 ◐ ♥ 24°C sg: 1.023 10 cm 100L

*Scartella cristata* 395
2, 13 ◐ ♥ 26°C sg: 1.022 11 cm 100L

*Stanulus talboti* 395
7-8 ◐ ♥ 26°C sg: 1.022 4 cm 50L

*Hypsoblennius gentilis* 395
3 ◐ ♥ 26°C sg: 1.022 15 cm 200L

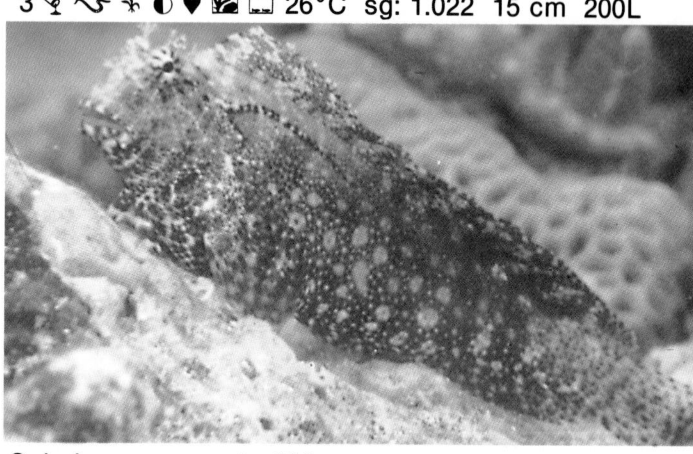

*Salarias ceramensis* 395
7 ◐ ♥ 26°C sg: 1.022 6 cm 60L

*Parablennius gattorugine* 395
13-15 ◐ ♥ 23°C sg: 1.024 30 cm 300L

*Stanulus seychellensis* 395
9 ◐ ♥ 26°C sg: 1.022 3.5 cm 40L

*Istiblennius edentulus* 395
6-9 ◐ ♥ 26°C sg: 1.022 18 cm 200L

*Istiblennius gibbifrons* 395
6-7, 9 ◐ ♥ 26°C sg: 1.022 13 cm 150L

*Istiblennius meleagris* 395
7 ◐ ♥ 26°C sg: 1.022 9 cm 100L

*Istiblennius chrysospilos* 395
6-8 ◐ ♥ 26°C sg: 1.022 10 cm 100L

*Istiblennius striatus* 395 ♂
7 ◐ ♥ 26°C sg: 1.022 9 cm 100L

*Istiblennius lineatus* 395 ♀
7 ◐ ♥ 26°C sg: 1.022 8 cm 100L

*Istiblennius zebra* 395 ♂
6 ◐ ♥ 26°C sg: 1.022 10 cm 100L

*Istiblennius chrysospilos* 395
6-8 ◐ ♥ 26°C sg: 1.022 10 cm 100L

*Aspidontus dussumieri* 395
6-10 26°C sg: 1.022 13 cm 150L

*Cirripectes variolosus* 395
6-7, 9 26°C sg: 1.022 8 cm 100L

*Plagiotremus tapeinosoma* 395
6-9 26°C sg: 1.022 16 cm 200L

*Ecsenius bicolor* 395
6-9 26°C sg: 1.022 8 cm 100L

*Aspidontus dussumieri* 395
6-10 26°C sg: 1.022 13 cm 150L

*Pereulixia kosiensis* 395
9 26°C sg: 1.022 24 cm 300L

*Meiacanthus mossambicus* 395
9 26°C sg: 1.022 9 cm 100L

*Ecsenius bicolor* 395
6-9 26°C sg: 1.022 8 cm 100L

*Ecsenius midas* 395
9-10 ◐ ♥ 26°C sg: 1.022 13 cm 150L

*Ecsenius midas* 395
9-10 ◐ ♥ 26°C sg: 1.022 13 cm 150L

*Ecsenius oculus* 395
6-7 ◐ ♥ 26°C sg: 1.022 7 cm 80L

*Ecsenius oculus* 395
6-7 ◐ ♥ 26°C sg: 1.022 7 cm 80L

*Ecsenius lineatus* 395
7 ◐ ♥ 26°C sg: 1.022 8 cm 100L

*Ecsenius lineatus* 395
7 ◐ ♥ 26°C sg: 1.022 8 cm 100L

*Ecsenius nalolo* 395
9-10 ◐ ♥ 26°C sg: 1.022 7 cm 80L

*Ecsenius gravieri* 395
9-10 ◐ ♥ 26°C sg: 1.022 8 cm 100L

*Istiblennius edentulus* 395
6-9 ◐ ♥ 26°C sg: 1.022 18 cm 200L

*Istiblennius periophthalmus* 395
6-9 ◐ ♥ 26°C sg: 1.022 16 cm 200L

*Istiblennius dussumieri* 395
6-9 ◐ ♥ 26°C sg: 1.022 14 cm 150L

*Istiblennius dussumieri* 395
6-9 ◐ ♥ 26°C sg: 1.022 14 cm 150L

*Omobranchus elongatus* 395
6-9 ◐ ♥ 26°C sg: 1.022 8 cm 100L

*Petroscirtes mitratus* 395
6-10 ◐ ♥ 26°C sg: 1.022 9 cm 100L

*Exallias brevis* 395
6-10 ◐ ♥ 26°C sg: 1.022 15 cm 200L

*Congrogadus subducens* 376
7 ◐ 26°C sg: 1.022 50 cm 500L

*#453*

*Synchiropus picturatus* 399
7 ∿ ◐ ♥ 26°C sg: 1.022 7 cm 80L

*Pterosynchiropus splendidus* 399
7 ∿ ◐ ♥ 26°C sg: 1.022 6 cm 80L

*Dactylopus dactylopus* 399
12 23°C sg: 1.024 18 cm 200L

*Dactylopus dactylopus* 399
12 23°C sg: 1.024 18 cm 200L

*Synchiropus papilio* 399
7-10 24°C sg: 1.023 12 cm 100L

*Repomucenus beniteguri* 399
7 26°C sg: 1.022 16 cm 200L

*Neosynchiropus* sp. 399
7-8 26°C sg: 1.022 10 cm 100L

*Diplogrammus xenicus* 399
7 26°C sg: 1.022 7 cm 80L

*Neosynchiropus ocellatus* 399
7, 9 26°C sg: 1.022 9 cm 100L

*Neosynchiropus ijimai* 399
5, 7 23°C sg: 1.023 7 cm 75L

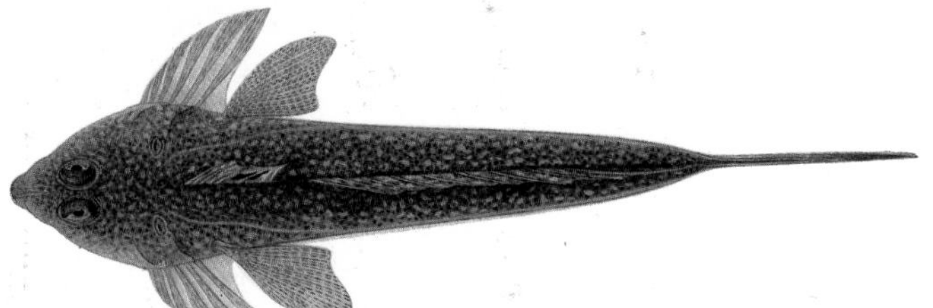

*Repomucenus richardsoni* 399 ♀
5, 7 ◐ ♥ 26°C sg: 1.022 20 cm 200L

*Repomucenus richardsoni* 399 ♂
5, 7 ◐ ♥ 26°C sg: 1.022 20 cm 200L

*Calliurichthys japonicus* 399
5, 7, 9 ◐ ♥ 26°C sg: 1.022 30 cm 300L

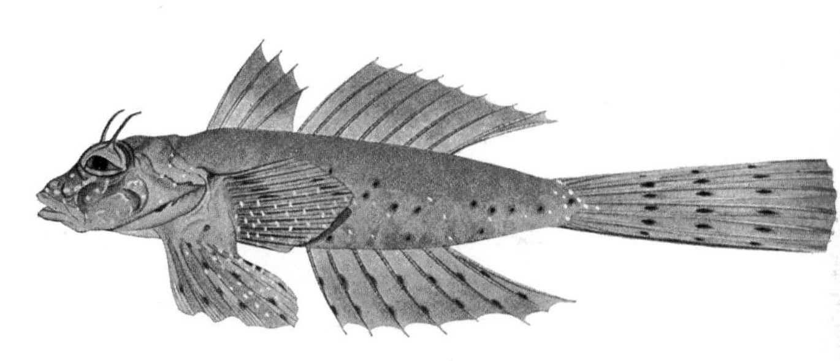

*Anaora tentaculata* 399
5, 7 ◐ ♥ 26°C sg: 1.022 4 cm 50L

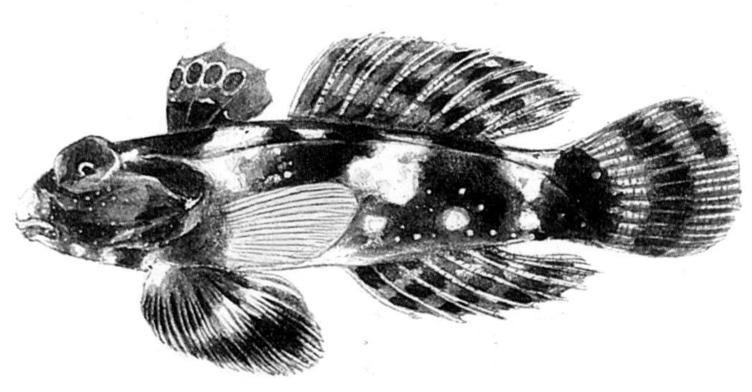

*Neosynchiropus ocellatus* 399
7, 9 ◐ ♥ 26°C sg: 1.022 9 cm 100L

*Foetorepus* sp. 399
5, 7 ◐ ♥ 25°C sg: 1.022 15 cm 200L

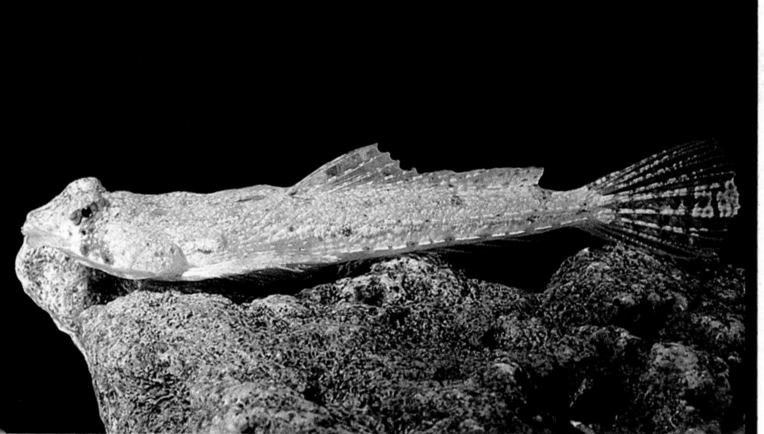

*Callionymus calcaratus* 399
12 ◐ ♥ 24°C sg: 1.023 7 cm 80L

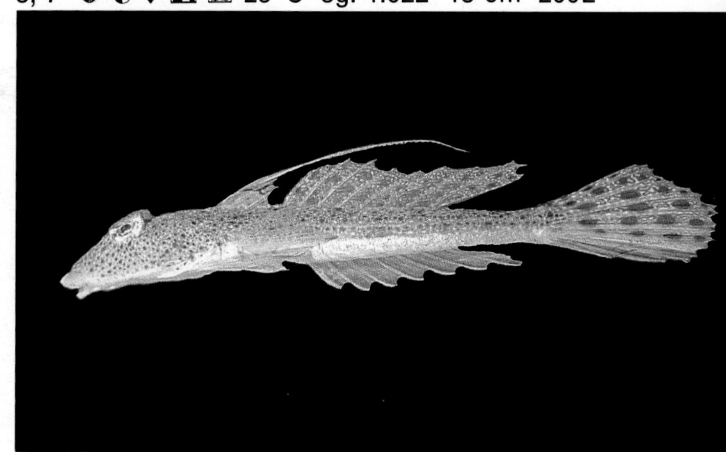

*Callionymus goodladi* 399
7, 12 ◐ ♥ 25°C sg: 1.022 14 cm 150L

*Synchiropus* sp. 399
7-9 ∿ ◐ ♥ ▣ ☐ 25°C sg: 1.022 7 cm 75L

*Synchiropus* sp. 399
7-9 ∿ ◐ ♥ ▣ ☐ 25°C sg: 1.022 7 cm 75L

*Paradiplogrammus bairdi* 399
2 ∿ ◐ ♥ ▣ ☐ 26°C sg: 1.022 11.4 cm 100L

*Paradiplogrammus bairdi* 399
2 ∿ ◐ ♥ ▣ ☐ 26°C sg: 1.022 11.4 cm 100L

*Synchiropus marmoratus* 399
9 ∿ ◐ ♥ ▣ ☐ 26°C sg: 1.022 13 cm 150L

*Synchiropus* sp. 399
7-8 ∿ ◐ ♥ ▣ ☐ 25°C sg: 1.022 8 cm 80L

*Diplogrammus pauciradiatus* 399
2 ∿ ◐ ♥ ▣ ☐ 25°C sg: 1.022 5 cm 50L

*Paradiplogrammus bairdi* 399
2 ∿ ◐ ♥ ▣ ☐ 26°C sg: 1.022 11.4 cm 100L

*Trichonotus setigerus* 384
7-9 ∿ ◐ ♥ ▣ ▭ 26°C sg: 1.022 25 cm 300L

*Dactyloptena orientalis* 260
7-9 ∿ ◐ ♥ ▣ ▭ 26°C sg: 1.022 35 cm 400L

*Synchiropus* sp. 399
7, 8 ∿ ◐ ♥ ▣ ▭ 26°C sg: 1.022 8 cm 100L

*Synchiropus* sp. 399
7, 8 ∿ ◐ ♥ ▣ ▭ 26°C sg: 1.022 9 cm 100L

*Trichonotus setigerus* 384
7-9 ∿ ◐ ♥ ▣ ▭ 26°C sg: 1.022 25 cm 300L

*Pterosynchiropus splendidus* 399
7 ∿ ○ ♥ ▣ ▭ 26°C sg: 1.022 6 cm 80L

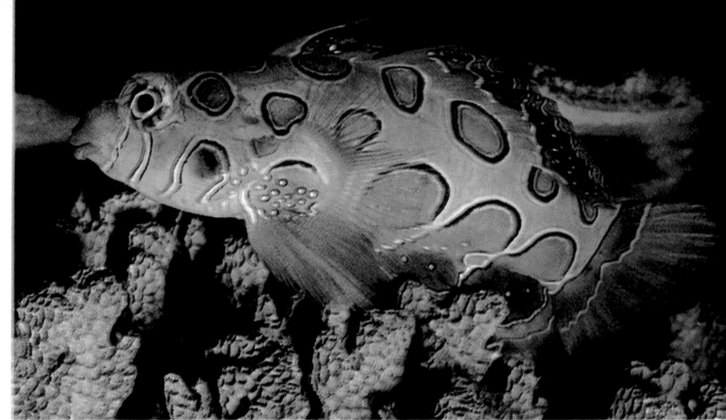

*Synchiropus picturatus* 399
7 ∿ ○ ♥ ▣ ▭ 26°C sg: 1.022 7 cm 80L

*Synchiropus* sp. 399
7, 8 ∿ ◐ ♥ ▣ ▭ 26°C sg: 1.022 8 cm 100L

*Cryptocentrus leptocephalus* 403
7-9 ~ ◐ ♥ 26°C sg: 1.022 10 cm 100L

*Signigobius biocellatus* 403
6 ~ ◐ ♥ 26°C sg: 1.022 5 cm 50L

#457A

*Nemateleotris magnifica* 403
6-9 ↝ ◐ ♥ 26°C sg: 1.022 9 cm 100L

*Cryptocentrus cinctus* 403
7, 9 ↝ ◐ ♥ 26°C sg: 1.022 8 cm 80L

*Oxymetopon* sp. 402
7 26°C sg: 1.022 20 cm 200L

*Oxymetopon cyanoctenosum* 402
7 26°C sg: 1.022 20 cm 200L

*Ophiocara porocephala* (juv.) 402
7, 9 26°C sg: 1.020 34 cm 400L

*Bostrychus sinensis* (adult) 402
7 26°C sg: 1.022 10 cm 100L

*Eleotris* cf *acanthopoma* 402
7 26°C sg: 1.022 18 cm 200L

*Butis amboinensis* 402
7 26°C sg: 1.017 8 cm 100L

*Ophiocara porocephala* 402
6-9 26°C sg: 1.018 16 cm 200L

*Bathygobius laddi* 403
7, 9 26°C sg: 1.022 5 cm 50L

*Amblyeleotris aurora* 403
9 26°C sg: 1.022 9 cm 100L

*Amblyeleotris fontanesii* 403
7 26°C sg: 1.022 15 cm 200L

*Amblyeleotris steinitzi* 403
7-10 26°C sg: 1.022 8 cm 80L

*Amblyeleotris* sp. 403
9 26°C sg: 1.022 6 cm 60L

*Amblyeleotris fasciatus* 403
9 26°C sg: 1.022 6 cm 60L

*Amblyeleotris periophthalmus* 403
12 24°C sg: 1.023 5 cm 50L

*Amblyeleotris sungami* 403
7-10 26°C sg: 1.022 10 cm 100L

*Amblyeleotris diagonalis* 403
7-9 26°C sg: 1.022 6 cm 60L

Goby sp. 5 403
13 ◐ ♥ 26°C sg: 1.022 2.5 cm

Goby sp. 1 403
13 ◐ ♥ 26°C sg: 1.022 2.5 cm

*Gnatholepis* sp. 403
13 ◐ ♥ 26°C sg: 1.022 3 cm

Goby sp. 2 403
13 ◐ ♥ 26°C sg: 1.022 2.5 cm

*Amblyeleotris* sp. 403
6-8 ◐ ♥ 26°C sg: 1.022 10 cm

*Amblyeleotris* sp. 403
6-8 ◐ ♥ 26°C sg: 1.022 10 cm

*Amblyeleotris callopareia* 403
7 ◐ ♥ 26°C sg: 1.022 8 cm

*Amblyeleotris latifasciata* 403
7-8 ◐ ♥ 26°C sg: 1.022 7 cm

*Amblyeleotris randalli* 403
7 ~ ◐ ♥ 26°C sg: 1.022 3 cm 40L

*Amblyeleotris* sp. aff *periophthalmus* 403
12 ~ ◐ ♥ 24°C sg: 1.023 5 cm 50L

*Amblyeleotris wheeleri* 403
7-9 ~ ◐ ♥ 26°C sg: 1.022 9 cm 100L

*Amblyeleotris wheeleri* 403
7-9 ~ ◐ ♥ 26°C sg: 1.022 9 cm 100L

*Amblyeleotris* sp. 403
8 ~ ◐ ♥ 26°C sg: 1.022 4 cm 40L

*Amblyeleotris guttata* 403
7 ~ ◐ ♥ 26°C sg: 1.022 7 cm 80L

*Amblyeleotris gymnocephala* 403
7, 9 ~ ◐ ♥ 26°C sg: 1.022 14 cm 150L

*Amblyeleotris gymnocephala* 403
7, 9 ~ ◐ ♥ 26°C sg: 1.022 14 cm 150L

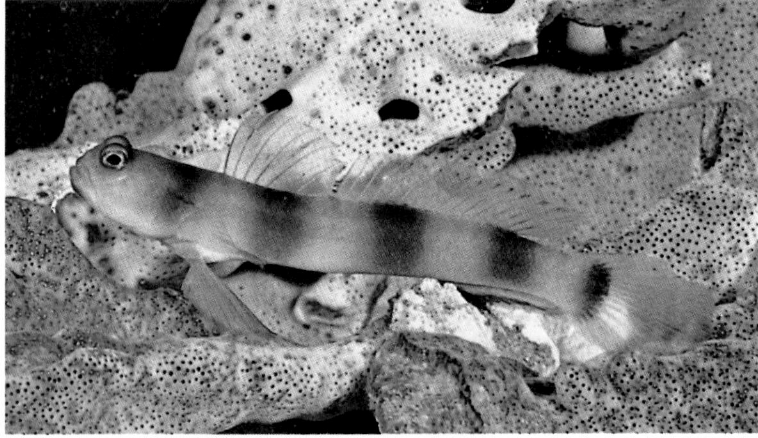

*Ambyeleotris* sp. 403
? 26°C sg: 1.022 13 cm 150L

*Amblyeleotris steinitzi* 403
7-10 26°C sg: 1.022 8 cm 100L

*Ambyeleotris sungami* 403
7-10 26°C sg: 1.022 10 cm 100L

*Amblyeleotris steinitzi* 403
7-10 26°C sg: 1.022 8 cm 100L

*Valenciennea puellaris* 403
7, 9 26°C sg: 1.022 14 cm 150L

*Ctenogobiops aurocingulus* 403
6-8 26°C sg: 1.022 4 cm 50L

*Sagamia geneionema* 403
5, 7 26°C sg: 1.022 9 cm 100L

*Amblygobius* sp. 403
7-8 26°C sg: 1.022 10 cm 100L

*Cryptocentrus cyanotaenia* 403
7 ◐ ♥ 26°C sg: 1.022 11.5 cm 100L

*Cryptocentrus cinctus* 403
7-8 ◐ ♥ 26°C sg: 1.022 8 cm 100L

*Redigobius balteata* 403
7 ◐ ♥ 26°C sg: 1.022 4.5 cm 50L

*Cryptocentrus aurora* 403
9 ◐ ♥ 26°C sg: 1.022 9 cm 100L

*Ctenogobiops aurocingulus* 403
6-8 ◐ ♥ 26°C sg: 1.022 4 cm 50L

*Ctenogobiops aurocingulus* 403
6-8 ◐ ♥ 26°C sg: 1.022 4 cm 50L

*Ctenogobiops pomastictus* 403
7-8 ◐ ♥ 26°C sg: 1.022 4.5 cm 50L

*Ctenogobiops pomastictus* 403
7-8 ◐ ♥ 26°C sg: 1.022 4.5 cm 50L

*Ctenogobiops tangaroai* 403
6 ∿ ◐ ♥ 26°C sg: 1.022 4 cm 50L

*Ctenogobiops pomastictus* 403
7-8 ∿ ◐ ♥ 26°C sg: 1.022 4.5 cm 50L

*Cryptocentrus ambanora* 403
8 ∿ ◐ ♥ 26°C sg: 1.022 5 cm 50L

*Gobius casamancus* 403
13 ∿ ◐ ♥ 26°C sg: 1.022 11.2 cm 100L

*Amblyeleotris* sp. cf *japonica* 403
8 ∿ ◐ ♥ 26°C sg: 1.022 6 cm 80L

*Amblyeleotris* sp. cf japonicus 403
7-8 ∿ ◐ ♥ 26°C sg: 1.022 10 cm 100L

Goby sp. #3 403
13 ∿ ◐ ♥ 26°C sg: 1.022 3 cm 50L

*Tomiyamichthys oni* 403
6-8 ∿ ◐ ♥ 26°C sg: 1.022 10 cm 100L

*Cryptocentrus caeruleomaculatus* 403
7-8 ∽ ◐ ♥ ⊡ ⊡ 26°C sg: 1.022 8 cm 100L

*Cryptocentrus cryptocentrus* 403
7, 9-10 ∽ ◐ ♥ ⊡ ⊡ 26°C sg: 1.022 13 cm 100L

*Cryptocentrus lutheri* 403
10 ∽ ◐ ♥ ⊡ ⊡ 26°C sg: 1.022 11 cm 100L

*Ctenogobiops crocineus* 403
9 ∽ ◐ ♥ ⊡ ⊡ 26°C sg: 1.022 6 cm 80L

*Cryptocentrus cinctus* 403
7, 9 ∽ ◐ ♥ ⊡ ⊡ 26°C sg: 1.022 8 cm 80L

*Cryptocentrus fasciatus* 403
7 ∽ ◐ ♥ ⊡ ⊡ 26°C sg: 1.022 8 cm 100L

*Cryptocentrus strigilliceps* 403
7, 9 ∽ ◐ ♥ ⊡ ⊡ 26°C sg: 1.022 5 cm 50L

*Ctenogobiops feroculus* 403
8-10 ∽ ◐ ♥ ⊡ ⊡ 26°C sg: 1.022 6 cm 80L

*Fusigobius* sp. 403
7 ~ ◐ ♥ 26°C sg: 1.022 5 cm 50L

*Fusigobius* sp. *(neophytus?)* 403
5(?) ~ ◐ ♥ 26°C sg: 1.022 3(?) cm 50L

*?Eviota* sp. 403
8 ~ ◐ ♥ 26°C sg: 1.022 3 cm 50L

*?Eviota* sp. 403
8 ~ ◐ ♥ 26°C sg: 1.022 3 cm 50L

*Oplopomus oplopomus* 403
6-10 ~ ◐ ♥ 26°C sg: 1.022 8 cm 100L

*Yongeichthys criniger?* 403
6-10 ~ ◐ ♥ 26°C sg: 1.022 13 cm 150L

*Nes longus* 403
2 ~ ◐ ♥ 26°C sg: 1.022 100L

*Nes l ongus* 403
2 ~ ◐ ♥ 26°C sg: 1.022 10 cm 100L

*Amblygobius rainfordi* 403
7 ∿ ◐ ♥ ▣ ▭ 26°C sg: 1.022 10 cm 100L

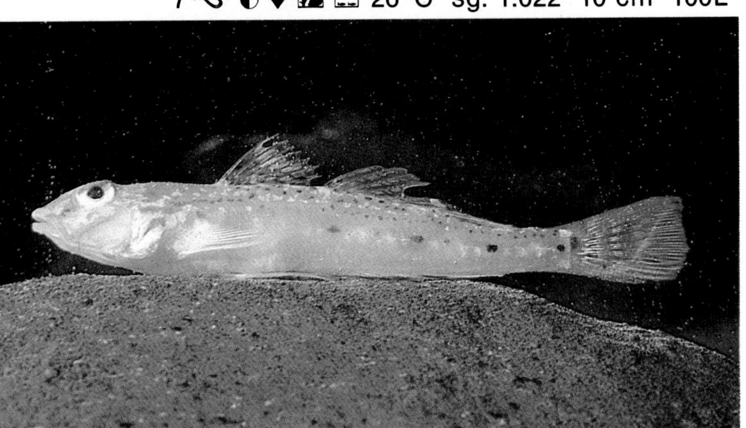

*Nesogobius* sp. 403
7 ∿ ◐ ♥ ▣ ▭ 26°C sg: 1.022 6 cm 80L

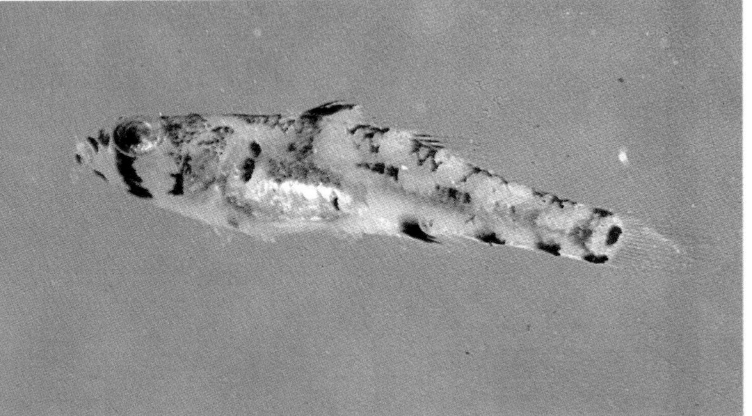

*Pandaka lidwilli* 403
7 ∿ ◐ ♥ ▣ ▭ 26°C sg: 1.022 4 cm 50L

*Kellogella cardinalis* 403
6 ∿ ◐ ♥ ▣ ▭ 26°C sg: 1.022 3 cm 50L

*Signigobius biocellatus* 403
6 ∿ ◐ ♥ ▣ ▭ 26°C sg: 1.022 5 cm 50L

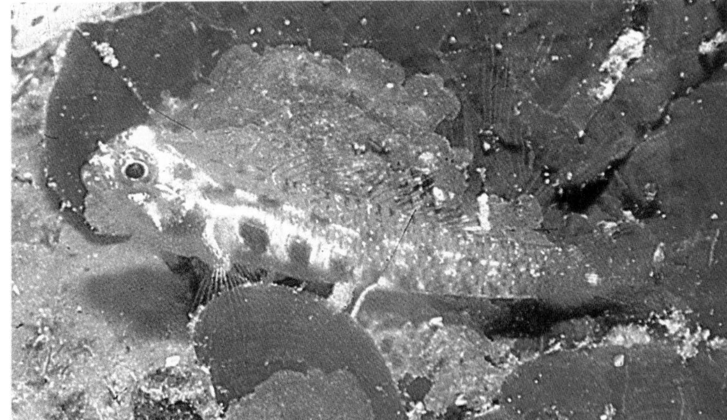

*Eviota* sp. 403
8 ∿ ◐ ♥ ▣ ▭ 26°C sg: 1.022 3.5 cm 50L

*Silhouettea insinuans* 403
7 ∿ ◐ ♥ ▣ ▭ 26°C sg: 1.022 4 cm 50L

*Acentrogobius gracilis* 403
7 ∿ ◐ ♥ ▣ ▭ 26°C sg: 1.018 6 cm 80L

*Rhinogobius brunneus* 403
5 ∿ ◐ ♥ 26°C sg: 1.018 10 cm 100L

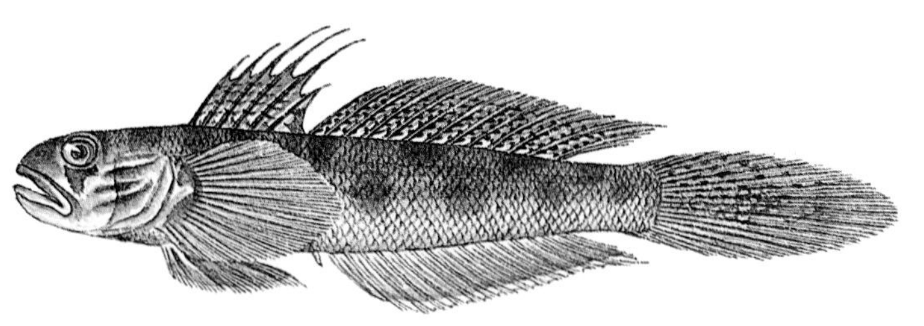

*Oxyurichthys microlepis* 403
7, 9 ∿ ◐ ♥ 26°C sg: 1.022 13.5 cm 150L

*Acanthogobius flavimanus* 403
5 ∿ ◐ ♥ 26°C sg: 1.022 10 cm 100L

*Myersina nigrivirgata* 403
8 ∿ ◐ ♥ 26°C sg: 1.022 8 cm 80L

*Yongeichthys criniger* 403
7-10 ∿ ◐ ♥ 26°C sg: 1.022 15 cm 200L

*Oxyurichthys papuensis* 403
6 ∿ ◐ ♥ 26°C sg: 1.022 17 cm 200L

*Stiphodon* sp. 403
7 ∿ ◐ ♥ 26°C sg: 1.022 4.5 cm 50L

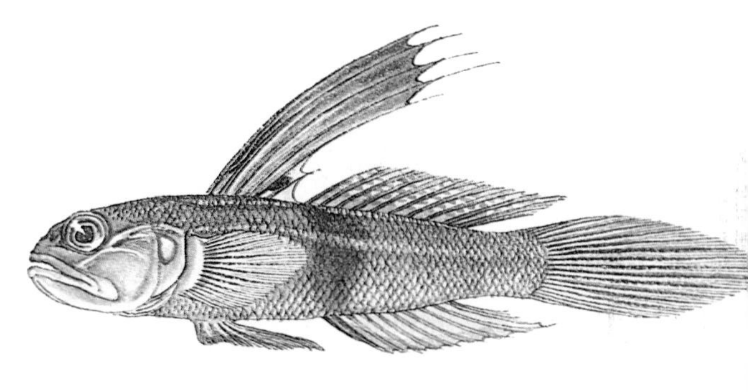

*Myersina macrostoma* 403
7 ∿ ◐ ♥ 26°C sg: 1.022 6 cm 80L

*Tridentiger trigonocephalus* 403
5 ∿ ◐ ♥ ▣ ⌴ 26°C sg: 1.022 4 cm 50L

*Asterropteryx* sp. 403
7, 9 ∿ ◐ ♥ ▣ ⌴ 26°C sg: 1.022 7 cm 80L

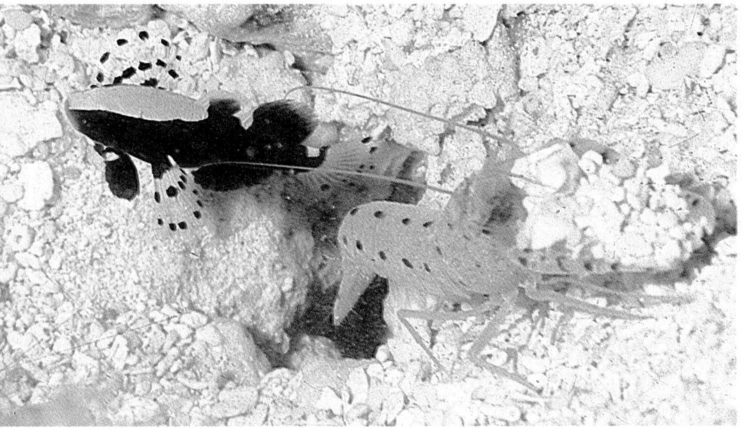

*Lotilia graciliosa* 403
7-10 ∿ ◐ ♥ ▣ ⌴ 26°C sg: 1.022 4 cm 50L

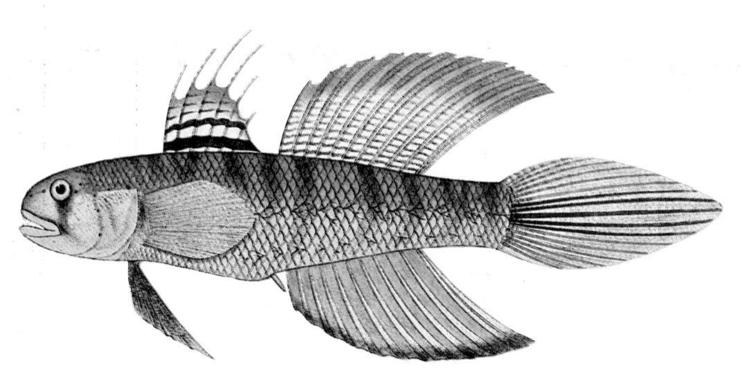

*Stenogobius lachrymosus* 403
6-9 ∿ ◐ ♥ ▣ ⌴ 26°C sg: 1.022 12 cm 150L

*Stonogobiops xanthorhinica* 403
7-8 ∿ ◐ ♥ ▣ ⌴ 26°C sg: 1.022 10 cm 100L

*Mahidolia mystacina* 403
7-9 ∿ ◐ ♥ ▣ ⌴ 26°C sg: 1.022 8 cm 100L

*Gobulus myersi* 403
2 ∿ ◐ ♥ ▣ ⌴ 26°C sg: 1.022 3 cm 50L

*Yongeichthys criniger* 403
7-10 ∿ ◐ ♥ ▣ ⌴ 26°C sg: 1.022 15 cm 200L

*Amblygobius phalaena* 403
7 ◐ ♥ 26°C sg: 1.022 10 cm 100L

*Amblygobius phalaena* 403
7 ◐ ♥ 26°C sg: 1.022 10 cm 100L

*Amblygobius albimacula* 403
7-10 ◐ ♥ 26°C sg: 1.022 18 cm 200L

*Amblygobius phalaena* 403
7 ◐ ♥ 26°C sg: 1.022 10 cm 100L

*Amblygobius phalaena* 403
7 ◐ ♥ 26°C sg: 1.022 10 cm 100L

*Amblygobius sphynx* 403
7, 9 ◐ ♥ 26°C sg: 1.022 18 cm 200L

*Amblygobius bynoensis* 403
6-7 ◐ ♥ 26°C sg: 1.022 10 cm 100L

*Amblygobius bynoensis* 403
6-7 ◐ ♥ 26°C sg: 1.022 10 cm 100L

*Amblygobius decussatus* 403
7 ◐ ♥ 26°C sg: 1.022 7.5 cm 80L

*Amblygobius hectori* 403
10 ◐ ♥ 26°C sg: 1.022 5 cm 50L

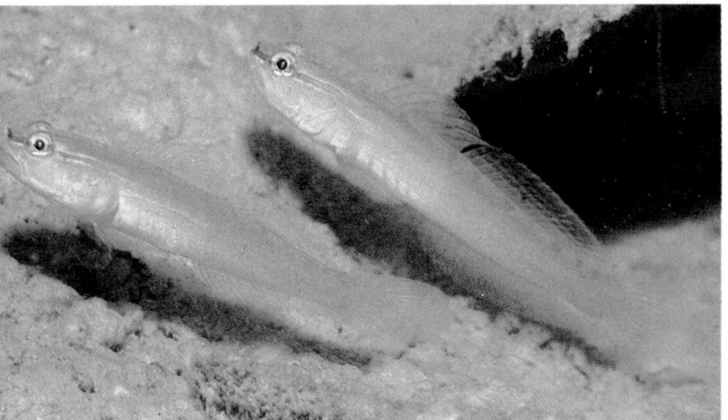

*Amblygobius nocturnus* 403
9 ◐ ♥ 26°C sg: 1.022 10 cm 100L

*Amblygobius phalaena* 403
7 ◐ ♥ 26°C sg: 1.022 10 cm 100L

*Amblygobius seminctus* 403
9 ◐ ♥ 26°C sg: 1.022 10 cm 100L

*Amblygobius sphynx* 403
7, 9 ◐ ♥ 26°C sg: 1.022 18 cm 200L

*Asterropteryx semipunctatus* 403
6-9 ◐ ♥ 26°C sg: 1.022 6 cm 60L

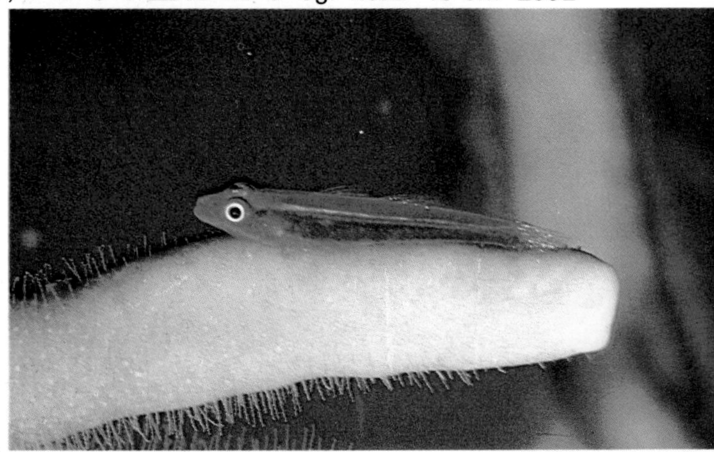

*Bryaninops* sp. 403
8 ◐ ♥ 26°C sg: 1.022 3 cm 50L

*Cryptocentrus* sp. 403
7-8 ◐ ♥ 26°C sg: 1.022 8 cm 80L

*Amblyeleotris steinitzi* 403
7-10 ◐ ♥ 26°C sg: 1.022 8 cm 100L

*Cryptocentrus leptocephalus* 403
7-9 ◐ ♥ 26°C sg: 1.022 10 cm 100L

*Cryptocentrus leptocephalus* 403
7-9 ◐ ♥ 26°C sg: 1.022 10 cm 100L

*Cryptocentrus fasciatus* 403
7 ◐ ♥ 26°C sg: 1.022 8 cm 80L

*Cryptocentrus fasciatus* 403
7 ◐ ♥ 26°C sg: 1.022 8 cm 80L

*Cryptocentrus niveatus* 403
7 ◐ ♥ 26°C sg: 1.022 11 cm 100L

*Cryptocentrus niveatus* 403
7 ◐ ♥ 26°C sg: 1.022 11 cm 100L

*Cryptocentrus* sp. 403
7 ∿ ◐ ♥ ▭ ▭ 26°C sg: 1.022 7 cm 80L

*Cryptocentrus caeruleomaculatus* 403
7-8 ∿ ◐ ♥ ▭ ▭ 26°C sg: 1.022 8 cm 100L

*Cryptocentrus leptocephalus* 403
7-9 ∿ ◐ ♥ ▭ ▭ 26°C sg: 1.022 10 cm 100L

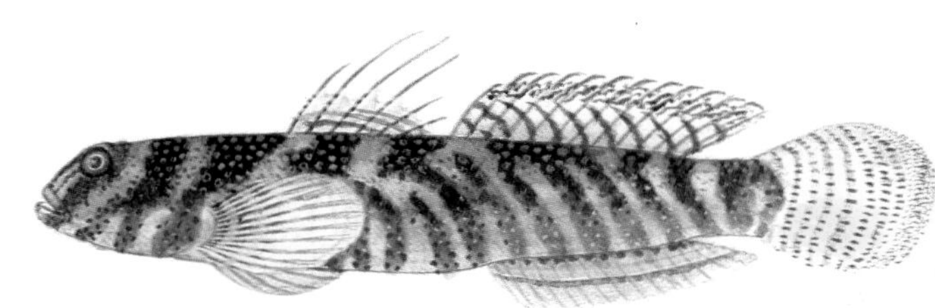

*Cryptocentroides insignis* 403
7 ∿ ◐ ♥ ▭ ▭ 26°C sg: 1.022 9 cm 100L

*Cryptocentrus cinctus* 403
7-8 ∿ ◐ ♥ ▭ ▭ 26°C sg: 1.022 8 cm 100L

*Cryptocentrus albidorsus* 403
7 ∿ ◐ ♥ ▭ ▭ 26°C sg: 1.022 6 cm 60L

*Cryptocentrus* sp. 403
8 ∿ ◐ ♥ ▭ ▭ 26°C sg: 1.022 8 cm 100L

? Unidentified Goby 403
8 ∿ ◐ ♥ ▭ ▭ 26°C sg: 1.022 11 cm 100L

*Gnatholepis thompsoni* 403
2 ∽ ◐ ♥ 26°C sg: 1.022 7.5 cm 80L

*Gnatholepis deltoides* 403
7 ∽ ◐ ♥ 26°C sg: 1.022 8 cm 100L

*Gnatholepis* sp. 1 403
7, 9 ∽ ◐ ♥ 26°C sg: 1.022 11 cm 100L

*Gnatholepis inconsequens* 403
7 ∽ ◐ ♥ 26°C sg: 1.022 6 cm 80L

*Favonigobius lateralis* 403
7 ∽ ◐ ♥ 26°C sg: 1.022 6 cm 60L

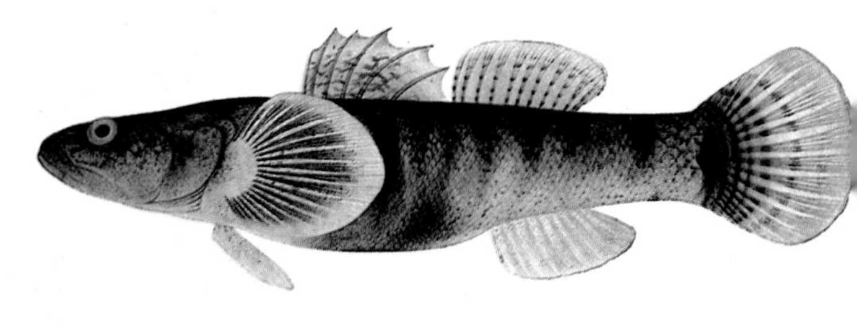

*Chaenogobius urotaenia* 403
5, 7 ∽ ◐ ♥ 24°C sg: 1.023 11 cm 100L

*Caffrogobius caffer* 403
9 ∽ ◐ ♥ 26°C sg: 1.022 18 cm 200L

*Pomatoschistus microps* 403
14 ∽ ◐ ♥ 26°C sg: 1.022 7 cm 80L

*Gobius niger* 403
13-15 ~ ◐ ♥ ▣ ▭ 26°C sg: 1.024 15 cm 150L

*Gobius cruentatus* 403
13-15 ~ ◐ ♥ ▣ ▭ 26°C sg: 1.024 18 cm 200L

*Gobius vittatus* 403
15 ~ ◐ ♥ ▣ ▭ 26°C sg: 1.024 4 cm 50L

*Gobius auratus* 403
14-15 ~ ◐ ♥ ▣ ▭ 26°C sg: 1.024 12 cm 100L

*Caffrogobius caffer* 403
9 ~ ◐ ♥ ▣ ▭ 26°C sg: 1.022 18 cm 200L

*Gobius elanthematicus* 403
15 ~ ◐ ♥ ▣ ▭ 26°C sg: 1.024 12 cm 100L

*Gobius bucchichii* 403
15 ~ ◐ ♥ ▣ ▭ 26°C sg: 1.024 10 cm 100L

*Gobius niger* 403
13-15 ~ ◐ ♥ ▣ ▭ 26°C sg: 1.024 15 cm 150L

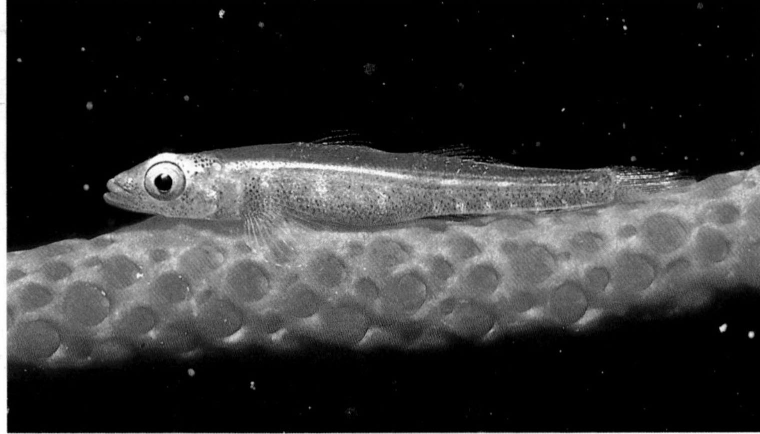

*Bryaninops amphis* 403
8 ∿ ◐ ♥ ▨ ▭ 26°C sg: 1.022 3 cm 50L

*Bryaninops* sp.403
8 ∿ ◐ ♥ ▨ ▭ 26°C sg: 1.022 3 cm 50L

*Bryaninops natans* 403
8 ∿ ◐ ♥ ▨ ▭ 26°C sg: 1.022 3 cm 50L

*Bryaninops tigris* 403
8 ∿ ◐ ♥ ▨ ▭ 26°C sg: 1.022 3 cm 50L

*Parioglossus formosus* 403
7 ∿ ◐ ♥ ▨ ▭ 26°C sg: 1.022 2.8 cm 50L

*Parioglossus lineatus* 403
7 ∿ ◐ ♥ ▨ ▭ 26°C sg: 1.022 3 cm 50L

*Favonigobius reichei* 403
7-9 ∿ ◐ ♥ ▨ ▭ 26°C sg: 1.022 7 cm 80L

*Eviota bifasciata* 403
7 ∿ ◐ ♥ ▨ ▭ 26°C sg: 1.022 3 cm 50L

*Ptereleotris* sp. 403
7 〰 ◐ ♥ ▨ ⊔ 26°C sg: 1.022 7 cm 80L

*Ptereleotris hanae* 403
7 〰 ◐ ♥ ▨ ⊔ 26°C sg: 1.022 8 cm 80L

*Ptereleotris microlepis* and *P. monoptera* 403
6-9 〰 ◐ ♥ ▨ ⊔ 26°C sg: 1.022 11 cm 100L

*Gobionellus saepepallens?* 403
2 〰 ◐ ♥ ▨ ⊔ 26°C sg: 1.022 5 cm 50L

*Nematelotris helfrichi* 403
6 〰 ◐ ♥ ▨ ⊟ 26°C sg: 1.022 5 cm 50L

*Ptereleotris monoptera* 403
7 〰 ◐ ♥ ▨ ⊟ 26°C sg: 1.022 11 cm 100L

*Ptereleotris zebra* 403
6-9 〰 ◐ ♥ ▨ ⊔ 26°C sg: 1.022 10 cm 100L

*Vomerogobius flavus* 403
2 〰 ◐ ♥ ▨ ⊔ 26°C sg: 1.022 4 cm 50L

*Vanderhorstia ornatissima* 403
7-9 ◐ ♥ 26°C sg: 1.022 7 cm 80L

*Vanderhorstia ornatissima* 403
7-9 ◐ ♥ 26°C sg: 1.022 7 cm 80L

*Callogobius snelliusi* 403
7 ◐ ♥ 26°C sg: 1.022 5 cm 50L

*Callogobius* sp. 403
7 ◐ ♥ 26°C sg: 1.022 6 cm 60L

*Callogobius mucosus* 403
7 ◐ ♥ 26°C sg: 1.022 6 cm 80L

*Callogobius hasselti* 403
7-8 ◐ ♥ 26°C sg: 1.022 8 cm 100L

*Arenigobius bifrenatus* 403
12 ◐ ♥ 24°C sg: 1.023 8 cm 100L

*Arenigobius bifrenatus* 403
12 ◐ ♥ 24°C sg: 1.023 8 cm 100L

*Istigobius ornatus* 403
6-9 ∿ ◐ ♥ ⌂ ⊔ 26°C sg: 1.022 8 cm 80L

*Istigobius ornatus* 403
6-9 ∿ ◐ ♥ ⌂ ⊔ 26°C sg: 1.022 8 cm 80L

*Istigobius nigroocellatus* 403
5, 7 ∿ ◐ ♥ ⌂ ⊔ 26°C sg: 1.022 8 cm 80L

*Istigobius decoratus* 403
7 ∿ ◐ ♥ ⌂ ⊔ 26°C sg: 1.022 10 cm 100L

*Istigobius goldmanni* 403
7-10 ∿ ◐ ♥ ⌂ ⊔ 26°C sg: 1.022 8 cm 80L

*Istigobius ornatus* 403
6-9 ∿ ◐ ♥ ⌂ ⊔ 26°C sg: 1.022 8 cm 80L

*Redigobius tessellatus* 403
7 ∿ ◐ ♥ ⌂ ⊔ 26°C sg: 1.022 5.2 cm 50L

Unidentified Goby 403
7 ∿ ◐ ♥ ⌂ ⊔ 26°C sg: 1.022 8 cm 80L

*Exyrias puntang* 403
7 ∿ ◐ ♥ 26°C sg: 1.022 13 cm 150L

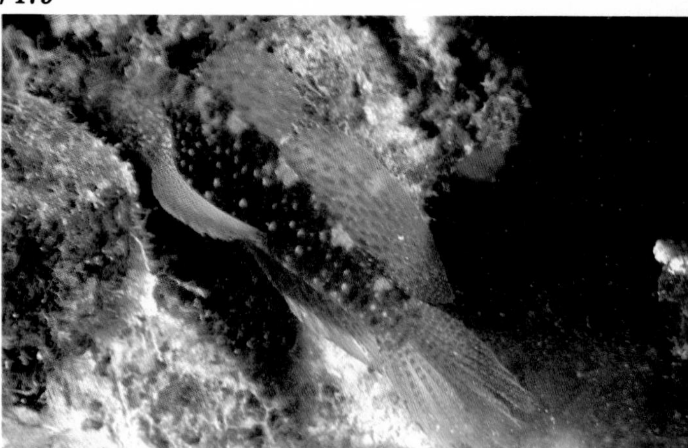

*Exyrias belissimus* 403
7, 9 ∿ ◐ ♥ 26°C sg: 1.022 11 cm 100L

*Aruma histrio* 403
3 ∿ ◐ ♥ 26°C sg: 1.022 6.4 cm 80L

*Exyrias puntang* 403
7 ∿ ◐ ♥ 26°C sg: 1.022 13 cm 150L

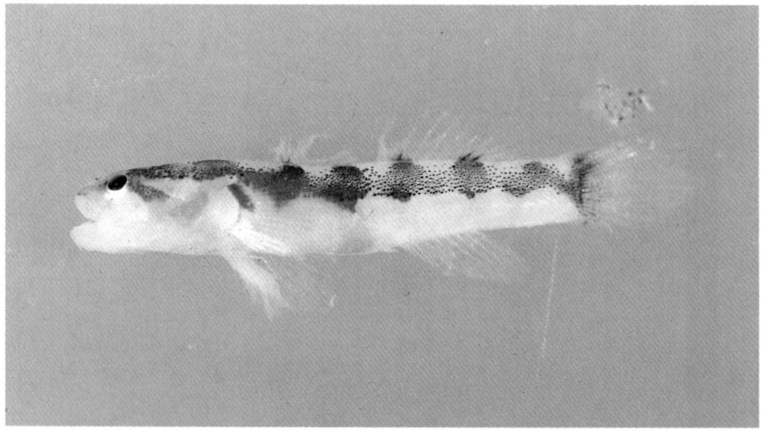

*Barbulifer ceuthoecus* 403
2 ∿ ◐ ♥ 26°C sg: 1.022 3 cm 50L

*Barbulifer pantherinus* 403
3 ∿ ◐ ♥ 26°C sg: 1.022 5 cm 50L

***Bathygobius cocosensis*** **403**
**7, 9 ∿ ◐ ♥ 26°C sg: 1.022 8 cm 80L**

*Bathygobius ramosus* 403
3 ∿ ◐ ♥ 26°C sg: 1.022 11.4 cm 100L

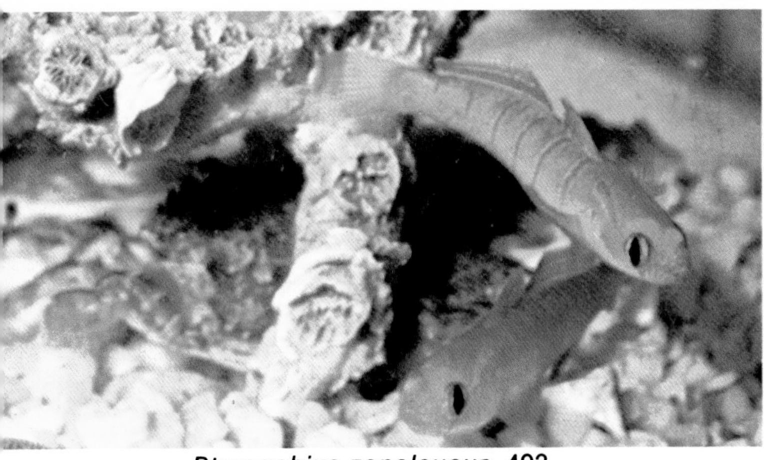

*Pterogobius zonoleucus* 403
5, 7 ◐ ♥ 23°C sg: 1.024 9 cm 100L

*Pterogobius virgo* 403
5, 7 ◐ ♥ 23°C sg: 1.024 16 cm 200L

*Pterogobius elapoides* 403
5, 7 ◐ ♥ 23°C sg: 1.024 8.5 cm 100L

*Gobionellus stigmalophius* 403
2 ◐ ♥ 26°C sg: 1.022 16.5 cm 200L

*Gobionellus stigmaticus* 403
2 ◐ ♥ 26°C sg: 1.022 8 cm 100L

*Gobionellus saepepallens* 403
2 ◐ ♥ 26°C sg: 1.022 5 cm 50L

*Chasmichthys gulosus* 403
5, 7 ◐ 23°C sg: 1.024 10 cm 100L

*Chasmichthys dolichognathus* 403
5 ◐ ♥ 26°C sg: 1.022 3 cm 50L

*Valenciennea longipinnis* 403
7 ∿ ◐ ♥ ▣ ⊔ 26°C sg: 1.022 17 cm 200L

*Valenciennea puellaris* 403
7 ∿ ◐ ♥ ▣ ⊔ 26°C sg: 1.022 12 cm 100L

*Valenciennea sexguttata* 403
7, 9 ∿ ◐ ♥ ▣ ⊔ 26°C sg: 1.022 13 cm 150L

*Valenciennea muralis* 403
7 ∿ ◐ ♥ ▣ ⊔ 26°C sg: 1.022 10 cm 100L

*Valenciennea helsdingenii* 403
7, 9 ∿ ◐ ♥ ▣ ⊔ 26°C sg: 1.022 16 cm 200L

*Valenciennea puellaris* 403
7 ∿ ◐ ♥ ▣ ⊔ 26°C sg: 1.022 12 cm 100L

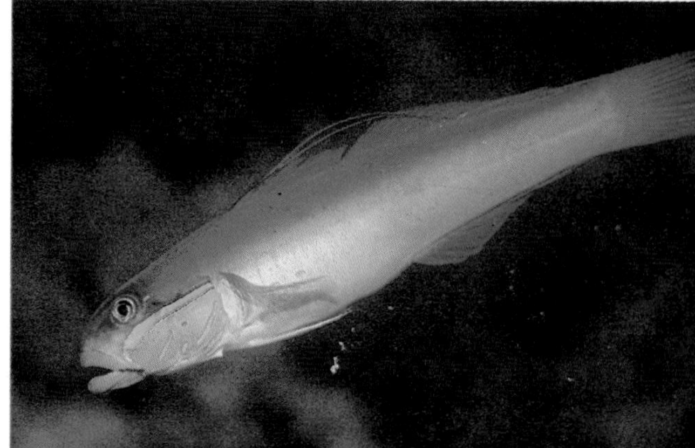

*Valenciennea strigata* 403
7, 9 ∿ ◐ ♥ ▣ ⊔ 26°C sg: 1.022 18 cm 200

*Priolepis cincta* 403
7, 9 ∿ ◐ ♥ ▣ ⊔ 26°C sg: 1.022 4 cm 50L

Unidentified Goby 403
8 ∿ ◐ ♥ 26°C sg: 1.022 4 cm 50L

*Chriolepis fisheri* 403
2 ∿ ◐ ♥ 26°C sg: 1.022 4 cm 50L

*Priolepis semidoliatus* 403
7 ∿ ◐ ♥ 26°C sg: 1.022 3 cm 50L

*Priolepis boreus* 403
5 ∿ ◐ ♥ 26°C sg: 1.022 2.5 cm 50L

*Gymneleotris seminudus* 403
3 ∿ ◐ ♥ 26°C sg: 1.022 5 cm 50L

*Chriolepis zebra* 403
3 ∿ ◐ ♥ 26°C sg: 1.022 6 cm 60L

*Priolepis cinctus* 403
7-9 ∿ ◐ ♥ 26°C sg: 1.022 6 cm 80L

*Priolepis hipoliti* 403
2 ∿ ◐ ♥ 26°C sg: 1.022 3.5 cm 50L

*Periophthalmus koelruteri* 403
9 ◐ ♥ 26°C sg: 1.022 10 cm 100L

*Pleurosicya* sp. 403
9 ◐ ♥ 26°C sg: 1.022 2.5 cm 30L

*Ptereleotris evides* 403
7-10 ◐ ♥ 26°C sg: 1.022 12 cm 150L

*Ptereleotris evides* 403
7-10 ◐ ♥ 26°C sg: 1.022 12 cm 150L

*Ptereleotris heteropterus* 403
7-9 ◐ ♥ 26°C sg: 1.022 9 cm 100L

*Ptereleotris microlepis* 403
6-9 ◐ ♥ 26°C sg: 1.022 11 cm 100L

*Vanderhorstia ambonoro* 403
7-8 ◐ ♥ 26°C sg: 1.022 8 cm 100L

*Vanderhorstia ornatissima* 403
7-9 ◐ ♥ 26°C sg: 1.022 7 cm 80L

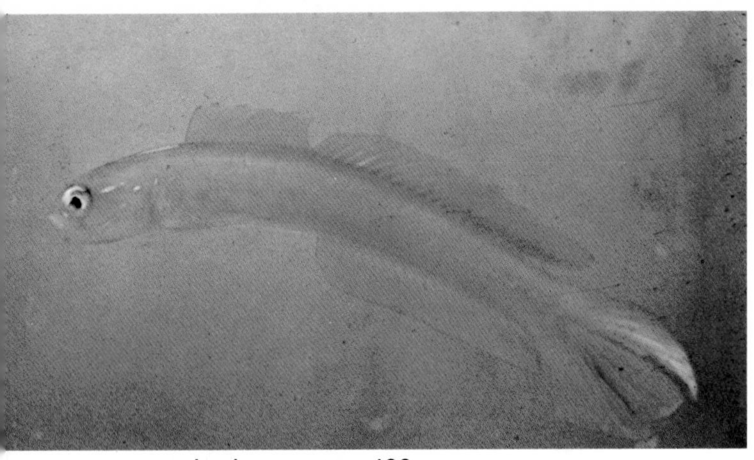

*Ioglossus* sp. 403
3 ◐ ♥ 26°C sg: 1.022 10 cm 100L

*Ioglossus helenae* 403
2 ◐ ♥ 26°C sg: 1.022 24 cm 300L

*Ioglossus calliurus* 403
2 ◐ ♥ 26°C sg: 1.022 10 cm 100L

*Ioglossus calliurus* 403
2 ◐ ♥ 26°C sg: 1.022 10 cm 100L

*Microgobius carri* 403
2 ◐ ♥ 26°C sg: 1.022 7.5 cm 80L

*Microgobius carri* 403
2 ◐ ♥ 26°C sg: 1.022 7.5 cm 80L

*Bollmannia boqueronensis* 403
2 ◐ ♥ 26°C sg: 1.022 10 cm 100L

*Microgobius signatus* 403
2 ◐ ♥ 26°C sg: 1.022 6 cm 60L

*Ctenogobiops maculosus* 403
8 26°C sg: 1.022 7 cm 80L

*Fusigobius neophytus* 403
5 26°C sg: 1.022 7.5 cm 80L

*Fusigobius* sp. 403
7 26°C sg: 1.022 6 cm 80L

*Gnatholepis* sp. 403
7 26°C sg: 1.022 5 cm 50L

*Gobiodon citrinus* 403
7-9 26°C sg: 1.022 6 cm 80L

*Nemateleotris magnifica* 403
6-9 26°C sg: 1.022 9 cm 100L

*Nemateleotris decora* 403
7-8 26°C sg: 1.022 7.5 cm 80L

*Nemateleotris decora* 403
7-8 26°C sg: 1.022 7.5 cm 80L

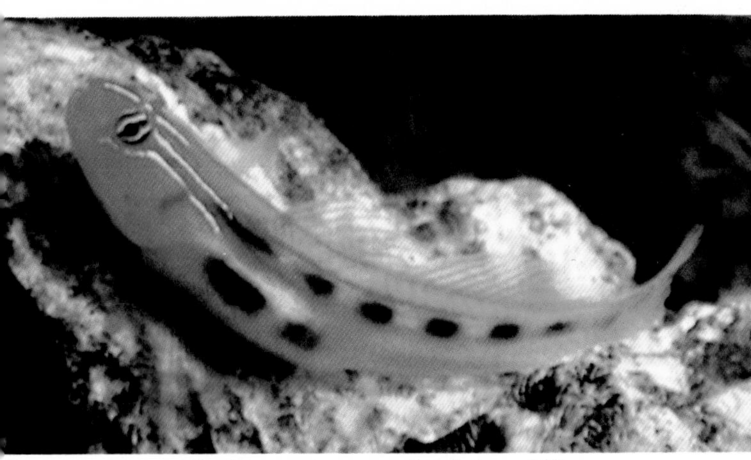

*Gobiosoma puncticulatus* 403
3 26°C sg: 1.022 3 cm 40L

*Gobiosoma saucrum* 403
2 26°C sg: 1.022 3 cm 40L

*Gobiosoma macrodon* 403
2 26°C sg: 1.022 5 cm 50L

*Gobiosoma multifasciatum* 403
2 26°C sg: 1.022 4.5 cm 50L

*Gobiosoma aff. limbaughi* 403
3 26°C sg: 1.022 3 cm 40L

*Gobiosoma digueti* 403
3 26°C sg: 1.022 3 cm 40L

*Gobiosoma tenox* 403
2 26°C sg: 1.022 3.2 cm 40L

*Gobiosoma* sp. 403
3 26°C sg: 1.022 2.5 cm 40L

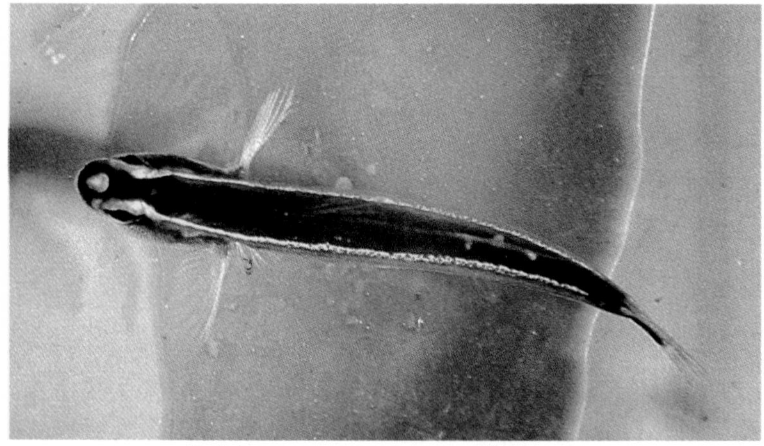

*Gobiosoma atronasum* 403
2 26°C sg: 1.022 2.5 cm 40L

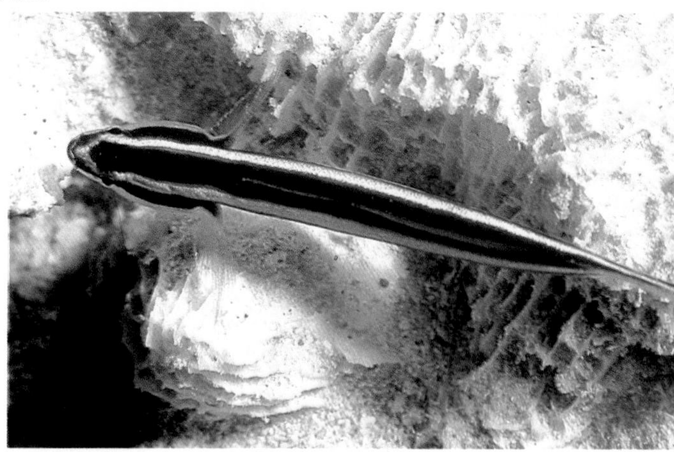

*Gobiosoma prochilus* 403
2 26°C sg: 1.022 2.7 cm 40L

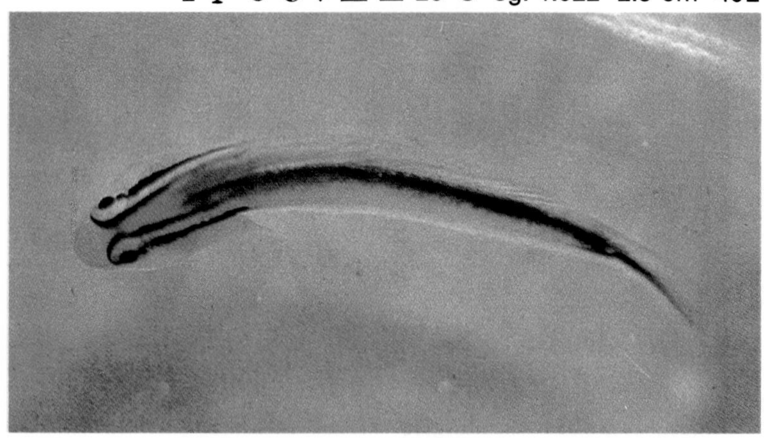

*Gobiosoma chancei* 403
2 26°C sg: 1.022 4.3 cm 50L

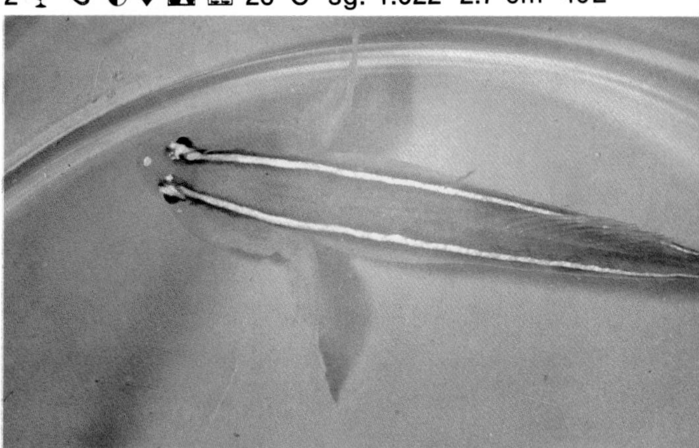

*Gobiosoma horsti* 403
2 26°C sg: 1.022 5 cm 50L

*Gobiosoma louisae* 403
2 26°C sg: 1.022 3.5 cm 40L

*Gobiosoma chiquita* 403
3 26°C sg: 1.022 3 cm 40L

*Eviota nigriventris* 403
7 26°C sg: 1.022 2.5 cm 40L

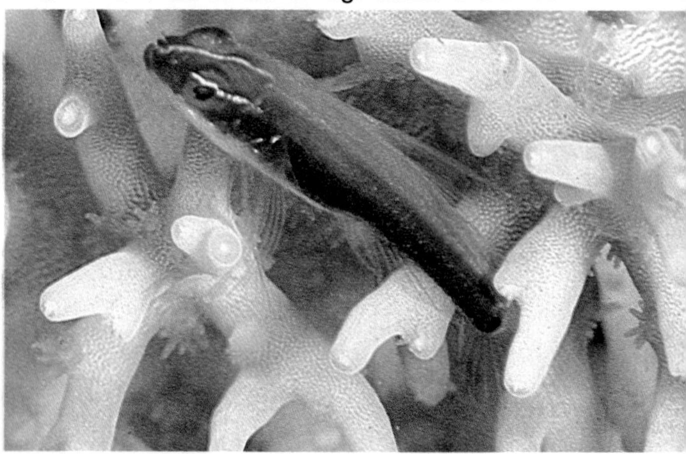

*Eviota nigriventris* 403
7 26°C sg: 1.022 2.5 cm 40L

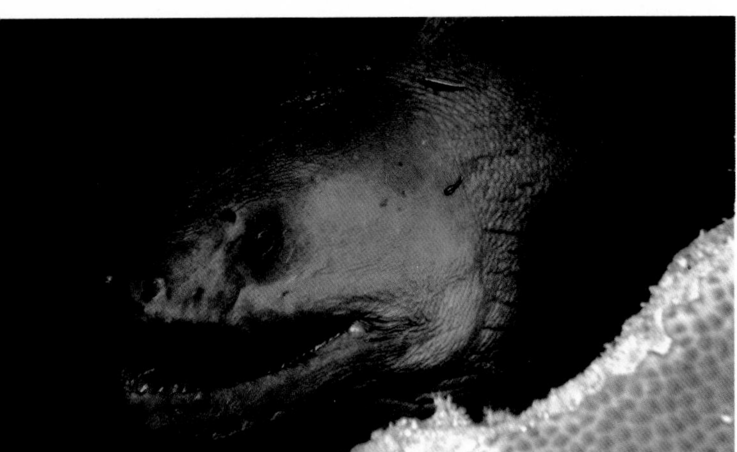

*Gobiosoma oceanops* 403
2 26°C sg: 1.022 5 cm 50L

*Gobiosoma oceanops* 403
2 26°C sg: 1.022 5 cm 50L

*Gobiosoma illecebrosum* 403
2 26°C sg: 1.022 3.5 cm 40L

*Gobiosoma randalli* 403
2 26°C sg: 1.022 2.5 cm 30L

*Gobiosoma evelynae* 403
2 26°C sg: 1.022 6 cm 80L

*Gobiosoma evelynae* 403
2 26°C sg: 1.022 6 cm 80L

*Gobiosoma xanthiprora* 403
2 26°C sg: 1.022 3.7 cm 40L

*Gobiosoma genie* 403
2 26°C sg: 1.022 3.6 cm 40L

*Coryphopterus dicrus* 403
2 ◐ ♥ 26°C sg: 1.022 5 cm 50L

*Coryphopterus personatus* 403
2 ◐ ♥ 26°C sg: 1.022 3 cm 40L

*Coryphopterus* sp. 403
2 ◐ ♥ 26°C sg: 1.022 3 cm 40L

*Coryphopterus eidolon* 403
2 ◐ ♥ 26°C sg: 1.022 5.5 cm 60L

*Coryphopterus lipernes* 403
2 ◐ ♥ 26°C sg: 1.022 3 cm 40L

*Coryphopterus glaucofrenum* 403
2 ◐ ♥ 26°C sg: 1.022 7.5 cm 80L

*Coryphopterus nicholsi* 403
3 ◐ ♥ 24°C sg: 1.022 15 cm 150L

*Coryphopterus urospilus* 403
3 ◐ ♥ 26°C sg: 1.022 3 cm 40L

*Lythrypnus zebra* 403
3 26°C sg: 1.022 5.7 cm 60L

*Lythrypnus dalli* 403
3 26°C sg: 1.022 3 cm 40L

*Lythrypnus spilus* 403
2 26°C sg: 1.022 2.5 cm 40L

*Lythrypnus pulchellus* 403
3 26°C sg: 1.022 2.5 cm 40L

*Lythrypnus phorellus* 403
2 26°C sg: 1.022 2 cm 40L

*Lythrypnus nesiotes* 403
2 26°C sg: 1.022 1.5 cm 40L

*Lythrypnus spilus* 403
2 26°C sg: 1.022 2.5 cm 40L

*Ginsburgellus novemlineatus* 403
2 26°C sg: 1.022 2.5 cm 40L

*Eviota* sp. 403
7 ◐ ♥ 26°C sg: 1.022 3 cm 40L

*Eviota* sp. 403
7 ◐ ♥ 26°C sg: 1.022 3 cm 40L

*Eviota bimaculata* 403
12 ◐ ♥ 26°C sg: 1.022 2.3 cm 40L

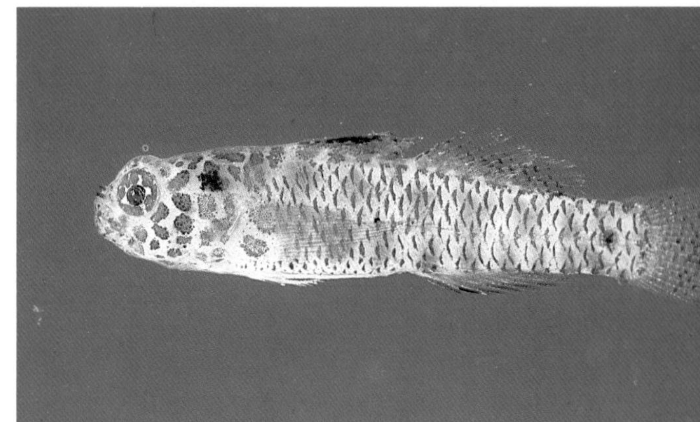

*Eviota* sp. 403
7 ◐ ♥ 26°C sg: 1.022 3 cm 40L

*Eviota abax* 403
5 ◐ ♥ 26°C sg: 1.022 3.6 cm 40L

*Eviota fasciola* 403
8 ◐ ♥ 26°C sg: 1.022 3 cm 40L

*Eviota infulata* 403
6-9 ◐ ♥ 26°C sg: 1.022 2 cm 40L

*Eviota bifasciata* 403
7-10 ◐ ♥ 26°C sg: 1.022 2.3 cm 40L

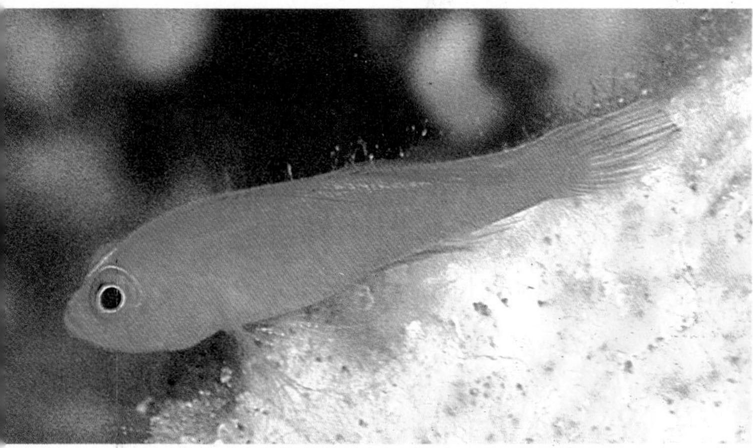

*Trimma* sp. 403
7-8 26°C sg: 1.022 3.5 cm 40L

*Trimma striata* 403
7-8 26°C sg: 1.022 3 cm 40L

*Trimma caesiura* 403
7 26°C sg: 1.022 3.5 cm 40L

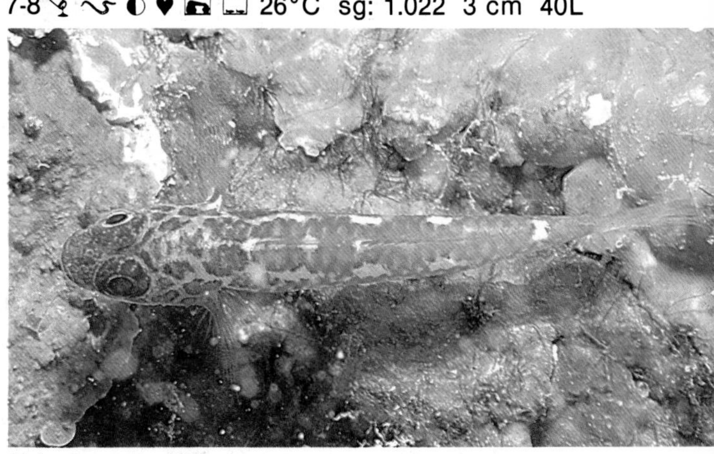

*Trimma* sp. 403
7-8 26°C sg: 1.022 3.5 cm 40L

*Trimma macrophthalma* 403
7-9 26°C sg: 1.022 2.5 cm 40L

*Trimma* sp. 403
7-8 26°C sg: 1.022 3.5 cm 40L

*Trimma* sp. 403
7 26°C sg: 1.022 3 cm 40L

*Trimma* sp. 403
7 26°C sg: 1.022 3 cm 40L

*Gobiodon atrangulatus* 403
6-7 26°C sg: 1.022 3.5 cm 40L

*Gobiodon okinawae* 403
5, 7 26°C sg: 1.022 3.5 cm 40L

*Gobiodon histrio* 403
7 26°C sg: 1.022 7 cm 80L

*Gobiodon rivulatus* 403
7, 9 26°C sg: 1.022 5 cm 50L

*Gobiodon multilineatus* 403
7 26°C sg: 1.022 3.5 cm 40L

*Paragobiodon xanthosomus* 403
7-9 26°C sg: 1.022 3.5 cm 40L

*Paragobiodon echinocephalus* 403
7 26°C sg: 1.022 3 cm 40L

*Gobiodon quinquestrigatus* 403
5, 7, 9 26°C sg: 1.022 4 cm 50L

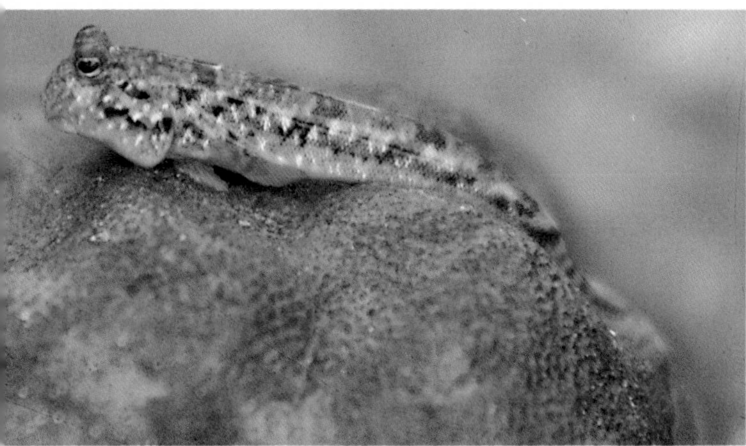

*Periophthalmus sobrinus?* 403
9 ◐ ♥ 26°C sg: 1.015 14 cm 200L

*Periophthalmus* sp. 403
7 ◐ ♥ 26°C sg: 1.015 12 cm 100L

*Periophthalmus koelreuteri* 403
8 ◐ ♥ 26°C sg: 1.015 15 cm 200L

Unidentified Mudskipper 403
7 ◐ ♥ 26°C sg: 1.015 20 cm 200L

*Periophthalmus argentilineatus* 403
7-8 ◐ ♥ 26°C sg: 1.015 10 cm 100L

*Periophthalmus regius* 403
7 ◐ ♥ 26°C sg: 1.015 10 cm 100L

*Periophthalmus cantonensis* 403
5, 7 ◐ ♥ 26°C sg: 1.015 12 cm 100L

*Periophthalmus papilio?* 403
9 ◐ ♥ 26°C sg: 1.015 25 cm 300L

*Boleophthalmus pectinirostris* 403
5, 7 ◐ ♥ 26°C sg: 1.018 20 cm 200L

*Boleophthalmus polyophthalmus* 403
5, 7 ◐ ♥ 26°C sg: 1.022 20 cm 200L

*Ctenotrypauchen microcephalus* 405
7 ● ♥ 26°C sg: 1.022 17.5 cm 200L

*Brachyamblyopus coecus* 404
7 ◐ ♥ 26°C sg: 1.022 7 cm 80L

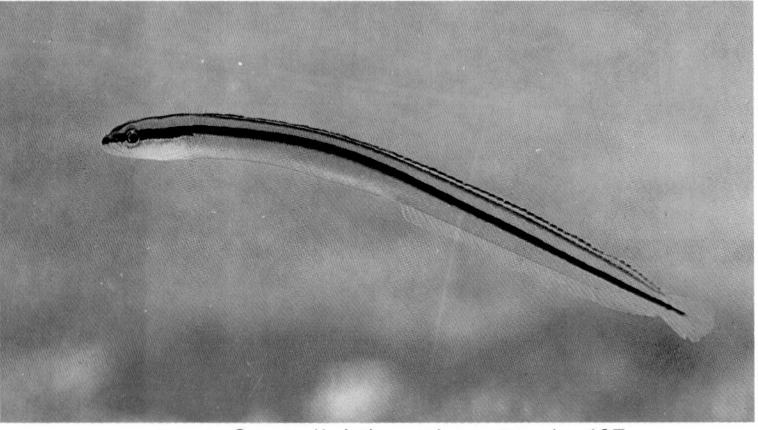

*Gunnelichthys pleurotaenia* 407
7 ◐ ♥ 26°C sg: 1.022 6 cm 60L

*Gunnelichthys monostigma* 407
7 ◐ ♥ 26°C sg: 1.022 9 cm 100L

*Cerdale floridana* 407
2 ◐ ♥ 26°C sg: 1.022 5 cm 50L

*Gunnelichthys curiosus* 407
6 ◐ ♥ 26°C sg: 1.022 13 cm 150L

*Acanthurus achilles* 409
5-7 26°C sg: 1.022 28 cm 300L

*Acanthurus leucosternon* 409
7-9 26°C sg: 1.022 23 cm 300L

*Acanthurus chirurgus* 409
2 ◐ ♥ 26°C sg: 1.022 25 cm 300L

*Acanthurus bahianus* 409
2 ◐ ♥ 26°C sg: 1.022 30 cm 300L

*Acanthurus coeruleus* 409
2 ◐ ♥ 26°C sg: 1.022 23 cm 300L

*Acanthurus coeruleus* 409
2 ◐ ♥ 26°C sg: 1.022 23 cm 300L

*Acanthurus blochii* 409
6-7, 9 ◐ ♥ 26°C sg: 1.022 42 cm 500L

*Acanthurus monroviae* 409
13 ◐ ♥ 26°C sg: 1.022 24 cm 300L

*Acanthurus achilles* 409
5-7 ◐ ♥ 26°C sg: 1.022 28 cm 300L

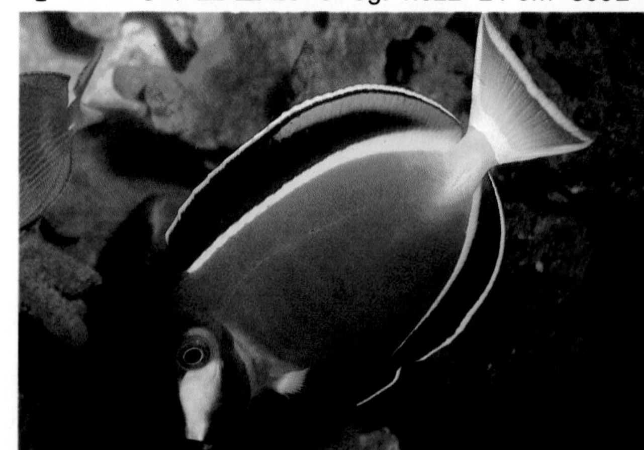

*Acanthurus japonicus* 409
7 ◐ ♥ 26°C sg: 1.022 20 cm 200L

*Acanthurus mata* 409
6-9 26°C sg: 1.022 50 cm 500L

*Acanthurus glaucopareius* 409
3, 6-8 26°C sg: 1.022 17 cm 200L

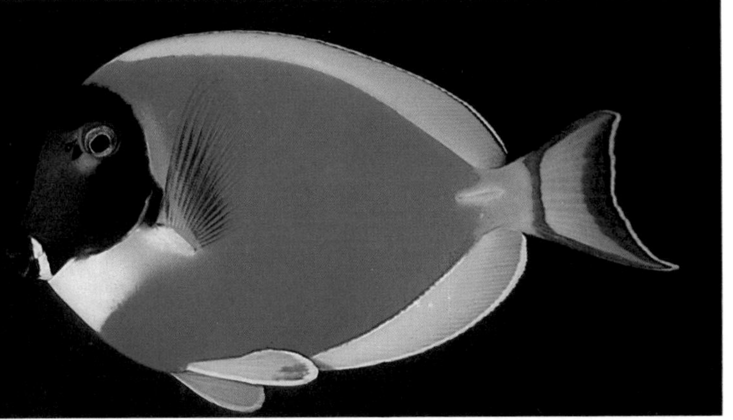

*Acanthurus leucosternon* 409
7-9 26°C sg: 1.022 23 cm 300L

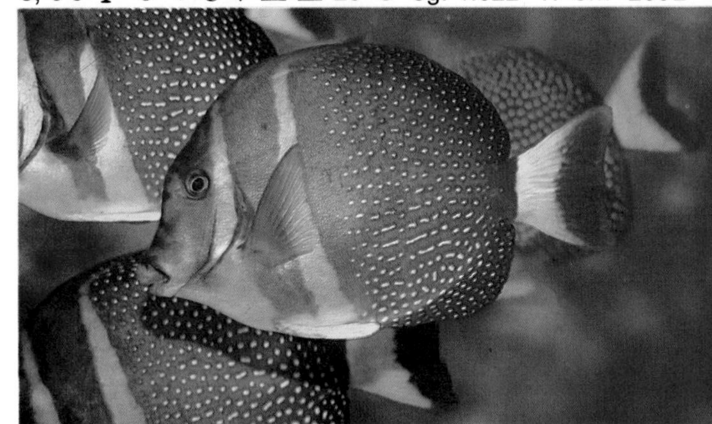

*Acanthurus guttatus* 409
6-9 26°C sg: 1.022 23 cm 300L

*Acanthurus leucosternon* 409
7-9 26°C sg: 1.022 23 cm 300L

*Acanthurus nigrofuscus* 409
7-10 ◐ ♥ 26°C sg: 1.022 21 cm 200L

*Acanthurus olivaceus* 409
6-7 ◐ ♥ 26°C sg: 1.022 25 cm 300L

*Acanthurus pyroferus* 409
6-7 ◐ ♥ 26°C sg: 1.022 19 cm 200L

*Acanthurus pyroferus* 409
6-7 ◐ ♥ 26°C sg: 1.022 19 cm 200L

*Acanthurus sohal* 358
10 ◐ ♥ 26°C sg: 1.028 40 cm 400L

*Acanthurus tennenti* 409
9 ◐ ♥ 26°C sg: 1.022 31 cm 300L

*Acanthurus thompsoni* 409
6-7 ◐ ♥ 26°C sg: 1.022 27 cm 300L

*Acanthurus xanthopterus* 409
3, 6-9 ◐ ♥ 26°C sg: 1.022 62.5 cm 600L

*Acanthurus lineatus* 409
6-9 [symbols] 26°C sg: 1.022 38 cm 400L

*Acanthurus chronixis* 409
7 26°C sg: 1.022 19 cm 200L

*Acanthurus pyroferus* 409
6-7 26°C sg: 1.022 19 cm 200L

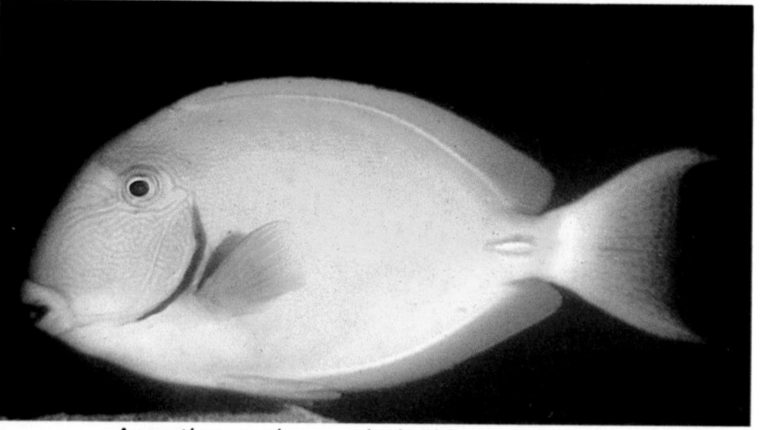

*Acanthurus dussumieri* 409
6-9 26°C sg: 1.022 54 cm 600L

*Acanthurus olivaceous* 409
6-7 26°C sg: 1.022 25 cm 300L

*Acanthurus chronix is* 409
7 26°C sg: 1.022 19 cm 200L

*Acanthurus pyroferus* 409
6-7 26°C sg: 1.022 19 cm 200L

*Acanthurus bariene* 409
7, 9 26°C sg: 1.022 30 cm 300L

*Acanthurus mata* 409
6-9 26°C sg: 1.022 50 cm 500L

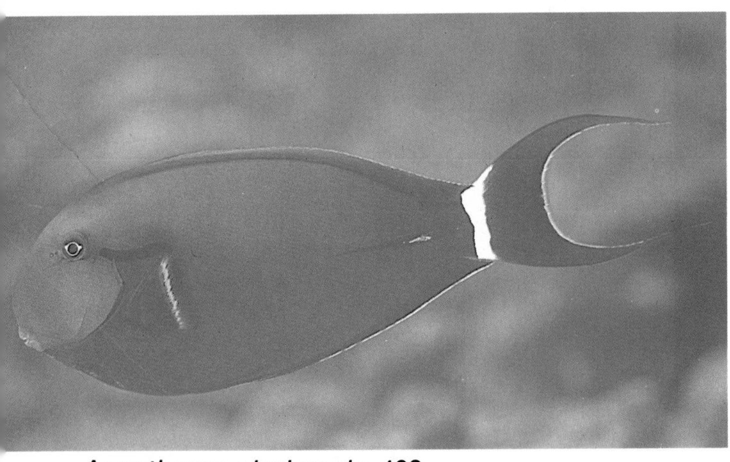

*Acanthurus nigricauda* 409
6-9 26°C sg: 1.022 40 cm 400L

*Acanthurus lineatus* 409
6-9 26°C sg: 1.022 38 cm 400L

*Acanthurus maculiceps* 409
7 26°C sg: 1.022 19 cm 200L

*Acanthurus blochii* 409
6-7, 9 26°C sg: 1.022 42 cm 500L

*Ctenochaetus strigosus* 409
6-10 26°C sg: 1.022 18 cm 200L

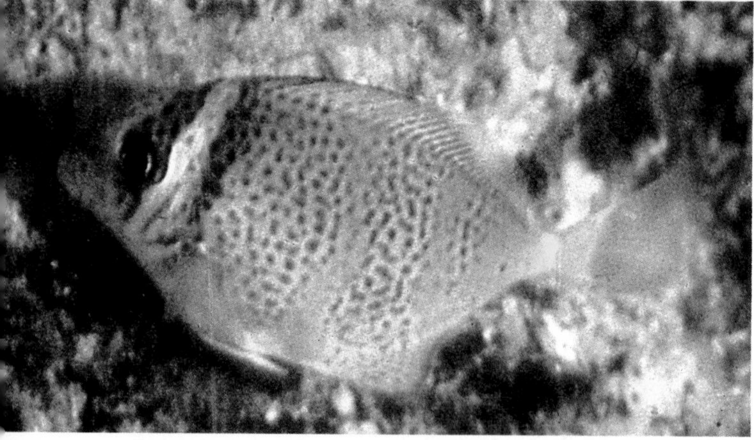

*Prionurus punctatus* (juv.) 409
3 26°C sg: 1.022 60 cm 600L

*Prionurus laticlavius* 409
3 26°C sg: 1.022 50 cm 500L

*Acanthurus leucopareius* 409
6-7 26°C sg: 1.022 20 cm 200L

*Acanthurus nigroris* (juv.) 409
6-7 26°C sg: 1.022 20 cm 200L

*Prionurus punctatus* 409
3 26°C sg: 1.022 60 cm 600L

*Prionurus scalprus* 409
7 26°C sg: 1.022 40 cm 400L

*Acanthurus triostegus* 409
6-9 26°C sg: 1.022 27 cm 300L

*Acanthurus nigroris* 409
6-7 26°C sg: 1.022 20 cm 200L

*Paracanthurus hepatus* 409
6-9 26°C sg: 1.022 26 cm 300L

*Paracanthurus hepatus* 409
6-9 26°C sg: 1.022 26 cm 300L

*Ctenochaetus marginatus* 409
7-9 26°C sg: 1.022 20 cm 200L

*Ctenochaetus striatus* 409
6-10 26°C sg: 1.022 26 cm 300L

*Ctenochaetus tominiensis* (juv.) 409
7 26°C sg: 1.022 15 cm 150L

*Ctenochaetus tominiensis* 409
7 26°C sg: 1.022 15 cm 150L

*Ctenochaetus hawaiiensis* 409
6 26°C sg: 1.022 21 cm 200L

*Ctenochaetus hawaiiensis* (juv.) 409
6 26°C sg: 1.022 21 cm 200L

*Ctenochaetus strigosus* 409
6-9 26°C sg: 1.022 18 cm 200L

*Paracanthurus hepatus* 409
6-9 26°C sg: 1.022 26 cm 300L

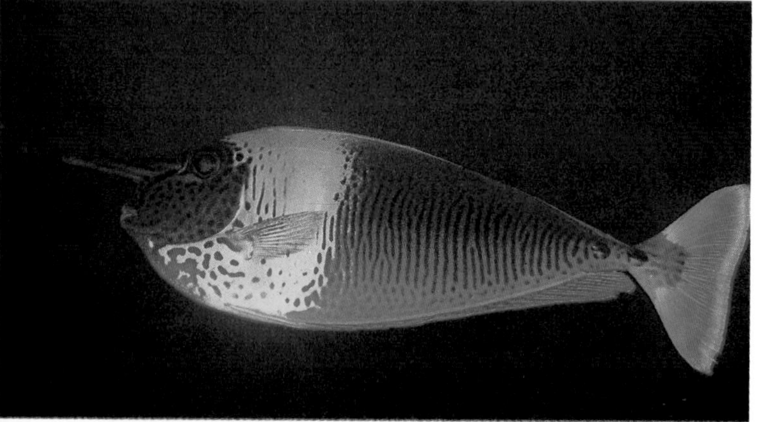

*Naso brevirostris* 409
6-10 26°C sg: 1.022 60 cm 600L

*Naso vlamingi* 409
6-9 26°C sg: 1.022 60 cm 600L

*Ctenochaetus strigosus* (juv.) 409
6-9 26°C sg: 1.022 18 cm 200L

*Naso tuberosus* 409
6-9 26°C sg: 1.022 60 cm 600L

*Naso lituratus* 409
6-10 26°C sg: 1.022 45 cm 500L

*Naso vlamingi* 409
6-9 26°C sg: 1.022 60 cm 600L

*Naso lopezi* 409
6-7 ◐ ♥ 26°C sg: 1.022 45 cm 500L

*Naso brevirostris* (juv.) 409
6-10 ◐ ♥ 26°C sg: 1.022 60 cm 600L

*Naso lituratus* (juv.) 409
6-10 ◐ ♥ 26°C sg: 1.022 45 cm 500L

*Naso unicornis* (juv.) 409
6-10 ◐ ♥ 26°C sg: 1.022 70 cm 700L

*Naso brachycentron* 409
7-9 ◐ ♥ 26°C sg: 1.022 60 cm 600L

*Naso hexacanthus* 409
7-10 ◐ ♥ 26°C sg: 1.022 75 cm 800L

*Naso lituratus* 409
◐ ♥ 26°C sg: 1.022 45 cm 500L

*Naso unicornis* 409
6-10 ◐ ♥ 26°C sg: 1.022 70 cm 700L

*Zebrasoma scopas* 409
6-10 26°C sg: 1.022 20 cm 200L

*Zebrasoma veliferum* 409
6-8 26°C sg: 1.022 40 cm 400L

*Zebrasoma gemmatum* 409
9 26°C sg: 1.022 22 cm 200L

*Zebrasoma flavescens* 409
6-8 26°C sg: 1.022 15 cm 150L

*Zebrasoma rostratum* 409
6 26°C sg: 1.022 20 cm 200L

*Zebrasoma veliferum* 409
6-8 26°C sg: 1.022 40 cm 400L

*Zebrasoma flavescens* 409
6-8 26°C sg: 1.022 15 cm 150L

*Zebrasoma flavescens* 409
6-8 26°C sg: 1.022 15 cm 150L

*Zebrasoma veliferum* 409
6-8 ♀ ∿ ⚘ ◐ ♥ ▨ ☷ 26°C sg: 1.022 40 cm 400L

*Zebrasoma scopas* 409
6-10 26°C sg: 1.022 20 cm 200L

*Zebrasoma gemmatum* 409
9 26°C sg: 1.022 22 cm 200L

*Zebrasoma desjardinii* 409
9-10 26°C sg: 1.022 40 cm 400L

*Zanclus canescens* 409
3, 6-9 26°C sg: 1.022 22 cm 200L

*Zebrasoma scopas* 409
6-10 26°C sg: 1.022 20 cm 200L

*Zebrasoma desjardinii* 409
9-10 26°C sg: 1.022 40 cm 400L

*Zebrasoma xanthurus* 409
10 26°C sg: 1.022 22 cm 200L

*Zanclus canescens* 409
3, 6-10 ~ ⚘ ◐ ♥ ▨ ⊡ 26°C sg: 1.022 22 cm 200L

*Lo magnifica* 410
9 26°C sg: 1.022 18 cm 200L

*Lo vulpinus* 410
6-7 26°C sg: 1.022 19 cm 200L

*Lo vulpinus* (juv.) 410
6-7 26°C sg: 1.022 19 cm 200L

*Siganus argenteus* 410
6-10 26°C sg: 1.022 35 cm 400L

*Siganus fuscescens* 410
7, 9 26°C sg: 1.022 30 cm 300L

*Lo vulpinus* 410
6-7 26°C sg: 1.022 19 cm 200L

*Lo uspi* 410
6 26°C sg: 1.022 18 cm 200L

*Siganus canaliculatus* 410
7, 9 26°C sg: 1.022 30 cm 300L

*Siganus canaliculatus* 410
7, 9 26°C sg: 1.022 30 cm 300L

*Lo magnifica* 410
9 ◐ ♥ 26°C sg: 1.022 18 cm 200L

*Siganus canaliculatus* 410
7, 9 ◐ ♥ 26°C sg: 1.022 30 cm 300L

*Siganus guttatus* 410
7-8 ◐ ♥ 26°C sg: 1.022 35 cm 400L

*Siganus lineatus* 410
7-9 ◐ ♥ 26°C sg: 1.022 40 cm 400L

*Siganus corallinus* 410
7-9 ◐ ♥ 26°C sg: 1.022 25 cm 300L

*Siganus javus* 410
7, 9 ◐ ♥ 26°C sg: 1.022 45 cm 500L

*Siganus puelloides* 410
9 ◐ ♥ 26°C sg: 1.022 30 cm 300L

*Siganus chrysospilos* 410
8 ◐ ♥ 26°C sg: 1.022 40 cm 400L

*Siganus doliatus* 410
7-8 26°C sg: 1.022 30 cm 300L

*Siganus stellatus* 410
9-10 26°C sg: 1.022 40 cm 400L

*Siganus trispilos* 410
7, 12 26°C sg: 1.022 25 cm 300L

*Siganus vermiculatus* 410
6-8 26°C sg: 1.022 45 cm 500L

*Siganus virgatus* 410
7-8 26°C sg: 1.022 30 cm 300L

*Siganus puellus* 410
6-7 26°C sg: 1.022 30 cm 300L

*Siganus chrysospilos* 410
8 26°C sg: 1.022 40 cm 400L

*Siganus spinus* 410
6-9 26°C sg: 1.022 21 cm 200L

*Siganus lineatus* 410
7-9 ♀ ~ ⚘ ◐ ♥ ▣ ▣ 26°C sg: 1.022 40 cm 400L

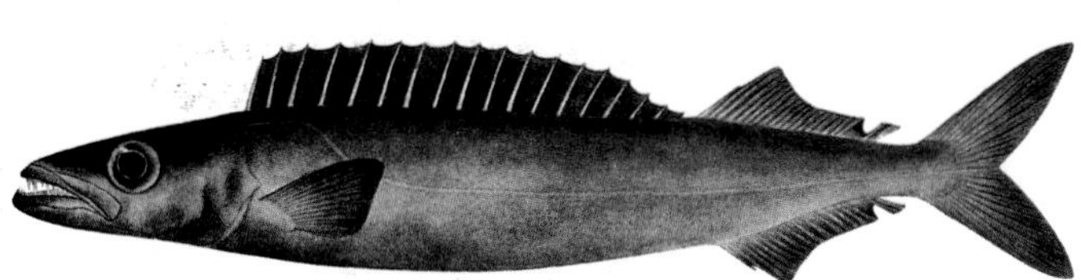

*Promethichthys prometheus* 412
Circumtrop. 26°C sg: 1.022 60 cm 600L

*Ruvettus pretiosus* 412
Circumtrop. 26°C sg: 1.022 300 cm 3000L

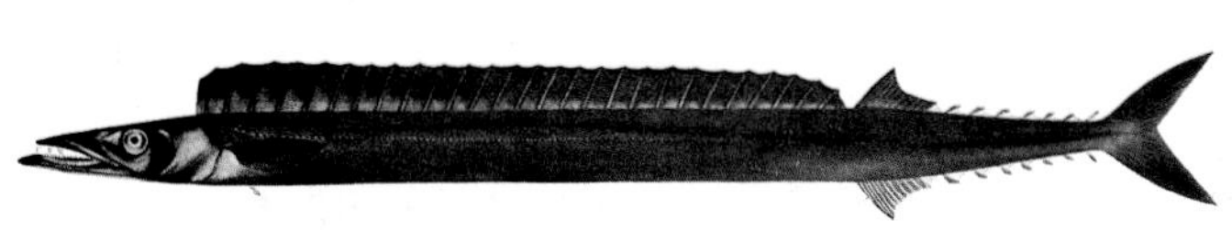

*Gempylus serpens* 412
Circumtrop. 26°C sg: 1.022 100 cm

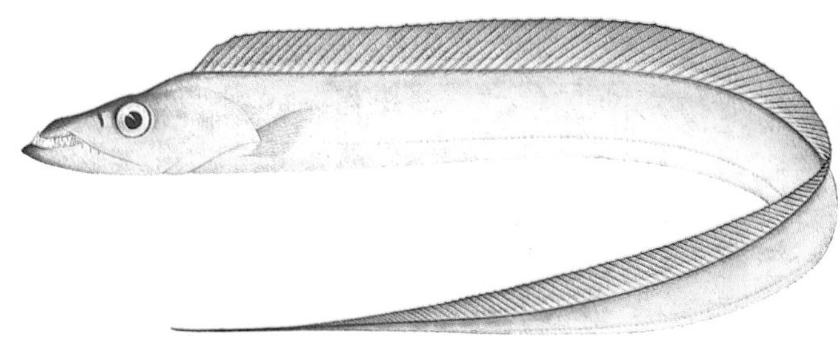

*Trichiurus lepturus* 413
Circumtrop. 26°C sg: 1.022 120 cm 1200L

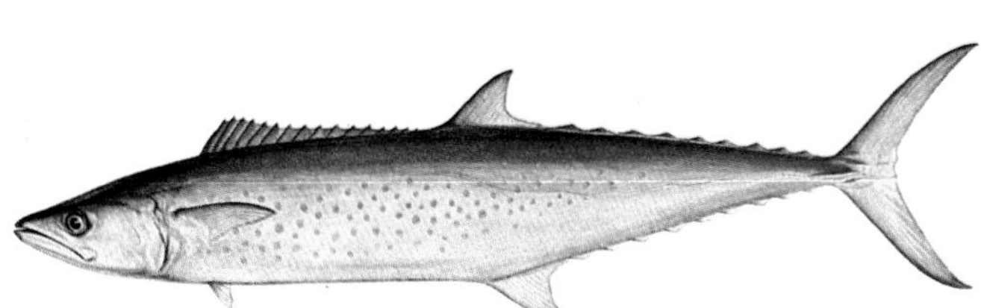

*Scomberomorus sierra* 414
3 26°C sg: 1.022 81 cm 800L

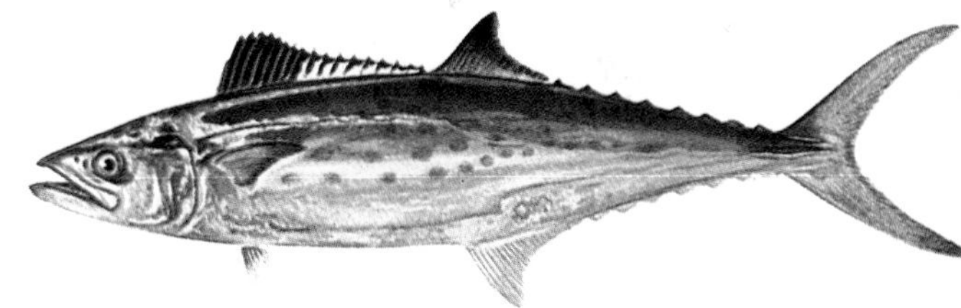

*Scomberomorus maculatus* 414
1-2 26°C sg: 1.022 70 cm 800L

*Scomber australasicus* 414
8, 12 25°C sg: 1.022 40 cm 400L

*Thunnus thynnus* 414
Circumglobal 300 cm 3000L

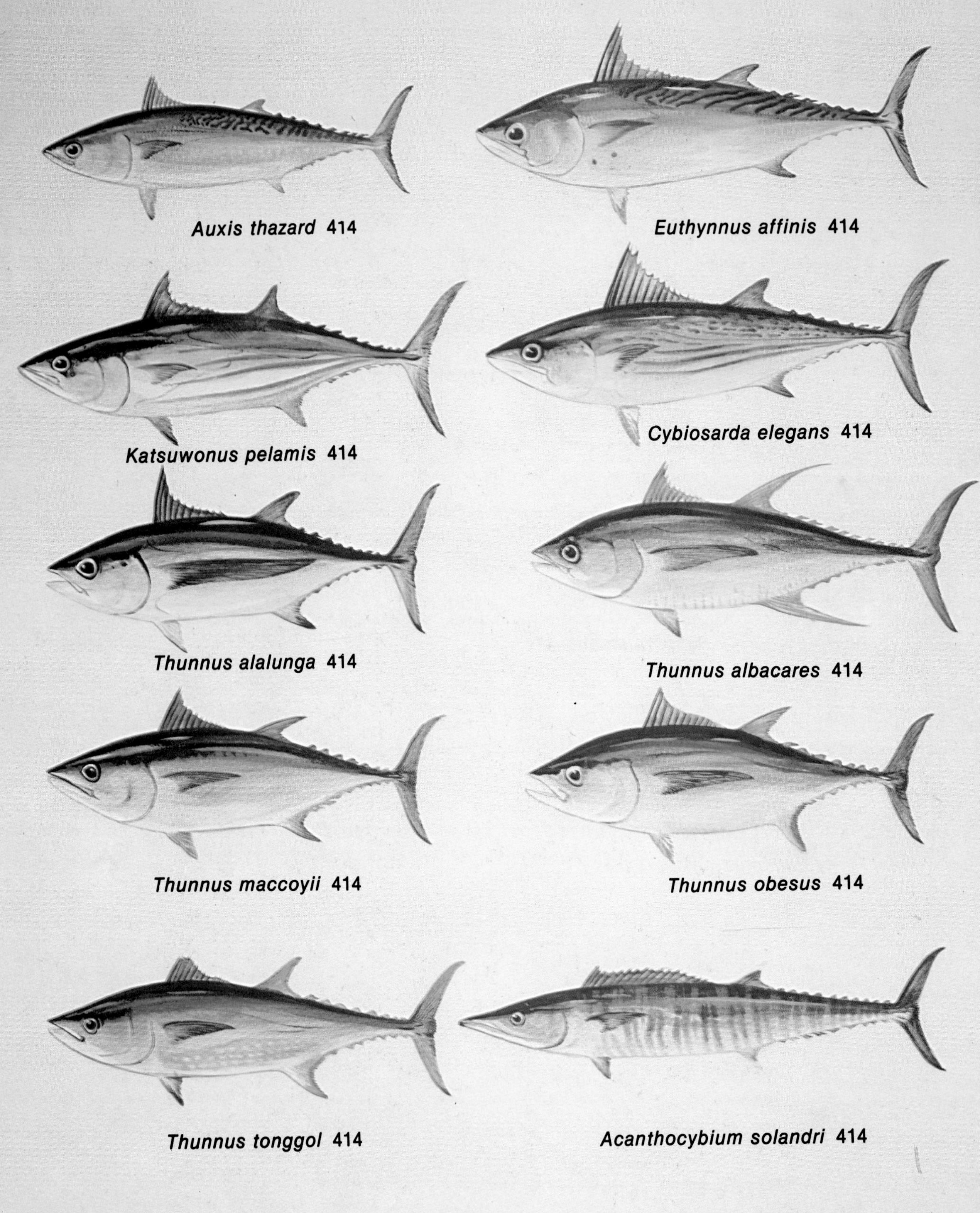
*Auxis thazard* 414
*Euthynnus affinis* 414
*Katsuwonus pelamis* 414
*Cybiosarda elegans* 414
*Thunnus alalunga* 414
*Thunnus albacares* 414
*Thunnus maccoyii* 414
*Thunnus obesus* 414
*Thunnus tonggol* 414
*Acanthocybium solandri* 414

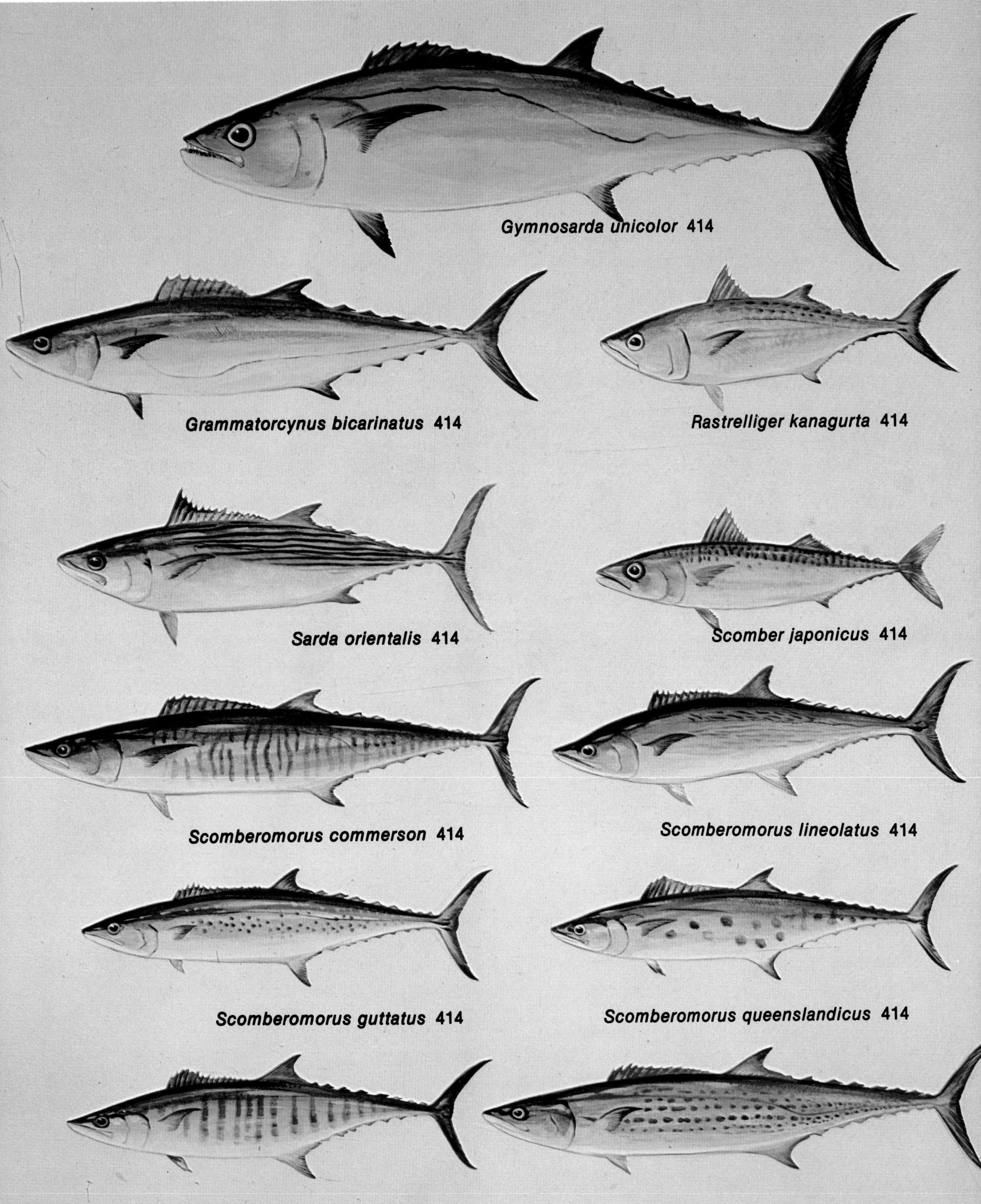

Gymnosarda unicolor 414

Grammatorcynus bicarinatus 414

Rastrelliger kanagurta 414

Sarda orientalis 414

Scomber japonicus 414

Scomberomorus commerson 414

Scomberomorus lineolatus 414

Scomberomorus guttatus 414

Scomberomorus queenslandicus 414

Scomberomorus semifasciatus 414

Scomberomorus niphonius 414

#517

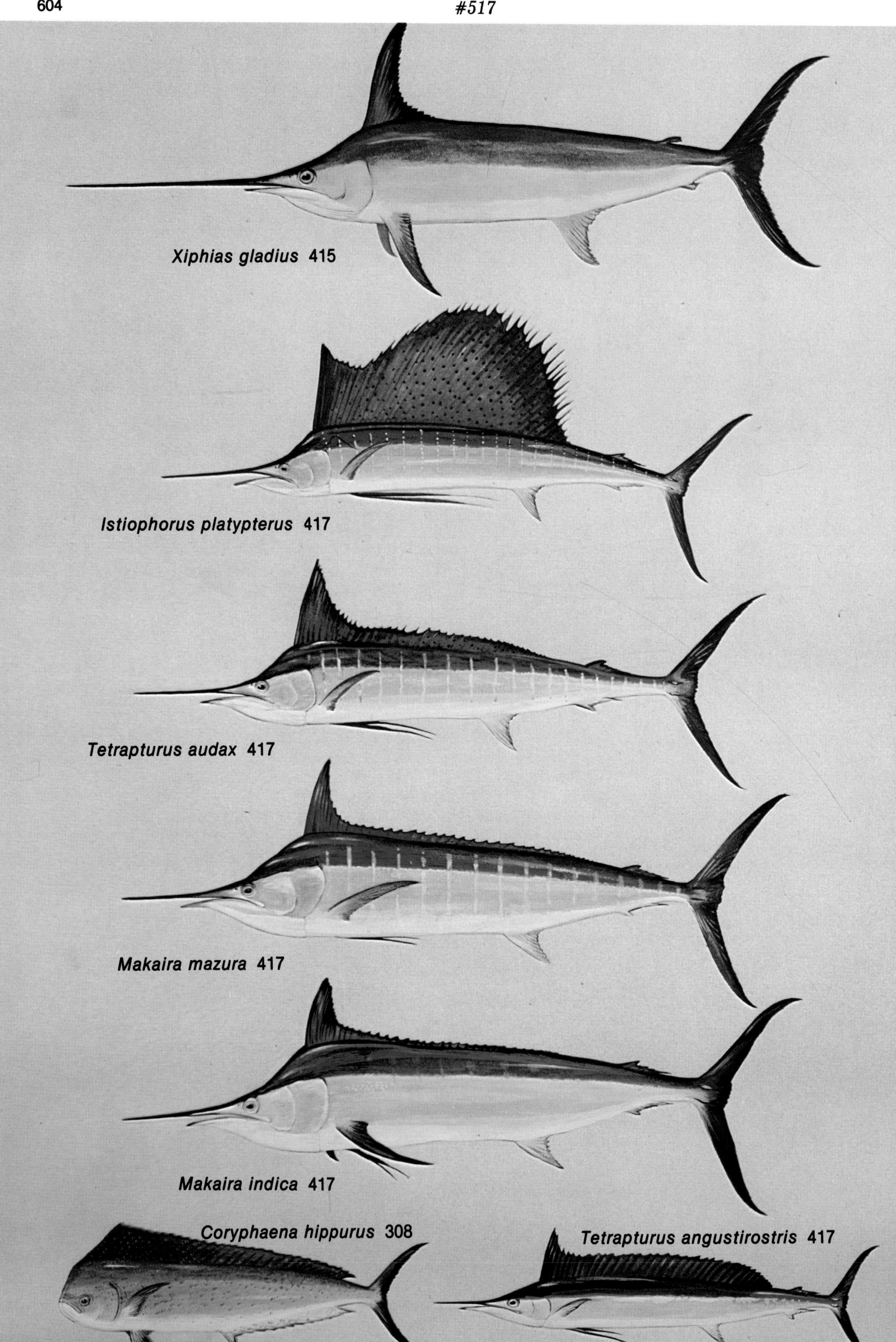
Xiphias gladius 415
Istiophorus platypterus 417
Tetrapturus audax 417
Makaira mazura 417
Makaira indica 417
Coryphaena hippurus 308
Tetrapturus angustirostris 417

#517A

*Makaira* sp. 417
7-10 ↘ ◐ ☠ ▭ ▭ 26°CX sg: 1.022 4500 cm >5000L

*Nomeus gronovii* 420
Circumtrop. ~ ◐ ☠ ▭ ▭ 26°C sg: 1.022 39 cm 400L

*Psenes pellucidus* 420
Circumtrop. 26°C sg: 1.022 80 cm 1000L

*Nomeus gronovii* 420
Circumtrop. 26°C sg: 1.022 39 cm 400L

*Hyperoglyphe japonica* 419
7 26°C sg: 1.022 90 cm 1000L

*Ariomma indica* 420
7, 9 26°C sg: 1.022 25 cm 300L

*Psenopsis anomala* 419
7 26°C sg: 1.022 30 cm 500L

*Pampas argenteus* 423
7, 9 26°C sg: 1.022 60 cm 600L

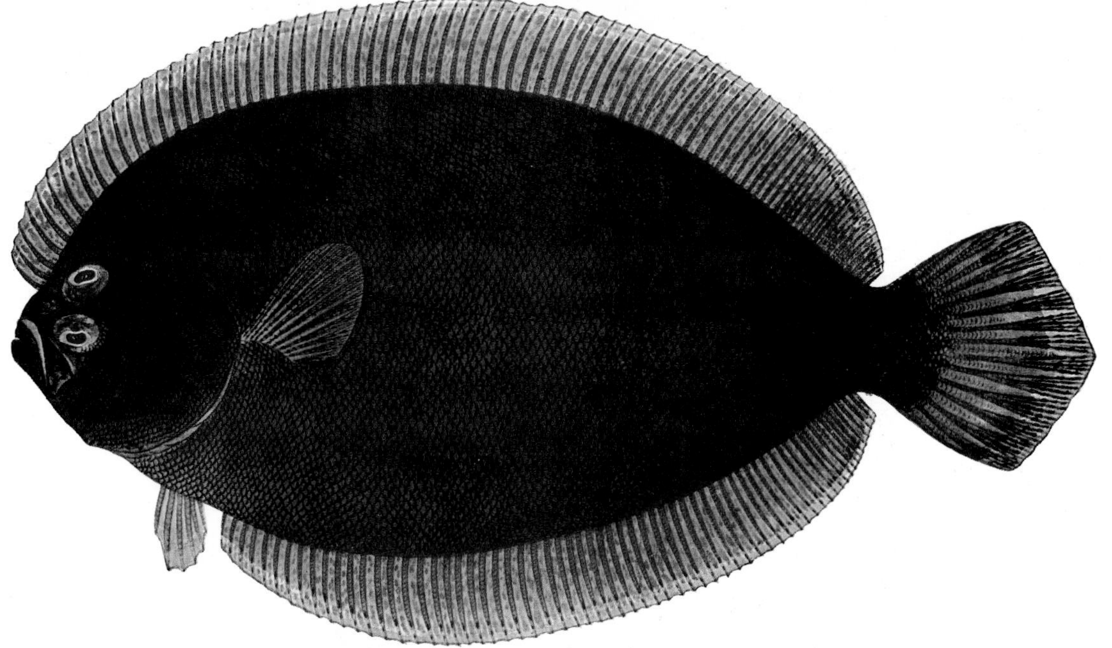

*Pseudorhombus cinnamoneus* 434
7 ◐ ♥ 26°C sg: 1.022 30 cm 300L

*Platichthys stellatus* 435
4-5 ◐ 24°C sg: 1.023 91 cm 1000L

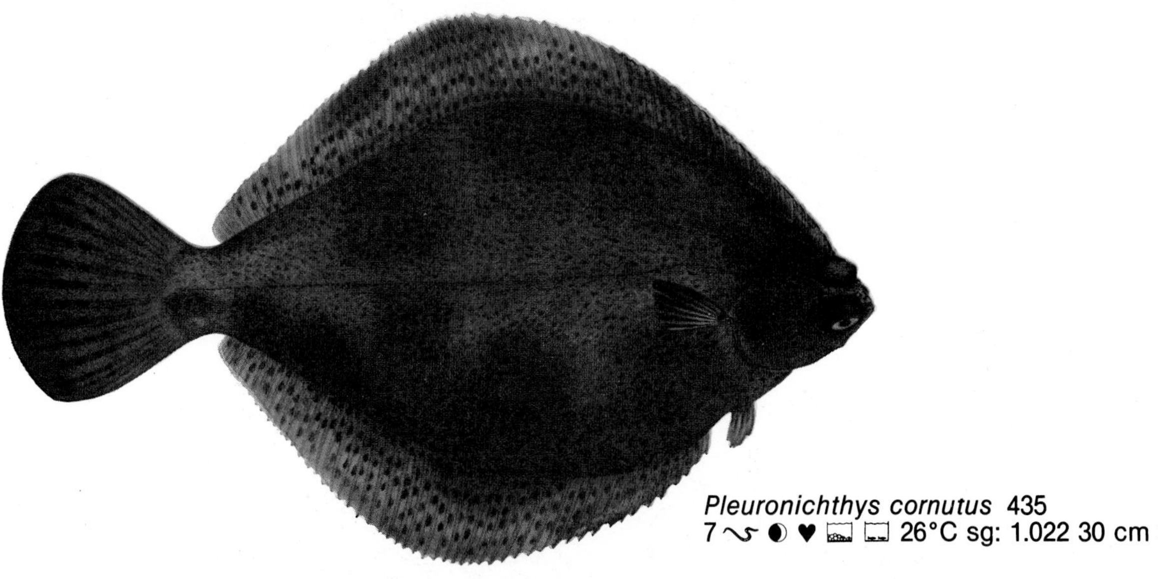

*Pleuronichthys cornutus* 435
7 ◐ ♥ 26°C sg: 1.022 30 cm 300L

*Cleisthenes pinetorum herzensteini* 435
5, 7 ◐ 26°C sg: 1.022 45 cm 500L

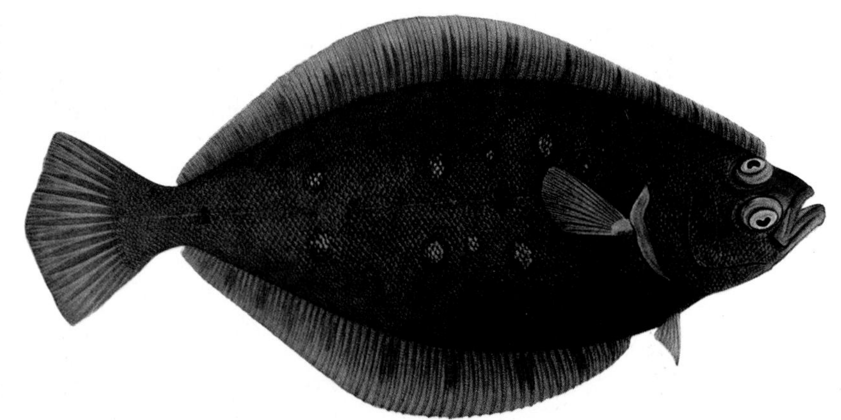

*Eopsetta grigorjewi* 435
5, 7 ◐ ♥ 26°C sg: 1.022 40 cm 400L

*Clidoderma asperrimum* 435
4, 5, 7 ◐ 26°C sg: 1.022 55 cm 600L

*Psettodes erumei* 432
7-10 ◐ ♥ 26°C sg: 1.022 60 cm 600L

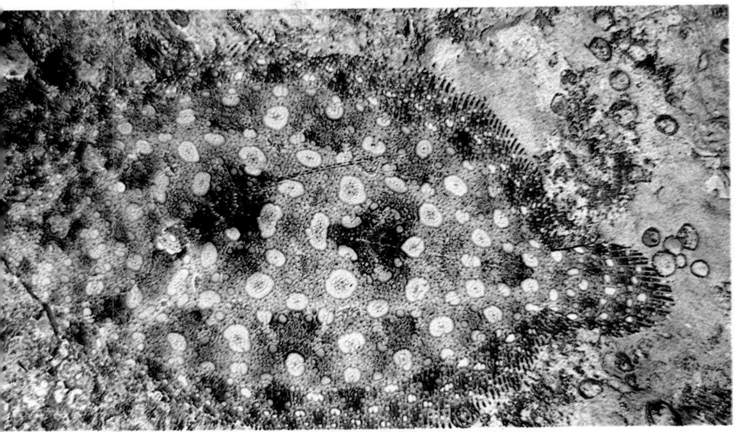

*Bothus pantherinus* 434
6-10 ◐ ♥ 26°C sg: 1.022 30 cm 300L

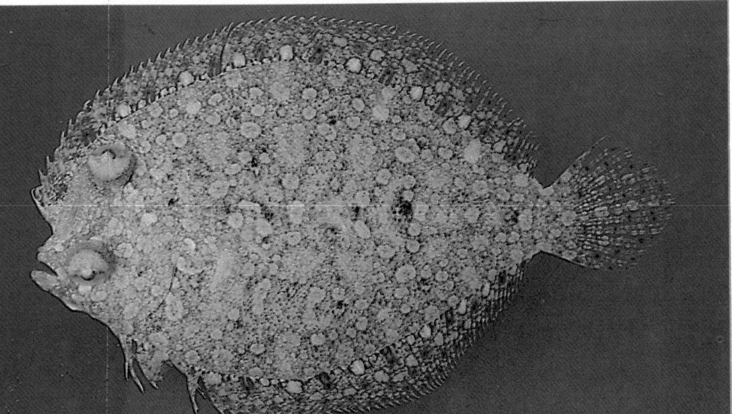

*Bothus ocellatus* 434
1-2 ◐ ♥ 26°C sg: 1.022 15 cm 150L

*Citharichthys gilberti* 434
3 ◐ ♥ 25°C sg: 1.022 20 cm 200L

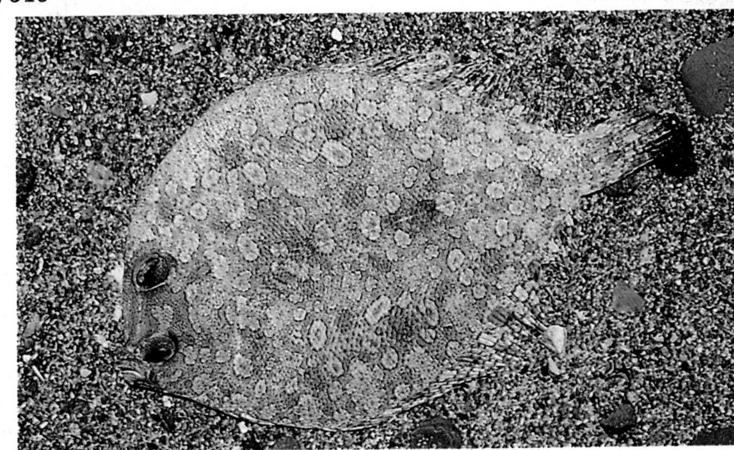

*Bothus leopardus* 434
3 ◐ ♥ 26°C sg: 1.022 20 cm 200L

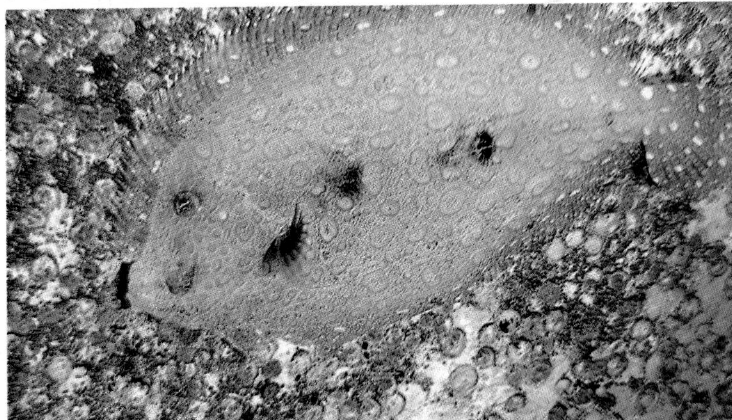

*Bothus pantherinus* 434
6-10 ◐ ♥ 26°C sg: 1.022 30 cm 300L

*Bothus lunatus* 434
2 ◐ ♥ 26°C sg: 1.022 45 cm 500L

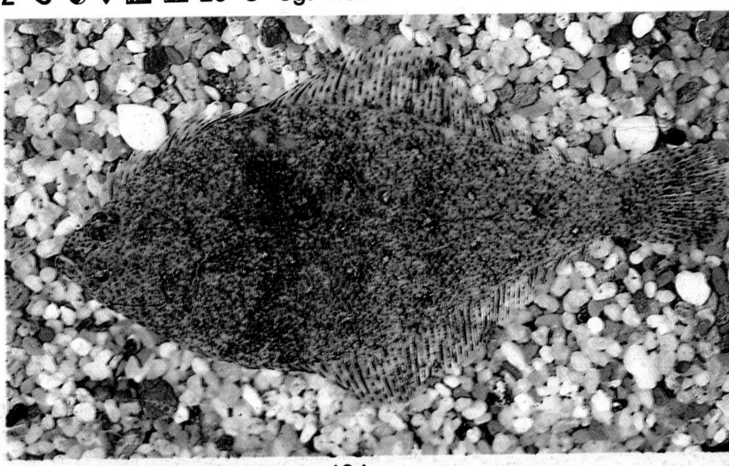

*Citharichthys stigmaeus* 434
4 ◐ ♥ 23°C sg: 1.024 17 cm 200L

*Paralichthys olivaceus* 434
7 26°C sg: 1.022 80 cm 1000L

*Paralichthys dentatus* 434
1 23°C sg: 1.024 94 cm 1000L

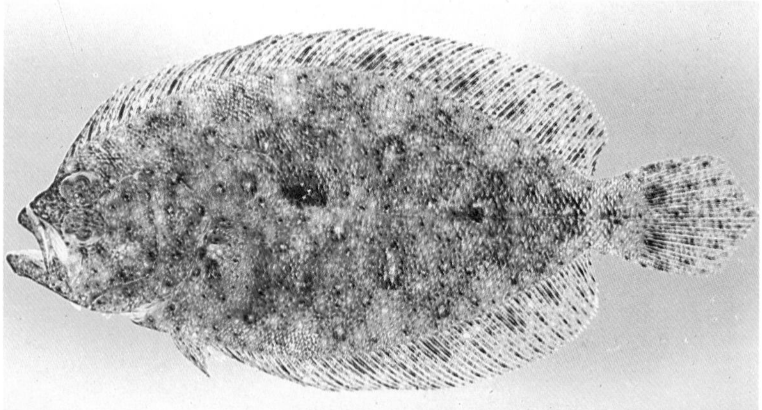

*Pseudorhombus cinnamoneus* 434
7 26°C sg: 1.022 30 cm 300L

*Pseudorhombus* sp. 434
7 26°C sg: 1.022 30 cm 300L

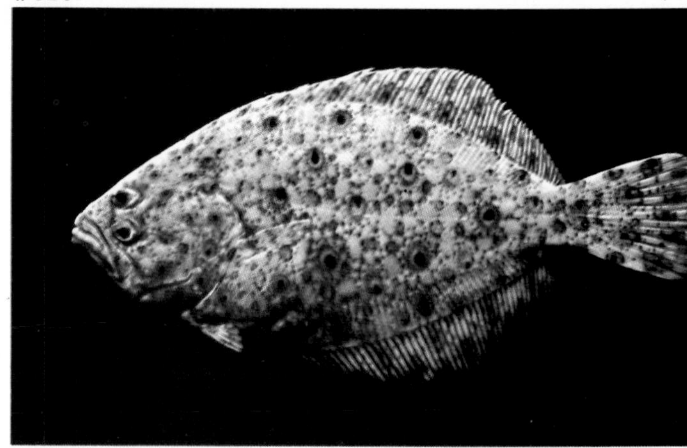

*Paralichthys woolmani* 434
3 26°C sg: 1.022 80 cm 1000L

*Xystreurys liolepis* 434
3-4 26°C sg: 1.022 53 cm 500L

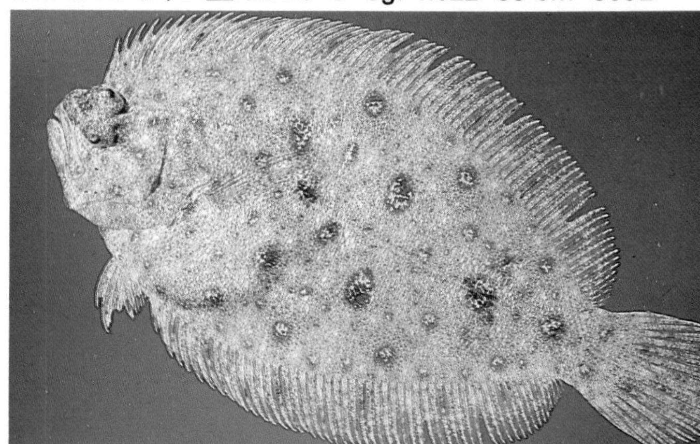

*Pseudorhombus jenynsii* 434
7 26°C sg: 1.022 27 cm 300L

*Zeugopterus punctatus* 434
14 20°C sg: 1.024 25 cm 300L

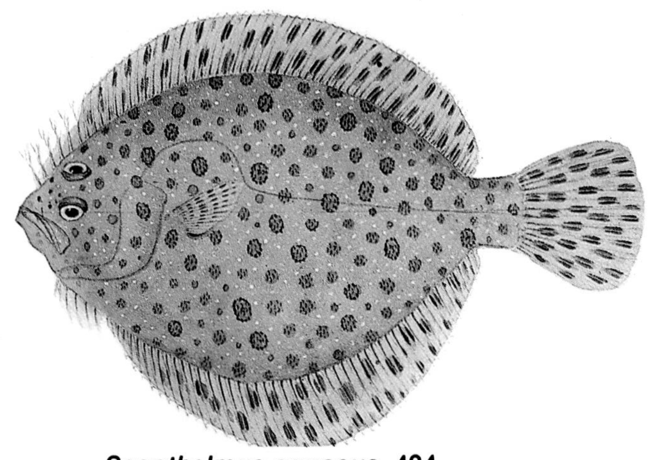

*Scopthalmus aquosus* 434
1 23°C sg: 1.023 45 cm 500L

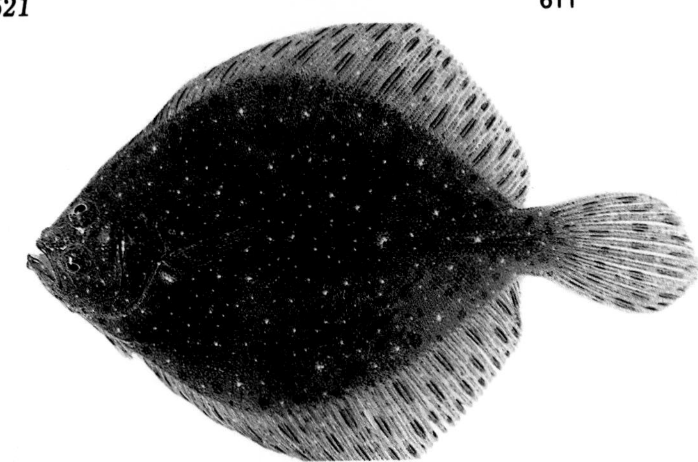

*Scopthalmus aquosus* 434
1 23°C sg: 1.023 45 cm 500L

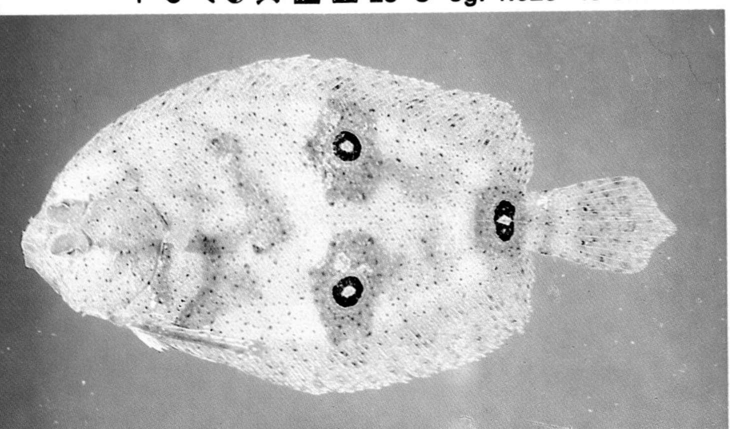

*Ancylopsetta dilecta* 434
2 26°C sg: 1.022 25 cm 300L

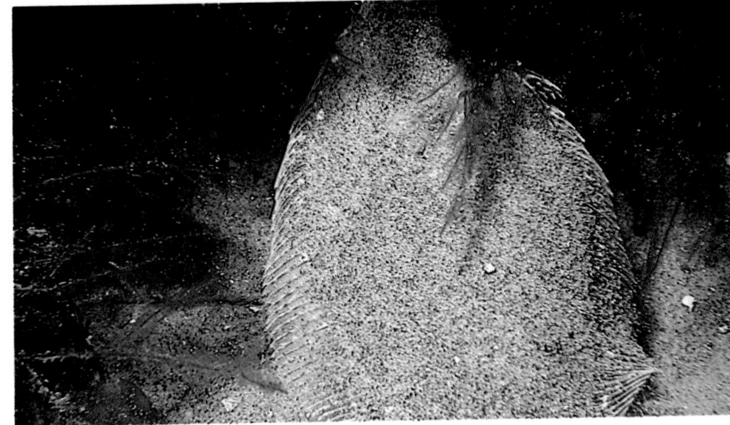

*Scophthalmus rhombus* 434
14 16°C sg: 1.024 61 cm 600L

*Pseudopleuronectes americanus* 435
1 10°C sg: 1.024 64 cm 600L

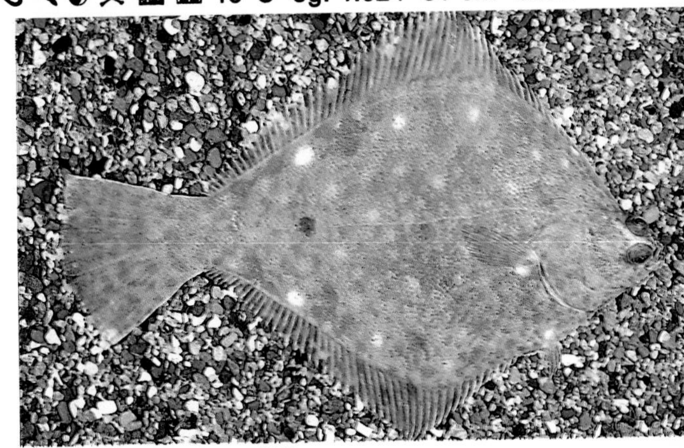

*Hypsopsetta guttulata* 435
3 26°C sg: 1.022 46 cm 500L

*Lepidopsetta bilineata* 435
3 26°C sg: 1.022 60 cm 600L

*Eopsetta grigorjewi* 435
5, 7 26°C sg: 1.022 40 cm 400L

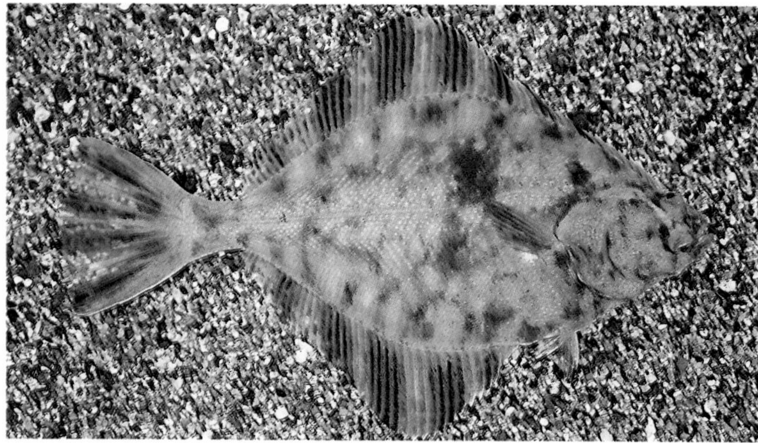

*Platichthys stellatus* 435
4-5 ◐ 24°C sg: 1.023 91 cm 1000L

*Platichthys flesus* 435
14 ◐ 16°C sg: 1.024 51 cm 500L

*Pleuronichthys cornutus* 435
7 ◐ ♥ 26°C sg: 1.022 30 cm 300L

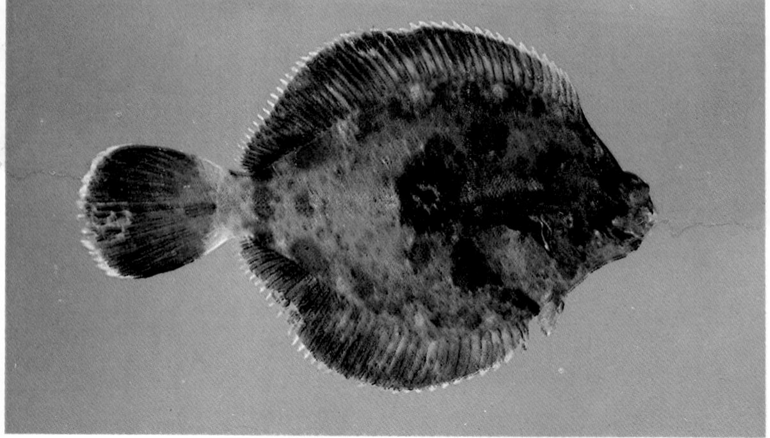

*Pleuronichthys ocellatus* 435
3 ◐ ♥ 26°C sg: 1.022 30 cm 300L

*Pleuronectes platessa* 435
14 ◐ ♥ 25°C sg: 1.022 71 cm 800L

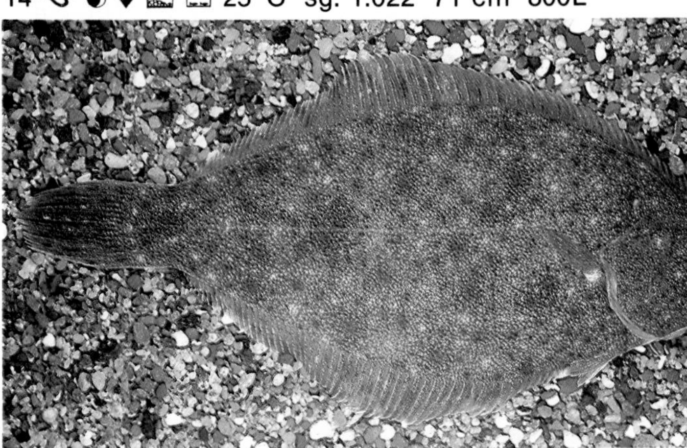

*Psettichthys melanostictus* 435
4 ◐ ♥ 22°C sg: 1.024 63 cm 600L

*Pleuronichthys coenosus* 435
4 ◐ ♥ 22°C sg: 1.024 36 cm 400L

*Pleuronichthys verticalis* 435
3 ◐ ♥ 26°C sg: 1.022 37 cm 400L

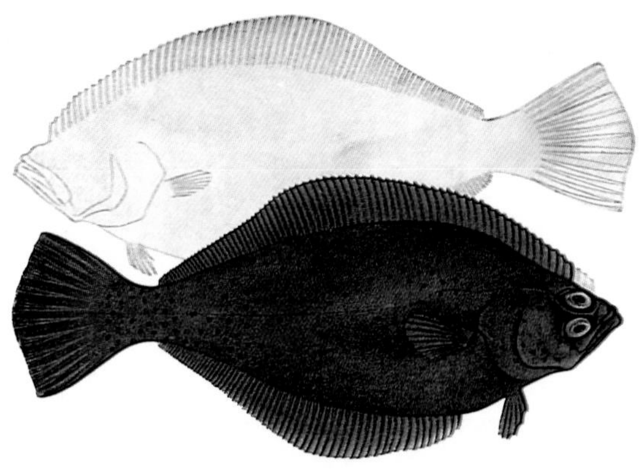

*Hippoglossoides robustus* 435
5 26°C sg: 1.022 30 cm 300L

*Samaris cristatus* 435
7-10 26°C sg: 1.022 17 cm 200L

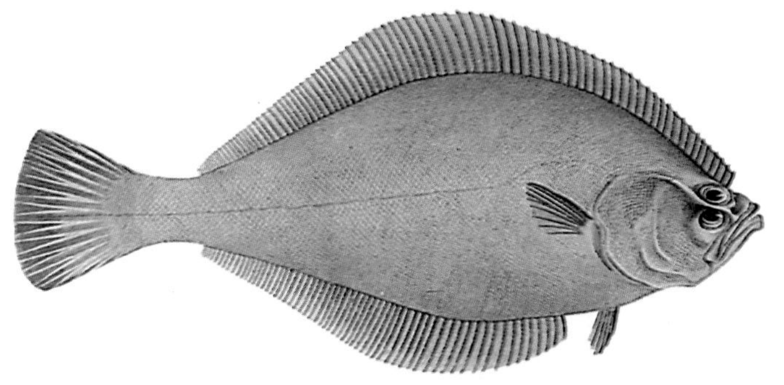

*Hippoglossoides dubius* 435
5 26°C sg: 1.022 45 cm 500L

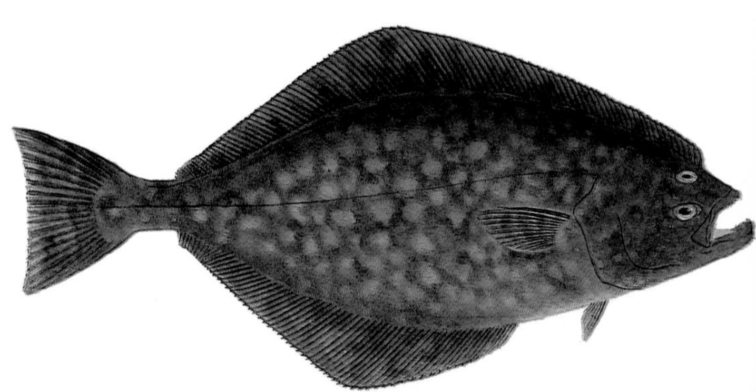

*Hippoglossus stenolepis* 435
5 26°C sg: 1.022 250 cm 3000L

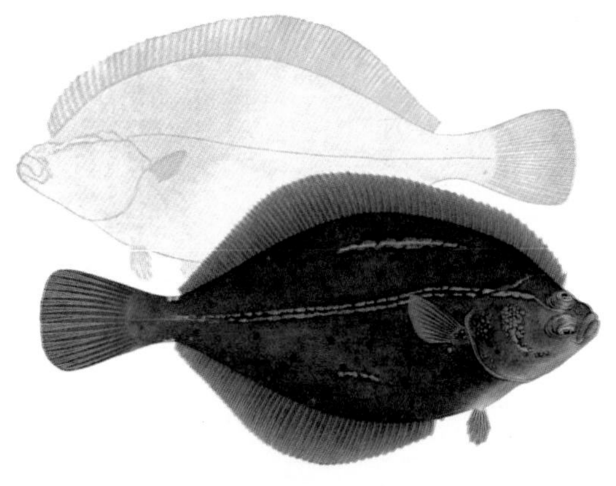

*Kareius bicoloratus* 435
5 26°C sg: 1.022 50 cm 500L

*Pleuronectes pallasii* 435
7 26°C sg: 1.022 25 cm 300L

*Limanda schrenki* 435
5 26°C sg: 1.022 50 cm 500L

*Verasper variegatus* 435
5 26°C sg: 1.022 60 cm 600L

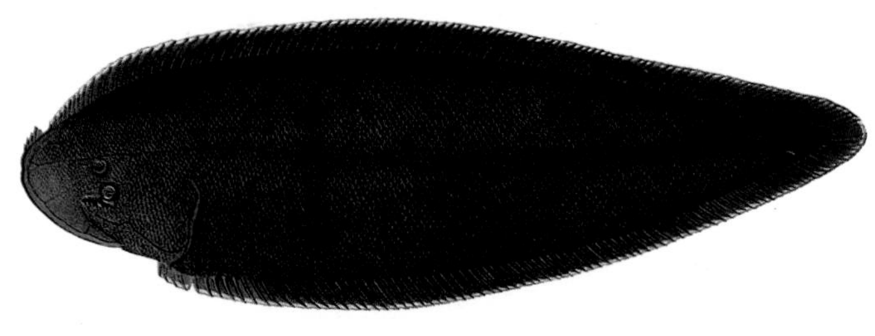

*Paraplagusia japonica* 436
7 ∿ ◐ ♥ ▭ ▭ 26°C sg: 1.022 35 cm 400L

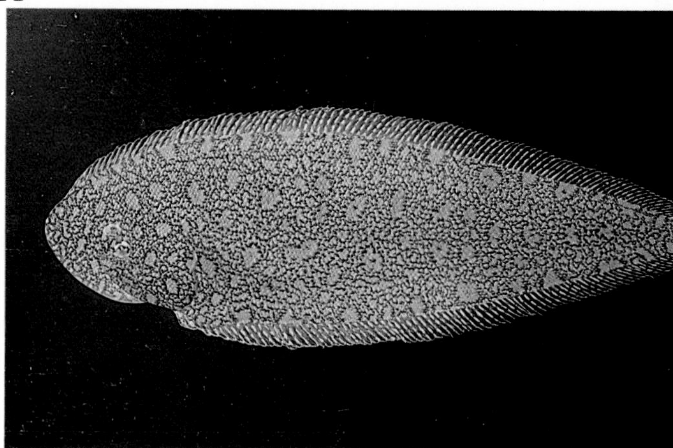

*Paraplagusia bilineata* 436
7-9 ∿ ◐ ♥ ▭ ▭ 26°C sg: 1.022 30 cm 300L

*Symphurus elongatus* 436
3 ∿ ◐ ♥ ▭ ▭ 26°C sg: 1.022 22.5 cm 300L

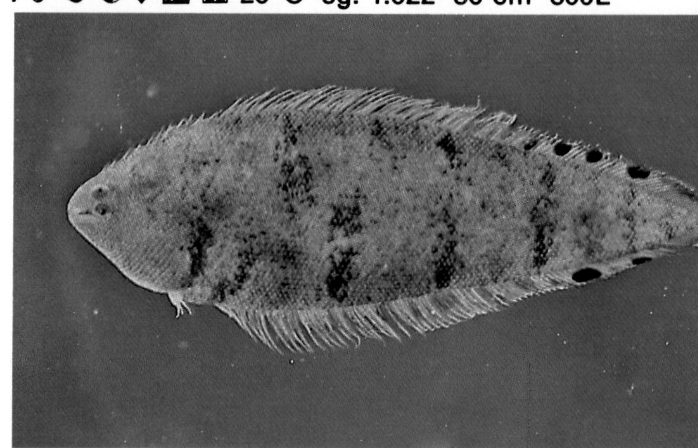

*Symphurus fasciolaris* 436
3 ∿ ◐ ♥ ▭ ▭ 26°C sg: 1.022 25 cm 300L

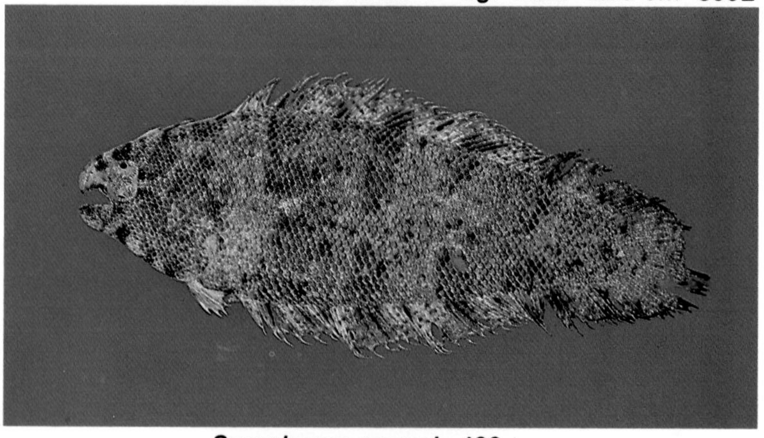

*Symphurus arawak* 436
2 ∿ ◐ ♥ ▭ ▭ 26°C sg: 1.022 51 cm 300L

*Symphurus arawak* 436
2 ∿ ◐ ♥ ▭ ▭ 26°C sg: 1.022 51 cm 500L

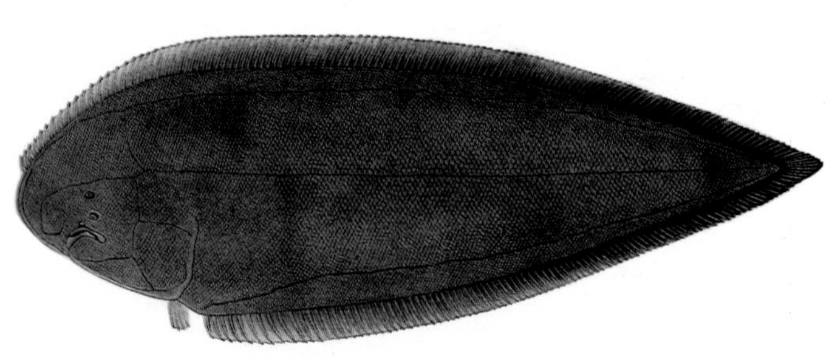

*Cynoglossus joyneri* 436
5, 7 ∿ ◐ ♥ ▭ ▭ 26°C sg: 1.022 35 cm 400L

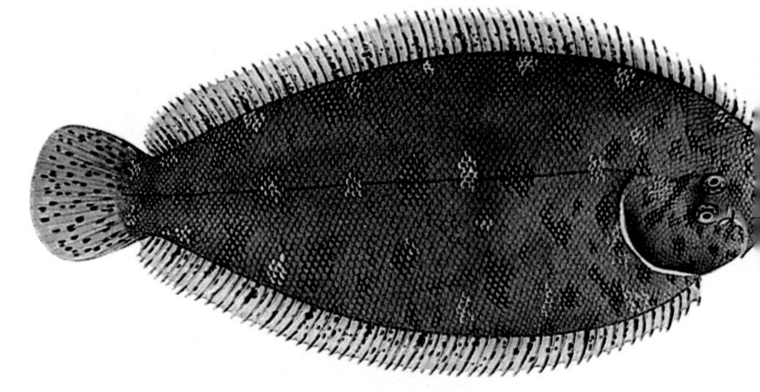

*Heteromycteris japonicus* 437
7 ∿ ◐ ♥ ▭ ▭ 26°C sg: 1.022 13.5 cm 150L

*Zebrias zebra* 437
7-8 ~ ◐ ♥ ▭ ▭ 26°C sg: 1.022 19 cm 200L

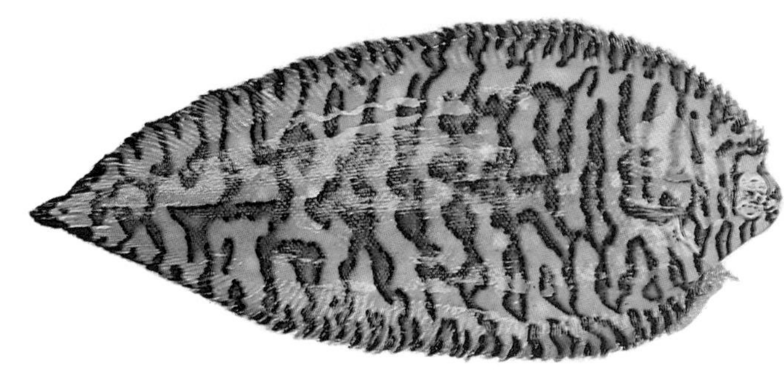

*Soleichthys heterorhinos* 437
6-9 ~ ◐ ♥ ▭ ▭ 26°C sg: 1.022 11 cm 100L

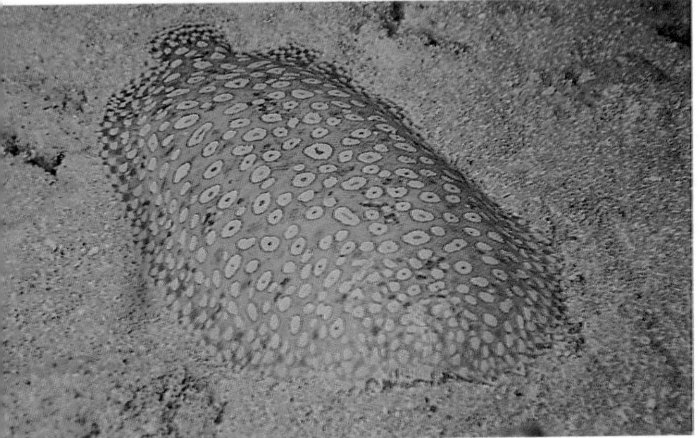

*Pardachirus pavoninus* 437
6-9 ~ ◐ ♥ ▭ ▭ 26°C sg: 1.022 25 cm 300L

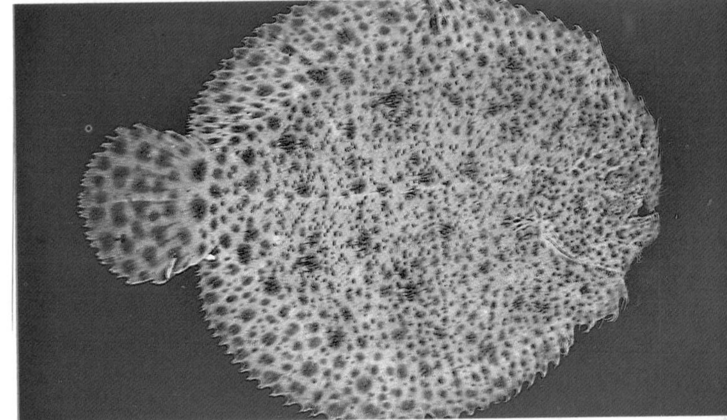

*Achirus lineatus* 437
2 ~ ◐ ♥ ▭ ▭ 26°C sg: 1.022 10 cm 100L

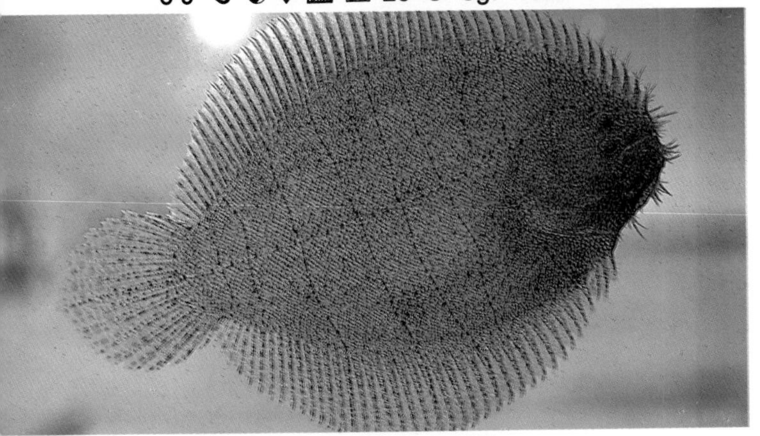

*Trinectes maculatus* 437
2 ~ ◐ ♥ ▭ ▭ 26°C sg: 1.022 20 cm 200L

*Trinectes maculatus* 437
2 ~ ◐ ♥ ▭ ▭ 26°C sg: 1.022 20 cm 200L

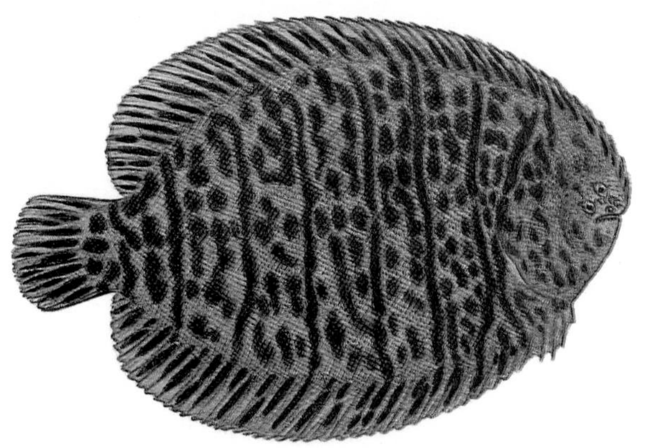

*Trinectes maculatus?* 437
2 ~ ◐ ♥ ▭ ▭ 26°C sg: 1.022 20 cm 200L

*Trinectes maculatus?* 437
2 ~ ◐ ♥ ▭ ▭ 26°C sg: 1.022 20 cm 200L

*#526*

*Pseudobalistes fuscus* 440
7-10 26°C sg: 1.022 55 cm 500L

*#526A*

*Ostracion meleagris meleagris* 441
7-9 ◐ ♥ 26°C sg: 1.022 15 cm 150L

*Anaplocapros lenticularis* 441
12 ◐ ♥ 24°C sg: 1.023 15 cm 150L

#526B

*Canthigaster amboinensis* 443
6-9 26°C sg: 1.022 15 cm 150L

*Diodon Hystrix* 444
Circumtrop. 26°C sg: 1.022 60 cm 600L

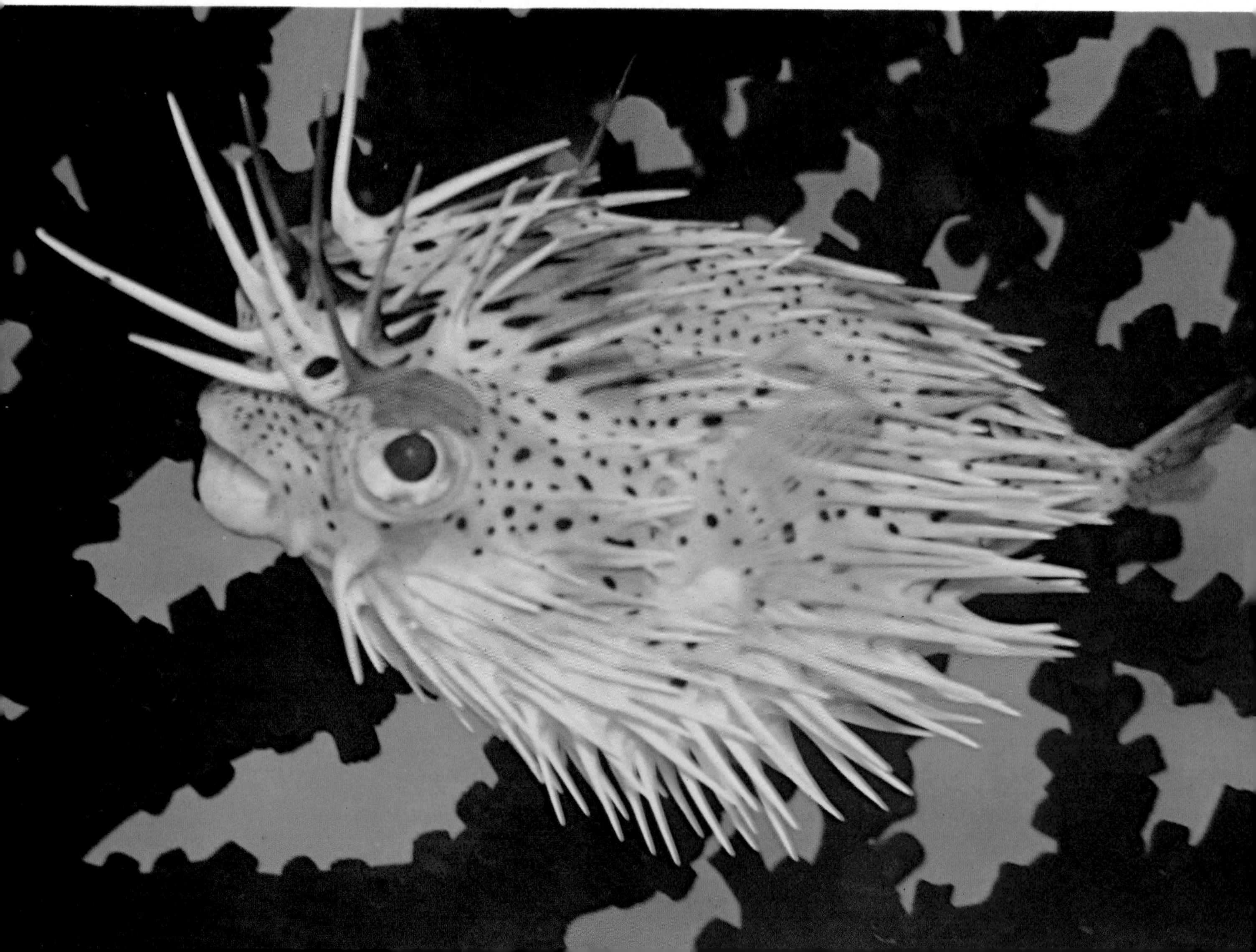

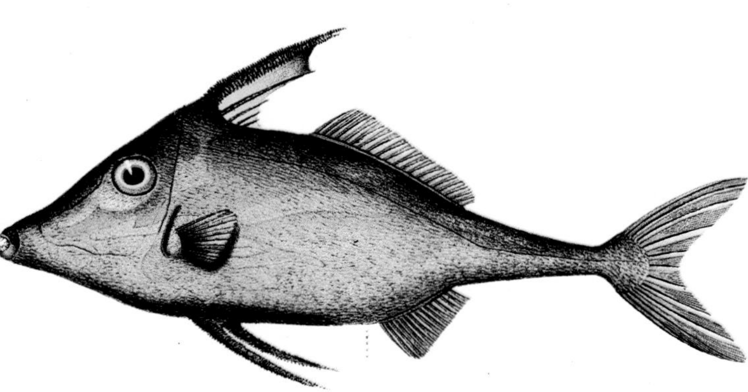

*Tripodichthys strigilifer* 439
7, 9 ~ ◐ ♥ 26°C sg: 1.022 20 cm 200L

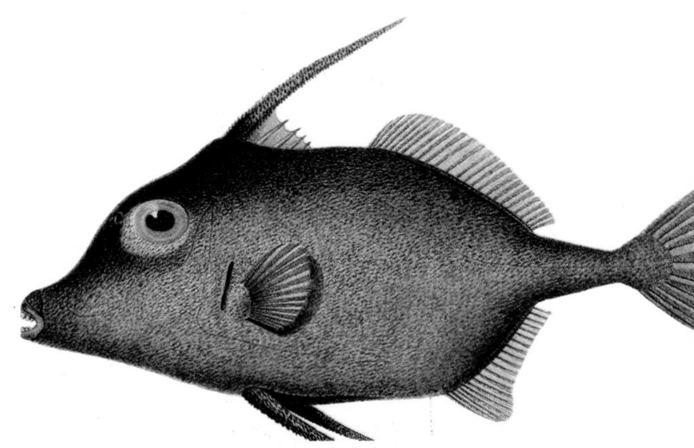

*Tripodichthys oxycephalus* 439
7, 9 ~ ◐ ♥ 26°C sg: 1.022 15 cm 150L

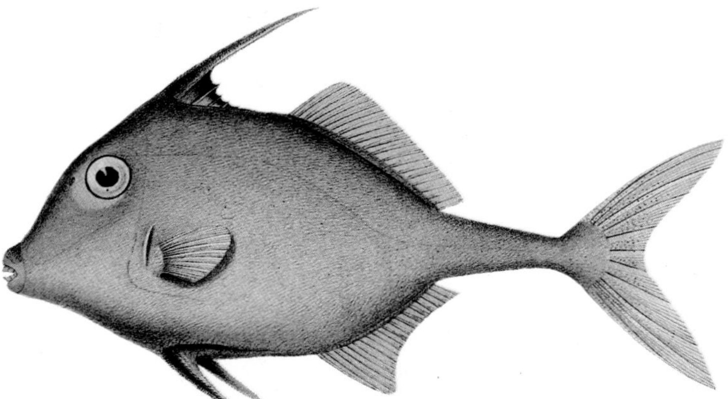

*Triacanthus nieuhofi* 439
7 ~ ◐ ♥ 26°C sg: 1.022 14 cm 150L

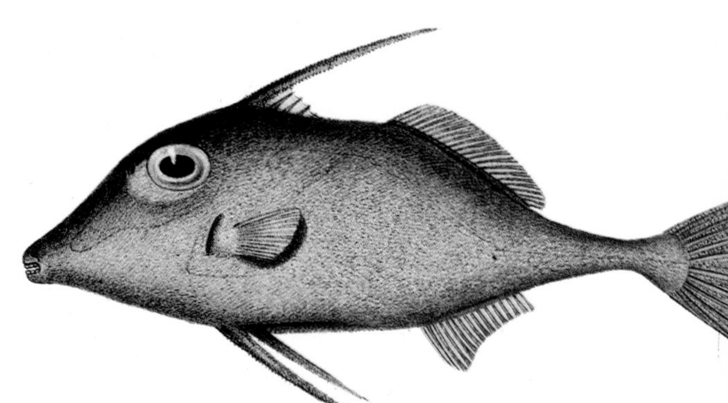

*Tripodichthys blochii* 439
7, 9 ~ ◐ ♥ 26°C sg: 1.024 15 cm 150L

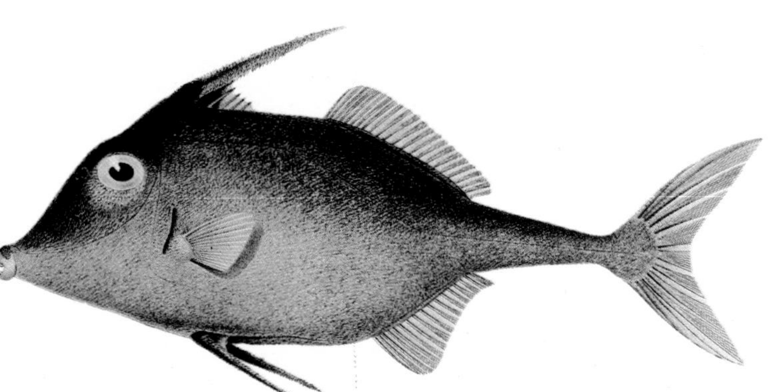

*Tripodichthys angustifrons* 439
7, 12 ~ ◐ ♥ 24°C sg: 1.024 18 cm 200L

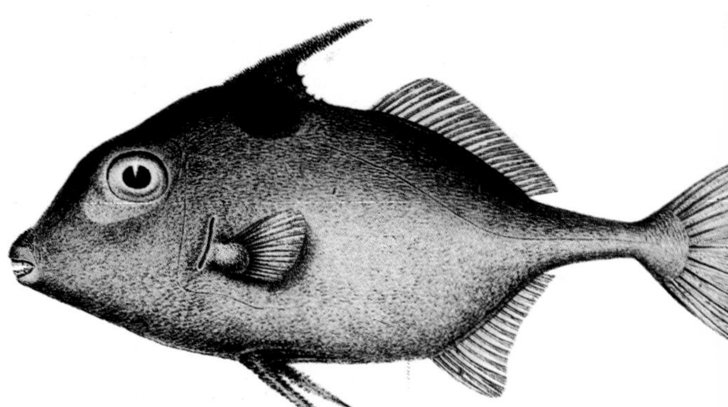

*Triacanthus biaculeatus* 439
7-9 ~ ◐ ♥ 26°C sg: 1.024 24 cm 250L

*Tripodichthys* sp. 439
?7 ~ ◐ ♥ 24°C sg: 1.024 15 cm 150L

*Trixiphichthys weberi?* 439
7 ~ ◐ ♥ 26°C sg: 1.022 16 cm 200L

*Johnsonina eriomma* 438
2∿ ◐ ♥ ▣ ☷ 26°C sg: 1.022 13 cm 150L

*Triacanthodes anomalus* 438
7∿ ◐ ♥ ▣ ☷ 26°C sg: 1.022 10 cm 100L

*Tripodichthys blochii* 439
7, 9∿ ◐ ♥ ▣ ☷ 26°C sg: 1.022 15 cm 150L

*Tripodichthys blochii* 439
7, 9∿ ◐ ♥ ▣ ⊔ 26°C sg: 1.022 15 cm 150L

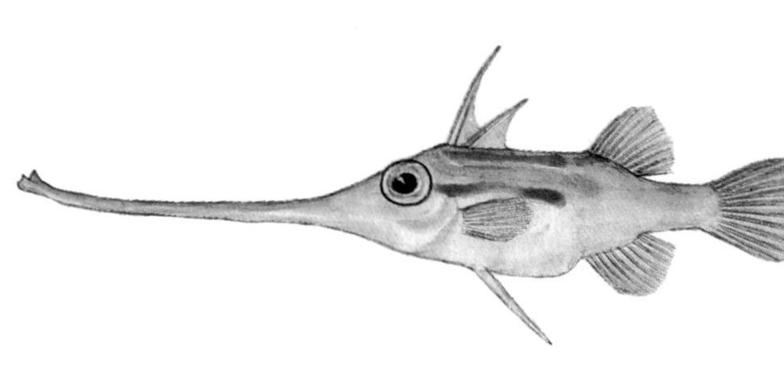

*Halimochirurgus alcocki* 438
7∿ ◐ ♥ ▣ ⊔ 26°C sg: 1.022 17 cm 200L

*Paratriacanthodes retrospinis* 438
7, 9∿ ◐ ♥ ▣ ☷ 26°C sg: 1.022 9 cm 100L

*Tripodichthys strigilifer* 439
7, 9∿ ◐ ♥ ▣ ☷ 26°C sg: 1.022 20 cm 200L

*Tripodichthys strigilifer* 439
7, 9∿ ◐ ♥ ▣ ⊔ 26°C sg: 1.022 20 cm 200L

*Balistoides conspicillum* 440
7-9 26°C sg: 1.022 50 cm 500L

*Pseudobalistes flavimarginatus* 440
6-10 26°C sg: 1.022 60 cm 600L

*Balistoides conspicillum* 440
7-9 26°C sg: 1.022 50 cm 500L

*Melichthys niger* 440
Circumtrop. 26°C sg: 1.022 35 cm 400L

*Melichthys niger* (var.) 440
Circumtrop. 26°C sg: 1.022 35 cm 400L

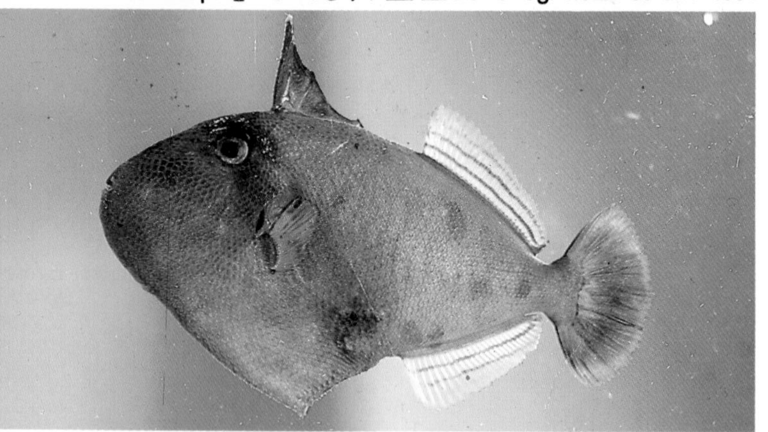

*Melichthys vidua* 440
6-10 26°C sg: 1.022 40 cm 400L

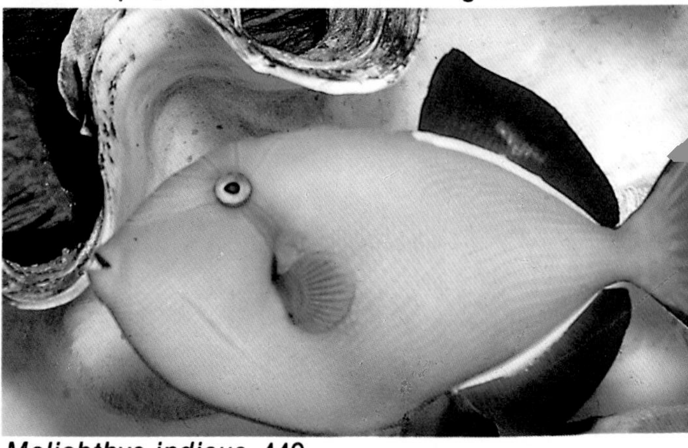

*Melichthys indicus* 440
9 26°C sg: 1.022 25 cm 300L

*Pseudobalistes flavimarginatus* 440
6-10 26°C sg: 1.022 60 cm 600L

*Pseudobalistes naufragium* 440
3 26°C sg: 1.022 40 cm 400L

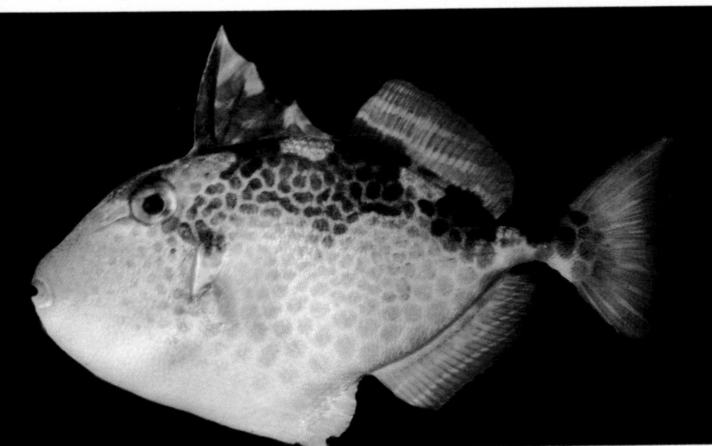

*Abalistes stellatus* 440
7-10 26°C sg: 1.022 60 cm 600L

*Balistoides conspicillum* 440
7-9 26°C sg: 1.022 50 cm 500L

*Melichthys indicus* 440
9 26°C sg: 1.022 25 cm 300L

*Xanthichthys auromarginatus* 440
6-9 26°C sg: 1.022 20 cm 200L

*Balistapus undulatus* 440
7-10 26°C sg: 1.022 30 cm 300L

*Melichthys vidua* 440
6-10 26°C sg: 1.022 40 cm 400L

*Melichthys indicus* 440
9 26°C sg: 1.022 25 cm 300L

*Xanthichthys auromarginatus* 440
6-9 26°C sg: 1.022 20 cm 200L

*Xanthichthys ringens* 440
2 26°C sg: 1.022 25 cm 300L

*Sufflamen* 440
7, 9 26°C sg: 1.022 25 cm 300L

*Sufflamen albicaudatus* 440
10 26°C sg: 1.022 30 cm 300L

*Sufflamen bursa* 440
7-9 26°C sg: 1.022 25 cm 300L

*Xanthichthys ringens* 440
2 26°C sg: 1.022 25 cm 300L

*Xanthichthys mento* 440
3, 6-7 26°C sg: 1.022 30 cm 300L

*Sufflamen chrysopterus* (juv.) 440
7-9 26°C sg: 1.022 30 cm 300L

*Sufflamen fraenatus* 440
7-9 26°C sg: 1.022 40 cm 400L

*Canthidermis maculatus* 440
Circumtemp. 26°C sg: 1.022 50 cm 500L

*Odonus niger* 440
7-10 26°C sg: 1.022 50 cm 500L

*Balistes polylepis* 440
3 26°C sg: 1.022 76 cm 800L

*Balistes forcipitus* 440
13 26°C sg: 1.022 44 cm 500L

*Canthidermis maculatus* (juv.) 440
Circumtrop. 26°C sg: 1.022 50 cm 500L

*Canthidermis sufflamen* 440
2 26°C sg: 1.022 25 cm 300L

*Balistes capriscus* 440
2, 13 26°C sg: 1.022 30 cm 300L

*Balistes vetula* 440
2 26°C sg: 1.022 60 cm 600L

*Pseudobalistes fuscus* 440
7-10 26°C sg: 1.022 55 cm 500L

*Balistoides viridescens* 440
7-10 26°C sg: 1.022 70 cm 700L

*Rhinecanthus assasi* 440
7-10 26°C sg: 1.022 30 cm 300L

*Pseudobalistes fuscus* (juv.) 440
7-10 26°C sg: 1.022 55 cm 50

*Pseudobalistes fuscus* 440
7-10 26°C sg: 1.022 55 cm 50

*Rhinecanthus aculeatus* 440
7-9 26°C sg: 1.022 30 cm 300

*Rhinecanthus rectangulus* 440
7-9 26°C sg: 1.022 30 cm 300

*Sufflamen bursa* 440
7-9 26°C sg: 1.022 25 cm 300L

*Sufflamen fraenatus* 440
7-9 26°C sg: 1.022 40 cm 400L

*Amanses scopas* 440
7-10 26°C sg: 1.022 20 cm 200L

*Cantherhines dumerili* 440
7-9 26°C sg: 1.022 35 cm 400L

*Sufflamen chrysopterus* 440
7-9 26°C sg: 1.022 30 cm 300L

*Odonus niger* 440
7-10 26°C sg: 1.022 50 cm 500L

*Cantherhines pardalis* 440
7-10 26°C sg: 1.022 27 cm 300L

*Cantherhines dumerili* 440
7-9 26°C sg: 1.022 35 cm 400L

*Rhinecanthus lunula* 440
6-8 26°C sg: 1.022 19.4 cm 200L

*Monacanthus tuckeri* 440
2 26°C sg: 1.022 9 cm 100L

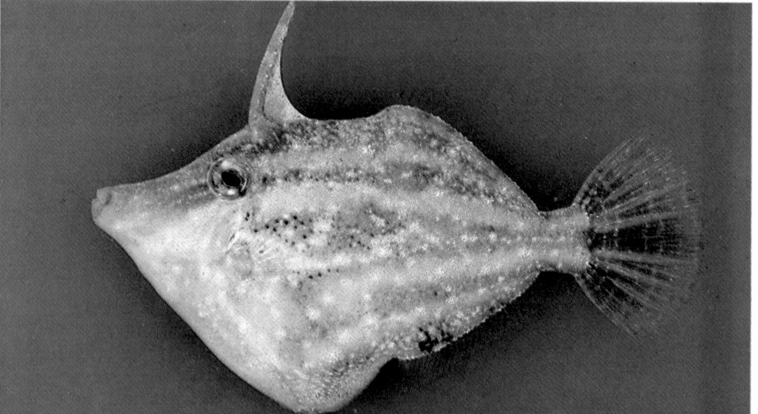

*Monacanthus ciliatus* 440
2, 13 26°C sg: 1.022 20 cm 200L

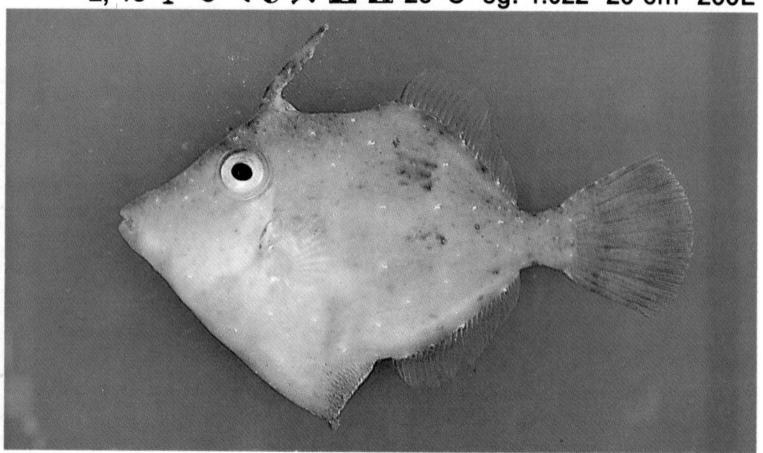

*Monacanthus hispidus* 440
2, 13 26°C sg: 1.022 25 cm 300L

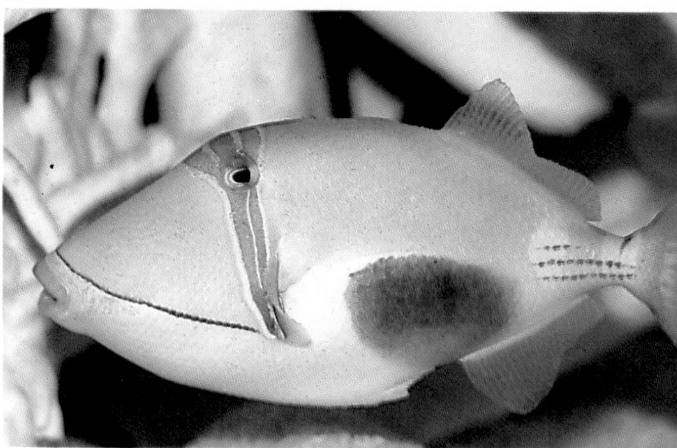

*Rhinecanthus verrucosus* 440
7 26°C sg: 1.022 30 cm 300L

*Monacanthus tuckeri* 440
2 26°C sg: 1.022 9 cm 100L

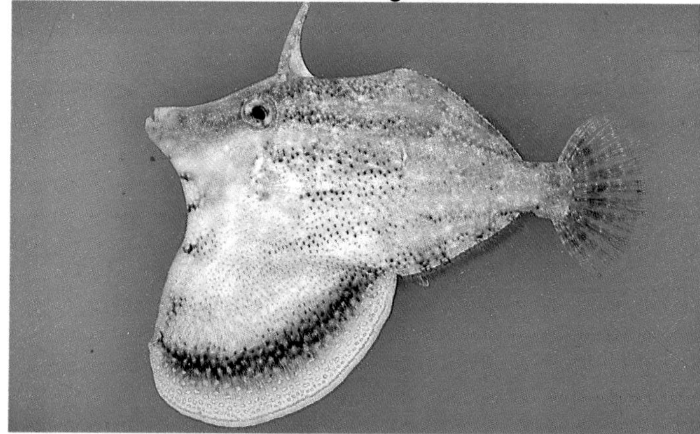

*Monacanthus ciliatus* 440
2, 13 26°C sg: 1.022 20 cm 200L

*Monacanthus hispidus* 440
2, 13 26°C sg: 1.022 25 cm 300L

*Monacanthus chinensis* 440
7, 8 26°C sg: 1.022 25 cm 300L

*Monacanthus filicauda* 440
7-8 26°C sg: 1.022 25 cm 250L

*Cantherhines sandwichensis* 440
6 26°C sg: 1.022 13 cm 150L

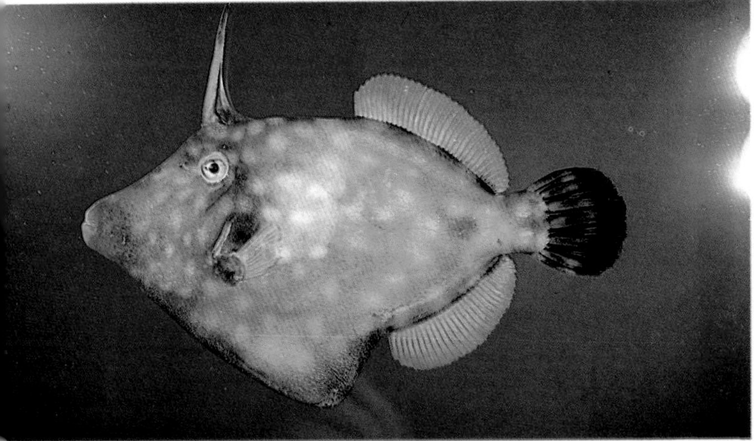

*Cantherhines macroceros* 440
1-2 24°C sg: 1.023 46 cm 500L

*Monacanthus chinensis* 440
7-8 26°C sg: 1.022 25 cm 300L

*Cantherhines pullus* 440
1-2 24°C sg: 1.023 20 cm 200L

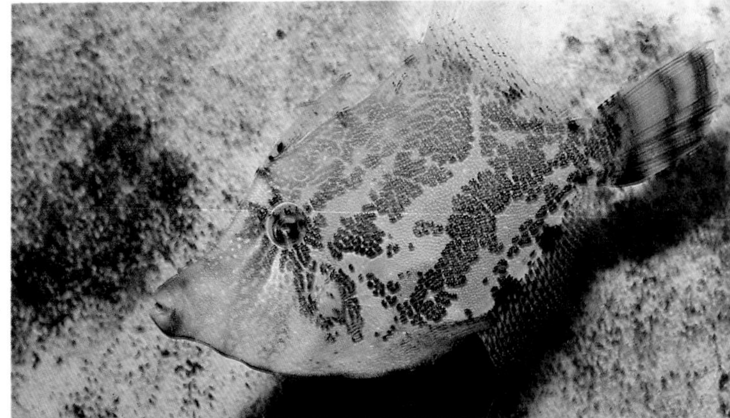

*Monacanthus chinensis* 440
7-8 26°C sg: 1.022 25 cm 300L

*Cantherhines macroceros* 440
1-2 24°C sg: 1.023 46 cm 500L

*Meuschenia flavolineata* 440
12 23°C sg: 1.024 20 cm 200L

*Meuschenia hippocrepis* 440
12 24°C sg: 1.023 50 cm 500L

*Pervagor melanocephalus* 440
7-10 26°C sg: 1.022 16 cm 200L

*Chaetodermis penicilligerus* 440
5, 7-9 26°C sg: 1.022 18 cm 200L

*Meuschenia galii* 440
12 24°C sg: 1.022 23 cm 300L

*Oxymonacanthus longirostris* 440
6-10 26°C sg: 1.022 7 cm 80L

*Scobinichthys granulatus* 440
8, 12 24°C sg: 1.022 25 cm 300L

*Aluterus scriptus* 440
Circumtrop. 26°C sg: 1.022 100 cm 1000L

*Oxymonacanthus longirostris* 440
7-9 ~ ◐ ♥ ▨ ▤ 26°C sg: 1.022 10 cm 100L

*Stephanolepis cirrhifer* 440
5, 7-9 ◐ 26°C sg: 1.022 40 cm 400L

*Cantherhines howensis* 440
8 ◐ ♥ 26°C sg: 1.022 20 cm 200L

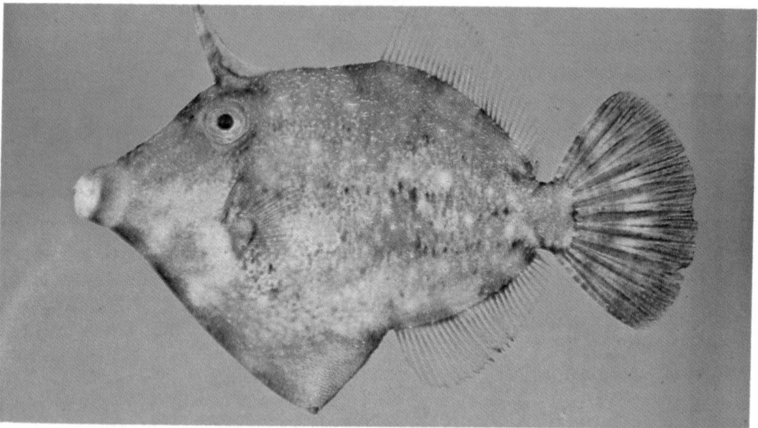

*Cantherhines verrucundus* 440
6 ◐ ♥ 26°C sg: 1.022 12.5 cm 150L

*Cantherhines fronticinctus* 440
7-9 ◐ ♥ 26°C sg: 1.022 14 cm 150L

? *Paramonacanthus japonicus* 440
5, 7 ◐ ♥ 25°C sg: 1.022 16 cm 200L

*Meuschenia flavolineata* 440
12 ◐ ♥ 24°C sg: 1.023 20 cm 200L

*Meuschenia hippocrepis* 440
12 ◐ ♥ 24°C sg: 1.023 50 cm 500L

*Meuschenia venusta* 440
12 ◐ ♥ 24°C sg: 1.023 18 cm 200L

*Pervagor melanocephalus* 440
7-9 26°C sg: 1.022 16 cm 200L

*Pervagor melanocephalus* 440
7-9 26°C sg: 1.022 16 cm 200L

*Pervagor aspricaudus* 440
6 26°C sg: 1.022 15 cm 150L

*Pervagor spilosoma* 440
6 26°C sg: 1.022 13 cm 150L

*Rudarius ercodes* 440
5, 7 26°C sg: 1.022 10 cm 100L

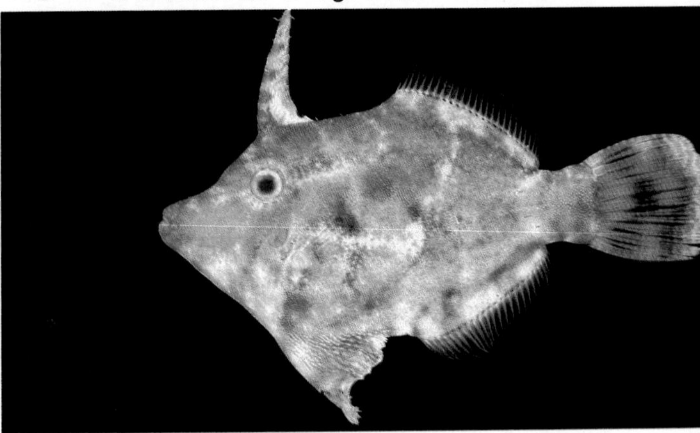

*Acreichthys tomentosus* 440
6-7 26°C sg: 1.022 9 cm 100L

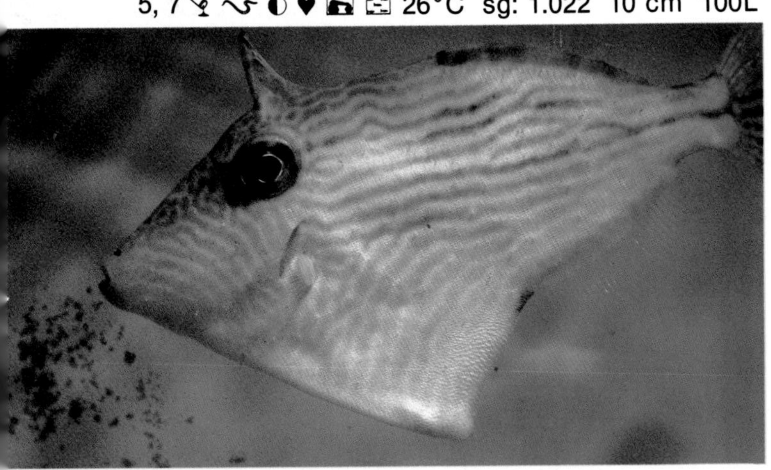

*Pseudomonacanthus garretti* 440
6 26°C sg: 1.022 9.4 cm 100L

*Rudarius minutus* 440 ♀
8 26°C sg: 1.022 5 cm 50L

*Paramonacanthus oblongus* 440
5, 7, 9 26°C sg: 1.022 16 cm 200L

***Pencipelta vittiger*** **440**
**12 24°C sg: 1.023 10 cm 100L**

*Paramonacanthus barnardi* 440
9 26°C sg: 1.022 9 cm 100L

**? *Paramonacanthus* sp. 440**
**7-8 26°C sg: 1.022 20 cm 200L**

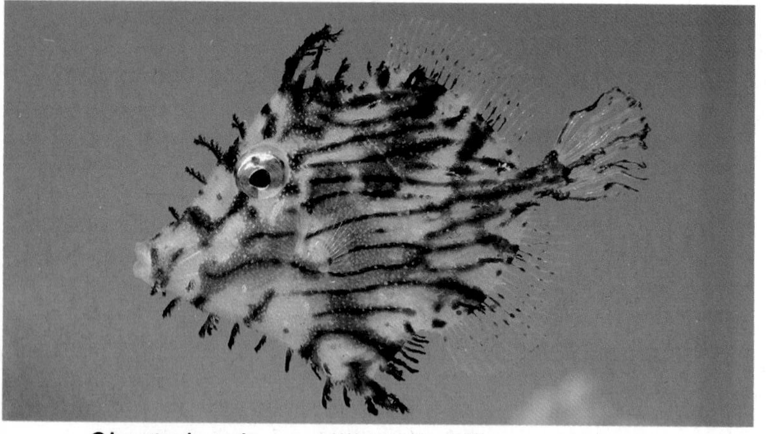

*Chaetodermis pencilligerus* 440
5, 7-9 26°C sg: 1.022 25 cm 250L

*Scobinichthys granulatus* 440
8, 12 24°C sg: 1.022 25 cm 300L

*Eubalichthys mosaicus* 440
12 24°C sg: 1.023 30 cm 300L

*Brachaluteres jacksonianus* 440
12 24°C sg: 1.022 10 cm 100L

*Aluterus schoepfi* 440
1-2 24°C sg: 1.023 60 cm 600L

*Thamnaconus modestus* 440
5, 7-9 24°C sg: 1.023 30 cm 300L

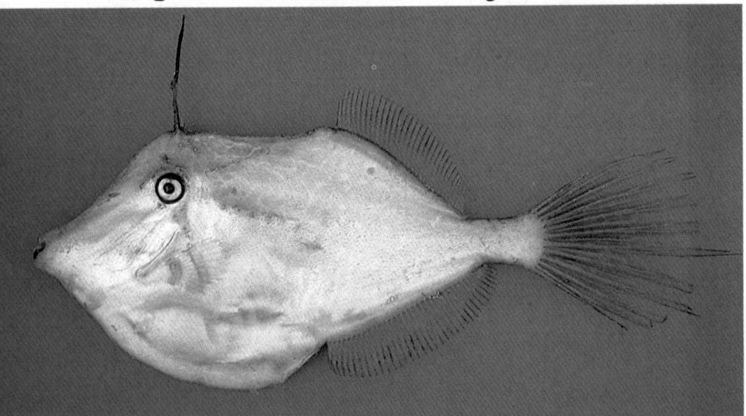

*Aluterus monoceros* 440
Circumtrop. 26°C sg: 1.022 75 cm 800L

*Aluterus monoceros* 440
Circumtrop. 26°C sg: 1.022 75 cm 800L

?*Aluterus* sp. 440
8 26°C sg: 1.022 40 cm 400L

*Pseudalutarius nasicornis* 440
7-9 26°C sg: 1.022 18 cm 200L

*Acanthaluterus spilomelanura* 440
12 24°C sg: 1.022 8 cm 80L

*Amanses scopas* 440
7-10 26°C sg: 1.022 30 cm 300L

*Thamnaconus modestus* 440
5, 7-9 ◐ ♥ 24°C sg: 1.023 30 cm 300L

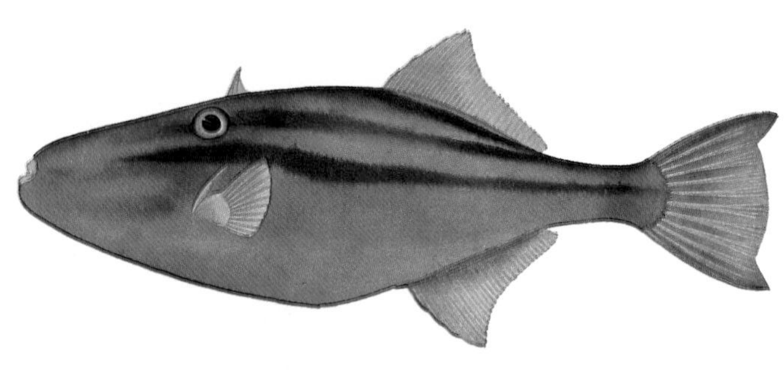

*Nelusetta ayraudi* 440
7, 12 ◐ ♥ 26°C sg: 1.022 50 cm 500L

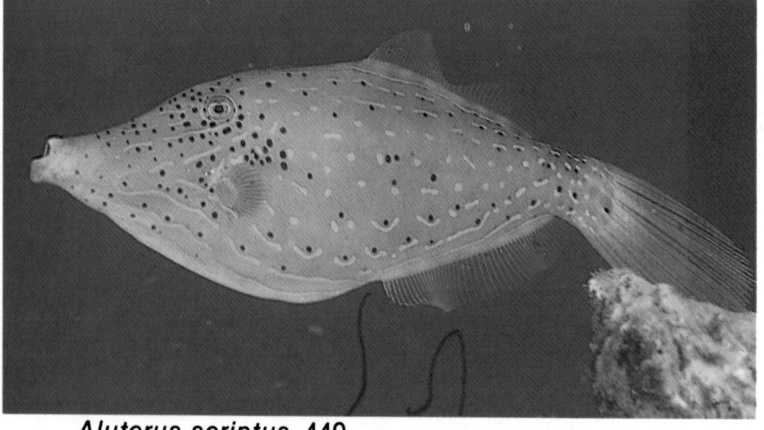

*Aluterus scriptus* 440
Circumtrop. ◐ ♥ 26°C sg: 1.022 100 cm 1000L

*Paraluterus prionurus* 440
7-9 ◐ ♥ 26°C sg: 1.022 9.5 cm 100L

*Thamnaconus australis* 440
12 ◐ ♥ 24°C sg: 1.022 27.5 cm 300L

*Parika scaber* 440
11 ◐ ♥ 22°C sg: 1.024 20 cm 200L

*Paraluterus prionurus* (juv.) 440
7-9 ◐ ♥ 26°C sg: 1.024 9.5 cm 100L

*Paraluterus prionurus* 440
7-9 ◐ ♥ 26°C sg: 1.024 9.5 cm 100L

*Aracana aurita* 441
12 ◐ ♥ 24°C sg: 1.023 18 cm 200L

*Anoplocapros lenticularis* 441
12 ◐ ♥ 24°C sg: 1.023 15 cm 150L

*Lactoria cornuta* 441
8, 12 ◐ ♥ 25°C sg: 1.023 50 cm 500L

*Anaplocapros lenticularis* 441
12 ◐ ♥ 24°C sg: 1.023 15 cm 150L

*Ostracion cubicus* 441
7-10 ◐ ♥ 26°C sg: 1.022 45 cm 500L

*Ostracion meleagris meleagris* 441 ♂
7-9 ◐ ♥ 26°C sg: 1.022 14 cm 150L

*Ostracion trachys* 441
7, 9 ◐ ♥ 26°C sg: 1.022 15 cm 150L

*Lactoria fornasini* 441
5 ◐ ♥ 23°C sg: 1.024 40 cm 400L

*Ostracion cubicus* 441
7-10 ◐ ♥ 26°C sg: 1.022 45 cm 500L

*Ostracion meleagris meleagris* 441 ♀
7-9 ◐ ♥ 26°C sg: 1.022 15 cm 150L

*Tetrosomus gibbosus* 441
7-10 ◐ ♥ 26°C sg: 1.022 30 cm 300L

*Lactoria diaphanus* 441
6-9 ◐ ♥ 26°C sg: 1.022 25 cm 300L

*Kentrocapros aculeatus* 441
5, 7 ◐ ♥ 26°C sg: 1.022 13 cm 150L

*Ostracion immaculatus* 441
6-10 ◐ ♥ 26°C sg: 1.022 45 cm 500L

*Ostracion cubicus?* 441
7-10 ◐ ♥ 26°C sg: 1.022 45 cm 500L

*Strophiurichthys robustus* 441
12 ◐ ♥ 24°C sg: 1.023 25 cm 300L

*Lactoria cornuta* 441
8, 12 ◐ ♥ 25°C sg: 1.023 50 cm 500L

*Ostracion cubicus* 441
7-10 ◐ ♥ 26°C sg: 1.022 45 cm 500L

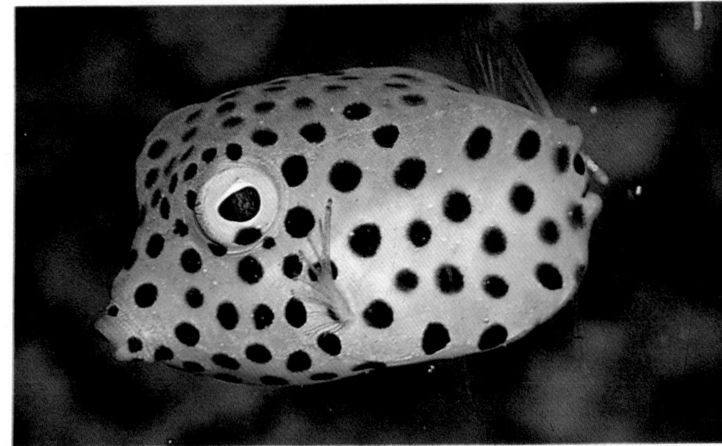

(juv.)
*Ostracion cubicus* 441
7-10 ◐ ♥ 26°C sg: 1.022 45 cm 500L

*Ostracion solorensis* (juv.) 441
7 26°C sg: 1.022 15 cm 200L

*Ostracion solorensis* 441 ♂
7 26°C sg: 1.022 15 cm 200L

*Ostracion whitleyi* 441 ♀
6 26°C sg: 1.022 13 cm 150L

*Ostracion whitleyi* 441 ♂
6 26°C sg: 1.022 13 cm 150L

*Ostracion meleagris camurum* 441 ♀
6 26°C sg: 1.022 14 cm 150L

*Ostracion meleagris camurum* 441 ♂
6 26°C sg: 1.022 14 cm 150L

*Ostracion cyanurus* 441
9-10 26°C sg: 1.022 15 cm 150L

*Ostracion cyanurus* 441
9-10 26°C sg: 1.022 15 cm 150L

*Lactophrys quadricornis* 441
2 ♀ ∿ ◐ ♥ ▧ ⊡ 26°C sg: 1.022 43 cm 500L

*Lactophrys quadricornis* 441
2 ♀ ∿ ◐ ♥ ▧ ⊡ 26°C sg: 1.022 43 cm 500L

*Lactophrys polygonia* 441
2 ♀ ∿ ◐ ♥ ▧ ⊡ 26°C sg: 1.022 48 cm 500L

*Lactophrys polygonia* 441
2 ♀ ∿ ◐ ♥ ▧ ⊡ 26°C sg: 1.022 48 cm 500L

*Lactophrys bicaudalis* (juv.) 441
2 ♀ ∿ ◐ ♥ ▧ ⊡ 26°C sg: 1.022 43 cm 500L

*Lactophrys bicaudalis* 441
2 ♀ ∿ ◐ ♥ ▧ ⊡ 26°C sg: 1.022 43 cm 500L

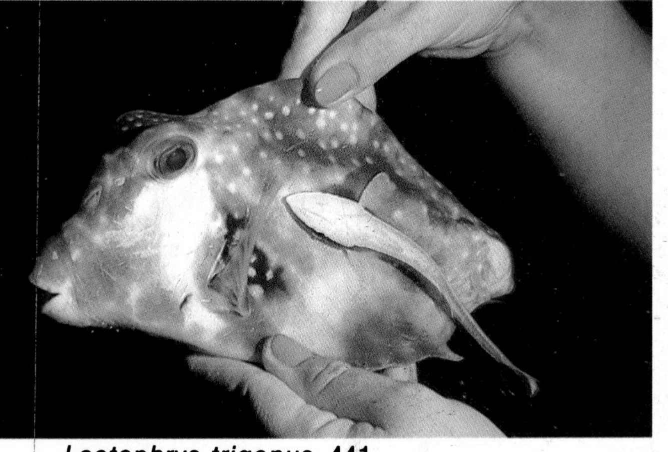

*Lactophrys trigonus* 441
2 ♀ ∿ ◐ ♥ ▧ ⊡ 26°C sg: 1.022 45 cm 500L

*Lactophrys triqueter* 441
2 ♀ ∿ ◐ ♥ ▧ ⊡ 26°C sg: 1.022 28 cm 300L

#549

*Ostracion cubicus* 441

*Ostracion cubicus* 441

*Ostracion cubicus* 441

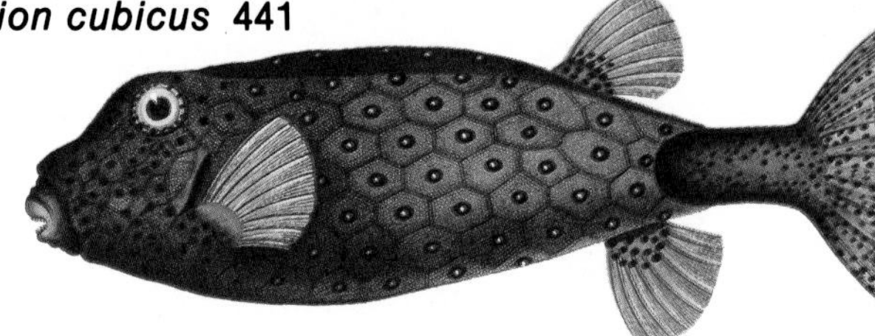

*Ostracion cubicus* 441

*Ostracion cubicus* 441

*Ostracion meleagris* 441

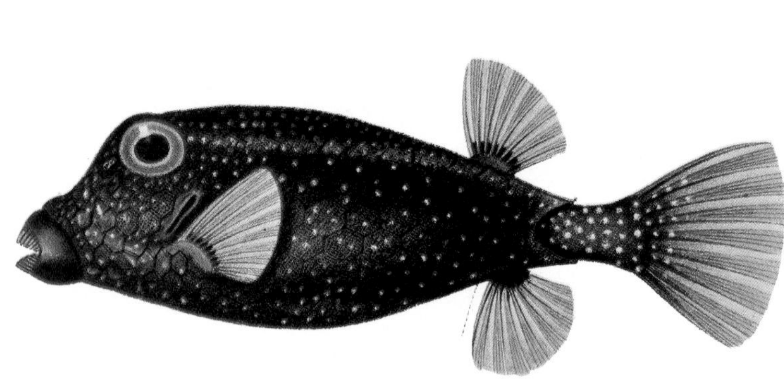

*Ostracion meleagris* 441

*Ostracion cubicus* 441

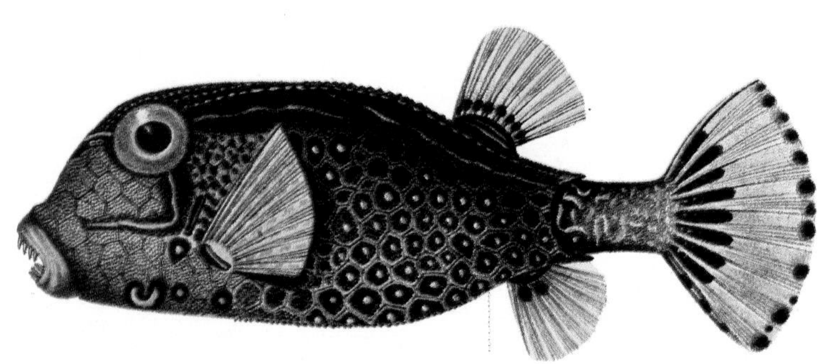

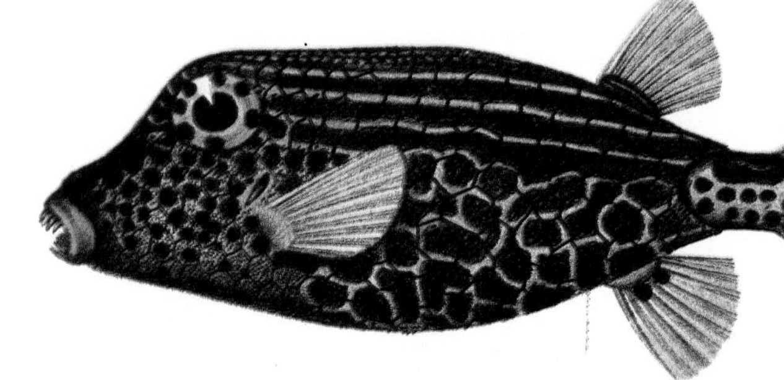

*Ostracion solorensis* 441

*Ostracion solorensis* 441

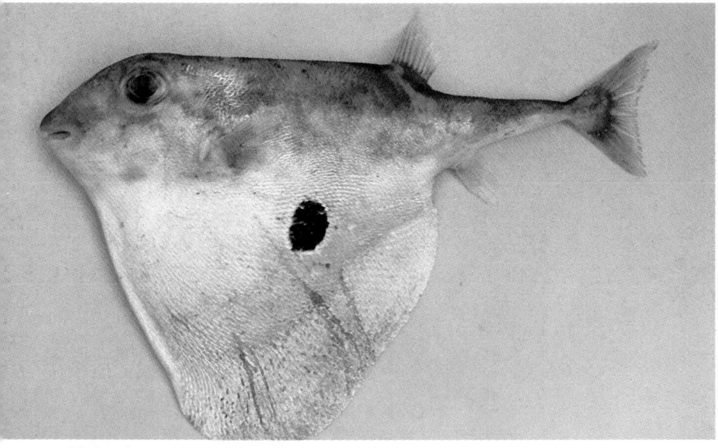

*Triodon macropterus* 442
5, 7, 9 26°C sg: 1.022 50 cm 500L

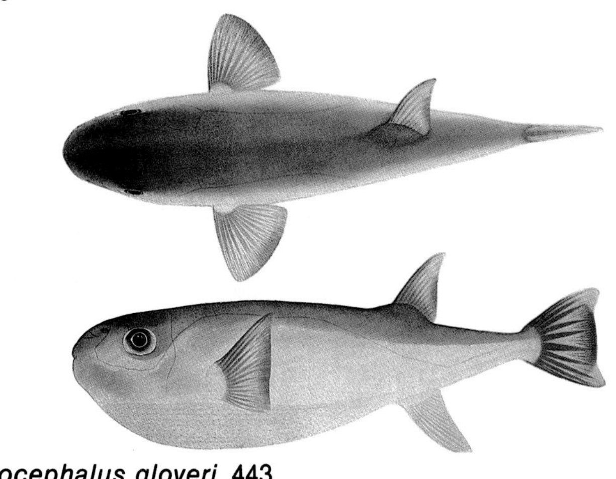

*Lagocephalus gloveri* 443
7-10 26°C sg: 1.022 40 cm 400L

*Amblyrhynchotes honckenii* 443
5, 7, 9 26°C sg: 1.022 30 cm 300L

*Amblyrhynchotes* sp. 443
7 26°C sg: 1.022 25 cm 300L

*Torquigener pleurogramma* 443
12 24°C sg: 1.022 15 cm 200L

*Amblyrhynchotes hypselogenion* 443
6-10 26°C sg: 1.022 18 cm 200L

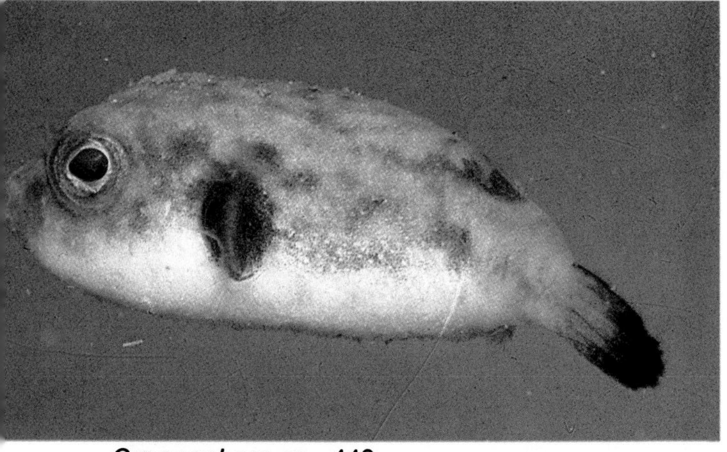

*Omegophora* sp. 443
12 24°C sg: 1.022 15 cm 200L

*Omegophora armilla* 443
12 26°C sg: 1.022 14 cm 150L

*Arothron hispidus* 443
7-10 26°C sg: 1.022 50 cm 500L

*Arothron meleagris* 443
3, 6-9 26°C sg: 1.022 15 cm 200L

*Arothron meleagris* 443
3, 6-9 26°C sg: 1.022 15 cm 200L

*Arothron meleagris* (yellow phase) 443
3, 6-9 26°C sg: 1.022 15 cm 200L

*Arothron meleagris* (black phase) 443
3, 6-9 26°C sg: 1.022 15 cm 200L

*Arothron nigropunctatus* (gray) 443
7-9 26°C sg: 1.022 40 cm 400L

*Arothron nigropunctatus* (½ yellow) 443
7-9 26°C sg: 1.022 40 cm 400L

*Arothron hispidus* 443
7-10 26°C sg: 1.022 50 cm 500L

*Arothron hispidus* (var) 443
7-10 26°C sg: 1.022 50 cm 500L

*Arothron hispidus* 443
7-10 26°C sg: 1.022 50 cm 500L

*Arothron nigropunctatus* 443
7-9 26°C sg: 1.022 40 cm 400L

*Arothron stellatus* 443
7-10 26°C sg: 1.022 100 cm 1000L

*Omegophora cyanopunctata* 443
12 24°C sg: 1.022 12 cm 150L

*Arothron meleagris* 443
3, 6-9 26°C sg: 1.022 15 cm 200L

***Arothron nigropunctatus*** **443**
**7-9** 26°C sg: 1.022 40 cm 400L

*Arothron inconditus* 443
9 26°C sg: 1.022 40 cm 400L

*Amblyrhinchotes hypselogenion* 443
6-10 26°C sg: 1.022 18 cm 200L

*Arothron diadematus* 443
6-10 26°C sg: 1.022 30 cm 300L

*Arothron stellatus* 443
6-10 26°C sg: 1.022 90 cm 1000L

*Arothron stellatus* (adult) 443
6-10 26°C sg: 1.022 90 cm 1000L

*Canthigaster leopardus* 443
7 26°C sg: 1.022 5 cm 50L

*Arothron mappa* 443
7, 9 26°C sg: 1.022 70 cm 700L

*Arothron stellatus* 443
6-10 26°C sg: 1.022 90 cm 1000L

*Arothron reticularis* 443
7, 9 26°C sg: 1.022 35 cm 400L

*Canthigaster tyleri* 443
7, 9 26°C sg: 1.022 7 cm 80L

*Arothron manilensis* 443
6-9 26°C sg: 1.022 50 cm 500L

*Takifugu rubripes* 443
5, 7 26°C sg: 1.022 80 cm 800L

*Takifugu pardalis* 443
5, 7 26°C sg: 1.022 35 cm 400L

*Takifugu niphobles* 443
5 24°C sg: 1.023 20 cm 200L

*Arothron manilensis* 443
6-9 26°C sg: 1.022 50 cm 500L

*Arothron immaculatus* 443
7-10 26°C sg: 1.022 30 cm 300L

*Takifugu pardalis* 443
5, 7 26°C sg: 1.022 35 cm 400L

*Takifugu stictonotus* 443
5, 7 26°C sg: 1.022 35 cm 350L

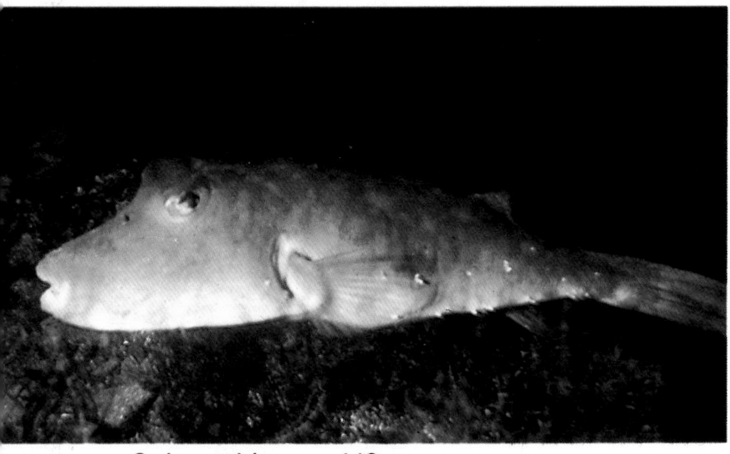

*Sphoeroides* sp. 443
3 26°C sg: 1.022 20 cm 200L

*Sphoeroides marmoratus* 443
13 26°C sg: 1.022 30 cm 300L

*Sphoeroides spengleri* 443
1, 2 24°C sg: 1.022 20 cm 200L

*Sphoeroides hamiltoni* 443
8 26°C sg: 1.018 12.5 cm 150L

*Sphoeroides annulatus* 443
3 26°C sg: 1.022 10 cm 100L

*Sphoeroides erythrotaenia* 443
7 26°C sg: 1.022 9 cm 100L

? *Chelonodon laticeps* 443
9 26°C sg: 1.022 20 cm 200L

?*Takifugu oblongus* 443
7 26°C sg: 1.022 20 cm 200L

*Canthigaster ambionensis* 443
6-9 26°C sg: 1.022 15 cm 150L

*Canthigaster bennetti* 443
7, 9 26°C sg: 1.022 10 cm 100L

*Canthigaster epilamprus* 443
6-8 26°C sg: 1.022 7 cm 80L

*Canthigaster leopardus* 443
7 26°C sg: 1.022 5 cm 50L

*Canthigaster amboinensis* 443
6-9 26°C sg: 1.022 15 cm 150L

*Canthigaster coronata* 443
6-10 26°C sg: 1.022 13 cm 150L

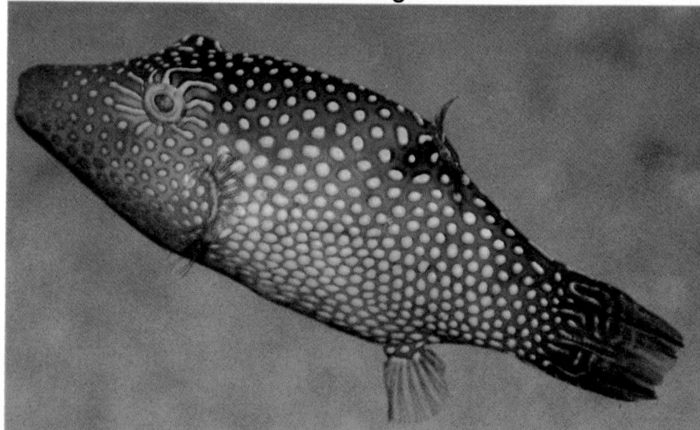

*Canthigaster janthinoptera* 443
7, 9 26°C sg: 1.022 9 cm 100L

*Canthigaster smithae* 443
7, 9 26°C sg: 1.022 13 cm 150L

*Canthigaster punctatissimus* 443
3 26°C sg: 1.022 7.5 cm 100L

*Canthigaster compressus* 443
7 26°C sg: 1.022 10 cm 100L

*Canthigaster bennetti* 443
7, 9 26°C sg: 1.022 10 cm 100L

*Canthigaster coronata* 443
6-10 26°C sg: 1.022 13 cm 150L

*Canthigaster jactator* 443
5, 6-7 26°C sg: 1.022 8 cm 100L

*Canthigaster callisterna* 443
12 24°C sg: 1.024 23 cm 250L

*Canthigaster rostrata* 443
2, 13 26°C sg: 1.022 11 cm 100L

*Canthigaster valentini* 443
7-9 26°C sg: 1.022 20 cm 200L

*Canthigaster ocellicincta* 443
7-8 26°C sg: 1.022 10 cm 100L

*Canthigaster rivulata* 443
6-7, 9 26°C sg: 1.022 20 cm 200L

*Canthigaster margaritata* 443
10 26°C sg: 1.022 12 cm 150L

*Canthigaster capistratus* 443
13 26°C sg: 1.022 6 cm 60L

*Canthigaster marquesensis* 443
6 26°C sg: 1.022 15 cm 150L

*Canthigaster rapaensis* 443
6 26°C sg: 1.022 10 cm 100L

*Canthigaster inframacula* 443
6 26°C sg: 1.022 15 cm 150L

*Canthigaster sanctaehelenae* 443
13 26°C sg: 1.022 12 cm 150L

*Canthigaster natalensis* 443
9 26°C sg: 1.022 15 cm 150L

*Canthigaster natalensis* 443
9 26°C sg: 1.022 15 cm 150L

*Canthigaster solandri* 443
6-7, 9 26°C sg: 1.022 11 cm 100L

*Canthigaster tyleri* 443
9 26°C sg: 1.022 14 cm 150L

*Chilomycterus affinis* 444
3 26°C sg: 1.022 51 cm 500L

*Cyclichthys orbicularis* 444
7-9 26°C sg: 1.022 14 cm 150L

*Diodon hystrix* 444
Circumtrop. 26°C sg: 1.022 60 cm 600L

*Diodon nicthemerus* 444
12 24°C sg: 1.023 28 cm 300L

*Diodon hystrix* 444
Circumtrop. 26°C sg: 1.022 60 cm 600L

*Diodon nicthemerus* 444
12 24°C sg: 1.023 28 cm 300L

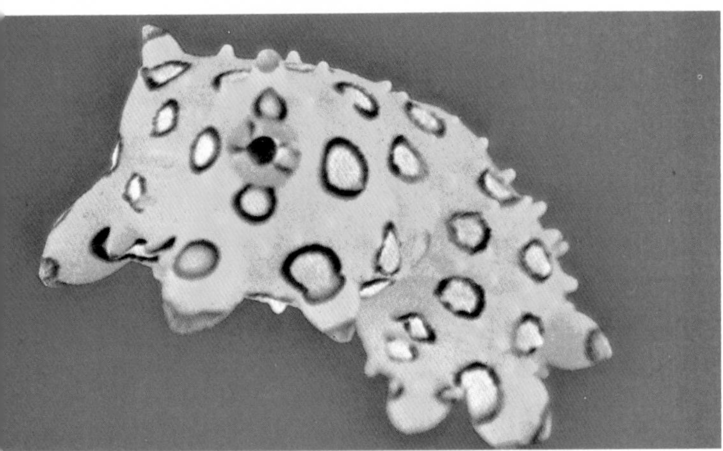

*Chilomycterus antillarum* 444
2 26°C sg: 1.022 25 cm 300L

*Chilomycterus schoepfi* 444
2 26°C sg: 1.022 25 cm 300L

*Chilomycterus schoepfi* 444
2 26°C sg: 1.022 25 cm 300L

*Chilomycterus schoepfi* 444
2 26°C sg: 1.022 25 cm 300L

*Chilomycterus antennatus* 444
2, 13 26°C sg: 1.022 23 cm 250L

*Chilomycterus antennatus* 444
2, 13 26°C sg: 1.022 23 cm 250L

*Chilomycterus atinga* 444
1-2, 13 26°C sg: 1.022 46 cm 500L

*Chilomycterus spilostylus* 444
7, 9-10 26°C sg: 1.022 34 cm 400L

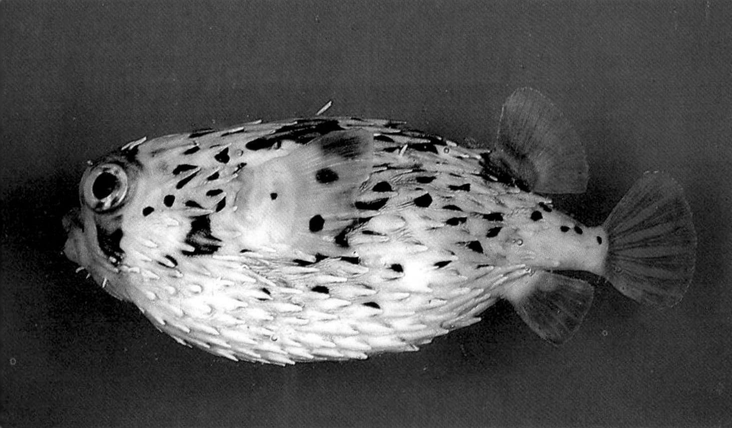
*Diodon holacanthus* 444
Circumtrop. 26°C sg: 1.022 50 cm 500L

*Diodon holacanthus* 444
Circumtrop. 26°C sg: 1.022 50 cm 500L

*Lophodiodon calori* 444
7-9 26°C sg: 1.022 20 cm 200L

*Diodon liturosus* 444
5-9 26°C sg: 1.022 50 cm 500L

*Diodon hystrix* 444
Circumtrop. 26°C sg: 1.022 50 cm 500L

*Diodon myersi* 444
8 26°C sg: 1.022 41 cm 400L

*Mola mola* 444
Circumtrop. 26°C sg: 1.022 300 cm 3000L

*Ranzania laevis* 445
Circumtrop. 26°C sg: 1.022 81 cm 800L

# *Family Discussions*

The following discussions of families of fishes portrayed in this book are provided in order to give some additional information about the families and to act as an introduction to them. The discussions are necessarily brief, and for more information it is suggested that Nelson's book *Fishes of the World* be sought out.

Plate numbers referred to in the text appear (preceded by the number symbol, #) at center top of photo pages.

## Jawless Fishes (Plates 1 & 2)

The hagfishes (class Myxini, family Myxinidae) are jawless cartilaginous fishes, eel-like or worm-like in general shape, that are voracious scavengers feeding on the internal tissues and organs of dead or dying invertebrates and fishes. Commercial fishermen examining their catch, whether it is haddock, cod, mackerel, flatfishes, etc., may sometimes discover that some of the fishes are virtually hollow. The hagfish has bored its way into the fish with a set of rasp-like teeth. Polychaete worms may form a part of their diet in some areas.

Although not usually kept as aquarium fishes by home aquarists, hagfishes may sometimes be seen in public aquariums. They are cool- to cold-water fishes that become distressed if the water temperature rises to more than 10-13° C. The water should be marine in character, hagfishes usually not surviving well in fresh or brackish conditions. They are commonly found almost completely buried in soft mud or clay bottoms.

Although both male and female sex organs are contained in the same individual, only one or the other functions at one time (i.e., they are not synchronous hermaphrodites). There is no particular spawning season, and as many as 30 eggs can be laid by a single female in any month of the year. The eggs are large (up to 2.5 cm in diameter), yolky, and covered with a horny material. Unlike the lampreys, which have a distinct larval stage, the hagfishes do not undergo a metamorphosis.

Aquarists should be warned that the name "slime eel" is well earned as they can turn an aquarium into a slimy mess if suitably disturbed. Under the confined conditions of the aquarium the slime can have poisonous qualities.

## Sharks, Rays, and Chimaeras (Plates 1-16)

The sharks, rays, and chimaeras are all grouped into the class Chondrichthys, commonly called the cartilaginous fishes (although as noted above the hagfishes and lampreys are also cartilaginous fishes). They are divided into two main evolutionary lines, the subclass Holocephali (chimaeras) and subclass Elasmobranchii (sharks and rays), with the former being the most primitive.

The chimaeras are grouped into 1-3 families, the divisions usually based on the shape of the snout (plownose, shortnose, and longnose chimaeras). There are usually two dorsal fins, the first being preceded by a spine that in some cases has a poison gland associated with it.

The males have paired claspers used for internal fertilization. They also may have an accessory clasper-like structure in front of the eyes, the function of which is still not well known. The eggs are encased in brown horny capsules.

Most chimaeras are found in cool to cold deep marine waters. They grow to fairly large sizes (normally to 1 m but up to 1.5 m) and do not take to handling very well. All this causes difficulties to those wishing to keep any in captivity. They normally do not last more than a few months in public aquariums although one has been kept alive for more than two years by University of Washington aquarists. These rather poor swimmers eat small invertebrates and fishes and are sometimes caught on hook and line, perishing quickly once removed from the water.

Sharks are a fairly large (approximately 250 species) and highly diversified (about 13 families in the superorder Selachimorpha) group. Most people are familiar with some sharks, particularly since the popular motion picture *Jaws* and its sequels were released. Almost every public aquarium or oceanarium keeps their share of sharks in large tanks that are preferably circular or doughnut-shaped so that the larger free-swimming species can be in constant motion, a requirement for such species. Even with such facilities many sharks fare quite poorly in captivity, ceasing to feed and often almost blindly ramming into the sides of the tank. Certain sharks do well in captivity, and exhibitions of their feeding draw considerable crowds. Home aquarists are more limited in their selection and normally must choose small, bottom-dwelling sharks for their aquaria.

Almost all sharks are marine. There are a few species that are able to ascend rivers into pure fresh water; the almost land-locked shark of Lake Nicaragua is quite well known. They are found around the world, mostly in tropical and subtropical waters with fewer numbers in the temperate regions and practically none in the cold polar waters. They vary considerably in size from those barely 46 cm long to giants 15-20 m long.

Shark reproduction involves internal fertilization. Males are provided with claspers on the inner edges of the pelvic fins. Development in most cases is ovoviviparous, while in others it may be oviparous or viviparous. In those that deposit eggs, the eggs are encased in horny capsules, sometimes highly ornamented, with long tendrils at the ends that become entangled (and thus anchored) with objects on the ocean floor. Some of the egg capsules have been successfully hatched in captivity.

Sharks are, without exception, carnivorous. Many are provided with very sharp, often serrated teeth that can do considerable damage to objects a lot harder than human flesh. Most sharks feed primarily on fishes, while others are scavengers feeding on whatever becomes available. Still others have teeth modified to feed on hard-shelled molluscs or crustaceans. The huge whale shark and basking shark, on the other hand, feed on small planktonic forms, primarily crustaceans. As for attacks on man, these are usually few and far between. Even then, in many cases the shark was provoked or it was a case of mistaken identity, the human victim appearing to the shark as its more natural prey (ex. seals).

Aquarists should be warned that even the small sharks that are kept in home aquaria have the potential of inflicting a severe bite on anyone foolish enough to become careless when handling them. These sharks are surprisingly strong and often are able to twist enough to bite at anything close enough, usually an arm. They are also quite adept at getting tangled in nets and slashing at the fingers that are freeing it from the mesh.

The two families of the order Hexanchiformes (frill sharks, Chlamydoselachidae, and cow sharks, Hexanchidae) have a single, spineless dorsal fin and six or seven gill slits. The Frill Shark (*Chlamydoselachus anguineus*) is snake-like in appearance and lives in deep water where it feeds mainly on squids. Of the cow sharks, the one most likely to be seen is the Sevengill Shark (*Notorynchus maculatus*), which is common in California bays as well as in the western Pacific. Sharks of both families are ovoviviparous.

The single family in the order Heterodontiformes, Heterodontidae, contains species that find their way into marine aquarists' tanks. *Heterodontus portusjacksoni*, the Port Jackson Shark, is one of these. It is also called the oyster-crusher because of its feeding habits. Aquarists should be wary of the sharp spines preceding each of its two dorsal fins. Horny egg cases with spiral flanges are laid by members of this family.

The order Lamniformes (with about seven families) contains most of the sharks. There are two spineless dorsal fins, an anal fin, and five gill slits. Some of the sharks in this order are small and very colorful or have interesting patterns and so are of interest to aquarists. Some of the carpet or nurse sharks, for example, are generally available to aquarists. First among these is probably the Atlantic Nurse Shark (*Ginglymostoma cirratum*), although it soon outgrows the tank in which it is housed. It is not very colorful but is quite docile, comparatively speaking. The carpet sharks are very colorful and in addition have fringes or lappets that add to their appeal. Most of these sharks also outgrow their tanks quite rapidly.

The family Scyliorhinidae (cat sharks) is by far the most important family of sharks to aquarists. It contains the smaller, more colorful species that do well in captivity. Almost all are bottom-dwellers feeding on the invertebrates and small fishes that are found there. Aquarists should be aware that some species grow large (over a yard) and many are from temperate regions, requiring cooler tank water. Most of the species kept in aquaria are from the Indo-West Pacific. Included in this family are the swell sharks that can fill their stomachs with air if they are removed from the water, much like a pufferfish. The species are ovoviviparous. No special care is needed for these small sharks other than a suitably large tank, plenty of good food, and perhaps an open area of sand.

Other members of the Lamniformes include the whale shark (family Rhincodontidae), the sand tigers (family Odontaspididae), the thresher, basking, and mackerel sharks (family Lamnidae), the hammerhead sharks (family Sphyrnidae), and the smooth dogfishes and requiem sharks (family Carcharhinidae). Almost all of these are too large for private tanks, and only a few are regularly seen in public aquariums. Among the better known sharks in this group are the Whale Shark, a monster that is said to reach as much as 15 m in length, the Gray Nurse Shark (perhaps responsible for many of the shark attacks in Australian waters), the thresher sharks with their unusually elongate upper tail lobes, the Great White Shark ("Jaws"), the Mako, and of course the Tiger Shark with its tiger-like stripes and reputation to match. Stomachs of Tiger Sharks have contained a wide variety of items from indigestible, inanimate garbage items to human body parts. With such a reputation many public aquariums have tried (mostly unsuccessfully) to keep them alive. Among the more unusual sharks can be included the hammerheads, so-called because of the bizarre development of their heads, with the eyes on the end of lateral extensions.

The order Squaliformes contains sharks with two dorsal fins (with or without spines), no anal fin, and five gill slits. Three families are currently included, the dogfish sharks (family

Squalidae), the saw sharks (family Pristiophoridae), and the angel sharks (family Squatinidae). Only some of the smaller squalids are kept in home aquaria, such as species of *Squalus* and *Cephaloscyllium*, and it is *Squalus acanthias* that is the shark commonly used in comparative anatomy labs. The smallest shark, *Squaliolus laticaudus*, which grows to about 25 cm, belongs to the Squalidae. The saw sharks should not be confused with the sawfishes (family Pristidae), which are rays, although the saw sharks have many ray-like characters and have a great superficial similarity to those fishes. The saw sharks have laterally positioned gill slits while those of the sawfishes are ventrally located. The angel sharks also are somewhat ray-like but they also have the gill slits laterally positioned. The angel sharks are also called monkfish. As their flattened body might lead one to guess, they live on or close to the bottom, often partially hidden in the sand.

The superorder Batidoidimorpha, Order Rajiformes, contains the rays (in the broad sense including the sawfishes, guitarfishes, skates, etc.). Only a few colorful species are kept by marine aquarists. All of these fishes are characterized in part by having the gill slits opening on the underside of the body.

Small members of the sawfishes (family Pristidae) are sometimes kept in home aquaria and commonly in public aquariums. They should be handled with care as the elongate snout provided with rows of sharp teeth (actually modified scales) along each side can cause considerable damage. Many an unlucky person who thought it was safe to hold one by the tail has scars to prove the fallacy of this idea. Normally the saw is used to slash through schools of fishes (mullets, etc.), impaling some on the saw teeth. Sawfishes are found around the world in shallow tropical waters. They may stray into brackish or even fresh water, and, like a shark cousin, one species has become almost land-locked in Lake Nicaragua. The guitarfishes (family Rhinobatidae) are similar in shape to the sawfishes but are without the saw. They are too big for home aquarists but may find their way into public aquariums. More fascinating to aquarists are the electric rays (family Torpedinidae). These ovoviviparous fishes can generate electrical charges, some quite intense, and should be handled with great care. Most encounters are by swimmers or waders who inadvertently step on one on a sandy bottom. These rays are poor swimmers and rely mostly on their shocking ability rather than flight for protection. Some of the species are quite colorful and, regardless of the risk, are kept in home tanks. Their food is mainly bottom invertebrates or fishes. The eagle rays (family Myliobatidae) and manta rays (family Mobulidae) are much too large for home aquaria, but some smaller ones are kept in oceanariums. They always attract attention with their graceful "flying" motions. Both eagle and manta rays are noted for their ability to leap from the water and come down with a resounding crash. The two most speciose families are the skates (family Rajidae) and stingrays (family Dasyatidae), and it is from these families, particularly the latter, that aquarium species are selected. Most skates and rays live inshore on the bottom, feeding on shellfish and/or crustaceans. Skates prefer more temperate waters and in many areas are fished for commercially. Males have long claspers for use in internal fertilization. They lay eggs encased in horny capsules that have tendrils or projections that help anchor them to objects on the bottom. Many are washed up on shore and have been given the names sailor's purse and mermaid's purse. Stingrays are more tropical fishes, spending much of their time almost completely buried in the sand or soft bottom material. In addition to the crustaceans and molluscs, they will readily feed on worms when available. Stingrays have the base of their tail armed with one or more spines provided with venom-producing tissue. Perhaps the most commonly kept stingray is *Taeniura lymma*, a colorful species with blue spots scattered over its upper surface.

The remaining fishes all belong to the bony fishes (class Osteichthys), which have skeletons composed, at least in part, of true bone.

## The Coelacanth (Plate 17)

The Comoro Islands Coelacanth (order Coelacanthiformes, family Latimeriidae, *Latimeria chalumnae*) is the only known survivor of the crossopterygians, fishes usually considered to be ancestors to the entire lineage of present-day vertebrates. All the Coelacanths have been collected in relatively deep water (to 360 m) where there is a rocky bottom. Their large scales are mostly a deep metallic blue. They feed exclusively on other fishes. What makes them very unique is their lobed fins. The second dorsal, pectoral, and pelvic fins are supported by fleshy stalk-like structures earning them the common name of lobefins. Most public aquariums and oceanariums would love to have a living Coelacanth on display, but they have not been very successful in their endeavors. Obviously a rare 1.2-1.5-m fish reaching a weight of 72 kilos would not be available to private aquarists. These ovoviviparous fishes were found to contain eggs up to 9.1 cm in diameter and young in the oviduct with a length of up to 33.5 cm total length.

## Tarpons, Ladyfish, and Bonefish (Plate 17)

The tarpons (Megalopidae), ladyfishes (Elopidae), and bonefishes (Albulidae) are all included in the order Elopiformes where the pelvic fins are abdominal, the tail is deeply forked, and all have a fork-tailed leptocephalus-like larva. None are of great interest to aquarists, although all are sought after avidly by fishermen. Often called the silver king, the Atlantic Tarpon (*Megalops atlanticus*) grows the largest, attaining up to 2.4 m in length and a weight of 135 kilos. Once hooked, the tarpon puts up a tremendous battle (especially on relatively light tackle) with spectacular leaps, giving the fisherman the time of his life. The bony mouth makes it hard to set the hook and many fish are lost. Even when landed, however, this fish is often released, partly in respect for the pleasure it has just given. Bonefish (*Albula vulpes*) are smaller and instead of leaping make powerful runs stripping line from the reel at a fast clip. Like the others just mentioned, the Atlantic Ladyfish (*Elops saurus*) is a game fish. It resembles the tarpon more in appearance and fighting characteristics but averages closer to 2.25 kilos. It also lacks the filamentous last ray characterizing the tarpon. Most of these species are found in shallow inshore waters where they feed on small fishes and invertebrates. There is a deep-water genus of bonefish (*Pterothrissus*) with a long dorsal fin.

## Eels (Plates 18-29)

All the true eels, comprising about 20 families, are included in the order Anguilliformes. The body is elongate, and the dorsal and anal fins are usually connected to the caudal fin, while the pelvic fins (occasionally also the pectoral fins) are absent. There is a leptocephalus larva (elongate, very flattened, and almost transparent) but, contrary to that of the Elopiformes, it has a tail tapering to a point rather than a forked one. The elongate form of the eels has been suggested as being an adaptation for moving through small openings and in some cases there are further adaptations for burrowing. Although most eels are bottom-dwellers, there are at least some adapted to a bathypelagic mode of life.

Of the many eel families, only a few contribute species to the marine aquarium on a regular basis. Others may be kept as curiosities as the occasion allows. Freshwater eels (which usually spend much of their life in fully marine waters) of the family Anguillidae are collected occasionally and may find their way to home aquaria of marine enthusiasts but are then usually released again when the novelty wears off. The freshwater eels generally spawn far out in the open ocean where as many as 20 million eggs are released by each female. After spawning the adults die. The leptocephali then travel back to the continental shores (this trip may be up to several thousand kilometers) where they ultimately metamorphose into young eels called elvers that move toward fresh water. The snake eels (family Ophichthidae) are burrowers, the tails of some genera being modified into a hard, fleshy point without fins. Burrowing is done tail-first. Several species from this family, especially the colorful members of the genus *Myrichthys*, are regularly kept in marine aquaria. The worm or spaghetti eels (family Moringuidae) are extremely thread-like, without or with only feeble pectoral fins, and with eyes that are small and covered with skin.

The conger eels (family Congridae) are distinguishable from the moray eels by possessing pectoral fins. The larger species are usually passed over by aquarists, but several members of the garden eels (subfamily Heterocongrinae) make interesting aquarium inhabitants and are seen from time to time. Garden eels are found in nature usually in rather large colonies (gardens) where there are many burrows. The garden eels will be seen hovering just above the burrows feeding on small organisms that are carried to them in the current. At the approach of some threat the eels will retreat tail-first into their burrows only to appear again slowly when the danger is past.

The moray eels (family Muraenidae) lack pectoral fins, have small, restricted lateral gill openings, and most have long, fang-like teeth. Most live on tropical and subtropical reefs in relatively shallow water and are quite colorful. Most are large, generally up to a meter in length, with others reaching a length of over two meters. Divers frequently encounter morays that are in holes in the reef with only their heads sticking out. As they respire the mouth opens and closes exhibiting the formidable teeth. Although this deters any diver from messing with them, unfortunate divers have been bitten when they stuck a hand into a hole after a fish or shell and were unaware that it was occupied by a moray eel. Normal food of morays includes small fishes and some invertebrates. Apparently squid are a delicacy for most morays, and aquarists able to supply such food should do so. Morays of the genus *Echidna* generally have teeth modified for crushing the shells and carapaces of crustaceans and molluscs. Some morays even feed on sea urchins. Even with such a bad reputation (or possibly because of it) aquarists keep many species of morays (mostly from the genus *Gymnothorax*) in their home tanks. Public aquariums almost always have several species on exhibit as well.

## Herrings and Herring-like Fishes (Plates 30-32)

The herrings and herring-like fishes (order Clupeiformes) are among the most important food fishes in the world, both for human consumption and as an important link in the food chain of many fishes. They occur in vast schools that may extend for kilometers. Thus the various predators (other fishes, birds, marine mammals, etc.) can usually take their fill without seriously depleting the population. Only man, with his high-tech equipment, can seriously threaten the species as a whole. The fishes, in turn, feed on planktonic organisms that they strain out by means of their numerous long gill rakers. The herrings (family Clupeidae) are usually silvery fishes that possess abdominal scutes. Besides the herrings themselves, such well-known fishes as shad, sardines, and menhaden are included. Spawning is usually in relatively shallow water where each female may shed many thousands of eggs into the open water. The eggs are demersal (sinking to the bottom) and are coated with mucus so that they stick to objects when they reach the bottom.

The anchovies (family Engraulidae) are also commercially important food fishes. They are generally recognizable by the snout overhanging the mouth and the silvery stripe along the side. They also strain planktonic organisms with their numerous slender gill rakers, occur in massive schools, and are mostly found in tropical or temperate waters.

The wolf herrings (family Chirocentridae) grow much larger than their cousins, attaining an average length of about 1.5 m. They are voracious predators with large fang-like teeth.

None of the clupeiform fishes are generally kept by aquarists. Indeed, anchovies are so fragile they usually die if touched or taken out of the water even for a second. Add to this their lack of color, and they have little if anything to make them appealing to aquarists. Public aquariums will keep them mainly as food for the larger fishes.

## Milkfish (Plate 32)

A member of the order Gonorynchiformes, *Chanos chanos* (family Chanidae) looks somewhat like the ladyfish or bonefish discussed previously but possesses a suprabranchial organ (lateral pouches in the posterior part of the branchial chamber). It is a very important food fish in Southeast Asia and the subject of intense aquaculture (particularly in the Philippines, Taiwan, and Indonesia). The fry are collected along the shore and removed to growing-out ponds until they reach marketable size. Those seeking higher returns on their investment by raising the Milkfish to a larger size may often lose most of their fish in typhoons (causing flooding and/or destruction of the ponds) if they are unlucky.

## Smelts and Noddlefishes (Plate 33)

The smelts (family Osmeridae) and noddlefishes (family Salangidae) have very little in common other than they both belong to the order Salmoniformes. As such the maxilla is included in the gape of the mouth and they possess an adipose fin between the dorsal fin and the tail. The smelts are small and silvery like herrings but, like salmon, make spawning runs into freshwater streams. They are cooler water fishes occurring in the Northern Hemisphere in both the Atlantic and Pacific Oceans. Most of the species are commercially important food fishes; none are usually kept as aquarium fishes. The icefishes or noddlefishes have almost scaleless, transparent bodies with a strongly depressed head. They are found from Sakhalin to China and perhaps even further south.

## Deep-sea Bristlemouths and Viperfishes (Plate 33)

The deep-sea order Stomiiformes contains about nine families of fishes. These normally possess luminescent organs in the form of photophores. In some groups there is a chin barbel that is often used in specific identification. The mouth is usually well provided with teeth and the dominant color is usually black or brown, although there are silvery forms. Most are deep-sea fishes living in areas of perpetual darkness while some approach upper water layers at night, retreating to the darker regions with the approach of dawn. Many attempts have been made to keep species of this group alive as they make spectacular displays in public aquariums, but they are difficult to bring up to the surface alive or to keep alive once captured.

## Lizardfishes and Their Relatives (Plates 34-37)

The sailfin lizardfishes (family Aulopodidae) and the lizardfishes (family Synodontidae) are only two of the dozen families of the order Aulopiformes, which is characterized by a specialization in the gill arches involving the second pharyngobranchial. These two families (plus a third, Chlorophthalmidae) are benthic, the others pelagic. An adipose fin is commonly present.

The sailfin lizardfishes resemble the typical lizardfishes but have larger dorsal fins that earned them their common name. They are found in tropical and subtropical waters and are predators on small fishes and invertebrates. Although attractive species that would be welcome in hobbyists' tanks, they are only rarely seen offered. Far more common are the members of the family Synodontidae. These fishes spend a great deal of time sitting on the bottom propped up by the ventral fins waiting for prey to come within reach. This might be small fishes or invertebrates that they dispatch quite easily as one might guess by noting the rows of sharp teeth in the jaws and the rather large mouth. Some species blend well with the sandy bottom upon which they sit while others go a step further and partially bury themselves in the substrate, making themselves almost invisible to the approaching prey. Most of the aquarium species are selected from the subfamily Synodontinae; the remaining subfamily, Harpadontinae, contains the Bombay ducks, genera *Saurida* and *Harpadon*.

The lancetfishes (family Alepisauridae) may grow to a length of almost two meters and are slender pelagic fishes with a large sail-like dorsal fin. The mouth is large and provided with well-developed teeth.

## Lanternfishes (Plate 37)

The order Myctophiformes includes only two families, the lanternfishes (family Myctophidae) and the family Neoscopelidae. The lanternfishes are so-called because of the presence of groups and rows of photophores on the head and body. They live in the twilight to dark regions of the open oceans but make vertical migrations daily to the surface at night (where they are often taken by dip-netting). They are small fishes less than 15 cm in length and may be black, brown, silvery, blue, etc., some with iridescent reflections. They are very common and occasionally are caught for public aquarium displays. Private aquarists rarely encounter them unless they collect them themselves.

## Codfishes and Rattails (Plates 38 & 39)

The order Gadiformes contains seven families of fishes including the codfishes (family Gadidae) and the grenadiers or rattails (family Macrouridae). These fishes have thoracic or jugular pelvic fins that contain up to 17 rays. There are no true spines in the fins.

The codfishes, which also include the hakes, haddock, and burbot, are cold-water fishes of the Northern Hemisphere. They are very important commercial food fishes, most of the catch nowadays being processed as frozen fillets. They are generally bottom feeders preying on small fishes, worms, crustaceans, and molluscs. A very large number of eggs are produced, a 9-kilo female Cod releasing up to 5 million eggs per season. The eggs and larvae are pelagic. These fishes are not readily available to marine aquarists and there is practically no interest in them anyway. Most public aquariums, especially those in the colder regions of the United States and Europe, have displays of these important food fishes.

The family Moridae (morid cods) includes quite variable fishes with one to three dorsal fins and one or two anal fins. The chin barbels present in many cods may or may not be present in members of this family. Most of the species are deep-water fishes and rarely available for aquaria, private or public.

The grenadiers or rattails are deep-water fishes rarely found at less than 185 m depth and often in water greater than 750 m deep. The body tapers posteriorly to a point, and the second dorsal and anal fins are many-rayed and continuous with the long tail; a chin barbel is usually present. The eyes are usually large for vision in the low-light depths they inhabit. Special conditions are needed to keep these fishes in captivity (cold water, low light levels, etc.) and few, if any, are ever seen even in public aquariums.

## Cusk Eels, Pearlfishes, and Their Relatives (Plates 40 & 41)

The cusk eels, pearlfishes, etc. (order Ophidiiformes) have many-rayed dorsal and anal fins extending to the caudal fin and often united with it. The pelvic fins are usually well forward, even mental or jugular in position, and are composed of only one or two rays.

The cusk eels and brotulas (family Ophidiidae) inhabit tropical and temperate waters where they live on the bottom or even burrow into it. The far anterior pelvic fins are used as sensory "barbels" to search the bottom for food. These brotulas are egg-layers. Brotulas may be found in shallow to very deep water, with some even extending down in the oceanic trenches in excess of 7000 m. Those living in deep waters usually have small eyes. The pearlfishes (family Carapidae) are mostly tropical shallow-water fishes of small size. They have very interesting symbiotic relationships with assorted invertebrate animals. The most publicized of these associations is the one in which the pearlfish lives in the gut or respiratory organs of sea cucumbers, but they also find refuge in other animals such as giant clams and sea squirts. At least one species, *Onuxodon margaritiferae*, shelters only in pearl oysters. Pearlfishes feed at night outside their host and find their way back by following a chemical scent. Because of these strange actions, pearlfishes are often sought out (with their hosts) for home aquaria.

The viviparous brotulas (family Bythitidae) are, as the common name implies, fishes that give birth to living young. Some species are well known to serious aquarists, such as the Black Widow (*Stygnobrotula latebricola*) and various species of *Ogilbia* and *Dinematichthys*. The family includes mostly fishes that inhabit shallow waters and even move into brackish or fresh waters. There are some species that are cave-dwellers. Because these brotulas give birth to living young, some are sought for home aquaria, where they do reasonably well on a diet of mixed bottom invertebrates.

## Toadfishes and Anglerfishes (Plates 42-51)

The toadfishes (family Batrachoididae) and the anglerfishes—some 16 families including the goosefishes (family Lophiidae), frogfishes (family Antennariidae), and batfishes (family Ogcocephalidae)—are generally grouped into the order Batrachoidiformes, although some workers use another order, Lophiiformes, for the families of anglerfishes, which are characterized by the first ray of the spinous dorsal fin being transformed into an illicium, a lure-bearing spine.

The toadfishes are bottom dwelling coastal fishes that commonly bury themselves in the soft substrate in wait for prey. Many are able to produce rather loud croaking noises (during courtship, when disturbed, etc.) that have earned them their common name. Some can enter brackish waters, and a few are confined to purely fresh water. Several species have turned up in the marine aquarium trade as curiosities, but almost all, save the reef-dwelling brightly patterned *Sanopus*, are drably colored. Some midshipmans possess photophores. Members of the subfamily Thalassophryninae have two dorsal spines and an opercular spine connected to venom glands, so aquarists beware. *Opsanus tau* can be very pugnacious, especially during breeding season. The eggs usually are laid on solid objects on the bottom (rocks, shells, even tin cans) and are vigorously defended by the male toadfish for about a month.

The goosefishes (Lophiidae) have a broad, flattened head with a big mouth and the characteristic "fishing pole" used to attract prey. They are large fishes found in cold to Arctic waters and are not kept in home aquaria. The frogfishes (Antennariidae), on the other hand, have many representatives in the marine aquarium trade. They are quite rounded, almost balloon-shaped, in contrast to the goosefishes and are most commonly encountered around coral reefs or rocky areas. Most are relatively small. The "fishing pole" and "lure" of frogfishes are well developed and used as a means of identification. The pectoral and pelvic fins are somewhat stalked and are moved as if they were tiny hands and feet as they move around obstacles over the bottom. Many colorful species are available and provide hours of entertainment for their owners as they "fish" for their prey. This is captured in a surprisingly rapid movement when the prey animal comes close to investigate the "bait." One of the most popular antennariids is the Sargassumfish (*Histrio histrio*). This species lives in sargassum weed as it floats in the open ocean waters. It "crawls" about on its floating home looking for fishes or crustaceans. Its pattern resembles the sargassum weed so closely that it is extremely hard to detect. Their appetites are prodigious and they can and will swallow animals that are quite large, comparatively speaking. Any fishes kept with any of the frogfishes should be larger than the frogfishes for safety. It is often said that a tankful of Sargassumfish will be reduced to one large contented Sargassumfish in a very short time.

The batfishes (Ogcocephalidae) have a very depressed, hard, and usually rough-textured body. Their pectoral fins are used to "walk" over the soft bottom on which they live. Like the frogfishes they can swim, but only awkwardly. The illicium is relatively short and is thrust from beneath the snout when the batfish is fishing for prey. Most batfishes, although quite appealing fishes, are usually passed over for more colorful reef-dwelling species.

## Clingfishes (Plates 52-54)

The clingfishes share the order Gobiesociformes with only one other family, the singleslits (family Alabetidae). This latter family is restricted to Australia (primarily the southern parts), including Tasmania, and lacks the sucking disc of the clingfishes. It is a small family of four species grouped into a single genus (*Alabes*) with reduced or absent pelvic fins and no dorsal or anal fin rays.

The clingfishes (family Gobiesocidae) contain over 100 species distributed in warm to temperate waters around the world. Their common name is derived from the modified pelvic fins that form a characteristic sucking disc that is used to anchor them to objects in a strong current. Almost all of them are less than 10 cm in length, but a few species grow larger and one attains a length of almost 30 cm in length. The most common shape is somewhat tear-drop-like with a large head and tapering tail. However, there are many modifications on this theme, particularly in the length of the snout. Eggs are usually laid on a firm substrate (rocks, etc.) and guarded by the parent(s?). The diet includes small invertebrates for the most part. One species, *Sicyases sanguineus*, commonly leaves the water while foraging for food, which consists of a variety of items including algae and small molluscs. Although there are a number of quite colorful species and the size is small, these fishes have not found favor with marine aquarists, with few exceptions. Clingfishes that live among the feathery arms of crinoids have been kept, but the difficulty of keeping the crinoid itself places severe restrictions on setting up a truly natural situation.

## Flyingfishes, Halfbeaks, and Needlefishes (Plates 55 & 56)

The order Cyprinodontiformes contains about 13 families grouped into three suborders. Only one suborder, Exocoetoidei, with four families, is mostly marine; the other two, Adrianichthyoidei and Cyprinodontoidei, contain mostly freshwater or brackish water fishes.

The flyingfishes (family Exocoetidae) are the most appealing to aquarists because of their ability to glide for some distance over the water's surface. This is accomplished mainly by means of enlarged pectoral fins and in some cases abetted by enlarged pelvic fins (the so-called four-winged species). The lower lobe of the caudal fin is also enlarged and aids in the flight by dipping into the water while vibrating rapidly almost like an outboard motor. A succession of flights can keep the fish out of water for a considerable distance, which may deter the predators that sent them into the flight panic in the first place. Juvenile flyingfishes are quite colorful and are sometimes kept by marine aquarists, but they are not very hardy (being open ocean fishes) and soon die.

The halfbeaks (family Hemiramphidae) usually have an elongated lower jaw and lack the enlarged pectoral (and pelvic) fins of flyingfishes. The lower caudal lobe is often elongated. Like the flyingfishes, they are tropical and travel in schools. They are more inclined to live in shallow water, and there are some halfbeaks that are live entirely in fresh water. Only the freshwater species are commonly kept in captivity.

The needlefishes (family Belonidae) have both jaws elongated and provided with numerous needle-like teeth. Like the above families they are surface fishes of tropical (and sometimes temperate) seas, but with representatives in brackish and pure fresh waters. They can also leap from the water like projectiles and, because they are attracted to light at night, have injured fishermen working with lanterns or other lights. Unlike the halfbeaks, which have most freshwater species restricted to the Indo-Australian region, the needlefishes have their freshwater representatives mostly in the Neotropical region. Only the freshwater species are generally kept by aquarists.

## Silversides and Their Relatives (Plate 57)

The silversides (family Atherinidae) belong to the order Atheriniformes along with four other families, including the Melanotaeniidae (rainbowfishes and their relatives). They are usually schooling fishes found in shallow waters of temperate and tropical seas, although some species are strictly freshwater fishes. The silversides normally have a broad silver band along the sides, two dorsal fins, and abdominal pelvic fins. The most famous silverside is the California Grunion (*Leuresthes tenuis*), which spawns at night on the beaches during the highest tides from March through August. Crowds gather to watch the millions of little fish go through their act—and to gather them for food. The precision of their timing is remarkable. The eggs incubate in the warm sand for two weeks, then hatch out as the tides reach another peak, washing the fry back out to sea. Although silversides are quite hardy, the marine representatives are not very colorful and are passed over by marine aquarists. Some of the freshwater species are kept.

A closely related family, the Isonidae, includes only two genera and six species.

## Opah and Related Fishes (Plate 58)

The Lampriformes contains 11 families of mostly oceanic or pelagic (some deep-water) fishes. Of these perhaps the best known are the Opah (*Lampris guttatus*, family Lampridae), the ribbonfishes (family Trachipteridae), and the oarfishes (family Regalecidae).The Opah is a very colorful deep-bodied fish that may grow to a weight of over 225 kilos. Ribbonfishes are deep-water fishes with a ribbon-like body and a many-rayed dorsal fin. The oarfishes are similar in shape but possess long, slender pelvic fins that are their "oars." The oarfishes, reaching lengths exceeding 3 m (unconfirmed reports to twice that), are probably responsible for some of the sightings of sea serpents.

## Squirrelfishes, Lanterneye Fishes, Pineconefishes, and Their Relatives (Plates 58-69)

Fourteen families comprise the order Beryciformes, including such diverse groups as the squirrelfishes (family Holocentridae), lanterneye fishes (family Anomalopidae), beardfishes (family Polymixiidae), and the pineconefishes (family Monocentrididae). The composition of this order is commonly in a state of flux as workers in the groups add or subtract families as they see fit.

The pineconefishes are well known to aquarists. They are encased in an armor composed of large, plate-like scales and possess phosphorescent light organs on the lower jaw. Although thought rare a few years back, they are being imported into the hobby almost regularly nowadays. Public aquariums seek out these fishes for displays, usually a darkened tank or one with periods of darkness when the light organs can be seen.

The lanterneye fishes have a light organ beneath each eye that is provided with a mechanism (in different species the organ can either be rotated or covered) to control the amount of light emitted. As for pineconefishes, public aquariums construct for these fishes tanks that are darkened. The lanterneyes are able to control their light, and the darkened tank looks like it is populated with fireflies blinking on and off.

The slimeheads (family Trachichthyidae) have a preopercular spine and a row of abdominal scutes. The mucous pores on the head are well developed (as is normal in the Beryciformes). Some species have luminescence. Few species of this family are available to aquarists. One, *Trachichthys australis*, is occasionally seen in shipments from Australia and makes an excellent aquarium subject.

The alfonsinos (family Berycidae) lack a notched dorsal fin and have a spine and 7-13 rays in each pelvic fin. Only eight species are included in the family, and only rarely are they seen in public aquariums.

The beardfishes (Polymixiidae) are so-called because of the pair of hyoid barbels. The pelvic fins are farther back (subabdominal) than in the other groups and have a spine and only six soft rays. They generally inhabit depths from 180 to 640 m.

One of the largest families of the order, the Holocentridae includes the squirrelfishes and soldierfishes. The dorsal fin has a spiny portion and a soft-rayed portion separated by a notch. The eyes and scales are large, and the color usually includes a great deal of red. These are nocturnal fishes hiding in caves or beneath coral heads during the daytime but moving out at night to forage for food. Unlike most other members of the order, these fishes are generally found in relatively shallow water (although there are some deeper water representatives) of the tropical and subtropical regions. Adults remain close to the bottom but produce a pelagic larva that aids in their dispersal. The family is readily divided into two large groups (subfamilies) generally called the squirrelfishes and the soldierfishes, the former possessing a large spine at the angle of the preoperculum. Both squirrelfishes and soldierfishes are well represented in the aquarium trade and do well in hobbyists' tanks. They feed on a variety of foods, especially crustaceans and small fishes.

## Dories and Boarfishes (Plate 70)

The dories (family Zeidae) and boarfishes (family Caproidae) along with four other families belong to the order Zeiformes. Most of the fishes of this order are deep-sea fishes, although the dories are more midwater.

The dories have small spines or bucklers at the bases of the dorsal and anal fin rays as well as eight or nine plates along the abdomen. The most well known species have a large black lateral spot ocellated with yellow and long filaments extending from the anterior dorsal fin spines. These fishes are only rarely seen in public aquariums.

The boarfishes include two genera, red-colored fishes with extremely deep bodies (*Antigonia*), and *Capros aper*, a species similar to the dories but without the abdominal plates. They live at depths of more than 240 m.

## Tubesnouts and Sticklebacks (Plate 70)

The tubesnouts (family Aulorhynchidae) and sticklebacks (family Gasterosteidae) belong to the order Gasterosteiformes along with an obscure family (Hypoptychidae) from Japan and Korea containing a single species. The tubesnouts are elongate, with lateral scutes and a series of 24-26 short, isolated dorsal spines. They are coastal fishes of the North Pacific that may appear in aquaria on the West Coast of the United States and possibly in Japan. The sticklebacks may or may not be elongate, may have lateral scutes or not, and have 3-16 well-developed isolated dorsal fin spines. They are small (maximum length 18 cm in the European *Spinachia spinachia*) marine, brackish, or pure freshwater fishes and have gained considerable fame from the behavioral studies conducted on them. Most aquarists tend to keep the brackish or freshwater species to observe the spawning antics. The sticklebacks are primarily inhabitants of cool northern waters throughout the Northern Hemisphere.

## Sea Moths (Plate 71)

Sea moths (family Pegasidae) are small fishes encased in bony plates. They have large, horizontal pectoral fins and a long, flattened rostrum. The mouth is tiny and located at the base of the rostrum. These bottom-fishes are welcomed by aquarists when they appear in the trade, but unfortunately this is not very often.

## Sea Horses, Pipefishes, and Their Relatives (Plates 71-82)

The order Syngnathiformes contains half a dozen families of very interesting and very unusual fishes. The trumpetfishes (family Aulostomidae) are elongate, compressed fishes with 8-12 isolated dorsal fin spines and a short barbel at the tip of the lower jaw. They occur around reefs in tropical seas where they are often seen swimming close (almost touching) to a larger fish or orienting themselves with some gorgonians (sometimes even vertically). Most people believe that this is a ruse to make them less noticeable so they can more easily attack their prey (mostly small fishes). The cornetfishes (family Fistulariidae) occur in tropical and subtropical waters. They resemble the trumpetfishes but have no dorsal fin spines, no barbel on the lower jaw, shorter dorsal and anal fin bases, and possess an elongate filament extending from the middle of the caudal fin. They can reach a length of 1.8 m, about double that of the trumpetfishes.

The snipefishes (family Macrorhamphosidae) are deep-bodied and compressed, usually possessing bony plates on each side of the back. The second dorsal spine is very long, as is the snout in some species. Orientation in the water is usually vertical, with the head pointing downward. The tiny mouth is used for selecting small planktonic prey. The shrimpfishes (family Centriscidae) are almost entirely encased in thin bony plates. They are very compressed, with a sharp ventral edge, and are also commonly referred to as razorfishes. All the unpaired fins are at the extreme end of the body, and the tail is actually at an angle to the body. Small groups of these fishes can be seen swimming vertically in the water (head down) among the coral or even among the spines of long-spined sea urchins. It is amazing how fast these fishes move. The small, toothless mouth is used for snatching up small planktonic animals.

The ghost pipefishes (family Solenostomidae ) are also tropical and have large stellate bony plates. The dorsal fins are separate, the first comparatively large. The pelvic fins are large and the snout and caudal fin are elongate, creating an unusual shape that seems to be the rule for members of this order. Only a single genus with five species is included in this family.

All of the above families contribute members to the aquarium trade, but not to the extent of the family Syngnathidae. This family contains the sea horses and pipefishes, almost any of which may be kept by home aquarists. Certainly any sea horse is welcomed and many pipefishes are quite colorful, creating a demand for them as well. The body is elongate and encased in a series of bony rings; there are no pelvic fins. In the sea horses the head is bent at an angle to the body and the tail (which lacks a caudal fin) is prehensile. Both groups have tiny mouths and pick small animals from the plankton. In captivity newly hatched brine shrimp are excellent for the smaller species. Most species are found in shallow tropical waters, although there are representatives that range into temperate seas. The breeding habits are unusual in that the female will lay her eggs in a brood pouch located on the male's abdomen. Some species of pipefishes lack a true pouch and have the eggs attached to the abdomen open to the surrounding water. The young hatch inside the pouch and emerge as miniature adults. It is best to keep sea horses by themselves or wth similarly slow-moving fishes.

Some of the Australian forms (sea dragons, etc.) are quite bizarre in shape with numerous leafy appendages and/or gaudy coloration. These command a high price when they are available but usually are well worth it.

## Flying Gurnards (Plate 83)

The flying gurnards (order Dactyliformes, family Dactylopteridae) have large bony heads and large wing-like pectoral fins with free inner rays. They are bottom-fishes that use their pelvic fins alternately to "walk" along the sandy substrate. With a few vibrations of the tail they can gain momentum so they can glide through the water with the pectoral fins outspread. The hyomandibular bone is also used to produce sounds. Young flying gurnards are sometimes kept by marine aquarists.

## Scorpionfishes, Sea Robins, Sculpins, and Their Relatives (Plates 34, 83-114)

The Scorpaeniformes is a large order of fishes encompassing some twenty families and more than a thousand species. They are all characterized by a posterior extension of the third suborbital bone (suborbital stay) and are commonly called the mail-cheeked fishes. Many of the fishes are spiny, and often the spines have venom glands associated with them.

The scorpionfish or rockfish family (Scorpaenidae) is one of the largest families of this order with more than 300 species. The body is generally stocky and the head normally is supplied with ridges and spines. The dorsal, anal, and pelvic spines are usually supplied with venom glands. Fertilization is mostly internal. Among the unusual reproductive modes of these fishes are the production of a large gelatinous balloon bearing the eggs and the birth of living young. These bottom-living fishes are mostly found around reef or rocky areas in tropical to temperate waters. They are predators that lie in wait for their prey, pouncing on them with a swift motion combined with suction caused by the rapid opening of the large mouth. Although these fishes commonly are red or have a great deal of red color on them, many have patterns that effectively camouflage them against the substrate. This large family is divided into eight subfamilies in some classifications, while in others one or more of these groups are considered as full families. Among the more unusual are the Pteroidichthyinae, containing the genus *Rhinopias*, and the Tetraroginae with the genera *Ablabys*, *Paracentropogon*, *Tetraroge*, etc. The Sebastinae is one of the larger subfamilies, with one of its genera, *Sebastes*, having almost all of its 100 or so species occurring in the North Pacific, with California having a good representation of these. The Scorpaeninae is represented by the genera *Scorpaena*, *Scorpaenodes*, *Pontinus*, etc.

Of most interest to aquarists is the subfamily Pteroinae with *Pterois* and related genera. These turkeyfishes, lionfishes, zebrafishes, or whatever else they are known as in different areas are very attractive fishes with long filamentous extensions to the dorsal and pectoral fin rays and spines. The dorsal fin spines are still quite pungent and are provided with venom glands. The extent of the pain and suffering caused by a "sting" depends on the species involved, the amount of venom that gets into the bloodstream, the type of reaction a person has to the particular venom (similar to allergies to bee stings), and the type and speed of care given to the person who has come into contact with the spines. Treatment usually involves immersing the punctured foot or finger in water as hot as the person can stand. Severe reaction to a sting should be treated by a physician knowledgeable about such injuries. Most injuries occur when aquarists carelessy handle the fish (like trying to untangle one from a net) or when capturing the fish in the wild. Lionfishes are hardy and long-lived in captivity if provided with sufficient space and a variety of nutritious foods (small live fishes for example).

The stonefishes (family Synanceiidae, subfamily Synanceiinae) are seen mainly in public aquariums where they are handled only by experts, for the neurotoxin they possess is among the most deadly and can cause fatalities in humans. They are not very attractive and, indeed, look very much like a stone. This camouflage aids in their prey capturing but also is dangerous to people because waders in shallow water not recognizing the fish for what it is might step on it. Among the other genera in the subfamily are *Erosa* and *Dampierosa*. Other subfamilies of the stonefish family include Choridactylinae (with *Inimicus* and *Choridactylus*) and Minoinae (with *Minous*).

The orbicular velvetfishes (family Caracanthidae) have an oval, extremely compressed body that is covered with small papillae. This gives them the velvety appearance and has lead to another common name that is quite descriptive—furry half dollars. These are attractive little fishes that only rarely are seen in the aquarium trade.

The velvetfishes (family Aploactinidae) are coastal fishes of the Indo-Pacific. The body is generally covered with modified prickly scales and the head is provided with knob-like lumps. The dorsal fin originates well forward.

The family Pataecidae is sometimes known as the prowfishes. Members of this exclusively Australian family are scaleless, but the body may have tubercles or papillae. The dorsal fin originates far forward over the eyes.

The racehorses or pigfishes (family Congiopodidae) are Southern Hemisphere fishes without scales and with a reduced gill opening. A South African species has been reported to shed its skin, like reptiles. (This also has been reported for members of the family Scorpaenidae, among others). Few members of these last three families enter the aquarium trade.

The sea robins (family Triglidae) have a boxy bony head, separate dorsal fins, and two or three free lower pectoral fin rays that are used for detecting food. The remaining pectoral rays form a large wing-like fin (though not quite so large as in the flying gurnards). Sea robins also "walk" on the bottom with their pelvic fins. They inhabit tropical and temperate seas, most commonly in deep water. All are carnivorous and most produce sounds. Two subfamilies include the unarmored sea robins (Triglinae) and the armored sea robins (Peristediinae). Few sea robins are kept by aquarists.

The flatheads (family Platycephalidae) have an elongate, cylindrical body and a flat head. The mouth is large, able to engulf small fishes and invertebrates. Flatheads are mostly marine fishes (some are brackish) that occur in the Indo-Pacific.

The sablefishes (family Anoplopomatidae) occur in the cool waters of the North Pacific. There are two dorsal fins, and the head is not provided with ridges, spines, or papillae. Only two species are included in this family.

The greenlings (family Hexagrammidae) are also endemic to the North Pacific, where most occur close to shore and among the kelp and rocks. The head is provided with cirri only, and the dorsal fin is single but provided with a notch between the spines and soft rays. Sexual dichromatism is seen at least in some of the better known species.

Combfishes of the family Zaniolepidae have a single dorsal fin with a notch. They have earned their common name by the elongate anterior dorsal fin spines (the second spine very elongate in *Zaniolepis latipinnis*). The two species often are placed with the greenlings as a subfamily.

There about 300 species of sculpins (family Cottidae) inhabiting marine (most species) and fresh waters of the Northern Hemisphere and New Zealand, with the greatest diversity in the North Pacific. The head is usually provided with spines and ridges, there are two dorsal fins, and the pectoral fins are usually very large, often wing-like. The eyes are large. Sculpins are bottom-fishes normally living close to shore, even entering tide-pools. There are some deep-water species as well. Most sculpins are carnivorous, preferring to remain in a camouflaged position until they can make a quick strike at some prey (small fishes and invertebrates). Although many have drab mottled coloration, some species are quite colorful (ex. *Leiocottus hirundo*). One of the most sought-after species of cottids for aquaria is the Grunt Sculpin (*Rhamphocottus richardsoni*). Not only is it very attractive, but it has an unusual shape. Unfortunately it is a cool-water species that cannot (or should not) be housed in a tropical reef tank.

The family Psychrolutidae has no common name and the species are commonly included with the Cottidae. Even so, these fishes are usually divided into two subfamilies, one with a rigid interorbital region and spiny heads and the other without head spines that because of their general shape are generally referred to as tadpole sculpins.

Poachers (family Agonidae) are elongate armored fishes from the cold waters of the North Pacific, North Atlantic, and southern South America. The depth range is considerable, as they occur in tide-pools and to depths of 610 m. One or two dorsal fins may be present.

Lumpfishes and snailfishes (family Cyclopteridae) have pelvic fins (when present) modified into a thoracic sucking disc. Lumpfishes, as their name suggests, have a globose, flabby body commonly covered with bumps or tubercles. There may be two dorsal fins or a single one that is deeply notched. *Cyclopterus lumpus* is one of the largest and best known lumpfishes, attaining a length of about 30 cm. The females may lay 20,000 or more adhesive demersal (sinking) eggs that are guarded by the male. Snailfishes are more elongate, some species having their flabby body covered with prickles. The dorsal fin is low and single, sometimes confluent with the caudal fin. Snailfishes are generally small and range in color from shades of brown to pink and red. Some species are well patterned with spots, blotches, or stripes. The snailfishes are sometimes placed in their own family, the Liparididae.

## THE ORDER PERCIFORMES

The order Perciformes contains about 150 families and more than 7,500 species (in both fresh and salt water) and is thus the largest and most diversified of any of the fish orders. The composition of this order will vary as controversial issues are settled and others arise. Among the largest families are the Cichlidae (fresh water), Gobiidae, Labridae, Serranidae, Blenniidae, Pomacentridae, and Apogonidae.

### Snooks and Glassfishes (Plates 115, 254)

The snooks (family Centropomidae) have the lateral line extending onto the tail, two dorsal fins or a single one deeply divided, and a scaly process in the pelvic axis. They are marine to brackish or even freshwater fishes of tropical waters. Most are well respected game fishes. Snooks are predators with a diet including other fishes and crustaceans. Inshore waters (including estuaries and especially mangrove areas) are nurseries for the young of many species. Because development of these areas by man is destroying the habitat, snooks are becoming more and more threatened.

The glassfishes (family Ambassidae) are similar in general appearance to the snooks and are commonly included in the same family. They are small fishes that have become popular in the aquarium trade, particularly with the recent ability of Southeast Asian fish farmers to brighten them up by artificially adding fluorescent color to them. However, these colors are temporary and they soon return to the nearly transparent state that earned them their common name. Some workers do not accept *Ambassis* as a full genus and consider the proper family name to be Chandidae.

### Groupers and Their Relatives (Plates 116–158)

The temperate basses (family Percichthyidae) occur in marine, brackish, and fresh waters in tropical and temperate regions of the world. They are very much like serranids and at one time were placed in that family. The opercle has two rounded spines, the caudal fin is usually forked, and the sexes are separate. Perhaps the best known member of the family is the Striped Bass (*Morone saxatilis*), a very valuable sport and commercial fish. These "stripers" move into fresh water to spawn, where large females may lay up to five million eggs. At an age of about two years the stripers move toward the sea. One of the largest members of the family is the Giant Sea Bass (*Stereolepis gigas*), which grows to more than 2 m in length and weighs a quarter ton.

Groupers and sea basses (family Serranidae) inhabit mostly marine waters in tropical and temperate regions. They have three opercular spines, the dorsal fin is single (sometimes notched), and the caudal fin is normally rounded to lunate. They are hermaphroditic with the two sexes not functioning simultaneously except in the genus *Serranus* and its immediate relatives. The 350 to 400 species are commonly divided into several subfamilies. Most of the species in the marine aquarium trade are brightly colored members of the subfamily Anthiinae. These are commonly sexually dimorphic, with the males usually more brightly colored and usually with one or more elongate anterior dorsal fin spines. Juvenile groupers of the genus *Epinephelus* are also kept as they are hardy and feed well. Unfortunately, these soon do so well they outgrow even the largest aquaria. Other colorful species kept belong to the genus *Cephalopholis*, the dominant hue being red, often with blue spots or markings. The hamlets, *Hypoplectrus*, (whether a single polymorphic species or ten different species) commonly appear in the trade and are synchronously hermaphroditic (both sexes not only occurring in the same fish at the same time but both being functional at the same time). Species of the genus *Serranus* and *Liopropoma* are also welcome aquarium inhabitants, and *Cromileptes altivelis*, known to aquarists as the Leopard Grouper, has become a common sight in home aquaria.

The soapfishes (family Grammistidae) are grouper-like fishes with the opercle having three distinct spines, the dorsal with 2-9 spines, and the anal fin with 0-3 short spines. The lower jaw generally projects and is provided with a short, fleshy appendage. Members of the Grammistinae (one of the two subfamilies) secrete a body mucus that can turn into a sudsy froth when the fish is agitated or attacked. This mucus contains the toxin grammistin. Besides *Grammistes sexlineatus*, an attractively striped species, aquarists also keep members of the genus *Diploprion*, *Belonoperca chabanaudi*, and occasionally a blue fish with a bright yellow stripe down its back, *Aulacocephalus temmincki*. *Pogonoperca punctata* is called the Butterfly Grouper in the trade because of its beautiful coloration. It changes patterns with growth, but all of these patterns are attractive. The second subfamily (Pseudogrammatinae) contains the genus *Pseudogramma*, among others.

The dottybacks belong to the family Pseudochromidae. The dorsal and anal fins contain 1-3 often inconspicuous spines, with the dorsal rays numbering 21-37. Most species are small and colorful and well represented in the aquarium trade. The large genus *Pseudochromis* contains about 40 species displaying colors such as solid magenta, magenta and yellow, blue and yellow, etc. Members of the closely related genus *Labracinus* are also kept.

The basslets (family Grammidae) have an interrupted lateral line or it may be absent entirely. There are 11-13 spines in the dorsal fin. Contained in this family is the extremely popular Royal Gramma, *Gramma loreto*. This purple and yellow fish hails from the western Atlantic along with a few closely related species. A couple of other members of the family occur in Australia, and one (known only from the holotype) is from Hawaii.

The roundheads (family Plesiopidae) have 11-15 spines in the dorsal fin and include such well known species as *Calloplesiops altivelis* (Comet Grouper) and *Paraplesiops altivelis* (Blue-spotted Comet). Also included in this family are the lesser known genera *Assessor* and *Trachinops*.

Acanthoclinidae and Glaucosomatidae are small families (about five species each) of grouper-related fishes, the first very dottyback-like, the second more like serranids. Few if any of the species are kept by aquarists.

## Grunters or Tigerperches and Aholeholes (Plates 159–161)

The grunters and tigerperches (family Teraponidae) inhabit coastal marine, brackish, and freshwater areas of the Indo-West Pacific. Most of the freshwater species occur in Australia. The opercle has two spines and the dorsal fin has a notch; the spinous dorsal fin is depressible into a sheath composed of scales. The species most commonly kept in aquaria is *Terapon jarbua* (Three-striped Tigerfish). It attains a length of about 30 cm. Incidentally, the correct spelling is now considered to be *Terapon*, not *Therapon*. The grunters and tigerfishes have specially adapted muscles associated with the swim bladder for sound production, hence the common name grunter.

The aholeholes (family Kuhliidae) are also marine, brackish, and freshwater fishes of the Indo-West Pacific. They also have a scaly sheath for the spiny portion of the notched dorsal fin but lack the specialized sound production mechanism of the teraponids. Of the two subfamilies contained in this family, the Nannopercinae includes brackish and freshwater fishes of southern Australia while the Kuhliinae includes the widely distributed genus *Kuhlia*. It is from this genus that aquarists obtain their specimens, particularly the Flagtail Aholehole, *Kuhlia taeniura*.

## Bigeyes (Plates 161–162)

Bigeyes (family Priacanthidae) occur in tropical and subtropical waters in all oceans. The eyes are large, the dorsal fin is continuous, and the inner ray of the pelvic fin is connected to the body by a membrane. The large eyes and dominant red color of these fishes indicate their preference for low light levels and, indeed, they are nocturnal and found in relatively deep water. The large mouth indicates their predatory nature. The favorite species of aquarists is the Deep Bigeye, *Pristigenys alta,* which, when young, is quite attractive.

## Cardinalfishes (Plates 163–178, 254)

The cardinalfishes (family Apogonidae) have two separate dorsal fins, the anal fin has two spines, and the predominant color throughout the family is red, prompting the common name. Most are small reef dwellers, attaining lengths of 10 cm or less, from tropical and subtropical regions of the Atlantic, Pacific, and Indian Oceans. Most are relatively shallow-water species. Many cardinalfishes are mouthbrooders, with the male incubating the eggs in some species, the female in others, and in some instances the duties are shared. Some cardinalfishes enter into a symbiotic relationship with various invertebrates, primarily molluscs but in some cases sponges as well, where they gain shelter. One cardinalfish is named the Conchfish (*Astrapogon stellatus*) due to its association with conch. Almost any of the cardinalfishes can and do become aquarium residents, and of course the most colorful species are the ones most desired. One of particular popularity is the Pajama Cardinalfish (*Sphaeramia nematoptera*), which not only has an attractive pattern but also will remain out in the open tank, a feature not always present in the shy, nocturnal species. Of the almost 200 species in the family, most are included in the genus *Apogon.*

## Tilefishes and Smelt-whitings (Plates 179–181, 429)

The smelt-whitings (family Sillaginidae) have an elongate body, two dorsal fins, and two spines in the anal fin. They inhabit marine and brackish waters of the Indo-Pacific. They are almost never kept by marine aquarists but occasionally are seen in public aquariums.

Tilefishes (family Malacanthidae) have a long, continuous dorsal fin and a relatively long anal fin. There is only one opercular spine. Occurring in tropical to temperate waters of the Atlantic, Pacific, and Indian Oceans, the tilefishes are strictly marine. Most of the aquarium species come from the subfamily Malacanthinae, which includes the genera *Malacanthus* and *Hoplolatilus.* Although members of both genera are kept in aquaria, those of *Hoplolatilus* are more commonly maintained. One of the best known species, the western Atlantic Tilefish (*Lopholatilus chamaeleonticeps*), supports a sizable commercial fishery and is the object of a sports fishery. They live in deep water (to 370 m deep) and fishermen usually have to travel a fair distance to reach an area where they can be caught. Tilefish are bottom-fishes feeding on crustaceans and fishes.

## Jacks, Cobia, Remoras, Etc. (Plates 182–192, 194)

The Labracoglossidae has no common name for the five species (three genera) of this western and South Pacific family. They have a single dorsal fin and no canine teeth in the jaws. The false trevallies (family Lactariidae) from the Indo-Pacific have two dorsal fins, the soft-rayed portion of both dorsal and anal fins covered with scales. Two small canine teeth are present in each jaw. The single genus has up to two species. Neither of these families is commonly represented in the aquarium trade.

The bluefishes (family Pomatomidae) have two dorsal fins, the soft dorsal and anal fins covered with scales. The Bluefish (*Pomatomus saltatrix*) is quite famous as a sports fish. It is a schooling fish with the reputation of being vicious and bloodthirsty, killing just for the sake of killing. The schools of Bluefish trail schools of fishes such as herrings, menhadens, etc., charging into them violently enough to at times cause the water to boil with turbulence and usually killing more than they can consume. In the North Atlantic these schools migrate northward in the summer and southward when cooler temperatures arrive. Eggs are released into the water to develop as part of the plankton.

The Cobia (*Rachycentrum canadum*, family Rachycentridae) occurs in tropical waters around the world. It closely resembles the remoras, but instead of the sucking disc on top of the head it has a normal dorsal fin of 6-9 short, free spines. It feeds on fishes and crustaceans near the bottom and has been given the common name Crab-eater in some locales.

The remoras (family Echeneididae) possess a sucking disc, a modification of the spinous dorsal fin that is used to attach themselves to larger fishes, turtles, or marine mammals. They thus hitch a ride and are able to feed off the scraps of their host's dinner. Suction is increased if the remora moves back "against the grain" of the laminae of the disc and released if the remora swims forward. This suction effect has been used to catch turtles. A remora is released into the water after a line has been attached to its tail. After a time the line and remora are hauled in with the remora hopefully attached to a turtle. The disc develops at an early age, for specimens as small as 2.5 cm or so have been found with fully formed discs.

The jacks and pompanos (family Carangidae) are generally streamlined, silvery, fast-moving fishes of temperate and tropical seas of the world. The body may be deep to fusiform, and there are usually two dorsal fins, the first with 3-9 sometimes very short, detached spines, and three anal spines, the first two usually detached from the rest of the fin. Commonly there are modified scales (scutes) along the posterior portion of the lateral line. The tail is forked and the caudal peduncle slender. A number of species are commonly in the aquarium trade and many more are normally present in public aquariums. One of the favorites is *Gnathanodon speciosus* with its golden color set off by black bars. Others include the deep-bodied members of the genera *Alectis* and *Selene,* some of which have long trailing filaments to the dorsal and anal fins. *Naucrates ductor* is called the Pilotfish as it is normally seen in company with large sharks — often swimming in the bow wave of the shark's snout. A number of carangids are also found under the bells of floating jellyfish, some of which possess tentacles armed with stinging nematocysts. Small carangids will also shelter next to floating debris and are able to travel across open pelagic waters in relative safety. Most carangids are considered sports fishes and anglers are usually provided with a good fight for their troubles. In addition, most species are good eating, the pompanos being exceptionally good eating and commanding considerably higher prices than most food fishes.

The Roosterfish (family Nematistiidae) is the only member of its family. *Nematistius pectoralis* occurs in the tropical eastern Pacific and is distinctive by having the seven spines of the first dorsal fin elongate and filamentous. When folded back they fit into a groove. The Roosterfish is a good fighter and good to eat, thus making it a target for fishermen.

The dolphins (family Coryphaenidae) are more commonly being called dolphinfishes or even by the Hawaiian name mahimahis to help distinguish them from the porpoise-like mammals also called dolphins. The two species are very similar, with long, spineless dorsal and anal fins and a forked caudal fin. The males of the larger Dolphin *(Coryphaena hippurus)* develop a very high blunt forehead giving the fish a distinctive appearance. Mahimahis are excellent game fishes and excellent food fishes, so they are actively sought out by fishermen. They travel in small schools and once one is hooked others usually are also. Living fishes are quite beautiful, with blues, greens, and yellow predominating. Once landed, the fishes in their death throes change color, going through a rainbow of hues until they are dead and a dull silvery gray.

The family Apolectidae contains a single species, *Apolectus niger,* from the Indo-West Pacific. Formerly known under the name *Formio niger* (family Formionidae), individuals over 9.1 cm have no pelvic fins. The dorsal fin has 2-6 rudimentary spines and 41-46 rays. The scales are small and numerous, and a few enlarged scutes adorn the posterior end of the lateral line. Recently some authors have synonymized *Apolectus* with *Parastromateus* and have at the same time included the family Apolectidae in the Carangidae. It seems likely that these steps will be accepted.

## Moonfish and Slipmouths (Plate 193)

The Moonfish (*Mene maculata,* family Menidae) is very compressed with a sharp breast. The dorsal and anal fins are many-rayed (43-45 and 30-33 rays respectively) and have no spines.

Members of the family Leiognathidae are called by many names, the most common being ponyfishes, slipmouths, and slimys. They occur in marine and brackish waters of the Indo-West Pacific. The body is very compressed and the scales are small. The dorsal and anal fins are many-rayed, with spines, and fold back into scaly sheaths. Most species are small, the largest attaining a length of only a foot. They exude a slimy mucus when handled and the small mouths are highly protrusible, accounting for two of the common names. Although some of the species make interesting aquarium fishes, the basic silvery color places them low on the desirable list.

## Pomfrets (Plate 194)

Pomfrets (family Bramidae) are oceanic fishes from tropical oceans. Deep-bodied and with a single dorsal fin, the pomfrets are divided into two subfamilies. The Braminae contains *Brama, Taractes*, etc., while the Pteraclinae contains the genera *Pteraclis* and *Pterycombus*. Although the latter species are quite attractive (silvery body and long black sail-like dorsal and anal fins), they are never available.

## Australian Salmons (Plate 194)

The Australian salmons (family Arripidae) occur in southern Australia and New Zealand. Only a single genus and two species are known. They are not true salmons, but apparently arrived at the name through confusion of early settlers in Australia who likened them to the European salmon.

## Rovers, Snappers, and Fusiliers (Plates 195–209)

Rovers (family Emmelichthyidae) are warm-water fishes of most oceans. The dorsal fin may be continuous with but a shallow notch, so it appears to be in two separate parts but with the gap filled with short spines. The two lobes of the forked caudal fin fold in scissor-like fashion.

The snappers (family Lutjanidae) are quite well known, and a number of the almost 200 species are commonly kept in aquarists' tanks. Certainly snappers are well represented in public aquariums. The dorsal fin is continuous (some have a shallow notch), and most species have characteristic enlarged canine teeth on the jaws. They are important food fishes, and anglers consider some of them prize catches. Most are bottom-dwelling schooling fishes feeding on small fishes and invertebrates. The largest genus, *Lutjanus*, contains many species that are welcome in aquarists' tanks, especially the more colorful ones like the bright yellow species with blue stripes (mostly *Lutjanus kasmira* but others as well) and many juveniles. *Lutjanus sebae* has always been an aquarium favorite, as has the black and white patterned juvenile of *Macolor niger*. Although not common, juveniles of *Symphorus nematophorus* have filamentous dorsal fin rays and often are kept. The Yellowtail Snapper (*Ocyurus chrysurus*) has a yellow stripe that extends from the snout backward to include the entire tail. It differs behaviorally from other snappers by occurring solitarily and swimming higher in the water column.

Fusiliers (family Caesionidae) occur in the warm waters of the Indo-West Pacific. They are streamlined fishes with a deeply forked caudal fin and a small mouth. They are planktivorous (feeding on small drifting organisms) and commonly are seen in large schools over the reef. Only an occasional fusilier is seen in marine hobbyists' tanks, but they are more common in public aquariums.

## Tripletails (Plate 209)

Tripletails (family Lobotidae) occur in marine, brackish, and fresh waters of tropical seas. The name does not imply that they have three tails, but the posterior edges of the dorsal and anal fins plus the true tail give that appearance. Two genera are included in this family, the freshwater and brackish *Datnioides* that freshwater aquarists should know, and the marine *Lobotes*, the true Tripletail. Juvenile *Lobotes* are very good at pretending to be dead leaves or other floating material along the shoreline. They lie on their side and float among the debris until prey animals are encountered. Juveniles are mottled brown or dark brownish black, aiding in the illusion. These small fish are occasionally in the trade.

## Mojarras (Plates 210, 211)

Mojarras (family Gerreidae) occur in marine, brackish, and even some fresh waters in tropical and subtropical seas, the majority in American waters. They inhabit sandy shore areas. These relatively small (most less than 25 cm), silvery fishes have a highly protrusible mouth and sheaths that accept the dorsal and anal fins. The caudal fin is forked. The basic silver of these fishes may be complemented by dark markings and, in some species, yellow fins. Nevertheless, they are only occasionally present in the aquarium trade.

## Grunts, Porgies, and Their Relatives (Plates 212–242, 245)

The grunts (family Haemulidae) inhabit tropical and subtropical waters around the world, usually close to the bottom in reefy areas. Although most are strictly marine, some species occur in brackish water. The dorsal fin is continuous and the small mouth is normally provided with cardiform teeth. Two subfamilies are commonly employed, the Haemulinae (the true grunts) and Plectorhynchinae, the latter subfamily (common name sweetlips because of the thick, fleshy lips) sometimes being raised to family status. Grunts are predominantly an Atlantic group while sweetlips are more Indo-Pacific. The grunts get their name because of the grunting noise they make by grinding their pharyngeal teeth together and amplifying the sound with the swim bladder. They commonly school and may be seen on the reef in company with large schools of snappers. Juvenile Atlantic grunts are only occasionally offered for sale to hobbyists, but sweetlips are almost always available. Young sweetlips are usually brightly colored, and very small individuals move with a sort of sinuous motion. The most popular aquarium species are *Plectorinchus chaetodonoides* (Clown Sweetlips) and *P. orientalis* in the Plectorhynchinae and *Anisotremus virginicus* (Porkfish) in the Haemulinae. This large family includes about 175 species.

The bonnetmouths (family Inermiidae) have the dorsal fin divided by a deep notch and the caudal fin is forked. The upper jaw is highly protrusible. Bonnetmouths are planktivorous, feeding on the small drifting organisms of the plankton. Only two monotypic genera are included.

Porgies (family Sparidae) are marine (rarely brackish or freshwater) fishes of tropical to occasionally temperate waters, the greatest proportion of the 100 or so species occurring in the Atlantic. They resemble grunts in having a continuous dorsal fin, but the maxilla is covered by a sheath when the mouth is closed. Habitats include reefs and rocky and sandy areas. Like the grunts, the porgies commonly aggregate into schools. Food items are varied in these omnivorous fishes, some species crushing molluscs with molar-like teeth. Few of the porgies are in the aquarium trade. They are mostly caught as food fishes both commercially and by sport fishermen.

The emperors (family Lethrinidae) inhabit coastal waters of the Indo-West Pacific and West Africa. They have a continuous dorsal fin and the eyes (at least in *Lethrinus*) are commonly set high on the head, the resulting elongate snout being used to dig into the sand for small invertebrates (sort of marine *Geophagus*). These are common food fishes that rarely are seen in the aquarium trade.

The threadfin breams (family Nemipteridae) are closely related to the emperors. They have a continuous dorsal fin and the caudal fin may have a filament extending from the upper lobe. Most of the three dozen species are quite colorful, with species of *Scolopsis* and *Pentapodus* appearing regularly in the hobby. The third genus of the family, *Nemipterus*, contains delicately colored species, but for some reason they do not enter the marine aquarium trade.

## Drums and Croakers (Plates 242–244)

There are over 200 species of drums and croakers included in the family Sciaenidae that inhabit marine, brackish, and fresh waters of the tropical to temperate zones of the world. The largest number of freshwater drums occur in South America. The dorsal fin is long and has a deep notch between the spinous and soft portions. The lateral line scales extend to the end of the caudal fin, and some species possess a barbel or barbels on the chin. Most drums are found in shallow inshore waters over sandy bottoms. The common names are derived from their ability to make sounds using muscular contractions amplified by the swim bladder. Included in this family are such well known food and sports fishes as the weakfishes, Spotted Sea Trout, White Seabass, kingfishes, Corbina, and Black Drum. Aquarists keep the young of the genus *Equetus*, which often have the first dorsal and pelvic fins greatly elongated. These are the high-hats, cubbyus, and jackknife-fishes.

## Goatfishes (Plates 245–251)

Goatfishes (family Mullidae) are so-called because of their two long chin barbels that are used in detecting food as they move over the bottom substrate. They also have two widely separated dorsal fins and a forked tail. The dominant color is red with yellow, white, and black often providing contrast in various patterns. Goatfishes inhabit tropical seas usually near reefs, where they feed on the associated crustaceans and other invertebrates. They are important food fishes occurring occasionally in moderately large schools. Aquarists keep goatfishes not only for their coloration but also as a means of having the food on the bottom removed, much as do the catfishes in freshwater aquaria. The drawback is that they are so vigorous that at times the bottom is stirred up, causing a cloudy tank.

## Moonfishes (Plate 252, 344)

Moonfishes (family Monodactylidae) are marine and brackish water fishes (although they can exist in pure fresh water if necessary) from the Indo-West Pacific and West African coasts. The body is very deep and compressed, and the dorsal and anal fins are long-based and continuous, with graduated spines. These fins are covered with scales. The Common Moonfish (*Monodactylus argenteus*) is prized by both freshwater and marine aquarists, though most specimens are kept in brackish water with scats and other similar fishes.

## Sweepers (Plates 252–254)

Sweepers (family Pempherididae) are marine and brackish water fishes inhabiting the Indo-Pacific and the western Atlantic. The body is deep and compresed, and there is a single short-based dorsal fin and a long-based anal fin. These fishes normally are seen in large schools around reefs, commonly seeking shelter in caves or among the spines of sea urchins along with cardinalfishes and other small fishes. A few of the species are provided with luminescent organs. Sweepers are not usually seen in the aquarium trade.

## Butterflyfishes, Angelfishes, and Their Allies (Plates 255–296)

Sea chubs (family Kyphosidae) are marine fishes of tropical to temperate waters of the Atlantic, Pacific, and Indian Oceans. Most are compressed fishes with small mouths. The family is currently divided into three subfamilies, the Girellinae (nibblers), Kyphosinae (rudderfishes), and Scorpidinae (halfmoons). The halfmoons are commonly placed in their own family. The rudderfishes obtained their common name through their habit of following ships at sea. The nibblers are inshore fishes perhaps most commonly known through one of our West Coast species, the Opaleye (*Girella nigricans*). The halfmoons contain some popular aquarium fishes, especially the Stripey (*Microcanthus strigatus*) and the Moonlighter (*Tilodon sexfasciatus*, formerly *Vinculum sexfasciatum*). Some of the Australian species are quite colorful but have not appeared very often in the aquarium trade.

Spadefishes (family Ephippididae) have a deep, laterally compressed body and a small mouth. The dorsal fin is continuous in *Platax* but notched between the spinous and soft-rayed portions in the other genera. They occur in tropical and subtropical oceans mostly around reefs. Young spadefishes commonly occur in inshore waters among the mangroves.

Young *Chaetodipterus*, for example, are great mimics of dead leaves floating along the shore. Although most ephippids grow quite large with respect to home aquaria, several species are commonly maintained. Species of batfishes (*Platax*) are the favorites and are almost always available. The three most common batfishes kept (as juveniles) range from easy to keep but not especially colorful (*Platax orbicularis*) to fairly difficult to maintain but quite pretty (*P. pinnatus*).

Scats (family Scatophagidae) inhabit marine and brackish inshore waters in tropical regions of the Indo-West Pacific. The body is deep and compressed and the dorsal fin is deeply notched; there are four anal fin spines. It has been reported that a toxin is associated with the spines of the dorsal fin, so these fishes should be handled with care. All scats, when available, are suitable fishes for the aquarium although *Scatophagus argus* is by far the most common species available. Most aquarists house them in brackish water tanks as these are most suitable for the young. Larger individuals do better in more marine environments and are seen in harbors feeding on excrement and other refuse from the ships that dock there, earning them the rather unflattering common name dung eaters.

The butterflyfishes (family Chaetodontidae) are tropical marine fishes mostly found in reef situations. They are compressed and deep-bodied bodied with attractive colors and patterns. The dorsal fin is continuous, and a number of species have the snout produced to a greater or lesser extent. Common elements of the color pattern may include an eyeband and a false eyespot in the soft portion of the dorsal fin. A larval stage called the tholichthys is present. Butterflyfishes are among the most popular of aquarium fishes, and many species are always available where marine fishes are sold. Longevity in aquaria, however, is dependent almost entirely upon the species as some are very specific in their dietary requirements (needing live coral, for example) while others are omnivorous and will accept a variety of foods.

Angelfishes (family Pomacanthidae) inhabit tropical marine waters of the world, usually around reefs. The body is commonly deep and compressed, the dorsal fin is continuous, the soft portion often provided with a filament, and there is a characteristic spine at the angle of the preopercular bone. Most species are very colorful, some undergoing vast changes from juvenile to adult patterns and thereby confusing early workers in the group. Like butterflyfishes, they are extremely popular with marine aquarists and almost every species is a potential aquarium inhabitant. But also like butterflyfishes, certain angelfishes are more difficult to keep than others, mostly due to the inability of the aquarist to provide proper nourishment. The pygmy angelfishes of the genus *Centropyge* are best suited for home aquaria, while members of the genus *Pomacanthus* are best kept only when young as they grow quite large. The adults make excellent displays in public aquariums.

The Oldwife, *Enoplosus armatus* (family Enoplosidae), is a southern Australian species that is compressed and deep-bodied with a deeply notched dorsal fin, both portions being somewhat extended. It makes an excellent aquarium fish when available (which isn't very often).

The armorheads (family Pentacerotidae) are deep- to very deep-bodied, compressed fishes with the head usually encased in exposed, rough, striated bone. They occur in the Indo-Pacific and southwestern Atlantic oceans. They are rarely available to home aquarists and only occasionally may be seen in public aquariums.

## Knifejaws (Plate 297)

Knifejaws (family Oplegnathidae) are so-called because of the parrot-like beak of fused teeth with which they are capable of crushing molluscs and crustaceans. The spinous dorsal fin is continuous, and the scales are small (in the parrotfishes, the other major family with fused teeth, the scales are large). Knifejaws are marine fishes with an unusual distribution — Japan, southern Australia, Peru and the Galapagos, and South Africa. A single genus with half a dozen species comprises the family.

## Surfperches (Plates 297–298)

The surfperches (family Embiotocidae) are marine fishes (with one exception, *Hysterocarpus traski*) inhabiting the coastal areas of the North Pacific. The dorsal fin is continuous and the scales are relatively small (35-75 in the lateral line). Surfperches are viviparous, giving birth to living young. The male impregnates the female by use of thickened anterior rays of the anal fin. Few surfperches are kept by marine aquarists except perhaps on a local basis in California, where they are common. One of the drawbacks is their need for cooler temperatures. Surfperches are normally present in West Coast public aquariums.

## Damselfishes and Clownfishes (Plates 299–336)

Damselfishes and clownfishes or anemonefishes (family Pomacentridae) are mostly marine fishes from shallow tropical waters around the world. The nostril is single in most species and the mouth is small. The dorsal fin is continuous (somewhat notched in some anemonefishes) and the anal fin has two spines instead of the usual three of perciform fishes. Most species are small (usually less than 15 cm ) and colorful (at least in the younger stages) with an aggressive, territorial nature. All these attributes endear them to marine aquarists, many of whom started in the hobby by keeping one or more species of damselfish or anemonefish. The anemonefishes (*Amphiprion* and *Premnas*) stand out from the rest of the family not only by their general appearance (most are white and orange or orange-red in color) but by their association with anemones. These fishes live unharmed among the stinging tentacles of anemones, thus receiving protection for themselves and their eggs. They are colorful fishes that beginners are able to keep for relatively long periods of time. Humbugs (members of the genus *Dascyllus*) have attractive black and white color patterns and are also quite popular with aquarists. Some species also are able to have a commensal association with anemones, but most simply shelter among the sharp branches of living coral. Of the rest of the family, almost any species would fare well in aquaria. Several favorites have emerged such as the Garibaldi (*Hypsypops rubicunda*), the Beaugregory (*Stegastes leucostictus*), the Jewelfish (*Microspathodon chrysurus*), and the Blue Devil (*Chrysiptera cyaneus*).

## Hawkfishes and Their Relatives (Plates 337–344)

Hawkfishes (family Cirrhitidae) occur in tropical regions of the world (although most are Indo-Pacific), usually in coral reef or rocky areas. They are usually small fishes with pleasing patterns, with reds predominating. The dorsal fin is continuous, and there sometimes are cirri on the interspinous membrane. The pectoral fins are large, the lower rays thickened and sometimes extended as sensory feelers. The name hawkfishes is derived from their habit of "perching" on the highest point of a coral head waiting for prey much as a hawk woud do. Most common hawkfishes are kept by marine aquarists.

Kelpfishes (family Chironemidae) are marine fishes from the coastal waters of Australia and New Zealand. Only two genera with about four species are included in the family. The family Aplodactylidae (no common name) has three genera with five species. These fishes are coastal marine fishes with a disjunct distribution, southern Australia, New Zealand, Peru, and Chile. Both these families are similar in general aspect to the morwongs.

Morwongs (family Cheilodactylidae) are marine fishes of both the Southern Hemisphere (all oceans) and Northern Hemisphere (China, Japan, and the Hawaiian Islands). The dorsal fin is continuous but may be notched, and the lower four to seven pectoral fin rays are generally thickened, elongated, and detached in adults. The generic name *Cheilodactylus* is currently preferred to *Goniistius*. Morwongs are only occasionally seen in the aquarium hobby.

Trumpeters (family Latrididae) are similar fishes from the coastal areas of southern Australia, New Zealand, and Chile. There are three genera with a total of about 10 species.

## Bandfishes and Owstoniids (Plate 345)

The family Owstoniidae is a small one of about a dozen species. The body is elongate and compressed, the dorsal fin continuous, and the caudal fin somewhat elongate but not connected to the other vertical fins. The lateral line runs along the base of the dorsal fin. Bandfishes (family Cepolidae) are marine fishes of the eastern Atlantic and Indo-West Pacific. The body is elongate and tapers to the tail. The many-rayed dorsal and anal fins are connected with the caudal fin and are without spines. The predominant color in both families is red or pinkish. None of the seven species are regularly available to the marine aquarist, and it is even unusual to see one displayed at public aquariums.

## Mullets, Barracudas, and Threadfins (Plates 345–347)

The mullets (family Mugilidae) occur in all temperate and tropical seas in coastal marine and brackish waters. There are two separate dorsal fins, and the pelvic fins are subabdominal. The stomach is thick-walled and muscular and the intestine is very long. These are schooling fishes commonly found near the surface, and they are prone to leaping from the water only to fall back with an audible splat. Mud is picked up from the bottom and strained by the elongate gill rakers. Mullets are not usually considered for home aquaria.

Barracudas (family Sphyraenidae) are elongate streamlined fishes with two widely separated dorsal fins. The lower jaw is projecting, and the mouth is provided with large, fang-like teeth earning these species a reputation of being ferocious predators that will even attack man. This reputation is enhanced by their habit of following swimmers and boats, perhaps attracted by the commotion and expecting to find something to eat. Most (but not all) reports of attacks on man by barracudas are untrue or greatly exaggerated. Barracudas are attracted by shining objects (like silvery bait fishes) and may inadvertently snap at a finger with a shiny ring on it if it is dangled from a boat in water of low visibility. Although most barracudas are relatively small, the great barracuda (*Sphyraena barracuda*) may attain a length of more than 1.8 m. Barracudas are kept by some marine aquarists as novelties and every public aquarium has a complement of them, especially if there is a large reef tank.

Threadfins (family Polynemidae) occur in marine and brackish waters of all tropical and subtropical areas. They have two separate dorsal fins, a subterminal mouth, and pectoral fins that are divided into two sections, the lower portion normally with 3-7 unattached, elongate rays that are use for detecting food.

## Wrasses, Parrotfishes, and Odacids (Plates 348–415)

The wrasses (family Labridae) are a highly diversified group of fishes found primarily in the warm tropical seas of the world. With some 500 species in about 57 genera, they run the gamut from deep-bodied and compressed to nearly terete, from species a few centimeters long to giants up to 3 m or more, and from drab colorless species to very gaudy fishes with a rainbow of colors. The mouth is protractile, the teeth are separate, some projecting outward, and the lips in some species are thick and blubbery. The dorsal fin is continuous, the soft rays of some species with long filaments. Behavioral patterns are often quite interesting. Many wrasses are parasite pickers (feeding on the ectoparasites of larger fishes) as juveniles, while members of one genus (*Labroides*) do it as a full-time job. Some wrasses dive into the sand to escape predators, and a number of species sleep under the sand at night. Still others build a cocoon around themselves for sleeping much as do some parrotfishes. The coloration of the wrasses is usually quite spectacular, endearing them to marine aquarists, and commonly changes from juvenile to adult. This change may be toward a less colorful adult but also may be from one gaudy pattern to another. For example, the Clown Wrasse (*Coris gaimard*) is bright orange with black-edged white markings. The adult is covered (particularly posteriorly) with brilliant blue spots. Sexual dichromatism is very common in the family, and this may reflect the two distinct spawning methods that may be present in the same species — a male-female one-on-one situation and group spawning. The single spawning male normally has a completely different livery. Many wrasses swim primarily by movement of their pectoral fins, giving them an odd sort of swimming motion. Many wrasses are in the aquarium trade.

The odacids (family Odacidae) are sometimes called weed whitings and have individual common names such as Herring Cale, Rainbowfish, and Tubemouth. The mouth is not protractile. The teeth in the jaws are fused into a parrot-like beak. The dorsal fin is continuous. Six genera with about a dozen species occur in the coastal marine waters of southern Australia and New Zealand. Mostly because of the long shipping distance and the cool water required, these fishes are not usually seen in the aquarium trade.

The parrotfishes (family Scaridae) are marine fishes of primarily tropical waters. The teeth are coalesced into a parrot-like beak (hence their common name) and the mouth is not protractile. The dorsal fin is continuous. There are about 75 species, but the exact number is not known because of confusion in parrotfish systematics. This is caused in large part by coloration changes from juvenile to adult, great coloration differences between the sexes, and by the very similar meristics of most of the species. Parrotfishes are herbivorous, commonly nibbling at living or dead coral to fed on the algae that is growing just below the surface layers or in the polyps themselves. Many are schooling fishes moving over the reef and stopping to graze as a unit as they go. Substantial amounts of calcareous material are ingested with the algae, broken down, and excreted back into the reef. Parrotfishes are thus considered one of the major factors in sediment production on the reef.

## Eelpouts, Pricklebacks, and Their Relatives (Plates 416–417)

Ronquils (family Bathymasteridae) are marine coastal fishes of the North Pacific. The dorsal fin is continuous and the large pectoral fins have a vertical base. Only three genera with seven species are included in this family. Normally these fishes are not seen in the aquarium trade.

Eelpouts (family Zoarcidae) are marine fishes of the cold waters of the Arctic and Antarctic. They have an elongate, tapering body with the long-based dorsal and anal fins confluent with the caudal fin. Pelvic fins are often lacking and when present are reduced and located far forward. Some members of the family are viviparous. Few aquarists can provide the cold water they need, although public aquariums on the West Coast of the U.S. usually have several representatives of this family on display. It is a fairly large family of 40 genera and 150 species.

Pricklebacks (family Stichaeidae) are marine fishes primarily of the North Pacific (plus a few in the North Atlantic). The dorsal and anal fins are long-based, the dorsal entirely spinous in most species (hence the common name). Among the better known species are the Monkeyface Prickleback (*Cebidichthys violaceous*) and Decorated Warbonnet (*Chirolophis polyactocephalus*) of the Pacific, and the Longsnout Prickleback (*Lumpenella longirostris*) of the Atlantic.

Gunnels (family Pholididae) are also marine fishes occurring in the shallow waters of the North Pacific and North Atlantic. The dorsal fin is about twice as long as the anal, with up to 100 spines. The pectoral fins may be absent, rudimentary, or small, while the pelvic fins may be rudimentary or absent. *Pholis gunnellus* is a representative species. The spawners take turns guarding the eggs, which are rolled into a ball by the curled bodies of the parents.

Wolffishes (family Anarhichadidae) are marine fishes of the North Atlantic and North Pacific. The dorsal fin contains only spines, the pectoral fins are large, and the pelvic fins are absent. The powerful jaws typically are provided with large molariform teeth for use in crushing the shells of molluscs and crustaceans and with large canine teeth, making them dangerous to handle. Only two genera with a total of seven species are included.

## Jawfishes, Stargazers, Sandperches, and Their Relatives (Plates 418–424)

Jawfishes (family Opistognathidae) inhabit tropical and subtropical waters. The dorsal and anal fins are long-based and continuous, and the lateral line is high on the body. The mouth is large and is used to excavate the burrows and to incubate the eggs (males are the oral incubators in this family). Most of the species are no larger than 15 cm in length. Some species of jawfishes are found in the aquarium trade, particularly the Yellowhead Jawfish (*Opistognathus aurifrons*) of the tropical western Atlantic. Aquarists must remember that a deep substrate is required for their well-being as they must be able to construct their burrows.

Eelblennies (family Congrogadidae) occur in the Indo-Pacific region. The body is elongate with long-based dorsal and anal fins confluent with the caudal fin. The pelvic fins may be present and located well forward (jugular) or absent. Eelblennies occur on mud and gravel bottoms and on coral reefs.

Only one genus with two species makes up the family Notograptidae of southern New Guinea and northern Australia. The body is elongate (eel-like) with long-based dorsal and anal fins that are confluent with the caudal fin. The pectoral fins are well developed, but the pelvics are reduced to a small spine and two rays. A mental barbel is present.

A single species, *Pholidichthys leucotaenia*, the Convict Blenny, comprises the family Pholidichthyidae. It occurs from the southwesternmost Philippines to the Solomon Islands. The body is eel-like, and the long-based dorsal and anal fins are confluent with the caudal fin.

Pectoral and pelvic fins are present, the latter with a slender spine and 2-3 soft rays. This species occasionally appears in the aquarium trade.

Sandfishes (family Trichodontidae) are marine fishes of the North Pacific. There are two dorsal fins and the pectoral fins are quite large. The mouth opens almost vertically and the lips are fringed. The two species of this family normally lie in wait for passing food while partially buried in the sand.

Weeverfishes (family Trachinidae) occur mostly in the Mediterranean but also in other parts of the eastern Atlantic, the Black Sea, and off Chile. There are two dorsal fins, the second dorsal and anal fins being long-based. Like the sandfishes, the weevers will lie on the bottom partially buried in the sand. They are dangerous because they are virtually invisible and thus are likely to be stepped upon, and there are venom glands associated with the spines of the first dorsal and the gill cover.

Stargazers (family Uranoscopidae) occur in temperate to tropical oceans. The mouth is nearly vertical and the lips are fringed. The eyes are dorsal or close to it, earning them their common name. There are two dorsal fins or the first may be absent; the second dorsal and anal have moderately long bases. Like the weeverfishes there are venom glands but these are associated with two large grooved spines just above the pectoral fins. Some stargazers also can produce an electrical shock of 50 volts or more. These fishes lie buried in the sand with just the anterior part of the head exposed. The mouth when opened reveals a worm-like filament on its floor used to entice prey.

Sanddivers (family Trichonotidae) occur in warm marine waters of the Indo-West Pacific. The dorsal and anal fins are long-based with the anterior rays of the dorsal fin often prolonged and filamentous.

The sandburrowers (family Creediidae) also occur in the warm to temperate waters of the Indo-West Pacific. The dorsal fin is continuous and the dorsal and anal fins are long-based. The fleshy snout projects beyond the lower jaw, which is bordered by a row of cirri.

Three species included in two genera comprise the family Leptoscopidae. The mouth is moderately oblique and the lips are fringed. The dorsal and anal fins are long-based and the eyes are dorsal in position like the stargazers. These fishes occur around Australia and New Zealand.

The sandperches (family Mugiloididae) occur on the Atlantic coasts of South America and Africa and throughout the Indo-Pacific. The dorsal fin is long-based, preceded by about four or five short spines that may or may not be separated from the soft rays by a notch. The pelvic fins are below and just anterior to the pectorals and are used to prop up the anterior end of the fish as it sits on the sand substrate. Of all the families of fishes discussed together here, the sandperches are the most likely to be seen in the aquarium trade.

## Blennies and Their Relatives (Plates 425–452)

People generally speak of blennies as if they were all included in a single family. The truth is that the suborder Blennioidei is composed of six families at present with some 675 species in about 127 genera. They are generally small, benthic fishes that often have cirri on their head. Many species are in the marine aquarium trade.

The triplefin blennies (family Tripterygiidae) are primarily tropical marine fishes of all oceans. The dorsal fin is divided into three distinct segments, the first two composed of spines, the third of soft rays. The pelvics are reduced and jugular in position, and there are no cirri on the nape. This family includes somewhat over 100 species in such genera as *Tripterygion* and *Enneanectes.*

The sand stargazers (family Dactyloscopidae) are warm temperate to tropical fishes from North and South America. The dorsal fin is continuous or divided and the jugular pelvic fins have a spine and three soft rays. The very oblique mouth usually has fringed lips, and the upper edge of the gill cover has finger-like elements. Sand stargazers commonly bury themselves in the sand bottom, breathing by means of a specialized branchiostegal pump.

Members of the family Labrisomidae (no common name as yet) are mostly tropical marine fishes from the Atlantic and Pacific Oceans. The dorsal fin is continuous (but with the rays longer than the spines) and has more spines than soft rays. Cirri are often present on the nape, nostrils, and above the eyes. Sixteen genera are included containing 100 or more species. Only *Xenomedea* and some *Starksia* are viviparous.

The clinid blennies (family Clinidae) also have a continuous dorsal fin with more spines than soft rays, with all the rays being simple. Like the previous families of the suborder, scales are present. About 75 species in 20 genera are divided into three tribes. The Ophiclinini from southern Australia are eel-shaped with a continuous dorsal fin that is united with the caudal fin as is the anal fin. They have many more spines than rays (36-84 and 1-4 respectively). They are mostly ovoviviparous, the males having an intromittent organ. The Myxodini are from temperate waters of the Western Hemisphere and the Mediterranean Sea. The continuous dorsal fin does not have the anterior few spines separated by a notch, and the anal fin is not attached to the caudal. Orbital and nasal cirri are present. The species are oviparous, the males lacking an intromittent organ. The Clinini are widespread mainly in the temperate Indo-West Pacific. The dorsal fin is continuous, but the anterior three spines are usually longer than the rest and separated from them by a small notch. The anal fin is rarely attached to the caudal. The species are ovoviviparous, the males having an intromittent organ.

Members of the family Chaenopsidae are commonly referred to by several common names, including pikeblennies, tubeblennies, and flagblennies. The body is naked (scaleless) and the dorsal fin is continuous (although some species have the anterior portion of the spinous dorsal fin much higher than the remainder of the fin). The dorsal and/or the anal fin may be united with the caudal, or all may be separate. The head is generally spiny or rough, and orbital and/or nasal cirri may be present or absent. These blennies are commonly known for their fierce territorial defense, displays with flag-like dorsal fins; at least one species has been shown to enter a symbiotic relationship with a stony coral.

The combtooth blennies (family Blenniidae) are what most people regard as "blennies." They are mostly marine (a few are brackish or freshwater species) fishes from tropical and subtropical waters around the world. They are naked or with modified scales. The dorsal fin is continuous, and the jaws are provided with comb-like teeth. About 300 species are divided into five tribes. The Salariini are mostly from the Indo-West Pacific. The caudal fin rays may or may not be branched. Some species are able to remain out of the water for considerable periods of time. About half the species of the Blenniidae are in the Salariini, including genera such as *Ecsenius, Istiblennius, Salarius, Entomacrodus,* etc. The Blenniini are mostly marine, and their caudal rays are branched. The 70 species are divided among fifteen genera, including *Blennius, Scartella,* and *Hypsoblennius.* The Omobranchini are also mostly marine, but their caudal fin rays are not branched. About 30 species are in this tribe. Phenablenniini includes the freshwater and brackish water *Phenablennius heyligeri* from Cambodia to Borneo. All the fin rays are unbranched. The tribe Nemophini includes the saber-toothed blennies. These occur in the Indian and Pacific Oceans, with one species, *Meiacanthus anema,* from brackish and fresh water. All fin rays are unbranched. These blennies are known for their more open-water existence and the habit of some of the species of mimicking more harmless fishes (such as cleaner wrasses) so that they can approach wary fishes that they then attack.

## Dragonets (Plates 453–456)

Dragonets (family Callionymidae) are marine benthic fishes from tropical waters around the world, although most occur in the Indo-West Pacific. There are two dorsal fins, the first usually composed of four spines. The mouth is generally small, the lips large, and the gill openings are reduced to a small aperture dorsally. The preoperculum is provided with a strong spine that commonly becomes entangled in nets. About 130 species are included in this family. Some of the species are regularly maintained in home aquaria, especially members of the genus *Synchiropus.* Sexual dimorphism in the form of the size and shape of the spinous dorsal fin and coloration is present.

## Gobies and Their Relatives (Plates 429, 457–495)

Seven families make up the suborder Gobioidei. These encompass some 263 genera that include almost 2,000 species, making it one of the most speciose groups of fishes. Some workers are of the opinion that the gobies should have full ordinal status; others relegate some of the families to subfamilies of the family Gobiidae. These are benthic fishes that usually are quite small, although some species reach 30 cm in length.

The sleepers (family Eleotrididae) are gobies of marine, brackish, and fresh waters of most tropical and subtropical areas. The pelvic fins are separate and do not form a sucking disc. However, the bases of these fins may be united and the variation in degree of fusion encountered leaves a question as to the advisability of keeping the sleepers separate from the "true" gobies. This discussion will probably go on for some time. There are two dorsal fins, the first with up to 8 spines. The mouth is never inferior in position. Only about 150 species are included in this family, including such genera as *Dormitator* and *Eleotris*. Some species are kept in captivity, although most are not very colorful.

The true gobies (family Gobiidae) are tropical to subtropical fishes of marine, fresh, and brackish waters around the world. The pelvic fins are united, forming a sucking disc. There are two separate dorsal fins, the first composed of up to 8 flexible spines. About 1,500 species in 200 genera make this the most speciose family of marine fishes. Most species are less than 10 cm long, although some may grow to 50 cm. Gobies have insinuated themselves into many different niches and may be seen in virtually every habitat. Some are able to live for extended periods out of water, returning only to wet down their gill chambers. Others are parasite-pickers, the most well-known of these being the Neon Goby, *Gobiosoma oceanops*. Still others have developed symbiotic relationships with various invertebrate animals, among which are sponges, corals, sea urchins, and of course the burrowing shrimp. Coloration ranges from drab, cryptic patterns to brilliant, almost unbelievable colors such as the red-orange and electric blue Catalina Goby, *Lythrypnus dalli*, from our West Coast and members of the genera *Nemateleotris* and *Ptereleotris* from the Indo-Pacific.

The eel-like gobies (family Gobioididae) occur in marine, fresh, and brackish waters of the Indo-Pacific, tropical America, and the tropical West African coast. The body is eel-like, the dorsal and anal fins confluent or nearly so with the caudal. The pelvic fins usually form an adhesive disc.

The burrowing gobies (family Trypauchenidae) are marine, brackish, and freshwater fishes from the Indo-Pacific region. They have an eel-like body with the continuous dorsal and anal fins confluent or nearly so with the caudal. The pelvic fins usually form an adhesive disc. The eyes are very small. These shallow-water gobies burrow into the soft muddy substrate.

The wormfishes (family Microdesmidae) occur in marine tropical waters. The body is very elongate to eel-like with small, embedded scales. The lower jaw is protruding. The dorsal fin is continuous but not united with the caudal fin. Occasional individuals of *Microdesmus* and *Gunnelichthys* turn up in the aquarium trade.

## Surgeonfishes (Plates 496–509)

The surgeonfishes (family Acanthuridae) are strictly marine fishes from all tropical seas. They are compressed, usually deep-bodied fishes with a continuous dorsal fin. Two subfamilies are currently recognized. The Acanthurinae contains all the species in the family save one. They are normally characterized by one or more spines or scalpel-like blades along the caudal peduncle that gave rise to their common name. Most species are found in reef habitats where they form aggregations browsing on the surface of the corals, substrate, or whatever. Many species are quite colorful, and several species are commonly found in the aquarium trade. Species of *Acanthurus*, *Paracanthurus*, and *Zebrasoma* are popular members of the disc-shaped group, while some species of *Naso* with their protuberances on the frontal region are also popular. The second subfamily, Zanclinae, the Moorish Idol, has commonly been regarded as a separate family (and many ichthyologists still regard the single species included—*Zanclus canescens* — as such). This species not only has an attractive color pattern but a pleasing shape as well and frequently has been used (along with the seahorse) as a decorative motif.

## Rabbitfishes (Plates 510–513)

The rabbitfishes (family Siganidae) are marine fishes from the Indo-Pacific region. The body is compressed and generally oval in shape. The dorsal fin is continuous and provided with 13 strong spines and ten soft rays; the anal fin has seven spines and nine soft rays, and the pelvic fins each have two spines (very unusual) and three soft rays. All the spines are grooved and associated with venom glands so that stab wounds are very painful and slow to heal. Of the two genera, *Lo* provides the aquarium trade with just about as many species as *Siganus* even though it is a much smaller genus.

## Tunas, Mackerels, Billfishes, and Their Relatives (Plates 514–517)

Seven families make up the suborder Scombroidei, which includes some of the world's fastest swimming fishes. Most are pelagic species, and some are found in deep oceanic waters. Altogether there are about 100 species included in 45 genera. None of the species are regularly in the aquarium trade, although many are seen in public aquariums in the larger tanks.

The snake mackerels (family Gempylidae) are tropical to temperate marine fishes often found at depths to 2,000 feet or more. The body is elongate and compressed, and the dorsal and anal fins are usually followed by isolated finlets. A forked caudal fin is present, but the pelvics are reduced or absent. Strong teeth are usually present in the jaws. About 22 species comprise this family.

The cutlassfishes (family Trichiuridae) also have a very elongate, very compressed body. The caudal fin may be small or absent and the pelvic fins are reduced. No finlets are present. The jaws are usually provided with fang-like teeth. About 17 species are included in this family. Cutlassfishes are good swimmers that usually stay near the bottom.

The largest family by far is the Scombridae, which includes the mackerels and tunas. About fifteen genera contain about 50 species. These streamlined fishes have two dorsal fins and detached finlets behind both the dorsal and anal fins. The caudal peduncle is tapering and is provided with two keels. The tunas and mackerels are fast swimming fishes that are highly regarded as food and sport fishes around the world. They are mainly schooling fishes of the open seas. Most are bluish to greenish on the back shading to silvery or white ventrally, making them very difficult to see.

The Swordfish (*Xiphias gladius*, family Xiphiidae) has the premaxillae and nasal bones prolonged to form the "sword." The pelvic fins and girdle are absent, and there is a single median keel on the peduncle of adults. The dorsal fin is short-based but high, and there is a single finlet posteriorly above and below on the caudal peduncle. Scales and jaw teeth are absent.

The billfishes (family Istiophoridae) are similar in aspect to the Swordfish but have scales and jaw teeth as well as pelvic fins. The caudal peduncle has two keels on each side. The dorsal fin is long-based and in the sailfishes is sail-shaped and higher than the body depth. In the spearfishes it is not sail-like and is about as high as the body depth while, in the marlins it is not sail-like and is not so high as the body depth. All these fishes are big-game fishes of sportsmen, their fighting abilities legendary.

## Driftfishes, Butterfishes, and Medusafishes (Plate 518)

Medusafishes (family Centrolophidae) are marine fishes of tropical and temperate seas. The dorsal fin is continuous, the spines weakly developed and graduating into the soft rays or stout and noticeably shorter than the soft rays. Seven genera are included with about 22 species.

The driftfishes (family Nomeidae) are marine fishes of tropical and subtropical seas. There are two dorsal fins and well developed pelvic fins. Most notable of the 15 species of this family is the small brightly colored Man-o'-war Fish (*Nomeus gronovii*), which can be seen swimming unharmed among the stinging tentacles of the jellyfish-like Man-o'-war (*Physalia*). Attempts to keep both the fish and the invertebrate in aquaria have usually met with failure.

The butterfishes (family Stromateidae) are marine coastal fishes of North and South America, western Africa, and southern Asia. The dorsal fin is continuous, usually taller anteriorly, and the body is deep and compressed. Adults lack pelvic fins. Only three genera with about a dozen species are included in this family. These schooling fishes are good eating and larger ones are harvested commercially.

## Flatfishes (Plates 519–525)

The six families of flatfishes are included in the order Pleuronectiformes. All of these fishes are quite distinctive in that the eyes both migrate to one side of the head and only that side becomes fully pigmented. The fishes lie on their uncolored side on the bottom substrate, usually nearly invisible by virtue of their coloration and pattern (which can be modified within limits) and because they partially cover themselves with the substrate. The pelagic larvae are bilaterally symmetrical and colorless. One eye (which one depends upon the species involved) migrates toward the one on the opposite side by either going around the edge of the fish or in some cases passing through it. As this is happening the colors start to become evident on one side and the fish takes up a bottom-living existence. Most flatfishes are carnivorous, their camouflage hiding them from potential prey animals. Many species are commercially valuable, for example the halibuts that may attain lengths of up to 3 m. The flatfishes include such well known fishes as the flounders, soles, halibuts, plaice, and tonguefishes.

The family Psettodidae is a small family of only one genus with two species from the Indo-Pacific and West Africa. The eyes may be either sinistral (left-sided) or dextral (right-sided). The pelvic fins are symmetrical, and the mouth is large. This family is by itself in a suborder because the dorsal fin does not extend onto the head, the anterior dorsal rays are spinous, and the palatine is toothed. The pelvic fins are nearly symmetrical and are each provided with a spine and five soft rays.

In the suborder Pleuronectoidei the dorsal fin extends onto the head at least to the eyes, the dorsal and anal fins are without spines, and the palatine is toothless. Three families, Citharidae, Bothidae, and Pleuronectidae, are included.

The Citharidae is a small family of five species included in four genera occurring in the Indo-West Pacific and the Mediterranean. The pelvic fins have a spine and five soft rays and their bases are short; the branchiostegal membranes are separated from each other. In one subfamily the eyes are sinistral while in the other they are dextral.

The lefteye flounders (family Bothidae) occur in the Atlantic, Pacific, and Indian Oceans. The eyes are sinistral and the pelvic fins are spineless. The eggs have a single oil globule in the yolk. The family is relatively large, with 37 genera and more than 200 species. Three subfamilies are presently admitted based partly on whether the pelvic fin bases are elongate (Scophthalminae), short and nearly symmetrical (Paralichthyinae), or the blind side base is shorter than that of the eyed side (Bothinae).

The righteye flounders (family Pleuronectidae) occur in the Arctic, Atlantic, and Pacific Oceans mostly in marine waters. No oil globule is seen in the yolk of the eggs. The 41 genera include some 100 species in four subfamilies. In the Poecilopsettinae the dorsal fin origin is above the eyes, the pelvic fins are symmetrical, and the lateral line of the blind side is rudimentary. In the Samarinae the dorsal fin origin is in front of the eyes, the pelvic fins are symmetrical, and the lateral lines are well developed or rudimentary. The Rhombosoleinae have asymmetrical pelvic fins and the lateral lines are equally developed on blind and eyed sides. The Pleuronectinae have the dorsal fin origin above the eyes, symmetrical pelvic fins, and the lateral lines well developed on both sides.

The suborder Soleoidei contains only two families (Cynoglossidae, Soleidae) where the pelvic fins are usually absent in the adults (the right one may be developed in some species), the mouth is small, and the jaws on the blind side are strongly curved and toothed.

The tonguefishes (family Cynoglossidae) are mostly marine fishes from tropical and subtropical seas. The eyes are sinistral, the dorsal and anal fins are confluent with the pointed caudal fin, and normally only the left pelvic fin is developed. The pectoral fins are absent. The mouth is asymmetrical, and the eyes are normally very small and close together. More than 100 species are included in three genera. Two subfamilies are recognized in which the snout may be hooked (Cynoglossinae) or not (Symphurinae).

The soles (family Soleidae) are mostly marine fishes of tropical to temperate seas. The eyes are dextral. Some 117 species are included in 31 genera. Two subfamilies are recognized, the Achirinae and the Soleinae. The Achirinae are American in distribution and provide the freshwater soles of the aquarium trade. The dorsal and anal fins are free from the caudal and the right pelvic fin is joined to the anal fin. The Soleinae are mostly found from Europe to Japan and Australia. The dorsal and anal fins are free from or united with the caudal fin and the pelvic fins are free from the anal fin.

## Puffers, Triggerfishes, Boxfishes, and Their Relatives (Plates 526–563)

The order Tetraodontiformes includes eight families of sometimes rather unusual fishes. The scales are often modified into spines, plates, or shields, and the gill openings are restricted. Most species are able to produce sounds by use of the swim bladder or by grinding their jaws or pharyngeal teeth. Tetraodontiforms (sometimes also called plectognaths) are divided into eight families that include more than 300 species.

The spikefishes (family Triacanthodidae) are deep-water benthic fishes from the tropical and subtropical western Atlantic and Indo-Pacific regions. They have a relatively normal dorsal fin divided into spines and soft rays, and the caudal fin is rounded to truncate.

The very similar triplespines (family Triacanthidae) are more shallow-water benthic fishes from the Indo-Pacific. They are readily distinguished from the species of the previous family by their forked caudal fin and higher number of dorsal and anal fin rays. There are only about 20 species of spikefishes and seven species of triplespines. Only one or two species are occasionally seen in the marine aquarium trade.

The leatherjackets (including the triggerfishes and filefishes) are members of the family Balistidae. These are marine fishes found around the world in tropical and subtropical waters. The body is coverd with heavy scales giving them a leathery or very rough texture. The pelvic fins are absent and the first dorsal fin is provided with a trigger or locking mechanism. The upper jaw has two rows of protruding incisor-like teeth that can be formidable weapons in some species. The soft dorsal and anal fins are usually long-based. The 135 species are generally included in 42 genera. Two subfamilies (often regarded as separate families) are currently recognized. The triggerfishes (subfamily Balistinae) have three dorsal fin spines, plate-like scales in regular series, and all soft fins with branched rays. The jaw teeth are heavy and strong, more developed for crushing than for nibbling. Many aquarium fishes are found in this subfamily including perhaps the most prized marine species of all — the Clown Triggerfish (*Balistoides conspicillum*). The filefishes (subfamily Monacanthinae) usually have only two dorsal spines, the second very small or even absent. The scales are small and in regular series but rough, giving the skin a prickly or furry feel. The soft dorsal, anal, and pectoral rays are all unbranched. The teeth in the jaws (three outer and two inner as compared with the four outer and three inner of the triggerfishes) are more developed for nibbling than for crushing. Many species of this subfamily have also found their way into the aquarium trade. One of the favorites is the Long-nosed Filefish, *Oxymonacanthus longirostris*, with its orange spots on a bluish to greenish background.

The boxfishes (including the trunkfishes and cowfishes) belong to the family Ostraciidae. These are marine fishes from the tropical oceans of the world. The body is enclosed in a bony carapace that is commonly box-shaped but may be very angular and provided with sharp edges and long spines. There is no spinous dorsal fin. The fins stick out from openings in the carapace to provide the meager propulsion for these fishes. Some species are so slow they can be easily caught by hand. Some species are dangerous in marine tanks, for when they are upset they exude a toxic substance that can kill any living thing in the tank including themselves. Even so several species have become standard importations for home aquaria. One of the most popular is *Ostracion cubicus*, which, when young, is bright yellow with black spots.

The Three-toothed Puffer (family Triodontidae) is called that by virtue of the three fused teeth in the jaws. There is a small spiny dorsal fin in most specimens, and the dorsal and anal fins each have 11 rays. The single species occurs in the Indo-West Pacific.

The puffers (family Tetraodontidae) are mostly marine fishes (some freshwater species are known in the aquarium trade) of tropical and subtropical waters of the world. The body is without scales or with some prickles in the belly area. There are four fused teeth in the jaws. Some species of puffers produce toxic substances that are dangerous if eaten. Instances of death caused by improperly prepared puffers are reported each year in Japan, where they regularly are eaten. The puffers have the ability to inflate themselves (with water or air depending on where they are) into a balloon-like shape when disturbed, a defense mechanism apparently helping to prevent them from being eaten. When left to their own devices they eventually return to their previous shape and beat a hasty retreat. Most of the aquarium puffers come from the genus *Canthigaster*. Several of these sharpnose puffers may be seen in any well stocked marine aquarium store.

The porcupinefishes (family Diodontidae) are also distributed worldwide in tropical seas. No freshwater or brackish water species are known. They are similar to the puffers but the body is covered with well developed spines. In some species the spines are permanently erected, in other they become erect only when the fish is inflated. There are two fused teeth in the jaws. Porcupinefishes are not as popular as the puffers but may occasionally be seen in dealers' tanks.

Finally, the molas (family Molidae) are marine tropical and subtropical fishes from around the world. They are sometimes called headfish as they seem to be composed almost entirely of a very large head. There is no swim bladder, no pelvic fins, no caudal peduncle, and the caudal fin may be absent as well. There are two fused teeth in the jaws. The dorsal and anal fins are set well back and provide the locomotory thrust. The young swim upright like most fishes, but the giant adults are more apt to spend their time floating or feebly swimming on their side. The largest species, *Mola mola*, may grow to 3 m and 270 kilos. It is also very fecund, producing up to 300 million eggs.

# INDEX

## A

*Abalistes stellatus*, Starry Triggerfish, 623
Abax Goby, *Eviota abax*, 576
*abax, Eviota*, Abax Goby, 576
*abbreviatus, Gerres*, Blue-backed Silver-Biddy, 276
*abdominalis, Abudefduf*, Maomao, 382
*abdominalis, Hippocampus*, Big-belly Seahorse, 129
*abei, Chaunax*, Abe's Sea Toad, 91
Abe's Sea Toad, *Chaunax abei*, 91
*Ablabys taenianotus*, Cockatoo Waspfish, 137
*Ablennes hians*, Flat Needlefish, 100
Abrolhos Scorpionfish, *Scorpaena* sp., 146
Abrolhos Triplefin, *Vauclusella* sp., 507
*Abudefduf abdominalis*, Maomao, 382
*Abudefduf bengalensis*, Bengal Sergeant, 381
*Abudefduf declevifrons*, Slope-head Sergeant, 380
*Abudefduf lorenzi*, Black-tail Sergeant, 382
*Abudefduf margariteus*, Pearl Sergeant, 381
*Abudefduf notatus*, Yellowtail Sergeant, 381
*Abudefduf saxatilis*, Sergeant Major, 380
*Abudefduf septemfasciatus*, Sevenbar Damsel, 382
*Abudefduf sexfasciatus*, Stripetail Damsel, 381
*Abudefduf sordidus*, Black Spot Sergeant, 380
*Abudefduf sparoides*, False-eye Damsel, 381
*Abudefduf taurus*, Night Sergeant, 380
*Abudefduf troscheli*, Panamic Sergeant Major, 380
*Abudefduf vaigiensis*, South Seas Sergeant Major, 380
*Abudefduf whitleyi*, Whitley's Sergeant, 382
Academy Eel, *Apterichtus ansp*, 62
*Acanthaluterus spilomelanura*, Bridled Leatherjacket, 635
*Acanthemblemaria aspera*, Roughhead Blenny, 518
*Acanthemblemaria balanorum*, Clubhead Blenny, 518
*Acanthemblemaria crockeri*, Browncheek Blenny, 518
*Acanthemblemaria exilispinis*, Slender-spined Blenny, 518
*Acanthemblemaria hancocki*, Hancock's Blenny, 518
*Acanthemblemaria macrospilus*, Barnacle Blenny, 518
*Acanthemblemaria spinosa*, Spiny Blenny, 518
*Acanthistius cinctus*, Yellow-banded Perch, 202
*Acanthistius pardalotus*, Australian Brown Grouper, 179
*Acanthistius serratus*, Wirrah, 202
*acanthistius, Epinephelus*, Gulf Coney, 191
*Acanthocepola indica*, Philippine Bandfish, 420
*Acanthocepola limbata*, Spotfin Bandfish, 420
*Acanthochromis polyacanthus*, Spiny Chromis, 397
*Acanthocybium solandri*, Wahoo, 602
*Acanthogobius flavimanus*, Yellowfin Goby, 552
*Acanthopagrus australis*, Australian Black Porgy, 292
*Acanthopagrus berda*, Black Bream, 289
*Acanthopagrus bifasciatus*, Twobar Seabream, 292
*Acanthopagrus latus*, Japanese Silver Bream, 292
*Acanthopagrus schlegeli*, Schlegel's Bream, 292
*acanthops, Centropyge*, African Pygmy Angelfish, 354
*Acanthurus achilles*, Achilles Tang, 581, 582
*Acanthurus bahianus*, Ocean Surgeon, 582
*Acanthurus bariene*, Black-spot Surgeon, 586
*Acanthurus blochii*, Tailring Surgeonfish, 582, 587
*Acanthurus chirurgus*, Doctorfish, 582
*Acanthurus chronixis*, Mimic Surgeonfish, 586
*Acanthurus coeruleus*, Blue Tang, 582
*Acanthurus dussumieri*, Dussumier's Surgeonfish, 586
*Acanthurus glaucopareius*, Gold-rimmed Surgeonfish, 583
*Acanthurus guttatus*, Mustard Surgeonfish, 583
*Acanthurus japonicus*, White-faced Surgeonfish, 582
*Acanthurus leucopareius*, Whiteband Surgeonfish, 588
*Acanthurus leucosternon*, Powder-blue Tang, 581, 583
*Acanthurus lineatus*, Clown Surgeonfish, 585, 587
*Acanthurus maculiceps*, Black-eared Surgeonfish, 587
*Acanthurus mata*, Mata Tang, 583, 586
*Acanthurus monroviae*, Monrovian Surgeonfish, 582
*Acanthurus nigricauda*, Brown-eared Surgeonfish, 587
*Acanthurus nigrofuscus*, Spot-cheeked Surgeonfish, 584
*Acanthurus nigroris*, Cuvier's Surgeonfish, 588
*Acanthurus olivaceus*, Orange-epaulette Surgeonfish, 584, 586
*Acanthurus pyroferus*, Chocolate Surgeonfish, 584, 586
*Acanthurus sohal*, Red Sea Clown Surgeon, 584
*Acanthurus tennenti*, Lieutenant Surgeonfish, 584
*Acanthurus thompsoni*, Yellow-tailed Surgeonfish, 584
*Acanthurus triostegus*, Convict Surgeonfish, 588

*Acanthurus xanthopterus*, Purple Surgeonfish, 584
*acares, Chromis*, Midget Chromis, 385
*acarne, Pagellus*, Spanish Bream, 290
*Acentrogobius gracilis*, Mangrove Goby, 551
Achilles Tang, *Acanthurus achilles*, 581, 582
*achilles, Acanthurus*, Achilles Tang, 581, 582
*Achirus lineatus*, Lined Sole, 615
*Achoerodus gouldii*, Blue Groper, 429
*aciminatus, Myrichthys*, Sharptail Eel, 61
*acinaces, Gerres*, Smallscale Pursemouth, 275, 276
*acipenserinus, Agonus*, Sturgeon Poacher, 168
*Acreichthys tomentosus*, Matted Leatherjacket, 633
*acroptilus, Odax*, Rainbow Fish, 478
*aculeatus, Chaetodon*, Poey's Butterflyfish, 346
*aculeatus, Halieutichthys*, Pancake Batfish, 93
*aculeatus, Kentrocapros*, Sawtooth Boxfish, 639
*aculeatus, Rhinecanthus*, Painted Triggerfish, 626
*acuminatus, Equetus*, High-hat, 308
*acuminatus, Heniochus*, Bannerfish, 348, 352
*acutidens, Negaprion*, Lemon Shark, 40
*acutirostris, Evistias*, Banded Boarhead, 335
Adalah, *Psettodes erumei*, 609
*adelaidae, Heteroclinus*, Adelaide Weedfish, 517
Adelaide Weedfish, *Heteroclinus adelaidae*, 517
*adetii, Lutjanus*, Gold-eyed Snapper, 261
*adiergastos, Chaetodon*, Bantayan Butterflyfish, 338
Adorned Wrasse, *Halichoeres cosmetus*, 442
Adriatic Blenny, *Lipophrys adriaticus*, 524
*adriaticus, Lipophrys*, Adriatic Blenny, 524
*adscensiones, Holocentrus*, Longjaw Squirrelfish, 109
*adscensionis, Epinephelus*, Rock Hind, 192
*adspersa, Pempheris*, Glowlight Bullseye, 322
*adspersus, Tautogolabrus*, Cunner, 468
*adustus, Gobiesox*, Panamic Clingfish, 97
*adustus, Myripristis*, Blacktip Soldierfish, 113, 114, 116
Aeneus Sculpin, *Myoxocephalus aeneus*, 165
*aeneus, Myoxocephalus*, Aeneus Sculpin, 165
*Aeoliscus punctulatus*, Spotted Shrimpfish, 122
*Aeoliscus strigatus*, Shrimpfish, 122
*aequalis, Ecsenius*, Lined Blenny, 528.16
*aequipinnis, Scorpis*, Blue Maomao, 328
*aequoreus, Entelurus*, Snake Pipefish, 126
*Aethaloperca rogaa*, Redflush Rockcod, 179
*Aetobatus narinari*, Spotted Eagle Ray, 47, 48, 49
*afer, Alphestes*, Mutton Hamlet, 203
aff *limbaughi, Gobiosoma*, Widebanded Cleaning Goby, 571
*affinis, Apogon*, Bigtooth Cardinalfish, 234
*affinis, Atherinops*, Topsmelt, 102
*affinis, Chilomycterus*, Pacific Burrfish, 653
*affinis, Euthynnus*, Kawakawa, 602
*affinis, Trachichthodes*, Nannygai, 106
African Angelfish, *Holacanthus africanus*, 366
African Butterflyfish, *Chaetodon dolosus*, 341
African Clown Wrasse, *Coris gaimard africana*, 439
African Goatfish, *Pseudupeneus prayensis*, 315
African Pompano, *Alectis ciliaris*, 251
African Pygmy Angelfish, *Centropyge acanthops*, 354
*africanus, Holacanthus*, African Angelfish, 366
*africanus, Urogymnus*, Porcupine Ray, 46
*aggregata, Cymatogaster*, Shiner Surfperch, 369
*agilis, Chromis*, Reef Chromis, 385
*Agonomalus proboscidalis*, Barbed Hunchback Poacher, 168
*Agonus acipenserinus*, Sturgeon Poacher, 168
*Aidablennius sphynx*, Sphinx Blenny, 524
*akaara, Epinephelus*, Red Spotted Grouper, 190
*akajei, Dasyatis*, Japanese Stingray, 45
*akallopisos, Amphiprion*, Skunk-striped Anemonefish, 373
*akindynos, Amphiprion*, Barrier Reef Anemonefish, 372
*Alabes parvulus*, Eel Clingfish, 97
*alalunga, Thunnus*, Albacore, 602
*alascanus, Sebastolobus*, Shortspine Thornyhead, 138
*albacares, Thunnus*, Yellowfin Tuna, 602
Albacore, *Thunnus alalunga*, 602
*albescens, Remorina*, White Remora, 244
*albicaudatus, Sufflamen*, Whitetail Triggerfish, 624
*albidorsus, Cryptocentrus*, White-backed Goby, 557
*albifasciatus, Stegastes*, White-bar Gregory, 403, 404
*albifimbria, Scorpaena*, Coral Scorpionfish, 145
*albimacula, Amblygobius*, Butterfly Goby, 554
*albimaculus, Pomacentrus*, Bronzeback Damsel, 401
*albimarginatus, Carcharhinus*, Silvertip Shark, 40
*albisella, Dascyllus*, Hawaiian Threespot Damsel, 378
*alboapicalis, Cirripectes*, Snowflake Blenny, 528
*albofasciatus, Sebasticus*, Yellow-barred Red Rockfish, 138
*albomarginata, Gracila*, Blue-striped Grouper, 182
*albomarginata, Variola*, Crescent Tailed Grouper, 203
*alboscapularis, Parma*, White Shoulder Parma, 379
*albovittata, Stethojulis*, Bluelined Wrasse, 455
*albovittatus, Plectorhinchus*, Yellow-lined Sweetlips, 283
*Albula vulpes*, Bonefish, 50
*album, Haemulon*, Margate, 279
*albus, Branchiostegus*, White Tilefish, 239
*alcocki, Halimochirurgus*, Alcock's Longnose Tripodfish, 620
Alcock's Longnose Tripodfish, *Halimochirurgus alcocki*, 620
*Aldrichetta forsteri*, Yellow-eyed Mullet, 421
*Alectis ciliaris*, African Pompano, 251
*Alectis indicus*, Indian Threadfin, 242, 247, 251
*alepidota, Chaenopsis*, Orangethroat Pikeblenny, 519
*Alepisaurus borealis*, Northern Lancetfish, 75
Alfonsino, *Beryx splendens*, 106
*allardi, Amphiprion*, Allard's Clownfish, 372
Allard's Clownfish, *Amphiprion allardi*, 372
*alleni, Creedia*, Slender Sandfish, 501
*alleni, Ecsenius*, Allen's Blenny, 528.14
*alleni, Labropsis*, Allen's Wrasse, 454
*alleni, Pomacentrus*, Allen's Pomacentrus, 399
Allen's Blenny, *Ecsenius alleni*, 528.14
Allen's Pomacentrus, *Pomacentrus alleni*, 399
Allen's Wrasse, *Labropsis alleni*, 454
Alligator Pipefish, *Syngnathoides biaculeatus*, 125
Allis, *Porocottus allisi*, 166
*allisi, Porocottus*, Allis, 166
*allporti, Callanthias*, Splendid Perch, 186
Almaco Jack, *Seriola rivoliana*, 250, 252
*Alopias superciliosus*, Bigeye Thresher, 37
*Alphestes afer*, Mutton Hamlet, 203
*Alphestes multiguttatus*, Pacific Hamlet, 203
*alta, Apopterygion*, Kuiter's Tall Triplefin, 510
*alta, Pristigenys*, Short Bigeye, 219
*altipinnis, Rabaulichthys*, Sailfin Bass, 200
*altivelis, Calloplesiops*, Comet, 214, 215
*altivelis, Coradion*, Tawneygirdled Butterflyfish, 347
*altivelis, Cromileptes*, Panther Grouper, 194, 195, 205
*altivelis, Enneanectes*, Lofty Triplefin, 507

*altus, Chromis,* Silverstripe Chromis, 389
*altus, Oligoplites,* Small-mouthed Leatherjacket, 251
*alula, Synanceia,* Littlewing Stonefish, 158
*Aluterus monoceros,* Unicorn Leatherjacket, 635
*Aluterus schoepfi,* Orange Filefish, 635
*Aluterus scriptus,* Scribbled Filefish, 630, 636
?*Aluterus* sp., Spotted Fantail Filefish, 635
*Aluterus* sp., Filefish, unidentified, 635
*amaenus, Myripristis,* Castelnau's Soldierfish, 115
*Amanses scopas,* Broom Filefish, 627, 635
Ambanora Goby, *Cryptocentrus ambanora,* 548
*ambanora, Cryptocentrus,* Ambanora Goby, 548
*Ambassis interruptus,* Long-spined Perchlet, 170
*Ambassis macracanthus,* Perchlet, 170
*Ambassis natalensis,* Slender Glassy, 323
Amberfish, *Decapterus muruadsi,* 245
Amberjack, *Seriola hippos,* 252
*ambionensis, Canthigaster,* Spotted Toby, 618, 650
*Amblyapistus taenionotus,* Rogue Fish, 58
*amblycephalum, Thalassoma,* Rainbow Wrasse, 465
*amblycephalus, Epinephelus,* Blunt-headed Grouper, 190
*amblycephalus, Thalassoma,* Rainbow Wrasse, 476
*Amblycirrhites bimacula,* Two-spot Hawkfish, 415
*Amblycirrhitus earnshawi,* Earnshaw's Hawkfish, 415
*Amblycirrhitus oxyrhynchus,* Brown-barred Rosy Hawkfish, 414
*Amblycirrhitus pinos,* Redspotted Hawkfish, 415
*Amblyeleotris aurora,* Pinkbar Goby, 543
*Amblyeleotris callopareia,* Beautiful Cheek Prawn Goby, 544
*Amblyeleotris diagonalis,* Diagonal Bar Prawn Goby, 543
*Amblyeleotris fasciatus,* Red-necked Goby, 543
*Amblyeleotris fontanesii,* Fontanes Goby, 543
*Amblyeleotris guttata,* Orange-spotted Prawn Goby, 545
*Amblyeleotris gymnocephala,* Brownstreak Prawn Goby, 545
*Amblyeleotris latifasciata,* Wideband Prawn Goby, 544
*Amblyeleotris periophthalmus,* Slender Shrimp Goby, 543
*Amblyeleotris randalli,* Orangestripe Prawn Goby, 545
*Amblyeleotris* sp., Banded Prawn Goby, 543; Orange-spotted Dorsal Goby, 545, 546; Prawn Goby, unidentified, 544
*Amblyeleotris* sp. aff *periophthalmus,* Slender Shrimp Goby, 545
*Amblyeleotris* sp. cf *japonicus,* Barrier Reef Prawn Goby, 548; Pretty Cheek Goby, 548
*Amblyeleotris steinitzi,* Steinitz's Goby, 543, 546, 556
*Amblyeleotris sungami,* Magnus' Goby, 543, 546
*Amblyeleotris wheeleri,* Wheeler's Prawn Goby, 545
*Amblygaster leiogaster,* Sharp-nosed Trench Sardine, 66
*Amblygaster sirm,* Sirm, 66
*Amblyglyphidodon aureus,* Golden Damsel, 382
*Amblyglyphidodon curacao,* Staghorn Damsel, 382
*Amblyglyphidodon flavilatus,* Yellow-flank Damselfish, 381
*Amblyglyphidodon leucogaster,* White-belly Damsel, 381, 382
*Amblyglyphidodon ternatensis,* Ternate Damsel, 382
*Amblygobius albimacula,* Butterfly Goby, 554
*Amblygobius bynoensis,* Spottyhead Goby, 554
*Amblygobius decussatus,* Orangemarked Goby, 555
*Amblygobius hectori,* Hector's Goby, 555
*Amblygobius nocturnus,* Nocturnal Goby, 555
*Amblygobius phalaena,* Banded Goby, 551, 554, 555
*Amblygobius seminctus,* Half-banded Goby, 555
*Amblygobius* sp., Prawn Goby, unidientified, 547
*Amblygobius sphynx,* Sphinx Goby, 554, 555
*Amblypomacentrus breviceps,* Black-banded Demoiselle, 397
*amblyrhynchos, Carcharhinus,* Gray Reef Shark, 39, 40
*Amblyrhynchotes honckenii,* Evileye Pufferfish, 643
*Amblyrhynchotes hypselogenion,* Bar-cheeked Toadfish, 643, 646
*Amblyrhynchotes* sp., Pufferfish, unidentified, 643
*amblyuroptera, Pseudamia,* Spottail Cardinalfish, 237
Amboina Cardinalfish, *Apogon amboinensis,* 227
Amboina Porgy, *Lethrinus amboinensis,* 294
*amboinensis, Apogon,* Amboina Cardinalfish, 227
*amboinensis, Butis,* Ambon Sleeper, 542
*amboinensis, Chromis,* Ambon Chromis, 386
*amboinensis, Halichoeres,* Ambon Wrasse, 473
*amboinensis, Lethrinus,* Amboina Porgy, 294
*amboinensis, Pomacentrus,* Ambon Damsel, 402
Ambon Chromis, *Chromis amboinensis,* 386
Ambon Damsel, *Pomacentrus amboinensis,* 402
Ambon Sleeper, *Butis amboinensis,* 542
Ambon Wrasse, *Halichoeres amboinensis,* 473
Ambonor Goby, *Vanderhorstia ambonoro,* 568
*ambonoro, Vanderhorstia,* Ambonor Goby, 568
*americana, Dasyatis,* Southern Stingray, 46
*americanus, Hemitripteris,* Sea Raven, 165
*americanus, Macrozoarces,* Ocean Pout, 494
*americanus, Pseudopleuronectes,* Winter Flounder, 611
*Amniataba caudavittatus,* Bartail Grunter, 217
*Amphichaetodon howensis,* Broad-barred Butterflyfish, 350
*Amphichaetodon melbae,* Narrow-barred Butterflyfish, 350
*Amphiprion akallopisos,* Skunk-striped Anemonefish, 373
*Amphiprion akindynos,* Barrier Reef Anemonefish, 372
*Amphiprion allardi,* Allard's Clownfish, 372
*Amphiprion bicinctus,* Two-banded Anemonefish, 374
*Amphiprion chrysogaster,* Yellow-bellied Anemonefish, 373
*Amphiprion chrysopterus,* Orange-finned Anemonefish, 376
*Amphiprion clarkii,* Clark's Anemonefish, 373
*Amphiprion ephippium,* Saddle Anemonefish, 373, 374
*Amphiprion frenatus,* Red Clown, 376
*Amphiprion fuscocaudatus,* Dusky-tail Anemonefish, 373
*Amphiprion latezonatus,* Wide-band Anemonefish, 372
*Amphiprion leucokranos,* Whitecap Anemonefish, 372
*Amphiprion mccullochi,* McCulloch's Anemonefish, 374
*Amphiprion melanopus,* Black Anemonefish, 374
*Amphiprion nigripes,* Black-finned Anemonefish, 377
*Amphiprion ocellaris,* Anemone Demoiselle, 377
*Amphiprion percula,* Clown Anemonefish, 372
*Amphiprion perideraion,* False Skunk-striped Anemonefish, 375, 376
*Amphiprion polymnus,* Saddleback Clown, 372
*Amphiprion rubrocinctus,* Red Anemonefish, 376
*Amphiprion sandaracinos,* Orange Anemonefish, 376
*Amphiprion sebae,* Seba's Anemonefish, 377
*Amphiprion thiellei,* Thielle's Anemonefish, 374
*Amphiprion tricinctus,* Three-banded Anemonefish, 376
*amphis, Bryaninops,* Sea Whip Goby, 560
*Amphistichus argenteus,* Barred Surfperch, 369
*Amphistichus rhodoterus,* Redtail Surfperch, 369
*Amphotistius kuhlii,* Blue-spotted Stingray, 45
*amplexus, Corythoichthys,* Banded Pipefish, 127, 128
*Anago anago,* Yellow Conger Eel, 62
*anago, Anago,* Yellow Conger Eel, 62
*analis, Antennarius,* Tail-jet Frogfish, 92
*analis, Cephalopholis,* Golden Orange Rockcod, 184
*analis, Chromis,* Yellow Chromis, 385
*analis, Clinocottus,* Wooly Sculpin, 164
*analis, Lutjanus,* Mutton Snapper, 265

*analis, Pempheris,* Blacktip Bullseye, 321, 322
*analogus, Epinephelus,* Spotted Cabrilla, 191
*analogus, Kyphosus,* Blue-bronze Sea Chub, 328
Analspot Demoiselle, *Pomacentrus stigma,* 401
*Anampses caeruleopunctatus,* Bluespotted Tamarin, 425, 426
*Anampses chrysocephalus,* Red-tailed Tamarin, 425
*Anampses cuvier,* Cuvier's Tamarin, 425
*Anampses elegans,* Lord Howe Tamarin, 427
*Anampses femininus,* Blue-striped Orange Tamarin, 427
*Anampses geographicus,* Black-spotted Tamarin, 425, 477
*Anampses lennardi,* Lennard's Tamarin, 426, 427
*Anampses lineatus,* Lined Tamarin, 426
*Anampses melanurus melanurus,* Yellow Tailband Wrasse, 477
*Anampses meleagrides,* Yellow-tail Tamarin, 425, 477
*Anampses neoguinaicus,* New Guinea Tamarin, 425
*Anampses twistii,* Yellowbreasted Tamarin, 426, 477
*ananassa, Sorosichthys,* Little Pineapplefish, 103
*Anaora tentaculata,* Tentacled dragonet, 537
*Anaplocapros lenticularis,* White-barred Boxfish, 617, 637
*Anarhichas lupus,* Wolffish, 495
*Anarrhichthys ocellatus,* Wolf-eel, 495
*anastomella, Strongylura,* Greengar, 100
*anchorago, Choerodon,* Orange-dotted Tuskfish, 431; Orange-dotted Wrasse, 474
*Anchovia commersoniana,* Market Anchovy, 68
*Anchoviella* sp., Anchovy, unidentified, 68
Anchovy, unidentified, *Anchoviella* sp., 68
*Ancylopsetta dilecta,* Three-eye Flounder, 611
*aneitensis, Xyrichthys,* White-marked Razorfish, 457
*anema, Meiacanthus,* Double Banded Forktail Blenny, 523
Anemone Demoiselle, *Amphiprion ocellaris,* 377
Angel Blenny, *Coralliozetus angelica,* 519
*angelica, Coralliozetus,* Angel Blenny, 519
Angle-mouthed Lanternfish, *Gonostoma elongatum,* 70
*anglicus, Chrysoblephus,* Englishman, 293
*Anguilla anguilla,* European Eel, 53
*Anguilla australis,* Southern Eel, 53
*Anguilla dieffenbachii,* Long-finned Eel, 53
*Anguilla japonica,* Japanese Eel, 53
*anguilla, Anguilla,* European Eel, 53
*anguineus, Chlamydoselachus,* Frill Shark, 33
*angustatus, Apogon,* Broad-striped Cardinalfish, 223
*angustifrons, Tripodichthys,* Narrow Snouted Tripodfish, 619
*angustipes, Eupetrichthys,* Australian Slender Wrasse, 463
*angustirostris, Tetrapturus,* Shortbill Spearfish, 604
*angustus, Hippocampus,* Tigersnout Seahorse, 128
*anisolepis, Apogon,* Oddscale Cardinalfish, 231
*Anisotremus davidsonii,* Sargo, 280
*Anisotremus surinamensis,* Black Margate, 280
*Anisotremus taeniatus,* Panamic Porkfish, 280
*Anisotremus virginicus,* Atlantic Porkfish, 280
*annularis, Pomacanthus,* Blue King Angelfish, 363
*annularis, Serranus,* Orangeback Bass, 197
*annulata, Chrysiptera,* Footballer, 391
*annulata, Ellerkeldia,* Ringed Seaperch, 199
*annulatus, Hologymnosus,* Finescale Wrasse, 449, 450
*annulatus, Sphoeroides,* Bullseye Puffer, 649
*Anodontostoma chacunda,* Indies Gizzard Shad, 67
*anomala, Psenopsis,* Blackspot Butterfish, 606
*Anomalops katoptron,* Lantern-eye, 106
Anomalus Tripodfish, *Triacanthodes anomalus,* 620
*anomalus, Triacanthodes,* Anomalus Tripodfish, 620
*Anoplopoma fimbria,* Sablefish, 162
*Anoxypristis cuspidata,* Pointed Sawfish, 42
*ansp, Apterichtus,* Academy Eel, 62
Antenna Featherfin Scorpionfish, *Hipposcorpaena* sp., 156
*Antennarius analis,* Tail-jet Frogfish, 92
*Antennarius avalonis,* Roughjaw Frogfish, 88
*Antennarius biocellatus,* Brackish-water Frogfish, 85, 87, 90
*Antennarius coccineus,* Scarlet Frogfish, 86, 91
*Antennarius commersoni,* Commerson's Frogfish, 87, 90, 91, 92
*Antennarius hispidus,* Fishing Frog, 83, 87, 91
*Antennarius indicus,* Indian Frogfish, 91
*Antennarius maculatus,* Warty Frogfish, 85, 86, 89, 92
*Antennarius multiocellatus,* Longlure Frogfish, 88
*Antennarius nummifer,* Coin-bearing Frogfish, 90, 91
*Antennarius ocellatus,* Ocellated Frogfish, 88
*Antennarius pardalis,* Leopard Frogfish, 88
*Antennarius pauciradiatus,* Dwarfed Frogfish, 88
*Antennarius pictus,* Painted Frogfish, 87, 90
*Antennarius sanguineus,* Bloody Frogfish, 88
*Antennarius striatus,* Striated Frogfish, 82, 86, 90, 91
*Antennarius strigatus,* Bandtail Frogfish, 88
*Antennarius tuberosus,* Tuberculated Frogfish, 88, 90
*antennata, Pterois,* Spotfin Lionfish, 141, 142
*antennatus, Chilomycterus,* Bridled Burrfish, 655
*Anthias anthias,* Barbier, 174
*anthias, Anthias,* Barbier, 174
*anthioides, Bodianus,* Lyretail Hogfish, 429, 473
*Antigonia capros,* Boarfish, 118
*antillarum, Chilomycterus,* Web Burrfish, 655
*Anyperodon leucogrammicus,* White-lined Rockcod, 179
*aphanes, Rhinopias,* Merlet Scorpionfish, 139
*Aphareus furcatus,* Blue Smalltooth Jobfish, 260
*apicalis, Stegastes,* Australian Gregory, 404
*apicalis, Triaenodon,* White-tip Shark, 38
*Apistus carinatus,* Ocellated Waspfish, 137
*Aploactis aspera,* Japanese Velvetfish, 156
*Aplodactylus meandritus,* Marblefish, 416
*apodus, Lutjanus,* Schoolmaster, 265
*Apogon affinis,* Bigtooth Cardinalfish, 234
*Apogon amboinensis,* Amboina Cardinalfish, 227
*Apogon angustatus,* Broad-striped Cardinalfish, 223
*Apogon anisolepis,* Oddscale Cardinalfish, 231
*Apogon apogonides,* Short-tooth Cardinalfish, 233
*Apogon aureus,* Band-tailed Cardinalfish, 233
*Apogon aurolineatus,* Bridle Cardinalfish, 230
*Apogon binotatus,* Barred Cardinalfish, 231
*Apogon ceramensis,* Ceram Cardinalfish, 227
*Apogon chrysotaenia,* Many-lined Cardinalfish, 225
*Apogon coccineus,* Little Ruby Red Cardinalfish, 232
*Apogon compressus,* Split-banded Cardinalfish, 224
*Apogon cookii,* Cook's Black-banded Cardinalfish, 223, 224
*Apogon crassiceps,* Big Red Cardinalfish, 232
*Apogon cyanosoma,* Gold-striped Cardinalfish, 222, 223
*Apogon darnleyensis,* Darnley Cardinalfish, 228
*Apogon dispar,* Startailed Cardinalfish, 228
*Apogon doederleini,* Doederlein's Cardinalfish, 224
*Apogon dovii,* Tailspot Cardinalfish, 230
*Apogon elliotti,* Flag-fin Cardinalfish, 232
*Apogon endekataenia,* Black-banded Cardinalfish, 224
*Apogon evermanni,* Evermann's Cardinalfish, 232
*Apogon exostigma,* One-lined Cardinalfish, 226
*Apogon fasciatus,* Four-banded Cardinalfish, 224

*Apogon fraenatus,* Spiny-eyed Cardinalfish, 223
*Apogon gilberti,* Gilbert's Cardinalfish, 226
*Apogon guamensis,* Pearl Cardinalfish, 229
*Apogon hartzfeldii,* Hartzfeld's Cardinalfish, 225
*Apogon hyalosoma,* Translucent Cardinalfish, 227
*Apogon ishigakiensis,* Japanese Cardinalfish, 226
*Apogon kallopterus,* Spinyhead Cardinalfish, 226, 233
*Apogon kiensis,* Rifle Cardinalfish, 227
*Apogon lachneri,* Whitestar Cardinalfish, 231
*Apogon leptacanthus,* Longspine Cardinalfish, 228
*Apogon leptocaulus,* Fairy Cardinalfish, 230
*Apogon lineatus,* Lined Cardinalfish, 228
*Apogon maculatus,* Flamefish, 230
*Apogon maculifera,* Spotted Cardinalfish, 229
*Apogon margaritiphora,* Lattice Cardinalfish, 224
*Apogon melas,* Dusky Cardinalfish, 228
*Apogon menesemus,* Prettytail Cardinalfish, 229
*Apogon niger,* Black Cardinalfish, 228
*Apogon nigripes,* Blackfoot Cardinalfish, 232
*Apogon nigrofasciatus,* Black-striped Cardinalfish, 224
*Apogon nitidus,* Bluespot Cardinalfish, 223
*Apogon norfolcensis,* Norfolk Cardinalfish, 229
*Apogon notatus,* Blackspot Cardinalfish, 226
*Apogon novaeguinea (?cyanosoma),* New Guinea Cardinalfish, 225
*Apogon novemfasciatus,* Nine-banded Cardinalfish, 224
*Apogon pacifici,* Pink Cardinalfish, 230
*Apogon phenax,* Mimic Cardinalfish, 231
*Apogon pillionatus,* Broadsaddle Cardinalfish, 231
*Apogon planifrons,* Pale Cardinalfish, 231
*Apogon pseudomaculatus,* Twospot Cardinalfish, 230
*Apogon quadrifasciatus,* Two-striped Cardinalfish, 229
*Apogon quadrisquamatus,* Sawcheek Cardinalfish, 230
*Apogon retrosella,* Barspot Cardinalfish, 230
*Apogon robinsi,* Roughlip Cardinalfish, 231
*Apogon robustus,* Cook's Cardinalfish, 223
*Apogon ruppelli,* Gobbleguts, 229
*Apogon sangiensis,* Bar-cheeked Cardinalfish, 227
*Apogon savayensis,* Ghost Cardinalfish, 229
*Apogon sealei,* Seale's Cardinalfish, 228
*Apogon semilineatus,* Indian Little Fish, 226
*Apogon semiornatus,* Oblique-banded Cardinalfish, 225
*Apogon* sp., Cardinalfish, unidentified, 225, 227, 233; Orange-stripe Cardinalfish, 232
*Apogon taeniatus,* Two-belted Cardinalfish, 228, 233
*Apogon taeniopterus,* Belted Cardinalfish, 229
*Apogon thermalis,* Masked Cardinalfish, 227
*Apogon townsendi,* Belted Cardinalfish, 231
*Apogon trimaculatum,* Three-spot Cardinalfish, 228
*Apogon victoriae,* Victoria Cardinalfish, 223
*Apogonichthys ocellatus,* Ocellated Cardinalfish, 237
*apogonides, Apogon,* Short-tooth Cardinalfish, 233
*Apolemichthys arcuatus,* Hawaiian Pearlyscale Angelfish, 366
*Apolemichthys trimaculatus,* Three-spot Angelfish, 354
*Apolemichthys xanthopunctatus,* Gold-spangled Angelfish, 366
*Apolemichthys xanthotis,* Red Sea Angelfish, 366
*Apolemichthys xanthurus,* Yellowtail Black Angelfish, 354
*Apopterygion alta,* Kuiter's Tall Triplefin, 510
*aprinus, Cirrhitichthys,* Spotted Hawkfish, 410, 411, 414
*Aprion virescens,* Green Jobfish, 259
*Aprognathodon platyventris,* One-stripe Snake Eel, 62
*Apsilus dentatus,* Black Snapper, 259
*Apsilus fuscus,* Cape Verde Snapper, 259
*Apterichtus ansp,* Academy Eel, 62
*apterygia, Conniella,* Connie's Wrasse, 436
*aquosus, Scopthalmus,* Windowpane, 611
Arabian Angelfish, *Arusetta asfur,* 364
Arabian Blenny, *Ecsenius pulcher,* 528.04
*Aracana aurita,* Shaw's Cowfish, 637
*aratus, Lutjanus,* Mullet Snapper, 268
*arawak, Symphurus,* Caribbean Tonguefish, 614
Arc-eyed Hawkfish, *Paracirrhites arcatus,* 413, 414
*arcatus, Paracirrhites,* Arc-eyed Hawkfish, 413, 414
*Archamia biguttata,* Spot-tail Cardinalfish, 235
*Archamia fucata,* Redbarred Cardinalfish, 235
*Archamia leai,* Lea's Cardinalfish, 235
*Archamia lineolata,* Bronze-streaked Cardinalfish, 235
*Archamia melasma,* Black-spot Cardinalfish, 235
*Archamia mozambiquensis,* Mozambique Cardinal, 323
*Archamia zosterophora,* Girdled Cardinalfish, 235
*Archosargus probatocephalus,* Sheepshead, 292
*Arcos robiginosus,* Red Clingfish, 96
*Arctoscopus japonicus,* Sailfin Sandfish, 500
*arctus, Cosmocampus,* Snubnose Pipefish, 125
*arcuatus, Apolemichthys,* Hawaiian Pearlyscale Angelfish, 366
*arcuatus, Pomacanthus,* Gray Angelfish, 362
*arenarius, Crapatalus,* Sandfish, 501
*arenarius, Pomacentrus,* Specklefin Damsel, 401
*arenatus, Priacanthus,* Bigeye, 220
*Arenigobius bifrenatus,* Double-striped Goby, 562
*areolatus, Epinephelus,* Squaretail Grouper, 190
*areolatus, Plectropomus,* Squaretail Leopard Grouper, 203
*argalus, Platybelone,* Gill-rakered Needlefish, 100
*argentatus, Chaetodon,* Silver and Black Butterflyfish, 336
*argentea, Sphyraena,* Pacific Barracuda, 422
*argenteus, Amphistichus,* Barred Surfperch, 369
*argenteus, Eucinostomus,* Spotfin Mojarra, 275
*argenteus, Mesopristes,* Silver Grunter, 217, 218
*argenteus, Monodactylus,* Silver Mono, 320, 418
*argenteus, Neoniphon,* Silver Squirrelfish, 110, 112
*argenteus, Pampas,* Silver Pomfret, 606
*argenteus, Siganus,* Streamlined Spinefoot, 597
*argentilineatus, Periophthalmus,* Silverline Mudskipper, 579
*argentimaculatus, Lutjanus,* Silver Snapper, 260, 261, 266
*argentiventris, Labracoglossa,* Yellow-striped Butterfish, 241
*argi, Centropyge,* Cherubfish, 356
*argoliba, Rhinopias,* Weeping Scorpionfish, 139
Argus Comet, *Calloplesiops argus,* 214
Argus Grouper, *Cephalopholis argus,* 182
Argus Wrasse, *Halichoeres argus,* 443, 474
*argus, Calloplesiops,* Argus Comet, 214
*argus, Cephalopholis,* Argus Grouper, 182
*argus, Halichoeres,* Argus Wrasse, 443, 474
*argus, Scatophagus,* Spotted Scat, 329
*argus, Stigmatopora,* Australian Spotted Pipefish, 125
*argyreus, Pomadasys,* Silver Grunt, 281
*Argyrocottus zanderi,* Zander's Cottid, 166
*argyrophanes, Siphonognathus,* Tubemouth, 478
*Argyrops bleekeri,* Bleeker's Sea Bream, 289, 290
*Argyrops spinifer,* Longspine Sea Bream, 289
*Ariomma indica,* Indian Driftfish, 606
*Ariosoma impressa,* Bandtooth Conger, 63
*armatus, Carangoides,* Longfin Trevally, 247
*armatus, Enoplosus,* Old Wife, 334
*armatus, Epinephelides,* Breaksea Grouper, 187

*armatus, Neocirrhitus,* Brilliant Red Hawkfish, 412
*armatus, Rhinobatos,* Clearnose Guitarfish, 44
*armatus, Solenostomus,* Armored Pipefish, 124
*armilla, Omegophora,* Ringed Puffer, 643
Armored Pipefish, *Solenostomus armatus,* 124
*aroni, Ecsenius,* Khaki Blenny, 528.04
*Arothron diadematus,* Masked Puffer, 647
*Arothron hispidus,* Stars and Stripes Puffer, 644, 645, 646
*Arothron immaculatus,* Black-edged Puffer, 648
*Arothron inconditus,* Bellystriped Puffer, 646
*Arothron manilensis,* Narrow-lined Toadfish, 648
*Arothron mappa,* Scribbled Toadfish, 647
*Arothron meleagris,* Golden Puffer, 645, 646
*Arothron nigropunctatus,* Black-spotted Puffer, 645, 646
*Arothron reticularis,* Reticulated Pufferfish, 647
*Arothron stellatus,* Starry Pufferfish, 646, 647
*Arripes georgianus,* King George's Salmon, 257
*Arripes trutta,* Australian Salmon, 257
Arrow Blenny, *Lucayablennius zingaro,* 518
Arrow Cardinal, *Rhabdamia gracilis,* 222
Arrow Stargazer, *Gillelus greyae,* 512
Arrowhead Soapfish, *Belonoperca chabanaudi,* 205
Arrowhead Wrasse, *Wetmorella nigropinnata,* 454
Arrowtooth Cardinalfish, *Cheilodipterus lachneri,* 234
*Artedius harringtoni,* Scalyhead Sculpin, 164
*artus, Cheilodipterus,* Wolf Cardinalfish, 233
*aruanus, Dascyllus,* White-tailed Damselfish, 377
*Aruma histrio,* Slow Goby, 564
*Arusetta asfur,* Arabian Angelfish, 364
Ascencion Cherubfish, *Centropyge resplendens,* 356
*asfur, Arusetta,* Arabian Angelfish, 364
Ash-colored Rudderfish, *Kyphosus fuscus,* 329
Ashen Conger-eel, *Conger cinereus,* 63
Ashen Drummer, *Kyphosus cinerascens,* 328
Asian Trumpetfish, *Aulostomus chinensis,* 117, 119
*Aspasmichthys ciconiae,* Yellow Clingfish, 96
*Aspasmogaster tasmaniensis,* Tasmanian Clingfish, 96
*asper, Coryphaenoides,* Slaty Grenadier, 78
*asper, Exerpes,* Sargassum Blenny, 512
*asper, Uranoscopus,* Stinging Stargazer, 501
*aspera, Acanthemblemaria,* Roughhead Blenny, 518
*aspera, Aploactis,* Japanese Velvetfish, 156
*asperrimum, Clidoderma,* Peppered Righteye Flounder, 608
*Aspidontus dussumieri,* Floating Blenny, 532
*Aspidontus taeniatus,* False Cleanerfish, 522
*apricaudus, Pervagor,* Hawaiian Redtail Filefish, 633
Assarius Butterflyfish, *Chaetodon assarius,* 341
*assarius, Chaetodon,* Assarius Butterflyfish, 341
*assasi, Rhinecanthus,* Picasso Triggerfish, 626
*Assessor flavissimus,* Golden Mini-Grouper, 213
*Assessor macneilli,* MacNeill's Mini-grouper, 213
*Asterropteryx semipunctatus,* Starry Fin Goby, 555
*Asterropteryx* sp., Starry Goby, 553
*Astrapogon punticulatus,* Spotted Conchfish, 236
*Astrapogon stellatus,* Starry Conchfish, 236
Astrolabe Wrasse, *Halichoeres margaritaceus,* 444
*Atelomycterus macleayi,* Marbled Cat Shark, 38
*Atherina boyeri,* Boyer's Smelt, 102
*Atherinomorus endrachtensis,* Spotted Hardyhead, 102
*Atherinomorus lacunosus,* Slender Hardyhead, 102
*Atherinomorus ogilbyi,* Ogilby's Hardyhead, 102
*Atherinops affinis,* Topsmelt, 102
*Atherinosoma elongata,* Elongate Hardyhead, 102
*atinga, Chilomycterus,* Spotted Burrfish, 655
Atlantic Bearded Goby, *Barbulifer ceuthoecus,* 564
Atlantic Bumper, *Chloroscombrus chrysurus,* 253
Atlantic Clown Wrasse, *Halichoeres maculipinna,* 446
Atlantic Cod, *Gadus morhua,* 78
Atlantic Fanged Blenny, *Ophioblennius atlanticus,* 528
Atlantic Hawkfish, *Cirrhitus atlanticus,* 412
Atlantic Moonfish, *Selene setapinnis,* 251
Atlantic Needlefish, *Strongylura timucu,* 100
Atlantic Porkfish, *Anisotremus virginicus,* 280
Atlantic Rainbow Wrasse, *Halichoeres pictus,* 446
Atlantic Spadefish, *Chaetodipterus faber,* 330
Atlantic Tarpon, *Megalops atlanticus,* 50
Atlantic Thread Herring, *Opisthonema oglinum,* 69
Atlantic Torpedo Ray, *Torpedo nobiliana,* 43
*atlanticus, Cirrhitus,* Atlantic Hawkfish, 412
*atlanticus, Megalops,* Atlantic Tarpon, 50
*atlanticus, Ophioblennius,* Atlantic Fanged Blenny, 528
*atomarium, Sparisoma,* Greenblotch Parrotfish, 487
*atrangulatus, Gobiodon,* Earspot Coral Goby, 578
*atrilobata, Chromis,* Scissor Damselfish, 389
*atrilunula, Scarus,* Blue Moon Parrotfish, 482
*atripectoralis, Chromis,* Black-axil Chromis, 383
*atripes, Chromis,* Dark-fin Chromis, 386
*atrisignis, Cheilopogon,* Flying Fish, 99
*atrocingulatus, Parupeneus,* Three-striped Goatfish, 312, 315, 316
*atrodorsalis, Meiacanthus,* Forktail Blenny, 523
*atronasum, Gobiosoma,* Exuma Cleaning Goby, 572
*atrorus, Enneanectes,* Blackedge Triplefin, 508
*Atrosalarias fuscus,* Dusky Blenny, 527
*atrovirens, Sebastes,* Kelp Rockfish, 149
*Atule mate,* Yellowtail Scad, 246, 247
*Atypichthys latus,* White-bellied Stripey, 325, 326
*Atypichthys strigatus,* Australian Stripey, 326
*audax, Tetrapturus,* Striped Marlin, 604
*Aulacocephalus temmincki,* Goldribbon Soapfish, 204
*Aulichthys japonicus,* Japanese Tubesnout, 118
*Aulopus japonicus,* Japanese Aulopus, 73
*Aulopus purpurissatus,* Sergeant Baker, 71, 72
*Aulorhynchus flavidus,* Tubesnout, 118
*Aulostomus chinensis,* Asian Trumpetfish, 117, 119
*Aulostomus maculatus,* Caribbean Trumpetfish, 119
*aurantia, Cephalopholis,* Garrupa, 182
*aurantiacus, Cristiceps,* Yellow Crested Weedfish, 517
*aurantiacus, Dotalabrus,* Castelnau's Golden Wrasse, 463
*aurantiacus, Urolophus,* Sepia Stingray, 46
*aurantica, Parapercis,* Golden Grubfish, 502
*aurantonotus, Centropyge,* Flameback Angelfish, 356
*auratus, Gobius,* Golden Goby, 559
*auratus, Pagrus,* Golden Sea Bream, 290
*aureofasciatus, Chaetodon,* Sunburst Butterflyfish, 340
*aureolineatum, Haemulon,* Tomtate, 279
*aureus, Amblyglyphidodon,* Golden Damsel, 382
*aureus, Apogon,* Band-tailed Cardinalfish, 233
*aureus, Cirrhitichthys,* Golden Yellow Hawkfish, 412
*aureus, Pseudochromis,* Golden Dottyback, 209
*aureus, Stegastes,* Golden Gregory, 405
*auricularis, Coris,* King Coris, 436, 438
*auriculatus, Sebastes,* Brown Rockfish, 149
*aurifrons, Opistognathus,* Yellow Head Jawfish, 497, 499
*auriga, Chaetodon,* Threadfin Butterflyfish, 345

*auripes, Chaetodon,* Golden Butterflyfish, 338
*aurita, Aracana,* Shaw's Cowfish, 637
*aurita, Fowleria,* Crosseyed Cardinalfish, 235
*aurocingulus, Ctenogobiops,* Herre's Samoan Prawn Goby, 546, 547
*aurofrenatum, Sparisoma,* Redband Parrotfish, 487
*auroguttatus, Paralabrax,* Golden Spotted Rock Bass, 202
*aurolineatus, Apogon,* Bridle Cardinalfish, 230
*aurolineatus, Gnathodentex,* Gold-lined Sea Bream, 296, 298
*aurolineatus, Neoniphon,* Yellow-striped Squirrelfish, 110
*auromarginatus, Xanthichthys,* Blue-throat Triggerfish, 623
*aurora, Amblyeleotris,* Pinkbar Goby, 543
*aurora, Cryptocentrus,* Pinkbar Goby, 547
*aurora, Micrometrus,* Reef Surfperch, 370
*aurora, Pikea,* Hawaiian Basslet, 200
*aurorubens, Rhomboplites,* Vermillion Snapper, 259
*australasicus, Scomber,* Slimy Mackerel, 601
Australian Banded Pipefish, *Corythoichthys intestinalis,* 127
Australian Bandfish, *Cepola australis,* 420
Australian Black Porgy, *Acanthopagrus australis,* 292
Australian Blenny, *Ecsenius australianus,* 528.14
Australian Blowfish, *Torquigener pleurogramma,* 643
Australian Brown Grouper, *Acanthistius pardalotus,* 179
Australian Damsel, *Pomacentrus australis,* 400
Australian Globefish, *Diodon nicthemerus,* 653, 654
Australian Gregory, *Stegastes apicalis,* 404
Australian Guitarfish, *Rhinobatos vincentiana,* 44
Australian Numbfish, *Hypnos subnigrum,* 42
Australian Salmon, *Arripes trutta,* 257
Australian Slender Wrasse, *Eupetrichthys angustipes,* 463
Australian Spotted Pipefish, *Stigmatopora argus,* 125
Australian Stripey, *Atypichthys strigatus,* 326
*australianus, Ecsenius,* Australian Blenny, 528.14
*australis, Acanthopagrus,* Australian Black Porgy, 292
*australis, Anguilla,* Southern Eel, 53
*australis, Centropogon,* Waspfish, 137
*australis, Cepola,* Australian Bandfish, 420
*australis, Cristiceps,* Crested Weedfish, 517
*australis, Pomacentrus,* Australian Damsel, 400
*australis, Thamnaconus,* Velvet Leatherjacket, 636
*australis, Trachichthys,* Roughy, 103
*austriacus, Chaetodon,* Red Sea Melon Butterflyfish, 341
*Auxis thazard,* Frigate Tuna, 602
*avalonis, Antennarius,* Roughjaw Frogfish, 88
*averruncus, Kathetostoma,* Smooth Stargazer, 500
*awoara, Epinephelus,* Green Hata, 186
*axelrodi, Ecsenius,* Axelrod's Blenny, 528.12
Axelrod's Blenny, *Ecsenius axelrodi,* 528.12
*axillaris, Bodianus,* Coral Hogfish, 426
*axillaris, Chromis,* Gray Chromis, 383
*axillaris, Myripristis,* White-edge Soldierfish, 115
*aya, Chaetodon,* Bank Butterflyfish, 347
*aygula, Coris,* Clown Coris, 436
*ayraudi, Nelusetta,* Chinaman Leatherjacket, 636
*azaleus, Plagiotremus,* Sabretooth Blenny, 521
*azonus, Pleurogrammus,* Greenling, 163
Azure Damsel, *Chrysiptera parasema,* 392
*azurea, Hermosilla,* Zebraperch, 326
*azurio, Choerodon,* Scarbreast Tuskfish, 431
*azysron, Neopomacentrus,* Yellowtail Demoiselle, 398

## B

*baconensis, Gerres,* Ghost Mojarra, 274
*bahianus, Acanthurus,* Ocean Surgeon, 582
*baillonii, Trachinotus,* Smallspot Pompano, 250, 254
*bairdi, Microspathodon,* Bumphead Damselfish, 408
*bairdi, Paradiplogrammus,* Lancer Dragonet, 538
*Bairdiella batabana,* Blue Croaker, 311
*bajonado, Calamus,* Jolthead Porgy, 291
*balanorum, Acanthemblemaria,* Clubhead Blenny, 518
Baldchin Tuskfish, *Choerodon rubescens,* 429
*baldwini, Serranus,* Lantern Bass, 197
Bali Threadfin Bream, *Nemipterus balinensis,* 305
*balinensis, Nemipterus,* Bali Threadfin Bream, 305
*Balistapus undulatus,* Undulate Triggerfish, 623
*Balistes capriscus,* Gray Triggerfish, 625
*Balistes forcipitus,* West African Triggerfish, 625
*Balistes polylepis,* East Pacific Triggerfish, 625
*Balistes vetula,* Queen Triggerfish, 625
*Balistoides conspicillum,* Clown Triggerfish, 621, 622, 623
*Balistoides viridescens,* Dotty Triggerfish, 626
Ballan Wrasse, *Labrus bergylta,* 469
*ballieui, Coris,* Malamalama, 438
*ballieui, Scorpaena,* Ballieu's Scorpionfish, 154
*ballieui, Thalassoma,* Hinalea Luahine, 466
Ballieu's Scorpionfish, *Scorpaena ballieui,* 154
Balloonfish, *Diodon holacanthus,* 656
Ballyhoo, *Hemiramphus brasiliensis,* 100
Balteata, *Redigobius balteata,* 547
*balteata, Redigobius,* Balteata, 547
*balteata, Stethojulis,* Orange Band Wrasse, 455
*balteatus, Neodax,* Little Weed Whiting, 478
Band-tailed Cardinalfish, *Apogon aureus,* 233
Band-tailed Goatfish, *Upeneus vittatus,* 314, 318
Banda Blenny, *Ecsenius bandanus,* 528.15
*bandanensis, Stethojulis,* Orange-axil Wrasse, 455, 465
*bandanus, Ecsenius,* Banda Blenny, 528.15
Banded African Goby, Gobiidae sp. 5, 548
Banded Basslet, *Liopropoma fasciatum,* 198
Banded Blanquillo, *Malacanthus brevirostris,* 241, 511
Banded Blenny, *Paraclinus fasciatus,* 515
Banded Boarhead, *Evistias acutirostris,* 335
Banded Butterflyfish, *Chaetodon striatus,* 343
Banded Cardinalfish, *Cheilodipterus zonatus,* 234
Banded Catshark, *Chiloscyllium plagiosum,* 36
Banded Cleaner Goby, *Gobiosoma digueti,* 571
Banded Coral Goby, *Eviota fasciola,* 576
Banded Damsel, *Dischistodus fasciatus,* 409
Banded Fairy Basslet, *Pseudanthias fasciatus,* 177
Banded Goby, *Amblygobius phalaena,* 551, 554, 555
Banded Guitarfish, *Zapteryx exasperata,* 43
Banded Hawkfish, *Cirrhitops fasciatus,* 413
Banded Jawfish, *Opistognathus macrognathus,* 499
Banded Knifejaw, *Oplegnathus fasciatus,* 368, 369
Banded Longfin, *Belonepterygion fasciolatum,* 212
Banded Moray, *Gymnothorax rueppelliae,* 54
Banded Parma, *Parma polylepis,* 379
Banded Pipefish, *Corythoichthys amplexus,* 127, 128; *Doryrhamphus dactyliophorus,* 127
Banded Pony Fish, *Leiognathus fasciata,* 256
Banded Prawn Goby, *Amblyeleotris* sp., 543
Banded Rudderfish, *Seriola zonata,* 253
Banded Sweep, *Scorpis georgianus,* 327
Banded Threadfin Bream, *Pentapodus caninus,* 299, 300, 307
Banded Triplefin, *Tripterygion bucknilli,* 510

Banded Wobbegong, *Orectolobus ornatus,* 36
Banded-head Goby, *Priolepis boreus,* 567
Banded-tail Coral-cod, *Cephalopholis urodelus,* 183
Bandtail Frogfish, *Antennarius strigatus,* 88
Bandtail Puffer, *Sphoeroides spengleri,* 649
Bandtail Searobin, *Prionotus ophryas,* 161
Bandtooth Conger, *Ariosoma impressa,* 63
Bank Butterflyfish, *Chaetodon aya,* 347
*bankanensis, Pomacentrus,* Speckled Damsel, 402
Bannerfish, *Heniochus acuminatus,* 348, 352
Bantayan Butterflyfish, *Chaetodon adiergastos,* 338
Bar Jack, *Carangoides ruber,* 248
Bar-cheeked Cardinalfish, *Apogon sangiensis,* 227
Bar-cheeked Toadfish, *Amblyrhynchotes hypselogenion,* 643, 646
Bar-faced Weever, *Parapercis nebulosa,* 502
Bar-head Damsel, *Paraglyphidodon thoracotaeniatus,* 396
Bar-tail Moray, *Gymnothorax zonipectus,* 58
Bar-tailed Goatfish, *Upeneus tragula,* 313, 314, 318
*baramenuke, Sebastes,* Japanese Scorpionfish, 152
*barbata, Brotula,* Bearded Brotula, 80
*barbatus, Scorpaenopsis,* Bearded Scorpionfish, 147
Barbed Hunchback Poacher, *Agonomalus proboscidalis,* 168
Barber Perch, *Caesioperca rasor,* 181
*barberi, Dendochirus,* Barber's Lionfish, 140
*barberinoides, Parupeneus,* Bicolor Goatfish, 317, 319
*barberinus, Parupeneus,* Dash-dot Goatfish, 317, 319
Barber's Lionfish, *Dendochirus barberi,* 140
Barbier, *Anthias anthias,* 174
Barbu, *Polydactylus virginicus,* 420
*Barbulifer ceuthoecus,* Atlantic Bearded Goby, 564
*Barbulifer pantherinus,* Panther Goby, 564
Barchin Scorpionfish, *Sebastapistes strongia,* 147
Barfin Sculpin, *Gymnocanthus detrisus,* 164
*bargibanti, Hippocampus,* Bargibant's Seahorse, 129
Bargibant's Seahorse, *Hippocampus bargibanti,* 129
*bariene, Acanthurus,* Black-spot Surgeon, 586
Barnacle Bill Blenny, *Hypsoblennius brevipinnis,* 530
Barnacle Blenny, *Acanthemblemaria macrospilus,* 518
*barnardi, Paramonacanthus,* Wedgetail Filefish, 634
Baroness Butterflyfish, *Chaetodon baronessa,* 336
*baronessa, Chaetodon,* Baroness Butterflyfish, 336
*barracuda, Sphyraena,* Great Barracuda, 422, 423
Barramundi, *Lates calcarifer,* 170
Barred Blenny, *Hypleurochilus bermudensis,* 530
Barred Cardinalfish, *Apogon binotatus,* 231
Barred Flagtail, *Kuhlia mugil,* 217, 219
Barred Garfish, *Hemiramphus far,* 99
Barred Grunt, *Conodon nobilis,* 281
Barred Hamlet, *Hypoplectrus puella,* 201
Barred Morwong, *Cheilodactylus quadricornis,* 417
Barred Pargo, *Hoplopagrus guentheri,* 269
Barred Sandperch, *Parapercis multifasciata,* 502
Barred Serrano, *Serranus fasciatus,* 197
Barred Snake Eel, *Myrichthys colubrinus,* 61
Barred Surfperch, *Amphistichus argenteus,* 369
Barred Thicklip, *Hemigymnus fasciatus,* 450
Barrier Reef Anemonefish, *Amphiprion akindynos,* 372
Barrier Reef Chromis, *Chromis nitida,* 387
Barrier Reef Prawn Goby, *Amblyeleotris* sp. cf *japonicus,* 548
Barspot Cardinalfish, *Apogon retrosella,* 230
Bartail Flathead, *Platycephalus indicus,* 162
Bartail Fusilier, *Pterocaesio tile,* 271
Bartail Grunter, *Amniataba caudavittatus,* 217
*bartholomei, Carangoides,* Yellow Jack, 249
*bartletti, Mirolabrichthys,* Bartlett's Fairy Basslet, 178
Bartlett's Fairy Basslet, *Mirolabrichthys bartletti,* 178
Basking Shark, *Cetorhinus maximus,* 37
*batabana, Bairdiella,* Blue Croaker, 311
Batavian Batfish, *Platax batavianus,* 331, 332
Batavian Parrotfish, *Scarus bataviensis,* 490
*batavianus, Platax,* Batavian Batfish, 331, 332
*bataviensis, Scarus,* Batavian Parrotfish, 490
Batesian Mimic, *Petroscirtes fallax,* 522
*bathi, Ecsenius,* Bath's Blenny, 528.13
Bath's Blenny, *Ecsenius bathi,* 528.13
*Bathygobius cocosensis,* Coco Frillgoby, 564
*Bathygobius laddi,* Ladd's Goby, 542
*Bathygobius ramosus,* Panamic Frillfin Goby, 564
*Bathymaster derjugini,* Derjugin's Ronquil, 494
*bathyphilus, Halichoeres,* Greenband Wrasse, 446
*Batrachomoeus trispinosus,* Threespine Toadfish, 84
*batuensis, Coris,* Heliotrope Eyeband Wrasse, 475
Bay Blenny, *Hypsoblennius gentilis,* 530
*bayeri, Enchelycore,* Bayer's Moray, 59
Bayer's Moray, *Enchelycore bayeri,* 59
Beach Conger, *Conger japonicus,* 63
Beady Pipefish, *Hippichthys penicillus,* 126
Bearded Brotula, *Brotula barbata,* 80
Bearded Codfish, *?Lotella* sp., 77
Bearded Goby, *Sagamia geneionema,* 546
Bearded Rock Cod, *Pseudophycis breviusculus,* 77
Bearded Scorpionfish, *Scorpaenopsis barbatus,* 147
Beardie, *Lotella fuliginosa,* 77
Beau Brummel, *Stegastes flavilatus,* 407
Beau Gregory, *Stegastes leucostictus,* 407
Beautiful Angelfish, *Holacanthus venustus,* 366
Beautiful Cheek Prawn Goby, *Amblyeleotris callopareia,* 544
Beautiful Fusilier, *Caesio teres,* 271, 273
*beddomei, Siphonognathus,* Pencil Weed Whiting, 478
*belissimus, Exyrias,* Flowing Finned Goby, 564
*Bellator gymnostethius,* Searobin, 160
Bellus Lyretail Angelfish, *Genicanthus bellus,* 359
*bellus, Genicanthus,* Bellus Lyretail Angelfish, 359
Bellyband Damselfish, *Plectroglyphidodon leucozona,* 394
Bellystriped Puffer, *Arothron inconditus,* 646
*Belonepterygion fasciolatum,* Banded Longfin, 212
*Belonoperca chabanaudi,* Arrowhead Soapfish, 205
Belted Cardinalfish, *Apogon taeniopterus,* 229; *Apogon townsendi,* 231
Belted Morwong, *Cheilodactylus zonatus,* 416, 419
Belted Sandfish, *Serranus subligarius,* 197
*Bembras japonicus,* Japanese Flathead, 161
Bengal Sergeant, *Abudefduf bengalensis,* 381
Bengal Snapper, *Lutjanus bengalensis,* 260
*bengalensis, Abudefduf,* Bengal Sergeant, 381
*bengalensis, Lutjanus,* Bengal Snapper, 260
Beniteguri, *Repomucenus beniteguri,* 536
*beniteguri, Repomucenus,* Beniteguri, 536
*bennetti, Canthigaster,* Bennett's Toby, 650, 651
*bennetti, Chaetodon,* Bennett's Butterflyfish, 341
Bennett's Butterflyfish, *Chaetodon bennetti,* 341
Bennett's Toby, *Canthigaster bennetti,* 650, 651
*bensasi, Upeneus,* Salmonet, 314
*berda, Acanthopagrus,* Black Bream, 289

*bergi, Scorpaena,* Goosehead Scorpionfish, 145
*bergylta, Labrus,* Ballan Wrasse, 469
Bermuda Chub, *Kyphosus sectatrix,* 328
Bermuda Porgy, *Diplodus bermudensis,* 288
*bermudensis, Carapus,* Pearlfish, 79, 80
*bermudensis, Diplodus,* Bermuda Porgy, 288
*bermudensis, Hypleurochilus,* Barred Blenny, 530
*berndti, Myripristis,* Bigscale Soldierfish, 115
*berndti, Polymixia,* Pacific Beardfish, 106
*berycoides, Doederleinia,* Blackthroat Seaperch, 173
*Beryx decadactylus,* Broad Alfonsino, 106
*Beryx splendens,* Alfonsino, 106
*beta, Schultzea,* Slide-mouth Bass, 200
*biaculeatus, Premnas,* Spine-cheeked Anemonefish, 372
*biaculeatus, Syngnathoides,* Alligator Pipefish, 125
*biaculeatus, Triacanthus,* Common Tripodfish, 619
*bicarinatus, Grammatorcynus,* Double-lined Mackerel, 603
*bicaudalis, Lactophrys,* Spotted Trunkfish, 641
*bicinctus, Amphiprion,* Two-banded Anemonefish, 374
*bicinctus, Uranoscopus,* Two-banded Stargazer, 501
*bicirrhis, Protemblemaria,* Warthead Blenny, 520
Bicolor Basslet, *Lipogramma klayi,* 213
Bicolor Chromis, *Chromis bicolor,* 387
Bicolor Damselfish, *Stegastes partitus,* 406
Bicolor Fairy Basslet, *Mirolabrichthys bicolor,* 174
Bicolor Goatfish, *Parupeneus barberinoides,* 317, 319
Bicolor Parrotfish, *Cetoscarus bicolor,* 480, 489, 490
Bicolor Scorpionfish, *Scorpaenodes* sp., 154
*bicolor, Centropyge,* Two-colored Angelfish, 354
*bicolor, Cetoscarus,* Bicolor Parrotfish, 480, 489, 490
*bicolor, Chromis,* Bicolor Chromis, 387
*bicolor, Ecsenius,* Two-colored Blenny, 532
*bicolor, Labroides,* Bicolored Cleaner Wrasse, 469
*bicolor, Mirolabrichthys,* Bicolor Fairy Basslet, 174
*bicolor, Parma,* Bicolored Parma, 377
*bicolor?, Rypticus,* Cortez Soapfish, 207
*bicoloratus, Kareius,* Stone Flounder, 613
Bicolored Butterflyfish, *Chaetodon dichrous,* 346
Bicolored Cleaner Wrasse, *Labroides bicolor,* 469
Bicolored Coral Goby, *Gobiodon quinquestrigatus,* 578
Bicolored Parma, *Parma bicolor,* 377
Bicolored Toby, *Canthigaster smithae,* 650
*bifasciata, Eviota,* Two-striped Coral Goby, 560, 576
*bifasciatum, Thalassoma,* Bluehead Wrasse, 466
*bifasciatus, Acanthopagrus,* Twobar Seabream, 292
*bifasciatus, Diploprion,* Two-banded Grouper, 206
*bifasciatus, Parupeneus,* Two-barred Goatfish, 317
*bifasciatus, Pentapodus,* Two-striped Bream, 307
*bifrenatus, Arenigobius,* Double-striped Goby, 562
Big Lip Damsel, *Cheiloprion labiatus,* 397
Big Red Cardinalfish, *Apogon crassiceps,* 232
Big-belly Seahorse, *Hippocampus abdominalis,* 129
Big-eye, *Monotaxis grandoculis,* 296, 301
Big-scaled Parma, *Parma oligolepis,* 379
Bigeye, *Priacanthus arenatus,* 220
Bigeye Kingfish, *Caranx sexfasciatus,* 247, 249
Bigeye Scad, *Selar crumenophthalmus,* 245, 250
Bigeye Soldierfish, *Myripristis murdjan,* 114, 116
Bigeye Stumpnose, *Rhabdosargus thorpei,* 293
Bigeye Thresher, *Alopias superciliosus,* 37
Bigeye Tuna, *Thunnus obesus,* 602
Bighand Thornyhead, *Sebastolobus macrochir,* 138
Bigscale Goatfish, *Pseudupeneus grandisquammis,* 314
Bigscale Scorpionfish, *Scorpaena scrofa,* 144
Bigscale Soldierfish, *Myripristis berndti,* 115
Bigtooth Cardinalfish, *Apogon affinis,* 234
*biguttata, Archamia,* Spot-tail Cardinalfish, 235
*biguttatus, Lutjanus,* Doublebar Snapper, 258, 262
*bilineata, Lepidopsetta,* Rock Sole, 611
*bilineata, Paraplagusia,* Doubleline Tongue Sole, 614
*bilineatus, Scolopsis,* Two-lined Monocle Bream, 293, 302, 304
*bilunulatus, Bodianus,* Saddleback Hogfish, 428, 429, 473
*bimacula, Amblycirrhites,* Two-spot Hawkfish, 415
*bimaculata, Eviota,* Doublespot Goby, 576
*bimaculatus, Bodianus,* Twospot Hogfish, 426
*bimaculatus, Cheilinus,* Two-spot Wrasse, 432
*bimaculatus, Ecsenius,* Double-spot Blenny, 528.15
*bimaculatus, Halichoeres,* Double-spot Wrasse, 443
*bimaculatus, Scolopsis,* Double Blotch Spinecheek, 293
*binotatus, Apogon,* Barred Cardinalfish, 231
*biocellata, Chrysiptera,* Two-spot Demoiselle, 394
*biocellatus, Antennarius,* Brackish-water Frogfish, 85, 87, 90
*biocellatus, Dendrochirus,* Twinspot Lionfish, 143
*biocellatus, Halichoeres,* Red-lined Wrasse, 440, 443
*biocellatus, Signigobius,* Two-spot Goby, 540, 551
*bipartitus, Macropharyngodon,* Divided Wrasse, 451
*bipinnulata, Elagatis,* Rainbow Runner, 245, 247
Bird Wrasse, *Gomphosus varius,* 439, 449
*birostris, Manta,* Manta Ray, 47, 48, 49
*biserialis, Pseudolabrus,* Red-banded Wrasse, 462, 465
*bison, Enophrys,* Buffalo Sculpin, 164
*bispinosus, Centropyge,* Coral Beauty, 354
*bistrispinus, Rypticus,* Freckled Soapfish, 207
*bitaeniata, Pseudochromis,* Two-banded Dottyback, 209
*bitorquatus, Gymnocranius,* Collared Sea Bream, 290
*bivittata, Parapercis,* Black Dorsal Grubfish, 504
*bivittatus, Halichoeres,* Slippery Dick, 447
Blach-and-White Chromis, *Chromis iomelas,* 387
Black and White Striped Blenny, *Meiacanthus kamoharai,* 522
Black and Yellow Butterflyfish, *Chaetodon mitratus,* 345
Black Anemonefish, *Amphiprion melanopus,* 374
Black Back Butterflyfish, *Chaetodon melannotus,* 337
Black Beauty, *Macolor niger,* 269, 270
Black Belt Flagfin Goby, *Pterogobius elapoides,* 565
Black Bream, *Acanthopagrus berda,* 289
Black Cardinalfish, *Apogon niger,* 228
Black Damsel, *Paraglyphidodon melas,* 396
Black Demoiselle, *Chrysiptera niger,* 390
Black Dorsal Grubfish, *Parapercis bivittata,* 504
Black Dragonfish, *Melanostomias* sp., 70
Black Grouper, *Mycteroperca bonaci,* 193
Black Hamlet, *Hypoplectrus nigricans,* 201
Black Jack, *Caranx lugubris,* 247, 248
Black Long-nosed Butterflyfish, *Forcipiger longirostris,* 351
Black Margate, *Anisotremus surinamensis,* 280
Black Marlin, *Makaira indica,* 604
Black Patch Triggerfish, *Rhinecanthus verrucosus,* 628
Black Pomfret, *Parastromateus niger,* 257
Black Rockfish, *Sebastes melanops,* 150
Black Scraper, *Thamnaconus modestus,* 635, 636
Black Sea Goby, *Gobius elanthematicus,* 559
Black Snapper, *Apsilus dentatus,* 259
Black Snook, *Centropomus nigrescens,* 170
Black Spot Sergeant, *Abudefduf sordidus,* 380

Black Surfperch, *Embiotoca jacksoni,* 370
Black Sweetlips, *Plectorhinchus nigrus,* 284
Black Triggerfish, *Melichthys niger,* 622
Black Velvet Angelfish, *Chaetodontoplus melanosoma,* 360
Black Widow, *Stygnobrotula latibricola,* 81
Black-and-White Striped Bream, *Pentapodus* sp., 300
Black-and-Yellow Rockfish, *Sebastes chrysomelas,* 149
Black-axil Chromis, *Chromis atripectoralis,* 383
Black-axil Damsel, *Pomacentrus nigromanus,* 401
Black-backed Damsel, *Dischistodus melanotus,* 409
Black-banded Cardinalfish, *Apogon endekataenia,* 224
Black-banded Demoiselle, *Amblypomacentrus breviceps,* 397
Black-banded Seaperch, *Hypoplectrodes nigrorubrum,* 199
Black-bar Chromis, *Chromis retrofasciata,* 387
Black-eared Moray, *Muraena clepsydra,* 60
Black-eared Surgeonfish, *Acanthurus maculiceps,* 587
Black-eared Wrasse, *Halichoeres melasmopomas,* 442
Black-edged Puffer, *Arothron immaculatus,* 648
Black-edged Sculpin, *Gymnocanthus herzensteini,* 164
Black-eyed Spinefoot, *Siganus puelloides,* 598
Black-finned Anemonefish, *Amphiprion nigripes,* 377
Black-finned Butterflyfish, *Chaetodon decussatus,* 344
Black-finned Grunt, *Hapalogenys nigripinnis,* 283
Black-finned Melon Butterflyfish, *Chaetodon melapterus,* 341
Black-finned Morwong, *Cheilodactylus nigripes,* 418
Black-headed Blenny, *Lipophrys nigriceps,* 525
Black-lined Blenny, *Meiacanthus nigrolineatus,* 523
Black-margined Damsel, *Pomacentrus nigromarginatus,* 401
Black-mouth Damsel, *Paraglyphidodon nigroris,* 396
Black-nosed Butterflyfish, *Pseudochaetodon nigrirostris,* 347
Black-nosed Cardinalfish, *Rhabdamia cypselurus,* 222
Black-saddled Leopard Grouper, *Plectropomus laevis,* 204
Black-saddled Toby, *Canthigaster valentini,* 651
Black-shoulderspot Threadfin Bream, *Nemipterus upeneoides,* 305
Black-spot Cardinalfish, *Archamia melasma,* 235
Black-spot Emperor, *Lethrinus harak,* 295, 298
Black-spot Snapper, *Lutjanus ehrenbergii,* 260
Black-spot Surgeon, *Acanthurus bariene,* 586
Black-spotted Goby, *Istigobius nigroocellatus,* 563
Black-spotted Puffer, *Arothron nigropunctatus,* 645, 646
Black-spotted Ray, *Taeniura melanospila,* 47
Black-spotted Rubberlip, *Plectorhinchus gaterinus,* 282, 285
Black-spotted Tamarin, *Anampses geographicus,* 425, 477
Black-stripe Sweeper, *Pempheris schwenki,* 322
Black-striped Cardinalfish, *Apogon nigrofasciatus,* 224
Black-striped Worm Eel, *Gunnelichthys pleurotaenia,* 580
Black-tail Sergeant, *Abudefduf lorenzi,* 382
Black-tailed Chromis, *Chromis nigrura,* 383
Black-tailed Wrasse, *Symphodus melanocercus,* 471
Black-throated Threefin, *Helcogramma decurrens,* 507, 511
Blackband Threadfin Bream, *Pentapodus* sp., 300
Blackbanded Amberjack, *Seriolina nigrofasciata,* 250, 253
Blackbar Soldierfish, *Myripristis jacobus,* 113
Blackbelly Eelpout, *Lycodes pacifcus,* 494
Blackbottom Goby, *Eviota nigriventris,* 572
*blackburnii, Chaetodon,* Blackburn's Butterflyfish, 340
Blackburn's Butterflyfish, *Chaetodon blackburnii,* 340
Blackcap Basslet, *Gramma melacara,* 213
Blackcheek Moray, *Gymnothorax breedeni,* 58
Blackear Wrasse, *Halichoeres poeyi,* 446
Blackedge Fairy Wrasse, *Cirrhilabrus melanomarginatus,* 434
Blackedge Triplefin, *Enneanectes atrorus,* 508
Blackeye Goby, *Coryphopterus nicholsi,* 574
Blackfin Barracuda, *Sphyraena qenie,* 422
Blackfin Blenny, *Paraclinus nigripinnis,* 515
Blackfin Gurnard, *Lepidotrigla microptera,* 160
Blackfin Hogfish, *Bodianus macrourus,* 428, 429
Blackfin Snapper, *Lutjanus buccanella,* 265
Blackfin Squirrelfish, *Neoniphon opercularis,* 108, 110, 112
Blackfin Sweeper, *Pempheris* cf *japonicus,* 322; *Pempheris japonicus,* 321
Blackfish, *Girella tricuspidatus,* 325, 369
Blackfoot Cardinalfish, *Apogon nigripes,* 232
Blackfoot Lionfish, *Parapterois heterurus,* 140
Blackloin Butterflyfish, *Chaetodon nippon,* 346
Blackmouth Goosefish, *Lophiomus setigerus,* 84
Blackrag, *Psenes pellucidus,* 606
Blacksaddle Goatfish, *Parupeneus rubescens,* 313
Blacksmith, *Chromis punctipinnis,* 389
Blackspot Butterfish, *Psenopsis anomala,* 606
Blackspot Cardinalfish, *Apogon notatus,* 226
Blackspot Demoiselle, *Chrysiptera melanomaculata,* 390
Blackspot Goatfish, *Parupeneus pleurostigma,* 315, 319
Blackspot Lyretail Angelfish, *Genicanthus melanospilus,* 358
Blackspot Moray, *Gymnothorax melatremus,* 56
Blackspot Tuskfish, *Choerodon schoenleinii,* 431
Blackspot Wrasse, *Decodon melasma,* 470
Blackstripe Parrotfish, *Scarus tricolor,* 484
Blacktail Humbug, *Dascyllus melanurus,* 378
Blackthorn Sawtail, *Prionurus scalprus,* 588
Blackthroat Seaperch, *Doederleinia berycoides,* 173
Blacktip Bullseye, *Pempheris analis,* 321, 322
Blacktip Grouper, *Epinephelus fasciatus,* 184, 187
Blacktip Reef Shark, *Carcharhinus melanopterus,* 39, 40
Blacktip Soldierfish, *Myripristis adustus,* 113, 114, 116
Blacktongue Unicornfish, *Naso hexacanthus,* 591
Blackwing Searobin, *Prionotus rubio,* 161
*blatteus, Cirrhilabrus,* Lancetail Fairy Wrasse, 462
*bleekeri, Argyrops,* Bleeker's Sea Bream, 289, 290
*bleekeri, Cirrhitichthys,* Bleeker's Hawkfish, 411
*bleekeri, Pseudocoris,* Bleeker's Rainbowfish, 427
*bleekeri, Scarus,* Pacific Whitecheek Parrotfish, 483, 492, 493
*bleekeri, Scolopsis,* Bleeker's Monocle Bream, 302, 304
Bleeker's Coralline Velvetfish, *Cocotropus dermacanthus,* 156
Bleeker's Damsel, *Stegastes simsiang,* 404
Bleeker's Hawkfish, *Cirrhitichthys bleekeri,* 411
Bleeker's Monocle Bream, *Scolopsis bleekeri,* 302, 304
Bleeker's Rainbowfish, *Pseudocoris bleekeri,* 427
Bleeker's Sea Bream, *Argyrops bleekeri,* 289, 290
*Blennodesmus scapularis,* Ocellate Eel Blenny, 500
Blenny, *Cirripectes* sp., 528.02
Blenny, unidentified, *Istiblennius* sp., 526; *Salarias* sp., 527, 528.01
Blenny, unidentified, *Cirripectes* sp., 528.02
*Blepsias* sp., Sailfin Sculpin, 166
Blind Goby, *Brachyamblyopus coesus,* 580
*blochii, Acanthurus,* Tailring Surgeonfish, 582, 587
*blochii, Trachinotus,* Round Pompano, 254, 255
*blochii, Tripodichthys,* Bloch's Tripodfish, 619, 620
Bloch's Tripodfish, *Tripodichthys blochii,* 619, 620
Bloody Frogfish, *Antennarius sanguineus,* 88
Blotched African Goby, *Gnatholepis* sp., 558
Blotchy Grouper, *Epinephelus fuscoguttatus,* 187
Blotchy Mudskipper, *Periophthalmus koelreuteri,* 568, 579

Blotchy Sillago, *Sillago maculata,* 239
Blue and Gold Snapper, *Lutjanus viridis,* 264
Blue and Yellow Grouper, *Epinephelus flavocoeruleus,* 190
Blue Angelfish, *Holacanthus isabelita,* 367
Blue Bird Wrasse, *Gomphosus caeruleus,* 449
Blue Blanquillo, *Malacanthus latovittatus,* 241
Blue Bumphead Parrotfish, *Scarus cyanescens,* 481
Blue Cheekline Triggerfish, *Xanthichthys mento,* 624
Blue Chromis, *Chromis cyaneus,* 388
Blue Croaker, *Bairdiella batabana,* 311
Blue Damsel, *Pomacentrus pavo,* 403
Blue Damselfish, *Pomacentrus coelestis,* 399, 400
Blue Devil, *Chrysiptera cyanea,* 392
Blue Groper, *Achoerodus gouldii,* 429
Blue Gudgeon, *Ptereleotris microlepis,* 561, 568
Blue Hamlet, *Hypoplectrus gemma,* 201
Blue Hana Goby, *Ptereleotris hanae,* 561
Blue King Angelfish, *Pomacanthus annularis,* 363
Blue Maomao, *Scorpis aequipinnis,* 328
Blue Marlin, *Makaira mazura,* 604
Blue Moki, *Latridopsis ciliaris,* 416
Blue Moon Angelfish, *Pomacanthus maculosus,* 362, 363
Blue Moon Parrotfish, *Scarus atrilunula,* 482
Blue Parrotfish, *Scarus coeruleus,* 486; *Scarus frontalis,* 483
Blue Rockfish, *Sebastes mystinus,* 150
Blue Runner, *Caranx crysos,* 248
Blue Sleeper, *Ioglossus calliurus,* 569
Blue Smalltooth Jobfish, *Aphareus furcatus,* 260
Blue Spangled Angelfish, *Chaetodontoplus cyanopunctatus,* 361
Blue Sprat, *Spratelloides robustus,* 66
Blue Surgeonfish, *Paracanthurus hepatus,* 589, 590
Blue Tang, *Acanthurus coeruleus,* 582
Blue-and-gold Blenny, *Ecsenius lividanalis,* 528.04
Blue-and-Gold Fin Goby, *Cryptocentrus* sp., 557
Blue-and-Gold Fusilier, *Caesio caerulaurea,* 271, 273
Blue-and-Gold Striped Snapper, *Symphorichthys spilurus,* 267, 268
Blue-and-Gold Triggerfish, *Pseudobalistes fuscus,* 616, 626
Blue-backed Silver-Biddy, *Gerres abbreviatus,* 276
Blue-barred Orange Parrotfish, *Scarus ghobban,* 482, 485
Blue-blotched Butterflyfish, *Chaetodon plebeius,* 339
Blue-bronze Sea Chub, *Kyphosus analogus,* 328
Blue-dorsal Mudskipper, *Periophthalmus papilio?,* 579
Blue-eared Wrasse, *Halichoeres pardaleocephalus,* 475
Blue-finned Shrimp Goby, *Cryptocentrus fasciatus,* 549, 556
Blue-girdled Angelfish, *Euxiphipops navarchus,* 361, 364
Blue-green Reeffish, *Chromis viridis,* 371, 383, 388
Blue-line Demoiselle, *Chrysiptera caeruleolineata,* 391
Blue-lined Angelfish, *Chaetodontoplus septentrionalis,* 360
Blue-lined Leatherjacket, *Meuschenia galii,* 630
Blue-lined Parrotfish, *Scarus cyanotaenia,* 492
Blue-lined Snapper, *Symphorus nematophorus,* 268, 270
Blue-nosed Monocle Bream, *Scolopsis personatus,* 303
Blue-sided Fairy Wrasse, *Cirrhilabrus cyanopleura,* 433, 434
Blue-sided Wrasse, *Leptojulis cyanopleura,* 462, 475
Blue-spot Blenny, *Salarias guttatus,* 527
Blue-spot Damsel, *Pomacentrus grammorhynchus,* 402
Blue-spotted Coral Goby, *Gobiodon histrio,* 578
Blue-spotted Dascyllus, *Dascyllus carneus,* 377, 378
Blue-spotted Goatfish, *Upeneichthys lineatus,* 314
Blue-spotted Puffer, *Omegophora cyanopunctata,* 646
Blue-spotted Ray, *Taeniura lymma,* 44, 47
Blue-spotted Sharp-nosed Puffer, *Canthigaster epilamprus,* 650
Blue-spotted Shrimp Goby, *Cryptocentrus caeruleomaculatus,* 549, 557
Blue-spotted Snapper, *Lutjanus rivulatus,* 266
Blue-spotted Spinefoot, *Siganus corallinus,* 598
Blue-spotted Stingray, *Amphotistius kuhlii,* 45
Blue-spotted Trevally, *Caranx bucculentus,* 248
Blue-streak Devil, *Paraglyphidodon oxyodon,* 396
Blue-striped Butterflyfish, *Chaetodon fremblii,* 342
Blue-striped Dottyback, *Pseudochromis cyanotaenia,* 208, 211
Blue-striped Grouper, *Gracila albomarginata,* 182
Blue-striped Orange Tamarin, *Anampses femininus,* 427
Blue-striped Snapper, *Lutjanus kasmira,* 260; *Lutjanus notatus,* 260
Blue-throat Triggerfish, *Xanthichthys auromarginatus,* 623
Blue-tip Longfin, *Paraplesiops poweri,* 214
Blueback Pygmy Angelfish, *Centropyge colini,* 355
Bluebacked Puffer, *Takifugu stictonotus,* 648
Bluedotted Damselfish, *Pristotis cyanostigma,* 408
Bluefin Kingfish, *Carangoides caeruleopinnatus,* 249
Bluefin Searobin, *Chelidonichthys spinosus,* 160
Bluefin Trevally, *Caranx melampygus,* 247, 248
Bluefin Tuna, *Thunnus thynnus,* 601
Bluefish Tailor, *Pomatomus saltatrix,* 241
Bluehead Wrasse, *Thalassoma bifasciatum,* 466
Bluejean Squirrelfish, *Neoniphon laeve,* 111
Bluelined Wrasse, *Stethojulis albovittata,* 455
Bluemask Angelfish, *Chaetodontoplus personifer,* 360
Bluespot Cardinalfish, *Apogon nitidus,* 223
Bluespotted Boxfish, *Ostracion immaculatus,* 639
Bluespotted Cornetfish, *Fistularia tabacaria,* 119
Bluespotted Jawfish, *Opistognathus* sp., 497
Bluespotted Mudskipper, *Boleophthalmus polyophthalmus,* 580
Bluespotted Stargazer, *Gnathagnus elongatus,* 501
Bluespotted Tamarin, *Anampses caeruleopunctatus,* 425, 426
Bluespotted Wrasse, *Macropharyngodon cyanoguttatus,* 451
Bluestreak Cleaner Wrasse, *Labroides dimidiatus,* 469
Bluestreak Mudskipper, *Periophthalmus* sp., 579
Bluestreak Prawn Goby, *Cryptocentrus cyanotaenia,* 547
Bluestreak Weever, *Parapercis pulchella,* 502
Bluestripe Pipefish, *Doryrhamphus excisus excisus,* 127
Bluestriped Grunt, *Haemulon sciurus,* 278, 279
Bluetail Trunkfish, *Ostracion cyanurus,* 640
Bluethroat Pikeblenny, *Chaenopsis ocellata,* 519
Blunt-headed Grouper, *Epinephelus amblycephalus,* 190
Blunt-snout Gregory, *Stegastes lividus,* 404
Blunthead Triggerfish, *Pseudobalistes naufragium,* 622
Blushing Hogfish, *Bodianus* sp., 427
Boarfish, *Antigonia capros,* 118
Bocaccio, *Sebastes paucispinis,* 150
*Bodianus anthioides,* Lyretail Hogfish, 429, 473
*Bodianus axillaris,* Coral Hogfish, 426
*Bodianus bilunulatus,* Saddleback Hogfish, 428, 429, 473
*Bodianus bimaculatus,* Twospot Hogfish, 426
*Bodianus diana,* Diana's Hogfish, 428, 429, 473
*Bodianus diplotaenia,* Mexican Hogfish, 430
*Bodianus eclancheri,* Galapagos Hogfish, 430
*Bodianus frenchii,* Foxfish, 429
*Bodianus macrourus,* Blackfin Hogfish, 428, 429
*Bodianus masudai,* Masuda's Hogfish, 427
*Bodianus mesothorax,* Eclipse Hogfish, 428
*Bodianus opercularis,* Candystripe Hogfish, 426
*Bodianus oxycephalus,* Linespot Hogfish, 427

*Bodianus perdito*, Goldsaddle Hogfish, 428
*Bodianus pulchellus*, Spotfin Hogfish, 430
*Bodianus rufus*, Spanish Hogfish, 430
*Bodianus* sp., Blushing Hogfish, 427; Redfin Hogfish, 427
*Bodianus speciosus*, Darkbar Hogfish, 427
*boehlkei, Enneanectes*, Roughhead Triplefin, 507
*boehlkei, Malacoctenus*, Diamond Blenny, 515
*boenack, Cephalopholis*, Boenacki Grouper, 182
Boenacki Grouper, *Cephalopholis boenack*, 182
Boga, *Inermia vittata*, 288
*bohar, Lutjanus*, Red Mumea, 262, 263
*Bolbometopon muricatus*, Humphead Parrotfish, 484
*Boleophthalmus pectinirostris*, Comb-toothed Mudskipper, 580
*Boleophthalmus polyophthalmus*, Bluespotted Mudskipper, 580
*Bollmannia boqueronensis*, White-eye Goby, 569
*bonaci, Mycteroperca*, Black Grouper, 193
Bonefish, *Albula vulpes*, 50
Boomerang Triggerfish, *Sufflamen bursa*, 624, 627
*Boops salpa*, Saupe, 288
*boops, Scombrops*, Gnomefish, 244
*boqueronensis, Bollmannia*, White-eye Goby, 569
Borbon Fairy Basslet, *Holanthias borbonius*, 180
*borbonius, Holanthias*, Borbon Fairy Basslet, 180
*borealis, Alepisaurus*, Northern Lancetfish, 75
*boreus, Priolepis*, Banded-head Goby, 567
*Bothus leopardus*, Leopard Flounder, 609
*Bothus lunatus*, Peacock Flounder, 609
*Bothus ocellatus*, Eyed Flounder, 609
*Bothus pantherinus*, Panther Flounder, 609
*bottomei, Emblemaria*, Bottome's Blenny, 520
Bottome's Blenny, *Emblemaria bottomei*, 520
*bougainvillei, Histophryne*, Bougainville's Frogfish, 85
Bougainville's Frogfish, *Histophryne bougainvillei*, 85
Bow-tailed Dottyback, *Pseudochromis melanotaenia*, 210
*boyeri, Atherina*, Boyer's Smelt, 102
Boyer's Smelt, *Atherina boyeri*, 102
*Brachaluteres jacksonianus*, Pygmy Leatherjacket, 634
*brachialis, Pomacentrus*, Charcoal Damsel, 401
*Brachyamblyopus coesus*, Blind Goby, 580
*brachycentron, Naso*, Humpback Unicornfish, 591
*brachydactylus, Chirodactylus*, Two-tone Fingerfin, 418
*brachylepis, Norfolkia*, Schultz's Triplefin, 508
*brachypterus, Dendrochirus*, Shortfin Lionfish, 143
*Brachysomophis cirrhocheilus*, Ghost Snake Eel, 64
*brachysomus, Calamus*, Pacific Porgy, 291
*brachyurus, Microphis*, Shorttail Pipefish, 125
Brackish-water Frogfish, *Antennarius biocellatus*, 85, 87, 90
*Brama japonicus*, Pacific Pomfret, 257
*Branchiostegus albus*, White Tilefish, 239
*Branchiostegus japonicus*, Japanese Tilefish, 239
*Branchiostegus* sp., Yellow-lined Tilefish, 239
*brasiliensis, Hemiramphus*, Ballyhoo, 100
*brasiliensis, Narcine*, Lesser Electric Ray, 42
*brauni, Bulbonaricus*, Eel Pipefish, 125
*brauni, Trachinops*, Braun's Hulafish, 215
Braun's Hulafish, *Trachinops brauni*, 215
Breaksea Grouper, *Epinephelides armatus*, 187
*breedeni, Gymnothorax*, Blackcheek Moray, 58
*brevicaudata, Dasyatis*, Short-tail Stingray, 45
*breviceps, Amblypomacentrus*, Black-banded Demoiselle, 397
*breviceps, Hippocampus*, Knobby Seahorse, 129
*breviceps, Petroscirtes*, Dandy Blenny, 522
*breviceps, Setipinna*, Bristle-feathered Anchovy, 68
*brevifilis, Scarus*, Tattooed Parrotfish, 483
*brevifrons, Scorpaenopsis*, Short-browed Scorpionfish, 147
*brevipinnis, Hypsoblennius*, Barnacle Bill Blenny, 530
*brevirostris, Malacanthus*, Banded Blanquillo, 241, 511
*brevirostris, Naso*, Spotted Unicornfish, 590, 591
*brevirostris, Negaprion*, Lemon Shark, 39
*brevis, Exallias*, Leopard Rockskipper, 534
*breviusculus, Pseudophycis*, Bearded Rock Cod, 77
*brevoortii, Selene*, Mexican Lookdown, 251
Bridle Cardinalfish, *Apogon aurolineatus*, 230
Bridle Triggerfish, *Sufflamen fraenatus*, 624, 627
Bridled Burrfish, *Chilomycterus antennatus*, 655
Bridled Goby, *Coryphopterus glaucofrenum*, 574
Bridled Leatherjacket, *Acanthaluterus spilomelanura*, 635
Bridled Weed Whiting, *Siphonognathus radiatus*, 478
Bright Eye, *Plectroglyphidodon imparipennis*, 395
Bright-saddled Goatfish, *Parupeneus pleurotaenia*, 316
Brill, *Scopthalmus rhombus*, 611
Brilliant Red Hawkfish, *Neocirrhitus armatus*, 412
Brindlebass, *Epinephelus lanceolatus*, 194
Bristle-feathered Anchovy, *Setipinna breviceps*, 68
Broad Alfonsino, *Beryx decadactylus*, 106
Broad-barred Butterflyfish, *Amphichaetodon howensis*, 350
Broad-barred Spanish Mackerel, *Scomberomorus semifasciatus*, 603
Broad-striped Cardinalfish, *Apogon angustatus*, 223
Broadnose Sevengill Shark, *Notorynchus cepedianus*, 33
Broadsaddle Cardinalfish, *Apogon pillionatus*, 231
Bronze-streaked Cardinalfish, *Archamia lineolata*, 235
Bronzeback Damsel, *Pomacentrus albimaculus*, 401
Broom Filefish, *Amanses scopas*, 627, 635
Broom Grouper, *Epinephelus cometae*, 190
Broomtail Wrasse, *Cheilinus lunulatus*, 432
*Brosmophycis marginata*, Red Brotula, 81
*Brotula barbata*, Bearded Brotula, 80
*Brotula erythrea?*, Scaled-cheek Brotula, 81
*Brotula multibarbata*, Whiskered Brotula, 80
*Brotulina fusca*, Dusky Brotulid, 81
Brown and Yellow Blenny, *Enchelyurus flavipes*, 526
Brown Blenny, *Ernogrammus hexagrammus*, 494
Brown Carpet Shark, *Chiloscyllium griseum*, 36
Brown Comber, *Serranus hepatus*, 196
Brown Demoiselle, *Neopomacentrus filamentosus*, 398
Brown Dottyback, *Pseudochromis fuscus*, 209
Brown Electric Ray, *Narcine brunneus*, 42
Brown Hakeling, *Physiculus maximowiczi*, 77
Brown Moray, *Gymnothorax prasinus*, 58, 60
Brown Puller, *Chromis hypselepis*, 386
Brown Rockfish, *Sebastes auriculatus*, 149
Brown Sailfin Tang, *Zebrasoma scopas*, 592, 594
Brown Smoothhound, *Mustelus henlei*, 38
Brown Triggerfish, *Sufflamen* sp., 624
Brown-and-White Butterflyfish, *Hemitaurichthys zoster*, 351
Brown-backed Puffer, *Lagocephalus gloveri*, 643
Brown-banded Dottyback, *Pseudochromis perspicillatus*, 211
Brown-banded Razorfish, *Xyrichthys* sp., 457
Brown-banded Rockcod, *Cephalopholis pachycentron*, 182, 194
Brown-barred Rosy Hawkfish, *Amblycirrhitus oxyrhynchus*, 414
Brown-eared Surgeonfish, *Acanthurus nigricauda*, 587
Brown-gold Blenny, *Ecsenius frontalis*, 528.06
Brown-spot Blenny, *Ecsenius paroculus*, 528.09
Brown-spotted Cat Shark, *Chiloscyllium punctatum*, 36, 38

Brown-spotted Spinefoot, *Siganus stellatus,* 599
Brown-spotted Wrasse, *Pseudolabrus parilus,* 465
Browncheek Blenny, *Acanthemblemaria crockeri,* 518
*brownfieldi, Halichoeres,* Brownfield's Wrasse, 441
Brownfield's Wrasse, *Halichoeres brownfieldi,* 441
Brownstreak Prawn Goby, *Amblyeleotris gymnocephala,* 545
Brownstripe Wrasse, *Suezichthys gracilis,* 464
*brunneus, Narcine,* Brown Electric Ray, 42
*brunneus, Rhinogobius,* Lake Goby, 552
*Bryaninops amphis,* Sea Whip Goby, 560
*Bryaninops natans,* Pink-eye Sea Whip Goby, 560
*Bryaninops* sp., Violet Sea Whip Goby, 555, 560
*Bryaninops tigris,* Tiger Sea Whip Goby, 560
*bryope, Neoclinus,* Neoclinus bryope, 512
*Bryx dunckeri,* Pugnose Pipefish, 125
*bubalis, Taurulus,* Rock Sculpin, 167
*buccanella, Lutjanus,* Blackfin Snapper, 265
*bucchichii, Gobius,* Bucchichi's Goby, 559
Bucchichi's Goby, *Gobius bucchichii,* 559
*bucciferus, Labrisomus,* Puffcheek Blenny, 513
*bucculentus, Caranx,* Blue-spotted Trevally, 248
*bucknilli, Tripterygion,* Banded Triplefin, 510
Bucktooth Parrotfish, *Sparisoma radians,* 488
*buergeri, Halaelurus,* Burger's Spotted Cat Shark, 37
Buffalo Sculpin, *Enophrys bison,* 164
*bulbifrons, Coris,* Bumphead Coris, 437
*Bulbonaricus brauni,* Eel Pipefish, 125
Bullethead Rockskipper, *Istiblennius periophthalmus,* 534
Bullis' Squirrelfish, *Sargocentron bullisi,* 107
*bullisi, Sargocentron,* Bullis' Squirrelfish, 107
Bullseye, *Johnsonina eriomma,* 620; *Pempheris multiradiata,* 322
Bullseye Jawfish, *Opistognathus scops,* 499
Bullseye Puffer, *Sphoeroides annulatus,* 649
Bullseye Stingray, *Urolophus concentricus,* 46
Bumphead Coris, *Coris bulbifrons,* 437
Bumphead Damselfish, *Microspathodon bairdi,* 408
Bumphead Parrotfish, *Scarus gibbus,* 480, 482, 484, 491, 492
Bumpytail Ragged-tooth, *Odontaspis ferox,* 37
Bundoon, *Meiacanthus bundoon,* 523
*bundoon, Meiacanthus,* Bundoon, 523
*burgeri, Dictyosoma,* Skunk Blenny, 494
Burger's Spotted Cat Shark, *Halaelurus buergeri,* 37
*burgessi, Chaetodon,* Burgess's Butterflyfish, 346
Burgess's Butterflyfish, *Chaetodon burgessi,* 346
*bursa, Sufflamen,* Boomerang Triggerfish, 624, 627
*Butis amboinensis,* Ambon Sleeper, 542
*butleri, Tathicarpus,* Butler's Frogfish, 85
Butler's Frogfish, *Tathicarpus butleri,* 85
Butterfly Bream, *Pentapodus setosus,* 299, 300
Butterfly Dragonet, *Synchiropus papilio,* 536
Butterfly Goby, *Amblygobius albimacula,* 554
Butterfly Gurnard, *Paratrigla vanessa,* 160
Butterfly Ray, *Gymnura micrura,* 45
Butterfly Threadfin Bream, *Nemipterus zysron,* 305
Butterflyfin Goby, *Fusigobius* sp., 570
*bynoensis, Amblygobius,* Spottyhead Goby, 554

# C

C-O Turbot, *Pleuronichthys coenosus,* 612
*caballus, Caranx,* Green Jack, 249
Cabezon, *Scorpaenichthys marmoratus,* 167
*cabrilla, Serranus,* Comber, 196
*cadenati, Chromis,* Cadenat's Chromis, 388
Cadenat's Chromis, *Chromis cadenati,* 388
*caerulaurea, Caesio,* Blue-and-Gold Fusilier, 271, 273
*caeruleolineata, Chrysiptera,* Blue-line Demoiselle, 391
*caeruleomaculatus, Cryptocentrus,* Blue-spotted Shrimp Goby, 549, 557
*caeruleopinnatus, Carangoides,* Bluefin Kingfish, 249
*caeruleopunctatus, Anampses,* Bluespotted Tamarin, 425, 426
*caeruleopunctatus, Epinephelus,* White-spotted Reef Cod, 187
*caeruleus, Gomphosus,* Blue Bird Wrasse, 449
*caeruleus, Pomacentrus,* Yellow-bellied Blue Damsel, 399
*Caesio caerulaurea,* Blue-and-Gold Fusilier, 271, 273
*Caesio cuning,* Yellow-tailed Fusilier, 273
*Caesio erythrogaster,* Redbelly Fusilier, 273
*Caesio lunaris,* Lunar Fusilier, 272, 273
*Caesio pisang,* Yellowstriped Fusilier, 272, 273
*Caesio teres,* Beautiful Fusilier, 271, 273
*Caesio varilineata,* Yellow-lined Fusilier, 270
*Caesio xanthonotus,* Redfin Fusilier, 270, 271, 272
*Caesioperca lepidoptera,* Red Butterfly Perch, 181
*Caesioperca rasor,* Barber Perch, 181
Caesiura Goby, *Trimma caesiura,* 577
*caesiura, Trimma,* Caesiura Goby, 577
Caffer Goby, *Caffrogobius caffer,* 558, 559
*caffer, Caffrogobius,* Caffer Goby, 558, 559
*Caffrogobius caffer,* Caffer Goby, 558, 559
*Calamus bajonado,* Jolthead Porgy, 291
*Calamus brachysomus,* Pacific Porgy, 291
*Calamus calamus,* Saucereye Porgy, 291
*Calamus nodosus,* Knobbed Porgy, 291
*Calamus pennatula,* Pluma, 291
*calamus, Calamus,* Saucereye Porgy, 291
*calcaratus, Callionymus,* Sand Dragonet, 537
*calcarifer, Lates,* Barramundi, 170
Caledonian Devilfish, *Inimicus caledonicus,* 155
*caledonicus, Inimicus,* Caledonian Devilfish, 155
Calico Rockfish, *Sebastes dallii,* 149
California Corbina, *Menticirrhus undulatus,* 311
California Kelp Bass, *Paralabrax clathratus,* 202
California Moray, *Gymnothorax mordax,* 55
California Sand Bass, *Paralabrax nebulifer,* 202
California Scorpionfish, *Scorpaena guttata,* 145
California Sheephead, *Semicossyphus pulcher,* 463
*californica, Oxyjulis,* Senorita, 470
*californica, Squatina,* Pacific Angel Shark, 41
*californiensis, Medialuna,* Halfmoon, 328
*Callanthias allporti,* Splendid Perch, 186
*Callanthias japonica,* Pastel Fairy Basslet, 186
*Callechelys marmoratus,* Leopard Snake-eel, 61
*Callionymus calcaratus,* Sand Dragonet, 537
*Callionymus goodladi,* Goodlad's Dragonet, 537
*callisterna, Canthigaster,* Freckleback Sharp-nosed Puffer, 651
*Calliurichthys japonicus,* Japanese Dragonet, 537
*calliurus, Ioglossus,* Blue Sleeper, 569
*Callogobius hasselti,* Hasselt's Goby, 562
*Callogobius mucosus,* Sculptured Goby, 562
*Callogobius snelliusi,* Dusky Finned Goby, 562
*Callogobius* sp., Whiskered Goby, 562
*callopareia, Amblyeleotris,* Beautiful Cheek Prawn Goby, 544
*Calloplesiops altivelis,* Comet, 214, 215
*Calloplesiops argus,* Argus Comet, 214
*calori, Lophodiodon,* Four-bar Porcupinefish, 656

*Calotomus japonicus,* Japanese Parrotfish, 488
*Calotomus spinidens,* Spinytooth Parrotfish, 488, 491
*Calotomus zonarchia,* Jenkin's Parrotfish, 488
Camouflage Grouper, *Epinephelus microdon,* 189
*campechanus, Lutjanus,* Red Snapper, 265
*canadum, Rachycentron,* Cobia, 244
*canaliculatus, Siganus,* White-spotted Spinefoot, 597, 598
Canary Demoiselle, *Chrysiptera galba,* 390
Canary Rockfish, *Sebastes pinniger,* 150
*cancellatus, Mesopristes,* Tapiroid Grunter, 218
*cancellatus, Scolopsis,* Latticed Monocle Bream, 302, 304
*cancrivorus, Pisodonophis,* Long-finned Snake Eel, 61
*candollei, Lepadogaster,* Condolle's Lepadogaster, 97
Candy Basslet, *Liopropoma carmabi,* 198
Candystripe Hogfish, *Bodianus opercularis,* 426
*canescens, Zanclus,* Moorish Idol, 594, 595
*canevae, Lipophrys,* Caneva's Blenny, 525
Caneva's Blenny, *Lipophrys canevae,* 525
*canicula, Scyliorhinus,* Lesser Spotted Dogfish, 38
*caninus, Pentapodus,* Banded Threadfin Bream, 299, 300, 307
*Cantherhines dumerili,* Vagabond Filefish, 627
*Cantherhines fronticinctus,* Indo-Pacific Leatherjacket, 632
*Cantherhines howensis,* Lord Howe Leatherjacket, 632
*Cantherhines macroceros,* Whitespotted Filefish, 629
*Cantherhines pardalis,* Honeycomb Filefish, 627
*Cantherhines pullus,* Orange-spotted Filefish, 629
*Cantherhines sandwichensis,* Wire-netting Leatherjacket, 629
*Cantherhines verrucundus,* Shy Filefish, 632
*Canthidermis maculatus,* Rough Triggerfish, 625
*Canthidermis sufflamen,* Ocean Triggerfish, 625
*Canthigaster ambionensis,* Spotted Toby, 618, 650
*Canthigaster bennetti,* Bennett's Toby, 650, 651
*Canthigaster callisterna,* Freckleback Sharp-nosed Puffer, 651
*Canthigaster capistratus,* Madeira Sharp-nosed Puffer, 652
*Canthigaster compressus,* Sharp-nosed Puffer, 651
*Canthigaster coronata,* Four-barred Toby, 650, 651
*Canthigaster epilamprus,* Blue-spotted Sharp-nosed Puffer, 650
*Canthigaster inframacula,* Low Spot Sharpnosed Pufferfish, 652
*Canthigaster jactator,* Whitespotted Toby, 651
*Canthigaster janthinoptera,* Honeycomb Toby, 650
*Canthigaster leopardus,* Leopard Pufferfish, 647, 650
*Canthigaster margaritata,* Pearl Toby, 652
*Canthigaster marquesensis,* Marquesan Sharpnosed Pufferfish, 652
*Canthigaster natalensis,* Natal Sharpnosed Pufferfish, 653
*Canthigaster ocellicincta,* Saddled-ocellated Sharpnosed Puffer, 652
*Canthigaster punctatissimus,* Spotted Sharpnose Puffer, 651
*Canthigaster rapaensis,* Rapa Sharpnose Pufferfish, 652
*Canthigaster rivulata,* Doubleline Toby, 652
*Canthigaster rostrata,* Sharpnose Puffer, 651
*Canthigaster sanctaehelenae,* Saint Helena Sharpnose Puffer, 652
*Canthigaster smithae,* Bicolored Toby, 650
*Canthigaster solandri,* False-eye Toby, 653
*Canthigaster tyleri,* Tyler's Sharpnosed Pufferfish, 647, 653
*Canthigaster valentini,* Black-saddled Toby, 651
Canton Mudskipper, *Periophthalmus cantonensis,* 579
*cantonensis, Periophthalmus,* Canton Mudskipper, 579
Cape Conger, *Conger wilsoni,* 63
Cape Mono, *Monodactylus falciformes,* 418
Cape Verde Chromis, *Chromis cauta?,* 388
Cape Verde Snapper, *Apsilus fuscus,* 259
*capistratus, Canthigaster,* Madeira Sharp-nosed Puffer, 652
*capistratus, Chaetodon,* Four-eyed Butterflyfish, 343
*capriscus, Balistes,* Gray Triggerfish, 625
*Caprodon longimanus,* Pink Maomao, 181
*Caprodon schlegeli,* Schlegel's Red Bass, 181
*capros, Antigonia,* Boarfish, 118
*Caracanthus maculatus,* Pacific Spotted Velvetfish, 158
*Caracanthus madagascariensis,* Velvetfish, 158
*Carangoides armatus,* Longfin Trevally, 247
*Carangoides bartholomei,* Yellow Jack, 249
*Carangoides caeruleopinnatus,* Bluefin Kingfish, 249
*Carangoides chrysophrys,* Longnose Trevally, 247
*Carangoides dinema,* Goldband Trevally, 246
*Carangoides equula,* Horse Crevalle, 246
*Carangoides ferdau,* Yellow-spotted Crevalle, 247, 248
*Carangoides fulvoguttatus,* Yellowspotted Kingfish, 247, 249
*Carangoides malabaricus,* Malabar Trevally, 247
*Carangoides orthogrammus,* Yellowspotted Crevalle, 246
*Carangoides ruber,* Bar Jack, 248
*Carangoides* sp., Trevally, unidentified, 246
*Carangoides* sp. *(?armatus),* Longfinned Trevally, 248
*Carangoides vinctus,* Striped Trevally, 246
*Caranx bucculentus,* Blue-spotted Trevally, 248
*Caranx caballus,* Green Jack, 249
*Caranx crysos,* Blue Runner, 248
*Caranx hippos,* Crevalle Jack, 249
*Caranx ignobilis,* Giant Trevally, 247, 249
*Caranx latus,* Horse-eye Jack, 249
*Caranx lugubris,* Black Jack, 247, 248
*Caranx melampygus,* Bluefin Trevally, 247, 248
*Caranx sexfasciatus,* Bigeye Kingfish, 247, 249
*Carapus bermudensis,* Pearlfish, 79, 80
*Carapus homei,* Pen Shell Pearlfish, 80
*carberryi, Nemanthias,* Threadfin Goldie, 175
*Carcharhinus albimarginatus,* Silvertip Shark, 40
*Carcharhinus amblyrhynchos,* Gray Reef Shark, 39, 40
*Carcharhinus longimanus,* Oceanic Whitetip Shark, 40
*Carcharhinus melanopterus,* Blacktip Reef Shark, 39, 40
*Carcharhinus plumbeus,* Sandbar Shark, 39
*Carcharhinus wheeleri,* Shortnose Blacktail Shark, 39
Cardinal Scorpionfish, *Scorpaena cardinalis,* 138
Cardinal Soldierfish, *Plectrypops retrospinis,* 113
Cardinalfin Goby, *Kellogella cardinalis,* 551
Cardinalfish, unidentified, *Apogon* sp., 225, 227, 233; *Cheilodipterus* sp., 234; *Siphamia* sp., 237
*cardinalis, Evynnis,* Crimson Sea-Bream, 291
*cardinalis, Kellogella,* Cardinalfin Goby, 551
*cardinalis, Scorpaena,* Cardinal Scorpionfish, 138
Caribbean Garden Eel, *Heteroconger halis,* 63
Caribbean Tonguefish, *Symphurus arawak,* 614
Caribbean Trumpetfish, *Aulostomus maculatus,* 119
*carinatus, Apistus,* Ocellated Waspfish, 137
*carmabi, Liopropoma,* Candy Basslet, 198
*carnatus, Sebastes,* Gopher Rockfish, 149
*carneus, Dascyllus,* Blue-spotted Dascyllus, 377, 378
*carolinus, Prionotus,* Northern Searobin, 161
*carolinus, Trachinotus,* Florida Pompano, 254
*carpenteri, Paracheilinus,* Carpenter's Wrasse, 459
Carpenter's Wrasse, *Paracheilinus carpenteri,* 459
*carponotatus, Lutjanus,* Striped Snapper, 261
*carri, Microgobius,* Seminole Goby, 569
*carribbaeus, Scorpaenodes,* Reef Scorpionfish, 153
*caryi, Hypsurus,* Rainbow Surfperch, 368, 370

Casamance River Goby, *Gobius casamancus*, 548
*casamancus, Gobius*, Casamance River Goby, 548
*castaneus, Cirripectes*, Chestnut Blenny, 528
*castaneus, Gymnothorax*, Panamic Green Moray, 55
Castelnau's Golden Wrasse, *Dotalabrus aurantiacus*, 463
Castelnau's Soldierfish, *Myripristis amaenus*, 115
Cat Shark, *Chiloscyllium confusum*, 36
Catalina Goby, *Lythrypnus dalli*, 575
*catenata, Echidna*, Chain Moray, 53
*caudalis, Lissocampus*, Smooth Pipefish, 126
*caudavittatus, Amniataba*, Bartail Grunter, 217
*caudimacula, Coris*, Spottail Coris, 436, 438, 475
*caudimaculatum, Sargocentron*, Silverspot Squirrelfish, 108, 109, 111, 112
*caudovittatus, Genicanthus*, Zebra Lyretail Angelfish, 357
*caudovittatus, Hipposcarus*, Whitecrescent Parrotfish, 482
*Caulolatilus princeps*, Ocean Whitefish, 239
*caurinus, Sebastes*, Copper Rockfish, 149
*cauta?, Chromis*, Cape Verde Chromis, 388
Cave Bass, *Liopropoma mowbrayi*, 198
Cave Goby, *Fusigobius* sp., 550
Cavebass, *Dinoperca petersi*, 205
*cayorum, Ogilbia*, Key Brotutid, 81
*Cebidichthys violaceous*, Monkeyface Prickleback, 495
Celebes Butterfly Bream, *Nemipterus celebicus*, 307
Celebes Sweetlips, *Plectorhinchus celebicus*, 284
Celebes Wrasse, *Cheilinus celebicus*, 477
*celebicus, Cheilinus*, Celebes Wrasse, 477
*celebicus, Nemipterus*, Celebes Butterfly Bream, 307
*celebicus, Plectorhinchus*, Celebes Sweetlips, 284
*celidotus, Pseudolabrus*, New Zealand Spotty, 464
*Centriscus scutatus*, Grooved Razorfish, 123
*Centropogon australis*, Waspfish, 137
*Centropomus nigrescens*, Black Snook, 170
*Centropomus undecimalis*, Snook, 170
*Centropyge acanthops*, African Pygmy Angelfish, 354
*Centropyge argi*, Cherubfish, 356
*Centropyge aurantonotus*, Flameback Angelfish, 356
*Centropyge bicolor*, Two-colored Angelfish, 354
*Centropyge bispinosus*, Coral Beauty, 354
*Centropyge colini*, Blueback Pygmy Angelfish, 355
*Centropyge eibli*, Eibl-Eibesfeldt's Pygmy Angelfish, 354
*Centropyge ferrugatus*, Rusty Angelfish, 355
*Centropyge fisheri*, Fisher's Angelfish, 356
*Centropyge flavicauda*, Royal Blue Pygmy Angelfish, 356
*Centropyge flavissimus*, Lemonpeel, 357
*Centropyge flavopectoralis*, Yellow-finned Pygmy Angelfish, 354
*Centropyge heraldi*, Golden Angelfish, 355
*Centropyge hotumatua*, Easter Island Pygmy Angelfish, 356
*Centropyge interruptus*, Japanese Pygmy Angelfish, 356
*Centropyge joculator*, Half Yellow Pygmy Angelfish, 357
*Centropyge loriculus*, Flame Angelfish, 355
*Centropyge multicolor*, Pastel Pygmy Angelfish, 356
*Centropyge multifasciatus*, Many Banded Angelfish, 357
*Centropyge multispinis*, Dusky Cherub, 354
*Centropyge nox*, Midnight Angelfish, 355
*Centropyge potteri*, Potter's Angelfish, 355
*Centropyge resplendens*, Ascencion Cherubfish, 356
*Centropyge shepardi*, Shepard's Angelfish, 355
*Centropyge tibicin*, Keyhole Angelfish, 357
*Centropyge vroliki*, Pearl-scaled Angelfish, 357
*Centroscyllium ritteri*, Ritter's Catshark, 41
*cepedianus, Notorynchus*, Broadnose Sevengill Shark, 33
*Cephalopholis analis*, Golden Orange Rockcod, 184
*Cephalopholis argus*, Argus Grouper, 182
*Cephalopholis aurantia*, Garrupa, 182
*Cephalopholis boenack*, Boenacki Grouper, 182
*Cephalopholis cruentatus*, Grayshy, 184
*Cephalopholis fulva*, Coney, 184
*Cephalopholis hemistiktos*, Halfspotted Grouper, 184
*Cephalopholis leopardus*, Leopard Rockcod, 182
*Cephalopholis miniata*, Coral Rockcod, 183
*Cephalopholis nigripinnis*, Duskyfin Rockcod, 182
*Cephalopholis pachycentron*, Brown-banded Rockcod, 182, 194
*Cephalopholis panamensis*, Enjambre, 184
*Cephalopholis polleni*, Harlequin Rockcod, 182
*Cephalopholis sexmaculata*, Six-barred Grouper, 183, 185
*Cephalopholis sonnerati*, Tomato Rockcod, 183
*Cephalopholis taeniops*, Ghana Rockcod, 184
*Cephalopholis urodelus*, Banded-tail Coral-cod, 183
*cephalopunctata?, Parapercis*, Spothead Grubfish, 504
*cephalopunctata, Parapercis*, Spothead Grubfish, 504
*Cephaloscyllium ventriosum*, Swell Shark, 38
*cephalotaenia, Plesiops*, Northern Devilfish, 214
*cephalotes, Siphamia*, Southern Siphonfish, 237
*cephalus, Mugil*, Striped Mullet, 421
*Cepola australis*, Australian Bandfish, 420
Ceram Blenny, *Salarias ceramensis*, 530
Ceram Cardinalfish, *Apogon ceramensis*, 227
*ceramensis, Apogon*, Ceram Cardinalfish, 227
*ceramensis, Salarias*, Ceram Blenny, 530
*cerasinus, Pseudojuloides*, Smalltail Wrasse, 460, 461
*Cerdale floridana*, Pugjaw Wormfish, 580
*cervinus, Diplodus*, Thick-lipped Bream, 293
*Cetorhinus maximus*, Basking Shark, 37
*Cetoscarus bicolor*, Bicolor Parrotfish, 480, 489, 490
*ceuthoecus, Barbulifer*, Atlantic Bearded Goby, 564
cf *acanthopoma, Eleotris*, Yellowfin Sleeper, 542
cf *japonicus, Pempheris*, Blackfin Sweeper, 322
cf *jussieu, Sardinella*, Gold-striped Sardine, 66
cf *variegata, Fowleria*, False Variegated Cardinalfish, 235
*chabanaudi, Belonoperca*, Arrowhead Soapfish, 205
*chacunda, Anodontostoma*, Indies Gizzard Shad, 67
*Chaenogobius urotaenia*, Dusky Goby, 558
*Chaenopsis alepidota*, Orangethroat Pikeblenny, 519
*Chaenopsis limbaughi*, Yellowface Pikeblenny, 519
*Chaenopsis ocellata*, Bluethroat Pikeblenny, 519
*Chaetodermis penicilligerus*, Prickly Leatherjacket, 630, 634
*Chaetodipterus faber*, Atlantic Spadefish, 330
*Chaetodipterus zonatus*, Pacific Spadefish, 330
*Chaetodon aculeatus*, Poey's Butterflyfish, 346
*Chaetodon adiergastos*, Bantayan Butterflyfish, 338
*Chaetodon argentatus*, Silver and Black Butterflyfish, 336
*Chaetodon assarius*, Assarius Butterflyfish, 341
*Chaetodon aureofasciatus*, Sunburst Butterflyfish, 340
*Chaetodon auriga*, Threadfin Butterflyfish, 345
*Chaetodon auripes*, Golden Butterflyfish, 338
*Chaetodon austriacus*, Red Sea Melon Butterflyfish, 341
*Chaetodon aya*, Bank Butterflyfish, 347
*Chaetodon baronessa*, Baroness Butterflyfish, 336
*Chaetodon bennetti*, Bennett's Butterflyfish, 341
*Chaetodon blackburnii*, Blackburn's Butterflyfish, 340
*Chaetodon burgessi*, Burgess's Butterflyfish, 346
*Chaetodon capistratus*, Four-eyed Butterflyfish, 343

*Chaetodon citrinellus,* Citron Butterflyfish, 341
*Chaetodon collare,* Red-tailed Butterflyfish, 341
*Chaetodon daedalma,* Wrought-iron Butterflyfish, 335
*Chaetodon declevis,* Marquesas Butterflyfish, 336
*Chaetodon decussatus,* Black-finned Butterflyfish, 344
*Chaetodon dichrous,* Bicolored Butterflyfish, 346
*Chaetodon dolosus,* African Butterflyfish, 341
*Chaetodon ehippium,* Saddleback Butterflyfish, 345
*Chaetodon excelsa,* Hawaiian Gold-barred Butterflyfish, 346
*Chaetodon falcifer,* Scythe-marked Butterflyfish, 347
*Chaetodon falcula,* Sickle Butterflyfish, 340
*Chaetodon fasciatus,* Red Sea Raccoon Butterflyfish, 340
*Chaetodon flavirostris,* Yellow-face Butterflyfish, 338
*Chaetodon flavocoronatus,* Yellow-crowned Butterflyfish, 340
*Chaetodon fremblii,* Blue-striped Butterflyfish, 342
*Chaetodon gardneri,* Gardner's Butterflyfish, 338
*Chaetodon guentheri,* Guenther's Butterflyfish, 343
*Chaetodon guttatissimus,* Peppered Butterflyfish, 344
*Chaetodon guyanensis,* Guyana Butterflyfish, 347
*Chaetodon hemichrysus,* Half-yellow Butterflyfish, 342
*Chaetodon hoefleri,* Hoefler's Butterflyfish, 343
*Chaetodon humeralis,* East Pacific Banded Butterflyfish, 343
*Chaetodon jayakari,* Indian Golden-barred Butterflyfish, 346
*Chaetodon kleini,* Klein's Butterflyfish, 340
*Chaetodon larvatus,* Masked Butterflyfish, 337
*Chaetodon leucopleura,* Somali Butterflyfish, 337
*Chaetodon lineolatus,* Lined Butterflyfish, 339
*Chaetodon litus,* White-tip Butterflyfish, 342
*Chaetodon lunula,* Raccoon Butterflyfish, 340
*Chaetodon madagascariensis,* Indian Ocean Chevron Butterflyfish, 337
*Chaetodon marcellae,* French Butterflyfish, 347
*Chaetodon marleyi,* Marley's Butterflyfish, 345
*Chaetodon melannotus,* Black Back Butterflyfish, 337
*Chaetodon melapterus,* Black-finned Melon Butterflyfish, 341
*Chaetodon mertensii,* Mertens's Butterflyfish, 336
*Chaetodon mesoleucos,* Red Sea Butterflyfish, 338
*Chaetodon meyeri,* Meyer's Butterflyfish, 339
*Chaetodon miliaris,* Millet-seed Butterflyfish, 343
*Chaetodon mitratus,* Black and Yellow Butterflyfish, 345
*Chaetodon modestus,* Japanese Golden-barred Butterflyfish, 346
*Chaetodon multicinctus,* Pebbled Butterflyfish, 342
*Chaetodon nigropunctatus,* Mystery Butterflyfish, 338, 339
*Chaetodon nippon,* Blackloin Butterflyfish, 346
*Chaetodon ocellatus,* Spotfin Butterflyfish, 335
*Chaetodon ocellicaudus,* Spot-tail Butterflyfish, 337
*Chaetodon octofasciatus,* Eight-striped Butterflyfish, 339
*Chaetodon ornatissimus,* Ornate Butterflyfish, 339
*Chaetodon oxycephalus,* False Lined Butterflyfish, 339
*Chaetodon paucifasciatus,* Red Sea Chevron Butterflyfish, 337
*Chaetodon pelewensis,* Sunset Butterflyfish, 342
*Chaetodon plebeius,* Blue-blotched Butterflyfish, 339
*Chaetodon punctatofasciatus,* Spot-band Butterflyfish, 344
*Chaetodon quadrimaculatus,* Four-spot Butterflyfish, 335
*Chaetodon rafflesi,* Raffle's Butterflyfish, 345
*Chaetodon rainfordi,* Rainford's Butterflyfish, 343
*Chaetodon reticulatus,* Mailed Butterflyfish, 336
*Chaetodon robustus,* Ghana Butterflyfish, 335
*Chaetodon sanctaehelenae,* Saint Helena Butterflyfish, 342
*Chaetodon sedentarius,* Reef Butterflyfish, 342
*Chaetodon selene,* Moon Butterflyfish, 338
*Chaetodon semeion,* Decorated Butterflyfish, 344
*Chaetodon semilarvatus,* Red-lined Butterflyfish, 344
*Chaetodon speculum,* Mirror Butterflyfish, 344
*Chaetodon striatus,* Banded Butterflyfish, 343
*Chaetodon tinkeri,* Tinker's Butterflyfish, 346
*Chaetodon triangulum,* Triangle Butterflyfish, 337
*Chaetodon trichrous,* Tahitian Butterflyfish, 342
*Chaetodon tricinctus,* Lord Howe Butterflyfish, 343
*Chaetodon trifascialis,* Chevron Butterflyfish, 336, 337
*Chaetodon trifasciatus,* Melon Butterflyfish, 336, 341
*Chaetodon ulietensis,* Saddled Butterflyfish, 340
*Chaetodon unimaculatus,* Teardrop Butterflyfish, 345
*Chaetodon vagabundus,* Vagabond Butterflyfish, 344
*Chaetodon wiebeli,* Pocket Butterflyfish, 338
*Chaetodon xanthocephalus,* Yellowhead Butterflyfish, 345
*Chaetodon xanthurus,* Philippine Chevron Butterflyfish, 336
*Chaetodon zanzibariensis,* Zanzibar Butterflyfish, 344
*chaetodonoides, Plectorhinchus,* Harlequin Sweetlips, 282, 283, 287
*Chaetodontoplus chrysocephalus,* Yellow-headed Angelfish, 360
*Chaetodontoplus conspicillatus,* Spectacled Angelfish, 361
*Chaetodontoplus cyanopunctatus,* Blue Spangled Angelfish, 361
*Chaetodontoplus duboulayi,* Duboulay's Angelfish, 360
*Chaetodontoplus melanosoma,* Black Velvet Angelfish, 360
*Chaetodontoplus mesoleucus,* Vermiculated Angelfish, 361
*Chaetodontoplus personifer,* Bluemask Angelfish, 360
*Chaetodontoplus septentrionalis,* Blue-lined Angelfish, 360
Chain Moray, *Echidna catenata,* 53
Chain Pipefish, *Syngnathus louisianae,* 125
*chalcogramma, Theragra,* Wall-eye Pollock, 78
Chalk Bass, *Serranus tortugarum,* 196
*chalumnae, Latimeria,* Coelacanth, 50
Chameleon Tilefish, *Hoplolatilus chlupatyi,* 240
Chameleon Wrasse, *Halichoeres dispilus,* 448
*chameleonticeps, Lopholatilus,* Tilefish, 239
*chancei, Gobiosoma,* Shortstripe Cleaning Goby, 572
*Chanda ranga,* Glassfish, 170
*Chanos chanos,* Milkfish, 68
*chanos, Chanos,* Milkfish, 68
Charcoal Damsel, *Pomacentrus brachialis,* 401
*Chasmichthys dolichognathus,* Snakeskin Goby, 565
*Chasmichthys gulosus,* Gluttonous Goby, 565
*Chauliodus sloani,* Sloan's Viperfish, 70
*Chaunax abei,* Abe's Sea Toad, 91
Checkerboard Wrasse, *Halichoeres hortulanus,* 445, 472
Checkered Blenny, *Starksia ocellata,* 512
Checkered Snapper, *Lutjanus decussatus,* 260
Cheeklined Wrasse, *Cheilinus digrammus,* 432, 433, 477
*Cheilinus bimaculatus,* Two-spot Wrasse, 432
*Cheilinus celebicus,* Celebes Wrasse, 477
*Cheilinus chlorourus,* Floral Wrasse, 433
*Cheilinus digrammus,* Cheeklined Wrasse, 432, 433, 477
*Cheilinus fasciatus,* Redbreasted Wrasse, 432, 477
*Cheilinus lunulatus,* Broomtail Wrasse, 432
*Cheilinus oxycephalus,* Snooty Wrasse, 431
*Cheilinus trilobatus,* Tripletail Wrasse, 432
*Cheilinus undulatus,* Humphead Wrasse, 433, 477
*Cheilinus unifasciatus,* One-band Wrasse, 431
*Cheilio inermis,* Cigar Wrasse, 451, 472
*Cheilodactylus douglasi,* Porae, 416
*Cheilodactylus ephippium,* Painted Moki, 417
*Cheilodactylus fuscus,* Red Morwong, 416
*Cheilodactylus gibbosus,* Magpie Morwong, 417
*Cheilodactylus nigripes,* Black-finned Morwong, 418

*Cheilodactylus quadricornis,* Barred Morwong, 417
*Cheilodactylus rubrolabiatus,* Red-lipped Morwong, 418
*Cheilodactylus spectabilis,* Red Moki, 416
*Cheilodactylus vittatus,* Striped Hawkfish, 417
*Cheilodactylus zonatus,* Belted Morwong, 416, 419
*Cheilodipterus artus,* Wolf Cardinalfish, 233
*Cheilodipterus lachneri,* Arrowtooth Cardinalfish, 234
*Cheilodipterus lineatus,* Tiger Cardinalfish, 233
*Cheilodipterus macrodon,* Eight-lined Cardinalfish, 234
*Cheilodipterus quinquelineatus,* Sharptooth Cardinalfish, 233
*Cheilodipterus* sp., Cardinalfish, unidentified, 234
*Cheilodipterus zonatus,* Banded Cardinalfish, 234
*Cheilopogon atrisignis,* Flying Fish, 99
*Cheilopogon pinnatibarbatus japonicus,* Japanese Feather-finned Flying Fish, 99
*Cheilopogon suttoni,* Sutton's Flying Fish, 99
*Cheiloprion labiatus,* Big Lip Damsel, 397
*Chelidonichthys spinosus,* Bluefin Searobin, 160
*Chelidoperca hirundinacea,* Japanese Sand Bass, 200
*Chelmon marginalis,* Willemawillum, 348
*Chelmon muelleri,* Mueller's Butterflyfish, 349
*Chelmon rostratus,* Copperband Butterflyfish, 349, 350
*Chelmonops truncatus,* Truncate Coralfish, 348, 350
*chelomatus, Cirripectes,* Yellow-headed Blenny, 528
*Chelonodon laticeps,* Gold-spotted Puffer, 649
Cherry Bass, *Sacura margaritacea,* 180
Cherubfish, *Centropyge argi,* 356
Chestnut Blenny, *Cirripectes castaneus,* 528
Chevron Barracuda, *Sphyraena obtusata,* 422
Chevron Butterflyfish, *Chaetodon trifascialis,* 336, 337
*chierchiae, Halichoeres,* Wounded Wrasse, 448
*Chilara taylori,* Spotted Cusk-eel, 80
*Chilomycterus affinis,* Pacific Burrfish, 653
*Chilomycterus antennatus,* Bridled Burrfish, 655
*Chilomycterus antillarum,* Web Burrfish, 655
*Chilomycterus atinga,* Spotted Burrfish, 655
*Chilomycterus schoepfi,* Striped Burrfish, 655
*Chilomycterus spilostylus,* Yellowspotted Burrfish, 655
*Chiloscyllium confusum,* Cat Shark, 36
*Chiloscyllium griseum,* Brown Carpet Shark, 36
*Chiloscyllium plagiosum,* Banded Catshark, 36
*Chiloscyllium punctatum,* Brown-spotted Cat Shark, 36, 38
*Chimaera phantasma,* Ghost Shark, 33
China Rockfish, *Sebastes nebulosus,* 150
Chinaman Leatherjacket, *Nelusetta ayraudi,* 636
*chinensis, Aulostomus,* Asian Trumpetfish, 117, 119
*chinensis, Monacanthus,* Fan-bellied Leatherjacket, 629
Chinese Zebra Goby, *Ptereleotris zebra,* 561
*chionaraia, Serranus,* Snow Bass, 197
*chiquita, Gobiosoma,* Sonora Goby, 572
*Chirocentrus nudus,* Smooth Wolf Herring, 68
*Chirodactylus brachydactylus,* Two-tone Fingerfin, 418
*Chirolophis decoratus,* Decorated Warbonnet, 495
*Chirolophis japonicus,* Fringed Blenny, 495
*Chirolophis nugator,* Mosshead Warbonnet, 495
*Chironemus marmoratus,* Kelpfish, 415
*chirurgus, Acanthurus,* Doctorfish, 582
Chiseltooth Wrasse, *Pseudodax moluccanus,* 467
*Chlamydoselachus anguineus,* Frill Shark, 33
*chloropterus, Halichoeres,* Green Wrasse, 443, 445, 475
*Chloroscombrus chrysurus,* Atlantic Bumper, 253
*chlorourus, Cheilinus,* Floral Wrasse, 433
*chlorurus, Hypoplectrus,* Yellowtail Hamlet, 201
*chlupatyi, Hoplolatilus,* Chameleon Tilefish, 240
*choati, Macropharyngodon,* Choat's Wrasse, 452
Choat's Wrasse, *Macropharyngodon choati,* 452
Chocolate Surgeonfish, *Acanthurus pyroferus,* 584, 586
*Choerodon anchorago,* Orange-dotted Tuskfish, 431; Orange-dotted Wrasse, 474
*Choerodon azurio,* Scarbreast Tuskfish, 431
*Choerodon cyanodus,* Whitespot Tuskfish, 431
*Choerodon jordani,* Jordan's Tuskfish, 431
*Choerodon rubescens,* Baldchin Tuskfish, 429
*Choerodon schoenleinii,* Blackspot Tuskfish, 431
*Chriolepis fisheri,* Translucent Goby, 567
*Chriolepis zebra,* Gecko Goby, 567
Christmas Island Scorpionfish, *Scorpaenopsis* sp., 146, 148
Christmas Wrasse, *Thalassoma trilobatum,* 468
*Chromis acares,* Midget Chromis, 385
*Chromis agilis,* Reef Chromis, 385
*Chromis altus,* Silverstripe Chromis, 389
*Chromis amboinensis,* Ambon Chromis, 386
*Chromis analis,* Yellow Chromis, 385
*Chromis atrilobata,* Scissor Damselfish, 389
*Chromis atripectoralis,* Black-axil Chromis, 383
*Chromis atripes,* Dark-fin Chromis, 386
*Chromis axillaris,* Gray Chromis, 383
*Chromis bicolor,* Bicolor Chromis, 387
*Chromis cadenati,* Cadenat's Chromis, 388
*Chromis cauta?,* Cape Verde Chromis, 388
*Chromis chromis,* Mediterranean Damselfish, 388
*Chromis chrysura,* Stout-body Chromis, 385
*Chromis cinerascens,* Peppered Chromis, 384
*Chromis cyaneus,* Blue Chromis, 388
*Chromis dimidiata,* Half-and-Half Chromis, 383
*Chromis elerae,* Twin-spot Chromis, 383
*Chromis enchrysura,* Yellowtail Reeffish, 384
*Chromis flavicauda,* Cobalt Chromis, 388
*Chromis flavomaculata,* Yellow-freckled Reeffish, 384
*Chromis fumea,* Smoky Chromis, 386
*Chromis hanui,* Hawaiian Bicolor Chromis, 387
*Chromis hypselepis,* Brown Puller, 386
*Chromis insolatus,* Sunshinefish, 388
*Chromis iomelas,* Blach-and-White Chromis, 387
*Chromis klunzingeri,* Klunzinger's Chromis, 383
*Chromis lepidolepis,* Scaly Chromis, 386
*Chromis leucura,* White-tail Chromis, 387
*Chromis limbaughi,* Limbaugh's Chromis, 389
*Chromis lineata,* Lined Chromis, 385
*Chromis mirationis,* Wonder Chromis, 385
*Chromis multilineatus,* Yellow-edge Chromis, 389
*Chromis nigrura,* Black-tailed Chromis, 383
*Chromis nitida,* Barrier Reef Chromis, 387
*Chromis notata,* Tail-light Damselfish, 384
*Chromis opercularis,* Double Bar Chromis, 383, 386
*Chromis ovalis,* Hawaiian Chromis, 384
*Chromis punctipinnis,* Blacksmith, 389
*Chromis randalli,* Randall's Chromis, 384
*Chromis retrofasciata,* Black-bar Chromis, 387
*Chromis scotti,* Purple Reeffish, 388
*Chromis* sp., Damselfish, unidentified, 384
*Chromis* sp. "D", Deep-reef Chromis, 387
*Chromis ternatensis,* Ternate Chromis, 386
*Chromis vanderbilti,* Vanderbilt's Chromis, 385

*Chromis verater,* Three-spot Chromis, 385
*Chromis viridis,* Blue-green Reeffish, 371, 383, 388
*Chromis weberi,* Weber's Chromis, 386
*Chromis westaustralis,* Westralian Puller, 384
*Chromis xanthura,* Pale-tail Chromis, 387
*chromis, Chromis,* Mediterranean Damselfish, 388
*chronixis, Acanthurus,* Mimic Surgeonfish, 586
*chrysargyreum, Haemulon,* Smallmouth Grunt, 279
*Chrysiptera annulata,* Footballer, 391
*Chrysiptera biocellata,* Two-spot Demoiselle, 394
*Chrysiptera caeruleolineata,* Blue-line Demoiselle, 391
*Chrysiptera cyanea,* Blue Devil, 392
*Chrysiptera flavipinnis,* Yellow-fin Demoiselle, 392
*Chrysiptera galba,* Canary Demoiselle, 390
*Chrysiptera glauca,* Gray Demoiselle, 390, 394
*Chrysiptera hemicyanea,* Half-blue Demoiselle, 393
*Chrysiptera leucopoma,* White-banded Damselfish, 391
*Chrysiptera melanomaculata,* Blackspot Demoiselle, 390
*Chrysiptera niger,* Black Demoiselle, 390
*Chrysiptera notialis,* Southern Demoiselle, 390
*Chrysiptera parasema,* Azure Damsel, 392
*Chrysiptera rapanui,* Easter Island Demoiselle, 390
*Chrysiptera rex,* King Demoiselle, 390
*Chrysiptera rollandi,* Rolland's Demoiselle, 392, 394
*Chrysiptera springeri,* Springer's Demoiselle, 392
*Chrysiptera starcki,* Starck's Demoiselle, 392
*Chrysiptera talboti,* Talbot's Demoiselle, 391
*Chrysiptera taupou,* Village Belle, 392
*Chrysiptera traceyi,* Tracey's Demoiselle, 391
*Chrysiptera tricincta,* Three-band Demoiselle, 391
*Chrysiptera unimaculata,* One-spot Demoiselle, 394
*Chrysoblephus anglicus,* Englishman, 293
*chrysocephalus, Anampses,* Red-tailed Tamarin, 425
*chrysocephalus, Chaetodontoplus,* Yellow-headed Angelfish, 360
*chrysogaster, Amphiprion,* Yellow-bellied Anemonefish, 373
*chrysomelas, Sebastes,* Black-and-Yellow Rockfish, 149
*chrysophrys, Carangoides,* Longnose Trevally, 247
*chrysopleuron, Parupeneus,* Red Blush Goatfish, 316
*chrysopoecilus, Dischistodus,* White-spot Damsel, 409
*chrysopterum, Sparisoma,* Redtail Parrotfish, 487
*chrysopterus, Amphiprion,* Orange-finned Anemonefish, 376
*chrysopterus, Sufflamen,* Halfmoon Triggerfish, 624, 627
*chrysospilos, Istiblennius,* Orange-spotted Blenny, 531
*chrysospilos, Siganus,* Gold-spotted Spinefoot, 598, 599
*chrysostomus, Heniochus,* Threeband Pennant Coralfish, 352
*chrysostomus, Lethrinus,* Sweetlip Emperor, 298
*chrysotaenia, Apogon,* Many-lined Cardinalfish, 225
*chrysotaenia, Leptojulis,* Yellow Ribbon Wrasse, 462
*chrysozona, Pterocaesio,* Goldband Fusilier, 272
*chrysozonus, Coradion,* Golden-girdled Coralfish, 347, 348
*chrysura, Chromis,* Stout-body Chromis, 385
*chrysurus, Chloroscombrus,* Atlantic Bumper, 253
*chrysurus, Microspathodon,* Jewelfish, 408
*chrysurus, Ocyurus,* Yellowtail Snapper, 269
*chrysurus, Pomacanthus,* Goldtail Angelfish, 364
*chrysurus, Pomacentrus,* Whitetail Damsel, 400, 403
*chrysus, Halichoeres,* Golden Rainbowfish, 440
Chub Mackerel, *Scomber japonicus,* 603
Chub, unidentified, *Kyphosus* sp., 328
Chubby Soldierfish, *Myripristis melanostictus,* 114, 116
*chuss, Urophycis,* Red Hake, 78
*ciconiae, Aspasmichthys,* Yellow Clingfish, 96
Cigar Wrasse, *Cheilio inermis,* 451, 472
*ciliaris, Alectis,* African Pompano, 251
*ciliaris, Holacanthus,* Queen Angelfish, 367
*ciliaris, Latridopsis,* Blue Moki, 416
*ciliatus, Monacanthus,* Fringed Filefish, 628
*ciliatus, Scolopsis,* Saw-jawed Monocle Bream, 293, 303
*cincta, Priolepis,* Girdled Goby, 566
*cinctus, Acanthistius,* Yellow-banded Perch, 202
*cinctus, Cryptocentrus,* Yellow Prawn Goby, 541, 547, 549, 557
*cinctus, Plectorhinchus,* Three-banded Sweetlip, 284
*cinctus, Priolepis,* Pacific Convict Goby, 567
*cinerascens, Chromis,* Peppered Chromis, 384
*cinerascens, Kyphosus,* Ashen Drummer, 328
*cinereus, Conger,* Ashen Conger-eel, 63
*cinereus, Gerres,* Yellowfin Mojarra, 275
*cinereus, Muraenesox,* Silver Conger Eel, 62
*cinereus, Symphodus,* Mediterranean Gray Wrasse, 471
*cinnabarinus, Parupeneus,* Two-saddle Goatfish, 316
Cinnamon Flounder, *Pseudorhombus cinnamoneus,* 607, 610
*cinnamoneus, Pseudorhombus,* Cinnamon Flounder, 607, 610
*cirratum, Ginglymostoma,* Nurse Shark, 35
*cirrhifer, Stephanolepis,* Thread Sailfin Filefish, 632
*Cirrhilabrus blatteus,* Lancetail Fairy Wrasse, 462
*Cirrhilabrus cyanopleura,* Blue-sided Fairy Wrasse, 433, 434
*Cirrhilabrus exquisitus,* Exquisite Wrasse, 433
*Cirrhilabrus jordani,* Jordan's Fairy Wrasse, 435
*Cirrhilabrus labouti,* Laboute's Fairy Wrasse, 434
*Cirrhilabrus lineatus,* Lined Fairy Wrasse, 434
*Cirrhilabrus lubbocki,* Lubbock's Fairy Wrasse, 435
*Cirrhilabrus melanomarginatus,* Blackedge Fairy Wrasse, 434
*Cirrhilabrus rubripinnis,* Red-finned Fairy Wrasse, 435
*Cirrhilabrus rubriventralis,* Social Fairy Wrasse, 434
*Cirrhilabrus scottorum,* Greenback Fairy Wrasse, 435
*Cirrhilabrus* sp., Tahitian Fairy Wrasse, 434; Wrasse, unidentified, 433
*Cirrhilabrus* sp. "D", Red-sided Fairy Wrasse, 434
*Cirrhilabrus temmincki,* Temminck's Wrasse, 434
*Cirrhitichthys aprinus,* Spotted Hawkfish, 410, 411, 414
*Cirrhitichthys aureus,* Golden Yellow Hawkfish, 412
*Cirrhitichthys bleekeri,* Bleeker's Hawkfish, 411
*Cirrhitichthys falco,* Falco Hawkfish, 412
*Cirrhitichthys guichenoti,* Guichenot's Hawkfish, 411
*Cirrhitichthys oxycephalus,* Pixy Hawkfish, 411, 414
*Cirrhitops fasciatus,* Banded Hawkfish, 413
*Cirrhitus atlanticus,* Atlantic Hawkfish, 412
*Cirrhitus pinnulatus,* Freckled Hawkfish, 413, 414
*Cirrhitus rivulatus,* Giant Hawkfish, 412
*Cirrhitus splendens,* Splendid Hawkfish, 412
*cirrhocheilus, Brachysomophis,* Ghost Snake Eel, 64
*Cirripectes alboapicalis,* Snowflake Blenny, 528
*Cirripectes castaneus,* Chestnut Blenny, 528
*Cirripectes chelomatus,* Yellow-headed Blenny, 528
*Cirripectes filamentosus,* Filament Blenny, 528
*Cirripectes* sp., Blenny, unidentified, 528.02
*Cirripectes stigmaticus,* Ember Blenny, 528, 528.02
*Cirripectes variolosus,* Red-tipped Fringed-blenny, 532
*Citharichthys gilberti,* Gilbert's Sanddab, 609
*Citharichthys stigmaeus,* Speckled Sanddab, 609
*citrinellus, Chaetodon,* Citron Butterflyfish, 341
*citrinus, Gobiodon,* Citron Goby, 570
Citron Butterflyfish, *Chaetodon citrinellus,* 341
Citron Goby, *Gobiodon citrinus,* 570

Clarion Angelfish, *Holacanthus clarionensis,* 367
Clarion Damselfish, *Stegastes redemptus,* 406
*clarionensis, Holacanthus,* Clarion Angelfish, 367
*clarkei, Norfolkia,* Clark's Triplefin, 510
*clarkii, Amphiprion,* Clark's Anemonefish, 373
Clark's Anemonefish, *Amphiprion clarkii,* 373
Clark's Triplefin, *Norfolkia clarkei,* 510
*clathratus, Paralabrax,* California Kelp Bass, 202
Cleaner Mimic, *Plagiotremus rhinorhynchos,* 506, 521
Clearnose Guitarfish, *Rhinobatos armatus,* 44
*Cleidopus gloriamaris,* Knight-fish, 101, 103
*Cleisthenes pinetorum herzensteini,* Herzenstein's Righteye Flounder, 608
*clepsydra, Muraena,* Black-eared Moray, 60
*Clepticus parrae,* Creole Wrasse, 470
*Clidoderma asperrimum,* Peppered Righteye Flounder, 608
Clingfish, unidentified, *Gobiesocidae* sp., 96
*Clinocottus analis,* Wooly Sculpin, 164
*Clinus superciliosus,* Super Klipfish, 516
Cloister Blenny, *Omobranchus elongatus,* 534
Cloudy Dory, *Zenopsis nebulosa,* 118
Clown Anemonefish, *Amphiprion percula,* 372
Clown Coris, *Coris aygula,* 436
Clown Grouper, *Pogonoperca punctata,* 204
Clown Surgeonfish, *Acanthurus lineatus,* 585, 587
Clown Triggerfish, *Balistoides conspicillum,* 621, 622, 623
Clown Wrasse, *Coris gaimard,* 472
Clubhead Blenny, *Acanthemblemaria balanorum,* 518
*Clupea harengus pallasi,* Pacific Herring, 66
Coachwhip Ray, *Himantura uarnak,* 45, 47
Cobalt Chromis, *Chromis flavicauda,* 388
Cobia, *Rachycentron canadum,* 244
*coccineus, Antennarius,* Scarlet Frogfish, 86, 91
*coccineus, Apogon,* Little Ruby Red Cardinalfish, 232
*Cochleoceps spatula,* Cockburn Sound Clingfish, 96
*Cociella crocodila,* Spotted Flathead, 72, 161
Cockatoo Waspfish, *Ablabys taenianotus,* 137
Cockburn Sound Clingfish, *Cochleoceps spatula,* 96
Cocktail Fish, *Pteragogus flagellifer,* 449
Coco Frillgoby, *Bathygobius cocosensis,* 564
Cocoa Damselfish, *Stegastes variabilis,* 407
*cocosensis, Bathygobius,* Coco Frillgoby, 564
*Cocotropus dermacanthus,* Bleeker's Coralline Velvetfish, 156
Cod Scorpionfish, *Peristrominous dolosus,* 137
Coelacanth, *Latimeria chalumnae,* 50
*coelestinus, Scarus,* Midnight Parrotfish, 486
*coelestis, Pomacentrus,* Blue Damselfish, 399, 400
*Coelorhinchus tokiensis,* Tokien Grenadier, 78
*coenosus, Pleuronichthys,* C-O Turbot, 612
*coeruleus, Acanthurus,* Blue Tang, 582
*coeruleus, Scarus,* Blue Parrotfish, 486
*coesus, Brachyamblyopus,* Blind Goby, 580
Coin-bearing Frogfish, *Antennarius nummifer,* 90, 91
*colini, Centropyge,* Blueback Pygmy Angelfish, 355
*collare, Chaetodon,* Red-tailed Butterflyfish, 341
Collared Sea Bream, *Gymnocranius bitorquatus,* 290
*collei, Hydrolagus,* Spotted Ratfish, 34
*collettei, Ecsenius,* Collette's Blenny, 528.16
Collette's Blenny, *Ecsenius collettei,* 528.16
*Cololabias saira,* Pacific Saury, 100
Colon Goby, *Coryphopterus dicrus,* 574
Colonial Salmon, *Eleutheronema tetradactylum,* 420
*colonus, Paranthias,* Pacific Creole-fish, 178
Colorado Snapper, *Lutjanus colorado,* 268
*colorado, Lutjanus,* Colorado Snapper, 268
*colubrinus, Myrichthys,* Barred Snake Eel, 61
Comb Grouper, *Mycteroperca rubra,* 193
Comb-toothed Mudskipper, *Boleophthalmus pectinirostris,* 580
Comber, *Serranus cabrilla,* 196
Combfish, *Coris picta,* 437
Comet, *Calloplesiops altivelis,* 214, 215
*cometae, Epinephelus,* Broom Grouper, 190
*commerson, Scomberomorus,* Narrow-barred Spanish Mackerel, 603
*commersoni, Antennarius,* Commerson's Frogfish, 87, 90, 91, 92
*commersoni, Pomadasys,* Spotted Grunter, 313
*commersoniana, Anchovia,* Market Anchovy, 68
*commersonii, Fistularia,* Commerson's Cornetfish, 119
*commersonnianus, Scomberoides,* Talang Queenfish, 250
Commerson's Cornetfish, *Fistularia commersonii,* 119
Commerson's Frogfish, *Antennarius commersoni,* 87, 90, 91, 92
Common Buffalo Bream, *Kyphosus sydneyanus,* 327, 329
Common European Bass, *Dicentrarchus labrax,* 170
Common Mediterranean Triplefin, *Tripterygion tripteronotus,* 509
Common Sea Bass, *Lateolabrax japonicus,* 173
Common Slipmouth, *Leiognathus equulus,* 256
Common Sweeper, *Parapriacanthus dispar,* 321
Common Triplefin, *Enneapterygius etheostomus,* 509
Common Tripodfish, *Triacanthus biaculeatus,* 619
*compressa, Pempheris,* Compressed Sweeper, 322
Compressed Sweeper, *Pempheris compressa,* 322
*compressus, Apogon,* Split-banded Cardinalfish, 224
*compressus, Canthigaster,* Sharp-nosed Puffer, 651
*concentricus, Urolophus,* Bullseye Stingray, 46
*concolor, Nebrius,* Giant Sleepy Shark, 35
*concolor, Uropterygius,* Uniform Reef Eel, 54
Condolle's Lepadogaster, *Lepadogaster candollei,* 97
Coney, *Cephalopholis fulva,* 184
*confusum, Chiloscyllium,* Cat Shark, 36
*Conger cinereus,* Ashen Conger-eel, 63
*Conger japonicus,* Beach Conger, 63
*Conger wilsoni,* Cape Conger, 63
*Congrogadus subducens,* Eared Eel-blenny, 534
*coniorta, Scorpaena,* Small Scorpionfish, 146
*conklini, Phaeoptyx,* Freckled Cardinalfish, 236
*Conniella apterygia,* Connie's Wrasse, 436
Connie's Wrasse, *Conniella apterygia,* 436
*Conodon nobilis,* Barred Grunt, 281
*conspicillatus, Chaetodontoplus,* Spectacled Angelfish, 361
*conspicillum, Balistoides,* Clown Triggerfish, 621, 622, 623
*constellatus, Sebastes,* Starry Rockfish, 149
Convict Blenny, *Pholidichthys leucotaenia,* 500
Convict Goby, *Lythrypnus phorellus,* 575
Convict Surgeonfish, *Acanthurus triostegus,* 588
*cooki, Scorpaena,* Cook's Scorpionfish, 154
*cookii, Apogon,* Cook's Black-banded Cardinalfish, 223, 224
Cook's Black-banded Cardinalfish, *Apogon cookii,* 223, 224
Cook's Cardinalfish, *Apogon robustus,* 223
Cook's Scorpionfish, *Scorpaena cooki,* 154
Copper Rockfish, *Sebastes caurinus,* 149
Copper Sweeper, *Pempheris schomburgki,* 322
Copperband Butterflyfish, *Chelmon rostratus,* 349, 350
*Coradion altivelis,* Tawneygirdled Butterflyfish, 347
*Coradion chrysozonus,* Golden-girdled Coralfish, 347, 348
*Coradion melanopus,* Two-spot Coralfish, 347

Coral Beauty, *Centropyge bispinosus,* 354
Coral Demoiselle, *Neopomacentrus nemurus,* 398
Coral Hogfish, *Bodianus axillaris,* 426
Coral Rockcod, *Cephalopholis miniata,* 183
Coral Scorpionfish, *Scorpaena albifimbria,* 145
Coral Sea Gregory, *Stegastes gascoynei,* 405
Coral Toadfish, *Sanopus splendidus,* 84
Coral-dwelling Cleaning Goby, *Gobiosoma illecebrosum,* 573
*corallicola, Epinephelus,* East Indian Red Hind, 186
*corallicola, Plesiops,* Ocellated Longfin, 214
*corallinus, Siganus,* Blue-spotted Spinefoot, 598
*Coralliozetus angelica,* Angel Blenny, 519
*Coralliozetus diaphanus,* Glass Blenny, 520
*Coralliozetus micropes,* Scarletfin Blenny, 519
*cordyla, Megalaspis,* Torpedo Scad, 250, 253
*Coreoperca kawamebari,* Kawamebar's Bass, 172
*Coris auricularis,* King Coris, 436, 438
*Coris aygula,* Clown Coris, 436
*Coris ballieui,* Malamalama, 438
*Coris batuensis,* Heliotrope Eyeband Wrasse, 475
*Coris bulbifrons,* Bumphead Coris, 437
*Coris caudimacula,* Spottail Coris, 436, 438, 475
*Coris dorsomacula,* Twinspot Coris, 437
*Coris flavovittata,* Hinalea, 438
*Coris formosa,* Queen Coris, 439
*Coris gaimard,* Clown Wrasse, 472
*Coris gaimard africana,* African Clown Wrasse, 439
*Coris julis,* Mediterranean Rainbow Wrasse, 437
*Coris picta,* Combfish, 437
*Coris pictoides,* False Combfish, 437
*Coris sandageri,* Sandager's Coris, 437
*Coris variegata,* Dapple Coris, 436, 475
*Coris venusta,* Elegant Coris, 438
*cornelii, Kyphosus,* Western Buffalo Bream, 327
*Corniger spinosus,* Spinycheek Soldierfish, 106
*corniger, Ogcocephalus,* Longnose Batfish, 93
*cornuta, Lactoria,* Long-horned Cowfish, 637, 639
*cornutus, Pleuronichthys,* Fine-spotted Flounder, 607, 612
*coronata, Canthigaster,* Four-barred Toby, 650, 651
*coronatus, Hippocampus,* Crowned Seahorse, 131
Cortez Angelfish, *Pomacanthus zonipectus,* 362
Cortez Chromis, *Stegastes rectifraenum,* 405
Cortez Chub, *Kyphosus elegans,* 328
Cortez Garden Eel, *Taenioconger digueti,* 63
Cortez Hovering Goby, *Ioglossus* sp., 569
Cortez Rainbow Wrasse, *Thalassoma lucasanum,* 466
Cortez Soapfish, *Rypticus bicolor?,* 207
*coruscum, Sargocentron,* Reef Squirrelfish, 107
*corvinaeformis, Pomadasys,* Roughneck Grunt, 281
*Coryphaena hippurus,* Dolphinfish, 257, 604
*Coryphaenoides asper,* Slaty Grenadier, 78
*Coryphopterus dicrus,* Colon Goby, 574
*Coryphopterus eidolon,* Pallid Goby, 574
*Coryphopterus glaucofrenum,* Bridled Goby, 574
*Coryphopterus lipernes,* Peppermint Goby, 574
*Coryphopterus nicholsi,* Blackeye Goby, 574
*Coryphopterus personatus,* Masked Goby, 574
*Coryphopterus* sp., Goby, unidentified, 574
*Coryphopterus urospilus,* Orangespot Goby, 574
*Corythoichthys amplexus,* Banded Pipefish, 127, 128
*Corythoichthys haematopterus,* Messmate Pipefish, 128
*Corythoichthys intestinalis,* Australian Banded Pipefish, 127
*Corythoichthys paxtoni,* Paxton's Pipefish, 127
*Corythoichthys schultzi,* Gilded Pipefish, 128
*cosmetus, Halichoeres,* Adorned Wrasse, 442
*Cosmocampus arctus,* Snubnose Pipefish, 125
*cottoides, Pseudoblennius,* Painted Blenny, 167, 169
Cottonwick, *Haemulon melanurum,* 278
*Cottus kazika,* Kazika Sculpin, 164
*Cottus pollux,* Gunther's Sculpin, 164
Cow-nose Ray, *Rhinoptera neglecta,* 47
Cowtail Ray, *Dasyatis sephen,* 45
*Crapatalus arenarius,* Sandfish, 501
*crassiceps, Apogon,* Big Red Cardinalfish, 232
*Craterocephalus pauciradiatus,* Few-rayed Hardyhead, 102
*Creedia alleni,* Slender Sandfish, 501
Creole Wrasse, *Clepticus parrae,* 470
Creole-fish, *Paranthias furcifer,* 178
Crescent Snapper, *Lutjanus lunulatus,* 262
Crescent Tailed Grouper, *Variola albomarginata,* 203
Crescent Throat Blenny, *Glyptoparus delicatulus,* 527
Crescent Triggerfish, *Rhinecanthus lunula,* 628
Crescent-tail Bigeye, *Priacanthus hamrur,* 220
Crested Flounder, *Limanda schrenki,* 613
Crested Triplefin, *Norfolkia cristata,* 510
Crested Weedfish, *Cristiceps australis,* 517
Crevalle Jack, *Caranx hippos,* 249
Crimson Cleaner Wrasse, *Suezichthys* sp., 468
Crimson Goby, *Trimma* sp., 577
Crimson Sea-Bream, *Evynnis cardinalis,* 291
Crimson-eyed Coral Goby, Gobiidae sp., 567
*criniger?, Yongeichthys,* Fringyfin Goby, 550
*criniger, Yongeichthys,* Fringyfin Goby, 552, 553
*crinophila, Discotrema,* Feather Star Clingfish, 94, 95, 97
*cristata, Norfolkia,* Crested Triplefin, 510
*cristata, Scartella,* Molly Miller, 529, 530
*cristatus, Histiogamphelus,* Macleay's Crested Pipefish, 126
*cristatus, Samaris,* Gray's Crested Flounder, 613
*Cristiceps aurantiacus,* Yellow Crested Weedfish, 517
*Cristiceps australis,* Crested Weedfish, 517
*crocineus, Ctenogobiops,* Seychelles Goby, 549
*crocineus, Lethrinus,* Yellowfin Emperor, 294
*crockeri, Acanthemblemaria,* Browncheek Blenny, 518
*crocodila, Cociella,* Spotted Flathead, 72, 161
*crocodilus, Tylosurus,* Houndfish, 100
*croicensis, Scarus,* Striped Parrotfish, 486
*Cromileptes altivelis,* Panther Grouper, 194, 195, 205
Crosseyed Cardinalfish, *Fowleria aurita,* 235
Crown Squirrelfish, *Sargocentron diadema,* 107, 108, 111
Crown-of-thorns Cardinalfish, *Siphamia fuscolineata,* 237
Crowned Seahorse, *Hippocampus coronatus,* 131
*cruentatus, Cephalopholis,* Grayshy, 184
*cruentatus, Gobius,* Redmouth Goby, 559
*cruentatus, Heteropriacanthus,* Dusky-finned Bullseye, 220, 695
*cruentatus, Priacanthus,* Dusky-finned Bullseye, 220
*crumenophthalmus, Selar,* Bigeye Scad, 245, 250
*Cryptocentroides insignis,* Diagonal Striped Goby, 557
*Cryptocentrus albidorsus,* White-backed Goby, 557
*Cryptocentrus ambanora,* Ambanora Goby, 548
*Cryptocentrus aurora,* Pinkbar Goby, 547
*Cryptocentrus caeruleomaculatus,* Blue-spotted Shrimp Goby, 549, 557
*Cryptocentrus cinctus,* Yellow Prawn Goby, 541, 547, 549, 557
*Cryptocentrus cryptocentrus,* Eightbar Goby, 549

*Cryptocentrus cyanotaenia*, Bluestreak Prawn Goby, 547
*Cryptocentrus fasciatus*, Blue-finned Shrimp Goby, 549, 556
*Cryptocentrus leptocephalus*, Pink-and-Blue Spotted Goby, 540, 556, 557
*Cryptocentrus lutheri*, Luther's Goby, 549
*Cryptocentrus niveatus*, Snowpatch Goby, 556
*Cryptocentrus* sp., Blue-and-Gold Fin Goby, 557; Fancytail Goby, 557; Whitecheek Prawn Goby, 556
*Cryptocentrus strigilliceps*, Target Goby, 549
*cryptocentrus, Cryptocentrus*, Eightbar Goby, 549
*Cryptotomus roseus*, Manytooth Parrotfish, 488
*crysos, Caranx*, Blue Runner, 248
*Ctenochaetus hawaiiensis*, Hawaiian Bristletooth, 589
*Ctenochaetus marginatus*, Yelloweye Bristletooth, 589
*Ctenochaetus striatus*, Striped Bristletooth, 589
*Ctenochaetus strigosus*, Spotted Bristletooth, 587, 590
*Ctenochaetus tominiensis*, Tomini Bristletooth, 589
*Ctenogobiops aurocingulus*, Herre's Samoan Prawn Goby, 546, 547
*Ctenogobiops crocineus*, Seychelles Goby, 549
*Ctenogobiops feroculus*, Ferocious Goby, 549
*Ctenogobiops maculosus*, Spotted Prawn Goby, 570
*Ctenogobiops pomastictus*, Lizard Island Goby, 547, 548
*Ctenogobiops tangaroai*, Tangaroa Goby, 548
*Ctenotrypauchen microcephalus*, Small-headed Blind Goby, 580
Cuban Goby, *Microgobius signatus*, 569
Cubbyu, *Equetus umbrosus*, 308, 309
Cubera Snapper, *Lutjanus cyanopterus*, 265
*cubicus, Ostracion*, Polka Dot Boxfish, 638, 639, 642
*cuniculus, Hoplolatilus*, Dusky Tilefish, 240, 511
*cuning, Caesio*, Yellow-tailed Fusilier, 273
Cunner, *Tautogolabrus adspersus*, 468
Cupido Wrasse, *Thalassoma cupido*, 476
*cupido, Thalassoma*, Cupido Wrasse, 476
*curacao, Amblyglyphidodon*, Staghorn Damsel, 382
*curiosus, Gunnelichthys*, Yellow-striped Worm Eel, 511, 580
Curry-comb Tripodfish, *Tripodichthys strigilifer*, 619, 620
Cusk-eel, unidentified, *Lepophidium* sp., 80
*cuspidata, Anoxypristis*, Pointed Sawfish, 42
Cut-ribbon Rainbowfish, *Stethojulis interrupta*, 454
*cuvier, Anampses*, Cuvier's Tamarin, 425
*cuvieri, Galeocerdo*, Tiger Shark, 39, 40
*cuvieri, Opistognathus*, Cuvier's Jawfish, 499
Cuvier's Jawfish, *Opistognathus cuvieri*, 499
Cuvier's Surgeonfish, *Acanthurus nigroris*, 588
Cuvier's Tamarin, *Anampses cuvier*, 425
*cyanea, Chrysiptera*, Blue Devil, 392
*cyanescens, Scarus*, Blue Bumphead Parrotfish, 481
*cyaneus, Chromis*, Blue Chromis, 388
*cyanocephalus, Halichoeres*, Yellowcheek Wrasse, 446
*cyanoctenosum, Oxymetopon*, Feathertail Sleeper, 542
*cyanodus, Choerodon*, Whitespot Tuskfish, 431
*cyanoguttatus, Macropharyngodon*, Bluespotted Wrasse, 451
*cyanomelas, Odax*, Herring Cale, 478
*cyanomos, Neopomacentrus*, Regal Demoiselle, 398
*cyanopleura, Cirrhilabrus*, Blue-sided Fairy Wrasse, 433, 434
*cyanopleura, Leptojulis*, Blue-sided Wrasse, 462, 475
*cyanopodus, Epinephelus*, Freckled Grouper, 190
*cyanopterus, Lutjanus*, Cubera Snapper, 265
*cyanopterus, Solenostomus*, Variegated Ghost Pipefish, 123, 124
*cyanopunctata, Omegophora*, Blue-spotted Puffer, 646
*cyanopunctatus, Chaetodontoplus*, Blue Spangled Angelfish, 361
*cyanosoma, Apogon*, Gold-striped Cardinalfish, 222, 223
*cyanostigma, Pristotis*, Bluedotted Damselfish, 408
*cyanostigma, Sebastapistes*, Yellow-spotted Scorpionfish, 146, 148
*cyanotaenia, Cryptocentrus*, Bluestreak Prawn Goby, 547
*cyanotaenia, Pseudochromis*, Blue-striped Dottyback, 208, 211
*cyanotaenia, Scarus*, Blue-lined Parrotfish, 492
*cyanurus, Ostracion*, Bluetail Trunkfish, 640
*Cybiosarda elegans*, Leaping Bonito, 602
*Cyclichthys orbicularis*, Orbiculate Burrfish, 653
*cyclophthalmus, Labracinus*, Spottysail Dottyback, 207
Cyclops Electric Ray, *Diplobatos ommata*, 42
*Cyclopterus lumpus*, Lumpsucker, 168
*cyclostomus, Parupeneus*, Yellowsaddle Goatfish, 316, 317
*Cymatogaster aggregata*, Shiner Surfperch, 369
*Cynoglossus joyneri*, Joyner's Tonguefish, 614
*Cyprinocirrhites polyactus*, Soaring Hawkfish, 413
*Cyprinocirrhites* sp., Hawaiian Hawkfish, 412
*cyprinoides, Megalops*, Oxeye Herring, 50
*Cypselurus hiraii*, Hirai's Flying Fish, 99
*Cypselurus poecilopterus*, Yellow-winged Flying Fish, 99
*cypselurus, Rhabdamia*, Black-nosed Cardinalfish, 222
*Cyttopsis rosea?*, Rosy Dory, 118

## D

*dactyliophorus, Doryrhamphus*, Banded Pipefish, 127
*Dactylophora nigricans*, Dusky Morwong, 418
*Dactyloptena orientalis*, Oriental Flying Gurnard, 136, 539
*Dactyloptena peterseni*, Orange Gurnard, 137
*Dactylopterus volitans*, Flying Gurnard, 137
*Dactylopus dactylopus*, Fingered Dragonet, 536
*dactylopus, Dactylopus*, Fingered Dragonet, 536
*Dactylosargus* sp., Sea Carp, 418
*Dactyloscopus pectoralis*, Red-saddled Sand Stargazer, 512
*daedalma, Chaetodon*, Wrought-iron Butterflyfish, 335
*dalli, Lythrypnus*, Catalina Goby, 575
*dallii, Sebastes*, Calico Rockfish, 149
Dalmatian Blenny, *Lipophrys dalmatinus*, 524
*dalmatinus, Lipophrys*, Dalmatian Blenny, 524
*Damalichthys vacca*, Pile Surfperch, 370
*damelii, Epinephelus*, Saddled Rock-cod, 186
Dampier Stonefish, *Dampierosa daruma*, 155
*Dampierosa daruma*, Dampier Stonefish, 155
Damselfish, unidentified, *Chromis* sp., 384; *Pomacentridae* sp., 390; *Pomacentrus* sp., 403; *Stegastes* sp., 403, 404
Dandy Blenny, *Petroscirtes breviceps*, 522
Dane, *Porcostoma dentata*, 293
Dapple Coris, *Coris variegata*, 436, 475
Dappled Cardinalfish, *Phaeoptyx pigmentaria*, 236
Dark Dottyback, *Pseudochromis melas*, 212
Dark-backed Snake Blenny, *Ophiclinus graclis*, 516
Dark-fin Chromis, *Chromis atripes*, 386
Dark-spotted Moray, *Gymnothorax fimbriatus*, 54
Darkbar Hogfish, *Bodianus speciosus*, 427
Darkfin Sleeper, *Oxymetopon* sp., 542
Darnley Cardinalfish, *Apogon darnleyensis*, 228
*darnleyensis, Apogon*, Darnley Cardinalfish, 228
*daruma, Dampierosa*, Dampier Stonefish, 155
Darwin Jawfish, *Opistognathus darwiniensis*, 498
*darwiniensis, Opistognathus*, Darwin Jawfish, 498
Darwin's Damselfish, *Stegastes imbricata*, 407
*Dascyllus albisella*, Hawaiian Threespot Damsel, 378
*Dascyllus aruanus*, White-tailed Damselfish, 377
*Dascyllus carneus*, Blue-spotted Dascyllus, 377, 378

*Dascyllus flavicauda,* Yellow-tailed Dascyllus, 371, 378
*Dascyllus marginatus,* Marginate Damselfish, 378
*Dascyllus melanurus,* Blacktail Humbug, 378
*Dascyllus reticulatus,* Reticulated Damselfish, 378
*Dascyllus strasburgi,* Strasburg's Dascyllus, 378
*Dascyllus trimaculatus,* Threespot Damselfish, 377, 378
Dash Goby, *Gobionellus saepepallens?,* 561; *Gobionellus saepepallens,* 565
Dash-dot Goatfish, *Parupeneus barberinus,* 317, 319
*Dasyatis akajei,* Japanese Stingray, 45
*Dasyatis americana,* Southern Stingray, 46
*Dasyatis brevicaudata,* Short-tail Stingray, 45
*Dasyatis hawaiiensis,* Hawaiian Stingray, 45
*Dasyatis sephen,* Cowtail Ray, 45
*Dasycottus japonicus,* Japanese Sculpin, 167
*dasypogon, Eucrossorhinus,* Tassled Wobbegong, 36
*dasyrhynchus, Dinematichthys,* Orange Eelpout, 81
*davidsonii, Anisotremus,* Sargo, 280
*dea, Xyrichthys,* Goddess Rainbowfish, 457
*decadactylus, Beryx,* Broad Alfonsino, 106
*decagrammus, Hexagrammos,* Kelp Greenling, 163
*Decapterus muruadsi,* Amberfish, 245
*Decapterus punctatus,* Round Scad, 245
*Decapterus russelli,* Indian Scad, 247
*Decapterus tabl,* TABL Scad, 245
*declevifrons, Abudefduf,* Slope-head Sergeant, 380
*declevis, Chaetodon,* Marquesas Butterflyfish, 336
*Decodon melasma,* Blackspot Wrasse, 470
*Decodon puellaris,* Red Hogfish, 470
*decora, Nemateleotris,* Decorated Firefish, 570
Decorated Butterflyfish, *Chaetodon semeion,* 344
Decorated Firefish, *Nemateleotris decora,* 570
Decorated Goby, *Istigobius decoratus,* 563
Decorated Guitarfish, *Rhinobatos hynnicephalus,* 44
Decorated Sole, *Soleichthys heterorhinos,* 615
Decorated Spinefoot, *Siganus puellus,* 599
Decorated Warbonnet, *Chirolophis decoratus,* 495
*decoratus, Chirolophis,* Decorated Warbonnet, 495
*decoratus, Istigobius,* Decorated Goby, 563
*decurrens, Helcogramma,* Black-throated Threefin, 507, 511
*decussatus, Amblygobius,* Orangemarked Goby, 555
*decussatus, Chaetodon,* Black-finned Butterflyfish, 344
*decussatus, Entomacrodus,* Wavy-lined Blenny, 529
*decussatus, Lutjanus,* Checkered Snapper, 260
Deep-bodied Emperor, *Lethrinus haematopterus,* 295
Deep-bodied Silver-Biddy, *Gerres poeti,* 276
Deep-reef Chromis, *Chromis* sp. "D", 387
Deepreef Scorpionfish, *Scorpaenodes tredecimspinosus,* 145
Deepsea Bonefish, *Pterothrissus gissu,* 50
Deepsea Fairy Basslet, *Pseudanthias rubrizonatus,* 174
Deepwater Sculpin, *Nautichthys oculofasciatus,* 167
Delicate Triplefin, *Enneanectes sexmaculatus,* 507
*delicatulus, Glyptoparus,* Crescent Throat Blenny, 527
*deltoides, Gnatholepis,* Peacockfin Goby, 558
*Dendochirus barberi,* Barber's Lionfish, 140
*Dendrochirus biocellatus,* Twinspot Lionfish, 143
*Dendrochirus brachypterus,* Shortfin Lionfish, 143
*Dendrochirus zebra,* Zebra Lionfish, 140, 143
*dentata, Porcostoma,* Dane, 293
*dentatus, Apsilus,* Black Snapper, 259
*dentatus, Mulloides,* Mexican Goatfish, 315
*dentatus, Paralichthys,* Summer Flounder, 610
*Dentex tumifrons,* Yellowback Sea Bream, 289
*dentex, Ecsenius,* Many-toothed Blenny, 528.10
*dentex, Odontoscion,* Reef Croaker, 311
*dentex, Othos,* Harlequin Fish, 205
*dentex, Pseudocaranx,* Striped Jack, 243, 253
*denticulata, Nicholsina,* Loosetooth Parrotfish, 488
*derjugini, Bathymaster,* Derjugin's Ronquil, 494
Derjugin's Ronquil, *Bathymaster derjugini,* 494
*dermacanthus, Cocotropus,* Bleeker's Coralline Velvetfish, 156
*dermatogenys, Saurida,* Slender Grinner, 73
*dermatolepis, Epinephelus,* Leather Bass, 191
*dermopterus, Trisotropis,* Plain Grouper, 202
*desjardinii, Zebrasoma,* Desjardin's Sailfin Tang, 594
Desjardin's Sailfin Tang, *Zebrasoma desjardinii,* 594
*detrisus, Gymnocanthus,* Barfin Sculpin, 164
Devil Frogfish, *Halophryne diemensis,* 84
Devil Lionfish, *Pterois miles,* 142
Devil Scorpionfish, *Scorpaenopsis diabolus,* 147, 148, 154
Devilfish, *Inimicus* sp., 155
*diabolis, Mobula,* Lesser Devil Ray, 48
*diabolus, Scorpaenopsis,* Devil Scorpionfish, 147, 148, 154
*diacanthus, Epinephelus,* Six-barred Reef Grouper, 189
*diacanthus, Johnius,* Spotted Jewfish, 311
*diacanthus, Pygoplites,* Regal Angelfish, 353, 361, 364
Diadem Basslet, *Pseudochromis diadema,* 211
*diadema, Pseudochromis,* Diadem Basslet, 211
*diadema, Sargocentron,* Crown Squirrelfish, 107, 108, 111
*diadematus, Arothron,* Masked Puffer, 647
*Diademichthys lineatus,* Yellowstripe Clingfish, 95
Diagonal Bar Prawn Goby, *Amblyeleotris diagonalis,* 543
Diagonal Striped Goby, *Cryptocentroides insignis,* 557
*diagonalis, Amblyeleotris,* Diagonal Bar Prawn Goby, 543
*diagramma, Pterocaesio,* Yellow Lateral Line Fusilier, 272, 273
*diagrammus, Plectorhinchus,* Silver-banded Sweetlips, 284
*Dialommus fuscus,* Higheye Blenny, 515
Diamond Blenny, *Malacoctenus boehlkei,* 515
Diamond Turbot, *Hypsopsetta guttulata,* 611
Diamond Wrasse, *Halichoeres nigrescens,* 444, 473
*diana, Bodianus,* Diana's Hogfish, 428, 429, 473
Diana's Hogfish, *Bodianus diana,* 428, 429, 473
Diaphanous Cowfish, *Lactoria diaphanus,* 638
*diaphanus, Coralliozetus,* Glass Blenny, 520
*diaphanus, Lactoria,* Diaphanous Cowfish, 638
*Dicentrarchus labrax,* Common European Bass, 170
*diceraus, Enophrys,* Stripe-fin Sculpin, 164
*dichrous, Chaetodon,* Bicolored Butterflyfish, 346
*dickii, Plectroglyphidodon,* Narrow-bar Damsel, 395
*dicrus, Coryphopterus,* Colon Goby, 574
*Dictyosoma burgeri,* Skunk Blenny, 494
*didactylus, Inimicus,* Popeyed Sea Goblin, 156
*dieffenbachii, Anguilla,* Long-finned Eel, 53
*diemensis, Halophryne,* Devil Frogfish, 84
*diencaeus, Stegastes,* Longfin Damselfish, 407
*digrammus, Cheilinus,* Cheeklined Wrasse, 432, 433, 477
*digueti, Gobiosoma,* Banded Cleaner Goby, 571
*digueti, Taenioconger,* Cortez Garden Eel, 63
*dilecta, Ancylopsetta,* Three-eye Flounder, 611
*dilectus, Pseudochromis,* Sri Lanka Dottyback, 210
*dilemma, Ecsenius,* Philippine Blenny, 528.13
*dimidiata, Chromis,* Half-and-Half Chromis, 383
*dimidiatus, Labroides,* Bluestreak Cleaner Wrasse, 469
*dimidiatus, Scarus,* Fivesaddle Parrotfish, 482

*dinema, Carangoides,* Goldband Trevally, 246
*Dinematichthys dasyrhynchus,* Orange Eelpout, 81
*Dinoperca petersi,* Cavebass, 205
*Diodon holacanthus,* Balloonfish, 656
*Diodon hystrix,* Porcupinefish, 618, 653, 654, 656
*Diodon liturosus,* Shortspine Porcupinefish, 656
*Diodon myersi,* Myer's Balloonfish, 656
*Diodon nicthemerus,* Australian Globefish, 653, 654
*Diplectrum formosum,* Sand Perch, 200
*Diplectrum pacificum,* Pacific Sand Perch, 200
*Diplobatos ommata,* Cyclops Electric Ray, 42
*Diplodus bermudensis,* Bermuda Porgy, 288
*Diplodus cervinus,* Thick-lipped Bream, 293
*Diplodus puntazzo,* Sheepshead Bream, 288
*Diplodus sargus,* White Bream, 293
*Diplodus vulgaris,* Two-banded Bream, 288
*Diplogrammus pauciradiatus,* Few-rayed Dragonet, 538
*Diplogrammus xenicus,* Northern Dragonet, 536
*Diploprion bifasciatus,* Two-banded Grouper, 206
*Diploprion drachi,* Yellow-face Soapfish, 206
*diplotaenia, Bodianus,* Mexican Hogfish, 430
*Diproctacanthus xanthurus,* Yellow-tailed Cleaner, 439
Disappearing Wrasse, *Pseudocheilinus evanidus,* 458
*Dischistodus chrysopoecilus,* White-spot Damsel, 409
*Dischistodus fasciatus,* Banded Damsel, 409
*Dischistodus melanotus,* Black-backed Damsel, 409
*Dischistodus perspicillatus,* White Damsel, 409
*Dischistodus prosopotaenia,* Honey-head Damsel, 409
*Dischistodus pseudochrysopoecilus,* Monarch Damsel, 400, 409
*Discotrema crinophila,* Feather Star Clingfish, 94, 95, 97
*Discotrema* sp., Feather Star Clingfish, 94
*dispar, Apogon,* Startailed Cardinalfish, 228
*dispar, Mirolabrichthys,* Madder Seaperch, 171, 179
*dispar, Parapriacanthus,* Common Sweeper, 321
*dispilus, Halichoeres,* Chameleon Wrasse, 448
*Ditrema temmincki,* Japanese Seaperch, 369
Divided Wrasse, *Macropharyngodon bipartitus,* 451
*Dixiphichthys hoplites,* Doublesword Sea Robin, 160
*dixurus, Pseudochromis,* Forktail Dottyback, 210
*djeddensis, Rhynchobatus,* White-spotted Shovelnose Ray, 47
Doctorfish, *Acanthurus chirurgus,* 582
*doderleini, Symphodus,* Doderlein's Wrasse, 471
Doderlein's Wrasse, *Symphodus doderleini,* 471
*doederleini, Apogon,* Doederlein's Cardinalfish, 224
*Doederleinia berycoides,* Blackthroat Seaperch, 173
Doederlein's Cardinalfish, *Apogon doederleini,* 224
Dog Snapper, *Lutjanus jocu,* 264
Dogtooth Tuna, *Gymnosarda unicolor,* 603
*doliatus, Hologymnosus,* Ringed Wrasse, 450, 476
*dolichognathus, Chasmichthys,* Snakeskin Goby, 565
*dolosus, Chaetodon,* African Butterflyfish, 341
*dolosus, Peristrominous,* Cod Scorpionfish, 137
Dolphinfish, *Coryphaena hippurus,* 257, 604
*Doratonotus megalepis,* Dwarf Wrasse, 470
*Dorosoma petenense,* Threadfin Shad, 67
*dorsale, Sticharium,* Multicolor Snake Blenny, 516
*dorsalis, Microspathodon,* Giant Damselfish, 408
*dorsomacula, Coris,* Twinspot Coris, 437
*dorsopunicans, Stegastes,* Orangeback Damsel, 406
*Doryrhamphus dactyliophorus,* Banded Pipefish, 127
*Doryrhamphus excisus excisus,* Bluestripe Pipefish, 127
*Doryrhamphus janssi,* Janss' Pipefish, 127
*Doryrhamphus japonicus,* Japanese Blue-striped Pipefish, 127
*Doryrhamphus multiannulatus,* Many Banded Pipefish, 128
Dot-dash Blenny, *Ecsenius melarchus,* 528.05
Dot-dash Cusk-eel, *Lepophidium prorates,* 80
Dot-dash Goby, *Exyrias puntang,* 564
*Dotalabrus aurantiacus,* Castelnau's Golden Wrasse, 463
*Dotalabrus* sp., Little Rainbow Wrasse, 463
Dotted Cardinalfish, *Vincentia punctatus,* 236
Dotted Gizzard Shad, *Konosirus punctatus,* 67
Dotted Goatfish, *Pseudupeneus maculatus,* 314
Dotted-reef Eel, *Muraena lentiginosa,* 60
Dotty Triggerfish, *Balistoides viridescens,* 626
Double Banded Forktail Blenny, *Meiacanthus anema,* 523
Double Bar Chromis, *Chromis opercularis,* 383, 386
Double Blotch Spinecheek, *Scolopsis bimaculatus,* 293
Double-barred Spinefoot, *Siganus virgatus,* 599
Double-lined Mackerel, *Grammatorcynus bicarinatus,* 603
Double-spot Blenny, *Ecsenius bimaculatus,* 528.15
Double-spot Wrasse, *Halichoeres bimaculatus,* 443
Double-striped Goby, *Arenigobius bifrenatus,* 562
Doublebar Snapper, *Lutjanus biguttatus,* 258, 262
Doubleline Clingfish, *Lepadichthys lineatus,* 95
Doubleline Toby, *Canthigaster rivulata,* 652
Doubleline Tongue Sole, *Paraplagusia bilineata,* 614
Doublespot Goby, *Eviota bimaculata,* 576
Doublespotted Queenfish, *Scomberoides lysan,* 250, 251
Doublesword Sea Robin, *Dixiphichthys hoplites,* 160
Doublewhip Threadfin Bream, *Nemipterus nematophorus,* 305, 307
Doubtful Flounder, *Hippoglossoides dubius,* 613
*douglasi, Cheilodactylus,* Porae, 416
*dovii, Apogon,* Tailspot Cardinalfish, 230
Dowager Angelfish, *Pomacanthus striatus,* 364
Downy Blenny, *Labrisomus kalisherae,* 513
*drachi, Diploprion,* Yellow-face Soapfish, 206
*draconis, Eurypegasus,* Sea Moth, 92
Dragon Moray Eel, *Muraena pardalis,* 58
Dragon Wrasse, *Novaculichthys taeniourus,* 458, 472
Dragonet, unidentified, *Neosynchiropus* sp., 536; *Synchiropus* sp., 538, 539
Dragonfish, *Stomias* sp., 70
*Drepane punctata,* Spotted Drepane, 330, 334
*dubiosus, Scolopsis,* Yellow-streaked Monocle Bream, 302, 304
*dubius, Hippoglossoides,* Doubtful Flounder, 613
*dubius, Scarus,* Green Parrotfish, 484
*duboulayi, Chaetodontoplus,* Duboulay's Angelfish, 360
Duboulay's Angelfish, *Chaetodontoplus duboulayi,* 360
*ductor, Naucrates,* Pilot Fish, 253
*dumerili, Cantherhines,* Vagabond Filefish, 627
*dumerili, Seriola,* Greater Amberjack, 250, 252
*danckeri, Bryx,* Pugnose Pipefish, 125
*duperreyi, Thalassoma,* Saddle Wrasse, 466
Dusky Blenny, *Atrosalarias fuscus,* 527
Dusky Brotulid, *Brotulina fusca,* 81
Dusky Cardinalfish, *Apogon melas,* 228
Dusky Cherub, *Centropyge multispinis,* 354
Dusky Finned Goby, *Callogobius snelliusi,* 562
Dusky Fusegoby, *Fusigobius neophytus,* 570
Dusky Goby, *Chaenogobius urotaenia,* 558
Dusky Gregory, *Stegastes nigricans,* 405
Dusky Jawfish, *Opistognathus whitehursti,* 499
Dusky Morwong, *Dactylophora nigricans,* 418
Dusky Parrotfish, *Scarus niger,* 481, 489

Dusky Ray, *Trygonoptena testaceus*, 44
Dusky Spinefoot, *Siganus fuscescens*, 597
Dusky Tilefish, *Hoplolatilus cuniculus*, 240, 511
Dusky Wrasse, *Halichoeres marginatus*, 440, 444
Dusky-finned Bullseye, *Heteropriacanthus cruentatus*, 220, 695; *Priacanthus cruentatus*, 220
Dusky-tail Anemonefish, *Amphiprion fuscocaudatus*, 373
Duskyfin Rockcod, *Cephalopholis nigripinnis*, 182
*dussumieri, Acanthurus*, Dussumier's Surgeonfish, 586
*dussumieri, Aspidontus*, Floating Blenny, 532
*dussumieri, Hyporhamphus*, Dussumier's Halfbeak, 100
*dussumieri, Istiblennius*, Streaky Rockskipper, 526, 534
*Dussumieria hasselti*, Hasselt's Round Herring, 65
Dussumier's Halfbeak, *Hyporhamphus dussumieri*, 100
Dussumier's Surgeonfish, *Acanthurus dussumieri*, 586
*dutoiti, Pseudochromis*, Dutorti, 212
Dutorti, *Pseudochromis dutoiti*, 212
Dwarf Blenny, *Ecsenius minutus*, 528.11
Dwarf Leatherjacket, *Rudarius minutus*, 633
Dwarf Scorpionfish, *Scorpaena elachys*, 145
Dwarf Surfperch, *Micrometrus minimus*, 370
Dwarf Wrasse, *Doratonotus megalepis*, 470
Dwarfed Frogfish, *Antennarius pauciradiatus*, 88

## E

Eagle Ray, *Myliobatis tobijei*, 48
Eared Eel-blenny, *Congrogadus subducens*, 534
*earnshawi, Amblycirrhitus*, Earnshaw's Hawkfish, 415
Earnshaw's Hawkfish, *Amblycirrhitus earnshawi*, 415
Earspot Coral Goby, *Gobiodon atrangulatus*, 578
East Indian Red Hind, *Epinephelus corallicola*, 186
East Pacific Banded Butterflyfish, *Chaetodon humeralis*, 343
East Pacific Red Snapper, *Lutjanus peru*, 268
East Pacific Triggerfish, *Balistes polylepis*, 625
Easter Island Demoiselle, *Chrysiptera rapanui*, 390
Easter Island Pygmy Angelfish, *Centropyge hotumatua*, 356
*ebisui, Malacoctenus*, Fishgod Blenny, 514
*Echeneis naucrates*, White-tailed Remora, 244
*Echeneis naucratoides*, Whitefin Sharksucker, 244
*Echeneis* sp., Remora, unidentified, 244
*Echidna catenata*, Chain Moray, 53
*Echidna nebulosa*, Snowflake Moray, 59
*Echidna pozyzona*, Girdled Moray, 53
*echinocephalus, Paragobiodon*, Prickly-headed Goby, 578
Ecklonia Weedfish, *Heteroclinus eckloniae*, 517
*eckloniae, Heteroclinus*, Ecklonia Weedfish, 517
*eclancheri, Bodianus*, Galapagos Hogfish, 430
Eclipse Hogfish, *Bodianus mesothorax*, 428
*Ecsenius aequalis*, Lined Blenny, 528.16
*Ecsenius alleni*, Allen's Blenny, 528.14
*Ecsenius aroni*, Khaki Blenny, 528.04
*Ecsenius australianus*, Australian Blenny, 528.14
*Ecsenius axelrodi*, Axelrod's Blenny, 528.12
*Ecsenius bandanus*, Banda Blenny, 528.15
*Ecsenius bathi*, Bath's Blenny, 528.13
*Ecsenius bicolor*, Two-colored Blenny, 532
*Ecsenius bimaculatus*, Double-spot Blenny, 528.15
*Ecsenius collettei*, Collette's Blenny, 528.16
*Ecsenius dentex*, Many-toothed Blenny, 528.10
*Ecsenius dilemma*, Philippine Blenny, 528.13
*Ecsenius fijiensis*, Fiji Blenny, 528.14
*Ecsenius fourmanoiri*, Fourmanoir's Blenny, 528.14
*Ecsenius frontalis*, Brown-gold Blenny, 528.06
*Ecsenius gravieri*, Red Sea Mimic Blenny, 523, 533
*Ecsenius isos*, Iso Blenny, 528.15
*Ecsenius lineatus*, Klausewitz's Blenny, 533
*Ecsenius lividanalis*, Blue-and-gold Blenny, 528.04
*Ecsenius mandibularis*, White-dot Blenny, 528.16
*Ecsenius melarchus*, Dot-dash Blenny, 528.05
*Ecsenius midas*, Midas Blenny, 533
*Ecsenius minutus*, Dwarf Blenny, 528.11
*Ecsenius monoculus*, One-eyed Blenny, 528.09
*Ecsenius nalolo*, Nalolo, 533
*Ecsenius namiyei*, Yellow-tailed Blenny, 528.07
*Ecsenius oculatus*, Eyespot Blenny, 528.09
*Ecsenius oculus*, Ocellated Blenny, 533
*Ecsenius opsifrontalis*, Latticed Blenny, 528.14
*Ecsenius pardus*, Leopard Blenny, 528.09
*Ecsenius paroculus*, Brown-spot Blenny, 528.09
*Ecsenius pictus*, Painted Blenny, 528.15
*Ecsenius portenoyi*, Portenoy's Blenny, 528.10
*Ecsenius pulcher*, Arabian Blenny, 528.04
*Ecsenius schroederi*, Schroeder's Blenny, 528.16
*Ecsenius stictus*, Spotted Blenny, 528.11
*Ecsenius stigmatura*, Tail-spot Blenny, 528.06
*Ecsenius tessera*, Paving-tile Blenny, 528.09
*Ecsenius tigris*, Tiger Blenny, 528.13
*Ecsenius trilineatus*, Three-lined Blenny, 528.15
*Ecsenius yaeyamaensis*, Yaeyama Blenny, 528.11
*edentulus, Istiblennius*, Rippled Rockskipper, 531, 534
Eel Clingfish, *Alabes parvulus*, 97
Eel Pipefish, *Bulbonaricus brauni*, 125
*ehippium, Chaetodon*, Saddleback Butterflyfish, 345
*ehrenbergii, Lutjanus*, Black-spot Snapper, 260
Eibl-Eibesfeldt's Pygmy Angelfish, *Centropyge eibli*, 354
*eibli, Centropyge*, Eibl-Eibesfeldt's Pygmy Angelfish, 354
*eidolon, Coryphopterus*, Pallid Goby, 574
Eight-armed Snailfish, *Liparis ochotenis*, 168
Eight-lined Cardinalfish, *Cheilodipterus macrodon*, 234
Eight-striped Butterflyfish, *Chaetodon octofasciatus*, 339
Eight-toothed Parrotfish, *Scarus oktodon*, 490
Eightbar Goby, *Cryptocentrus cryptocentrus*, 549
Eightline Wrasse, *Paracheilinus octotaenia*, 460
Eightstripe Wrasse, *Pseudocheilinus octotaenia*, 458
*Ekemblemaria* sp. *(myersi?)*, Reefsand Blenny, 519
*elachys, Scorpaena*, Dwarf Scorpionfish, 145
*Elagatis bipinnulata*, Rainbow Runner, 245, 247
*elanthematicus, Gobius*, Black Sea Goby, 559
*elapoides, Pterogobius*, Black Belt Flagfin Goby, 565
*elator, Zalieutes*, Spotted Batfish, 93
Electric Ray, *Torpedo marmoratus*, 47
*elegans, Anampses*, Lord Howe Tamarin, 427
*elegans, Cybiosarda*, Leaping Bonito, 602
*elegans, Kyphosus*, Cortez Chub, 328
*elegans, Omobranchus*, Elegant Blenny, 525
Elegant Blenny, *Omobranchus elegans*, 525
Elegant Coris, *Coris venusta*, 438
*Eleginus gracilis*, Saffron Cod, 77
*Eleotris* cf *acanthopoma*, Yellowfin Sleeper, 542
*elerae, Chromis*, Twin-spot Chromis, 383
*Eleutheronema tetradactylum*, Colonial Salmon, 420
*elevatus, Zanclistius*, Longfinned Boarfish, 335
*elizabethae, Odontanthias*, Elizabeth's Fairy Basslet, 180
Elizabeth's Fairy Basslet, *Odontanthias elizabethae*, 180

*Ellerkeldia annulata,* Ringed Seaperch, 199
*Ellerkeldia hunti,* Half-banded Seaperch, 199
*Ellerkeldia maccullochi,* McCulloch's Seaperch, 199
*Ellerkeldia rubra,* Red Seaperch, 199
*Ellerkeldia wilsoni,* Western Sea Perch, 199, 205
*elliotti, Apogon,* Flag-fin Cardinalfish, 232
*ellipticum, Hyperprosopon,* Silver Surfperch, 370
*elongata, Atherinosoma,* Elongate Hardyhead, 102
*elongata, Ilisha,* Elongate Scute Herring, 67
Elongate Hardyhead, *Atherinosoma elongata,* 102
Elongate Scute Herring, *Ilisha elongata,* 67
Elongate Tonguefish, *Symphurus elongatus,* 614
Elongate Wrasse, *Pseudojuloides elongatus,* 461
*elongatum, Gonostoma,* Angle-mouthed Lanternfish, 70
*elongatus, Gnathagnus,* Bluespotted Stargazer, 501
*elongatus, Hoplostethus,* Slender Roughy, 103
*elongatus, Omobranchus,* Cloister Blenny, 534
*elongatus, Ophiodon,* Lingcod, 163
*elongatus, Pseudojuloides,* Elongate Wrasse, 461
*elongatus, Symphurus,* Elongate Tonguefish, 614
*Elops hawaiiensis,* Pacific Ladyfish, 50
*Elops machnata,* Ladyfish, 50
Elusive Blenny, *Emblemaria walkeri,* 520
*emarginatus, Pomacentrus,* Outer-reef Damsel, 400
Ember Blenny, *Cirripectes stigmaticus,* 528, 528.02
Ember Parrotfish, *Scarus rubroviolaceus,* 481, 483, 490
*Embiotoca jacksoni,* Black Surfperch, 370
*Emblemaria bottomei,* Bottome's Blenny, 520
*Emblemaria hypacanthus,* Signae Blenny, 520
*Emblemaria pandionis,* Sailfin Blenny, 520
*Emblemaria piratula,* Pirate Blenny, 520
*Emblemaria walkeri,* Elusive Blenny, 520
*emeryi, Stegastes,* Emery's Gregory, 405
Emery's Gregory, *Stegastes emeryi,* 405
*Emmelichthyops ruber,* Red Bonnetmouth, 288
Emperor Angelfish, *Pomacanthus imperator,* 363
Emperor Snapper, *Lutjanus sebae,* 270
*Encheliophis gracilis,* Graceful Pearlfish, 81
*Enchelycore bayeri,* Bayer's Moray, 59
*Enchelyurus flavipes,* Brown and Yellow Blenny, 526
*enchrysura, Chromis,* Yellowtail Reeffish, 384
*endekataenia, Apogon,* Black-banded Cardinalfish, 224
*endrachtensis, Atherinomorus,* Spotted Hardyhead, 102
*engelhardi, Pseudanthias,* Engelhard's Goldie, 177
Engelhard's Goldie, *Pseudanthias engelhardi,* 177
*engelmani, Synodus,* Redband Lizardfish, 74
Englishman, *Chrysoblephus anglicus,* 293
*Engraulis japonicus,* Japanese Anchovy, 68
*Engraulis mordax,* Northern Anchovy, 68, 69
*enigmaticus, Lethrinus,* Seychelles Emperor, 298
Enjambre, *Cephalopholis panamensis,* 184
*Enneanectes altivelis,* Lofty Triplefin, 507
*Enneanectes atrorus,* Blackedge Triplefin, 508
*Enneanectes boehlkei,* Roughhead Triplefin, 507
*Enneanectes pectoralis,* Redeye Triplefin, 507
*Enneanectes sexmaculatus,* Delicate Triplefin, 507
*Enneanectes* sp., Triplefin, unidentified, 507
*Enneapterygius etheostomus,* Common Triplefin, 509
*Enophrys bison,* Buffalo Sculpin, 164
*Enophrys diceraus,* Stripe-fin Sculpin, 164
*Enoplosus armatus,* Old Wife, 334
*ensenadae, Micrognathus,* Harlequin Pipefish, 125
*ensifer, Sargocentron,* Hawaiian Squirrelfish, 110
*ensis, Gaidropsarus,* Threebeard Rockling, 78
*Entelurus aequoreus,* Snake Pipefish, 126
*Entomacrodus decussatus,* Wavy-lined Blenny, 529
*Entomacrodus nigricans,* Pearl Blenny, 529
*Entomacrodus striatus,* Pearly Rockskipper, 529
*Eopsetta grigorjewi,* Grigorjew's Halibut, 608, 611
Epaulette Shark, *Hemiscyllium ocellatum,* 35
*ephippium, Amphiprion,* Saddle Anemonefish, 373, 374
*ephippium, Cheilodactylus,* Painted Moki, 417
*Ephippus orbis,* Spadefish, 330
*Epibulus insidiator,* Slingjaw Wrasse, 439, 449
*epilamprus, Canthigaster,* Blue-spotted Sharp-nosed Puffer, 650
*Epinephelides armatus,* Breaksea Grouper, 187
*Epinephelus acanthistius,* Gulf Coney, 191
*Epinephelus adscensionis,* Rock Hind, 192
*Epinephelus akaara,* Red Spotted Grouper, 190
*Epinephelus amblycephalus,* Blunt-headed Grouper, 190
*Epinephelus analogus,* Spotted Cabrilla, 191
*Epinephelus areolatus,* Squaretail Grouper, 190
*Epinephelus awoara,* Green Hata, 186
*Epinephelus caeruleopunctatus,* White-spotted Reef Cod, 187
*Epinephelus cometae,* Broom Grouper, 190
*Epinephelus corallicola,* East Indian Red Hind, 186
*Epinephelus cyanopodus,* Freckled Grouper, 190
*Epinephelus damelii,* Saddled Rock-cod, 186
*Epinephelus dermatolepis,* Leather Bass, 191
*Epinephelus diacanthus,* Six-barred Reef Grouper, 189
*Epinephelus epistictus,* Freckleback Grouper, 190
*Epinephelus fario,* Trout Reef Cod, 187
*Epinephelus fasciatus,* Blacktip Grouper, 184, 187
*Epinephelus flavocoeruleus,* Blue and Yellow Grouper, 190
*Epinephelus fuscoguttatus,* Blotchy Grouper, 187
*Epinephelus guttatus,* Red Hind, 192
*Epinephelus hexagonatus,* White Speckled Rock Cod, 187
*Epinephelus inermis,* Marbled Grouper, 192
*Epinephelus itajara,* Jewfish, 191
*Epinephelus labriformis,* Flag Cabrilla, 191
*Epinephelus lanceolatus,* Brindlebass, 194
*Epinephelus latifasciatus,* Laterally Banded Grouper, 190
*Epinephelus maculatus,* Spotted Grouper, 189
*Epinephelus malabaricus,* Malabar Rockcod, 188
*Epinephelus megachir,* Long-finned Grouper, 189
*Epinephelus merra,* Honeycomb Grouper, 186, 189
*Epinephelus microdon,* Camouflage Grouper, 189
*Epinephelus moara,* Kelp Grouper, 189
*Epinephelus morio,* Red Grouper, 192
*Epinephelus multinotatus,* White-blotched Rockcod, 188, 205
*Epinephelus mystacinus,* Misty Grouper, 192
*Epinephelus niveatus,* Snowy Grouper, 191
*Epinephelus rivulatus,* Halfmoon Rock Cod, 187
*Epinephelus septemfasciatus,* Seven-banded Grouper, 189
*Epinephelus socialis,* White-dotted Grouper, 188
*Epinephelus* sp., Grouper, unidentified, 188
*Epinephelus striatus,* Nassau Grouper, 192
*Epinephelus summana,* Speckled Fin Grouper, 205
*Epinephelus tauvina,* Greasy Rock Cod, 188
*Epinephelus truncatus,* Red-tipped Rock Cod, 189
*Epinephelus tukula,* Potato Bass, 188
*Epinephelus undulostriatus,* Wavy-lined Grouper, 117
*Epinephelus undulosus,* Midwater Rockcod, 188
*epistictus, Epinephelus,* Freckleback Grouper, 190

*Eptatretus* sp. *(stouti?)*, Pacific Hagfish, 33
*Eptatretus stouti*, Pacific Hagfish, 33
*eques, Phycodurus*, Leafy Seadragon, 121, 124
*Equetus acuminatus*, High-hat, 308
*Equetus lanceolatus*, Jackknife-fish, 310
*Equetus punctatus*, Spotted Drum, 309, 310
*Equetus umbrosus*, Cubbyu, 308, 309
*Equetus viola*, Rock Croaker, 310
*equula, Carangoides*, Horse Crevalle, 246
*equulus, Leiognathus*, Common Slipmouth, 256
*ercodes, Rudarius*, Japanese Filefish, 633
*erectus, Hippocampus*, Northern Seahorse, 131, 132
*Erilepis zonifer*, Skilfish, 162
*eriomma, Johnsonina*, Bullseye, 620
*Ernogrammus hexagrammus*, Brown Blenny, 494
*Erosa erosa*, Monkeyfish, 155, 156
*erosa, Erosa*, Monkeyfish, 155, 156
*erumei, Psettodes*, Adalah, 609
*erythrea?, Brotula*, Scaled-cheek Brotula, 81
*erythrodon, Scarus*, Slopehead Parrotfish, 490
*erythrogaster, Caesio*, Redbelly Fusilier, 273
*erythrops, Pseudojuloides*, Redeye Wrasse, 460
*erythropterus, Lutjanus*, Gold-striped Snapper, 266
*erythrotaenia, Sphoeroides*, Redline Puffer, 649
*eschmeyeri, Rhinopias*, Eschmeyer's Scorpionfish, 139
Eschmeyer's Scorpionfish, *Rhinopias eschmeyeri*, 139
*Etelis marshi*, Yellowstripe Ruby Snapper, 259
*Etelis oculatus*, Queen Snapper, 259
*etheostomus, Enneapterygius*, Common Triplefin, 509
*Etrumeus teres*, Round Herring, 66
*Eubalichthys mosaicus*, Mosaic Leatherjacket, 634
*Eucinostomus argenteus*, Spotfin Mojarra, 275
*Eucinostomus gracilis*, Pacific Flagfin Mojarra, 275
*Eucinostomus gula*, Silver Jenny, 275
*Eucrossorhinus dasypogon*, Tassled Wobbegong, 36
*eukrines, Liopropoma*, Wrasse Basslet, 198
*Eupetrichthys angustipes*, Australian Slender Wrasse, 463
European Eel, *Anguilla anguilla*, 53
European Flounder, *Platichthys flesus*, 612
European Scorpionfish, *Scorpaena porcus*, 144
European Seahorse, *Hippocampus hippocampus*, 130
*eurostus, Gymnothorax*, Wakanoura Moray, 54
*Eurypegasus draconis*, Sea Moth, 92
*Euthynnus affinis*, Kawakawa, 602
*Euxiphipops navarchus*, Blue-girdled Angelfish, 361, 364
*Euxiphipops sexstriatus*, Six-banded Angelfish, 364
*Euxiphipops xanthometapon*, Yellow-faced Angelfish, 361
*Euxiphipops xanthometopon*, Yellow-faced Angelfish, 364
*evanidus, Pseudocheilinus*, Disappearing Wrasse, 458
*evansi, Mirolabrichthys*, Yellowtail Goldie, 175
*evelynae, Gobiosoma*, Sharknose Goby, 573
*evermanni, Apogon*, Evermann's Cardinalfish, 232
Evermann's Cardinalfish, *Apogon evermanni*, 232
*evides, Ptereleotris*, Spottail Gudgeon, 568
Evileye Pufferfish, *Amblyrhynchotes honckenii*, 643
*Eviota abax*, Abax Goby, 576
*Eviota bifasciata*, Two-striped Coral Goby, 560, 576
*Eviota bimaculata*, Doublespot Goby, 576
*Eviota fasciola*, Banded Coral Goby, 576
*Eviota infulata*, Smith's Coral Goby, 576
*Eviota nigriventris*, Blackbottom Goby, 572
*Eviota* sp., Mini-goby, unidentified, 550; Orange-banded Goby, 576; Palespot Goby, 550; Red Coral Goby, 551
*Evistias acutirostris*, Banded Boarhead, 335
*Evynnis cardinalis*, Crimson Sea-Bream, 291
*Evynnis japonica*, Japanese Sea Bream, 289, 291
*Exallias brevis*, Leopard Rockskipper, 534
*exasperata, Zapteryx*, Banded Guitarfish, 43
*excelsa, Chaetodon*, Hawaiian Gold-barred Butterflyfish, 346
*excisus excisus, Doryrhamphus*, Bluestripe Pipefish, 127
*Exerpes asper*, Sargassum Blenny, 512
*exilis, Pomachromis*, Slender Reef-damsel, 395
*exilispinis, Acanthemblemaria*, Slender-spined Blenny, 518
Exocoetidae sp., Flying fish, 98
*exostigma, Apogon*, One-lined Cardinalfish, 226
Exquisite Wrasse, *Cirrhilabrus exquisitus*, 433
*exquisitus, Cirrhilabrus*, Exquisite Wrasse, 433
Exuma Cleaning Goby, *Gobiosoma atronasum*, 572
*Exyrias belissimus*, Flowing Finned Goby, 564
*Exyrias puntang*, Dot-dash Goby, 564
Eyed Flounder, *Bothus ocellatus*, 609
Eyespot Blenny, *Ecsenius oculatus*, 528.09

# F

*faber, Chaetodipterus*, Atlantic Spadefish, 330
Fairy Basslet, unidentified, *Pseudanthias* sp., 174, 177
Fairy Cardinalfish, *Apogon leptocaulus*, 230
*falcatus, Trachinotus*, PermitGreat Pompano, 254
*falcifer, Chaetodon*, Scythe-marked Butterflyfish, 347
*falciformes, Monodactylus*, Cape Mono, 418
Falco Hawkfish, *Cirrhitichthys falco*, 412
*falco, Cirrhitichthys*, Falco Hawkfish, 412
*falcula, Chaetodon*, Sickle Butterflyfish, 340
Fall Parrotfish, *Scarus frenatus*, 479, 482, 485
*fallax, Petroscirtes*, Batesian Mimic, 522
False Batfish, *Parachaetodon ocellatus*, 348, 350
False Bluestreak Wrasse, *Labroides pectoralis*, 469
False Cleanerfish, *Aspidontus taeniatus*, 522
False Combfish, *Coris pictoides*, 437
False Lined Butterflyfish, *Chaetodon oxycephalus*, 339
False Senator Wrasse, *Pictilabrus* sp., 462
False Skunk-striped Anemonefish, *Amphiprion perideraion*, 375, 376
False Variegated Cardinalfish, *Fowleria* cf *variegata*, 235
False-eye Damsel, *Abudefduf sparoides*, 381
False-eye Toby, *Canthigaster solandri*, 653
Fan-bellied Leatherjacket, *Monacanthus chinensis*, 629
Fancytail Goby, *Cryptocentrus* sp., 557
Fantail Filefish, *Pervagor spilosoma*, 633
Fantail Sole, *Xystreurys liolepis*, 610
*far, Hemiramphus*, Barred Garfish, 99
*fario, Epinephelus*, Trout Reef Cod, 187
*fasciata, Leiognathus*, Banded Pony Fish, 256
*fasciata, Lienardella*, Harlequin Tuskfish, 452, 453
*fasciata, Trygonorhina*, Fiddler Ray, 43
*fasciatum, Liopropoma*, Banded Basslet, 198
*fasciatus, Amblyeleotris*, Red-necked Goby, 543
*fasciatus, Apogon*, Four-banded Cardinalfish, 224
*fasciatus, Chaetodon*, Red Sea Raccoon Butterflyfish, 340
*fasciatus, Cheilinus*, Redbreasted Wrasse, 432, 477
*fasciatus, Cirrhitops*, Banded Hawkfish, 413
*fasciatus, Cryptocentrus*, Blue-finned Shrimp Goby, 549, 556
*fasciatus, Dischistodus*, Banded Damsel, 409

*fasciatus, Epinephelus,* Blacktip Grouper, 184, 187
*fasciatus, Hemigymnus,* Barred Thicklip, 450
*fasciatus, Limnichthys,* Tommy Fish, 501
*fasciatus, Oplegnathus,* Banded Knifejaw, 368, 369
*fasciatus, Paraclinus,* Banded Blenny, 515
*fasciatus, Pseudanthias,* Banded Fairy Basslet, 177
*fasciatus, Salarias,* Jewelled Rockskipper, 526, 527, 528.01
*fasciatus, Serranus,* Barred Serrano, 197
*fasciola, Eviota,* Banded Coral Goby, 576
*fasciolaris, Symphurus,* Spotfin Tonguefish, 614
*fasciolatum, Belonepterygion,* Banded Longfin, 212
*fasciolatus, Stegastes,* Pacific Gregory, 403, 404
Fat Barracuda, *Sphyraena pinguis,* 422
*favagineus, Gymnothorax,* Honeycomb Moray, 58, 59
*Favonigobius lateralis,* Long-finned Goby, 558
*Favonigobius reichei,* Tropical Sand Goby, 560
Feather Star Clingfish, *Discotrema crinophila,* 94, 95, 97; *Discotrema* sp., 94
Featherfin Scorpionfish, *Hipposcorpaena* sp., 156
Feathertail Sleeper, *Oxymetopon cyanoctenosum,* 542
*femininus, Anampses,* Blue-striped Orange Tamarin, 427
*ferdau, Carangoides,* Yellow-spotted Crevalle, 247, 248
Ferocious Goby, *Ctenogobiops feroculus,* 549
*feroculus, Ctenogobiops,* Ferocious Goby, 549
*ferox, Odontaspis,* Bumpytail Ragged-tooth, 37
*ferox, Omobranchus,* Gossamer Blenny, 525
*ferrugatus, Centropyge,* Rusty Angelfish, 355
*ferrugineus, Scarus,* Rusty Parrotfish, 483, 485
Few-rayed Dragonet, *Diplogrammus pauciradiatus,* 538
Few-rayed Hardyhead, *Craterocephalus pauciradiatus,* 102
Fiddler Ray, *Trygonorhina fasciata,* 43
Fifteen-spine Stickleback, *Spinachia spinachia,* 118
Fiji Blenny, *Ecsenius fijiensis,* 528.14
*fijiensis, Ecsenius,* Fiji Blenny, 528.14
Filament Blenny, *Cirripectes filamentosus,* 528
Filament Devilfish, *Inimicus filamentosus,* 135, 155
Filament-fin Wrasse, *Paracheilinus filamentosus,* 424, 459
Filamented Sand Eel, *Trichonotus setigerus,* 539
*filamentosus, Cirripectes,* Filament Blenny, 528
*filamentosus, Gerres,* Long-rayed Silver-Biddy, 275, 276
*filamentosus, Inimicus,* Filament Devilfish, 135, 155
*filamentosus, Labrisomus,* Filamentous Blenny, 513
*filamentosus, Neopomacentrus,* Brown Demoiselle, 398
*filamentosus, Paracheilinus,* Filament-fin Wrasse, 424, 459
*filamentosus, Pristipomoides,* Rosy Jobfish, 269
Filamentous Blenny, *Labrisomus filamentosus,* 513
Filefish, unidentified, *Aluterus* sp., 635; *Paramonacanthus* sp., 634
*filicauda, Monacanthus,* Thread-tailed Filefish, 629
*fimbria, Anoplopoma,* Sablefish, 162
*fimbriatus, Gymnothorax,* Dark-spotted Moray, 54
Fine-spotted Flounder, *Pleuronichthys cornutus,* 607, 612
Finescale Wrasse, *Hologymnosus annulatus,* 449, 450
Fingered Dragonet, *Dactylopus dactylopus,* 536
Fingerfish, *Monodactylus sebae,* 321
Firefish, *Nemateleotris magnifica,* 541, 570
*fisheri, Centropyge,* Fisher's Angelfish, 356
*fisheri, Chriolepis,* Translucent Goby, 567
Fisher's Angelfish, *Centropyge fisheri,* 356
Fishgod Blenny, *Malacoctenus ebisui,* 514
Fishing Frog, *Antennarius hispidus,* 83, 87, 91
*Fistularia commersonii,* Commerson's Cornetfish, 119
*Fistularia tabacaria,* Bluespotted Cornetfish, 119
Five-banded Parrotfish, *Scarus venosus,* 482
Five-line Snapper, *Lutjanus quinquelineatus,* 261
Five-spotted Wrasse, *Symphodus roissali,* 471
Five-striped Pigface, *Rhyncopelates oxyrhynchus,* 217
Fivefinger Wrasse, *Xyrichthys pentadactylus,* 457
Fivelined Threadfin Bream, *Nemipterus tambuloides,* 306
Fivesaddle Parrotfish, *Scarus dimidiatus,* 482
Fivestripe Wrasse, *Thalassoma quinquevittatum,* 467
Flag Cabrilla, *Epinephelus labriformis,* 191
Flag Rockfish, *Sebastes rubrovinctus,* 151
Flag Squirrelfish, *Sargocentron vexillarium,* 107
Flag-fin Cardinalfish, *Apogon elliotti,* 232
Flag-finned Goby, *Pterogobius zonoleucus,* 565
*flagellifer, Pteragogus,* Cocktail Fish, 449
Flame Angelfish, *Centropyge loriculus,* 355
Flame Basslet, *Mirolabrichthys ignitus,* 174
Flame Goby, *Trimma macrophthalma,* 577
Flameback Angelfish, *Centropyge aurantonotus,* 356
Flamefish, *Apogon maculatus,* 230
*flammicauda, Pseudochromis,* Red-tailed Dottyback, 211
Flashlight Fish, *Photoblepharon palpebratus,* 106
Flat Needlefish, *Ablennes hians,* 100
Flathead, unidentified, *Platycephalus* sp., 166
*flavescens, Zebrasoma,* Yellow Sailfin Tang, 592
*flavicauda, Centropyge,* Royal Blue Pygmy Angelfish, 356
*flavicauda, Chromis,* Cobalt Chromis, 388
*flavicauda, Dascyllus,* Yellow-tailed Dascyllus, 371, 378
*flavicauda, Sphagebranchus,* Yellow-tailed Snake Eel, 62
*flavicauda, Sphyraena,* Yellow-tailed Barracuda, 422
*flavidus, Aulorhynchus,* Tubesnout, 118
*flavidus, Sebastes,* Yellowtail Rockfish, 151
*flaviguttatum, Haemulon,* Pacific Lined Grunt, 280
*flavilatus, Amblyglyphidodon,* Yellow-flank Damselfish, 381
*flavilatus, Stegastes,* Beau Brummel, 407
*flavimanus, Acanthogobius,* Yellowfin Goby, 552
*flavimarginatus, Gymnothorax,* Yellow-edged Moray, 55, 56, 58
*flavimarginatus, Pseudobalistes,* Yellowface Triggerfish, 622
*flavipectoralis, Scarus,* Yellowfin Parrotfish, 484
*flavipes, Enchelyurus,* Brown and Yellow Blenny, 526
*flavipinnis, Chrysiptera,* Yellow-fin Demoiselle, 392
*flavirostris, Chaetodon,* Yellow-face Butterflyfish, 338
*flavissimus, Assessor,* Golden Mini-Grouper, 213
*flavissimus, Centropyge,* Lemonpeel, 357
*flavissimus, Forcipiger,* Long-nosed Butterflyfish, 351
*flaviventris, Serranus,* Twinspot Bass, 197
*flavivertex, Pseudochromis,* Sunrise Dottyback, 212
*flavocoeruleus, Epinephelus,* Blue and Yellow Grouper, 190
*flavocoronatus, Chaetodon,* Yellow-crowned Butterflyfish, 340
*flavolineata, Meuschenia,* Yellow-striped Leatherjacket, 630, 632
*flavolineatum, Haemulon,* French Grunt, 277, 278
*flavolineatus, Mulloides,* Yellowstripe Goatfish, 315, 318
*flavomaculata, Chromis,* Yellow-freckled Reeffish, 384
*flavomaculatus, Plectorhinchus,* Lemon Sweetlips, 282, 283, 287
*flavopectoralis, Centropyge,* Yellow-finned Pygmy Angelfish, 354
*flavovittata, Coris,* Hinalea, 438
*flavus, Vomerogobius,* Yellow Goby, 561
*flesus, Platichthys,* European Flounder, 612
Floating Blenny, *Aspidontus dussumieri,* 532
Floral Blenny, *Petroscirtes mitratus,* 534
Floral Wrasse, *Cheilinus chlorourus,* 433
Florida Pompano, *Trachinotus carolinus,* 254

*floridana, Cerdale,* Pugjaw Wormfish, 580
Flowerspot Flounder, *Pseudorhombus* sp., 610
Flowing Finned Goby, *Exyrias belissimus,* 564
Flying fish, Exocoetidae sp., 98
Flying Fish, *Cheilopogon atrisignis,* 99
Flying Gurnard, *Dactylopterus volitans,* 137
*fo, Foa,* Samoan Cardinalfish, 234
*Foa fo,* Samoan Cardinalfish, 234
*foetens, Synodus,* Inshore Lizardfish, 74
*Foetorepus* sp., Spotted Dragonet, 537
Fontanes Goby, *Amblyeleotris fontanesii,* 543
*fontanesii, Amblyeleotris,* Fontanes Goby, 543
Footballer, *Chrysiptera annulata,* 391
Footballer Trout, *Plectropomus maculatus,* 203
*Forcipiger flavissimus,* Long-nosed Butterflyfish, 351
*Forcipiger longirostris,* Black Long-nosed Butterflyfish, 351
*forcipitus, Balistes,* West African Triggerfish, 625
Forktail Blenny, *Meiacanthus atrodorsalis,* 523
Forktail Dottyback, *Pseudochromis dixurus,* 210
Forktailed Sea Bass, *Mirolabrichthys pascalus,* 178
*formosa, Coris,* Queen Coris, 439
Formosan Goby, *Parioglossus formosus,* 560
*formosensis, Rhinobatos,* Taiwan Guitarfish, 44
*formosum, Diplectrum,* Sand Perch, 200
*formosus, Parioglossus,* Formosan Goby, 560
*fornasini, Lactoria,* Thornback Cowfish, 638
*forsskalii, Parupeneus,* Forsskal's Goatfish, 316
Forsskal's Goatfish, *Parupeneus forsskalii,* 316
*forsteri, Aldrichetta,* Yellow-eyed Mullet, 421
*forsteri, Paracirrhites,* Forster's Hawkfish, 410, 413, 414, 415
Forster's Hawkfish, *Paracirrhites forsteri,* 410, 413, 414, 415
Forster's Parrotfish, *Scarus japanensis,* 492
Four-banded Cardinalfish, *Apogon fasciatus,* 224
Four-bar Porcupinefish, *Lophodiodon calori,* 656
Four-barred Toby, *Canthigaster coronata,* 650, 651
Four-barred Weever, *Parapercis tetracantha,* 504, 505
Four-eyed Butterflyfish, *Chaetodon capistratus,* 343
Four-lined Terapon, *Pelates quadrilineatus,* 217, 289
Four-lined Wrasse, *Pseudocheilinus tetrataenia,* 461
Four-spot Butterflyfish, *Chaetodon quadrimaculatus,* 335
Four-spot Wrasse, *Halichoeres trispilus,* 440, 441
Fourline Wrasse, *Larabicus quadrilineatus,* 451
*fourmanoiri, Ecsenius,* Fourmanoir's Blenny, 528.14
*fourmanoiri, Hoplolatilus,* Spotted Tilefish, 240
Fourmanoir's Blenny, *Ecsenius fourmanoiri,* 528.14
*Fowleria aurita,* Crosseyed Cardinalfish, 235
*Fowleria* cf *variegata,* False Variegated Cardinalfish, 235
*Fowleria variegata,* Variegated Cardinalfish, 234
Foxface, *Lo vulpinus,* 597
Foxfish, *Bodianus frenchii,* 429
*fraenatus, Apogon,* Spiny-eyed Cardinalfish, 223
*fraenatus, Sufflamen,* Bridle Triggerfish, 624, 627
*francisci, Heterodontus,* Horn Shark, 34
Freckleback Grouper, *Epinephelus epistictus,* 190
Freckleback Sharp-nosed Puffer, *Canthigaster callisterna,* 651
Freckled Cardinalfish, *Phaeoptyx conklini,* 236
Freckled Grouper, *Epinephelus cyanopodus,* 190
Freckled Hawkfish, *Cirrhitus pinnulatus,* 413, 414
Freckled Head Midshipman, *Porichthys margaritatus,* 84
Freckled Soapfish, *Rypticus bistrispinus,* 207
Freckled Waspfish, *Paracentropogon vespa,* 159
Freckletail Lyretail Angelfish, *Genicanthus lamarck,* 359
*fremblii, Chaetodon,* Blue-striped Butterflyfish, 342
*frenata, Zaniolepis,* Shortspine Combfish, 163
*frenatus, Amphiprion,* Red Clown, 376
*frenatus, Lepadichthys,* Green Clingfish, 97
*frenatus, Scarus,* Fall Parrotfish, 479, 482, 485
*frenatus, Scolopsis,* Seychelles Spinecheek, 293
French Angelfish, *Pomacanthus paru,* 362
French Butterflyfish, *Chaetodon marcellae,* 347
French Grunt, *Haemulon flavolineatum,* 277, 278
*frenchii, Bodianus,* Foxfish, 429
Freshwater Demoiselle, *Neopomacentrus taeniurus,* 398
*fridmani, Pseudochromis,* Orchid Dottyback, 212
Frigate Tuna, *Auxis thazard,* 602
Frill Shark, *Chlamydoselachus anguineus,* 33
Fringe-finned Trevally, *Pantolabus radiatus,* 253
Fringe-lipped Flathead, *Thysanophrys otaitensis,* 161
Fringed Blenny, *Chirolophis japonicus,* 495
Fringed Filefish, *Monacanthus ciliatus,* 628
Fringyfin Goby, *Yongeichthys criniger,* 552, 553; *Yongeichthys criniger?,* 550
Fringyhead Scorpionfish, *Scorpaena neglecta,* 146
*frondosa, Rhinopias,* Goose Scorpionfish, 139
*frontalis, Ecsenius,* Brown-gold Blenny, 528.06
*frontalis, Microspathodon,* Ghana Yellowtail Damselfish, 408
*frontalis, Scarus,* Blue Parrotfish, 483
*fronticinctus, Cantherhines,* Indo-Pacific Leatherjacket, 632
*fronticinctus, Hoplolatilus,* Pastel Tilefish, 238
*fronto, Pataecus,* Red Indianfish, 159
*fucata, Archamia,* Redbarred Cardinalfish, 235
*fuliginosa, Lotella,* Beardie, 77
*fulva, Cephalopholis,* Coney, 184
*fulviflammus, Lutjanus,* Golden Snapper, 260
*fulvoguttatus, Carangoides,* Yellowspotted Kingfish, 247, 249
*fulvus, Lutjanus,* Red and Green Snapper, 262
*fumea, Chromis,* Smoky Chromis, 386
*funebris, Gymnothorax,* Green Moray, 55
*furcatus, Aphareus,* Blue Smalltooth Jobfish, 260
*furcatus, Phanerodon,* White Surfperch, 370
*furcatus, Pomadasys,* Grey Grunter, 281
*furcifer, Paranthias,* Creole-fish, 178
*fusca, Brotulina,* Dusky Brotulid, 81
*fuscescens, Siganus,* Dusky Spinefoot, 597
*fuscidorsalis, Pomachromis,* Tahitian Reef-damsel, 395
*fuscipinnis, Odontanthias,* Lyretail Fairy Grouper, 180
*fuscocaudatus, Amphiprion,* Dusky-tail Anemonefish, 373
*fuscoguttatus, Epinephelus,* Blotchy Grouper, 187
*fuscolineata, Siphamia,* Crown-of-thorns Cardinalfish, 237
*fuscus, Apsilus,* Cape Verde Snapper, 259
*fuscus, Atrosalarias,* Dusky Blenny, 527
*fuscus, Cheilodactylus,* Red Morwong, 416
*fuscus, Dialommus,* Higheye Blenny, 515
*fuscus, Kyphosus,* Ash-colored Rudderfish, 329
*fuscus, Pseudobalistes,* Blue-and-Gold Triggerfish, 616, 626
*fuscus, Pseudochromis,* Brown Dottyback, 209
*Fusigobius neophytus,* Dusky Fusegoby, 570
*Fusigobius* sp., Butterflyfin Goby, 570; Cave Goby, 550
*Fusigobius* sp.*(neophytus?),* Goby, unidentified, 550
Fusilier Damsel, *Lepidozygus tapeinosoma,* 381

## G

*Gadus macrocephalus,* Gray Cod, 78
*Gadus morhua,* Atlantic Cod, 78

Gafftopsail Pompano, *Trachinotus rhodopus*, 254
Gag, *Mycteroperca microlepis*, 194
*Gaidropsarus ensis*, Threebeard Rockling, 78
*gaimard africana, Coris*, African Clown Wrasse, 439
*gaimard, Coris*, Clown Wrasse, 472
Galapagos Hogfish, *Bodianus eclancheri*, 430
Galapagos Sawtail, *Prionurus laticlavius*, 588
*galba, Chrysiptera*, Canary Demoiselle, 390
*Galeocerdo cuvieri*, Tiger Shark, 39, 40
*Galeus sauteri*, Gecko Shark, 37
*galii, Meuschenia*, Blue-lined Leatherjacket, 630
*gardneri, Chaetodon*, Gardner's Butterflyfish, 338
Gardner's Butterflyfish, *Chaetodon gardneri*, 338
Garibaldi, *Hypsypops rubicunda*, 397
Garnet Red Parrotfish, *Scarus sordidus*, 482, 490
*garnoti, Halichoeres*, Yellowhead Wrasse, 447
*garretti, Pseudomonacanthus*, Garrett's Slender Filefish, 633
Garrett's Slender Filefish, *Pseudomonacanthus garretti*, 633
Garrupa, *Cephalopholis aurantia*, 182
*gascoynei, Stegastes*, Coral Sea Gregory, 405
*gaterinus, Plectorhinchus*, Black-spotted Rubberlip, 282, 285
*gattorugine, Parablennius*, Tompot Blenny, 530
*Gazza minuta*, Toothed Pony Fish, 256
Gecko Goby, *Chriolepis zebra*, 567
Gecko Shark, *Galeus sauteri*, 37
*gelatinosa, Pseudamia*, Jelly Cardinalfish, 237
*gemma, Hypoplectrus*, Blue Hamlet, 201
*gemmatum, Zebrasoma*, Spotted Sailfin Tang, 592, 594
*Gempylus serpens*, Snake Mackerel, 601
*geneionema, Sagamia*, Bearded Goby, 546
*Genicanthus bellus*, Bellus Lyretail Angelfish, 359
*Genicanthus caudovittatus*, Zebra Lyretail Angelfish, 357
*Genicanthus lamarck*, Freckletail Lyretail Angelfish, 359
*Genicanthus melanospilus*, Blackspot Lyretail Angelfish, 358
*Genicanthus personatus*, Masked Lyretail Angelfish, 359
*Genicanthus semicinctus*, Half-striped Lyretail Angelfish, 358
*Genicanthus semifasciatus*, Half-banded Lyretail Angelfish, 358
*Genicanthus watanabei*, Watanabe's Lyretail Angelfish, 358
*genie, Gobiosoma*, Genie's Cleaning Goby, 573
Genie's Cleaning Goby, *Gobiosoma genie*, 573
*genivittatum, Thalassoma*, Redcheek Wrasse, 465, 467
*gentilis, Hypsoblennius*, Bay Blenny, 530
*Genyonemus lineatus*, White Croaker, 311
*geoffroyi, Macropharyngodon*, Geoffroy's Wrasse, 452
Geoffroy's Wrasse, *Macropharyngodon geoffroyi*, 452
*geographicus, Anampses*, Black-spotted Tamarin, 425, 477
Geometric Moray, *Siderea grisea*, 59
*georgianus, Arripes*, King George's Salmon, 257
*georgianus, Scorpis*, Banded Sweep, 327
*Gephyroberyx japonicus*, Japanese Slimefish, 103
*germaini, Omobranchus*, Germain's Blenny, 525
Germain's Blenny, *Omobranchus germaini*, 525
*Gerres abbreviatus*, Blue-backed Silver-Biddy, 276
*Gerres acinaces*, Smallscale Pursemouth, 275, 276
*Gerres baconensis*, Ghost Mojarra, 274
*Gerres cinereus*, Yellowfin Mojarra, 275
*Gerres filamentosus*, Long-rayed Silver-Biddy, 275, 276
*Gerres kapas*, Singapore Silver-Biddy, 276
*Gerres macracanthus*, Thread-fin Silver-Biddy, 276
*Gerres macrosoma*, Large-bodied Silver-Biddy, 276
*Gerres oyena*, Slenderspine Pursemouth, 274, 276
*Gerres poeti*, Deep-bodied Silver-Biddy, 276
Ghana Butterflyfish, *Chaetodon robustus*, 335
Ghana Goby, Gobiidae sp. 2, 548; Gobiidae sp. 3, 548
Ghana Rockcod, *Cephalopholis taeniops*, 184
Ghana Yellowtail Damselfish, *Microspathodon frontalis*, 408
*ghanam, Scolopsis*, Paleband Spinecheek, 282
*ghobban, Scarus*, Blue-barred Orange Parrotfish, 482, 485
Ghost Cardinalfish, *Apogon savayensis*, 229
Ghost Goby, *Ptereleotris monoptera*, 561
Ghost Mojarra, *Gerres baconensis*, 274
Ghost Pipefish, *Solenostomus paegnis*, 123
Ghost Shark, *Chimaera phantasma*, 33
Ghost Snake Eel, *Brachysomophis cirrhocheilus*, 64
Giant Chilean Clingfish, *Sicyases sanguineus*, 96
Giant Damselfish, *Microspathodon dorsalis*, 408
Giant Hawkfish, *Cirrhitus rivulatus*, 412
Giant Jawfish, *Opistognathus rhomaleus*, 497, 498
Giant Kelpfish, *Heterostichus rostratus*, 516
Giant Moray, *Gymnothorax javanicus*, 59, 60
Giant Sea Bass, *Stereolepis gigas*, 172, 173
Giant Sleepy Shark, *Nebrius concolor*, 35
Giant Trevally, *Caranx ignobilis*, 247, 249
*gibbifrons, Istiblennius*, Hump-headed Blenny, 531
*Gibbonsia metzi*, Striped Kelpfish, 516
*gibbosa, Scorpaenopsis*, Humpback Scorpionfish, 147
*gibbosus, Cheilodactylus*, Magpie Morwong, 417
*gibbosus, Tetrasomus*, Thornbacked Boxfish, 638
*gibbus, Lutjanus*, Humpback Snapper, 262, 266
*gibbus, Scarus*, Bumphead Parrotfish, 480, 482, 484, 491, 492
Gibert's Irish Lord, *Hemilepidotus gilberti*, 165
*gibsoni, Kyphosus*, Northern Buffalo Bream, 329
*gigas, Malacoctenus*, Sonara Blenny, 514
*gigas, Stereolepis*, Giant Sea Bass, 172, 173
*gilberti, Apogon*, Gilbert's Cardinalfish, 226
*gilberti, Citharichthys*, Gilbert's Sanddab, 609
*gilberti, Hemilepidotus*, Gibert's Irish Lord, 165
*gilberti, Opistognathus*, Yellow Jawfish, 496, 499
*gilberti, Scombrops*, Japanese Bluefish, 244
Gilbert's Cardinalfish, *Apogon gilberti*, 226
Gilbert's Sanddab, *Citharichthys gilberti*, 609
Gilded Pipefish, *Corythoichthys schultzi*, 128
Gill-rakered Needlefish, *Platybelone argalus*, 100
*Gillelus greyae*, Arrow Stargazer, 512
*gilli, Malacoctenus*, Gill's Blenny, 515
*Gilloblennius tripennis*, Spectacled Blenny, 508
Gill's Blenny, *Malacoctenus gilli*, 515
*Ginglymostoma cirratum*, Nurse Shark, 35
*Ginsburgellus novemlineatus*, Nineline Goby, 575
*girardi, Pseudojulis*, Girard's Wrasse, 476
Girard's Wrasse, *Pseudojulis girardi*, 476
Girdled Blenny, *Malacoctenus zonifer*, 514
Girdled Cardinalfish, *Archamia zosterophora*, 235
Girdled Goby, *Priolepis cincta*, 566
Girdled Moray, *Echidna pozyzona*, 53
*Girella mezina*, Yellow-striped Blackfish, 326
*Girella nigricans*, Opaleye, 326
*Girella punctata*, Rudderfish, 326
*Girella simplicidens*, Gulf Opaleye, 326
*Girella tephraeops*, Western Rock Blackfish, 326
*Girella tricuspidatus*, Blackfish, 325, 369
*Girella zebra*, Zebrafish, 326
*gissu, Pterothrissus*, Deepsea Bonefish, 50
*gladius, Xiphias*, Swordfish, 604

Glass Blenny, *Coralliozetus diaphanus,* 520
Glassfish, *Chanda ranga,* 170
Glassy Bombay Duck, *Harpadon translucens,* 73
*glauca, Chrysiptera,* Gray Demoiselle, 390, 394
*glaucofrenum, Coryphopterus,* Bridled Goby, 574
*glaucopareius, Acanthurus,* Gold-rimmed Surgeonfish, 583
*Glaucosoma hebraicum,* West Australian Jewfish, 212
*glesne, Regalecus,* Long Oarfish, 103
*gloriamaris, Cleidopus,* Knight-fish, 101, 103
*gloveri, Lagocephalus,* Brown-backed Puffer, 643
*gloveri, Rhycherus,* Glover's Frogfish, 85
Glover's Frogfish, *Rhycherus gloveri,* 85
Glowlight Bullseye, *Pempheris adspersa,* 322
Gluttonous Goby, *Chasmichthys gulosus,* 565
*Glyptauchen panduratus,* Goblinfish, 158
*Glyptoparus delicatulus,* Crescent Throat Blenny, 527
*Gnathagnus elongatus,* Bluespotted Stargazer, 501
*Gnathanodon speciosus,* Golden Trevally, 246, 247
*Gnathodentex aurolineatus,* Gold-lined Sea Bream, 296, 298
*Gnatholepis deltoides,* Peacockfin Goby, 558
*Gnatholepis inconsequens,* Orange-ear Goby, 558
*Gnatholepis* sp., Blotched African Goby, 558; Goby, unidentified, 544, 570
*Gnatholepis thompsoni,* Thompson's Goby, 558
*Gnathophis nystromi,* Nystrom's Conger Eel, 62
Gnomefish, *Scombrops boops,* 244
Gobbleguts, *Apogon ruppelli,* 229
Gobiesocidae sp., Recherche Clingfish, 96
*Gobiesocidae* sp., Clingfish, unidentified, 96
*Gobiesox adustus,* Panamic Clingfish, 97
*Gobiesox maeandricus,* Northern Clingfish, 97
Gobiidae sp., Crimson-eyed Coral Goby, 567; Goby, unidentified, 544, 557, 563
Gobiidae sp. 2, Ghana Goby, 548
Gobiidae sp. 1, Orange-spotted African Goby, 548
Gobiidae sp. 3, Ghana Goby, 548
Gobiidae sp. 5, Banded African Goby, 548
*Gobiodon atrangulatus,* Earspot Coral Goby, 578
*Gobiodon citrinus,* Citron Goby, 570
*Gobiodon histrio,* Blue-spotted Coral Goby, 578
*Gobiodon multilineatus,* Manylined Coral Goby, 578
*Gobiodon okinawae,* Yellow Coral Goby, 578
*Gobiodon quinquestrigatus,* Bicolored Coral Goby, 578
*Gobiodon rivulatus,* Rippled Coral Goby, 578
*Gobionellus saepepallens?,* Dash Goby, 561
*Gobionellus saepepallens,* Dash Goby, 565
*Gobionellus stigmalophius,* Spotfin Goby, 565
*Gobionellus stigmaticus,* Mashed Goby, 565
*Gobiosoma* aff *limbaughi,* Widebanded Cleaning Goby, 571
*Gobiosoma atronasum,* Exuma Cleaning Goby, 572
*Gobiosoma chancei,* Shortstripe Cleaning Goby, 572
*Gobiosoma chiquita,* Sonora Goby, 572
*Gobiosoma digueti,* Banded Cleaner Goby, 571
*Gobiosoma evelynae,* Sharknose Goby, 573
*Gobiosoma genie,* Genie's Cleaning Goby, 573
*Gobiosoma horsti,* Yellowline Goby, 572
*Gobiosoma illecebrosum,* Coral-dwelling Cleaning Goby, 573
*Gobiosoma louisae,* Spotlight Goby, 572
*Gobiosoma macrodon,* Tiger Goby, 571
*Gobiosoma multifasciatum,* Greenband Goby, 571
*Gobiosoma oceanops,* Neon Goby, 573
*Gobiosoma prochilus,* West Indian Cleaning Goby, 572
*Gobiosoma puncticulatus,* Redhead Goby, 571
*Gobiosoma randalli,* Yellownose Goby, 573
*Gobiosoma saucrum,* Goldspot Goby, 571
*Gobiosoma* sp., Goby, unidentified, 571; Orangehead Goby, 571
*Gobiosoma tenox,* Slaty Goby, 571
*Gobiosoma xanthiprora,* Yellowstripe Cleaning Goby, 573
*Gobius auratus,* Golden Goby, 559
*Gobius bucchichii,* Bucchichi's Goby, 559
*Gobius casamancus,* Casamance River Goby, 548
*Gobius cruentatus,* Redmouth Goby, 559
*Gobius elanthematicus,* Black Sea Goby, 559
*Gobius niger,* Mediterranean Black Goby, 559
*Gobius vittatus,* Mediterranean Banded Goby, 559
Goblin Devilfish, *Inimicus sinensis,* 158
Goblinfish, *Glyptauchen panduratus,* 158
*Gobulus myersi,* Paleback Goby, 553
Goby, unidentified, *Coryphopterus* sp., 574; *Fusigobius* sp.*(neophytus?),* 550; *Gnatholepis* sp., 544, 570; Gobiidae sp., 544, 557, 563; *Gobiosoma* sp., 571
Goddess Rainbowfish, *Xyrichthys dea,* 457
Gold-band Fusilier, *Pterocaesio lativittata,* 271
Gold-bar Snapper, *Tropidinus zonatus,* 269
Gold-eyed Snapper, *Lutjanus adetii,* 261
Gold-lined Sea Bream, *Gnathodentex aurolineatus,* 296, 298
Gold-lined Threadfin Bream, *Nemipterus gracilis,* 306
Gold-rimmed Surgeonfish, *Acanthurus glaucopareius,* 583
Gold-spangled Angelfish, *Apolemichthys xanthopunctatus,* 366
Gold-spotted Puffer, *Chelonodon laticeps,* 649
Gold-spotted Spinefoot, *Siganus chrysospilos,* 598, 599
Gold-spotted Sweetlips, *Plectorhinchus multivittatus,* 283
Gold-striped Cardinalfish, *Apogon cyanosoma,* 222, 223
Gold-striped Sardine, *Sardinella* cf *jussieu,* 66
Gold-striped Snapper, *Lutjanus erythropterus,* 266
Goldband Fusilier, *Pterocaesio chrysozona,* 272
Goldband Trevally, *Carangoides dinema,* 246
Goldbar Wrasse, *Thalassoma hebraicum,* 467
Goldcheek Devilfish, *Plesiops oxycephalus,* 214
Golden Angelfish, *Centropyge heraldi,* 355
Golden Butterflyfish, *Chaetodon auripes,* 338
Golden Damsel, *Amblyglyphidodon aureus,* 382
Golden Dottyback, *Pseudochromis aureus,* 209; *Pseudochromis luteus,* 207
Golden Goby, *Gobius auratus,* 559
Golden Gregory, *Stegastes aureus,* 405
Golden Grubfish, *Parapercis aurantica,* 502
Golden Hawkfish, *Paracirrhites xanthus,* 415
Golden Mimic Blenny, *Plagiotremus laudandus flavus,* 521
Golden Mini-Grouper, *Assessor flavissimus,* 213
Golden Orange Rockcod, *Cephalopholis analis,* 184
Golden Pollock, *Pollachius pollachius,* 76, 77
Golden Puffer, *Arothron meleagris,* 645, 646
Golden Rainbowfish, *Halichoeres chrysus,* 440
Golden Redfish, *Sebastes marinus,* 151
Golden Sea Bream, *Pagrus auratus,* 290
Golden Snapper, *Lutjanus fulviflammus,* 260
Golden Spotted Rock Bass, *Paralabrax auroguttatus,* 202
Golden Threadfin Bream, *Nemipterus virgatus,* 308
Golden Trevally, *Gnathanodon speciosus,* 246, 247
Golden Wrasse, *Pseudojulis melanotus,* 461
Golden Yellow Hawkfish, *Cirrhitichthys aureus,* 412
Golden-girdled Coralfish, *Coradion chrysozonus,* 347, 348
Golden-lined Spinefoot, *Siganus lineatus,* 598, 600

Golden-spotted Goatfish, *Parupeneus luteus*, 319
Goldentail Moray, *Muraena miliaris*, 60
*goldmanni, Istigobius*, Goldmann's Goby, 563
*goldmanni, Plectorhinchus*, Goldman's Sweetlips, 284, 286
Goldmann's Goby, *Istigobius goldmanni*, 563
Goldman's Sweetlips, *Plectorhinchus goldmanni*, 284, 286
Goldribbon Soapfish, *Aulacocephalus temmincki*, 204
Goldsaddle Hogfish, *Bodianus perdito*, 428
Goldspot Goby, *Gobiosoma saucrum*, 571
Goldspotted Snake Eel, *Myrichthys oculatus*, 61
Goldtail Angelfish, *Pomacanthus chrysurus*, 364
*Gomphosus caeruleus*, Blue Bird Wrasse, 449
*Gomphosus varius*, Bird Wrasse, 439, 449
*Gonioplectrus hispanus*, Spanish Flag, 181
*Gonostoma elongatum*, Angle-mouthed Lanternfish, 70
*goodei, Trachinotus*, Palometa, 254, 255
*goodladi, Callionymus*, Goodlad's Dragonet, 537
Goodlad's Dragonet, *Callionymus goodladi*, 537
Goose Scorpionfish, *Rhinopias frondosa*, 139
Goosehead Scorpionfish, *Scorpaena bergi*, 145
Gopher Rockfish, *Sebastes carnatus*, 149
*Gorgasia maculata*, Spotted Garden Eel, 64
*Gorgasia preclara*, Philippine Garden Eel, 63, 64
Gorgeous Goby, *Lythrypnus pulchellus*, 575
*goslinei, Plagiotremus*, Gosline's Mimic Blenny, 521
Gosline's Mimic Blenny, *Plagiotremus goslinei*, 521
Gossamer Blenny, *Omobranchus ferox*, 525
*gouldii, Achoerodus*, Blue Groper, 429
Gowan's Clingfish, *Lepadogaster lepadogaster*, 97
Graceful Lizardfish, *Saurida gracilis*, 72, 75
Graceful Pearlfish, *Encheliophis gracilis*, 81
*Gracila albomarginata*, Blue-striped Grouper, 182
*graciliosa, Lotilia*, White-capped Prawn Goby, 553
*gracilis, Acentrogobius*, Mangrove Goby, 551
*gracilis, Eleginus*, Saffron Cod, 77
*gracilis, Encheliophis*, Graceful Pearlfish, 81
*gracilis, Eucinostomus*, Pacific Flagfin Mojarra, 275
*gracilis, Hymenocephalus*, Grenadier, 78
*gracilis, Nemipterus*, Gold-lined Threadfin Bream, 306
*gracilis, Rhabdamia*, Arrow Cardinal, 222
*gracilis, Saurida*, Graceful Lizardfish, 72, 75
*gracilis, Suezichthys*, Brownstripe Wrasse, 464
*graclis, Ophiclinus*, Dark-backed Snake Blenny, 516
*Gramma linki*, Yellowlined Basslet, 213
*Gramma loreto*, Royal Gramma, 213
*Gramma melacara*, Blackcap Basslet, 213
*Grammatorcynus bicarinatus*, Double-lined Mackerel, 603
Grammistes Blenny, *Meiacanthus grammistes*, 522
*Grammistes sexlineatus*, Sixstripe Soapfish, 204, 206
*grammistes, Meiacanthus*, Grammistes Blenny, 522
*Grammistops ocellatus*, Ocellated Soapfish, 206
*grammodon?, Owstonia*, Owstonia, 420
*grammorhynchus, Pomacentrus*, Blue-spot Damsel, 402
*grandicornis, Scorpaena*, Grass Scorpionfish, 144
*grandisquammis, Pseudupeneus*, Bigscale Goatfish, 314
*grandoculis, Monotaxis*, Big-eye, 296, 301
*granulatus, Scobinichthys*, Rough Leatherjacket, 630, 634
Grass Puffer, *Takifugu niphobles*, 648
Grass Scorpionfish, *Scorpaena grandicornis*, 144
*gravieri, Ecsenius*, Red Sea Mimic Blenny, 523, 533
Gray Angelfish, *Pomacanthus arcuatus*, 362
Gray Chromis, *Chromis axillaris*, 383
Gray Cod, *Gadus macrocephalus*, 78
Gray Demoiselle, *Chrysiptera glauca*, 390, 394
Gray Lance, *Haliophis guttatus*, 500
Gray Moray, *Gymnothorax nubilis*, 57
Gray Reef Shark, *Carcharhinus amblyrhynchos*, 39, 40
Gray Snapper, *Lutjanus griseus*, 265
Gray Triggerfish, *Balistes capriscus*, 625
Graybar Grunt, *Haemulon sexfasciatum*, 280
*grayi, Halicampus*, Gray's Pipefish, 126
Gray's Crested Flounder, *Samaris cristatus*, 613
Gray's Pipefish, *Halicampus grayi*, 126
Grayshy, *Cephalopholis cruentatus*, 184
Greasy Rock Cod, *Epinephelus tauvina*, 188
Great Barracuda, *Sphyraena barracuda*, 422, 423
Greater Amberjack, *Seriola dumerili*, 250, 252
Greater Soapfish, *Rypticus saponaceus*, 207
Green Clingfish, *Lepadichthys frenatus*, 97
Green Hata, *Epinephelus awoara*, 186
Green Jack, *Caranx caballus*, 249
Green Jobfish, *Aprion virescens*, 259
Green Moray, *Gymnothorax funebris*, 55
Green Parrotfish, *Scarus dubius*, 484
Green Razorfish, *Xyrichthys splendens*, 456
Green Wrasse, *Halichoeres chloropterus*, 443, 445, 475
Greenback Fairy Wrasse, *Cirrhilabrus scottorum*, 435
Greenband Goby, *Gobiosoma multifasciatum*, 571
Greenband Wrasse, *Halichoeres bathyphilus*, 446
Greenbeak Parrotfish, *Scarus prasiognathos*, 481, 485, 490, 492
Greenblotch Parrotfish, *Sparisoma atomarium*, 487
Greengar, *Strongylura anastomella*, 100
Greenling, *Pleurogrammus azonus*, 163
Greenling, unidentified, *Hexagrammos* sp., 162
*gregoryi, Pseudogramma*, Reef Bass, 206
Grenadier, *Hymenocephalus gracilis*, 78
Grey Grunter, *Pomadasys furcatus*, 281
*greyae, Gillelus*, Arrow Stargazer, 512
*grigorjewi, Eopsetta*, Grigorjew's Halibut, 608, 611
*grigorjewi, Stichaeus*, Grigorjew's Shanny, 501
Grigorjew's Halibut, *Eopsetta grigorjewi*, 608, 611
Grigorjew's Shanny, *Stichaeus grigorjewi*, 501
*grisea, Siderea*, Geometric Moray, 59
*griseum, Chiloscyllium*, Brown Carpet Shark, 36
*griseus, Gymnocranius*, Naked-head Sea Bream, 293, 296
*griseus, Lutjanus*, Gray Snapper, 265
*gronovii, Nomeus*, Portuguese Man-O-War Fish, 605, 606
Grooved Razorfish, *Centriscus scutatus*, 123
Grouper, unidentified, *Epinephelus* sp., 188
Grunt Sculpin, *Rhamphocottus richardsoni*, 166
*guacamaia, Scarus*, Rainbow Parrotfish, 485
Guamanian Damsel, *Pomachromis guamensis*, 395
*guamensis, Apogon*, Pearl Cardinalfish, 229
*guamensis, Pomachromis*, Guamanian Damsel, 395
*guentheri, Chaetodon*, Guenther's Butterflyfish, 343
*guentheri, Hoplopagrus*, Barred Pargo, 269
Guenther's Butterflyfish, *Chaetodon guentheri*, 343
*guichenoti, Cirrhitichthys*, Guichenot's Hawkfish, 411
Guichenot's Hawkfish, *Cirrhitichthys guichenoti*, 411
Guinea Fowl Wrasse, *Macropharyngodon meleagris*, 452, 473
Guineafowl Moray, *Gymnothorax meleagris*, 56
*gula, Eucinostomus*, Silver Jenny, 275
Gulf Coney, *Epinephelus acanthistius*, 191
Gulf Damsel, *Pristotis jerdoni*, 408

Gulf Opaleye, *Girella simplicidens*, 326
*gulosus, Chasmichthys*, Gluttonous Goby, 565
*gummigutta, Hypoplectrus*, Orange Hamlet, 201
*Gunnelichthys curiosus*, Yellow-striped Worm Eel, 511, 580
*Gunnelichthys monostigma*, One-spot Worm Eel, 511, 580
*Gunnelichthys pleurotaenia*, Black-striped Worm Eel, 580
*gunnellus, Pholis*, Rock Gunnel, 495
*guntheri, Pseudolabrus*, Gunther's Rainbowfish, 464
Gunther's Rainbowfish, *Pseudolabrus guntheri*, 464
Gunther's Sculpin, *Cottus pollux*, 164
Gurnard Scorpion Perch, *Neosebastes pandus*, 137
*guttata, Amblyeleotris*, Orange-spotted Prawn Goby, 545
*guttata, Inegocia*, Spotted Crocodile Flathead, 162
*guttata, Scorpaena*, California Scorpionfish, 145
*guttatissimus, Chaetodon*, Peppered Butterflyfish, 344
*guttatus, Acanthurus*, Mustard Surgeonfish, 583
*guttatus, Epinephelus*, Red Hind, 192
*guttatus, Haliophis*, Gray Lance, 500
*guttatus, Lampris*, Moonfish, 103
*guttatus, Lutjanus*, Spotted Rose Snapper, 264
*guttatus, Salarias*, Blue-spot Blenny, 527
*guttatus, Scomberomorus*, King Spanish Mackerel, 603
*guttatus, Siganus*, Yellow-blotch Spinefoot, 598
*guttavarius, Hypoplectrus*, Shy Hamlet, 201
*guttulata, Hypsopsetta*, Diamond Turbot, 611
Guyana Butterflyfish, *Chaetodon guyanensis*, 347
*guyanensis, Chaetodon*, Guyana Butterflyfish, 347
*Gymnapogon urospilotus*, Spotted-tail Cardinalfish, 222
*Gymneleotris seminudus*, Split-banded Goby, 567
*Gymnocaesio gymnopterus*, Torpedo, 272
*Gymnocanthus detrisus*, Barfin Sculpin, 164
*Gymnocanthus herzensteini*, Black-edged Sculpin, 164
*gymnocephala, Amblyeleotris*, Brownstreak Prawn Goby, 545
*Gymnocranius bitorquatus*, Collared Sea Bream, 290
*Gymnocranius griseus*, Naked-head Sea Bream, 293, 296
*Gymnocranius japonicus*, Silver Large-eye Bream, 290
*Gymnocranius lethrinoides*, Red-tailed Sea Bream, 290, 296
*gymnogenis, Pseudolabrus*, White-spotted Rainbowfish, 464
*Gymnomuraena zebra*, Zebra Moray, 54
*gymnopterus, Gymnocaesio*, Torpedo, 272
*Gymnosarda unicolor*, Dogtooth Tuna, 603
*gymnostethius, Bellator*, Searobin, 160
*Gymnothorax breedeni*, Blackcheek Moray, 58
*Gymnothorax castaneus*, Panamic Green Moray, 55
*Gymnothorax eurostus*, Wakanoura Moray, 54
*Gymnothorax favagineus*, Honeycomb Moray, 58, 59
*Gymnothorax fimbriatus*, Dark-spotted Moray, 54
*Gymnothorax flavimarginatus*, Yellow-edged Moray, 55, 56, 58
*Gymnothorax funebris*, Green Moray, 55
*Gymnothorax javanicus*, Giant Moray, 59, 60
*Gymnothorax kidako*, Kidako Moray Eel, 51, 57
*Gymnothorax leucostigma*, Yellowblotch Moray, 57
*Gymnothorax margaritophorus*, Trunk-eyed Moray, 56
*Gymnothorax melatremus*, Blackspot Moray, 56
*Gymnothorax meleagris*, Guineafowl Moray, 56
*Gymnothorax mordax*, California Moray, 55
*Gymnothorax moringa*, Spotted Moray, 55
*Gymnothorax nubilis*, Gray Moray, 57
*Gymnothorax nudivomer*, Starry Moray, 56
*Gymnothorax obesus*, Speckled Moray, 57
*Gymnothorax panamensis*, Masked Moray, 55
*Gymnothorax permistus*, Reticulated Moray, 56
*Gymnothorax prasinus*, Brown Moray, 58, 60
*Gymnothorax prionodon*, Mottled Moray, 57
*Gymnothorax ramosus*, Mosaic Moray, 57
*Gymnothorax rueppelliae*, Banded Moray, 54
*Gymnothorax* sp., Moray eel, unidentified, 52, 57
*Gymnothorax steindachneri*, Steindachner's Moray Eel, 54
*Gymnothorax thyrsoideus*, Yellow-lined Moray, 54
*Gymnothorax undulatus*, Leopard Moray, 58
*Gymnothorax vicinus*, Purplemouth Moray, 55
*Gymnothorax woodwardi*, Woodward's Moray, 54
*Gymnothorax zonipectus*, Bar-tail Moray, 58
*Gymnura japonica*, Japanese Butterfly Ray, 45
*Gymnura micrura*, Butterfly Ray, 45

## H

*haackei, Parapercis*, Wavy Grubfish, 504
*haackei, Platycephalus*, Haacke's Flathead, 72
Haacke's Flathead, *Platycephalus haackei*, 72
*haematopterus, Corythoichthys*, Messmate Pipefish, 128
*haematopterus, Lethrinus*, Deep-bodied Emperor, 295
*Haemulon album*, Margate, 279
*Haemulon aureolineatum*, Tomtate, 279
*Haemulon chrysargyreum*, Smallmouth Grunt, 279
*Haemulon flaviguttatum*, Pacific Lined Grunt, 280
*Haemulon flavolineatum*, French Grunt, 277, 278
*Haemulon macrostomum*, Spanish Grunt, 279
*Haemulon melanurum*, Cottonwick, 278
*Haemulon parrai*, Sailor's Choice, 278
*Haemulon plumieri*, White Grunt, 278
*Haemulon sciurus*, Bluestriped Grunt, 278, 279
*Haemulon sexfasciatum*, Graybar Grunt, 280
*Haemulon striatum*, Striped Grunt, 278
Hairy Blenny, *Labrisomus nuchipinnis*, 513
Hairy Stingfish, *Scorpaenopsis oxycephala*, 136, 138, 146, 147
*haitiensis, Labrisomus*, Longfin Blenny, 513
Hakeling, unidentified, *Physiculus* sp., 77
*Halaelurus buergeri*, Burger's Spotted Cat Shark, 37
Half Yellow Pygmy Angelfish, *Centropyge joculator*, 357
Half-and-Half Chromis, *Chromis dimidiata*, 383
Half-and-Half Thicklip, *Hemigymnus melapterus*, 450
Half-banded Goby, *Amblygobius semictus*, 555
Half-banded Lyretail Angelfish, *Genicanthus semifasciatus*, 358
Half-banded Seaperch, *Ellerkeldia hunti*, 199
Half-banded Snake Eel, *Leiuranus semicinctus*, 61
Half-banded Snapper, *Lutjanus semicinctus*, 266
Half-blue Demoiselle, *Chrysiptera hemicyanea*, 393
Half-dotted Hawkfish, *Paracirrhites hemistictus*, 413
Half-striped Lyretail Angelfish, *Genicanthus semicinctus*, 358
Half-tail Blenny, *Xiphasia setifer*, 526
Half-yellow Butterflyfish, *Chaetodon hemichrysus*, 342
Halfmoon, *Medialuna californiensis*, 328
Halfmoon Rock Cod, *Epinephelus rivulatus*, 187
Halfmoon Triggerfish, *Sufflamen chrysopterus*, 624, 627
Halfspotted Grouper, *Cephalopholis hemistiktos*, 184
*Halicampus grayi*, Gray's Pipefish, 126
*Halicampus macrorhynchus*, Whiskered Pipefish, 127
*Halicampus spinirostris*, Spiny-nosed Pipefish, 128
*Halichoeres amboinensis*, Ambon Wrasse, 473
*Halichoeres argus*, Argus Wrasse, 443, 474
*Halichoeres bathyphilus*, Greenband Wrasse, 446
*Halichoeres bimaculatus*, Double-spot Wrasse, 443
*Halichoeres biocellatus*, Red-lined Wrasse, 440, 443

*Halichoeres bivittatus,* Slippery Dick, 447
*Halichoeres brownfieldi,* Brownfield's Wrasse, 441
*Halichoeres chierchiae,* Wounded Wrasse, 448
*Halichoeres chloropterus,* Green Wrasse, 443, 445, 475
*Halichoeres chrysus,* Golden Rainbowfish, 440
*Halichoeres cosmetus,* Adorned Wrasse, 442
*Halichoeres cyanocephalus,* Yellowcheek Wrasse, 446
*Halichoeres dispilus,* Chameleon Wrasse, 448
*Halichoeres garnoti,* Yellowhead Wrasse, 447
*Halichoeres hartzfeldii,* Hartzfeld's Wrasse, 441, 475
*Halichoeres hoeveni,* Yellow-lined Wrasse, 443, 474
*Halichoeres hortulanus,* Checkerboard Wrasse, 445, 472
*Halichoeres iridis,* Radiant Wrasse, 441, 442
*Halichoeres kallochroma,* Kallochrome Wrasse, 474
*Halichoeres maculipinna,* Atlantic Clown Wrasse, 446
*Halichoeres margaritaceus,* Astrolabe Wrasse, 444
*Halichoeres marginatus,* Dusky Wrasse, 440, 444
*Halichoeres melanochir,* Masked Rainbowfish, 442, 445
*Halichoeres melanurus,* Orange-tipped Rainbowfish, 442, 443
*Halichoeres melasmopomas,* Black-eared Wrasse, 442
*Halichoeres miniatus,* Spotted-finned Rainbowfish, 445
*Halichoeres nebulosus,* Picture Wrasse, 440, 444, 473
*Halichoeres nicholsi,* Spinster Wrasse, 448
*Halichoeres nigrescens,* Diamond Wrasse, 444, 473
*Halichoeres ornatissimus,* Red Checkerboard Wrasse, 445
*Halichoeres pardaleocephalus,* Blue-eared Wrasse, 475
*Halichoeres pelicieri,* Pelicier's Wrasse, 442
*Halichoeres pictus,* Atlantic Rainbow Wrasse, 446
*Halichoeres podostigma,* Pale-headed Checkerboard Wrasse, 445, 476
*Halichoeres poecilopterus,* Multicolorfin Rainbowfish, 444
*Halichoeres poeyi,* Blackear Wrasse, 446
*Halichoeres prosopeion,* Purpleheaded Wrasse, 441, 473
*Halichoeres radiatus,* Pudding Wife, 447
*Halichoeres scapularis,* Zigzag Wrasse, 440, 472
*Halichoeres semicinctus,* Rock Wrasse, 448
*Halichoeres* sp., Pacific Yellowcheek Wrasse, 448
*Halichoeres timorensis,* Timor Wrasse, 442
*Halichoeres trimaculatus,* Spottail Rainbowfish, 444, 472
*Halichoeres trispilus,* Four-spot Wrasse, 440, 441
*Halichoeres zeylonicus,* Zeylon Wrasse, 441
*Halieutaea retifera,* Net Batfish, 93
*Halieutaea stellata,* Starry Batfish, 93
*Halieutichthys aculeatus,* Pancake Batfish, 93
*Halimochirurgus alcocki,* Alcock's Longnose Tripodfish, 620
*Haliophis guttatus,* Gray Lance, 500
*halis, Heteroconger,* Caribbean Garden Eel, 63
*halleri, Urolophus,* Round Stingray, 46
*Halophryne diemensis,* Devil Frogfish, 84
*hamiltoni, Manta,* Hamilton's Manta, 48
*hamiltoni, Sphoeroides,* Hamilton's Puffer, 649
*hamiltoni, Thryssa,* Hamilton's Anchovy, 68
Hamilton's Anchovy, *Thryssa hamiltoni,* 68
Hamilton's Manta, *Manta hamiltoni,* 48
Hamilton's Puffer, *Sphoeroides hamiltoni,* 649
Hamlet, *Hypoplectrus unicolor,* 201
*hamrur, Priacanthus,* Crescent-tail Bigeye, 220
*hanae, Ptereleotris,* Blue Hana Goby, 561
*hancocki, Acanthemblemaria,* Hancock's Blenny, 518
Hancock's Blenny, *Acanthemblemaria hancocki,* 518
*hanui, Chromis,* Hawaiian Bicolor Chromis, 387
*Hapalogenys mucronatus,* Yellowtail Barred Grunt, 283
*Hapalogenys nigripinnis,* Black-finned Grunt, 283
*harak, Lethrinus,* Black-spot Emperor, 295, 298
*hardwicke, Thalassoma,* Sixbar Wrasse, 465
*Harengula koningsbergeri,* Koningsberg's Herring, 67
*harengus pallasi, Clupea,* Pacific Herring, 66
*harid, Hipposcarus,* Red-lined Parrotfish, 480, 489
Harlequin Bass, *Serranus tigrinis,* 197
Harlequin Filefish, *Oxymonacanthus longirostris,* 630, 631
Harlequin Fish, *Othos dentex,* 205
Harlequin Pipefish, *Micrognathus ensenadae,* 125
Harlequin Rockcod, *Cephalopholis polleni,* 182
Harlequin Sweetlips, *Plectorhinchus chaetodonoides,* 282, 283, 287
Harlequin Tuskfish, *Lienardella fasciata,* 452, 453
*Harpadon microchir,* Slender Bombay Duck, 73
*Harpadon translucens,* Glassy Bombay Duck, 73
*harringtoni, Artedius,* Scalyhead Sculpin, 164
*hartzfeldii, Apogon,* Hartzfeld's Cardinalfish, 225
*hartzfeldii, Halichoeres,* Hartzfeld's Wrasse, 441, 475
Hartzfeld's Cardinalfish, *Apogon hartzfeldii,* 225
Hartzfeld's Wrasse, *Halichoeres hartzfeldii,* 441, 475
*hasselti, Callogobius,* Hasselt's Goby, 562
*hasselti, Dussumieria,* Hasselt's Round Herring, 65
Hasselt's Goby, *Callogobius hasselti,* 562
Hasselt's Round Herring, *Dussumieria hasselti,* 65
*hassi, Taenioconger,* Hass's Garden Eel, 64
Hass's Garden Eel, *Taenioconger hassi,* 64
*hasta, Pomadasys,* Lined Silver Grunt, 281
*hastatus, Holocentrus,* West African Squirrelfish, 109
Hawaiian Aholehole, *Kuhlia sandvicensis,* 219
Hawaiian Basslet, *Pikea aurora,* 200
Hawaiian Bicolor Chromis, *Chromis hanui,* 387
Hawaiian Blood Red Wrasse, *Verriculus sanguineus,* 435
Hawaiian Blue Parrotfish, *Scarus perspicillatus,* 483
Hawaiian Bristletooth, *Ctenochaetus hawaiiensis,* 589
Hawaiian Chromis, *Chromis ovalis,* 384
Hawaiian Cleaner Wrasse, *Labroides phthirophagus,* 469
Hawaiian Fairy Basslet, *Pseudanthias ventralis hawaiiensis,* 174
Hawaiian Gold-barred Butterflyfish, *Chaetodon excelsa,* 346
Hawaiian Hawkfish, *Cyprinocirrhites* sp., 412
Hawaiian Lionfish, *Pterois sphex,* 140
Hawaiian Pearlyscale Angelfish, *Apolemichthys arcuatus,* 366
Hawaiian Redtail Filefish, *Pervagor aspricaudus,* 633
Hawaiian Rock Damsel, *Plectroglyphidodon sindonis,* 395
Hawaiian Soapfish, *Suttonia lineata,* 207
Hawaiian Squirrelfish, *Sargocentron ensifer,* 110
Hawaiian Stingray, *Dasyatis hawaiiensis,* 45
Hawaiian Threespot Damsel, *Dascyllus albisella,* 378
*hawaiiensis, Ctenochaetus,* Hawaiian Bristletooth, 589
*hawaiiensis, Dasyatis,* Hawaiian Stingray, 45
*hawaiiensis, Elops,* Pacific Ladyfish, 50
*hebraicum, Glaucosoma,* West Australian Jewfish, 212
*hebraicum, Thalassoma,* Goldbar Wrasse, 467
*hectori, Amblygobius,* Hector's Goby, 555
Hector's Goby, *Amblygobius hectori,* 555
*Helcogramma decurrens,* Black-throated Threefin, 507, 511
*Helcogramma* sp., Triplefin, unidentified, 508
*Helcogramma striata,* White Lined Triplefin, 511
*helena, Muraena,* St. Helena Moray, 60
*helenae, Ioglossus,* Hovering Goby, 569
*helfrichi, Nemateleotris,* Helfrich's Firefish, 561
Helfrich's Firefish, *Nemateleotris helfrichi,* 561
*Helicolenus hilgendorfi,* Hilgendorf Saucord, 138

*Helicolenus papillosus,* Jock Stuart Scorpionfish, 138
Heliotrope Eyeband Wrasse, *Coris batuensis,* 475
*hellmuthi, Pentapodus,* Hellmuth's Threadfin Bream, 299
Hellmuth's Threadfin Bream, *Pentapodus hellmuthi,* 299
*helsdingenii, Valenciennea,* Railway Glider, 566
*helvola, Uraspis,* White-tongued Crevalle, 246, 250
*hemichrysus, Chaetodon,* Half-yellow Butterflyfish, 342
*hemicyanea, Chrysiptera,* Half-blue Demoiselle, 393
*Hemiemblemaria simulus,* Mimic Blenny, 519
*Hemiglyphidodon plagiometopon,* Lagoon Damsel, 397
*Hemigymnus fasciatus,* Barred Thicklip, 450
*Hemigymnus melapterus,* Half-and-Half Thicklip, 450
*Hemilepidotus gilberti,* Gibert's Irish Lord, 165
*Hemilepidotus hemilepidotus,* Red Irish Lord, 165
*hemilepidotus, Hemilepidotus,* Red Irish Lord, 165
*Hemiramphus brasiliensis,* Ballyhoo, 100
*Hemiramphus far,* Barred Garfish, 99
*Hemiscyllium ocellatum,* Epaulette Shark, 35
*Hemiscyllium trispeculare,* Speckled Catshark, 35
*hemistictus, Paracirrhites,* Half-dotted Hawkfish, 413
*hemistiktos, Cephalopholis,* Halfspotted Grouper, 184
*Hemitaurichthys multispinus,* Spiny Butterflyfish, 351
*Hemitaurichthys polylepis,* Shy Butterflyfish, 351
*Hemitaurichthys thompsoni,* Thompson's Butterflyfish, 351
*Hemitaurichthys zoster,* Brown-and-White Butterflyfish, 351
*Hemitripteris americanus,* Sea Raven, 165
*Hemitripteris villosus,* Shaggy Sea Raven, 165
*hemphilli, Stathmonotus,* Hemphill's Blenny, 516
Hemphill's Blenny, *Stathmonotus hemphilli,* 516
*Heniochus acuminatus,* Bannerfish, 348, 352
*Heniochus chrysostomus,* Threeband Pennant Coralfish, 352
*Heniochus intermedius,* Red Sea Bannerfish, 352
*Heniochus monoceros,* Masked Bannerfish, 352
*Heniochus pleurotaenia,* Indian Ocean Bannerfish, 348
*Heniochus singularius,* Philippine Pennant Coralfish, 352
*Heniochus varius,* Humphead Bannerfish, 352
*henlei, Mustelus,* Brown Smoothhound, 38
*hepatus, Paracanthurus,* Blue Surgeonfish, 589, 590
*hepatus, Serranus,* Brown Comber, 196
*Heptranchias perlo,* Sharpnose Sevengill Shark, 33
*heraldi, Centropyge,* Golden Angelfish, 355
*Heraldia nocturna,* Herald's Pipefish, 126
Herald's Pipefish, *Heraldia nocturna,* 126
*Hermosilla azurea,* Zebraperch, 326
Herre's Samoan Prawn Goby, *Ctenogobiops aurocingulus,* 546, 547
Herring Cale, *Odax cyanomelas,* 478
Herring, unidentified, *Jenkinsia* sp., 66
*herzensteini, Gymnocanthus,* Black-edged Sculpin, 164
Herzenstein's Righteye Flounder, *Cleisthenes pinetorum herzensteini,* 608
*Heteristius rubrocinctus,* Saddle Stargazer, 512
*Heteroclinus adelaidae,* Adelaide Weedfish, 517
*Heteroclinus eckloniae,* Ecklonia Weedfish, 517
*Heteroclinus roseus,* Pink Weedfish, 517
*Heteroclinus* sp. cf *roseus,* Weedfish, 517
*Heteroclinus whitleyi,* Whitley's Weedfish, 517
*Heteroconger halis,* Caribbean Garden Eel, 63
*Heterodontus francisci,* Horn Shark, 34
*Heterodontus japonicus,* Japanese Horned Shark, 33
*Heterodontus mexicanus,* Mexican Horned Shark, 34
*Heterodontus portusjacksoni,* Port Jackson Shark, 33
*Heterodontus zebra,* Zebra Horn Shark, 34
*Heteromycteris japonicus,* Japanese Sole, 614
*Heteropriacanthus cruentatus,* Dusky-finned Bullseye, 220, 695
*heteropterus, Ptereleotris,* Pale Gudgeon, 568
*heterorhinos, Soleichthys,* Decorated Sole, 615
*Heterostichus rostratus,* Giant Kelpfish, 516
*heterurus, Parapterois,* Blackfoot Lionfish, 140
*heterurus, Serranus,* West African Sea Bass, 196
*hexacanthus, Naso,* Blacktongue Unicornfish, 591
*hexagonatus, Epinephelus,* White Speckled Rock Cod, 187
*hexagonatus, Myripristis,* Oval Soldierfish, 114, 116
*Hexagrammos decagrammus,* Kelp Greenling, 163
*Hexagrammos otakis,* Otakii's Greenling, 162
*Hexagrammos* sp., Greenling, unidentified, 162
*hexagrammus, Ernogrammus,* Brown Blenny, 494
*hexataenia, Pseudocheilinus,* Sixstripe Wrasse, 458
*hexodon, Nemipterus,* Ornate Threadfin Bream, 306, 307, 308
*hexophthalma, Parapercis,* Sharp-nosed Weever, 504
*hians, Ablennes,* Flat Needlefish, 100
Hifin Goby, *Myersina macrostoma,* 552
High-hat, *Equetus acuminatus,* 308
High-middle Pretty Fish, *Hypomesus pretioses japonicus,* 70
Higheye Blenny, *Dialommus fuscus,* 515
Hilgendorf Saucord, *Helicolenus hilgendorfi,* 138
*hilgendorfi, Helicolenus,* Hilgendorf Saucord, 138
*Hilsa reevesii,* Reeve's Shad, 65
*Himantura uarnak,* Coachwhip Ray, 45, 47
Hinalea, *Coris flavovittata,* 438
Hinalea Luahine, *Thalassoma ballieui,* 466
*hipoliti, Priolepis,* Rusty Goby, 567
*Hippichthys penicillus,* Beady Pipefish, 126
*Hippocampus abdominalis,* Big-belly Seahorse, 129
*Hippocampus angustus,* Tigersnout Seahorse, 128
*Hippocampus bargibanti,* Bargibant's Seahorse, 129
*Hippocampus breviceps,* Knobby Seahorse, 129
*Hippocampus coronatus,* Crowned Seahorse, 131
*Hippocampus erectus,* Northern Seahorse, 131, 132
*Hippocampus hippocampus,* European Seahorse, 130
*Hippocampus ingens,* Pacific Seahorse, 130
*Hippocampus japonicus,* Japanese Seahorse, 130
*Hippocampus kuda,* Oceanic Seahorse, 128, 130
*Hippocampus ramulosus,* Mediterranean Seahorse, 130
*Hippocampus reidi,* Longsnout Seahorse, 131
*Hippocampus* sp., Lattice Seahorse, 130
*hippocampus, Hippocampus,* European Seahorse, 130
*hippocrepis, Meuschenia,* Horseshoe Leatherjacket, 630, 632
*Hippoglossoides dubius,* Doubtful Flounder, 613
*Hippoglossoides robustus,* Robust Flounder, 613
*Hippoglossus stenolepis,* Pacific Halibut, 613
*hippos, Caranx,* Crevalle Jack, 249
*hippos, Seriola,* Amberjack, 252
*Hipposcarus caudovittatus,* Whitecrescent Parrotfish, 482
*Hipposcarus harid,* Red-lined Parrotfish, 480, 489
*Hipposcorpaena* sp., Antenna Featherfin Scorpionfish, 156; Featherfin Scorpionfish, 156
*hippurus, Coryphaena,* Dolphinfish, 257, 604
*hiraii, Cypselurus,* Hirai's Flying Fish, 99
Hirai's Flying Fish, *Cypselurus hiraii,* 99
*Hirundichthys* sp., Striped Wing Flying Fish, 99
*hirundinacea, Chelidoperca,* Japanese Sand Bass, 200
*hirundo, Leiocottus,* Lavender Sculpin, 165
*hispanus, Gonioplectrus,* Spanish Flag, 181
*hispidus, Antennarius,* Fishing Frog, 83, 87, 91

*hispidus, Arothron,* Stars and Stripes Puffer, 644, 645, 646
*hispidus, Monacanthus,* Planehead Filefish, 628
*Histiogamphelus cristatus,* Macleay's Crested Pipefish, 126
*Histophryne bougainvillei,* Bougainville's Frogfish, 85
*Histrio histrio,* Sargassum Fish, 85
*histrio, Aruma,* Slow Goby, 564
*histrio, Gobiodon,* Blue-spotted Coral Goby, 578
*histrio, Histrio,* Sargassum Fish, 85
*hoefleri, Chaetodon,* Hoefler's Butterflyfish, 343
Hoefler's Butterflyfish, *Chaetodon hoefleri,* 343
*hoeveni, Halichoeres,* Yellow-lined Wrasse, 443, 474
Hogchoker, *Trinectes maculatus,* 615
Hogfish, *Lachnolaimus maximus,* 470
*Holacanthus africanus,* African Angelfish, 366
*Holacanthus ciliaris,* Queen Angelfish, 367
*Holacanthus clarionensis,* Clarion Angelfish, 367
*Holacanthus isabelita,* Blue Angelfish, 367
*Holacanthus passer,* King Angelfish, 367
*Holacanthus tricolor,* Rock Beauty, 366
*Holacanthus venustus,* Beautiful Angelfish, 366
*holacanthus, Diodon,* Balloonfish, 656
*Holanthias borbonius,* Borbon Fairy Basslet, 180
*Holanthias martinicensis,* Martinique Fairy Basslet, 180
*Holocentrus adscensiones,* Longjaw Squirrelfish, 109
*Holocentrus hastatus,* West African Squirrelfish, 109
*Holocentrus rufus,* Longspine Squirrelfish, 109
*Hologymnosus annulatus,* Finescale Wrasse, 449, 450
*Hologymnosus doliatus,* Ringed Wrasse, 450, 476
*hololepis, Zenion,* Whole-scaled Dory, 118
*homei, Carapus,* Pen Shell Pearlfish, 80
*honckenii, Amblyrhynchotes,* Evileye Pufferfish, 643
Honey Damselfish, *Stegastes mellis,* 407
Honey-head Damsel, *Dischistodus prosopotaenia,* 409
Honeycomb Filefish, *Cantherhines pardalis,* 627
Honeycomb Grouper, *Epinephelus merra,* 186, 189
Honeycomb Moray, *Gymnothorax favagineus,* 58, 59
Honeycomb Podge, *Pseudogramma polycantha,* 206
Honeycomb Rockfish, *Sebastes umbrosus,* 151
Honeycomb Toby, *Canthigaster janthinoptera,* 650
Honeycomb Trunkfish, *Lactophrys polygonia,* 641
*hoplites, Dixiphichthys,* Doublesword Sea Robin, 160
*Hoplolatilus chlupatyi,* Chameleon Tilefish, 240
*Hoplolatilus cuniculus,* Dusky Tilefish, 240, 511
*Hoplolatilus fourmanoiri,* Spotted Tilefish, 240
*Hoplolatilus fronticinctus,* Pastel Tilefish, 238
*Hoplolatilus marcosi,* Redstripe Tilefish, 240
*Hoplolatilus purpureus,* Purple Tilefish, 240
*Hoplolatilus starcki,* Stark's Tilefish, 238, 240
*Hoplopagrus guentheri,* Barred Pargo, 269
*Hoplostethus elongatus,* Slender Roughy, 103
Horn Shark, *Heterodontus francisci,* 34
Horned Squirrelfish, *Sargocentron melanospilus,* 110, 111
Hornyhead Turbot, *Pleuronichthys verticalis,* 612
Horse Crevalle, *Carangoides equula,* 246
Horse Mackerel, *Trachurus japonicus,* 245
Horse-eye Jack, *Caranx latus,* 249
Horseshoe Leatherjacket, *Meuschenia hippocrepis,* 630, 632
*horsti, Gobiosoma,* Yellowline Goby, 572
*hortulanus, Halichoeres,* Checkerboard Wrasse, 445, 472
*hotumatua, Centropyge,* Easter Island Pygmy Angelfish, 356
Houndfish, *Tylosurus crocodilus,* 100
Hovering Goby, *Ioglossus helenae,* 569
*howensis, Amphichaetodon,* Broad-barred Butterflyfish, 350
*howensis, Cantherhines,* Lord Howe Leatherjacket, 632
*humeralis, Chaetodon,* East Pacific Banded Butterflyfish, 343
*humeralis, Tomicodon,* Sonora Clingfish, 97
Hump-headed Blenny, *Istiblennius gibbifrons,* 531
Humpback Scorpionfish, *Scorpaenopsis gibbosa,* 147
Humpback Snapper, *Lutjanus gibbus,* 262, 266
Humpback Unicornfish, *Naso brachycentron,* 591
Humphead Bannerfish, *Heniochus varius,* 352
Humphead Parrotfish, *Bolbometopon muricatus,* 484
Humphead Wrasse, *Cheilinus undulatus,* 433, 477
Humpnose Unicornfish, *Naso tuberosus,* 590
Hunchback Scorpionfish, *Scorpaena* sp., 145
*hunti, Ellerkeldia,* Half-banded Seaperch, 199
*hutchi, Pseudanthias,* Sea Goldie, 177
*hyalosoma, Apogon,* Translucent Cardinalfish, 227
*Hydrolagus colliei,* Spotted Ratfish, 34
*Hymenocephalus gracilis,* Grenadier, 78
*hynnicephalus, Rhinobatos,* Decorated Guitarfish, 44
*hypacanthus, Emblemaria,* Signae Blenny, 520
*Hyperoglyphe japonica,* Japanese Butterfish, 606
*Hyperprosopon ellipticum,* Silver Surfperch, 370
*Hypleurochilus bermudensis,* Barred Blenny, 530
*Hypnos monopterygium,* South Australian Numbfish, 42
*Hypnos subnigrum,* Australian Numbfish, 42
*Hypodytes leucogaster,* Whitebelly Sailfin Scorpionfish, 159
*Hypodytes longispinis,* Longspine Sailfin Scorpionfish, 156
*Hypodytes rubripinnis,* Redfin Sailfin Scorpionfish, 159
*Hypodytes* sp., Sailfin Scorpionfish, 159
*Hypomesus olidus,* Pond Smelt, 70
*Hypomesus pretioses japonicus,* High-middle Pretty Fish, 70
*hypoplecta, Rathbunella,* Smooth Ronqiul, 494
*Hypoplectrodes nigrorubrum,* Black-banded Seaperch, 199
*Hypoplectrus chlorurus,* Yellowtail Hamlet, 201
*Hypoplectrus gemma,* Blue Hamlet, 201
*Hypoplectrus gummigutta,* Orange Hamlet, 201
*Hypoplectrus guttavarius,* Shy Hamlet, 201
*Hypoplectrus indigo,* Indigo Hamlet, 201
*Hypoplectrus nigricans,* Black Hamlet, 201
*Hypoplectrus puella,* Barred Hamlet, 201
*Hypoplectrus unicolor,* Hamlet, 201
*Hyporhamphus dussumieri,* Dussumier's Halfbeak, 100
*Hyporhamphus melanochir,* Southern Sea Garfish, 100
*Hyporhamphus sajori,* Japanese Halfbeak, 100
*hypselepis, Chromis,* Brown Puller, 386
*hypselogenion, Amblyrhynchotes,* Bar-cheeked Toadfish, 643, 646
*hypselopterus, Lethrinus,* Mozambique Emperor, 295, 297
*Hypsoblennius brevipinnis,* Barnacle Bill Blenny, 530
*Hypsoblennius gentilis,* Bay Blenny, 530
*Hypsopsetta guttulata,* Diamond Turbot, 611
*Hypsurus caryi,* Rainbow Surfperch, 368, 370
*Hypsypops rubicunda,* Garibaldi, 397
*hystrix, Diodon,* Porcupinefish, 618, 653, 654, 656

# I

*Ichthyoscopus lebeck,* Stargazer, 500
*ignitus, Mirolabrichthys,* Flame Basslet, 174
*ignobilis, Caranx,* Giant Trevally, 247, 249
*ijimai, Neosynchiropus,* Ijima's Dragonet, 536
Ijima's Dragonet, *Neosynchiropus ijimai,* 536
*Ilisha elongata,* Elongate Scute Herring, 67
*illecebrosum, Gobiosoma,* Coral-dwelling Cleaning Goby, 573

*imbricata, Stegastes,* Darwin's Damselfish, 407
*imeldae, Mirolabrichthys,* Imelda's Seaperch, 175, 178
Imelda's Seaperch, *Mirolabrichthys imeldae,* 175, 178
*immaculatus, Arothron,* Black-edged Puffer, 648
*immaculatus, Mecaenichthys,* Ogilby's Puller, 409
*immaculatus, Ostracion,* Bluespotted Boxfish, 639
*imparipennis, Plectroglyphidodon,* Bright Eye, 395
*imperator, Pomacanthus,* Emperor Angelfish,' 363
Impostor Boxfish, *Ostracion trachys,* 638
*impressa, Ariosoma,* Bandtooth Conger, 63
*incisa, Norfolkia,* Incised Triplefin, 510
Incised Triplefin, *Norfolkia incisa,* 510
*incisor, Kyphosus,* Yellow Chub, 328
*incognitus, Parablennius,* Pontif Blenny, 525
*inconditus, Arothron,* Bellystriped Puffer, 646
*inconsequens, Gnatholepis,* Orange-ear Goby, 558
Indian Driftfish, *Ariomma indica,* 606
Indian Frogfish, *Antennarius indicus,* 91
Indian Goatfish, *Parupeneus indicus,* 316, 319
Indian Golden-barred Butterflyfish, *Chaetodon jayakari,* 346
Indian Little Fish, *Apogon semilineatus,* 226
Indian Mackerel, *Trachurus indicus,* 250
Indian Ocean Bannerfish, *Heniochus pleurotaenia,* 348
Indian Ocean Chevron Butterflyfish, *Chaetodon madagascariensis,* 337
Indian Scad, *Decapterus russelli,* 247
Indian Threadfin, *Alectis indicus,* 242, 247, 251
Indian Triggerfish, *Melichthys indicus,* 622, 623
*indica, Acanthocepola,* Philippine Bandfish, 420
*indica, Ariomma,* Indian Driftfish, 606
*indica, Makaira,* Black Marlin, 604
*indicus, Alectis,* Indian Threadfin, 242, 247, 251
*indicus, Antennarius,* Indian Frogfish, 91
*indicus, Melichthys,* Indian Triggerfish, 622, 623
*indicus, Parupeneus,* Indian Goatfish, 316, 319
*indicus, Platycephalus,* Bartail Flathead, 162
*indicus, Trachurus,* Indian Mackerel, 250
Indies Gizzard Shad, *Anodontostoma chacunda,* 67
Indigo Hamlet, *Hypoplectrus indigo,* 201
*indigo, Hypoplectrus,* Indigo Hamlet, 201
Indo-Pacific Leatherjacket, *Cantherhines fronticinctus,* 632
Indo-Pacific Squirrelfish, *Sargocentron tieroides,* 107
*Inegocia guttata,* Spotted Crocodile Flathead, 162
*Inermia vittata,* Boga, 288
*inermis, Cheilio,* Cigar Wrasse, 451, 472
*inermis, Epinephelus,* Marbled Grouper, 192
*inermis, Scolopsis,* Unarmed Monocle Bream, 303
*inermis, Scorpaena,* Mushroom Scorpionfish, 145
*inermis, Sebastes,* Japanese Black Rockfish, 152
*inframacula, Canthigaster,* Low Spot Sharpnosed Pufferfish, 652
*infulata, Eviota,* Smith's Coral Goby, 576
*ingens, Hippocampus,* Pacific Seahorse, 130
*Inimicus caledonicus,* Caledonian Devilfish, 155
*Inimicus didactylus,* Popeyed Sea Goblin, 156
*Inimicus filamentosus,* Filament Devilfish, 135, 155
*Inimicus sinensis,* Goblin Devilfish, 158
*Inimicus* sp., Devilfish, 155
*inornatus, Pseudoplesiops,* Plain Dottyback, 211
*inscriptus, Pseudolabrus,* Poor Knights Wrasse, 464
Inshore Lizardfish, *Synodus foetens,* 74
*insidiator, Epibulus,* Slingjaw Wrasse, 439, 449
*insignis, Cryptocentroides,* Diagonal Striped Goby, 557
*insinuans, Silhouettea,* Silhouette Goby, 551
*insolatus, Chromis,* Sunshinefish, 388
*insularis, Scorpaenodes,* St. Helena Scorpionfish, 153
*intermedius, Heniochus,* Red Sea Bannerfish, 352
*intermedius, Synodus,* Sanddiver Lizardfish, 73, 74
*interrupta, Stethojulis,* Cut-ribbon Rainbowfish, 454
*interruptus, Ambassis,* Long-spined Perchlet, 170
*interruptus, Centropyge,* Japanese Pygmy Angelfish, 356
*interstitialis, Mycteroperca,* Yellowmouth Grouper, 193
*intestinalis, Corythoichthys,* Australian Banded Pipefish, 127
*Ioglossus calliurus,* Blue Sleeper, 569
*Ioglossus helenae,* Hovering Goby, 569
*Ioglossus* sp., Cortez Hovering Goby, 569
*iomelas, Chromis,* Blach-and-White Chromis, 387
*Iracundus signifier,* Spot-bearing Scorpionfish, 148
*iridis, Halichoeres,* Radiant Wrasse, 441, 442
*irroratus, Salarias,* Spotted Blenny, 527
*isabelita, Holacanthus,* Blue Angelfish, 367
*ischinagi, Stereolepis,* Striped Grouper, 173
*ishigakiensis, Apogon,* Japanese Cardinalfish, 226
Island Goby, *Lythrypnus nesiotes,* 575
Iso Blenny, *Ecsenius isos,* 528.15
*Iso rhothophilus,* Surge Silverside, 102
*isos, Ecsenius,* Iso Blenny, 528.15
*Istiblennius chrysospilos,* Orange-spotted Blenny, 531
*Istiblennius dussumieri,* Streaky Rockskipper, 526, 534
*Istiblennius edentulus,* Rippled Rockskipper, 531, 534
*Istiblennius gibbifrons,* Hump-headed Blenny, 531
*Istiblennius lineatus,* Lined Blenny, 531
*Istiblennius meleagris,* Painted Blenny, 531
*Istiblennius periophthalmus,* Bullethead Rockskipper, 534
*Istiblennius* sp., Blenny, unidentified, 526
*Istiblennius zebra,* Zebra Blenny, 531
*Istigobius decoratus,* Decorated Goby, 563
*Istigobius goldmanni,* Goldmann's Goby, 563
*Istigobius nigroocellatus,* Black-spotted Goby, 563
*Istigobius ornatus,* Ornate Goby, 563
*Istiophorus platypterus,* Sailfish, 604
*Isurus oxyrinchus,* Shortfin Mako Shark, 37, 40
*itajara, Epinephelus,* Jewfish, 191
*ittodai, Sargocentron,* Japanese Squirrelfish, 107

## J

Jackknife-fish, *Equetus lanceolatus,* 310
*jacksoni, Embiotoca,* Black Surfperch, 370
*jacksonianus, Brachaluteres,* Pygmy Leatherjacket, 634
*jacobus, Myripristis,* Blackbar Soldierfish, 113
*jactator, Canthigaster,* Whitespotted Toby, 651
*jaculum, Synodus,* Leaping Lizardfish, 72
*jamaicensis, Urolophus,* Yellow Stingray, 46
*jansenii, Thalassoma,* Jansen's Wrasse, 466
Jansen's Wrasse, *Thalassoma jansenii,* 466
Janss' Pipefish, *Doryrhamphus janssi,* 127
*janssi, Doryrhamphus,* Janss' Pipefish, 127
*janthinoptera, Canthigaster,* Honeycomb Toby, 650
*japanensis, Scarus,* Forster's Parrotfish, 492
Japanese Anchovy, *Engraulis japonicus,* 68
Japanese Angel Shark, *Squatina japonica,* 41
Japanese Aulopus, *Aulopus japonicus,* 73
Japanese Basslet, *Liopropoma susumi,* 198
Japanese Bigeye, *Pristigenys niphonia,* 219
Japanese Black Rockfish, *Sebastes inermis,* 152

Japanese Blue Sprat, *Spratelloides japonicus,* 66
Japanese Blue-striped Pipefish, *Doryrhamphus japonicus,* 127
Japanese Bluefish, *Scombrops gilberti,* 244
Japanese Boarfish, *Pentaceros japonicus,* 335
Japanese Bonyhead, *Ostichthys japonicus,* 113
Japanese Butterfish, *Hyperoglyphe japonica,* 606
Japanese Butterfly Ray, *Gymnura japonica,* 45
Japanese Cardinalfish, *Apogon ishigakiensis,* 226
Japanese Coral Trout, *Plectranthias japonicus,* 181
Japanese Dragonet, *Calliurichthys japonicus,* 537
Japanese Eel, *Anguilla japonica,* 53
Japanese Fairy Basslet, *Pseudanthias taira,* 177
Japanese Feather-finned Flying Fish, *Cheilopogon pinnatibarbatus japonicus,* 99
Japanese Filefish, *Rudarius ercodes,* 633
Japanese Flathead, *Bembras japonicus,* 161
Japanese Golden-barred Butterflyfish, *Chaetodon modestus,* 346
Japanese Halfbeak, *Hyporhamphus sajori,* 100
Japanese Horned Shark, *Heterodontus japonicus,* 33
Japanese Leopard Shark, *Triakis scyllia,* 39
Japanese Numbfish, *Narke japonica,* 42
Japanese Parrotfish, *Calotomus japonicus,* 488
Japanese Pygmy Angelfish, *Centropyge interruptus,* 356
Japanese Sand Bass, *Chelidoperca hirundinacea,* 200
Japanese Scorpionfish, *Sebastes baramenuke,* 152
Japanese Sculpin, *Dasycottus japonicus,* 167
Japanese Sea Bream, *Evynnis japonica,* 289, 291
Japanese Seahorse, *Hippocampus japonicus,* 130
Japanese Seaperch, *Ditrema temmincki,* 369
Japanese Silver Bream, *Acanthopagrus latus,* 292
Japanese Slimefish, *Gephyroberyx japonicus,* 103
Japanese Smoothhound, *Mustelus manazo,* 38
Japanese Sole, *Heteromycteris japonicus,* 614
Japanese Spanish Mackerel, *Scomberomorus niphonius,* 603
Japanese Squirrelfish, *Sargocentron ittodai,* 107
Japanese Stargazer, *Uranoscopus japonicus,* 501
Japanese Stingray, *Dasyatis akajei,* 45
Japanese Threadfin Bream, *Nemipterus japonicus,* 305
Japanese Threadfin Shad, *Nematalosa japonica,* 67
Japanese Tilefish, *Branchiostegus japonicus,* 239
Japanese Tonguefish, *Paraplagusia japonica,* 614
Japanese Torpedo Ray, *Torpedo tokionis,* 43
Japanese Tubesnout, *Aulichthys japonicus,* 118
Japanese Velvetfish, *Aploactis aspera,* 156
Japanese Wobbegong, *Orectolobus japonicus,* 35
Japanese Wrasse, *Pseudolabrus japonicus,* 464
Japanese Yellowtail, *Seriola quinqueradiata,* 252
*japonica, Anguilla,* Japanese Eel, 53
*japonica, Callanthias,* Pastel Fairy Basslet, 186
*japonica, Evynnis,* Japanese Sea Bream, 289, 291
*japonica, Gymnura,* Japanese Butterfly Ray, 45
*japonica, Hyperoglyphe,* Japanese Butterfish, 606
*japonica, Narke,* Japanese Numbfish, 42
*japonica, Nematalosa,* Japanese Threadfin Shad, 67
*japonica, Paraplagusia,* Japanese Tonguefish, 614
*japonica, Squatina,* Japanese Angel Shark, 41
*japonicus, Acanthurus,* White-faced Surgeonfish, 582
*japonicus, Arctoscopus,* Sailfin Sandfish, 500
*japonicus, Aulichthys,* Japanese Tubesnout, 118
*japonicus, Aulopus,* Japanese Aulopus, 73
*japonicus, Bembras,* Japanese Flathead, 161
*japonicus, Brama,* Pacific Pomfret, 257
*japonicus, Branchiostegus,* Japanese Tilefish, 239
*japonicus, Calliurichthys,* Japanese Dragonet, 537
*japonicus, Calotomus,* Japanese Parrotfish, 488
*japonicus, Chirolophis,* Fringed Blenny, 495
*japonicus, Conger,* Beach Conger, 63
*japonicus, Dasycottus,* Japanese Sculpin, 167
*japonicus, Doryrhamphus,* Japanese Blue-striped Pipefish, 127
*japonicus, Engraulis,* Japanese Anchovy, 68
*japonicus, Gephyroberyx,* Japanese Slimefish, 103
*japonicus, Gymnocranius,* Silver Large-eye Bream, 290
*japonicus, Heterodontus,* Japanese Horned Shark, 33
*japonicus, Heteromycteris,* Japanese Sole, 614
*japonicus, Hippocampus,* Japanese Seahorse, 130
*japonicus, Lateolabrax,* Common Sea Bass, 173
*japonicus, Monocentris,* Pineapplefish, 92, 103
*japonicus, Nemipterus,* Japanese Threadfin Bream, 305
*japonicus, Orectolobus,* Japanese Wobbegong, 35
*japonicus, Ostichthys,* Japanese Bonyhead, 113
*japonicus, Paramonacanthus,* Striped Filefish, 632
*japonicus, Pempheris,* Blackfin Sweeper, 321
*japonicus, Pentaceros,* Japanese Boarfish, 335
*japonicus, Plectranthias,* Japanese Coral Trout, 181
*japonicus, Pseudolabrus,* Japanese Wrasse, 464
*japonicus, Scomber,* Chub Mackerel, 603
*japonicus, Spratelloides,* Japanese Blue Sprat, 66
*japonicus, Trachurus,* Horse Mackerel, 245
*japonicus, Uranoscopus,* Japanese Stargazer, 501
*japonicus, Zeus,* John Dory, 118
*jarbua, Terapon,* Targetfish, 216, 218
Java Parrotfish, *Scarus javanicus,* 489
*javanicus, Gymnothorax,* Giant Moray, 59, 60
*javanicus, Scarus,* Java Parrotfish, 489
*javus, Siganus,* Streaked Spinefoot, 598
*jayakari, Chaetodon,* Indian Golden-barred Butterflyfish, 346
*jello, Sphyraena,* Pickhandle Barracuda, 422
Jelly Cardinalfish, *Pseudamia gelatinosa,* 237
Jenkin's Parrotfish, *Calotomus zonarchia,* 488
*Jenkinsia* sp., Herring, unidentified, 66
Jenyns' Flounder, *Pseudorhombus jenynsii,* 610
*jenynsii, Pseudorhombus,* Jenyns' Flounder, 610
*jerdoni, Pristotis,* Gulf Damsel, 408
Jet Black Dottyback, *Pseudochromis paranox,* 210
Jewel Damsel, *Paraglyphidodon lacrymatus,* 391, 396
Jewel Goby, *Stiphodon* sp., 552
Jewelfish, *Microspathodon chrysurus,* 408
Jewelled Rockskipper, *Salarias fasciatus,* 526, 527, 528.01
Jewfish, *Epinephelus itajara,* 191
Jock Stuart Scorpionfish, *Helicolenus papillosus,* 138
*jocu, Lutjanus,* Dog Snapper, 264
*joculator, Centropyge,* Half Yellow Pygmy Angelfish, 357
John Dory, *Zeus japonicus,* 118
*Johnius diacanthus,* Spotted Jewfish, 311
*Johnsonina eriomma,* Bullseye, 620
Johnston Damsel, *Plectroglyphidodon johnstonianus,* 395
*johnstonianus, Plectroglyphidodon,* Johnston Damsel, 395
Jolthead Porgy, *Calamus bajonado,* 291
*jordani, Choerodon,* Jordan's Tuskfish, 431
*jordani, Cirrhilabrus,* Jordan's Fairy Wrasse, 435
Jordan's Fairy Wrasse, *Cirrhilabrus jordani,* 435
Jordan's Squirrelfish, *Neoniphon scythrops,* 110
Jordan's Tuskfish, *Choerodon jordani,* 431
*joyneri, Cynoglossus,* Joyner's Tonguefish, 614

*joyneri, Sebastes,* Joyner's Stingfish, 152
Joyner's Stingfish, *Sebastes joyneri,* 152
Joyner's Tonguefish, *Cynoglossus joyneri,* 614
*julis, Coris,* Mediterranean Rainbow Wrasse, 437
Jumping Blenny, *Lepidoblennius marmoratus,* 508

## K

*kalisherae, Labrisomus,* Downy Blenny, 513
*kallochroma, Halichoeres,* Kallochrome Wrasse, 474
Kallochrome Wrasse, *Halichoeres kallochroma,* 474
*kallopterus, Apogon,* Spinyhead Cardinalfish, 226, 233
*kallopterus, Lethrinus,* Yellow-spotted Emperor, 295, 298
*kamoharai, Meiacanthus,* Black and White Striped Blenny, 522
*kanagurta, Rastrelliger,* Rake-gilled Mackerel, 603
*kapas, Gerres,* Singapore Silver-Biddy, 276
*Kareius bicoloratus,* Stone Flounder, 613
*kashiwae, Pseudanthias,* Red Fairy Basslet, 174
*kasmira, Lutjanus,* Blue-striped Snapper, 260
*Kathetostoma averruncus,* Smooth Stargazer, 500
*katoptron, Anomalops,* Lantern-eye, 106
*Katsuwonus pelamis,* Skipjack Tuna, 602
Kawakawa, *Euthynnus affinis,* 602
*kawamebari, Coreoperca,* Kawamebar's Bass, 172
Kawamebar's Bass, *Coreoperca kawamebari,* 172
Kazika Sculpin, *Cottus kazika,* 164
*kazika, Cottus,* Kazika Sculpin, 164
*Kellogella cardinalis,* Cardinalfin Goby, 551
*kelloggi, Scorpaenodes,* Kellogg's Scorpionfish, 154
Kellogg's Scorpionfish, *Scorpaenodes kelloggi,* 154
Kelp Greenling, *Hexagrammos decagrammus,* 163
Kelp Grouper, *Epinephelus moara,* 189
Kelp Rockfish, *Sebastes atrovirens,* 149
Kelpfish, *Chironemus marmoratus,* 415
*kennedyi, Trachinotus,* Pacific Palometa, 254
*Kentrocapros aculeatus,* Sawtooth Boxfish, 639
Key Blenny, *Starksia starcki,* 513
Key Brotutid, *Ogilbia cayorum,* 81
Keyhole Angelfish, *Centropyge tibicin,* 357
Keys Jawfish, *Opistognathus* sp., 499
Khaki Blenny, *Ecsenius aroni,* 528.04
Kidako Moray Eel, *Gymnothorax kidako,* 51, 57
*kidako, Gymnothorax,* Kidako Moray Eel, 51, 57
*kiensis, Apogon,* Rifle Cardinalfish, 227
King Angelfish, *Holacanthus passer,* 367
King Coris, *Coris auricularis,* 436, 438
King Demoiselle, *Chrysiptera rex,* 390
King George's Salmon, *Arripes georgianus,* 257
King Spanish Mackerel, *Scomberomorus guttatus,* 603
Klausewitz's Blenny, *Ecsenius lineatus,* 533
*klayi, Lipogramma,* Bicolor Basslet, 213
*kleini, Chaetodon,* Klein's Butterflyfish, 340
Klein's Butterflyfish, *Chaetodon kleini,* 340
*klunzinger, Pempheris,* Rough Bullseye, 322
*klunzingeri, Chromis,* Klunzinger's Chromis, 383
*klunzingeri, Thalassoma,* Klunzinger's Wrasse, 467
Klunzinger's Chromis, *Chromis klunzingeri,* 383
Klunzinger's Wrasse, *Thalassoma klunzingeri,* 467
Knight-fish, *Cleidopus gloriamaris,* 101, 103
Knobbed Porgy, *Calamus nodosus,* 291
Knobby Seahorse, *Hippocampus breviceps,* 129
*koelreuteri, Periophthalmus,* Blotchy Mudskipper, 568, 579
*koningsbergeri, Harengula,* Koningsberg's Herring, 67
Koningsberg's Herring, *Harengula koningsbergeri,* 67
*Konosirus punctatus,* Dotted Gizzard Shad, 67
Koran Angelfish, *Pomacanthus semicirculatus,* 362, 364, 365
Kosi Rockskipper, *Pereulixia kosiensis,* 532
*kosiensis, Pereulixia,* Kosi Rockskipper, 532
*kuda, Hippocampus,* Oceanic Seahorse, 128, 130
*Kuhlia marginata,* Sported Flagtail, 219
*Kuhlia mugil,* Barred Flagtail, 217, 219
*Kuhlia rupestris,* Rock Flagtail, 219
*Kuhlia sandvicensis,* Hawaiian Aholehole, 219
*kuhlii, Amphotistius,* Blue-spotted Stingray, 45
Kuiter's Tall Triplefin, *Apopterygion alta,* 510
*kuntee, Myripristis,* Shoulderbar Soldierfish, 114, 115
*Kyphosus analogus,* Blue-bronze Sea Chub, 328
*Kyphosus cinerascens,* Ashen Drummer, 328
*Kyphosus cornelii,* Western Buffalo Bream, 327
*Kyphosus elegans,* Cortez Chub, 328
*Kyphosus fuscus,* Ash-colored Rudderfish, 329
*Kyphosus gibsoni,* Northern Buffalo Bream, 329
*Kyphosus incisor,* Yellow Chub, 328
*Kyphosus sectatrix,* Bermuda Chub, 328
*Kyphosus* sp., Chub, unidentified, 328
*Kyphosus sydneyanus,* Common Buffalo Bream, 327, 329

## L

*labiatus, Cheiloprion,* Big Lip Damsel, 397
Laboute's Fairy Wrasse, *Cirrhilabrus labouti,* 434
*labouti, Cirrhilabrus,* Laboute's Fairy Wrasse, 434
*Labracinus cyclophthalmus,* Spottysail Dottyback, 207
*Labracinus lineatus,* Lined Cichlops, 212
*Labracoglossa argentiventris,* Yellow-striped Butterfish, 241
*labrax, Dicentrarchus,* Common European Bass, 170
*Labrichthys unilineatus,* Tubelip Wrasse, 451
*labriformis, Epinephelus,* Flag Cabrilla, 191
*Labrisomus bucciferus,* Puffcheek Blenny, 513
*Labrisomus filamentosus,* Filamentous Blenny, 513
*Labrisomus haitiensis,* Longfin Blenny, 513
*Labrisomus kalisherae,* Downy Blenny, 513
*Labrisomus nigricinctus,* Spotcheek Blenny, 513
*Labrisomus nuchipinnis,* Hairy Blenny, 513
*Labroides bicolor,* Bicolored Cleaner Wrasse, 469
*Labroides dimidiatus,* Bluestreak Cleaner Wrasse, 469
*Labroides pectoralis,* False Bluestreak Wrasse, 469
*Labroides phthirophagus,* Hawaiian Cleaner Wrasse, 469
*Labroides rubrolabiatus,* Redlip Cleaner Wrasse, 469
*Labropsis alleni,* Allen's Wrasse, 454
*Labropsis manabei,* Oriental Wrasse, 454
*Labropsis micronesica,* Micronesian Wrasse, 454
*Labropsis xanthonota,* Yellowback Wrasse, 451, 454
*Labrus bergylta,* Ballan Wrasse, 469
*Labrus merula,* Mediterranean Brown Wrasse, 469
*lacertinus, Synodus,* Panamanian Lizardfish, 75
*lachneri, Apogon,* Whitestar Cardinalfish, 231
*lachneri, Cheilodipterus,* Arrowtooth Cardinalfish, 234
*Lachnolaimus maximus,* Hogfish, 470
*lachrymosus, Stenogobius,* Teary Goby, 553
*lacrymatus, Paraglyphidodon,* Jewel Damsel, 391, 396
*Lactarius lactarius,* Milk Trevally, 241
*lactarius, Lactarius,* Milk Trevally, 241
*lacteoguttatus, Sargocentron,* White-spotted Squirrelfish, 111
*Lactophrys bicaudalis,* Spotted Trunkfish, 641
*Lactophrys polygonia,* Honeycomb Trunkfish, 641

*Lactophrys quadricornis,* Scrawled Cowfish, 641
*Lactophrys trigonus,* Trunkfish, 641
*Lactophrys triqueter,* Smooth Trunkfish, 641
*Lactoria cornuta,* Long-horned Cowfish, 637, 639
*Lactoria diaphanus,* Diaphanous Cowfish, 638
*Lactoria fornasini,* Thornback Cowfish, 638
*lacunosus, Atherinomorus,* Slender Hardyhead, 102
Ladder Glider, *Valenciennea sexguttata,* 566
*laddi, Bathygobius,* Ladd's Goby, 542
Ladd's Goby, *Bathygobius laddi,* 542
Ladyfish, *Elops machnata,* 50
*laeve, Neoniphon,* Bluejean Squirrelfish, 111
*laevis, Plectropomus,* Black-saddled Leopard Grouper, 204
*laevis, Ranzania,* Slender Mola, 656
*Lagocephalus gloveri,* Brown-backed Puffer, 643
*Lagodon rhomboides,* Pinfish, 292
Lagoon Damsel, *Hemiglyphidodon plagiometopon,* 397
*Laiphognathus multimaculatus,* Many-spotted Blenny, 527
Lake Goby, *Rhinogobius brunneus,* 552
*lalandi dorsalis, Seriola,* Yellowtail, 252
*lalandi lalandi, Seriola,* Yellowtail, 252
*lamarck, Genicanthus,* Freckletail Lyretail Angelfish, 359
*Lampris guttatus,* Moonfish, 103
Lance-like Smelt, *Spirinchus lanceolatus,* 70
*lanceolatus, Epinephelus,* Brindlebass, 194
*lanceolatus, Equetus,* Jackknife-fish, 310
*lanceolatus, Spirinchus,* Lance-like Smelt, 70
Lancer, *Lethrinus nematacanthus,* 295
Lancer Dragonet, *Paradiplogrammus bairdi,* 538
Lancetail Fairy Wrasse, *Cirrhilabrus blatteus,* 462
Lane Snapper, *Lutjanus synagris,* 264
Lantern Bass, *Serranus baldwini,* 197
Lantern-eye, *Anomalops katoptron,* 106
Lanternfish, unidentified, *Myctophidae* sp., 75
*Larabicus quadrilineatus,* Fourline Wrasse, 451
Large-bodied Silver-Biddy, *Gerres macrosoma,* 276
Large-headed Scorpionfish, *Pontinus macrocephalus,* 146
Large-scaled Grinner, *Saurida undosquamis,* 73
Large-scaled Mullet, *Liza oligolepis,* 421
Large-scaled Whiting, *Sillago macrolepis,* 239
Largehead Hairtail, *Trichiurus lepturus,* 601
*larvatus, Chaetodon,* Masked Butterflyfish, 337
*Lateolabrax japonicus,* Common Sea Bass, 173
*lateralis, Favonigobius,* Long-finned Goby, 558
Laterally Banded Grouper, *Epinephelus latifasciatus,* 190
*Lates calcarifer,* Barramundi, 170
*latezonatus, Amphiprion,* Wide-band Anemonefish, 372
*latibricola, Stygnobrotula,* Black Widow, 81
*laticephalus, Satyrichthys,* Offshore Crocodilefish, 160
*laticeps, Chelonodon,* Gold-spotted Puffer, 649
*laticlavius, Pictilabrus,* Senator Wrasse, 462
*laticlavius, Prionurus,* Galapagos Sawtail, 588
*latifasciata, Amblyeleotris,* Wideband Prawn Goby, 544
*latifasciatus, Epinephelus,* Laterally Banded Grouper, 190
*Latimeria chalumnae,* Coelacanth, 50
*latipinnis, Zaniolepis,* Longspine Combfish, 163
*latitabunda, Tandya,* Spotted Pug, 498
*lativittata, Pterocaesio,* Gold-band Fusilier, 271
*latovittatus, Malacanthus,* Blue Blanquillo, 241
*Latridopsis ciliaris,* Blue Moki, 416
Lattice Cardinalfish, *Apogon margaritiphora,* 224
Lattice Monocle Bream, *Scolopsis taeniopterus,* 303
Lattice Seahorse, *Hippocampus* sp., 130
Lattice Soldierfish, *Myripristis violacea,* 112, 114, 115
Latticed Blenny, *Ecsenius opsifrontalis,* 528.14
Latticed Monocle Bream, *Scolopsis cancellatus,* 302, 304
*latus, Acanthopagrus,* Japanese Silver Bream, 292
*latus, Atypichthys,* White-bellied Stripey, 325, 326
*latus, Caranx,* Horse-eye Jack, 249
*latus, Serranocirrhitus,* Sunburst Basslet, 180
*laudandus flavus, Plagiotremus,* Golden Mimic Blenny, 521
Lavender Sculpin, *Leiocottus hirundo,* 165
Leafy Seadragon, *Phycodurus eques,* 121, 124
*leai, Archamia,* Lea's Cardinalfish, 235
Leaping Bonito, *Cybiosarda elegans,* 602
Leaping Lizardfish, *Synodus jaculum,* 72
Lea's Cardinalfish, *Archamia leai,* 235
Leather Bass, *Epinephelus dermatolepis,* 191
Leatherjacket, *Oligoplites saurus,* 251
*lebeck, Ichthyoscopus,* Stargazer, 500
*Leiocottus hirundo,* Lavender Sculpin, 165
*leiogaster, Amblygaster,* Sharp-nosed Trench Sardine, 66
*Leiognathus equulus,* Common Slipmouth, 256
*Leiognathus fasciata,* Banded Pony Fish, 256
*Leiognathus nuchalis,* Spotnape Pony Fish, 256
*Leiognathus rivulatus,* Offshore Pony Fish, 256
*leiognathus, Myripristis,* Panamic Soldierfish, 113
*Leiuranus semicinctus,* Half-banded Snake Eel, 61
*leiurus, Tylosurus,* Needlefish, 100
*lemniscatus, Lutjanus,* Sweetlips Snapper, 266
Lemon Shark, *Negaprion acutidens,* 40; *Negaprion brevirostris,* 39
Lemon Sweetlips, *Plectorhinchus flavomaculatus,* 282, 283, 287
Lemonpeel, *Centropyge flavissimus,* 357
*lennardi, Anampses,* Lennard's Tamarin, 426, 427
Lennard's Tamarin, *Anampses lennardi,* 426, 427
*lenticularis, Anaplocapros,* White-barred Boxfish, 617, 637
*lentiginosa, Muraena,* Dotted-reef Eel, 60
*lentjan, Lethrinus,* Red-spotted Emperor, 294, 297
Leonard's Common Goby, *Pomatoschistus microps,* 558
Leopard Blenny, *Ecsenius pardus,* 528.09
Leopard Flounder, *Bothus leopardus,* 609
Leopard Frogfish, *Antennarius pardalis,* 88
Leopard Grouper, *Plectropomus leopardus,* 203, 204
Leopard Moray, *Gymnothorax undulatus,* 58
Leopard Pufferfish, *Canthigaster leopardus,* 647, 650
Leopard Rockcod, *Cephalopholis leopardus,* 182
Leopard Rockskipper, *Exallias brevis,* 534
Leopard Searobin, *Prionotus scitulus,* 161
Leopard Shark, *Triakis semifasciatus,* 39
Leopard Snake-eel, *Callechelys marmoratus,* 61
*leopardus, Bothus,* Leopard Flounder, 609
*leopardus, Canthigaster,* Leopard Pufferfish, 647, 650
*leopardus, Cephalopholis,* Leopard Rockcod, 182
*leopardus, Plectropomus,* Leopard Grouper, 203, 204
*Lepadichthys frenatus,* Green Clingfish, 97
*Lepadichthys lineatus,* Doubleline Clingfish, 95
*Lepadogaster candollei,* Condolle's Lepadogaster, 97
*Lepadogaster lepadogaster,* Gowan's Clingfish, 97
*lepadogaster, Lepadogaster,* Gowan's Clingfish, 97
*Lepidoblennius marmoratus,* Jumping Blenny, 508
*lepidogenys, Pomacentrus,* Scaly Damsel, 400
*lepidolepis, Chromis,* Scaly Chromis, 386
*Lepidopsetta bilineata,* Rock Sole, 611
*lepidoptera, Caesioperca,* Red Butterfly Perch, 181

*Lepidotrigla microptera,* Blackfin Gurnard, 160
*Lepidozygus tapeinosoma,* Fusilier Damsel, 381
*Lepophidium prorates,* Dot-dash Cusk-eel, 80
*Lepophidium* sp., Cusk-eel, unidentified, 80
*lepros, Sargocentron,* Rough-scaled Squirrelfish, 109
*leptacanthus, Apogon,* Longspine Cardinalfish, 228
*leptocaulus, Apogon,* Fairy Cardinalfish, 230
*leptocephalus, Cryptocentrus,* Pink-and-Blue Spotted Goby, 540, 556, 557
*Leptojulis chrysotaenia,* Yellow Ribbon Wrasse, 462
*Leptojulis cyanopleura,* Blue-sided Wrasse, 462, 475
*leptolepis, Selaroides,* Yellowstripe Scad, 250
*Leptoscarus vaigiensis,* Marbled Parrotfish, 488, 491
*lepturus, Trichiurus,* Largehead Hairtail, 601
Lesser Devil Ray, *Mobula diabolis,* 48
Lesser Electric Ray, *Narcine brasiliensis,* 42
Lesser Spotted Dogfish, *Scyliorhinus canicula,* 38
*lethrinoides, Gymnocranius,* Red-tailed Sea Bream, 290, 296
*Lethrinus amboinensis,* Amboina Porgy, 294
*Lethrinus chrysostomus,* Sweetlip Emperor, 298
*Lethrinus crocineus,* Yellowfin Emperor, 294
*Lethrinus enigmaticus,* Seychelles Emperor, 298
*Lethrinus haematopterus,* Deep-bodied Emperor, 295
*Lethrinus harak,* Black-spot Emperor, 295, 298
*Lethrinus hypselopterus,* Mozambique Emperor, 295, 297
*Lethrinus kallopterus,* Yellow-spotted Emperor, 295, 298
*Lethrinus lentjan,* Red-spotted Emperor, 294, 297
*Lethrinus mahsena?,* Mahsena, 297
*Lethrinus mahsena,* Mahsena, 296
*Lethrinus miniatus,* Long-snouted Bream, 297
*Lethrinus nebulosus,* Spangled Emperor, 295, 296, 297
*Lethrinus nematacanthus,* Lancer, 295
*Lethrinus ornatus,* Ornate Emperor, 295, 296
*Lethrinus ramak,* Orange-striped Emperor, 297
*Lethrinus reticulatus,* Reticulated Emperor, 294
*Lethrinus rostratus,* Longsnout Emperor, 294
*Lethrinus rubrioperculatus,* Red Opercled Snapper, 297
*Lethrinus variegatus,* Variegated Emperor, 294, 298
*Lethrinus xanthochilus,* Yellow-lip Snapper, 297
*leucogaster, Amblyglyphidodon,* White-belly Damsel, 381, 382
*leucogaster, Hypodytes,* Whitebelly Sailfin Scorpionfish, 159
*leucogrammicus, Anyperodon,* White-lined Rockcod, 179
*leucokranos, Amphiprion,* Whitecap Anemonefish, 372
*leucometopon, Perryena,* Whitenose Pigfish, 158
*leucopareius, Acanthurus,* Whiteband Surgeonfish, 588
*leucopleura, Chaetodon,* Somali Butterflyfish, 337
*leucopoma, Chrysiptera,* White-banded Damselfish, 391
*leucorus, Stegastes,* Pale-tailed Damselfish, 405
*leucosternon, Acanthurus,* Powder-blue Tang, 581, 583
*leucostictus, Stegastes,* Beau Gregory, 407
*leucostigma, Gymnothorax,* Yellowblotch Moray, 57
*leucotaenia, Pholidichthys,* Convict Blenny, 500
*leucotaenia, Scolopsis,* Whiteribbon Spinecheek, 302
*leucozona, Plectroglyphidodon,* Bellyband Damselfish, 394
*leucura, Chromis,* White-tail Chromis, 387
*lewini, Sphyrna,* Scalloped Hammerhead, 40, 41
Libertad Thread Herring, *Opisthonema libertate,* 67
*libertate, Opisthonema,* Libertad Thread Herring, 67
*lidwilli, Pandaka,* Pygmy Goby, 551
*Lienardella fasciata,* Harlequin Tuskfish, 452, 453
Lieutenant Surgeonfish, *Acanthurus tennenti,* 584
*lima, Plectrypops,* Rough-scaled Soldierfish, 113
*Limanda schrenki,* Crested Flounder, 613
*limbata, Acanthocepola,* Spotfin Bandfish, 420
*limbaughi, Chaenopsis,* Yellowface Pikeblenny, 519
*limbaughi, Chromis,* Limbaugh's Chromis, 389
Limbaugh's Chromis, *Chromis limbaughi,* 389
*Limnichthys fasciatus,* Tommy Fish, 501
*lineata, Chromis,* Lined Chromis, 385
*lineata, Liopropoma,* Lined Basslet, 198
*lineata, Suttonia,* Hawaiian Soapfish, 207
*lineatus, Acanthurus,* Clown Surgeonfish, 585, 587
*lineatus, Achirus,* Lined Sole, 615
*lineatus, Anampses,* Lined Tamarin, 426
*lineatus, Apogon,* Lined Cardinalfish, 228
*lineatus, Cheilodipterus,* Tiger Cardinalfish, 233
*lineatus, Cirrhilabrus,* Lined Fairy Wrasse, 434
*lineatus, Diademichthys,* Yellowstripe Clingfish, 95
*lineatus, Ecsenius,* Klausewitz's Blenny, 533
*lineatus, Genyonemus,* White Croaker, 311
*lineatus, Istiblennius,* Lined Blenny, 531
*lineatus, Labracinus,* Lined Cichlops, 212
*lineatus, Lepadichthys,* Doubleline Clingfish, 95
*lineatus, Meiacanthus,* Striped Blenny, 522
*lineatus, Parioglossus,* Lined Goby, 560
*lineatus, Plectorhinchus,* Yellow-banded Sweetlips, 285, 286
*lineatus, Siganus,* Golden-lined Spinefoot, 598, 600
*lineatus, Upeneichthys,* Blue-spotted Goatfish, 314
Lined Basslet, *Liopropoma lineata,* 198
Lined Blenny, *Ecsenius aequalis,* 528.16; *Istiblennius lineatus,* 531
Lined Butterflyfish, *Chaetodon lineolatus,* 339
Lined Cardinalfish, *Apogon lineatus,* 228
Lined Chromis, *Chromis lineata,* 385
Lined Cichlops, *Labracinus lineatus,* 212
Lined Fairy Wrasse, *Cirrhilabrus lineatus,* 434
Lined Goby, *Parioglossus lineatus,* 560
Lined Silver Grunt, *Pomadasys hasta,* 281
Lined Sole, *Achirus lineatus,* 615
Lined Tamarin, *Anampses lineatus,* 426
*lineolata, Archamia,* Bronze-streaked Cardinalfish, 235
*lineolatus, Chaetodon,* Lined Butterflyfish, 339
*lineolatus, Ophthalmolepis,* Maori Wrasse, 460
*lineolatus, Scomberomorus,* Streaked Spanish Mackerel, 603
*lineopunctatus, Paracheilinus,* Scarletfin Wrasse, 459
Linespot Hogfish, *Bodianus oxycephalus,* 427
Lingcod, *Ophiodon elongatus,* 163
*linki, Gramma,* Yellowlined Basslet, 213
*Liocranium praepositum,* One-spot Waspfish, 495
*liolepis, Xystreurys,* Fantail Sole, 610
Lionfish, *Pterois volitans,* 134, 140, 142
*Liopropoma carmabi,* Candy Basslet, 198
*Liopropoma eukrines,* Wrasse Basslet, 198
*Liopropoma fasciatum,* Banded Basslet, 198
*Liopropoma lineata,* Lined Basslet, 198
*Liopropoma mowbrayi,* Cave Bass, 198
*Liopropoma pallidum,* Palefin Basslet, 199
*Liopropoma rubre,* Peppermint Basslet, 198
*Liopropoma* sp., Red-tailed Yellow Bass, 199
*Liopropoma susumi,* Japanese Basslet, 198
*Liopropoma swalesi,* Swales's Basslet, 198
*Liparis ochotenis,* Eight-armed Snailfish, 168
*Liparis pulchellus,* Showy Snailfish, 168
*lipernes, Coryphopterus,* Peppermint Goby, 574
*Lipogramma klayi,* Bicolor Basslet, 213

*Lipogramma regia,* Royal Basslet, 213
*Lipogramma trilineata,* Threeline Basslet, 213
*Lipophrys adriaticus,* Adriatic Blenny, 524
*Lipophrys canevae,* Caneva's Blenny, 525
*Lipophrys dalmatinus,* Dalmatian Blenny, 524
*Lipophrys nigriceps,* Black-headed Blenny, 525
*Lissocampus caudalis,* Smooth Pipefish, 126
*Lithognathus mormyrus,* Sand Steenbras, 288
Little Fairy Basslet, *Sacura parva,* 180
Little Pineapplefish, *Sorosichthys ananassa,* 103
Little Rainbow Wrasse, *Dotalabrus* sp., 463
Little Ruby Red Cardinalfish, *Apogon coccineus,* 232
Little Spinefoot, *Siganus spinus,* 599
Little Weed Whiting, *Neodax balteatus,* 478
Little-scaled Parma, *Parma microlepis,* 379
Littlewing Stonefish, *Synanceia alula,* 158
*littoralis, Scorpaenodes,* Shore Rockfish, 154
*lituratus, Naso,* Orange-spine Unicornfish, 590, 591
*liturosus, Diodon,* Shortspine Porcupinefish, 656
*litus, Chaetodon,* White-tip Butterflyfish, 342
*lividanalis, Ecsenius,* Blue-and-gold Blenny, 528.04
*lividus, Stegastes,* Blunt-snout Gregory, 404
*livingstonei, Notograptus,* Livingstone's Eel Blenny, 500
Livingstone's Eel Blenny, *Notograptus livingstonei,* 500
*Liza oligolepis,* Large-scaled Mullet, 421
*Liza saliens,* Skipper, 421
*Liza* sp., Mullet, unidentified, 421
*Liza vaigiensis,* Squaretail Mullet, 421
Lizard Island Goby, *Ctenogobiops pomastictus,* 547, 548
Lizard Triplefin, Tripterygiidae sp., 509
Lizardfish, unidentified, *Synodus* sp., 71, 75
*Lo magnifica,* Magnificent Foxface, 596, 598
*Lo uspi,* Uspi Spinefoot, 597
*Lo vulpinus,* Foxface, 597
*lobatus, Urolophus,* Lobed Stingaree, 46
Lobed Stingaree, *Urolophus lobatus,* 46
*Lobotes surinamensis,* Tripletail, 273
Lofty Triplefin, *Enneanectes altivelis,* 507
*Lonchopisthus micrognathus,* Pastel Jawfish, 498
*lonchurus, Opistognathus,* Moustache Jawfish, 498
Long Oarfish, *Regalecus glesne,* 103
Long-barbeled Goatfish, *Parupeneus macronema,* 313, 319
Long-finned Batfish, *Platax pinnatus,* 330, 332
Long-finned Dottyback, *Pseudochromis longipinnis,* 209
Long-finned Eel, *Anguilla dieffenbachii,* 53
Long-finned Goby, *Favonigobius lateralis,* 558
Long-finned Grouper, *Epinephelus megachir,* 189
Long-finned Silver-Biddy, *Pentaprion longimanus,* 275
Long-finned Snake Eel, *Pisodonophis cancrivorus,* 61
Long-horned Cowfish, *Lactoria cornuta,* 637, 639
Long-nosed Butterflyfish, *Forcipiger flavissimus,* 351
Long-nosed Wrasse, *Symphodus rostratus,* 471
Long-rayed Silver-Biddy, *Gerres filamentosus,* 275, 276
Long-snouted Boarfish, *Pentaceropsis recurvirostris,* 334
Long-snouted Bream, *Lethrinus miniatus,* 297
Long-spined Perchlet, *Ambassis interruptus,* 170
Long-tailed Dragonfish, *Parapegasus natans,* 119
Longfin Blenny, *Labrisomus haitiensis,* 513
Longfin Damselfish, *Stegastes diencaeus,* 407
Longfin Trevally, *Carangoides armatus,* 247
Longfinned Boarfish, *Zanclistius elevatus,* 335
Longfinned Trevally, *Carangoides* sp. (*?armatus*), 248
*longimanus, Caprodon,* Pink Maomao, 181
*longimanus, Carcharhinus,* Oceanic Whitetip Shark, 40
*longimanus, Pentaprion,* Long-finned Silver-Biddy, 275
*longipinnis, Pseudochromis,* Long-finned Dottyback, 209
*longipinnis, Valenciennea,* Ocellated Gudgeon, 566
*longirostris, Forcipiger,* Black Long-nosed Butterflyfish, 351
*longirostris, Oxymonacanthus,* Harlequin Filefish, 630, 631
*longispinis, Hypodytes,* Longspine Sailfin Scorpionfish, 156
Longjaw Squirrelfish, *Holocentrus adscensiones,* 109
Longlure Frogfish, *Antennarius multiocellatus,* 88
Longnose Batfish, *Ogcocephalus corniger,* 93
Longnose Hawkfish, *Oxycirrhites typus,* 413, 414
Longnose Sailfin Tang, *Zebrasoma rostratum,* 592
Longnose Spiny Dogfish, *Squalus mitsukurii,* 41
Longnose Trevally, *Carangoides chrysophrys,* 247
Longsnout Emperor, *Lethrinus rostratus,* 294
Longsnout Seahorse, *Hippocampus reidi,* 131
Longspine Cardinalfish, *Apogon leptacanthus,* 228
Longspine Combfish, *Zaniolepis latipinnis,* 163
Longspine Sailfin Scorpionfish, *Hypodytes longispinis,* 156
Longspine Sea Bream, *Argyrops spinifer,* 289
Longspine Snipefish, *Macrorhamphosus scolopax,* 123
Longspine Squirrelfish, *Holocentrus rufus,* 109
Longtail Seamoth, *Pegasus volitans,* 119
Longtail Tuna, *Thunnus tonggol,* 602
*Longus, Nes,* Orange-spotted Goby, 550
Lookdown, *Selene vomer,* 251
Loosetooth Parrotfish, *Nicholsina denticulata,* 488
*lopezi, Naso,* Lopez's Unicornfish, 591
Lopez's Unicornfish, *Naso lopezi,* 591
*Lophiocharon trisignatus,* Three-spot Frogfish, 85, 90
*Lophiomus setigerus,* Blackmouth Goosefish, 84
*Lophodiodon calori,* Four-bar Porcupinefish, 656
*Lopholatilus chameleonticeps,* Tilefish, 239
Lord Howe Butterflyfish, *Chaetodon tricinctus,* 343
Lord Howe Leatherjacket, *Cantherhines howensis,* 632
Lord Howe Scorpionfish, *Scorpaenopsis* sp., 146
Lord Howe Tamarin, *Anampses elegans,* 427
*lorenzi, Abudefduf,* Black-tail Sergeant, 382
*loreto, Gramma,* Royal Gramma, 213
*loriculus, Centropyge,* Flame Angelfish, 355
*Lotella fuliginosa,* Beardie, 77
*Lotella rhacinus,* Rock Cod, 77
*?Lotella* sp., Bearded Codfish, 77
*Lotilia graciliosa,* White-capped Prawn Goby, 553
*louisae, Gobiosoma,* Spotlight Goby, 572
*louisianae, Syngnathus,* Chain Pipefish, 125
*louti, Variola,* Lyretail Grouper, 203, 204
Low Spot Sharpnosed Pufferfish, *Canthigaster inframacula,* 652
*lowei, Polymixia,* Lowe's Beardfish, 106
Lowe's Beardfish, *Polymixia lowei,* 106
*lubbocki, Cirrhilabrus,* Lubbock's Fairy Wrasse, 435
Lubbock's Fairy Wrasse, *Cirrhilabrus lubbocki,* 435
*lucasana, Protemblemaria,* Plume Blenny, 520
*lucasanum, Thalassoma,* Cortez Rainbow Wrasse, 466
*Lucayablennius zingaro,* Arrow Blenny, 518
*luciopercanus, Serranus,* Walleye Basslet, 196
*luculentus, Pseudolabrus,* Orange Wrasse, 464
*lugubris, Caranx,* Black Jack, 247, 248
Lumpsucker, *Cyclopterus lumpus,* 168
*lumpus, Cyclopterus,* Lumpsucker, 168
Lunar Fusilier, *Caesio lunaris,* 272, 273

*lunare, Thalassoma,* Lyretail Wrasse, 467, 476
*lunaris, Caesio,* Lunar Fusilier, 272, 273
*lunatus, Bothus,* Peacock Flounder, 609
*lunula, Chaetodon,* Raccoon Butterflyfish, 340
*lunula, Rhinecanthus,* Crescent Triggerfish, 628
*lunulatus, Cheilinus,* Broomtail Wrasse, 432
*lunulatus, Lutjanus,* Crescent Snapper, 262
*lupus, Anarhichas,* Wolffish, 495
*lutescens, Thalassoma,* Yellow Wrasse, 467, 468
*luteus, Parupeneus,* Golden-spotted Goatfish, 319
*luteus, Pseudochromis,* Golden Dottyback, 207
*lutheri, Cryptocentrus,* Luther's Goby, 549
Luther's Goby, *Cryptocentrus lutheri,* 549
*Lutjanus adetii,* Gold-eyed Snapper, 261
*Lutjanus analis,* Mutton Snapper, 265
*Lutjanus apodus,* Schoolmaster, 265
*Lutjanus aratus,* Mullet Snapper, 268
*Lutjanus argentimaculatus,* Silver Snapper, 260, 261, 266
*Lutjanus bengalensis,* Bengal Snapper, 260
*Lutjanus biguttatus,* Doublebar Snapper, 258, 262
*Lutjanus bohar,* Red Mumea, 262, 263
*Lutjanus buccanella,* Blackfin Snapper, 265
*Lutjanus campechanus,* Red Snapper, 265
*Lutjanus carponotatus,* Striped Snapper, 261
*Lutjanus colorado,* Colorado Snapper, 268
*Lutjanus cyanopterus,* Cubera Snapper, 265
*Lutjanus decussatus,* Checkered Snapper, 260
*Lutjanus ehrenbergii,* Black-spot Snapper, 260
*Lutjanus erythropterus,* Gold-striped Snapper, 266
*Lutjanus fulviflammus,* Golden Snapper, 260
*Lutjanus fulvus,* Red and Green Snapper, 262
*Lutjanus gibbus,* Humpback Snapper, 262, 266
*Lutjanus griseus,* Gray Snapper, 265
*Lutjanus guttatus,* Spotted Rose Snapper, 264
*Lutjanus jocu,* Dog Snapper, 264
*Lutjanus kasmira,* Blue-striped Snapper, 260
*Lutjanus lemniscatus,* Sweetlips Snapper, 266
*Lutjanus lunulatus,* Crescent Snapper, 262
*Lutjanus lutjanus,* Rosy Snapper, 261
*Lutjanus madras,* Madras Yellow-lined Snapper, 262
*Lutjanus mahogoni,* Mahogany Snapper, 264
*Lutjanus malabaricus,* Malabar Snapper, 263
*Lutjanus monostigma,* One-spot Snapper, 262, 263
*Lutjanus notatus,* Blue-striped Snapper, 260
*Lutjanus novemfasciatus,* Pacific Dog Snapper, 268
*Lutjanus peru,* East Pacific Red Snapper, 268
*Lutjanus quinquelineatus,* Five-line Snapper, 261
*Lutjanus rivulatus,* Blue-spotted Snapper, 266
*Lutjanus rufolineatus,* Rufous Snapper, 261
*Lutjanus russelli,* Russell's One-spot Snapper, 263
*Lutjanus sebae,* Emperor Snapper, 270
*Lutjanus semicinctus,* Half-banded Snapper, 266
*Lutjanus* sp. *(lemniscatus?),* Sweetlips Snapper, 266
*Lutjanus stellatus,* Spotted Snapper, 263
*Lutjanus synagris,* Lane Snapper, 264
*Lutjanus timorensis,* Timor Snapper, 263
*Lutjanus vaigiensis,* Vaigeu Snapper, 263
*Lutjanus viridis,* Blue and Gold Snapper, 264
*Lutjanus vitta,* Olive-striped Snapper, 261, 270
*Lutjanus vivanus,* Silk Snapper, 264
*lutjanus, Lutjanus,* Rosy Snapper, 261
*luzonensis, Pseudanthias,* Philippine Fairy Basslet, 174
*Luzonichthys microlepis,* Slender Splitfin, 205
*Luzonichthys waitei,* Pink Basslet, 200
*Lycodes pacifcus,* Blackbelly Eelpout, 494
*Lycogramma zesta,* Pouter, 494
*lymma, Taeniura,* Blue-spotted Ray, 44, 47
Lyretail Coralfish, *PseudaAthias squamipinnis,* 174, 179
Lyretail Fairy Grouper, *Odontanthias fuscipinnis,* 180
Lyretail Grouper, *Variola louti,* 203, 204
Lyretail Hogfish, *Bodianus anthioides,* 429, 473
Lyretail Wrasse, *Thalassoma lunare,* 467, 476
*lysan, Scomberoides,* Doublespotted Queenfish, 250, 251
*Lythrypnus dalli,* Catalina Goby, 575
*Lythrypnus nesiotes,* Island Goby, 575
*Lythrypnus phorellus,* Convict Goby, 575
*Lythrypnus pulchellus,* Gorgeous Goby, 575
*Lythrypnus spilus,* Spotwing Goby, 575
*Lythrypnus zebra,* Zebra Goby, 575

## M

*maccoyii, Thunnus,* Southern Bluefin Tuna, 602
*maccullochi, Ellerkeldia,* McCulloch's Seaperch, 199
*machnata, Elops,* Ladyfish, 50
*macleayi, Atelomycterus,* Marbled Cat Shark, 38
Macleay's Crested Pipefish, *Histiogamphelus cristatus,* 126
*macneilli, Assessor,* MacNeill's Mini-grouper, 213
MacNeill's Mini-grouper, *Assessor macneilli,* 213
*Macolor niger,* Black Beauty, 269, 270
*macracantha, Trachypoma,* Toadstool Groper, 202
*macracanthus, Ambassis,* Perchlet, 170
*macracanthus, Gerres,* Thread-fin Silver-Biddy, 276
*macracanthus, Priacanthus,* Red Bullseye, 220
*macrocephalus, Gadus,* Gray Cod, 78
*macrocephalus, Pontinus,* Large-headed Scorpionfish, 146
*macroceros, Cantherhines,* Whitespotted Filefish, 629
*macrocheilus, Scarus,* Plain Parrotfish, 490, 492
*macrochir, Sebastolobus,* Bighand Thornyhead, 138
*macrodon, Cheilodipterus,* Eight-lined Cardinalfish, 234
*macrodon, Gobiosoma,* Tiger Goby, 571
*macrognathus, Opistognathus,* Banded Jawfish, 499
*macrolepidotus, Novaculichthys,* Seagrass Wrasse, 458, 472
*macrolepis, Onigocia,* Northern Bigscale Flathead, 162
*macrolepis, Sillago,* Large-scaled Whiting, 239
*macronema, Parupeneus,* Long-barbeled Goatfish, 313, 319
*Macropharyngodon bipartitus,* Divided Wrasse, 451
*Macropharyngodon choati,* Choat's Wrasse, 452
*Macropharyngodon cyanoguttatus,* Bluespotted Wrasse, 451
*Macropharyngodon geoffroyi,* Geoffroy's Wrasse, 452
*Macropharyngodon meleagris,* Guinea Fowl Wrasse, 452, 473
*Macropharyngodon negrosensis,* Yellowspotted Wrasse, 452
*Macropharyngodon ornatus,* Ornate Wrasse, 451
*macrophthalma, Trimma,* Flame Goby, 577
*macrophthalmus, Pristipomoides,* Yellowline Bananafish, 269
*macropterus, Nemadactylus,* Tarakihi, 416
*macropterus, Triodon,* Threetooth Puffer, 643
*macropus, Malacoctenus,* Rosy Blenny, 515
*Macrorhamphosus scolopax,* Longspine Snipefish, 123
*macrorhynchus, Halicampus,* Whiskered Pipefish, 127
*macrosoma, Gerres,* Large-bodied Silver-Biddy, 276
*macrospilus, Acanthemblemaria,* Barnacle Blenny, 518
*macrostoma, Myersina,* Hifin Goby, 552
*macrostomum, Haemulon,* Spanish Grunt, 279
*macrourus, Bodianus,* Blackfin Hogfish, 428, 429

*Macrozoarces americanus,* Ocean Pout, 494
*macrurus, Pentapodus,* Yellow-striped Whiptail, 299
*maculata, Gorgasia,* Spotted Garden Eel, 64
*maculata, Mene,* Moonfish, 256
*maculata, Sillago,* Blotchy Sillago, 239
*maculatofasciatus, Paralabrax,* Red Spotted Rock Bass, 202
*maculatum, Orectolobus,* Spotted Wobbegong, 35
*maculatum, Pomadasys,* Spotted Javelin Fish, 281
*maculatus, Antennarius,* Warty Frogfish, 85, 86, 89, 92
*maculatus, Apogon,* Flamefish, 230
*maculatus, Aulostomus,* Caribbean Trumpetfish, 119
*maculatus, Canthidermis,* Rough Triggerfish, 625
*maculatus, Caracanthus,* Pacific Spotted Velvetfish, 158
*maculatus, Epinephelus,* Spotted Grouper, 189
*maculatus, Plectropomus,* Footballer Trout, 203
*maculatus, Pseudupeneus,* Dotted Goatfish, 314
*maculatus, Scomberomorus,* Spotted Spanish Mackerel, 601
*maculatus, Trinectes,* Hogchoker, 615
*maculiceps, Acanthurus,* Black-eared Surgeonfish, 587
*maculifera, Apogon,* Spotted Cardinalfish, 229
*maculipinna, Halichoeres,* Atlantic Clown Wrasse, 446
*maculosus, Ctenogobiops,* Spotted Prawn Goby, 570
*maculosus, Myrichthys,* Tiger Snake Eel, 61, 64
*maculosus, Pomacanthus,* Blue Moon Angelfish, 362, 363
*maculosus, Threpterius,* Silverspot, 415
*madagascariensis, Caracanthus,* Velvetfish, 158
*madagascariensis, Chaetodon,* Indian Ocean Chevron Butterflyfish, 337
Madder Seaperch, *Mirolabrichthys dispar,* 171, 179
Madeira Sharp-nosed Puffer, *Canthigaster capistratus,* 652
Madras Yellow-lined Snapper, *Lutjanus madras,* 262
*madras, Lutjanus,* Madras Yellow-lined Snapper, 262
*maeandricus, Gobiesox,* Northern Clingfish, 97
*maena flexuosa, Spicara,* Picarel, 288
Magenta Dottyback, *Pseudochromis porphyreus,* 211
*magnifica, Lo,* Magnificent Foxface, 596, 598
*magnifica, Nemateleotris,* Firefish, 541, 570
Magnificent Foxface, *Lo magnifica,* 596, 598
Magnus' Goby, *Amblyeleotris sungami,* 543, 546
Magpie Morwong, *Cheilodactylus gibbosus,* 417
*Mahidolia mystacina,* Smiling Goby, 553
Mahogany Snapper, *Lutjanus mahogoni,* 264
*mahogoni, Lutjanus,* Mahogany Snapper, 264
Mahsena, *Lethrinus mahsena,* 296; *Lethrinus mahsena?,* 297
*mahsena, Lethrinus,* Mahsena, 296
*mahsena?, Lethrinus,* Mahsena, 297
Mailed Butterflyfish, *Chaetodon reticulatus,* 336
*major, Pagrus,* Red Tai, 290
*Makaira indica,* Black Marlin, 604
*Makaira mazura,* Blue Marlin, 604
*Makaira* sp., Marlin, 605
Malabar Rockcod, *Epinephelus malabaricus,* 188
Malabar Snapper, *Lutjanus malabaricus,* 263
Malabar Trevally, *Carangoides malabaricus,* 247
*malabaricus, Carangoides,* Malabar Trevally, 247
*malabaricus, Epinephelus,* Malabar Rockcod, 188
*malabaricus, Lutjanus,* Malabar Snapper, 263
*Malacanthus brevirostris,* Banded Blanquillo, 241, 511
*Malacanthus latovittatus,* Blue Blanquillo, 241
*Malacanthus plumieri,* Sand Tilefish, 241
*Malacoctenus boehlkei,* Diamond Blenny, 515
*Malacoctenus ebisui,* Fishgod Blenny, 514
*Malacoctenus gigas,* Sonara Blenny, 514
*Malacoctenus gilli,* Gill's Blenny, 515
*Malacoctenus macropus,* Rosy Blenny, 515
*Malacoctenus margaritae,* Margarita Blenny, 514
*Malacoctenus tetranemus,* Throatspotted Blenny, 514
*Malacoctenus triangulatus,* Saddled Blenny, 515
*Malacoctenus zonifer,* Girdled Blenny, 514
*Malakichthys wakiyai,* Wakiya's Perch, 173
Malamalama, *Coris ballieui,* 438
*maliger, Sebastes,* Quillback Rockfish, 149
*manabei, Labropsis,* Oriental Wrasse, 454
*manazo, Mustelus,* Japanese Smoothhound, 38
Mandarin Fish, *Pterosynchiropus splendidus,* 535, 539
*mandibularis, Ecsenius,* White-dot Blenny, 528.16
Maned Goby, *Oxyurichthys microlepis,* 552
Mangrove Goby, *Acentrogobius gracilis,* 551
*manilensis, Arothron,* Narrow-lined Toadfish, 648
*Manta birostris,* Manta Ray, 47, 48, 49
*Manta hamiltoni,* Hamilton's Manta, 48
Manta Ray, *Manta birostris,* 47, 48, 49
Many Banded Angelfish, *Centropyge multifasciatus,* 357
Many Banded Pipefish, *Doryrhamphus multiannulatus,* 128
Many Banded Scat, *Selenotoca multifasciata,* 329
Many-banded Goatfish, *Parupeneus multifasciata,* 315
Many-lined Cardinalfish, *Apogon chrysotaenia,* 225
Many-spotted Blenny, *Laiphognathus multimaculatus,* 527
Many-striped Sweetlips, *Plectorhinchus polytaenia,* 286
Many-toothed Blenny, *Ecsenius dentex,* 528.10
Manylined Coral Goby, *Gobiodon multilineatus,* 578
Manytooth Parrotfish, *Cryptotomus roseus,* 488
Maomao, *Abudefduf abdominalis,* 382
Maori Wrasse, *Ophthalmolepis lineolatus,* 460
*mappa, Arothron,* Scribbled Toadfish, 647
Marbled Blenny, *Paraclinus marmoratus,* 515
Marbled Cat Shark, *Atelomycterus macleayi,* 38
Marbled Dragonet, *Synchiropus marmoratus,* 538
Marbled Electric Ray, *Torpedo sinuspersici,* 43
Marbled Grouper, *Epinephelus inermis,* 192
Marbled Parrotfish, *Leptoscarus vaigiensis,* 488, 491
Marbled Puffer, *Sphoeroides marmoratus,* 649
Marbled Rockfish, *Sebasticus marmoratus,* 138
Marblefish, *Aplodactylus meandritus,* 416
*marcellae, Chaetodon,* French Butterflyfish, 347
*marcosi, Hoplolatilus,* Redstripe Tilefish, 240
Margarita Blenny, *Malacoctenus margaritae,* 514
*margaritacea, Sacura,* Cherry Bass, 180
*margaritaceous, Xenojulis,* Pink Speckled Wrasse, 469
*margaritaceus, Halichoeres,* Astrolabe Wrasse, 444
*margaritae, Malacoctenus,* Margarita Blenny, 514
*margaritata, Canthigaster,* Pearl Toby, 652
*margaritatus, Porichthys,* Freckled Head Midshipman, 84
*margariteus, Abudefduf,* Pearl Sergeant, 381
*margaritifera, Scolopsis,* Pearly Monocle Bream, 303, 308
*margaritiferae, Onuxodon,* Sharp-tailed Pearlfish, 79, 80
*margaritiphora, Apogon,* Lattice Cardinalfish, 224
*margaritophorus, Gymnothorax,* Trunk-eyed Moray, 56
Margate, *Haemulon album,* 279
*marginalis, Chelmon,* Willemawillum, 348
*marginata, Brosmophycis,* Red Brotula, 81
*marginata, Kuhlia,* Sported Flagtail, 219
Marginate Damselfish, *Dascyllus marginatus,* 378
*marginatus, Ctenochaetus,* Yelloweye Bristletooth, 589

*marginatus, Dascyllus,* Marginate Damselfish, 378
*marginatus, Halichoeres,* Dusky Wrasse, 440, 444
*marginatus, Nemipterus,* Palefinned Threadfin Bream, 306
Marianas Squirrelfish, *Neoniphon marianus,* 110
*marianus, Neoniphon,* Marianas Squirrelfish, 110
*marinus, Petromyzon,* Sea Lamprey, 34
*marinus, Sebastes,* Golden Redfish, 151
Market Anchovy, *Anchovia commersoniana,* 68
*marleyi, Chaetodon,* Marley's Butterflyfish, 345
Marley's Butterflyfish, *Chaetodon marleyi,* 345
Marlin, *Makaira* sp., 605
*marmoratus, Callechelys,* Leopard Snake-eel, 61
*marmoratus, Chironemus,* Kelpfish, 415
*marmoratus, Lepidoblennius,* Jumping Blenny, 508
*marmoratus, Paraclinus,* Marbled Blenny, 515
*marmoratus, Scorpaenichthys,* Cabezon, 167
*marmoratus, Sebasticus,* Marbled Rockfish, 138
*marmoratus, Sphoeroides,* Marbled Puffer, 649
*marmoratus, Synchiropus,* Marbled Dragonet, 538
*marmoratus, Torpedo,* Electric Ray, 47
*marmoreus, Parablennius,* Seaweed Blenny, 529
*Maroubra perserrata,* Sawtooth Pipefish, 126
Marquesan Sharpnosed Pufferfish, *Canthigaster marquesensis,* 652
Marquesas Butterflyfish, *Chaetodon declevis,* 336
*marquesensis, Canthigaster,* Marquesan Sharpnosed Pufferfish, 652
*marshallensis, Pseudochromis,* Marshall's Dottyback, 207
Marshall's Dottyback, *Pseudochromis marshallensis,* 207
*marshi, Etelis,* Yellowstripe Ruby Snapper, 259
*martinicensis, Holanthias,* Martinique Fairy Basslet, 180
*martinicensis, Xyrichthys,* Straight-tail Razorfish, 456
*martinicus, Mulloides,* Yellow Goatfish, 315
Martinique Fairy Basslet, *Holanthias martinicensis,* 180
Mashed Goby, *Gobionellus stigmaticus,* 565
Masked Bannerfish, *Heniochus monoceros,* 352
Masked Butterflyfish, *Chaetodon larvatus,* 337
Masked Cardinalfish, *Apogon thermalis,* 227
Masked Goby, *Coryphopterus personatus,* 574
Masked Lyretail Angelfish, *Genicanthus personatus,* 359
Masked Moray, *Gymnothorax panamensis,* 55
Masked Puffer, *Arothron diadematus,* 647
Masked Rainbowfish, *Halichoeres melanochir,* 442, 445
*masudai, Bodianus,* Masuda's Hogfish, 427
Masuda's Hogfish, *Bodianus masudai,* 427
Mata Tang, *Acanthurus mata,* 583, 586
*mata, Acanthurus,* Mata Tang, 583, 586
*mate, Atule,* Yellowtail Scad, 246, 247
*matsubarae, Sebastes,* Matsubara's Red Rockfish, 152
Matsubara's Red Rockfish, *Sebastes matsubarae,* 152
Matted Leatherjacket, *Acreichthys tomentosus,* 633
*maximowiczi, Physiculus,* Brown Hakeling, 77
*maximus, Cetorhinus,* Basking Shark, 37
*maximus, Lachnolaimus,* Hogfish, 470
*mazura, Makaira,* Blue Marlin, 604
*mccullochi, Amphiprion,* McCulloch's Anemonefish, 374
*mccullochi, Parma,* McCulloch's Scalyfin, 379
*mccullochi, Pseudochromis,* McCulloch's Dottyback, 209
McCulloch's Anemonefish, *Amphiprion mccullochi,* 374
McCulloch's Dottyback, *Pseudochromis mccullochi,* 209
McCulloch's Scalyfin, *Parma mccullochi,* 379
McCulloch's Seaperch, *Ellerkeldia maccullochi,* 199
*meandritus, Aplodactylus,* Marblefish, 416
*Mecaenichthys immaculatus,* Ogilby's Puller, 409
*Medialuna californiensis,* Halfmoon, 328
Mediterranean Banded Goby, *Gobius vittatus,* 559
Mediterranean Black Goby, *Gobius niger,* 559
Mediterranean Brown Wrasse, *Labrus merula,* 469
Mediterranean Damselfish, *Chromis chromis,* 388
Mediterranean Gray Wrasse, *Symphodus cinereus,* 471
Mediterranean Ocellated Wrasse, *Symphodus ocellatus,* 471
Mediterranean Rainbow Wrasse, *Coris julis,* 437
Mediterranean Seahorse, *Hippocampus ramulosus,* 130
Mediterranean Wrasse, *Symphodus mediterraneus,* 471
*mediterraneus, Symphodus,* Mediterranean Wrasse, 471
*megachir, Epinephelus,* Long-finned Grouper, 189
*Megalaspis cordyla,* Torpedo Scad, 250, 253
*megalepis, Doratonotus,* Dwarf Wrasse, 470
*Megalops atlanticus,* Atlantic Tarpon, 50
*Megalops cyprinoides,* Oxeye Herring, 50
*Meiacanthus anema,* Double Banded Forktail Blenny, 523
*Meiacanthus atrodorsalis,* Forktail Blenny, 523
*Meiacanthus bundoon,* Bundoon, 523
*Meiacanthus grammistes,* Grammistes Blenny, 522
*Meiacanthus kamoharai,* Black and White Striped Blenny, 522
*Meiacanthus lineatus,* Striped Blenny, 522
*Meiacanthus mossambicus,* Mozambique Blenny, 532
*Meiacanthus nigrolineatus,* Black-lined Blenny, 523
*Meiacanthus oualanensis,* Oualan Forktail Blenny, 523
*Meiacanthus smithii,* Smith's Blenny, 523
*Meiacanthus vittatus,* Singleband Forktail Blenny, 523
*melacara, Gramma,* Blackcap Basslet, 213
*melampygus, Caranx,* Bluefin Trevally, 247, 248
*melannotus, Chaetodon,* Black Back Butterflyfish, 337
*melanocephalus, Pervagor,* Redtail Filefish, 630, 633
*melanocercus, Symphodus,* Black-tailed Wrasse, 471
*melanochir, Halichoeres,* Masked Rainbowfish, 442, 445
*melanochir, Hyporhamphus,* Southern Sea Garfish, 100
*melanomaculata, Chrysiptera,* Blackspot Demoiselle, 390
*melanomarginatus, Cirrhilabrus,* Blackedge Fairy Wrasse, 434
*melanops, Sebastes,* Black Rockfish, 150
*melanopterus, Carcharhinus,* Blacktip Reef Shark, 39, 40
*melanopus, Amphiprion,* Black Anemonefish, 374
*melanopus, Coradion,* Two-spot Coralfish, 347
*melanosoma, Chaetodontoplus,* Black Velvet Angelfish, 360
*melanospila, Taeniura,* Black-spotted Ray, 47
*melanospilus, Genicanthus,* Blackspot Lyretail Angelfish, 358
*melanospilus, Sargocentron,* Horned Squirrelfish, 110, 111
*melanostictus, Myripristis,* Chubby Soldierfish, 114, 116
*melanostictus, Psettichthys,* Sand Sole, 612
*Melanostomias* sp., Black Dragonfish, 70
*melanotaenia, Pseudochromis,* Bow-tailed Dottyback, 210
*melanotis, Muraena,* Spotted Reef Moray, 57, 60
*melanotus, Dischistodus,* Black-backed Damsel, 409
*melanotus, Pseudojulis,* Golden Wrasse, 461
*melanurum, Haemulon,* Cottonwick, 278
*melanurus melanurus, Anampses,* Yellow Tailband Wrasse, 477
*melanurus, Dascyllus,* Blacktail Humbug, 378
*melanurus, Halichoeres,* Orange-tipped Rainbowfish, 442, 443
*melapterus, Chaetodon,* Black-finned Melon Butterflyfish, 341
*melapterus, Hemigymnus,* Half-and-Half Thicklip, 450
*melarchus, Ecsenius,* Dot-dash Blenny, 528.05
*melas, Apogon,* Dusky Cardinalfish, 228
*melas, Paraglyphidodon,* Black Damsel, 396
*melas, Pseudochromis,* Dark Dottyback, 212
*melasma, Archamia,* Black-spot Cardinalfish, 235

*melasma, Decodon,* Blackspot Wrasse, 470
*melasmopomas, Halichoeres,* Black-eared Wrasse, 442
*melatremus, Gymnothorax,* Blackspot Moray, 56
*melbae, Amphichaetodon,* Narrow-barred Butterflyfish, 350
Melbourne Mojarra, *Parequula melbournenses,* 275
*melbournenses, Parequula,* Melbourne Mojarra, 275
*meleagrides, Anampses,* Yellow-tail Tamarin, 425, 477
*meleagris camurum, Ostracion,* Spotted Boxfish, 640
*meleagris meleagris, Ostracion,* Spotted Boxfish, 617, 638
*meleagris, Arothron,* Golden Puffer, 645, 646
*meleagris, Gymnothorax,* Guineafowl Moray, 56
*meleagris, Istiblennius,* Painted Blenny, 531
*meleagris, Macropharyngodon,* Guinea Fowl Wrasse, 452, 473
*meleagris, Ostracion,* Spotted Boxfish, 642
*meleagris, Paraplesiops,* Western Blue Devil, 215
*Melichthys indicus,* Indian Triggerfish, 622, 623
*Melichthys niger,* Black Triggerfish, 622
*Melichthys vidua,* Pinktail Triggerfish, 622, 623
*mellis, Stegastes,* Honey Damselfish, 407
Melon Butterflyfish, *Chaetodon trifasciatus,* 336, 341
*Mene maculata,* Moonfish, 256
*menesemus, Apogon,* Prettytail Cardinalfish, 229
*Menticirrhus undulatus,* California Corbina, 311
*mento, Xanthichthys,* Blue Cheekline Triggerfish, 624
Merlet Scorpionfish, *Rhinopias aphanes,* 139
*merra, Epinephelus,* Honeycomb Grouper, 186, 189
*mertensii, Chaetodon,* Mertens's Butterflyfish, 336
Mertens's Butterflyfish, *Chaetodon mertensii,* 336
*merula, Labrus,* Mediterranean Brown Wrasse, 469
*mesoleucos, Chaetodon,* Red Sea Butterflyfish, 338
*mesoleucus, Chaetodontoplus,* Vermiculated Angelfish, 361
*mesoprion, Nemipterus,* Redfilament Threadfin Bream, 306
*Mesopristes argenteus,* Silver Grunter, 217, 218
*Mesopristes cancellatus,* Tapiroid Grunter, 218
*mesothorax, Bodianus,* Eclipse Hogfish, 428
Messmate Pipefish, *Corythoichthys haematopterus,* 128
Metallic Demoiselle, *Neopomacentrus metallicus,* 398
*metallicus, Neopomacentrus,* Metallic Demoiselle, 398
*metopias, Nemipterus,* Slender Threadfin Bream, 305
*metzi, Gibbonsia,* Striped Kelpfish, 516
*Meuschenia flavolineata,* Yellow-striped Leatherjacket, 630, 632
*Meuschenia galii,* Blue-lined Leatherjacket, 630
*Meuschenia hippocrepis,* Horseshoe Leatherjacket, 630, 632
*Meuschenia venusta,* Stars and Stripes Leatherjacket, 632
Mexican Blenny, *Paraclinus mexicanus,* 514
Mexican Goatfish, *Mulloides dentatus,* 315
Mexican Hogfish, *Bodianus diplotaenia,* 430
Mexican Horned Shark, *Heterodontus mexicanus,* 34
Mexican Lookdown, *Selene brevoortii,* 251
Mexican Parrotfish, *Scarus perrico,* 485
*mexicanus, Heterodontus,* Mexican Horned Shark, 34
*mexicanus, Paraclinus,* Mexican Blenny, 514
*meyeri, Chaetodon,* Meyer's Butterflyfish, 339
Meyer's Butterflyfish, *Chaetodon meyeri,* 339
*mezina, Girella,* Yellow-striped Blackfish, 326
*Microcanthus strigatus,* Stripey, 324, 327
*microcephalus, Ctenotrypauchen,* Small-headed Blind Goby, 580
*microchir, Harpadon,* Slender Bombay Duck, 73
*microchir, Moringa,* Spaghetti Eel, 53
*microdon, Epinephelus,* Camouflage Grouper, 189
*microdon, Pentapodus,* Small-toothed Threadfin Bream, 299
*microdon, Salangichthys,* Noddlefish, 70
*Micrognathus ensenadae,* Harlequin Pipefish, 125
*micrognathus, Lonchopisthus,* Pastel Jawfish, 498
*Microgobius carri,* Seminole Goby, 569
*Microgobius signatus,* Cuban Goby, 569
*microlepis, Luzonichthys,* Slender Splitfin, 205
*microlepis, Mycteroperca,* Gag, 194
*microlepis, Oxyurichthys,* Maned Goby, 552
*microlepis, Parma,* Little-scaled Parma, 379
*microlepis, Ptereleotris,* Blue Gudgeon, 561, 568
*Micrometrus aurora,* Reef Surfperch, 370
*Micrometrus minimus,* Dwarf Surfperch, 370
Micronesian Wrasse, *Labropsis micronesica,* 454
*micronesica, Labropsis,* Micronesian Wrasse, 454
*micropes, Coralliozetus,* Scarletfin Blenny, 519
*Microphis brachyurus,* Shorttail Pipefish, 125
*microps, Pomatoschistus,* Leonard's Common Goby, 558
*microptera, Lepidotrigla,* Blackfin Gurnard, 160
*Microspathodon bairdi,* Bumphead Damselfish, 408
*Microspathodon chrysurus,* Jewelfish, 408
*Microspathodon dorsalis,* Giant Damselfish, 408
*Microspathodon frontalis,* Ghana Yellowtail Damselfish, 408
*microstoma, Sargocentron,* Smallmouthed Squirrelfish, 108
*micrura, Gymnura,* Butterfly Ray, 45
Midas Blenny, *Ecsenius midas,* 533
*midas, Ecsenius,* Midas Blenny, 533
Midget Chromis, *Chromis acares,* 385
Midnight Angelfish, *Centropyge nox,* 355
Midnight Parrotfish, *Scarus coelestinus,* 486
Midwater Rockcod, *Epinephelus undulosus,* 188
*miles, Pterois,* Devil Lionfish, 142
*milesi, Pseudolabrus,* Scarlet Wrasse, 463
*miliaris, Chaetodon,* Millet-seed Butterflyfish, 343
*miliaris, Muraena,* Goldentail Moray, 60
Milk Trevally, *Lactarius lactarius,* 241
Milkfish, *Chanos chanos,* 68
*milleri, Pomacentrus,* Miller's Damselfish, 404
Miller's Damselfish, *Pomacentrus milleri,* 404
Millet-seed Butterflyfish, *Chaetodon miliaris,* 343
Mimic Blenny, *Hemiemblemaria simulus,* 519
Mimic Cardinalfish, *Apogon phenax,* 231
Mimic Surgeonfish, *Acanthurus chronixis,* 586
Mini-goby, unidentified, *Eviota* sp., 550
*miniata, Cephalopholis,* Coral Rockcod, 183
*miniatus, Halichoeres,* Spotted-finned Rainbowfish, 445
*miniatus, Lethrinus,* Long-snouted Bream, 297
*miniatus, Sebastes,* Vermillion Rockfish, 151
*Minilabrus striatus,* Red Sea Multicolor Wrasse, 459
*minimus, Micrometrus,* Dwarf Surfperch, 370
*Minous quincarinatus,* Whitetail Goblinfish, 155
*Minous versicolor,* Striped Scorpionfish, 155
*minuta, Gazza,* Toothed Pony Fish, 256
*minutus, Ecsenius,* Dwarf Blenny, 528.11
*minutus, Rudarius,* Dwarf Leatherjacket, 633
*mirationis, Chromis,* Wonder Chromis, 385
*mirifica, Pterapogon,* Sailfin Cardinalfish, 236
*Mirolabrichthys bartletti,* Bartlett's Fairy Basslet, 178
*Mirolabrichthys bicolor,* Bicolor Fairy Basslet, 174
*Mirolabrichthys dispar,* Madder Seaperch, 171, 179
*Mirolabrichthys evansi,* Yellowtail Goldie, 175
*Mirolabrichthys ignitus,* Flame Basslet, 174
*Mirolabrichthys imeldae,* Imelda's Seaperch, 175, 178
*Mirolabrichthys pascalus,* Forktailed Sea Bass, 178

*Mirolabrichthys smithvanizi,* Smith-vaniz's Fairy Basslet, 179
*Mirolabrichthys thompsoni,* Thompson's Fairy Basslet, 176
*Mirolabrichthys tuka,* Purple Queen, 178
Mirror Butterflyfish, *Chaetodon speculum,* 344
*miryae, Neopomacentrus,* Miry's Damselfish, 394
Miry's Damselfish, *Neopomacentrus miryae,* 394
Misty Grouper, *Epinephelus mystacinus,* 192
*mitratus, Chaetodon,* Black and Yellow Butterflyfish, 345
*mitratus, Petroscirtes,* Floral Blenny, 534
Mitsukuri Croaker, *Nibea mitsukurii,* 311
*mitsukurii, Nibea,* Mitsukuri Croaker, 311
*mitsukurii, Squalus,* Longnose Spiny Dogfish, 41
*moara, Epinephelus,* Kelp Grouper, 189
*Mobula diabolis,* Lesser Devil Ray, 48
*modestus, Chaetodon,* Japanese Golden-barred Butterflyfish, 346
*modestus, Thamnaconus,* Black Scraper, 635, 636
Moens Parrotfish, *Scarus moensi,* 489
*moensi, Scarus,* Moens Parrotfish, 489
*Mola mola,* Ocean Sunfish, 656
*mola, Mola,* Ocean Sunfish, 656
Molly Miller, *Scartella cristata,* 529, 530
Molucca Damsel, *Pomacentrus moluccensis,* 371, 402
Moluccan Goatfish, *Upeneus moluccensis,* 314, 318
*moluccanus, Pseudodax,* Chiseltooth Wrasse, 467
*moluccensis, Pomacentrus,* Molucca Damsel, 371, 402
*moluccensis, Upeneus,* Moluccan Goatfish, 314, 318
*Monacanthus chinensis,* Fan-bellied Leatherjacket, 629
*Monacanthus ciliatus,* Fringed Filefish, 628
*Monacanthus filicauda,* Thread-tailed Filefish, 629
*Monacanthus hispidus,* Planehead Filefish, 628
*Monacanthus tuckeri,* Slender Filefish, 628
Monarch Damsel, *Dischistodus pseudochrysopoecilus,* 400, 409
Monkeyface Prickleback, *Cebidichthys violaceous,* 495
Monkeyfish, *Erosa erosa,* 155, 156
*Monocentris japonicus,* Pineapplefish, 92, 103
*monoceros, Aluterus,* Unicorn Leatherjacket, 635
*monoceros, Heniochus,* Masked Bannerfish, 352
*monoculus, Ecsenius,* One-eyed Blenny, 528.09
*Monodactylus argenteus,* Silver Mono, 320, 418
*Monodactylus falciformes,* Cape Mono, 418
*Monodactylus sebae,* Fingerfish, 321
*monogramma, Scolopsis,* Monogrammed Monocle Bream, 302, 304
Monogrammed Monocle Bream, *Scolopsis monogramma,* 302, 304
*monoptera, Ptereleotris,* Ghost Goby, 561
*monopterygium, Hypnos,* South Australian Numbfish, 42
*monostigma, Gunnelichthys,* One-spot Worm Eel, 511, 580
*monostigma, Lutjanus,* One-spot Snapper, 262, 263
*Monotaxis grandoculis,* Big-eye, 296, 301
*monroviae, Acanthurus,* Monrovian Surgeonfish, 582
Monrovian Surgeonfish, *Acanthurus monroviae,* 582
Moon Butterflyfish, *Chaetodon selene,* 338
Moonfish, *Lampris guttatus,* 103; *Mene maculata,* 256
Moonlighter, *Tilodon sexfasciatum,* 327
*moorei, Pseudochromis,* Moore's Dottyback, 209
Moore's Dottyback, *Pseudochromis moorei,* 209
Moorish Idol, *Zanclus canescens,* 594, 595
Moray eel, unidentified, *Gymnothorax* sp., 52, 57
*mordax, Engraulis,* Northern Anchovy, 68, 69
*mordax, Gymnothorax,* California Moray, 55
*morhua, Gadus,* Atlantic Cod, 78
*Moringa microchir,* Spaghetti Eel, 53
*moringa, Gymnothorax,* Spotted Moray, 55
*morio, Epinephelus,* Red Grouper, 192
*mormyrus, Lithognathus,* Sand Steenbras, 288
*Morone saxatilis,* Striped Bass, 173
Mosaic Leatherjacket, *Eubalichthys mosaicus,* 634
Mosaic Moray, *Gymnothorax ramosus,* 57
*mosaicus, Eubalichthys,* Mosaic Leatherjacket, 634
*mossambica?, Siphamia,* Sea Urchin Cardinalfish, 237
*mossambicus, Meiacanthus,* Mozambique Blenny, 532
Mosshead Warbonnet, *Chirolophis nugator,* 495
Mottled Goby, *Trimma* sp., 577
Mottled Jawfish, *Opistognathus* sp., 498
Mottled Moray, *Gymnothorax prionodon,* 57
Moustache Jawfish, *Opistognathus lonchurus,* 498
*mowbrayi, Liopropoma,* Cave Bass, 198
Mozambique Blenny, *Meiacanthus mossambicus,* 532
Mozambique Cardinal, *Archamia mozambiquensis,* 323
Mozambique Emperor, *Lethrinus hypselopterus,* 295, 297
*mozambiquensis, Archamia,* Mozambique Cardinal, 323
*mucosus, Callogobius,* Sculptured Goby, 562
*mucosus, Urolophus,* Slimy Stingray, 46
*mucronatus, Hapalogenys,* Yellowtail Barred Grunt, 283
Mudskipper, unidentified, *Periophthalmidae* sp., 579
*muelleri, Chelmon,* Mueller's Butterflyfish, 349
Mueller's Butterflyfish, *Chelmon muelleri,* 349
*Mugil cephalus,* Striped Mullet, 421
*mugil, Kuhlia,* Barred Flagtail, 217, 219
Mullet Snapper, *Lutjanus aratus,* 268
Mullet, unidentified, *Liza* sp., 421
*Mulloides dentatus,* Mexican Goatfish, 315
*Mulloides flavolineatus,* Yellowstripe Goatfish, 315, 318
*Mulloides martinicus,* Yellow Goatfish, 315
*Mulloides pflugeri,* Pflueger's Goatfish, 315
*Mulloides vanicolensis,* Vanikolo Goatfish, 317, 318
Multi-spotted Searobin, *Pterygotrigla multiocellatus,* 160
*multiannulatus, Doryrhamphus,* Many Banded Pipefish, 128
*multibarbata, Brotula,* Whiskered Brotula, 80
*multicinctus, Chaetodon,* Pebbled Butterflyfish, 342
Multicolor Snake Blenny, *Sticharium dorsale,* 516
*multicolor, Centropyge,* Pastel Pygmy Angelfish, 356
Multicolorfin Rainbowfish, *Halichoeres poecilopterus,* 444
*multidens, Pristipomoides,* Striped Jobfish, 269
*multifasciata, Parapercis,* Barred Sandperch, 502
*multifasciata, Parupeneus,* Many-banded Goatfish, 315
*multifasciata, Pristigenys,* Red-striped Bigeye, 219
*multifasciata, Selenotoca,* Many Banded Scat, 329
*multifasciatum, Gobiosoma,* Greenband Goby, 571
*multifasciatus, Centropyge,* Many Banded Angelfish, 357
*multiguttatus, Alphestes,* Pacific Hamlet, 203
*multilineatus, Chromis,* Yellow-edge Chromis, 389
*multilineatus, Gobiodon,* Manylined Coral Goby, 578
*multimaculatus, Laiphognathus,* Many-spotted Blenny, 527
*multinotatus, Epinephelus,* White-blotched Rockcod, 188, 205
*multiocellatus, Antennarius,* Longlure Frogfish, 88
*multiocellatus, Pterygotrigla,* Multi-spotted Searobin, 160
*multiradiata, Pempheris,* Bullseye, 322
Multispined Damsel, *Paraglyphidodon polyacanthus,* 396
*multispinis, Centropyge,* Dusky Cherub, 354
*multispinus, Hemitaurichthys,* Spiny Butterflyfish, 351
*multivittatus, Plectorhinchus,* Gold-spotted Sweetlips, 283
*Muraena clepsydra,* Black-eared Moray, 60
*Muraena helena,* St. Helena Moray, 60
*Muraena lentiginosa,* Dotted-reef Eel, 60

*Muraena melanotis,* Spotted Reef Moray, 57, 60
*Muraena miliaris,* Goldentail Moray, 60
*Muraena pardalis,* Dragon Moray Eel, 58
*Muraenesox cinereus,* Silver Conger Eel, 62
*Muraenichthys* sp., Snake eel, unidentified, 53
*Muraenichthys tasmaniensis,* Tasmanian Golden Eel, 61
*muralis, Valenciennea,* Valencienne's Goby, 566
*murdjan, Myripristis,* Bigeye Soldierfish, 114, 116
*muricatus, Bolbometopon,* Humphead Parrotfish, 484
*muruadsi, Decapterus,* Amberfish, 245
Mushroom Scorpionfish, *Scorpaena inermis,* 145
Mustard Surgeonfish, *Acanthurus guttatus,* 583
*Mustelus henlei,* Brown Smoothhound, 38
*Mustelus manazo,* Japanese Smoothhound, 38
Mutton Hamlet, *Alphestes afer,* 203
Mutton Snapper, *Lutjanus analis,* 265
*Mycteroperca bonaci,* Black Grouper, 193
*Mycteroperca interstitialis,* Yellowmouth Grouper, 193
*Mycteroperca microlepis,* Gag, 194
*Mycteroperca prionura,* Sawtail Grouper, 193
*Mycteroperca rosacea,* Rosy Grouper, 193, 194
*Mycteroperca rubra,* Comb Grouper, 193
*Mycteroperca tigris,* Tiger Grouper, 194
*Mycteroperca venenosa,* Yellowfin Grouper, 193
*Myctophidae* sp., Lanternfish, unidentified, 75
Myer's Balloonfish, *Diodon myersi,* 656
*myersi, Diodon,* Myer's Balloonfish, 656
*myersi, Gobulus,* Paleback Goby, 553
*Myersina macrostoma,* Hifin Goby, 552
*Myersina nigrivirgata,* Myers's Goby, 552
Myers's Goby, *Myersina nigrivirgata,* 552
*Myliobatis tobijei,* Eagle Ray, 48
*myops, Trachinocephalus,* Shortheaded Lizardfish, 73
*Myoxocephalus aeneus,* Aeneus Sculpin, 165
*Myoxocephalus scorpius,* Short-finned Sculpin, 165
*Myrichthys aciminatus,* Sharptail Eel, 61
*Myrichthys colubrinus,* Barred Snake Eel, 61
*Myrichthys maculosus,* Tiger Snake Eel, 61, 64
*Myrichthys oculatus,* Goldspotted Snake Eel, 61
*Myripristis adustus,* Blacktip Soldierfish, 113, 114, 116
*Myripristis amaenus,* Castelnau's Soldierfish, 115
*Myripristis axillaris,* White-edge Soldierfish, 115
*Myripristis berndti,* Bigscale Soldierfish, 115
*Myripristis hexagonatus,* Oval Soldierfish, 114, 116
*Myripristis jacobus,* Blackbar Soldierfish, 113
*Myripristis kuntee,* Shoulderbar Soldierfish, 114, 115
*Myripristis leiognathus,* Panamic Soldierfish, 113
*Myripristis melanostictus,* Chubby Soldierfish, 114, 116
*Myripristis murdjan,* Bigeye Soldierfish, 114, 116
*Myripristis pralinia,* Scarlet Soldierfish, 112, 115
*Myripristis* sp., Pacific Soldierfish, 113; Soldierfish, unidentified, 104, 112, 113
*Myripristis trachyacron,* Rough-peaked Soldierfish, 116
*Myripristis violacea,* Lattice Soldierfish, 112, 114, 115
*Myripristis vittatus,* Ribbon-striped Soldierfish, 114
*Myripristis xanthacrus,* Yellowtip Soldierfish, 115
*mystacina, Mahidolia,* Smiling Goby, 553
*mystacinus, Epinephelus,* Misty Grouper, 192
Mystery Butterflyfish, *Chaetodon nigropunctatus,* 338, 339
Mystery Wrasse, *Pseudocheilinus* sp., 461
*mystinus, Sebastes,* Blue Rockfish, 150

## N

Naked-head Sea Bream, *Gymnocranius griseus,* 293, 296
Nalolo, *Ecsenius nalolo,* 533
*nalolo, Ecsenius,* Nalolo, 533
*namiyei, Ecsenius,* Yellow-tailed Blenny, 528.07
Nannygai, *Trachichthodes affinis,* 106
*Narcine brasiliensis,* Lesser Electric Ray, 42
*Narcine brunneus,* Brown Electric Ray, 42
*narinari, Aetobatus,* Spotted Eagle Ray, 47, 48, 49
*Narke japonica,* Japanese Numbfish, 42
Narrow Snouted Tripodfish, *Tripodichthys angustifrons,* 619
Narrow-bar Damsel, *Plectroglyphidodon dickii,* 395
Narrow-barred Butterflyfish, *Amphichaetodon melbae,* 350
Narrow-barred Spanish Mackerel, *Scomberomorus commerson,* 603
Narrow-lined Toadfish, *Arothron manilensis,* 648
*nasicornis, Pseudalutarius,* Rhino Leatherjacket, 635
*Naso brachycentron,* Humpback Unicornfish, 591
*Naso brevirostris,* Spotted Unicornfish, 590, 591
*Naso hexacanthus,* Blacktongue Unicornfish, 591
*Naso lituratus,* Orange-spine Unicornfish, 590, 591
*Naso lopezi,* Lopez's Unicornfish, 591
*Naso tuberosus,* Humpnose Unicornfish, 590
*Naso unicornis,* Unicorn Tang, 591
*Naso vlamingi,* Vlaming's Unicornfish, 590
Nassau Grouper, *Epinephelus striatus,* 192
*nasutus, Ogcocephalus,* Shortnose Batfish, 93
Natal Sharpnosed Pufferfish, *Canthigaster natalensis,* 653
Natal Stumpnose, *Rhabdosargus sarba,* 292
*natalensis, Ambassis,* Slender Glassy, 323
*natalensis, Canthigaster,* Natal Sharpnosed Pufferfish, 653
*natans, Bryaninops,* Pink-eye Sea Whip Goby, 560
*natans, Parapegasus,* Long-tailed Dragonfish, 119
*Naucrates ductor,* Pilot Fish, 253
*naucrates, Echeneis,* White-tailed Remora, 244
*naucratoides, Echeneis,* Whitefin Sharksucker, 244
*naufragium, Pseudobalistes,* Blunthead Triggerfish, 622
*Nautichthys oculofasciatus,* Deepwater Sculpin, 167
*navarchus, Euxiphipops,* Blue-girdled Angelfish, 361, 364
*Neatypus obliquus,* Western Footballer, 327
*Nebrius concolor,* Giant Sleepy Shark, 35
*nebulifer, Paralabrax,* California Sand Bass, 202
*nebulosa, Echidna,* Snowflake Moray, 59
*nebulosa, Parapercis,* Bar-faced Weever, 502
*nebulosa, Zenopsis,* Cloudy Dory, 118
*nebulosus, Halichoeres,* Picture Wrasse, 440, 444, 473
*nebulosus, Lethrinus,* Spangled Emperor, 295, 296, 297
*nebulosus, Sebastes,* China Rockfish, 150
Needlefish, *Tylosurus leiurus,* 100
Needlescaled Queenfish, *Scomberoides tol,* 250
*Negaprion acutidens,* Lemon Shark, 40
*Negaprion brevirostris,* Lemon Shark, 39
*neglecta, Rhinoptera,* Cow-nose Ray, 47
*neglecta, Scorpaena,* Fringyhead Scorpionfish, 146
*negrosensis, Macropharyngodon,* Yellowspotted Wrasse, 452
*Nelusetta ayraudi,* Chinaman Leatherjacket, 636
*Nemadactylus macropterus,* Tarakihi, 416
*Nemadactylus valenciennesi,* Valenciennes's Morwong, 416
*Nemanthias carberryi,* Threadfin Goldie, 175
*nematacanthus, Lethrinus,* Lancer, 295
*Nematalosa japonica,* Japanese Threadfin Shad, 67
*Nemateleotris decora,* Decorated Firefish, 570
*Nemateleotris helfrichi,* Helfrich's Firefish, 561

*Nemateleotris magnifica*, Firefish, 541, 570
*Nematistius pectoralis*, Roosterfish, 257
*nematophorus, Nemipterus*, Doublewhip Threadfin Bream, 305, 307
*nematophorus, Symphorus*, Blue-lined Snapper, 268, 270
*nematophthalmus, Pontinus*, Spinythroat Scorpionfish, 137
*nematoptera, Sphaeramia*, Polka-dot Cardinalfish, 221, 232
*Nemipterus balinensis*, Bali Threadfin Bream, 305
*Nemipterus celebicus*, Celebes Butterfly Bream, 307
*Nemipterus gracilis*, Gold-lined Threadfin Bream, 306
*Nemipterus hexodon*, Ornate Threadfin Bream, 306, 307, 308
*Nemipterus japonicus*, Japanese Threadfin Bream, 305
*Nemipterus marginatus*, Palefinned Threadfin Bream, 306
*Nemipterus mesoprion*, Redfilament Threadfin Bream, 306
*Nemipterus metopias*, Slender Threadfin Bream, 305
*Nemipterus nematophorus*, Doublewhip Threadfin Bream, 305, 307
*Nemipterus nemurus*, Redspine Threadfin Bream, 307
*Nemipterus ovenii*, Owen's Threadfin Bream, 305
*Nemipterus peronii*, Peron's Butterfly Bream, 306
*Nemipterus sumbawensis*, Sumbawa Threadfin Bream, 306
*Nemipterus tambuloides*, Fivelined Threadfin Bream, 306
*Nemipterus tolu*, Notched Threadfin Bream, 305, 306
*Nemipterus upeneoides*, Black-shoulderspot Threadfin Bream, 305
*Nemipterus virgatus*, Golden Threadfin Bream, 308
*Nemipterus zysron*, Butterfly Threadfin Bream, 305
*nemurus, Nemipterus*, Redspine Threadfin Bream, 307
*nemurus, Neopomacentrus*, Coral Demoiselle, 398
*nemurus, Pentapodus*, Whiptail Threadfin Bream, 299, 300
*Neocirrhitus armatus*, Brilliant Red Hawkfish, 412
Neoclinus bryope, *Neoclinus bryope*, 512
*Neoclinus bryope*, Neoclinus bryope, 512
*Neodax balteatus*, Little Weed Whiting, 478
*Neoditrema ransonneti*, Ransonet's Surfperch, 370
*neoguinaicus, Anampses*, New Guinea Tamarin, 425
Neon Goby, *Gobiosoma oceanops*, 573
*Neoniphon argenteus*, Silver Squirrelfish, 110, 112
*Neoniphon aurolineatus*, Yellow-striped Squirrelfish, 110
*Neoniphon laeve*, Bluejean Squirrelfish, 111
*Neoniphon marianus*, Marianas Squirrelfish, 110
*Neoniphon opercularis*, Blackfin Squirrelfish, 108, 110, 112
*Neoniphon sammara*, Spotfin Squirrelfish, 108, 110, 112
*Neoniphon sammara?*, Spotfin Squirrelfish, 111
*Neoniphon scythrops*, Jordan's Squirrelfish, 110
*Neopataecus waterhausi*, Whiskered Prowfish, 159
*neophytus, Fusigobius*, Dusky Fusegoby, 570
*Neopomacentrus azysron*, Yellowtail Demoiselle, 398
*Neopomacentrus cyanomos*, Regal Demoiselle, 398
*Neopomacentrus filamentosus*, Brown Demoiselle, 398
*Neopomacentrus metallicus*, Metallic Demoiselle, 398
*Neopomacentrus miryae*, Miry's Damselfish, 394
*Neopomacentrus nemurus*, Coral Demoiselle, 398
*Neopomacentrus taeniurus*, Freshwater Demoiselle, 398
*Neopomacentrus violascens*, Violet Demoiselle, 398
*Neosebastes pandus*, Gurnard Scorpion Perch, 137
*Neosynchiropus ijimai*, Ijima's Dragonet, 536
*Neosynchiropus ocellatus*, Scooter Dragonet, 536, 537
*Neosynchiropus* sp., Dragonet, unidentified, 536
*Nes Longus*, Orange-spotted Goby, 550
*nesiotes, Lythrypnus*, Island Goby, 575
*Nesogobius* sp., White Goby, 307, 551
Net Batfish, *Halieutaea retifera*, 93
New Guinea Cardinalfish, *Apogon novaeguinea (?cyanosoma)*, 225
New Guinea Tamarin, *Anampses neoguinaicus*, 425
New Zealand Red Mullet, *Upeneichthys porosus*, 312, 314
New Zealand Spotty, *Pseudolabrus celidotus*, 464
*Nibea mitsukurii*, Mitsukuri Croaker, 311
*nicholsi, Coryphopterus*, Blackeye Goby, 574
*nicholsi, Halichoeres*, Spinster Wrasse, 448
*Nicholsina denticulata*, Loosetooth Parrotfish, 488
*nicthemerus, Diodon*, Australian Globefish, 653, 654
*nieuhofi, Triacanthus*, Nieuhof's Tripodfish, 619
Nieuhof's Tripodfish, *Triacanthus nieuhofi*, 619
*niger, Apogon*, Black Cardinalfish, 228
*niger, Chrysiptera*, Black Demoiselle, 390
*niger, Gobius*, Mediterranean Black Goby, 559
*niger, Macolor*, Black Beauty, 269, 270
*niger, Melichthys*, Black Triggerfish, 622
*niger, Odonus*, Redtooth Triggerfish, 625, 627
*niger, Parastromateus*, Black Pomfret, 257
*niger, Scarus*, Dusky Parrotfish, 481, 489
Night Sergeant, *Abudefduf taurus*, 380
*nigra, Stigmatopora*, Wide-bodied Pipefish, 125
*nigrescens, Centropomus*, Black Snook, 170
*nigrescens, Halichoeres*, Diamond Wrasse, 444, 473
*nigricans, Dactylophora*, Dusky Morwong, 418
*nigricans, Entomacrodus*, Pearl Blenny, 529
*nigricans, Girella*, Opaleye, 326
*nigricans, Hypoplectrus*, Black Hamlet, 201
*nigricans, Stegastes*, Dusky Gregory, 405
*nigricauda, Acanthurus*, Brown-eared Surgeonfish, 587
*nigriceps, Lipophrys*, Black-headed Blenny, 525
*nigricinctus, Labrisomus*, Spotcheek Blenny, 513
*nigripes, Amphiprion*, Black-finned Anemonefish, 377
*nigripes, Apogon*, Blackfoot Cardinalfish, 232
*nigripes, Cheilodactylus*, Black-finned Morwong, 418
*nigripinnis, Cephalopholis*, Duskyfin Rockcod, 182
*nigripinnis, Hapalogenys*, Black-finned Grunt, 283
*nigripinnis, Paraclinus*, Blackfin Blenny, 515
*nigrirostris, Pseudochaetodon*, Black-nosed Butterflyfish, 347
*nigriventris, Eviota*, Blackbottom Goby, 572
*nigrivirgata, Myersina*, Myers's Goby, 552
*nigrocinctus, Sebastes*, Tiger Rockfish, 150
*nigrofasciata, Seriolina*, Blackbanded Amberjack, 250, 253
*nigrofasciatus, Apogon*, Black-striped Cardinalfish, 224
*nigrofuscus, Acanthurus*, Spot-cheeked Surgeonfish, 584
*nigrolineatus, Meiacanthus*, Black-lined Blenny, 523
*nigromanus, Pomacentrus*, Black-axil Damsel, 401
*nigromarginatus, Pomacentrus*, Black-margined Damsel, 401
*nigroocellatus, Istigobius*, Black-spotted Goby, 563
*nigropinnata, Wetmorella*, Arrowhead Wrasse, 454
*nigropunctatus, Arothron*, Black-spotted Puffer, 645, 646
*nigropunctatus, Chaetodon*, Mystery Butterflyfish, 338, 339
*nigroris, Acanthurus*, Cuvier's Surgeonfish, 588
*nigroris, Paraglyphidodon*, Black-mouth Damsel, 396
*nigrorubrum, Hypoplectrodes*, Black-banded Seaperch, 199
*nigrura, Chromis*, Black-tailed Chromis, 383
*nigrus, Plectorhinchus*, Black Sweetlips, 284
Nine-banded Cardinalfish, *Apogon novemfasciatus*, 224
Nine-spined Batfish, *Zabidius novemaculeatus*, 330
Nineline Goby, *Ginsburgellus novemlineatus*, 575
*niphobles, Takifugu*, Grass Puffer, 648
*Niphon spinosus*, Saw-edged Perch, 173
*niphonia, Pristigenys*, Japanese Bigeye, 219
*niphonius, Scomberomorus*, Japanese Spanish Mackerel, 603

*nippon, Chaetodon,* Blackloin Butterflyfish, 346
*nitida, Chromis,* Barrier Reef Chromis, 387
*nitidus, Apogon,* Bluespot Cardinalfish, 223
*niveatus, Cryptocentrus,* Snowpatch Goby, 556
*niveatus, Epinephelus,* Snowy Grouper, 191
*nivosus, Sebastes,* Snowy Rockfish, 152
*noarlungae, Trachinops,* Southern Hulafish, 214
*nobiliana, Torpedo,* Atlantic Torpedo Ray, 43
*nobilis, Conodon,* Barred Grunt, 281
*nocturna, Heraldia,* Herald's Pipefish, 126
Nocturnal Goby, *Amblygobius nocturnus,* 555
*nocturnus, Amblygobius,* Nocturnal Goby, 555
Noddlefish, *Salangichthys microdon,* 70
*nodosus, Calamus,* Knobbed Porgy, 291
*Nomeus gronovii,* Portuguese Man-O-War Fish, 605, 606
*norfolcensis, Apogon,* Norfolk Cardinalfish, 229
Norfolk Cardinalfish, *Apogon norfolcensis,* 229
*Norfolkia brachylepis,* Schultz's Triplefin, 508
*Norfolkia clarkei,* Clark's Triplefin, 510
*Norfolkia cristata,* Crested Triplefin, 510
*Norfolkia incisa,* Incised Triplefin, 510
*Norfolkia* sp., Northwest Triplefin, 508; Rosy Triplefin, 507
*normani, Saurida,* Shortjaw Lizardfish, 74
Northern Anchovy, *Engraulis mordax,* 68, 69
Northern Bigscale Flathead, *Onigocia macrolepis,* 162
Northern Buffalo Bream, *Kyphosus gibsoni,* 329
Northern Clingfish, *Gobiesox maeandricus,* 97
Northern Devilfish, *Plesiops cephalotaenia,* 214
Northern Dragonet, *Diplogrammus xenicus,* 536
Northern Lancetfish, *Alepisaurus borealis,* 75
Northern Seahorse, *Hippocampus erectus,* 131, 132
Northern Searobin, *Prionotus carolinus,* 161
Northern Wobbegong, *Sutorectus wardi,* 36
Northwest Triplefin, *Norfolkia* sp., 508
*notata, Chromis,* Tail-light Damselfish, 384
*notata, Scorpaena,* Red Scorpionfish, 144
*notatus, Abudefduf,* Yellowtail Sergeant, 381
*notatus, Apogon,* Blackspot Cardinalfish, 226
*notatus, Lutjanus,* Blue-striped Snapper, 260
*notatus, Porichthys,* Plainfin Midshipman, 84
Notched Threadfin Bream, *Nemipterus tolu,* 305, 306
*notialis, Chrysiptera,* Southern Demoiselle, 390
*notochir, Quassiremus,* Red-diamond Eel, 62
*Notograptus livingstonei,* Livingstone's Eel Blenny, 500
*Notorynchus cepedianus,* Broadnose Sevengill Shark, 33
*notospilus, Pseudojulis,* Senorita De Cintas, 461
*novacula, Xyrichthys,* Pearly Razorfish, 456
*Novaculichthys macrolepidotus,* Seagrass Wrasse, 458, 472
*Novaculichthys taeniourus,* Dragon Wrasse, 458, 472
*novaeguinea (?cyanosoma), Apogon,* New Guinea Cardinalfish, 225
*novaehollandiae, Pseudochromis,* Red and Green Dottyback, 209
*novemaculeatus, Zabidius,* Nine-spined Batfish, 330
*novemfasciatus, Apogon,* Nine-banded Cardinalfish, 224
*novemfasciatus, Lutjanus,* Pacific Dog Snapper, 268
*novemlineatus, Ginsburgellus,* Nineline Goby, 575
*nox, Centropyge,* Midnight Angelfish, 355
*nubilis, Gymnothorax,* Gray Moray, 57
*nuchalis, Leiognathus,* Spotnape Pony Fish, 256
*nuchipinnis, Labrisomus,* Hairy Blenny, 513
*nudivomer, Gymnothorax,* Starry Moray, 56
*nudus, Chirocentrus,* Smooth Wolf Herring, 68
*nugator, Chirolophis,* Mosshead Warbonnet, 495
*nummifer, Antennarius,* Coin-bearing Frogfish, 90, 91
Nurse Shark, *Ginglymostoma cirratum,* 35
*nystromi, Gnathophis,* Nystrom's Conger Eel, 62
Nystrom's Conger Eel, *Gnathophis nystromi,* 62

## O

*obbesi?, Paraploactis,* Weber's Coralline Velvetfish, 159
*obesus, Gymnothorax,* Speckled Moray, 57
*obesus, Thunnus,* Bigeye Tuna, 602
*obesus, Triaenodon,* Whitetip Reef Shark, 38, 40
Oblique-banded Cardinalfish, *Apogon semiornatus,* 225
*obliquus, Neatypus,* Western Footballer, 327
Oblong Filefish, *Paramonacanthus oblongus,* 634
Oblong Rockfish, *Sebastes oblongus,* 152
*oblongus, Paramonacanthus,* Oblong Filefish, 634
*oblongus, Sebastes,* Oblong Rockfish, 152
*oblongus, Takifugu,* Shy Puffer, 649
*obreptus, Stegastes,* Western Gregory, 405
*obtusata, Sphyraena,* Chevron Barracuda, 422
*Occella verrucosa,* Warty Poacher, 168
*occidentalis, Parma,* Western Scalyfin, 379
Ocean Pout, *Macrozoarces americanus,* 494
Ocean Sunfish, *Mola mola,* 656
Ocean Surgeon, *Acanthurus bahianus,* 582
Ocean Triggerfish, *Canthidermis sufflamen,* 625
Ocean Whitefish, *Caulolatilus princeps,* 239
Oceanic Seahorse, *Hippocampus kuda,* 128, 130
Oceanic Whitetip Shark, *Carcharhinus longimanus,* 40
*oceanops, Gobiosoma,* Neon Goby, 573
*ocellaris, Amphiprion,* Anemone Demoiselle, 377
*ocellata, Chaenopsis,* Bluethroat Pikeblenny, 519
*ocellata, Starksia,* Checkered Blenny, 512
Ocellate Damselfish, *Pomacentrus vaiuli,* 402
Ocellate Eel Blenny, *Blennodesmus scapularis,* 500
Ocellate Goby, *Vanderhorstia ornatissima,* 562, 568
Ocellated Blenny, *Ecsenius oculus,* 533
Ocellated Cardinalfish, *Apogonichthys ocellatus,* 237
Ocellated Frogfish, *Antennarius ocellatus,* 88
Ocellated Gudgeon, *Valenciennea longipinnis,* 566
Ocellated Longfin, *Plesiops corallicola,* 214
Ocellated Soapfish, *Grammistops ocellatus,* 206
Ocellated Turbot, *Pleuronichthys ocellatus,* 612
Ocellated Waspfish, *Apistus carinatus,* 137
*ocellatum, Hemiscyllium,* Epaulette Shark, 35
*ocellatus, Anarrhichthys,* Wolf-eel, 495
*ocellatus, Antennarius,* Ocellated Frogfish, 88
*ocellatus, Apogonichthys,* Ocellated Cardinalfish, 237
*ocellatus, Bothus,* Eyed Flounder, 609
*ocellatus, Chaetodon,* Spotfin Butterflyfish, 335
*ocellatus, Grammistops,* Ocellated Soapfish, 206
*ocellatus, Neosynchiropus,* Scooter Dragonet, 536, 537
*ocellatus, Parachaetodon,* False Batfish, 348, 350
*ocellatus, Pleuronichthys,* Ocellated Turbot, 612
*ocellatus, Symphodus,* Mediterranean Ocellated Wrasse, 471
*ocellicaudus, Chaetodon,* Spot-tail Butterflyfish, 337
*ocellicincta, Canthigaster,* Saddled-ocellated Sharpnosed Puffer, 652
*ochotenis, Liparis,* Eight-armed Snailfish, 168
Ochreband Goatfish, *Upeneus sundaicus,* 318
*octofasciatus, Chaetodon,* Eight-striped Butterflyfish, 339
*octotaenia, Paracheilinus,* Eightline Wrasse, 460
*octotaenia, Pseudocheilinus,* Eightstripe Wrasse, 458

*oculatus, Ecsenius,* Eyespot Blenny, 528.09
*oculatus, Etelis,* Queen Snapper, 259
*oculatus, Myrichthys,* Goldspotted Snake Eel, 61
*oculofasciatus, Nautichthys,* Deepwater Sculpin, 167
*oculus, Ecsenius,* Ocellated Blenny, 533
*Ocyurus chrysurus,* Yellowtail Snapper, 269
*Odax acroptilus,* Rainbow Fish, 478
*Odax cyanomelas,* Herring Cale, 478
Oddscale Cardinalfish, *Apogon anisolepis,* 231
*Odontanthias elizabethae,* Elizabeth's Fairy Basslet, 180
*Odontanthias fuscipinnis,* Lyretail Fairy Grouper, 180
*Odontaspis ferox,* Bumpytail Ragged-tooth, 37
*Odontaspis taurus,* Sand Tiger, 37
*Odontoscion dentex,* Reef Croaker, 311
*Odonus niger,* Redtooth Triggerfish, 625, 627
Offshore Crocodilefish, *Satyrichthys laticephalus,* 160
Offshore Lizardfish, *Synodus poeyi,* 74
Offshore Pony Fish, *Leiognathus rivulatus,* 256
*Ogcocephalus corniger,* Longnose Batfish, 93
*Ogcocephalus nasutus,* Shortnose Batfish, 93
*Ogcocephalus radiatus,* Polka-dot Batfish, 93
*Ogilbia cayorum,* Key Brotutid, 81
*Ogilbia* sp., Sonora Brotulid, 81
*ogilbyi, Atherinomorus,* Ogilby's Hardyhead, 102
Ogilby's Hardyhead, *Atherinomorus ogilbyi,* 102
Ogilby's Puller, *Mecaenichthys immaculatus,* 409
*oglinum, Opisthonema,* Atlantic Thread Herring, 69
Oilfish, *Ruvettus pretiosus,* 601
*okinawae, Gobiodon,* Yellow Coral Goby, 578
*oktodon, Scarus,* Eight-toothed Parrotfish, 490
Old Wife, *Enoplosus armatus,* 334
*olidus, Hypomesus,* Pond Smelt, 70
*oligacanthus, Plectropomus,* Striped Coral Trout, 203
*oligolepis, Liza,* Large-scaled Mullet, 421
*oligolepis, Parma,* Big-scaled Parma, 379
*oligolepis, Pristilepis,* Slender Soldierfish, 113
*Oligoplites altus,* Small-mouthed Leatherjacket, 251
*Oligoplites saurus,* Leatherjacket, 251
*olivaceous, Pseudochromis,* Olive Dottyback, 211
*olivaceus, Acanthurus,* Orange-epaulette Surgeonfish, 584, 586
*olivaceus, Paralichthys,* Olive Flounder, 610
Olive Dottyback, *Pseudochromis olivaceous,* 211
Olive Flounder, *Paralichthys olivaceus,* 610
Olive Rockfish, *Sebastes serranoides,* 151
Olive-spotted Monocle Bream, *Scolopsis xenochrous,* 304
Olive-striped Snapper, *Lutjanus vitta,* 261, 270
*Omegophora armilla,* Ringed Puffer, 643
*Omegophora cyanopunctata,* Blue-spotted Puffer, 646
*Omegophora* sp., Puffer, unidentified, 643
*ommata, Diplobatos,* Cyclops Electric Ray, 42
*Omobranchus elegans,* Elegant Blenny, 525
*Omobranchus elongatus,* Cloister Blenny, 534
*Omobranchus ferox,* Gossamer Blenny, 525
*Omobranchus germaini,* Germain's Blenny, 525
One-band Wrasse, *Cheilinus unifasciatus,* 431
One-eyed Blenny, *Ecsenius monoculus,* 528.09
One-lined Cardinalfish, *Apogon exostigma,* 226
One-spot Demoiselle, *Chrysiptera unimaculata,* 394
One-spot Snapper, *Lutjanus monostigma,* 262, 263
One-spot Waspfish, *Liocranium praepositum,* 495
One-spot Worm Eel, *Gunnelichthys monostigma,* 511, 580
One-stripe Snake Eel, *Aprognathodon platyventris,* 62
*oni, Tomiyamichthys,* Tomiyama's Shrimp Goby, 548
*Onigocia macrolepis,* Northern Bigscale Flathead, 162
*Onigocia spinosa,* Speckle-finned Flathead, 161
*Onuxodon margaritiferae,* Sharp-tailed Pearlfish, 79, 80
Opaleye, *Girella nigricans,* 326
*opercularis, Bodianus,* Candystripe Hogfish, 426
*opercularis, Chromis,* Double Bar Chromis, 383, 386
*opercularis, Neoniphon,* Blackfin Squirrelfish, 108, 110, 112
*opercularis, Rainfordia,* Rainford's Perch, 200
Ophichthid eel, Ophichthidae sp., 62
Ophichthidae sp., Ophichthid eel, 62
*Ophichthus ophis,* Spotted Snake Eel, 62
*Ophiclinus graclis,* Dark-backed Snake Blenny, 516
*Ophioblennius atlanticus,* Atlantic Fanged Blenny, 528
*Ophioblennius steindachneri,* Panamic Fanged Blenny, 528
*Ophiocara porocephala,* Spangled Gudgeon, 542
*Ophiodon elongatus,* Lingcod, 163
*ophis, Ophichthus,* Spotted Snake Eel, 62
*ophryas, Prionotus,* Bandtail Searobin, 161
*Ophthalmolepis lineolatus,* Maori Wrasse, 460
*Opisthonema libertate,* Libertad Thread Herring, 67
*Opisthonema oglinum,* Atlantic Thread Herring, 69
*Opisthopterus tartoor,* Snake-eyed Tartoor, 67
*Opistognathus aurifrons,* Yellow Head Jawfish, 497, 499
*Opistognathus cuvieri,* Cuvier's Jawfish, 499
*Opistognathus darwiniensis,* Darwin Jawfish, 498
*Opistognathus gilberti,* Yellow Jawfish, 496, 499
*Opistognathus lonchurus,* Moustache Jawfish, 498
*Opistognathus macrognathus,* Banded Jawfish, 499
*Opistognathus rhomaleus,* Giant Jawfish, 497, 498
*Opistognathus scops,* Bullseye Jawfish, 499
*Opistognathus* sp., Bluespotted Jawfish, 497; Keys Jawfish, 499; Mottled Jawfish, 498
*Opistognathus whitehursti,* Dusky Jawfish, 499
*Oplegnathus fasciatus,* Banded Knifejaw, 368, 369
*Oplegnathus punctatus,* Spotted Knifejaw, 369
*Oplopomus oplopomus,* Spinecheek Goby, 550
*oplopomus, Oplopomus,* Spinecheek Goby, 550
*opsifrontalis, Ecsenius,* Latticed Blenny, 528.14
Orange Anemonefish, *Amphiprion sandaracinos,* 376
Orange Band Wrasse, *Stethojulis balteata,* 455
Orange Eelpout, *Dinematichthys dasyrhynchus,* 81
Orange Filefish, *Aluterus schoepfi,* 635
Orange Gurnard, *Dactyloptena peterseni,* 137
Orange Hamlet, *Hypoplectrus gummigutta,* 201
Orange Wrasse, *Pseudolabrus luculentus,* 464
Orange-axil Wrasse, *Stethojulis bandanensis,* 455, 465
Orange-banded Goby, *Eviota* sp., 576
Orange-dotted Tuskfish, *Choerodon anchorago,* 431
Orange-dotted Wrasse, *Choerodon anchorago,* 474
Orange-ear Goby, *Gnatholepis inconsequens,* 558
Orange-epaulette Surgeonfish, *Acanthurus olivaceus,* 584, 586
Orange-finned Anemonefish, *Amphiprion chrysopterus,* 376
Orange-spine Unicornfish, *Naso lituratus,* 590, 591
Orange-spotted African Goby, Gobiidae sp. 1, 548
Orange-spotted Blenny, *Istiblennius chrysospilos,* 531
Orange-spotted Dorsal Goby, *Amblyeleotris* sp., 545, 546
Orange-spotted Filefish, *Cantherhines pullus,* 629
Orange-spotted Goby, *Nes Longus,* 550
Orange-spotted Prawn Goby, *Amblyeleotris guttata,* 545
Orange-stripe Cardinalfish, *Apogon* sp., 232
Orange-striped Emperor, *Lethrinus ramak,* 297

Orange-tipped Rainbowfish, *Halichoeres melanurus,* 442, 443
Orangeback Bass, *Serranus annularis,* 197
Orangeback Damsel, *Stegastes dorsopunicans,* 406
Orangecheek Parrotfish, *Scarus* sp., 484
Orangehead Goby, *Gobiosoma* sp., 571
Orangemarked Goby, *Amblygobius decussatus,* 555
Orangespot Goby, *Coryphopterus urospilus,* 574
Orangestripe Prawn Goby, *Amblyeleotris randalli,* 545
Orangethroat Pikeblenny, *Chaenopsis alepidota,* 519
*orbicularis, Cyclichthys,* Orbiculate Burrfish, 653
*orbicularis, Platax,* Orbiculate Batfish, 330, 332, 333
*orbicularis, Sphaeramia,* Orbiculate Cardinalfish, 323
Orbiculate Batfish, *Platax orbicularis,* 330, 332, 333
Orbiculate Burrfish, *Cyclichthys orbicularis,* 653
Orbiculate Cardinalfish, *Sphaeramia orbicularis,* 323
*orbis, Ephippus,* Spadefish, 330
Orchid Dottyback, *Pseudochromis fridmani,* 212
*Orectolobus japonicus,* Japanese Wobbegong, 35
*Orectolobus maculatum,* Spotted Wobbegong, 35
*Orectolobus ornatus,* Banded Wobbegong, 36
Oriental Flying Gurnard, *Dactyloptena orientalis,* 136, 539
Oriental Sweetlips, *Plectorhinchus picus,* 283, 285
Oriental Thornback, *Platyrhina sinensis,* 43
Oriental Wrasse, *Labropsis manabei,* 454
*orientalis, Dactyloptena,* Oriental Flying Gurnard, 136, 539
*orientalis, Sarda,* Striped Bonito, 603
Ornate Butterflyfish, *Chaetodon ornatissimus,* 339
Ornate Emperor, *Lethrinus ornatus,* 295, 296
Ornate Goby, *Istigobius ornatus,* 563
Ornate Scorpionfish, *Scorpaenodes varipinnis,* 153
Ornate Threadfin Bream, *Nemipterus hexodon,* 306, 307, 308
Ornate Wrasse, *Macropharyngodon ornatus,* 451
*ornatissima, Vanderhorstia,* Ocellate Goby, 562, 568
*ornatissimus, Chaetodon,* Ornate Butterflyfish, 339
*ornatissimus, Halichoeres,* Red Checkerboard Wrasse, 445
*ornatus, Istigobius,* Ornate Goby, 563
*ornatus, Lethrinus,* Ornate Emperor, 295, 296
*ornatus, Macropharyngodon,* Ornate Wrasse, 451
*ornatus, Orectolobus,* Banded Wobbegong, 36
*orthogrammus, Carangoides,* Yellowspotted Crevalle, 246
*Ostichthys japonicus,* Japanese Bonyhead, 113
*Ostracion cubicus,* Polka Dot Boxfish, 638, 639, 642
*Ostracion cyanurus,* Bluetail Trunkfish, 640
*Ostracion immaculatus,* Bluespotted Boxfish, 639
*Ostracion meleagris,* Spotted Boxfish, 642
*Ostracion meleagris camurum,* Spotted Boxfish, 640
*Ostracion meleagris meleagris,* Spotted Boxfish, 617, 638
*Ostracion solorensis,* Scribbled Boxfish, 640, 642
*Ostracion trachys,* Impostor Boxfish, 638
*Ostracion whitleyi,* Whitley's Boxfish, 640
*otaitensis, Thysanophrys,* Fringe-lipped Flathead, 161
Otakii's Greenling, *Hexagrammos otakis,* 162
*otakis, Hexagrammos,* Otakii's Greenling, 162
*Othos dentex,* Harlequin Fish, 205
Oualan Forktail Blenny, *Meiacanthus oualanensis,* 523
*oualanensis, Meiacanthus,* Oualan Forktail Blenny, 523
*oualensis, Pempheris,* Silver Sweeper, 321, 323
Outer-reef Damsel, *Pomacentrus emarginatus,* 400
Oval Soldierfish, *Myripristis hexagonatus,* 114, 116
*ovalis, Chromis,* Hawaiian Chromis, 384
*ovenii, Nemipterus,* Owen's Threadfin Bream, 305
*oviceps, Scarus,* Variable Parrotfish, 489
Owen's Threadfin Bream, *Nemipterus ovenii,* 305
Owstonia, *Owstonia grammodon?,* 420
*Owstonia grammodon?,* Owstonia, 420
Oxeye Herring, *Megalops cyprinoides,* 50
*oxycephala, Scorpaenopsis,* Hairy Stingfish, 136, 138, 146, 147
*oxycephalus, Bodianus,* Linespot Hogfish, 427
*oxycephalus, Chaetodon,* False Lined Butterflyfish, 339
*oxycephalus, Cheilinus,* Snooty Wrasse, 431
*oxycephalus, Cirrhitichthys,* Pixy Hawkfish, 411, 414
*oxycephalus, Plesiops,* Goldcheek Devilfish, 214
*oxycephalus, Tripodichthys,* Sharphead Tripodfish, 619
*Oxycirrhites typus,* Longnose Hawkfish, 413, 414
*oxygeneiosus, Polyprion,* Saw-tooth Grouper, 173
*Oxyjulis californica,* Senorita, 470
*Oxylebias pictus,* Painted Greenling, 163
*Oxymetopon cyanoctenosum,* Feathertail Sleeper, 542
*Oxymetopon* sp., Darkfin Sleeper, 542
*Oxymonacanthus longirostris,* Harlequin Filefish, 630, 631
*oxyodon, Paraglyphidodon,* Blue-streak Devil, 396
*oxyrhynchus, Amblycirrhitus,* Brown-barred Rosy Hawkfish, 414
*oxyrhynchus, Rhyncopelates,* Five-striped Pigface, 217
*oxyrinchus, Isurus,* Shortfin Mako Shark, 37, 40
*Oxyurichthys microlepis,* Maned Goby, 552
*Oxyurichthys papuensis,* Papuan Goby, 552
*oyena, Gerres,* Slenderspine Pursemouth, 274, 276

# P

*paccagnellae, Pseudochromis,* Royal Dottyback, 211
*pachycentron, Cephalopholis,* Brown-banded Rockcod, 182, 194
*pachycephalus, Sebastes,* Spotbelly Rockfish, 152
*pacifcus, Lycodes,* Blackbelly Eelpout, 494
Pacific Angel Shark, *Squatina californica,* 41
Pacific Barracuda, *Sphyraena argentea,* 422
Pacific Beardfish, *Polymixia berndti,* 106
Pacific Burrfish, *Chilomycterus affinis,* 653
Pacific Convict Goby, *Priolepis cinctus,* 567
Pacific Creole-fish, *Paranthias colonus,* 178
Pacific Dog Snapper, *Lutjanus novemfasciatus,* 268
Pacific Flagfin Mojarra, *Eucinostomus gracilis,* 275
Pacific Gregory, *Stegastes fasciolatus,* 403, 404
Pacific Hagfish, *Eptatretus* sp. *(stouti?),* 33; *Eptatretus stouti,* 33
Pacific Halibut, *Hippoglossus stenolepis,* 613
Pacific Hamlet, *Alphestes multiguttatus,* 203
Pacific Herring, *Clupea harengus pallasi,* 66
Pacific Ladyfish, *Elops hawaiiensis,* 50
Pacific Lined Grunt, *Haemulon flaviguttatum,* 280
Pacific Palometa, *Trachinotus kennedyi,* 254
Pacific Pomfret, *Brama japonicus,* 257
Pacific Porgy, *Calamus brachysomus,* 291
Pacific Sailfin Tang, *Zebrasoma veliferum,* 592, 593
Pacific Sand Perch, *Diplectrum pacificum,* 200
Pacific Saury, *Cololabias saira,* 100
Pacific Seahorse, *Hippocampus ingens,* 130
Pacific Sierra, *Scomberomorus sierra,* 601
Pacific Soldierfish, *Myripristis* sp., 113
Pacific Spadefish, *Chaetodipterus zonatus,* 330
Pacific Spotted Velvetfish, *Caracanthus maculatus,* 158
Pacific Threadfin, *Polydactylus sexfilis,* 420
Pacific Whitecheek Parrotfish, *Scarus bleekeri,* 483, 492, 493
Pacific Yellowcheek Wrasse, *Halichoeres* sp., 448
*pacifici, Apogon,* Pink Cardinalfish, 230
*pacificum, Diplectrum,* Pacific Sand Perch, 200

*paegnis, Solenostomus*, Ghost Pipefish, 123
*Pagellus acarne*, Spanish Bream, 290
*Pagrus auratus*, Golden Sea Bream, 290
*Pagrus major*, Red Tai, 290
*Pagrus pagrus*, Red Tai, 291
*pagrus, Pagrus*, Red Tai, 291
Painted Blenny, *Ecsenius pictus*, 528.15; *Istiblennius meleagris*, 531; *Pseudoblennius cottoides*, 167, 169
Painted Comber, *Serranus scriba*, 196
Painted Frogfish, *Antennarius pictus*, 87, 90
Painted Goldie, *Pseudanthias pictilis*, 177
Painted Greenling, *Oxylebias pictus*, 163
Painted Moki, *Cheilodactylus ephippium*, 417
Painted Scorpionfish, *Scorpaena picta*, 148
Painted Sweetlips, *Plectorhinchus pictus*, 287, 313
Painted Triggerfish, *Rhinecanthus aculeatus*, 626
Painted Wrasse, *Symphodus tinca*, 471
Paintspotted Moray, *Siderea picta*, 55, 58
Pale Cardinalfish, *Apogon planifrons*, 231
Pale Dottyback, *Pseudochromis pesi*, 210
Pale Gudgeon, *Ptereleotris heteropterus*, 568
Pale-headed Checkerboard Wrasse, *Halichoeres podostigma*, 445, 476
Pale-tail Chromis, *Chromis xanthura*, 387
Pale-tailed Damselfish, *Stegastes leucorus*, 405
Paleback Goby, *Gobulus myersi*, 553
Paleband Spinecheek, *Scolopsis ghanam*, 282
Palefin Basslet, *Liopropoma pallidum*, 199
Palefinned Threadfin Bream, *Nemipterus marginatus*, 306
Palespot Goby, *?Eviota* sp., 550
*pallasii, Pleuronectes*, Pallas's Flounder, 613
Pallas's Flounder, *Pleuronectes pallasii*, 613
Pallid G by, *Coryphopterus eidolon*, 574
*pallidum, Liopropoma*, Palefin Basslet, 199
Palmate Horned Blenny, *Parablennius sanguinolentus*, 524
Palometa, *Trachinotus goodei*, 254, 255
*palpebratus, Photoblepharon*, Flashlight Fish, 106
*Pampas argenteus*, Silver Pomfret, 606
Panamanian Lizardfish, *Synodus lacertinus*, 75
*panamensis, Cephalopholis*, Enjambre, 184
*panamensis, Gymnothorax*, Masked Moray, 55
Panamic Clingfish, *Gobiesox adustus*, 97
Panamic Fanged Blenny, *Ophioblennius steindachneri*, 528
Panamic Frillfin Goby, *Bathygobius ramosus*, 564
Panamic Green Moray, *Gymnothorax castaneus*, 55
Panamic Porkfish, *Anisotremus taeniatus*, 280
Panamic Sergeant Major, *Abudefduf troscheli*, 380
Panamic Soldierfish, *Myripristis leiognathus*, 113
Pancake Batfish, *Halieutichthys aculeatus*, 93
*Pandaka lidwilli*, Pygmy Goby, 551
*pandionis, Emblemaria*, Sailfin Blenny, 520
*panduratus, Glyptauchen*, Goblinfish, 158
*pandus, Neosebastes*, Gurnard Scorpion Perch, 137
Panther Flounder, *Bothus pantherinus*, 609
Panther Goby, *Barbulifer pantherinus*, 564
Panther Grouper, *Cromileptes altivelis*, 194, 195, 205
Panther Puffer, *Takifugu pardalis*, 648
*pantherinus, Barbulifer*, Panther Goby, 564
*pantherinus, Bothus*, Panther Flounder, 609
*Pantolabus radiatus*, Fringe-finned Trevally, 253
*papilio?, Periophthalmus*, Blue-dorsal Mudskipper, 579
*papilio, Synchiropus*, Butterfly Dragonet, 536
*papillosus, Helicolenus*, Jock Stuart Scorpionfish, 138
Papuan Goby, *Oxyurichthys papuensis*, 552
*papuensis, Oxyurichthys*, Papuan Goby, 552
*Parablennius gattorugine*, Tompot Blenny, 530
*Parablennius incognitus*, Pontif Blenny, 525
*Parablennius marmoreus*, Seaweed Blenny, 529
*Parablennius rouxi*, Roux's Blenny, 524
*Parablennius sanguinolentus*, Palmate Horned Blenny, 524
*Parablennius tasmanianus*, Tasmanian Blenny, 529
*Parablennius tentacularis*, Tentacled Blenny, 524
*Parablennius zvonimiri*, Zvonimiri's Blenny, 525
*Paracaesio xanthura*, Southern Fusilier, 259
*Paracanthurus hepatus*, Blue Surgeonfish, 589, 590
*Paracentropogon vespa*, Freckled Waspfish, 159
*Parachaetodon ocellatus*, False Batfish, 348, 350
*Paracheilinus carpenteri*, Carpenter's Wrasse, 459
*Paracheilinus filamentosus*, Filament-fin Wrasse, 424, 459
*Paracheilinus lineopunctatus*, Scarletfin Wrasse, 459
*Paracheilinus octotaenia*, Eightline Wrasse, 460
*Paracirrhites arcatus*, Arc-eyed Hawkfish, 413, 414
*Paracirrhites forsteri*, Forster's Hawkfish, 410, 413, 414, 415
*Paracirrhites hemistictus*, Half-dotted Hawkfish, 413
*Paracirrhites xanthus*, Golden Hawkfish, 415
*Paraclinus fasciatus*, Banded Blenny, 515
*Paraclinus marmoratus*, Marbled Blenny, 515
*Paraclinus mexicanus*, Mexican Blenny, 514
*Paraclinus nigripinnis*, Blackfin Blenny, 515
*Paradiplogrammus bairdi*, Lancer Dragonet, 538
*paradoxus, Psychrolutes*, Tadpole Sculpin, 167
*paradoxus, Solenostomus*, Short-bodied Ghost Pipefish, 120, 123
*Paraglyphidodon lacrymatus*, Jewel Damsel, 391, 396
*Paraglyphidodon melas*, Black Damsel, 396
*Paraglyphidodon nigroris*, Black-mouth Damsel, 396
*Paraglyphidodon oxyodon*, Blue-streak Devil, 396
*Paraglyphidodon polyacanthus*, Multispined Damsel, 396
*Paraglyphidodon thoracotaeniatus*, Bar-head Damsel, 396
*Paragobiodon echinocephalus*, Prickly-headed Goby, 578
*Paragobiodon xanthosomus*, Yellow Prickly-headed Coral Goby, 578
*Paralabrax auroguttatus*, Golden Spotted Rock Bass, 202
*Paralabrax clathratus*, California Kelp Bass, 202
*Paralabrax maculatofasciatus*, Red Spotted Rock Bass, 202
*Paralabrax nebulifer*, California Sand Bass, 202
*Paralichthys dentatus*, Summer Flounder, 610
*Paralichthys olivaceus*, Olive Flounder, 610
*Paralichthys woolmani*, Woolman's Halibut, 610
*Paraluterus prionurus*, Valentini Mimic, 636
*Paramonacanthus barnardi*, Wedgetail Filefish, 634
*Paramonacanthus japonicus*, Striped Filefish, 632
*Paramonacanthus oblongus*, Oblong Filefish, 634
*Paramonacanthus* sp., Filefish, unidentified, 634
*paranox, Pseudochromis*, Jet Black Dottyback, 210
*Paranthias colonus*, Pacific Creole-fish, 178
*Paranthias furcifer*, Creole-fish, 178
*Parapegasus natans*, Long-tailed Dragonfish, 119
*Parapegasus* sp.?, Seamoth, 119
*Parapercis aurantica*, Golden Grubfish, 502
*Parapercis bivittata*, Black Dorsal Grubfish, 504
*Parapercis cephalopunctata*, Spothead Grubfish, 504
*Parapercis cephalopunctata?*, Spothead Grubfish, 504
*Parapercis haackei*, Wavy Grubfish, 504
*Parapercis hexophthalma*, Sharp-nosed Weever, 504

*Parapercis multifasciata*, Barred Sandperch, 502
*Parapercis nebulosa*, Bar-faced Weever, 502
*Parapercis pulchella*, Bluestreak Weever, 502
*Parapercis schuinslandi*, Red Grubfish, 502
*Parapercis sexfasciata*, Six-banded Weever, 502
*Parapercis snyderi*, Snyder's Weever, 503, 505
*Parapercis* sp., Weever, unidentified, 502
*Parapercis* sp. (*cylindrica?*), Weever, unidentified, 504
*Parapercis tetracantha*, Four-barred Weever, 504, 505
*Parapercis trispilota*, Three-spotted Weever, 504
*Parapercis xanthozona*, Whitebar Weever, 502
*Paraplagusia bilineata*, Doubleline Tongue Sole, 614
*Paraplagusia japonica*, Japanese Tonguefish, 614
*Paraplesiops meleagris*, Western Blue Devil, 215
*Paraplesiops poweri*, Blue-tip Longfin, 214
*Paraploactis obbesi?*, Weber's Coralline Velvetfish, 159
*Parapriacanthus dispar*, Common Sweeper, 321
*Parapriacanthus ransonneti*, Slender Sweeper, 323
*Parapriacanthus unwini*, Slender Bullseye, 321
*Parapristipoma trilineatum*, Three-lined Grunt, 281
*Parapterois heterurus*, Blackfoot Lionfish, 140
*parasema*, *Chrysiptera*, Azure Damsel, 392
*Parastromateus niger*, Black Pomfret, 257
*Paratriacanthodes retrospinis*, Striped Tripodfish, 620
*Paratrigla vanessa*, Butterfly Gurnard, 160
*Pardachirus pavoninus*, Peacock Sole, 615
*pardaleocephalus*, *Halichoeres*, Blue-eared Wrasse, 475
*pardalis*, *Antennarius*, Leopard Frogfish, 88
*pardalis*, *Cantherhines*, Honeycomb Filefish, 627
*pardalis*, *Muraena*, Dragon Moray Eel, 58
*pardalis*, *Takifugu*, Panther Puffer, 648
*pardalotus*, *Acanthistius*, Australian Brown Grouper, 179
*pardus*, *Ecsenius*, Leopard Blenny, 528.09
*Parequula melbournenses*, Melbourne Mojarra, 275
Parika, *Parika scaber*, 636
*Parika scaber*, Parika, 636
*parilus*, *Pseudolabrus*, Brown-spotted Wrasse, 465
*Parioglossus formosus*, Formosan Goby, 560
*Parioglossus lineatus*, Lined Goby, 560
*Parma alboscapularis*, White Shoulder Parma, 379
*Parma bicolor*, Bicolored Parma, 377
*Parma mccullochi*, McCulloch's Scalyfin, 379
*Parma microlepis*, Little-scaled Parma, 379
*Parma occidentalis*, Western Scalyfin, 379
*Parma oligolepis*, Big-scaled Parma, 379
*Parma polylepis*, Banded Parma, 379
*Parma victoriae*, Victorian Scalyfin, 379
*paroculus*, *Ecsenius*, Brown-spot Blenny, 528.09
*parrae*, *Clepticus*, Creole Wrasse, 470
*parrai*, *Haemulon*, Sailor's Choice, 278
Parrotfish, unidentified, *Scarus* sp., 483, 493
*partitus*, *Stegastes*, Bicolor Damselfish, 406
*paru*, *Pomacanthus*, French Angelfish, 362
*Parupeneus atrocingulatus*, Three-striped Goatfish, 312, 315, 316
*Parupeneus barberinoides*, Bicolor Goatfish, 317, 319
*Parupeneus barberinus*, Dash-dot Goatfish, 317, 319
*Parupeneus bifasciatus*, Two-barred Goatfish, 317
*Parupeneus chrysopleuron*, Red Blush Goatfish, 316
*Parupeneus cinnabarinus*, Two-saddle Goatfish, 316
*Parupeneus cyclostomus*, Yellowsaddle Goatfish, 316, 317
*Parupeneus forsskalii*, Forsskal's Goatfish, 316
*Parupeneus indicus*, Indian Goatfish, 316, 319
*Parupeneus luteus*, Golden-spotted Goatfish, 319
*Parupeneus macronema*, Long-barbeled Goatfish, 313, 319
*Parupeneus multifasciata*, Many-banded Goatfish, 315
*Parupeneus pleurospilus*, Spotted Goatfish, 319
*Parupeneus pleurostigma*, Blackspot Goatfish, 315, 319
*Parupeneus pleurotaenia*, Bright-saddled Goatfish, 316
*Parupeneus porphyreus*, Purple Goatfish, 316
*Parupeneus rubescens*, Blacksaddle Goatfish, 313
*parva*, *Sacura*, Little Fairy Basslet, 180
*parvipinnis*, *Scorpaenodes*, Short-spined Scorpionfish, 143
*parvulus*, *Alabes*, Eel Clingfish, 97
*pascalus*, *Mirolabrichthys*, Forktailed Sea Bass, 178
*passer*, *Holacanthus*, King Angelfish, 367
Pastel Fairy Basslet, *Callanthias japonica*, 186
Pastel Jawfish, *Lonchopisthus micrognathus*, 498
Pastel Pygmy Angelfish, *Centropyge multicolor*, 356
Pastel Tilefish, *Hoplolatilus fronticinctus*, 238
*Pataecus fronto*, Red Indianfish, 159
*paucifasciatus*, *Chaetodon*, Red Sea Chevron Butterflyfish, 337
*pauciradiatus*, *Antennarius*, Dwarfed Frogfish, 88
*pauciradiatus*, *Craterocephalus*, Few-rayed Hardyhead, 102
*pauciradiatus*, *Diplogrammus*, Few-rayed Dragonet, 538
*paucispinis*, *Sebastes*, Bocaccio, 150
Paving-tile Blenny, *Ecsenius tessera*, 528.09
*pavo*, *Pomacentrus*, Blue Damsel, 403
*pavo*, *Salaria*, Peacock Blenny, 524
*pavo*, *Xyrichthys*, Peacock Wrasse, 456, 457, 458
*pavoninus*, *Pardachirus*, Peacock Sole, 615
*paxtoni*, *Corythoichthys*, Paxton's Pipefish, 127
Paxton's Pipefish, *Corythoichthys paxtoni*, 127
Peacock Blenny, *Salaria pavo*, 524
Peacock Flounder, *Bothus lunatus*, 609
Peacock Sole, *Pardachirus pavoninus*, 615
Peacock Wrasse, *Xyrichthys pavo*, 456, 457, 458
Peacockfin Goby, *Gnatholepis deltoides*, 558
Pearl Blenny, *Entomacrodus nigricans*, 529
Pearl Cardinalfish, *Apogon guamensis*, 229
Pearl Sergeant, *Abudefduf margariteus*, 381
Pearl Toby, *Canthigaster margaritata*, 652
Pearl-scaled Angelfish, *Centropyge vroliki*, 357
Pearlfish, *Carapus bermudensis*, 79, 80
Pearly Monocle Bream, *Scolopsis margaritifera*, 303, 308
Pearly Razorfish, *Xyrichthys novacula*, 456
Pearly Rockskipper, *Entomacrodus striatus*, 529
Pebbled Butterflyfish, *Chaetodon multicinctus*, 342
*pectinata*, *Pristis*, Smalltooth Sawfish, 42
*pectinirostris*, *Boleophthalmus*, Comb-toothed Mudskipper, 580
*pectoralis*, *Dactyloscopus*, Red-saddled Sand Stargazer, 512
*pectoralis*, *Enneanectes*, Redeye Triplefin, 507
*pectoralis*, *Labroides*, False Bluestreak Wrasse, 469
*pectoralis*, *Nematistius*, Roosterfish, 257
*Pegasus volitans*, Longtail Seamoth, 119
*pelamis*, *Katsuwonus*, Skipjack Tuna, 602
*Pelates quadrilineatus*, Four-lined Terapon, 217, 289
*Pelates sexlineatus*, Six-lined Trumpeter, 217, 218
*pelewensis*, *Chaetodon*, Sunset Butterflyfish, 342
*pelicieri*, *Halichoeres*, Pelicier's Wrasse, 442
Pelicier's Wrasse, *Halichoeres pelicieri*, 442
*pellucidus*, *Psenes*, Blackrag, 606
*pelycus*, *Pteragogus*, Sideburn Wrasse, 449, 450
*Pempheris adspersa*, Glowlight Bullseye, 322
*Pempheris analis*, Blacktip Bullseye, 321, 322

*Pempheris* cf *japonicus*, Blackfin Sweeper, 322
*Pempheris compressa*, Compressed Sweeper, 322
*Pempheris japonicus*, Blackfin Sweeper, 321
*Pempheris klunzinger*, Rough Bullseye, 322
*Pempheris multiradiata*, Bullseye, 322
*Pempheris oualensis*, Silver Sweeper, 321, 323
*Pempheris schomburgki*, Copper Sweeper, 322
*Pempheris schwenki*, Black-stripe Sweeper, 322
*Pempheris vanicolensis*, Vanikoro Sweeper, 323
Pen Shell Pearlfish, *Carapus homei*, 80
Pencil Weed Whiting, *Siphonognathus beddomei*, 478
*Pencipelta vittiger*, Toothbrush Leatherjacket, 634
*penicilligerus, Chaetodermis*, Prickly Leatherjacket, 630, 634
*penicillus, Hippichthys*, Beady Pipefish, 126
Pennant Glider, *Valenciennea strigata*, 566
*pennatula, Calamus*, Pluma, 291
*Pentaceropsis recurvirostris*, Long-snouted Boarfish, 334
*Pentaceros japonicus*, Japanese Boarfish, 335
*pentadactylus, Xyrichthys*, Fivefinger Wrasse, 457
*Pentapodus bifasciatus*, Two-striped Bream, 307
*Pentapodus caninus*, Banded Threadfin Bream, 299, 300, 307
*Pentapodus hellmuthi*, Hellmuth's Threadfin Bream, 299
*Pentapodus macrurus*, Yellow-striped Whiptail, 299
*Pentapodus microdon*, Small-toothed Threadfin Bream, 299
*Pentapodus nemurus*, Whiptail Threadfin Bream, 299, 300
*Pentapodus porosus*, Yellowstreak Whiptail, 300
*Pentapodus setosus*, Butterfly Bream, 299, 300
*Pentapodus* sp., Black-and-White Striped Bream, 300; Blackband Threadfin Bream, 300; Threeline Bream, 300; Yellowstripe Threadfin Bream, 299
*Pentapodus vitta*, Threadfin Bream, 293, 300
*Pentaprion longimanus*, Long-finned Silver-Biddy, 275
Peppered Butterflyfish, *Chaetodon guttatissimus*, 344
Peppered Chromis, *Chromis cinerascens*, 384
Peppered Righteye Flounder, *Clidoderma asperrimum*, 608
Peppermint Basslet, *Liopropoma rubre*, 198
Peppermint Goby, *Coryphopterus lipernes*, 574
Perch Sculpin, *Pseudoblennius percoides*, 167
Perchlet, *Ambassis macracanthus*, 170
*percoides, Pseudoblennius*, Perch Sculpin, 167
*percula, Amphiprion*, Clown Anemonefish, 372
*perdito, Bodianus*, Goldsaddle Hogfish, 428
*Pereulixia kosiensis*, Kosi Rockskipper, 532
*perideraion, Amphiprion*, False Skunk-striped Anemonefish, 375, 376
*Periophthalmidae* sp., Mudskipper, unidentified, 579
*Periophthalmus argentilineatus*, Silverline Mudskipper, 579
*Periophthalmus cantonensis*, Canton Mudskipper, 579
*Periophthalmus koelreuteri*, Blotchy Mudskipper, 568, 579
*Periophthalmus papilio?*, Blue-dorsal Mudskipper, 579
*Periophthalmus regius*, Regal Mudskipper, 579
*Periophthalmus sobrinus?*, Seychelles Mudskipper, 579
*Periophthalmus* sp., Bluestreak Mudskipper, 579
*periophthalmus, Amblyeleotris*, Slender Shrimp Goby, 543
*periophthalmus, Istiblennius*, Bullethead Rockskipper, 534
*?Peristedion* sp., Sea Robin, unidentified, 160
*Peristrominous dolosus*, Cod Scorpionfish, 137
*perlo, Heptranchias*, Sharpnose Sevengill Shark, 33
*permistus, Gymnothorax*, Reticulated Moray, 56
PermitGreat Pompano, *Trachinotus falcatus*, 254
*peronii, Nemipterus*, Peron's Butterfly Bream, 306
Peron's Butterfly Bream, *Nemipterus peronii*, 306
*perrico, Scarus*, Mexican Parrotfish, 485
*Perryena leucometopon*, Whitenose Pigfish, 158
*perserrata, Maroubra*, Sawtooth Pipefish, 126
*personatus, Coryphopterus*, Masked Goby, 574
*personatus, Genicanthus*, Masked Lyretail Angelfish, 359
*personatus, Scolopsis*, Blue-nosed Monocle Bream, 303
*personifer, Chaetodontoplus*, Bluemask Angelfish, 360
*perspicillatus, Dischistodus*, White Damsel, 409
*perspicillatus, Pseudochromis*, Brown-banded Dottyback, 211
*perspicillatus, Scarus*, Hawaiian Blue Parrotfish, 483
*peru, Lutjanus*, East Pacific Red Snapper, 268
*Pervagor aspricaudus*, Hawaiian Redtail Filefish, 633
*Pervagor melanocephalus*, Redtail Filefish, 630, 633
*Pervagor spilosoma*, Fantail Filefish, 633
*pesi, Pseudochromis*, Pale Dottyback, 210
*petenense, Dorosoma*, Threadfin Shad, 67
*peterseni, Dactyloptena*, Orange Gurnard, 137
*petersi, Dinoperca*, Cavebass, 205
*petersii, Pterycombus*, Prickly Fanfish, 257
*Petromyzon marinus*, Sea Lamprey, 34
*Petroscirtes breviceps*, Dandy Blenny, 522
*Petroscirtes fallax*, Batesian Mimic, 522
*Petroscirtes mitratus*, Floral Blenny, 534
*Petroscirtes xestus*, Zesty Blenny, 522
Pflueger's Goatfish, *Mulloides pflugeri*, 315
*pflugeri, Mulloides*, Pflueger's Goatfish, 315
*Phaeoptyx conklini*, Freckled Cardinalfish, 236
*Phaeoptyx pigmentaria*, Dappled Cardinalfish, 236
*Phaeoptyx xenus*, Sponge Cardinalfish, 236
*phalaena, Amblygobius*, Banded Goby, 551, 554, 555
Phallic Blenny, *Starksia spinipenis*, 512
*Phanerodon furcatus*, White Surfperch, 370
*phantasma, Chimaera*, Ghost Shark, 33
Phenax, *Plagiotremus phenax*, 521
*phenax, Apogon*, Mimic Cardinalfish, 231
*phenax, Plagiotremus*, Phenax, 521
Philippine Bandfish, *Acanthocepola indica*, 420
Philippine Blenny, *Ecsenius dilemma*, 528.13
Philippine Chevron Butterflyfish, *Chaetodon xanthurus*, 336
Philippine Damsel, *Pomacentrus philippinus*, 399, 401
Philippine Fairy Basslet, *Pseudanthias luzonensis*, 174
Philippine Garden Eel, *Gorgasia preclara*, 63, 64
Philippine Pennant Coralfish, *Heniochus singularius*, 352
*philippinus, Pomacentrus*, Philippine Damsel, 399, 401
*phoebe, Serranus*, Tattler, 196
Phoenix Damsel, *Plectroglyphidodon phoenixensis*, 394
*phoenixensis, Plectroglyphidodon*, Phoenix Damsel, 394
*Pholidichthys leucotaenia*, Convict Blenny, 500
*Pholis gunnellus*, Rock Gunnel, 495
*phorellus, Lythrypnus*, Convict Goby, 575
*Photoblepharon palpebratus*, Flashlight Fish, 106
*phthirophagus, Labroides*, Hawaiian Cleaner Wrasse, 469
*Phycodurus eques*, Leafy Seadragon, 121, 124
*Phyllopteryx taeniolatus*, Weedy Seadragon, 120, 124
*Physiculus maximowiczi*, Brown Hakeling, 77
*Physiculus* sp., Hakeling, unidentified, 77
Piano Blenny, *Plagiotremus tapeinosoma*, 532
Picarel, *Spicara maena flexuosa*, 288
Picasso Triggerfish, *Rhinecanthus assasi*, 626
Pickhandle Barracuda, *Sphyraena jello*, 422
*picta, Coris*, Combfish, 437
*picta, Scorpaena*, Painted Scorpionfish, 148

*picta, Siderea,* Paintspotted Moray, 55, 58
*Pictilabrus laticlavius,* Senator Wrasse, 462
*Pictilabrus* sp., False Senator Wrasse, 462
*pictilis, Pseudanthias,* Painted Goldie, 177
*pictoides, Coris,* False Combfish, 437
*picturatus, Synchiropus,* Psychedelic Fish, 535, 539
Picture Wrasse, *Halichoeres nebulosus,* 440, 444, 473
*pictus, Antennarius,* Painted Frogfish, 87, 90
*pictus, Ecsenius,* Painted Blenny, 528.15
*pictus, Halichoeres,* Atlantic Rainbow Wrasse, 446
*pictus, Oxylebias,* Painted Greenling, 163
*pictus, Plectorhinchus,* Painted Sweetlips, 287, 313
*picus, Plectorhinchus,* Oriental Sweetlips, 283, 285
*pigmentaria, Phaeoptyx,* Dappled Cardinalfish, 236
*Pikea aurora,* Hawaiian Basslet, 200
*pikei, Pomacentrus,* Scintillating Damsel, 403
Pile Surfperch, *Damalichthys vacca,* 370
*pillionatus, Apogon,* Broadsaddle Cardinalfish, 231
Pilot Fish, *Naucrates ductor,* 253
Pineapplefish, *Monocentris japonicus,* 92, 103
*pinetorum herzensteini, Cleisthenes,* Herzenstein's Righteye Flounder, 608
Pinfish, *Lagodon rhomboides,* 292
*pinguis, Sphyraena,* Fat Barracuda, 422
Pink Basslet, *Luzonichthys waitei,* 200
Pink Cardinalfish, *Apogon pacifici,* 230
Pink Maomao, *Caprodon longimanus,* 181
Pink Speckled Wrasse, *Xenojulis margaritaceous,* 469
Pink Weedfish, *Heteroclinus roseus,* 517
Pink-and-Blue Spotted Goby, *Cryptocentrus leptocephalus,* 540, 556, 557
Pink-eye Sea Whip Goby, *Bryaninops natans,* 560
Pinkbar Goby, *Amblyeleotris aurora,* 543; *Cryptocentrus aurora,* 547
Pinktail Triggerfish, *Melichthys vidua,* 622, 623
*pinnatibarbatus japonicus, Cheilopogon,* Japanese Feather-finned Flying Fish, 99
*pinnatus, Platax,* Long-finned Batfish, 330, 332
*pinniger, Sebastes,* Canary Rockfish, 150
*pinnulatus, Cirrhitus,* Freckled Hawkfish, 413, 414
*pinos, Amblycirrhitus,* Redspotted Hawkfish, 415
Pipefish, unidentified, *Syngnathus* sp., 125
Pirate Blenny, *Emblemaria piratula,* 520
*piratula, Emblemaria,* Pirate Blenny, 520
*pisang, Caesio,* Yellowstriped Fusilier, 272, 273
*Pisodonophis cancrivorus,* Long-finned Snake Eel, 61
Pixy Hawkfish, *Cirrhitichthys oxycephalus,* 411, 414
*plagiometopon, Hemiglyphidodon,* Lagoon Damsel, 397
*plagiosum, Chiloscyllium,* Banded Catshark, 36
*Plagiotremus azaleus,* Sabretooth Blenny, 521
*Plagiotremus goslinei,* Gosline's Mimic Blenny, 521
*Plagiotremus laudandus flavus,* Golden Mimic Blenny, 521
*Plagiotremus phenax,* Phenax, 521
*Plagiotremus rhinorhynchos,* Cleaner Mimic, 506, 521
*Plagiotremus tapeinosoma,* Piano Blenny, 532
*Plagiotremus townsendi,* Townsend's Mimic Blenny, 521
Plaice, *Pleuronectes platessa,* 612
Plain Dottyback, *Pseudoplesiops inornatus,* 211
Plain Grouper, *Trisotropis dermopterus,* 202
Plain Parrotfish, *Scarus macrocheilus,* 490, 492
Plainfin Midshipman, *Porichthys notatus,* 84
Planehead Filefish, *Monacanthus hispidus,* 628
*planifrons, Apogon,* Pale Cardinalfish, 231
*planifrons, Stegastes,* Three Spot Damselfish, 406
*Platax batavianus,* Batavian Batfish, 331, 332
*Platax orbicularis,* Orbiculate Batfish, 330, 332, 333
*Platax pinnatus,* Long-finned Batfish, 330, 332
*Platax teira,* Round-faced Batfish, 334
*platessa, Pleuronectes,* Plaice, 612
*Platichthys flesus,* European Flounder, 612
*Platichthys stellatus,* Starry Flounder, 607, 612
*Platybelone argalus,* Gill-rakered Needlefish, 100
*Platycephalus haackei,* Haacke's Flathead, 72
*Platycephalus indicus,* Bartail Flathead, 162
*Platycephalus* sp., Flathead, unidentified, 166
*platypterus, Istiophorus,* Sailfish, 604
*Platyrhina sinensis,* Oriental Thornback, 43
*Platyrhinoidis triseriata,* Thornback, 43
*platyventris, Aprognathodon,* One-stripe Snake Eel, 62
*plebeius, Chaetodon,* Blue-blotched Butterflyfish, 339
*Plectorhinchus albovittatus,* Yellow-lined Sweetlips, 283
*Plectorhinchus celebicus,* Celebes Sweetlips, 284
*Plectorhinchus chaetodonoides,* Harlequin Sweetlips, 282, 283, 287
*Plectorhinchus cinctus,* Three-banded Sweetlip, 284
*Plectorhinchus diagrammus,* Silver-banded Sweetlips, 284
*Plectorhinchus flavomaculatus,* Lemon Sweetlips, 282, 283, 287
*Plectorhinchus gaterinus,* Black-spotted Rubberlip, 282, 285
*Plectorhinchus goldmanni,* Goldman's Sweetlips, 284, 286
*Plectorhinchus lineatus,* Yellow-banded Sweetlips, 285, 286
*Plectorhinchus multivittatus,* Gold-spotted Sweetlips, 283
*Plectorhinchus nigrus,* Black Sweetlips, 284
*Plectorhinchus pictus,* Painted Sweetlips, 287, 313
*Plectorhinchus picus,* Oriental Sweetlips, 283, 285
*Plectorhinchus polytaenia,* Many-striped Sweetlips, 286
*Plectorhinchus schotaf,* Sombre Sweetlips, 282, 284
*Plectorhinchus sordidus,* Redlip Rubberlip, 284, 285
*Plectranthias japonicus,* Japanese Coral Trout, 181
*Plectroglyphidodon dickii,* Narrow-bar Damsel, 395
*Plectroglyphidodon imparipennis,* Bright Eye, 395
*Plectroglyphidodon johnstonianus,* Johnston Damsel, 395
*Plectroglyphidodon leucozona,* Bellyband Damselfish, 394
*Plectroglyphidodon phoenixensis,* Phoenix Damsel, 394
*Plectroglyphidodon sindonis,* Hawaiian Rock Damsel, 395
*Plectropomus areolatus,* Squaretail Leopard Grouper, 203
*Plectropomus laevis,* Black-saddled Leopard Grouper, 204
*Plectropomus leopardus,* Leopard Grouper, 203, 204
*Plectropomus maculatus,* Footballer Trout, 203
*Plectropomus oligacanthus,* Striped Coral Trout, 203
*Plectrypops lima,* Rough-scaled Soldierfish, 113
*Plectrypops retrospinis,* Cardinal Soldierfish, 113
*Plesiops cephalotaenia,* Northern Devilfish, 214
*Plesiops corallicola,* Ocellated Longfin, 214
*Plesiops oxycephalus,* Goldcheek Devilfish, 214
*pleurogramma, Torquigener,* Australian Blowfish, 643
*Pleurogrammus azonus,* Greenling, 163
*Pleuronectes pallasii,* Pallas's Flounder, 613
*Pleuronectes platessa,* Plaice, 612
*Pleuronichthys coenosus,* C-O Turbot, 612
*Pleuronichthys cornutus,* Fine-spotted Flounder, 607, 612
*Pleuronichthys ocellatus,* Ocellated Turbot, 612
*Pleuronichthys verticalis,* Hornyhead Turbot, 612
*Pleurosicya* sp., Similan Goby, 568
*pleurospilus, Parupeneus,* Spotted Goatfish, 319
*pleurostigma, Parupeneus,* Blackspot Goatfish, 315, 319
*pleurotaenia, Gunnelichthys,* Black-striped Worm Eel, 580

*pleurotaenia, Heniochus,* Indian Ocean Bannerfish, 348
*pleurotaenia, Parupeneus,* Bright-saddled Goatfish, 316
*pleurotaenia, Pseudanthias,* Purple Blotch Basslet, 174, 178
Pluma, *Calamus pennatula,* 291
*plumbeus, Carcharhinus,* Sandbar Shark, 39
Plume Blenny, *Protemblemaria lucasana,* 520
*plumieri mystes, Scorpaena,* Stone Scorpionfish, 144
*plumieri plumieri, Scorpaena,* Spotted Scorpionfish, 144
*plumieri, Haemulon,* White Grunt, 278
*plumieri, Malacanthus,* Sand Tilefish, 241
Pocket Butterflyfish, *Chaetodon wiebeli,* 338
*podostigma, Halichoeres,* Pale-headed Checkerboard Wrasse, 445, 476
*Podothecus sachi,* Sailfin Poacher, 168
*poecilopterus, Cypselurus,* Yellow-winged Flying Fish, 99
*poecilopterus, Halichoeres,* Multicolorfin Rainbowfish, 444
*poeti, Gerres,* Deep-bodied Silver-Biddy, 276
*poeyi, Halichoeres,* Blackear Wrasse, 446
*poeyi, Synodus,* Offshore Lizardfish, 74
Poey's Butterflyfish, *Chaetodon aculeatus,* 346
*Pogonoperca punctata,* Clown Grouper, 204
Pointed Sawfish, *Anoxypristis cuspidata,* 42
Polka Dot Boxfish, *Ostracion cubicus,* 638, 639, 642
Polka-dot Batfish, *Ogcocephalus radiatus,* 93
Polka-dot Cardinalfish, *Sphaeramia nematoptera,* 221, 232
*Pollachius pollachius,* Golden Pollock, 76, 77
*pollachius, Pollachius,* Golden Pollock, 76, 77
*polleni, Cephalopholis,* Harlequin Rockcod, 182
*pollux, Cottus,* Gunther's Sculpin, 164
*polyacanthus, Acanthochromis,* Spiny Chromis, 397
*polyacanthus, Paraglyphidodon,* Multispined Damsel, 396
*polyactus, Cyprinocirrhites,* Soaring Hawkfish, 413
*polycantha, Pseudogramma,* Honeycomb Podge, 206
*Polydactylus sexfilis,* Pacific Threadfin, 420
*Polydactylus* sp., Threadfin, unidentified, 420
*Polydactylus virginicus,* Barbu, 420
*polygonia, Lactophrys,* Honeycomb Trunkfish, 641
*polylepis, Balistes,* East Pacific Triggerfish, 625
*polylepis, Hemitaurichthys,* Shy Butterflyfish, 351
*polylepis, Parma,* Banded Parma, 379
*Polymixia berndti,* Pacific Beardfish, 106
*Polymixia lowei,* Lowe's Beardfish, 106
*polymnus, Amphiprion,* Saddleback Clown, 372
*polyophthalmus, Boleophthalmus,* Bluespotted Mudskipper, 580
*Polyprion oxygeneiosus,* Saw-tooth Grouper, 173
*polytaenia, Plectorhinchus,* Many-striped Sweetlips, 286
*Pomacanthus annularis,* Blue King Angelfish, 363
*Pomacanthus arcuatus,* Gray Angelfish, 362
*Pomacanthus chrysurus,* Goldtail Angelfish, 364
*Pomacanthus imperator,* Emperor Angelfish, 363
*Pomacanthus maculosus,* Blue Moon Angelfish, 362, 363
*Pomacanthus paru,* French Angelfish, 362
*Pomacanthus semicirculatus,* Koran Angelfish, 362, 364, 365
*Pomacanthus striatus,* Dowager Angelfish, 364
*Pomacanthus zonipectus,* Cortez Angelfish, 362
*Pomacentridae* sp., Damselfish, unidentified, 390
*Pomacentrus albimaculus,* Bronzeback Damsel, 401
*Pomacentrus alleni,* Allen's Pomacentrus, 399
*Pomacentrus amboinensis,* Ambon Damsel, 402
*Pomacentrus arenarius,* Specklefin Damsel, 401
*Pomacentrus australis,* Australian Damsel, 400
*Pomacentrus bankanensis,* Speckled Damsel, 402
*Pomacentrus brachialis,* Charcoal Damsel, 401
*Pomacentrus caeruleus,* Yellow-bellied Blue Damsel, 399
*Pomacentrus chrysurus,* Whitetail Damsel, 400, 403
*Pomacentrus coelestis,* Blue Damselfish, 399, 400
*Pomacentrus emarginatus,* Outer-reef Damsel, 400
*Pomacentrus grammorhynchus,* Blue-spot Damsel, 402
*Pomacentrus lepidogenys,* Scaly Damsel, 400
*Pomacentrus milleri,* Miller's Damselfish, 404
*Pomacentrus moluccensis,* Molucca Damsel, 371, 402
*Pomacentrus nigromanus,* Black-axil Damsel, 401
*Pomacentrus nigromarginatus,* Black-margined Damsel, 401
*Pomacentrus pavo,* Blue Damsel, 403
*Pomacentrus philippinus,* Philippine Damsel, 399, 401
*Pomacentrus pikei,* Scintillating Damsel, 403
*Pomacentrus reidi,* Reid's Damsel, 400
*Pomacentrus smithi,* Smith's Damsel, 402
*Pomacentrus* sp., Damselfish, unidentified, 403
*Pomacentrus stigma,* Analspot Demoiselle, 401
*Pomacentrus sulfureus,* Sulphur Damselfish, 402
*Pomacentrus trichourus,* Yellowtail Damsel, 399
*Pomacentrus trilineatus,* Three-line Damsel, 403
*Pomacentrus tripunctatus,* Three-spot Damsel, 400
*Pomacentrus vaiuli,* Ocellate Damselfish, 402
*Pomacentrus wardi,* Ward's Damsel, 401
*Pomachromis exilis,* Slender Reef-damsel, 395
*Pomachromis fuscidorsalis,* Tahitian Reef-damsel, 395
*Pomachromis guamensis,* Guamanian Damsel, 395
*Pomachromis richardsoni,* Richardson's Reef-damsel, 395
*Pomadasys argyreus,* Silver Grunt, 281
*Pomadasys commersoni,* Spotted Grunter, 313
*Pomadasys corvinaeformis,* Roughneck Grunt, 281
*Pomadasys furcatus,* Grey Grunter, 281
*Pomadasys hasta,* Lined Silver Grunt, 281
*Pomadasys maculatum,* Spotted Javelin Fish, 281
*Pomadasys* sp., Yellowfinned Grunt, 313
*pomastictus, Ctenogobiops,* Lizard Island Goby, 547, 548
*Pomatomus saltatrix,* Bluefish Tailor, 241
*Pomatoschistus microps,* Leonard's Common Goby, 558
Pond Smelt, *Hypomesus olidus,* 70
Pontif Blenny, *Parablennius incognitus,* 525
*Pontinus macrocephalus,* Large-headed Scorpionfish, 146
*Pontinus nematophthalmus,* Spinythroat Scorpionfish, 137
Pony Fish, *Secutor ruconius,* 256
Poor Knights Wrasse, *Pseudolabrus inscriptus,* 464
Popeye Catalufa, *Pristigenys serrula,* 219
Popeyed Sea Goblin, *Inimicus didactylus,* 156
Porae, *Cheilodactylus douglasi,* 416
*Porcostoma dentata,* Dane, 293
Porcupine Ray, *Urogymnus africanus,* 46
Porcupinefish, *Diodon hystrix,* 618, 653, 654, 656
*porcus, Scorpaena,* European Scorpionfish, 144
*Porichthys margaritatus,* Freckled Head Midshipman, 84
*Porichthys notatus,* Plainfin Midshipman, 84
*porocephala, Ophiocara,* Spangled Gudgeon, 542
*Porocottus allisi,* Allis, 166
*porosa, Raja,* Roughback, 44
*porosus, Pentapodus,* Yellowstreak Whiptail, 300
*porosus, Upeneichthys,* New Zealand Red Mullet, 312, 314
*porphyreus, Parupeneus,* Purple Goatfish, 316
*porphyreus, Pseudochromis,* Magenta Dottyback, 211
Port Jackson Shark, *Heterodontus portusjacksoni,* 33
*portenoyi, Ecsenius,* Portenoy's Blenny, 528.10

Portenoy's Blenny, *Ecsenius portenoyi*, 528.10
Portuguese Man-O-War Fish, *Nomeus gronovii*, 605, 606
*portusjacksoni, Heterodontus*, Port Jackson Shark, 33
Potato Bass, *Epinephelus tukula*, 188
*potteri, Centropyge*, Potter's Angelfish, 355
Potter's Angelfish, *Centropyge potteri*, 355
Pouter, *Lycogramma zesta*, 494
Powder-blue Tang, *Acanthurus leucosternon*, 581, 583
*poweri, Paraplesiops*, Blue-tip Longfin, 214
*pozyzona, Echidna*, Girdled Moray, 53
*praepositum, Liocranium*, One-spot Waspfish, 495
*pralinia, Myripristis*, Scarlet Soldierfish, 112, 115
*prasinus, Gymnothorax*, Brown Moray, 58, 60
*prasiognathos, Scarus*, Greenbeak Parrotfish, 481, 485, 490, 492
Prawn Goby, unidentified, *Amblyeleotris* sp., 544
Prawn Goby, unidientified, *Amblygobius* sp., 547
*prayensis, Pseudupeneus*, African Goatfish, 315
*preclara, Gorgasia*, Philippine Garden Eel, 63, 64
*Premnas biaculeatus*, Spine-cheeked Anemonefish, 372
*pretioses japonicus, Hypomesus*, High-middle Pretty Fish, 70
*pretiosus, Ruvettus*, Oilfish, 601
Pretty Cheek Goby, *Amblyeleotris* sp. cf *japonicus*, 548
Pretty Prawn Goby, *Valenciennea puellaris*, 546, 566
Prettytail Cardinalfish, *Apogon menesemus*, 229
*Priacanthus arenatus*, Bigeye, 220
*Priacanthus cruentatus*, Dusky-finned Bullseye, 220
*Priacanthus hamrur*, Crescent-tail Bigeye, 220
*Priacanthus macracanthus*, Red Bullseye, 220
*Priacanthus tayenus*, Purple-spotted Bullseye, 220
Prickly Fanfish, *Pterycombus petersii*, 257
Prickly Leatherjacket, *Chaetodermis penicilligerus*, 630, 634
Prickly-headed Goby, *Paragobiodon echinocephalus*, 578
*princeps, Caulolatilus*, Ocean Whitefish, 239
Princess Parrotfish, *Scarus taeniopterus*, 486
*Priolepis boreus*, Banded-head Goby, 567
*Priolepis cincta*, Girdled Goby, 566
*Priolepis cinctus*, Pacific Convict Goby, 567
*Priolepis hipoliti*, Rusty Goby, 567
*Priolepis semidoliatus*, Redhead Goby, 567
*prionodon, Gymnothorax*, Mottled Moray, 57
*Prionotus carolinus*, Northern Searobin, 161
*Prionotus ophryas*, Bandtail Searobin, 161
*Prionotus rubio*, Blackwing Searobin, 161
*Prionotus scitulus*, Leopard Searobin, 161
*prionura, Mycteroperca*, Sawtail Grouper, 193
*Prionurus laticlavius*, Galapagos Sawtail, 588
*Prionurus punctatus*, Yellowtail Sawtail, 588
*Prionurus scalprus*, Blackthorn Sawtail, 588
*prionurus, Paraluterus*, Valentini Mimic, 636
*Pristigenys alta*, Short Bigeye, 219
*Pristigenys multifasciata*, Red-striped Bigeye, 219
*Pristigenys niphonia*, Japanese Bigeye, 219
*Pristigenys serrula*, Popeye Catalufa, 219
*Pristilepis oligolepis*, Slender Soldierfish, 113
*Pristipomoides filamentosus*, Rosy Jobfish, 269
*Pristipomoides macrophthalmus*, Yellowline Bananafish, 269
*Pristipomoides multidens*, Striped Jobfish, 269
*Pristis pectinata*, Smalltooth Sawfish, 42
*Pristotis cyanostigma*, Bluedotted Damselfish, 408
*Pristotis jerdoni*, Gulf Damsel, 408
*probatocephalus, Archosargus*, Sheepshead, 292
*proboscidalis, Agonomalus*, Barbed Hunchback Poacher, 168
*prochilus, Gobiosoma*, West Indian Cleaning Goby, 572
*productus, Rhinobatos*, Shovelnose Guitarfish, 43
Promethean Escolar, *Promethichthys prometheus*, 601
*prometheus, Promethichthys*, Promethean Escolar, 601
*Promethichthys prometheus*, Promethean Escolar, 601
*prorates, Lepophidium*, Dot-dash Cusk-eel, 80
*prosopeion, Halichoeres*, Purpleheaded Wrasse, 441, 473
*prosopotaenia, Dischistodus*, Honey-head Damsel, 409
*Protemblemaria bicirrhis*, Warthead Blenny, 520
*Protemblemaria lucasana*, Plume Blenny, 520
*Psammoperca waigiensis*, Sea Perch, 170
*Psenes pellucidus*, Blackrag, 606
*Psenopsis anomala*, Blackspot Butterfish, 606
*Psettichthys melanostictus*, Sand Sole, 612
*Psettodes erumei*, Adalah, 609
*PseudaAthias squamipinnis*, Lyretail Coralfish, 174, 179
*Pseudalutarius nasicornis*, Rhino Leatherjacket, 635
*Pseudamia amblyuroptera*, Spottail Cardinalfish, 237
*Pseudamia gelatinosa*, Jelly Cardinalfish, 237
*Pseudanthias engelhardi*, Engelhard's Goldie, 177
*Pseudanthias fasciatus*, Banded Fairy Basslet, 177
*Pseudanthias hutchi*, Sea Goldie, 177
*Pseudanthias kashiwae*, Red Fairy Basslet, 174
*Pseudanthias luzonensis*, Philippine Fairy Basslet, 174
*Pseudanthias pictilis*, Painted Goldie, 177
*Pseudanthias pleurotaenia*, Purple Blotch Basslet, 174, 178
*Pseudanthias rubrizonatus*, Deepsea Fairy Basslet, 174
*Pseudanthias* sp., Fairy Basslet, unidentified, 174, 177
*Pseudanthias taeniatus*, Silver Streak Goldie, 177
*Pseudanthias taira*, Japanese Fairy Basslet, 177
*Pseudanthias tenuis*, Threadnose Fairy Basslet, 177
*Pseudanthias truncatus*, Truncate Fairy Basslet, 174
*Pseudanthias ventralis hawaiiensis*, Hawaiian Fairy Basslet, 174
*Pseudanthias ventralis ventralis*, Rainbow Fairy Basslet, 174
*Pseudobalistes flavimarginatus*, Yellowface Triggerfish, 622
*Pseudobalistes fuscus*, Blue-and-Gold Triggerfish, 616, 626
*Pseudobalistes naufragium*, Blunthead Triggerfish, 622
*Pseudoblennius cottoides*, Painted Blenny, 167, 169
*Pseudoblennius percoides*, Perch Sculpin, 167
*Pseudocaranx dentex*, Striped Jack, 243, 253
*Pseudochaetodon nigrirostris*, Black-nosed Butterflyfish, 347
*Pseudocheilinus evanidus*, Disappearing Wrasse, 458
*Pseudocheilinus hexataenia*, Sixstripe Wrasse, 458
*Pseudocheilinus octotaenia*, Eightstripe Wrasse, 458
*Pseudocheilinus* sp., Mystery Wrasse, 461
*Pseudocheilinus tetrataenia*, Four-lined Wrasse, 461
*Pseudochromis aureus*, Golden Dottyback, 209
*Pseudochromis bitaeniata*, Two-banded Dottyback, 209
*Pseudochromis cyanotaenia*, Blue-striped Dottyback, 208, 211
*Pseudochromis diadema*, Diadem Basslêt, 211
*Pseudochromis dilectus*, Sri Lanka Dottyback, 210
*Pseudochromis dixurus*, Forktail Dottyback, 210
*Pseudochromis dutoiti*, Dutorti, 212
*Pseudochromis flammicauda*, Red-tailed Dottyback, 211
*Pseudochromis flavivertex*, Sunrise Dottyback, 212
*Pseudochromis fridmani*, Orchid Dottyback, 212
*Pseudochromis fuscus*, Brown Dottyback, 209
*Pseudochromis longipinnis*, Long-finned Dottyback, 209
*Pseudochromis luteus*, Golden Dottyback, 207
*Pseudochromis marshallensis*, Marshall's Dottyback, 207
*Pseudochromis mccullochi*, McCulloch's Dottyback, 209
*Pseudochromis melanotaenia*, Bow-tailed Dottyback, 210

*Pseudochromis melas,* Dark Dottyback, 212
*Pseudochromis moorei,* Moore's Dottyback, 209
*Pseudochromis novaehollandiae,* Red and Green Dottyback, 209
*Pseudochromis olivaceous,* Olive Dottyback, 211
*Pseudochromis paccagnellae,* Royal Dottyback, 211
*Pseudochromis paranox,* Jet Black Dottyback, 210
*Pseudochromis perspicillatus,* Brown-banded Dottyback, 211
*Pseudochromis pesi,* Pale Dottyback, 210
*Pseudochromis porphyreus,* Magenta Dottyback, 211
*Pseudochromis sankeyi,* Striped Dottyback, 210
*Pseudochromis springeri,* Springer's Dottyback, 210
*Pseudochromis tapeinosoma,* Yellow-head Dottyback, 208
*Pseudochromis veliferus,* Sailfin Dottyback, 208
*Pseudochromis wilsoni,* Yellow-fin Dottyback, 208
*Pseudochromis xanthochir,* Yellow-tail Dottyback, 208
*pseudochrysopoecilus, Dischistodus,* Monarch Damsel, 400, 409
*Pseudocoris bleekeri,* Bleeker's Rainbowfish, 427
*Pseudocoris yamashiroi,* Yamashiro's Rainbowfish, 459, 460
*Pseudodax moluccanus,* Chiseltooth Wrasse, 467
*Pseudogramma gregoryi,* Reef Bass, 206
*Pseudogramma polycantha,* Honeycomb Podge, 206
*Pseudojulis girardi,* Girard's Wrasse, 476
*Pseudojulis melanotus,* Golden Wrasse, 461
*Pseudojulis notospilus,* Senorita De Cintas, 461
*Pseudojuloides cerasinus,* Smalltail Wrasse, 460, 461
*Pseudojuloides elongatus,* Elongate Wrasse, 461
*Pseudojuloides erythrops,* Redeye Wrasse, 460
*Pseudojuloides* sp., Yellowband Wrasse, 461
*Pseudojuloides trifasciatus,* Threestripe Wrasse, 460
*Pseudolabrus biserialis,* Red-banded Wrasse, 462, 465
*Pseudolabrus celidotus,* New Zealand Spotty, 464
*Pseudolabrus guntheri,* Gunther's Rainbowfish, 464
*Pseudolabrus gymnogenis,* White-spotted Rainbowfish, 464
*Pseudolabrus inscriptus,* Poor Knights Wrasse, 464
*Pseudolabrus japonicus,* Japanese Wrasse, 464
*Pseudolabrus luculentus,* Orange Wrasse, 464
*Pseudolabrus milesi,* Scarlet Wrasse, 463
*Pseudolabrus parilus,* Brown-spotted Wrasse, 465
*pseudomaculatus, Apogon,* Twospot Cardinalfish, 230
*Pseudomonacanthus garretti,* Garrett's Slender Filefish, 633
*Pseudophycis breviusculus,* Bearded Rock Cod, 77
*Pseudoplesiops inornatus,* Plain Dottyback, 211
*Pseudoplesiops rosae,* Rose Devilfish, 207
*Pseudopleuronectes americanus,* Winter Flounder, 611
*Pseudorhombus cinnamoneus,* Cinnamon Flounder, 607, 610
*Pseudorhombus jenynsii,* Jenyns' Flounder, 610
*Pseudorhombus* sp., Flowerspot Flounder, 610
*Pseudupeneus grandisquammis,* Bigscale Goatfish, 314
*Pseudupeneus maculatus,* Dotted Goatfish, 314
*Pseudupeneus prayensis,* African Goatfish, 315
*psittacus, Scarus,* Yellow-sided Parrotfish, 481, 485, 489, 492
Psychedelic Fish, *Synchiropus picturatus,* 535, 539
*Psychrolutes paradoxus,* Tadpole Sculpin, 167
*Pteragogus flagellifer,* Cocktail Fish, 449
*Pteragogus pelycus,* Sideburn Wrasse, 449, 450
*Pterapogon mirifica,* Sailfin Cardinalfish, 236
*Ptereleotris evides,* Spottail Gudgeon, 568
*Ptereleotris hanae,* Blue Hana Goby, 561
*Ptereleotris heteropterus,* Pale Gudgeon, 568
*Ptereleotris microlepis,* Blue Gudgeon, 561, 568
*Ptereleotris monoptera,* Ghost Goby, 561
*Ptereleotris zebra,* Chinese Zebra Goby, 561
*Pterocaesio chrysozona,* Goldband Fusilier, 272
*Pterocaesio diagramma,* Yellow Lateral Line Fusilier, 272, 273
*Pterocaesio lativittata,* Gold-band Fusilier, 271
*Pterocaesio randalli,* Randall's Fusilier, 271
*Pterocaesio striatus,* Striated Fusilier, 571
*Pterocaesio tile,* Bartail Fusilier, 271
*Pterocaesio trilineata,* Three-lined Fusilier, 271
*Pterogobius elapoides,* Black Belt Flagfin Goby, 565
*Pterogobius virgo,* Red-and-Blue Goby, 565
*Pterogobius zonoleucus,* Flag-finned Goby, 565
*Pterois antennata,* Spotfin Lionfish, 141, 142
*Pterois miles,* Devil Lionfish, 142
*Pterois radiata,* Tailbar Lionfish, 142
*Pterois sphex,* Hawaiian Lionfish, 140
*Pterois volitans,* Lionfish, 134, 140, 142
*Pterosynchiropus splendidus,* Mandarin Fish, 535, 539
*Pterothrissus gissu,* Deepsea Bonefish, 50
*Pterycombus petersii,* Prickly Fanfish, 257
*Pterygotrigla multiocellatus,* Multi-spotted Searobin, 160
Pudding Wife, *Halichoeres radiatus,* 447
*puella, Hypoplectrus,* Barred Hamlet, 201
*puellaris, Decodon,* Red Hogfish, 470
*puellaris, Valenciennea,* Pretty Prawn Goby, 546, 566
*puelloides, Siganus,* Black-eyed Spinefoot, 598
*puellus, Siganus,* Decorated Spinefoot, 599
Puffcheek Blenny, *Labrisomus bucciferus,* 513
Puffer, unidentified, *Omegophora* sp., 643; *Sphoeroides* sp., 649
Pufferfish, unidentified, *Amblyrhynchotes* sp., 643
Pugjaw Wormfish, *Cerdale floridana,* 580
Pugnose Pipefish, *Bryx dunckeri,* 125
*pulchella, Parapercis,* Bluestreak Weever, 502
*pulchellus, Bodianus,* Spotfin Hogfish, 430
*pulchellus, Liparis,* Showy Snailfish, 168
*pulchellus, Lythrypnus,* Gorgeous Goby, 575
*pulcher, Ecsenius,* Arabian Blenny, 528.04
*pulcher, Semicossyphus,* California Sheephead, 463
*pullus, Cantherhines,* Orange-spotted Filefish, 629
*pumilio, Serraniculus,* Pygmy Sea Bass, 196
*punctata, Drepane,* Spotted Drepane, 330, 334
*punctata, Girella,* Rudderfish, 326
*punctata, Pogonoperca,* Clown Grouper, 204
*punctatissimum, Sargocentron,* Speckled Squirrelfish, 109
*punctatissimus, Canthigaster,* Spotted Sharpnose Puffer, 651
*punctatofasciatus, Chaetodon,* Spot-band Butterflyfish, 344
*punctatum, Chiloscyllium,* Brown-spotted Cat Shark, 36, 38
*punctatus, Decapterus,* Round Scad, 245
*punctatus, Equetus,* Spotted Drum, 309, 310
*punctatus, Konosirus,* Dotted Gizzard Shad, 67
*punctatus, Oplegnathus,* Spotted Knifejaw, 369
*punctatus, Prionurus,* Yellowtail Sawtail, 588
*punctatus, Vincentia,* Dotted Cardinalfish, 236
*punctatus, Zeugopterus,* Topknot Flounder, 610
*puncticulatus, Gobiosoma,* Redhead Goby, 571
*punctipinnis, Chromis,* Blacksmith, 389
*punctulatus, Aeoliscus,* Spotted Shrimpfish, 122
*puntang, Exyrias,* Dot-dash Goby, 564
*puntazzo, Diplodus,* Sheepshead Bream, 288
*punticulatus, Astrapogon,* Spotted Conchfish, 236
Purple Blotch Basslet, *Pseudanthias pleurotaenia,* 174, 178
Purple Goatfish, *Parupeneus porphyreus,* 316
Purple Queen, *Mirolabrichthys tuka,* 178
Purple Reeffish, *Chromis scotti,* 388

Purple Surgeonfish, *Acanthurus xanthopterus,* 584
Purple Tilefish, *Hoplolatilus purpureus,* 240
Purple-spotted Bullseye, *Priacanthus tayenus,* 220
Purpleheaded Wrasse, *Halichoeres prosopeion,* 441, 473
Purplemouth Moray, *Gymnothorax vicinus,* 55
*purpureum, Thalassoma,* Surge Wrasse, 468
*purpureus, Hoplolatilus,* Purple Tilefish, 240
*purpurissatus, Aulopus,* Sergeant Baker, 71, 72
Pygmy Goby, *Pandaka lidwilli,* 551
Pygmy Leatherjacket, *Brachaluteres jacksonianus,* 634
Pygmy Sea Bass, *Serraniculus pumilio,* 196
*Pygoplites diacanthus,* Regal Angelfish, 353, 361, 364
*pyroferus, Acanthurus,* Chocolate Surgeonfish, 584, 586

## Q

*qenie, Sphyraena,* Blackfin Barracuda, 422
*quadricornis, Cheilodactylus,* Barred Morwong, 417
*quadricornis, Lactophrys,* Scrawled Cowfish, 641
*quadrifasciatus, Apogon,* Two-striped Cardinalfish, 229
*quadrilineatus, Larabicus,* Fourline Wrasse, 451
*quadrilineatus, Pelates,* Four-lined Terapon, 217, 289
*quadrimaculatus, Chaetodon,* Four-spot Butterflyfish, 335
*quadrisquamatus, Apogon,* Sawcheek Cardinalfish, 230
*quaesita, Rhinomuraena,* Ribbon Eel, 52, 64
*Quassiremus notochir,* Red-diamond Eel, 62
Queen Angelfish, *Holacanthus ciliaris,* 367
Queen Coris, *Coris formosa,* 439
Queen Parrotfish, *Scarus vetula,* 486
Queen Snapper, *Etelis oculatus,* 259
Queen Triggerfish, *Balistes vetula,* 625
Queensland Spanish Mackerel, *Scomberomorus queenslandicus,* 603
*queenslandicus, Scomberomorus,* Queensland Spanish Mackerel, 603
Quillback Rockfish, *Sebastes maliger,* 149
*quincarinatus, Minous,* Whitetail Goblinfish, 155
*quinquelineatus, Cheilodipterus,* Sharptooth Cardinalfish, 233
*quinquelineatus, Lutjanus,* Five-line Snapper, 261
*quinqueradiata, Seriola,* Japanese Yellowtail, 252
*quinquestrigatus, Gobiodon,* Bicolored Coral Goby, 578
*quinquevittatum, Thalassoma,* Fivestripe Wrasse, 467

## R

*Rabaulichthys altipinnis,* Sailfin Bass, 200
Raccoon Butterflyfish, *Chaetodon lunula,* 340
*Rachycentron canadum,* Cobia, 244
*radians, Sparisoma,* Bucktooth Parrotfish, 488
Radiant Wrasse, *Halichoeres iridis,* 441, 442
*radiata, Pterois,* Tailbar Lionfish, 142
*radiatus, Halichoeres,* Pudding Wife, 447
*radiatus, Ogcocephalus,* Polka-dot Batfish, 93
*radiatus, Pantolabus,* Fringe-finned Trevally, 253
*radiatus, Siphonognathus,* Bridled Weed Whiting, 478
Raffle's Butterflyfish, *Chaetodon rafflesi,* 345
*rafflesi, Chaetodon,* Raffle's Butterflyfish, 345
Railway Glider, *Valenciennea helsdingenii,* 566
Rainbow Fairy Basslet, *Pseudanthias ventralis ventralis,* 174
Rainbow Fish, *Odax acroptilus,* 478
Rainbow Monocle Bream, *Scolopsis temporalis,* 303
Rainbow Parrotfish, *Scarus guacamaia,* 485
Rainbow Runner, *Elagatis bipinnulata,* 245, 247
Rainbow Scorpionfish, *Scorpaenodes xyris,* 153
Rainbow Surfperch, *Hypsurus caryi,* 368, 370
Rainbow Wrasse, *Thalassoma amblycephalus,* 465, 476
*rainfordi, Chaetodon,* Rainford's Butterflyfish, 343
*Rainfordia opercularis,* Rainford's Perch, 200
Rainford's Butterflyfish, *Chaetodon rainfordi,* 343
Rainford's Perch, *Rainfordia opercularis,* 200
*Raja porosa,* Roughback, 44
Rake-gilled Mackerel, *Rastrelliger kanagurta,* 603
*ramak, Lethrinus,* Orange-striped Emperor, 297
*ramosus, Bathygobius,* Panamic Frillfin Goby, 564
*ramosus, Gymnothorax,* Mosaic Moray, 57
*ramulosus, Hippocampus,* Mediterranean Seahorse, 130
*randalli, Amblyeleotris,* Orangestripe Prawn Goby, 545
*randalli, Chromis,* Randall's Chromis, 384
*randalli, Gobiosoma,* Yellownose Goby, 573
*randalli, Pterocaesio,* Randall's Fusilier, 271
Randall's Chromis, *Chromis randalli,* 384
Randall's Fusilier, *Pterocaesio randalli,* 271
*ranga, Chanda,* Glassfish, 170
Ransonet's Surfperch, *Neoditrema ransonneti,* 370
*ransonneti, Neoditrema,* Ransonet's Surfperch, 370
*ransonneti, Parapriacanthus,* Slender Sweeper, 323
*Ranzania laevis,* Slender Mola, 656
Rapa Sharpnose Pufferfish, *Canthigaster rapaensis,* 652
*rapaensis, Canthigaster,* Rapa Sharpnose Pufferfish, 652
*rapanui, Chrysiptera,* Easter Island Demoiselle, 390
*rasor, Caesioperca,* Barber Perch, 181
*Rastrelliger kanagurta,* Rake-gilled Mackerel, 603
*Rathbunella hypoplecta,* Smooth Ronqiul, 494
Recherche Clingfish, Gobiesocidae sp., 96
Rectangle Triggerfish, *Rhinecanthus rectangulus,* 626
*rectangulus, Rhinecanthus,* Rectangle Triggerfish, 626
*rectifraenum, Stegastes,* Cortez Chromis, 405
*recurvirostris, Pentaceropsis,* Long-snouted Boarfish, 334
Red and Green Dottyback, *Pseudochromis novaehollandiae,* 209
Red and Green Snapper, *Lutjanus fulvus,* 262
Red Anemonefish, *Amphiprion rubrocinctus,* 376
Red Blush Goatfish, *Parupeneus chrysopleuron,* 316
Red Bonnetmouth, *Emmelichthyops ruber,* 288
Red Brotula, *Brosmophycis marginata,* 81
Red Bullseye, *Priacanthus macracanthus,* 220
Red Butterfly Perch, *Caesioperca lepidoptera,* 181
Red Checkerboard Wrasse, *Halichoeres ornatissimus,* 445
Red Clingfish, *Arcos robiginosus,* 96
Red Clown, *Amphiprion frenatus,* 376
Red Coral Goby, *Eviota* sp., 551
Red Fairy Basslet, *Pseudanthias kashiwae,* 174
Red Grouper, *Epinephelus morio,* 192
Red Grubfish, *Parapercis schuinslandi,* 502
Red Hake, *Urophycis chuss,* 78
Red Hind, *Epinephelus guttatus,* 192
Red Hogfish, *Decodon puellaris,* 470
Red Indianfish, *Pataecus fronto,* 159
Red Irish Lord, *Hemilepidotus hemilepidotus,* 165
Red Lizardfish, *Synodus synodus,* 73, 74, 75
Red Moki, *Cheilodactylus spectabilis,* 416
Red Morwong, *Cheilodactylus fuscus,* 416
Red Mumea, *Lutjanus bohar,* 262, 263
Red Opercled Snapper, *Lethrinus rubrioperculatus,* 297
Red Scorpin, *Scorpaena sumptuosa,* 146
Red Scorpionfish, *Scorpaena notata,* 144
Red Sea Angelfish, *Apolemichthys xanthotis,* 366

Red Sea Bannerfish, *Heniochus intermedius,* 352
Red Sea Butterflyfish, *Chaetodon mesoleucos,* 338
Red Sea Chevron Butterflyfish, *Chaetodon paucifasciatus,* 337
Red Sea Clown Surgeon, *Acanthurus sohal,* 584
Red Sea Melon Butterflyfish, *Chaetodon austriacus,* 341
Red Sea Mimic Blenny, *Ecsenius gravieri,* 523, 533
Red Sea Multicolor Wrasse, *Minilabrus striatus,* 459
Red Sea Raccoon Butterflyfish, *Chaetodon fasciatus,* 340
Red Seaperch, *Ellerkeldia rubra,* 199
Red Snapper, *Lutjanus campechanus,* 265
Red Spotted Grouper, *Epinephelus akaara,* 190
Red Spotted Rock Bass, *Paralabrax maculatofasciatus,* 202
Red Tai, *Pagrus major,* 290, 291
Red-and-Blue Goby, *Pterogobius virgo,* 565
Red-banded Wrasse, *Pseudolabrus biserialis,* 462, 465
Red-brown Lizardfish, *Synodus ulae,* 74
Red-diamond Eel, *Quassiremus notochir,* 62
Red-finned Fairy Wrasse, *Cirrhilabrus rubripinnis,* 435
Red-lined Butterflyfish, *Chaetodon semilarvatus,* 344
Red-lined Parrotfish, *Hipposcarus harid,* 480, 489
Red-lined Wrasse, *Halichoeres biocellatus,* 440, 443
Red-lipped Morwong, *Cheilodactylus rubrolabiatus,* 418
Red-marbled Lizardfish, *Synodus rubromarmoratus,* 74
Red-necked Goby, *Amblyeleotris fasciatus,* 543
Red-saddled Sand Stargazer, *Dactyloscopus pectoralis,* 512
Red-sided Fairy Wrasse, *Cirrhilabrus* sp. "D", 434
Red-spotted Emperor, *Lethrinus lentjan,* 294, 297
Red-spotted Razorfish, *Xyrichthys verrens,* 457
Red-striped Bigeye, *Pristigenys multifasciata,* 219
Red-tailed Butterflyfish, *Chaetodon collare,* 341
Red-tailed Dottyback, *Pseudochromis flammicauda,* 211
Red-tailed Sea Bream, *Gymnocranius lethrinoides,* 290, 296
Red-tailed Tamarin, *Anampses chrysocephalus,* 425
Red-tailed Yellow Bass, *Liopropoma* sp., 199
Red-tipped Fringed-blenny, *Cirripectes variolosus,* 532
Red-tipped Rock Cod, *Epinephelus truncatus,* 189
Redband Lizardfish, *Synodus engelmani,* 74
Redband Parrotfish, *Sparisoma aurofrenatum,* 487
Redbarred Cardinalfish, *Archamia fucata,* 235
Redbelly Fusilier, *Caesio erythrogaster,* 273
Redbreasted Wrasse, *Cheilinus fasciatus,* 432, 477
Redcheek Wrasse, *Thalassoma genivittatum,* 465, 467
*redemptus, Stegastes,* Clarion Damselfish, 406
Redeye Triplefin, *Enneanectes pectoralis,* 507
Redeye Wrasse, *Pseudojuloides erythrops,* 460
Redfilament Threadfin Bream, *Nemipterus mesoprion,* 306
Redfin Fusilier, *Caesio xanthonotus,* 270, 271, 272, 273
Redfin Hogfish, *Bodianus* sp., 427
Redfin Sailfin Scorpionfish, *Hypodytes rubripinnis,* 159
Redflush Rockcod, *Aethaloperca rogaa,* 179
Redhead Goby, *Gobiosoma puncticulatus,* 571; *Priolepis semidoliatus,* 567
*Redigobius balteata,* Balteata, 547
*Redigobius tessellatus,* Tessellated Goby, 563
Redline Puffer, *Sphoeroides erythrotaenia,* 649
Redlip Cleaner Wrasse, *Labroides rubrolabiatus,* 469
Redlip Rubberlip, *Plectorhinchus sordidus,* 284, 285
Redmouth Goby, *Gobius cruentatus,* 559
Redrump Blenny, *Xenomedia rhodopyga,* 516
Redspine Threadfin Bream, *Nemipterus nemurus,* 307
Redspotted Hawkfish, *Amblycirrhitus pinos,* 415
Redstripe Tilefish, *Hoplolatilus marcosi,* 240
Redtail Filefish, *Pervagor melanocephalus,* 630, 633
Redtail Parrotfish, *Sparisoma chrysopterum,* 487
Redtail Surfperch, *Amphistichus rhodoterus,* 369
Redtooth Triggerfish, *Odonus niger,* 625, 627
Reef Bass, *Pseudogramma gregoryi,* 206
Reef Butterflyfish, *Chaetodon sedentarius,* 342
Reef Chromis, *Chromis agilis,* 385
Reef Croaker, *Odontoscion dentex,* 311
Reef Scorpionfish, *Scorpaenodes carribbaeus,* 153
Reef Squirrelfish, *Sargocentron coruscum,* 107
Reef Surfperch, *Micrometrus aurora,* 370
Reefsand Blenny, *Ekemblemaria* sp. *(myersi?),* 519
Reeve's Shad, *Hilsa reevesii,* 65
*reevesii, Hilsa,* Reeve's Shad, 65
Regal Angelfish, *Pygoplites diacanthus,* 353, 361, 364
Regal Demoiselle, *Neopomacentrus cyanomos,* 398
Regal Mudskipper, *Periophthalmus regius,* 579
*Regalecus glesne,* Long Oarfish, 103
*regia, Lipogramma,* Royal Basslet, 213
*regius, Periophthalmus,* Regal Mudskipper, 579
*reichei, Favonigobius,* Tropical Sand Goby, 560
*reidi, Hippocampus,* Longsnout Seahorse, 131
*reidi, Pomacentrus,* Reid's Damsel, 400
Reid's Damsel, *Pomacentrus reidi,* 400
Remora, unidentified, *Echeneis* sp., 244
*Remorina albescens,* White Remora, 244
*Repomucenus beniteguri,* Beniteguri, 536
*Repomucenus richardsoni,* Richardson's Dragonet, 537
*resplendens, Centropyge,* Ascencion Cherubfish, 356
*reticularis, Arothron,* Reticulated Pufferfish, 647
Reticulated Bumphead Wrasse, *Semicossyphus reticulatus,* 463
Reticulated Damselfish, *Dascyllus reticulatus,* 378
Reticulated Emperor, *Lethrinus reticulatus,* 294
Reticulated Moray, *Gymnothorax permistus,* 56
Reticulated Pufferfish, *Arothron reticularis,* 647
*reticulatus, Chaetodon,* Mailed Butterflyfish, 336
*reticulatus, Dascyllus,* Reticulated Damselfish, 378
*reticulatus, Lethrinus,* Reticulated Emperor, 294
*reticulatus, Semicossyphus,* Reticulated Bumphead Wrasse, 463
*retifera, Halieutaea,* Net Batfish, 93
*retrofasciata, Chromis,* Black-bar Chromis, 387
*retrosella, Apogon,* Barspot Cardinalfish, 230
*retrospinis, Paratriacanthodes,* Striped Tripodfish, 620
*retrospinis, Plectrypops,* Cardinal Soldierfish, 113
*rex, Chrysiptera,* King Demoiselle, 390
*Rhabdamia cypselurus,* Black-nosed Cardinalfish, 222
*Rhabdamia gracilis,* Arrow Cardinal, 222
*Rhabdamia* sp., Slender Cardinalfish, 222
*Rhabdosargus sarba,* Natal Stumpnose, 292
*Rhabdosargus thorpei,* Bigeye Stumpnose, 293
*rhacinus, Lotella,* Rock Cod, 77
*Rhamphocottus richardsoni,* Grunt Sculpin, 166
*Rhincodon typus,* Whale Shark, 34, 40
*Rhinecanthus aculeatus,* Painted Triggerfish, 626
*Rhinecanthus assasi,* Picasso Triggerfish, 626
*Rhinecanthus lunula,* Crescent Triggerfish, 628
*Rhinecanthus rectangulus,* Rectangle Triggerfish, 626
*Rhinecanthus verrucosus,* Black Patch Triggerfish, 628
Rhino Leatherjacket, *Pseudalutarius nasicornis,* 635
*Rhinobatos armatus,* Clearnose Guitarfish, 44
*Rhinobatos formosensis,* Taiwan Guitarfish, 44
*Rhinobatos hynnicephalus,* Decorated Guitarfish, 44

*Rhinobatos productus*, Shovelnose Guitarfish, 43
*Rhinobatos schlegeli*, Schlegel's Guitarfish, 44
*Rhinobatos vincentiana*, Australian Guitarfish, 44
*Rhinogobius brunneus*, Lake Goby, 552
*Rhinomuraena quaesita*, Ribbon Eel, 52, 64
*Rhinopias aphanes*, Merlet Scorpionfish, 139
*Rhinopias argoliba*, Weeping Scorpionfish, 139
*Rhinopias eschmeyeri*, Eschmeyer's Scorpionfish, 139
*Rhinopias frondosa*, Goose Scorpionfish, 139
*Rhinoptera neglecta*, Cow-nose Ray, 47
*rhinorhynchos, Plagiotremus*, Cleaner Mimic, 506, 521
*rhodopus, Trachinotus*, Gafftopsail Pompano, 254
*rhodopyga, Xenomedia*, Redrump Blenny, 516
*rhodoterus, Amphistichus*, Redtail Surfperch, 369
*rhodurupterus, Scarus*, Rosefinned Parrotfish, 492
*rhomaleus, Opistognathus*, Giant Jawfish, 497, 498
*rhomboides, Lagodon*, Pinfish, 292
*Rhomboplites aurorubens*, Vermillion Snapper, 259
*rhombus, Scopthalmus*, Brill, 611
*rhothophilus, Iso*, Surge Silverside, 102
*Rhycherus gloveri*, Glover's Frogfish, 85
*Rhynchobatus djeddensis*, White-spotted Shovelnose Ray, 47
*Rhyncopelates oxyrhynchus*, Five-striped Pigface, 217
Ribbon Eel, *Rhinomuraena quaesita*, 52, 64
Ribbon-striped Soldierfish, *Myripristis vittatus*, 114
*richardsoni, Pomachromis*, Richardson's Reef-damsel, 395
*richardsoni, Repomucenus*, Richardson's Dragonet, 537
*richardsoni, Rhamphocottus*, Grunt Sculpin, 166
Richardson's Dragonet, *Repomucenus richardsoni*, 537
Richardson's Reef-damsel, *Pomachromis richardsoni*, 395
Rifle Cardinalfish, *Apogon kiensis*, 227
Ringed Puffer, *Omegophora armilla*, 643
Ringed Seaperch, *Ellerkeldia annulata*, 199
Ringed Wrasse, *Hologymnosus doliatus*, 450, 476
*ringens, Xanthichthys*, Sargassum Triggerfish, 624
Rippled Coral Goby, *Gobiodon rivulatus*, 578
Rippled Rockskipper, *Istiblennius edentulus*, 531, 534
*ritteri, Centroscyllium*, Ritter's Catshark, 41
Ritter's Catshark, *Centroscyllium ritteri*, 41
*rivoliana, Seriola*, Almaco Jack, 250, 252
*rivulata, Canthigaster*, Doubleline Toby, 652
*rivulatus, Cirrhitus*, Giant Hawkfish, 412
*rivulatus, Epinephelus*, Halfmoon Rock Cod, 187
*rivulatus, Gobiodon*, Rippled Coral Goby, 578
*rivulatus, Leiognathus*, Offshore Pony Fish, 256
*rivulatus, Lutjanus*, Blue-spotted Snapper, 266
*robiginosus, Arcos*, Red Clingfish, 96
*robinsi, Apogon*, Roughlip Cardinalfish, 231
Robust Boxfish, *Strophiurichthys robustus*, 639
Robust Flounder, *Hippoglossoides robustus*, 613
*robustus, Apogon*, Cook's Cardinalfish, 223
*robustus, Chaetodon*, Ghana Butterflyfish, 335
*robustus, Hippoglossoides*, Robust Flounder, 613
*robustus, Spratelloides*, Blue Sprat, 66
*robustus, Strophiurichthys*, Robust Boxfish, 639
Rock Beauty, *Holacanthus tricolor*, 366
Rock Cod, *Lotella rhacinus*, 77
Rock Croaker, *Equetus viola*, 310
Rock Flagtail, *Kuhlia rupestris*, 219
Rock Gunnel, *Pholis gunnellus*, 495
Rock Hind, *Epinephelus adscensionis*, 192
Rock Sculpin, *Taurulus bubalis*, 167
Rock Sole, *Lepidopsetta bilineata*, 611
Rock Wrasse, *Halichoeres semicinctus*, 448
Rockfish, *Sebastes* sp., 151
*rogaa, Aethaloperca*, Redflush Rockcod, 179
Rogue Fish, *Amblyapistus taenionotus*, 58
*roissali, Symphodus*, Five-spotted Wrasse, 471
*rollandi, Chrysiptera*, Rolland's Demoiselle, 392, 394
Rolland's Demoiselle, *Chrysiptera rollandi*, 392, 394
*Roncador stearnsi*, Spotfin Croaker, 311
*roncador, Umbrina*, Yellowfin Croaker, 311
Roosterfish, *Nematistius pectoralis*, 257
*rosacea, Mycteroperca*, Rosy Grouper, 193, 194
*rosaceus, Sebastes*, Rosy Rockfish, 150
*rosae, Pseudoplesiops*, Rose Devilfish, 207
Rose Devilfish, *Pseudoplesiops rosae*, 207
*rosea?, Cyttopsis*, Rosy Dory, 118
Rosefinned Parrotfish, *Scarus rhodurupterus*, 492
*roseus, Cryptotomus*, Manytooth Parrotfish, 488
*roseus, Heteroclinus*, Pink Weedfish, 517
*rostrata, Canthigaster*, Sharpnose Puffer, 651
*rostratum, Zebrasoma*, Longnose Sailfin Tang, 592
*rostratus, Chelmon*, Copperband Butterflyfish, 349, 350
*rostratus, Heterostichus*, Giant Kelpfish, 516
*rostratus, Lethrinus*, Longsnout Emperor, 294
*rostratus, Symphodus*, Long-nosed Wrasse, 471
Rosy Blenny, *Malacoctenus macropus*, 515
Rosy Dory, *Cyttopsis rosea?*, 118
Rosy Grouper, *Mycteroperca rosacea*, 193, 194
Rosy Jobfish, *Pristipomoides filamentosus*, 269
Rosy Rockfish, *Sebastes rosaceus*, 150
Rosy Snapper, *Lutjanus lutjanus*, 261
Rosy Triplefin, *Norfolkia* sp., 507
Rough Bullseye, *Pempheris klunzinger*, 322
Rough Leatherjacket, *Scobinichthys granulatus*, 630, 634
Rough Scorpionfish, *Scorpaenodes scaber*, 153
Rough Triggerfish, *Canthidermis maculatus*, 625
Rough-peaked Soldierfish, *Myripristis trachyacron*, 116
Rough-scaled Soldierfish, *Plectrypops lima*, 113
Rough-scaled Squirrelfish, *Sargocentron lepros*, 109
Roughback, *Raja porosa*, 44
Roughhead Blenny, *Acanthemblemaria aspera*, 518
Roughhead Triplefin, *Enneanectes boehlkei*, 507
Roughjaw Frogfish, *Antennarius avalonis*, 88
Roughlip Cardinalfish, *Apogon robinsi*, 231
Roughneck Grunt, *Pomadasys corvinaeformis*, 281
Roughy, *Trachichthys australis*, 103
Round Herring, *Etrumeus teres*, 66
Round Pompano, *Trachinotus blochii*, 254, 255
Round Scad, *Decapterus punctatus*, 245
Round Stingray, *Urolophus halleri*, 46
Round-faced Batfish, *Platax teira*, 334
*rouxi, Parablennius*, Roux's Blenny, 524
Roux's Blenny, *Parablennius rouxi*, 524
Royal Basslet, *Lipogramma regia*, 213
Royal Blue Pygmy Angelfish, *Centropyge flavicauda*, 356
Royal Dottyback, *Pseudochromis paccagnellae*, 211
Royal Gramma, *Gramma loreto*, 213
*ruber, Carangoides*, Bar Jack, 248
*ruber, Emmelichthyops*, Red Bonnetmouth, 288
*ruberrimus, Sebastes*, Yelloweye Rockfish, 150
*rubescens, Choerodon*, Baldchin Tuskfish, 429
*rubescens, Parupeneus*, Blacksaddle Goatfish, 313

*rubicunda, Hypsypops,* Garibaldi, 397
*rubio, Prionotus,* Blackwing Searobin, 161
*rubra, Ellerkeldia,* Red Seaperch, 199
*rubra, Mycteroperca,* Comb Grouper, 193
*rubre, Liopropoma,* Peppermint Basslet, 198
*rubrioperculatus, Lethrinus,* Red Opercled Snapper, 297
*rubripes, Takifugu,* Tiger Puffer, 648
*rubripinne, Sparisoma,* Yellowtail Parrotfish, 488
*rubripinnis, Cirrhilabrus,* Red-finned Fairy Wrasse, 435
*rubripinnis, Hypodytes,* Redfin Sailfin Scorpionfish, 159
*rubriventralis, Cirrhilabrus,* Social Fairy Wrasse, 434
*rubrizonatus, Pseudanthias,* Deepsea Fairy Basslet, 174
*rubrocinctus, Amphiprion,* Red Anemonefish, 376
*rubrocinctus, Heteristius,* Saddle Stargazer, 512
*rubrolabiatus, Cheilodactylus,* Red-lipped Morwong, 418
*rubrolabiatus, Labroides,* Redlip Cleaner Wrasse, 469
*rubromarmoratus, Synodus,* Red-marbled Lizardfish, 74
*rubrovinctus, Sebastes,* Flag Rockfish, 151
*rubroviolaceus, Scarus,* Ember Parrotfish, 481, 483, 490
*rubrum, Sargocentron,* Russet Squirrelfish, 109
*ruconius, Secutor,* Pony Fish, 256
*Rudarius ercodes,* Japanese Filefish, 633
*Rudarius minutus,* Dwarf Leatherjacket, 633
Rudderfish, *Girella punctata,* 326
*rueppelliae, Gymnothorax,* Banded Moray, 54
*rufolineatus, Lutjanus,* Rufous Snapper, 261
Rufous Snapper, *Lutjanus rufolineatus,* 261
*rufus, Bodianus,* Spanish Hogfish, 430
*rufus, Holocentrus,* Longspine Squirrelfish, 109
*rupestris, Kuhlia,* Rock Flagtail, 219
*ruppelli, Apogon,* Gobbleguts, 229
*russelli, Decapterus,* Indian Scad, 247
*russelli, Lutjanus,* Russell's One-spot Snapper, 263
Russell's One-spot Snapper, *Lutjanus russelli,* 263
Russet Squirrelfish, *Sargocentron rubrum,* 109
Rusty Angelfish, *Centropyge ferrugatus,* 355
Rusty Goby, *Priolepis hipoliti,* 567
Rusty Parrotfish, *Scarus ferrugineus,* 483, 485
*Ruvettus pretiosus,* Oilfish, 601
*Rypticus bicolor?,* Cortez Soapfish, 207
*Rypticus bistrispinus,* Freckled Soapfish, 207
*Rypticus saponaceus,* Greater Soapfish, 207
*Rypticus subbifrenatus,* Spotted Soapfish, 207

## S

Sablefish, *Anoplopoma fimbria,* 162
Sabretooth Blenny, *Plagiotremus azaleus,* 521
*sachi, Podothecus,* Sailfin Poacher, 168
*Sacura margaritacea,* Cherry Bass, 180
*Sacura parva,* Little Fairy Basslet, 180
Saddle Anemonefish, *Amphiprion ephippium,* 373, 374
Saddle Stargazer, *Heteristius rubrocinctus,* 512
Saddle Wrasse, *Thalassoma duperreyi,* 466
Saddleback Butterflyfish, *Chaetodon ehippium,* 345
Saddleback Clown, *Amphiprion polymnus,* 372
Saddleback Hogfish, *Bodianus bilunulatus,* 428, 429, 473
Saddled Blenny, *Malacoctenus triangulatus,* 515
Saddled Butterflyfish, *Chaetodon ulietensis,* 340
Saddled Rock-cod, *Epinephelus damelii,* 186
Saddled-ocellated Sharpnosed Puffer, *Canthigaster ocellicincta,* 652
*saepepallens, Gobionellus,* Dash Goby, 565
*saepepallens?, Gobionellus,* Dash Goby, 561
Saffron Cod, *Eleginus gracilis,* 77
*Sagamia geneionema,* Bearded Goby, 546
Sailfin Bass, *Rabaulichthys altipinnis,* 200
Sailfin Blenny, *Emblemaria pandionis,* 520
Sailfin Cardinalfish, *Pterapogon mirifica,* 236
Sailfin Dottyback, *Pseudochromis veliferus,* 208
Sailfin Leaffish, *Taenianotus triacanthus,* 143
Sailfin Poacher, *Podothecus sachi,* 168
Sailfin Sandfish, *Arctoscopus japonicus,* 500
Sailfin Scorpionfish, *Hypodytes* sp., 159
Sailfin Sculpin, *Blepsias* sp., 166
Sailfish, *Istiophorus platypterus,* 604
Sailor's Choice, *Haemulon parrai,* 278
Saint Helena Butterflyfish, *Chaetodon sanctaehelenae,* 342
Saint Helena Sharpnose Puffer, *Canthigaster sanctaehelenae,* 652
*saira, Cololabias,* Pacific Saury, 100
*sajori, Hyporhamphus,* Japanese Halfbeak, 100
*Salangichthys microdon,* Noddlefish, 70
*Salaria pavo,* Peacock Blenny, 524
*Salarias ceramensis,* Ceram Blenny, 530
*Salarias fasciatus,* Jewelled Rockskipper, 526, 527, 528.01
*Salarias guttatus,* Blue-spot Blenny, 527
*Salarias irroratus,* Spotted Blenny, 527
*Salarias* sp., Blenny, unidentified, 527, 528.01; Starry Blenny, 527
*saliens, Liza,* Skipper, 421
Salmonet, *Upeneus bensasi,* 314
*salpa, Boops,* Saupe, 288
*saltatrix, Pomatomus,* Bluefish Tailor, 241
*Samaris cristatus,* Gray's Crested Flounder, 613
*sammara, Neoniphon,* Spotfin Squirrelfish, 112
*sammara?, Neoniphon,* Spotfin Squirrelfish, 111
*sammara, Neoniphon,* Spotfin Squirrelfish, 108, 110
Samoan Cardinalfish, *Foa fo,* 234
*sanctaehelenae, Canthigaster,* Saint Helena Sharpnose Puffer, 652
*sanctaehelenae, Chaetodon,* Saint Helena Butterflyfish, 342
Sand Dragonet, *Callionymus calcaratus,* 537
Sand Perch, *Diplectrum formosum,* 200
Sand Sole, *Psettichthys melanostictus,* 612
Sand Steenbras, *Lithognathus mormyrus,* 288
Sand Tiger, *Odontaspis taurus,* 37
Sand Tilefish, *Malacanthus plumieri,* 241
*sandageri, Coris,* Sandager's Coris, 437
Sandager's Coris, *Coris sandageri,* 437
*sandaracinos, Amphiprion,* Orange Anemonefish, 376
Sandbar Shark, *Carcharhinus plumbeus,* 39
Sanddiver Lizardfish, *Synodus intermedius,* 73, 74
Sandfish, *Crapatalus arenarius,* 501
*sandvicensis, Kuhlia,* Hawaiian Aholehole, 219
*sandwichensis, Cantherhines,* Wire-netting Leatherjacket, 629
*sangiensis, Apogon,* Bar-cheeked Cardinalfish, 227
*sanguineus, Antennarius,* Bloody Frogfish, 88
*sanguineus, Sicyases,* Giant Chilean Clingfish, 96
*sanguineus, Verriculus,* Hawaiian Blood Red Wrasse, 435
*sanguinolentus, Parablennius,* Palmate Horned Blenny, 524
*sankeyi, Pseudochromis,* Striped Dottyback, 210
*Sanopus splendidus,* Coral Toadfish, 84
*saponaceus, Rypticus,* Greater Soapfish, 207
*sarba, Rhabdosargus,* Natal Stumpnose, 292
*Sarda orientalis,* Striped Bonito, 603
*Sardinella* cf *jussieu,* Gold-striped Sardine, 66

Sargassum Blenny, *Exerpes asper,* 512
Sargassum Fish, *Histrio histrio,* 85
Sargassum Triggerfish, *Xanthichthys ringens,* 624
Sargo, *Anisotremus davidsonii,* 280
*Sargocentron bullisi,* Bullis' Squirrelfish, 107
*Sargocentron caudimaculatum,* Silverspot Squirrelfish, 108, 109, 111, 112
*Sargocentron coruscum,* Reef Squirrelfish, 107
*Sargocentron diadema,* Crown Squirrelfish, 107, 108, 111
*Sargocentron ensifer,* Hawaiian Squirrelfish, 110
*Sargocentron ittodai,* Japanese Squirrelfish, 107
*Sargocentron lacteoguttatus,* White-spotted Squirrelfish, 111
*Sargocentron lepros,* Rough-scaled Squirrelfish, 109
*Sargocentron melanospilus,* Horned Squirrelfish, 110, 111
*Sargocentron microstoma,* Smallmouthed Squirrelfish, 108
*Sargocentron punctatissimum,* Speckled Squirrelfish, 109
*Sargocentron rubrum,* Russet Squirrelfish, 109
*Sargocentron seychellensis,* Seychelles Squirrelfish, 108
*Sargocentron spiniferum,* Scarlet-fin Squirrelfish, 104, 108, 112
*Sargocentron suborbitalis,* Tinsel Squirrelfish, 109
*Sargocentron tiere,* Tahitian Squirrelfish, 108, 111
*Sargocentron tieroides,* Indo-Pacific Squirrelfish, 107
*Sargocentron vexillarium,* Flag Squirrelfish, 107
*Sargocentron violaceum,* Violet Squirrelfish, 105, 107, 111
*Sargocentron xantherythrus,* Yellow-red Squirrelfish, 107
*sargus, Diplodus,* White Bream, 293
*Satyrichthys laticephalus,* Offshore Crocodilefish, 160
Saucereye Porgy, *Calamus calamus,* 291
*saucrum, Gobiosoma,* Goldspot Goby, 571
Saupe, *Boops salpa,* 288
*Saurida dermatogenys,* Slender Grinner, 73
*Saurida gracilis,* Graceful Lizardfish, 72, 75
*Saurida normani,* Shortjaw Lizardfish, 74
*Saurida undosquamis,* Large-scaled Grinner, 73
*saurus, Oligoplites,* Leatherjacket, 251
*sauteri, Galeus,* Gecko Shark, 37
*savayensis, Apogon,* Ghost Cardinalfish, 229
Saw-edged Perch, *Niphon spinosus,* 173
Saw-jawed Monocle Bream, *Scolopsis ciliatus,* 293, 303
Saw-tooth Grouper, *Polyprion oxygeneiosus,* 173
Sawcheek Cardinalfish, *Apogon quadrisquamatus,* 230
Sawtail Grouper, *Mycteroperca prionura,* 193
Sawtooth Boxfish, *Kentrocapros aculeatus,* 639
Sawtooth Pipefish, *Maroubra perserrata,* 126
*saxatilis, Abudefduf,* Sergeant Major, 380
*saxatilis, Morone,* Striped Bass, 173
*scaber, Parika,* Parika, 636
*scaber, Scorpaenodes,* Rough Scorpionfish, 153
Scaled-cheek Brotula, *Brotula erythrea?,* 81
Scalloped Hammerhead, *Sphyrna lewini,* 40, 41
*scalprus, Prionurus,* Blackthorn Sawtail, 588
Scaly Chromis, *Chromis lepidolepis,* 386
Scaly Damsel, *Pomacentrus lepidogenys,* 400
Scalyhead Sculpin, *Artedius harringtoni,* 164
*scapularis, Blennodesmus,* Ocellate Eel Blenny, 500
*scapularis, Halichoeres,* Zigzag Wrasse, 440, 472
Scarbreast Tuskfish, *Choerodon azurio,* 431
Scarlet Frogfish, *Antennarius coccineus,* 86, 91
Scarlet Soldierfish, *Myripristis pralinia,* 112, 115
Scarlet Wrasse, *Pseudolabrus milesi,* 463
Scarlet-fin Squirrelfish, *Sargocentron spiniferum,* 104, 108, 112
Scarletfin Blenny, *Coralliozetus micropes,* 519
Scarletfin Wrasse, *Paracheilinus lineopunctatus,* 459
*Scartella cristata,* Molly Miller, 529, 530
*Scarus atrilunula,* Blue Moon Parrotfish, 482
*Scarus bataviensis,* Batavian Parrotfish, 490
*Scarus bleekeri,* Pacific Whitecheek Parrotfish, 483, 492, 493
*Scarus brevifilis,* Tattooed Parrotfish, 483
*Scarus coelestinus,* Midnight Parrotfish, 486
*Scarus coeruleus,* Blue Parrotfish, 486
*Scarus croicensis,* Striped Parrotfish, 486
*Scarus cyanescens,* Blue Bumphead Parrotfish, 481
*Scarus cyanotaenia,* Blue-lined Parrotfish, 492
*Scarus dimidiatus,* Fivesaddle Parrotfish, 482
*Scarus dubius,* Green Parrotfish, 484
*Scarus erythrodon,* Slopehead Parrotfish, 490
*Scarus ferrugineus,* Rusty Parrotfish, 483, 485
*Scarus flavipectoralis,* Yellowfin Parrotfish, 484
*Scarus frenatus,* Fall Parrotfish, 479, 482, 485
*Scarus frontalis,* Blue Parrotfish, 483
*Scarus ghobban,* Blue-barred Orange Parrotfish, 482, 485
*Scarus gibbus,* Bumphead Parrotfish, 480, 482, 484, 491, 492
*Scarus guacamaia,* Rainbow Parrotfish, 485
*Scarus japanensis,* Forster's Parrotfish, 492
*Scarus javanicus,* Java Parrotfish, 489
*Scarus macrocheilus,* Plain Parrotfish, 490, 492
*Scarus moensi,* Moens Parrotfish, 489
*Scarus niger,* Dusky Parrotfish, 481, 489
*Scarus oktodon,* Eight-toothed Parrotfish, 490
*Scarus oviceps,* Variable Parrotfish, 489
*Scarus perrico,* Mexican Parrotfish, 485
*Scarus perspicillatus,* Hawaiian Blue Parrotfish, 483
*Scarus prasiognathos,* Greenbeak Parrotfish, 481, 485, 490, 492
*Scarus psittacus,* Yellow-sided Parrotfish, 481, 485, 489, 492
*Scarus rhodurupterus,* Rosefinned Parrotfish, 492
*Scarus rubroviolaceus,* Ember Parrotfish, 481, 483, 490
*Scarus schlegeli,* Schlegel's Parrotfish, 484
*Scarus sordidus,* Garnet Red Parrotfish, 482, 490
*Scarus* sp., Orangecheek Parrotfish, 484; Parrotfish, unidentified, 483, 493
*Scarus taeniopterus,* Princess Parrotfish, 486
*Scarus tricolor,* Blackstripe Parrotfish, 484
*Scarus venosus,* Five-banded Parrotfish, 482
*Scarus vetula,* Queen Parrotfish, 486
*Scatophagus argus,* Spotted Scat, 329
*Scatophagus tetracanthus,* Striped Scat, 329
*schlegeli, Acanthopagrus,* Schlegel's Bream, 292
*schlegeli, Caprodon,* Schlegel's Red Bass, 181
*schlegeli, Rhinobatos,* Schlegel's Guitarfish, 44
*schlegeli, Scarus,* Schlegel's Parrotfish, 484
Schlegel's Bream, *Acanthopagrus schlegeli,* 292
Schlegel's Guitarfish, *Rhinobatos schlegeli,* 44
Schlegel's Parrotfish, *Scarus schlegeli,* 484
Schlegel's Red Bass, *Caprodon schlegeli,* 181
*schoenleinii, Choerodon,* Blackspot Tuskfish, 431
*schoepfi, Aluterus,* Orange Filefish, 635
*schoepfi, Chilomycterus,* Striped Burrfish, 655
*schomburgki, Pempheris,* Copper Sweeper, 322
Schoolmaster, *Lutjanus apodus,* 265
*schotaf, Plectorhinchus,* Sombre Sweetlips, 282, 284
*schrenki, Limanda,* Crested Flounder, 613
*schroederi, Ecsenius,* Schroeder's Blenny, 528.16
Schroeder's Blenny, *Ecsenius schroederi,* 528.16
*Schuettea woodwardi,* Woodward's Pomfret, 321

*schuinslandi, Parapercis,* Red Grubfish, 502
*Schultzea beta,* Slide-mouth Bass, 200
*schultzi, Corythoichthys,* Gilded Pipefish, 128
Schultz's Triplefin, *Norfolkia brachylepis,* 508
*schwanefeldi, Thalassoma,* Six-bar Wrasse, 476
*schwenki, Pempheris,* Black-stripe Sweeper, 322
Scintillating Damsel, *Pomacentrus pikei,* 403
Scissor Damselfish, *Chromis atrilobata,* 389
*scitulus, Prionotus,* Leopard Searobin, 161
*sciurus, Haemulon,* Bluestriped Grunt, 278, 279
*Scobinichthys granulatus,* Rough Leatherjacket, 630, 634
*scolopax, Macrorhamphosus,* Longspine Snipefish, 123
*Scolopsis bilineatus,* Two-lined Monocle Bream, 293, 302, 304
*Scolopsis bimaculatus,* Double Blotch Spinecheek, 293
*Scolopsis bleekeri,* Bleeker's Monocle Bream, 302, 304
*Scolopsis cancellatus,* Latticed Monocle Bream, 302, 304
*Scolopsis ciliatus,* Saw-jawed Monocle Bream, 293, 303
*Scolopsis dubiosus,* Yellow-streaked Monocle Bream, 302, 304
*Scolopsis frenatus,* Seychelles Spinecheek, 293
*Scolopsis ghanam,* Paleband Spinecheek, 282
*Scolopsis inermis,* Unarmed Monocle Bream, 303
*Scolopsis leucotaenia,* Whiteribbon Spinecheek, 302
*Scolopsis margaritifera,* Pearly Monocle Bream, 303, 308
*Scolopsis monogramma,* Monogrammed Monocle Bream, 302, 304
*Scolopsis personatus,* Blue-nosed Monocle Bream, 303
*Scolopsis taeniopterus,* Lattice Monocle Bream, 303
*Scolopsis temporalis,* Rainbow Monocle Bream, 303
*Scolopsis trilineatus,* Three-line Monocle Bream, 303
*Scolopsis vosmeri,* Whitecheek Monocle Bream, 293, 302
*Scolopsis xenochrous,* Olive-spotted Monocle Bream, 304
*Scomber australasicus,* Slimy Mackerel, 601
*Scomber japonicus,* Chub Mackerel, 603
*Scomberoides commersonnianus,* Talang Queenfish, 250
*Scomberoides lysan,* Doublespotted Queenfish, 250, 251
*Scomberoides tol,* Needlescaled Queenfish, 250
*Scomberomorus commerson,* Narrow-barred Spanish Mackerel, 603
*Scomberomorus guttatus,* King Spanish Mackerel, 603
*Scomberomorus lineolatus,* Streaked Spanish Mackerel, 603
*Scomberomorus maculatus,* Spotted Spanish Mackerel, 601
*Scomberomorus niphonius,* Japanese Spanish Mackerel, 603
*Scomberomorus queenslandicus,* Queensland Spanish Mackerel, 603
*Scomberomorus semifasciatus,* Broad-barred Spanish Mackerel, 603
*Scomberomorus sierra,* Pacific Sierra, 601
*Scombrops boops,* Gnomefish, 244
*Scombrops gilberti,* Japanese Bluefish, 244
Scooter Dragonet, *Neosynchiropus ocellatus,* 536, 537
*scopas, Amanses,* Broom Filefish, 627, 635
*scopas, Zebrasoma,* Brown Sailfin Tang, 592, 594
*scops, Opistognathus,* Bullseye Jawfish, 499
*Scopthalmus aquosus,* Windowpane, 611
*Scopthalmus rhombus,* Brill, 611
*Scorpaena albifimbria,* Coral Scorpionfish, 145
*Scorpaena ballieui,* Ballieu's Scorpionfish, 154
*Scorpaena bergi,* Goosehead Scorpionfish, 145
*Scorpaena cardinalis,* Cardinal Scorpionfish, 138
*Scorpaena coniorta,* Small Scorpionfish, 146
*Scorpaena cooki,* Cook's Scorpionfish, 154
*Scorpaena elachys,* Dwarf Scorpionfish, 145
*Scorpaena grandicornis,* Grass Scorpionfish, 144
*Scorpaena guttata,* California Scorpionfish, 145
*Scorpaena inermis,* Mushroom Scorpionfish, 145
*Scorpaena neglecta,* Fringyhead Scorpionfish, 146
*Scorpaena notata,* Red Scorpionfish, 144
*Scorpaena picta,* Painted Scorpionfish, 148
*Scorpaena plumieri mystes,* Stone Scorpionfish, 144
*Scorpaena plumieri plumieri,* Spotted Scorpionfish, 144
*Scorpaena porcus,* European Scorpionfish, 144
*Scorpaena scrofa,* Bigscale Scorpionfish, 144
*Scorpaena sonorae,* Sonora Scorpionfish, 145
*Scorpaena* sp., Abrolhos Scorpionfish, 146; Hunchback Scorpionfish, 145; Spotted Scorpionfish, 148
*Scorpaena sumptuosa,* Red Scorpin, 146
*Scorpaenichthys marmoratus,* Cabezon, 167
*Scorpaenidae* sp., Scorpionfish, unidentified, 154
*Scorpaenodes carribbaeus,* Reef Scorpionfish, 153
*Scorpaenodes insularis,* St. Helena Scorpionfish, 153
*Scorpaenodes kelloggi,* Kellogg's Scorpionfish, 154
*Scorpaenodes littoralis,* Shore Rockfish, 154
*Scorpaenodes parvipinnis,* Short-spined Scorpionfish, 143
*Scorpaenodes scaber,* Rough Scorpionfish, 153
*Scorpaenodes* sp., Bicolor Scorpionfish, 154; Scorpionfish, 153
*Scorpaenodes steenei,* Steene's Scorpionfish, 143
*Scorpaenodes tredecimspinosus,* Deepreef Scorpionfish, 145
*Scorpaenodes varipinnis,* Ornate Scorpionfish, 153
*Scorpaenodes xyris,* Rainbow Scorpionfish, 153
*Scorpaenopsis barbatus,* Bearded Scorpionfish, 147
*Scorpaenopsis brevifrons,* Short-browed Scorpionfish, 147
*Scorpaenopsis diabolus,* Devil Scorpionfish, 147, 148, 154
*Scorpaenopsis gibbosa,* Humpback Scorpionfish, 147
*Scorpaenopsis oxycephala,* Hairy Stingfish, 136, 138, 146, 147
*Scorpaenopsis* sp., Christmas Island Scorpionfish, 146, 148; Lord Howe Scorpionfish, 146; Scorpionfish, unidentified, 148, 153
Scorpionfish, *Scorpaenodes* sp., 153
Scorpionfish, unidentified, *Sebastapistes* sp., 147; *Scorpaenidae* sp., 154; *Scorpaenopsis* sp., 148, 153
*Scorpis aequipinnis,* Blue Maomao, 328
*Scorpis georgianus,* Banded Sweep, 327
*scorpius, Myoxocephalus,* Short-finned Sculpin, 165
*scotti, Chromis,* Purple Reeffish, 388
*scottorum, Cirrhilabrus,* Greenback Fairy Wrasse, 435
Scrawled Cowfish, *Lactophrys quadricornis,* 641
*scriba, Serranus,* Painted Comber, 196
Scribbled Boxfish, *Ostracion solorensis,* 640, 642
Scribbled Filefish, *Aluterus scriptus,* 630, 636
Scribbled Toadfish, *Arothron mappa,* 647
*scriptus, Aluterus,* Scribbled Filefish, 630, 636
*scrofa, Scorpaena,* Bigscale Scorpionfish, 144
Sculptured Goby, *Callogobius mucosus,* 562
*scutatus, Centriscus,* Grooved Razorfish, 123
*Scyliorhinus canicula,* Lesser Spotted Dogfish, 38
*scyllia, Triakis,* Japanese Leopard Shark, 39
Scythe-marked Butterflyfish, *Chaetodon falcifer,* 347
*scythrops, Neoniphon,* Jordan's Squirrelfish, 110
Sea Carp, *Dactylosargus* sp., 418
Sea Goldie, *Pseudanthias hutchi,* 177
Sea Lamprey, *Petromyzon marinus,* 34
Sea Moth, *Eurypegasus draconis,* 92
Sea Perch, *Psammoperca waigiensis,* 170
Sea Raven, *Hemitripteris americanus,* 165
Sea Robin, unidentified, *?Peristedion* sp., 160
Sea Urchin Cardinalfish, *Siphamia mossambica?,* 237
Sea Whip Goby, *Bryaninops amphis,* 560
Seagrass Wrasse, *Novaculichthys macrolepidotus,* 458, 472
*sealei, Apogon,* Seale's Cardinalfish, 228

Seale's Cardinalfish, *Apogon sealei*, 228
Seamoth, *Parapegasus* sp.?, 119
Searobin, *Bellator gymnostethius*, 160
Seaweed Blenny, *Parablennius marmoreus*, 529
*sebae, Amphiprion*, Seba's Anemonefish, 377
*sebae, Lutjanus*, Emperor Snapper, 270
*sebae, Monodactylus*, Fingerfish, 321
Seba's Anemonefish, *Amphiprion sebae*, 377
*Sebastapistes cyanostigma*, Yellow-spotted Scorpionfish, 146, 148
*Sebastapistes* sp., Scorpionfish, unidentified, 147
*Sebastapistes strongia*, Barchin Scorpionfish, 147
*Sebastes atrovirens*, Kelp Rockfish, 149
*Sebastes auriculatus*, Brown Rockfish, 149
*Sebastes baramenuke*, Japanese Scorpionfish, 152
*Sebastes carnatus*, Gopher Rockfish, 149
*Sebastes caurinus*, Copper Rockfish, 149
*Sebastes chrysomelas*, Black-and-Yellow Rockfish, 149
*Sebastes constellatus*, Starry Rockfish, 149
*Sebastes dallii*, Calico Rockfish, 149
*Sebastes flavidus*, Yellowtail Rockfish, 151
*Sebastes inermis*, Japanese Black Rockfish, 152
*Sebastes joyneri*, Joyner's Stingfish, 152
*Sebastes maliger*, Quillback Rockfish, 149
*Sebastes marinus*, Golden Redfish, 151
*Sebastes matsubarae*, Matsubara's Red Rockfish, 152
*Sebastes melanops*, Black Rockfish, 150
*Sebastes miniatus*, Vermillion Rockfish, 151
*Sebastes mystinus*, Blue Rockfish, 150
*Sebastes nebulosus*, China Rockfish, 150
*Sebastes nigrocinctus*, Tiger Rockfish, 150
*Sebastes nivosus*, Snowy Rockfish, 152
*Sebastes oblongus*, Oblong Rockfish, 152
*Sebastes pachycephalus*, Spotbelly Rockfish, 152
*Sebastes paucispinis*, Bocaccio, 150
*Sebastes pinniger*, Canary Rockfish, 150
*Sebastes rosaceus*, Rosy Rockfish, 150
*Sebastes ruberrimus*, Yelloweye Rockfish, 150
*Sebastes rubrovinctus*, Flag Rockfish, 151
*Sebastes serranoides*, Olive Rockfish, 151
*Sebastes serriceps*, Treefish, 151
*Sebastes* sp., Rockfish, 151
*Sebastes trivittatus*, Threestripe Rockfish, 152
*Sebastes umbrosus*, Honeycomb Rockfish, 151
*Sebasticus albofasciatus*, Yellow-barred Red Rockfish, 138
*Sebasticus marmoratus*, Marbled Rockfish, 138
*Sebastolobus alascanus*, Shortspine Thornyhead, 138
*Sebastolobus macrochir*, Bighand Thornyhead, 138
*sectatrix, Kyphosus*, Bermuda Chub, 328
*Secutor ruconius*, Pony Fish, 256
*sedentarius, Chaetodon*, Reef Butterflyfish, 342
*Selar crumenophthalmus*, Bigeye Scad, 245, 250
*Selaroides leptolepis*, Yellowstripe Scad, 250
*Selene brevoortii*, Mexican Lookdown, 251
*Selene setapinnis*, Atlantic Moonfish, 251
*Selene vomer*, Lookdown, 251
*selene, Chaetodon*, Moon Butterflyfish, 338
*Selenotoca multifasciata*, Many Banded Scat, 329
*semeion, Chaetodon*, Decorated Butterflyfish, 344
*semicinctus, Genicanthus*, Half-striped Lyretail Angelfish, 358
*semicinctus, Halichoeres*, Rock Wrasse, 448
*semicinctus, Leiuranus*, Half-banded Snake Eel, 61
*semicinctus, Lutjanus*, Half-banded Snapper, 266
*semicirculatus, Pomacanthus*, Koran Angelfish, 362, 364, 365
*Semicossyphus pulcher*, California Sheephead, 463
*Semicossyphus reticulatus*, Reticulated Bumphead Wrasse, 463
*semidoliatus, Priolepis*, Redhead Goby, 567
*semifasciatus, Genicanthus*, Half-banded Lyretail Angelfish, 358
*semifasciatus, Scomberomorus*, Broad-barred Spanish Mackerel, 603
*semifasciatus, Triakis*, Leopard Shark, 39
*semilarvatus, Chaetodon*, Red-lined Butterflyfish, 344
*semilineatus, Apogon*, Indian Little Fish, 226
*seminctus, Amblygobius*, Half-banded Goby, 555
Seminole Goby, *Microgobius carri*, 569
*seminudus, Gymneleotris*, Split-banded Goby, 567
*semiornatus, Apogon*, Oblique-banded Cardinalfish, 225
*semipunctatus, Asterropteryx*, Starry Fin Goby, 555
Senator Wrasse, *Pictilabrus laticlavius*, 462
Senorita, *Oxyjulis californica*, 470
Senorita De Cintas, *Pseudojulis notospilus*, 461
*sephen, Dasyatis*, Cowtail Ray, 45
Sepia Stingray, *Urolophus aurantiacus*, 46
*septemfasciatum, Thalassoma*, Sevenband Wrasse, 468
*septemfasciatus, Abudefduf*, Sevenbar Damsel, 382
*septemfasciatus, Epinephelus*, Seven-banded Grouper, 189
*septentrionalis, Chaetodontoplus*, Blue-lined Angelfish, 360
Sergeant Baker, *Aulopus purpurissatus*, 71, 72
Sergeant Major, *Abudefduf saxatilis*, 380
*Seriola dumerili*, Greater Amberjack, 250, 252
*Seriola hippos*, Amberjack, 252
*Seriola lalandi dorsalis*, Yellowtail, 252
*Seriola lalandi lalandi*, Yellowtail, 252
*Seriola quinqueradiata*, Japanese Yellowtail, 252
*Seriola rivoliana*, Almaco Jack, 250, 252
*Seriola zonata*, Banded Rudderfish, 253
*Seriolina nigrofasciata*, Blackbanded Amberjack, 250, 253
*serpens, Gempylus*, Snake Mackerel, 601
*Serraniculus pumilio*, Pygmy Sea Bass, 196
*Serranocirrhitus latus*, Sunburst Basslet, 180
*serranoides, Sebastes*, Olive Rockfish, 151
*Serranus annularis*, Orangeback Bass, 197
*Serranus baldwini*, Lantern Bass, 197
*Serranus cabrilla*, Comber, 196
*Serranus chionaraia*, Snow Bass, 197
*Serranus fasciatus*, Barred Serrano, 197
*Serranus flaviventris*, Twinspot Bass, 197
*Serranus hepatus*, Brown Comber, 196
*Serranus heterurus*, West African Sea Bass, 196
*Serranus luciopercanus*, Walleye Basslet, 196
*Serranus phoebe*, Tattler, 196
*Serranus scriba*, Painted Comber, 196
*Serranus subligarius*, Belted Sandfish, 197
*Serranus tabacarius*, Tobacco Fish, 197
*Serranus tigrinis*, Harlequin Bass, 197
*Serranus tortugarum*, Chalk Bass, 196
*serratus, Acanthistius*, Wirrah, 202
*serriceps, Sebastes*, Treefish, 151
*serrula, Pristigenys*, Popeye Catalufa, 219
*setapinnis, Selene*, Atlantic Moonfish, 251
*setifer, Xiphasia*, Half-tail Blenny, 526
*setigerus, Lophiomus*, Blackmouth Goosefish, 84
*setigerus, Trichonotus*, Filamented Sand Eel, 539
*Setipinna breviceps*, Bristle-feathered Anchovy, 68
*setosus, Pentapodus*, Butterfly Bream, 299, 300

Seven-banded Grouper, *Epinephelus septemfasciatus,* 189
Sevenband Wrasse, *Thalassoma septemfasciatum,* 468
Sevenbar Damsel, *Abudefduf septemfasciatus,* 382
*sexfasciata, Parapercis,* Six-banded Weever, 502
*sexfasciatum, Haemulon,* Graybar Grunt, 280
*sexfasciatum, Tilodon,* Moonlighter, 327
*sexfasciatus, Abudefduf,* Stripetail Damsel, 381
*sexfasciatus, Caranx,* Bigeye Kingfish, 247, 249
*sexfilis, Polydactylus,* Pacific Threadfin, 420
*sexguttata, Valenciennea,* Ladder Glider, 566
*sexlineatus, Grammistes,* Sixstripe Soapfish, 204, 206
*sexlineatus, Pelates,* Six-lined Trumpeter, 217, 218
*sexmaculata, Cephalopholis,* Six-barred Grouper, 183, 185
*sexmaculatus, Enneanectes,* Delicate Triplefin, 507
*sexstriatus, Euxiphipops,* Six-banded Angelfish, 364
Seychelle Blenny, *Stanulus seychellensis,* 530
*seychellensis, Sargocentron,* Seychelles Squirrelfish, 108
*seychellensis, Stanulus,* Seychelle Blenny, 530
Seychelles Emperor, *Lethrinus enigmaticus,* 298
Seychelles Goby, *Ctenogobiops crocineus,* 549
Seychelles Mudskipper, *Periophthalmus sobrinus?,* 579
Seychelles Spinecheek, *Scolopsis frenatus,* 293
Seychelles Squirrelfish, *Sargocentron seychellensis,* 108
Shaggy Sea Raven, *Hemitripteris villosus,* 165
Sharknose Goby, *Gobiosoma evelynae,* 573
Sharp-nosed Puffer, *Canthigaster compressus,* 651
Sharp-nosed Trench Sardine, *Amblygaster leiogaster,* 66
Sharp-nosed Weever, *Parapercis hexophthalma,* 504
Sharp-tailed Pearlfish, *Onuxodon margaritiferae,* 79, 80
Sharphead Tripodfish, *Tripodichthys oxycephalus,* 619
Sharpnose Puffer, *Canthigaster rostrata,* 651
Sharpnose Sevengill Shark, *Heptranchias perlo,* 33
Sharptail Eel, *Myrichthys aciminatus,* 61
Sharptooth Cardinalfish, *Cheilodipterus quinquelineatus,* 233
Shaw's Cowfish, *Aracana aurita,* 637
Sheepshead, *Archosargus probatocephalus,* 292
Sheepshead Bream, *Diplodus puntazzo,* 288
*shepardi, Centropyge,* Shepard's Angelfish, 355
Shepard's Angelfish, *Centropyge shepardi,* 355
Shimmering Cardinalfish, *Siphamia versicolor,* 237
Shiner Surfperch, *Cymatogaster aggregata,* 369
Shore Rockfish, *Scorpaenodes littoralis,* 154
Short Bigeye, *Pristigenys alta,* 219
Short-bodied Ghost Pipefish, *Solenostomus paradoxus,* 120, 123
Short-browed Scorpionfish, *Scorpaenopsis brevifrons,* 147
Short-finned Sculpin, *Myoxocephalus scorpius,* 165
Short-spined Scorpionfish, *Scorpaenodes parvipinnis,* 143
Short-tail Stingray, *Dasyatis brevicaudata,* 45
Short-tooth Cardinalfish, *Apogon apogonides,* 233
Shortbill Spearfish, *Tetrapturus angustirostris,* 604
Shortfin Lionfish, *Dendrochirus brachypterus,* 143
Shortfin Mako Shark, *Isurus oxyrinchus,* 37, 40
Shortheaded Lizardfish, *Trachinocephalus myops,* 73
Shortjaw Lizardfish, *Saurida normani,* 74
Shortnose Batfish, *Ogcocephalus nasutus,* 93
Shortnose Blacktail Shark, *Carcharhinus wheeleri,* 39
Shortspine Combfish, *Zaniolepis frenata,* 163
Shortspine Porcupinefish, *Diodon liturosus,* 656
Shortspine Thornyhead, *Sebastolobus alascanus,* 138
Shortstripe Cleaning Goby, *Gobiosoma chancei,* 572
Shorttail Pipefish, *Microphis brachyurus,* 125
Shoulderbar Soldierfish, *Myripristis kuntee,* 114, 115
Shovelnose Guitarfish, *Rhinobatos productus,* 43
Showy Snailfish, *Liparis pulchellus,* 168
Shrimpfish, *Aeoliscus strigatus,* 122
Shy Butterflyfish, *Hemitaurichthys polylepis,* 351
Shy Filefish, *Cantherhines verrucundus,* 632
Shy Hamlet, *Hypoplectrus guttavarius,* 201
Shy Puffer, *Takifugu oblongus,* 649
Sickle Butterflyfish, *Chaetodon falcula,* 340
Sickle Pomfret, *Taractichthys steindachneri,* 257
*Sicyases sanguineus,* Giant Chilean Clingfish, 96
Sideburn Wrasse, *Pteragogus pelycus,* 449, 450
*Siderea grisea,* Geometric Moray, 59
*Siderea picta,* Paintspotted Moray, 55, 58
*sierra, Scomberomorus,* Pacific Sierra, 601
*Siganus argenteus,* Streamlined Spinefoot, 597
*Siganus canaliculatus,* White-spotted Spinefoot, 597, 598
*Siganus chrysospilos,* Gold-spotted Spinefoot, 598, 599
*Siganus corallinus,* Blue-spotted Spinefoot, 598
*Siganus fuscescens,* Dusky Spinefoot, 597
*Siganus guttatus,* Yellow-blotch Spinefoot, 598
*Siganus javus,* Streaked Spinefoot, 598
*Siganus lineatus,* Golden-lined Spinefoot, 598, 600
*Siganus puelloides,* Black-eyed Spinefoot, 598
*Siganus puellus,* Decorated Spinefoot, 599
*Siganus spinus,* Little Spinefoot, 599
*Siganus stellatus,* Brown-spotted Spinefoot, 599
*Siganus trispilos,* Three-spot Spinefoot, 599
*Siganus vermiculatus,* Vermiculated Spinefoot, 599
*Siganus virgatus,* Double-barred Spinefoot, 599
Signae Blenny, *Emblemaria hypacanthus,* 520
*signatus, Microgobius,* Cuban Goby, 569
*signifier, Iracundus,* Spot-bearing Scorpionfish, 148
*Signigobius biocellatus,* Two-spot Goby, 540, 551
*sihama, Sillago,* Silver Sillago, 239
Silhouette Goby, *Silhouettea insinuans,* 551
*Silhouettea insinuans,* Silhouette Goby, 551
Silk Snapper, *Lutjanus vivanus,* 264
*Sillago macrolepis,* Large-scaled Whiting, 239
*Sillago maculata,* Blotchy Sillago, 239
*Sillago sihama,* Silver Sillago, 239
Silver and Black Butterflyfish, *Chaetodon argentatus,* 336
Silver Conger Eel, *Muraenesox cinereus,* 62
Silver Grunt, *Pomadasys argyreus,* 281
Silver Grunter, *Mesopristes argenteus,* 217, 218
Silver Jenny, *Eucinostomus gula,* 275
Silver Large-eye Bream, *Gymnocranius japonicus,* 290
Silver Mono, *Monodactylus argenteus,* 320, 418
Silver Pomfret, *Pampas argenteus,* 606
Silver Sillago, *Sillago sihama,* 239
Silver Snapper, *Lutjanus argentimaculatus,* 260, 261, 266
Silver Squirrelfish, *Neoniphon argenteus,* 110, 112
Silver Streak Goldie, *Pseudanthias taeniatus,* 177
Silver Surfperch, *Hyperprosopon ellipticum,* 370
Silver Sweeper, *Pempheris oualensis,* 321, 323
Silver-banded Sweetlips, *Plectorhinchus diagrammus,* 284
Silverline Mudskipper, *Periophthalmus argentilineatus,* 579
Silverspot, *Threpterius maculosus,* 415
Silverspot Squirrelfish, *Sargocentron caudimaculatum,* 108, 109, 111, 112
Silverstripe Chromis, *Chromis altus,* 389
Silvertip Shark, *Carcharhinus albimarginatus,* 40
Similan Goby, *Pleurosicya* sp., 568

*simplicidens, Girella,* Gulf Opaleye, 326
*simsiang, Stegastes,* Bleeker's Damsel, 404
*simulus, Hemiemblemaria,* Mimic Blenny, 519
*sindonis, Plectroglyphidodon,* Hawaiian Rock Damsel, 395
*sinensis, Inimicus,* Goblin Devilfish, 158
*sinensis, Platyrhina,* Oriental Thornback, 43
Singapore Silver-Biddy, *Gerres kapas,* 276
Singleband Forktail Blenny, *Meiacanthus vittatus,* 523
*singularius, Heniochus,* Philippine Pennant Coralfish, 352
*sinuscalifornici, Stathmonotus,* Worm Blenny, 516
*sinuspersici, Torpedo,* Marbled Electric Ray, 43
*Siphamia cephalotes,* Southern Siphonfish, 237
*Siphamia fuscolineata,* Crown-of-thorns Cardinalfish, 237
*Siphamia mossambica?,* Sea Urchin Cardinalfish, 237
*Siphamia* sp., Cardinalfish, unidentified, 237
*Siphamia versicolor,* Shimmering Cardinalfish, 237
*Siphonognathus argyrophanes,* Tubemouth, 478
*Siphonognathus beddomei,* Pencil Weed Whiting, 478
*Siphonognathus radiatus,* Bridled Weed Whiting, 478
Sirm, *Amblygaster sirm,* 66
*sirm, Amblygaster,* Sirm, 66
Six-banded Angelfish, *Euxiphipops sexstriatus,* 364
Six-banded Weever, *Parapercis sexfasciata,* 502
Six-bar Wrasse, *Thalassoma schwanefeldi,* 476
Six-barred Grouper, *Cephalopholis sexmaculata,* 183, 185
Six-barred Reef Grouper, *Epinephelus diacanthus,* 189
Six-lined Trumpeter, *Pelates sexlineatus,* 217, 218
Sixbar Wrasse, *Thalassoma hardwicke,* 465
Sixstripe Soapfish, *Grammistes sexlineatus,* 204, 206
Sixstripe Wrasse, *Pseudocheilinus hexataenia,* 458
Skilfish, *Erilepis zonifer,* 162
Skipjack Tuna, *Katsuwonus pelamis,* 602
Skipper, *Liza saliens,* 421
Skunk Blenny, *Dictyosoma burgeri,* 494
Skunk-striped Anemonefish, *Amphiprion akallopisos,* 373
Slaty Goby, *Gobiosoma tenox,* 571
Slaty Grenadier, *Coryphaenoides asper,* 78
Slender Bombay Duck, *Harpadon microchir,* 73
Slender Bullseye, *Parapriacanthus unwini,* 321
Slender Cardinalfish, *Rhabdamia* sp., 222
Slender Filefish, *Monacanthus tuckeri,* 628
Slender Glassy, *Ambassis natalensis,* 323
Slender Grinner, *Saurida dermatogenys,* 73
Slender Hardyhead, *Atherinomorus lacunosus,* 102
Slender Mola, *Ranzania laevis,* 656
Slender Reef-damsel, *Pomachromis exilis,* 395
Slender Roughy, *Hoplostethus elongatus,* 103
Slender Sandfish, *Creedia alleni,* 501
Slender Shrimp Goby, *Amblyeleotris periophthalmus,* 543; *Amblyeleotris* sp. aff *periophthalmus,* 545
Slender Soldierfish, *Pristilepis oligolepis,* 113
Slender Splitfin, *Luzonichthys microlepis,* 205
Slender Sweeper, *Parapriacanthus ransonneti,* 323
Slender Threadfin Bream, *Nemipterus metopias,* 305
Slender-spined Blenny, *Acanthemblemaria exilispinis,* 518
Slenderspine Pursemouth, *Gerres oyena,* 274, 276
Slide-mouth Bass, *Schultzea beta,* 200
Slimy Mackerel, *Scomber australasicus,* 601
Slimy Stingray, *Urolophus mucosus,* 46
Slingjaw Wrasse, *Epibulus insidiator,* 439, 449
Slippery Dick, *Halichoeres bivittatus,* 447
*sloani, Chauliodus,* Sloan's Viperfish, 70
Sloan's Viperfish, *Chauliodus sloani,* 70
Slope-head Sergeant, *Abudefduf declevifrons,* 380
Slopehead Parrotfish, *Scarus erythrodon,* 490
Slow Goby, *Aruma histrio,* 564
Small Scorpionfish, *Scorpaena coniorta,* 146
Small-headed Blind Goby, *Ctenotrypauchen microcephalus,* 580
Small-mouthed Leatherjacket, *Oligoplites altus,* 251
Small-toothed Threadfin Bream, *Pentapodus microdon,* 299
Smallmouth Grunt, *Haemulon chrysargyreum,* 279
Smallmouthed Squirrelfish, *Sargocentron microstoma,* 108
Smallscale Pursemouth, *Gerres acinaces,* 275, 276
Smallspot Pompano, *Trachinotus baillonii,* 250, 254
Smalltail Wrasse, *Pseudojuloides cerasinus,* 460, 461
Smalltooth Sawfish, *Pristis pectinata,* 42
Smiling Goby, *Mahidolia mystacina,* 553
Smith-vaniz's Fairy Basslet, *Mirolabrichthys smithvanizi,* 179
*smithae, Canthigaster,* Bicolored Toby, 650
*smithi, Pomacentrus,* Smith's Damsel, 402
*smithii, Meiacanthus,* Smith's Blenny, 523
Smith's Blenny, *Meiacanthus smithii,* 523
Smith's Coral Goby, *Eviota infulata,* 576
Smith's Damsel, *Pomacentrus smithi,* 402
*smithvanizi, Mirolabrichthys,* Smith-vaniz's Fairy Basslet, 179
Smoky Chromis, *Chromis fumea,* 386
Smooth Hammerhead, *Sphyrna zygaena,* 40, 41
Smooth Pipefish, *Lissocampus caudalis,* 126
Smooth Ronqiul, *Rathbunella hypoplecta,* 494
Smooth Stargazer, *Kathetostoma averruncus,* 500
Smooth Trunkfish, *Lactophrys triqueter,* 641
Smooth Wolf Herring, *Chirocentrus nudus,* 68
Snake eel, unidentified, *Muraenichthys* sp., 53
Snake Mackerel, *Gempylus serpens,* 601
Snake Pipefish, *Entelurus aequoreus,* 126
Snake-eyed Tartoor, *Opisthopterus tartoor,* 67
Snakeskin Goby, *Chasmichthys dolichognathus,* 565
*snelliusi, Callogobius,* Dusky Finned Goby, 562
Snook, *Centropomus undecimalis,* 170
Snooty Wrasse, *Cheilinus oxycephalus,* 431
Snow Bass, *Serranus chionaraia,* 197
Snowflake Blenny, *Cirripectes alboapicalis,* 528
Snowflake Moray, *Echidna nebulosa,* 59
Snowpatch Goby, *Cryptocentrus niveatus,* 556
Snowy Grouper, *Epinephelus niveatus,* 191
Snowy Rockfish, *Sebastes nivosus,* 152
Snubnose Pipefish, *Cosmocampus arctus,* 125
*snyderi, Parapercis,* Snyder's Weever, 503, 505
Snyder's Weever, *Parapercis snyderi,* 503, 505
Soaring Hawkfish, *Cyprinocirrhites polyactus,* 413
*sobrinus?, Periophthalmus,* Seychelles Mudskipper, 579
Social Fairy Wrasse, *Cirrhilabrus rubriventralis,* 434
*socialis, Epinephelus,* White-dotted Grouper, 188
*sohal, Acanthurus,* Red Sea Clown Surgeon, 584
*solandri, Acanthocybium,* Wahoo, 602
*solandri, Canthigaster,* False-eye Toby, 653
Soldierfish, unidentified, *Myripristis* sp., 104, 112, 113
*Soleichthys heterorhinos,* Decorated Sole, 615
*Solenostomus armatus,* Armored Pipefish, 124
*Solenostomus cyanopterus,* Variegated Ghost Pipefish, 123, 124
*Solenostomus paegnis,* Ghost Pipefish, 123
*Solenostomus paradoxus,* Short-bodied Ghost Pipefish, 120, 123
*solorensis, Ostracion,* Scribbled Boxfish, 640, 642
Somali Butterflyfish, *Chaetodon leucopleura,* 337

Sombre Sweetlips, *Plectorhinchus schotaf,* 282, 284
Sonara Blenny, *Malacoctenus gigas,* 514
*sonnerati, Cephalopholis,* Tomato Rockcod, 183
Sonora Brotulid, *Ogilbia* sp., 81
Sonora Clingfish, *Tomicodon humeralis,* 97
Sonora Goby, *Gobiosoma chiquita,* 572
Sonora Scorpionfish, *Scorpaena sonorae,* 145
*sonorae, Scorpaena,* Sonora Scorpionfish, 145
*sordidus, Abudefduf,* Black Spot Sergeant, 380
*sordidus, Plectorhinchus,* Redlip Rubberlip, 284, 285
*sordidus, Scarus,* Garnet Red Parrotfish, 482, 490
*Sorosichthys ananassa,* Little Pineapplefish, 103
South Australian Numbfish, *Hypnos monopterygium,* 42
South Seas Sergeant Major, *Abudefduf vaigiensis,* 380
Southern Bluefin Tuna, *Thunnus maccoyii,* 602
Southern Demoiselle, *Chrysiptera notialis,* 390
Southern Eel, *Anguilla australis,* 53
Southern Fusilier, *Paracaesio xanthura,* 259
Southern Hulafish, *Trachinops noarlungae,* 214
Southern Sea Garfish, *Hyporhamphus melanochir,* 100
Southern Siphonfish, *Siphamia cephalotes,* 237
Southern Stingray, *Dasyatis americana,* 46
Spadefish, *Ephippus orbis,* 330
Spaghetti Eel, *Moringa microchir,* 53
Spangled Emperor, *Lethrinus nebulosus,* 295, 296, 297
Spangled Gudgeon, *Ophiocara porocephala,* 542
Spanish Bream, *Pagellus acarne,* 290
Spanish Flag, *Gonioplectrus hispanus,* 181
Spanish Grunt, *Haemulon macrostomum,* 279
Spanish Hogfish, *Bodianus rufus,* 430
*Sparisoma atomarium,* Greenblotch Parrotfish, 487
*Sparisoma aurofrenatum,* Redband Parrotfish, 487
*Sparisoma chrysopterum,* Redtail Parrotfish, 487
*Sparisoma radians,* Bucktooth Parrotfish, 488
*Sparisoma rubripinne,* Yellowtail Parrotfish, 488
*Sparisoma viride,* Stoplight Parrotfish, 487
*sparoides, Abudefduf,* False-eye Damsel, 381
*spatula, Cochleoceps,* Cockburn Sound Clingfish, 96
*speciosus, Bodianus,* Darkbar Hogfish, 427
*speciosus, Gnathanodon,* Golden Trevally, 246, 247
Speckle-finned Flathead, *Onigocia spinosa,* 161
Speckled Catshark, *Hemiscyllium trispeculare,* 35
Speckled Damsel, *Pomacentrus bankanensis,* 402
Speckled Fin Grouper, *Epinephelus summana,* 205
Speckled Moray, *Gymnothorax obesus,* 57
Speckled Sanddab, *Citharichthys stigmaeus,* 609
Speckled Squirrelfish, *Sargocentron punctatissimum,* 109
Specklefin Damsel, *Pomacentrus arenarius,* 401
*spectabilis, Cheilodactylus,* Red Moki, 416
Spectacled Angelfish, *Chaetodontoplus conspicillatus,* 361
Spectacled Blenny, *Gilloblennius tripennis,* 508
*speculum, Chaetodon,* Mirror Butterflyfish, 344
*spengleri, Sphoeroides,* Bandtail Puffer, 649
*Sphaeramia nematoptera,* Polka-dot Cardinalfish, 221, 232
*Sphaeramia orbicularis,* Orbiculate Cardinalfish, 323
*Sphagebranchus flavicauda,* Yellow-tailed Snake Eel, 62
*sphex, Pterois,* Hawaiian Lionfish, 140
Sphinx Blenny, *Aidablennius sphynx,* 524
Sphinx Goby, *Amblygobius sphynx,* 554, 555
*Sphoeroides annulatus,* Bullseye Puffer, 649
*Sphoeroides erythrotaenia,* Redline Puffer, 649
*Sphoeroides hamiltoni,* Hamilton's Puffer, 649
*Sphoeroides marmoratus,* Marbled Puffer, 649
*Sphoeroides* sp., Puffer, unidentified, 649
*Sphoeroides spengleri,* Bandtail Puffer, 649
*sphynx, Aidablennius,* Sphinx Blenny, 524
*sphynx, Amblygobius,* Sphinx Goby, 554, 555
*Sphyraena argentea,* Pacific Barracuda, 422
*Sphyraena barracuda,* Great Barracuda, 422, 423
*Sphyraena flavicauda,* Yellow-tailed Barracuda, 422
*Sphyraena jello,* Pickhandle Barracuda, 422
*Sphyraena obtusata,* Chevron Barracuda, 422
*Sphyraena pinguis,* Fat Barracuda, 422
*Sphyraena qenie,* Blackfin Barracuda, 422
*Sphyrna lewini,* Scalloped Hammerhead, 40, 41
*Sphyrna zygaena,* Smooth Hammerhead, 40, 41
*Spicara maena flexuosa,* Picarel, 288
*spilomelanura, Acanthaluterus,* Bridled Leatherjacket, 635
*spilosoma, Pervagor,* Fantail Filefish, 633
*spilostylus, Chilomycterus,* Yellowspotted Burrfish, 655
*spilurus, Symphorichthys,* Blue-and-Gold Striped Snapper, 267, 268
*spilus, Lythrypnus,* Spotwing Goby, 575
*Spinachia spinachia,* Fifteen-spine Stickleback, 118
*spinachia, Spinachia,* Fifteen-spine Stickleback, 118
Spine-cheeked Anemonefish, *Premnas biaculeatus,* 372
Spinecheek Goby, *Oplopomus oplopomus,* 550
*spinidens, Calotomus,* Spinytooth Parrotfish, 488, 491
*spinifer, Argyrops,* Longspine Sea Bream, 289
*spiniferum, Sargocentron,* Scarlet-fin Squirrelfish, 104, 108, 112
*spinipenis, Starksia,* Phallic Blenny, 512
*spinirostris, Halicampus,* Spiny-nosed Pipefish, 128
*spinosa, Acanthemblemaria,* Spiny Blenny, 518
*spinosa, Onigocia,* Speckle-finned Flathead, 161
*spinosus, Chelidonichthys,* Bluefin Searobin, 160
*spinosus, Corniger,* Spinycheek Soldierfish, 106
*spinosus, Niphon,* Saw-edged Perch, 173
Spinster Wrasse, *Halichoeres nicholsi,* 448
*spinus, Siganus,* Little Spinefoot, 599
Spiny Blenny, *Acanthemblemaria spinosa,* 518
Spiny Butterflyfish, *Hemitaurichthys multispinus,* 351
Spiny Chromis, *Acanthochromis polyacanthus,* 397
Spiny-eyed Cardinalfish, *Apogon fraenatus,* 223
Spiny-nosed Pipefish, *Halicampus spinirostris,* 128
Spinycheek Soldierfish, *Corniger spinosus,* 106
Spinyhead Cardinalfish, *Apogon kallopterus,* 226, 233
Spinythroat Scorpionfish, *Pontinus nematophthalmus,* 137
Spinytooth Parrotfish, *Calotomus spinidens,* 488, 491
*Spirinchus lanceolatus,* Lance-like Smelt, 70
*splendens, Beryx,* Alfonsino, 106
*splendens, Cirrhitus,* Splendid Hawkfish, 412
*splendens, Xyrichthys,* Green Razorfish, 456
Splendid Hawkfish, *Cirrhitus splendens,* 412
Splendid Perch, *Callanthias allporti,* 186
*splendidus, Pterosynchiropus,* Mandarin Fish, 535, 539
*splendidus, Sanopus,* Coral Toadfish, 84
Split-banded Cardinalfish, *Apogon compressus,* 224
Split-banded Goby, *Gymneleotris seminudus,* 567
Sponge Cardinalfish, *Phaeoptyx xenus,* 236
Sported Flagtail, *Kuhlia marginata,* 219
Spot-band Butterflyfish, *Chaetodon punctatofasciatus,* 344
Spot-bearing Scorpionfish, *Iracundus signifier,* 148
Spot-cheeked Surgeonfish, *Acanthurus nigrofuscus,* 584
Spot-tail Butterflyfish, *Chaetodon ocellicaudus,* 337

Spot-tail Cardinalfish, *Archamia biguttata*, 235
Spotbelly Rockfish, *Sebastes pachycephalus*, 152
Spotcheek Blenny, *Labrisomus nigricinctus*, 513
Spotfin Bandfish, *Acanthocepola limbata*, 420
Spotfin Butterflyfish, *Chaetodon ocellatus*, 335
Spotfin Croaker, *Roncador stearnsi*, 311
Spotfin Flounder, *Verasper variegatus*, 613
Spotfin Goby, *Gobionellus stigmalophius*, 565
Spotfin Hogfish, *Bodianus pulchellus*, 430
Spotfin Lionfish, *Pterois antennata*, 141, 142
Spotfin Mojarra, *Eucinostomus argenteus*, 275
Spotfin Squirrelfish, *Neoniphon sammara*, 108, 110, 111, 112
Spotfin Tonguefish, *Symphurus fasciolaris*, 614
Spothead Grubfish, *Parapercis cephalopunctata*, 504; *Parapercis cephalopunctata?*, 504
Spotlight Goby, *Gobiosoma louisae*, 572
Spotnape Pony Fish, *Leiognathus nuchalis*, 256
Spottail Cardinalfish, *Pseudamia amblyuroptera*, 237
Spottail Coris, *Coris caudimacula*, 436, 438, 475
Spottail Gudgeon, *Ptereleotris evides*, 568
Spottail Rainbowfish, *Halichoeres trimaculatus*, 444, 472
Spotted Batfish, *Zalieutes elator*, 93
Spotted Blenny, *Ecsenius stictus*, 528.11; *Salarias irroratus*, 527
Spotted Boxfish, *Ostracion meleagris*, 642; *Ostracion meleagris camurum*, 640; *Ostracion meleagris meleagris*, 617, 638
Spotted Bristletooth, *Ctenochaetus strigosus*, 587, 590
Spotted Burrfish, *Chilomycterus atinga*, 655
Spotted Cabrilla, *Epinephelus analogus*, 191
Spotted Cardinalfish, *Apogon maculifera*, 229
Spotted Conchfish, *Astrapogon punticulatus*, 236
Spotted Crocodile Flathead, *Inegocia guttata*, 162
Spotted Cusk-eel, *Chilara taylori*, 80
Spotted Dragonet, *Foetorepus* sp., 537
Spotted Drepane, *Drepane punctata*, 330, 334
Spotted Drum, *Equetus punctatus*, 309, 310
Spotted Eagle Ray, *Aetobatus narinari*, 47, 48, 49
Spotted Fantail Filefish, *?Aluterus* sp., 635
Spotted Flathead, *Cociella crocodila*, 72, 161
Spotted Garden Eel, *Gorgasia maculata*, 64
Spotted Goatfish, *Parupeneus pleurospilus*, 319
Spotted Grouper, *Epinephelus maculatus*, 189
Spotted Grunter, *Pomadasys commersoni*, 313
Spotted Hardyhead, *Atherinomorus endrachtensis*, 102
Spotted Hawkfish, *Cirrhitichthys aprinus*, 410, 411, 414
Spotted Javelin Fish, *Pomadasys maculatum*, 281
Spotted Jewfish, *Johnius diacanthus*, 311
Spotted Knifejaw, *Oplegnathus punctatus*, 369
Spotted Moray, *Gymnothorax moringa*, 55
Spotted Prawn Goby, *Ctenogobiops maculosus*, 570
Spotted Pug, *Tandya latitabunda*, 498
Spotted Ratfish, *Hydrolagus collei*, 34
Spotted Reef Moray, *Muraena melanotis*, 57, 60
Spotted Rose Snapper, *Lutjanus guttatus*, 264
Spotted Sailfin Tang, *Zebrasoma gemmatum*, 592, 594
Spotted Scat, *Scatophagus argus*, 329
Spotted Scorpionfish, *Scorpaena plumieri plumieri*, 144; *Scorpaena* sp., 148
Spotted Sharpnose Puffer, *Canthigaster punctatissimus*, 651
Spotted Shrimpfish, *Aeoliscus punctulatus*, 122
Spotted Snake Eel, *Ophichthus ophis*, 62
Spotted Snapper, *Lutjanus stellatus*, 263
Spotted Soapfish, *Rypticus subbifrenatus*, 207
Spotted Spanish Mackerel, *Scomberomorus maculatus*, 601
Spotted Tilefish, *Hoplolatilus fourmanoiri*, 240
Spotted Toby, *Canthigaster ambionensis*, 618, 650
Spotted Trunkfish, *Lactophrys bicaudalis*, 641
Spotted Unicornfish, *Naso brevirostris*, 590, 591
Spotted Wobbegong, *Orectolobus maculatum*, 35
Spotted-finned Rainbowfish, *Halichoeres miniatus*, 445
Spotted-tail Cardinalfish, *Gymnapogon urospilotus*, 222
Spottyhead Goby, *Amblygobius bynoensis*, 554
Spottysail Dottyback, *Labracinus cyclophthalmus*, 207
Spotwing Goby, *Lythrypnus spilus*, 575
*Spratelloides japonicus*, Japanese Blue Sprat, 66
*Spratelloides robustus*, Blue Sprat, 66
*Springeratus xanthosoma*, Weed Blenny, 517
*springeri, Chrysiptera*, Springer's Demoiselle, 392
*springeri, Pseudochromis*, Springer's Dottyback, 210
Springer's Demoiselle, *Chrysiptera springeri*, 392
Springer's Dottyback, *Pseudochromis springeri*, 210
*Squalus mitsukurii*, Longnose Spiny Dogfish, 41
*Squalus suckleyi*, Suckley's Spiny Dogfish, 41
*squamipinnis, PseudaAthias*, Lyretail Coralfish, 174, 179
Squaretail Grouper, *Epinephelus areolatus*, 190
Squaretail Leopard Grouper, *Plectropomus areolatus*, 203
Squaretail Mullet, *Liza vaigiensis*, 421
*Squatina californica*, Pacific Angel Shark, 41
*Squatina japonica*, Japanese Angel Shark, 41
Sri Lanka Dottyback, *Pseudochromis dilectus*, 210
St. Helena Moray, *Muraena helena*, 60
St. Helena Scorpionfish, *Scorpaenodes insularis*, 153
Staghorn Damsel, *Amblyglyphidodon curacao*, 382
*Stanulus seychellensis*, Seychelle Blenny, 530
*Stanulus talboti*, Talbot's Blenny, 530
*starcki, Chrysiptera*, Starck's Demoiselle, 392
*starcki, Hoplolatilus*, Stark's Tilefish, 238, 240
*starcki, Starksia*, Key Blenny, 513
Starck's Demoiselle, *Chrysiptera starcki*, 392
Stargazer, *Ichthyoscopus lebeck*, 500
Stark's Tilefish, *Hoplolatilus starcki*, 238, 240
*Starksia ocellata*, Checkered Blenny, 512
*Starksia* sp., Wine Red Blenny, 512
*Starksia spinipenis*, Phallic Blenny, 512
*Starksia starcki*, Key Blenny, 513
Starry Batfish, *Halieutaea stellata*, 93
Starry Blenny, *Salarias* sp., 527
Starry Conchfish, *Astrapogon stellatus*, 236
Starry Fin Goby, *Asterropteryx semipunctatus*, 555
Starry Flounder, *Platichthys stellatus*, 607, 612
Starry Goby, *Asterropteryx* sp., 553
Starry Moray, *Gymnothorax nudivomer*, 56
Starry Pufferfish, *Arothron stellatus*, 646, 647
Starry Rockfish, *Sebastes constellatus*, 149
Starry Triggerfish, *Abalistes stellatus*, 623
Stars and Stripes Leatherjacket, *Meuschenia venusta*, 632
Stars and Stripes Puffer, *Arothron hispidus*, 644, 645, 646
Startailed Cardinalfish, *Apogon dispar*, 228
*Stathmonotus hemphilli*, Hemphill's Blenny, 516
*Stathmonotus sinuscalifornici*, Worm Blenny, 516
*stearnsi, Roncador*, Spotfin Croaker, 311
*steenei, Scorpaenodes*, Steene's Scorpionfish, 143
Steene's Scorpionfish, *Scorpaenodes steenei*, 143
*Stegastes albifasciatus*, White-bar Gregory, 403, 404
*Stegastes apicalis*, Australian Gregory, 404

*Stegastes aureus,* Golden Gregory, 405
*Stegastes diencaeus,* Longfin Damselfish, 407
*Stegastes dorsopunicans,* Orangeback Damsel, 406
*Stegastes emeryi,* Emery's Gregory, 405
*Stegastes fasciolatus,* Pacific Gregory, 403, 404
*Stegastes flavilatus,* Beau Brummel, 407
*Stegastes gascoynei,* Coral Sea Gregory, 405
*Stegastes imbricata,* Darwin's Damselfish, 407
*Stegastes leucorus,* Pale-tailed Damselfish, 405
*Stegastes leucostictus,* Beau Gregory, 407
*Stegastes lividus,* Blunt-snout Gregory, 404
*Stegastes mellis,* Honey Damselfish, 407
*Stegastes nigricans,* Dusky Gregory, 405
*Stegastes obreptus,* Western Gregory, 405
*Stegastes partitus,* Bicolor Damselfish, 406
*Stegastes planifrons,* Three Spot Damselfish, 406
*Stegastes rectifraenum,* Cortez Chromis, 405
*Stegastes redemptus,* Clarion Damselfish, 406
*Stegastes simsiang,* Bleeker's Damsel, 404
*Stegastes* sp., Damselfish, unidentified, 403, 404
*Stegastes variabilis,* Cocoa Damselfish, 407
*Stegastoma varium,* Zebra Shark, 40
*Stegostoma varium,* Zebra Shark, 34
*steindachneri, Gymnothorax,* Steindachner's Moray Eel, 54
*steindachneri, Ophioblennius,* Panamic Fanged Blenny, 528
*steindachneri, Taractichthys,* Sickle Pomfret, 257
Steindachner's Moray Eel, *Gymnothorax steindachneri,* 54
*steinitzi, Amblyeleotris,* Steinitz's Goby, 543, 546, 556
Steinitz's Goby, *Amblyeleotris steinitzi,* 543, 546, 556
*stellata, Halieutaea,* Starry Batfish, 93
*stellatus, Abalistes,* Starry Triggerfish, 623
*stellatus, Arothron,* Starry Pufferfish, 646, 647
*stellatus, Astrapogon,* Starry Conchfish, 236
*stellatus, Lutjanus,* Spotted Snapper, 263
*stellatus, Platichthys,* Starry Flounder, 607, 612
*stellatus, Siganus,* Brown-spotted Spinefoot, 599
*Stenogobius lachrymosus,* Teary Goby, 553
*stenolepis, Hippoglossus,* Pacific Halibut, 613
*Stephanolepis cirrhifer,* Thread Sailfin Filefish, 632
*Stereolepis gigas,* Giant Sea Bass, 172, 173
*Stereolepis ischinagi,* Striped Grouper, 173
*Stethojulis albovittata,* Bluelined Wrasse, 455
*Stethojulis balteata,* Orange Band Wrasse, 455
*Stethojulis bandanensis,* Orange-axil Wrasse, 455, 465
*Stethojulis interrupta,* Cut-ribbon Rainbowfish, 454
*Stethojulis strigiventer,* Three-ribbon Rainbowfish, 454, 465, 474
*Stethojulis trilineata,* Three-lined Wrasse, 455, 474
*Stichaeus grigorjewi,* Grigorjew's Shanny, 501
*Sticharium dorsale,* Multicolor Snake Blenny, 516
*stictonotus, Takifugu,* Bluebacked Puffer, 648
*stictus, Ecsenius,* Spotted Blenny, 528.11
*stigma, Pomacentrus,* Analspot Demoiselle, 401
*stigmaeus, Citharichthys,* Speckled Sanddab, 609
*stigmalophius, Gobionellus,* Spotfin Goby, 565
*stigmaticus, Cirripectes,* Ember Blenny, 528, 528.02
*stigmaticus, Gobionellus,* Mashed Goby, 565
*Stigmatopora argus,* Australian Spotted Pipefish, 125
*Stigmatopora nigra,* Wide-bodied Pipefish, 125
*stigmatura, Ecsenius,* Tail-spot Blenny, 528.06
Stinging Stargazer, *Uranoscopus asper,* 501
*Stiphodon* sp., Jewel Goby, 552
*Stomias* sp., Dragonfish, 70
Stone Flounder, *Kareius bicoloratus,* 613
Stone Scorpionfish, *Scorpaena plumieri mystes,* 144
Stonefish, *Synanceia verrucosa,* 157, 158
*Stonogobiops xanthorhinica,* Yellowrose Goby, 553
Stoplight Parrotfish, *Sparisoma viride,* 487
Stout-body Chromis, *Chromis chrysura,* 385
*stouti, Eptatretus,* Pacific Hagfish, 33
Straight-lined Thornfish, *Terapon theraps,* 216, 217, 218
Straight-tail Razorfish, *Xyrichthys martinicensis,* 456
*strasburgi, Dascyllus,* Strasburg's Dascyllus, 378
Strasburg's Dascyllus, *Dascyllus strasburgi,* 378
Streaked Spanish Mackerel, *Scomberomorus lineolatus,* 603
Streaked Spinefoot, *Siganus javus,* 598
Streaky Rockskipper, *Istiblennius dussumieri,* 526, 534
Streamlined Spinefoot, *Siganus argenteus,* 597
*striata, Helcogramma,* White Lined Triplefin, 511
*striata, Trimma,* Striped Coral Goby, 577
Striated Frogfish, *Antennarius striatus,* 82, 86, 90, 91
Striated Fusilier, *Pterocaesio striatus,* 571
*striatum, Haemulon,* Striped Grunt, 278
*striatus, Antennarius,* Striated Frogfish, 82, 86, 90, 91
*striatus, Chaetodon,* Banded Butterflyfish, 343
*striatus, Ctenochaetus,* Striped Bristletooth, 589
*striatus, Entomacrodus,* Pearly Rockskipper, 529
*striatus, Epinephelus,* Nassau Grouper, 192
*striatus, Minilabrus,* Red Sea Multicolor Wrasse, 459
*striatus, Pomacanthus,* Dowager Angelfish, 364
*striatus, Pterocaesio,* Striated Fusilier, 571
*strigata, Valenciennea,* Pennant Glider, 566
*strigatus, Aeoliscus,* Shrimpfish, 122
*strigatus, Antennarius,* Bandtail Frogfish, 88
*strigatus, Atypichthys,* Australian Stripey, 326
*strigatus, Microcanthus,* Stripey, 324, 327
*strigilifer, Tripodichthys,* Curry-comb Tripodfish, 619, 620
*strigilliceps, Cryptocentrus,* Target Goby, 549
*strigiventer, Stethojulis,* Three-ribbon Rainbowfish, 454, 465, 474
*strigosus, Ctenochaetus,* Spotted Bristletooth, 587, 590
Stripe-fin Sculpin, *Enophrys diceraus,* 164
Striped Bass, *Morone saxatilis,* 173
Striped Blenny, *Meiacanthus lineatus,* 522
Striped Bonito, *Sarda orientalis,* 603.
Striped Bristletooth, *Ctenochaetus striatus,* 589
Striped Burrfish, *Chilomycterus schoepfi,* 655
Striped Coral Goby, *Trimma striata,* 577
Striped Coral Trout, *Plectropomus oligacanthus,* 203
Striped Dottyback, *Pseudochromis sankeyi,* 210
Striped Filefish, *Paramonacanthus japonicus,* 632
Striped Goby, *Tridentiger trigonocephalus,* 553
Striped Grouper, *Stereolepis ischinagi,* 173
Striped Grunt, *Haemulon striatum,* 278
Striped Hawkfish, *Cheilodactylus vittatus,* 417
Striped Jack, *Pseudocaranx dentex,* 243, 253
Striped Jobfish, *Pristipomoides multidens,* 269
Striped Kelpfish, *Gibbonsia metzi,* 516
Striped Marlin, *Tetrapturus audax,* 604
Striped Mullet, *Mugil cephalus,* 421
Striped Parrotfish, *Scarus croicensis,* 486
Striped Scat, *Scatophagus tetracanthus,* 329
Striped Scorpionfish, *Minous versicolor,* 155
Striped Snapper, *Lutjanus carponotatus,* 261
Striped Trevally, *Carangoides vinctus,* 246
Striped Tripodfish, *Paratriacanthodes retrospinis,* 620

Striped Wing Flying Fish, *Hirundichthys* sp., 99
Stripetail Damsel, *Abudefduf sexfasciatus*, 381
Stripey, *Microcanthus strigatus*, 324, 327
*strongia, Sebastapistes*, Barchin Scorpionfish, 147
*Strongylura anastomella*, Greengar, 100
*Strongylura timucu*, Atlantic Needlefish, 100
*Strophiurichthys robustus*, Robust Boxfish, 639
Sturgeon Poacher, *Agonus acipenserinus*, 168
*Stygnobrotula latibricola*, Black Widow, 81
*subbifrenatus, Rypticus*, Spotted Soapfish, 207
*subducens, Congrogadus*, Eared Eel-blenny, 534
*subligarius, Serranus*, Belted Sandfish, 197
*subnigrum, Hypnos*, Australian Numbfish, 42
*suborbitalis, Sargocentron*, Tinsel Squirrelfish, 109
*suckleyi, Squalus*, Suckley's Spiny Dogfish, 41
Suckley's Spiny Dogfish, *Squalus suckleyi*, 41
*Suezichthys gracilis*, Brownstripe Wrasse, 464
*Suezichthys* sp., Crimson Cleaner Wrasse, 468
*Sufflamen albicaudatus*, Whitetail Triggerfish, 624
*Sufflamen bursa*, Boomerang Triggerfish, 624, 627
*Sufflamen chrysopterus*, Halfmoon Triggerfish, 624, 627
*Sufflamen fraenatus*, Bridle Triggerfish, 624, 627
*Sufflamen* sp., Brown Triggerfish, 624
*sufflamen, Canthidermis*, Ocean Triggerfish, 625
*sulfureus, Pomacentrus*, Sulphur Damselfish, 402
Sulphur Damselfish, *Pomacentrus sulfureus*, 402
Sulphur Goatfish, *Upeneus sulphureus*, 318
*sulphureus, Upeneus*, Sulphur Goatfish, 318
Sumbawa Threadfin Bream, *Nemipterus sumbawensis*, 306
*sumbawensis, Nemipterus*, Sumbawa Threadfin Bream, 306
*summana, Epinephelus*, Speckled Fin Grouper, 205
Summer Flounder, *Paralichthys dentatus*, 610
*sumptuosa, Scorpaena*, Red Scorpin, 146
Sunburst Basslet, *Serranocirrhitus latus*, 180
Sunburst Butterflyfish, *Chaetodon aureofasciatus*, 340
*sundaicus, Upeneus*, Ochreband Goatfish, 318
*sungami, Amblyeleotris*, Magnus' Goby, 543, 546
Sunrise Dottyback, *Pseudochromis flavivertex*, 212
Sunset Butterflyfish, *Chaetodon pelewensis*, 342
Sunshinefish, *Chromis insolatus*, 388
Super Klipfish, *Clinus superciliosus*, 516
*superciliosus, Alopias*, Bigeye Thresher, 37
*superciliosus, Clinus*, Super Klipfish, 516
Surge Silverside, *Iso rhothophilus*, 102
Surge Wrasse, *Thalassoma purpureum*, 468
*surinamensis, Anisotremus*, Black Margate, 280
*surinamensis, Lobotes*, Tripletail, 273
*susumi, Liopropoma*, Japanese Basslet, 198
*Sutorectus wardi*, Northern Wobbegong, 36
*suttoni, Cheilopogon*, Sutton's Flying Fish, 99
*Suttonia lineata*, Hawaiian Soapfish, 207
Sutton's Flying Fish, *Cheilopogon suttoni*, 99
*swalesi, Liopropoma*, Swales's Basslet, 198
Swales's Basslet, *Liopropoma swalesi*, 198
Sweetlip Emperor, *Lethrinus chrysostomus*, 298
Sweetlips Snapper, *Lutjanus lemniscatus*, 266; *Lutjanus* sp. *(lemniscatus?)*, 266
Swell Shark, *Cephaloscyllium ventriosum*, 38
Swordfish, *Xiphias gladius*, 604
*sydneyanus, Kyphosus*, Common Buffalo Bream, 327, 329
*Symphodus cinereus*, Mediterranean Gray Wrasse, 471
*Symphodus doderleini*, Doderlein's Wrasse, 471
*Symphodus mediterraneus*, Mediterranean Wrasse, 471
*Symphodus melanocercus*, Black-tailed Wrasse, 471
*Symphodus ocellatus*, Mediterranean Ocellated Wrasse, 471
*Symphodus roissali*, Five-spotted Wrasse, 471
*Symphodus rostratus*, Long-nosed Wrasse, 471
*Symphodus tinca*, Painted Wrasse, 471
*Symphorichthys spilurus*, Blue-and-Gold Striped Snapper, 267, 268
*Symphorus nematophorus*, Blue-lined Snapper, 268, 270
*Symphurus arawak*, Caribbean Tonguefish, 614
*Symphurus elongatus*, Elongate Tonguefish, 614
*Symphurus fasciolaris*, Spotfin Tonguefish, 614
*synagris, Lutjanus*, Lane Snapper, 264
*Synanceia alula*, Littlewing Stonefish, 158
*Synanceia verrucosa*, Stonefish, 157, 158
*Synchiropus marmoratus*, Marbled Dragonet, 538
*Synchiropus papilio*, Butterfly Dragonet, 536
*Synchiropus picturatus*, Psychedelic Fish, 535, 539
*Synchiropus* sp., Dragonet, unidentified, 538, 539
*Syngnathoides biaculeatus*, Alligator Pipefish, 125
*Syngnathus louisianae*, Chain Pipefish, 125
*Syngnathus* sp., Pipefish, unidentified, 125
*Synodus engelmani*, Redband Lizardfish, 74
*Synodus foetens*, Inshore Lizardfish, 74
*Synodus intermedius*, Sanddiver Lizardfish, 73, 74
*Synodus jaculum*, Leaping Lizardfish, 72
*Synodus lacertinus*, Panamanian Lizardfish, 75
*Synodus poeyi*, Offshore Lizardfish, 74
*Synodus rubromarmoratus*, Red-marbled Lizardfish, 74
*Synodus* sp., Lizardfish, unidentified, 71, 75
*Synodus synodus*, Red Lizardfish, 73, 74, 75
*Synodus ulae*, Red-brown Lizardfish, 74
*Synodus variegatus*, Variegated Lizardfish, 72
*synodus, Synodus*, Red Lizardfish, 73, 74, 75

# T

*tabacaria, Fistularia*, Bluespotted Cornetfish, 119
*tabacarius, Serranus*, Tobacco Fish, 197
TABL Scad, *Decapterus tabl*, 245
*tabl, Decapterus*, TABL Scad, 245
Tadpole Sculpin, *Psychrolutes paradoxus*, 167
*Taenianotus triacanthus*, Sailfin Leaffish, 143
*taenianotus, Ablabys*, Cockatoo Waspfish, 137
*taeniatus, Anisotremus*, Panamic Porkfish, 280
*taeniatus, Apogon*, Two-belted Cardinalfish, 228, 233
*taeniatus, Aspidontus*, False Cleanerfish, 522
*taeniatus, Pseudanthias*, Silver Streak Goldie, 177
*Taenioconger digueti*, Cortez Garden Eel, 63
*Taenioconger hassi*, Hass's Garden Eel, 64
*Taenioconger* sp., White-eared Garden Eel, 63
*taeniolatus, Phyllopteryx*, Weedy Seadragon, 120, 124
*taenionotus, Amblyapistus*, Rogue Fish, 58
*taeniops, Cephalopholis*, Ghana Rockcod, 184
*taeniopterus, Apogon*, Belted Cardinalfish, 229
*taeniopterus, Scarus*, Princess Parrotfish, 486
*taeniopterus, Scolopsis*, Lattice Monocle Bream, 303
*taeniourus, Novaculichthys*, Dragon Wrasse, 458, 472
*Taeniura lymma*, Blue-spotted Ray, 44, 47
*Taeniura melanospila*, Black-spotted Ray, 47
*taeniurus, Neopomacentrus*, Freshwater Demoiselle, 398
Tahitian Butterflyfish, *Chaetodon trichrous*, 342
Tahitian Fairy Wrasse, *Cirrhilabrus* sp., 434
Tahitian Reef-damsel, *Pomachromis fuscidorsalis*, 395

Tahitian Squirrelfish, *Sargocentron tiere,* 108, 111
Tail-jet Frogfish, *Antennarius analis,* 92
Tail-light Damselfish, *Chromis notata,* 384
Tail-spot Blenny, *Ecsenius stigmatura,* 528.06
Tailbar Lionfish, *Pterois radiata,* 142
Tailring Surgeonfish, *Acanthurus blochii,* 582, 587
Tailspot Cardinalfish, *Apogon dovii,* 230
*taira, Pseudanthias,* Japanese Fairy Basslet, 177
Taiwan Guitarfish, *Rhinobatos formosensis,* 44
*Takifugu niphobles,* Grass Puffer, 648
*Takifugu oblongus,* Shy Puffer, 649
*Takifugu pardalis,* Panther Puffer, 648
*Takifugu rubripes,* Tiger Puffer, 648
*Takifugu stictonotus,* Bluebacked Puffer, 648
Talang Queenfish, *Scomberoides commersonnianus,* 250
*talboti, Chrysiptera,* Talbot's Demoiselle, 391
*talboti, Stanulus,* Talbot's Blenny, 530
Talbot's Blenny, *Stanulus talboti,* 530
Talbot's Demoiselle, *Chrysiptera talboti,* 391
*tambuloides, Nemipterus,* Fivelined Threadfin Bream, 306
*Tandya latitabunda,* Spotted Pug, 498
Tangaroa Goby, *Ctenogobiops tangaroai,* 548
*tangaroai, Ctenogobiops,* Tangaroa Goby, 548
*tapeinosoma, Lepidozygus,* Fusilier Damsel, 381
*tapeinosoma, Plagiotremus,* Piano Blenny, 532
*tapeinosoma, Pseudochromis,* Yellow-head Dottyback, 208
Tapiroid Grunter, *Mesopristes cancellatus,* 218
*Taractichthys steindachneri,* Sickle Pomfret, 257
Tarakihi, *Nemadactylus macropterus,* 416
Target Goby, *Cryptocentrus strigilliceps,* 549
Targetfish, *Terapon jarbua,* 216, 218
*tartoor, Opisthopterus,* Snake-eyed Tartoor, 67
Tasmanian Blenny, *Parablennius tasmanianus,* 529
Tasmanian Clingfish, *Aspasmogaster tasmaniensis,* 96
Tasmanian Golden Eel, *Muraenichthys tasmaniensis,* 61
*tasmanianus, Parablennius,* Tasmanian Blenny, 529
*tasmaniensis, Aspasmogaster,* Tasmanian Clingfish, 96
*tasmaniensis, Muraenichthys,* Tasmanian Golden Eel, 61
Tassled Wobbegong, *Eucrossorhinus dasypogon,* 36
*Tathicarpus butleri,* Butler's Frogfish, 85
Tattler, *Serranus phoebe,* 196
Tattooed Parrotfish, *Scarus brevifilis,* 483
*taupou, Chrysiptera,* Village Belle, 392
*Taurulus bubalis,* Rock Sculpin, 167
*taurus, Abudefduf,* Night Sergeant, 380
*taurus, Odontaspis,* Sand Tiger, 37
*Tautogolabrus adspersus,* Cunner, 468
*tauvina, Epinephelus,* Greasy Rock Cod, 188
Tawneygirdled Butterflyfish, *Coradion altivelis,* 347
*tayenus, Priacanthus,* Purple-spotted Bullseye, 220
*taylori, Chilara,* Spotted Cusk-eel, 80
Teardrop Butterflyfish, *Chaetodon unimaculatus,* 345
Teary Goby, *Stenogobius lachrymosus,* 553
*teira, Platax,* Round-faced Batfish, 334
*temmincki, Aulacocephalus,* Goldribbon Soapfish, 204
*temmincki, Cirrhilabrus,* Temminck's Wrasse, 434
*temmincki, Ditrema,* Japanese Seaperch, 369
Temminck's Wrasse, *Cirrhilabrus temmincki,* 434
*temporalis, Scolopsis,* Rainbow Monocle Bream, 303
*tennenti, Acanthurus,* Lieutenant Surgeonfish, 584
*tenox, Gobiosoma,* Slaty Goby, 571
Tentacled Blenny, *Parablennius tentacularis,* 524
Tentacled dragonet, *Anaora tentaculata,* 537
*tentacularis, Parablennius,* Tentacled Blenny, 524
*tentaculata, Anaora,* Tentacled dragonet, 537
*tenuis, Pseudanthias,* Threadnose Fairy Basslet, 177
*tephraeops, Girella,* Western Rock Blackfish, 326
*Terapon jarbua,* Targetfish, 216, 218
*Terapon theraps,* Straight-lined Thornfish, 216, 217, 218
*teres, Caesio,* Beautiful Fusilier, 271, 273
*teres, Etrumeus,* Round Herring, 66
Ternate Chromis, *Chromis ternatensis,* 386
Ternate Damsel, *Amblyglyphidodon ternatensis,* 382
*ternatensis, Amblyglyphidodon,* Ternate Damsel, 382
*ternatensis, Chromis,* Ternate Chromis, 386
Tessellated Goby, *Redigobius tessellatus,* 563
*tessellatus, Redigobius,* Tessellated Goby, 563
*tessera, Ecsenius,* Paving-tile Blenny, 528.09
*testaceus, Trygonoptena,* Dusky Ray, 44
*tetracantha, Parapercis,* Four-barred Weever, 504, 505
*tetracanthus, Scatophagus,* Striped Scat, 329
*tetradactylum, Eleutheronema,* Colonial Salmon, 420
*tetranemus, Malacoctenus,* Throatspotted Blenny, 514
*Tetrapturus angustirostris,* Shortbill Spearfish, 604
*Tetrapturus audax,* Striped Marlin, 604
*Tetrasomus gibbosus,* Thornbacked Boxfish, 638
*tetrataenia, Pseudocheilinus,* Four-lined Wrasse, 461
*Thalassoma amblycephalum,* Rainbow Wrasse, 465
*Thalassoma amblycephalus,* Rainbow Wrasse, 476
*Thalassoma ballieui,* Hinalea Luahine, 466
*Thalassoma bifasciatum,* Bluehead Wrasse, 466
*Thalassoma cupido,* Cupido Wrasse, 476
*Thalassoma duperreyi,* Saddle Wrasse, 466
*Thalassoma genivittatum,* Redcheek Wrasse, 465, 467
*Thalassoma hardwicke,* Sixbar Wrasse, 465
*Thalassoma hebraicum,* Goldbar Wrasse, 467
*Thalassoma jansenii,* Jansen's Wrasse, 466
*Thalassoma klunzingeri,* Klunzinger's Wrasse, 467
*Thalassoma lucasanum,* Cortez Rainbow Wrasse, 466
*Thalassoma lunare,* Lyretail Wrasse, 467, 476
*Thalassoma lutescens,* Yellow Wrasse, 467, 468
*Thalassoma purpureum,* Surge Wrasse, 468
*Thalassoma quinquevittatum,* Fivestripe Wrasse, 467
*Thalassoma schwanefeldi,* Six-bar Wrasse, 476
*Thalassoma septemfasciatum,* Sevenband Wrasse, 468
*Thalassoma trilobatum,* Christmas Wrasse, 468
*Thamnaconus australis,* Velvet Leatherjacket, 636
*Thamnaconus modestus,* Black Scraper, 635, 636
*thazard, Auxis,* Frigate Tuna, 602
*Theragra chalcogramma,* Wall-eye Pollock, 78
*theraps, Terapon,* Straight-lined Thornfish, 216, 217, 218
*thermalis, Apogon,* Masked Cardinalfish, 227
Thick-lipped Bream, *Diplodus cervinus,* 293
*thiellei, Amphiprion,* Thielle's Anemonefish, 374
Thielle's Anemonefish, *Amphiprion thiellei,* 374
*thompsoni, Acanthurus,* Yellow-tailed Surgeonfish, 584
*thompsoni, Gnatholepis,* Thompson's Goby, 558
*thompsoni, Hemitaurichthys,* Thompson's Butterflyfish, 351
*thompsoni, Mirolabrichthys,* Thompson's Fairy Basslet, 176
Thompson's Butterflyfish, *Hemitaurichthys thompsoni,* 351
Thompson's Fairy Basslet, *Mirolabrichthys thompsoni,* 176
Thompson's Goby, *Gnatholepis thompsoni,* 558
*thoracotaeniatus, Paraglyphidodon,* Bar-head Damsel, 396
Thornback, *Platyrhinoidis triseriata,* 43

Thornback Cowfish, *Lactoria fornasini,* 638
Thornbacked Boxfish, *Tetrasomus gibbosus,* 638
*thorpei, Rhabdosargus,* Bigeye Stumpnose, 293
Thread Sailfin Filefish, *Stephanolepis cirrhifer,* 632
Thread-fin Silver-Biddy, *Gerres macracanthus,* 276
Thread-tailed Filefish, *Monacanthus filicauda,* 629
Threadfin Bream, *Pentapodus vitta,* 293, 300
Threadfin Butterflyfish, *Chaetodon auriga,* 345
Threadfin Goldie, *Nemanthias carberryi,* 175
Threadfin Shad, *Dorosoma petenense,* 67
Threadfin, unidentified, *Polydactylus* sp., 420
Threadnose Fairy Basslet, *Pseudanthias tenuis,* 177
Three Spot Damselfish, *Stegastes planifrons,* 406
Three-band Demoiselle, *Chrysiptera tricincta,* 391
Three-banded Anemonefish, *Amphiprion tricinctus,* 376
Three-banded Sweetlip, *Plectorhinchus cinctus,* 284
Three-eye Flounder, *Ancylopsetta dilecta,* 611
Three-line Damsel, *Pomacentrus trilineatus,* 403
Three-line Monocle Bream, *Scolopsis trilineatus,* 303
Three-lined Blenny, *Ecsenius trilineatus,* 528.15
Three-lined Fusilier, *Pterocaesio trilineata,* 271
Three-lined Grunt, *Parapristipoma trilineatum,* 281
Three-lined Wrasse, *Stethojulis trilineata,* 455, 474
Three-ribbon Rainbowfish, *Stethojulis strigiventer,* 454, 465, 474
Three-spot Angelfish, *Apolemichthys trimaculatus,* 354
Three-spot Cardinalfish, *Apogon trimaculatum,* 228
Three-spot Chromis, *Chromis verater,* 385
Three-spot Damsel, *Pomacentrus tripunctatus,* 400
Three-spot Frogfish, *Lophiocharon trisignatus,* 85, 90
Three-spot Spinefoot, *Siganus trispilos,* 599
Three-spotted Weever, *Parapercis trispilota,* 504
Three-striped Goatfish, *Parupeneus atrocingulatus,* 312, 315, 316
Threeband Pennant Coralfish, *Heniochus chrysostomus,* 352
Threebeard Rockling, *Gaidropsarus ensis,* 78
Threeline Basslet, *Lipogramma trilineata,* 213
Threeline Bream, *Pentapodus* sp., 300
Threespine Toadfish, *Batrachomoeus trispinosus,* 84
Threespot Damselfish, *Dascyllus trimaculatus,* 377, 378
Threestripe Rockfish, *Sebastes trivittatus,* 152
Threestripe Wrasse, *Pseudojuloides trifasciatus,* 460
Threetooth Puffer, *Triodon macropterus,* 643
*Threpterius maculosus,* Silverspot, 415
Throatspotted Blenny, *Malacoctenus tetranemus,* 514
*Thryssa hamiltoni,* Hamilton's Anchovy, 68
*Thunnus alalunga,* Albacore, 602
*Thunnus albacares,* Yellowfin Tuna, 602
*Thunnus maccoyii,* Southern Bluefin Tuna, 602
*Thunnus obesus,* Bigeye Tuna, 602
*Thunnus thynnus,* Bluefin Tuna, 601
*Thunnus tonggol,* Longtail Tuna, 602
*thynnus, Thunnus,* Bluefin Tuna, 601
*thyrsoideus, Gymnothorax,* Yellow-lined Moray, 54
*Thysanophrys otaitensis,* Fringe-lipped Flathead, 161
*tibicin, Centropyge,* Keyhole Angelfish, 357
*tiere, Sargocentron,* Tahitian Squirrelfish, 108, 111
*tieroides, Sargocentron,* Indo-Pacific Squirrelfish, 107
Tiger Blenny, *Ecsenius tigris,* 528.13
Tiger Cardinalfish, *Cheilodipterus lineatus,* 233
Tiger Goby, *Gobiosoma macrodon,* 571
Tiger Grouper, *Mycteroperca tigris,* 194
Tiger Puffer, *Takifugu rubripes,* 648
Tiger Reef Eel, *Uropterygius tigrinus,* 60
Tiger Rockfish, *Sebastes nigrocinctus,* 150
Tiger Sea Whip Goby, *Bryaninops tigris,* 560
Tiger Shark, *Galeocerdo cuvieri,* 39, 40
Tiger Snake Eel, *Myrichthys maculosus,* 61, 64
Tigersnout Seahorse, *Hippocampus angustus,* 128
*tigrinis, Serranus,* Harlequin Bass, 197
*tigrinus, Uropterygius,* Tiger Reef Eel, 60
*tigris, Bryaninops,* Tiger Sea Whip Goby, 560
*tigris, Ecsenius,* Tiger Blenny, 528.13
*tigris, Mycteroperca,* Tiger Grouper, 194
*tile, Pterocaesio,* Bartail Fusilier, 271
Tilefish, *Lopholatilus chameleonticeps,* 239
*Tilodon sexfasciatum,* Moonlighter, 327
Timor Snapper, *Lutjanus timorensis,* 263
Timor Wrasse, *Halichoeres timorensis,* 442
*timorensis, Halichoeres,* Timor Wrasse, 442
*timorensis, Lutjanus,* Timor Snapper, 263
*timucu, Strongylura,* Atlantic Needlefish, 100
*tinca, Symphodus,* Painted Wrasse, 471
*tinkeri, Chaetodon,* Tinker's Butterflyfish, 346
Tinker's Butterflyfish, *Chaetodon tinkeri,* 346
Tinsel Squirrelfish, *Sargocentron suborbitalis,* 109
Toadstool Groper, *Trachypoma macracantha,* 202
Tobacco Fish, *Serranus tabacarius,* 197
*tobijei, Myliobatis,* Eagle Ray, 48
Tokien Grenadier, *Coelorhinchus tokiensis,* 78
*tokiensis, Coelorhinchus,* Tokien Grenadier, 78
*tokionis, Torpedo,* Japanese Torpedo Ray, 43
*tol, Scomberoides,* Needlescaled Queenfish, 250
*tolu, Nemipterus,* Notched Threadfin Bream, 305, 306
Tomato Rockcod, *Cephalopholis sonnerati,* 183
*tomentosus, Acreichthys,* Matted Leatherjacket, 633
*Tomicodon humeralis,* Sonora Clingfish, 97
Tomini Bristletooth, *Ctenochaetus tominiensis,* 589
*tominiensis, Ctenochaetus,* Tomini Bristletooth, 589
Tomiyama's Shrimp Goby, *Tomiyamichthys oni,* 548
*Tomiyamichthys oni,* Tomiyama's Shrimp Goby, 548
Tommy Fish, *Limnichthys fasciatus,* 501
Tompot Blenny, *Parablennius gattorugine,* 530
Tomtate, *Haemulon aureolineatum,* 279
*tonggol, Thunnus,* Longtail Tuna, 602
Toothbrush Leatherjacket, *Pencipelta vittiger,* 634
Toothed Pony Fish, *Gazza minuta,* 256
Topknot Flounder, *Zeugopterus punctatus,* 610
Topsmelt, *Atherinops affinis,* 102
Torpedo, *Gymnocaesio gymnopterus,* 272
*Torpedo marmoratus,* Electric Ray, 47
*Torpedo nobiliana,* Atlantic Torpedo Ray, 43
Torpedo Scad, *Megalaspis cordyla,* 250, 253
*Torpedo sinuspersici,* Marbled Electric Ray, 43
*Torpedo tokionis,* Japanese Torpedo Ray, 43
*Torquigener pleurogramma,* Australian Blowfish, 643
*tortugarum, Serranus,* Chalk Bass, 196
*townsendi, Apogon,* Belted Cardinalfish, 231
*townsendi, Plagiotremus,* Townsend's Mimic Blenny, 521
Townsend's Mimic Blenny, *Plagiotremus townsendi,* 521
*traceyi, Chrysiptera,* Tracey's Demoiselle, 391
Tracey's Demoiselle, *Chrysiptera traceyi,* 391
*Trachichthodes affinis,* Nannygai, 106
*Trachichthys australis,* Roughy, 103
*Trachinocephalus myops,* Shortheaded Lizardfish, 73
*Trachinops brauni,* Braun's Hulafish, 215

*Trachinops noarlungae,* Southern Hulafish, 214
*Trachinops* sp., Yellowstripe Hulafish, 214
*Trachinotus baillonii,* Smallspot Pompano, 250, 254
*Trachinotus blochii,* Round Pompano, 254, 255
*Trachinotus carolinus,* Florida Pompano, 254
*Trachinotus falcatus,* PermitGreat Pompano, 254
*Trachinotus goodei,* Palometa, 254, 255
*Trachinotus kennedyi,* Pacific Palometa, 254
*Trachinotus rhodopus,* Gafftopsail Pompano, 254
*Trachurus indicus,* Indian Mackerel, 250
*Trachurus japonicus,* Horse Mackerel, 245
*trachyacron, Myripristis,* Rough-peaked Soldierfish, 116
*Trachypoma macracantha,* Toadstool Groper, 202
*trachys, Ostracion,* Impostor Boxfish, 638
*tragula, Upeneus,* Bar-tailed Goatfish, 313, 314, 318
*translucens, Harpadon,* Glassy Bombay Duck, 73
Translucent Cardinalfish, *Apogon hyalosoma,* 227
Translucent Goby, *Chriolepis fisheri,* 567
*tredecimspinosus, Scorpaenodes,* Deepreef Scorpionfish, 145
Treefish, *Sebastes serriceps,* 151
Trevally, unidentified, *Carangoides* sp., 246
*Triacanthodes anomalus,* Anomalus Tripodfish, 620
*Triacanthus biaculeatus,* Common Tripodfish, 619
*Triacanthus nieuhofi,* Nieuhof's Tripodfish, 619
*triacanthus, Taenianotus,* Sailfin Leaffish, 143
*Triaenodon apicalis,* White-tip Shark, 38
*Triaenodon obesus,* Whitetip Reef Shark, 38, 40
*Triakis scyllia,* Japanese Leopard Shark, 39
*Triakis semifasciatus,* Leopard Shark, 39
Triangle Butterflyfish, *Chaetodon triangulum,* 337
*triangulatus, Malacoctenus,* Saddled Blenny, 515
*triangulum, Chaetodon,* Triangle Butterflyfish, 337
*Trichiurus lepturus,* Largehead Hairtail, 601
*Trichonotus setigerus,* Filamented Sand Eel, 539
*trichourus, Pomacentrus,* Yellowtail Damsel, 399
*trichrous, Chaetodon,* Tahitian Butterflyfish, 342
*tricincta, Chrysiptera,* Three-band Demoiselle, 391
*tricinctus, Amphiprion,* Three-banded Anemonefish, 376
*tricinctus, Chaetodon,* Lord Howe Butterflyfish, 343
*tricolor, Holacanthus,* Rock Beauty, 366
*tricolor, Scarus,* Blackstripe Parrotfish, 484
*tricuspidatus, Girella,* Blackfish, 325, 369
*Tridentiger trigonocephalus,* Striped Goby, 553
*trifascialis, Chaetodon,* Chevron Butterflyfish, 336, 337
*trifasciatus, Chaetodon,* Melon Butterflyfish, 336, 341
*trifasciatus, Pseudojuloides,* Threestripe Wrasse, 460
*trigonocephalus, Tridentiger,* Striped Goby, 553
*trigonus, Lactophrys,* Trunkfish, 641
*trilineata, Lipogramma,* Threeline Basslet, 213
*trilineata, Pterocaesio,* Three-lined Fusilier, 271
*trilineata, Stethojulis,* Three-lined Wrasse, 455, 474
*trilineatum, Parapristipoma,* Three-lined Grunt, 281
*trilineatus, Ecsenius,* Three-lined Blenny, 528.15
*trilineatus, Pomacentrus,* Three-line Damsel, 403
*trilineatus, Scolopsis,* Three-line Monocle Bream, 303
*trilobatum, Thalassoma,* Christmas Wrasse, 468
*trilobatus, Cheilinus,* Tripletail Wrasse, 432
*trimaculatum, Apogon,* Three-spot Cardinalfish, 228
*trimaculatus, Apolemichthys,* Three-spot Angelfish, 354
*trimaculatus, Dascyllus,* Threespot Damselfish, 377, 378
*trimaculatus, Halichoeres,* Spottail Rainbowfish, 444, 472
*Trimma caesiura,* Caesiura Goby, 577
*Trimma macrophthalma,* Flame Goby, 577
*Trimma* sp., Crimson Goby, 577; Mottled Goby, 577; Whitespot Coral Goby, 577
*Trimma striata,* Striped Coral Goby, 577
*Trinectes maculatus,* Hogchoker, 615
*Triodon macropterus,* Threetooth Puffer, 643
*triostegus, Acanthurus,* Convict Surgeonfish, 588
*tripennis, Gilloblennius,* Spectacled Blenny, 508
Triplefin, unidentified, *Enneanectes* sp., 507; *Helcogramma* sp., 508; *Tripterygiidae* sp., 508; *Tripterygion* sp., 509, 510; *Vauclusella* sp., 508
Tripletail, *Lobotes surinamensis,* 273
Tripletail Wrasse, *Cheilinus trilobatus,* 432
*Tripodichthys angustifrons,* Narrow Snouted Tripodfish, 619
*Tripodichthys blochii,* Bloch's Tripodfish, 619, 620
*Tripodichthys oxycephalus,* Sharphead Tripodfish, 619
*Tripodichthys* sp., Yellow-spotted Tripodfish, 619
*Tripodichthys strigilifer,* Curry-comb Tripodfish, 619, 620
*tripteronotus, Tripterygion,* Common Mediterranean Triplefin, 509
*Tripterygiidae* sp., Triplefin, unidentified, 508
Tripterygiidae sp., Lizard Triplefin, 509
*Tripterygion bucknilli,* Banded Triplefin, 510
*Tripterygion* sp., Triplefin, unidentified, 509, 510
*Tripterygion tripteronotus,* Common Mediterranean Triplefin, 509
*tripunctatus, Pomacentrus,* Three-spot Damsel, 400
*triqueter, Lactophrys,* Smooth Trunkfish, 641
*triseriata, Platyrhinoidis,* Thornback, 43
*trisignatus, Lophiocharon,* Three-spot Frogfish, 85, 90
*Trisotropis dermopterus,* Plain Grouper, 202
*trispeculare, Hemiscyllium,* Speckled Catshark, 35
*trispilos, Siganus,* Three-spot Spinefoot, 599
*trispilota, Parapercis,* Three-spotted Weever, 504
*trispilus, Halichoeres,* Four-spot Wrasse, 440, 441
*trispinosus, Batrachomoeus,* Threespine Toadfish, 84
*trivittatus, Sebastes,* Threestripe Rockfish, 152
*Trixiphichthys weberi?,* Weber's Tripodfish, 619
Tropical Sand Goby, *Favonigobius reichei,* 560
*Tropidinus zonatus,* Gold-bar Snapper, 269
*troscheli, Abudefduf,* Panamic Sergeant Major, 380
Trout Reef Cod, *Epinephelus fario,* 187
Truncate Coralfish, *Chelmonops truncatus,* 348, 350
Truncate Fairy Basslet, *Pseudanthias truncatus,* 174
*truncatus, Chelmonops,* Truncate Coralfish, 348, 350
*truncatus, Epinephelus,* Red-tipped Rock Cod, 189
*truncatus, Pseudanthias,* Truncate Fairy Basslet, 174
Trunk-eyed Moray, *Gymnothorax margaritophorus,* 56
Trunkfish, *Lactophrys trigonus,* 641
*trutta, Arripes,* Australian Salmon, 257
*Trygonoptena testaceus,* Dusky Ray, 44
*Trygonorhina fasciata,* Fiddler Ray, 43
Tubelip Wrasse, *Labrichthys unilineatus,* 451
Tubemouth, *Siphonognathus argyrophanes,* 478
Tuberculated Frogfish, *Antennarius tuberosus,* 88, 90
*tuberosus, Antennarius,* Tuberculated Frogfish, 88, 90
*tuberosus, Naso,* Humpnose Unicornfish, 590
Tubesnout, *Aulorhynchus flavidus,* 118
*tuckeri, Monacanthus,* Slender Filefish, 628
*tuka, Mirolabrichthys,* Purple Queen, 178
*tukula, Epinephelus,* Potato Bass, 188
*tumifrons, Dentex,* Yellowback Sea Bream, 289
Twin-spot Chromis, *Chromis elerae,* 383
Twinspot Bass, *Serranus flaviventris,* 197

Twinspot Coris, *Coris dorsomacula,* 437
Twinspot Lionfish, *Dendrochirus biocellatus,* 143
*twistii, Anampses,* Yellowbreasted Tamarin, 426, 477
Two-banded Anemonefish, *Amphiprion bicinctus,* 374
Two-banded Bream, *Diplodus vulgaris,* 288
Two-banded Dottyback, *Pseudochromis bitaeniata,* 209
Two-banded Grouper, *Diploprion bifasciatus,* 206
Two-banded Stargazer, *Uranoscopus bicinctus,* 501
Two-barred Goatfish, *Parupeneus bifasciatus,* 317
Two-belted Cardinalfish, *Apogon taeniatus,* 228, 233
Two-colored Angelfish, *Centropyge bicolor,* 354
Two-colored Blenny, *Ecsenius bicolor,* 532
Two-lined Monocle Bream, *Scolopsis bilineatus,* 293, 302, 304
Two-saddle Goatfish, *Parupeneus cinnabarinus,* 316
Two-spot Coralfish, *Coradion melanopus,* 347
Two-spot Demoiselle, *Chrysiptera biocellata,* 394
Two-spot Goby, *Signigobius biocellatus,* 540, 551
Two-spot Hawkfish, *Amblycirrhites bimacula,* 415
Two-spot Wrasse, *Cheilinus bimaculatus,* 432
Two-striped Bream, *Pentapodus bifasciatus,* 307
Two-striped Cardinalfish, *Apogon quadrifasciatus,* 229
Two-striped Coral Goby, *Eviota bifasciata,* 560, 576
Two-tone Fingerfin, *Chirodactylus brachydactylus,* 418
Twobar Seabream, *Acanthopagrus bifasciatus,* 292
Twospot Cardinalfish, *Apogon pseudomaculatus,* 230
Twospot Hogfish, *Bodianus bimaculatus,* 426
*tyleri, Canthigaster,* Tyler's Sharpnosed Pufferfish, 647, 653
Tyler's Sharpnosed Pufferfish, *Canthigaster tyleri,* 647, 653
*Tylosurus crocodilus,* Houndfish, 100
*Tylosurus leiurus,* Needlefish, 100
*typus, Oxycirrhites,* Longnose Hawkfish, 413, 414
*typus, Rhincodon,* Whale Shark, 34, 40

## U

*uarnak, Himantura,* Coachwhip Ray, 45, 47
*ulae, Synodus,* Red-brown Lizardfish, 74
*ulietensis, Chaetodon,* Saddled Butterflyfish, 340
*Umbrina roncador,* Yellowfin Croaker, 311
*umbrosus, Equetus,* Cubbyu, 308, 309
*umbrosus, Sebastes,* Honeycomb Rockfish, 151
Unarmed Monocle Bream, *Scolopsis inermis,* 303
*undecimalis, Centropomus,* Snook, 170
*undosquamis, Saurida,* Large-scaled Grinner, 73
Undulate Triggerfish, *Balistapus undulatus,* 623
*undulatus, Balistapus,* Undulate Triggerfish, 623
*undulatus, Cheilinus,* Humphead Wrasse, 433, 477
*undulatus, Gymnothorax,* Leopard Moray, 58
*undulatus, Menticirrhus,* California Corbina, 311
*undulostriatus, Epinephelus,* Wavy-lined Grouper, 117
*undulosus, Epinephelus,* Midwater Rockcod, 188
*unicolor, Gymnosarda,* Dogtooth Tuna, 603
*unicolor, Hypoplectrus,* Hamlet, 201
Unicorn Leatherjacket, *Aluterus monoceros,* 635
Unicorn Tang, *Naso unicornis,* 591
*unicornis, Naso,* Unicorn Tang, 591
*unifasciatus, Cheilinus,* One-band Wrasse, 431
Uniform Reef Eel, *Uropterygius concolor,* 54
*unilineatus, Labrichthys,* Tubelip Wrasse, 451
*unimaculata, Chrysiptera,* One-spot Demoiselle, 394
*unimaculatus, Chaetodon,* Teardrop Butterflyfish, 345
*unwini, Parapriacanthus,* Slender Bullseye, 321
*Upeneichthys lineatus,* Blue-spotted Goatfish, 314
*Upeneichthys porosus,* New Zealand Red Mullet, 312, 314
*upeneoides, Nemipterus,* Black-shoulderspot Threadfin Bream, 305
*Upeneus bensasi,* Salmonet, 314
*Upeneus moluccensis,* Moluccan Goatfish, 314, 318
*Upeneus sulphureus,* Sulphur Goatfish, 318
*Upeneus sundaicus,* Ochreband Goatfish, 318
*Upeneus tragula,* Bar-tailed Goatfish, 313, 314, 318
*Upeneus vittatus,* Band-tailed Goatfish, 314, 318
*Uranoscopus asper,* Stinging Stargazer, 501
*Uranoscopus bicinctus,* Two-banded Stargazer, 501
*Uranoscopus japonicus,* Japanese Stargazer, 501
*Uraspis helvola,* White-tongued Crevalle, 246, 250
*urodelus, Cephalopholis,* Banded-tail Coral-cod, 183
*Urogymnus africanus,* Porcupine Ray, 46
*Urolophus aurantiacus,* Sepia Stingray, 46
*Urolophus concentricus,* Bullseye Stingray, 46
*Urolophus halleri,* Round Stingray, 46
*Urolophus jamaicensis,* Yellow Stingray, 46
*Urolophus lobatus,* Lobed Stingaree, 46
*Urolophus mucosus,* Slimy Stingray, 46
*Urophycis chuss,* Red Hake, 78
*Uropterygius concolor,* Uniform Reef Eel, 54
*Uropterygius tigrinus,* Tiger Reef Eel, 60
*urospilotus, Gymnapogon,* Spotted-tail Cardinalfish, 222
*urospilus, Coryphopterus,* Orangespot Goby, 574
*urotaenia, Chaenogobius,* Dusky Goby, 558
Uspi Spinefoot, *Lo uspi,* 597
*uspi, Lo,* Uspi Spinefoot, 597

## V

*vacca, Damalichthys,* Pile Surfperch, 370
Vagabond Butterflyfish, *Chaetodon vagabundus,* 344
Vagabond Filefish, *Cantherhines dumerili,* 627
*vagabundus, Chaetodon,* Vagabond Butterflyfish, 344
Vaigeu Snapper, *Lutjanus vaigiensis,* 263
*vaigiensis, Abudefduf,* South Seas Sergeant Major, 380
*vaigiensis, Leptoscarus,* Marbled Parrotfish, 488, 491
*vaigiensis, Liza,* Squaretail Mullet, 421
*vaigiensis, Lutjanus,* Vaigeu Snapper, 263
*vaiuli, Pomacentrus,* Ocellate Damselfish, 402
*Valenciennea helsdingenii,* Railway Glider, 566
*Valenciennea longipinnis,* Ocellated Gudgeon, 566
*Valenciennea muralis,* Valencienne's Goby, 566
*Valenciennea puellaris,* Pretty Prawn Goby, 546, 566
*Valenciennea sexguttata,* Ladder Glider, 566
*Valenciennea strigata,* Pennant Glider, 566
Valencienne's Goby, *Valenciennea muralis,* 566
*valenciennesi, Nemadactylus,* Valenciennes's Morwong, 416
Valenciennes's Morwong, *Nemadactylus valenciennesi,* 416
Valentini Mimic, *Paraluterus prionurus,* 636
*valentini, Canthigaster,* Black-saddled Toby, 651
*vanderbilti, Chromis,* Vanderbilt's Chromis, 385
Vanderbilt's Chromis, *Chromis vanderbilti,* 385
*Vanderhorstia ambonoro,* Ambonor Goby, 568
*Vanderhorstia ornatissima,* Ocellate Goby, 562, 568
*vanessa, Paratrigla,* Butterfly Gurnard, 160
*vanicolensis, Mulloides,* Vanikolo Goatfish, 317, 318
*vanicolensis, Pempheris,* Vanikoro Sweeper, 323
Vanikolo Goatfish, *Mulloides vanicolensis,* 317, 318
Vanikoro Sweeper, *Pempheris vanicolensis,* 323
*variabilis, Stegastes,* Cocoa Damselfish, 407
Variable Parrotfish, *Scarus oviceps,* 489

*variegata, Coris,* Dapple Coris, 436, 475
*variegata, Fowleria,* Variegated Cardinalfish, 234
Variegated Cardinalfish, *Fowleria variegata,* 234
Variegated Emperor, *Lethrinus variegatus,* 294, 298
Variegated Ghost Pipefish, *Solenostomus cyanopterus,* 123, 124
Variegated Lizardfish, *Synodus variegatus,* 72
*variegatus, Lethrinus,* Variegated Emperor, 294, 298
*variegatus, Synodus,* Variegated Lizardfish, 72
*variegatus, Verasper,* Spotfin Flounder, 613
*varilineata, Caesio,* Yellow-lined Fusilier, 270
*Variola albomarginata,* Crescent Tailed Grouper, 203
*Variola louti,* Lyretail Grouper, 203, 204
*variolosus, Cirripectes,* Red-tipped Fringed-blenny, 532
*varipinnis, Scorpaenodes,* Ornate Scorpionfish, 153
*varium, Stegastoma,* Zebra Shark, 40
*varium, Stegostoma,* Zebra Shark, 34
*varius, Gomphosus,* Bird Wrasse, 439, 449
*varius, Heniochus,* Humphead Bannerfish, 352
*Vauclusella* sp., Abrolhos Triplefin, 507; Triplefin, unidentified, 508
*veliferum, Zebrasoma,* Pacific Sailfin Tang, 592, 593
*veliferus, Pseudochromis,* Sailfin Dottyback, 208
Velvet Leatherjacket, *Thamnaconus australis,* 636
Velvetfish, *Caracanthus madagascariensis,* 158
*veneficus, Zoarchias,* Viviparous Eelpout, 494
*venenosa, Mycteroperca,* Yellowfin Grouper, 193
*venosus, Scarus,* Five-banded Parrotfish, 482
*ventralis hawaiiensis, Pseudanthias,* Hawaiian Fairy Basslet, 174
*ventralis ventralis, Pseudanthias,* Rainbow Fairy Basslet, 174
*ventriosum, Cephaloscyllium,* Swell Shark, 38
*venusta, Coris,* Elegant Coris, 438
*venusta, Meuschenia,* Stars and Stripes Leatherjacket, 632
*venustus, Holacanthus,* Beautiful Angelfish, 366
*Verasper variegatus,* Spotfin Flounder, 613
*verater, Chromis,* Three-spot Chromis, 385
Vermiculated Angelfish, *Chaetodontoplus mesoleucus,* 361
Vermiculated Spinefoot, *Siganus vermiculatus,* 599
*vermiculatus, Siganus,* Vermiculated Spinefoot, 599
Vermillion Rockfish, *Sebastes miniatus,* 151
Vermillion Snapper, *Rhomboplites aurorubens,* 259
*verrens, Xyrichthys,* Red-spotted Razorfish, 457
*Verriculus sanguineus,* Hawaiian Blood Red Wrasse, 435
*verrucosa, Occella,* Warty Poacher, 168
*verrucosa, Synanceia,* Stonefish, 157, 158
*verrucosus, Rhinecanthus,* Black Patch Triggerfish, 628
*verrucundus, Cantherhines,* Shy Filefish, 632
*versicolor, Minous,* Striped Scorpionfish, 155
*versicolor, Siphamia,* Shimmering Cardinalfish, 237
*verticalis, Pleuronichthys,* Hornyhead Turbot, 612
*vespa, Paracentropogon,* Freckled Waspfish, 159
*vetula, Balistes,* Queen Triggerfish, 625
*vetula, Scarus,* Queen Parrotfish, 486
*vexillarium, Sargocentron,* Flag Squirrelfish, 107
*vicinus, Gymnothorax,* Purplemouth Moray, 55
Victoria Cardinalfish, *Apogon victoriae,* 223
*victoriae, Apogon,* Victoria Cardinalfish, 223
*victoriae, Parma,* Victorian Scalyfin, 379
Victorian Scalyfin, *Parma victoriae,* 379
*vidua, Melichthys,* Pinktail Triggerfish, 622, 623
Village Belle, *Chrysiptera taupou,* 392
*villosus, Hemitripteris,* Shaggy Sea Raven, 165
*Vincentia punctatus,* Dotted Cardinalfish, 236
*Vincentia* sp., Western Cardinalfish, 236
*vincentiana, Rhinobatos,* Australian Guitarfish, 44
*vinctus, Carangoides,* Striped Trevally, 246
*viola, Equetus,* Rock Croaker, 310
*violacea, Myripristis,* Lattice Soldierfish, 112, 114, 115
*violaceous, Cebidichthys,* Monkeyface Prickleback, 495
*violaceum, Sargocentron,* Violet Squirrelfish, 105, 107, 111
*violascens, Neopomacentrus,* Violet Demoiselle, 398
Violet Demoiselle, *Neopomacentrus violascens,* 398
Violet Sea Whip Goby, *Bryaninops* sp., 555, 560
Violet Squirrelfish, *Sargocentron violaceum,* 105, 107, 111
*virescens, Aprion,* Green Jobfish, 259
*virgatus, Nemipterus,* Golden Threadfin Bream, 308
*virgatus, Siganus,* Double-barred Spinefoot, 599
*virginicus, Anisotremus,* Atlantic Porkfish, 280
*virginicus, Polydactylus,* Barbu, 420
*virgo, Pterogobius,* Red-and-Blue Goby, 565
*viride, Sparisoma,* Stoplight Parrotfish, 487
*viridescens, Balistoides,* Dotty Triggerfish, 626
*viridis, Chromis,* Blue-green Reeffish, 371, 383, 388
*viridis, Lutjanus,* Blue and Gold Snapper, 264
*vitta, Lutjanus,* Olive-striped Snapper, 261, 270
*vitta, Pentapodus,* Threadfin Bream, 293, 300
*vittata, Inermia,* Boga, 288
*vittatus, Cheilodactylus,* Striped Hawkfish, 417
*vittatus, Gobius,* Mediterranean Banded Goby, 559
*vittatus, Meiacanthus,* Singleband Forktail Blenny, 523
*vittatus, Myripristis,* Ribbon-striped Soldierfish, 114
*vittatus, Upeneus,* Band-tailed Goatfish, 314, 318
*vittiger, Pencipelta,* Toothbrush Leatherjacket, 634
*vivanus, Lutjanus,* Silk Snapper, 264
Viviparous Eelpout, *Zoarchias veneficus,* 494
*vlamingi, Naso,* Vlaming's Unicornfish, 590
Vlaming's Unicornfish, *Naso vlamingi,* 590
*volitans, Dactylopterus,* Flying Gurnard, 137
*volitans, Pegasus,* Longtail Seamoth, 119
*volitans, Pterois,* Lionfish, 134, 140, 142
*vomer, Selene,* Lookdown, 251
*Vomerogobius flavus,* Yellow Goby, 561
*vosmeri, Scolopsis,* Whitecheek Monocle Bream, 293, 302
*vroliki, Centropyge,* Pearl-scaled Angelfish, 357
*vulgaris, Diplodus,* Two-banded Bream, 288
*vulpes, Albula,* Bonefish, 50
*vulpinus, Lo,* Foxface, 597

## W

Wahoo, *Acanthocybium solandri,* 602
*waigiensis, Psammoperca,* Sea Perch, 170
*waitei, Luzonichthys,* Pink Basslet, 200
Wakanoura Moray, *Gymnothorax eurostus,* 54
*wakiyai, Malakichthys,* Wakiya's Perch, 173
Wakiya's Perch, *Malakichthys wakiyai,* 173
*walkeri, Emblemaria,* Elusive Blenny, 520
Wall-eye Pollock, *Theragra chalcogramma,* 78
Walleye Basslet, *Serranus luciopercanus,* 196
*wardi, Pomacentrus,* Ward's Damsel, 401
*wardi, Sutorectus,* Northern Wobbegong, 36
Ward's Damsel, *Pomacentrus wardi,* 401
Warthead Blenny, *Protemblemaria bicirrhis,* 520
Warty Frogfish, *Antennarius maculatus,* 85, 86, 89, 92
Warty Poacher, *Occella verrucosa,* 168
Waspfish, *Centropogon australis,* 137

*watanabei, Genicanthus,* Watanabe's Lyretail Angelfish, 358
Watanabe's Lyretail Angelfish, *Genicanthus watanabei,* 358
*waterhausi, Neopataecus,* Whiskered Prowfish, 159
Wavy Grubfish, *Parapercis haackei,* 504
Wavy-lined Blenny, *Entomacrodus decussatus,* 529
Wavy-lined Grouper, *Epinephelus undulostriatus,* 117
Web Burrfish, *Chilomycterus antillarum,* 655
*weberi, Chromis,* Weber's Chromis, 386
*weberi?, Trixiphichthys,* Weber's Tripodfish, 619
Weber's Chromis, *Chromis weberi,* 386
Weber's Coralline Velvetfish, *Paraploactis obbesi?,* 159
Weber's Tripodfish, *Trixiphichthys weberi?,* 619
Wedgetail Filefish, *Paramonacanthus barnardi,* 634
Weed Blenny, *Springeratus xanthosoma,* 517
Weedfish, *Heteroclinus* sp. cf *roseus,* 517
Weedy Seadragon, *Phyllopteryx taeniolatus,* 120, 124
Weeping Scorpionfish, *Rhinopias argoliba,* 139
Weever, unidentified, *Parapercis* sp., 502; *Parapercis* sp. *(cylindrica?),* 504
West African Sea Bass, *Serranus heterurus,* 196
West African Squirrelfish, *Holocentrus hastatus,* 109
West African Triggerfish, *Balistes forcipitus,* 625
West Australian Jewfish, *Glaucosoma hebraicum,* 212
West Indian Cleaning Goby, *Gobiosoma prochilus,* 572
*westaustralis, Chromis,* Westralian Puller, 384
Western Blue Devil, *Paraplesiops meleagris,* 215
Western Buffalo Bream, *Kyphosus cornelii,* 327
Western Cardinalfish, *Vincentia* sp., 236
Western Footballer, *Neatypus obliquus,* 327
Western Gregory, *Stegastes obreptus,* 405
Western Rock Blackfish, *Girella tephraeops,* 326
Western Scalyfin, *Parma occidentalis,* 379
Western Sea Perch, *Ellerkeldia wilsoni,* 199, 205
Westralian Puller, *Chromis westaustralis,* 384
*Wetmorella nigropinnata,* Arrowhead Wrasse, 454
Whale Shark, *Rhincodon typus,* 34, 40
*wheeleri, Amblyeleotris,* Wheeler's Prawn Goby, 545
*wheeleri, Carcharhinus,* Shortnose Blacktail Shark, 39
Wheeler's Prawn Goby, *Amblyeleotris wheeleri,* 545
Whiptail Threadfin Bream, *Pentapodus nemurus,* 299, 300
Whiskered Brotula, *Brotula multibarbata,* 80
Whiskered Goby, *Callogobius* sp., 562
Whiskered Pipefish, *Halicampus macrorhynchus,* 127
Whiskered Prowfish, *Neopataecus waterhausi,* 159
White Bream, *Diplodus sargus,* 293
White Croaker, *Genyonemus lineatus,* 311
White Damsel, *Dischistodus perspicillatus,* 409
White Goby, *Nesogobius* sp., 307, 551
White Grunt, *Haemulon plumieri,* 278
White Lined Triplefin, *Helcogramma striata,* 511
White Remora, *Remorina albescens,* 244
White Shoulder Parma, *Parma alboscapularis,* 379
White Speckled Rock Cod, *Epinephelus hexagonatus,* 187
White Surfperch, *Phanerodon furcatus,* 370
White Tilefish, *Branchiostegus albus,* 239
White-backed Goby, *Cryptocentrus albidorsus,* 557
White-banded Damselfish, *Chrysiptera leucopoma,* 391
White-bar Gregory, *Stegastes albifasciatus,* 403, 404
White-barred Boxfish, *Anaplocapros lenticularis,* 617, 637
White-bellied Stripey, *Atypichthys latus,* 325, 326
White-belly Damsel, *Amblyglyphidodon leucogaster,* 381, 382
White-blotched Rockcod, *Epinephelus multinotatus,* 188, 205
White-capped Prawn Goby, *Lotilia graciliosa,* 553
White-dot Blenny, *Ecsenius mandibularis,* 528.16
White-dotted Grouper, *Epinephelus socialis,* 188
White-eared Garden Eel, *Taenioconger* sp., 63
White-edge Soldierfish, *Myripristis axillaris,* 115
White-eye Goby, *Bollmannia boqueronensis,* 569
White-faced Surgeonfish, *Acanthurus japonicus,* 582
White-lined Rockcod, *Anyperodon leucogrammicus,* 179
White-marked Razorfish, *Xyrichthys aneitensis,* 457
White-spot Damsel, *Dischistodus chrysopoecilus,* 409
White-spotted Rainbowfish, *Pseudolabrus gymnogenis,* 464
White-spotted Reef Cod, *Epinephelus caeruleopunctatus,* 187
White-spotted Shovelnose Ray, *Rhynchobatus djeddensis,* 47
White-spotted Spinefoot, *Siganus canaliculatus,* 597, 598
White-spotted Squirrelfish, *Sargocentron lacteoguttatus,* 111
White-tail Chromis, *Chromis leucura,* 387
White-tailed Damselfish, *Dascyllus aruanus,* 377
White-tailed Remora, *Echeneis naucrates,* 244
White-tip Butterflyfish, *Chaetodon litus,* 342
White-tip Shark, *Triaenodon apicalis,* 38
White-tongued Crevalle, *Uraspis helvola,* 246, 250
Whiteband Surgeonfish, *Acanthurus leucopareius,* 588
Whitebar Weever, *Parapercis xanthozona,* 502
Whitebelly Sailfin Scorpionfish, *Hypodytes leucogaster,* 159
Whitecap Anemonefish, *Amphiprion leucokranos,* 372
Whitecheek Monocle Bream, *Scolopsis vosmeri,* 293, 302
Whitecheek Prawn Goby, *Cryptocentrus* sp., 556
Whitecrescent Parrotfish, *Hipposcarus caudovittatus,* 482
Whitefin Sharksucker, *Echeneis naucratoides,* 244
*whitehursti, Opistognathus,* Dusky Jawfish, 499
Whitenose Pigfish, *Perryena leucometopon,* 158
Whiteribbon Spinecheek, *Scolopsis leucotaenia,* 302
Whitespot Coral Goby, *Trimma* sp., 577
Whitespot Tuskfish, *Choerodon cyanodus,* 431
Whitespotted Filefish, *Cantherhines macroceros,* 629
Whitespotted Toby, *Canthigaster jactator,* 651
Whitestar Cardinalfish, *Apogon lachneri,* 231
Whitetail Damsel, *Pomacentrus chrysurus,* 400, 403
Whitetail Goblinfish, *Minous quincarinatus,* 155
Whitetail Triggerfish, *Sufflamen albicaudatus,* 624
Whitetip Reef Shark, *Triaenodon obesus,* 38, 40
*whitleyi, Abudefduf,* Whitley's Sergeant, 382
*whitleyi, Heteroclinus,* Whitley's Weedfish, 517
*whitleyi, Ostracion,* Whitley's Boxfish, 640
Whitley's Boxfish, *Ostracion whitleyi,* 640
Whitley's Sergeant, *Abudefduf whitleyi,* 382
Whitley's Weedfish, *Heteroclinus whitleyi,* 517
Whole-scaled Dory, *Zenion hololepis,* 118
Wide-band Anemonefish, *Amphiprion latezonatus,* 372
Wide-bodied Pipefish, *Stigmatopora nigra,* 125
Wideband Prawn Goby, *Amblyeleotris latifasciata,* 544
Widebanded Cleaning Goby, *Gobiosoma* aff *limbaughi,* 571
*wiebeli, Chaetodon,* Pocket Butterflyfish, 338
Willemawillum, *Chelmon marginalis,* 348
*wilsoni, Conger,* Cape Conger, 63
*wilsoni, Ellerkeldia,* Western Sea Perch, 199, 205
*wilsoni, Pseudochromis,* Yellow-fin Dottyback, 208
Windowpane, *Scopthalmus aquosus,* 611
Wine Red Blenny, *Starksia* sp., 512
Winter Flounder, *Pseudopleuronectes americanus,* 611
Wire-netting Leatherjacket, *Cantherhines sandwichensis,* 629
Wirrah, *Acanthistius serratus,* 202

Wolf Cardinalfish, *Cheilodipterus artus,* 233
Wolf-eel, *Anarrhichthys ocellatus,* 495
Wolffish, *Anarhichas lupus,* 495
Wonder Chromis, *Chromis mirationis,* 385
*woodwardi, Gymnothorax,* Woodward's Moray, 54
*woodwardi, Schuettea,* Woodward's Pomfret, 321
Woodward's Moray, *Gymnothorax woodwardi,* 54
Woodward's Pomfret, *Schuettea woodwardi,* 321
*woolmani, Paralichthys,* Woolman's Halibut, 610
Woolman's Halibut, *Paralichthys woolmani,* 610
Wooly Sculpin, *Clinocottus analis,* 164
Worm Blenny, *Stathmonotus sinuscalifornici,* 516
Wounded Wrasse, *Halichoeres chierchiae,* 448
Wrasse Basslet, *Liopropoma eukrines,* 198
Wrasse, unidentified, *Cirrhilabrus* sp., 433
Wrought-iron Butterflyfish, *Chaetodon daedalma,* 335

## X

*xanthacrus, Myripristis,* Yellowtip Soldierfish, 115
*xantherythrus, Sargocentron,* Yellow-red Squirrelfish, 107
*Xanthichthys auromarginatus,* Blue-throat Triggerfish, 623
*Xanthichthys mento,* Blue Cheekline Triggerfish, 624
*Xanthichthys ringens,* Sargassum Triggerfish, 624
*xanthiprora, Gobiosoma,* Yellowstripe Cleaning Goby, 573
*xanthocephalus, Chaetodon,* Yellowhead Butterflyfish, 345
*xanthochilus, Lethrinus,* Yellow-lip Snapper, 297
*xanthochir, Pseudochromis,* Yellow-tail Dottyback, 208
*xanthometapon, Euxiphipops,* Yellow-faced Angelfish, 361
*xanthometopon, Euxiphipops,* Yellow-faced Angelfish, 364
*xanthonota, Labropsis,* Yellowback Wrasse, 451, 454
*xanthonotus, Caesio,* Redfin Fusilier, 270, 271, 272, 273
*xanthopterus, Acanthurus,* Purple Surgeonfish, 584
*xanthopunctatus, Apolemichthys,* Gold-spangled Angelfish, 366
*xanthorhinica, Stonogobiops,* Yellowrose Goby, 553
*xanthosoma, Springeratus,* Weed Blenny, 517
*xanthosomus, Paragobiodon,* Yellow Prickly-headed Coral Goby, 578
*xanthotis, Apolemichthys,* Red Sea Angelfish, 366
*xanthozona, Parapercis,* Whitebar Weever, 502
*xanthura, Chromis,* Pale-tail Chromis, 387
*xanthura, Paracaesio,* Southern Fusilier, 259
*xanthurus, Apolemichthys,* Yellowtail Black Angelfish, 354
*xanthurus, Chaetodon,* Philippine Chevron Butterflyfish, 336
*xanthurus, Diproctacanthus,* Yellow-tailed Cleaner, 439
*xanthurus, Zebrasoma,* Yellowtail Sailfin Tang, 594
*xanthus, Paracirrhites,* Golden Hawkfish, 415
*xenicus, Diplogrammus,* Northern Dragonet, 536
*xenochrous, Scolopsis,* Olive-spotted Monocle Bream, 304
*Xenojulis margaritaceous,* Pink Speckled Wrasse, 469
*Xenomedia rhodopyga,* Redrump Blenny, 516
*xenus, Phaeoptyx,* Sponge Cardinalfish, 236
*xestus, Petroscirtes,* Zesty Blenny, 522
*Xiphasia setifer,* Half-tail Blenny, 526
*Xiphias gladius,* Swordfish, 604
*Xyrichthys aneitensis,* White-marked Razorfish, 457
*Xyrichthys dea,* Goddess Rainbowfish, 457
*Xyrichthys martinicensis,* Straight-tail Razorfish, 456
*Xyrichthys novacula,* Pearly Razorfish, 456
*Xyrichthys pavo,* Peacock Wrasse, 456, 457, 458
*Xyrichthys pentadactylus,* Fivefinger Wrasse, 457
*Xyrichthys* sp., Brown-banded Razorfish, 457
*Xyrichthys splendens,* Green Razorfish, 456
*Xyrichthys verrens,* Red-spotted Razorfish, 457
*xyris, Scorpaenodes,* Rainbow Scorpionfish, 153
*Xystreurys liolepis,* Fantail Sole, 610

## Y

Yaeyama Blenny, *Ecsenius yaeyamaensis,* 528.11
*yaeyamaensis, Ecsenius,* Yaeyama Blenny, 528.11
*yamashiroi, Pseudocoris,* Yamashiro's Rainbowfish, 459, 460
Yamashiro's Rainbowfish, *Pseudocoris yamashiroi,* 459, 460
Yellow Chromis, *Chromis analis,* 385
Yellow Chub, *Kyphosus incisor,* 328
Yellow Clingfish, *Aspasmichthys ciconiae,* 96
Yellow Conger Eel, *Anago anago,* 62
Yellow Coral Goby, *Gobiodon okinawae,* 578
Yellow Crested Weedfish, *Cristiceps aurantiacus,* 517
Yellow Goatfish, *Mulloides martinicus,* 315
Yellow Goby, *Vomerogobius flavus,* 561
Yellow Head Jawfish, *Opistognathus aurifrons,* 497, 499
Yellow Jack, *Carangoides bartholomei,* 249
Yellow Jawfish, *Opistognathus gilberti,* 496, 499
Yellow Lateral Line Fusilier, *Pterocaesio diagramma,* 272, 273
Yellow Prawn Goby, *Cryptocentrus cinctus,* 541, 547, 549, 557
Yellow Prickly-headed Coral Goby, *Paragobiodon xanthosomus,* 578
Yellow Ribbon Wrasse, *Leptojulis chrysotaenia,* 462
Yellow Sailfin Tang, *Zebrasoma flavescens,* 592
Yellow Stingray, *Urolophus jamaicensis,* 46
Yellow Tailband Wrasse, *Anampses melanurus melanurus,* 477
Yellow Wrasse, *Thalassoma lutescens,* 467, 468
Yellow-banded Perch, *Acanthistius cinctus,* 202
Yellow-banded Sweetlips, *Plectorhinchus lineatus,* 285, 286
Yellow-barred Red Rockfish, *Sebasticus albofasciatus,* 138
Yellow-bellied Anemonefish, *Amphiprion chrysogaster,* 373
Yellow-bellied Blue Damsel, *Pomacentrus caeruleus,* 399
Yellow-blotch Spinefoot, *Siganus guttatus,* 598
Yellow-crowned Butterflyfish, *Chaetodon flavocoronatus,* 340
Yellow-edge Chromis, *Chromis multilineatus,* 389
Yellow-edged Moray, *Gymnothorax flavimarginatus,* 55, 56, 58
Yellow-eyed Mullet, *Aldrichetta forsteri,* 421
Yellow-face Butterflyfish, *Chaetodon flavirostris,* 338
Yellow-face Soapfish, *Diploprion drachi,* 206
Yellow-faced Angelfish, *Euxiphipops xanthometopon,* 361, 364
Yellow-fin Demoiselle, *Chrysiptera flavipinnis,* 392
Yellow-fin Dottyback, *Pseudochromis wilsoni,* 208
Yellow-finned Pygmy Angelfish, *Centropyge flavopectoralis,* 354
Yellow-flank Damselfish, *Amblyglyphidodon flavilatus,* 381
Yellow-freckled Reeffish, *Chromis flavomaculata,* 384
Yellow-head Dottyback, *Pseudochromis tapeinosoma,* 208
Yellow-headed Angelfish, *Chaetodontoplus chrysocephalus,* 360
Yellow-headed Blenny, *Cirripectes chelomatus,* 528
Yellow-lined Fusilier, *Caesio varilineata,* 270
Yellow-lined Moray, *Gymnothorax thyrsoideus,* 54
Yellow-lined Sweetlips, *Plectorhinchus albovittatus,* 283
Yellow-lined Tilefish, *Branchiostegus* sp., 239
Yellow-lined Wrasse, *Halichoeres hoeveni,* 443, 474
Yellow-lip Snapper, *Lethrinus xanthochilus,* 297
Yellow-red Squirrelfish, *Sargocentron xantherythrus,* 107
Yellow-sided Parrotfish, *Scarus psittacus,* 481, 485, 489, 492
Yellow-spotted Crevalle, *Carangoides ferdau,* 247, 248
Yellow-spotted Emperor, *Lethrinus kallopterus,* 295, 298
Yellow-spotted Scorpionfish, *Sebastapistes cyanostigma,* 146, 148
Yellow-spotted Tripodfish, *Tripodichthys* sp., 619

Yellow-streaked Monocle Bream, *Scolopsis dubiosus,* 302, 304
Yellow-striped Blackfish, *Girella mezina,* 326
Yellow-striped Butterfish, *Labracoglossa argentiventris,* 241
Yellow-striped Leatherjacket, *Meuschenia flavolineata,* 630, 632
Yellow-striped Squirrelfish, *Neoniphon aurolineatus,* 110
Yellow-striped Whiptail, *Pentapodus macrurus,* 299
Yellow-striped Worm Eel, *Gunnelichthys curiosus,* 511, 580
Yellow-tail Dottyback, *Pseudochromis xanthochir,* 208
Yellow-tail Tamarin, *Anampses meleagrides,* 425, 477
Yellow-tailed Barracuda, *Sphyraena flavicauda,* 422
Yellow-tailed Blenny, *Ecsenius namiyei,* 528.07
Yellow-tailed Cleaner, *Diproctacanthus xanthurus,* 439
Yellow-tailed Dascyllus, *Dascyllus flavicauda,* 371, 378
Yellow-tailed Fusilier, *Caesio cuning,* 273
Yellow-tailed Snake Eel, *Sphagebranchus flavicauda,* 62
Yellow-tailed Surgeonfish, *Acanthurus thompsoni,* 584
Yellow-winged Flying Fish, *Cypselurus poecilopterus,* 99
Yellowback Sea Bream, *Dentex tumifrons,* 289
Yellowback Wrasse, *Labropsis xanthonota,* 451, 454
Yellowband Wrasse, *Pseudojuloides* sp., 461
Yellowblotch Moray, *Gymnothorax leucostigma,* 57
Yellowbreasted Tamarin, *Anampses twistii,* 426, 477
Yellowcheek Wrasse, *Halichoeres cyanocephalus,* 446
Yelloweye Bristletooth, *Ctenochaetus marginatus,* 589
Yelloweye Rockfish, *Sebastes ruberrimus,* 150
Yellowface Pikeblenny, *Chaenopsis limbaughi,* 519
Yellowface Triggerfish, *Pseudobalistes flavimarginatus,* 622
Yellowfin Croaker, *Umbrina roncador,* 311
Yellowfin Emperor, *Lethrinus crocineus,* 294
Yellowfin Goby, *Acanthogobius flavimanus,* 552
Yellowfin Grouper, *Mycteroperca venenosa,* 193
Yellowfin Mojarra, *Gerres cinereus,* 275
Yellowfin Parrotfish, *Scarus flavipectoralis,* 484
Yellowfin Sleeper, *Eleotris* cf *acanthopoma,* 542
Yellowfin Tuna, *Thunnus albacares,* 602
Yellowfinned Grunt, *Pomadasys* sp., 313
Yellowhead Butterflyfish, *Chaetodon xanthocephalus,* 345
Yellowhead Wrasse, *Halichoeres garnoti,* 447
Yellowline Bananafish, *Pristipomoides macrophthalmus,* 269
Yellowline Goby, *Gobiosoma horsti,* 572
Yellowlined Basslet, *Gramma linki,* 213
Yellowmouth Grouper, *Mycteroperca interstitialis,* 193
Yellownose Goby, *Gobiosoma randalli,* 573
Yellowrose Goby, *Stonogobiops xanthorhinica,* 553
Yellowsaddle Goatfish, *Parupeneus cyclostomus,* 316, 317
Yellowspotted Burrfish, *Chilomycterus spilostylus,* 655
Yellowspotted Crevalle, *Carangoides orthogrammus,* 246
Yellowspotted Kingfish, *Carangoides fulvoguttatus,* 247, 249
Yellowspotted Wrasse, *Macropharyngodon negrosensis,* 452
Yellowstreak Whiptail, *Pentapodus porosus,* 300
Yellowstripe Cleaning Goby, *Gobiosoma xanthiprora,* 573
Yellowstripe Clingfish, *Diademichthys lineatus,* 95
Yellowstripe Goatfish, *Mulloides flavolineatus,* 315, 318
Yellowstripe Hulafish, *Trachinops* sp., 214
Yellowstripe Ruby Snapper, *Etelis marshi,* 259
Yellowstripe Scad, *Selaroides leptolepis,* 250
Yellowstripe Threadfin Bream, *Pentapodus* sp., 299
Yellowstriped Fusilier, *Caesio pisang,* 272, 273
Yellowtail, *Seriola lalandi dorsalis,* 252; *Seriola lalandi lalandi,* 252
Yellowtail Barred Grunt, *Hapalogenys mucronatus,* 283
Yellowtail Black Angelfish, *Apolemichthys xanthurus,* 354
Yellowtail Damsel, *Pomacentrus trichourus,* 399
Yellowtail Demoiselle, *Neopomacentrus azysron,* 398
Yellowtail Goldie, *Mirolabrichthys evansi,* 175
Yellowtail Hamlet, *Hypoplectrus chlorurus,* 201
Yellowtail Parrotfish, *Sparisoma rubripinne,* 488
Yellowtail Reeffish, *Chromis enchrysura,* 384
Yellowtail Rockfish, *Sebastes flavidus,* 151
Yellowtail Sailfin Tang, *Zebrasoma xanthurus,* 594
Yellowtail Sawtail, *Prionurus punctatus,* 588
Yellowtail Scad, *Atule mate,* 246, 247
Yellowtail Sergeant, *Abudefduf notatus,* 381
Yellowtail Snapper, *Ocyurus chrysurus,* 269
Yellowtip Soldierfish, *Myripristis xanthacrus,* 115
*Yongeichthys criniger?,* Fringyfin Goby, 550
*Yongeichthys criniger,* Fringyfin Goby, 552, 553

## Z

*Zabidius novemaculeatus,* Nine-spined Batfish, 330
*Zalieutes elator,* Spotted Batfish, 93
*Zanclistius elevatus,* Longfinned Boarfish, 335
*Zanclus canescens,* Moorish Idol, 594, 595
*zanderi, Argyrocottus,* Zander's Cottid, 166
Zander's Cottid, *Argyrocottus zanderi,* 166
*Zaniolepis frenata,* Shortspine Combfish, 163
*Zaniolepis latipinnis,* Longspine Combfish, 163
Zanzibar Butterflyfish, *Chaetodon zanzibariensis,* 344
*zanzibariensis, Chaetodon,* Zanzibar Butterflyfish, 344
*Zapteryx exasperata,* Banded Guitarfish, 43
Zebra Blenny, *Istiblennius zebra,* 531
Zebra Goby, *Lythrypnus zebra,* 575
Zebra Horn Shark, *Heterodontus zebra,* 34
Zebra Lionfish, *Dendrochirus zebra,* 140, 143
Zebra Lyretail Angelfish, *Genicanthus caudovittatus,* 357
Zebra Moray, *Gymnomuraena zebra,* 54
Zebra Shark, *Stegostoma varium,* 34, 40
Zebra Sole, *Zebrias zebra,* 615
*zebra, Chriolepis,* Gecko Goby, 567
*zebra, Dendrochirus,* Zebra Lionfish, 140, 143
*zebra, Girella,* Zebrafish, 326
*zebra, Gymnomuraena,* Zebra Moray, 54
*zebra, Heterodontus,* Zebra Horn Shark, 34
*zebra, Istiblennius,* Zebra Blenny, 531
*zebra, Lythrypnus,* Zebra Goby, 575
*zebra, Ptereleotris,* Chinese Zebra Goby, 561
*zebra, Zebrias,* Zebra Sole, 615
Zebrafish, *Girella zebra,* 326
Zebraperch, *Hermosilla azurea,* 326
*Zebrasoma desjardinii,* Desjardin's Sailfin Tang, 594
*Zebrasoma flavescens,* Yellow Sailfin Tang, 592
*Zebrasoma gemmatum,* Spotted Sailfin Tang, 592, 594
*Zebrasoma rostratum,* Longnose Sailfin Tang, 592
*Zebrasoma scopas,* Brown Sailfin Tang, 592, 594
*Zebrasoma veliferum,* Pacific Sailfin Tang, 592, 593
*Zebrasoma xanthurus,* Yellowtail Sailfin Tang, 594
*Zebrias zebra,* Zebra Sole, 615
*Zenion hololepis,* Whole-scaled Dory, 118
*Zenopsis nebulosa,* Cloudy Dory, 118
*zesta, Lycogramma,* Pouter, 494
Zesty Blenny, *Petroscirtes xestus,* 522
*Zeugopterus punctatus,* Topknot Flounder, 610
*Zeus japonicus,* John Dory, 118
Zeylon Wrasse, *Halichoeres zeylonicus,* 441
*zeylonicus, Halichoeres,* Zeylon Wrasse, 441

Zigzag Wrasse, *Halichoeres scapularis,* 440, 472
*zingaro, Lucayablennius,* Arrow Blenny, 518
*Zoarchias veneficus,* Viviparous Eelpout, 494
*zonarchia, Calotomus,* Jenkin's Parrotfish, 488
*zonata, Seriola,* Banded Rudderfish, 253
*zonatus, Chaetodipterus,* Pacific Spadefish, 330
*zonatus, Cheilodactylus,* Belted Morwong, 416, 419
*zonatus, Cheilodipterus,* Banded Cardinalfish, 234
*zonatus, Tropidinus,* Gold-bar Snapper, 269
*zonifer, Erilepis,* Skilfish, 162
*zonifer, Malacoctenus,* Girdled Blenny, 514
*zonipectus, Gymnothorax,* Bar-tail Moray, 58
*zonipectus, Pomacanthus,* Cortez Angelfish, 362
*zonoleucus, Pterogobius,* Flag-finned Goby, 565
*zoster, Hemitaurichthys,* Brown-and-White Butterflyfish, 351
*zosterophora, Archamia,* Girdled Cardinalfish, 235
*zvonimiri, Parablennius,* Zvonimiri's Blenny, 525
Zvonimiri's Blenny, *Parablennius zvonimiri,* 525
*zygaena, Sphyrna,* Smooth Hammerhead, 40, 41
*zysron, Nemipterus,* Butterfly Threadfin Bream, 305